SO-AKC-886

The World Book Atlas

The World Book Atlas

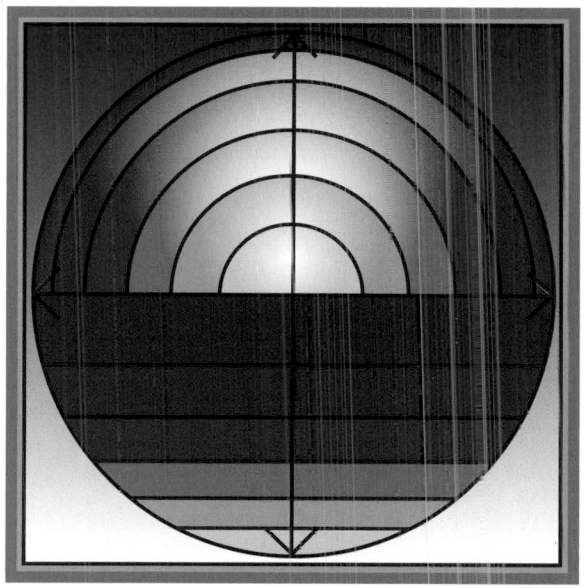

World Book, Inc.
a Scott Fetzer company
Chicago

Staff

President   *Robert C. Martin*

Vice president, Publisher   *Michael Ross*

Editorial

Managing editor
Maureen Mostyn Liebenson

Associate editor
Sharon Nowakowski

Permissions editor
Janet T. Peterson

Art

Executive director
Roberta Dimmer

Art director
Wilma Stevens

Senior photographs editor
Sandra Dyrlund

Product production

Manufacturing manager
Barbara Podczerwinski

Senior production manager
Madelyn Underwood

The World Book Atlas
© 2000, 1997, 1994 World Book, Inc. All rights reserved. This volume may not be reproduced in whole or in part in any form without prior written permission from the publisher.

World Book, Inc.
233 N. Michigan Ave.
Chicago, IL 60601

For information on other World Book products, call 1-800-WORLDBK (967-5325), or visit our Web site at http://www.worldbook.com

Maps of the world © Rand McNally & Company

Some illustrative material on pages vi-xxvi from *Goode's World Atlas*, © Rand McNally & Company

ISBN 0-7166-2650-0

Library of Congress Catalog Card Number 00-104754

Printed in the United States of America

1 2 3 4 5 6 7 8 9 09 08 07 06 05 04 03 02 01 00

Acknowledgments

Illustration credits read from top to bottom and from left to right on each page. Illustrations that extend over two pages are credited to the lefthand page.

vi, *Artwork* © Mitchell Beazley Pub. Ltd. 1973 as *The Good Earth.* **vii,** © John Eastcott/Yva Momatiuk, Woodfin Camp, Inc.; © Marty Snyderman; © Jeff Foott, Bruce Coleman Ltd. **viii,** © Leo Touchet, Woodfin Camp, Inc.; Henry Ausloss, World Wildlife Fund from Bruce Coleman Ltd. **ix,** World Book *diagrams;* Terraphotographics/BPS; Carlos Elmer, Shostal; Robert Glaze; © Loren McIntyre. **x,** *Artwork* Brian Delf. **xi,** Ronald Thompson/Frank W. Lane, Bruce Coleman Ltd.; © Jim Brandenburg Woodfin Camp, Inc.; Charlie Ott, Bruce Coleman Ltd. **xii,** © David Muench; World Book *Artwork.* **xiii,** © Dwight Kuhn; *Artwork* © Mitchell Beazley Pub. Ltd. 1973 as *The Good Earth.* **xiv,** Norman Tomalin, Bruce Coleman Ltd. **xv,** © David Muench; © Jeff Foott. **xvi,** *Animals* Ccral Mula; *Trees* Donald Myall. **xvii,** E. R. Degginger: Mike Price, Bruce Coleman Ltd. **xviii,** Hutchison Library; *Artwork* Bob Bampton/ The Garden Studio. **xix,** G. R. Plage, Bruce Coleman Ltd. **xx,** © Jodi Cobb, Woodfin Camp, Inc.; *Artwork* Jim Robins. **xxii,** © Dwight R. Kuhn; © J. Alsop, Bruce Coleman Inc.; © Dwight R. Kuhn. **xxiii,** E. R. Degginger; *Artwork* Donald Myall. **xxiv,** W. E. Ruth, Bruce Coleman Inc. **xxv,** Phil Degginger from E. R. Degginger; © Jim Brandenburg, Woodfin Camp, Inc.; *Wolf* Jean Hellmer for World Book; *Other animals* Coral Mula. **xxvi,** World Book *Artwork;* © B. and C. Alexander. **xxvii,** TSW/Chicago Ltd.; U.S. Naval Photographic Center; *Artwork* Jim Robins.

Locator maps on pages xvi, xviii, xxi, xxiii xxiv, xxvii were created exclusively for *The World Book Atlas.*

Contents

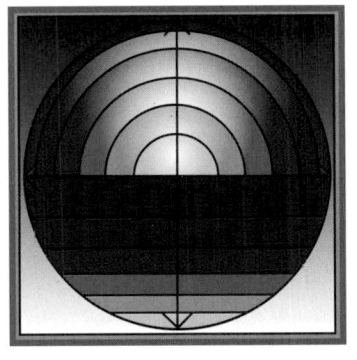

INTRODUCTORY SECTION
The Ocean   vi
Mountains   viii
Rivers and Streams   x
Lakes and Ponds   xii
Swamps, Marshes, and Bogs   xiv
Tropical Forests   xvi
Deserts   xviii
Grasslands   xx
Midlatitude Forests   xxii
Subarctic Cold Lands   xxiv
Polar Caps   xxvi

World Time Zones   xxviii

Using the Atlas   xxx

REFERENCE MAPS
Index Map and Legend   1

WORLD   2-5
World, Political   2-3
World, Physical   4-5

EUROPE   6-29
Europe, Political   6-7
Northern Europe and Scandinavia   8-9
Baltic Regions and Moscow   10-11
British Isles   12-13
Northern France, Belgium, and the
   Netherlands   14-15
Germany, Czech Republic, Slovakia, and
   Poland   16-17
Southern France and
   Switzerland   18-19
Spain and Portugal   20-21
Northern Italy, Austria, and the
   Balkans   22-23
Southern Italy   24-25
Hungary, Yugoslavia, Romania, and
   Bulgaria   26-27
Greece and Western Turkey   28-29

ASIA   30-59
Asia, Political   30-31
Northwestern Asia   32-33
Northeastern Asia   34-35
China, Korea, and Japan   36-37
Japan, Korea, and Northeastern China
   38-39
Central and Southern Japan   40-41
Eastern China   42-43
Southeast Asia   44-45
Southern Asia   46-47
Myanmar, Thailand, and Singapore   48-
   49
Borneo, Java, and Sumatra   50-51
Philippines   52
Southern India   53
Northern India   54-55
Southwestern Asia   56-57
Israel, Lebanon, and Jordan   58-59

AFRICA   60-71
Africa, Political   60-61
Northeastern Africa   62-63
Northwestern Africa   64-65
Central Africa   66-67
Southern Africa   68-69
South Africa   70-71

AUSTRALIA AND OCEANIA   72-80
Australia and Oceania, Political   72-73
Australia   74-75
Southeastern Australia   76-77
Islands of the Pacific   78-79
New Zealand   80

ANTARCTICA   81

SOUTH AMERICA   82-93
South America, Political   82-83
Northern South America   84-85
Venezuela and Colombia   86-87
Eastern Brazil   88-89
Southern South America   90-91
Central Argentina and Chile   92-93

NORTH AMERICA   94-141
North America, Political   94-95
Mexico, Central America, and the
   Caribbean   96-97
Northwestern Mexico and
   Southwestern United States   98-99
Central Mexico   100-101
Central America   102-103
Islands of the Caribbean   104-105
Canada   106-107
United States   108-109
Northeastern United States and
   Southeastern Canada   110-111
Great Lakes   112-113
Central Atlantic States   114-115
Southeastern United States   116-117
Northern Midwest   118-119
Midwest   120-121
Mississippi Delta   122-123
Northern Great Plains   124-125
Central Great Plains   126-127
Southern Great Plains   128-129
Southern Texas   130-131
Arizona and Utah   132-133
California, Nevada, and Hawaii   134-135
Northwestern United States   136-137
Southwestern Canada   138-139
Alaska and the Aleutians   140
Greenland   141

OCEANS   142-144
Pacific and Indian oceans   142-143
Atlantic Ocean   144

INDEX
Index to the Reference Maps   I•1-I•64

The Ocean

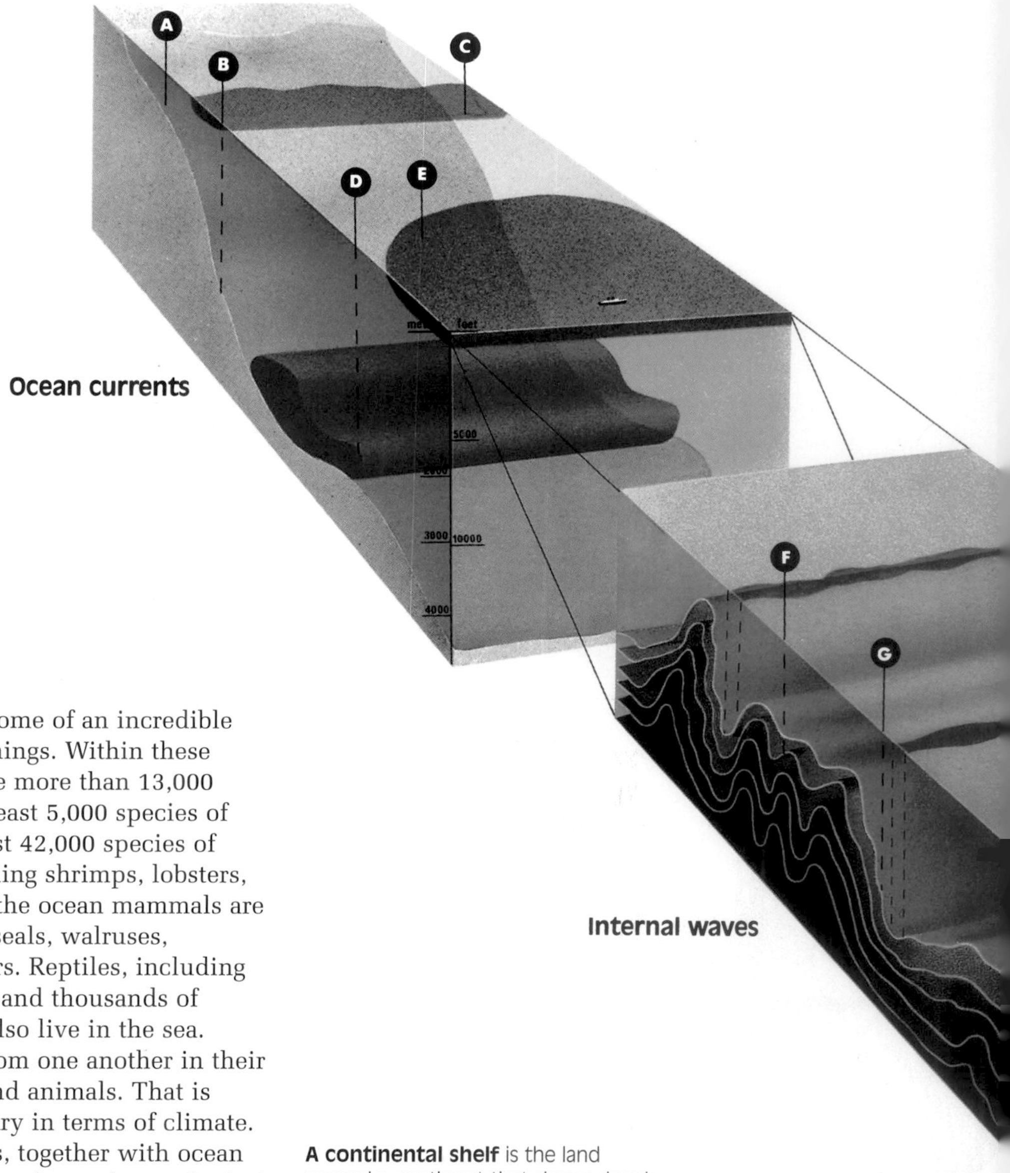

More than 70 percent of the world's surface is covered by oceans. Oceans have been given different names, such as Atlantic and Pacific, but they are actually all one large, interconnected body of water, swept by winds that create waves, and moved by tides caused by the tug of the moon.

Oceans, often known as seas, are deep as well as vast. The bottoms of some seas lie more than 6 miles (10 kilometers) below their surfaces. Great mountains can rise from their floors and stick out above the water as islands.

Oceans are very important parts of the earth. The action of the sun's heat pouring down on an ocean turns enormous amounts of its surface into water vapor. This vapor rises into the air, cools, and forms clouds, which are carried by wind. When clouds are cooled even more, much of the water vapor forming them turns back into water and falls as rain or snow. This moisture creates the fresh water of rivers and lakes. It also provides the ground water that helps plants to grow, and thus animal life to exist.

Ocean water moves constantly in streams called currents. Currents are caused by a combination of the wind, the sun's heat, the salinity of the water, and the earth's rotation. The temperature of a current affects the temperature of the air above it. Therefore, warm currents bring warm air and water to some places, and cool currents bring cool air and water to other places. Without the help of the Equatorial Current, the Gulf Stream, and other currents, the air around the planet would be hotter both day and night near the equator and cooler both day and night at high latitudes.

Ocean water is salty. There is enough salt in the sea to cover every bit of dry land with a layer of salt 150 feet (45 meters) high. Actually, much of this salt originally came from the land. For countless millions of years, rivers that were supplied by rainfall runoff moved down mountainsides and across rolling lands. These rivers washed millions of tons of minerals out of the channels through which they flowed. The minerals, mainly various kinds of salts, were carried along by the rivers. Eventually, the rivers flowed into the ocean and released their cargoes of mud and salt. This accumulation of salt in its water keeps the ocean salty. Only pure water evaporates from its surface when water vapor forms.

Oceans are the home of an incredible number of living things. Within these bodies of water live more than 13,000 species of fish; at least 5,000 species of sponges; and almost 42,000 species of crustaceans, including shrimps, lobsters, and crabs. Among the ocean mammals are whales, dolphins, seals, walruses, manatees, and otters. Reptiles, including turtles and snakes, and thousands of species of worms also live in the sea. Oceans do differ from one another in their species of plants and animals. That is because the seas vary in terms of climate.

All these animals, together with ocean plants, are members of complex ecological systems. The ocean food chain begins with microscopic plantlike organisms. These organisms, called phytoplankton, drift in masses near the sunlit surfaces and give the water a greenish tint. Like green plants, they use sunlight to manufacture food for themselves. As a by-product of this process, the phytoplankton produce tiny amounts of oxygen. This oxygen is used by sea animals and plants. It also helps replenish the oxygen in the earth's air.

Floating among the phytoplankton are trillions of microscopic animals called zooplankton. These creatures cannot make their own food. Instead they feed on phytoplankton. Zooplankton themselves are eaten by small fish and crustaceans, which are eaten by bigger fish and other creatures. They, in turn, are food for still larger animals, such as 60-foot-long (18-meter-long) sperm whales. But without the tiny phytoplankton, the earth's oceans could not support this complex food chain.

Ocean currents

Internal waves

A continental shelf is the land around a continent that slopes deeply underwater **(A)**. Farther offshore, the continental slope **(B)** plunges to the ocean bottom. Ocean characteristics vary greatly. Below the warm Gulf Stream **(C)** off the United States east coast, moves a cold current **(D)**. Near its source, the Gulf Stream borders the Sargasso Sea **(E)**, a region of slow ocean currents surrounded by a boundary of fast-moving currents. Waves beneath the ocean surface **(F)** are caused by differences in salt content, density, and temperature. These internal waves move up and down like surface waves **(G)**. Sometimes a dark band **(H)** on the surface marks an internal wave. The internal wave motion **(I)** shows how deep water is held back while surface waves lunge forward. A beach's breakpoint and foreshore determine where waves break. For example, a breakpoint at position **(J)** and foreshore at position **(K)** would cause waves to break at position **(L)**. When the moon is full or new, incoming tides are at their highest and outgoing tides at their lowest. These tides are called spring tides. In the diagram, **(M-M)** shows the spring tidal range. At the quarters of the moon, tides are neither high nor low. Such tides are called neap tides. The neap tidal range is shown at **(N-N)**. Location **(O)** shows the average tide level. Strong ocean waves wear away shoreline rocks, producing sand. Sand can be dry **(P)** or permanently wet **(Q)**. Surface sand often has ripple marks **(R)** created when water recedes after each wave.

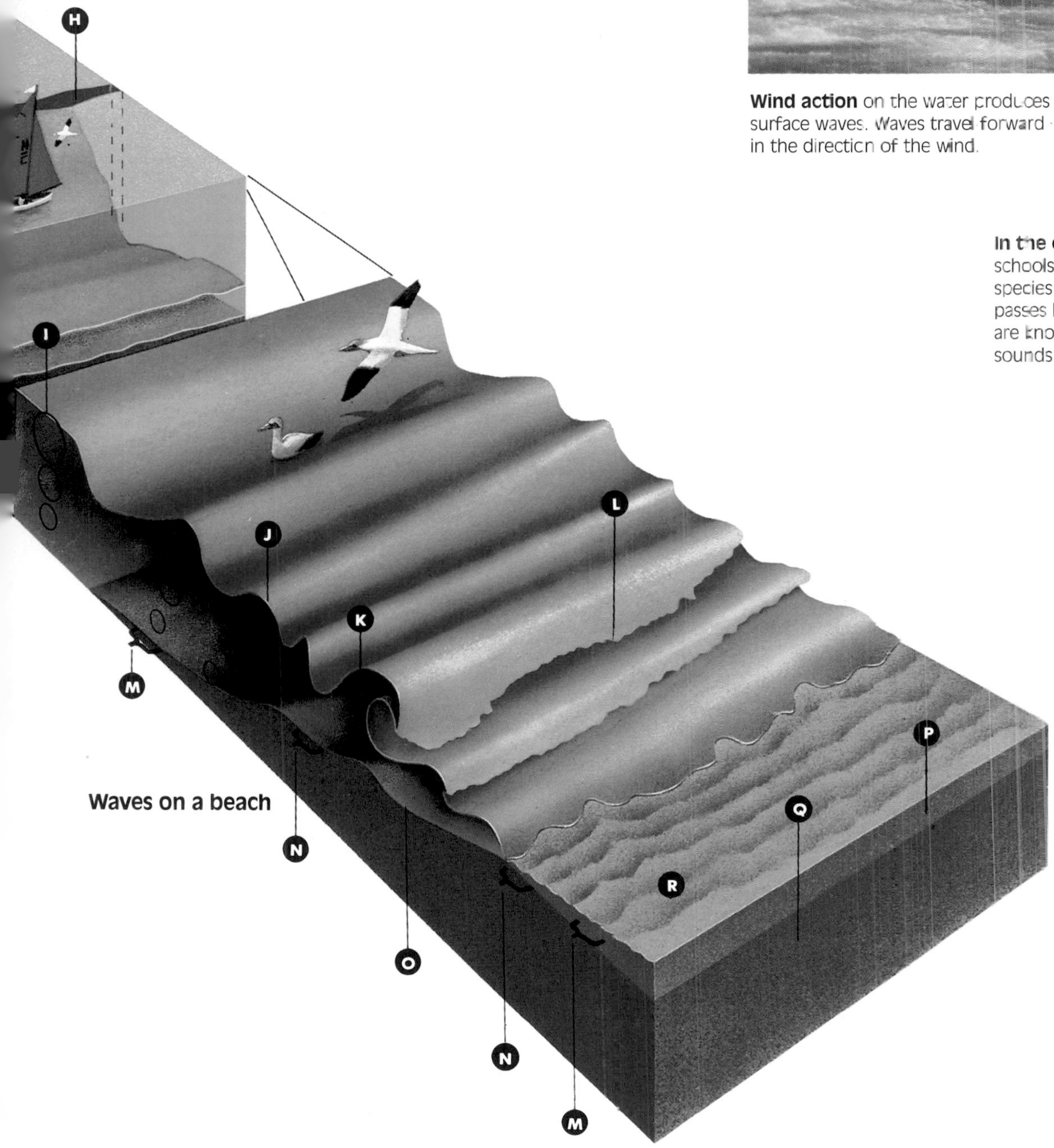

Wind action on the water produces surface waves. Waves travel forward in the direction of the wind.

In the ocean, fish often travel in schools—large groups of the same species. Here a school of grunts passes by coral formations. Grunts are known for making grunting sounds when taken from the water.

Waves on a beach

The sea otter swims, often on its back, in the North Pacific Ocean and near the shores of western North America and Siberia. This brown, furry animal floats in masses of seaweed called kelp.

Mountains

Mount Saint Elias, Alaska, is one of the highest peaks in North America. It stands in the Saint Elias Mountains, a rugged series of the highest coastal mountains in the world.

About one-fifth of the earth's land surface is made up of mountains. Mountains are composed of rock formations that rise 2,000 feet (610 meters) or more above the surrounding land. There are also mountains underwater. Those rock formations, called submarine mountains, form islands or are part of the ocean floor.

On land, mountains may be rocky and barren, or they may be green with vegetation. They may have high pointed peaks and narrow ridges. Their sides, or slopes, are long, broad, or slanting. Often mountains are cut by deep, wide indentations called canyons or valleys. Due to the decrease in temperature as elevation increases, mountainsides are made up of a number of different environments.

Mountains are formed over enormous amounts of time by movements of the earth's rocky crust. In some places, sideways shifts of the crust make huge wavelike wrinkles or folds. These movements result in fold mountains such as the Jura Mountains of Europe and the Appalachian Mountains of eastern North America. In other places, the crust is broken into gigantic blocks that are pushed upward along a fracture line called a fault to form fault-block mountains. The Sierra Nevada of California is an example of fault-block mountains. Dome mountains such as the Harlech Dome in Wales are created when molten rock called magma is forced upward under the surface rock to form a blisterlike swelling. The volcanic mountains of Washington and Oregon were created by volcanic activity.

The top of a very high mountain is generally covered with ice and snow. But a little farther down the slope, melted

An ibex climbs a rocky slope in the Italian Alps. The thinness of the forest shows that the animal is nearing the timber line.

snow can provide moisture for lichens, mosses, and low-growing flowering plants that flourish where soil develops. This region is called the alpine zone. A number of species of insects, particularly springtails and bristletails, thrive in this region. Brightly colored butterflies flit among the flowers. The American Rocky Mountain goat and the European ibex live here too. Small animals such as conies, chipmunks, and mountain ground hogs also make their homes near a mountain's top.

The animals of the high mountain regions are especially fitted for their environment. Many have enlarged hearts and lungs, and their blood contains extra oxygen-bearing red corpuscles. These features help the animals survive in a mountaintop's thin air. When winter comes, most of the smaller creatures take shelter in burrows and live on seeds and hay stored during summer. Larger animals and even some birds simply move a short way down the mountainside. There the temperature is not as cold and food is still available.

A little below the alpine region is the timber line. This is the highest point at which a tree can survive without freezing. The tallest trees in this region are often bush-size dwarf willows, birches, aspens, spruces, firs, and pines. Each winter they are mostly covered by snow, which actually protects them from the terrible freezing wind of the mountaintop. These trees may, however, have some shoots that reach above the snow. At lower levels of mountains, the same kinds of trees can reach full size and form forests. Birds, squirrels, deer, and bears are at home in openings in these wooded areas.

The lower the elevation, the higher the temperature. If a mountain is in a place that gets plenty of rainfall, there will generally be a forest growing on its lower slopes. But if the mountain is in a dry region, its lower slopes will be covered with grassy meadow or maybe even desert. The animals that live here are not true "mountain animals." The same kinds of creatures may be found in other environments that feature similar conditions.

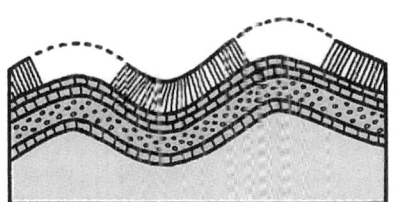

Fold mountains include the European Alps, *right*. The valleys and ridges that are characteristic of fold mountains are shown in the diagram above.

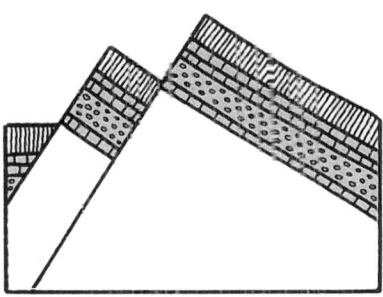

Fault-block mountains are found in the desert land near Las Vegas, Nevada, *right*. The diagram above shows the layers of cleanly broken sedimentary rock that are characteristic of fault-block mountains.

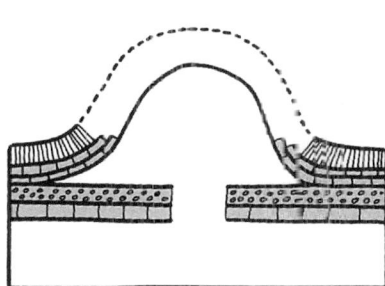

Dome mountains, such as Harlech Dome in Wales, *right*, are formed when the earth's crust rises into domes. The diagram above indicates that a dome's softer rock is eventually eroded.

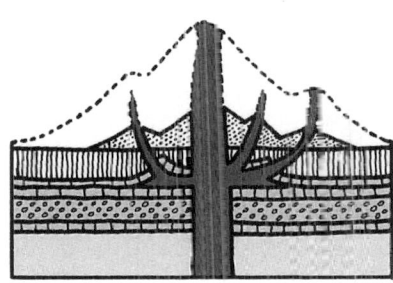

Volcanic mountains include the Cascade Mountains of Washington and Oregon, *right*. Such mountains form when molten rock, or lava, from deep within the earth erupts and piles up on the surface. The diagram above shows the vents through which the lava moves.

Rivers and Streams

Rivers and streams are bodies of water that flow through land in long passages called channels. They flow downhill and are fed by other waters that enrich them and increase their size. Eventually, they flow into another body of water, such as a larger river, a lake, or the ocean.

A river or stream channel is formed by the wearing away, or erosion, of the land by flowing water. The bottom of a channel is called the bed, and the sides are known as the banks. The channel of a small stream can be a few feet wide and less than a mile long. The channel of a large river, however, can be miles wide and can extend for thousands of miles.

A river often begins high on a mountain. It can start as trickles of water from melting snow, as a spring bubbling out of rocks, or as a stream flowing from a mountain lake. As the water flows along, it is fed by streams and smaller rivers. It becomes deeper and wider, and its size is increased further by rainfall.

A river or stream is a habitat for plant and animal life. The character of that life depends upon the temperature, depth, and speed of the water. A swift-moving, shallow mountain stream does not have much plant life. The exception is the jellylike algae that coat the rocky bottom. Black fly larvae inhabit the swift-moving stream. They use their tiny hooks to anchor themselves to rocks. These creatures have their food—microscopic plants and animals—delivered to them by the swift-flowing water. The larvae, in turn, are a source of nourishment for such species of birds as dippers, or water ouzels, of western North America. These birds spend much of their time wading in streams and feeding on the insects there.

A larger, slow-moving river that is far from its mountain beginnings is a very different environment. Unlike a swift-flowing stream that sweeps its floor clean, the bed of a slow-moving river is filled with mud and silt. These materials form soil for plant life. "Forests" of algae or eel-grass often cover a sluggish river's bottom. Cattails and bulrushes grow thickly along the banks. Water lilies and similar plants float on the surface. Fish such as pike and bass lurk among the bottom greenery and dart out to snap up frogs and smaller fishes. Muskrats use cattails and other plants both as food and to line the insides of riverbank burrows. Frogs attach their eggs to plants and rocks. Insects rely on the river plants as resting places.

Many kinds of insects burrow in the mud below the water. They are food for such fish as carp. Predatory swimming insects, including dragonfly nymphs and diving beetles, often thrive in surface waters where light is more plentiful. Small fish, frogs, otters, and such birds as kingfishers are also among the creatures that make these waters their regular hunting place. And in parts of Africa, warm, slow rivers are the natural habitat of hippopotamuses. Sometimes, a river changes its course to take a more direct path to the sea. The river may deposit earth in such a way that a river channel is cut off from the main stream. When this happens, an oxbow lake may form. Oxbow lakes are crescent-shaped, shallow, and often filled with sediment.

The place where a river empties into the sea is called the mouth. A low plain made up of clay, gravel, sand, and other sediments at a river's mouth is known as a delta, and a deep, broad mouth is called an estuary.

In an estuary, there is a mingling of fresh water and saltwater. This mixing creates a different kind of environment for life. The most common kind of estuary animal is the oyster. Hundreds of thousands of oysters may cover an estuary's bottom. Shrimps, crabs, and such fish as flounder are typical dwellers of this environment. Such sea plants as turtle grass and sea lettuce can also thrive in the quiet shallow, salty environment where a river and the ocean meet.

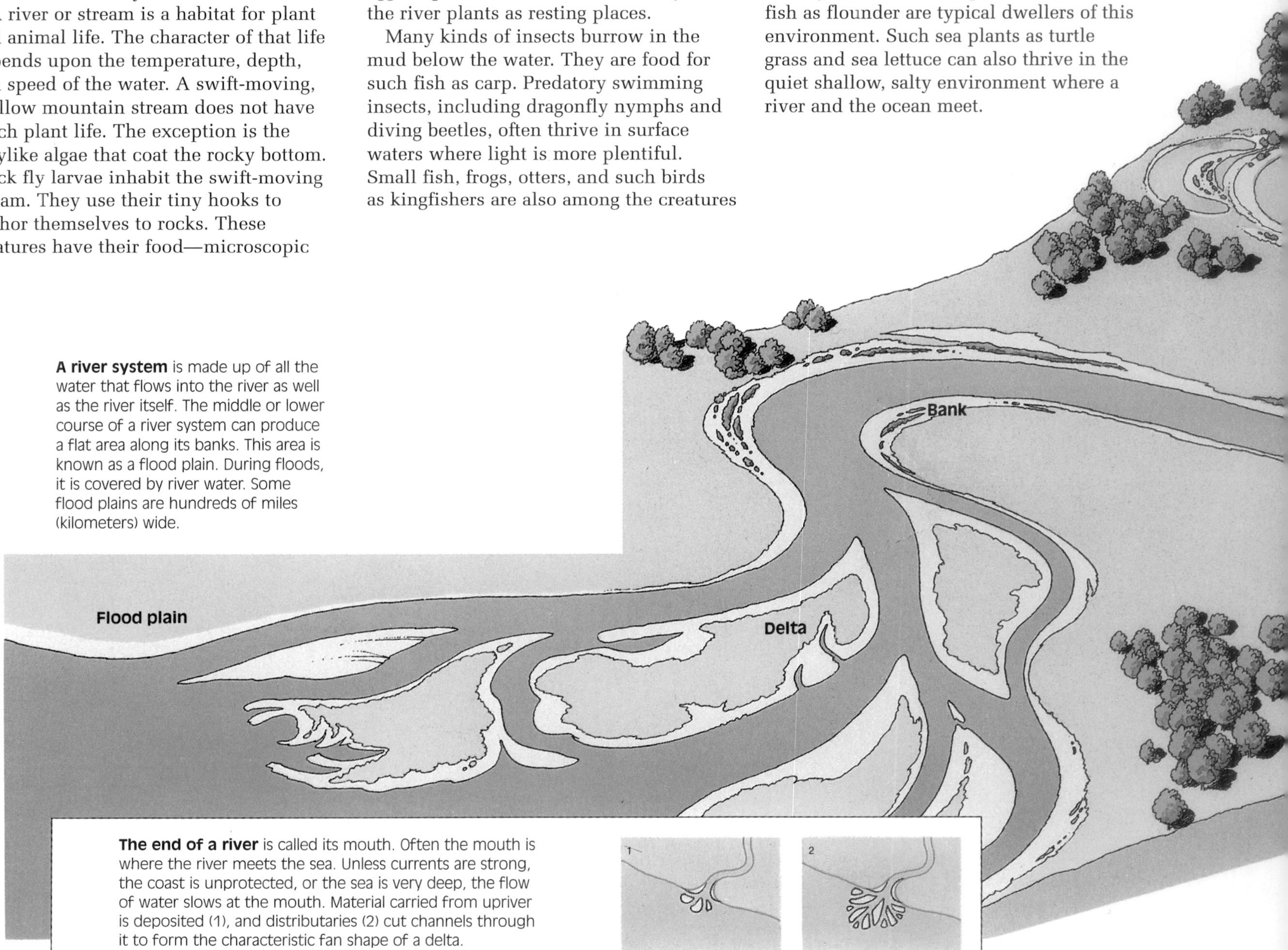

A river system is made up of all the water that flows into the river as well as the river itself. The middle or lower course of a river system can produce a flat area along its banks. This area is known as a flood plain. During floods, it is covered by river water. Some flood plains are hundreds of miles (kilometers) wide.

Flood plain

Bank

Delta

The end of a river is called its mouth. Often the mouth is where the river meets the sea. Unless currents are strong, the coast is unprotected, or the sea is very deep, the flow of water slows at the mouth. Material carried from upriver is deposited (1), and distributaries (2) cut channels through it to form the characteristic fan shape of a delta.

Oxbow lake

The muddy Klamath River enters the clean, blue water of the Pacific Ocean north of Redwood National Park in northern California

The flow of water in most rivers is fastest in the upper courses. Salmon have to fight to reach their upstream spawning grounds.

A river's slope tends to flatten near the mouth, and the water slows down. Painted turtles are at home in this environment.

Lakes and Ponds

Lakes and ponds are bodies of standing water that are surrounded by land. Lakes, which are larger than ponds, may be formed in many ways. Some lakes are made by stranded blocks of ice and blocked rivers that result when glaciers melt. Others are formed by the slow accumulation of rain water in volcanic craters. Still others are caused by the gradual filling in of sink holes with ground water. Sinkholes are depressions in the earth caused by the collapse of underground rock.

Lakes can be fed in many ways. Some are fed by rivers and mountain streams. Others are supplied by underground springs or streams, as well as ground water replenishment. Some lakes have inlets but no outlets. The excess waters of these kinds of lakes do not drain away. Instead, they slowly evaporate.

The presence of a large lake can affect weather conditions for the land around it. In summer, a lake does not get as warm as the surrounding land. Cool winds blowing off the water help hold down the temperature of the land. In winter, a lake does not cool off as fast as the land. This helps keep the nearby land warmer, at least until the lake freezes. Then, the lake acts the same way as a cold land surface.

Crater Lake is located in an inactive volcano in the Cascade Mountains of Oregon. It is the deepest lake in the United States, measuring 1,932 feet (589 meters).

Lake waters are divided into distinct layers, which are determined by the amount of penetrating sunlight. Each descending layer receives less sunlight than the one above it, unless the water is very clear. Therefore, the deeper a layer is, the colder and darker its waters.

The different layers of a lake are inhabited by distinct communities of animal and plant life. These communities depend on one another for food. For example, microscopic plants that drift in a lake's upper waters are eaten by microscopic animals. Both the tiny plants and the tiny animals are called plankton. Plankton is eaten by fish that live near a lake's surface.

Many kinds of insects live in the upper water of a lake. Whirligig beetles swim in this region. Their divided eyes look both above and below the water. Backswimmers, another type of insect, reside just at the surface, and they swim faceup. Water striders actually walk *upon* the water, which for them is like solid ground. All these insects feed on other insects that fall or alight upon the quiet surface water.

Many of a lake's plants and animals live near the shore, in what is called the littoral zone. Here, snails and worms creep on plant stems, and predatory fish lurk among bulrushes and other water plants. In the shallows near the shore, water birds often hunt and use bits of plants as nesting material.

Few of the littoral zone animals or water animals are found on the lake bottom. There is also little, if any, plant life there. The main inhabitants include snails and shrimplike crustaceans. These creatures eat the remains of dead plants and animals that drift down from the upper regions of the lake.

A pond is basically a miniature lake that is shallow enough for sunlight to reach the bottom and enable plants to grow there. Many ponds are formed naturally, but a great many are made by people. Most of the same creatures that are found in lakes are also found in ponds. Such creatures include fish, frogs, and water insects. In many cases, eggs and larvae of these animals are brought from one lake or pond to another by water birds. The birds carry the transported material on their feet or in their feathers. The wind is another transporter. It carries plant seeds from one water home to another. The seeds of water plants can also float to new locations.

Many ponds and small, shallow lakes are temporary features. Over time, the build-up of material on the water's floor and the spread of vegetation will fill in a small pond. Eventually, it will become a marsh or swamp. Over many hundreds or many thousands of years, climate change, sediment accumulation, and vegetation growth will turn even a large, shallow lake into a wetland.

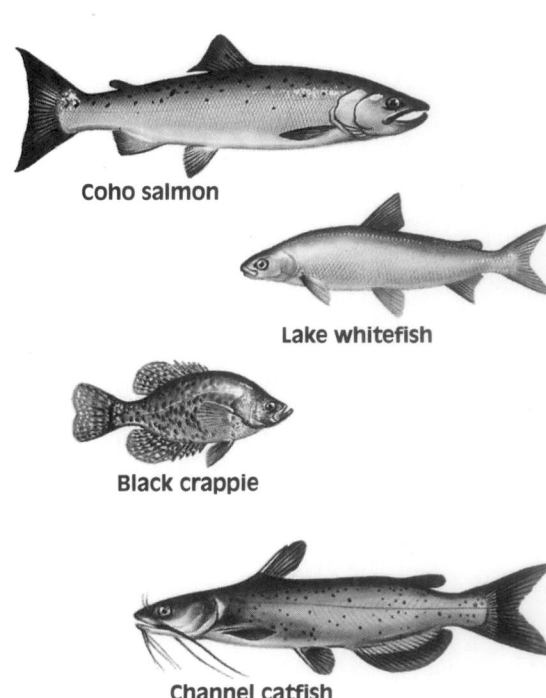

Many species of fish are found in lakes. If a lake freezes over in winter, the fish that live there can swim down to warmer water near the bottom until spring.

Coho salmon

Lake whitefish

Black crappie

Channel catfish

Eutrophication is a process that destroys the delicate balance of water life. This dying pond is naturally eutrophic, but there are other ponds that are killed by pollution.

Pond animal and plant life

In a pond, the primary food producers are microscopic plants that use sunlight to make food for primary consumers, such as tadpoles. A fish (secondary consumer) may eat the tadpole. Decomposers complete the food chain by cleaning up the waste and producing chemicals that primary producers use to make food.

The pond environment

The pond environment
1 Common frog (male, x 0.5)
2 Starwort (x 0.5)
3 Water crowfoot (x 0.25)
4 Aplecta hypnorum (x 2)
5 Wandering snail (x 0.75)
6 Keeled ramshorn snail (x 0.5)
7 Curled pondweed (x 0.25)
8 Bithynia (x 1)
9 Ramshorn snail (x 0.3)
10 Water lily root (x 0.25)
11 Great pond snail (x 0.8)

Near the surface
12 Pond skater (x 0.5)
13 Whirligig beetle (x 0.25)
14 Water boatman (x 1)
15 Nonbiting midge (x 5)
16 Mosquito pupa (x 5)
17 Dragonfly (male, x 0.65)
18 China-marks moth (x 0.75)
19 Mayfly (female, x 0.2)

Middle depths
20 Water flea (Daphnia, x 2.5)
21 Smooth newt (male, x 0.5)
22 Cyclops (typical of species, x 8)
23 Flagellate (x 650)
24 Great diving beetle (male, x 1)
25 Hydra (x 4)
26 Stickleback (male, x 0.5)
27 Common frog tadpole (x 1.5)
28 Flagellate (Euglena, x 180)
29 Water mite (x 5)

The bottom
30 Caddis-fly larva in case
31 Chaetonotus (x 150)
32 Horny-orb shell (x 1)
33 Tubifex worms (x 0.2)
34 Midge larva (x 3.5)
35 Pond sponge (x 0.2)
36 Leech (Helobdella sp., x 4)
37 Water hog-louse (x 2.5)
38 Flatworm (x 2)

Near the surface

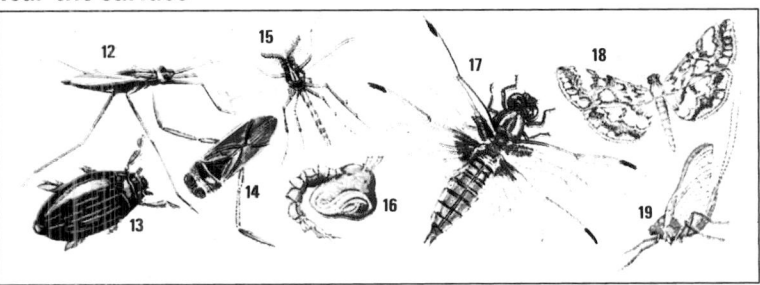

Middle depths

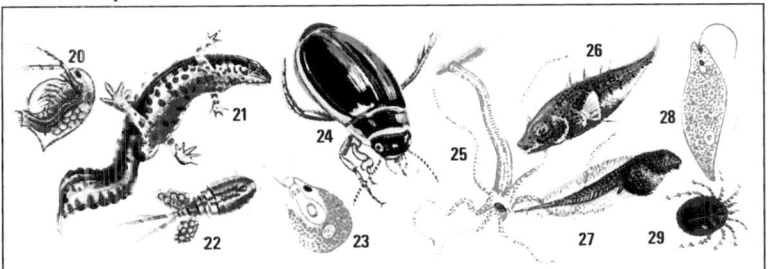

The bottom

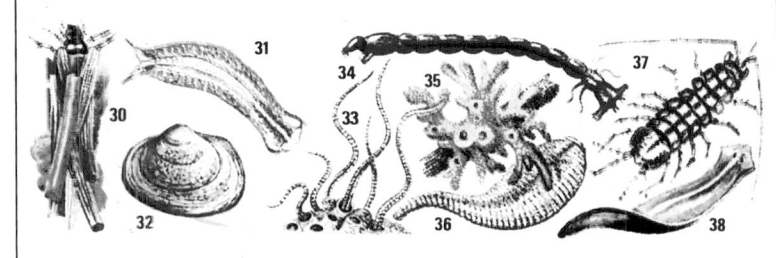

Swamps, Marshes, and Bogs

Okefenokee Swamp, in south-eastern Georgia and northeastern Florida, is the home of many animals, including deer, bears, wildcats, otters, raccoons, opossums, and alligators. About two-thirds of the swamp is a government wildlife preserve.

Swamps, marshes, and bogs are known as the earth's wetlands. A wetland is a land area where the water level remains near or above the surface of the ground for most of the year.

Swamps, the first type of wetland, are areas of muddy, watery land covered by trees and bushes. The major kinds of swamps are deepwater, shallow-water, and mangrove.

Deepwater swamps are near large, slow-flowing rivers that flood regularly. These floods spread water over adjoining land. Bald cypress and black gum trees, which thrive in muddy soil, grow easily in such areas. The thick foliage of these trees blocks out much of the sunlight. Thus, only certain kinds of plants can grow on the muddy ground.

Shallow-water swamps are usually found in areas where soil stays moist or water-covered for only part of the year. Bushes and trees, such as willows, oaks, and maples, flourish there. Water lilies and similar plants cover the surface of the standing water in springtime.

Unlike the other deepwater and shallow-water swamps that have fresh water, mangrove swamps have saltwater. These swamps lie along tropical seacoasts and are named for the mangrove shrubs that grow there.

Swamp water swarms with insects, frogs, and fish. These creatures are food for such long-legged birds as herons and egrets. The birds wade in the water and use their beaks to spear prey. In the tropics and subtropics, swamps are home to alligators, crocodiles, turtles, and snakes. Such animals prefer the combination of hot weather and watery conditions.

Many animals are equally at home in swamps and in inland marshes. Marshes, the second kind of wetland, are flat, treeless areas covered with water. There are, however, such animals as American redwinged blackbirds and muskrats that prefer marshes. Blackbirds nest among the cattails, bulrushes, and other water plants that grow thickly in this environment. Those same plants are food for muskrats and also nesting places for many kinds of waterfowl. Like muskrats, these birds are prey for mink, which live on marshland edges.

An inland marsh is also a major source of food for animals that do not actually inhabit it. Raccoons visit marshes to hunt fish and crayfish in the shallow water. Raccoons also dig up nests of turtle eggs and search for the egg-filled nests of ducks

and other waterfowl. Deer also visit marshes. There, they browse on water lilies, marsh marigolds, grasses, and grasslike plants called sedges.

In addition to inland marshes, there are also saltwater marshes. This type of marsh forms where river deltas empty into the sea. Fish, crabs, oysters, and mussels flourish in salt marshes where salt grasses are abundant. Such diving birds as ospreys are salt marsh dwellers, and gulls are frequent visitors.

Bogs, the third type of wetland, are wet, spongy areas. They are filled with mosses and large amounts of partly decayed plant matter called peat. These environments are usually found in the colder, northern parts of the world. Bogs generally evolve from deep lakes that have become filled with dead, compacted plant material. Sphagnum moss and sedges form a thick mat on the surface of the water. There, wild cranberries, other berry bushes, and a few dwarf trees may grow. Other species of plants that thrive in and around bogs are carnivorous plants such as the sundew, pitcher plant, and Venus's-flytrap. Aside from insects and frogs, few animals live permanently in this type of wetland. But many animals, among them moose and bear, visit bogs in search of food.

In addition to supporting plant and animal communities, wetlands are ecologically valuable in other ways. They can store large amounts of water for long periods of time. And because they hold back water, they help prevent floods.

Bogs, with their acidic soil and water, favor the growth of mosses—especially sphagnum moss, which absorbs water like a sponge.

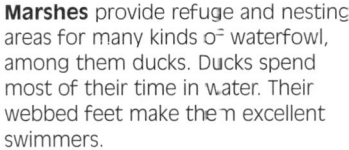

Marshes provide refuge and nesting areas for many kinds of waterfowl, among them ducks. Ducks spend most of their time in water. Their webbed feet make them excellent swimmers.

Tropical Forests

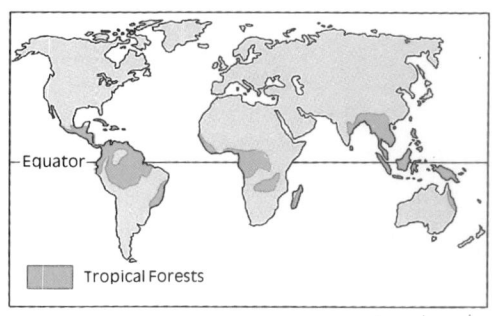

A broad band around the middle of the earth receives the planet's greatest amount of sunlight. This zone, known as the tropics, generally features year-round summer conditions. Humidity and temperatures are constantly high. Days are long and sunny, and many tropical regions are frequently rainy. In this climate, huge forests flourish. They are called tropical rain forests, and they almost always lie near the equator. These forests cover parts of the tropical portions of Africa, Asia, Australia, Central and South America, and the Pacific Islands.

Unlike a midlatitude forest, a tropical rain forest has few seasonal temperature changes. Because of the unending summer conditions, most trees in a tropical forest stay green all year. Such trees gradually lose old leaves as they grow new ones. However, there are some deciduous trees in tropical forests that shed all their leaves briefly during the dry season.

Generally, all the trees in a tropical rain forest have tall, straight trunks with branches only at the very top. The tops of the trees are called the crowns, and they merge to form a covering of leaves high in the air. This covering is known as the upper canopy. Its thickness blocks most of the sunlight from reaching the forest floor. Because the floor is so dim, few plants can grow there. Mushrooms and other fungi that need little light flourish in this environment.

Orchids, wild pineapples, other flowering plants, and ferns grow high up on the trunks of tropical trees. These plants begin as seeds that are carried by the wind. The seeds lodge within crevices in the tree bark and are warmed by sunlight. For water, the seeds soak up moisture from the air and rain that runs down the tree trunks.

Forest vines are rooted in the ground. Often, they wind up tree trunks and other vines until they reach the treetops. There they can spread out among the leafy branches of the upper canopy. Extremely tall trees called emergents thrust through the upper canopy's vines and branches.

Many kinds of insects and insect-eating birds live in the emergents. Large, predatory birds live there too. Such birds include harpy eagles, which prey on the monkeys that live below in the upper canopy.

Monkeys and many other creatures are attracted by the upper canopy's abundance of fruit and nuts. Fruit-eating birds, such as toucans, and leaf-eating mammals, such as sloths, also thrive in the crowns of tall trees. Hummingbirds and brilliantly colored butterflies flutter between the canopy's leaves and flowers. Tree frogs and lizards creep through the upper canopy branches, hunting insects. Snakes lurk among the leaves to capture these creatures. Other residents of the upper canopy include such gliding animals as the large bat called the flying fox and the flying dragon, a type of lizard.

Not all trees are tall enough to reach the upper canopy. Some full-grown trees can thrive at lower levels in the forest because they do not require an abundance of light. The crowns of these trees form one or two lower canopies that are generally quite sturdy. The lower canopies are inhabited by larger forest animals such as apes and leopards. These animals live both in trees and on the forest floor.

In many parts of tropical rain forest, tree trunks are spread far apart and few plants grow on the ground. But in places where abundant sunlight is able to reach the ground, there is a thick, tangled growth of bushes and low plants. Such areas are called jungles, and they grow frequently in former clearings and along the banks of wide rivers in the tropical regions of the world.

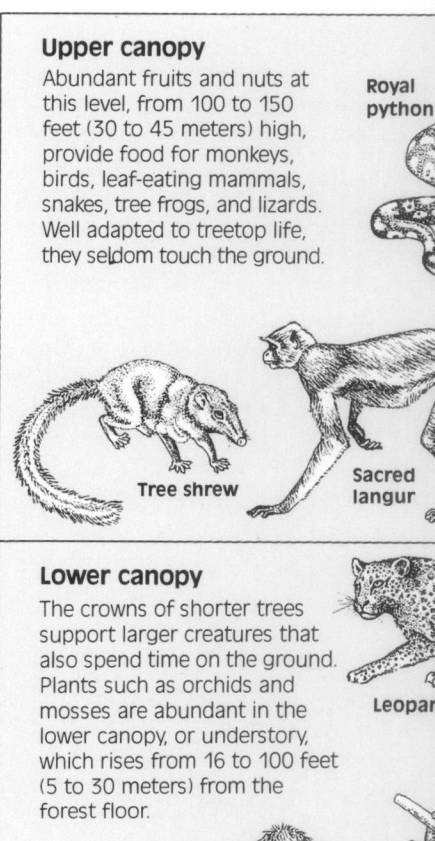

Upper canopy

Abundant fruits and nuts at this level, from 100 to 150 feet (30 to 45 meters) high, provide food for monkeys, birds, leaf-eating mammals, snakes, tree frogs, and lizards. Well adapted to treetop life, they seldom touch the ground.

Royal python

Tree shrew

Sacred langur

Lower canopy

The crowns of shorter trees support larger creatures that also spend time on the ground. Plants such as orchids and mosses are abundant in the lower canopy, or understory, which rises from 16 to 100 feet (5 to 30 meters) from the forest floor.

Leopard

Orangutan

Pouched tree frog

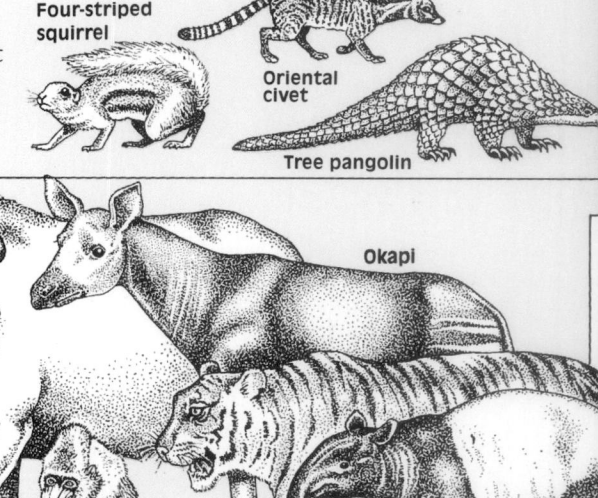

Shrub layer

Woody shrubs at this layer rarely reach higher than 16 feet (5 meters). The plants spring up to fill the space available between larger, taller trees.

Four-striped squirrel

Oriental civet

Tree pangolin

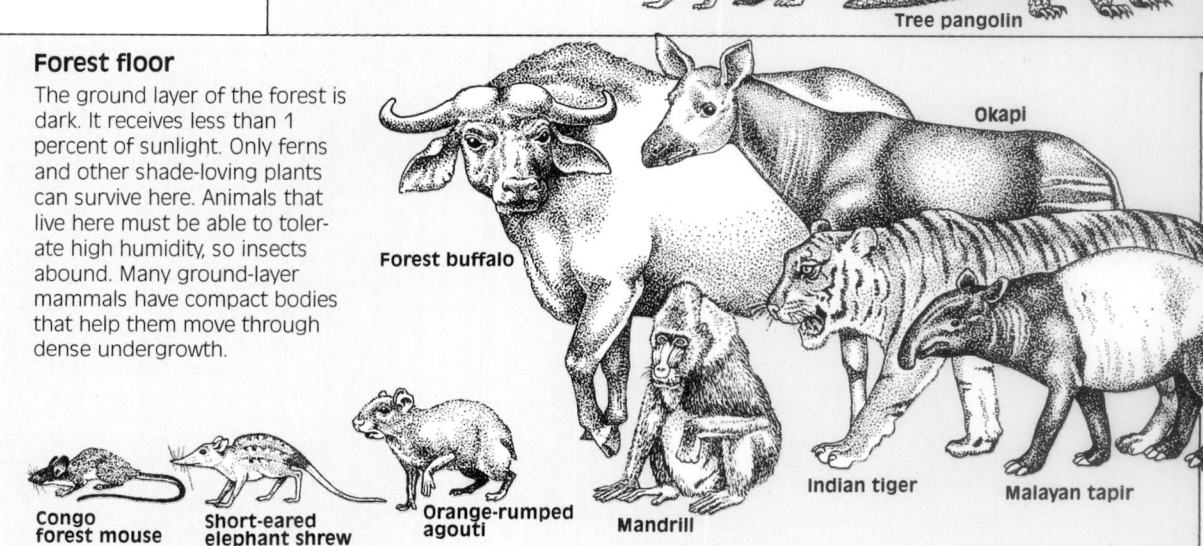

Forest floor

The ground layer of the forest is dark. It receives less than 1 percent of sunlight. Only ferns and other shade-loving plants can survive here. Animals that live here must be able to tolerate high humidity, so insects abound. Many ground-layer mammals have compact bodies that help them move through dense undergrowth.

Okapi

Forest buffalo

Indian tiger

Malayan tapir

Congo forest mouse

Short-eared elephant shrew

Orange-rumped agouti

Mandrill

Emergent layer

The tallest trees in a tropical forest form the emergent layer, up to 200 feet (61 meters) high. Animal life at this level is mostly birds and insects.

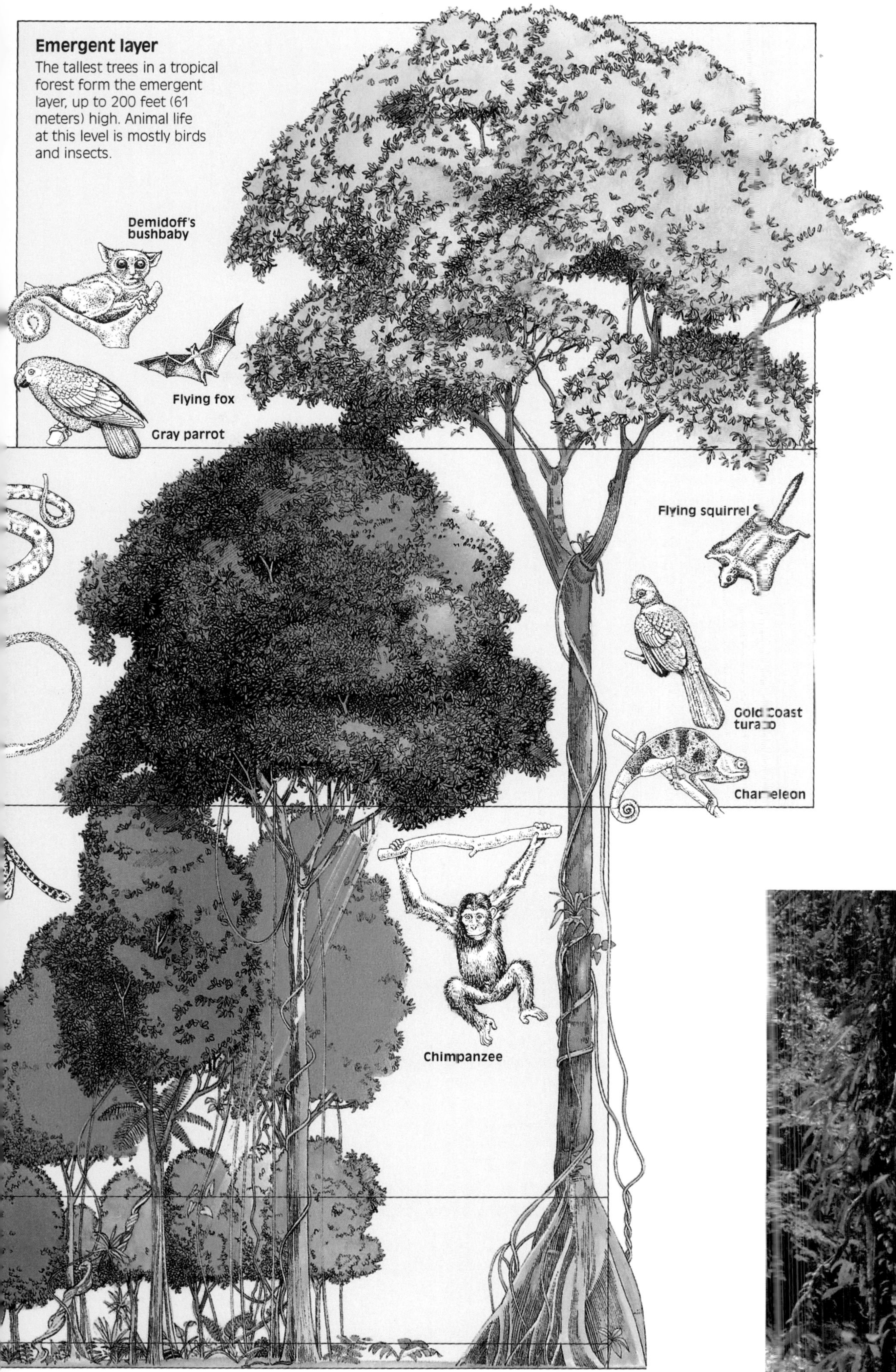

Demidoff's bushbaby

Flying fox

Gray parrot

Flying squirrel

Gold Coast turaco

Chameleon

Chimpanzee

Orchids, which thrive in humid conditions, abound in tropical forests. They range in size from small flowers to huge vines as long as 100 feet (30 meters).

In the dim light near the edge of a Sumatra rain forest, the forest floor is relatively free of plant life.

Layers of the forest

Living conditions at different heights determine what creatures inhabit different layers of the forest. The topmost layers are so high up that only birds and insects are found there. To survive in the dense canopy and middle layer, animals must be streamlined and adapted for climbing. In the high humidity and gloom of the ground layer, insects and fungi break down rotting fruit and leaves from above. These decomposers enrich the soil that feeds the forest.

Deserts

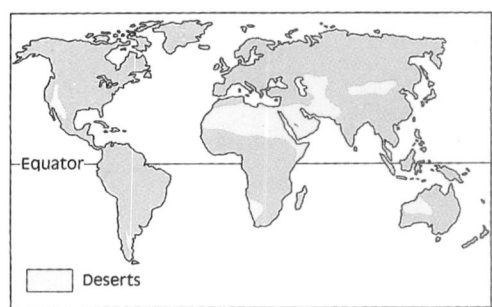

Deserts

About one-fifth of the earth's land is covered by deserts. In general, deserts are any areas that have little rainfall, dry soil, and a limited amount of very special kinds of plants. But there is no "typical" desert. Some, such as parts of the Sahara, consist mainly of lifeless, rocky surfaces and smaller areas of shifting piles of sand called dunes. Others are limited to rocky, dry areas full of plant and animal life. Those deserts, located in the subtropics, remain searingly hot throughout the year. But others such as the Great Basin and the Gobi Desert are bitterly cold in winter and very hot in summer.

Often a desert will gradually merge with a fertile grassland. But unlike the neighboring grasses, desert plants must cope with a minimal supply of water. Some of these plants have long roots that probe far underground to find water. Others have shallow, widespread roots that absorb the tiniest amounts of dew and rain that soak down from the surface. The leaves of these plants are small, and they often fall off during the dry season.

Many types of desert vegetation flourish only when there is a little rain. After a rainfall, previously inactive seeds quickly germinate and grow into plants. These plants—known as annuals—flower, form more seeds, then die. The new seeds lie dormant until it rains again. The next rainfall, however, may be years away.

Desert plants vary in form from the prickly pear cactus to giant cacti. Many shrub and low tree species also grow in deserts. Such desert plants enable wildlife to live among them. They do this by providing animals with food and moisture. Some desert plants also provide animals with shelter. For example, North American Gila woodpeckers drill holes in giant cacti. In these hollows, the birds raise their families. When they leave, the holes are taken over by other kinds of birds or by lizards, rats, or mice.

Extreme heat can kill an animal. That is why desert creatures must be able to keep their bodies from becoming too hot. There are various ways animals can control their body temperatures. Small creatures, among them insects, snakes, and tiny mammals, hide from the heat. They dig down into the sand and stay there. Or they keep cool in underground burrows or dark crevices in the rocks. Some creatures pant to cool themselves. Others escape the heat by going into a kind of hibernation for days or weeks. During this time, their bodies stay cool. Some desert animals have special body features that help them lose heat. The big ears of a desert fox or jack rabbit are examples of these features. Blood carries body heat up into the thin skin of these animals' ears. From the ears, heat radiates into the dry, hot air of the desert. Thus, the body temperature of the animals is lowered.

In addition to surviving the heat, desert animals must be adapted for an environment that has very little water. Desert larks of the Sahara, for example, can thrive for weeks without a drink. Camels and little furry dassies of South Africa can often live without drinking for months. These birds and mammals get moisture from the food they eat. They are also able to store this moisture in their bodies for a long time. There are also desert creatures, among them the kangaroo rat, that never need to drink. Their food gives them all the moisture they require.

Some desert dwellers, however, must find water each day. One such animal is the red kangaroo of the Australian Desert. This large mammal is known for grazing in the dry grasslands that border the desert. Each day, in search of water, the kangaroo must travel from the grasslands to one of the few watering holes in the almost waterless environment of the desert.

Long-nosed bat

Different deserts are home to different species of plants and animals. All desert creatures and vegetation, however, share the need to obtain and conserve water.

Scattered throughout the world's largest desert, the Sahara, are fertile areas known as oases. The water for Saharan oases comes mainly from springs or underground streams.

Agave

Esparto grass

Monument Valley, Utah, gets bitterly cold in winter. Red sandstone formations rise 1,000 feet (300 meters) from the desert floor.

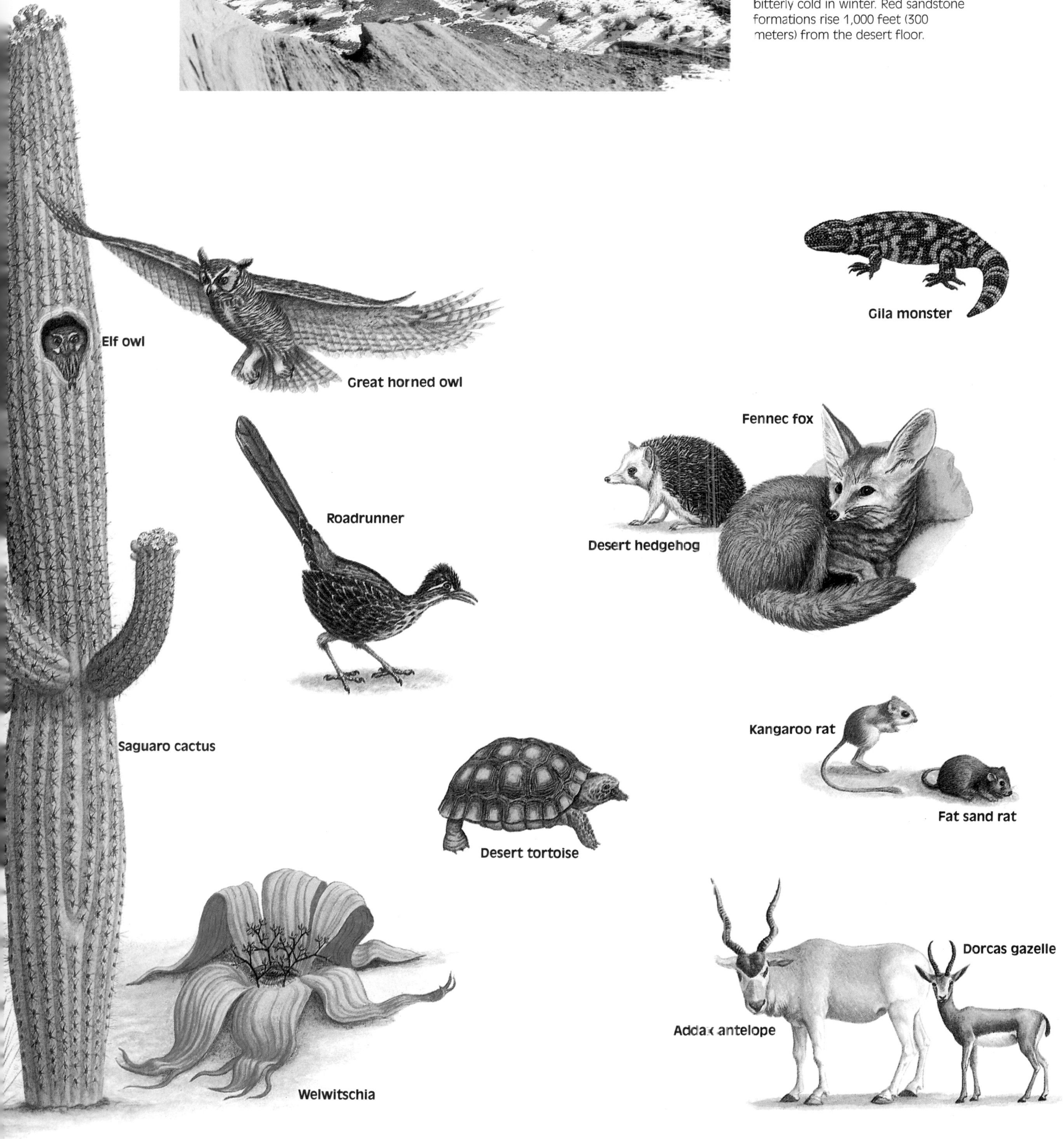

Gila monster

Elf owl

Great horned owl

Fennec fox

Roadrunner

Desert hedgehog

Saguaro cactus

Kangaroo rat

Desert tortoise

Fat sand rat

Welwitschia

Addax antelope

Dorcas gazelle

Grasslands

Between humid forests and arid deserts lie the earth's sun-filled grasslands. These areas, which may be flat or hilly, are literally seas of grasses.

The three types of grasslands are steppes, prairies, and savannas. A grassland is classified into one of these three types according to the average height of the grass that grows there. Plant height depends upon the amount of rainfall received.

Steppes, which are the driest grassland, are covered mainly by short grasses. Most plants in a steppe do not grow over 1 foot (30 centimeters) high. Steppes cover large areas of the interior of North America and Europe, and also extend into central Asia.

Prairies, which receive moderate rainfall, are blanketed chiefly by tall grasses. In moist prairies, grass may grow 6 feet (1.8 meters) high or even taller. The North American prairie reaches from central Texas to southern Saskatchewan. Saskatchewan, Alberta, and Manitoba are called Canada's "Prairie Provinces." Other prairies include the Pampa of Argentina.

Savannas are grasslands with widely scattered trees and shrubs. Most savannas are in the tropics, but some are in temperate regions. This type of grassland covers more than two-fifths of Africa and large parts of Australia, South America, and India.

One of the main types of grassland animals is the grazer, or grass-eater. The larger grazers are generally animals that live in herds, such as the American bison and antelope and the African gnu and zebra. In many places, however, wild grazers have been replaced by domesticated grazers such as sheep and cattle. The herds of grass-eaters roam across a grassland, eating as they go. The area they move across looks like a mowed lawn for a time, but the grass quickly grows again unless it is the dry season.

Actually, there are many more small grazers than big ones. Small grazers include many kinds of grasshoppers, ants, aphids, leaf hoppers, and other insects. Just as large predators prey on large grazers, such small predators as birds and mice prey on small grazers.

Many kinds of flowering plants such as sunflowers, prairie clover, and cornflowers grow in grasslands. They produce seeds and leaves that are eaten by the region's wildlife, which includes jack rabbits and colonies of prairie dogs. There are many predators of these seed- and leaf-eaters. All grasslands contain snakes, which hunt for prey among the grass stems. But in addition to being the hunter, snakes are also the hunted. The sky over a grassland is the natural range for hawks and other birds of prey that will swoop down to seize snakes, as well as rabbits.

In tropical savannas, the temperature stays hot all year, so life goes on unchanged, except for alternating rainy and dry seasons. But the steppes and prairies have warm summers and cool to cold winters. In most of these regions the grassland life is curtailed by cold weather. The ground freezes and the grass stops growing. Much of the insect life dies or burrows underground. The insect-eating birds migrate to other regions. Most of the smaller animals hibernate or remain in burrows through the cold season, living on stored food. But the coming of spring and the thawing of the ground, the grasslands quickly return to life.

Much of the world's grasslands have been turned into farmland where wheat and corn, which are actually grasses, are grown. Even in farmlands, however, much of the same life which may be found in a natural grassland exists. Insects, birds, small mammals, and other creatures thrive among the cultivated grasses.

Great herds of American buffalo,
or bison, once roamed and grazed on
the grasses and small plants found
on American prairies.

Short-grass prairies

Mid-grass prairies

Topsoil

Permanently moist subsoil

Lime layer

Permanently dry subsoil

Annual Rainfall	
mm	in
1,250	50
1,000	40
750	30
500	20
250	10

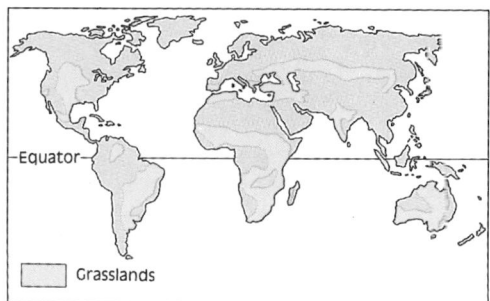

Equator

☐ Grasslands

Grassland creatures solve the problem of survival by adapting to the environment in various ways. Many, such as small burrowing animals and certain invertebrates, seek protection underground. The marsupial mole lives almost entirely underground, while the prairie dog surfaces to eat. Snakes, of course, are well adapted for the pursuit of burrowing creatures. Small carnivores like the pampas cat often surprise their victims. Certain grassland predators rely on speed for catching prey—as do some of the creatures they hunt in the race for survival. The sharp-eyed hawk rides thermal winds in search of food, while the meadowlark adapts to a mostly tree-less environment by singing to declare its territory. Camouflage protects many insects.

Red-tailed hawk

Western meadowlark

Burrowing owl

Rainfall determines what grasses grow where on the North American prairies. In general, the drier the climate, the shorter the grasses. In regions where annual rainfall is no more than 20 inches (500 millimeters), only short grass—with short root systems—can survive in the relatively narrow layer of permanently moist subsoil. As the depth of the subsoil increases, it can support the longer root systems of mid-grass and tall-grass prairies. Tall bluestem and Indian grass predominate in the regions where annual rainfall measures 40 inches (1,000 millimeters). The North American prairie includes most of Oklahoma, Kansas, Nebraska, Iowa, Illinois, South Dakota, and North Dakota, and parts of neighboring states and provinces. Alberta, Saskatchewan, and Manitoba are the "Prairie Provinces" of Canada.

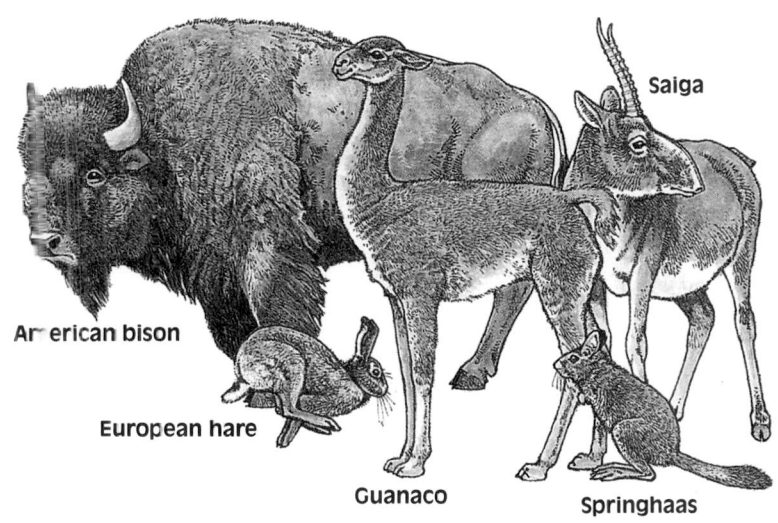

Saiga

American bison

European hare

Guanaco

Springhaas

Tall-grass prairies

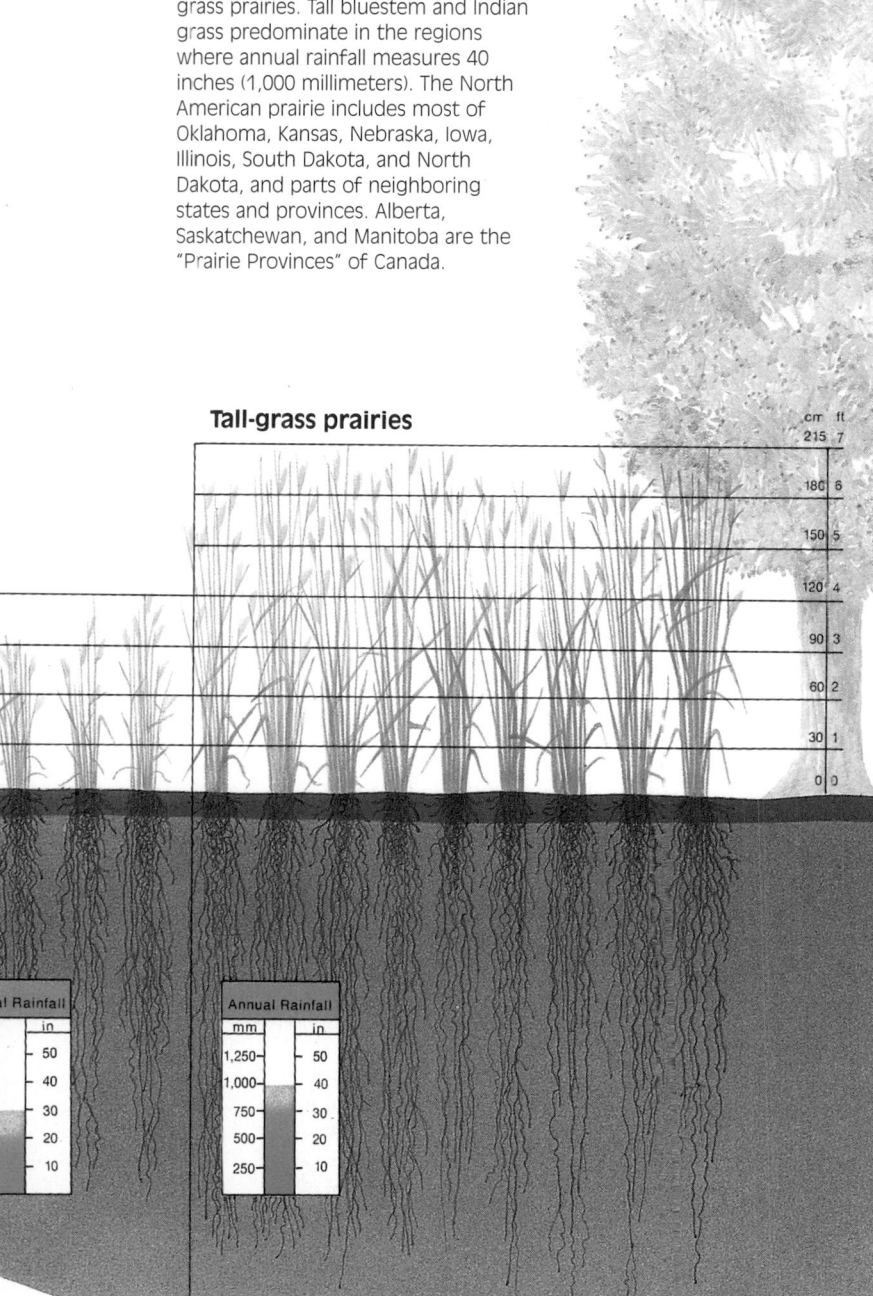

cm	ft
215	7
180	6
150	5
120	4
90	3
60	2
30	1
0	0

Annual Rainfall

mm	in
50	50
00	40
50	30
00	20
50	10

Annual Rainfall

mm	in
1,250	50
1,000	40
750	30
500	20
250	10

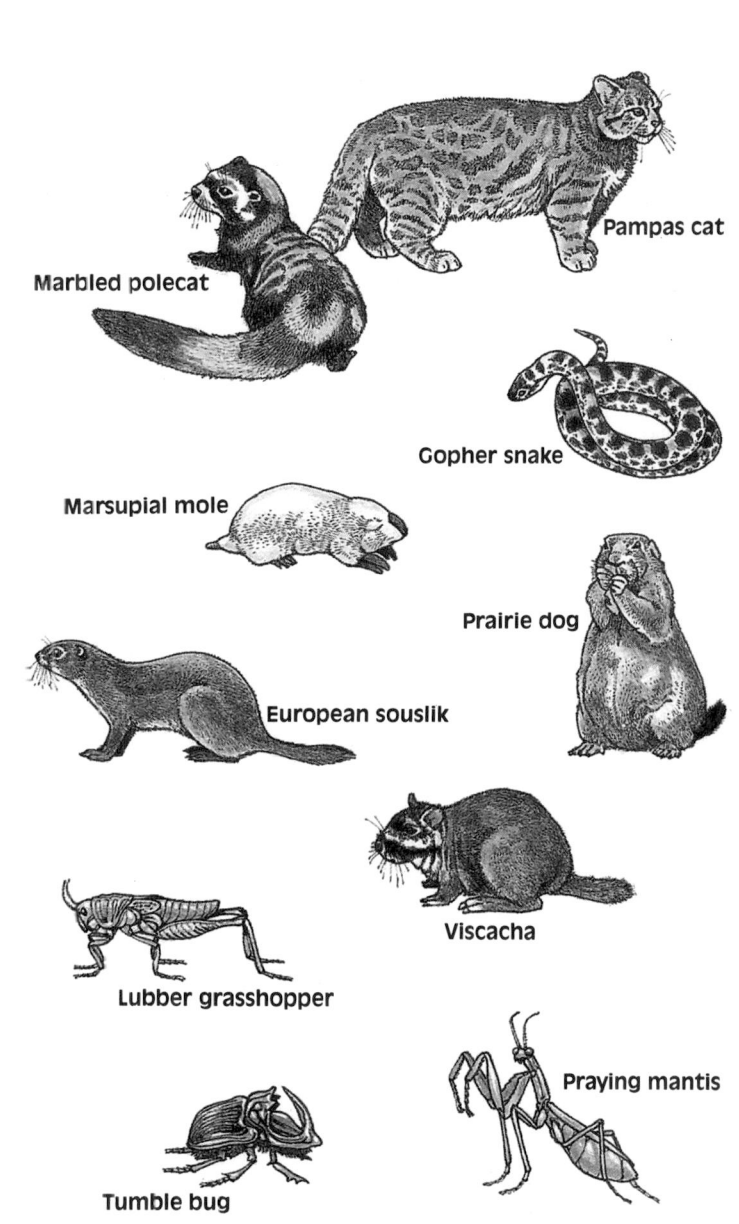

Marbled polecat

Pampas cat

Gopher snake

Marsupial mole

Prairie dog

European souslik

Viscacha

Lubber grasshopper

Tumble bug

Praying mantis

Midlatitude Forests

The earth's midlatitude regions lie between the polar circles and the tropics. Here, the seasonal climate ranges from warm summers to cold winters and, in some places, offers distinct dry and rainy seasons.

Deciduous trees, those with broad leaves that are shed annually, grow best in midlatitude regions where it is warm and moist at least four to five months a year. They are the main trees of most midlatitude forests, but many kinds of needle-leaved or broad-leaved evergreens also thrive in such a climate.

Midlatitude forests once covered eastern North America, western Europe, and eastern Asia. Changes in climate, together with activities such as forestry and farming, have reduced these forests to small areas.

Ground water generally freezes in midlatitude regions during winter. Thus, deciduous trees cannot draw up water into their leaves, and the leaves cannot tolerate freezing. This is why trees shed their leaves in autumn and stand bare during winter. However, evergreens can hold water in their needles throughout wintertime. This is how they can remain green all year.

In spring, when the ground begins to thaw, small flowers of the forest floor are first to bloom. Buds soon appear on trees and bushes and burst into pastel-colored flowers and tiny, pale-green leaves. Hibernating creatures stir. Birds return from the warm lands where they spent the winter. Insect and spider eggs, produced in autumn, now hatch by the millions.

Summer days are long and filled with sunshine and frequent rain. During this season, the tree leaves grow and become dark green with the substance called chlorophyll. Leaves are a tree's foodmakers. Using sunlight for power, their chlorophyll turns water absorbed by the roots and carbon dioxide from the air into sugars.

To get at this food in the leaves, leaf-eating insects, such as aphids, grasshoppers, and caterpillars, swarm among the upper branches of the trees. Many predatory insects and spiders live there too, preying on the leaf-eaters. And such a plentiful supply of insects and spiders attracts a variety of insect-eating birds.

The tops of the taller deciduous trees form the roof, or canopy, of the forest. The canopy is the home of insects, spiders, songbirds, squirrels, and nocturnal flying squirrels. Beneath the canopy is a second "layer" of trees called the understory. Some young trees in this layer must grow into the sunlight or they will die. Others are low-growing trees that do not need as much sunlight.

Beneath the understory is a layer of shrubs. These shrubs produce berries and seeds that are a source of food for mice and chipmunks. Under the bushes, upon the forest floor, are low-growing flowering plants, ferns, and mosses, which do not need much sunlight to make their food. Mushrooms also grow there. They need little sunlight, for they take their food from the rotting, decaying things on which they grow. Grouse, woodcocks, and pheasants feed on this vegetation. Deer also browse on the forest floor, and insects swarm there and are hunted by mice, frogs, and toads. They in turn are preyed upon by snakes, foxes, and raccoons.

In late summer, deciduous trees begin to prepare for winter. A layer of corklike substance grows where each leaf stem is attached to the branch. No more water can reach the leaves. Their green color fades and their true color, generally yellow or orange, is seen. After chlorophyll breaks down, red or purple pigments form in a dying leaf.

With no water, the leaves die, turn brown, and wither. Autumn wind and rains tear them loose to swirl to the ground. There, they become food for mushrooms, other fungi, and tiny animals. These will help turn the leaves into the soil of the forest floor. The seasonal cycle is now complete, and winter is approaching.

Seasonal climate is an important feature of midlatitude forests. Deciduous trees, which lose their leaves each autumn, flourish in such an environment.

Mushrooms get their nourishment from dead matter, such as decaying bark.

A paper wasp makes its nest from chewed-up wood.

A flying squirrel can spread its legs and glide through the air from tree to tree.

Equator

Midlatitude Forests

Midlatitude forests provide food and shelter for many animals and for a variety of plants.

Hazel mouse

American black bear

Acorn woodpecker

European woodcock

Stag beetle

Bluebell

Hepatica

Subarctic Cold Lands

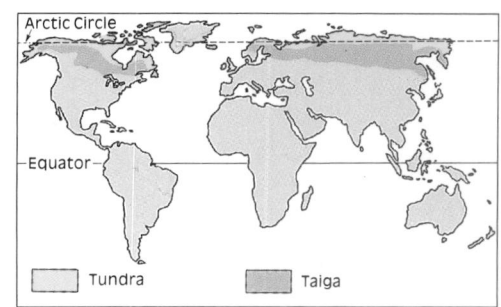

The transitional area between tundra and taiga is marked by shrubs, grasses, and the shoots of deciduous trees.

The dry, treeless, subarctic cold lands that lie near the Arctic Ocean are called arctic tundras. They include the northern parts of North America, Europe, and Asia. For three to four months a year, the sky over arctic tundras is dark both day and night. Beneath the darkened sky, snow blankets the frozen ground.

Change occurs on the tundra in spring, when the northern part of the earth is tilted toward the sun. This causes the tundra sky to lighten. Sunlight melts the snow and thaws the land's upper layer of soil, which is about 1-foot (30 centimeters) deep. Below this layer is the perpetually frozen ground known as permafrost.

Plants that have been dormant through the months of darkness abruptly burst into bloom in springtime. These plants are tough, low-growing, and ground-hugging. They include mosses, lichens, grasses, and small flowering plants such as bilberries and bearberries. The very cold winters with strong winds prevent plants from growing higher than the depth of the protective snow. Therefore, no full-size trees can survive on the tundra. Some willow shrubs, however, grow 3 to 10 feet (91 to 305 centimeters) high on slopes and valleys where winter snows are deep.

In spring and summer, the many flowering plants of the tundra turn the region into a sea of color. Arctic foxes, ermines, and snowy owls prey on the little mouselike lemming and arctic hare that search the tundra for tender leaves. Birds such as the willow ptarmigan nest and raise their young among the flowers. Mosquitoes, midges, and black flies are everywhere. Polar bears may leave the icepack and come on land to find food. Caribou, reindeer, and musk oxen browse on plants and are hunted by packs of wolves.

When earth tilts away from the sun, winter returns suddenly. In late August or early September, the ground freezes and snow begins to fall. Most birds and animals migrate southward during winter, but some live year-round on the tundra. Lemmings spend the winter in nests of leaves and feed on the green shoots of flowering plants and mosses. In winter, herds of shaggy musk oxen use their broad hoofs to search for grasses buried beneath the snow in patches.

The tundra regions spread southward for hundreds of miles until they reach regions that are slightly warmer. There, where the ground thaws more in summer, short trees

grow far apart from one another. A little farther south, taller trees grow closer and closer together until they form vast, thick stretches of forest. This is the northern boreal forest, or taiga. It covers much of Canada and the northern parts of the Scandinavian countries and Russia.

The trees of the taiga are mainly needle-leaf evergreens, such as the white spruce. A few species of hardy deciduous trees, among them birches, are also present. Mosses, lichens, and very few flowering plants cover the forest floor.

Throughout winter, trees in the taiga stand heaped with snow. Elk, caribou, reindeer, and moose graze through the forests. As they go, they eat shrubs, grasses, and shoots of deciduous trees. Snowshoe hare, squirrels, and ptarmigan are abundant and preyed on by lynxes, martins, and wolves. Bears spend their winters in the taiga in long periods of sleep or in complete hibernation.

In spring, the snow melts, soaking into the ground. This provides the taiga with a new supply of water for all the trees. Mosquitoes and horseflies swarm. Birds arrive. Hibernating animals become active. Like the tundra, the taiga teems with life through the short, warm summer.

With the spring thaws, bears emerge from their winter hibernation to forage along the banks of the McNeil River in Alaska.

Musk ox

Brant goose

Raven

Seasonal changes have tremendous effect on the animals of subarctic cold lands. Rock ptarmigans and arctic hares turn white in winter for warmth and camouflage. In spring, brant geese and 30 other species of birds migrate to the Arctic. Capercaillies move southward from the taiga each summer.

Wolf

Snowy owl

Arctic hare

Capercaillie

Brown lemming

Rock ptarmigan

Flowers, mosses, and lichens carpet the tundra when springtime relieves the long months of darkness. To survive, they must reproduce before the first snows come in September.

Polar Caps

The polar caps are regions of permanent ice and snow located at earth's North and South Poles. These regions are the parts of the planet that receive the least sunlight. During four months of winter, no sunlight touches either pole. In summer, much of the continuous light that does reach the poles is reflected into space by the glare of snow.

The two polar caps are very different from one another. The North Pole lies on a frozen sea, the Arctic Ocean. The South Pole sits upon the continent of Antarctica, which is covered by a layer of ice and snow at least a mile (1.6 kilometers) deep. The ice at the North Pole is frozen salty seawater, but the ice covering Antarctica is frozen fresh water—the largest concentration of fresh water in the world.

These frozen regions are deserts for plants. Animal life, however, does exist in the seas at both polar caps. Many kinds of fish, including the 8- to 14-foot (2.4 to 4.2-meter) long polar shark, live beneath the ice in the Arctic Ocean waters. Seals and walruses are also at home in the sea, and it is there that they find their food. Seals eat mainly fish, while walruses dive to the ocean floor to scoop up clams and other shellfish. Even in the coldest waters, these large mammals are kept warm by their

extremely thick skin and layer of blubber. Of course, seals and walruses are air breathers. Thus, they must find or make openings in the ice so they can put their noses above water and breathe.

At the north polar cap, polar bears roam over the ice hunting for seals and other animals. These bears are excellent swimmers, and their thick, dense fur keeps them warm in freezing water. The fur's white color helps the animals blend in with the environment. Thus camouflaged, a bear can wait on ice near a seal's breathing hole and seize an unsuspecting victim when it comes up for air.

Several kinds of whales also make the Arctic Ocean their home. Such whales include the beluga, or white whale, and the narwhal. The narwhal is a small whale that has a maximum length of 18 feet (5.4 meters). The male narwhal has a long, spiral tusk that juts out from its upper jaw. The much larger bowhead whale is also an inhabitant of the Arctic Ocean.

The sea around Antarctica is the summer home of several species of whales that feed on small, shrimplike creatures called krill. These include blue, fin, humpback, and right whales. Southern bottlenose and southern fourtooth whales, which feed on squid and fish, are also Antarctic residents. Killer whales swim all year around in the cold Antarctic waters, preying on penguins, seals, and smaller whales in addition to fish and

squid. A number of seal species, including krill-eating Antarctic fur seals and crabeater seals, aggressive leopard seals, and massive southern elephant seals, nest on the Antarctic coastline or on nearby islands.

The main creature found on land at the southern pole cap is the penguin, a flightless bird that walks with a clumsy waddle. One species of penguin, the emperor penguin, lays eggs and rears its young on the snow-covered slopes of Antarctica during winter. The birds' feathers and layers of fat keep them warm. To keep their eggs warm, the male birds hold them on their feet and cover them with their bellies.

Although they are at home on land for several months of the year, penguins are primarily sea creatures. Emperor penguins are superb swimmers that live on fish, and the birds spend months at a time in cold, polar waters.

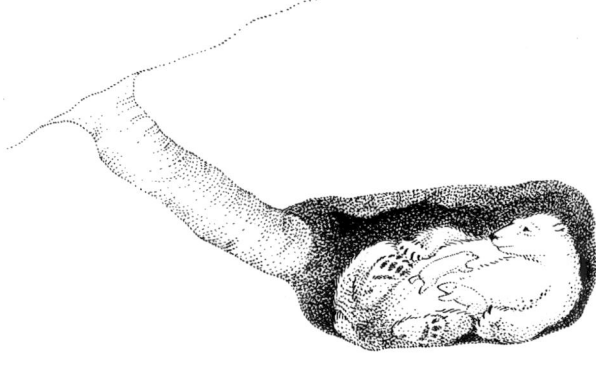

Polar bears live in underground shelters called dens during the colder months. Bears usually dig their dens in deep snowbanks.

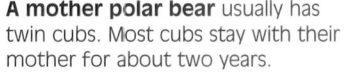

A mother polar bear usually has twin cubs. Most cubs stay with their mother for about two years.

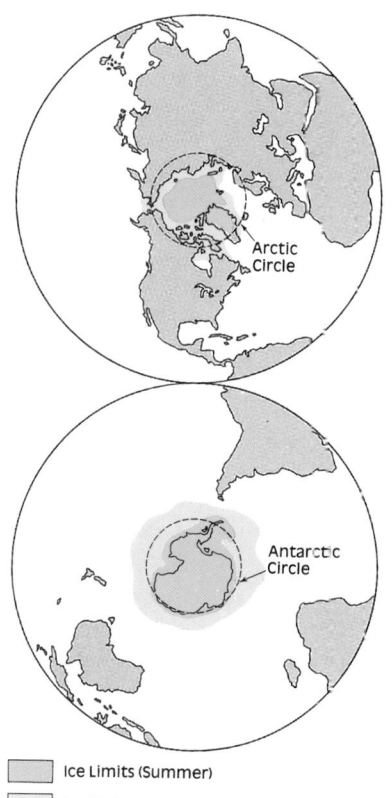

Arctic
Circle

Antarctic
Circle

Ice Limits (Summer)
Ice Limits (Winter)

Penguins have adapted to Antarctic conditions with short, dense feathers, thick layers of fat, webbed feet, and wings that serve as flippers.

The Antarctic landscape is made up of mountains, glaciers, and dry valleys, like those shown at the left. A dry valley is an ice-free rocky area carved out by a glacier that has retreated. Wind sweeps away most of the snow that falls in dry valleys.

Blue whales and crabeater seals eat millions of tons of krill, the Antarctic's chief food source. Leopard seals and killer whales prey on penguins.

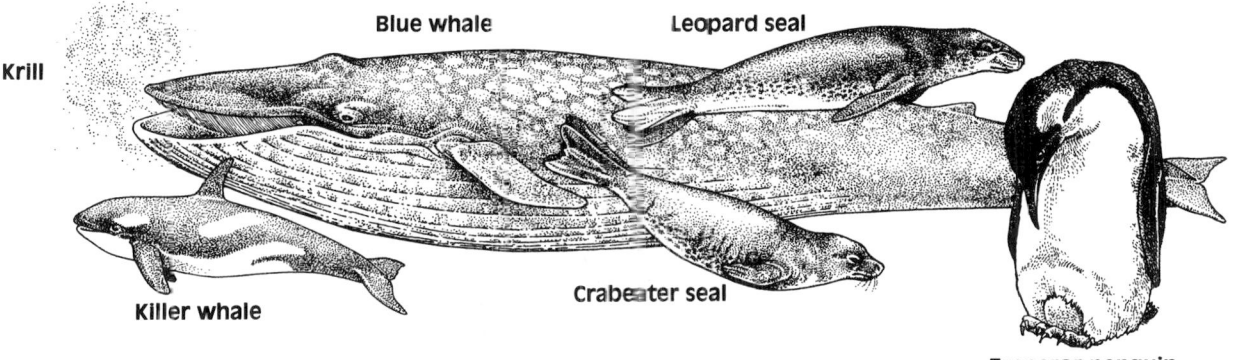

Krill

Blue whale

Leopard seal

Killer whale

Crabeater seal

Emperor penguin

World Time Zones

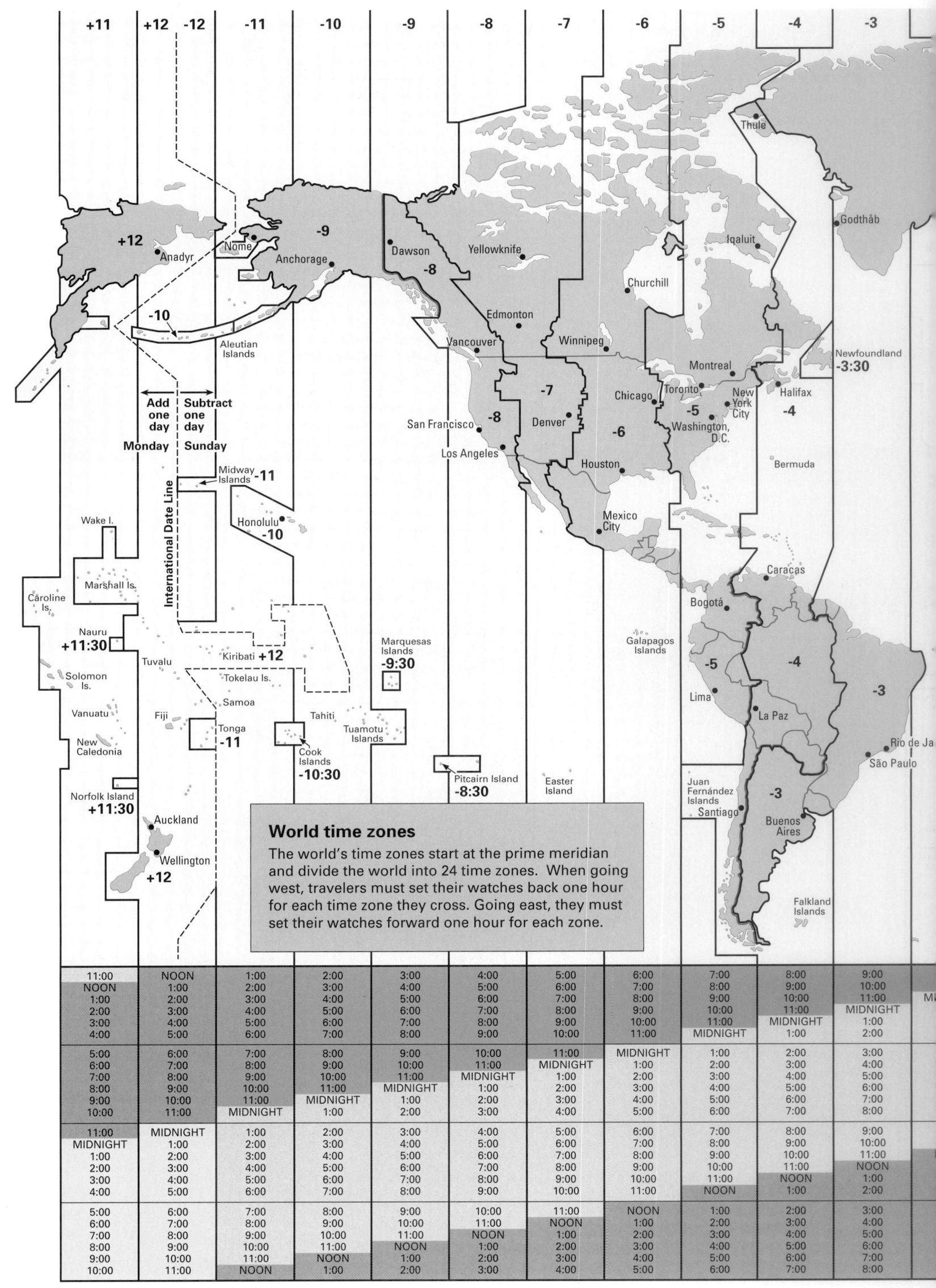

World time zones

The world's time zones start at the prime meridian and divide the world into 24 time zones. When going west, travelers must set their watches back one hour for each time zone they cross. Going east, they must set their watches forward one hour for each zone.

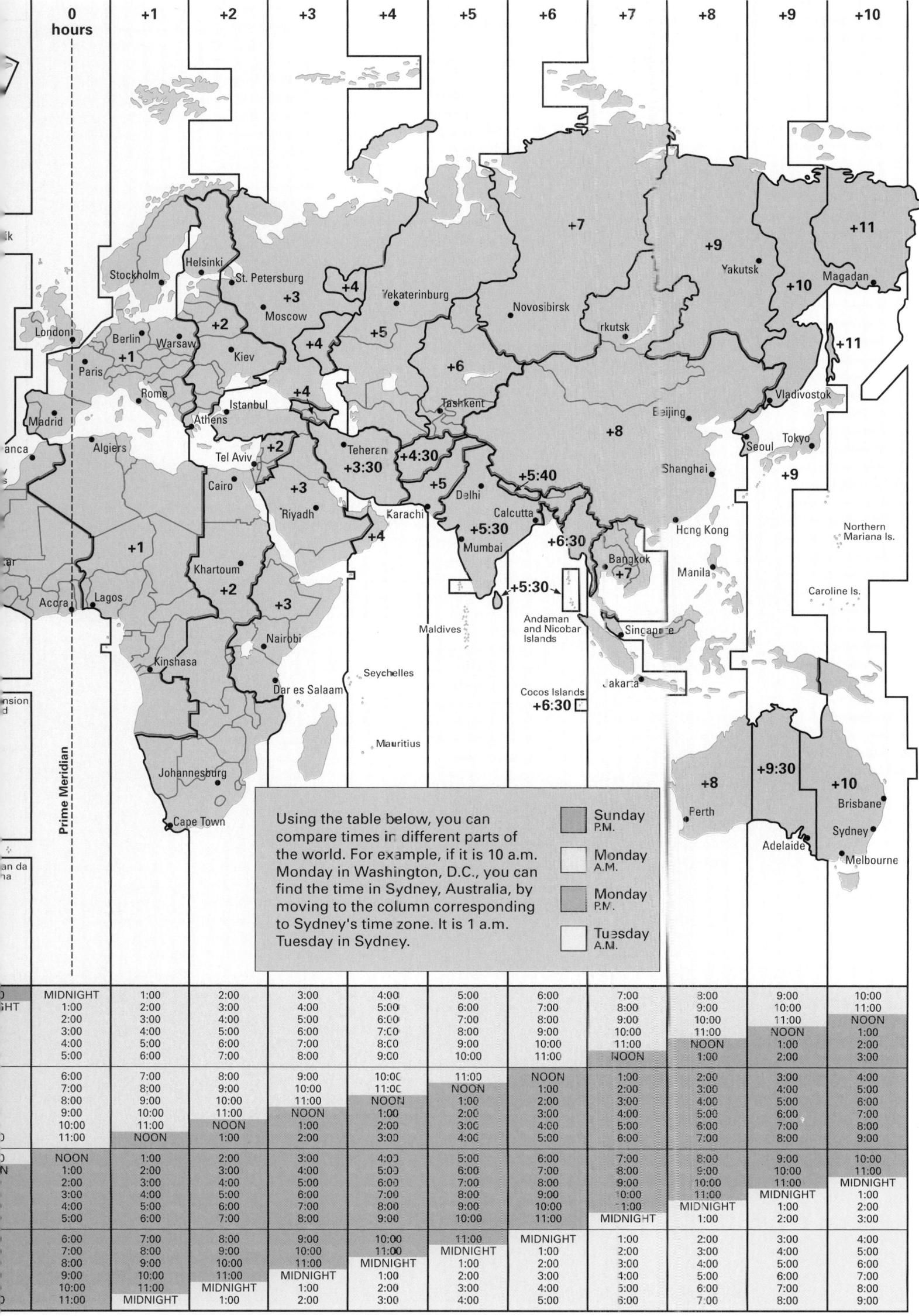

Using the table below, you can compare times in different parts of the world. For example, if it is 10 a.m. Monday in Washington, D.C., you can find the time in Sydney, Australia, by moving to the column corresponding to Sydney's time zone. It is 1 a.m. Tuesday in Sydney.

- Sunday P.M.
- Monday A.M.
- Monday P.M.
- Tuesday A.M.

0 hours	+1	+2	+3	+4	+5	+6	+7	+8	+9	+10
MIDNIGHT	1:00	2:00	3:00	4:00	5:00	6:00	7:00	8:00	9:00	10:00
1:00	2:00	3:00	4:00	5:00	6:00	7:00	8:00	9:00	10:00	11:00
2:00	3:00	4:00	5:00	6:00	7:00	8:00	9:00	10:00	11:00	NOON
3:00	4:00	5:00	6:00	7:00	8:00	9:00	10:00	11:00	NOON	1:00
4:00	5:00	6:00	7:00	8:00	9:00	10:00	11:00	NOON	1:00	2:00
5:00	6:00	7:00	8:00	9:00	10:00	11:00	NOON	1:00	2:00	3:00
6:00	7:00	8:00	9:00	10:00	11:00	NOON	1:00	2:00	3:00	4:00
7:00	8:00	9:00	10:00	11:00	NOON	1:00	2:00	3:00	4:00	5:00
8:00	9:00	10:00	11:00	NOON	1:00	2:00	3:00	4:00	5:00	6:00
9:00	10:00	11:00	NOON	1:00	2:00	3:00	4:00	5:00	6:00	7:00
10:00	11:00	NOON	1:00	2:00	3:00	4:00	5:00	6:00	7:00	8:00
11:00	NOON	1:00	2:00	3:00	4:00	5:00	6:00	7:00	8:00	9:00
NOON	1:00	2:00	3:00	4:00	5:00	6:00	7:00	8:00	9:00	10:00
1:00	2:00	3:00	4:00	5:00	6:00	7:00	8:00	9:00	10:00	11:00
2:00	3:00	4:00	5:00	6:00	7:00	8:00	9:00	10:00	11:00	MIDNIGHT
3:00	4:00	5:00	6:00	7:00	8:00	9:00	10:00	11:00	MIDNIGHT	1:00
4:00	5:00	6:00	7:00	8:00	9:00	10:00	11:00	MIDNIGHT	1:00	2:00
5:00	6:00	7:00	8:00	9:00	10:00	11:00	MIDNIGHT	1:00	2:00	3:00
6:00	7:00	8:00	9:00	10:00	11:00	MIDNIGHT	1:00	2:00	3:00	4:00
7:00	8:00	9:00	10:00	11:00	MIDNIGHT	1:00	2:00	3:00	4:00	5:00
8:00	9:00	10:00	11:00	MIDNIGHT	1:00	2:00	3:00	4:00	5:00	6:00
9:00	10:00	11:00	MIDNIGHT	1:00	2:00	3:00	4:00	5:00	6:00	7:00
10:00	11:00	MIDNIGHT	1:00	2:00	3:00	4:00	5:00	6:00	7:00	8:00
11:00	MIDNIGHT	1:00	2:00	3:00	4:00	5:00	6:00	7:00	8:00	9:00

Using the Atlas

WHAT IS AN ATLAS?

A set of maps bound together is called an atlas. Abraham Ortelius' *Theatrum orbis terrarum*, published in 1570, is considered to be the first modern "atlas," although it was not referred to as such for almost 20 years. In 1589, Gerardus Mercator (figure 1) coined the term when he named his collection of maps after Atlas, the mythological Titan who carried Earth on his shoulders as punishment for warring against Zeus. Since then, the definition of *atlas* has been expanded, and atlases often include additional geographic information in diagrams, tables, and text.

Figure 1

LATITUDE AND LONGITUDE

The terms *latitude* and *longitude* refer to the grid of horizontal and vertical lines found on most maps and globes. Any point on Earth can be located by its precise latitude and longitude coordinates.

The imaginary horizontal line that circles Earth halfway between the North and South poles is called the equator; it represents 0° latitude and lies 90° from either pole. The other lines of latitude, or parallels, measure distances north or south from the equator (figure 2). The imaginary vertical line that measures 0° longitude runs through the Greenwich Observatory in the United Kingdom, and is called the Prime Meridian. The other lines of longitude, or meridians, measure distances east or west from the prime meridian (figure 3), up to a maximum of 180°. Lines of latitude and longitude cross each other, forming a grid (figure 4).

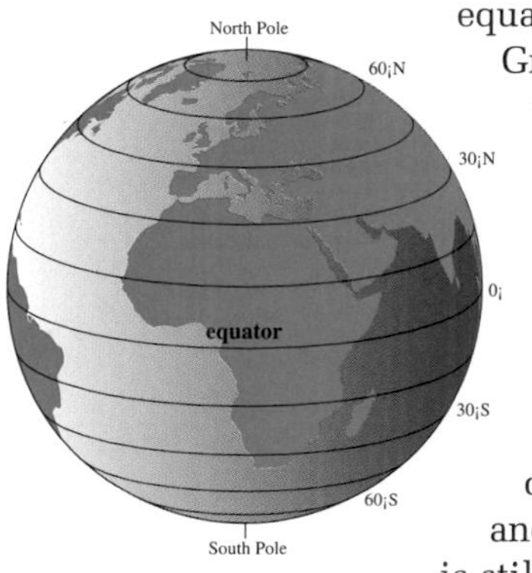

Figure 2

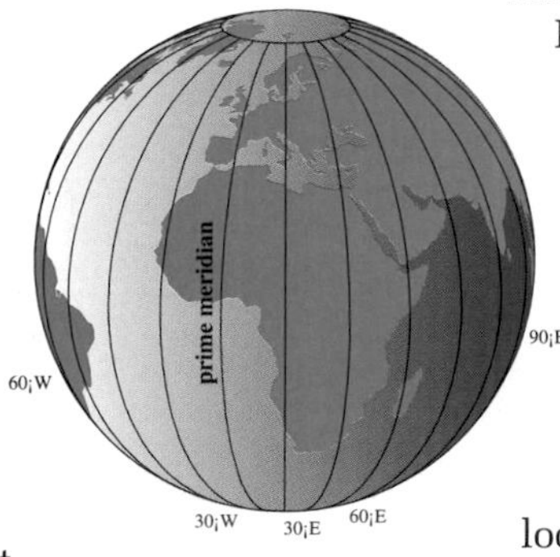

Figure 3

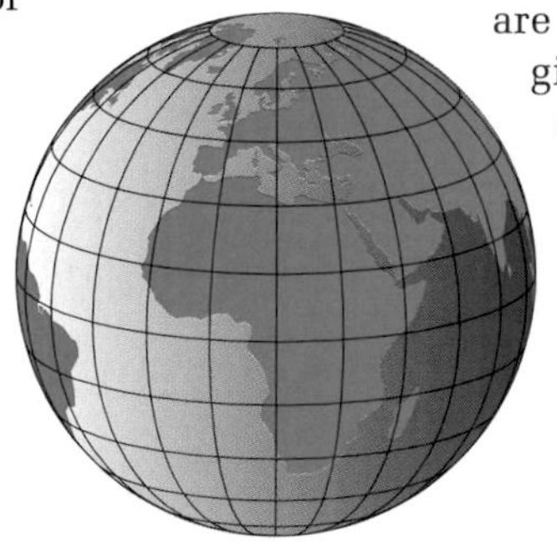

Figure 4

MAP PROJECTIONS

Every cartographer is faced with the problem of transforming the curved surface of Earth onto a flat plane with a minimum of distortion. The systematic transformation of locations on Earth (a spherical surface) to locations on a map (a flat surface) is called projection.

It is not possible to represent on a flat map the spatial relationships of angle, distance, direction, and area that only a globe can show faithfully. As a result, projections inevitably involve some distortion. On large-scale maps representing a few square miles, the distortion is generally negligible. But on maps depicting large countries, continents, or the entire world, the amount of distortion can be significant. On maps that use the Mercator Projection (figure 5), for example, distortion increases with distance from the equator. Thus the island of Greenland appears larger than the entire continent of South America, although South America is in fact nine times larger.

In contrast, the Robinson Projection (figure 6) renders the world's major land areas in generally correct proportion to one another, although distortion is still apparent in areas such as Antarctica, which is actually smaller than all of the continents except Europe and Australia.

There are an infinite number of possible map projections, all of which distort one or more of the characteristics of the globe in varying degrees. The projection that a cartographer chooses depends on the size and location of the area being projected and the purpose of the map. In this atlas, most of the maps are drawn on projections that give a consistent or only slightly distorted area scale, good land and ocean shape, parallels that are parallel, and as consistent a linear scale as possible throughout the projection.

Figure 5

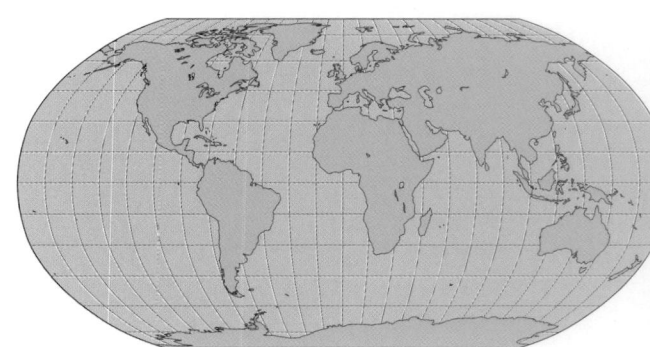

Figure 6

MAP SCALE

The scale of a map is the relationship between distances or areas shown on the map and the corresponding distances or areas on Earth's surface. Large-scale maps show relatively small areas in greater detail than do small-scale maps, such as those of individual continents or of the world.

There are three different ways to express scale. Most often scale is given as a fraction, such as 1:10,000,000, which means that the ratio of distances on the map to actual distances on Earth is 1 to 10,000,000. Scale can also be expressed as a phrase, such as "One inch represents approximately ten million miles." Finally, scale can be illustrated via a bar scale on which various distances are labeled (figure 7). Any of these three scale expressions can be used to calculate distances on a map.

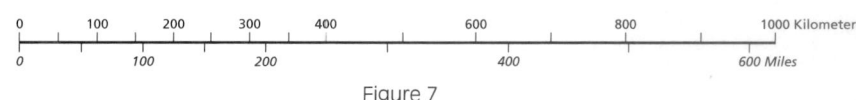

Figure 7

MEASURING DISTANCES

Using a bar scale, it is possible to calculate the distance between any two points on a map. To find the approximate distance between São Paulo and Rio de Janeiro, Brazil, for example, follow these steps:

1) Lay a piece of paper on the right-hand page of the "Eastern Brazil" map found on pages 88-89, lining up its edge with the city dots for São Paulo and Rio de Janeiro. Make a mark on the paper next to each dot (figure 8).

2) Place the paper along the scale bar found below the map, and position the first mark at 0. The second mark falls between the 200-mile (300-kilometer) tick and the 300-mile (400-kilometer) tick, indicating that the distance separating the two cities is approximately 225 miles (350 kilometers) (figure 9).

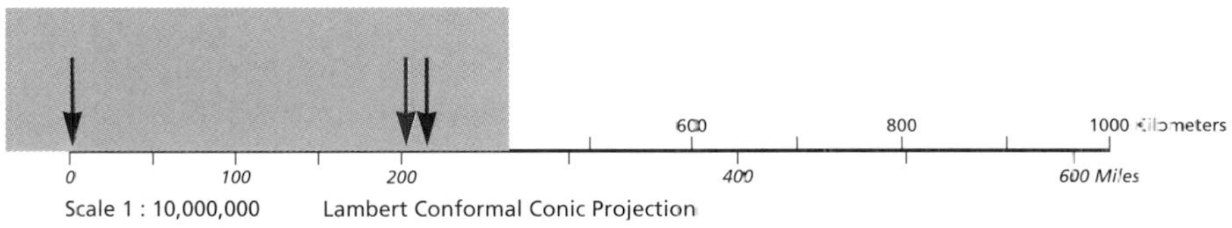

Figure 8

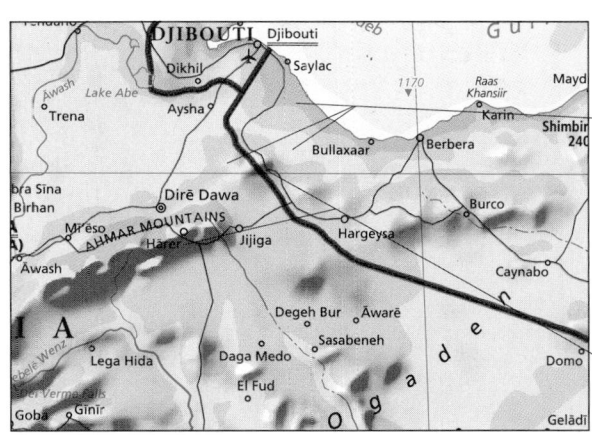

Figure 9

Scale 1 : 10,000,000   Lambert Conformal Conic Projection

3) To confirm this measurement in miles, make a third pencil mark (shown in red in figure 9) at the 200-mile tick. Slide the paper to the left so that this mark lines up with 0. The Rio de Janeiro mark now falls about halfway between the 0 tick and the 50-mile tick. Thus, São Paulo and Rio de Janeiro are indeed approximately 225 (200 + 25) miles apart.

USING THE INDEX TO FIND PLACES

One of the most important purposes of an atlas is to help the reader locate cities, towns, and geographic features, such as rivers, lakes, and mountains. This atlas uses a "bingo key" indexing system. In the index, found on pages I•1 through I•64, every entry is assigned an alpha-numeric code that consists of a letter and a number. This code relates to the red letters and numbers that run along the perimeter of each map. To locate places or features, follow the steps outlined in this example for the city of Bratsk, Russia.

1) Look up Bratsk in the index. The entry (figure 10) contains the following information: the place name (Bratsk), the name of the country (Russia) in which Bratsk is located, the map reference key

Brassey, Banjaran, mts.,		
Malay	A10	50
Brass Islands, is., V.I.U.S.	o7	104 b
Brasstown Bald, mtn., Ga.,		
U.S.	B2	116
Bratca, Rom.	C9	26
Bratislava, Slov.	H13	16
Bratislava, state, Slov.	H13	16
Bratsk, Russia	C18	32
Bratskoe vodohranilisce,		
res., Russia	C18	32

Figure 10

(C18) that corresponds to Bratsk's location on the map, and the page number (32) of the map on which Bratsk can be found.

2) Turn to the Northwestern Asia map on pages 32-33. Look along either the left- or right-hand margin for the red letter "C"—the letter code given for Bratsk. The "C" denotes a band that arcs horizontally across the map, between the grid lines representing 55° and 60° north latitude. Then, look along either the top or bottom margin for the red number "18"—the numerical part of the code given for Bratsk. The "18" denotes a widening vertical band, between the grid lines representing 100° and 105° east longitude, which angles from the top center of the map to right-hand edge.

3) Using your finger, follow the horizontal "C" band and the vertical "18" band to the area where they overlap (figure 11). Bratsk lies within this overlap area.

Figure 11

PHYSICAL MAPS AND POLITICAL MAPS

Most of the maps in *The World Book Atlas* are physical maps, like the one shown in figure 12, emphasizing terrain, landforms, and elevation. Political maps, as in figure 13, emphasize countries and other political units over topography. The atlas includes political maps of the world and each of the continents except Antarctica.

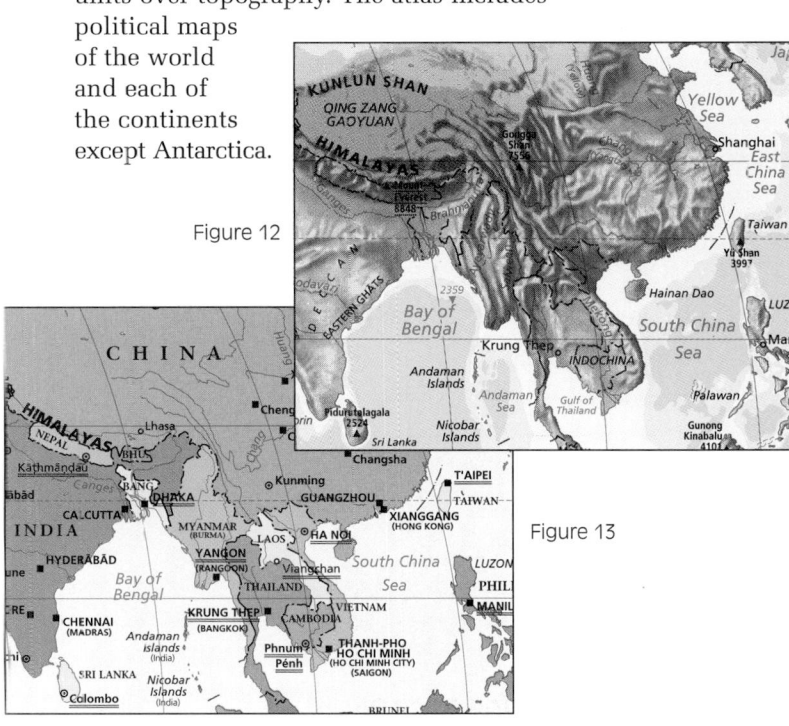

Figure 12

Figure 13

HOW MAPS SHOW TOPOGRAPHY

The physical maps in this atlas use two techniques to depict Earth's topography. Variations in elevation are shown through a series of colors called hypsometric tints. Areas below sea level appear as a dark green; as the elevation rises, the tints move successively through lighter green, yellow, and orange. Similarly, variations in ocean depth are represented by bathymetric tints. The shallowest areas appear as light blue; darker tints of blue indicate greater depths. The hypsometric/ bathymetric scale that accompanies each map identifies, in feet and meters, all of the elevation and depth categories that appear on the map.

Principal landforms, such as mountain ranges and valleys, are rendered in shades of gray, a technique known as shaded relief. The combination of hypsometric tints and shaded relief provides the map reader with a three-dimensional picture of Earth's surface (figure 14).

Hypsometric tints

Shaded relief

Figure 14

INDEX MAP AND LEGEND

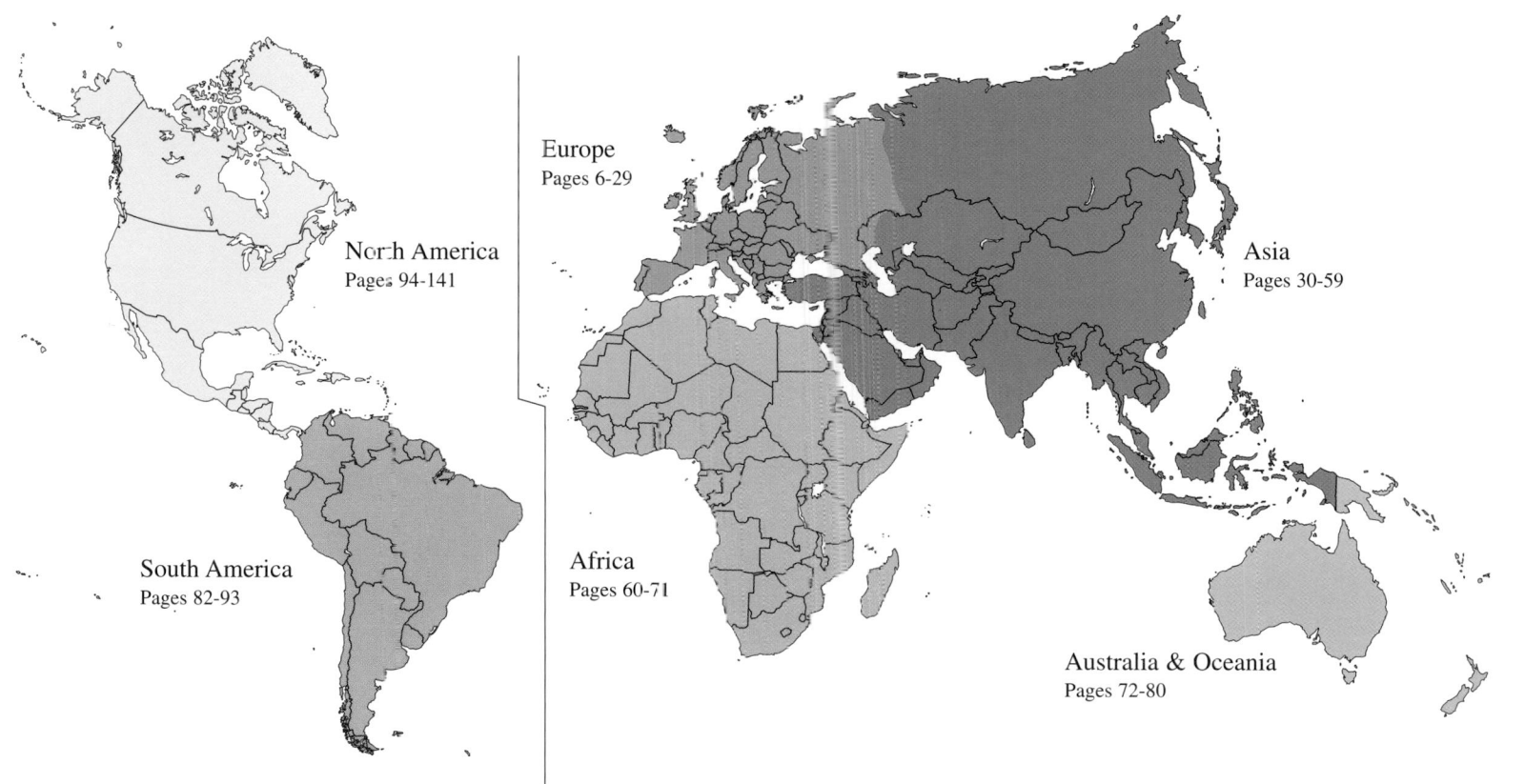

Europe
Pages 6-29

North America
Pages 94-141

Asia
Pages 30-59

South America
Pages 82-93

Africa
Pages 60-71

Australia & Oceania
Pages 72-80

Hydrographic Features

Perennial river

Seasonal river

 Dam

 Falls

 Aqueduct

Lake, reservoir

Seasonal lake

Salt lake

Seasonal salt lake

Dry lake

 Lake surface elevation

 Swamp, marsh

Reef

Glacier/ice sheet

Topographic Features

764 Depth of water

2278 Elevation above sea level

1700 Elevation below sea level

Mountain pass

Huo Shan 1774 Mountain peak/elevation

The highest elevation on each continent is underlined.

The highest elevation in each country is shown in boldface.

Transportation Features

Motorway/special highway

Major road

Other road

Trail

Major railway

Other railway

Navigable canal

Tunnel

Ferry

✈ International airport

✈ Other airport

Political Features

International boundaries (First-order political unit)

 Demarcated

 Disputed (de facto)

 Disputed (de jure)

 Indefinite/undefined

 Demarcation line

Internal boundaries

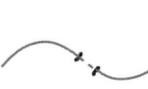 State/province

 Third-order (counties, oblasts, etc.)

NORMANDIE Cultural/historic region

(Denmark) Administering country

Cities and Towns

The size of symbol and type indicates the relative importance of the locality.

■ **LONDON**

▣ **CHICAGO**

◉ **Milwaukee**

◎ Tacna

⊙ Iquitos

○ Old Crow

∘ Mettawa

Urban area

Capitals

MEXICO CITY Bonn — Country, dependency

RIO DE JANEIRO Perth — State, province

MANCHESTER Chester — County

Cultural Features

or ▪ National park, reservation

▪ Point of interest

Wall

∴ Ruins

Military installation

● Polar research station

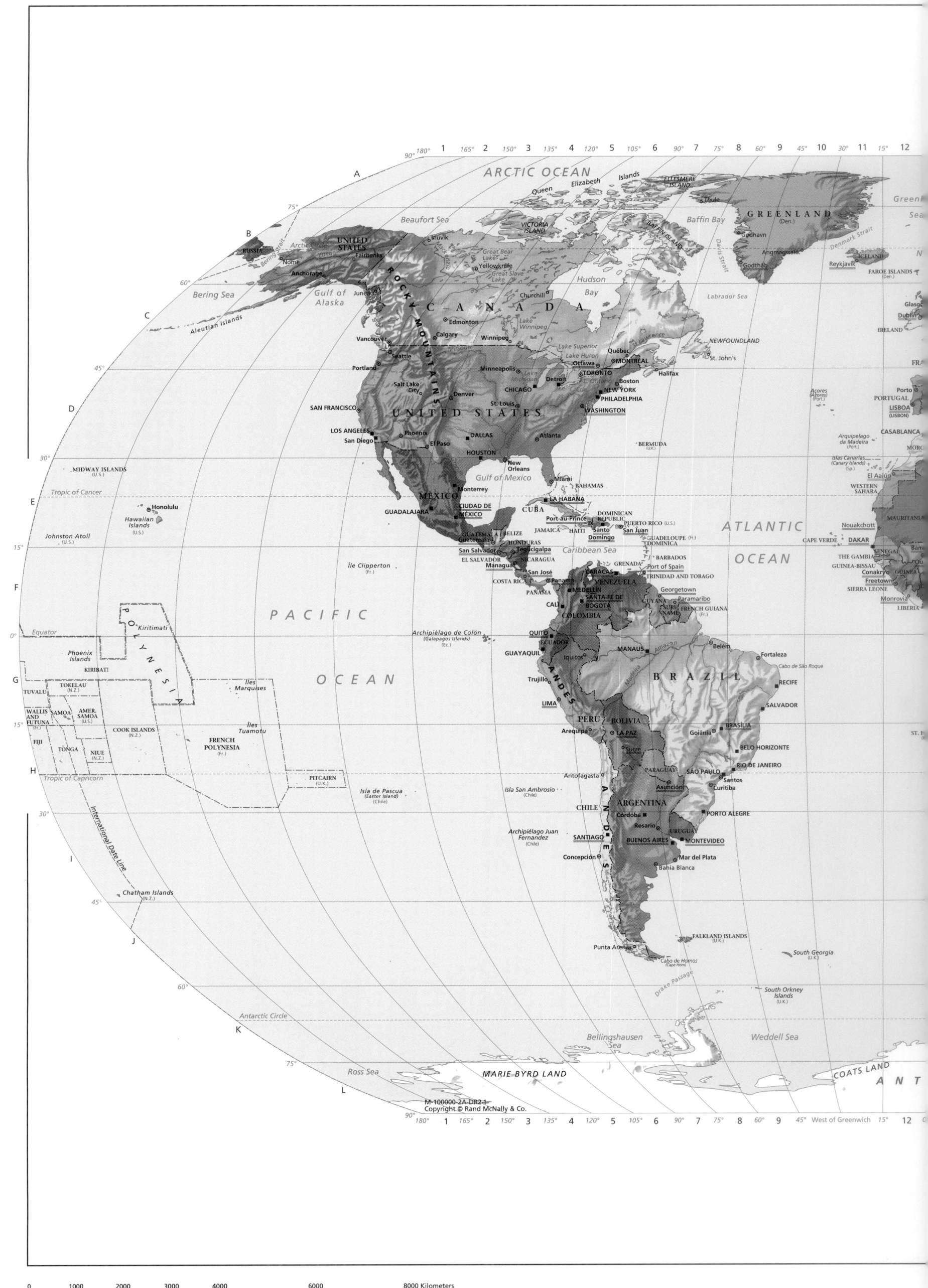

ARCTIC OCEAN

GREENLAND
(Den.)

Beaufort Sea

Baffin Bay

Bering Sea

UNITED STATES

RUSSIA

Nome

Anchorage

Gulf of
Alaska

Aleutian Islands

Juneau

ROCKY MOUNTAINS

CANADA

Inuvik

Yellowknife
Great Bear Lake
Great Slave Lake

Edmonton

Calgary

Vancouver
Seattle

Winnipeg
Lake Winnipeg

Hudson
Bay

Churchill

Labrador Sea

NEWFOUNDLAND

ICELAND

Reykjavik

FAROE ISLANDS
(Den.)

IRELAND

Dublin

Portland

Salt Lake
City

Minneapolis
Lake Superior
Lake Huron
Lake Michigan

Ottawa
Québec
MONTRÉAL
St. Lawrence

St. John's

Halifax

SAN FRANCISCO

UNITED STATES

Denver

St. Louis

CHICAGO
Detroit
Lake Erie
Lake Ontario
TORONTO

Boston
NEW YORK
PHILADELPHIA
WASHINGTON

PORTUGAL
LISBOA
(LISBON)

CASABLANCA

LOS ANGELES
San Diego

Phoenix

El Paso

DALLAS

HOUSTON

Atlanta

BERMUDA
(U.K.)

Açores
(Azores)
(Port.)

Porto

Arquipélago
da Madeira
(Port.)

MIDWAY ISLANDS
(U.S.)

Tropic of Cancer

Honolulu

Hawaiian
Islands
(U.S.)

Johnston Atoll
(U.S.)

MEXICO

New
Orleans

Monterrey

GUADALAJARA

Gulf of Mexico

Miami

BAHAMAS

CIUDAD DE
MÉXICO

CUBA
LA HABANA

Islas Canarias
(Canary Islands)
(Sp.)

El Aaiún

WESTERN
SAHARA

MOR

ATLANTIC

OCEAN

Nouakchott

MAURITANIA

Île Clipperton
(Fr.)

GUATEMALA BELIZE
Guatemala
SAN SALVADOR HONDURAS
Tegucigalpa
EL SALVADOR NICARAGUA
Managua

San José
COSTA RICA
PANAMÁ
Panamá

JAMAICA

Port-au-Prince
HAITI

DOMINICAN
REPUBLIC
Santo
Domingo

PUERTO RICO (U.S.)
San Juan
GUADELOUPE (Fr.)
DOMINICA

Caribbean Sea

BARBADOS

GRENADA

TRINIDAD AND TOBAGO

CARACAS
VENEZUELA

CAPE VERDE DAKAR
SENEGAL
THE GAMBIA
GUINEA-BISSAU
Conakry
GUINEA Freetown
SIERRA LEONE
Monrovia
LIBERIA

PACIFIC

OCEAN

POLYNESIA

Kiritimati

Equator

Phoenix
Islands

KIRIBATI

Archipiélago de Colón
(Galapagos Islands)
(Ec.)

MEDELLÍN
CALI
COLOMBIA
SANTA FE DE
BOGOTÁ

QUITO
ECUADOR
GUAYAQUIL
Iquitos

Georgetown
GUYANA
Paramaribo
SURINAME
FRENCH GUIANA
(Fr.)

MANAUS
Amazon
Belém

BRAZIL

Fortaleza

Cabo de São Roque

RECIFE

TUVALU

TOKELAU
(N.Z.)

WALLIS
AND SAMOA
FUTUNA
(Fr.)
AMER.
SAMOA
(U.S.)

COOK ISLANDS
(N.Z.)

Îles
Marquises

Îles
Tuamotu

FRENCH
POLYNESIA
(Fr.)

Trujillo

LIMA

PERÚ

Arequipa

BOLIVIA
LA PAZ
Sucre

Goiânia

Madeira

SÃO PAULO

SALVADOR

BRASÍLIA

BELO HORIZONTE

RIO DE JANEIRO

FIJI

TONGA

NIUE
(N.Z.)

PITCAIRN
(U.K.)

Tropic of Capricorn

Isla de Pascua
(Easter Island)
(Chile)

Isla San Ambrosio
(Chile)

Antofagasta

PARAGUAY
Asunción

CHILE

ARGENTINA

ANDES

Córdoba

Santos
Curitiba

PORTO ALEGRE

URUGUAY

International Date Line

Chatham Islands
(N.Z.)

Archipiélago Juan
Fernández
(Chile)

SANTIAGO

Concepción

Rosario

BUENOS AIRES MONTEVIDEO
Mar del Plata
Bahía Blanca

FALKLAND ISLANDS
(U.K.)

South Georgia
(U.K.)

Antarctic Circle

Punta Arenas

Cabo de Hornos
(Cape Horn)

Drake Passage

South Orkney
Islands
(U.K.)

Ross Sea

MARIE BYRD LAND

Bellingshausen
Sea

Weddell Sea

COATS LAND

M-100000-2A-DR21
Copyright © Rand McNally & Co.

| 0 | 1000 | 2000 | 3000 | 4000 | | 6000 | | 8000 Kilometers |

| 0 | 500 | 1000 | 1500 | 2000 | | 3000 | | 4000 | | 5000 Miles |

Scale 1 : 80,000,000

30° 15 45° 16 60° 17 75° 18 90° 19 105° 20 120° 21 135° 22 150° 23 165° 24 ~80°

A

ARCTIC OCEAN

Zemlja Franca-Iosifa

Barents Sea

Novosibirskie ostrova

more Laptevyh

Novaja Zemlja

Karskoe more

Vostočno-Sibirskoe more

90°

B

75°

Hammerfest

Murmansk

Arhangel'sk

Vorkuta

Berka

Iiki

Arctic Circle

Prohotnoy Kameohe

SWEDEN

FINLAND

Helsinki

SANKT-PETERBURG (ST. PETERSBURG)

R U S S I A

Ob

Jakutsk

60°

Sea of Okhotsk

Bering Sea

C

Stockholm

ESTONI

LATVIA

LITH.

NIŽNIJ NOVGOROD

Perm'

Ekaterinburg

Krasnojarsk

Magadan

ostrov Sahalin

Petropavlovsk-Kamčatskij

Aleutian Is. (U.S.)

International Date Line

POLAND

BELARUS

MOSKVA (MOSCOW)

Samara

Čeljabinsk

Omsk

Novosibirsk

ALTAI

Irkutsk

Habarovsk

Kuril'skie ostrova

45°

D

ANY

WARSZAWA

CZECH REP.

WIEN

BUDAPEST

KYÏV

UKRAINE

Volgograd

KAZAKSTAN

Astana (Akmola)

ozero Balhaš

Ulaanbaatar

MONGOLIA

Harbin

Vladivostok

Sapporo

Hokkaido

Sea of Japan

Sendai

HONSHU

TOKYO

JAPAN

OMA

HUNG.

Beograd

ROMANIA

BULGARIA

BOS.

YUGO.

CRO.

ITALY

Napoli

Black Sea

GEORGIA

Aral Sea

UZBEKISTAN

TAŠKENT

Ürümqi

TIEN SHAN

Hohhot

BEIJING

SHENYANG

NORTH KOREA

P'yongyang

Dalian

Qingdao

SEOUL

SOUTH KOREA

PUSAN

Fukuoka

OSAKA

30°

E

ALB.

GREECE

ATHINA (ATHENS)

İstanbul

ANKARA

İzmir

AZER.

BAKI

TURKMENISTAN

KYRGYZSTAN

GOBI DESERT

CHINA

Xi'an

SHANGHAI

Nansei-shotō

PACIFIC OCEAN

Tropic of Cancer

WAKE ISLAND (U.S.)

 abulus

Mediterranean Sea

TURKEY

CYPRUS

SYRIA

BAGHDAD

TEHRAN

KABOL

AFGHANISTAN

Chengdu

Chongqing

WUHAN

Changsha

LIBYA

LEBANON

ISRAEL

EL-ISKANDARÎYA (ALEXANDRIA)

EL-QAHIRA (CAIRO)

JORDAN

Amman

IRAQ

KUWAIT

Eşfahān

Abadan

IRAN

Islamabad

Rawalpindi

LAHORE

DELHI

New Delhi

Kāthmāndu

NEPAL

HIMALAYAS

Kunming

GUANGZHOU

T'AIPEI

TAIWAN

Changchun

HA NOI

XIANGGANG (HONG KONG)

Philippine

NORTHERN MARIANAS (U.S.)

30°

ARA

EGYPT

AR-RIYÂD (RIYADH)

BAHRAIN

QATAR

U.A.E.

Abu Zaby

PAKISTAN

Ahmadābād

KARACHI

Kāthmāndu

DHAKA

GANG

MYANMAR (BURMA)

LAOS

YANGON

Vientiane

HAI-PHO

HA NOI

T'AIPEI

NIGER

CHAD

Al-Khartûm (Khartoum)

SUDAN

ERITREA

Asmara

YEMEN

OMAN

Masqat

Red Sea

SAUDI ARABIA

San'a

MUMBAI (BOMBAY)

Pune

INDIA

HYDERABAD

CALCUTTA

Bay of Bengal

THAILAND

South China Sea

LUZON

PHILIPPINES

MANILA

15°

Philippine Sea

GUAM (U.S.)

MARSHALL ISLANDS

FEDERATED STATES OF MICRONESIA

N'Djamena

Kano

ERIA

Abuja

CAMEROON

CENTRAL AFRICAN REPUBLIC

Bangui

Lake Chad

DJIBOUTI

Djibouti

Adan

Gees Gwardafuy

Arabian Sea

BANGALORE

CHENNAI (MADRAS)

Kochi

Andaman Islands (India)

KRUNG THEP (BANGKOK)

CAMBODIA

Phnum Pénh

HO CHI MINH (HO CHI MINH CITY) (SAIGON)

F

Yaoundé

UGANDA

ETHIOPIA

ADÎS ABEBA

MALDIVES

SRI LANKA

Colombo

Nicobar Islands (India)

Medan

BRUNEI

Davao

MINDANAO

PALAU

0°

Equator

MICRONESIA

AT. NEA

GABON

Brazzaville

CONGO DEM. REP. OF THE CONGO

KINSHASA

Kampala

Kigali

RWANDA

BURUNDI

Bujumbura

KENYA

NAIROBI

SEYCHELLES

BRITISH INDIAN OCEAN TERRITORY

Kuala Lumpur

MALAYSIA

SINGAPORE

BORNEO (KALIMANTAN)

Banjarmasin

SUMATERA (SUMATRA)

SULAWESI (CELEBES)

Ujungpandang

PAPUA NEW GUINEA

NEW GUINEA

NAURU

KIRIBATI

TUVALU

G

LUANDA

Lubumbashi

TANZANIA

Dodoma

Zanzibar

Dar es Salaam

INDIAN OCEAN

JAKARTA

JAWA (JAVA)

INDONESIA

Surabaya

Port Moresby

SOLOMON ISLANDS

MELANESIA

ANGOLA

Lobito

ZAMBIA

MALAWI

Lilongwe

COMOROS

Cape York

Darwin

VANUATU

FIJI

Suva

15°

NAMIBIA

Windhoek

Walvis Bay

ZIMBABWE

Harare

Lusaka

BOTSWANA

Gaborone

MOZAMBIQUE

Mozambique Channel

MADAGASCAR

Antananarivo

MAURITIUS

REUNION (Fr.)

Cairns

Alice Springs

Coral Sea

NEW CALEDONIA (Fr.)

Nouméa

H

SOUTH AFRICA

JOHANNESBURG

Pretoria

SWAZILAND

Maputo

Durban

LESOTHO

AUSTRALIA

Rockhampton

Tropic of Capricorn

Cape Town

Cape of Good Hope

Port Elizabeth

Perth

Darling

Brisbane

30°

Adelaide

SYDNEY

Canberra

Tasman Sea

Auckland

NORTH ISLAND

MELBOURNE

TASMANIA

Hobart

NEW ZEALAND

Wellington

SOUTH ISLAND

Christchurch

I

SOUTHERN

OCEAN

Archipel de Kerguelen (Fr.)

45°

J

60°

Antarctic Circle

K

ENDERBY LAND

WILKES LAND

75°

L

ICA

of Greenwich 45° 16 60° 17 75° 18 90° 19 105° 20 120° 21 135° 22 150° 23 165° 24 180° 90°

M-100000-7A-DR2-1
Copyright © Rand McNally & Co.

Meters
Feet

6000
19680

4000
13120

3000
9840

2000
6560

1000
3280

500
1640

200
656

Sea Level

200
656

2000
6560

0   1000   2000   3000   4000   6000   8000 Kilometers

0   500   1000   1500   2000   3000   4000   5000 Miles

Scale 1 : 80,000,000   Robinson Projection

15° 45° 16° 60° 17° 75° 18° 90° 19° 105° 20° 120° 21° 135° 22° 150° 23° 165° 24° 180° 90°

A

Zemlja Franca-Iosifa
Severnaja Zemlja
ARCTIC OCEAN

Barents Sea
more Laptevyh
Novosibirskie ostrova

Nordkapp
Karskoe more
Vostočno-Sibirskoe more
75°

Novaja Zemlja
B
Arctic Circle

Korskij poluostrov
ZAPADNO-
gora Kamen 1701
gora Pobeda 3147
60°

Ladožskoe ozero
SIBIRSKAJA
Nižnjaja Tunguska
SIBIR (SIBERIA)
Sea of Okhotsk

Baltic Sea
RAVNINA
Ob'
(WEST SIBERIAN LOWLAND)
C

Moskva (Moscow)
Ekaterinberg
A Z I J A
ostrov Sahalin
Bering Sea
4097

Dnepr
URAL'SKIE GORY
Ishim
Irtyš
ALTAI
mys Lopatka

Kura
Aral
ozero Balhaš
Lena
Kuril'skie ostrova

PENNINO
gora El'brus 5642
Syr Darja
pik Pobedy 7439
45°

Black Sea
CAUCASUS
TIEN SHAN
Ulaanbaatar
Hokkaidō
D

Istanbul
Caspian Sea
pik Kommunizma 7495
Beijing
Sea of Japan
HONSHŪ

Sicilia (Sicily)
HINDU KUSH
KUNLUN SHAN
GOBI DESERT
Fuji-san 3776
Tōkyō

Kriti
Tehran
DASHT-E KAVIR 5604
QING ZANG GAOYUAN
Shikoku
Kyūshū
292

Mediterranean Sea
Cyprus
KUHHA-YE ZAGROS
HIMALAYAS
Gongga Shan 7556
Shanghai
9695

El-Qahira (Cairo)
Delhi
Mount Everest 8848
East China Sea
30°

SAHARA
A R A
Persian Gulf
Brahmaputra
Taiwan
PACIFIC
E

TIBESTI
Emi Koussi 3415
NUBIAN DESERT
ARABIAN PENINSULA
Godavari
EASTERN GHATS
3997
Nanzei-shotō
OCEAN
Tropic of Cancer

Gulf of Oman
Mumbai (Bombay)
Hainan Dao
LUZON
Mariana Islands
Wake Island

Lake Chad
Red Sea
AR-RUB' AL-KHALI
Arabian
Sea
Krung Thep
South China Sea
Manila
Philippine Sea
15°

N
Gulf of Aden
Ras Dashen Terara 4620
Andaman Islands
INDOCHINA
Palawan
Guam 10915
Marshall Islands
F

AFRICA
Adis Abeba
Suquṭrā
Gees Gwardafuy
Pidurutalagala 2524
Nicobar Islands
Andaman Sea
Gulf of Thailand
MINDANAO
Gunong Kinabalu 4101
Palau Islands
M I C R O N E S I A

Cape Comorin
Sri Lanka
Maldive Islands
5425
Malay Peninsula
Celebes Sea
Halmahera
Caroline Islands

Margherita Peak 5109
Kirinyaga 5199
Lake Victoria
5340
SUMATERA (SUMATRA)
BORNEO (KALIMANTAN)
SULAWESI
Seram
NEW GUINEA
New Britain
8940
Equator
0°

CONGO BASIN
Kilimanjaro 5895
Lake Tanganyika
Zanzibar
Les Amirantes
Seychelles
Greater Sunda Islands
Jakarta
Laut Jawa
Laut Banda
Mount Wilhelm 4509
Solomon Islands

RIFT VALLEY
Lake Rudolf
JAWA (JAVA)
Timor
Arafura Sea
Cape York
New Hebrides
G

Tanjona Bobaomby
Maromokotro 2876
INDIAN
6090
1706
Timor Sea
Gulf of Carpentaria
CAPE YORK PENINSULA
M E L A N E S I A
Fiji Islands
15°

KALAHARI DESERT
MADAGASCAR
Réunion
Mauritius
OCEAN
North West Cape
6658
Kimberley Plateau
Tanami Desert
Coral Sea
Nouvelle-Calédonie

Thabana-Ntlenyana 3482
DRAKENSBERG
Tanjona Vohimena
6400
Mount Meharry 1253
GREAT SANDY DESERT
AUSTRALIA
Mount Woodroffe 1435
GREAT DIVIDING RANGE
Tropic of Capricorn
H

Cape Town
Cape of Good Hope
5536
Île Amsterdam
GREAT VICTORIA DESERT
Darling
Sydney
North Cape
5301

Cape Leeuwin
Great Australian Bight
Melbourne
Mount Kosciusko 2229
Tasman Sea
NORTH ISLAND
Mount Ruapehu 2737
I

Prince Edward Islands
Iles de Crozet
Iles Kerguélen
2690
Mount Ossa 1617
TASMANIA
South East Cape
SOUTH ISLAND
Mount Cook 3754
45°

3079
Heard Island
6089
SOUTHERN
J

5124
4425
OCEAN
Macquarie Island
60°

Cape Poinsett
Antarctic Circle
K

ENDERBY LAND
WILKES LAND
VICTORIA LAND
Cape Adare
25°

MAUD LAND
Ross Sea
L

ANTARCTICA

Greenwich 45° 16° 60° 17° 75° 18° 90° 19° 105° 20° 120° 21° 135° 22° 150° 23° 165° 24° 180° 90°

GREENLAND SEA

N O R W E G I A N   S E A

Arctic Circle

VESTERÅLEN

LOFOTEN

ICELAND

Reykjavik

Horn

Kaflafjörður

Akureyri

Hvannadalshnúkur
2119

Seyðisfjörður

NORWAY

Namso

Mo i Rana

Bodø

Trondheim

Kristiansund

Ålesund

Molde

Dombås

Galdhøpiggen
2469

Bergen

Haugesund

Stavanger

Kristiansand

Oslo

Hamar

SWEDEN

Östersund

Härnösand

Sundsvall

Falun

Gävle

STOCKHOLM

FAROE ISLANDS
(Den.)
Tórshavn

SHETLAND
ISLANDS
(U.K.)

ORKNEY
ISLANDS

H E B R I D E S

Thurso

Inverness

Aberdeen

Dundee

GLASGOW

EDINBURGH

Londonderry

Belfast

Carlisle

NEWCASTLE
UPON TYNE

Middlesbrough

UNITED
KINGDOM

IRELAND

Sligo

Galway

Limerick

DUBLIN

Waterford

Cork

Mizen
Head

IRISH SEA

LIVERPOOL

LEEDS

MANCHESTER

Sheffield

Nottingham

Leicester

BIRMINGHAM

Swansea

Oxford

Cardiff

Bristol

Norwich

Ipswich

LONDON

Southampton

Brighton

Dover

Plymouth

Penzance

Land's End

ISLES OF
SCILLY

English Channel

Strait of Dover

Cherbourg

GUERNSEY
(U.K.)

JERSEY
(U.K.)

Le Havre

Amiens

Rouen

Caen

Saint-
Malo

Pointe de
Saint-Mathieu

Brest

Rennes

Le Mans

NORTH SEA

Skagerrak

DENMARK

Holstebro

Kattegat

Frederikshavn

Ålborg

Århus

Odense

Esbjerg

Kolding

Flensburg

Kiel

KØBENHAVN
(COPENHAGEN)

Helsingborg

Malmö

Karlskrona

ÖLAND

GOTLAND

Bornholm
(Den.)

BA...

Gdynia

Gdańsk

NETHERLANDS

Groningen

Bremerhaven

'S-Gravenhage
(The Hague)

AMSTERDAM

ROTTERDAM

Utrecht

Münster

ANTWERPEN

BRUXELLES

BELGIUM

LILLE

Liège

Bonn

ESSEN

KÖLN

DÜSSELDORF

Dortmund

Hannover

Bremen

HAMBURG

Lübeck

Rostock

Szczecin

Bydgoszcz

Poznań

BERLIN

Magdeburg

Leipzig

Dresden

Wrocław

GERMANY

Erfurt

Chemnitz

Wałbrzych

Częstochowa

POL...

Katowice

Ostrava

Olomouc

Brno

PRAHA

CZECH REP

Plzeň

FRANKFURT
AM MAIN

Wiesbaden

MANNHEIM

Würzburg

Nürnberg

Regensburg

LUXEMBOURG

Metz

Nancy

Saarbrücken

Strasbourg

STUTTGART

Augsburg

MÜNCHEN
(MUNICH)

Linz

Reims

Troyes

Orléans

PARIS

Nantes

FRANCE

Tours

Bourges

Dijon

Besançon

Mulhouse

Basel

Zürich

Bern

SWITZERLAND

LIECHT.

Innsbruck

Salzburg

AUSTRIA

WIEN
(VIENNA)

Klagenfurt

Graz

Győr

BUDAPE...

HUN...

SLO...

Bratislava

La Rochelle

Poitiers

Limoges

Clermont-
Ferrand

LYON

Saint-
Étienne

Grenoble

Genève

Lausanne

Mont Blanc
4807

Bolzano

SLOVENIA

Ljubljana

Zagreb

CROATIA

Bordeaux

Toulouse

Montpellier

Nîmes

Avignon

MARSEILLE

Toulon

Nice

MONACO

TORINO

MILANO

Brescia

Verona

Padova

Venézia
(Venice)

Trieste

Pes

GENOVA

Parma

Bologna

SAN
MARINO

Zadar

Split

BOSNIA AND
HERZEGOVINA

Sarajevo

PYRENEES

ANDORRA

Andorra
la Vella

Perpignan

Lleida

BARCELONA

Tarragona

A Coruña

Cabo de Estaca

Gijón

Oviedo

León

Burgos

Santander

Bilbao

Donostia

Bayonne

Vigo

Ourense

Braga

Porto

PORTUGAL

Coimbra

Salamanca

Valladolid

Segovia

MADRID

SPAIN

Zaragoza

Pamplona

Gasteiz

LISBOA
(LISBON)

Setúbal

Évora

Badajoz

Toledo

Castelló
de la Plana

VALÈNCIA

Albacete

CÓRDOBA

Jaén

Granada

Murcia

Alacant

Elx

ILLES BALEARS
(BALEARIC ISLANDS)

Menorca

Palma de
Mallorca

MALLORCA

Eivissa

Faro

Huelva

Sevilla

Cádiz

Málaga

Mulhacén
3482

Cartagena

Isla de
Alborán
(Sp.)

GIBRALTAR
(U.K.)

Ceuta (Sp.)

Tanger

Strait of Gibraltar

LIGURIAN SEA

Livorno

Pisa

CORSE
(CORSICA)
(Fr.)

Bastia

Ajaccio

VATICAN CITY

ROMA
(ROME)

Perugia

L'Aquila

Arezzo

A P E N N I N E S

Firenze

Ancona

Pescara

ITALY

Foggia

Bari

NAPOLI
(NAPLES)

Salerno

Brindisi

Taranto

A D R I A T I C   S E A

Dubrovnik

Podg...

SARDEGNA
(SARDINIA)
(It.)

Sassari

Nuoro

Olbia

Cagliari

Oristano

TYRRHENIAN
SEA

Cosenza

Catanzaro

Reggio
di Calabria

Messina

Palermo

SICILIA
(SICILY)

Trapani

Monte Etna
3323

Catania

Siracusa

Agrigento

Cap Bon

MALTA

Valletta

Isola di
Pantelleria
(It.)

ISOLE
PELAGIE
(It.)

IONIAN
SEA

M E D I T E R R A N E A N

EL DJAZAÏR
(ALGIERS)

El Boulaïda

Tizi-
Ouzou

Béjaïa

Skikda

Annaba

La Goulette

Bizerte

TUNIS

Nabeul

Sousse

Kairouan

Sfax

Gafsa

CASABLANCA

Rabat

Salé

El-Jadida

Larache

Tétouan

Al Hoceïma

Melilla
(Sp.)

Nador

Wahran

Mestghanem

Ech Cheliff

Ténès

Bouira

Sétif

Batna

Tébessa

TUNISIA

Meknès

Fès

Taza

Oujda

Sidi bel
Abbès

Tlemcen

Tihert

Biskra

Chott
Melrhir

MOROCCO

Safi

Khouribga

Essaouira

Marrakech

Jebel Toubkal
4165

Agadir

Taroudant

Er-Rachidia

A T L A S   M O U N T A I N S

ALGERIA

Laghouat

Chott ech Chergui

Chott el
Hodna

ATLANTIC
OCEAN

Rockall
(U.K.)

Bay of Biscay

Strasbourg

M-500000-2-A-DR2-1
Copyright © Rand McNally & Co.

West of Greenwich 0° East of Greenwich

0   200   400   800   1200 Kilometers

0   100   200   400   600   800 Miles

Scale 1 : 12,500,000   Conic Equidistant Projection

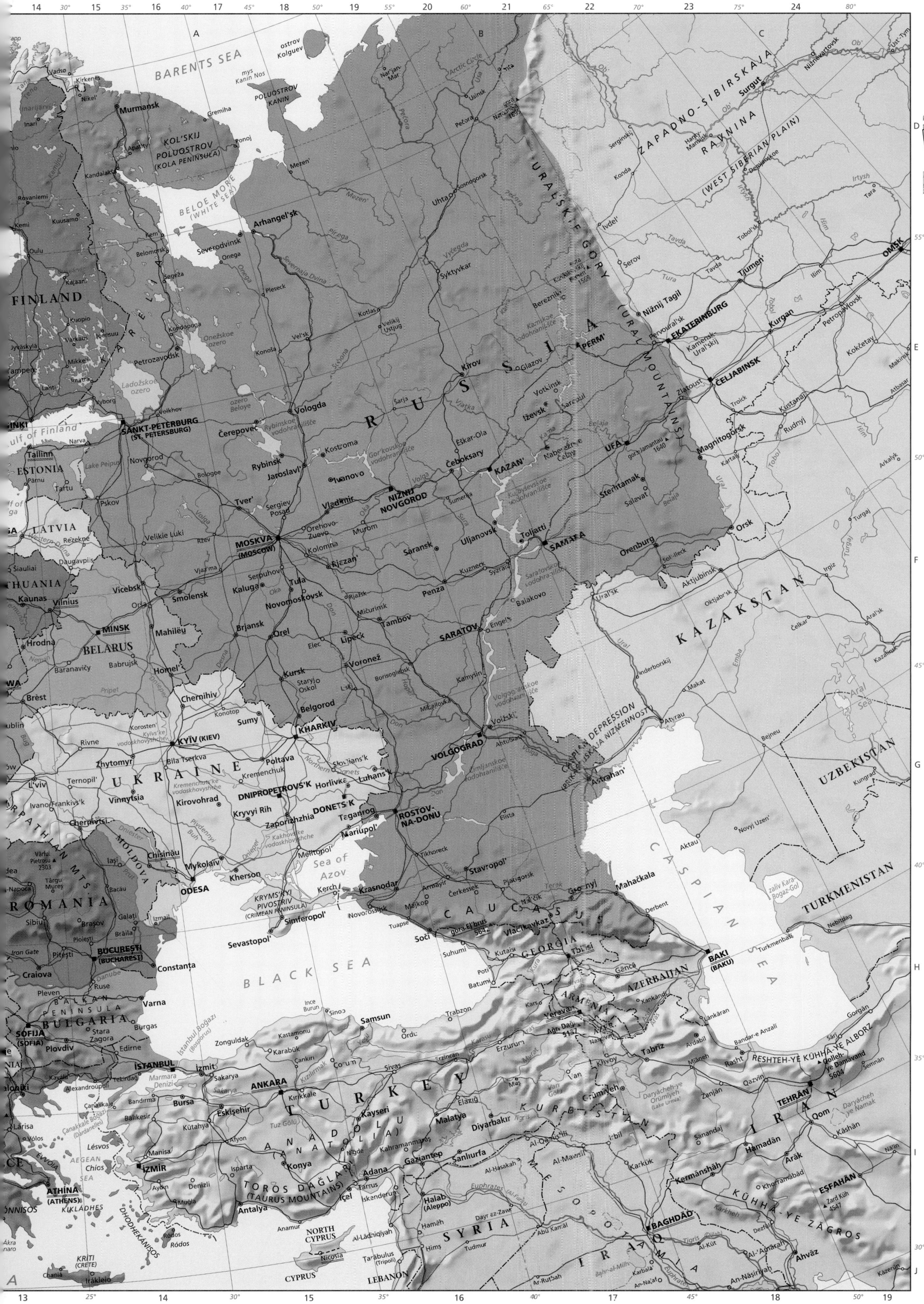

14 30° 15 35° 16 40° 17 45° 18 50° 19 55° 20 60° 21 65° 22 70° 23 75° 24 80°

A · B · C · D

BARENTS SEA

ostrov Kolguev
mys Kanin Nos
POLUOSTROV KANIN

Vadsø
Kirkenes
Nikel'
Murmansk
Gremiha
Inari
Ivalo
Rovaniemi
Kemi
Oulu
Kuusamo

KOL'SKIJ POLUOSTROV (KOLA PENINSULA)
Apatity
Kandalakša
Belomorsk
Segeža

Narjan-Mar
Usinsk
Pečora
Uhta
Kosnogorsk
Mezen'

ZAPADNO-SIBIRSKAJA RAVNINA (WEST SIBERIAN PLAIN)
Ob'
Surgut
Nižnevartovsk
Nižnevartovsk
Ust'-Tym

Arctic Circle

FINLAND
Kajaani
Kuopio
Jyväskylä
Vaasa
Tampere
Mikkeli
Lahti

BELOE MORE (WHITE SEA)
Onežskoe ozero
Petrozavodsk
Kem'
Onega
Arhangel'sk
Severodvinsk

Syktyvkar
Uhta
Berezniki

URAL'SKIE GORY (URAL MOUNTAINS)

Serov
Ivdel'
Konda
Tavda
Tjumen'
Tobol'sk
Irtyš
Tara
Om'

OMSK

R U S S I A

Ladožskoe ozero
Vyborg
SANKT-PETERBURG (ST. PETERSBURG)
Narva
Novgorod
Pskov
Lake Peipus

HELSINKI
Tallinn
ESTONIA
Pärnu
Tartu
Gulf of Finland

Volhov
Vologda
Čerepovec
Rybinsk
Jaroslavl'
Ivanovo

Kirov
Perm'
Glazov
Votkinsk
Iževsk
Serov
Pervoural'sk
EKATERINBURG
Nižnij Tagil
Kamensk-Ural'skij
Zlatoust
ČELJABINSK
Kurgan
Troick
Kustanaj
Petropavlovsk
Kokčetav
Makinsk

LATVIA
Rēzekne
Daugavpils
Velikie Luki

Kostroma
Rybinskoe vodohranilišče
Tver'
Sergiev Posad
Vladimir
Murom
NIŽNIJ NOVGOROD
Čeboksary
KAZAN'
Sumerlja
Naberežnye Čelny
UFA
Magnitogorsk
Sterlitamak
Salavat
Orsk

LITHUANIA
Šiauliai
Kaunas
Vilnius
Vicebsk
Smolensk
Orša
MINSK
BELARUS
Mahilëu
Hrodna
Baranaviči
Babrujsk
Homel'

MOSKVA (MOSCOW)
Serpuhov
Kaluga
Tula
Novomoskovsk
Orel
Brjansk
Rjazan'
Kolomna
Mičurinsk
Tambov
Lipeck
Penza
Saransk
Uljanovsk
Toljatti
SAMARA
Syzran'
Balakovo
Saratovskoe vodohranilišče
Orenburg
Sol'-Ileck
Aktjubinsk
Irgiz

WARSZAWA
Brèst
Pripet
Homel'

SARATOV
Voronež
Elec
Kursk
Staryj Oskol
Belgorod
Borisoglebsk
Kamyšin
Engels'
Volžskij
VOLGOGRAD

KAZAKSTAN
Čelkar
Aral'sk
Kazalinsk

UKRAINE
Kyïv (KIEV)
Korosten'
Rivne
Žytomyr
Konotop
Sumy
KHARKIV
Poltava
Slov'jans'k
Luhans'k
Horlivka
DNIPROPETROVS'K
DONETS'K
Kryvyj Rih
Zaporižžhia
Taganrog
ROSTOV-NA-DONU
Mariupol'
Melitopol'
Volgodonsk
Zimljanskoe vodohranilišče
Elista
Astrahan'
CASPIAN DEPRESSION

UZBEKISTAN
Kungrad
Nukus

MOLDOVA
Chişinău
Iaşi
Bălţi
ODESA
Mykolaïv
Kherson
Sea of Azov
Kerch
KRYMS'KYI PIVOSTRIV (CRIMEAN PENINSULA)
Simferopol'
Sevastopol'
Novorossijsk
Krasnodar
Armavir
Majkop
Stavropol'
Pjatigorsk
Mahačkala
Derbent
TURKMENISTAN
Nebitdag

ROMANIA
Sibiu
Braşov
Galaţi
Brăila
Ploieşti
Piteşti
BUCUREŞTI (BUCHAREST)
Craiova
Danube
Ruse
Pleven

CAUCASUS
gora El'brus 5642
Tuapse
Soči
Vlaďkavkaz
GEORGIA
Kutaisi
Suhumi
Poti
Batumi
Tbilisi
Gäncä
AZERBAIJAN
BAKI (BAKU)
Turkmenbaši
zaliv Kara-Bogaz-Gol

BLACK SEA

BALKAN PENINSULA
BULGARIA
SOFIJA (SOFIA)
Plovdiv
Stara Zagora
Edirne
Varna
Burgas
İstanbul Boğazı (Bosporus)
İSTANBUL
İzmit
Zonguldak
Samsun
Sinop
Trabzon
Ordu
Kars
ARMENIA
Yerevan
Ağrı 5131
Tabriz
Ardabıl
Bandar-e Anzalī
Rasht
RESHTEH-YE KŪHHĀ-YE ALBORZ
Gorgān

ANKARA
Kırıkkale
Bursa
Eskişehir
Kütahya
Kastamonu
Çankırı
Çorum
Yozgat
Sivas
Erzincan
Erzurum
Muş
Van
Urmia (Lake Urmia)
Daryācheh-ye Orūmīyeh
Mīāneh
Zanjān
Qazvīn
TEHRĀN
Qom

TURKEY
Kayseri
ANADOLU (ANATOLIA)
Malatya
Diyarbakır
Elazığ
Al-Qamishli
Al-Mawsil
Karkūk
Kermānshāh
Sanandaj
KŪHHĀ-YE ZAGROS
ESFAHĀN

İZMIR
Manisa
Aydın
Denizli
Muğla
Konya
Adana
Tarsus
İçel
İskenderun
Gaziantep
Şanlıurfa
Al-Ḥasakah
Euphrates (Al Furāt)
Tigris
MESOPOTAMIA
Arak
Khorramābād
Ahvāz

TOROS DAĞLARI (TAURUS MOUNTAINS)
Antalya
Anamur
NORTH CYPRUS
Nicosia
CYPRUS
Al-Lādhiqīyah
Ţarābulus (Tripoli)
LEBANON
SYRIA
Ḥalab (Aleppo)
Ḥamāh
Ḥimş
Dayr az-Zawr
IRAQ
BAGHDĀD
Karbalā'
An-Najaf
An-Nāşirīyah

AEGEAN SEA
ATHÍNA (ATHENS)
KIKLÁDHES
KRITI (CRETE)
Iráklio
Chaniá
DHODHEKANISOS
Ródhos (Rhodes)

13 25° 14 30° 15 35° 16 40° 17 45° 18 50° 19

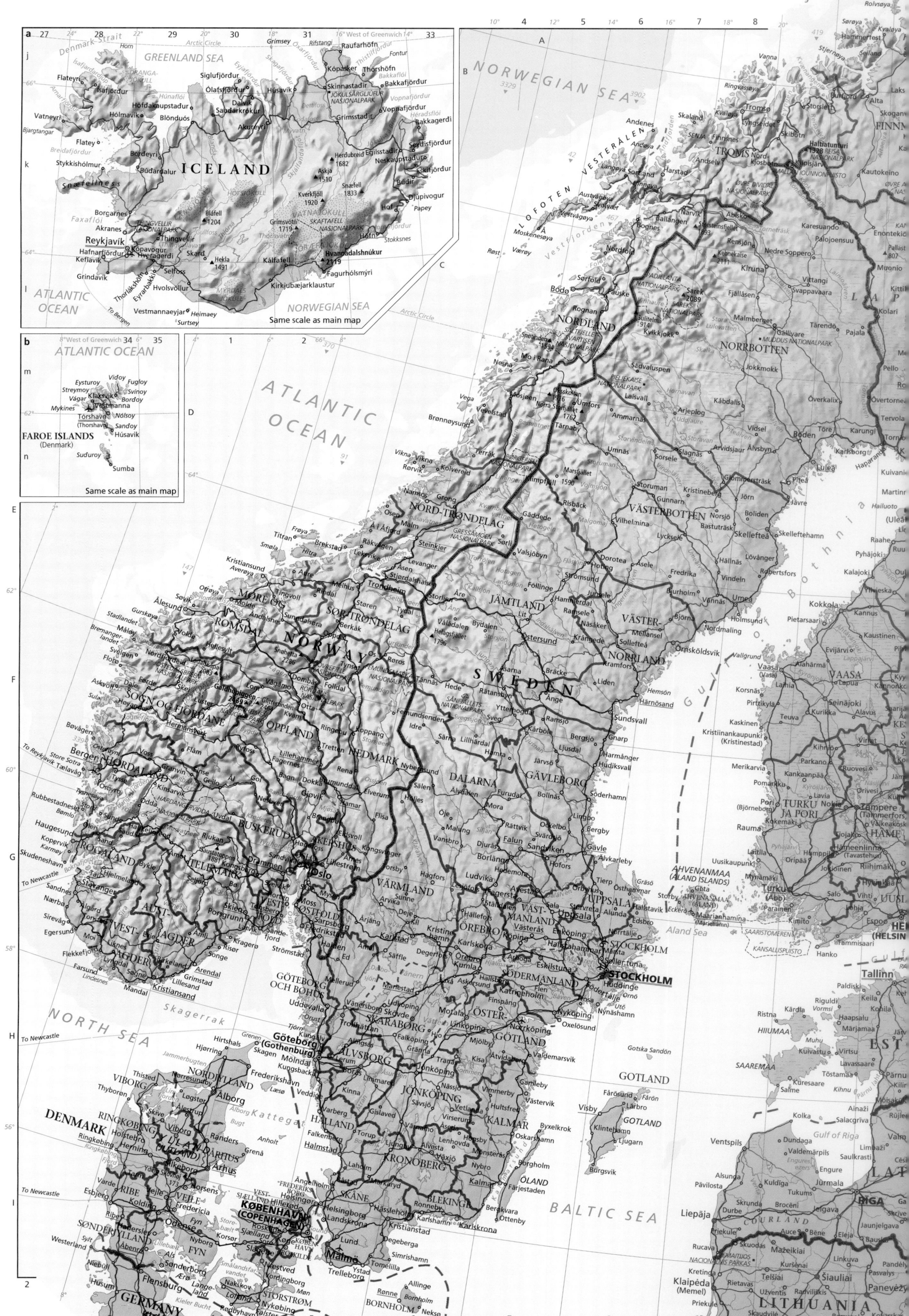

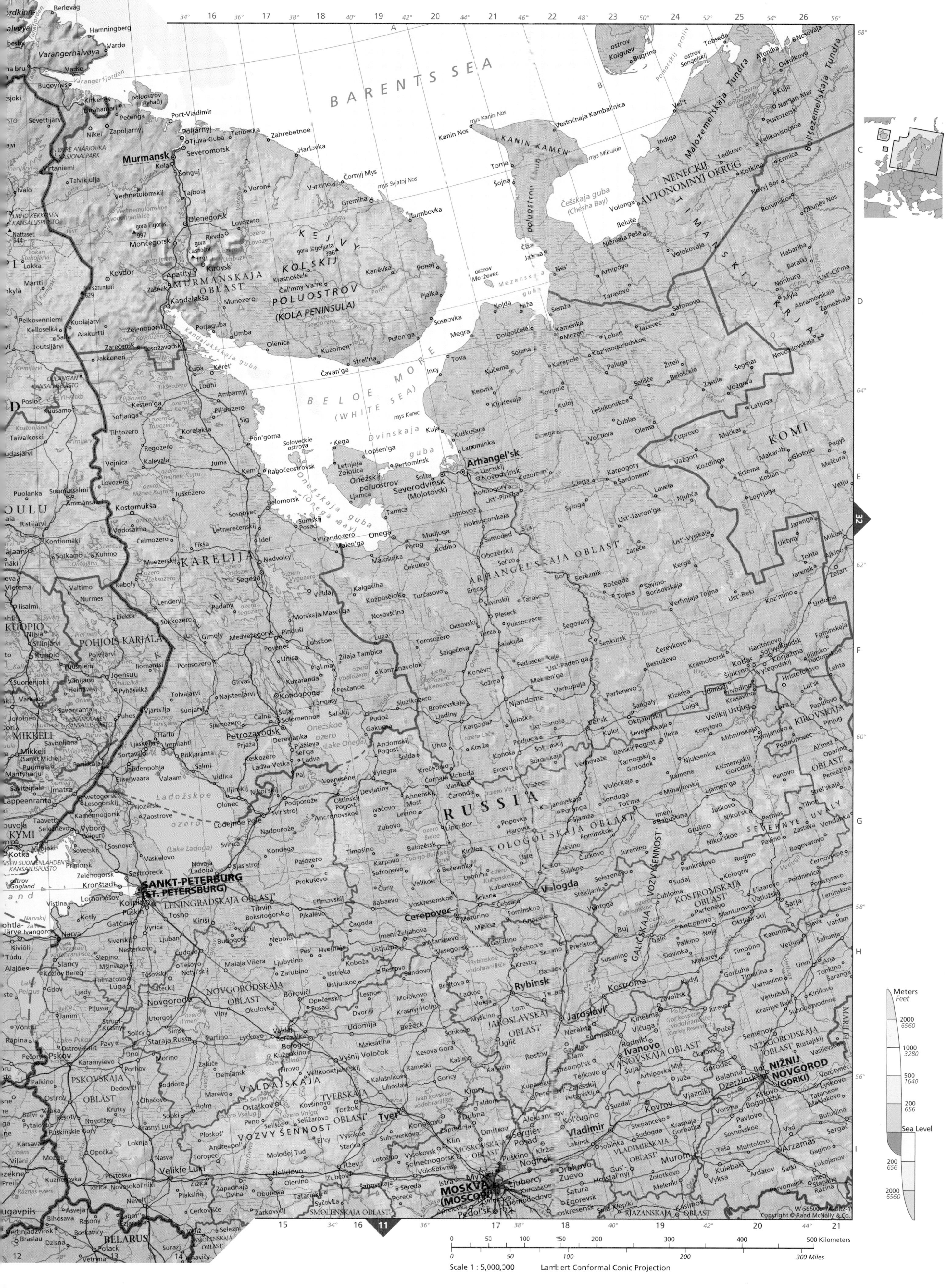

BARENTS SEA

KANIN KAMEN'

NENECKIJ
AVTONOMNYJ OKRUG

poluostrov
Kanin

Čéšskaja guba
(Chésha Bay)

T
I
M
A
N
S
K
I
J
K
R
J
A
Ž

Bol'šezemel'skaja Tundra
Malozemel'skaja Tundra

KEJVY

KOL'SKIJ
POLUOSTROV
(KOLA PENINSULA)

MURMANSKAJA
OBLAST

Murmansk

BELOE MORE
(WHITE SEA)

Dvinskaja
guba

Onežskaja guba
(Onega Bay)

Onežskij
poluostrov

Severodvinsk
(Molotovsk)

Arhangel'sk

KOMI

KARELIJA

POHJOIS-KARJALA

ARHANGEL'SKAJA OBLAST'

KUOPIO

Petrozavodsk

ozero
Onežskoe
(Lake Onega)

MIKKELI

Ladožskoe
ozero
(Lake Ladoga)

RUSSIA

VOLOGODSKAJA OBLAST'

KIROVSKAJA
OBLAST

SEVERNYE UVALY

SANKT-PETERBURG
(ST. PETERSBURG)

LENINGRADSKAJA OBLAST'

Vologda

KOSTROMSKAJA
OBLAST

GALIČSKAJA VOZVYŠENNOST'

Čerepovec

Rybinsk

NOVGORODSKAJA
OBLAST

Novgorod

Jaroslavl'

JAROSLAVSKAJA
OBLAST'

Ivanovo

IVANOVSKAJA OBLAST

NIZNIJ
NOVGOROD
(GORKI)

NIZEGORODSKAJA
OBLAST

PSKOVSKAJA
OBLAST

VALDAJSKAJA
VOZVYŠENNOST

TVERSKAJA
OBLAST'

Tver

Vladimir

VLADIMIRSKAJA
OBLAST

Velikie Luki

MOSKOVSKAJA
OBLAST

MOSKVA
(MOSCOW)

BELARUS

SMOLENSKAJA OBLAST'

RJAZANSKAJA OBLAST'

Copyright © Rand McNally & Co.
W-565000-74-GR2-11

Meters
Feet

2000
6560

1000
3280

500
1640

200
656

Sea Level

200
656

2000
6560

Scale 1 : 5,000,000   Lambert Conformal Conic Projection

0   50   100   200   300   400   500 Kilometers

0   50   100   200   300 Miles

Copyright © Rand McNally & Co.

12

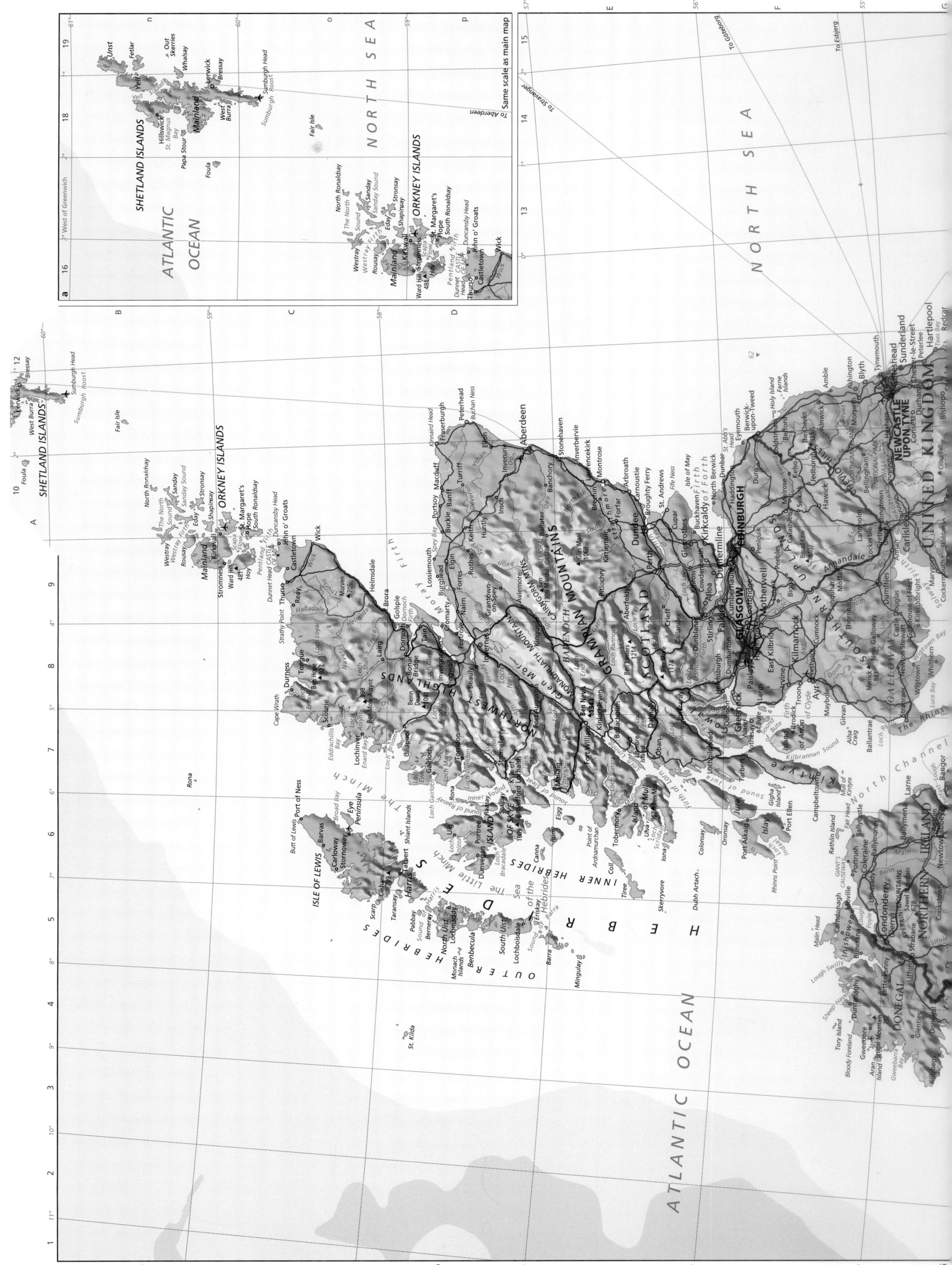

Inset map (top):

19 18

3° West of Greenwich

Unst
Fetlar
Out Skerries
Whalsay
Yell
Hillswick
Lerwick
St. Magnus Bay
Bressay
Papa Stour
West Burra
Sumburgh Head
Foula
Sumburgh Roost

SHETLAND ISLANDS

ATLANTIC OCEAN

NORTH SEA

Fair Isle

ORKNEY ISLANDS

North Ronaldsay
The North Sound
Sanday
Sanday Sound
Eday
Stronsay
Shapinsay
Westray
Westray Firth
Rousay
Kirkwall
St. Margaret's
Hope
South Ronaldsay
Duncansby Head
Stromness
Ward Hill
481
Hoy
Scapa Flow
Dunnet Head
CASTLE of MEY
Pentland Firth
John o' Groats
Mainland
Castletown
Thurso
Wick

Same scale as main map

To Aberdeen

a

To Goteborg
To Esbjerg
To Stranraer

NORTH SEA

Main map:

12

SHETLAND ISLANDS

Foula
Bressay
Sumburgh Head
West Burra
Sumburgh Roost
Fair Isle

ORKNEY ISLANDS

North Ronaldsay
The North Sound
Sanday
Sanday Sound
Eday
Stronsay
Shapinsay
Westray
Westray Firth
Rousay
Kirkwall
St. Margaret's
Hope
South Ronaldsay
Stromness
Ward Hill
Hoy
Scapa Flow
Dunnet Head
Pentland Firth
John o' Groats
Mainland
Castletown
Thurso
Wick

ATLANTIC OCEAN

Rona

Cape Wrath
Durness
Scourie
Lochinver
Ullapool
Gairloch

Butt of Lewis
Port of Ness
Broad Bay
Eye Peninsula
Barvas
ISLE OF LEWIS
Carloway
Stornoway
Shiant Islands
Tarbert
Harris
Scarp
Scalpay
Taransay
Pabbay
Berneray
North Uist
Lochmaddy
Monach Islands
Benbecula
South Uist
Lochboisdale
Barra
Mingulay

St. Kilda

OUTER HEBRIDES

The Minch

The Little Minch

Sea of the Hebrides

Rona
Raasay
Portree
Dunvegan
ISLE OF SKYE
Kyle of Lochalsh
Loch Bracadale

INNER HEBRIDES

Canna
Rum
Eigg
Point of Ardnamurchan
Coll
Tiree
Tobermory
Ulva
ISLAND OF MULL
Staffa
Iona
Colonsay
Oronsay
Islay
Port Askaig
Port Ellen
Gigha Island
Rhinns Point

Skerryvore
Dubh Artach

NORTH-WEST HIGHLANDS

Ben Hope
Loch Loyal
Strathy Point
Halladale
Reay
Morven
705
Helmsdale
Brora
Golspie
Dornoch
Dornoch Firth
Tain
Lairg
Bonar Bridge
Invergordon
Cromarty
Beauly
Inverness
Fortrose
Nairn
Forres
Elgin
Lossiemouth
Buckie
Portsoy
Banff
Macduff
Keith
Huntly
Turriff
Fraserburgh
Peterhead
Buchan Ness
Kinnaird Head

GRAMPIAN MOUNTAINS
CAIRNGORM MOUNTAINS
MONADHLIATH MOUNTAINS

Aviemore
Grantown-on-Spey
Ben Nevis
1343
Fort William
Kinlochleven
Ballachulish
Oban
Loch Awe

Ben More
1174
Callander
Stirling

GLASGOW
Paisley
Greenock
Dumbarton
East Kilbride
Kilmarnock
Troon
Irvine
Ayr
Girvan
Maybole
Newton Stewart
Wigtown
Stranraer
Portpatrick

SCOTLAND

EDINBURGH
Dunfermline
Kirkcaldy
Firth of Forth
Motherwell
Hamilton
Lanark
Biggar
Peebles
Galashiels
Hawick
Selkirk
Jedburgh
Dumfries
Castle Douglas
Kirkcudbright

Stonehaven
Inverbervie
Montrose
Brechin
Arbroath
Dundee
Broughty Ferry
St. Andrews
Cupar
Aberdeen
Ballater
Banchory
Forfar
Isle of May
North Berwick
Dunbar
St. Abb's Head

Aberfeldy
Pitlochry
Perth
Crieff

Balmoral
Gird Mial

Stranraer
The Rhins
Luce Bay
Solway Firth

Isle of Arran
Brodick
Firth of Clyde
Campbeltown
Mull of Kintyre
KINTYRE
Kilbrannan Sound
Sound of Jura
Firth of Lorn
Alba Craig
Ailsa Craig
Ballantrae

NORTH CHANNEL

NEWCASTLE UPON TYNE
Sunderland
Hartlepool
Redcar
Tynemouth
Whitley Bay
Blyth
Amble
Ashington
Morpeth
Alnwick
Berwick-upon-Tweed
Eyemouth
Holy Island
Farne Islands
Bamburgh
Bellingham
Hexham
Haltwhistle
Carlisle
Annan
Gretna
Kelso
Coldstream
Duns
Melrose
Moffat

UNITED KINGDOM

CHEVIOT HILLS
SOUTHERN UPLANDS

SCOTLAND

NORTH SEA

NORTHERN IRELAND

Londonderry
Coleraine
Portrush
Ballycastle
Rathlin Island
Fair Head
Ballymena
Larne
Bangor
Portstewart
Limavady
Strabane
Omagh
Cookstown
Magherafelt
Sawel
678
SPERRIN MOUNTAINS
GIANT'S CAUSEWAY

DONEGAL
Letterkenny
Lifford
Dungloe
Gweedore
Aran Island
Bloody Foreland
Tory Island
Gweebarra Bay
Glenties
Ardara
Errigal
752
Muckish Mountain
Lough Swilly
Malin Head
Inishowen
Buncrana
Moville
Carndonagh
Lough Foyle

ATLANTIC OCEAN

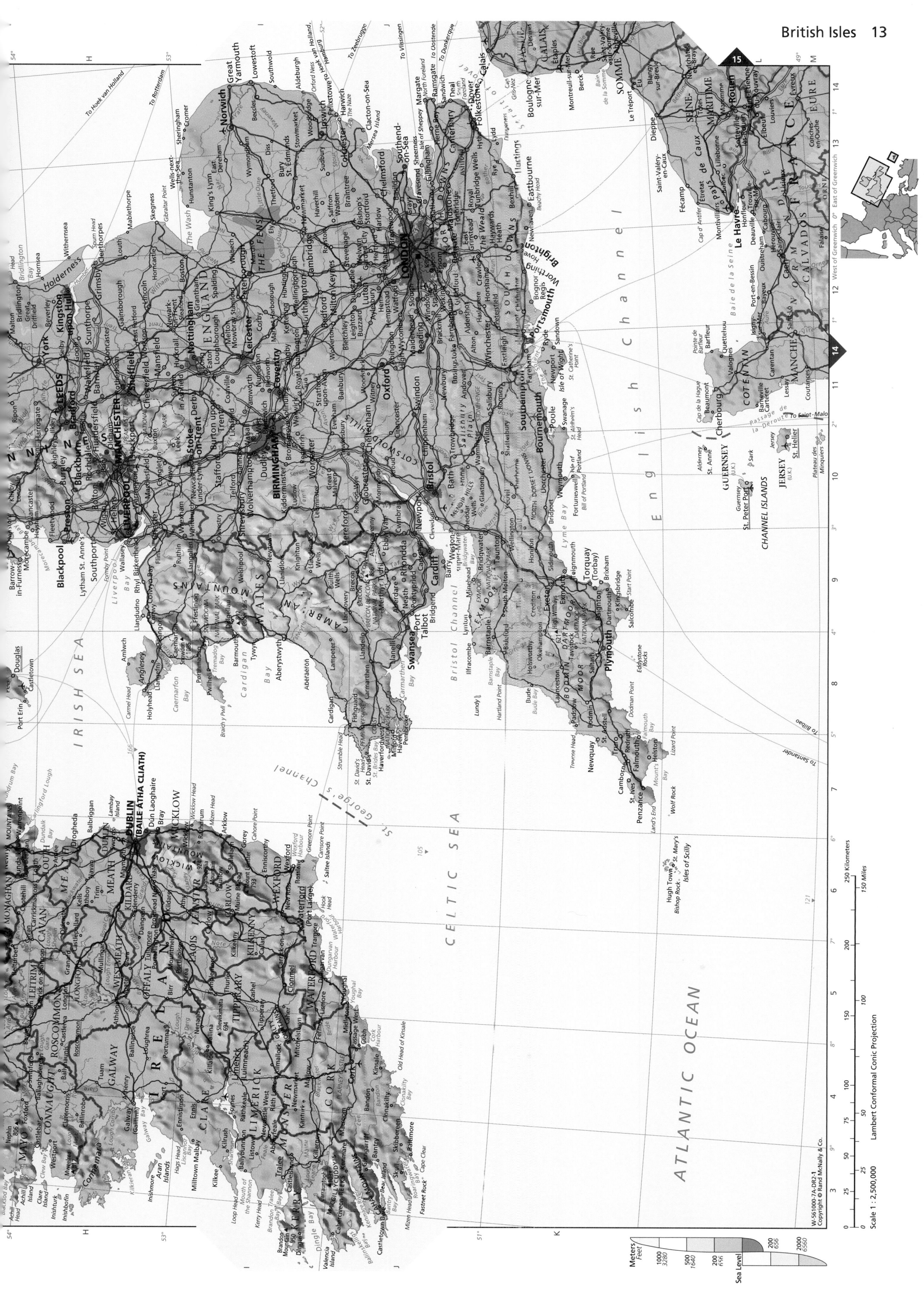

W-561000-7A-DR21
Copyright © Rand McNally & Co.

Scale 1 : 2,500,000

Lambert Conformal Conic Projection

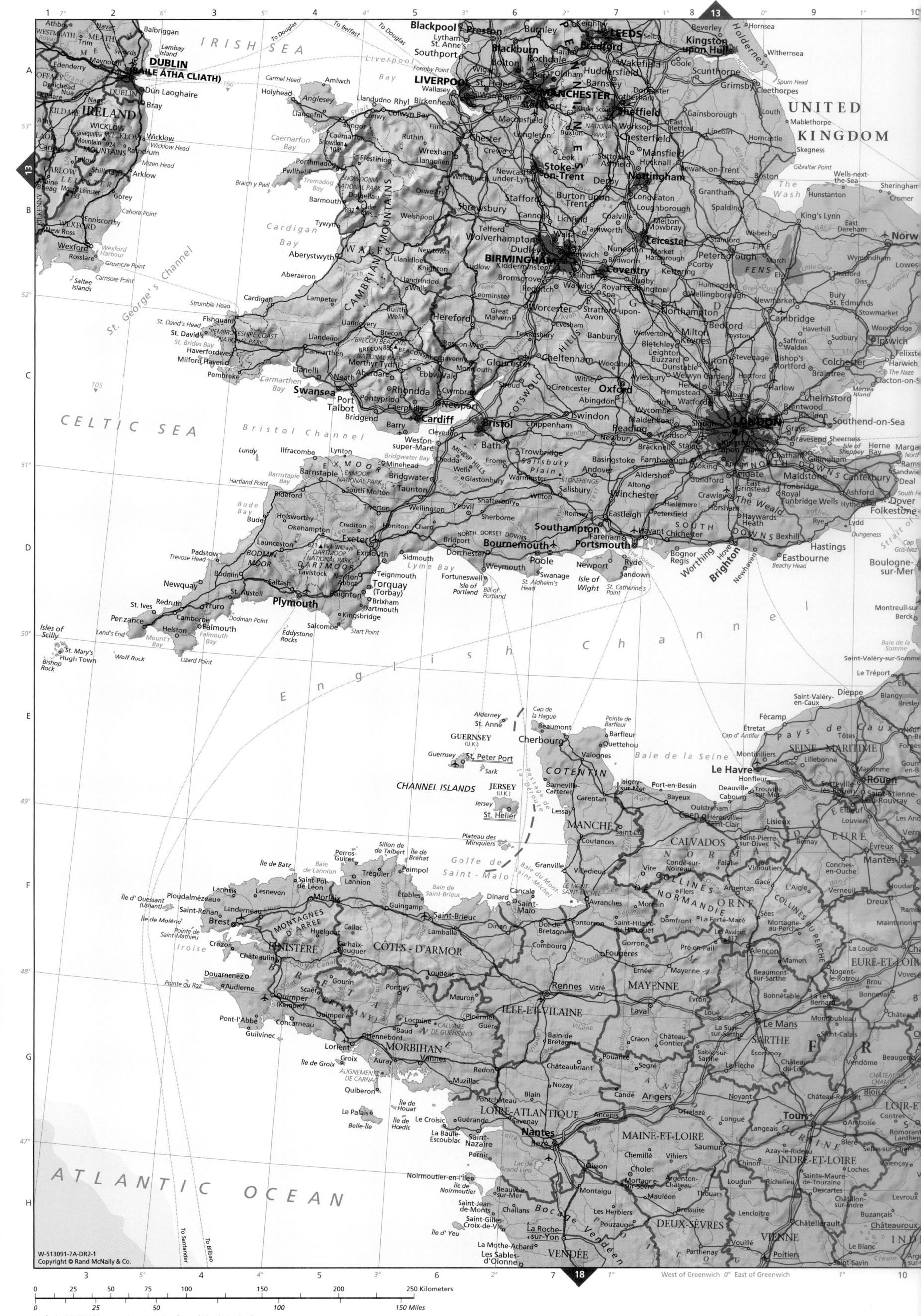

IRISH SEA

IRELAND

WALES

Cardigan
Bay

St. George's Channel

CELTIC SEA

Bristol Channel

UNITED
KINGDOM

ENGLAND

English Channel

ATLANTIC OCEAN

CHANNEL ISLANDS

GUERNSEY
(U.K.)

JERSEY
(U.K.)

MANCHE

NORMANDIE

BRETAGNE

FINISTÈRE

CÔTES-D'ARMOR

MORBIHAN

ILLE-ET-VILAINE

MAYENNE

SARTHE

LOIRE-ATLANTIQUE

MAINE-ET-LOIRE

VENDÉE

DEUX-SÈVRES

VIENNE

INDRE-ET-LOIRE

SEINE-MARITIME

EURE

CALVADOS

ORNE

EURE-ET-LOIR

Meters
Feet

4000
13120

3000
9842

2000
6560

1000
3280

500
1640

200
656

Sea Level

200
656

2000
6560

W-513091-7A-DR2-1
Copyright © Rand McNally & Co.

Scale 1 : 2,500,000   Lambert Conformal Conic Projection

0   25   50   75   100   150   200   250 Kilometers

0   25   50   100   150 Miles

West of Greenwich 0° East of Greenwich

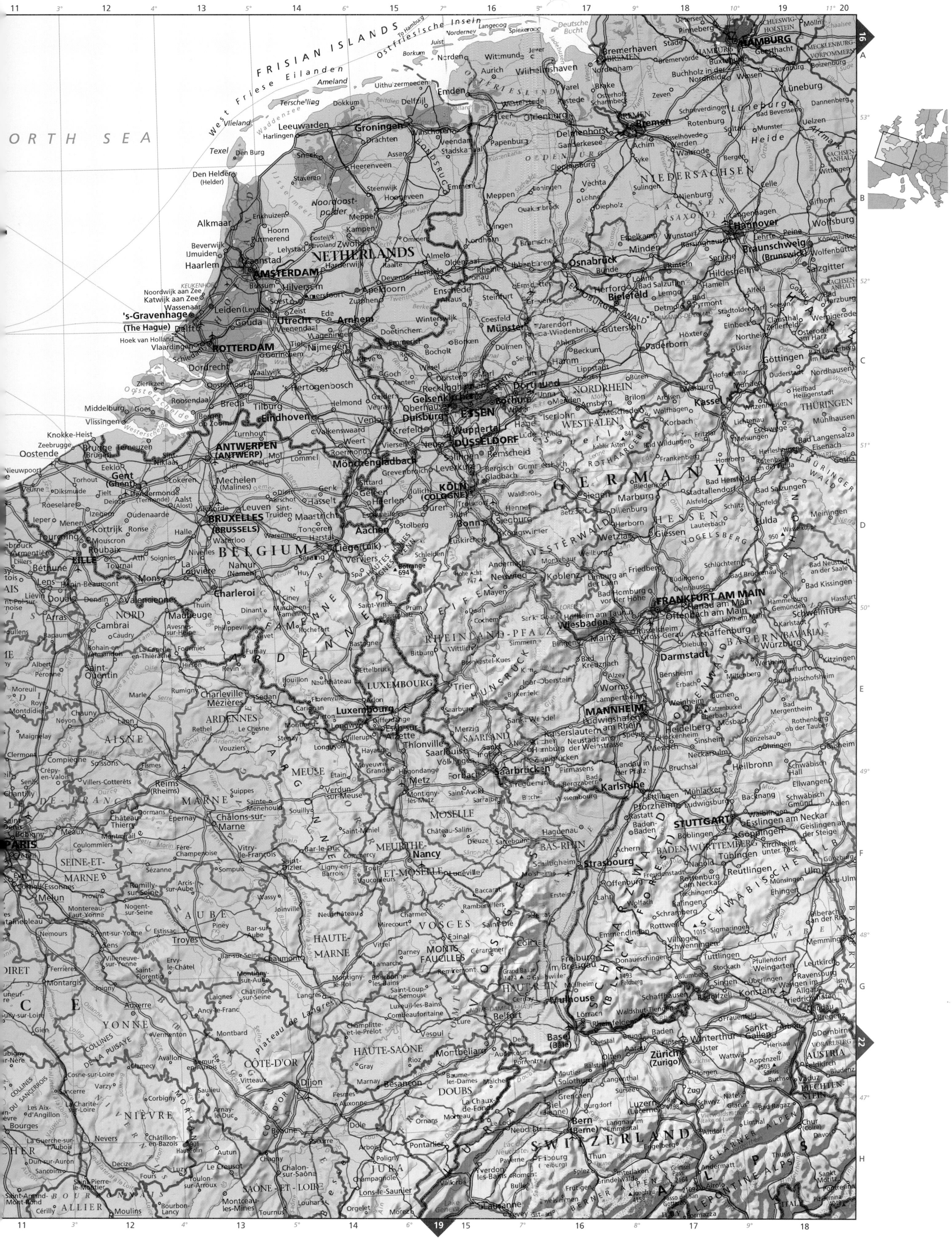

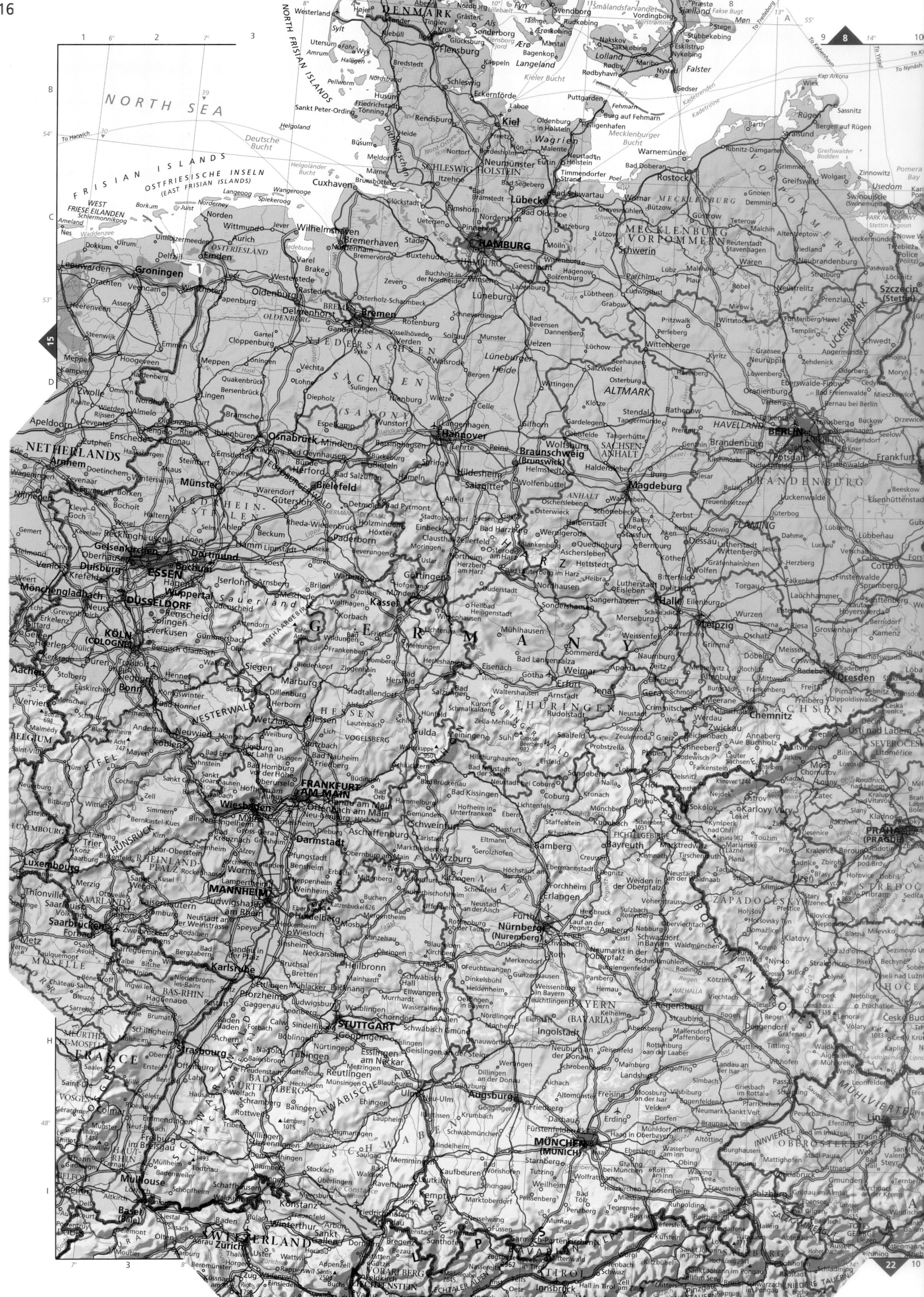

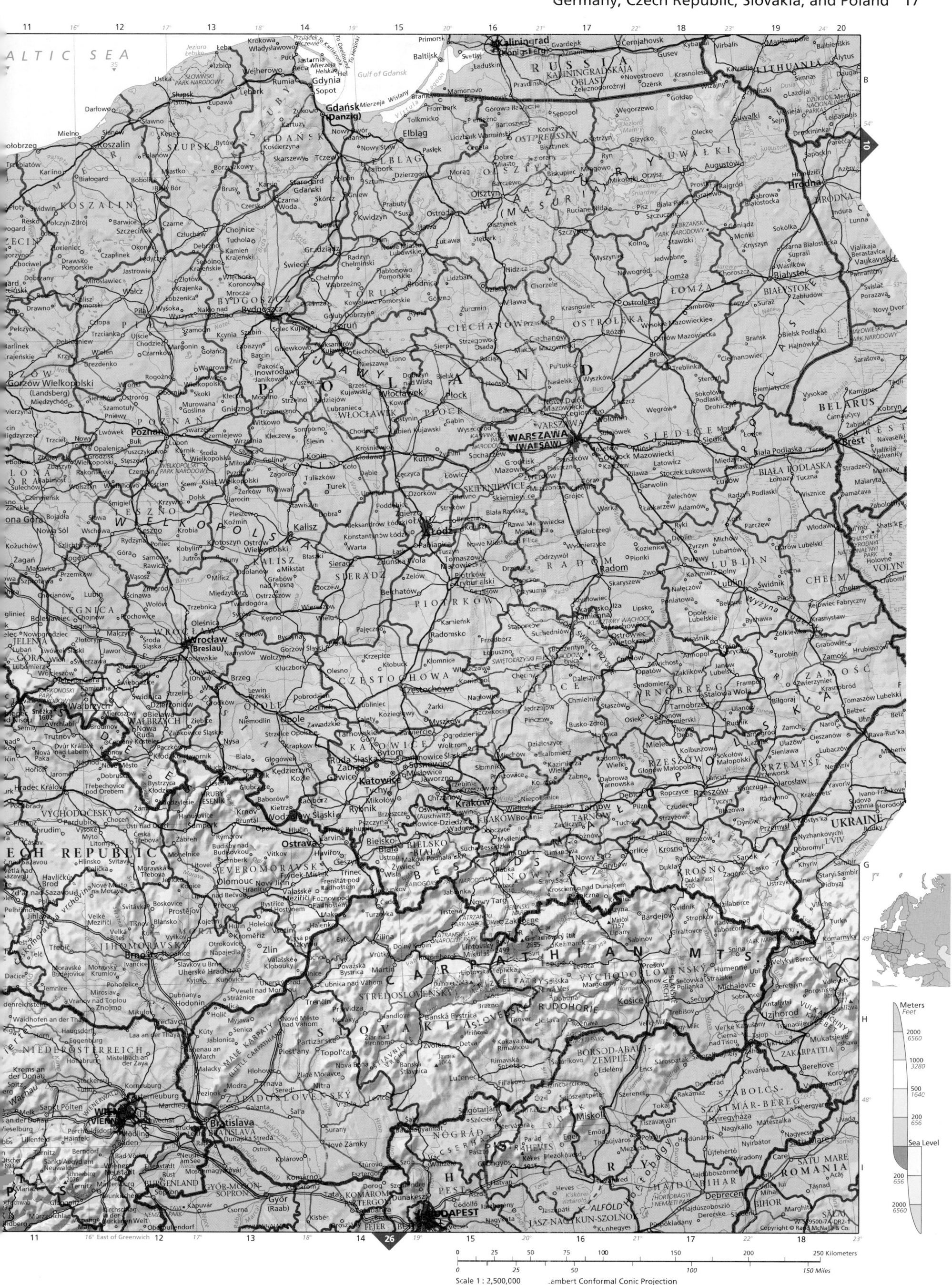

Scale 1 : 2,500,000
Lambert Conformal Conic Projection

0   25   50   75   100   150   200   250 Kilometers
0   25   50   100   150 Miles

ATLANTIC
OCEAN

Bay of Biscay

Meters
Feet

4000
13120

3000
9840

2000
6560

1300
3280

500
1540

200
556

Sea Level

200
656

2000
6560

Scale 1 : 2 500 000   Lambert Conformal Conic Projection

0   25   50   75   100   150   200   250 Kilometers

0   25   50   100   150 Miles

West of Greenwich   0°   East of Greenwch

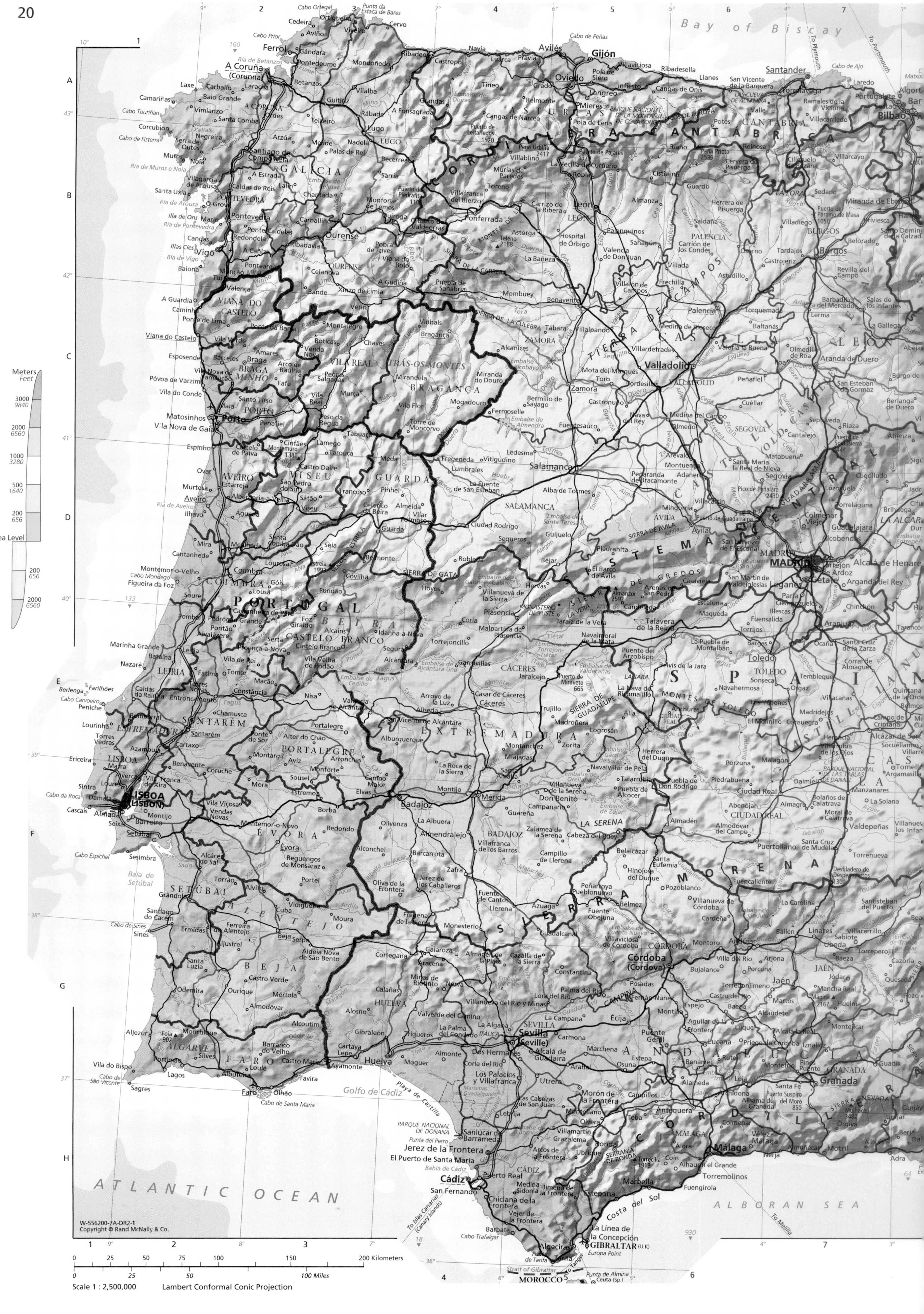

Bay of Biscay
ATLANTIC OCEAN
ALBORAN SEA
Golfo de Cádiz
PORTUGAL
SPAIN
GALICIA
ASTURIAS
CANTABRIA
CORDILLERA CANTÁBRICA
CASTILLA Y LEÓN
CASTILLA-LA MANCHA
EXTREMADURA
ANDALUCÍA
SISTEMA CENTRAL
SIERRA MORENA
MONTES DE TOLEDO
SIERRA DE GREDOS
ALENTEJO
ALGARVE
A Coruña (Corunna)
Ferrol
Santiago de Compostela
Lugo
Ourense
Pontevedra
Vigo
Oviedo
Gijón
Avilés
Santander
Bilbao
León
Palencia
Burgos
Valladolid
Zamora
Salamanca
Segovia
Ávila
MADRID
Toledo
Cáceres
Badajoz
Mérida
Ciudad Real
Córdoba (Cordova)
Jaén
Sevilla (Seville)
Huelva
Cádiz
Jerez de la Frontera
Málaga
Granada
Algeciras
GIBRALTAR (U.K.)
Ceuta (Sp.)
MOROCCO
Strait of Gibraltar
Viana do Castelo
Braga
Porto
Bragança
Vila Real
Aveiro
Viseu
Guarda
Coimbra
Leiria
Castelo Branco
Santarém
Portalegre
LISBOA (LISBON)
Setúbal
Évora
Beja
Faro
Cabo da Roca
Cabo de São Vicente
Cabo Trafalgar
Cabo de Finisterra
Cabo Ortegal
Meters
Feet
3000
9840
2000
6560
1000
3280
500
1640
200
656
Sea Level
200
656
2000
6560
W-556200-7A-DR2-1
Copyright © Rand McNally & Co.
0 25 50 75 100 150 200 Kilometers
0 25 50 100 Miles
Scale 1 : 2,500,000
Lambert Conformal Conic Projection

FRANCE

HAUTE-CORSE

Monte Cinto
2706

C O R S E
(CORSICA)

CORSE-DU-SUD

Ajaccio

Bonifacio

Gallura

La Nurra

Angiona
Logudoro
Sassari

Alghero

S A R D E G N A
(S A R D I N I A)

Oristano

MONTI DEL
GENNARGENTU
Punta La Marmora
1834

ITALY

Iglesias

Carbonia

Cagliari

Isola di
San Pietro

Isola di
Sant'Antioco

TOSCANA

Isola d' Elba

Piombino

Grosseto

UMBRIA
Perugia

Todi

Terni

MARCHE

Ascoli Piceno

ABRUZZO

L'Aquila

LAZIO

ROMA
(ROME)
VATICAN CITY

Frosinone

Latina

Gaeta

NAPOLI
(NAPLES)
Pozzuoli

Isola d' Ischia

APPENNINO

SICILIA
Palermo

Trapani
ISOLE EGADI

Marsala

Mazara del Vallo

Sciacca

Agrigento

TYRRHENIAN SEA

ISOLE EOLIE
(ISOLE LIPARI)

MEDITERRANEAN SEA

Strait of Sicily

Isola di Ustica

Isola di
Pantelleria

Pantelleria

TUNISIA

Bizerte (Binzert)

TUNIS

ALGERIA

Golfe de Tunis

Cap Bon

Golfe de
Hammamet

Sousse

Monastir

Kairouan

MALTA

ISOLE PELAGIE
(Italy)

Meters
Feet

3000
9840

2000
6560

1000
3280

500
1640

200
656

Sea Level

200
656

2000
6560

0   25   50   75   100   150   200   250 Kilometers

0   25   50   100   150 Miles

Scale 1 : 2,500,000   Lambert Conformal Conic Projection

CROATIA

Svetac
Otok Vis Vis
Otok Biševo
Vela Luka Otok Korčula
Lastovski Kanal
Otok Mljet
Otok Sušac
Otok Lastovo

BOSNIA AND
HERZEGOVINA
Stolac
Ljubinje
Trebinje
Dubrovnik
Cavtat

YUGOSLAVIA

CRNA GORA
(MONTENEGRO)

Nikšić
Kolašin
Andrijevica

Podgorica
Cetinje
Herceg-Novi
Kotor

Bar
Virpazar

Ulcinj

SRBIJA
SERBIA

KOSOVO-
METOHIJA

Priština

MACEDONIA

Skopje

ISOLE TREMITI
Isola San
Domino
Isola Pianosa

Lago di
Lesina
Lago di
Varano
Rodi Garganico
Vieste
PROMONTORIO
DEL
GARGANO
San Giovanni
Rotondo Monte Calvo
Monte Sant'Angelo
Testa del Gargano

ADRIATIC SEA

ALBANIA

Shkodër
Lezhë

Durrës

Tiranë

Elbasan

Manfredonia
Golfo di
Manfredonia
Margherita
di Sávoia
Barletta
Trani
Bisceglie
Molfetta
Andria
Corato
Canosa
di Púglia
Bitonto
Bari
Mola di Bari
PUGLIA

Cerignola
Ascoli Satriano
Foggia
Troia

Gravina
in Púglia
Altamura
Monopoli

Basilicata
Potenza

Salentina
Peninsola
Brindisi
Mesagne
Lecce
Gallipoli

Taranto
Golfo di Taranto

IONIAN SEA

Catanzaro
Calabria
Reggio
di Calabria
Messina

GREECE

Kérkyra
(Corfu)

Ioánnina

PELOPÓNNISOS
(Peloponnese)

Pátra

IONIAN SEA

W-520092-7A-DR2-1
Copyright © Rand McNally & Co.

0   25   50   75   100   150   200   250 Kilometers

0   25   50   100   150 Miles

Scale 1 : 2,500,000   Lambert Conformal Conic Projection

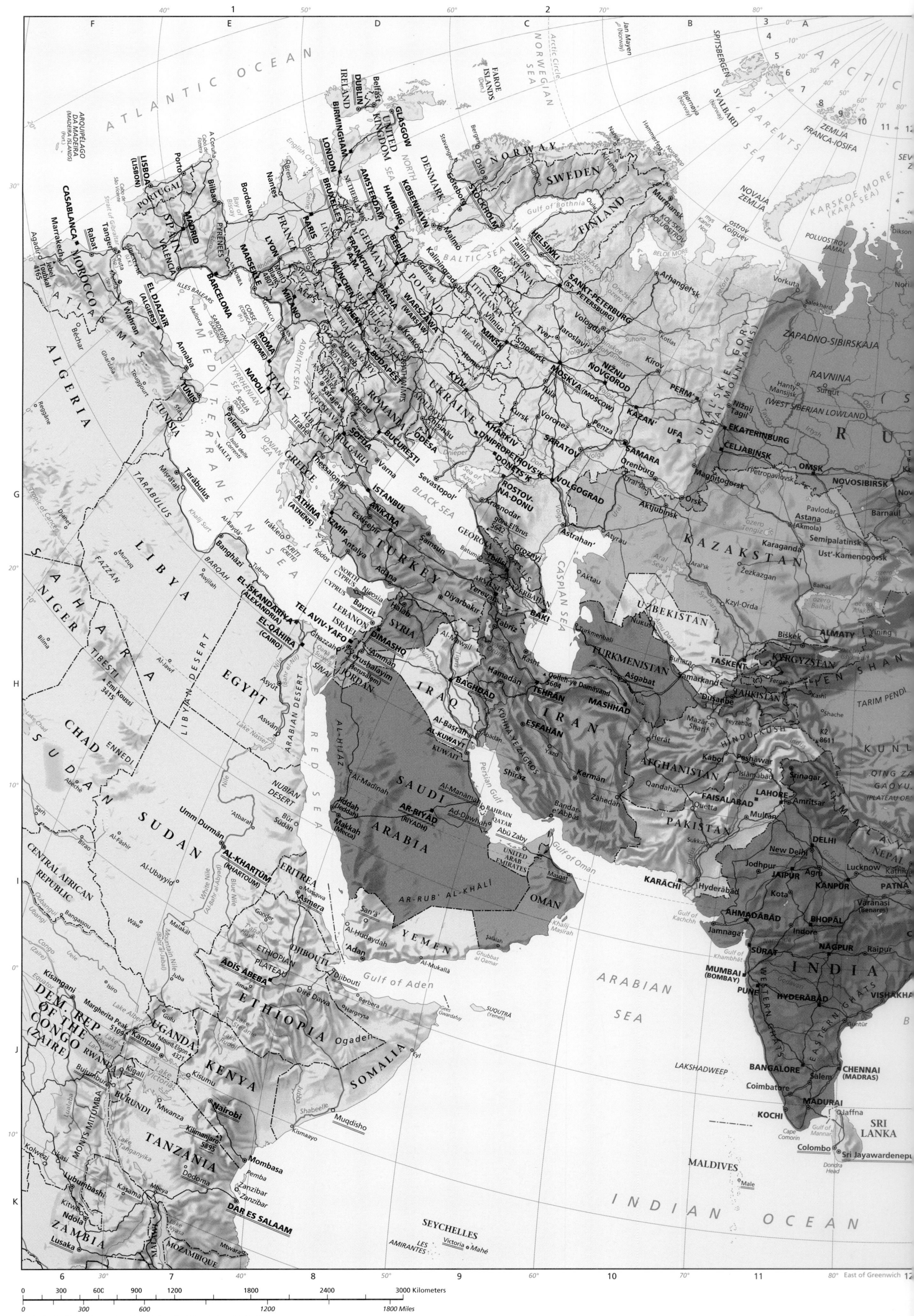

A 170° 21
80° 170°
160° 20
150° 19
140° 18
17
16

22 ostrov
Vrangelja

B

70°

proliv Longa

C

St.Lawrence
Island
(U.S.)

60°

mys
Navarin

D

50°

E 40° F 30°

HAWAIIAN
ISLANDS
(U.S.)

Bering Strait

VOSTOTNO-
SIBIRSKOE MORE

NOVOSIBIRSKIE
OSTROVA

Attu
Agattu

ALEUTIAN ISLANDS
(U.S.)

Kiska

KOMANDORSKIE
OSTROVA

Cape
Wrangell

BERING SEA

G

170°

MIDWAY
ISLANDS
(U.S.)

MORE
LAPTEVYH
(LAPTEV SEA)

ostrov
Karaginskij

mys Ozernoj

Petropavlovsk-
Kamčatskij

PACIFIC OCEAN

Tropic of Cancer

NESIBIRSKOE

VERHOJANSKIJ HREBET

HREBET CERSKOGO

SREDINNYJ HREBET

SEA OF
OKHOTSK

POLUOSTROV
KAMČATKA

OSKOGOR'E

S I B I R I J A
(AL SIBERIAN UPLANDS)

Jakutsk

Oha

H

20°

Bratsk

Angarsk

Irkutsk

Ulan-
Ude

Cita

STANOVOJ HREBET

Skovorodino

Blagoveščensk

Komsomol'sk-
na-Amure

Habarovsk

mys Elizavety

OSTROV
SAHALIN

Aleksandrovsk-
Sahalinskij

mys Terpenija

Južno-
Sahalinsk

SIHOTE-ALIN'

Tatarskij proliv

KURIL'SKIE OSTROVA
(KURIL ISLANDS)

ostrov
Iturup

ostrov
Kunašir

Minami-Tori-
Shima
(Japan)

WAKE
ISLAND
(U.S.)

H

170°

HANGAYN NURUU

Ulaanbaatar

Choybalsan

Hulun
Nur

Qiqihar

HARBIN

Ili

Vladivostok

Ch'ŏngjin

Asahikawa

Sapporo

HOKKAIDŌ

Hakodate

Aomori

SEA OF JAPAN

Akita

Niigata

HONSHŪ

Sendai

TŌKYŌ
YOKOHAMA

OGASAWARA-
GUNTO
(Japan)

20°

MONGOLIA

Hohhot

CHANGCHUN

SHENYANG

FUSHUN

Dandong

NORTH KOREA

P'yŏngyang

SŎUL
(SEOUL)

Kanazawa

KYŌTO NAGOYA
JAPAN

IZU-SHO
(Japan)

KAZAN-RETTO
(Japan)

GOBI DESERT

Zhangjiakou

BEIJING

DALIAN

SOUTH KOREA

Taegu

PUSAN

HIROSHIMA

OSAKA
SHIKOKU

Baotou

TIANJIN

Bo Hai

Mokp'o

Korea Strait

FUKUOKA

KYŪSHŪ

NORTHERN MARIANAS
(U.S.)

MARSHALL
ISLANDS

Enewetak

10°

TAIYUAN

JINAN

Shijiazhuang

Qingdao

YELLOW SEA

Cheju-do

Kagoshima

Farallon de Pajaros

Uujlang

Anxi

Yinchuan

Xi'ing

Lanzhou

Baoji

Zhengzhou

Xuzhou

Huainan

Nanjing

SHANGHAI

Ningbo

EAST
CHINA SEA

Amami-O-shima

NANSEI-SHOTO (RYUKYU ISLANDS)

Okinawa-Jima

Naha

Agrihan

Alamagan Pagan

Anatahan
Guguan

Saipan
Tinian
Rota

MARIANA
ISLANDS

Orolúk Kolonia

Pohnpei

MICRONESIA

HALL
ISLANDS

MORTLOCK
ISLANDS

SENYAVIN
ISLANDS

I

CHINA

XI'AN

WUHAN

Nanchang

Wenzhou

T'AIPEI

TAIWAN

T'ainan

KAOHSIUNG

GUAM
(U.S.)

Agana

Gaferut Ulul

CHUUK

Pulap

CAROLINE
ISLANDS

160°

CHENGDU

CHONGQING

CHANGSHA

Hengyang

Fuzhou

Xiamen

Taiwan Strait

Luzon Strait

Ngulu

YAP

Sorol Woleai

Eauripik

Ifalik Lamotrek

FEDERATED STATES
OF MICRONESIA

Zigong

Guiyang

Liuzhou

GUANGZHOU

XIANGGANG
(HONG KONG)

MACAU

Kapingamarangi

0°

Kunming

Nanning

Zhanjiang

Haikou

HAINAN
DAO

Babuyan

LUZON

Quezon City

Samar

PALAU ISLANDS

Koror

Equator

MYANMAR

Mandalay

HA NOI
(HANOI)

Hai Phong

Gulf of
Tonkin

MANILA

PHILIPPINES

Mindoro

Panay

Leyte

Cebu

Samar

SONSOROL
ISLANDS

PALAU

ADMIRALTY
ISLANDS

New
Hanover

Kavieng

NEW
IRELAND

J

BURMA

LAOS

VIETNAM

XISHA QUNDAO
(PARACEL ISLANDS)

Da Nang

Iloilo

Zamboanga

MINDANAO

Mount
Apo
2954

Davao

Moro
Gulf

Manus Island

BISMARCK
ARCHIPELAGO

NEW
BRITAIN

10°

YANGON
(RANGOON)

Gulf of
Martaban

THAILAND

KRUNG THEP
(BANGKOK)

SOUTH CHINA SEA

SPRATLY
ISLANDS

Palawan

SULU SEA

Jolo
Island

Balabac
Island

KEFULAUAN
TALAUD

BISMARCK
SEA

SOLOMON
SEA

COCO
ISLANDS

CAMBODIA

Phnum Pénh

THANH PHO
HO CHI MINH
(HO CHI MINH CITY)
(SAIGON)

Kâmpóng Saôm

Mui Ca Mau

Morotai

Gunong
Kinabalu
4101

KEPULAUAN
SANGIHE

HALMAHERA

Pulau Waigeo

Biak

Wewak

Jayapura

Madang

Mount Wilhelm
4509

Lae

Port Moresby

DAMAN
ISLANDS
(India)

ANDAMAN
SEA

Dawei

MALAY
PENINSULA

Pulau
Yapen

Puncak Jaya
5030

NEW GUINEA

PAPUA
NEW GUINEA

Gulf of
Papua

Torres Strait

Cape York

CORAL SEA

NICOBAR
ISLANDS
(India)

Phuket

George Town
(Penang)

MALAYSIA

KUALA LUMPUR

SINGAPORE

BRUNEI

Bandar Seri Begawan

Kuching

BORNEO
(KALIMANTAN)

KEPULAUAN
NATUNA
BESAR

Pontianak

CELEBES
SEA

Manado

SULAWESI
(CELEBES)

Teluk
Tomini

LAUT
MALUKU

KEPULAUAN
SULA

SERAM (CERAM)

Buru

MALUKU (MOLUCCAS)

LAUT BANDA

KEPULAUAN
KAI

KEPULAUAN
ARU

Pulau Yos
Sudarso

CAPE
YORK
PENINSULA

Gulf of
Carpentaria

K

Banda Aceh

MEDAN

Pulau Nias

KEPULAUAN
MENTAWAI

Pulau
Siberut

Strait of Malacca

SUMATERA
(SUMATRA)

Padang

Pulau
Bangka

Banjarmasin

Balikpapan

Pulau
Laut

Ujungpandang

Pulau
Buton

Selat Makasar

KEPULAUAN
TANIMBAR

Pulau
Wetar

ARAFURA SEA

Cape Arnhem

AUSTRALIA

Cape Wessel

Melville
Island

Cairns

Great Barrier Reef

20°

Palembang

Tanjungkarang-
Telukbetung

JAKARTA

BANDUNG

JAWA (JAVA)

SURABAYA

Madura

Bali

Lombok

Sumbawa

Sumba

LAUT JAWA

INDONESIA

LAUT FLORES

FLORES

LAUT SAWU

Kupang

TIMOR

Dili

TIMOR SEA

M-600000-2A-DR2-1
Copyright © Rand McNally & Co.

13 100° 14 110° 15 120° 16 17 130° 18 140° 19 150°

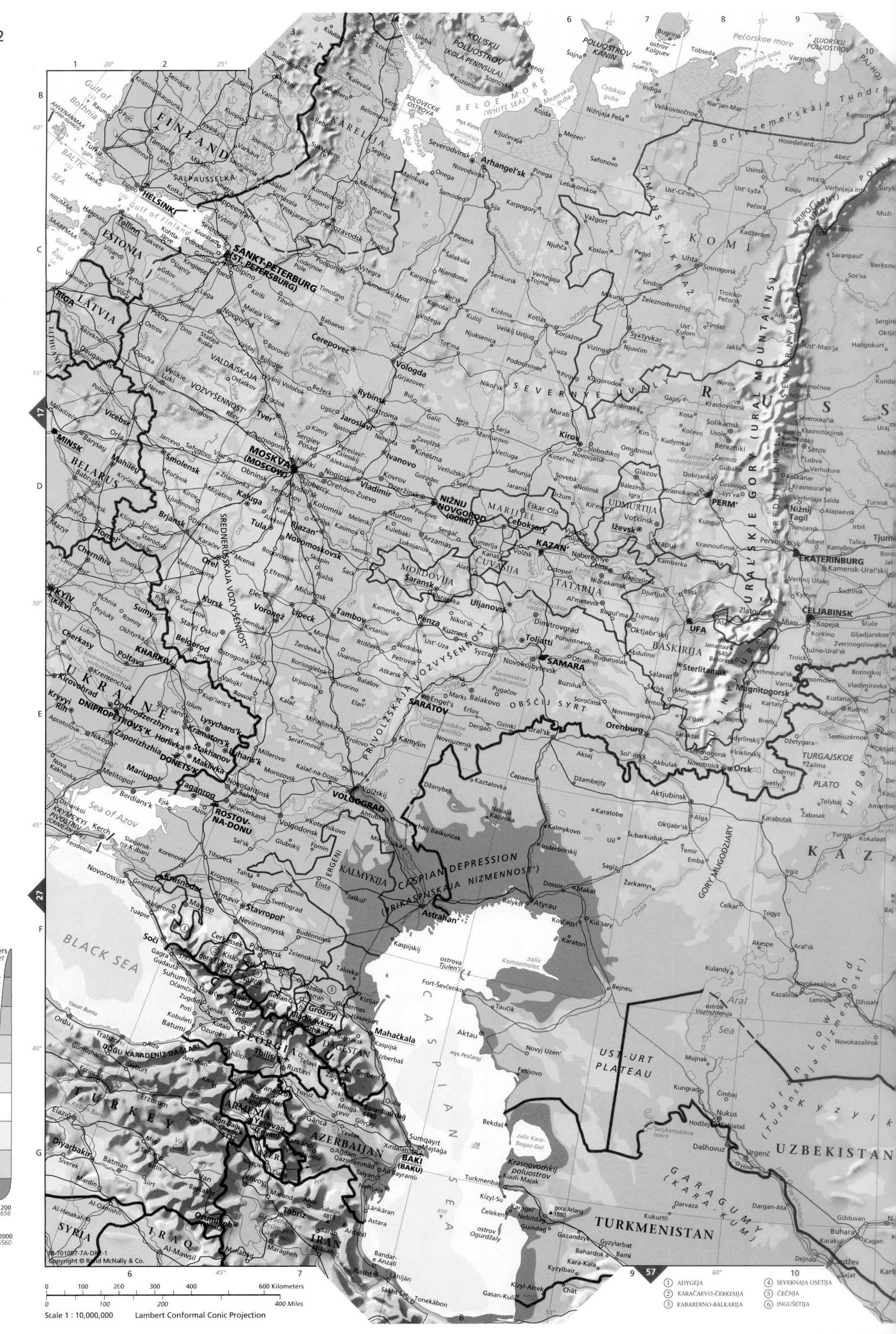

Meters
Feet

6000
19680

4000
13120

3000
9840

2000
6560

1000
3280

500
1640

200
656

Sea Level

200
656

2000
6560

0   100   200   300   400   600 Kilometers
0   100   200   400 Miles

Scale 1 : 10,000,000   Lambert Conformal Conic Projection

① ADYGEJA   ④ SEVERNAJA OSETIJA
② KARAČAEVO-ČERKESIJA ⑤ ČEČNJA
③ KABARDINO-BALKARIJA ⑥ INGUŠETIJA

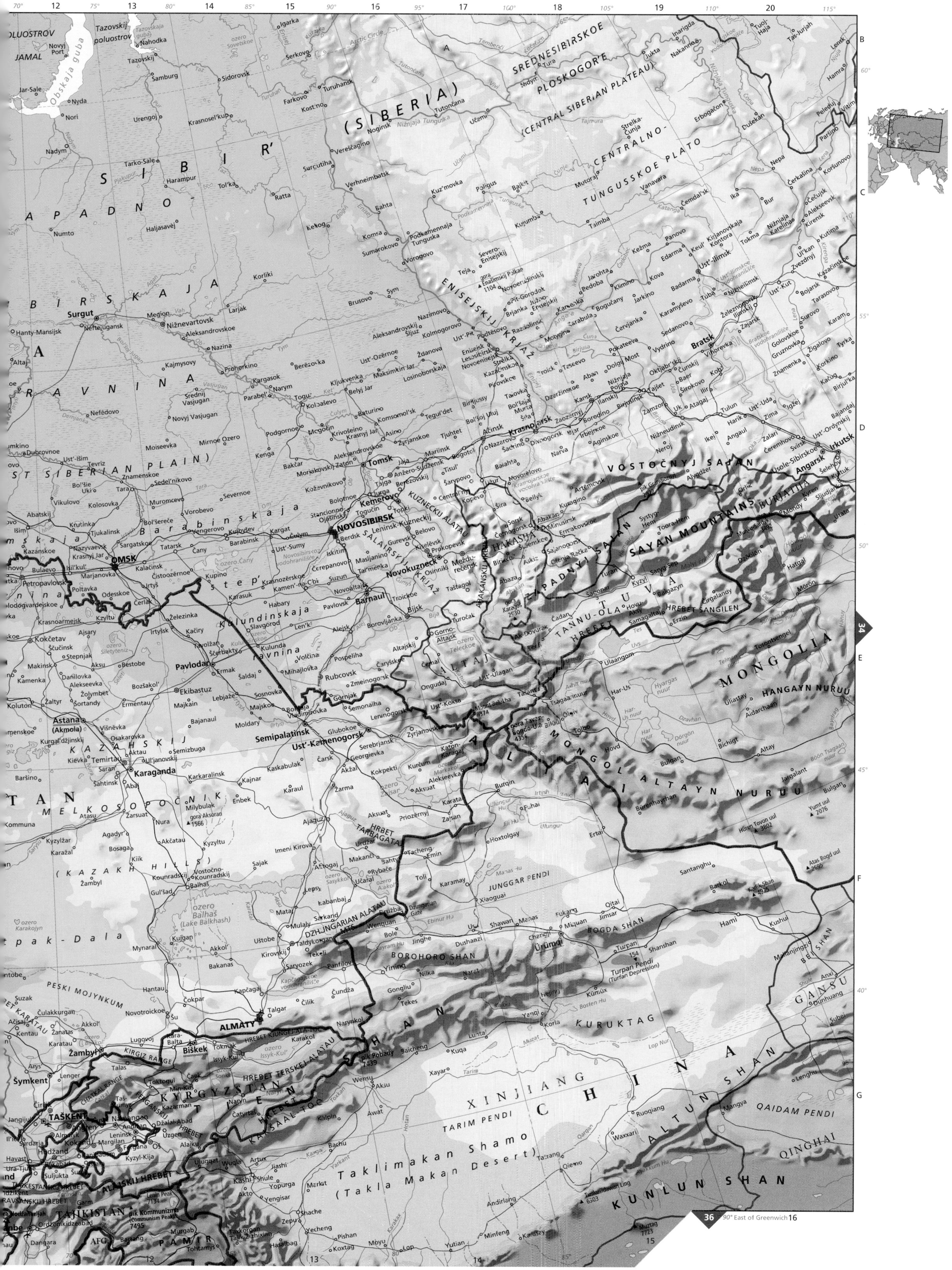

70° 12 75° 13 80° 14 85° 15 90° 16 95° 17 100° 18 105° 19 110° 20 115°

Grid references: A · B · C · D · E · F · G

Major labels

POLUOSTROV JAMAL

Obskaja guba

Tazovskij poluostrov

(SIBERIA)

SREDNESIBIRSKOE PLOSKOGOR'E (CENTRAL SIBERIAN PLATEAU)

CENTRALNO-TUNGUSSKOE PLATO

ZAPADNO-SIBIR' (WEST SIBERIAN PLAIN)

RAVNINA

BARABINSKAJA STEP'

KULUNDINSKAJA RAVNINA

ENISEJSKIJ KRJAŽ

HAKASIJA

ZAPADNYJ SAJAN

VOSTOČNYJ SAJAN

SAYAN MOUNTAINS

BURJATIJA

TUVA

TANNU-OLA

HREBET SANGILEN

MONGOLIA

HANGAYN NURUU

MONGOL ALTAYN NURUU

ALTAJ

KAZAHSKIJ MELKOSOPOČNIK (KAZAKH HILLS)

KAZAKHSTAN

ozero Balhaš (Lake Balkhash)

PESKI MOJYNKUM

DZUNGARIAN ALATAU

JUNGGAR PENDI

BOROHORO SHAN

BOGDA SHAN

TIEN SHAN

KYRGYZSTAN

KIRGIZ RANGE

HREBET TERSKEJ ALATAU

HREBET KUNGEJ-ALA-TOO

XINJIANG

TARIM PENDI

Taklimakan Shamo (Takla Makan Desert)

KURUKTAG

BEI SHAN

GANSU

CHINA

QINGHAI

QAIDAM PENDI

ALTUN SHAN

KUNLUN SHAN

PAMIR

TAJIKISTAN

Cities / towns (selected)

Surgut · Nefteugansk · Nižnevartovsk · Hanty-Mansijsk · OMSK · Tomsk · Kemerovo · NOVOSIBIRSK · Barnaul · Novokuzneck · Krasnojarsk · Abakan · Kyzyl · Irkutsk · Angarsk · Bratsk · Astana (Akmola) · Pavlodar · Karaganda · Semipalatinsk · Ust'-Kamenogorsk · Gorno-Altajsk · ALMATY · Biškek · Žambyl · TAŠKENT · Ürümqi · Mörön

90° East of Greenwich 16

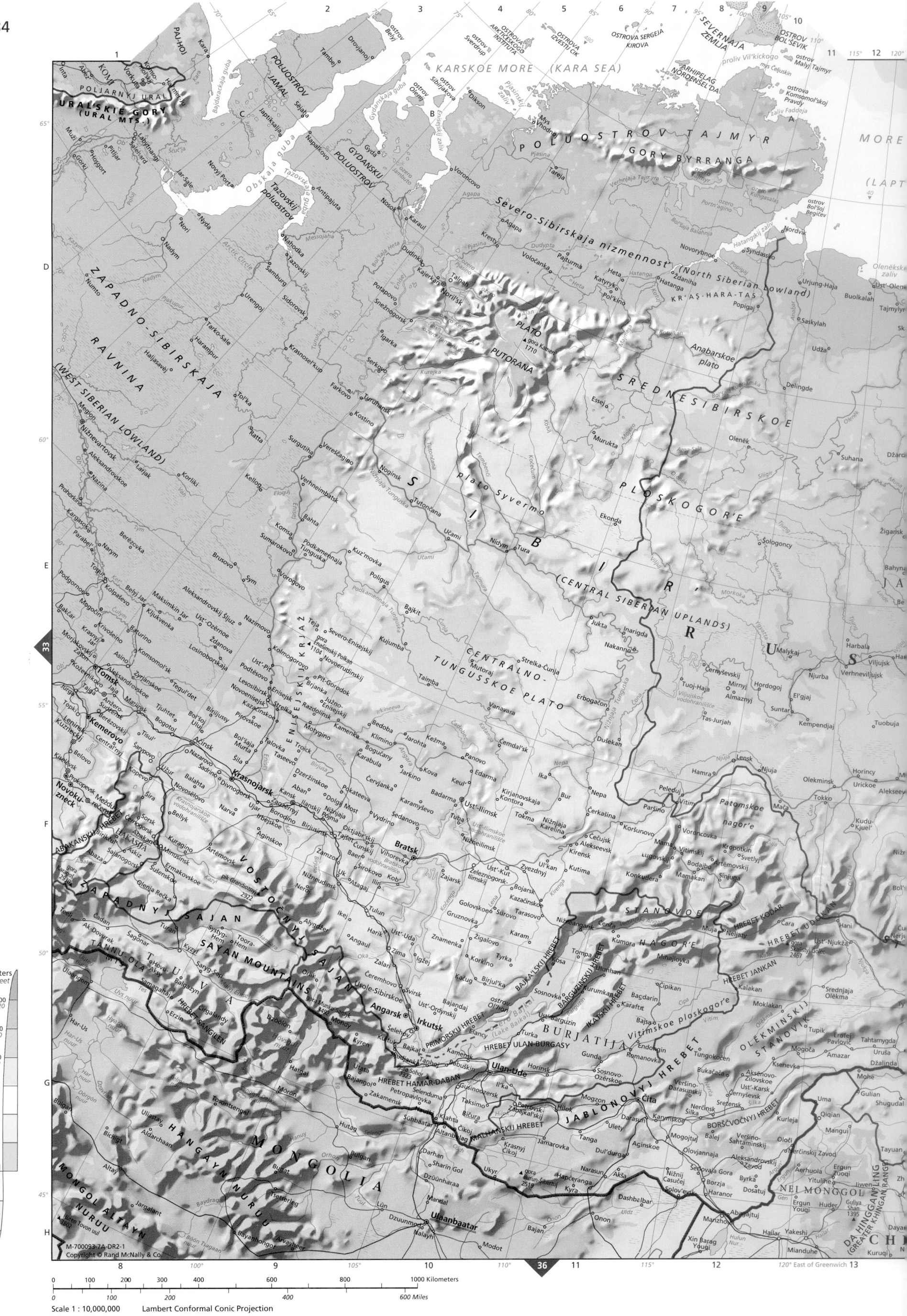

34

NOVOSIBIRSKIE OSTROVA

OSTROVA DE-LONGA
ostrov Genrietty
ostrov Bennetta
ostrov Žannetty
ostrov Žohova
ostrov Vil'kickogo

OSTROVA ANŽU
ostrov Bel'kovskij
OSTROV KOTEL'NYJ
OSTROV FADDEEVSKIJ
OSTROV NOVAJA SIBIR'
ostrov Stolbovoj
proliv Sannikova
LJAHOVSKIJE OSTROVA
LJAHOVSKIJE OSTROVA
OSTROV BOL'ŠOJ LJAHOVSKIJ

MEDVEŽJI OSTROVA

OSTROV VRANGELIA (WRANGEL ISLAND)

CHUKCHI SEA

U.S. ALASKA
Cape Wales
Teller
Bering Strait

proliv Longa

prošliv Dmitrija Lapteva
Svjatoj Nos
proliv Sannikova

VOSTOČNO-SIBIRSKOE MORE
(EAST SIBERIAN SEA)

Janskij zaliv
guba Buor-Haja
mys Buor-Haja

Bykovskij
Nižnejansk
Najba
Kular
Kazače
Tumat
Tenkeli
Ust'-Kujga
Tabor
Logaškino
Čokurdah
Srednekolymsk
Krest-Maёr
Svataj
Zyrjanka
Nelemnje

Ambarčik
Kolymskaja
Čerskij
Pohodsk
Anjujsk
Kolymskaja nizmennost' (Kolyma Plain)

ZUKOTSKIJ POLUOSTROV (CHUKOTSK PEN.)

Enmurino
Vankarem
Uelen
mys Deznova
Lavrentija
Providenija
Gambell
Cape Čaplino
Eneurmino

ANADYRSKOE PLOSKOGORE

HREBET PEKUL'NEJ

Anadyr
Ust'-Belaja
Markovo
Eropol

Anadyrskij zaliv (Gulf of Anadyr)

BERING SEA

KORJAKSKOE NAGORE

OLOJSKIJ HREBET
AN.UJS-II HREBET
Jukagirskoe ploskogor'e

VERHOJANSKIJ HREBET (VERHOJANSK MOUNTAINS)

HREBET KULAR
Batagaj-Alyta
Verhojansk
Batagaj
Bala
Tomtor
Junkjur
Batylas

Namy
Sajdy
Janskij
Suordah
Deputatskij
Syagannah
Družina

HREBET ČERSKOGO (ČERSKY MOUNTAINS)

MOMSKIJ HREBET
Honuu
gora Pobeda 3147
Moma
Ust'-Nera
Artyk

(SIBERIA)

Jakutsk
Namtcy
Borogoncy
Ytyk-Kjuёl'
Kangalassy
Bestjah
Majja
Pokrovsk
Čurapča
Myndagaj

Džebariki-Haja
Tompo
HREBET SETTE-DABAN
HREBET SUNTAR-HAJAT
gora Mus-Haja 2959
Ohotskij Pereval
Allah-Jun'
Ketanda
Arka

El'dikan
Ust'-Maja
Ynykčanskij
Nel'kan
Kemkara
Gonam

HREBET DŽUGDŽUR

Aim
Ust'-Judoma
Aldoma
Ajan

Oмjakon
Mjaundža
Adygalak
Bol'ševik
Susuman
Seimčan
Sporhoe
Ust'-Omčug
Omčak
Omsukčan
Jasačnaja
Balygyčan

Srednekan
Orotukan
Atka
Palatka
Talaja
Jagodnoe
Abориёn 2586

Oja
Ola
Sigljan
Magadan
Ust'-Hajrjuzovo
Tauisk
Motykleika
Taujskaja guba
mys Aleuna

Ohotsk
mys Duga-Zapadnaja
Ulja

ostrov Iony

SEA OF OKHOTSK

ŠANTARSKIE OSTROVA

POLUOSTROV KAMČATKA

SREDINNYJ HREBET

KAMČATSKIJ POLUOSTROV
KOMANDORSKIE OSTROVA
Nikol'skoe
ostrov Beringa
ostrov Karaginskij
KAMČATSKIJ zaliv
zaliv Ozernoj

Vulkan Ključevskaja Sopka 4750
Ključi
Ust'-Kamčatsk
Esso
Milkovo
Vulkan Kronockaja Sopka 3456
Kronockij zaliv
Sobolevo
Petropavlovsk-Kamčatskij
Jelizovo
Vulkan Korjakskaja Sopka 3456
Kihčik
Ust'-Bol'šereck
Oktjabr'skij
Ozernovskij
Pervyj Kuril'skij proliv
mys Lopatka

KURIL'SKIE OSTROVA (KURIL ISLANDS)
ostrov Atlasova
Severo-Kuril'sk
ostrov Paramušir
ostrov Onekotan
ostrov Slaškotan
ostrov Matua
ostrov Rasšua
ostrov Simušir
proliv Kruzenšterna
ostrov Ketoj
ostrov Urup
Aleutka
ostrov Simušir

HREBET DŽAGDY
Bomnak
Udskoe
Torom
Čumikan
Tugur
Baladёk

HREBET TUKURINGRA
Zejskoe vodohranilišče
Zeja
Jasnyj
Oktjabr'skij
Stojba
Bereja
Selemdžinsk
Norsk
Majskij
Šimanovsk
Svobodnyj
Belogorsk
Ivanovka
Ekaterinoslavka
Blagoveščensk
Rajčihinsk
Arhara
Obluč'e
Pompeevka
Bidžan
Leninskoe
Tongjiang

HREBET BUREINSKIJ
BADŽAL'SKIJ HREBET
Komsomol'sk-na-Amure

HREBET DŽAGDY

Aldoma
Ajan

Nikolaevsk-na-Amure
Mago
Moskal'vo
Oha
POLUOSTROV ŠMIDTA
Sahalinskij zaliv
OSTROV SAHALIN (SAKHALIN)

ZAPADNYJ HREBET
Nyvrovo
Susanino
Paromaj
Noglikoe
Katangli
De-Kastri
Lazarev
Bogorodskoe
Merinsk
Sofijsk
Aleksandrovsk-Sahalinskij
gora Lopatina 1609
Pobedino
Širokaja Pad'
Smirnyh
Bosnjakovo
Lesogorsk
Šahtёrsk
Uglegorsk
Makarov
Krasnogorsk
Tomari
Čehov
Holmsk
Nevel'sk
Anива
Korsakov
Ozёrskij
Dol'nsk
Južno-Sahalinsk
Adimi
Ne'ma
zaliv Terpenija
mys Terpenija
Poronajsk

SIHOTE-ALIN'
Habarovsk
Smidovič
Fuyuan
Muhen
Vjazemskij
Antun'
Tongjiang
Zhaoxing
Daotianji
Vanqing
wu
HEILONGJIANG

Scale 1 : 10,000,000   Lambert Conformal Conic Projection

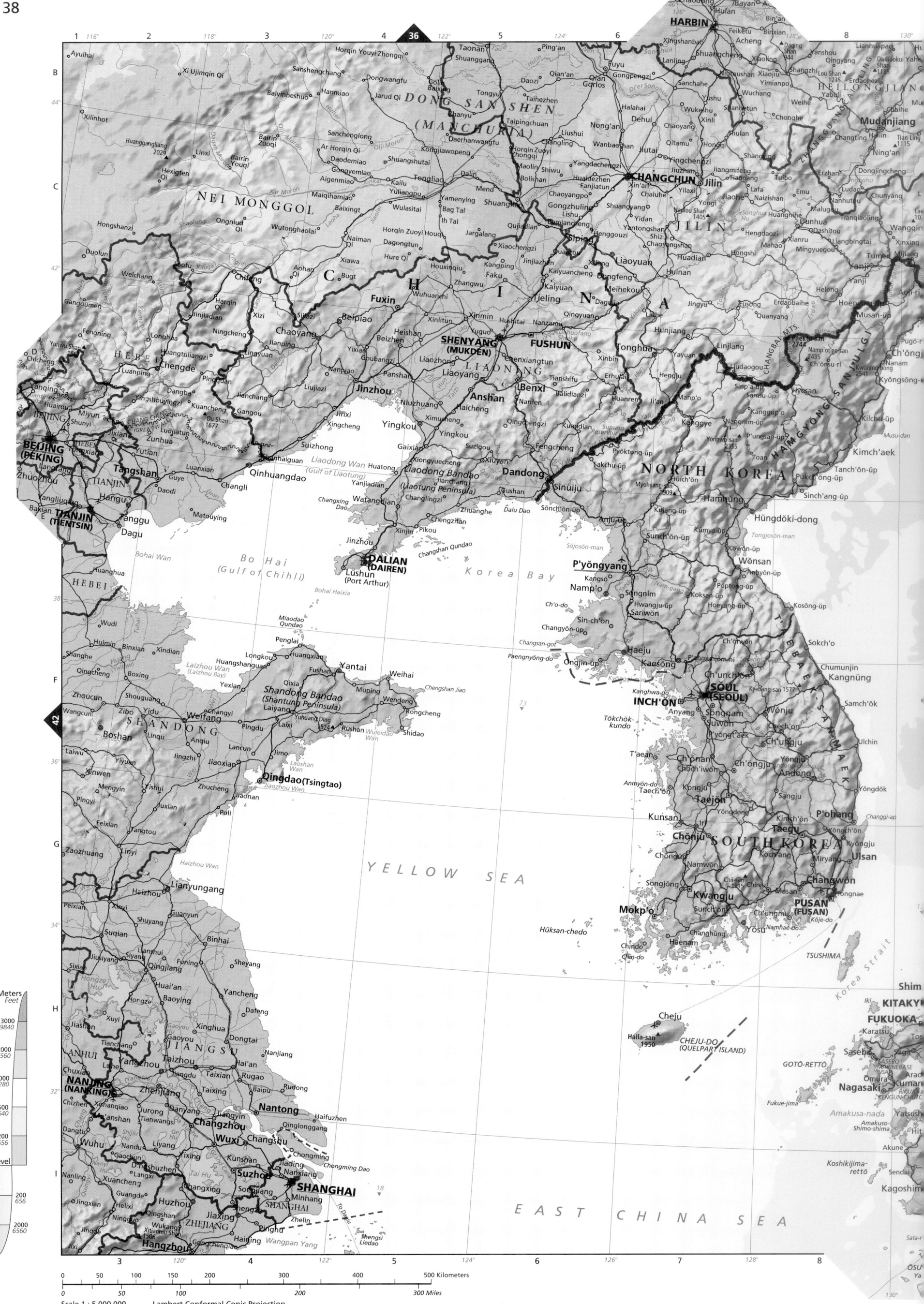

HARBIN

Xinshanbao Acheng Ningshou Lianhuapao

B Xi Ujimqin Qi Dongwangfu HEILONGJIANG

DONG SAN SHEN Daqing Shan 544

NEI MONGGOL (MANCHURIA) Mudanjiang

Changchun JILIN

C H I N A

Fuxin SHENYANG FUSHUN NORTH KOREA
(MUKDEN)

BEIJING Jinzhou
(PÉKING)

TIANJIN Dalian P'yŏngyang
(TIENTSIN) (DAIREN)
Lüshun
(Port Arthur)

Bo Hai Korea Bay
(Gulf of Chihli)

HEBEI

38

Yantai SÖUL
(SEOUL)

SHANDONG INCH'ŎN

Qingdao (Tsingtao) SOUTH KOREA

Taejon

YELLOW SEA Taegu

PUSAN
(FUSAN)

JIANGSU

NANJING Cheju
(NANKING) Halla-san CHEJU-DO
1950 (QUELPART ISLAND)

SHANGHAI

Hangzhou ZHEJIANG EAST CHINA SEA

Meters
Feet
3000
9840
2000
6560
1000
3280
500
1640
200
656
Sea Level
200
656
2000
6560

0 50 100 150 200 300 400 500 Kilometers
0 50 100 200 300 Miles
Scale 1 : 5,000,000 Lambert Conformal Conic Projection

Japan, Korea, and Northeastern China

W-566400-7A-D-72-1
Copyright © Rand McNally & Co

RUSSIA

Vladivostok
Nahodka
Ussurijsk

SIHOTÈ-ALIN'

SEA OF OKHOTSK

Habomai, Shikotan, Kunashiri and
Etorofu, occupied since 1945, are
claimed by Japan pending a final peace treaty.

KURIL'SKIE OSTROVA
(KURIL ISLANDS)

RUSSIA

ostrov
Iturup
(Etorofu-tō)

ostrov
Šikotan
(Shikotan-tō)

Malaja
Kuril'skaja
Grjada
(Habomai-shotō)

Wakkanai
Rishiri-tō
Rebun-tō

HOKKAIDŌ

Sapporo

Asahikawa

Hakodate

SEA OF JAPAN

(EAST SEA)

Take-shima
(by S. Korea and Japan)

Aomori

Akita

Sendai

J A P A N

SADO

Niigata

Kanazawa
Toyama

Fukui

OKI-SHOTŌ
Dōgo

Matsue
Tottori

Yonago
Izumo

CHŪGOKU-SANCHI

Gifu

KYŌTO
NAGOYA

KŌBE
OSAKA

Himeji

Okayama
Kurashiki

HIROSHIMA

Fukuyama

Matsuyama

Takamatsu
Tokushima

Kōchi

SHIKOKU

TŌKYŌ
Chiba

KAWASAKI
YOKOHAMA

Numazu

Shizuoka
Hamamatsu

Fuji-san
(Mount Fuji)
3776

HONSHŪ

IZU ISHOTŌ
(IZU ISLANDS)

Hachijō-jima

KYŪSHŪ

Miyazaki

P A C I F I C   O C E A N

EAST CHINA SEA

NANSEI-SHOTŌ
(RYUKYU ISLANDS)

AMAMI-SHOTŌ

Amami-Ō-shima

Naze

SATSUNAN-SHOTŌ

OKINAWA-SHOTŌ

Okinawa-jima

Naha

JAPAN

PACIFIC OCEAN

Same scale as main map

1   129°   2   130°   3   4   131°   5   133°   6   134°   7

NORTH KOREA

Kansŏng

Sohwa-ri
Sŏkch'o
Kangnŭng
Yŏyang-ni

KANGWON-DO

P'yŏngch'ang
Ch'ŏngsŏn
Mukho
Samch'ŏk
Imwŏn-ni

Ullŭng-do
(S. Korea)

Tok-to · Take-shima
(Claimed by S. Korea and Japan)

SEA OF JAPAN
(EAST SEA)

CH'UNGCH'ŎNG-BUKTO
Ulchin

SOUTH KOREA

OKI-SHOTŌ
Dōgo
Daimanji-san 608
Saigō
Dōzen

JAPAN

KYŎNGSANG-BUKTO

P'ohang

Taegu
Kyŏngju

PUSAN (FUSAN)

KYŎNGSANG-NAMDO
Changwŏn
Masan

KŌJE-DO

Western Channel
Korea Strait
Tsushima-kaikyō (Eastern channel)

TSUSHIMA

KITAKYŪSHŪ
FUKUOKA

GOTŌ-RETTŌ

NAGASAKI

SASEBO MARINEBASE
(USA)

Nagasaki

Fukue-Jima

Amakusa-nada
AMAKUSA-SHOTŌ
Amakuso-Shimo-shima

KYŪSHŪ

EAST CHINA SEA

Koshikijima-rettō

KAGOSHIMA

Kagoshima
YAKU-KOKURITSU-KŌEN
KIRISHIMA-YAKU-KOKURITSU-KŌEN

Uji-guntō

Matsue
TOTTORI
Yonago
SHIMANE
Hamada
Misumi

HIROSHIMA
Okayama
OKAYAMA
Kurashiki
Fukuyama

HIROSHIMA
Kure

YAMAGUCHI
Yamaguchi

Shimonoseki
Tokuyama
Iwakuni

INLAND SEA
SETO-NAIKAI

Takamatsu
KAGAWA
TOKUSHIMA

Matsuyama
EHIME
SHIKOKU
KŌCHI
Kōchi

ŌITA
Ōita
Beppu

KUMAMOTO
Kumamoto

MIYAZAKI

Miyazaki

Hyūga-nada

SHIKOKU

Tosa-wan
Muroto
Muroto-zaki

PACIFIC OCEAN

HONSHŪ

Scale 1 : 2,500,000   Lambert Conformal Conic Projection

W-561592-7A-DR2-1
Copyright © Rand McNally & Co.

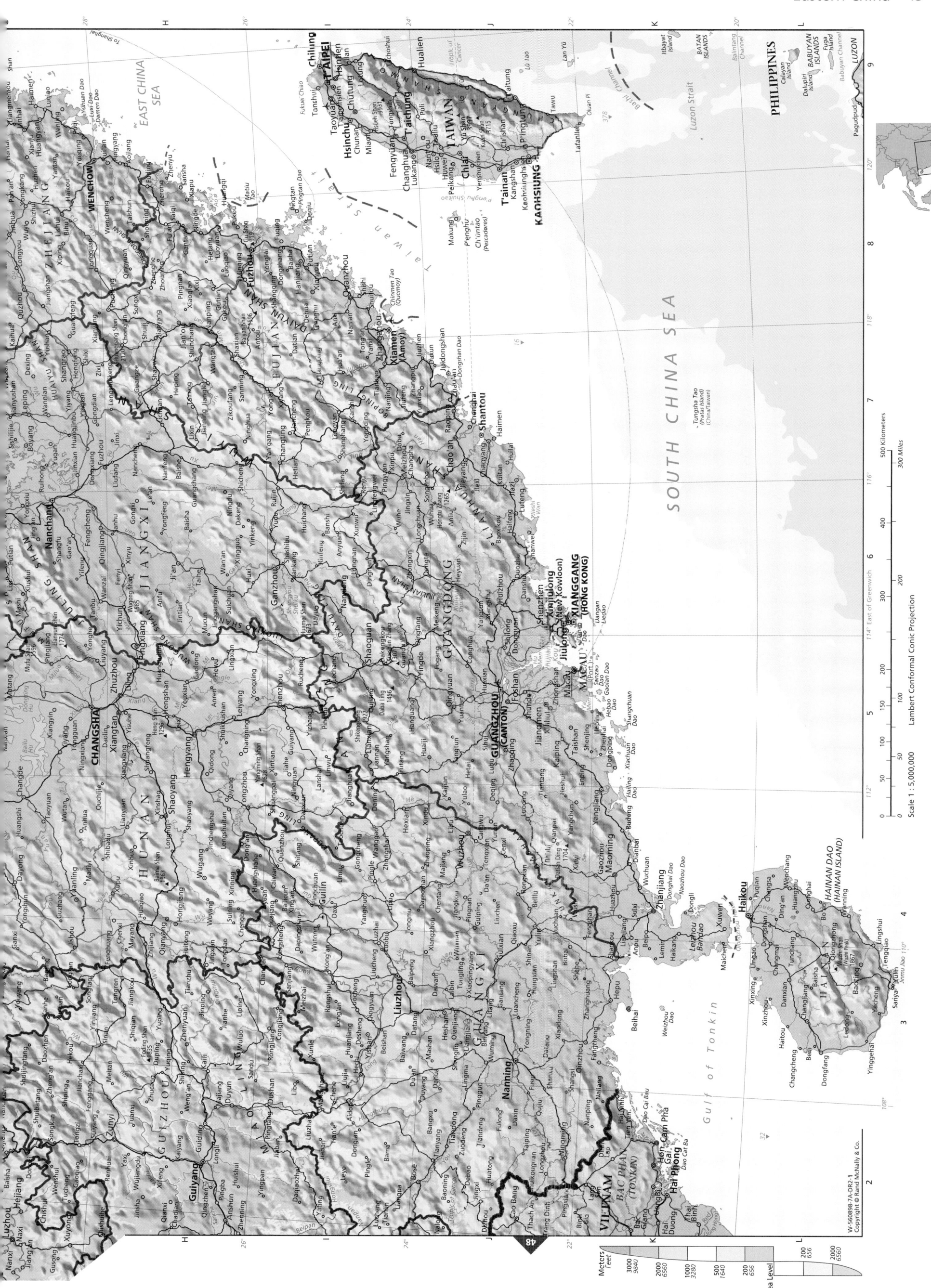

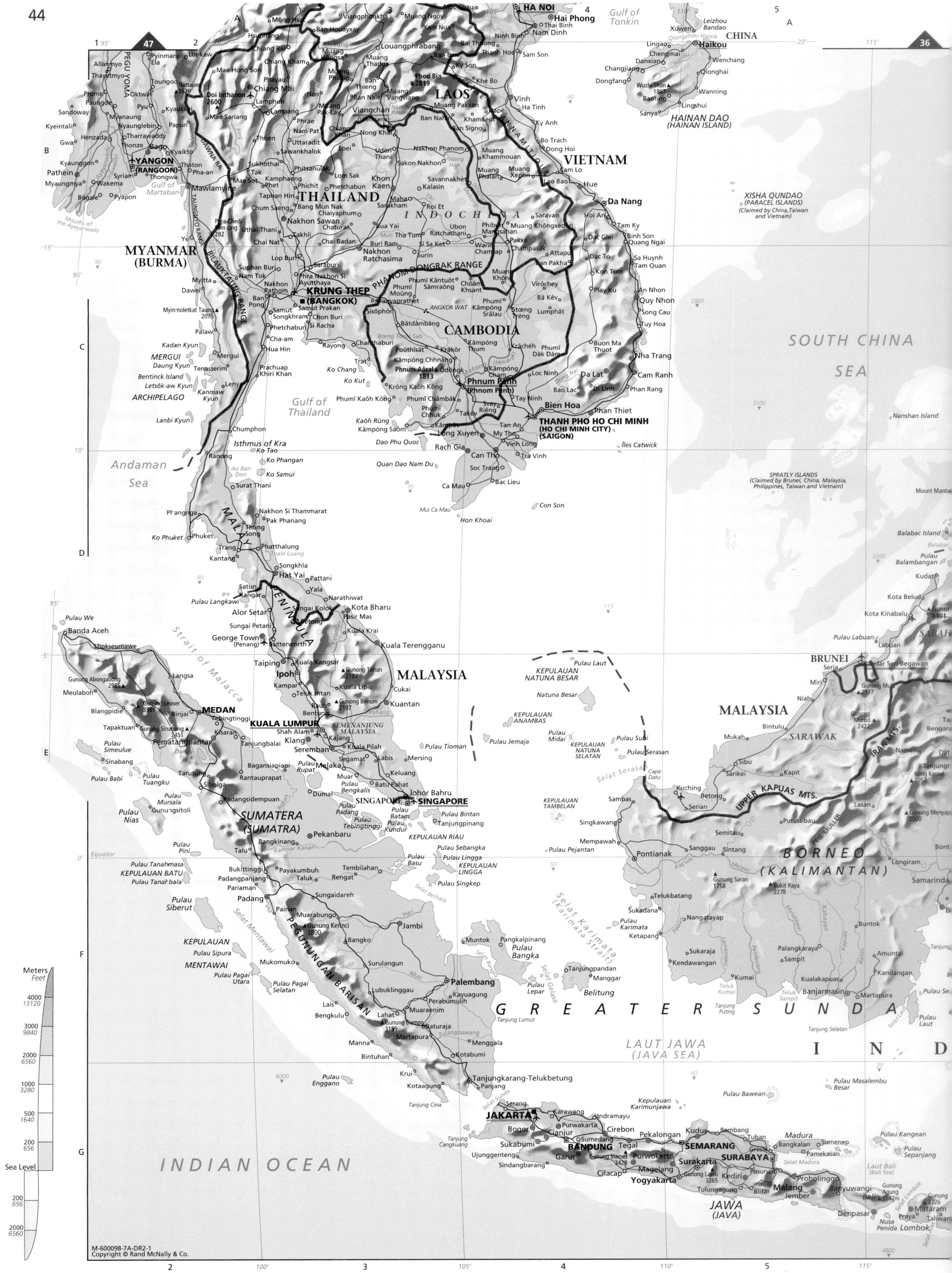

MYANMAR (BURMA)

THAILAND

LAOS

VIETNAM

CAMBODIA

CHINA

MALAYSIA

SUMATERA (SUMATRA)

BORNEO (KALIMANTAN)

SINGAPORE

JAWA (JAVA)

SOUTH CHINA SEA

Gulf of Tonkin

Andaman Sea

Gulf of Thailand

Gulf of Martaban

Strait of Malacca

INDIAN OCEAN

GREATER SUNDA

LAUT JAWA (JAVA SEA)

Laut Bali (Bali Sea)

HAINAN DAO (HAINAN ISLAND)

XISHA QUNDAO (PARACEL ISLANDS) (Claimed by China, Taiwan and Vietnam)

SPRATLY ISLANDS (Claimed by Brunei, China, Malaysia, Philippines, Taiwan and Vietnam)

INDOCHINA

DÔNGRAK RANGE

PHANOM

BILAUKTAUNG RANGE

TAUNGNYO RANGE

PEGU YOMA

SALWEEN RANGE

MALAY PENINSULA

PEGUNUNGAN BARISAN

UPPER KAPUAS MTS.

PEG. MULLER

IRAN MTS.

MERGUI ARCHIPELAGO

KEPULAUAN MENTAWAI

KEPULAUAN BATU

KEPULAUAN RIAU

KEPULAUAN LINGGA

KEPULAUAN NATUNA BESAR

KEPULAUAN ANAMBAS

KEPULAUAN NATUNA SELATAN

KEPULAUAN TAMBELAN

Selat Karimata (Karimata Strait)

Isthmus of Kra

Mouths of the Ayeyarwady

HA NOI
Hai Phong
Nam Dinh
Ninh Binh
Thai Binh

Haikou

BANGKOK (KRUNG THEP)

Phnum Pénh (Phnom Penh)

THANH PHO HO CHI MINH (HO CHI MINH CITY) (SAIGON)

YANGON (RANGOON)

KUALA LUMPUR

SINGAPORE

MEDAN

JAKARTA

BANDUNG

SEMARANG

SURABAYA

Surakarta

Yogyakarta

Palembang

Pontianak

BRUNEI
Bandar Seri Begawan

SARAWAK

SABAH

Kota Kinabalu

Da Nang

Nha Trang

Cam Ranh

Phan Rang

Phan Thiet

Bien Hoa

Da Lat

Hue

Quy Nhon

Chiang Mai

Mae Sariang

Doi Inthanon 2600

Phou Bia 2819

Gunung Kerinci 3800

Gunung Leuser 3381

Gunung Kinabalu 4101

Meters / Feet
4000 / 13120
3000 / 9840
2000 / 6560
1000 / 3280
500 / 1640
200 / 656
Sea Level
200 / 656
2000 / 6560

M-600098-7A-DR2-1
Copyright © Rand McNally & Co.

Scale 1 : 10,000,000   Sinusoidal Projection

0 100 200 300 400 600 800 1000 Kilometers
0 100 200 300 400 600 Miles

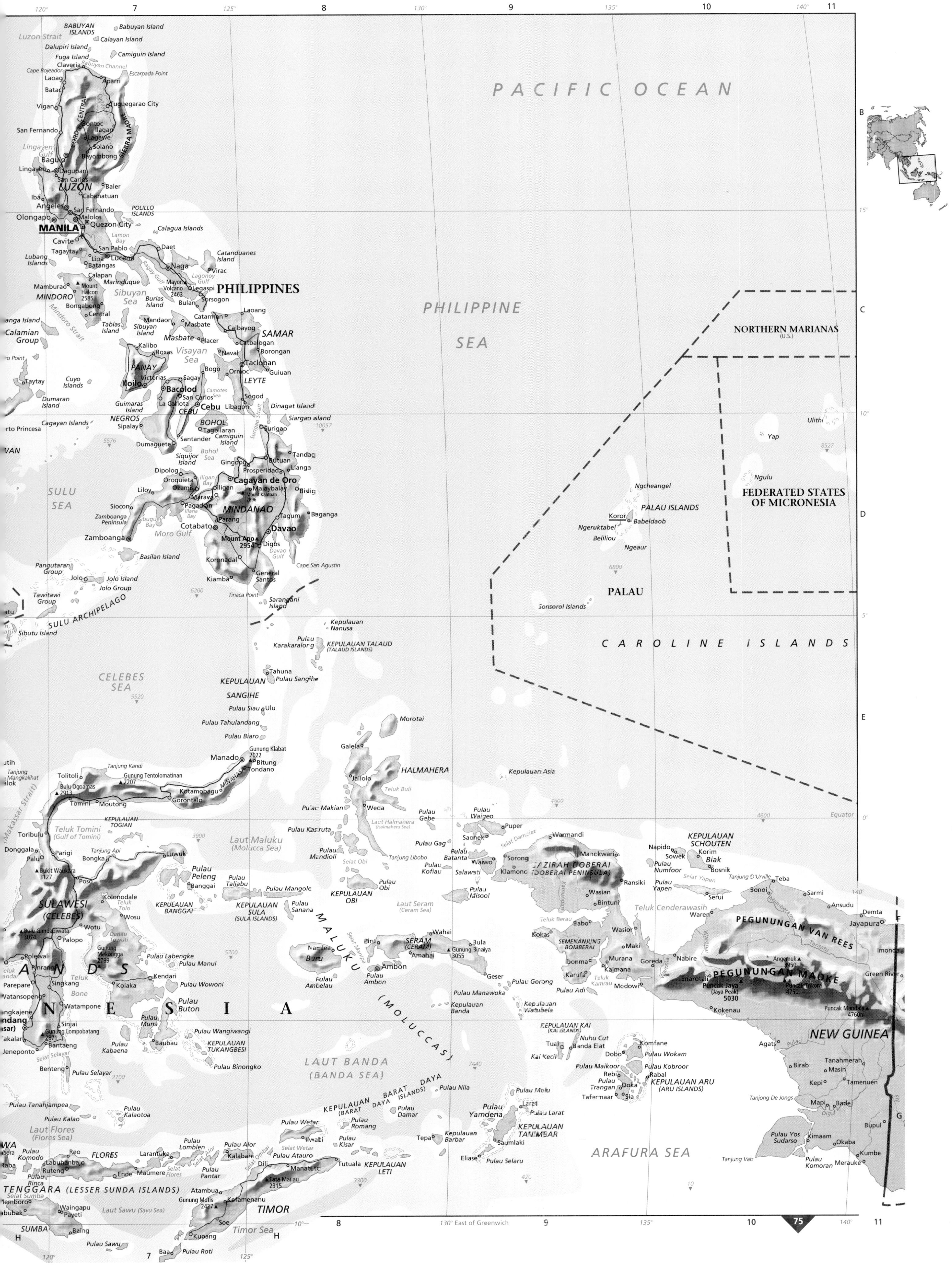

PACIFIC OCEAN

PHILIPPINE SEA

PHILIPPINES

CELEBES SEA

SULU SEA

NORTHERN MARIANAS (U.S.)

FEDERATED STATES OF MICRONESIA

PALAU ISLANDS

Koror
Babeldaob
Ngeruktabel
Beliliou
Ngeaur

PALAU

Yap
Ulithi
Ngulu
Ngcheangel

CAROLINE ISLANDS

Sonsorol Islands

Kepulauan Nanusa
Pulau Karakaralong
KEPULAUAN TALAUD (TALAUD ISLANDS)

Tahuna
Pulau Sangihe
KEPULAUAN SANGIHE
Pulau Siau
Ulu
Pulau Tahulandang
Pulau Biaro

Manado
Gunung Klabat 2022
Bitung
Tondano
MINAHASA
Galela
Morotai

HALMAHERA
Kepulauan Asia

Tolitoli
Tanjung Kandi
Bulu Ogoamas 2913
Gunung Tentolomatinan 2207
Kotamobagu
Gorontalo
Moutong
Tomini
TELUK TOMINI (Gulf of Tomini)
KEPULAUAN TOGIAN

Pu'au Makian
Weca
Jailolo
Teluk Buli

Pulau Gebe
Laut Halmahera (halmahera Sea)

Pulau Waigeo
Puper
Saoneк

Pulau Kasiruta
Pulau Mendioli
Selat Obi
Pulau Gag
Tanjung Libobo
Pulau Batanta
Waigeo
Selat Dampier
Warmandi
Manokwari
Napido
Sowek
KEPULAUAN SCHOUTEN
Korim
Biak
Bosnik

Toribulu
Donggala
Parigi
Palu
Bukit Wabula 3127
Poso
Tanjung Api
Bongka
Luwuk
Kolonedale
Teluk Tolo
Wosu
Wotu

Pulau Peleng
Banggai
KEPULAUAN BANGGAI
Pulau Taliabu
Pulau Mangole
KEPULAUAN SULA (SULA ISLANDS)
Pulau Sanana
Pulau Obi
KEPULAUAN OBI
Laut Seram (Ceram Sea)
Pulau Misool
Salawati
Kofiau
Pulau Kofiau
Sorong
Klamono
JAZIRAH DOBERAI (DOBERAI PENINSULA)
Wasian
Bintuni
Ransiki
Pulau Numfoor
Pulau Yapen
Selat Yapen
Teluk Cenderawasih
Waren
Serui
Bonoi
Sarmi
Ansudu
Demta
Jayapura

SULAWESI (CELEBES)
Bulu Gandadiwata 3074
Gunung Kolonodale
Danau Towuti
Palopo
Pulau Labengke
Pulau Manui
Kendari
Pulau Wowoni

PEGUNUNGAN VAN REES
Angemuk 3950
PEGUNUNGAN MAOKE
Puncak Jaya (Jaya Peak) 5030
Puncak Trikora 4750
Puncak Mandala 4760
Enarotali

Pinrang
Parepare
Watansopeng
Singkang
Kolaka
SERAM (CERAM)
Gunung Binaia 3055
Wahai
Bula
SEMENANJUNG BOMBERAI
Babo
Kokas
Maki
Wasior
Ibonuma
Murana
Kaimana
Goreda
Nabire
Kokenau

Makassar
Gunung Lompobatang
Bantaeng
Sinjai
Pulau Muna
Pulau Buton
Piru
Namlea
Buru
Amahai
Ambon
Pulau Ambon
Amelau
Geser
Pulau Gorong
Pulau Adi
Karufa
Mcdowi
Teluk Kamrau

NEW GUINEA
Agats
Tanahmerah
Birab
Masin
Kepi
Tamenuen

Jeneponto
Watampone
Teluk Bone
Benteng
Pulau Selayar
Pulau Kabaena
Baubau
KEPULAUAN TUKANGBESI
Pulau Wangiwangi
Pulau Manawoka
Kepulauan Watubela
Kepulauan Banda
KEPULAUAN KAI (KAI ISLANDS)
Nuhu Cut
Tual
Komfane
Pulau Wokam
Dobo
Pulau Kobroor
Kai Kecil
KEPULAUAN ARU (ARU ISLANDS)
Rebi
Pulau Trangan
Doka
Sia
Tafermaar

LAUT BANDA (BANDA SEA)

Pulau Tanahjampea
Pulau Kalaotoa
Laut Flores (Flores Sea)
Pulau Kalao

KEPULAUAN BARAT DAYA (BARAT DAYA ISLANDS)
Pulau Nila
Pulau Damar
Pulau Romang
Pulau Moa
Larat
Pulau Larat
Pulau Yamdena
KEPULAUAN TANIMBAR
Saumlaki
Pulau Maikoor
Pulau Maikoor

Pulau Wetar
Selat Wetar
Pulau Kisar
Tepa
Kepulauan Barbar
Eliase
Pulau Selaru

ARAFURA SEA

Pulau Yos Sudarso
Kimaam
Okaba
Kumbe
Merauke
Bade
Mapi
Kepi
Bupul
Tanjung De Jongs

FLORES
Larantuka
Ende
Maumere
NUSA TENGGARA (LESSER SUNDA ISLANDS)
Gunung Mutis 2427
Reo
Ruteng
Labuanbajo
Komodo
Rinca
Sumba
Waingapu
Payeti
SUMBA

TIMOR
Tata Mailau 3300
Dilli
Manatuto
Tutuala
KEPULAUAN LETI
Atambua
Soe
Kupang
Baa
Pulau Roti
Pulau Sawu
Laut Sawu (Savu Sea)
Timor Sea

Pulau Lomblen
Pulau Alor
Kalabahi
Pulau Atauro
Pulau Pantar

LUZON
Babuyan Islands
Babuyan Island
Calayan Island
Fuga Island
Dalupiri Island
Camiguin Island
Claveria
Aparri
Laoag
Batac
Vigan
Tuguegarao City
Bontoc
Bayombong
Baler
San Fernando
Baguio
Solano
Ilagan
San Carlos
Dagupan
Cabanatuan
Lingayen
Olongapo
Angeles
San Fernando
Malolos
Quezon City
MANILA
Cavite
Tagaytay
Lipa
Batangas
San Pablo
Lucena
Naga
Daet
Legaspi
Calapan
Marinduque
Mount Halcon 2585
MINDORO
Bongabong
Calamian Group
Taytay
Cuyo Islands
Dumaran Island
Mayon Volcano 2462
Sorsogon
Bulan
Catanduanes Island
Virac
Laoang
Catarman
Masbate
SAMAR
Calbayog
Catbalogan
Borongan
Guiuan
Naval
Tacloban
Ormoc
LEYTE
Sogod
Masbate
Placer
PANAY
Victorias
Iloilo
Bacolod
La Carlota
Sagay
San Carlos
Cebu
CEBU
Bogo
Libagon
Dinagat Island
Siargao Island
Guimaras Island
NEGROS
Sipalay
Dumaguete
Santander
Tagbilaran
BOHOL
Siquijor Island
Camiguin Island
Surigao
Butuan
Tandag
Lianga
Dipolog
Oroquieta
Ozamiz
Iligan
Iligan Bay
Marawi
Prosperidad
Cagayan de Oro
Malaybalay
Mount Kitanglad 2896
Bislig
Baganga
Pagadian
Iligan Bay
Parang
MINDANAO
Cotabato
Tagum
Davao
Zamboanga
Zamboanga Peninsula
Koronadal
Mount Apo 2954
Digos
Davao Gulf
Kiamba
General Santos
Cape San Agustin
Basilan Island
Pangutaran Group
Jolo
Jolo Island
Jolo Group
SULU ARCHIPELAGO
Tawitawi Group
Sibutu Island
Sarangani Island
Tinaca Point

Luzon Strait
Cape Bojeador
Lingayen Gulf
CORDILLERA CENTRAL
SIERRA MADRE
POLILLO ISLANDS
Lamon Bay
Lagonoy Gulf
Ragay Gulf
Sibuyan Sea
Visayan Sea
Bohol Sea
Camotes Sea
Surigao Strait
Moro Gulf
Illana Bay
Sibugay Bay
Mindoro Strait

130° East of Greenwich

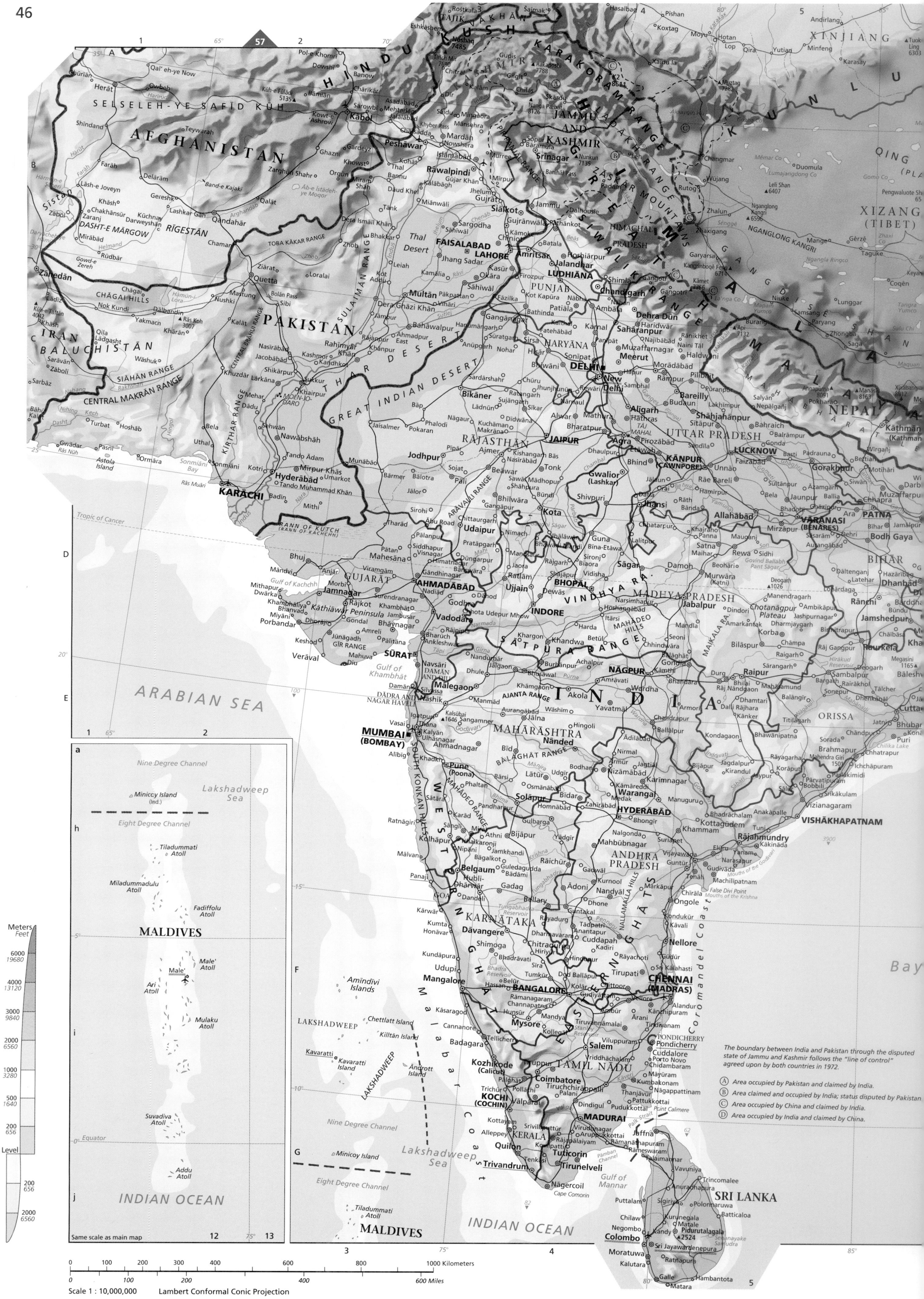

57

Countries / Regions

AFGHANISTAN
PAKISTAN
IRAN
BALUCHISTAN
INDIA
NEPAL
BHUTAN
XINJIANG
XIZANG (TIBET)
QING (PLATEAU)
SRI LANKA
MALDIVES
LAKSHADWEEP

Indian States / Regions

PUNJAB
HARYANA
RAJASTHAN
UTTAR PRADESH
GUJARAT
MADHYA PRADESH
BIHAR
ORISSA
MAHARASHTRA
ANDHRA PRADESH
KARNATAKA
GOA
KERALA
TAMIL NADU
HIMACHAL PRADESH
JAMMU AND KASHMIR
DĀDRA AND NAGAR HAVELI
DAMĀN AND DIU

Seas / Water bodies

ARABIAN SEA
Bay of (Bengal)
INDIAN OCEAN
Laccadive Sea / Lakshadweep Sea
Gulf of Kachchh
Gulf of Khambhāt
Gulf of Mannar
Palk Strait
Tropic of Cancer
Equator

Mountain ranges / Physical features

HINDU KUSH
KARAKORAM RANGE
KUN LUN
HIMALAYA
SELSELEH-YE SAFĪD KŪH
SULAIMAN RANGE
TOBA KĀKAR RANGE
CHĀGAI HILLS
CENTRAL MAKRĀN RANGE
KIRTHAR RANGE
SIĀHĀN RANGE
DASHT-E MARGOW
RĪGESTĀN
THAR DESERT
GREAT INDIAN DESERT
ARAVALLI RANGE
VINDHYA RANGE
SĀTPURA RANGE
MAHĀDEO HILLS
AJANTA RANGE
BĀLĀGHĀT RANGE
MAHĀDEO RANGE
WESTERN GHĀTS
EASTERN GHĀTS
NALLAMALA HILLS
KĀTHIĀWĀR Peninsula
GĪR RANGE
SOUTH KONKAN HILLS
Coromandel Coast
Malabar Coast
Cape Comorin

Major cities (selection)

Kābol, Herāt, Qandahār, Peshāwar, Rāwalpindi, Islāmābād, Srīnagar, Jammu, Lahore, FAISALABAD, Multān, Quetta, KARĀCHI, Hyderābād, Sukkur, LUDHIĀNA, Amritsar, Jalandhar, Chandīgarh, Shimla, DELHI, New Delhi, Meerut, Bīkāner, Jodhpur, JAIPUR, Agra, Gwalior, LUCKNOW, KĀNPUR (CAWNPORE), Allahābād, VĀRĀNASI (BENĀRES), PATNA, Bodh Gaya, Rānchi, Jamshedpur, Dhanbād, AHMADĀBĀD, Vadodara, SŪRAT, INDORE, BHOPAL, Jabalpur, NĀGPUR, Raipur, MUMBAI (BOMBAY), Pune (Poona), Solāpur, HYDERĀBĀD, Warangal, VISHĀKHAPATNAM, Vijayawada, Guntur, Kolhāpur, BELGAUM, Hubli-Dhārwār, Panaji, Mangalore, BANGALORE, Mysore, Salem, CHENNAI (MADRAS), PONDICHERRY, Coimbatore, KOCHI (COCHIN), MADURAI, Trivandrum, Tuticorin, Tirunelveli, Nāgercoil, Kozhikode (Calicut), Jaffna, Trincomalee, Colombo, Sri Jayawardenepura, Moratuwa, Galle, Hambantota, Anurādhapura

Inset maps

a

MALDIVES
Lakshadweep Sea
Nine Degree Channel
Eight Degree Channel
Minicoy Island (Ind.)
Tiladummati Atoll
Miladummadulu Atoll
Fadiffolu Atoll
Male' Atoll
Male'
Ari Atoll
Mulaku Atoll
Suvadiva Atoll
Addu Atoll
Equator
INDIAN OCEAN

Same scale as main map

LAKSHADWEEP
Amindivi Islands
Chettlatt Island
Kiltān Island
Kavaratti Island
Kavaratti
Andrott Island
Minicoy Island

Legend / boundary notes

The boundary between India and Pakistan through the disputed state of Jammu and Kashmir follows the "line of control" agreed upon by both countries in 1972.

Ⓐ Area occupied by Pakistan and claimed by India.
Ⓑ Area claimed and occupied by India; status disputed by Pakistan.
Ⓒ Area occupied by China and claimed by India.
Ⓓ Area occupied by India and claimed by China.

Elevation scale

Meters / Feet
6000 / 19680
4000 / 13120
3000 / 9840
2000 / 6560
1000 / 3280
500 / 1640
200 / 656
Sea Level
200 / 656
2000 / 6560

Scale

Scale 1 : 10,000,000   Lambert Conformal Conic Projection

0 100 200 300 400 600 800 1000 Kilometers
0 100 200 400 600 Miles

M-690000-7A-DR2-1
Copyright © Rand McNally & Co.

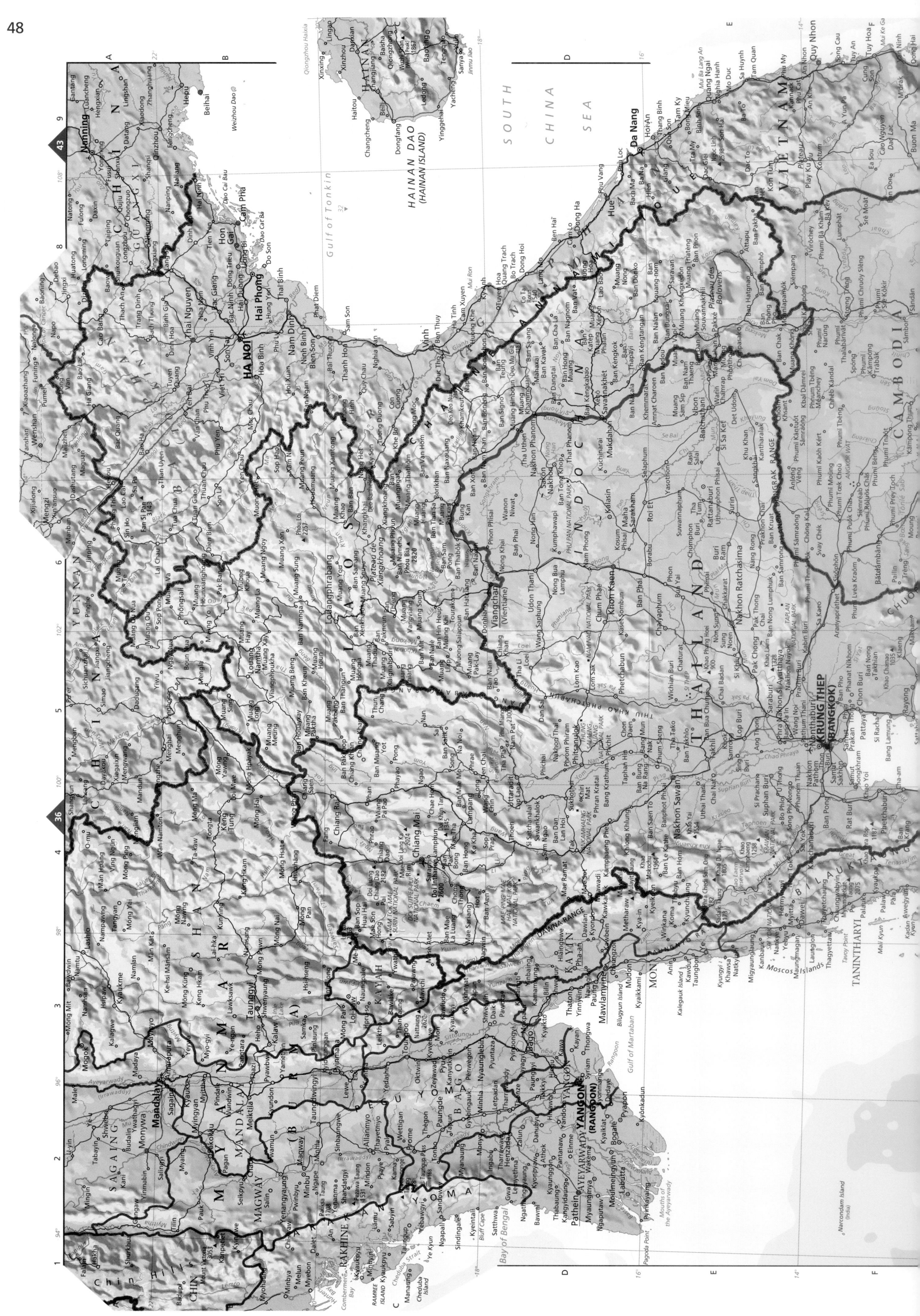

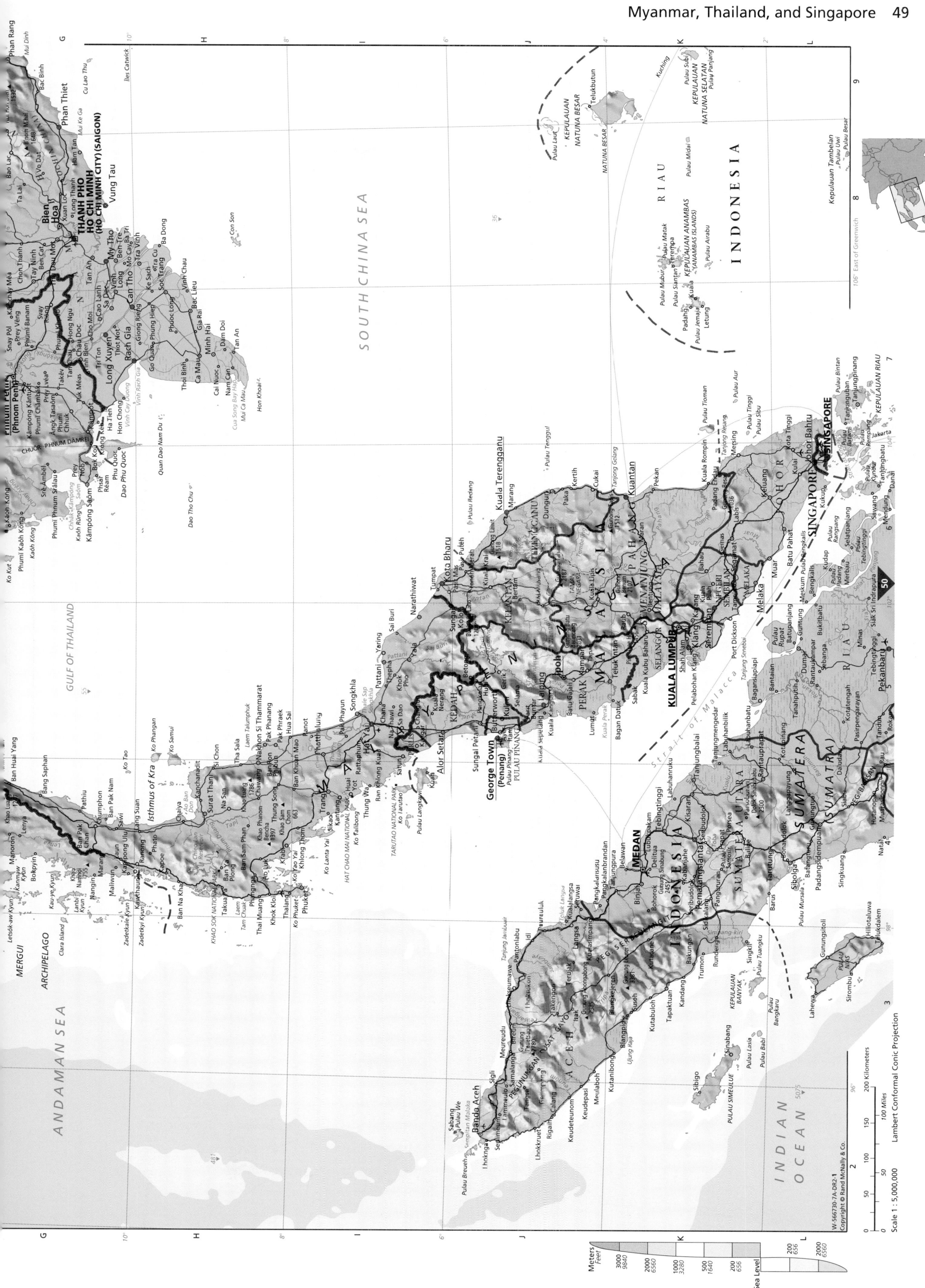

SULU SEA

PHILIPPINES

CELEBES SEA

BRUNEI

LABUAN

MALAYSIA

SARAWAK

SABAH

BORNEO

(KALIMANTAN)

KALIMANTAN BARAT

KALIMANTAN TIMUR

KALIMANTAN TENGAH

KALIMANTAN SELATAN

Samarinda

Balikpapan

Banjarmasin

Palangkaraya

SULAWESI TENGAH

Palu

SULAWESI (CELEBES)

SULAWESI SELATAN

SULAWESI TENGGARA

Teluk Tomini
(Gulf of Tomini)

Teluk Bone
(Gulf of Bone)

Ujungpandang
(Makasar)

Equator

Selat Makasar
(Makassar Strait)

DA ISLANDS

NESIA

WA (JAVA SEA)

SEMARANG

SURABAYA

MADURA

JAWA TIMUR

Surakarta

Malang

Denpasar

BALI

LOMBOK

Mataram

NUSA TENGGARA BARAT

SUMBAWA

FLORES

NUSA TENGGARA TIMUR
NUSA TENGGARA
(LESSER SUNDA ISLANDS)

SUMBA

Laut Flores
(Flores Sea)

Laut Bali
(Bali Sea)

Laut Sawu
(Savu Sea)

KEPULAUAN KANGEAN
(KANGEAN ISLANDS)

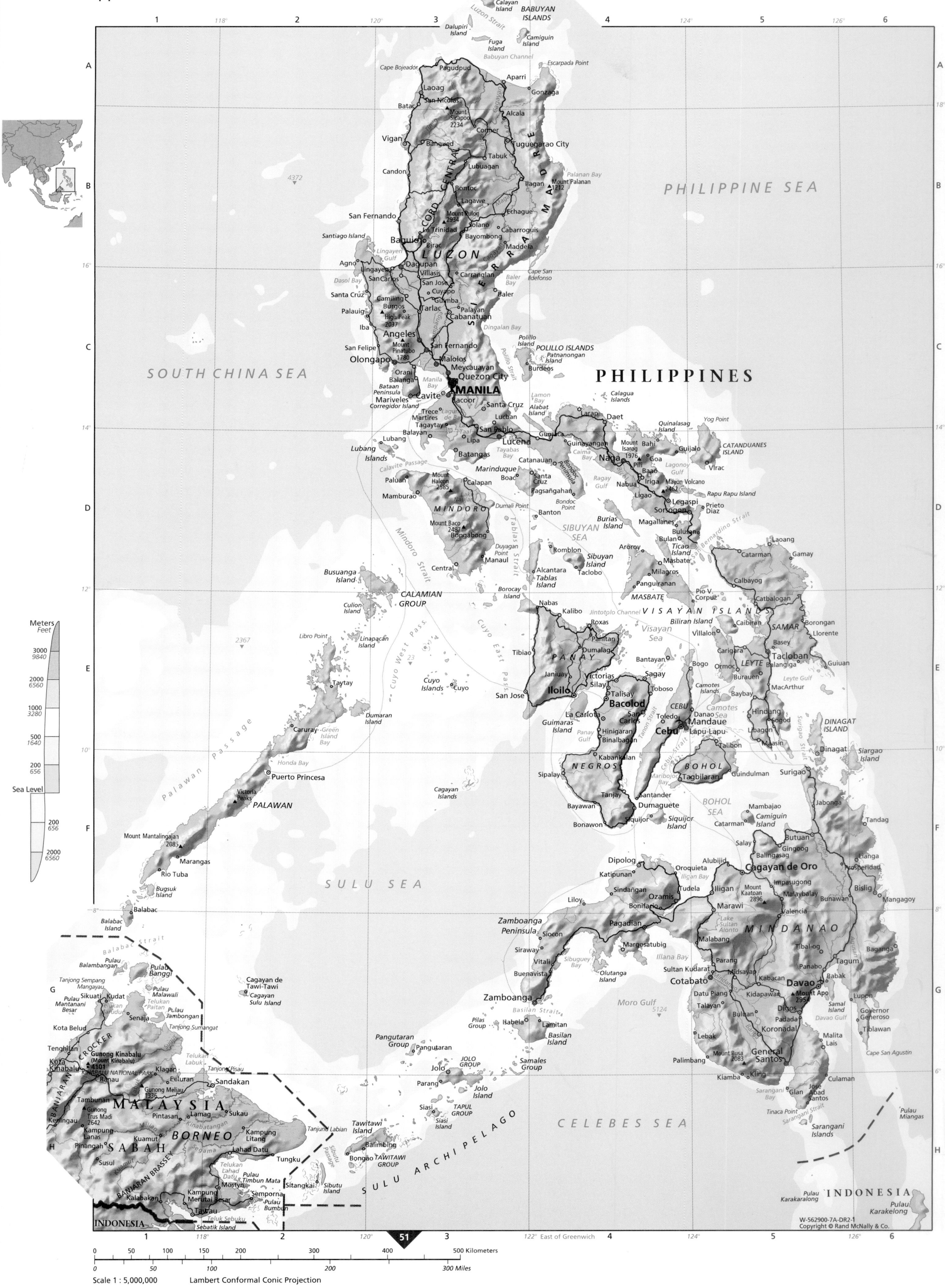

PHILIPPINES

PHILIPPINE SEA

SOUTH CHINA SEA

SULU SEA

CELEBES SEA

Meters / Feet
3000 / 9840
2000 / 6560
1000 / 3280
500 / 1640
200 / 656
Sea Level
200 / 656
2000 / 6560

LUZON

BABUYAN ISLANDS

Babuyan Island
Calayan Island
Dalupiri Island
Fuga Island
Camiguin Island
Luzon Strait
Babuyan Channel

Cape Bojeador
Pagudpud
Aparri
Gonzaga
Escarpada Point
Laoag
Batac
San Nicolas
Alcala
Claveria
Tuguegarao City
Vigan
Bangued
Tabuk
Lubuagan
Ilagan
Panalan Bay
Candon
Bontoc
Lagawe
Echague
San Fernando
Mount Pulog 2934
Solano
Cabarroguis
La Trinidad
Bayombong
Maddela
Baguio
Biri
Cape San Ildefonso
Agno
Dagupan
Carranglan
Baler Bay
Lingayen
Villasis
San Jose
Baler
Santa Cruz
San Carlos
Cuyapo
Palayan
Palauig
Camiling
Gumba
Dingalan Bay
Iba
Burgos
Tarlac
Cabanatuan
High Peak 2037
POLILLO ISLANDS
Angeles
San Fernando
Polillo Island
Patnanongan Island
San Felipe
Mount Pinatubo 1780
Malolos
Burdeos
Olongapo
Meycauayan
Orani
Quezon City
Calagua Islands
Balanga
MANILA
Bataan Peninsula
Manila Bay
Santa Cruz
Larap
Daet
Mariveles
Cavite
Bacoor
Lucban
Quinalasag Island
Corregidor Island
Trece Martires
Alabat Island
Yog Point
Tagaytay
San Pablo
Guinayangan
Mount Isarog 1976
CATANDUANES ISLAND
Balayan
Lipa
Lucena
Bahi
Goa
Guijalo
Lubang
Batangas
Catanauan
Naga
Pili
Virac
Lubang Islands
Tayabas Bay
Bagsanghan
Nabua
Iriga
Rapu Rapu Island
Calavite Passage
Santa Cruz
Boac
Ragay Gulf
Mayon Volcano 2462
Paluan
Marinduque
Magallanes
Legaspi
Mamburao
Mount Halcon 2585
Calapan
Banton
Bulusan
Sorsogon
Prieto Diaz
MINDORO
Dumali Point
Romblon
SIBUYAN SEA
Bulan
San Bernardino Strait
Mount Baco 2488
Bongabong
Sibuyan Island
Ticao Island
Laoang
Central
Tablas Island
Masbate
Catarman
Gamay
Busuanga Island
Duyagan Point
Alcantara
Milagros
MASBATE
Calbayog
Manaul
Tablas Strait
Panguiranan
Pio V Corpuz
Catbalogan
CALAMIAN GROUP
Borocay Island
Nabas
Kalibo
Biliran Island
SAMAR
Borongan
Culion Island
Roxas
Caibiran
Llorente
Libro Point
Linapacan Island
Tibiao
Janiuay
Bantayan
Carigara
Basey
Linacapan
PANAY
Dumalag
Capiz
VISAYAN ISLANDS
Ormoc
Tacloban
Taytay
Cuyo Islands
Cuyo
Victorias
Silay
Sagay
Bogo
LEYTE
Belanglang
Libro Point
San Jose
Iloilo
Talisay
Toboso
Danao
Camotes Islands
Baybay
MacArthur
Caruray
Dumaran Island
La Carlota
San Carlos
CEBU
Hindang
Guiuan
Honda Bay
Guimaras Island
Bacolod
Toledo
Mandaue
Leyte Gulf
Puerto Princesa
Panay Gulf
Binalbagan
Cebu
Lapu-Lapu
Hinunangan
Victoria Peaks
NEGROS
Kabankalan
Lubagon
Maasin
DINAGAT ISLAND
PALAWAN
Sipalay
Tanjay
BOHOL
Talibon
Dinagat
Siargao Island
Bayawan
Dumaguete
Tagbilaran
Guindulman
Surigao
Mount Mantalingajan 2085
Bonawon
Squijor
BOHOL SEA
Marangas
Siquijor Island
Mambajao
Rio Tuba
Camiguin Island
Jabonga
Bugsuk Island
Catarman
Salay
Butuan
Gingoog
Tandag
Balabac Island
Dipolog
Alubijid
Balingasag
Ilanga
Balabac
Katipunan
Oroquieta
CAGAYAN DE ORO
Prosperidad
Bislig
SULU SEA
Sindangan
Ozamis
Impasugong
Bunawan
Mangagoy
Tudela
Iligan
Mount Kaatoan 2896
Pulau Banggi
Tanjong Sempang Mangayau
Cagayan de Tawi-Tawi
Liloy
Bonifacio
Malaybalay
Valencia
Pulau Balambangan
Cagayan Sulu Island
Zamboanga Peninsula
Pagadian
Marawi
MINDANAO
Kudat
Siocon
Lake Sultan Alonto
Pulau Malawali
Malabang
Tibal-og
Baganga
Kota Belud
Siraway
Sultan Kudarat
Parang
Panabo
Tenghilan
Vitali
Illana Bay
Kabacan
Babak
BANJARAN CROCKER
Gunong Kinabalu (Mount Kinabalu) 4101
Buenavista
Olutanga Island
Cotabato
Kidapawan
Davao
Mount Apo 2954
Senaja
Klagan
Isabela
Lamitan
Datu Piang
Samal Island
Ranau
ZAMBOANGA
Basilan Island
Talayan
Digos
Davao Gulf
Kinabalu National Park
Pilas Group
Diatang
Kabacan
Padada
Tambunan
Pangutaran Group
Samales Group
Lebak
Bulatan
Malita
Gunong Meliau 1936
Pangutaran
Koronadal
Lais
Sandakan
JOLO GROUP
Palimbang
General Santos
Tiblawan
Lamag
MALAYSIA
Jolo
Mount Busa 2083
Kiamba
SABAH
Parang
Jolo Island
Kling
Cape San Agustin
Gunong Trus Madi 2642
BORNEO
Siasi
Glan
Jose Abad Santos
Kampung Lanas
Siasi Island
TAPUL GROUP
Sarangani Bay
Tinaca Point
Kuamut
Pintasan
Sarangani Islands
Pulau Miangas
Kampung Litang
Tawitawi Island
Pulau Karakaralong
Keningau
Balimbing
SULU ARCHIPELAGO
Lahad Datu
Bongao
Tungku
TAWITAWI GROUP
Tawitawi Island
CELEBES SEA
Pulau Karakelong
INDONESIA
Sitangkai
Sibutu Island
INDONESIA

SCALE 1 : 5,000,000
Lambert Conformal Conic Projection

0 50 100 150 200 300 400 500 Kilometers
0 50 100 200 300 Miles

W-562900-7A-DR2-1
Copyright © Rand McNally & Co.

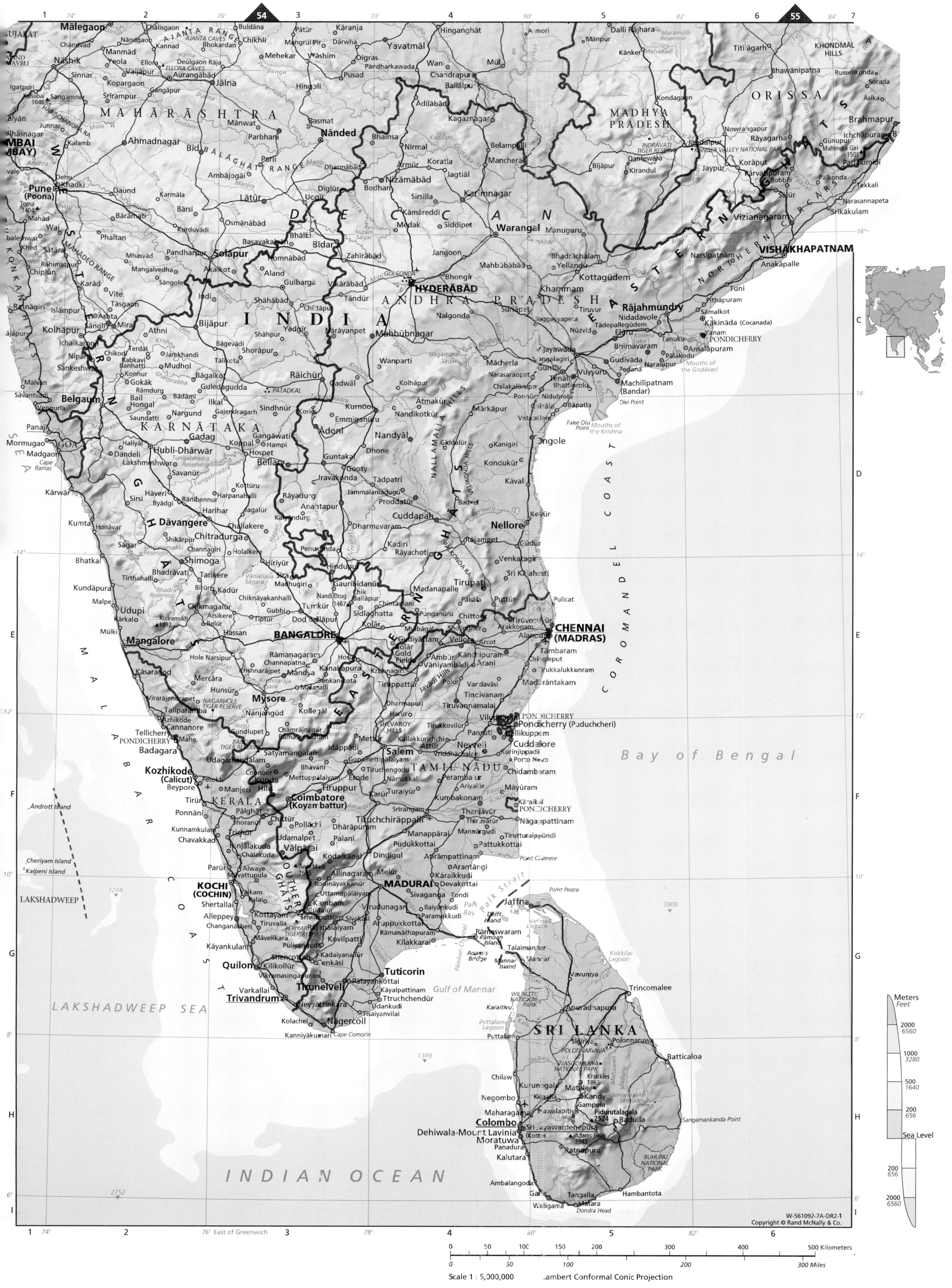

MAHĀRĀSHTRA
MADHYA PRADESH
ORISSA
ANDHRA PRADESH
KARNĀTAKA
KERALA
TAMIL NADU
INDIA
DECCAN
SRI LANKA
GOA
PONDICHERRY
Bay of Bengal
LAKSHADWEEP SEA
INDIAN OCEAN
Gulf of Mannar
Palk Strait
Palk Bay
MALABAR COAST
COROMANDEL COAST
KONKAN
NORTHERN CIRCARS
EASTERN GHATS
WESTERN GHATS
NALLAMALLA HILLS
VELIKONDA HILLS
LAKSHADWEEP
Andrott Island
Cheriyam Island
Kalpeni Island
HYDERĀBĀD
BANGALORE
CHENNAI (MADRAS)
VISHAKHAPATNAM
KOCHI (COCHIN)
Colombo
Sri Jayewardenepura (Kotte)
Mumbai (Bombay)
Pune (Poona)
Nāshik
Aurangābād
Jālna
Ahmadnagar
Solāpur
Kolhāpur
Belgaum
Hubli-Dhārwār
Bellary
Dāvangere
Shimoga
Mangalore
Mysore
Kozhikode (Calicut)
Coimbatore (Koyambattur)
Salem
Tiruchchirāppalli
MADURAI
Tuticorin
Tirunelveli
Trivandrum
Quilon
Nāgercoil
Cape Comorin
Pondicherry (Puducheri)
Cuddalore
Vellore
Tirupati
Nellore
Cuddapah
Kurnool
Guntūr
Vijayawāda
Rājahmundry
Kākināda (Cocanada)
Vizianagaram
Warangal
Nizāmābād
Nānded
Gulbarga
Bijāpur
Raichūr
Jaffna
Trincomalee
Anuradhapura
Kandy
Batticaloa
Galle
Hambantota
Pidurutalagala 2524
Adams Peak 2243
Scale 1 : 5,000,000 Lambert Conformal Conic Projection
0 50 100 150 200 300 400 500 Kilometers
0 50 100 200 300 Miles
Meters Feet
2000 6560
1000 3280
500 1640
200 656
Sea Level
W-561092-7A-DR2-1
Copyright © Rand McNally & Co.

Meters
Feet

6000
19680

4000
13120

3000
9840

2000
6560

1000
3280

500
1640

200
656

Sea Level

200
656

2000
6560

0 50 100 150 200   300   400   500 Kilometers

0   50   100   200   300 Miles

Scale 1 : 5,000,000   Lambert Conformal Conic Projection

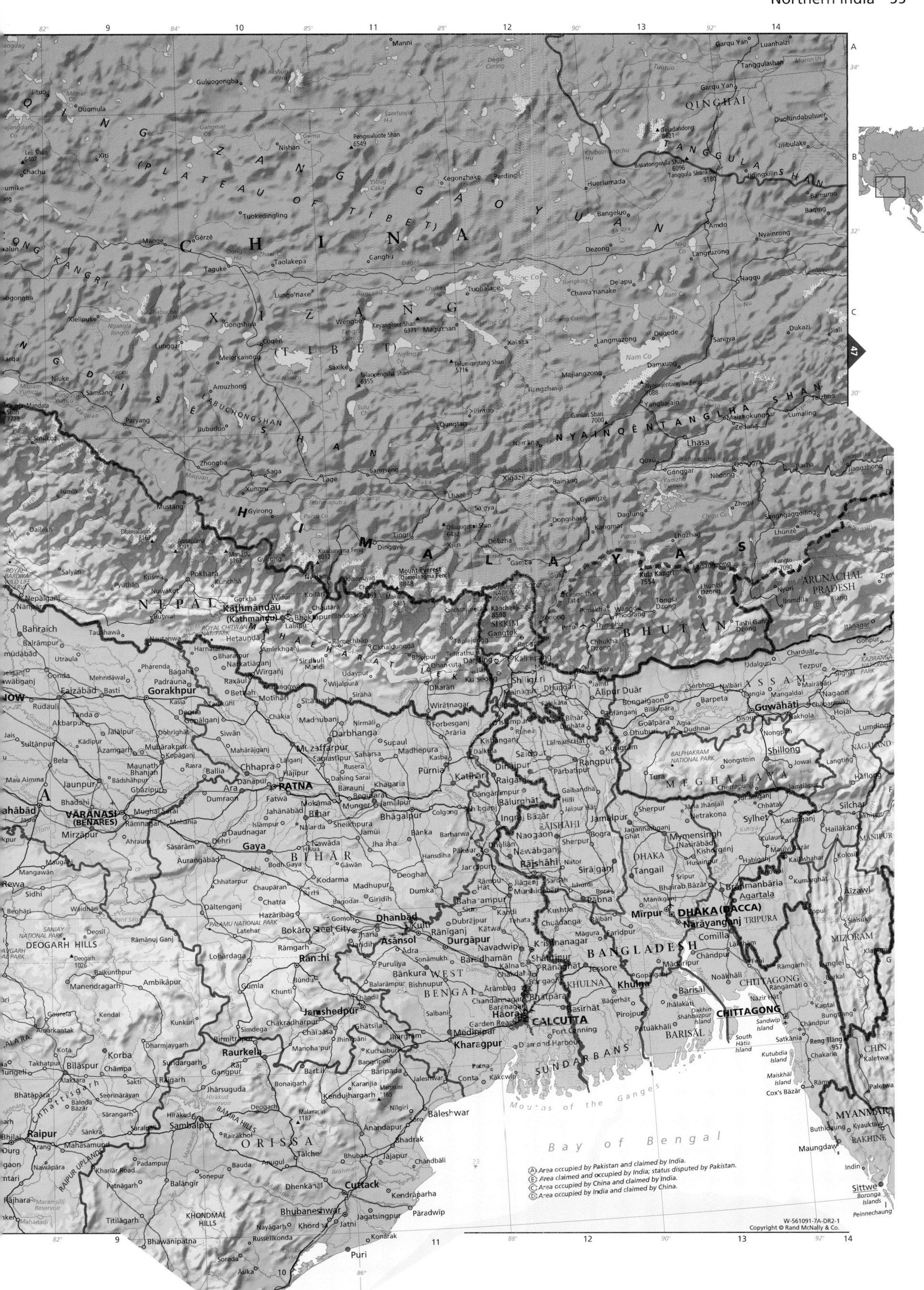

A Area occupied by Pakistan and claimed by India.
E Area claimed and occupied by India; status disputed by Pakistan.
C Area occupied by China and claimed by India.
D Area occupied by India and claimed by China.

W-561091-7A-DR2-1
Copyright © Rand McNally & Co.

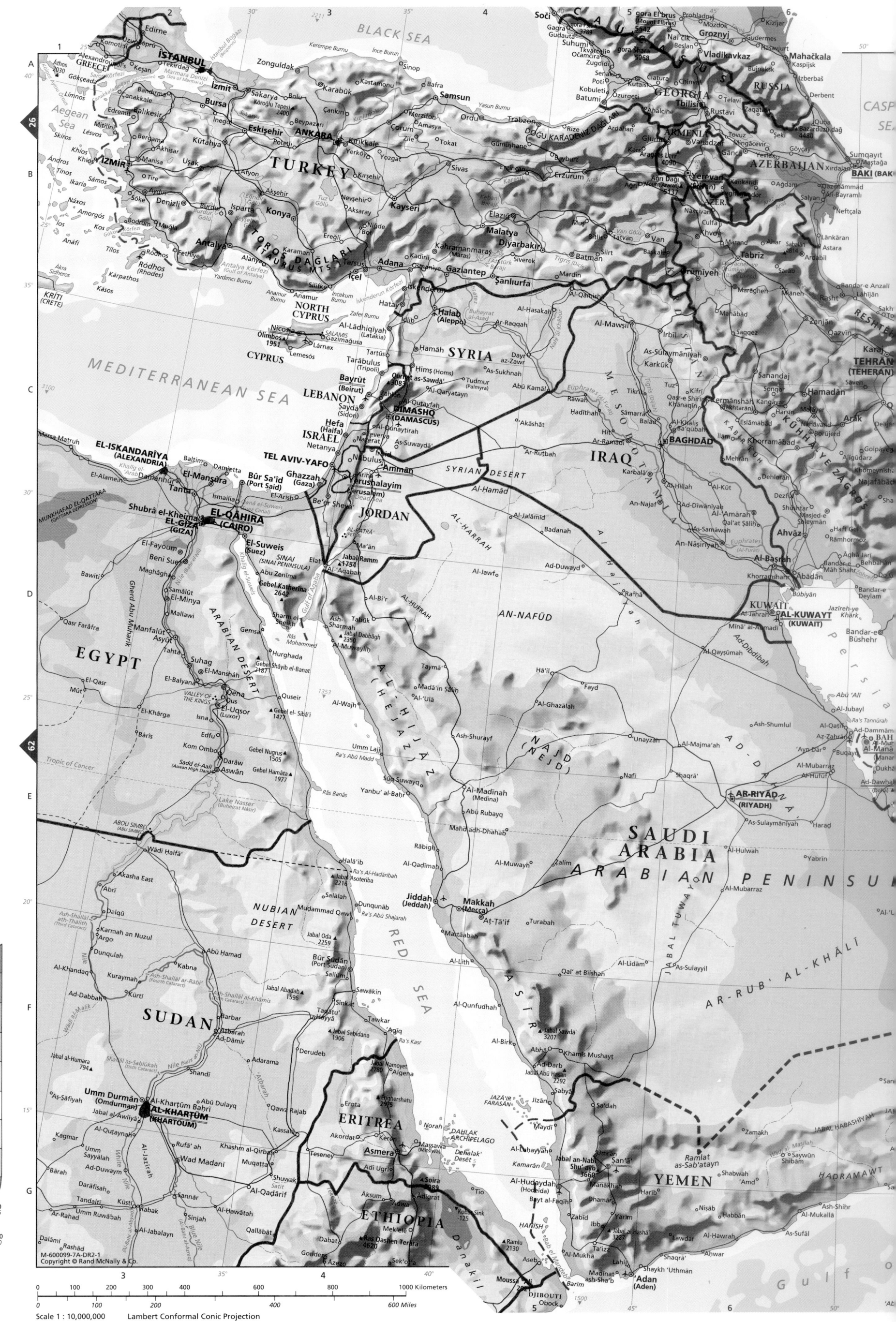

BLACK SEA

GREECE
İSTANBUL
İzmit
Edirne
Tekirdağ
Keşan
Kirklareli
Zonguldak
Karabük
Kastamonu
Sinop
Bafra
Samsun
Soči
CAUCASUS
gora El'brus
(Mount Elbrus)
5642
Prohladnyj
Mozdok
Kizljar

İzmir
İzmit
Marmara Denizi
(Sea of Marmara)
Bandırma
Bursa
İnegöl
Bilecik
Eskişehir
ANKARA
Kırıkkale
Polatlı
Yozgat
Çorum
Amasya
Tokat
Sivas
Erzincan
Gagra
Gudauta
Suhumi
Očamčira
Zugdidi
Senaki
Poti
Kobuleti
Batumi
Ozurgeti
GEORGIA
TBILISI
Telavi
Rustavi
Vladikavkaz
Groznyj
Gudermes
Nal'čik
Beslan
Mahačkala
Kaspijsk
RUSSIA
Bujnaksk
Izberbaš
Derbent

TURKEY
Balıkesir
Akhisar
Manisa
Uşak
Afyon
Kütahya
Eskişehir
Sakarya
Bolu
Köroğlu Tepesi
2400
Beypazarı
Çankırı
Kırşehir
Nevşehir
Kayseri
Elazığ
Malatya
Kahramanmaraş
(Maraş)
Diyarbakır
Van
Van Gölü
Bitlis
Siirt
Batman
Erzurum
Kars
Ardahan
Artvin
Rize
Trabzon
Giresun
Ordu
Gümüşhane
Bayburt
Ağrı Dağı
(Mount Ararat)
5137
ARMENIA
YEREVAN
Gyumri
Vanadzor
Aragats Lerr
4090
Naxçıvan
Tovuz
Gäncä
Yevlax
AZERBAIJAN
Şäki
BAKI (BAK)
Sumqayıt
Xırdalan

MEDITERRANEAN SEA

Aegean
Sea
Limnos
Lésvos
İzmir
Samos
Ikaria
Náxos
Amorgós
Kos
Anáfi
Astypálaia
Ródhos
(Rhodes)
Kárpathos
Kásos
KRITI
(CRETE)

TOROS DAĞLARI
(TAURUS MTS)
Antalya
Antalya Körfezi
(Gulf of Antalya)
Konya
Karaman
Silifke
İçel
Adana
Gaziantep
Şanlıurfa
Halab
(Aleppo)
Al-Hasakah
Al-Qamishli
Al-Mawsil
İrbil
As-Sulaymaniyah
Kirkük
Tuz
Kifri
Sanandaj
Kermanşah
(Bakhtaran)
Hamadan
Qazvin
TEHRAN
(TEHERAN)

NORTH
CYPRUS
Nicosia
Gazimağusa
Lárnax
CYPRUS
Lemesós
Tarábulus
(Tripoli)
Bayrüt
(Beirut)
LEBANON
Şaydā
(Sidon)
Hefa
(Haifa)
ISRAEL
TEL AVIV-YAFO
Nabulus
Yerushalayim
(Jerusalem)
Al-Ladhiqiyah
(Latakia)
Tartūs
Idlib
Hamah
Hims (Homs)
Qurnat as-Sawda
3083
Al-Qaryatayn
SYRIA
Ar-Raqqah
Nahr al-Khabur
Dayr az-Zawr
As-Sukhnah
Tudmur
(Palmyra)
Abū Kamāl
Rawah
Hadithah
Al-Mawsil
Balad
Samarra
Tikrit
Al-Khalis
MESOPOTAMIA
BAGHDAD
Euphrates

DIMASHQ
(DAMASCUS)
Al-Qutayfah
Akashat
Ar-Ramadi
Ar-Rutbah
Al-Hamad
SYRIAN DESERT
IRAQ
Karbalā
Al-Hillah
Ad-Diwaniyah
An-Najaf
As-Samawah
An-Nasiriyah
Al-Küt
Al-Amārah
Qal'at Salih
Ahvaz
ZAGROS

Nabulus
As-Sawdā
As-Salt
Amman
JORDAN
Al-Jalamid
Badanah
Rafha
KUWAIT
AL-KUWAYT
(KUWAIT)
Mina' al-Ahmadi

EL-ISKANDARĪYA
(ALEXANDRIA)
Baltim
Damietta
Būr Saʿīd
(Port Said)
El-Mansūra
Tanta
Shubrā el-Kheima
EL-QAHIRA
(CAIRO)
EL-GIZA
(GIZA)
El-Fayoum
El-Arish
Ghazzah
(Gaza)
Be'er Sheva'
Dead Sea
Al-Karak
Ma'an
Al-Bi'r
Al-Hufrah
AN-NAFŪD
Ad-Duwayd
Al-Qaysumah
Hafr al-Batin
Al-Jahrah
Bübiyan
Jazireh-ye
Khark
Bandar-e
Deylam

EGYPT
Mersa Matruh
El-Alamein
El-Qasr
Qasr Farâfra
Bawiti
El-Fayoum
Beni Suef
Maghāgha
Samālūt
El-Minya
Mallawi
Asyūt
Tahta
Suhag
El-Balyana
Qena
Luxor
(El-Uqsor)
Isna
Edfu
Kom Ombo
Darāw
Aswān
MUNKHAFAD EL-QATTÂRA
(QATTARA DEPRESSION)
ARABIAN DESERT
El-Suweis
(Suez)
SINAI
(SINAI PENINSULA)
Abu Zenima
Gebel Katherîna
2642
Sharm el-
Sheikh
Ras Mohammed
Hurghada
Gebel Shāyib el-Banat
2187
Quseir
Gebel el-Sibā'i
1477
Gebel Hamāta
1977
Gebel Nugrus
1505
Rās Bānās
Bur Safāga
Elat
Al-'Aqabah
Jabal Ramm
1754
Tabūk
Ash-Sharmah
Jabal Dabbagh
2350
Al-Muwaylih
Al-Jawf
Taymā'
Madā'in Sālih
Al-'Ulā
Hā'il
Fayd
Unayzah
Al-Ghazālah
Az-Zahrān
Ad-Dammam
Al-Qatīf
BAHRAIN
Al-Manā
Ad-Dawhah

AL-HEJĀZ
RED
SEA
Al-Wajh
Umm Lajj
Ra's Abū Madd
Sür Suwayq
Yanbu' al-Bahr
Al-Madīnah
(Medina)
Abū Rubayq
Rābigh
Jiddah
(Jeddah)
Makkah
(Mecca)
At-Tā'if
Qal'at Bīshah
As-Sulayyil
Yabrin
Al-Mubarraz
Al-Hufūf
AR-RIYĀD
(RIYADH)
As-Sulaymiyah
Harad
SAUDI
ARABIA
ARABIAN PENINSULA
AD-DAHNA
NAJD
(NEJD)
Nafī
Shaqrā'
Al-Majma'ah
Buraydah
Ash-Shumlul
Al-Jubayl
Ra's Tannūrah
Abū 'Alī
JABAL TUWAYQ

Tropic of Cancer
Sadd el-'Ali
(Aswan High Dam)
Lake Nasser
(Buheirat Nāsir)
ABOU SIMBEL
(ABU SIMBEL)
Wādi Halfa'
Akasha East
Abrī
Karmah an Nuzul
Dunqulah
Argo
Ad-Dabbah
Kuraymah
Abū Hamad
Kabna
Al-Khandaq
Kürti
Ash-Shallāl ar-Rābi'
(Fourth Cataract)
Ash-Shallāl al-Khāmis
(Fifth Cataract)
Halā'ib
Ra's Al-Hadāribah
Jabal Asoteriba
2216
Salālah
Mudammad Qawl
Ra's Abū Shajarah
Dunqunāb
Bür Sudān
(Port Sudan)
Sallum
Sawākin
Jabal Oda
2259
Tōkar
NUBIAN
DESERT
Al-Qadimah
Al-Lith
Al-Lidām
Al-Mubarraz
Al-Hulwah
Al-Muwayh
Zalim
Turabah
Ad-Darb
Al-Birk
Al-Qunfudhah
ASIR
Jabal Sawdā'
3207
Khamis Mushayt
Abhā
Jabal Abū Hasan
2292

SUDAN
Jabal al-Humara
794
Aş-Şāfiyah
Umm Durmān
(Omdurman)
Al-Qutaynah
AL-KHARTŪM
(KHARTOUM)
Al-Khartum Bahri
Abū Dulayq
Jabal al-Awliyā
Rufā'ah
Wad Madanī
Barbar
Ad-Dāmir
Atbarah
Adarama
Derudeb
Jabal Abadah
1596
Sinkat
Jabal Sabāna
1906
Taqatu'
Hayyā
'Agīg
Ra's Kasr
ERITREA
Akordat
Keren
Massawa
(Mitsiwa)
Asmera
Jabal Hamoyet
2780
Algena
Jabal al-Nabī
Shu'ayb
3660
San'ā'
Al-Luhayyah
JAZĀ'IR
FARASĀN
Jīzān
Sa'dah
Ramlat
as-Sab'atayn
YEMEN
Shabwah
Ma'rib
Harib
HADRAMAWT

Kagmar
Umm Sayyālah
Bārah
Dalāmi
Rashad
Ar-Rahad
Umm Ruwāba
Tandalti
Kūstī
Rabak
Sinjah
Al-Hawāta
Al-Qadārif
SUDAN
Sannār
Shuwak
Kassala
Teseney
Adi Ugri
Aksum
Adwa
Adigrat
Mekele
Dabat
Gondar
ETHIOPIA
Rās Dashen Terāra
4620
Sek'ot'a
Azezo
Dese
Soira
2989
Tio
DAHLAK
ARCHIPELAGO
Dese
Norah
Maydi
Kamaran
Al-Hudaydah
(Hodeida)
Dhamar
Ibb
Ta'izz
Zabid
Bayt al-Faqih
Al-Luhayyah
Manākhah
Dhī as-Sufāl
Yarīm
Qa'tabah
Al-Bayda'
Dālī'
Al-Hawban
HAMĪSH
Nişāb
Habbān
Al-Sufāl
Shaqrā'
Ahwar
Lawdar
Al-Mukallā
Ash-Shiḥr
Saywūn
Shibām
Tarīm

White Nile
Blue Nile
Qallābāt
Kassala
Gonder
DJIBOUTI
Obock
'Adan
(Aden)
Al-Mukhā
Moussa
Barīm
Aseb

M-600099-7A-DR2-1
Copyright © Rand McNally & Co.

Scale 1 : 10,000,000   Lambert Conformal Conic Projection

Meters
Feet
6000
19680
4000
13120
3000
9840
2000
6560
1000
3280
500
1640
200
656
Sea Level
200
656
2000
6560

0   100   200   300   400   500   600   700   800   900   1000 Kilometers
0   100   200   300   400   500   600 Miles

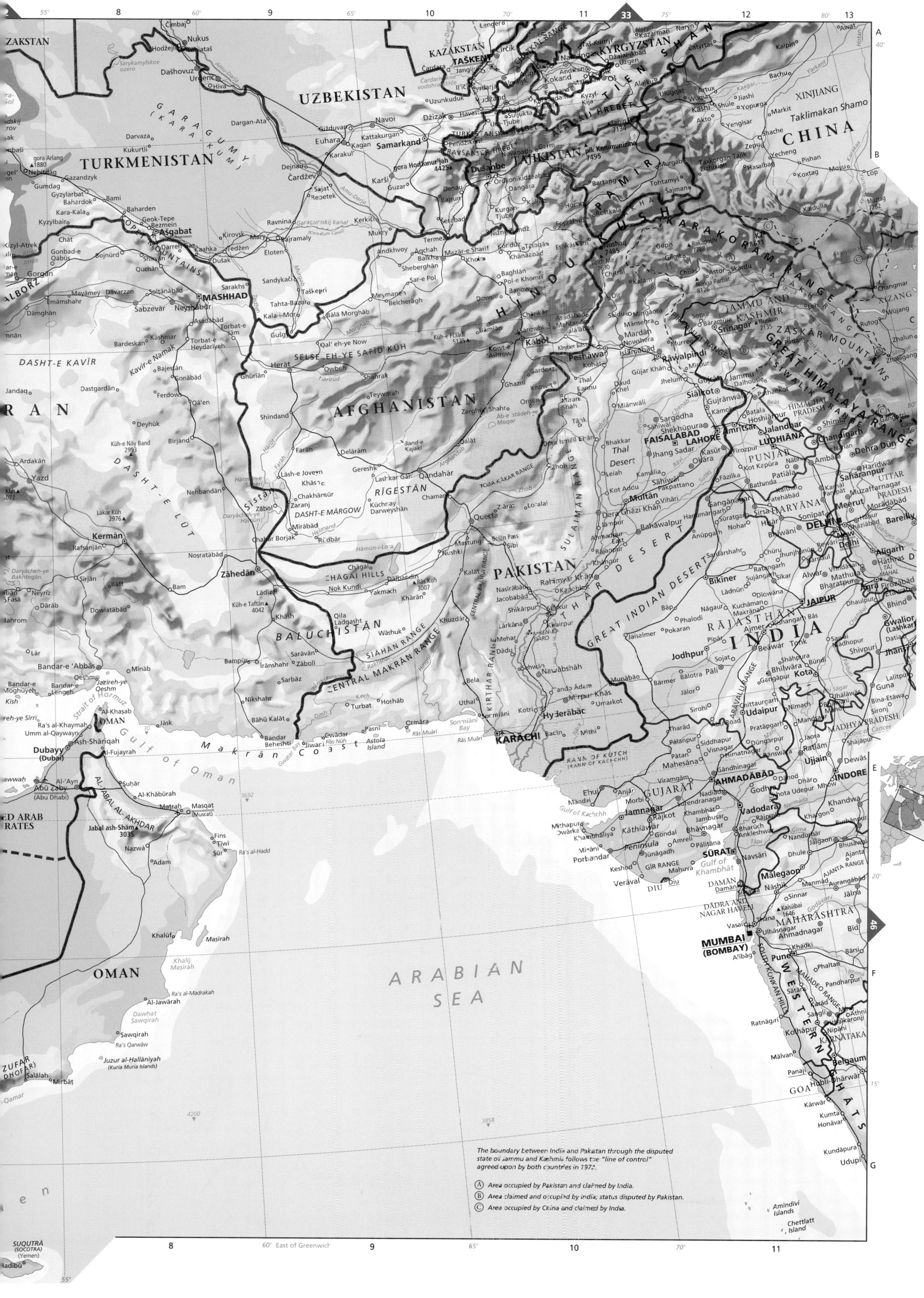

ZAKSTAN

KAZACHSTAN

TAŠKENT

UZBEKISTAN

TURKMENISTAN

KYRGYZSTAN

TIEN SHAN

TADŽIKISTAN

Dušanbe

pik Kommunizma 7495

XINJIANG

CHINA

Taklimakan Shamo

Samarkand

Urgenč
Hiva

Dašhovuz

Darvaza

Kara-Kala

Ašgabat

Geok-Tepe

KOPETDAG MOUNTAINS

MASHHAD

Neyshābūr

Sabzevār

HINDU KUSH

PAMIR

KARAKORAM RANGE

ZASKAR MOUNTAINS

GREAT HIMALAYA RANGE

JAMMU AND KASHMIR

Srīnagar

Mazār-e Sharīf

Kābol

Peshāwar

Islāmābād
Rāwalpindi

AFGHANISTAN

Herāt

SELSELEH-YE SAFĪD KŪH

Shindand

Farāh

Delārām

Qandahār

RĪGESTĀN

Quetta

PAKISTAN

Zābol

Zāhedān

DASHT-E KAVĪR

DASHT-E LŪT

Kermān

Bam

IRAN

Yazd

ČHAGAI HILLS

BALUCHISTĀN

CENTRAL MAKRĀN RANGE

SĪĀHAN RANGE

SULAIMĀN RANGE

KĪRTHAR RANGE

THAR DESERT

GREAT INDIAN DESERT

RĀJASTHĀN

Jaipur

Jodhpur

Bīkāner

DELHI
Delhi

PUNJAB

LAHORE
FAISALABAD

LUDHIĀNA

HARYĀNA

Multan

Sāhīwal

Bandar-e 'Abbās

Strait of Hormuz

OMAN

Masqat (Muscat)

Dubayy (Dubai)

Abū Zaby (Abu Dhabi)

Al-'Ayn

UNITED ARAB EMIRATES

JABAL AL-AKHDAR

Gulf of Oman

Makrān Coast

KARACHI

Hyderābād

RANN OF KUTCH (RANN OF KACHCHH)

GUJARAT

AHMADĀBĀD

Jāmnagar

Vadodara

Rājkot

SŪRAT

Jūnāgadh

Porbandar

GĪR RANGE

Gulf of Khambhāt

INDORE

MADHYA PRADESH

MAHĀRĀSHTRA

MUMBAI (BOMBAY)

Pune

WESTERN GHATS

ARABIAN SEA

Kolhāpur

Sāngli

GOA

Panaji

Belgaum

KARNĀTAKA

OMAN

ZUFAR (DHOFAR)

Şalālah

Mirbāţ

SUQUTRĀ (SOCOTRA) (Yemen)

Juzur al-Hallāniyah (Kuria Muria Islands)

Amīndīvī Islands

The boundary between India and Pakistan through the disputed state of Jammu and Kashmir follows the "line of control" agreed upon by both countries in 1972.

(A) Area occupied by Pakistan and claimed by India.

(B) Area claimed and occupied by India; status disputed by Pakistan.

(C) Area occupied by China and claimed by India.

East of Greenwich

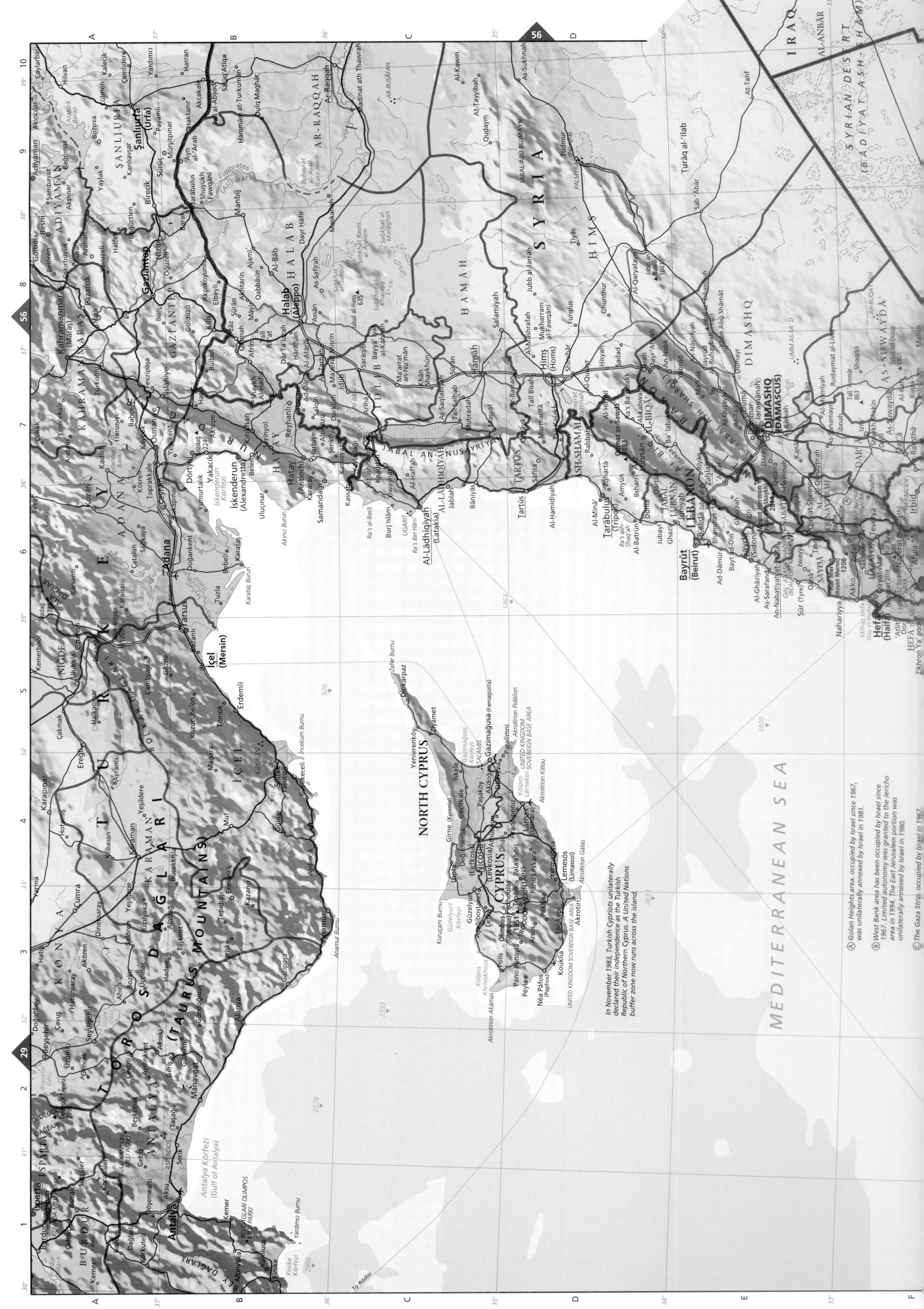

58

56

In November 1983, Turkish Cypriots unilaterally
declared their independence as the Turkish
Republic of Northern Cyprus. A United Nations
buffer zone now runs across the island.

(A) Golan Heights area, occupied by Israel since 1967,
was unilaterally annexed by Israel in 1981.

(B) West Bank area has been occupied by Israel since
1967. Limited autonomy was granted to the Jericho
area in 1994. The East Jerusalem portion was
unilaterally annexed by Israel in 1980.

(C) The Gaza Strip, occupied by Israel in 1967.

MEDITERRANEAN SEA

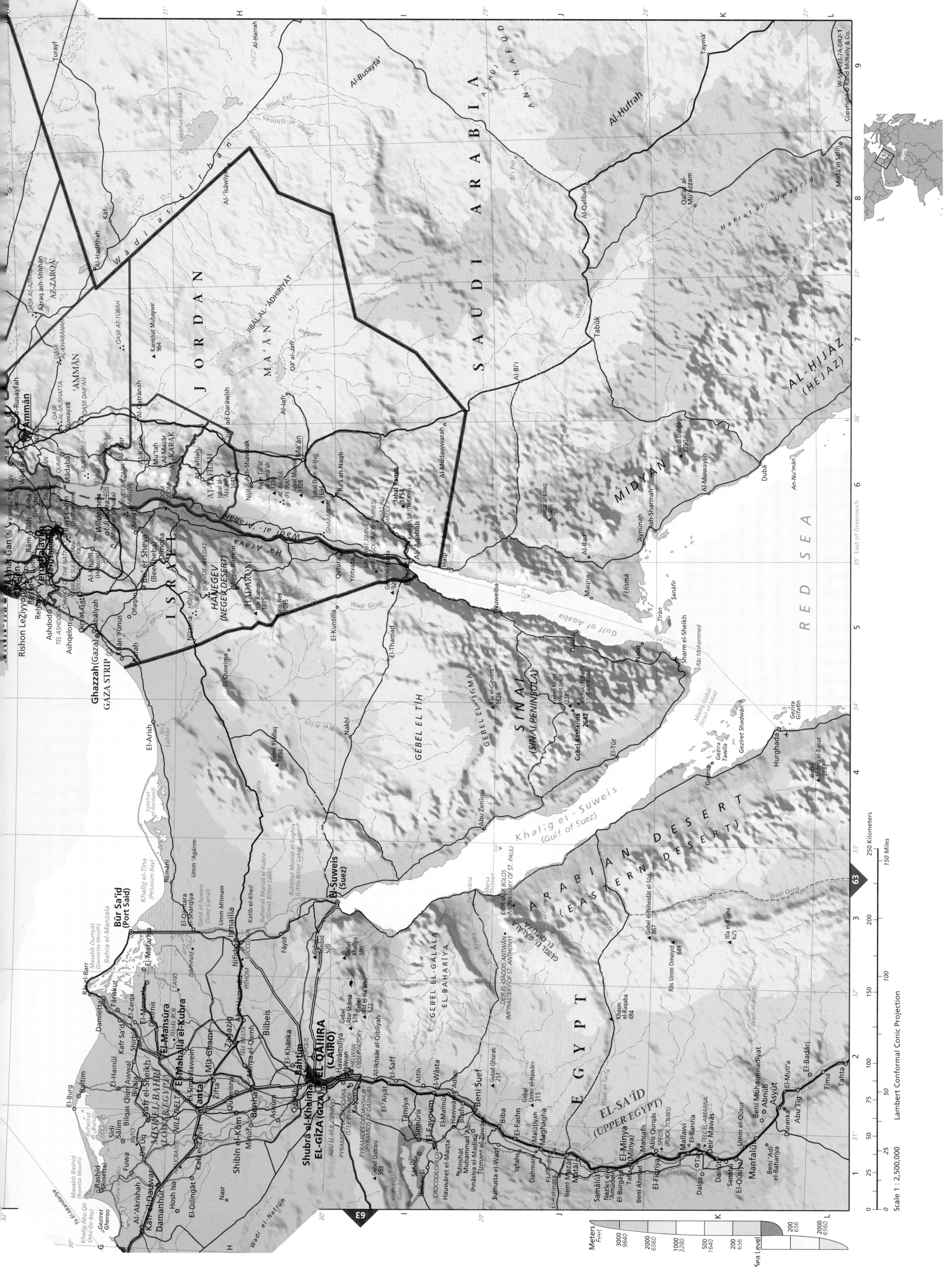

J O R D A N

S A U D I   A R A B I A

AL-HIJAZ
(HEJAZ)

MIDYAN

M A ' A N

JIBAL AL-'ADHIRIYAT

E G Y P T

SINAI
(SINAI PENINSULA)

GEBEL EL-TIH

GEBEL EL-IGMA

ARABIAN   DESERT
(EASTERN DESERT)

EL-SA'ID
(UPPER EGYPT)

ISRAEL

HANEGEV
(NEGEV DESERT)

HADAROM

GAZA STRIP

Wādī al-'Arabah

Ha-'Arava

Khalīg el-Suweis
(Gulf of Suez)

Gulf of Aqaba

RED SEA

Strait of Tiran

AN NAFUD

Gebel el-Galala
el-Bahariya

Gebel el-Galala
el-Qibliya

Azraq ash-Shīshān
AZ-ZARQĀ'

'AMMĀN

Al-'Aqabah

Nuweiba

Ras Muhammed

Sharm el-Sheikh

El-Tūr

Gebel Katherîna
2642

Gebel Mûsa
2285

El-Kuntilla

Nakhl

Abu Zenîma

El-Arîsh

Bûr Sa'īd
(Port Said)

El-Qantara

Ismâ'ilia

El-Suweis (Suez)

EL-QĀHIRA
(CAIRO)

EL-GÎZA (GÎZA)

El-Fayûm

Beni Suef

El-Minya

Asyût

El-Badâri

Mallawi

Deir Mawâs

Hurghada

Gebel Gharib

Tabûk

Al-Bi'r

Ras an-Naqb

Ma'ān

KARAK

AL-TAFÎLAH

Madabā

Bethlehem

Jerusalem

TEL AVIV-YAFO

Ashdod

Ashqelon

Ghazzah (Gaza)

Be'er Sheva
(Beersheba)

Dimona

Mizpe Ramon

Yotvata

Rafah

Khan Yunus

Damietta

El-Mansûra

El-Mahalla el-Kubra

Tanta

Zagazig

Bilbeis

Shibîn el-Kôm

Kafr el-Sheikh

Rosetta

Scale 1 : 2,500,000

Lambert Conformal Conic Projection

Meters   Feet
3000   9840
2000   6560
1000   3280
500   1640
200   656
Sea Level
200   656
2000   6560

Kilometers
0   25   50   75   100   150   200   250

Miles
0   25   50   75   100   150

W-SJ-05-7A-DR2.1
Copyright © Rand McNally & Co.

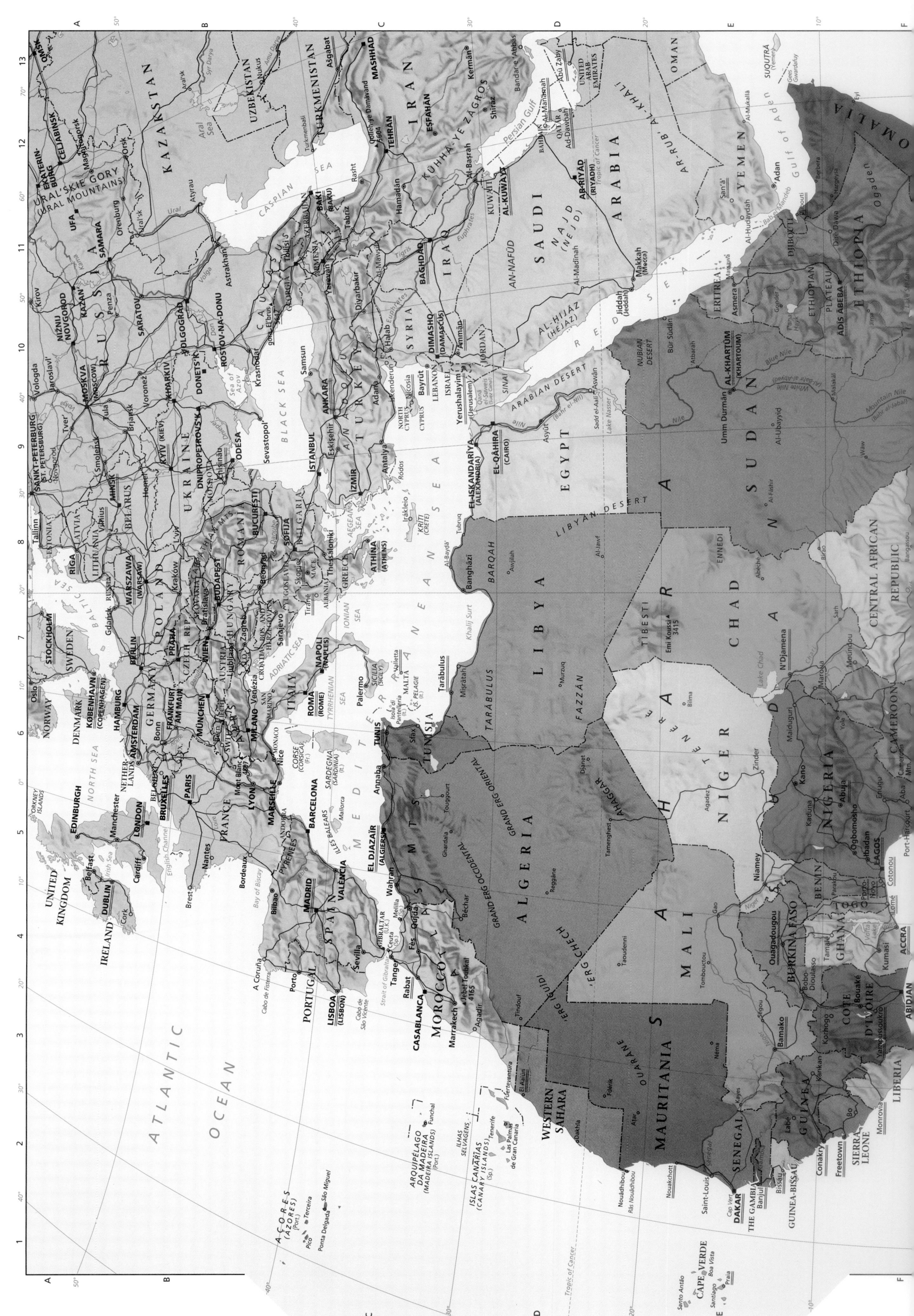

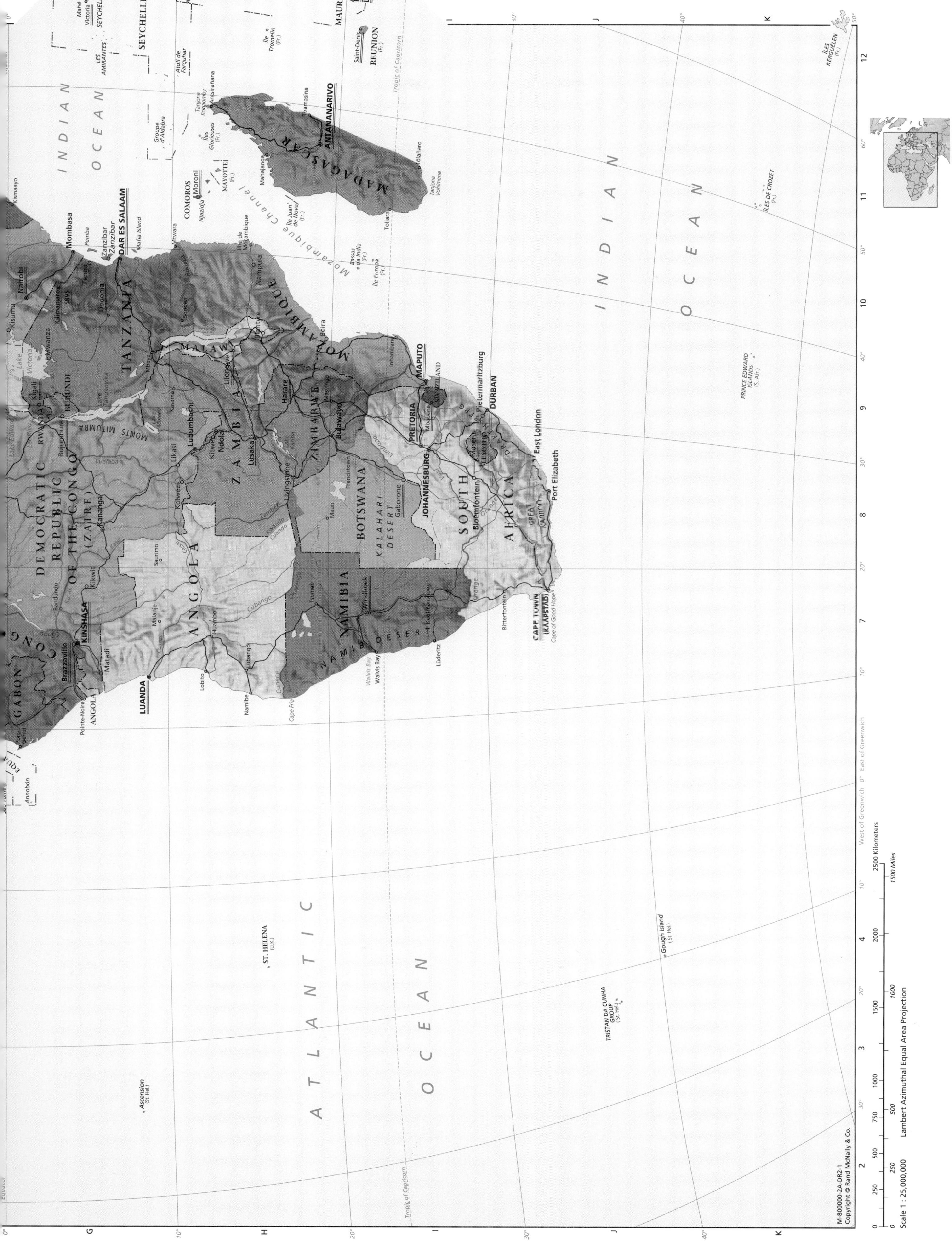

SEYCHELLES

Mahé
Victoria
LES
AMIRANTES
SEYCHELLES

Agalega
Islands
(Maur.)

G

H

MAURITIUS
Port
Louis

Île
Tromelin
(Fr.)

Atoll de
Farquhar

Saint-Denis
RÉUNION
(Fr.)

Tropic of Capricorn

12

LES
KERGUELEN
(Fr.)

Groupe
d'Aldabra

Îles
Glorieuses
(Fr.)

Tanjona
Bobaomby

Antsiranana

Tamatave

ANTANANARIVO

I N D I A N   O C E A N

Kismaayo

Mombasa

Pemba
Zanzibar
Zanzibar
DAR ES SALAAM

Tanga

Mafia Island

Mtwara

COMOROS
Moroni
Njazidja

MAYOTTE
(Fr.)

Île de
Moçambique

Nampula

MADAGASCAR

Mahajanga

Île Juan
de Nova (Fr.)

Toamasina

Antsirabe

Bassas
da India
(Fr.)
Île Europa
(Fr.)

Tanjona
Vohimena

Toliara

Fianarantsoa

Tôlanaro

ILES DE CROZET

Nairobi
Kisumu

Mwanza

Kilimanjaro
5895
Dodoma

Lake
Victoria

TANZANIA

MALAWI

Mozambique Channel

I N D I A N

O C E A N

RWANDA
Kigali
Bujumbura
BURUNDI

Lake
Kivu

MONTS MITUMBA

Lake
Tanganyika

Songea
Lake
Nyasa

Lilongwe

Nampula

MOZAMBIQUE

Beira

Lake
Edward

DEMOCRATIC
REPUBLIC
OF THE CONGO
(ZAÏRE)

Lubumbashi

Kolwezi

Likasi

Luapula

Kitwe
Ndola

ZAMBIA

Lusaka

Lake
Kariba

Kabwe

Livingstone

Harare

ZIMBABWE

Bulawayo

Masvingo

MAPUTO

SWAZILAND
Mbabane

PRETORIA
JOHANNESBURG
Maseru
LESOTHO

Pietermaritzburg
DURBAN

PRINCE EDWARD
ISLANDS
(S. Afr.)

Kananga

Bandundu

Kikwit

KINSHASA

Brazzaville

CONGO

GABON

Matadi
Pointe-Noire

Annobón

Lake
Mweru

Saurimo

Malanje

ANGOLA

Luena

LUANDA

Lobito

Namibe

Cape Frio

Kwango

Kasai

Cuanza

Cuango

Cubango

Cuito

Cunene

Huambo

Menongue

Zambeze

Maun

Francistown

BOTSWANA

Gaborone

KALAHARI
DESERT

Limpopo

SOUTH

AFRICA

Bloemfontein
Kimberley

Orange

Vaal

East London

Port Elizabeth

NAMIBIA

Windhoek

Tsumeb

NAMIB DESERT

Walvis Bay
Walvis Bay

Lüderitz

Keetmanshoop

Orange

CAPE TOWN
(KAAPSTAD)
Cape of Good Hope

Bitterfontein

West of Greenwich 0° East of Greenwich

ST. HELENA
(U.K.)

A T L A N T I C

O C E A N

Ascension
(St. Hel.)

Gough Island
(St. Hel.)

TRISTAN DA CUNHA
GROUP
(St. Hel.)

Tropic of Capricorn

Equator

M-800000-2A-0R2-1
Copyright © Rand McNally & Co.

Scale 1 : 25,000,000   Lambert Azimuthal Equal Area Projection

0 250 500 750 1000 1500 2000 2500 Kilometers
0 250 500 1000 1500 Miles

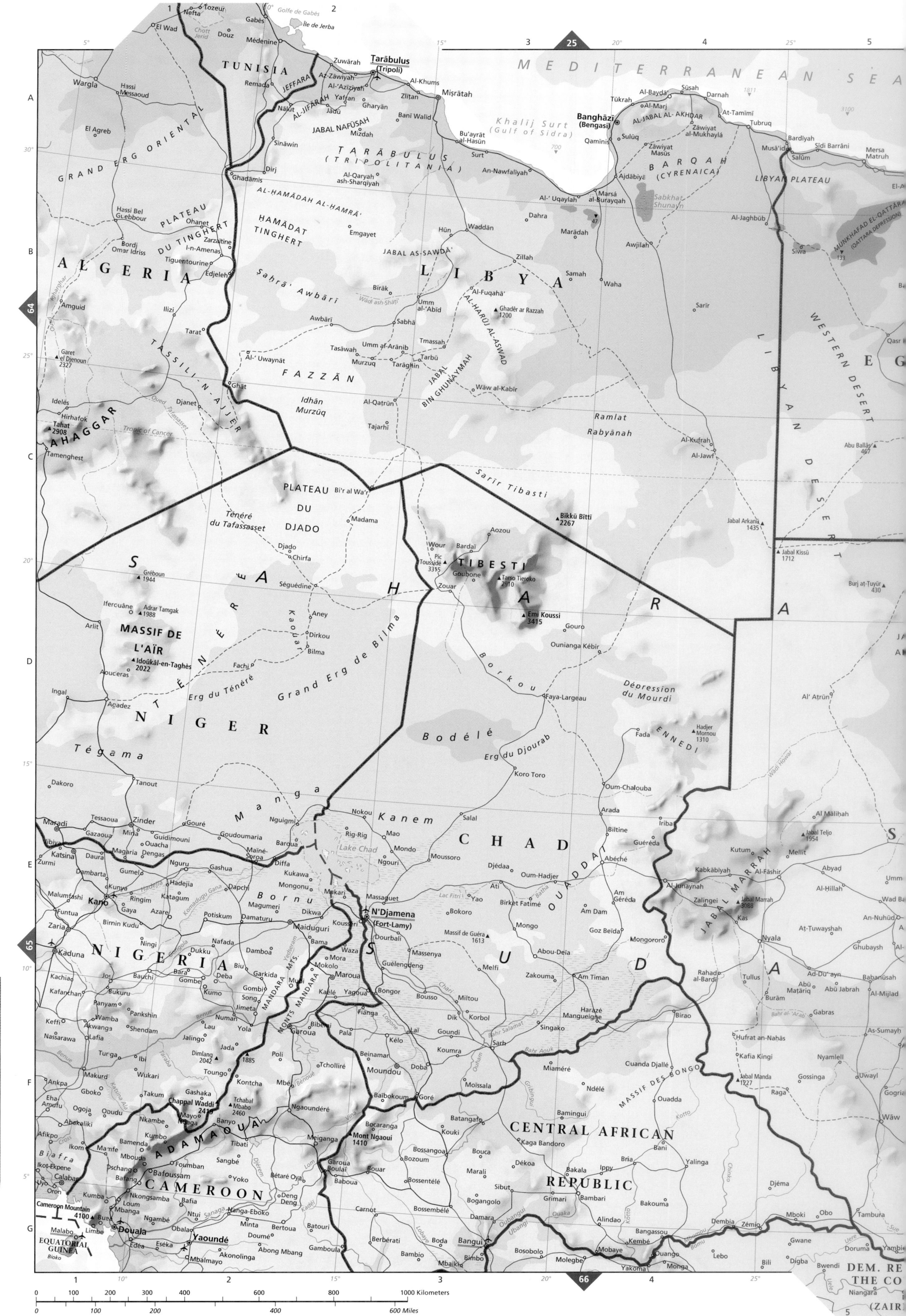

MEDITERRANEAN SEA

TUNISIA

ALGERIA

LIBYA

NIGER

CHAD

NIGERIA

CAMEROON

CENTRAL AFRICAN REPUBLIC

EQUATORIAL GUINEA

SAHARA

AHAGGAR

TIBESTI

FAZZĀN

PLATEAU DU DJADO

MASSIF DE L'AÏR

ADAMAOUA

WESTERN DESERT

LIBYAN PLATEAU

BARQAH (CYRENAICA)

TARĀBULUS (TRIPOLITANIA)

Tarābulus (Tripoli)
Banghāzī (Bengasi)
N'Djamena (Fort-Lamy)
Kano
Yaoundé
Douala

Meters
Feet

4000 / 13120
3000 / 9840
2000 / 6560
1000 / 3280
500 / 1640
200 / 656
Sea Level
200 / 656
2000 / 6560

0 100 200 300 400 500 600 800 1000 Kilometers
0 100 200 400 600 Miles

Scale 1 : 10,000,000   Lambert Conformal Conic Projection

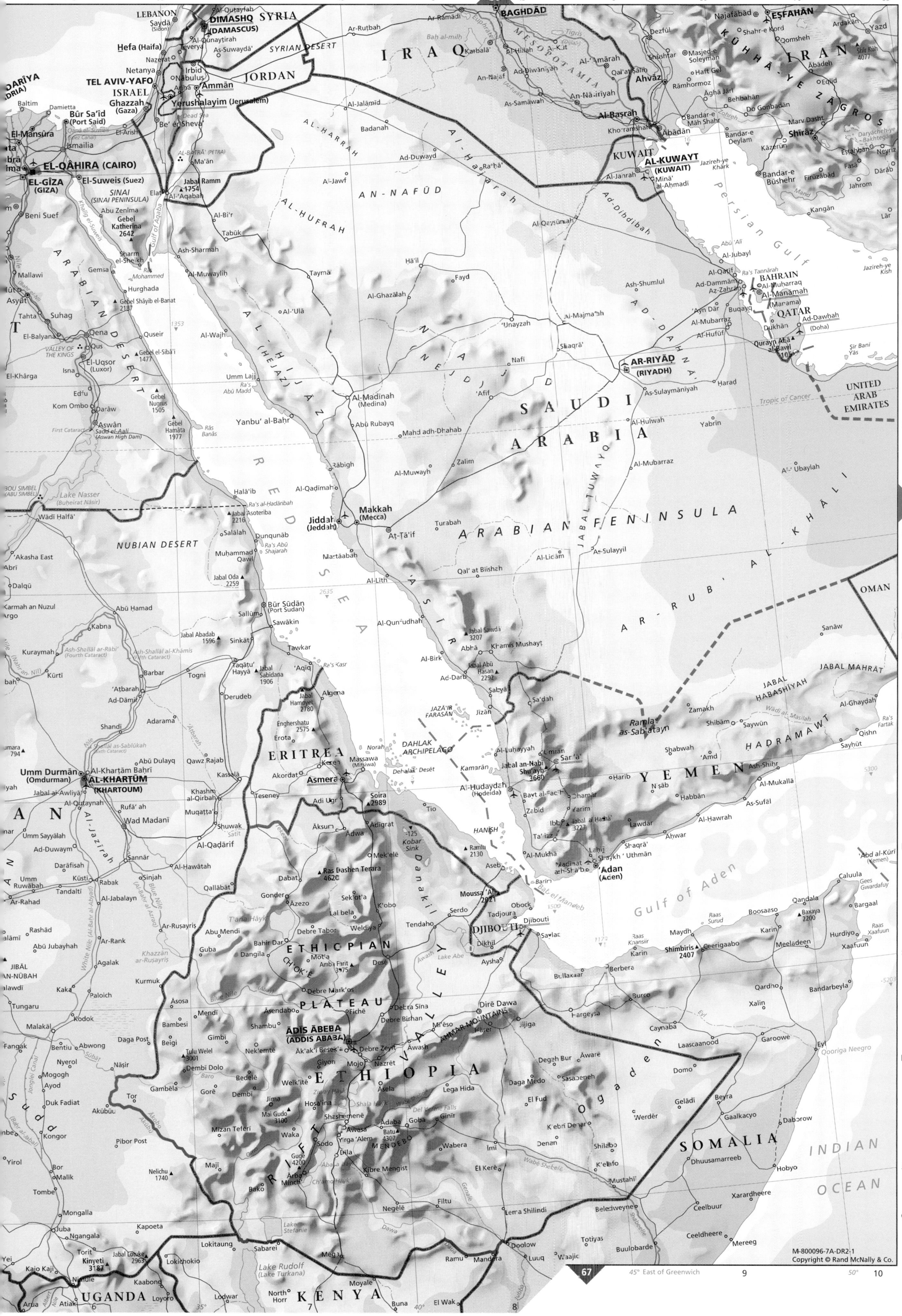

LEBANON
Saydā (Sidon)
DIMASHQ (DAMASCUS)   SYRIA
Al-Qutayfah
Hefa (Haifa)
Beyrut
As-Suwaydā'
Netanya
Irbid
As-Suwaydā'
Az-Zarqā'
TEL AVIV-YAFO
Amman
'Ajlūn
ISRAEL
Ghazzah (Gaza)
Yerushalayim (Jerusalem)
Be'er Sheva
JORDAN
SYRIAN DESERT
IRAQ
Ar-Ramadi
BAGHDAD
Ar-Rutbah
Karbalā'
Al-Hillah
Al-Kūt
Najafābād
EŞFAHĀN
Ardakān
Dezfūl
Shahr-e Kord
Qomsheh
KŪHHĀ-YE ZAGROS
Yazd
Shūshtar
Masjed-e Soleymān
Ahvāz
IRAN
Shūr Ru
4077
Ābādeh
Izadkhvāst
Haft Gel
Āghā Jārī
Ābādān
Eqlīd
Bandar-e Māh Shahr
Khorramshahr
Al-Başrah
Marv Dasht
Do Gonbadān
SAUDI ARABIA
Bandar-e Deylam
Behbahān
Bandar-e Būshehr
SHĪRĀZ
Kāzerūn
Eştahbān
Dārāb
Dead Sea
Ma'ān
Al-Jawf
Badanah
Ar-Rahhaliyah
Ar-Rab'a
An-Nāşiriyah
As-Samāwah
An-Najaf
Ad-Dīwānīyah
Qal'at Şālih
Al-'Amārah
Bandar-e 'Abbās
El-'Arīsh
Al-Qutranah
Al-Jālāmid
Jahrom
AL-HARRAH
Kangān
Lār
Al-Qaryatayn
Būr Sa'īd (Port Said)
El-Mansūra
(ALEXANDRIA)
Baltīm
Damietta
Ismailia
Suez Canal
EL-QAHIRA (CAIRO)
EL-GĪZA (GIZA)
El-Suweis (Suez)
SINAI (SINAI PENINSULA)
Jabal Ramm 1754
Elat
Al-'Aqabah
Abu Zenima
Sharm el-Sheikh
Gebel Katherīna 2642
Al-Bi'r
Tabūk
Al-Muwaylih
Ash-Sharmah
Mt. Sinai Mt. Mohammed
AL-HUFRAH
AN-NAFŪD
Hā'il
Fayd
'Unayzah
Al-Jubayl
Al-Qatif   Ra's Tannūrah
Ad-Dammām
BAHRAIN
Al-Muharraq
Az-Zahrān
Al-Manāmah
Al-Mubarraz
QATAR
Ad-Dawhah (Doha)
Dukhān
Şīr Banī Yās
UNITED ARAB EMIRATES
Beni Suef
ARABIAN DESERT
Mallawi
Asyūt
Gemsa
Hurghada
Gebel Shāyib el-Banāt 2187
Tahta
Suhag
Qena
El-Balyana
Nubt
Qūs
VALLEY OF THE KINGS
El-Uqsor (Luxor)
Isna
Edfu
Kom Ombo
Darāw
First Cataract
Aswān
Sadd el-'Ali (Aswan High Dam)
El-Khārga
Wādī Ramm
Umm Lajj
Ra's Abū Madd
Yanbu' al-Bahr
Al-Wajh
Gebel el-Sibā'ī 1477
Gebel Hamāta 1977
Ra's Banās
Taymā'
Al-Ghazālah
Al-'Ulā
NEJD
Nafī
'Afif
Ash-Shumlul
Al-Hufhah
Al-Majma'ah
Buraydah
Al-Hufūf
Yabrīn
Qurayn Mū'ammar
Al-Bāwī
SAUDI ARABIA
AR-RIYĀD (RIYADH)
As-Sulaymānīyah
Harad
Tropic of Cancer
Al-Mubarraz
Al-Hilwah
Al-'Ubaylah
Şāqrā'
ABU SIMBEL
Lake Nasser (Buheirat Nāsir)
Wādī Halfā'
Akasha East
Abri
Dalqū
NUBIAN DESERT
Rābigh
Hala'ib
Ra's al-Hadāribah
Jabal Asoteriba 2216
Salālah
Dunqunāb
Ra's Abū Shajarah
Muhammad Qawl
Jabal Oda 2259
MAKKAH (Mecca)
JIDDAH (Jeddah)
AL-MADINAH (Medina)
Abū Rubayq
Mahd adh-Dhahab
Al-Muwayh
Zalim
Turabah
AT-TĀ'IF
Al-Licām
As-Sulayyil
ARABIAN PENINSULA
JABAL TUWAYQ
AR-RUB' AL-KHĀLĪ
Sanāw
OMAN
Karmah an Nuzul
Argo
Kabna
Kuraymah
Ash-Shallāl ar-Rābi' (Fourth Cataract)
Kūrtī
Abū Hamad
Sawākin
BŪR SŪDĀN (Port Sudan)
Sallūm
Tawkar
Jabal Abadab 1596
Sinkāt
Martaabah
Al-Qunfudhah
Al-Lith
2635
Al-Birk
Jabal Sawdā' 3207
Khamīs Mushayt
Abhā
Jabal Abū Hasan 2292
Ad-Darb
Şalwah
JAZĀ'IR FARASAN
Ra's Kasr
'Aqīq
Taqatu' Hayyā
Jabal Sabidana 1906
Derudeb
Togni
Barbar
Ad-Dāmir
Shandi
Adarama
Abū Dulayq
Qawz Rajab
Kassala
Keren
Massawa (Mitsiwa)
Dehalak Deset
DAHLAK ARCHIPELAGO
Dehalak
Norah
Kamarān
Al-Luhayyah
'Imrān
Şan'ā'
Sa'dah
Zamakh
Shibām
Şaywūn
HADRAMAWT
JABAL HABASHIYAH
Al-Ghaydah
JABAL MAHRĀT
Ra's Fartak
Qishn
Sayhūt
Ramlat as-Sab'atayn
Shabwah
'Amd
Wādī al-Maşilah
5300
Umm Durmān (Omdurman)
Jabal al-Awlīyā'
AL-KHARTUM (KHARTOUM)
Al-Khartūm Bahrī
Khashm al-Qirbah
Teseney
Akordat
ERITREA
Enghershatu 2575
Erota
Soira 2989
Adi Ugri
Asmera
Adwa
Aksum
Adigrat
'Atbarah
Rufā'ah
Wad Madanī
Al-Gezira
Muqatta'
Shuwak
Al-Qadārif
Al-Hawātah
Sannār
Sinjah
Rabak
Kūstī
Tandaltī
Ar-Rahad
Rashād
Abū Jubayhah
JIBĀL AN-NŪBAH
Nuba Mts.
Zabīd
Bayt al-Faqīh
Al-Hudaydah (Hodeida)
Al-Mukhā
'Imrān
Harib
Ma'rib
Jabal an-Nabi Shu'ayb 3660
Warim
Dhamār
Ibb
Ta'izz
Habbān
Lawdar
N'şāb
Ash-Shihr
Al-Mukallā
As-Sufāl
As-Shu'aybah
Jabal al-Hashā 3227
YEMEN
'Ahwar
Al-Hawrah
Lahij
Shaykh 'Uthmān
Madīnat ash-Sha'b
'Adan (Aden)
'Abd al-Kūri (Yemen)
Gulf of Aden
Ra's Fartak
Caluula
Ra's Khansīyur
'Alūla
Ra's Gwardafuy
Bandarbeyla
Iy 'Abdī
Jabal al-Awlīyā'
SUDAN
Umm Sayyālah
Ad-Duwaym
Jabalayn
Al-Jabalayn
Ar-Ruşayriş
Khazzān ar-Ruşayriş
Guba
Dangila
Bahir Dar
ETHIOPIAN
CHOK'E
Debre Mark'os
Debre Tabor
Weldiya
K'obo
Sek'ot'a
Lal bela
Dabat
Gonder
Azezo
T'ana Hāyk'
Mek'elē
Ras Dashen Terara 4620
Amba Farit 3975
DANAKIL
Serdo
Tendaho
Aseb
Moussa 'Ali 2021
Tadjoura
Obock
DJIBOUTI
Djibouti
Dikhil
Aysha
Lake Abē
Hanish
Ramlu 2130
Bab el Mandeb
Zeila
Raas Surud
Raas Khansīyur
Maydh
Berbera
Shimbiris 2407
Ceerigaabo
Baxaya 2200
Hurdiyo
Qandala
Xaafuun
Boosaaso
Bargaal
Qardho
Xalin
Bandarbeyla
Kūrmuk
Asosa
Mendi
Bambesi
Gimbi
Daga Post
Beigi
Tulu Welel 3001
Dembi Dolo
Nek'emte
Guba
ADIS ĀBEBA (ADDIS ABABA)
Debre Zeyt
Debre Sina
Debre Birhan
Fichē
Giyon
Mojo
Nazrēt
AHMAR MOUNTAINS
Mī'eso
Dirē Dawa
Jijiga
Harer
Fiq
Degah Bur
Āware
Imī
Lega Hida
Sasabeneh
El Fud
Denan
Geladī
K'ebrī Dehar
Werdēr
Shilabo
Domo
Beyra
SOMALIA
Gaalkacyo
Galadī
Xarardheere
Dhuusamarreeb
Hobyo
INDIAN OCEAN
Jabal al-Awlīyā'
Rabak
Fangak
Nyerol
Nāşir
Abwong
Ayod
Malakāl
Kodok
Paloich
Kaka
Tungaru
Kurmuk
Baro
Gambēla
Gorē
Dembi
Mai Gudo 3100
Mizan Teferi
Waka
Jima
Hosa'ina
Sodō
Shashemenē
Āwasa
Adaba
Goba
Batu
Gīnīr
Wabera
Imī
Ginir
Daga Medo
El Kerē
El Fud
Wajir
RIFT VALLEY
Awash
'Ādola
ETHIOPIA
MENDEBO
Gugē 4200
Āreka
Dila
Yirga 'Alem
K'ibrē Mengist
Negēlē
Filtū
Mandera
Luuq
Waajid
Belet Weyne
Ceel Buur
Mereeg
Ceeldheere
Buulobarde
Mata Banu
Juba
Ngangala
Kapoeta
Tombe
Yirol
Bor
Malik
Mongalla
Torit
Kinyeti 3187
Jabal Tebek 2963
Lokichokio
Loyoro
UGANDA
Kaabong
Lodwar
Lake Stefanie
Mega
Moyale
North Horr
Ramu
El Wak
Buna
Lake Rudolf (Lake Turkana)
Sabarei
Luuq
Totiyas
KENYA
Garissa
45° East of Greenwich

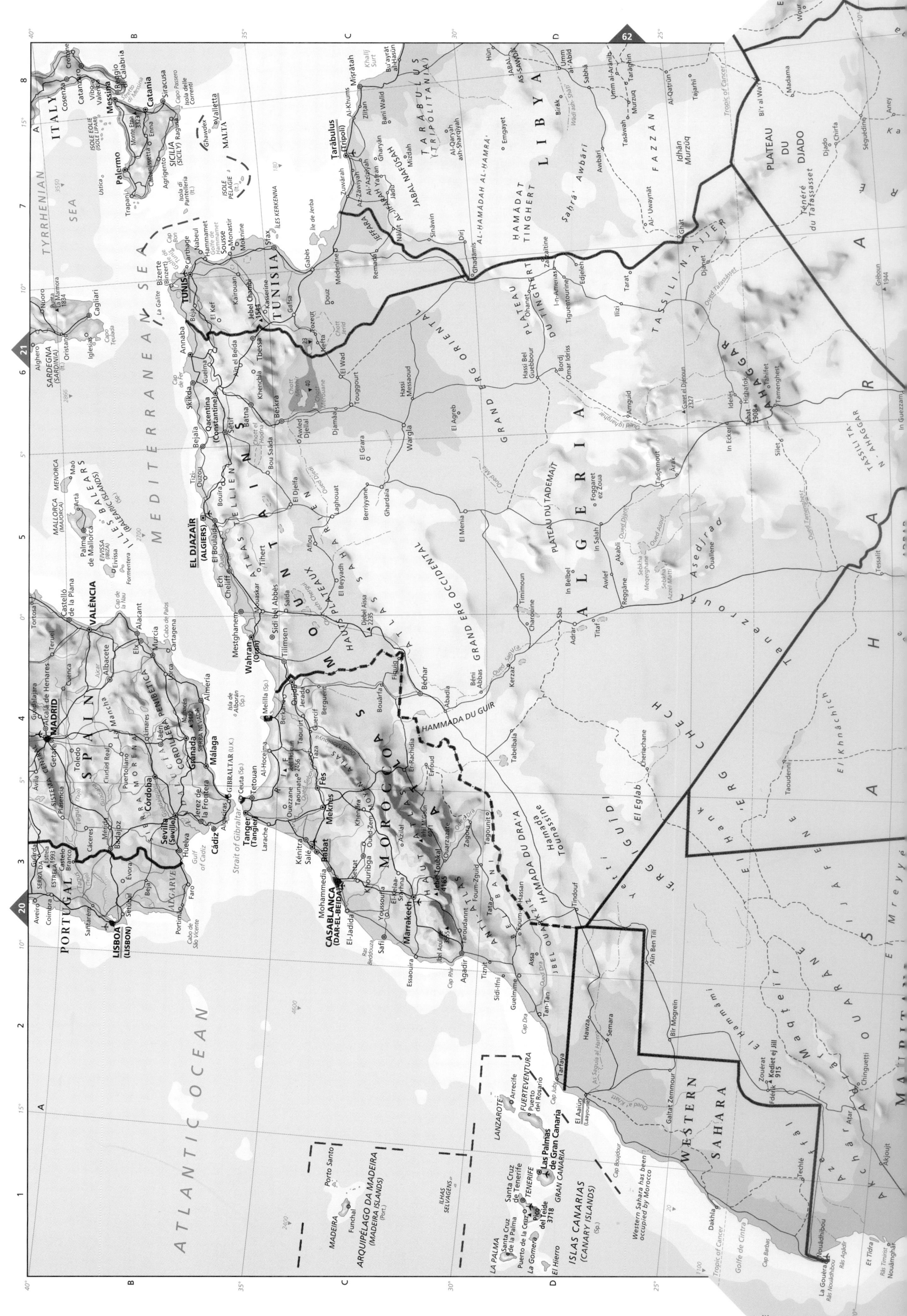

62
21
20

ITALY

TYRRHENIAN
SEA

SARDEGNA
(SARDINIA)

SICILIA
(SICILY)

MALTA

Palermo

Messina

Catania

Siracusa

MEDITERRANEAN SEA

TUNISIA

Tarābulus
(Tripoli)

TARĀBULUS
(TRIPOLITANIA)

FAZZĀN

PLATEAU
DU
DJADO

TUNIS

LIBYA

SPAIN

PORTUGAL

MADRID

LISBOA
(LISBON)

VALÈNCIA

MALLORCA
(MAJORCA)

MENORCA

ILES BALEARS
ILLES BALEARS
(BALEARIC ISLANDS)

EL DJAZAÏR
(ALGIERS)

ATLAS
TELLIEN
SAHARIEN
ATLAS

HAUTS PLATEAUX

GRAND ERG OCCIDENTAL

GRAND ERG ORIENTAL

ALGERIA

PLATEAU DU TADEMAÏT

MOROCCO

HAUT ATLAS

ANTI-ATLAS

Casablanca
(DAR-EL-BEIDA)

Marrakech

Agadir

Wahran
(Oran)

Tanger
(Tangier)

Rabat

Fès
Meknès

GIBRALTAR
(U.K.)

Ceuta (Sp.)

Melilla
(Sp.)

Málaga

Sevilla
(Seville)

Córdoba

HAMMADA DU GUIR

HAMMADA DU DRA'A

TASSILI-N-AJJER

HAGGAR

AHAGGAR

WESTERN
SAHARA

Western Sahara has been
occupied by Morocco

ISLAS CANARIAS
(CANARY ISLANDS)
(Sp.)

LANZAROTE

FUERTEVENTURA

GRAN CANARIA

TENERIFE

LA PALMA

LA GOMERA

EL HIERRO

Las Palmas
de Gran Canaria

ARQUIPÉLAGO DA MADEIRA
(MADEIRA ISLANDS)

MADEIRA

PORTO SANTO

ILHAS
SELVAGENS

ATLANTIC OCEAN

Tropic of Cancer

Tropic of Cancer

Gulf of Guinea

ATLANTIC OCEAN

Scale 1 : 10,000,000

Lambert Conformal Conic Projection

M-800097-7A-DR2-1
Copyright © Rand McNally & Co.

Meters Feet	
4000 13120	
3000 9840	
2000 6560	
1000 3280	
500 1640	
200 656	
Sea Level	
200 656	
2000 6560	

1000 Kilometers
600 Miles

a Same scale as main map

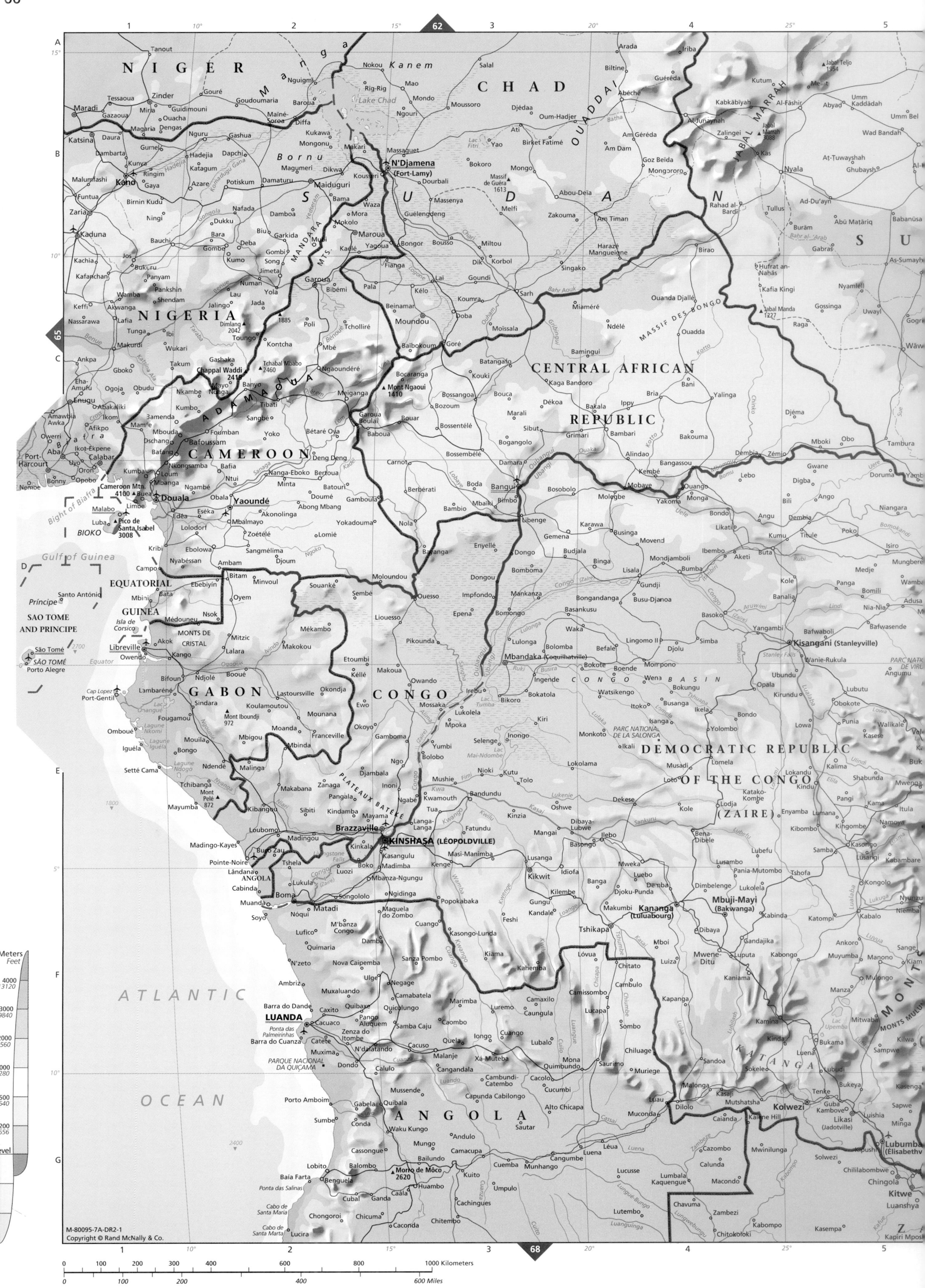

M-80095-7A-DR2-1
Copyright © Rand McNally & Co.

Meters
Feet

4000
13120

3000
9840

2000
6560

1000
3280

500
1640

200
656

Sea Level

200
656

2000
6560

0 100 200 300 400 500 600 700 800 900 1000 Kilometers

0 100 200 300 400 500 600 Miles

Scale 1 : 10,000,000 Sinusoidal Projection

RED SEA
ERITREA
Asmera
YEMEN
Ṣan'ā'
'Adan (Aden)
Gulf of Aden
Bab el Mandeb
DJIBOUTI
Djibouti
ETHIOPIAN PLATEAU
Danakil
ETHIOPIA
ĀDĪS ĀBEBA (ADDIS ABEBA)
AHMAR MOUNTAINS
Ogaden
SOMALIA
Muqdisho (Mogadiscio)
Lake Rudolf (Lake Turkana)
Chalbi Desert
KENYA
NAIROBI
Mombasa
UGANDA
Kampala
Lake Victoria
Serengeti Plain
Kilimanjaro 5895
Masai Steppe
TANZANIA
Dodoma
DAR ES SALAAM
Zanzibar
Pemba
Mafia Island
INDIAN OCEAN
SEYCHELLES
Groupe d'Aldabra
COMOROS
Moroni
Kartala 2361
Nzwani
Dzaoudzi
MAYOTTE (Fr.)
ARCHIPEL DES COMORES
MADAGASCAR
Antsirañana
Lake Nyasa
MALAWI
Lilongwe
MOZAMBIQUE
Niassa
RIFT VALLEY
Equator
63
69

A

B

C

D

E

F

G

1   2   66   3   4

10°   20°   25°

CONGO
Pointe-Noire
Buu Zau Tshela
Luozi   Kasangulu   Kenge
Lukula   Madimba   Kasangulu
Ländana   Boke   Kasangulu
Angola   Congololo   Mbanza-Ngungu
Cabinda   Ngidinga   Popokabaka
Muanda   Boma   Maquela do Zombo
Soyo   Matadi   M'banza   Kandale   Kahemba   Loange
N'zeto   Nóqui   Congo   Damba   Feshi   Dibaya   Mbuji-Mayi   Kabinda
Ambriz   Lufico   Camabatela   Kasongo-Lunda   Lóvua   Tshikapa   (Bakwanga)   Gandajika   Ankoro
Quimarie   Nova Caipemba   Uige   Kiama   Chitato   Luiza   Mwene-   Kaniama   Kabongo   Manono   Kiambi
Barra do Dande   Negage   Marimba   Caungula   Cambulo   Ditu   Kapanga   Manza   Mulongo
LUANDA   Caxito   Quibaxe   Samba Caju   Iongo   Cuango   Luremo   Saurimo   Chiluage   Sandoa   Bukama   Sampwe   Kilwa
Cacuaco   Pango   Malanje   Quela   Lubalo   Sombo   Chumbe   Muriege   Malonga   Mutshatsha   Kolwezi   Kambove   Luishia   Kasenga
Ponta das Palmeirinhas   Aluquem   Zenza   Quiculungo   DEMOCRATIC   Dilolo   Caianda   Kipushi   (Jadotville)   Minga
Barra do Cuanza   Catete   do Itombe   Xá-Muteba   Luau   REPUBLIC   Likasi   Lubumbashi
Muxima   Ndalatando   Cacuso   Cangandala   Mona Quimbundo   Cacolo   OF THE CONGO   Alto Chicapa   Mwinilunga   (Élisabethville)
Dondo   Calulu   Cambundi Catembo   Cacumbi   (ZAIRE)   Solwezi   Chililabombwe   Chingola
Mussende   Capunda Cabilongo   Cazombo   Kitwe
Porto Amboim   Quibala   Waku Kungo   Sautar   Lumbala   Zambezi   Kabompo   Kapiri Mposhi   Luanshya
Gabela   Andulo   Camacupa   Cuemba   Munhango   Kaquengue   Macondo   Kaoma   Mumbwa   Kabwe
Sumbe   Conda   Mungo   Cassongue   Bailundo   Cangumbe   Luena   Léua   Lutembo   Chavuma   ZAMBIA   Chisamba
Morro de Moco   Cuito   Umpulo   Lucusse   Lumbala   Lukulu
Lobito   Balombo   2620   Cáala   Chitembo   Luena   N'guimbo   Chitokoloki   Kasempa
Benguela   Cubal   Chicuma   Huambo   Cachingues   Muié   Mussuma   Kalabo   Senanga   Lusaka
Baía Farta   Ganda   Caconda   ANGOLA   Cangombe   Ninda   Mongu   Kataba   Namwala   Mazabuka
Ponta das Salinas   Chongoroi   Chicomba   Kuvango   Longa   Lupire   Chiume   Choma   Kalomo   Livingstone
Cabo de   SERRA DA NEVE   Quilengues   Cácula   Dongo   Menongue   Mavinga   Neriquinha   Luiana   Sesheke   Singalamwe   Victoria   Pemba
Santa Maria   Lucira   Quibala   Matala   Capelongo   Caiundo   Cuito-Cuanavale   Dirico   Caprivi Strip   Kasane   Falls   Zimba   Lake Kariba
Cabo de   1713   Cassinga   Cuangar   Rundu   Livingstone   Kalomo   Dete   Gokwe
Santa Marta   Bibala   Lubango   Chibia   Cahama   Xangongo   Okavango   Shakawe   Wankie   Binga
Namibe   SERRA DA CHELA   Chiange   Chibemba   Cunene   Ondjiva   Kwando
Ponta   Tombua   Humbe   Okavango Delta   Gcoverega   Nkayi   Inyathi
Albina   Iona   Oncócua   Chitado   Ruacana Falls   Ondangwa   OVAMBOLAND   Maun   Nata   Maitengwe   Bu
Foz do   Cunene   Opuwo   Tsintsabis   Nokaneng   Plumtree   West Nich
Cunene   Cunene   480   Okaukuejo   Tsumeb   KAUKAU VELD   Tsau   Lake   Makgadikgadi   Francistown   Old Tate
Cape Fria   Sesfontein   Etosha Pan   Grootfontein   Tsumkwe   Ngami   Toteng   Pan   Mmadinare   West N
KAOKO VELD   Namutoni   Otavi   Tsintsabis   Boteti   Rakops   Lake   Selebi-   Bobonong
480   Kamanjab   Otjikondo   Outjo   Sukses   Maun   Xau   Phikwe
NAMI   Fransfontein   Otjiwarongo   Otjinene   Serowe   Palapye
3700   Uis   Brandberg   Omatako   Hochfeld   Ghanzi   BOTSWANA   Mahalapye
Palgrave Point   2579   2289   Epukiro   Rietfontein   Shoshong   Baltimore
Okombahe   Omaruru   DAMARALAND   Okahandja   Witvlei   Gobabis   Tshootsha   KALAHARI   Lephephe   Pieters
Cape Cross   Usakos   Karibib   Tswaane   Okwa   Dinokwe   Potgietersru
Hentiesbaai   Windhoek   Kule   Mmadinare   Warmbad
Swakopmund   Rehoboth   DESERT   Gaborone   Thabazimbi   PRETOR
Walvis Bay   NAMIBIA   Aminuis   Lehututu   Letlhakeng   Mochudi
Walvis Bay   Kalkrand   Stampriet   Aranos   Tshane   Kang   Kanye   Zeerust   Warmbad
Conception Bay   Maltahöhe   Mariental   Khakhea   Werda   Lobatse   Krugersdorp
Tropic of Capricorn   Gochas   Kokong   Mmabatho   Rustenburg   Groble
GREAT NAMAQUALAND   Gibeon   Tses   Koës   Tshabong   JOHANNESBURG   Benoni
385   Helmeringhausen   Kuruman   Carletonville   Germiston   Vereenic
Lüderitz   Bethanien   Keetmanshoop   Ganyesa   Vryburg   Potchefstroom   Orkney   Klerksdorp   Parys
Aus   GROOT KARASBERGE   Aroab   Askham   Hotazel   Kuruman   Sisen   Wolmaransstad   Bothaville   Kroonstad
Humberge   Grünau   Olifantshoek   Bloemhof   Odendaalsrus   Heilbron   Bethlehem
1654   Karasburg   Upington   Postmasburg   Warrenton   Welkom   Virginia   Senekal
Sendelingsdrif   Warmbad   Augrabies-valle   Keimoes   Barkly West   Kimberley   Bultfontein   Ladybrand   Phofu
Oranjemund   Oranje (Orange)   Onseepkans   Kakamas   Douglas   BLOEMFONTEIN   Ficksburg   3299
Alexander Bay   LITTLE   Pofadder   Kenhardt   Hopetown   Koffiefontein   Ladybrand   LESOTHO
NAMAQUALAND   Steinkopf   Marydale   Strydenburg   Jagersfontein   Edenburg   Wepener   Mafeteng
Port Nolloth   BUSHMAN   Prieska   Philippolis   Springfontein   Bethulie   Outhing   Matat
LAND   SOUTH AFRICA   Marydale   Bethulie   Barkly
ATLANTIC OCEAN   Springbok   Kamieskroon   Brandvlei   Vanwyksvlei   Britstown   De Aar   Colesberg   Burgersdorp   King William's
Hondeklipbaai   Garies   Loeriesfontein   Sakrivier   Carnarvon   Hanover   Noupoort   Steynsburg   Dordrecht   Queenstow
Bitterfontein   Nieuwoudtville   Williston   Victoria   Richmond   Middelburg   Tarkastad   Sterkstroom   East Londo
Vanrhynsdorp   West   Loxton   Cradock   Winterberg   Oos-Lon
Klawer   Calvinia   Murraysburg   371   Stutterhe   King
Lambert's Bay   Clanwilliam   Fraserburg   Beaufort West   Aberdeen   Graaff-Reinet   Fort   Beaufort   Port Alfred
Citrusdal   Sutherland   GREAT KARROO   Somerset East   Adelaide   Grahamstown
Cape Columbine   Piketberg   Prince   Willowmore   Jansenville   Algoabaai
Sint Helenabaai   Laingsburg   Albert   Oudtshoorn   Uitenhage   Port
Saldanha   Tulbagh   Touwsrivier   LITTLE KARROO   George   Humansdorp   Elizabeth
Moorreesburg   Worcester   Swellendam   Knysna   Cape
Malmesbury   Paarl   Riversdale   Mosselbaai   St. Francis
CAPE TOWN   Stellenbosch   150
(KAAPSTAD)   Strand   4471
Simon's Town   Hermanus   Bredasdorp
Cape of Good Hope   False Bay   Kaap Agulhas
4080

East of Greenwich

5°   10°   15°   20°   25°

M-800092-7A-DR2-1
Copyright © Rand McNally & Co.

Meters
Feet
3000
9840
2000
6560
1000
3280
500
1640
200
656
Sea Level
200
656
2000
6560

0   100   200   300   400   500   600   800   1000 Kilometers
0   100   200   400   600 Miles

Scale 1 : 10,000,000   Lambert Conformal Conic Projection

INDIAN OCEAN

SEYCHELLES

Uruwira
Inyonga
Kitunda
Dodoma
Mpwapwa
Zanzibar
Zanzibar
Kasanga
Rungwa
Kipembawe
Kisiju
Mafia Island
Sao Hill
Utete
DAR ES SALAAM
Morogoro
Mikumi
Bagamoyo
Groupe
d'Aldabra
Assompton
Atoll de
Cosmoledo
St. Pierre
Atoll de
Providence
Astove   4030

COMOROS
Njazidja
Moroni
Kartala
2361
Nzwani
Mwali
Fomboni
Mutsamudu
Dzaoudzi
MAYOTTE
(Fr.)
Îles
Glorieuses
(Fr.)
Atoll de
Farquhar

TANZANIA

MALAWI

Niassa

MOZAMBIQUE

ARCHIPEL DES COMORES

Mozambique Channel

MADAGASCAR

INDIAN

OCEAN

Tropic of Capricorn

MAPUTO

DURBAN

INDIAN

OCEAN

a   Same scale as main map   b   Same scale as main map

INDIAN OCEAN
Port Louis   MAURITIUS
Piton de la Petite
Rivière Noire
828
Curepipe
Mahébourg
Saint-Denis
Saint-Paul
Saint-Pierre
Piton des Neiges
3070
REUNION
(Fr.)
MASCARENE ISLANDS

INDIAN OCEAN
SEYCHELLES
Groupe
d'Aldabra
St. Pierre
Atoll de
Providence
4406
Assomption
Atoll de
Cosmoledo
Astove
4030
Atoll de
Farquhar
Agalega
Islands
(Maur.)

Praslin
La Digue
Silhouette
Victoria
Mahé
SEYCHELLES
Poivre
Atoll
Desroches
Île Plate
LES
AMIRANTES
Alphonse
Coëtivy

Map labels

KAOKO VELD

KUNENE

Skeleton Coast

OTJOZONDJUPA

NGAMILAND

MAKGADIKGADI PANS GAME RES

Eransfontein
Khorixas
Outjo
Otjiwarongo
Waterberg Platopark
Eiseb
Otjozondjou
Rooibokklaagte
Sehithwa
Toteng

Sorris-Sorris
Kalkfeld
Sukses
Osire Süd
Otjinene
Mabeleapodi
Lake Ngami
Rakops
Khasebake

Brandberg 2579
Uis
Okombahe
Omaruru
Etjo 2085
Omatako 2789
Onbotozo 1916
Hochfeld
Epukiro
Epukiro
Rietfontein
Ghanzi
Khomodimo

DAMARALAND
Erongo 2305
Karibib
Wilhelmstal
Okahandja
Steinhausen
Rietfontein
OMAHEKE
GHANZI
CENTRAL KALAHARI GAME RESERVE

ERONGO
Hentiesbaai
Otjimbingwe
Khomas Hochland
Omitara
Seeis
Gobabis
Mamuno
Okwa
Tshootsha
Takachu
BOTS

Arandis
Swakopmund
Walvis Bay
Windhoek
Dordabis
NAMIBIA
KHOMAS
Witvlei
Okwa
Tswaane
Takachu
Kule

Walvis Bay (Wa.visbaai)
Sandwich Bay
Tropic of Capricorn
Ilhea Point
Rehoboth
Leonardville
Witvooi
KALAHARI
Lehututu
Kang
KWENE

Conception Bay
NAMIB-NAUKLUFT PARK
Uhlenhorst
Aminuis
Hukuntsi
Tshane
Kokong
Sekoma

Meobbaai
Kalkrand
Aranos
KGALAGADI DESERT
SOU

Hollandsbird Island
Nomtsas
HARDAP
Stampriet
Khakhea

214
GREAT NAMAQUALAND (GROOT NAMALAND)
Mariental
Gochas
GEMSBOK NATIONAL PARK
MABUASEHUBE GAME RESERVE
Werda

Maltahöhe
Gibeon
Witbooisvlei
KALAHARI GEMSBOK NATIONAL PARK
Tosca

Schwarz-rand
Tses
Maralaleng
Pomfret

Helmeringhausen
Berseba
Wee Rivieren
Tshabong
Morokweng
NO

Hottentotsbaai
Khuis
Van Zylsrus
Ganye

Bethanien
Keetmanshoop
Aroab
Askham
Kuruman
Mokhaweng

Diaz Point
Lüderitz
Aus
Seaheim
Khuis
Tsineng

Possession Island
HUIB-HOCH PLATEAU
Gawachab
Schoffenstein 2202
GROOT KARASBERGE
Hotazel
Dibeng
Reivi

KARAS
Holoog
Upington
Olifantshoek
Sishen 1855
Barkly

1654
Grünau
Kanus
BECHUANALAND
Postmasburg
Daniëlskuil
Ulée

Sendelingsdrif
Karasburg
Keimoes
GRIQUALAND WEST

Oranjemund
Warmbad
AUGRABIES FALLS NATIONAL PARK
Kakamas
Putonderwater
Campbell
Kimb

Alexander Bay
Vioolsdrif
Noordoewer
Onseepkans
Bladgrond-Noord
Grobblershoop
Griekwastad
Douglas

LITTLE NAMAQUALAND (KLEIN NAMALAND)
Goodhouse
Pofadder
Namies
Kenhardt
SOUTH A

Port Nolloth
Steinkopf
Aggeneys
BUSHMAN LAND
Marydale
Niekerkshoop

Nababeep
Okiep
Springbok
Gamoep
Grootvloer
Prieska
Hopetown

150
Kamieskroon
NORTHERN CAPE
Vanwyksvlei
Vosburg
Britstown
De Aar

Hondeklipbaai
Garies
Brandvlei
Sakrivier
Carnarvon
Myntontein
Hanover

Bitterfontein
Loeriesfontein
Williston
Hutchinson
Richmond

Nuwerus
Nieuwoudtville
Calvinia
Victoria West

1964
Lutzville
Vanrhynsdorp
ROGGEVELDBERGE
Loxton
Fraserburg

ATLANTIC OCEAN
Vredendal
Klawer
Nelspoort
Murraysburg
Bethe

Lambert's Bay
Clanwilliam
Elandsvlei
1596
Beaufort West
Aberdeen

Wuppertal
Bontberg 1922
Sutherland
GREAT KARROO (GROOT KARROO)
KAROO NATIONAL PARK

Citrusdal
Wadrif
Merweville
Leeu-Gamka

Cape Columbine
Aurora
Piketberg
Porterville
Laingsburg
Prince Albert
Willowmore
Steytlerville

Vredenburg
Velddrif
WESTERN CAPE
Touwsrivier
Ladismith
Calitzdorp
Uniondale

Saldanha
Hopefield
Moorreesburg
Ceres
Zeberg
Van Wyksdorp
Oudtshoorn
KOUGABERGE

Darling
Malmesbury
Tulbagh
De Doorns
LITTLE KARROO (KLEIN KARROO)
Avontuur
George

Wellington
Worcester
Montagu
Herbertsdale
Cape Seal

CAPE TOWN (KAAPSTAD)
Paarl
Robertson
Ashton
Riversdale
Brakrivier
Knysna

Bellville
Stellenbosch
Some st West
Caledon
Swellendam
Mosselbaai (Mossel Bay)

Simon's Town
Strand
Tipdale
Protem
BONTEBOK NATIONAL PARK
Albertinia
Stilbaai

False Bay
Hermanus
Witsand
St. Sebastian Bay

Cape of Good Hope (Kaap die Goeie Hoop)
1180
Gansbaai
Elim
Bredasdorp
Kaap Agulhas
Walker Bay
Danger Point

Scale / legend

Meters / Feet

3000 / 9840
2000 / 6560
1000 / 3280
500 / 1640
200 / 656
Sea Level
200 / 656
2000 / 6560

0 100 200 300 400 600 800 1000 Kilometer
0 200 400 600 Miles

Scale 1 : 5,000,000   Lambert Conformal Conic Projection

Countries/Regions: ZIMBABWE, MOZAMBIQUE, MANICA, GAZA, INHAMBANE, SOFALA, SWAZILAND, LESOTHO, KWAZULU-NATAL, FREE STATE, EASTERN CAPE, GAUTENG, MPUMALANGA, NORTHERN, TRANSKEI, MATABELELAND NORTH, MATABELELAND SOUTH, MIDLANDS, MASVINGO

Major cities: Bulawayo, Gaborone, PRETORIA, JOHANNESBURG, Soweto, Vereeniging, Bloemfontein, Maseru, Maputo, DURBAN, Pietermaritzburg, Richard's Bay, East London (Oos-Londen), Port Elizabeth, Beira, Messina, Beitbridge

Waters: INDIAN OCEAN, Mozambique Channel

Tropic of Capricorn

W-847000-7A-DR2-1
Copyright © Rand McNally & Co.

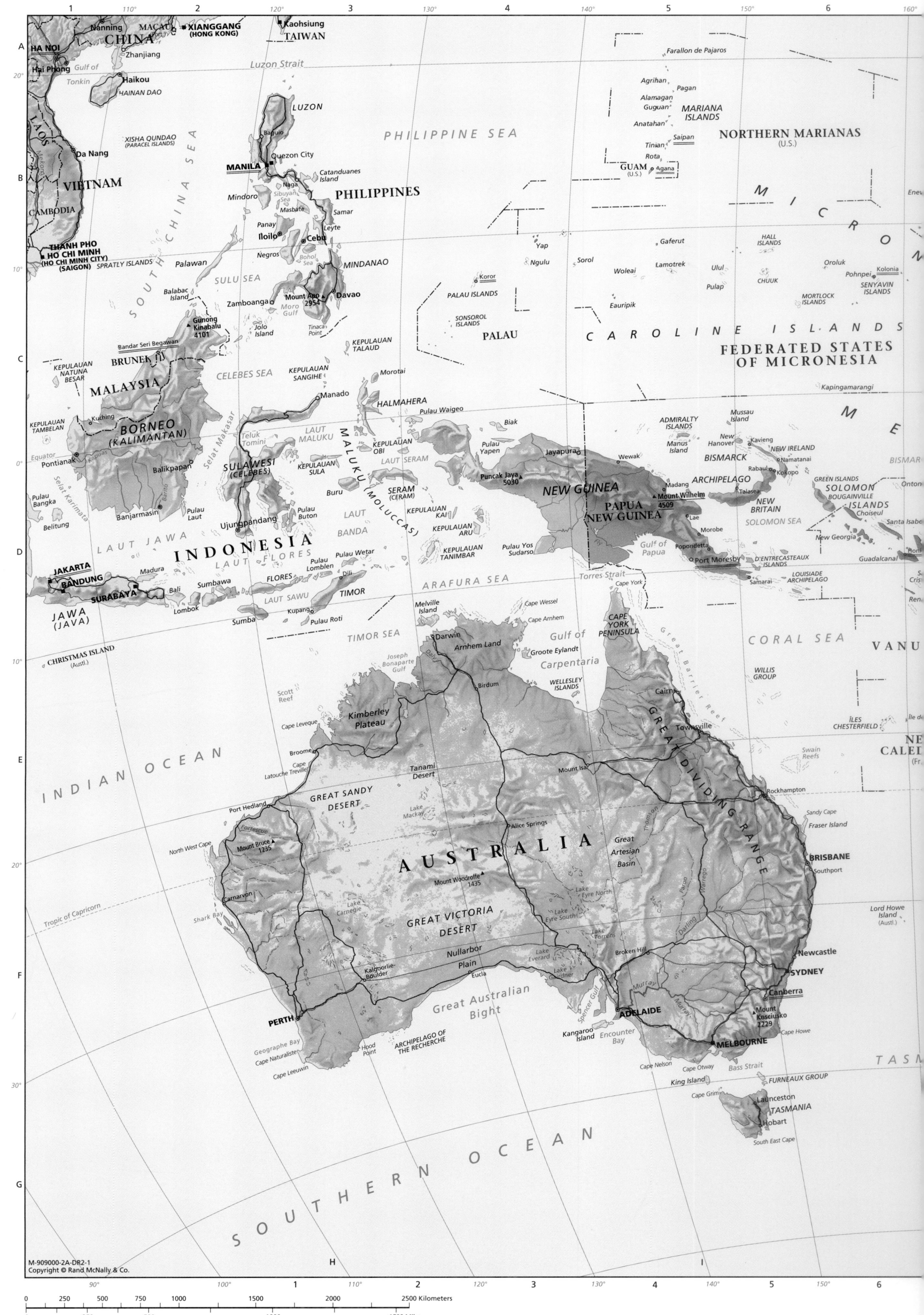

0   250   500   750   1000   1500   2000   2500 Kilometers

0   250   500   1000   1500 Miles

Scale 1 : 25,000,000   Lambert Azimuthal Equal Area Projection

KE ISLAND
(U.S.)

8   170°   180°   9   170°   10   160°   11   150°   12   140°   13

Fauai
Oahu
Mihau
Honolulu   Molokai   Maui
HAWAIIAN
ISLANDS   Mauna Kea ▲ Hilo
(U.S.)   4205
Ka Lae   HAWAII

A

Johnston Atoll
(U.S.)

B

SHALL ISLANDS

Taongi

Bikar
Rongelap
Utrik
RATAK
CHAIN
Kwajalein   Maloelap
RALIK
CHAIN
Ailinglaplap   Majuro   Arno
Jaluit   Mili

PACIFIC   OCEAN

Ebon

Kingman Reef
(U.S.)

Palmyra Atoll
(U.S.)
Teraina

10°

C

Butaritari

Tabuaeran

NAURU   Banaba

Tarawa ▪ Bairiki
Kuria   Abemama
GILBERT ISLANDS
Nonouti

Kiritimati
(Christmas Island)

Howland Island
(U.S.)
Baker Island (U.S.)

KIRIBATI

LINE ISLANDS

Jarvis
Island
(U.S.)

N   Nikunau
E   Onotoa   Arorae
S   Nanumea
I   Niutao
A   Nui

Kanton
Rawaki
Orona   Manra
Nikumaroro
PHOENIX ISLANDS

Malden

Equator   0°

OMON
DS   TUVALU   Funafuti

Starbuck

POLYNESIA

D

SANTA CRUZ
ISLANDS
Vanikolo

Niulakita

TOKELAU
(N.Z.)

Penrhyn

Vostok
Caroline
Flint

ÎLES BANKS
ua Lava
NEW
Pentecôte
Ambrym
alakula
HEBRIDES
Port Vila   Éfaté

Rotuma

WALLIS AND FUTUNA
(Fr.)
Île Futuna
ÎLES WALLIS
Île Alofi
Matā'utu

SAMOA   Swains
Island
Savai'i
Upolu   Apia
SAMOA   Tutuila
ISLANDS   Pago Pago

AMERICAN
SAMOA
(U.S.)

Nassau Island

Manihiki

NORTHERN COOK
ISLANDS

Suwarrow

Eiao
ÎLES
MARQUISES
Hiva Oa
Fatu Hiva

10°

E

FIJI
VANUA
LEVU

Île des
Pins

VITI
LEVU   Suva
KORO SEA
Kaduvu

LAU
GROUP

Ta'ahi

Vava'u

TONGA

Tongatapu   Nuku'alofa
'Eua
'Ata

NIUE
(N.Z.)

COOK ISLANDS
(N.Z.)

Palmerston

SOUTHERN
COOK
ISLANDS
Takutea
Rarotonga   Avarua

Aitutak
Manuae
Atiu

ÎLES MARIA

Manuae
Maupihaa

Rimatara
ILES AUSTRALES
Tubuai
Ralvavae

ÎLES DU
ROI GEORGES
Mataiva
Bora-Bora
ARCHIPEL DE LA SOCIÉTÉ
(SOCIETY ISLANDS)

Rurutu

Raraka
Anaa
Marutea

FRENCH POLYNESIA
(Fr.)

Tahiti   Papeete

ILES TUAMOTU

ÎLES DU
DÉSAPPOINTEMENT
Pukaruha
Ahunui   Reao

Tematangi   Mururoa   Tureia
Marutea
ÎLES
GAMBIER

Tropic of Capricorn   20°

NORFOLK ISLAND
(Austl.)

Raoul
Island
KERMADEC ISLANDS
(N.Z.)
Curtis
Island

F

PITCAIRN
(U.K.)
Adamstown

Rapa

THREE KINGS
ISLANDS
North
Cape
Great Barrier
Island
Auckland
Bay of
Plenty   East Cape
NORTH ISLAND
Cape Egmont   New Plymouth   Mount Ruapehu
▲2793   Hawke Bay   Napier
Cape Farewell   Wellington

PACIFIC   OCEAN

International Date Line

Ernest Legouvé
Reef

Maria Teresa
Reef

NEW
ZEALAND
SOUTH ISLAND
Mount Cook   Christchurch
▲3754
Canterbury
Bight
Dunedin
land   Invercargill
West Cape

Cook Strait

CHATHAM
ISLANDS
(N.Z.)

G

AUCKLAND ISLANDS
(N.Z.)

BOUNTY ISLANDS
(N.Z.)

ANTIPODES ISLANDS
(N.Z.)

Campbell Island
(N.Z.)

I   H

A.C.T. = AUSTRALIA CAPITAL TERRITORY

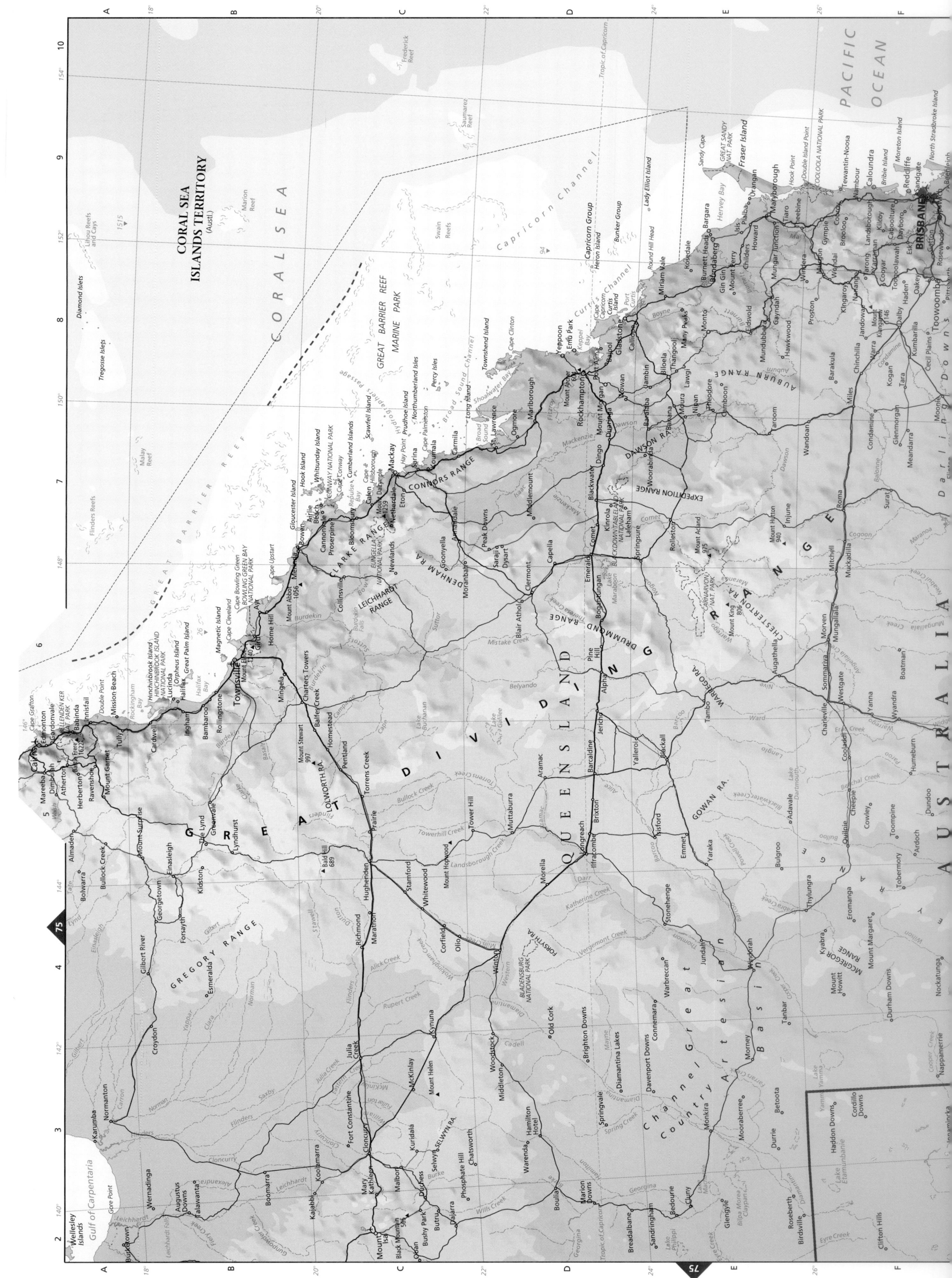

CORAL SEA
ISLANDS TERRITORY
(Austl.)

CORAL SEA

GREAT BARRIER REEF
MARINE PARK

PACIFIC
OCEAN

GULF of Carpentaria

QUEENSLAND

AUSTRALIA

BRISBANE

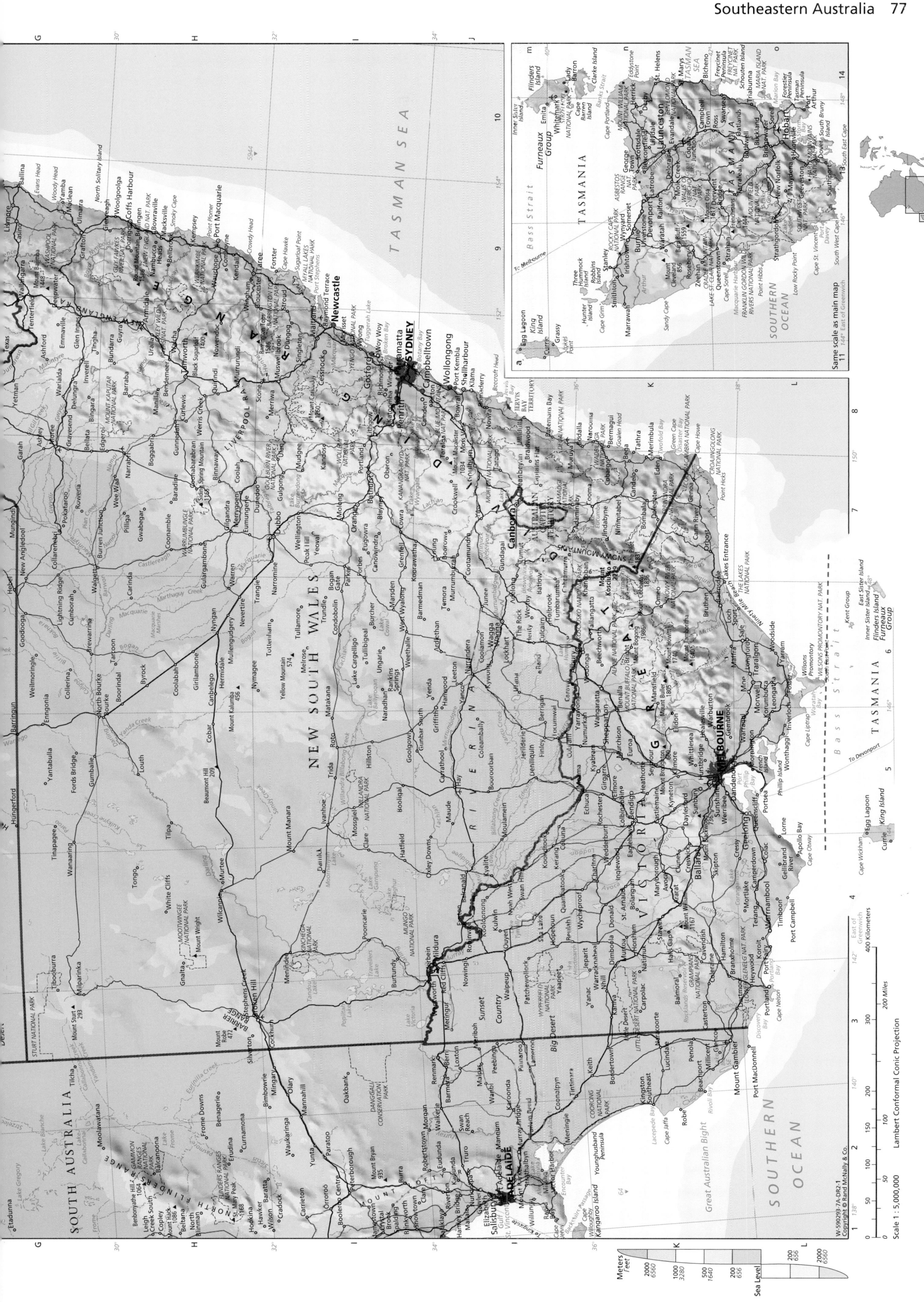

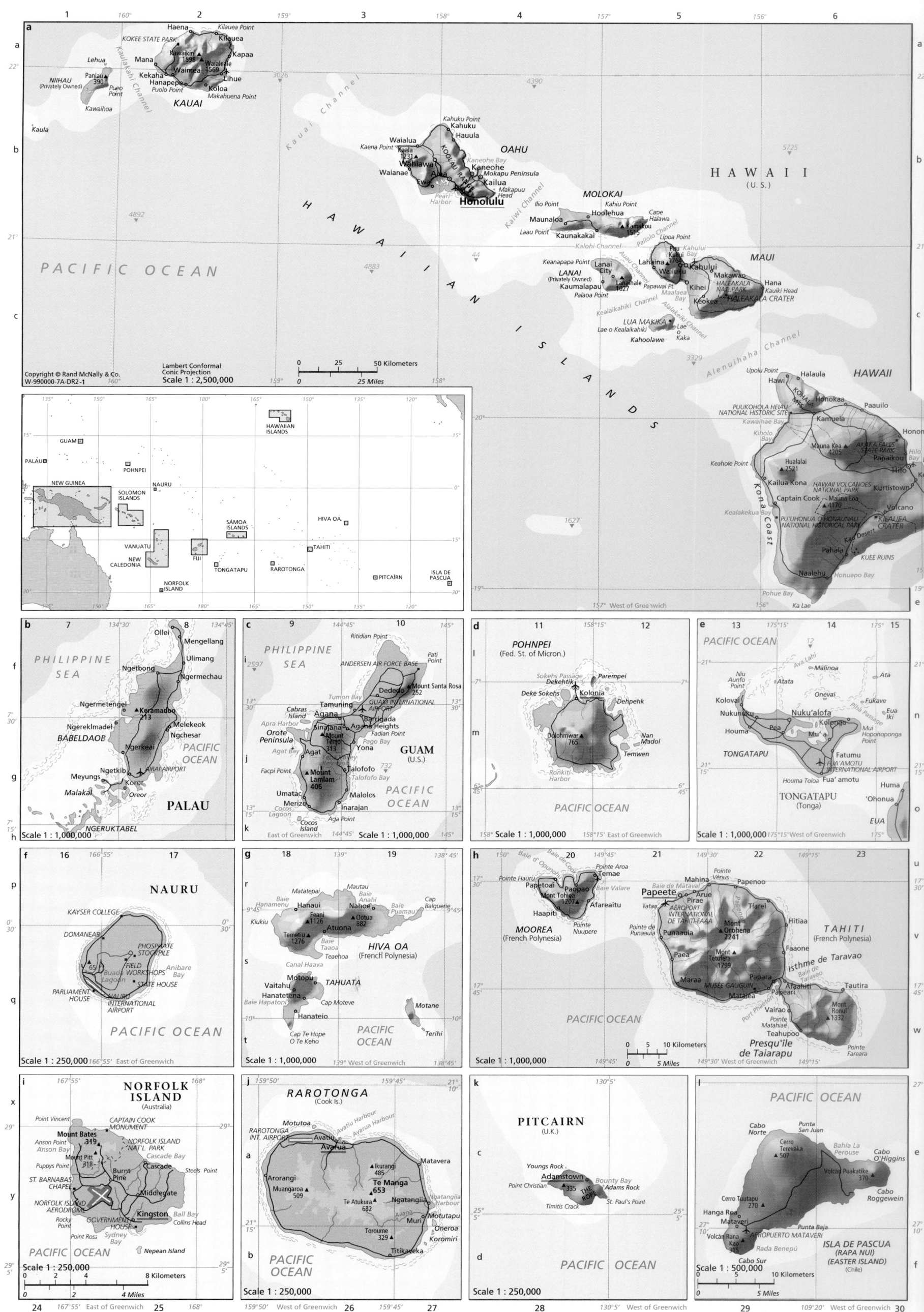

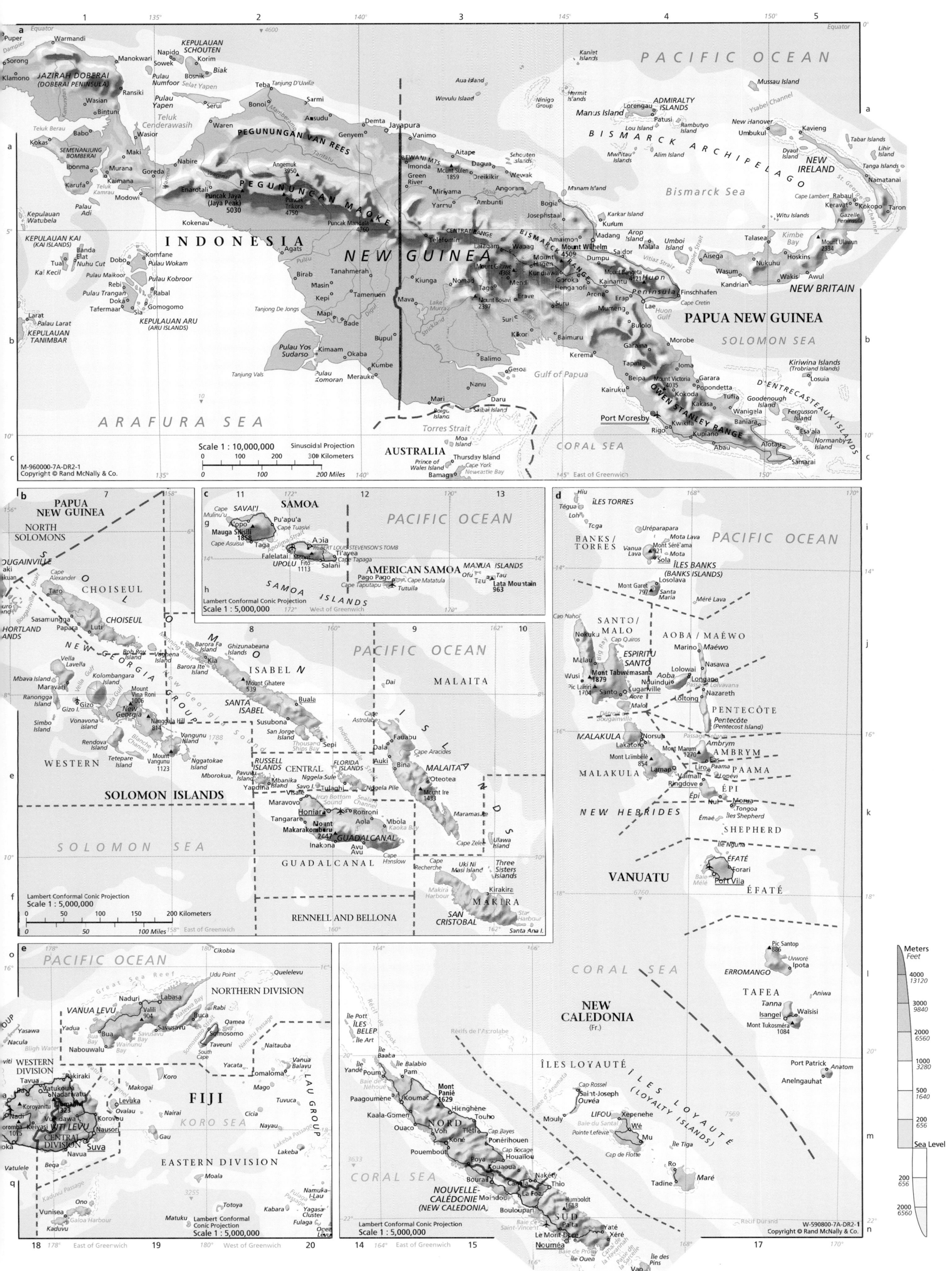

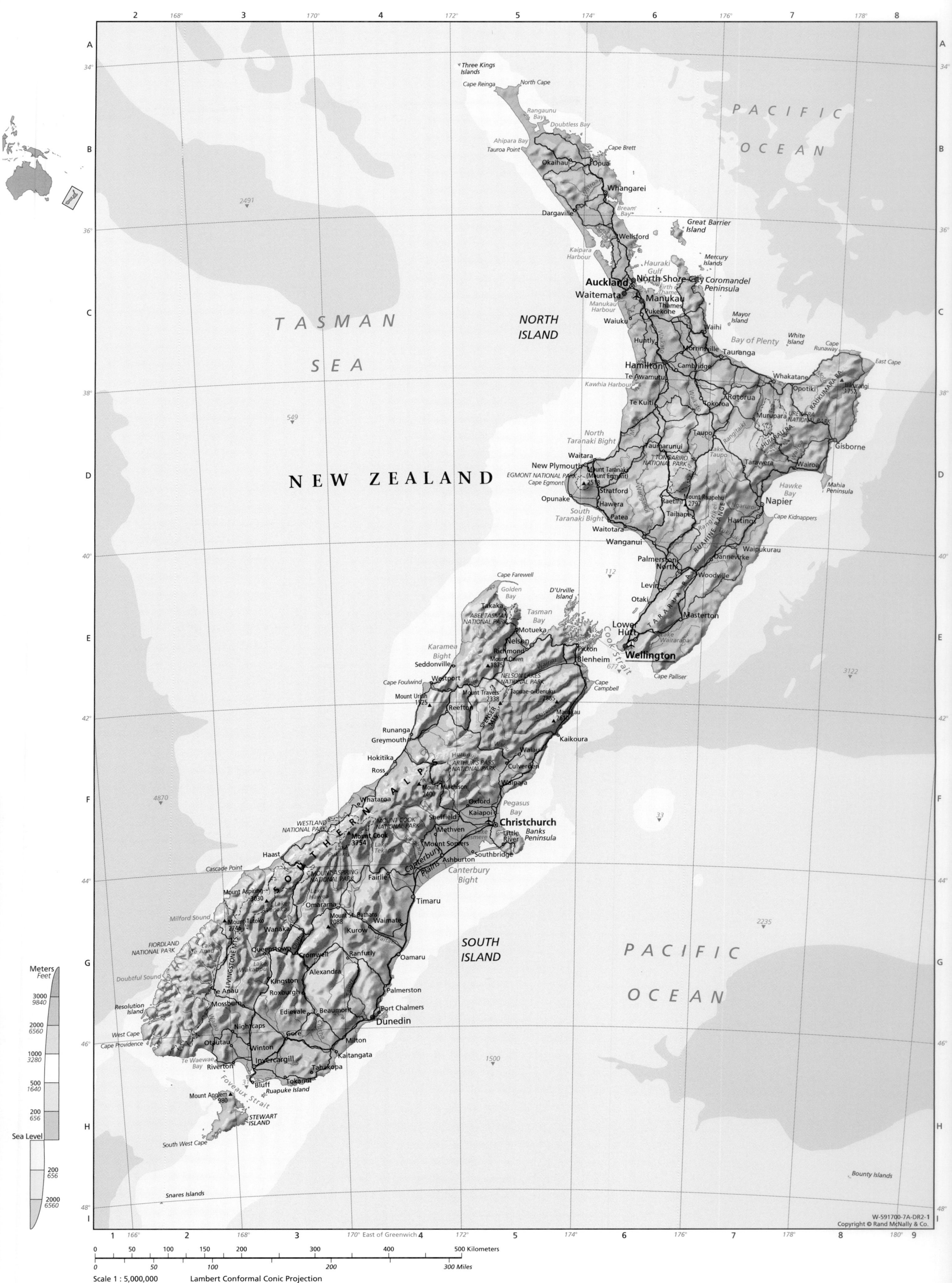

TASMAN

SEA

NEW ZEALAND

NORTH
ISLAND

PACIFIC

OCEAN

Auckland
Waitemata
Manukau

Hamilton

New Plymouth

Napier

Wellington
Lower
Hutt

SOUTH
ISLAND

Nelson
Blenheim

Christchurch

PACIFIC

OCEAN

Dunedin

Invercargill

Meters
Feet

3000
9840

2000
6560

1000
3280

500
1640

200
656

Sea Level

200
656

2000
6560

Scale 1 : 5,000,000   Lambert Conformal Conic Projection

0   50 100 150 200   300   400   500 Kilometers

0   50   100   200   300 Miles

W-591700-7A-DR2-1
Copyright © Rand McNally & Co.

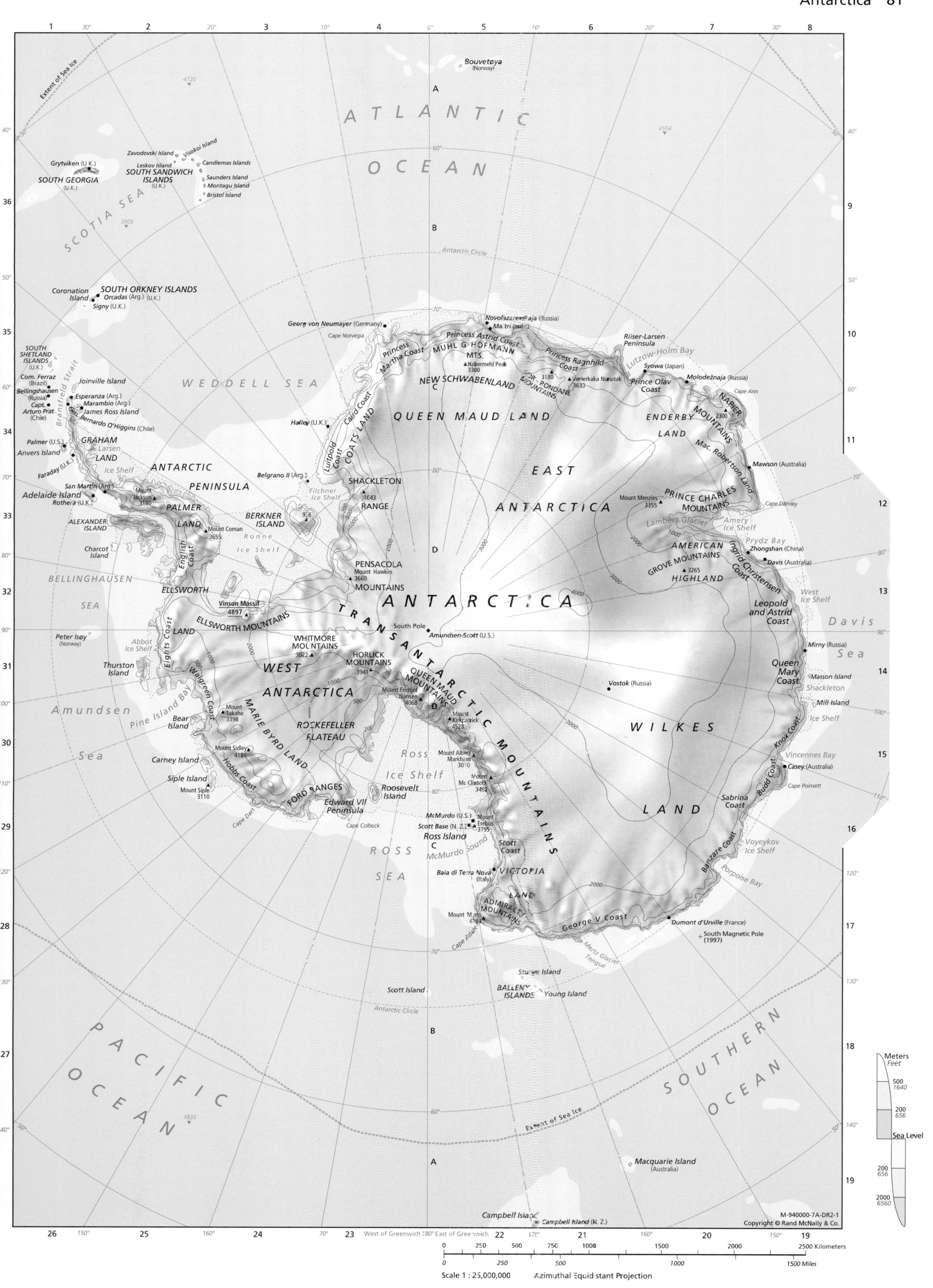

ATLANTIC OCEAN

Bouvetøya (Norway)

Grytviken (U.K.)
SOUTH GEORGIA (U.K.)

Zavodovski Island
Leskov Island
Visokoi Island
Candlemas Islands
Saunders Island
Montagu Island
Bristol Island
SOUTH SANDWICH ISLANDS (U.K.)

SCOTIA SEA

Coronation Island
SOUTH ORKNEY ISLANDS
Orcadas (Arg.)
Signy (U.K.)

SOUTH SHETLAND ISLANDS (U.K.)
Com. Ferraz (Brazil)
Bellingshausen (Russia)
Capt. Arturo Prat (Chile)
Esperanza (Arg.)
Marambio (Arg.)
James Ross Island
Bernardo O'Higgins (Chile)
Joinville Island

WEDDELL SEA

Palmer (U.S.)
Anvers Island
Faraday (U.K.)
San Martin (Arg.)
Adelaide Island
Rothera (U.K.)

GRAHAM LAND
ANTARCTIC PENINSULA
PALMER LAND
Larsen Ice Shelf

Halley (U.K.)

Georg von Neumayer (Germany)
Novolazarevskaja (Russia)
Ma tri Ind

Princess Astrid Coast
Cape Norvegia
Princess Martha Coast
MUHLIG-HOFMANN MTS.
Habermehl Peak 3300
NEW SCHWABENLAND

QUEEN MAUD LAND

Princess Ragnhild Coast
R. PONDANE MOUNTAINS 3180
Venerkaka Nunatak 3630

Riiser-Larsen Peninsula
Lützow-Holm Bay
Syowa (Japan)
Prince Olav Coast
Molodežnaja (Russia)
Cape Ann
NAPIER MOUNTAINS 2300
ENDERBY LAND

Caird Coast
COATS LAND
Luitpold Coast
Belgrano II (Arg.)
Filchner Ice Shelf
SHACKLETON RANGE 1643
BERKNER ISLAND 9 6

EAST ANTARCTICA

Mac. Robertson Land
Mawson (Australia)
Mount Menzies 3355
PRINCE CHARLES MOUNTAINS
Cape Darnley
Lambert Glacier
Amery Ice Shelf
Prydz Bay
Ingrid Christensen Coast
Zhongshan (China)
Davis (Australia)

Alexander Island
Mount Coman 3655
Charcot Island
ELLSWORTH LAND
Vinson Massif 4897
Mount Jackson 3180

Ronne Ice Shelf
PENSACOLA MOUNTAINS
Mount Hawkes 3660

ANTARCTICA

AMERICAN HIGHLAND
GROVE MOUNTAINS 3265
Leopold and Astrid Coast
West Ice Shelf

BELLINGHAUSEN SEA
English Coast
Eights Coast
Abbot Ice Shelf
Peter I Øy (Norway)
Thurston Island

ELLSWORTH MOUNTAINS
WHITMORE MOUNTAINS 3022
HORLICK MOUNTAINS 3941
WEST ANTARCTICA

TRANSANTARCTIC MOUNTAINS

South Pole
Amundsen-Scott (U.S.)

Vostok (Russia)

Davis Sea
Mirny (Russia)
Masson Island
Queen Mary Coast
Shackleton Ice Shelf
Mill Island

Amundsen Sea
Pine Island Bay
Bear Island
Carney Island
Siple Island
Mount Siple 3110

Walgreen Coast
Hobbs Coast
MARIE BYRD LAND
Mount Takahe 4181
Mount Sidley 4181
FORD RANGES
ROCKEFELLER PLATEAU
Edward VII Peninsula

QUEEN MAUD MOUNTAINS
Mount Fridtjof Nansen 4068
Mount Kirkpatrick 4528
Mount Albert Markham 3050
Mount Mc Clintock 3492

WILKES LAND

Vincennes Bay
Budd Coast
Casey (Australia)
Cape Poinsett
Sabrina Coast
Knox Coast

Ross Ice Shelf
Roosevelt Island
McMurdo (U.S.)
Scott Base (N.Z.)
Ross Island
Cape Colbeck
Cape Dart

ROSS SEA
McMurdo Sound
Baia di Terra Nova (Italy)
Mount Erebus 3795
Scott Coast
VICTORIA LAND
ADMIRALTY MOUNTAINS
Mount Minto 4165
Cape Adare

Banzare Coast
Voyeykov Ice Shelf
Porpoise Bay
George V Coast
Dumont d'Urville (France)
South Magnetic Pole (1997)
Mertz Glacier Tongue

PACIFIC OCEAN

Scott Island
Sturge Island
BALLENY ISLANDS
Young Island

SOUTHERN OCEAN

Campbell Island (N.Z.)

Macquarie Island (Australia)

Meters Feet
500 / 1640
200 / 656
Sea Level
200 / 656
2000 / 6560

M-940000-7A-DR2-1
Copyright © Rand McNally & Co.

0 250 500 750 1000 1500 2000 2500 Kilometers
0 250 500 1000 1500 Miles
Scale 1 : 25,000,000
Azimuthal Equidistant Projection

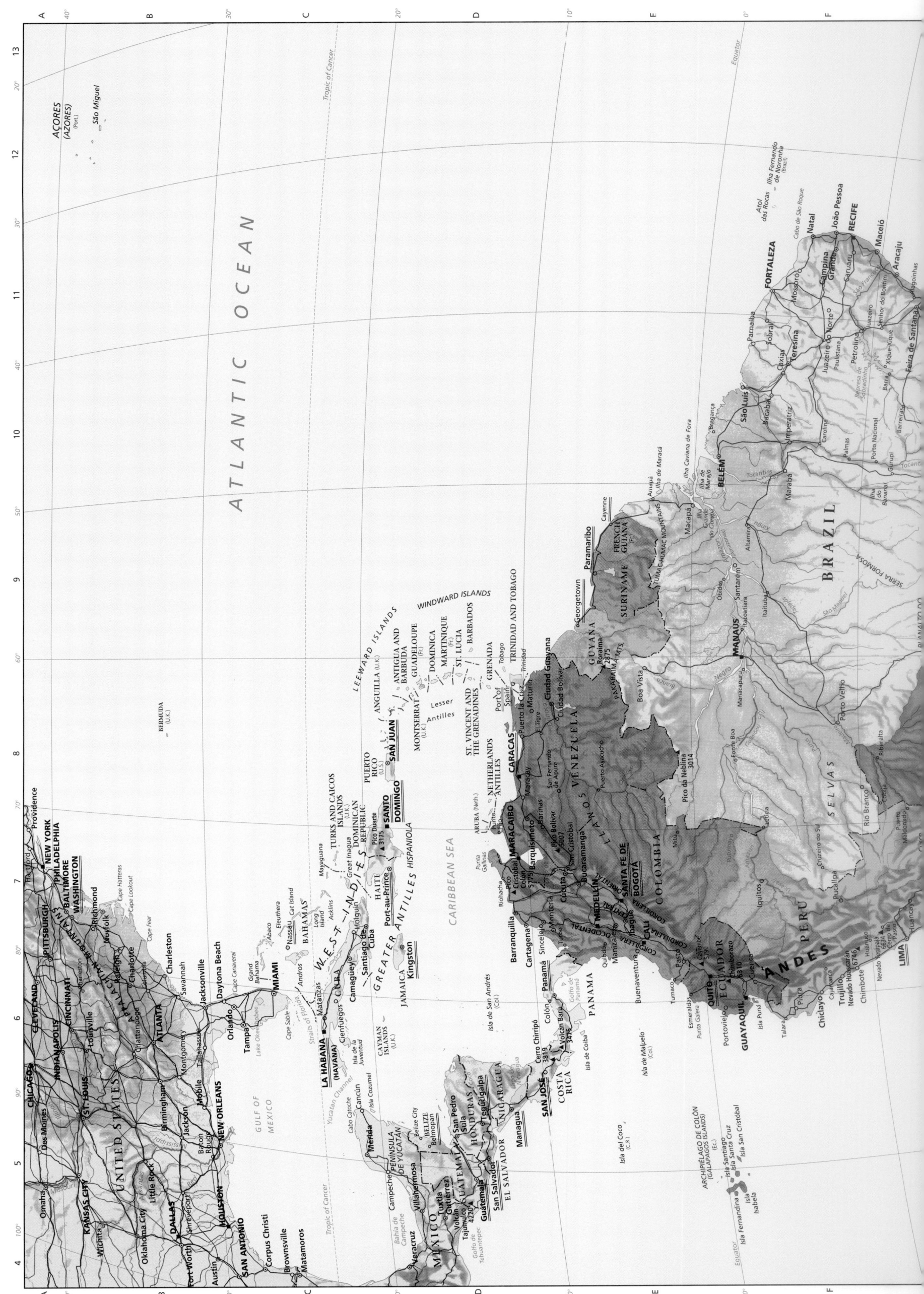

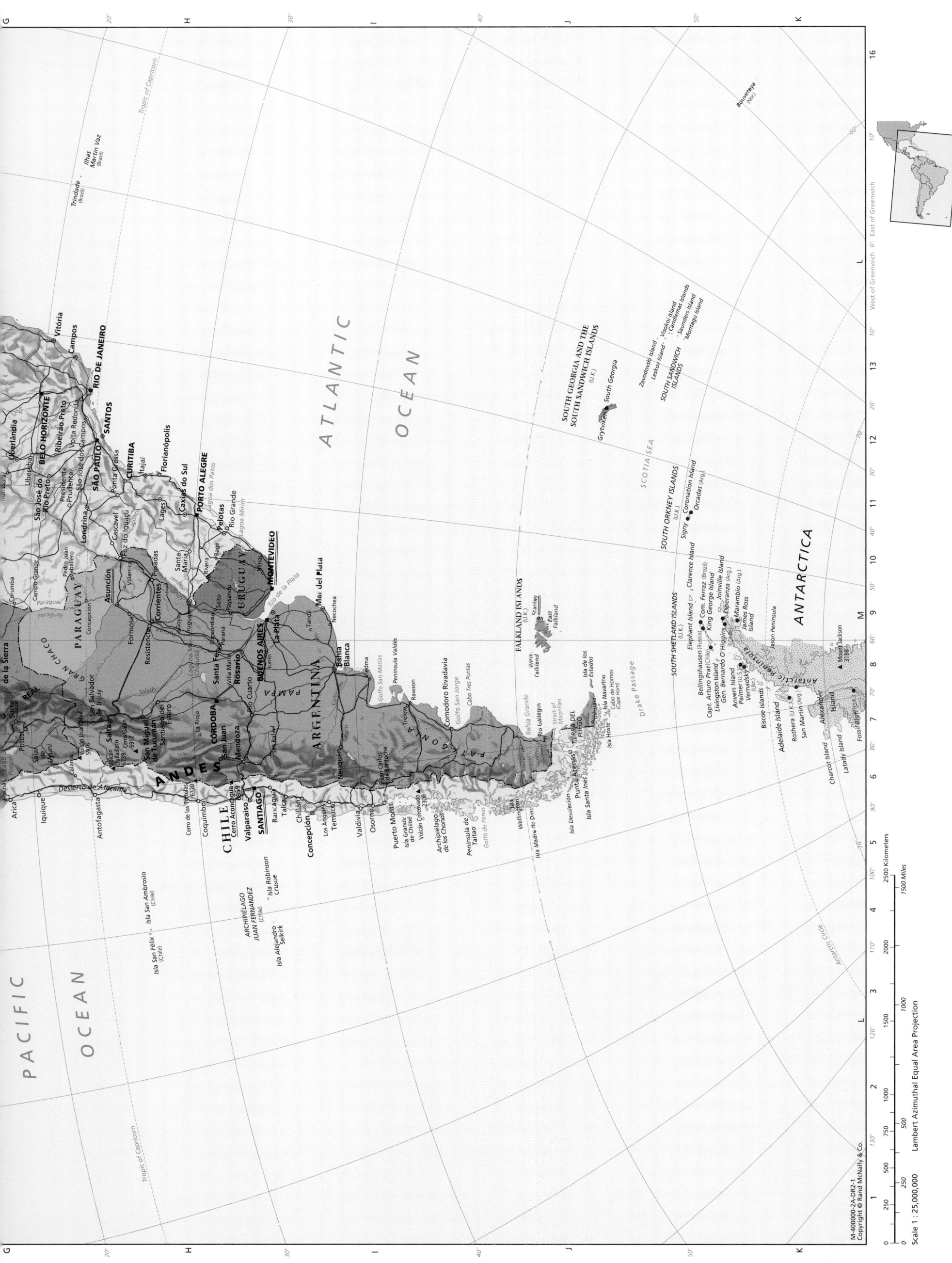

PACIFIC

OCEAN

ATLANTIC

OCEAN

SCOTIA SEA

Drake Passage

ANTARCTICA

ARGENTINA

CHILE

PARAGUAY

URUGUAY

ANDES

PAMPA

GRAN CHACO

PATAGONIA

TIERRA DEL FUEGO

Tropic of Capricorn

Antarctic Circle

Antarctic Peninsula

SOUTH GEORGIA AND THE
SOUTH SANDWICH ISLANDS
(U.K.)

SOUTH SANDWICH
ISLANDS

SOUTH ORKNEY ISLANDS
(U.K.)

SOUTH SHETLAND ISLANDS
(U.K.)

FALKLAND ISLANDS
(U.K.)

Rio de Janeiro
São Paulo
Belo Horizonte
Santos
Curitiba
Porto Alegre
Montevideo
Buenos Aires
Córdoba
Santiago
Valparaíso
Asunción
Rosario
Concepción

Vitória
Campos
Uberlândia
Ribeirão Preto
Volta Redonda
São José dos Campos
Florianópolis
Itajaí
Ponta Grossa
Caxias do Sul
Lages
Pelotas
Rio Grande
Londrina
Cascavel
Foz do Iguaçu
Posadas
Corrientes
Resistencia
Formosa
Santa Fe
Mar del Plata
Necochea
Tandil
Bahía Blanca
Neuquén
Comodoro Rivadavia
Trelew
Rawson
Río Gallegos
Punta Arenas
Puerto Montt
Valdivia
Osorno
Temuco
Chillán
Talca
Rancagua
Coquimbo
Antofagasta
Iquique
Arica
Mendoza
San Juan
La Rioja
Santiago del Estero
San Miguel de Tucumán
Salta
San Salvador de Jujuy
Río Cuarto
Santa María
Rivera
Salto
Paysandú
La Plata

Scale 1 : 25,000,000

Lambert Azimuthal Equal Area Projection

M-400000-2A-DR2-1
Copyright © Rand McNally & Co.

ATLANTIC

OCEAN

Equator

A
B
C
D
E
F
G

SURINAME

Amsterdam
Nieuw
Nickerie
Totness
Groningen
Onverwacht
Albina
Brokopondo
Kwakoegron
Paramaribo
Nieuw Amsterdam
Moengo
Iracoubo
Sinnamary
Île du Diable
Saint-Laurent du Maroni
Kourou
Cayenne
Saint-Élie
Tonate
Rémiré
Brokopondo Stuwmeer
Juliana Top △1230
HELMINA GEBERGTE
Gran Rio
ORANJE GEBERGTE

FRENCH GUIANA
Saül
Guisan Bourg
Cabo Orange
Ouanary
Saint-Georges
Cleveländia do Norte
Oiapoque
Cabo Cassiporé
Vila Velha

TUMUC-HUMAC MOUNTAINS
Cunani
Calçoene
Amapá
Ilha de Maracá
Cabo Norte

AMAPÁ
Lago Novo
Sucuriju
Serra do Navio
Aporema
Ferreira Gomes
Ilha do Curuá
Ilha Janaucu
Macapá
Ilha Caviana de Fora
Porto Grande
Porto Santana
Ilha Mexiana
Mazagão

Faro
Oriximiná
Terra Santa
Óbidos
Alenquer
Prainha
Juruti
Parintins
Monte Alegre
Ilha Grande do Gurupá
Itatupã
Ilha da Marajó
Boca do Jari
Gurupá
Breves
Curumu
Soure
Joanes
Salinópolis
Cabo Maguari
Baía de Marajó
Muaná
Curuçá
Marapanim
Açu
Bragança
Barreirinha
Santarém
Vitória
Altamira
Ilha da Laguna
Porto de Moz
Veiros
Portel
Carrazedo
Mojuí
Curralinho
BELÉM
Abaetetuba
São Domingos do Capim
Samiranga
Turiaçu
Curuçu
Cametá
Carapajó
Acará
Irituia
Santa Helena
Guimarã
Itaituba
Juaba
Baião
Tomé-Açu
Itamatare
Alcântara
Anil
Paulino
Neves
Tutóia
Parnaíba
Acaraú
Paracuru

PARÁ
Pinheiro
São Bento
São Luís
Rosário
Barreirinhas
Camocim
Granja
Marco
Tucuruí
Represa de Tucuruí
Jacundá
Viana
Monção
Anajatuba
Itapecuru-Mirim
Urbano Santos
Brejo
Chapadinha
Luzilândia
Piracuruca
Sobral
Itapipoca
Maranguape
Pindaré-Mirim
Cantanhede
Coreaú
Ipu
Pedro II
Tianguá
FORTALEZA
Maracanaú
Pacajus
Beberibe
Itapiúna
Aracati
Itupiranga
São João do Araguaia
Imperatriz
Laço da Pedra
Codó
Caxias
Timon
Teresina
Campo Maior
Crateús
Tamboril
CEARÁ
Baturité
Canindé
Quixadá
Quixeramobim
Russas
Areia Branca
Mossoró
Macau
São Bento do Norte

RIO GRANDE DO NORTE
Marabá
Araguatins
Presidente Dutra
Bacabal
Água Branca
São Miguel do Tapuio
Senador Pompeu
Piquet Carneiro
Iguatu
Acopiara
Tauá
Assu
Ceará-Mirim
Macaíba
Natal
Carrais Novos
Caicó

Santa Isabel do Araguaia
Montes Altos
Sítio Novo
Grajaú
Bar a do Corda
Colinas
Mirador
Amarante
Elesbão Veloso
Valença do Piauí
Picos
Campos Sales
Crato
Sousa
Juazeiro do Norte
Pombal
Campina Grande
João Pessoa

Carajás
Nazaré
Xambioá
Tocantinópolis
MARANHÃO
Barras
Oeiras
Pio IX
Jucás
Orós
Catolé do Rocha
Itaporanga
PARAÍBA

Araguaína
Babaçulândia
Riachão
Carolina
São João dos Patos
Floriano
São Raimundo das Mangabeiras
Benedito Leite
Fronteiras
Picos
Juazeiro do Norte
Ouricuri
Flores
Serra
Talhada
Arcoverde
Sertânia
Belo
Caruaru
Jardim
RECIFE

BRAZIL
Gradaús
Conceição do Araguaia
Itaporã de Goiás
Itacajá
Cristino Castro
São Raimundo Nonato
Simplício Mendes
Paulistana
Parnamirim
Salgueiro
Belém de São Francisco
PERNAMBUCO
Garanhuns
Ribeirão

Pequizeiro
Caro ina
Ealsas
Canto do Buriti
Alto Parnaíba
Bom Jesus
Caracol
Remanso
Casa Nova
Santa Maria da Boa Vista
Chorrochó
Petrolina
Paulo Afonso
Palmares
Porto de Pedras
Rio Largo
ALAGOAS
Maceió

Araguacema
Dois Irmãos de Goiás
Cachimbo
Miracema do Tocantins
Monte Alegre do Piauí
Gilbués
Santa Filomena
Curimatá
Juazeiro
Uauá
Propriá
Penedo
Brejo Grande

SERRA DO ESTRONDO
CHAPADA DAS MANGABEIRAS
Pedro Afonso
Tocantínia
Palmas
Sono
Parnaguá
Jaguarari
Senhor do Bonfim
Euclides da Cunha
Itabaiana
SERGIPE
Aracaju
Lagarto
Estância

Pium
Porto Nacional
Brejinho de Nazaré
Represa de Sobradinho
Campo Formoso
Jacobina
Queimadas
Tucano
Ribeira do Pombal
Olindina
Inhambupe
Esplanada

Cristalândia
Duere
Gurupi
Natividade
Dianópolis
Xique-Xique
Irecê
Serrinha
Riachão do Jacuípe
Alagoinhas

Ilha do Bananal
TOCANTINS
Ponte Alta do Bom Jesus
Peixe
Barra
Ibotirama
Morro do Chapéu
BAHIA
Feira de Santana
Santo Amaro
Camaçari

MATO GROSSO
Taguatinga
Araguaçu
Paranã
Arraias
Barreiras
Santana
Ibitiara
Itaberaba
Maragogipe
SALVADOR

PLANALTO DO MATO GROSSO
São Domingos
Correntina
Riacho de Santana
Bom Jesus da Lapa
Paramirim
Itaetê
Santo Antônio de Jesus
Nova Roma
Posse
Rio de Contas
Caetité
Maracás
Barra da Estiva
Jaguaquara
Ilha de Tinharé

São Miguel do Araguaia
Porangatu
Cavalcante
Colinas
Guanambi
Carinhanha
Urandi
Brumado
Ipiaú
Jequié
 Gandu
Camamu
Itacaré

GOIÁS
Mozarlândia
Aruanã
Itapaci
Pilar de Goiás
São João d'Aliança
Iaciara
Manga
Vitória da Conquista
Coaraci
Ilhéus
Itabuna

Cuiabá
Barra do Garças
Jussara
Goiás
Formoso
Jaíba
Itambé
Itapetinga
Itabuna

General Carneiro
Poxoréu
Ceres
São Gabriel de Goiás
Monte Azul
São João do Paraíso
Pau Brasil

Itapirapuã
Goianésia
São Francisco
Januária
Rio Pardo de Minas
Pedra Azul
Canavieiras
Belmonte

SERRA DE SÃO JERÔNIMO
Iporá
BRASÍLIA
Jacinto
Salto da Divisa

Baliza
Aragarças
Itaberaí
GOIÂNIA
Anápolis
DISTRITO FEDERAL
Unaí
São Romão
MINAS GERAIS
Montes Claros
Pirapora
Itaobim
Jequitinhonha
Almenara
Porto Seguro

Rondonópolis
Piranhas
Inhumas
Silvânia
Cristalina
Coronel Murta
Itamaraju

Alto Garças
Jandaia
Caiapônia
Pires do Rio
Paracatu
Bocaiuva
Minas Novas
Água
Formosa
Prado
Ponta da Baleia

Minaçu
Rio Verde
Campo Alegre de Goiás
Capelinha
Salinas
Carlos Chagas
Alcobaça
Caravelas

MATO GROSSO DO SUL
Pedro Gomes
Jataí
Santa Helena de Goiás
Morrinhos
João Pinheiro
Teófilo Otoni
Nanuque

M-400091-7A-DR2-1
Copyright © Rand McNally & Co.

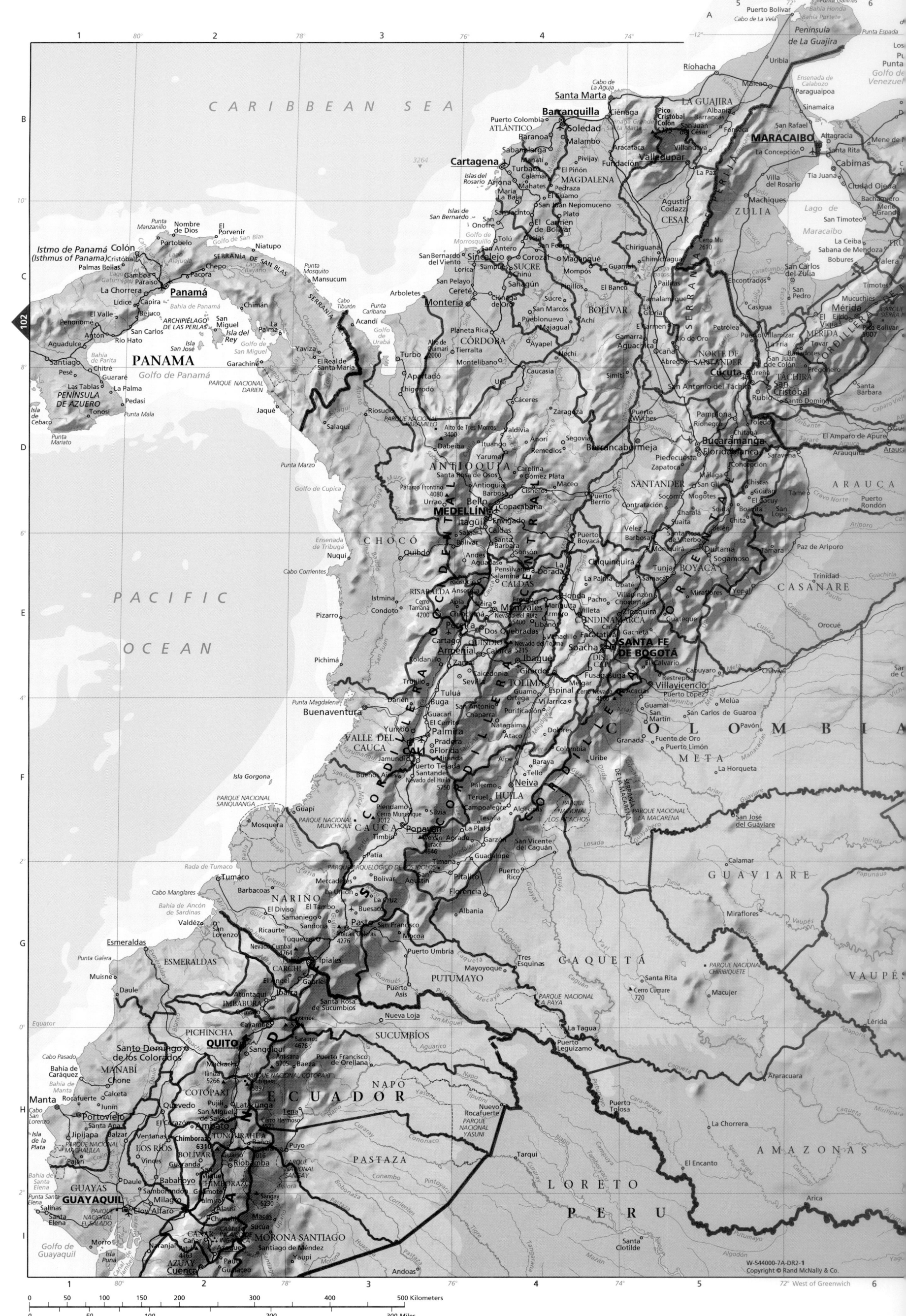

Meters
Feet

4000
13120

3000
9840

2000
6560

1000
3280

500
1640

200
656

Sea Level

200
656

2000
6560

0   50   100   150   200   250   300   400   500 Kilometers

0   50   100   200   300 Miles

Scale 1 : 5,000,000   Sinusoidal Projection

W-544000-7A-DR2-1
Copyright Rand McNally & Co.

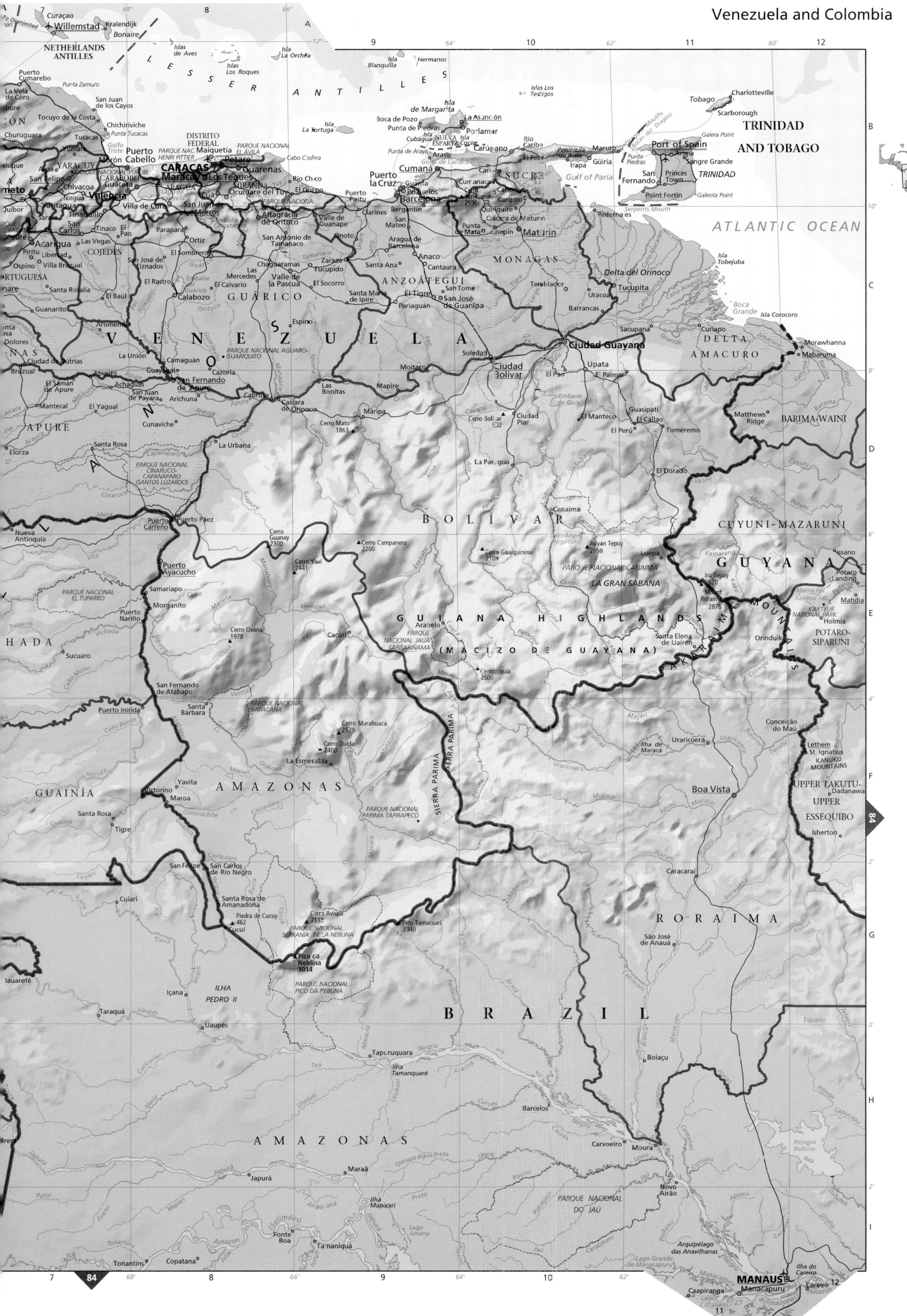

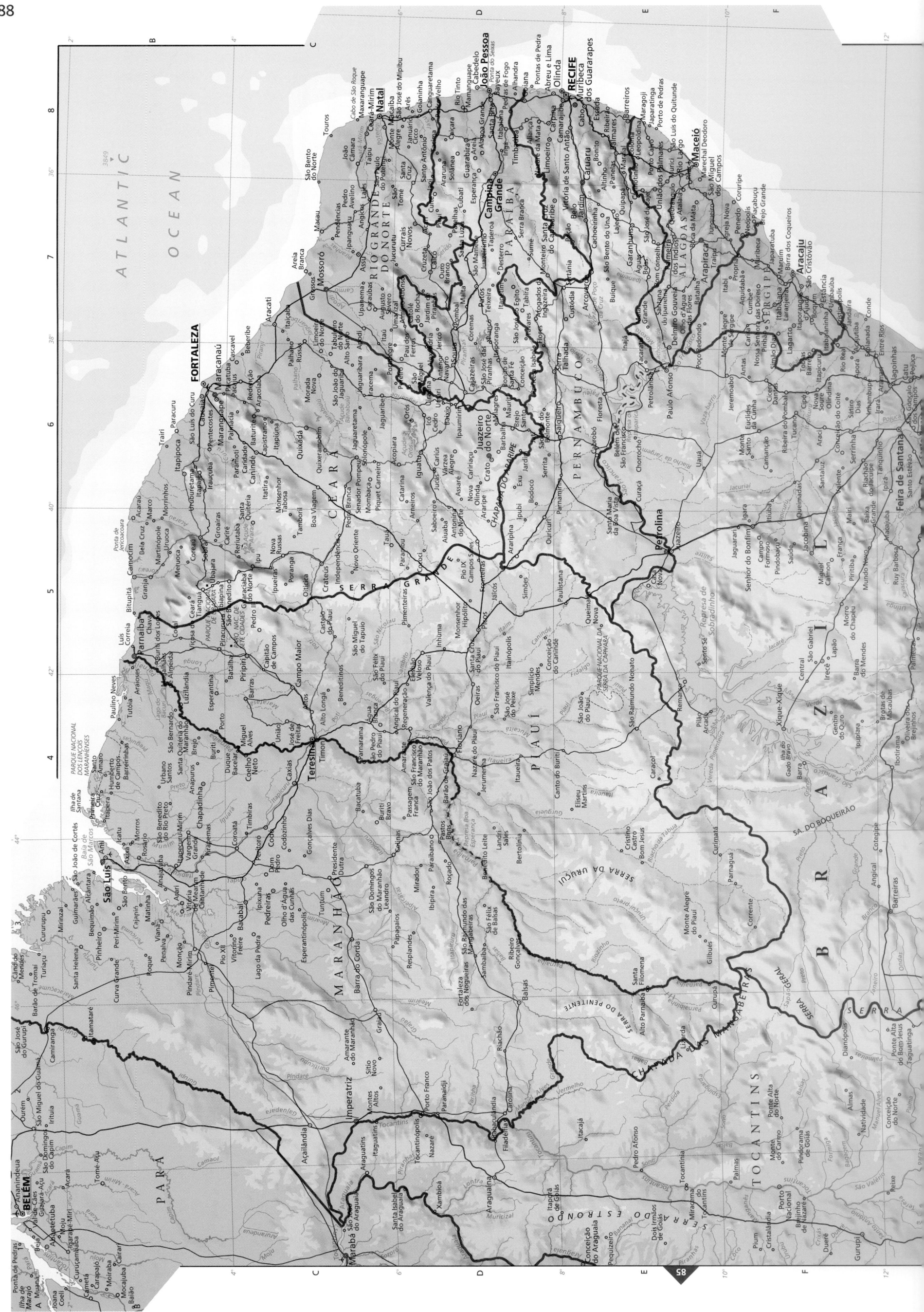

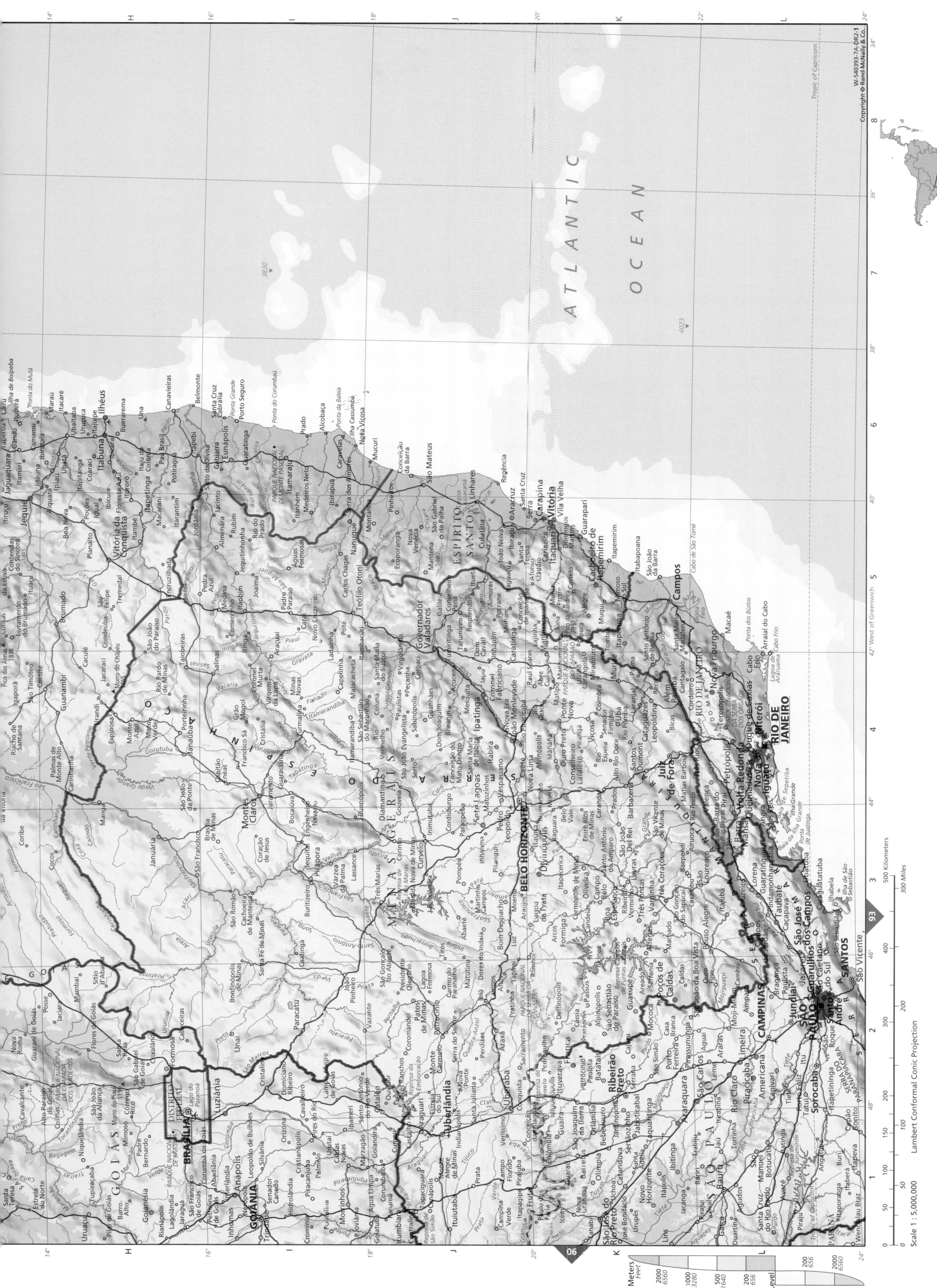

Scale 1 : 5,000,000

Lambert Conformal Conic Projection

Copyright © Rand McNally & Co.
W-540393-7A-DRZ-1

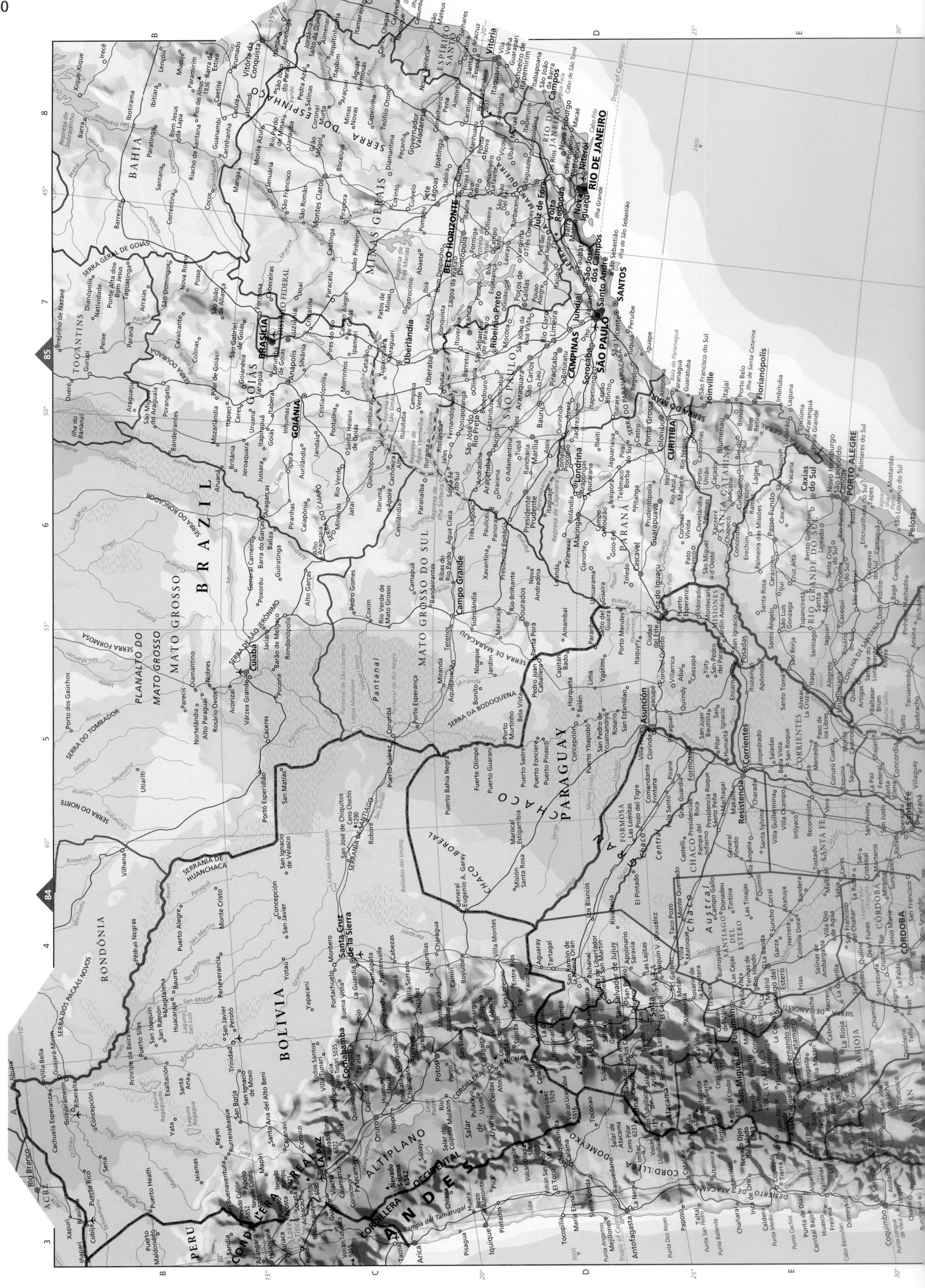

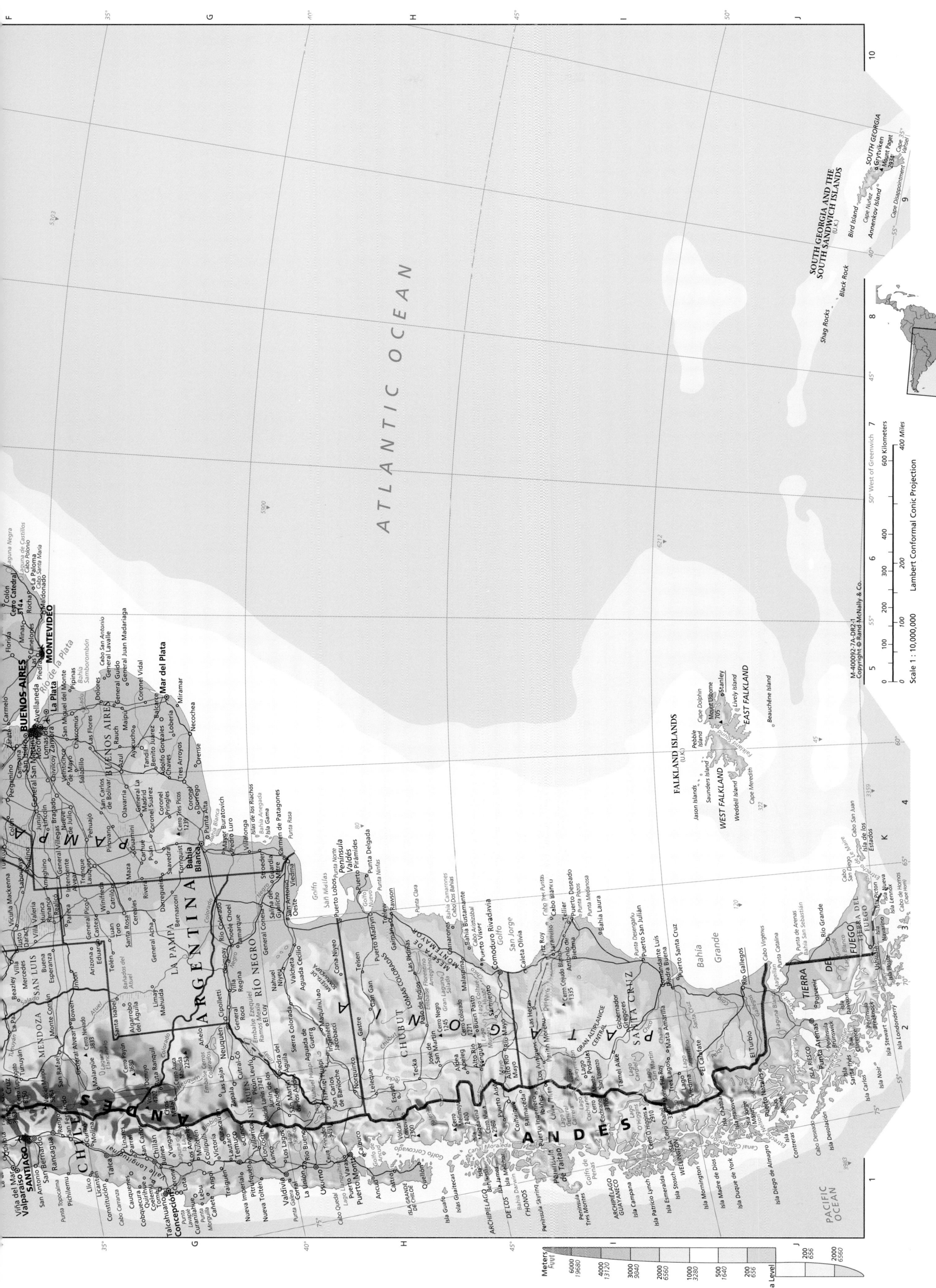

ATLANTIC OCEAN

PACIFIC OCEAN

ARGENTINA

CHILE

ANDES

PAMPA

LA PAMPA

NEUQUÉN

RÍO NEGRO

CHUBUT

SANTA CRUZ

TIERRA DEL FUEGO

BUENOS AIRES

MENDOZA

SAN LUIS

BUENOS AIRES
SANTIAGO
MONTEVIDEO

SOUTH GEORGIA AND THE
SOUTH SANDWICH ISLANDS
(U.K.)

FALKLAND ISLANDS
(U.K.)

WEST FALKLAND

EAST FALKLAND

Stanley

50° West of Greenwich

M-400092-7A-DR2-1
Copyright © Rand McNally & Co.

Lambert Conformal Conic Projection

Scale 1 : 10,000,000

| 0 | 100 | 200 | 300 | 400 | 500 | 600 Kilometers |

| 0 | 200 | 400 Miles |

Meters
Feet
6000 19680
4000 13120
3000 9840
2000 6560
1000 3280
500   1640
200   656
Sea Level
200   656
2000 6560

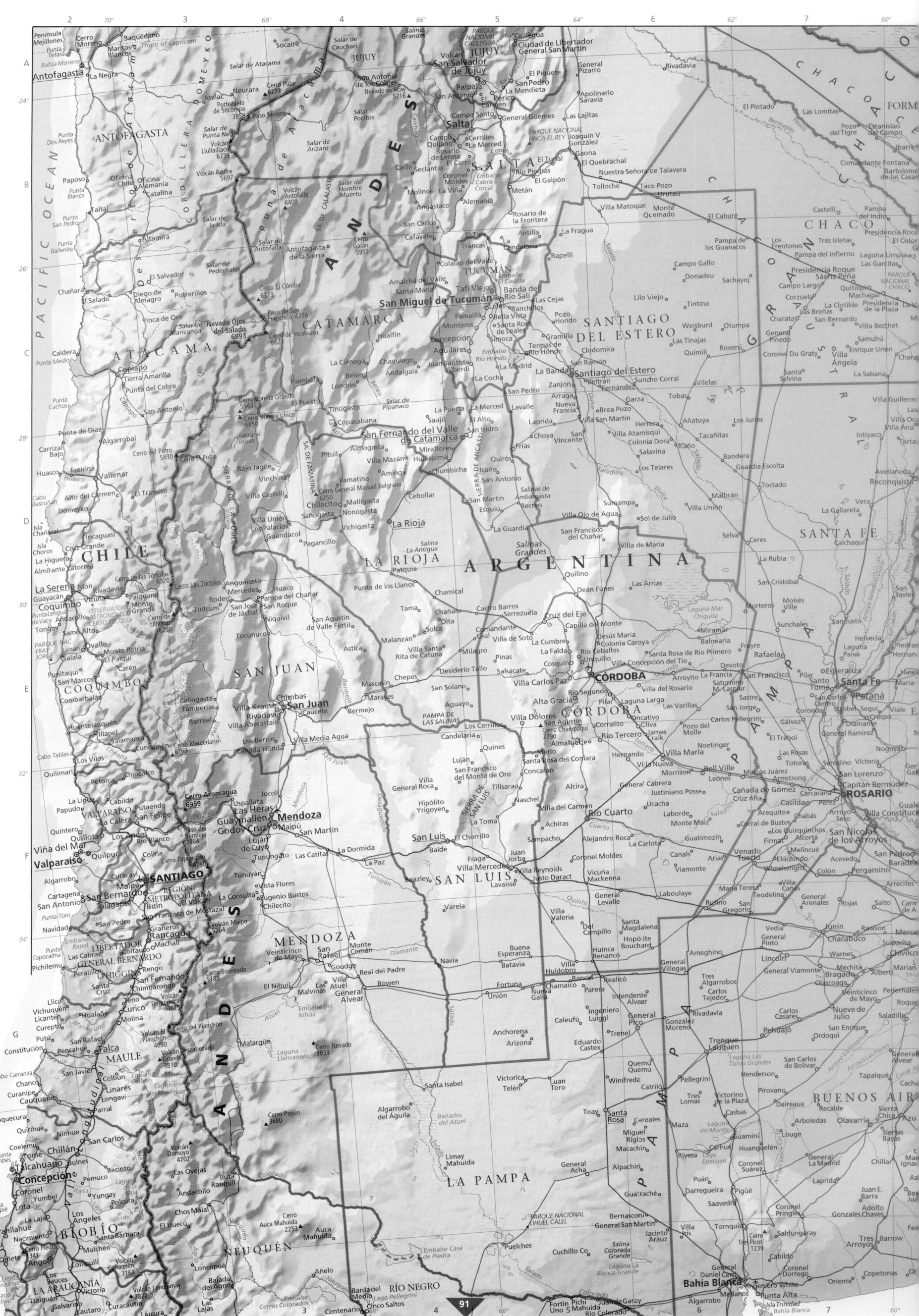

SWEDEN

NORWAY
Trondheim
Saldhöppigen
2469
Bergen
Stavanger

Göteborg
Oslo

DENMARK

UNITED
KINGDOM

Shetland Islands
(U.K.)

FAROE ISLANDS
(Den.)

NORWEGIAN

SEA

Arctic Circle

Jan Mayen
(Nor.)

Hvannadalshnúkur
2119

ICELAND

Reykjavík

Húni

Fontur

Denmark Strait

ATLANTIC

OCEAN

Kap Brewster

Gunnbjørn Fjeld
3700

GREENLAND
(Denmark)

Ammassalik

Julianehåb

Greenland Sea

25 24 23 22 21 20 19 18 17 16

SVALBARD
(Nor.)

Godthåb

Davis Strait

Disko

Godhavn

Cape Farvel

LABRADOR SEA

St. John's
NEWFOUNDLAND

ST. PIERRE
(Fr.)

Sable Island
Cape Race

Cape Sable

Gulf of
St. Lawrence

Halifax

Cape Cod

Île Anticosti
Prince Edward
Island
Cape Breton
Island

Les Escoumins

Portland
BOSTON
Providence

NEW YORK
PHILADELPHIA

North
Pole

ARCTIC

OCEAN

Kap York
Thule

Cape Columbia
Cape Dudley Alert

ELLESMERE
ISLAND

Devon
Island

Lancaster Sound

Baffin
Bay

BAFFIN ISLAND

Cumberland Sound

Iqaluit

Québec
Ottawa

MONTRÉAL

TORONTO

BUFFALO
CLEVELAND

DETROIT

RUSSIA

POLUOSTROV
KAMČATKA

SREDINNYJ HREBET

ostrov
Karaginskij

Anadyr'

zaliv
Šelichova

Kolyma

ostrov
Ajon

Uel Kal'
ČUKOTSKIJ POLUOSTROV

ostrov
Vrangelja
(Wrangel I.)

Arctic Circle

Bering Strait

Anadyrskij
zaliv

Provideniya

St. Lawrence
Island

St. Matthew
Island

Nunivak
Island

Nome
Bethel

Seward
Peninsula

Norton
Sound

Kuskokwim

Bristol
Bay

Alaska Peninsula

Kodiak
Island

Unalaska

ALEUTIAN ISLANDS

BERING SEA

International Date Line

Chukchi
Sea

Point Hope

Point Barrow

Barrow

Beaufort
Sea

Colville

BROOKS RANGE

Fairbanks

Mount McKinley
6194

ALASKA RANGE

Anchorage

Cook
Inlet

Gulf of Alaska

Mackenzie

Inuvik

Norman Wells

Amundsen Gulf

MACKENZIE MOUNTAINS

Yukon

Whitehorse

Mount Logan
5959

Juneau

COAST MOUNTAINS

Ketchikan
Prince Rupert

Queen
Charlotte
Islands

Hecate Strait

QUEEN ELIZABETH ISLANDS

Prince
Patrick
Island

Melville
Island

BANKS
ISLAND

Victoria
Island

15 14 13 12 11 10 9 8 7 6 5 4 3 2 1

Banks
Island

Axel
Heiberg
Island

PEARY LAND

Somerset
Island

Boothia
Prince of
Wales
Island

King
William
Island

VICTORIA
ISLAND

Kugluktuk

Gulf of Boothia

Foxe
Basin

Prince
Charles
Island

Southampton
Island

Coats Island

Mansel Island

Ivujivik

PENINSULE
D'UNGAVA

Belcher
Islands

Ungava
Bay

Labrador

Schefferville

Lac
Mistassini

Réservoir La
Grande Deux

Lac
Bienville

James
Bay

Churchill

Hudson
Bay

CANADA

Naujaat

Hudson Strait

Happy Valley

Sept-Îles

Timmins

Sudbury
Lansing

Lake Michigan

CHICAGO
MILWAUKEE

Uranium City

Lake
Athabasca

Fort
McMurray

Great
Slave
Lake

Yellowknife

Pine Point

Great Bear
Lake

Horn
Plateau

Peace

Fort Nelson

Liard

Fort
George

ROCKY

Edmonton

Calgary

Reindeer
Lake

Lynn Lake

Flin
Flon

La Ronge

Saskatoon

Regina

Winnipeg

Lake
Winnipeg

MINNEAPOLIS

St. Paul

Duluth

Thunder Bay

Lake Superior
Sault Sainte
Marie

Lake Huron

Lake Erie

Fargo

Bismarck

Billings

Great Falls

MOUNTAINS

Spokane

SEATTLE

VANCOUVER

PORTLAND

Victoria
VANCOUVER
ISLAND

Cape Flattery

CASCADE

Boise

Salt Lake
City

Reno

SACRAMENTO

SAN FRANCISCO

Cape Mendocino

GREAT

PLAINS

PACIFIC

OCEAN

Pacific

A B C D

E F

UNITED STATES

OKLAHOMA

TEXAS

Austin
HOUSTON
SAN ANTONIO

DALLAS
Fort Worth

ARIZONA
PHOENIX
Tucson

NEW MEXICO
El Paso
Ciudad Juárez

SAN DIEGO
Tijuana
Mexicali

BAJA CALIFORNIA

SONORA

CHIHUAHUA
Chihuahua

COAHUILA

MONTERREY
Saltillo
Torreón

BAJA CALIFORNIA SUR

La Paz

SINALOA
Culiacán

DURANGO
Durango

ZACATECAS
Zacatecas

SAN LUIS POTOSÍ
San Luis Potosí

TAMAULIPAS
Ciudad Victoria

Tampico
Ciudad Madero

Mazatlán

NAYARIT
Tepic

JALISCO
GUADALAJARA

AGUASCALIENTES
Aguascalientes

GUANAJUATO
León
Irapuato

QUERÉTARO
Querétaro

Puerto Vallarta

COLIMA

MICHOACÁN
Morelia

MEXICO
CIUDAD DE MÉXICO
Toluca
Cuernavaca
PUEBLA
Puebla

VERACRUZ
Veracruz
Xalapa

GUERRERO
Acapulco

OAXACA
Oaxaca de Juárez

CHIAPAS

Gulf of Mexico

PACIFIC OCEAN

ISLAS REVILLAGIGEDO

ISLAS TRES MARÍAS

WEST INDIES

ATLANTIC OCEAN

DOMINICAN REPUBLIC
SANTO DOMINGO

PUERTO RICO (U.S.)
SAN JUAN

VIRGIN ISLANDS (U.S.)

BRITISH VIRGIN ISLANDS

ANGUILLA (U.K.)

ANTIGUA AND BARBUDA
St. John's

ST. KITTS AND NEVIS
Basseterre

MONTSERRAT (U.K.)
Plymouth

GUADELOUPE (Fr.)
Basse-Terre
Pointe-à-Pitre
Marie-Galante

DOMINICA
Roseau
Morne Diablotins 1447

MARTINIQUE (Fr.)
Fort-de-France
Montagne Pelée 1397

ST. LUCIA
Castries
Mount Gimie 950

ST. VINCENT AND THE GRENADINES
Kingstown
Soufrière 1234

BARBADOS
Bridgetown
Mount Hillaby 340

GRENADA
St. George's

TRINIDAD AND TOBAGO
Port of Spain

LESSER ANTILLES

LEEWARD ISLANDS

WINDWARD ISLANDS

CARIBBEAN SEA

ARUBA (Neth.)
Oranjestad

NETHERLANDS ANTILLES
Willemstad
Bonaire

VENEZUELA
CARACAS
Maracaibo
Valencia
Barquisimeto

Meters / Feet
4000 / 13120
3000 / 9840
2000 / 6560
1000 / 3280
500 / 1640
200 / 656
Sea Level
200 / 656
2000 / 6560

0 100 200 300 400 600 800 1000 Kilometers
0 100 200 400 600 Miles

Scale 1 : 10,000,000 Lambert Conformal Conic Projection

M-300000-7A-DR2-1
Copyright © Rand McNally & Co.

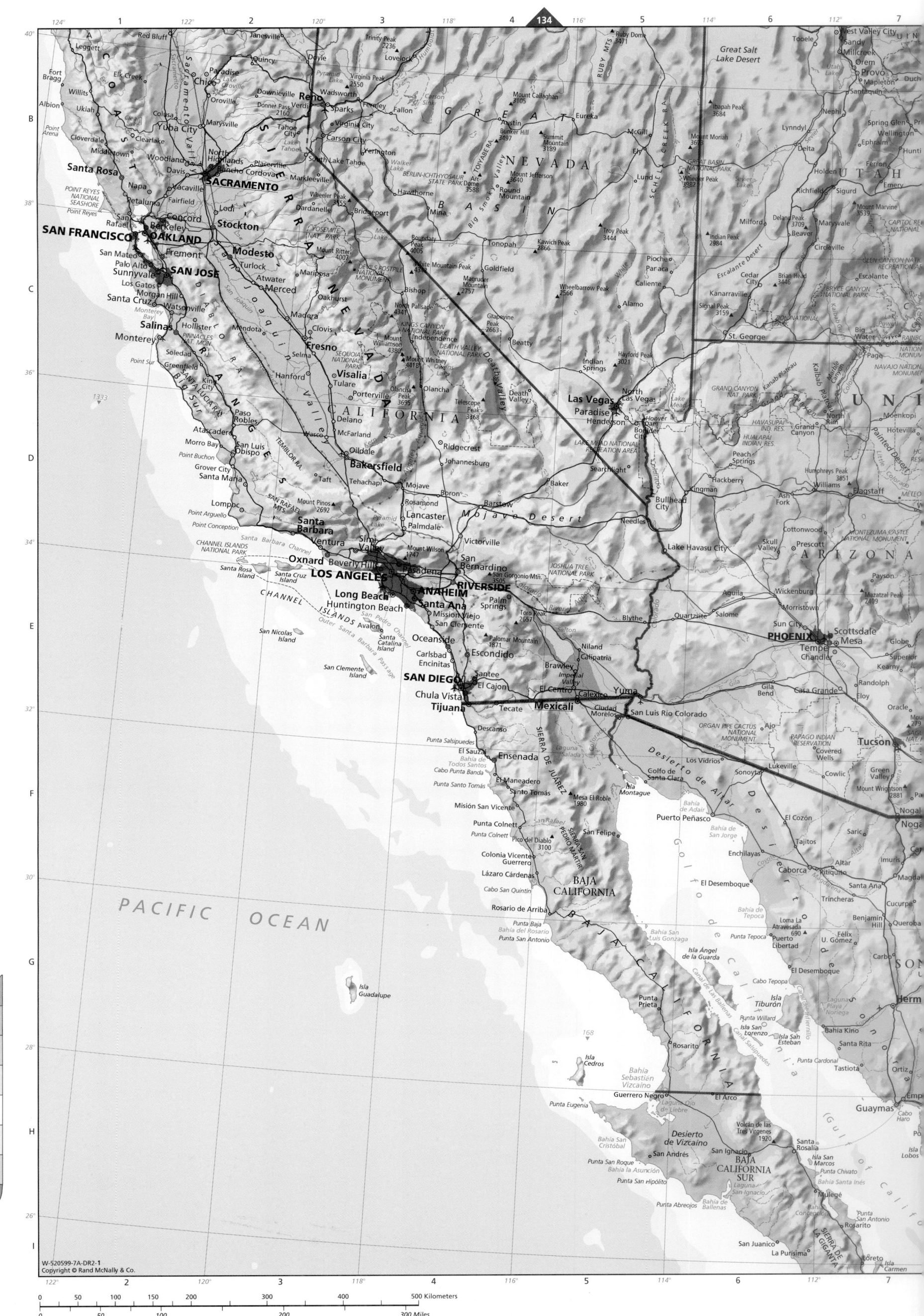

134

40°
38°
36°
34°
32°
30°
28°
26°

124° 122° 120° 118° 116° 114° 112°

1   2   3   4   5   6   7

CALIFORNIA

NEVADA

UTAH

ARIZONA

Great Salt Lake Desert

GREAT BASIN

SIERRA NEVADA

Mojave Desert

Death Valley

SAN FRANCISCO
OAKLAND
SAN JOSE
SACRAMENTO
Santa Rosa
Stockton
Modesto
Fresno
Visalia
Bakersfield
Santa Barbara
Oxnard
LOS ANGELES
Long Beach
Huntington Beach
ANAHEIM
Santa Ana
RIVERSIDE
San Bernardino
Oceanside
Escondido
Carlsbad
SAN DIEGO
Chula Vista
Tijuana
Mexicali

Reno
Sparks
Carson City
Las Vegas
Paradise
Henderson

PHOENIX
Scottsdale
Mesa
Tempe
Chandler
Tucson

Yuma

PACIFIC OCEAN

BAJA CALIFORNIA

BAJA CALIFORNIA SUR

Guaymas

Meters
Feet
4000
13120
3000
9840
2000
6560
1000
3280
500
1640
200
656
Sea Level
200
656
2000
6560

W-520599-7A-DR2-1
Copyright © Rand McNally & Co.

122° 120° 118° 116° 114° 112°
1   2   3   4   5   6   7

0 50 100 150 200 300 400 500 Kilometers
0 50 100 200 300 Miles

Scale 1 : 5,000,000   Lambert Conformal Conic Projection

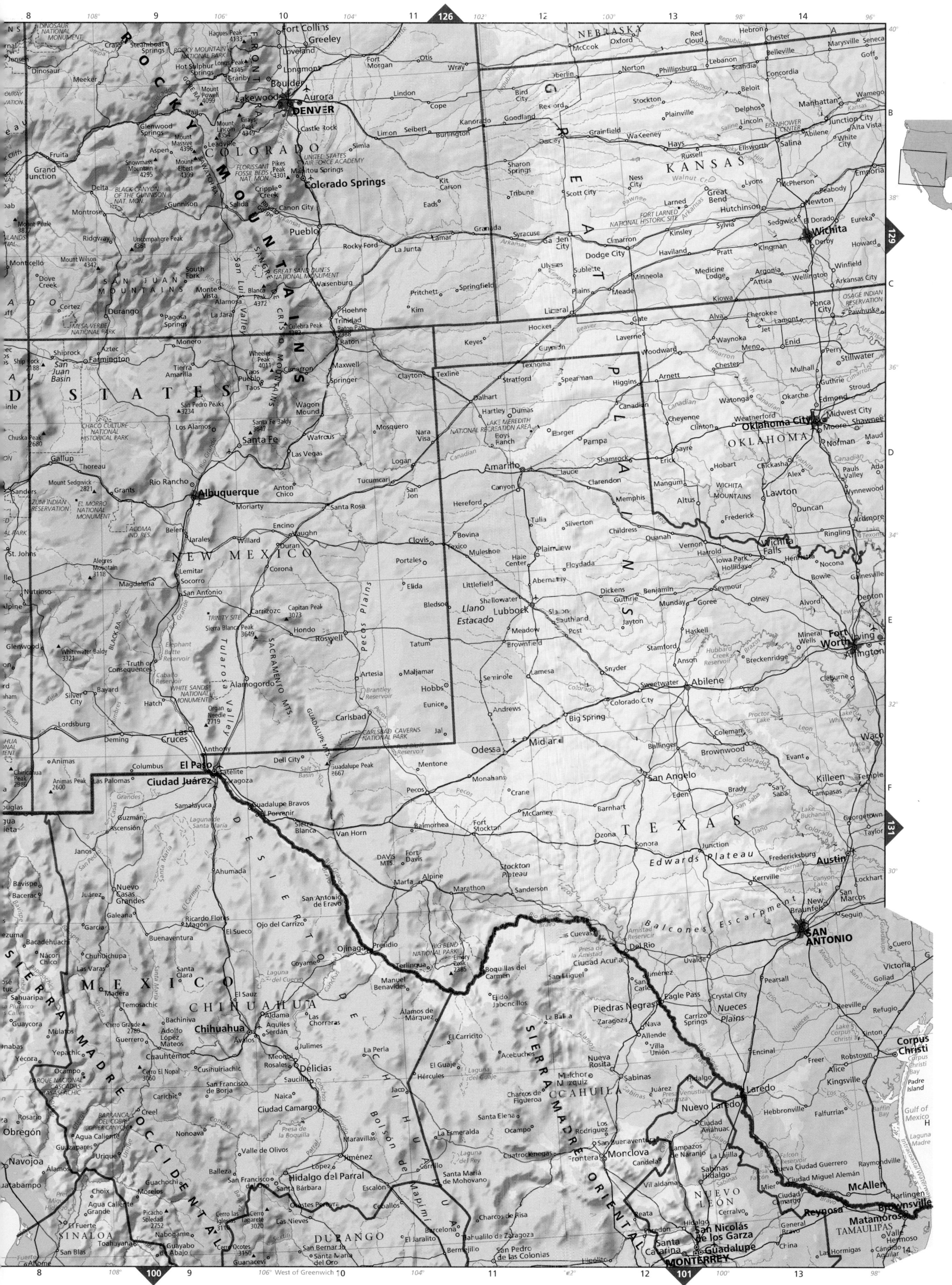

Scale 1 : 5,000,000   Lambert Conformal Conic Projection

W-532095-7A-DR2-1
Copyright © Rand McNally & Co.

UNITED STATES

TEXAS

GULF OF MEXICO

Bahía de Campeche

Golfo de Tehuantepec

SAN ANTONIO
Corpus Christi
Laredo
Nuevo Laredo
MONTERREY
Saltillo
Matamoros
Reynosa
McAllen
Brownsville
TAMAULIPAS
NUEVO LEÓN
Ciudad Victoria
Tampico
Ciudad Madero
San Luis Potosí
Aguascalientes
León
Guanajuato
Querétaro
Irapuato
Morelia
CIUDAD DE MÉXICO
(MEXICO CITY)
Toluca
PUEBLA
Cuernavaca
Veracruz
VERACRUZ
Xalapa (Jalapa)
Córdoba
Orizaba
Coatzacoalcos
Villahermosa
TABASCO
CAMPECHE
Ciudad del Carmen
CHIAPAS
Tuxtla Gutiérrez
San Cristóbal de las Casas
Acapulco
GUERRERO
Chilpancingo de los Bravo
OAXACA
Oaxaca de Juárez
Puerto Escondido
Salina Cruz
Tapachula
Puerto Madero
GUATEMALA
Tropic of Cancer
Padre Island
Laguna Madre
Isla del Carmen

Gulf of Mexico

CAYMAN IS (U.K.)

George Town   Grand Cayman

MEXICO

PENÍNSULA DE YUCATÁN

(YUCATAN PENINSULA)

CAMPECHE

QUINTANA ROO

YUCATÁN

Mérida

Cancún

Campeche

Chetumal

BELIZE

Belize City

Belmopan

GUATEMALA

GUATEMALA

HONDURAS

Tegucigalpa

San Pedro Sula

EL SALVADOR

San Salvador

NICARAGUA

Managua

COSTA RICA

SAN JOSÉ

PACIFIC

OCEAN

PANAMA

LA HABANA (HAVANA)

Pinar del Río

CHIAPAS

TABASCO

SIERRA MADRE

CORDILLERA DE MOSQUITOS

SAN ANDRÉS Y PROVIDENCIA (Col.)

Gulf of Honduras

ISLAS DE LA BAHÍA

Meters / Feet
3000 / 9840
2000 / 6560
1000 / 3280
500 / 1640
200 / 656
Sea Level
200 / 656
2000 / 6560

W-536000-7A-DR2-1
Copyright © Rand McNally & Co.

0   50 100   150   200   300   400   500 Kilometers
0   50   100   200   300 Miles

Scale 1 : 5,000,000   Lambert Conformal Conic Projection

BAHAMAS

Deadman Cay
Long Cay
Clarence Town
Cape Verde
Samana Cay
Ragged Island Range
Cay Lobos
Cay Coco
Cay Romano
Cayo Guajaba
Cay Sabinal
Bight of Acklins
Crooked Island
Long Cay
Acklins
North Ecs Point
Salina Point
Ragged Island
Matthew Town

TURKS AND CAICOS ISLANDS (U.K.)

Caico Passage
Providenciales
Kew
North Caicos
Middle Caicos
West Caicos
East Caicos
CAICOS ISLANDS
Little Inagua
South Caicos
Seal Cays
Grand Turk
TURKS ISLANDS
Palacca Point
Lake Rosa
Great Inagua

ATLANTIC OCEAN

Mouchoir Passage
Silver Bank Passage

CUBA

Caibarién
Placetas
Yaguajay
Morón
Bahía
Esmeralda
Ciego de Avila
Presa Zaza
Sancti Spíritus
Florida
Minas
Camagüey
Vertientes
Las Tunas
Guayabal
Golfo de Ana María
Archipiélago de los Jardines de la Reina
Campechuela
Niquero
Manzanillo
Bayamo
Jiguani
San Germán
Palma Soriano
Contramaestre
Santiago de Cuba
Pico Turquino 1972
Marea del Portillo
Cabo Cruz
Nuevitas
Puerto Manatí
Puerto Padre
Gibara
Holguín
Cueto
Mayarí
Sagua de Tánamo
Baracoa
Punta de Quemado
Guantánamo
Calmanera
GUANTÁNAMO BAY NAVAL STATION (U.S.)
Punta de Mulas
Banes
Antilla
Bahía de Nipe
Alto Cedro
San Luis
Tiguabos
Rafael Freyre

WEST INDIES

GREATER ANTILLES

HISPANIOLA

Monte Cristi
Manzanillo Bay
Cabo Isabela
Puerto Plata
Cabo Macoris
Cabo Francés Viejo
San Fernando
Cap-Haïtien
Fort-Liberté
Dajabón
Mao
Moca
Nagua
Cabo Samaná
SANS SOUCI LA CITADELLE
Limbe
Santiago de los Caballeros
La Vega
San Francisco de Macoris
Bahía Escocesa
Samaná
Bahía de Samaná

HAITI
Gonaïves
Morne Bonhomme 1788
Pico Duarte 3175
Bonao
Sabana de la Mar
Miches

Golfe de la Gonâve
Île de la Gonâve
Saint-Marc
Comendador
Alto Bandera 2630
El Seibo
Higüey
Cabo Engaño

Jérémie
Grande Cayemite
Pointe Fanchon
Anse-d'Hainault
Port-au-Prince
Pétion-Ville
San Juan de la Maguana
Azua
San Cristóbal
SANTO DOMINGO
San Pedro de Macoris
La Romana
Bahía de Yuma

Pic Macaya 2347
Les Cayes
Île à Vache
Léogâne
Morne La Selle 2674
Neiba
Lago Enriquillo
Barahona
Bahía de Ocoa
Bani
Punta Palenque
Isla Saona

DOMINICAN REPUBLIC

Coteaux
Pointe Abacou
Pedernales
Enriquillo
Cabo Falso
Isla Beata
Cabo Beata

Port-de-Paix
Île de la Tortue
Cap à Foux
Cap du Môle

JAMAICA

Montego Bay
Falmouth
Saint Ann's Bay
Ocho Rios
Port Maria
Port Antonio
South Negril Point
Mount Denham 986
Mandeville
Spanish Town
Kingston
Blue Mountain Peak 2256
Savanna-la-Mar
Portland Point
Portland Bight
Morant Bay
Morant Point

Pedro Cays
Morant Cays
2184

Navassa Island (U.S.)

Windward Passage
Jamaica Channel

CARIBBEAN SEA

Cayo de Serranilla (Col.)
Bajo Nuevo (Col.)
Roncador

LESSER ANTILLES

ARUBA (Neth.)
Oranjestad

NETHERLANDS ANTILLES (Neth.) Bonaire
Curaçao
Willemstad

Punta Gallinas
Bahía Honda
Puerto Bolívar
Cabo de La Vela
Cabo San Román
Peninsula de Paraguaná
Los Taques
Pueblo Nuevo
Puerto Cumarebo
Punta Zamuro
Punta Cardón
Punta Fijo
Coro
La Vela de Coro
Peninsula de La Guajira
Uribia
Golfo de Venezuela
Capatárida
Dabajuro
San Luis
Cabure
Churuguara
Richacha
Maicao
Paraguaipoa
Sinamaica
San Rafael
Pedregal
FALCÓN
Cabo de La Aguja
Santa Marta
Ciénaga
LA GUAJIRA
Albania
Altagracia
Mene de Mauroa
Siquisique
Barranquilla
Soledad
Malambo
Pico Cristóbal Colón 5775
Valledupar
MARACAIBO
Santa Rita
Mene Grande
ATLÁNTICO
Baranoa
Sabanalarga
Fonseca
Cabimas
Tía Juana
Ciudad Ojeda
Carora
Barquisimeto
VENEZUELA
San Felipe
YARACUY
PARQUE NACIONAL YURUBI
Cartagena
Islas del Rosario
Arjona
Turbaco
Manatí
El Piñón
Plato
Fundación
La Paz
Bachaquero
LARA
El Guamo
Mahates
Calamar
Agustín Codazzi
Villa del Rosario
Machiques
Trujillo
TRUJILLO
Acarigua
María La Baja
San Jacinto
San Onofre
Tolú
Islas de San Bernardo
Golfo de Morrosquillo
Nepomuceno
El Carmen de Bolívar
Magangué
MAGDALENA
CESAR
La Ceiba
Sabana de Mendoza
Valera
Ospino
Guanare
PORTUGUESA
87
Punta Mosquito
Mansucum
San Pelayo
SUCRE
Ciénaga de Oro
Sahagún
Corozal
Sincelejo
Pivijay
Pinillos
El Banco
Chiriguaná
San Pedro
Encontrados
Casigua
El Moral
Mérida
Barinas
BARINAS
Monteria
Cereté
Planeta Rica
Pijiño
Mompós
Cerro Murci 2610
Bobures
Santa Bárbara
Timotes
Mucuchíes
Barrancas
Guanaito
Santa Rosa
ANTIOQUIA
CÓRDOBA
Lorica
San Marcos
Achí
BOLÍVAR
ZULIA
Lago de Maracaibo
San Carlos del Zulia
Pico Bolívar 5007
SIERRA NEVADA
PARQUE NAC.
MÉRIDA
Ciudad Bolivia
Libertad
Ciudad de Nutrias
Arboletes
San Pelayo
Caucasia
Ayapel
Nechí
Montelíbano
Tierralta
Alto de Quimarí 2000
COLOMBIA
Gamarra
Aguachica
Ocaña
NORTE DE SANTANDER
Tovar
Bailadores
El Vigía
TÁCHIRA
CÓRDOBA
Turbo
Apartadó
Golfo de Urabá
Santa María
Garrapatas
CHOCÓ
Yaviza
El Real de Santa María
Cúcuta
San Cristóbal
Rubio
Santa Bárbara
Arauca
APURE

Panamá
Istmo de Panamá (Isthmus of Panama)
Nombre de Dios
El Porvenir
Golfo de San Blas
SERRANÍA DE SAN BLAS
Niatupo
Chepo
Lago Bayano
San Miguel
La Palma
Golfo de San Miguel
Isla del Rey
ARCHIPIÉLAGO DE LAS PERLAS
Isla San José
Garachiné
Bahía de Panamá
Golfo de Panamá
PARQUE NACIONAL DARIÉN

Canal de San Nicolás

Puerto Rico (map a)

ATLANTIC OCEAN

Punta Agujereada · Isabela · Camuy · Hatillo · Punta Las Tunas · Poblado Cerro Gordo · Poblado · Bahía de San Juan · **SAN JUAN**

San Antonio · Feliciano · Quebradillas · El Soto · Arecibo · Vega Baja · Dorado · Toa Baja · Toa Alta · AEROPUERTO INT. LUIS MUÑOZ MARIN · Loíza Aldea · Poblado Mediania Alta

Aguadilla · Moca · Pueblito de Ponce · Lago de Guajataca · Charco Hondo · Palo Blanco · Manati · Vega Alta · Levittown · Cataño · Carolina · Isla Vacia Talega · Punta Picúa · Soroco

La Cuesta · Indiera Alta · OBSERVATORIO DE ARECIBO · Dos Bocas · Asomante · Florida · Montebello · El Campamento · Bayamón · Guaynabo · Trujillo Alto · Río Grande · Palmer · Luquillo · Playa de Fajardo · Cabezas de San Juan

Punta Higüero · Rincón · Córcega · San Sebastián · Perchas · Lares · Utuado · Ciales · Morovis · Corozal · La Esperanza · El Polvorín · El Yunque 1065 · Sabana · Fajardo · Cayo de Luis Peña · Culebra

Punta Cadena · AEROPUERTO MAYAGÜEZ · Mayagüez · Las Marias · Javuya · Orocovis · Naranjito · Comerio · Gurabo · Aguas Buenas · El Toro 1074 · Juncos · Florida · Ceiba · Quebrada Seca · Isla de Culebra · Culebrita

Mani · Las Vegas · Maricao · Los Rábanos · Cerro de Punta 1338 · Adjuntas · Barranquitas · Aibonito · La Torrecilla 943 · Caguas · San Lorenzo · Las Piedras · Playa de Naguabo · Punta Puerca

PUERTO RICO (U.S.) · CORDILLERA CENTRAL · SIERRA DE CAYEY · Humacao · Punta Santiago · Punta Mulas · Vieques · Santa Maria · Isla de Vieques

Joyuda · San Germán · Sabana Grande · Peñuelas · Villalba · Coamo · Cerro La Santa 903 · Cayey · Yabucoa · Maunabo · Monte Pirata 301 · Esperanza · Punta Este

Puerto Real · Lajas · Yauco · Guayanilla · Juana Diaz · Los Llanos · Rio Jueyes · Cerro de la Tabla 890 · Patillas

Cabo Rojo · Palmarejo · Las Arenas · Guánica · Guayanilla · Ponce · Santa Isabel · Guayama · Las Palmas · Arroyo · Colonia Providencia

Bahía de Boquerón · Ensenada · Bahía de Guayanilla · Boca Chica · Paso Seco · Arenas · Salinas · Central Aguirre · Jobos

Cabo Rojo · Punta Brea · Isla Caja de Muertos · Punta Petrona · Bahía de Rincón · Bahía de Jobos · Las Mareas

CARIBBEAN SEA

Scale 1 : 1,000,000

Virgin Islands (map b)

ATLANTIC OCEAN

VIRGIN ISLANDS · Great Tobago · West End Point · Little Harbour · Necker Island · Mosquito Island · Pajaros Point · Guana Island · Great Camanoe · Virgin Gorda Peak 414

Little Tobago · Jost Van Dyke · Road Town · Long Swamp · Scrub Island · Dog Islands · Spanish Town · VIRGIN GORDA · South Sound · Copper Mine Point

Brass Islands · Hans Lollick Island · ST. THOMAS · Thatch Cay · Great Thatch Island · Mount Sage 521 · Beef Island · Fallen Jerusalem · Ginger Island

Fortuna · CYRIL E. KING AIRPORT · Crown Mountain 474 · Charlotte Amalie · Hassel Island · Pillsbury Sound · VIRGIN IS. NAT. PARK · Coral Bay · Cooper Island · Salt Island · Peter Island

To San Juan · Water Island · Long Point · Lind Point · Cruz Bay · Bordeaux Mtn. 390 · ST. JOHN · Flanagan Passage · Norman Island · BRITISH VIRGIN ISLANDS (U.K.)

Saba Island · Capella Islands · St. James Islands · Ram Head · VIRGIN ISLANDS (U.S.) · CARIBBEAN SEA

Frenchcap Cay · Sir Francis Drake Channel

0 5 10 Kilometers · 0 5 Miles · Scale 1 : 500,000

St. Croix (map c)

ST. CROIX (Virgin Islands–U.S.) · Hams Bluff · Baron Bluff · BUCK ISLAND REEF NATIONAL MONUMENT · Buck Island

Frederiksted · Mount Eagle 354 · Kingshill · Christiansted · ALEXANDER HAMILTON AIRPORT · Southwest Cape · CARIBBEAN SEA

Scale 1 : 500,000

Jamaica (map d)

Montego Bay · Duncans · St. Ann's Bay · Galina Point · 2711 · Lucea · Falmouth · Clark's Town · Ocho Rios · Port Maria · Port Antonio · Annotto Bay

South Negril Point · Dolphin Head 545 · Montpelier · Cockpit Country · Browns Town · Blue Mtn. Peak 2256 · Port Antonio

Little London · Whithorn · Mount Denham 986 · Frankfield · Linstead · Catherines Peak 1541 · Mandeville · Mavis Bank

Bluefields Bay · Savanna-la-Mar · Christiana · Porus · Chapelton · Spanish Town · **Kingston** · Morant Bay · Morant

Black River · Mandeville · Mount Ida 725 · May Pen · Portmore · Old Harbour · Port Royal · Morant Point

JAMAICA · Alligator Pond · Lionel Town · Portland Bight · Portland Point · Morant Channel

CARIBBEAN SEA · Scale 1 : 2,500,000

Bermuda (map e)

ATLANTIC OCEAN · St. George's Island · FORT VICTORIA · St. George · St. David's Island · KINDLEY FIELD · Castle Harbour · Harrington Sound · Town Hill 79

Ireland Island North · Somerset Island · Spanish Point · Flatts · Great Sound · Hamilton · Little Sound · High Point · **BERMUDA (U.K.)**

Scale 1 : 500,000

New Providence (map f)

ATLANTIC OCEAN · Northeast Providence Channel · North Cay · Long Cay · Paradise Island · Salt Cay

Old Fort Point · Delaport Point · NASSAU INTERNATIONAL AIRPORT · Nassau · Lake Killarney · Sandilands Village · Athol Island · East End Point

Adelaide · South West Bay · Coral Harbour · Cay Point · Long Point · **NEW PROVIDENCE (Bahamas)**

Scale 1 : 500,000

Aruba / Curaçao / Bonaire / Venezuela (map g)

Westpunt · **ARUBA (Neth.)** · CARIBBEAN SEA

Druif · Bushiribana · Hooiberg 167 · Oranjestad · Jamanota 188 · Sint Nicolaas · Lago Kolonie · Punt Basora

Cabo San Román · Puerto Escondido · San Lorenzo · Salina de Bangua · Las Cumaraguas · Noordpunt · Savonet · Sint Christoffelberg 375 · Sint Kruis · Solo

VENEZUELA · Peninsula de Paraguana · FALCON · El Vinculo · Santa Rita · **CURAÇAO** · Bocht van Hato · **NETHERLANDS ANTILLES (Neth.)** · Malmok · Brandaris 240 · Dos Pos · **BONAIRE** · Montagne

San José · Asaro · La Serena · Bullenbaai · Julianadorp · **Willemstad** · Tafelberg 194 · Nieuwpoort · Klein Bonaire · Kralendijk · Wanapa

Oostpunt · Klein Curaçao · To La Vela de Coro · Lacre Punt

Scale 1 : 1,000,000

W-537000-7A-DR2-1
Copyright © Rand McNally & Co.

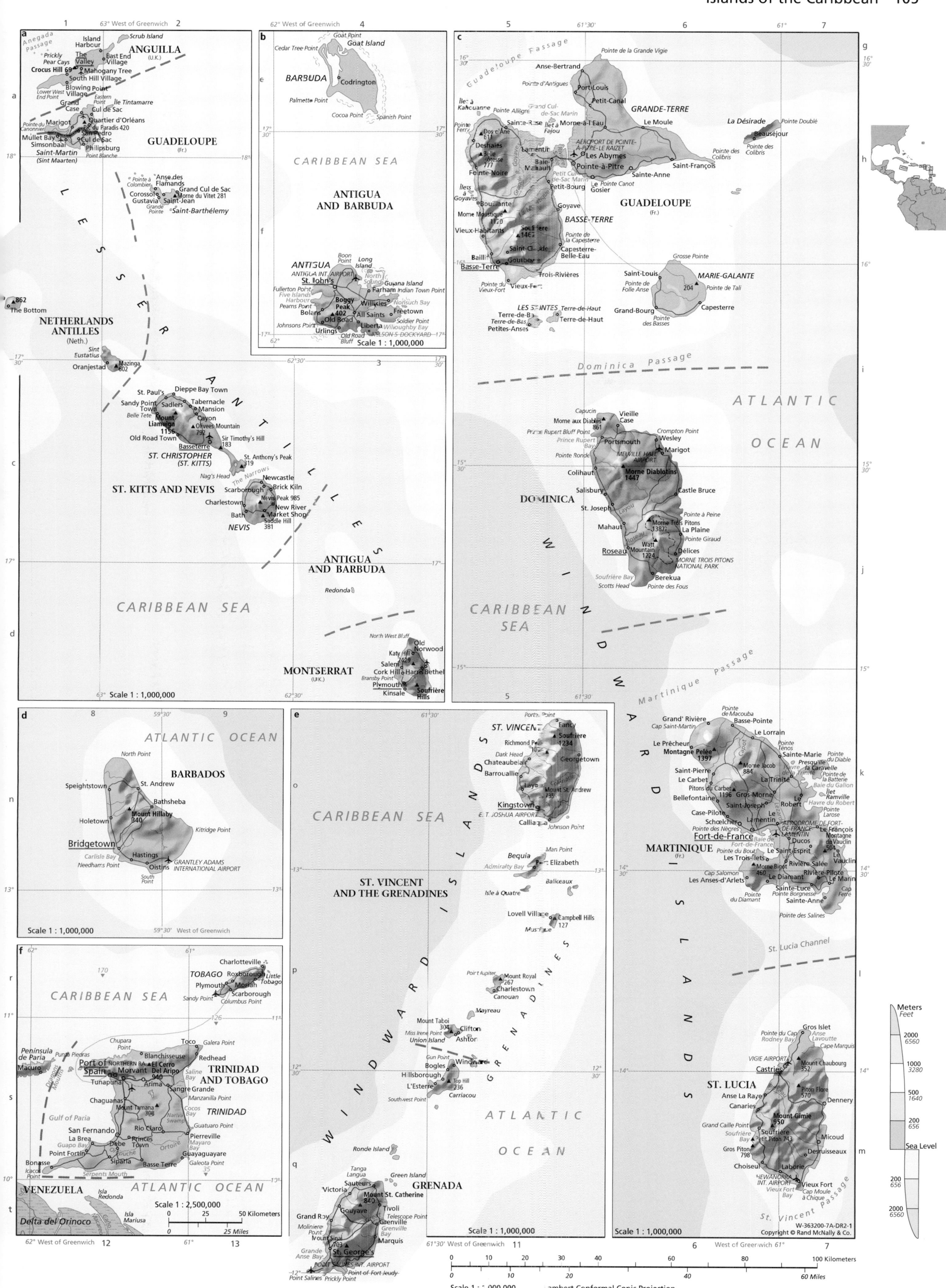

Scale 1 : 1,000,000

Scale 1 : 1,000,000

Scale 1 : 1,000,000

Scale 1 : 2,500,000

Scale 1 : 1,000,000

Scale 1 : 1,000,000

Scale 1 : 1,000,000

Lambert Conformal Conic Projection

W-363200-7A-DR2-1
Copyright © Rand McNally & Co.

Meters
Feet

2000
6560

1000
3280

500
1640

200
656

Sea Level

200
656

2000
6560

0   5   10   20   30   40   50 Kilometers
0   10   20   40   60 Miles

PACIFIC OCEAN

ALASKA

YUKON

NORTHWEST TERRITORIES

BRITISH COLUMBIA

ALBERTA

SASKATCHEWAN

MANITOBA

CANADA

UNITED STATES

WASHINGTON

OREGON

IDAHO

MONTANA

WYOMING

NORTH DAKOTA

SOUTH DAKOTA

MINNESOTA

NEVADA

UTAH

CALIFORNIA

VICTORIA ISLAND

BANKS ISLAND

PRINCE OF WALES ISLAND

KING WILLIAM ISLAND

STEFANSSON ISLAND

QUEEN CHARLOTTE ISLANDS

VANCOUVER ISLAND

ROCKY MOUNTAINS

COAST MOUNTAINS

MACKENZIE MOUNTAINS

SELWYN MOUNTAINS

OGILVIE MOUNTAINS

CASSIAR MOUNTAINS

OMINECA MTS.

SKEENA MOUNTAINS

CARIBOO MOUNTAINS

COLUMBIA MOUNTAINS

PURCELL MOUNTAINS

MONASHEE MOUNTAINS

BITTERROOT RANGE

SALMON RIVER MTS.

BLUE MTS.

CASCADE RANGE

PELLY MOUNTAINS

LOGAN MOUNTAINS

STIKINE RANGES

DAWSON RANGE

GREAT BASIN

WIND RIVER RANGE

BIGHORN MTS.

BIG BELT MTS.

CYPRESS HILLS

BLACK HILLS

CARIBOU MTS.

BIRCH MTS.

CAMERON HILLS

FRANKLIN MTS.

SHALER MOUNTAINS

Great Bear Lake

Great Slave Lake

Lake Athabasca

Reindeer Lake

Lake Winnipeg

Hudson Bay

Amundsen Gulf

Coronation Gulf

Queen Maud Gulf

VANCOUVER
SEATTLE
Tacoma
PORTLAND
Salem
Calgary
Edmonton
Saskatoon
Regina
Winnipeg
MINNEAPOLIS
Reno
Spokane
Boise
Helena
Bismarck

Meters / Feet
4000 / 13120
3000 / 9840
2000 / 6560
1000 / 3280
200 / 656
Sea Level
200 / 656
2000 / 6560

0 100 200 300 400 600 800 1000 Kilometers
0 100 200 400 600 Miles

Scale 1 : 10,000,000   Lambert Conformal Conic Projection

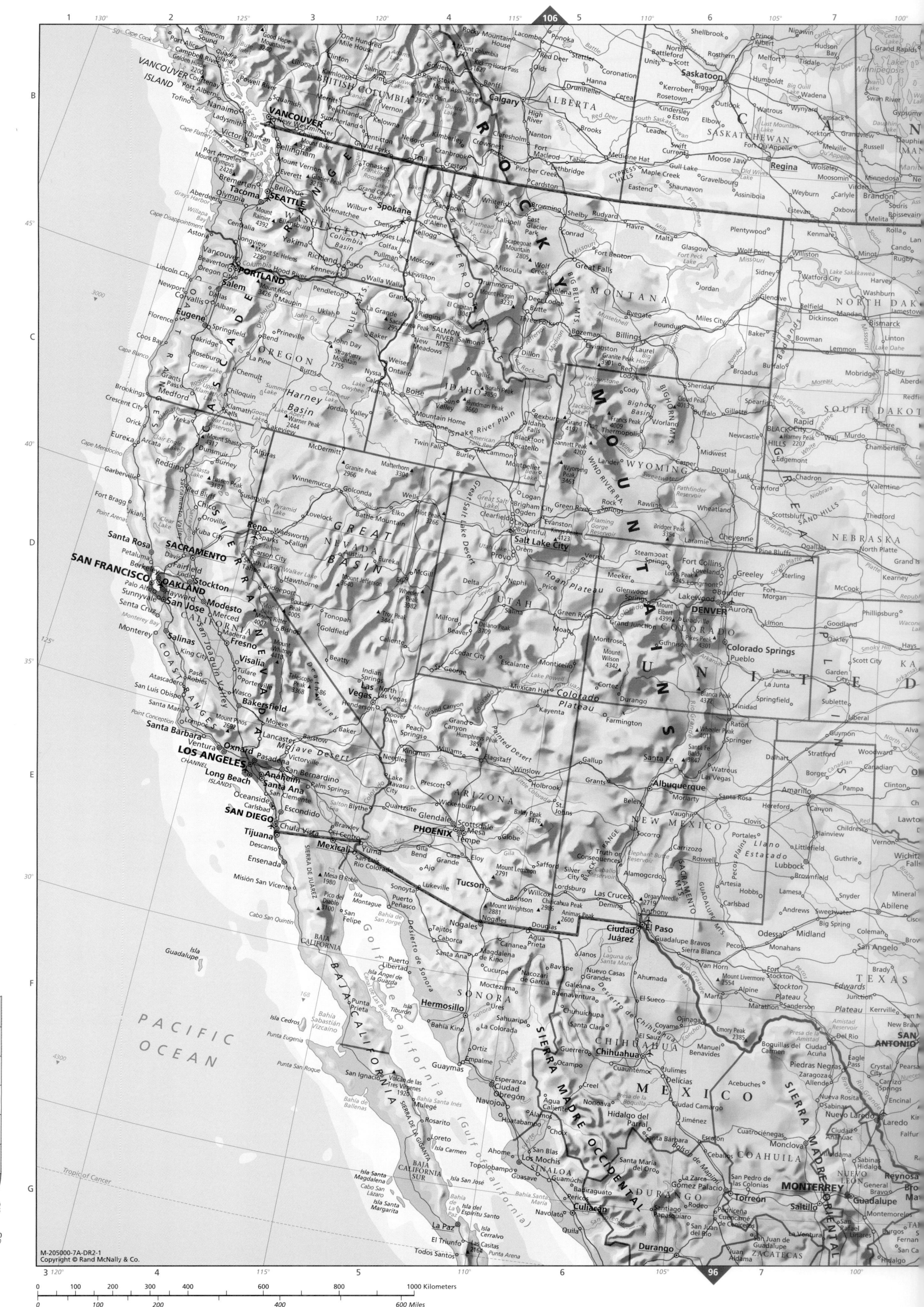

PACIFIC

OCEAN

Meters
Feet

3000
9840

2000
6560

1000
3280

500
1640

200
656

Sea Level

200
656

2000
6560

M-205000-7A-DR2-1
Copyright © Rand McNally & Co.

Scale 1 : 10,000,000   Lambert Conformal Conic Projection

0 100 200 300 400 600 800 1000 Kilometers

0 100 200 400 600 Miles

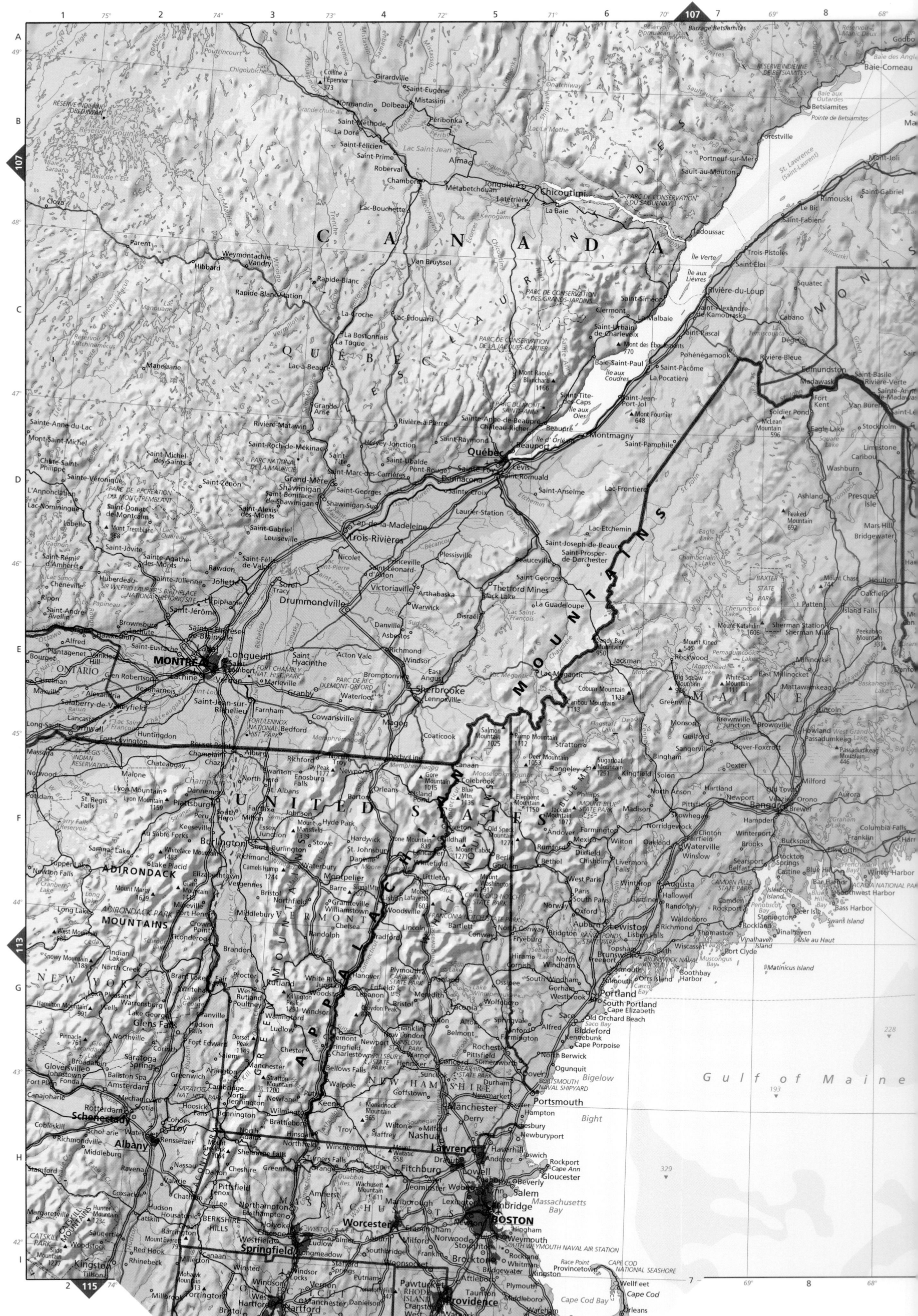

10   66°   11   65°   12   64°   13   63°   14   62°   15   61°   16   60°   17   59°

A

Pointe du Sud-Ouest
ÎLE D'ANTICOSTI
Rivière-de-la-Chaloupe
Detroit d'Honguedo
Pointe de l'Est
Pointe Heath

354
La Martre   Rivière-à-Claude   Madeleine-Centre   Saint-Yvon
Sainte-Anne-des-Monts   Pointe-à-la-Frégate
Cap-Chat
Mont Jacques-Cartier   1277
PARC PROVINCIAL   DE LA GASPÉSIE
PARC NATIONAL DE FORILLON
Fontenelle
Gaspé
Cap Gaspé
Baie de Gaspé
Port au Port Peninsula
Cape St. George

B

Mont Blanc   1059
MONTS   CHIC-CHOCS
PÉNINSULE DE LA GASPÉSIE   (GASPE PENINSULA)
Saint-Jean
NOTRE DAME
Saint-Gabriel-de-Gaspé
La Malbaie
Percé
Île Bonaventure

NEWFOUNDLAND

Gulf of St. Lawrence

Cape Anguille
Codroy
Doyles
Tompkins
Table Mountain   527
Cape Ray

New Richmond
Caplan
Bonaventure
New Carlisle
Grande-Rivière
Chandler
Newport
Pointe au Maquereau

C

Campbellton
Squaw Cap Mountain   483
Lorne
Blue Mountain   528
Beresford
Nepisiguit Bay
Grande-Anse
Caraquet
Shippegan
Île Lamèque
Lamèque
Miscou Point
Miscou Island
Miscou Centre
Chaleur Bay
Jacquet River

Île Brion
La Grosse Île
Grande-Entrée   Île de l'Est
ÎLES DE LA MADELEINE   (Que.)
Île du Cap aux Meules
Cap-aux-Meules
Baie de Plaisance
Île du Havre Aubert
Havre-Aubert

Cabot Strait
To Channel-Port-aux-Basques

Bathurst
MOUNT CARLETON PROVINCIAL PARK
Tetagouche
Mount Carleton   820
Saint-Isidore
Tracadie
Haut Sheila
Brantville

60

St. Paul Island

D

Big Bald Mountain   672
Nepisiguit
Lavillette
Neguac
Northwest Miramichi
Miramichi Bay
Point Escuminac

53

Cape St. Lawrence   Cape North
Aspy Bay
Dingwall   Long Point
Pleasant Bay
CAPE BRETON HIGHLANDS NATIONAL PARK
Ingonish
Chéticamp   Cape Smokey
Grand-Étang
Margaree Harbour   Margaree
Indian Brook
St. Anns Bay
Boularderie Island
New Waterford
Dominion

Newcastle
Chatham
Chatham Head
Little Southwest Miramichi
Point Sapin
Tignish
North Cape
Cape Kildare
Alberton
O'Leary
Conway
Cascumpec Bay

KOUCHIBOUGUAC NATIONAL PARK
Renous
Renous
Rogersville
St-Louis de Kent
Richibucto
St.-Ignace
Rexton
West Point
Cape Traverse

Upper Blackville
Doaktown
Boiestown
Bouctouche
Notre-Dame
Saint-Antoine
Wellington Station
Kensington
North Rustico
PRINCE EDWARD ISLAND NATIONAL PARK
Morell   Peters Bay
Emile
Souris
East Point

Inverness
CAPE BRETON ISLAND
Baddeck
Strathlorne
Sydney Mines
North Sydney
Sydney
Glace Bay
Port Morien

Stanley
NEW BRUNSWICK
Taymouth
Minto
Chipman
Grand Lake
Moncton
Lewisville
Dieppe
Summerside
Bedeque Bay
Hunter River
Victoria
Port Borden
PRINCE EDWARD ISLAND
Charlottetown
Cardigan
Mount Stewart
Vernon
Georgetown
Cardigan Bay

Margaree Harbour
Mabou
Lake Ainslie
Whycocomagh
Judique
Iona
Bras d'Or Lake
Loch Lomond
L'Ardoise
Gabarus

46°

E

Fredericton
Oromocto
Geary   Gagetown
CANADIAN FORCES BASE GAGETOWN
Fredericton Junction
Marysville
Petitcodiac
Turtle Creek
Hillsborough
Dorchester
FORT BEAUSÉJOUR NATIONAL HISTORIC PARK
Harvey
Memramcook
Cap-Pelé
Shemogue
Bayfield
Cape Tormentine
Port Elgin
Baie Verte
Northumberland Strait
Flat River
Wood Islands
Murray River
Murray Harbour
Smith Point
Amet Sound
Pictou Island
Caribou
Elmsdale

172

Geary
Norton
Jacquet
Amherst
Oxford
Malagash
River John
Westchester Station
Scotsburn
Pictou
Fismore
Antigonish
Pomquet
St. Georges Bay
West Bay
St. Peters
Fourchu

Marysville
Sussex
Joggins
River Hébert
Pugwash
Springhill
Nuttby Mountain   367
New Glasgow
Stellarton
Trenton
Westville
Cape George
Port Hood
Point Michaud
Isle Madame
Arichat

F

Welsford
Hampton
Rothesay   St. Martins
Grand Bay
Saint John
Cape Spencer   67
St. George
Point Lepreau
Andrews
Passamaquoddy Bay
Wilsons Beach
ROOSEVELT CAMPOBELLO INTERNATIONAL PARK
West Quoddy Head
Deer Island
FUNDY NATIONAL PARK
Alma
Southampton
Cape Chignecto
Advocate Harbour
Cape Split
Harbourville
Canning
Berwick
Kentville
COBEQUID MTS.
Five Islands
Bass River
Belmont
Cobequid Bay
Greville Bay
Parrsboro
Minas Channel
Minas Basin
GRAND PRÉ NATIONAL HISTORIC PARK
Walton
Maitland
Brookfield
Middle Stewiacke
Londonderry
Truro
Sunnybrae
NOVA SCOTIA
Guysborough
Goshen
Goldboro
Queensport
Larrys River
Canso
Chedabucto Bay
Strait of Canso
Port Hawkesbury
Mulgrave
Lundsdale
Goldboro
Sherbrooke

G

Grand Manan Island
Grand Manan
Digby Neck
Bear River
KEJIMKUJIK NATIONAL PARK
Weymouth
Long Island
Westport
Brier Island
St. Marys Bay
Cape St. Marys
Meteghan
Hectanooga
Digby
Clementsport
Annapolis Royal
PORT ROYAL NATIONAL HISTORIC PARK
FORT ANNE NAT HIST PARK
Bridgetown
Torbrook
Middleton
Springfield
New Germany
Caledonia
South Brookfield
Lake Rossignol
New Ross
Hemford
Bridgewater
Lunenburg
Mahone Bay
New Germany
Windsor
Milford Station
Mount Uniacke
Stewiacke
Shubenacadie
Middle Musquodoboit
Upper Musquodoboit
Moses River
Ecum Secum
Sheet Harbour
Tangier
Musquodoboit Harbour
New Road
Terence Bay
Pennant Point
Halifax
Dartmouth
Herring Cove
HALIFAX CITADEL NATIONAL HISTORIC PARK
Halifax Harbour
Margarets Bay
Prospect

106

162

257

18

Yarmouth
Wedgeport
Chebogue Point
Lower West Pubnico
Lower Woods Harbour
Seal Island
Cape Sable Island
Cape Sable
Pubnico
Barrington
Clark's Harbour
Great Pubnico Lake
Port Maitland
Port Mouton
Liverpool
Liverpool Bay
Brooklyn
Shelburne
Lockeport

44°

Sable Island   (N.S.)

ATLANTIC OCEAN

H

43°

Meters   Feet
1000   3280
500   1640
200   656
Sea Level
200   656
2000   6560

I

10   66°   West of Greenwich   11   65°   12   64°   13   63°   14   62°   15   61°   16   60°

W-520298-7A-DR2-1
Copyright © Rand McNally & Co.

0   25   50   75   100   150   200   250 Kilometers
0   25   50   100   150 Miles

Scale 1 : 2,500,000   Lambert Conformal Conic Projection

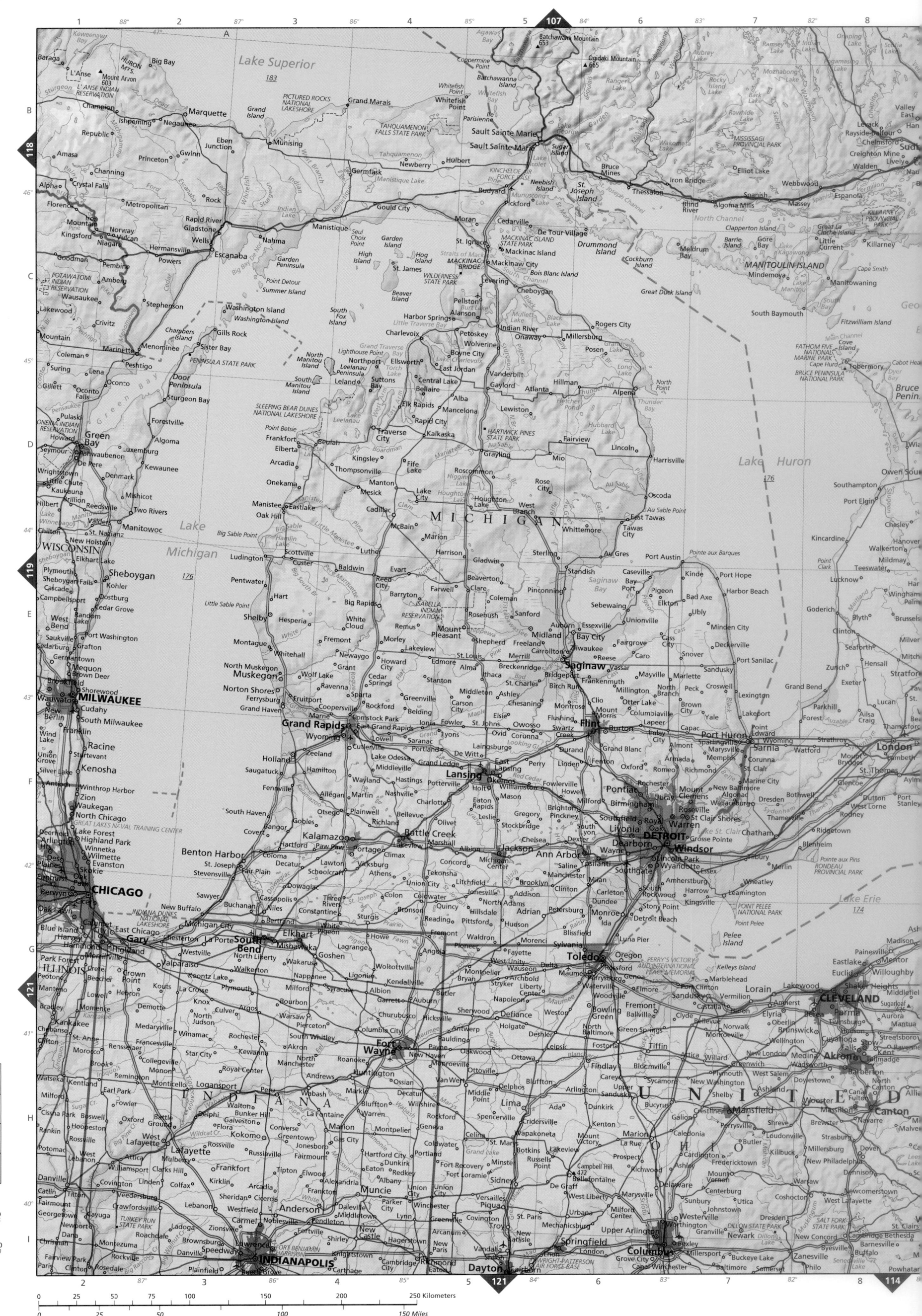

Meters
Feet

1000
3280

500
1640

200
656

Sea Level

200
656

2000
6560

0   25   50   75   100   150   200   250 Kilometers

0   25   50   100   150 Miles

Scale 1 : 2,500,000   Lambert Conformal Conic Projection

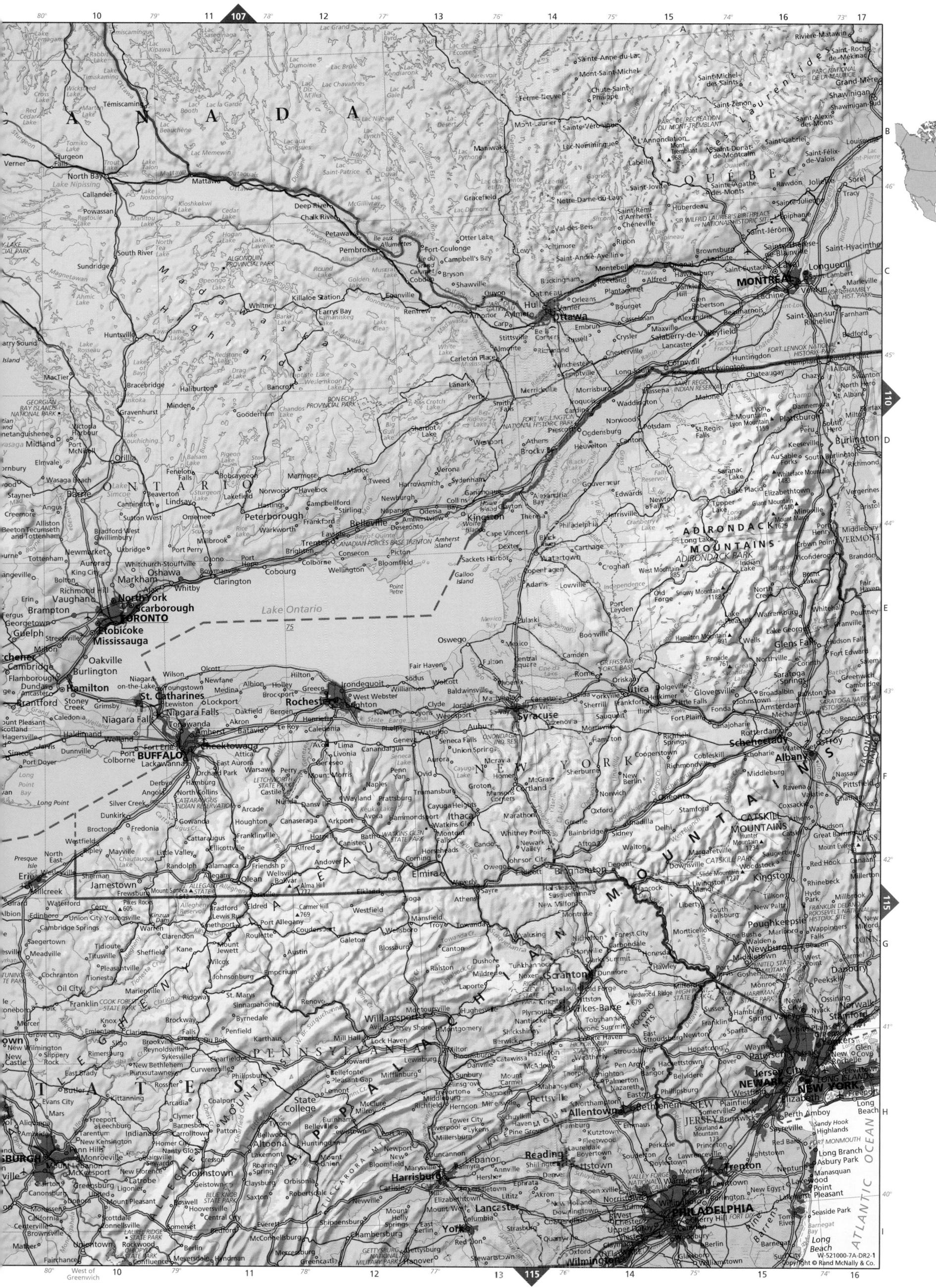

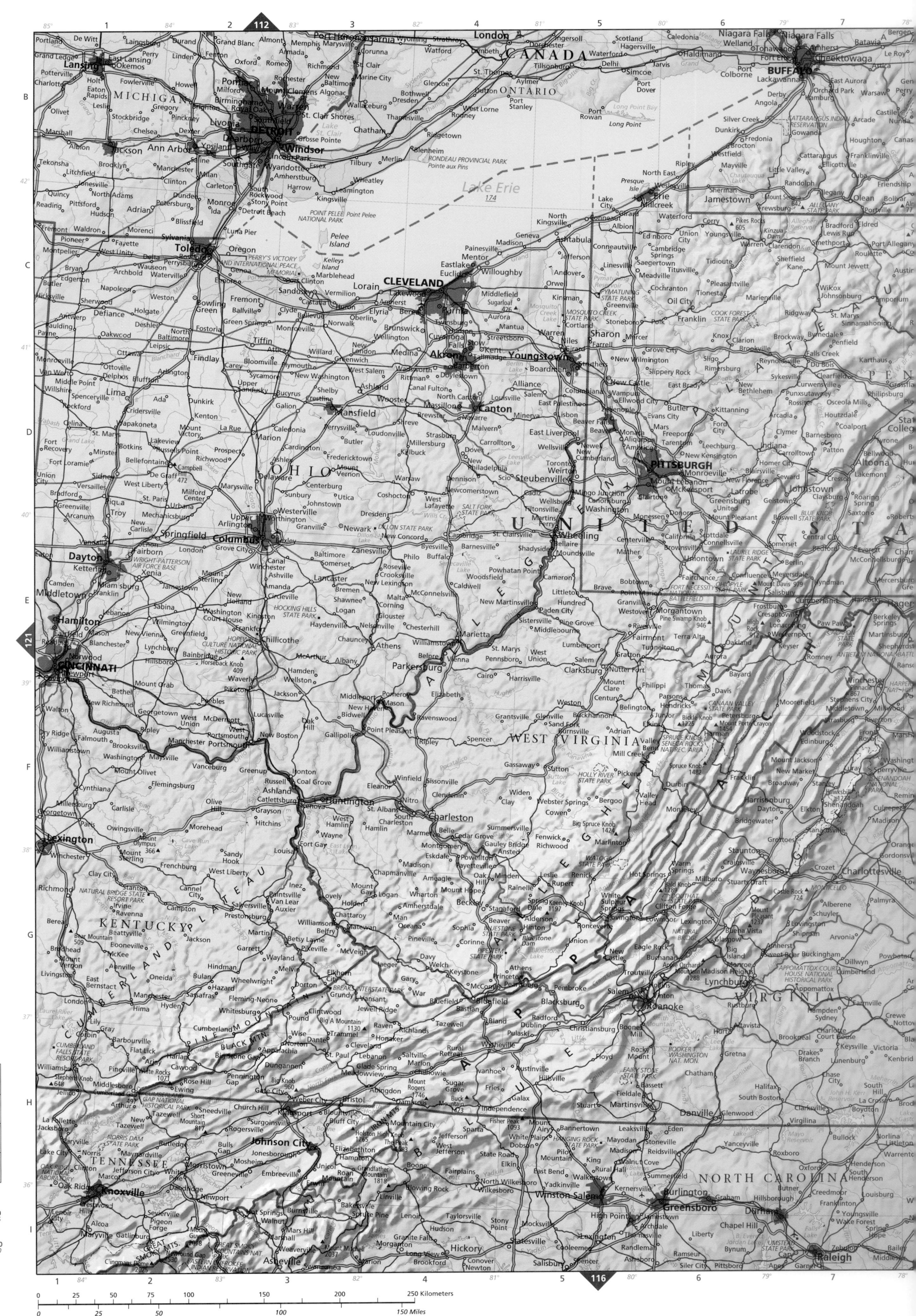

121

Meters
Feet

1000
3280

500
1640

200
656

Sea Level

200
656

2000
6560

0   25   50   75   100   150   200   250 Kilometers

0   25   50   100   150 Miles

Scale 1 : 2,500,000   Lambert Conformal Conic Projection

ATLANTIC OCEAN

W-520558-7A-DR2-1
Copyright © Rand McNally & Co.

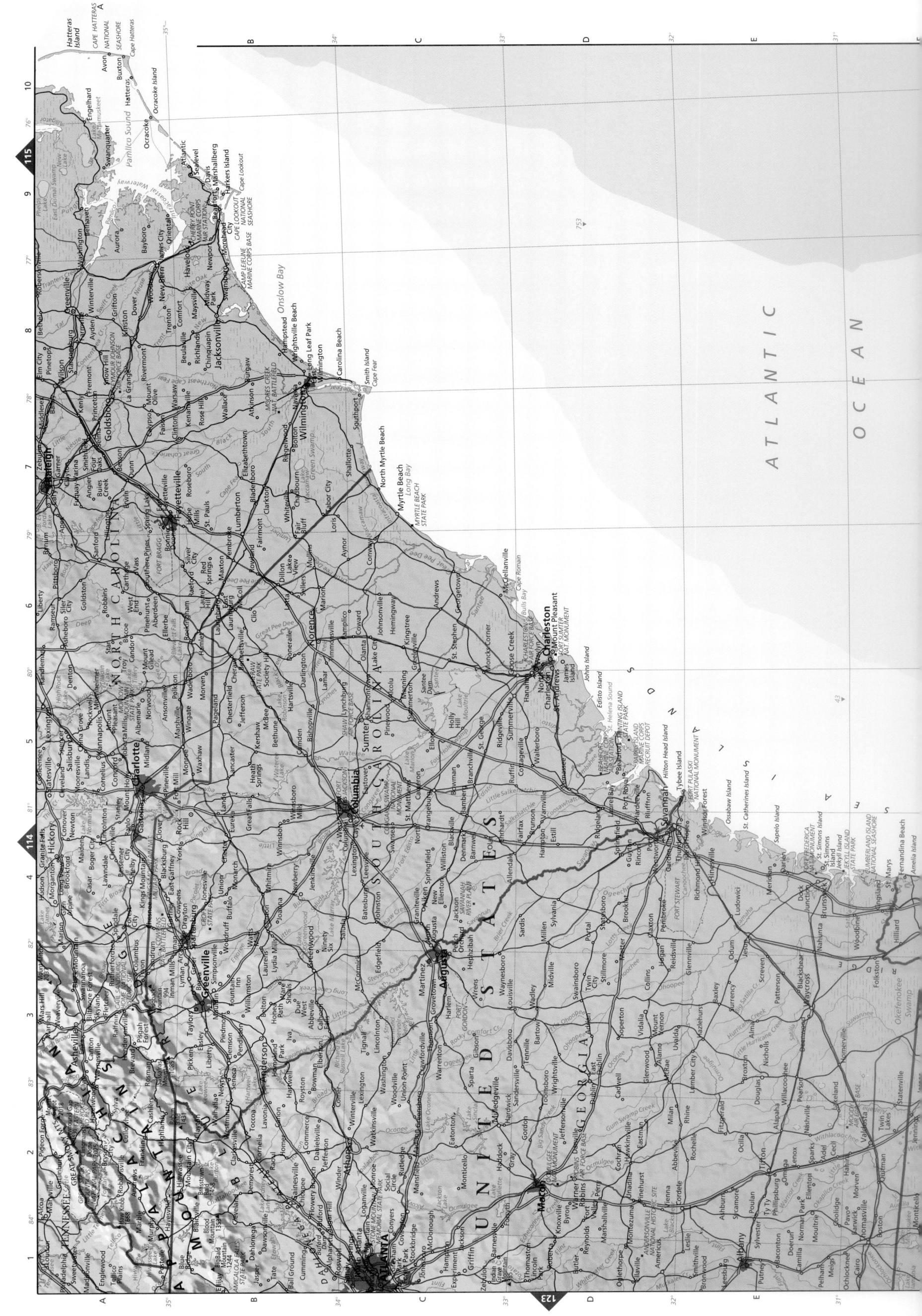

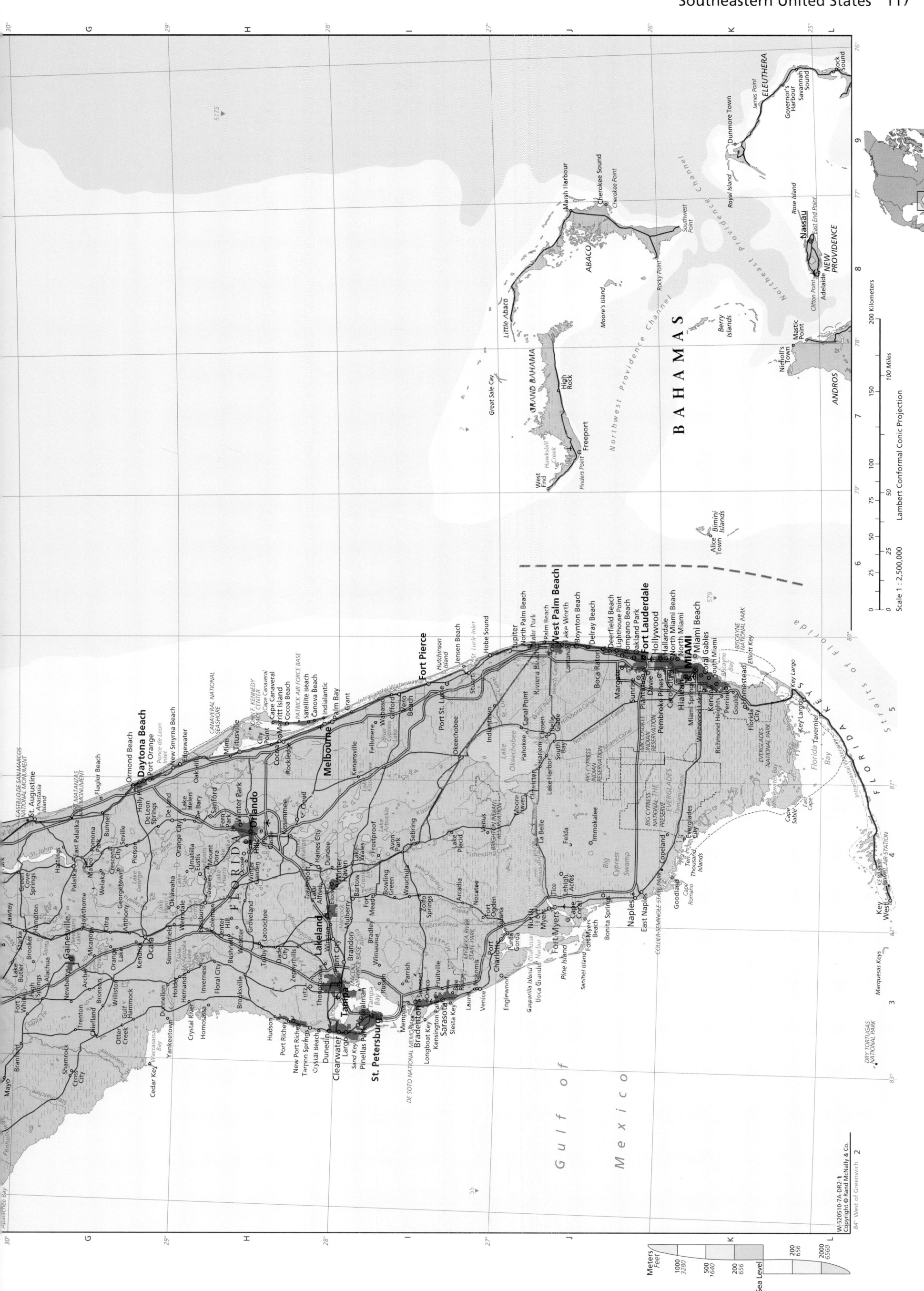

W:520510-7A-DR2-1
Copyright © Rand McNally & Co.

Lambert Conformal Conic Projection

Scale 1 : 2,500,000

84°   West of Greenwich   2

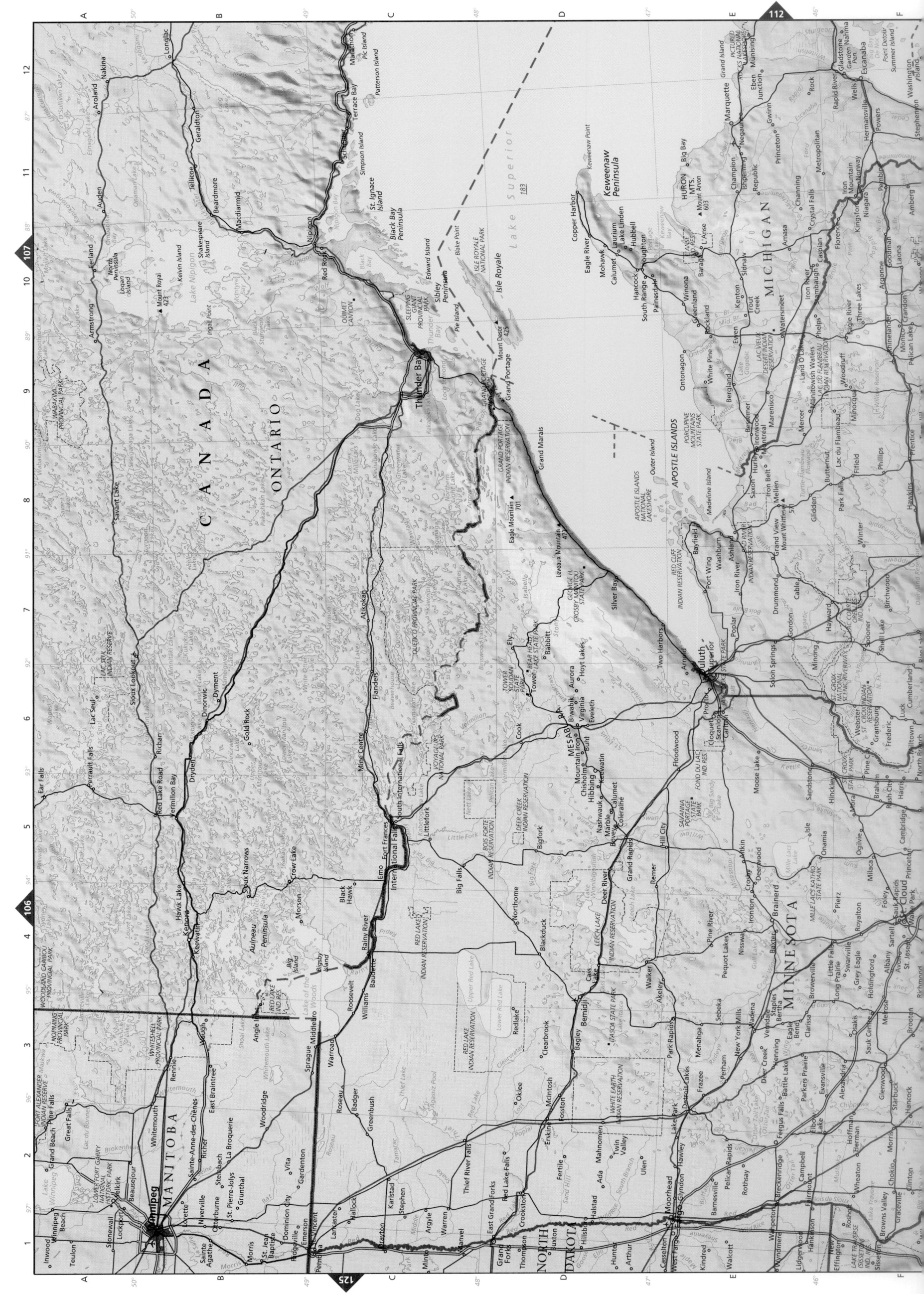

112
107
106
125

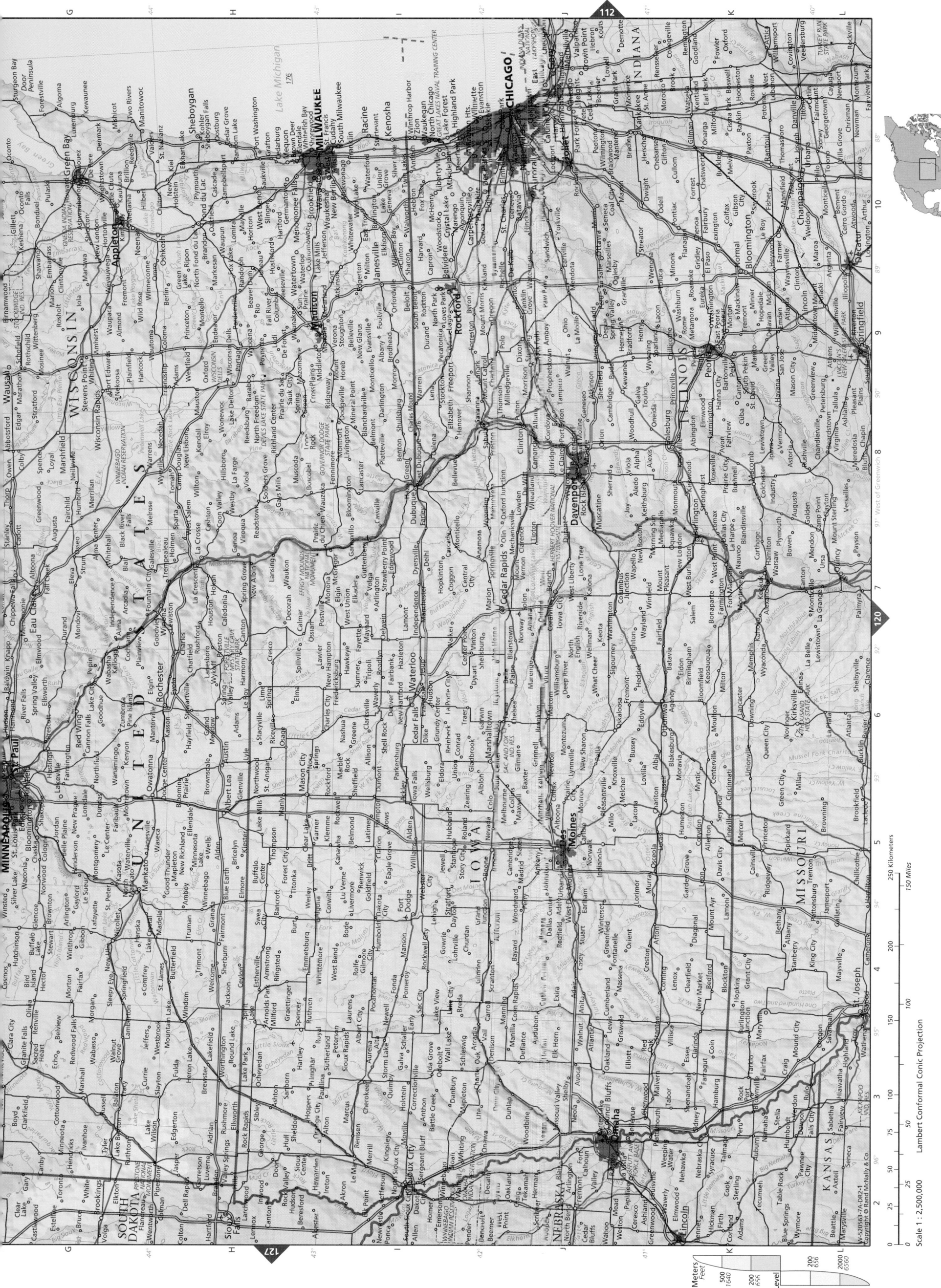

W-52D5G37A-DR2-1
Copyright © Rand McNally & Co.

Scale 1 : 2,500,000

Lambert Conformal Conic Projection

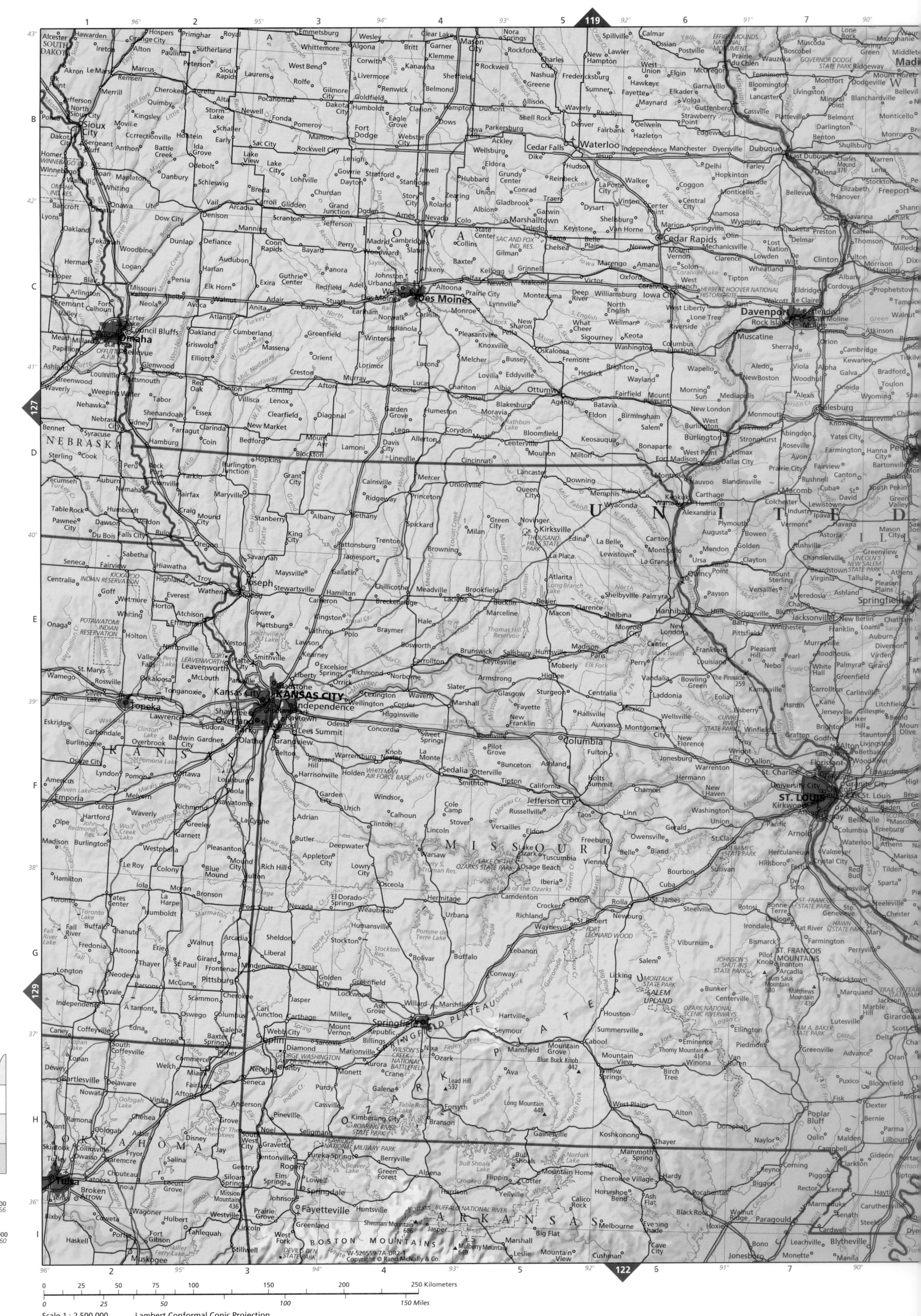

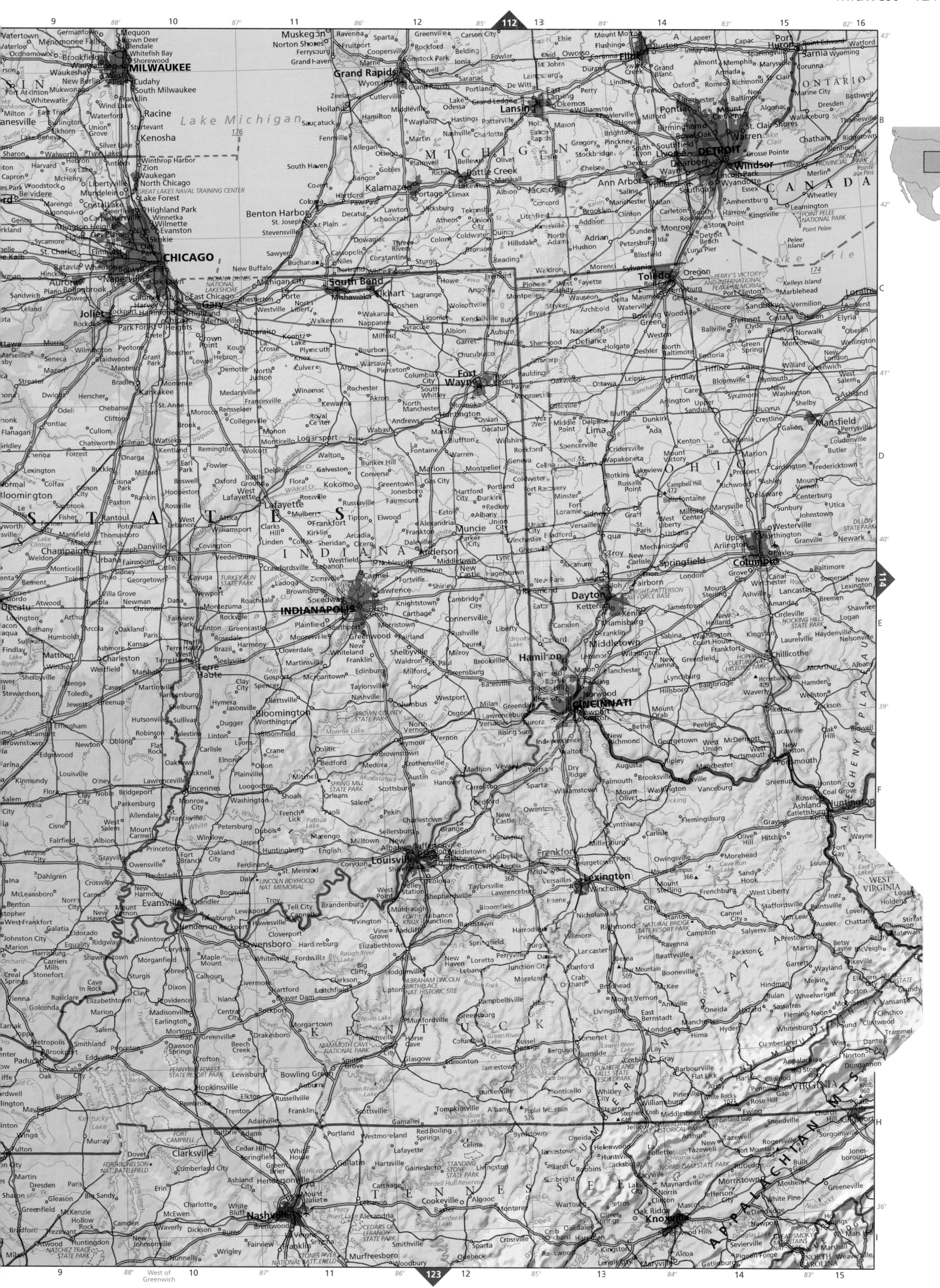

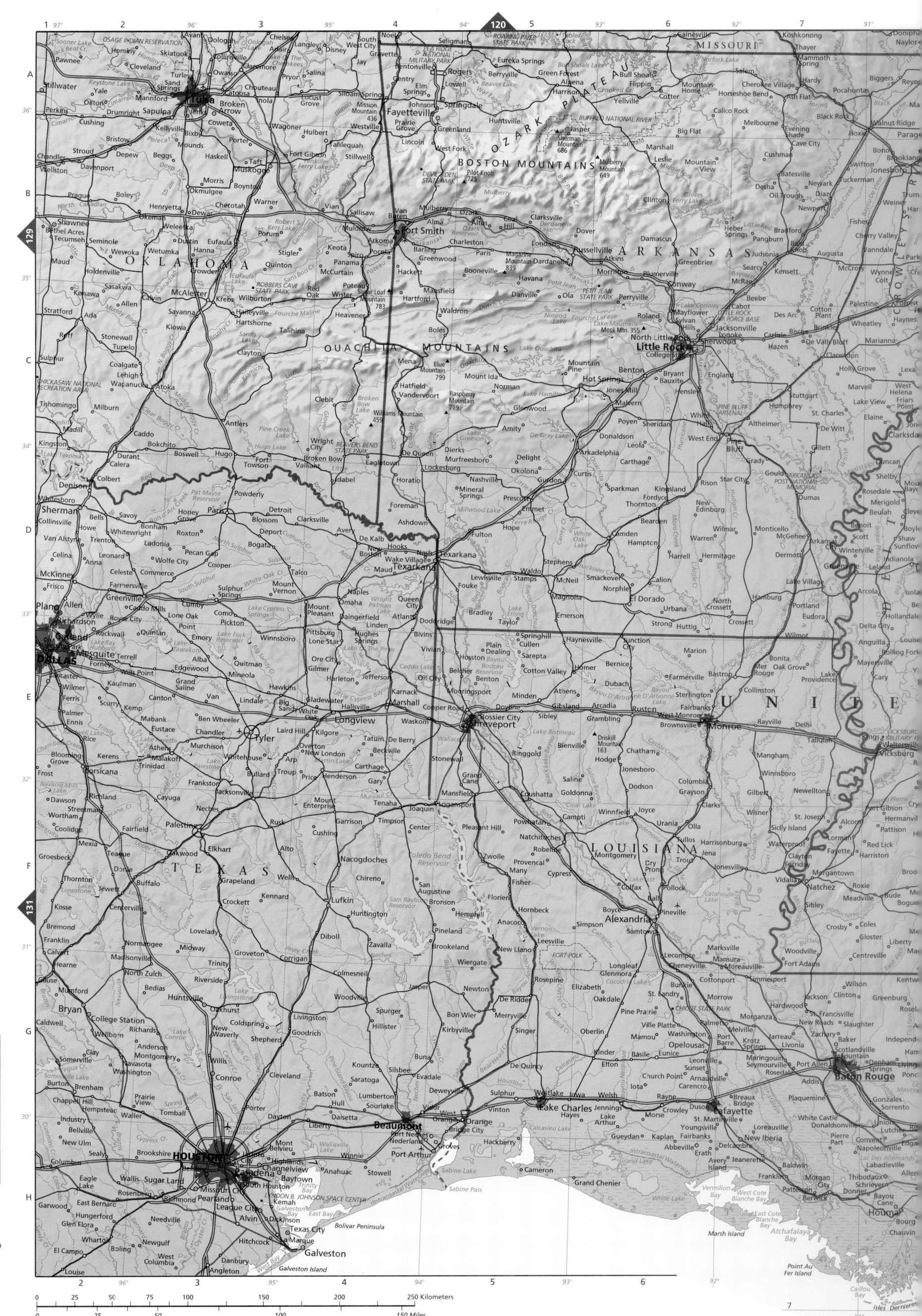

Meters
Feet

2000
6560

1000
3280

500
1640

200
656

Sea Level

200
656

2000
6560

0   25   50   75   100   150   200   250 Kilometers

0   25   50   100   150 Miles

Scale 1 : 2,500,000   Lambert Conformal Conic Projection

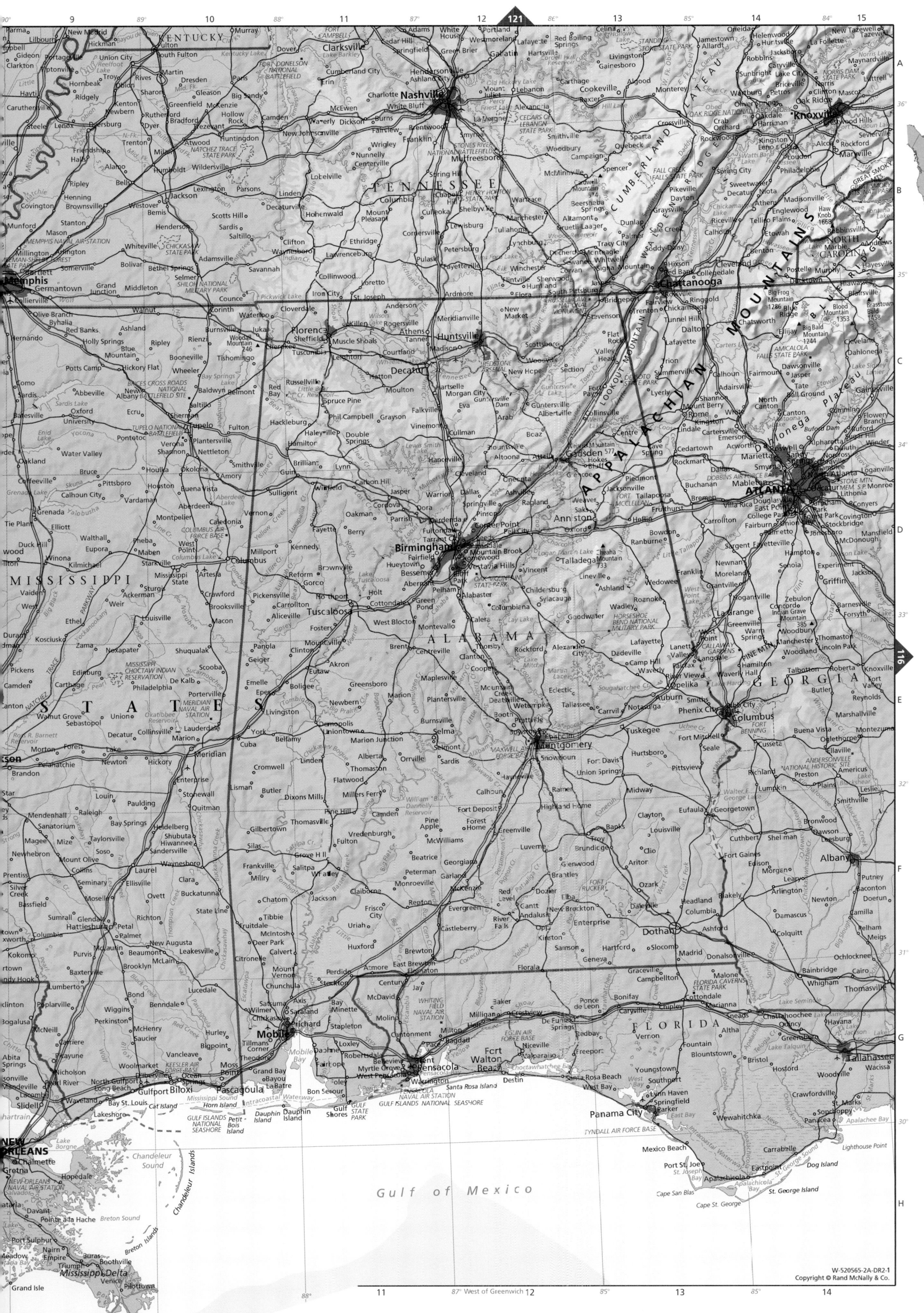

W-520565-2A-DR2-1
Copyright © Rand McNally & Co.

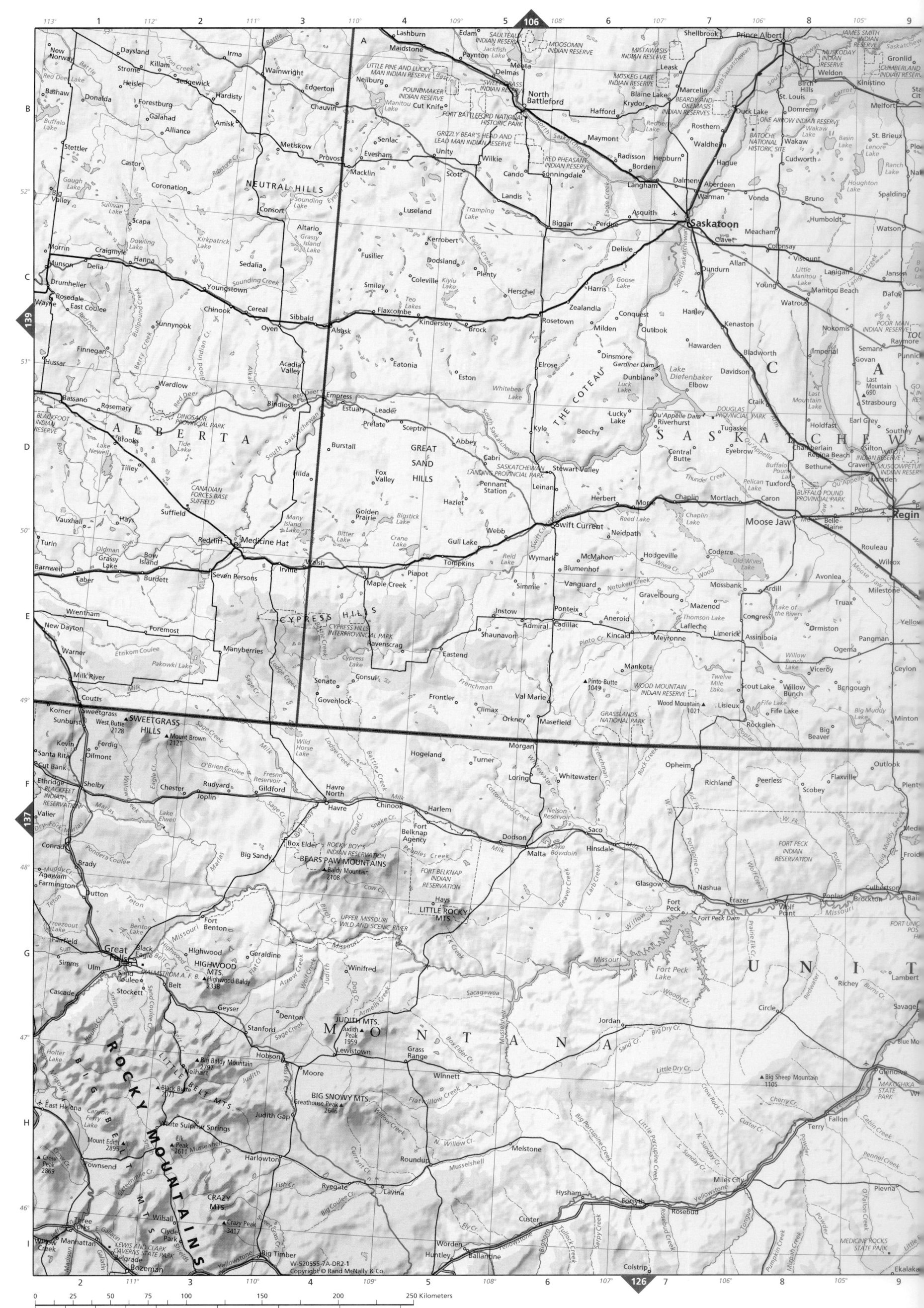

Scale 1 : 2,500,000   Lambert Conformal Conic Projection

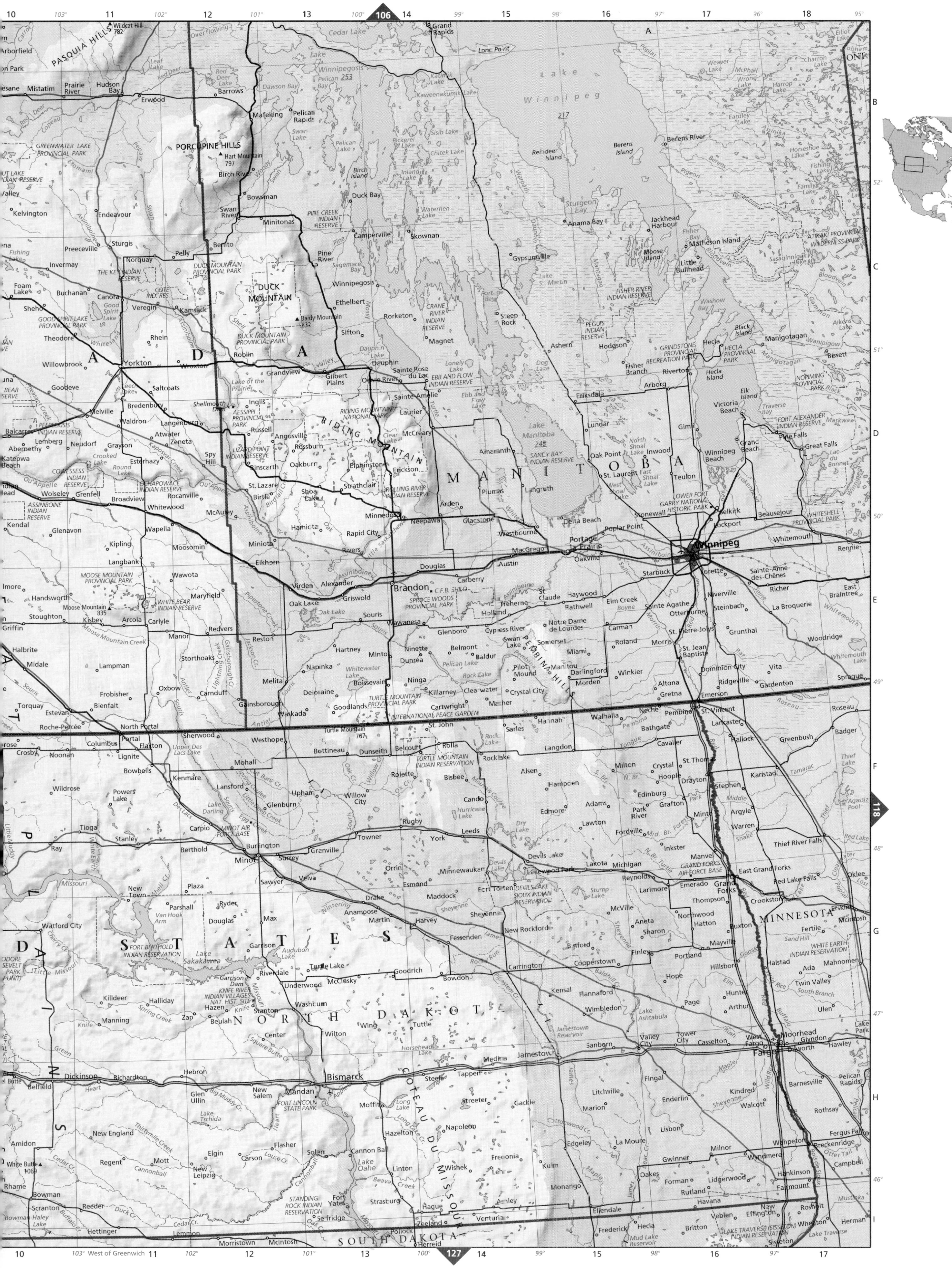

MANITOBA

Lake Winnipeg

SASKATCHEWAN

NORTH DAKOTA

SOUTH DAKOTA

MINNESOTA

UNITED STATES

CANADA

Winnipeg

Brandon

Bismarck

Fargo

Grand Forks

Minot

Moorhead

Dickinson

PASQUIA HILLS

PORCUPINE HILLS

DUCK MOUNTAIN

RIDING MOUNTAIN NATIONAL PARK

MOOSE MOUNTAIN PROVINCIAL PARK

TURTLE MOUNTAIN PROVINCIAL PARK

GREENWATER LAKE PROVINCIAL PARK

DUCK MOUNTAIN PROVINCIAL PARK

HECLA PROVINCIAL PARK

GRINDSTONE PROVINCIAL RECREATION PARK

NOPIMING PROVINCIAL PARK

WHITESHELL PROVINCIAL PARK

ATIKAKI PROVINCIAL WILDERNESS PARK

SPRUCE WOODS PROVINCIAL PARK

THEODORE ROOSEVELT NATIONAL PARK

FORT BERTHOLD INDIAN RESERVATION

TURTLE MOUNTAIN INDIAN RESERVATION

DEVILS LAKE SIOUX INDIAN RESERVATION

STANDING ROCK INDIAN RESERVATION

LAKE TRAVERSE (SISSETON) INDIAN RESERVATION

WHITE EARTH INDIAN RESERVATION

PEMBINA HILLS

COTEAU DU MISSOURI

Lake Manitoba

Lake Winnipegosis

Lake Sakakawea

Lake Oahe

ONT.

Meters
Feet

6000	19680
4000	13120
3000	9840
2000	6560
1000	3280
500	1640
200	656
Sea Level	
200	656
2000	6560

0   25   50   75   100   150   200   250 Kilometers

0   25   50   100   150 Miles

Scale 1 : 2,500,000   Lambert Conformal Conic Projection

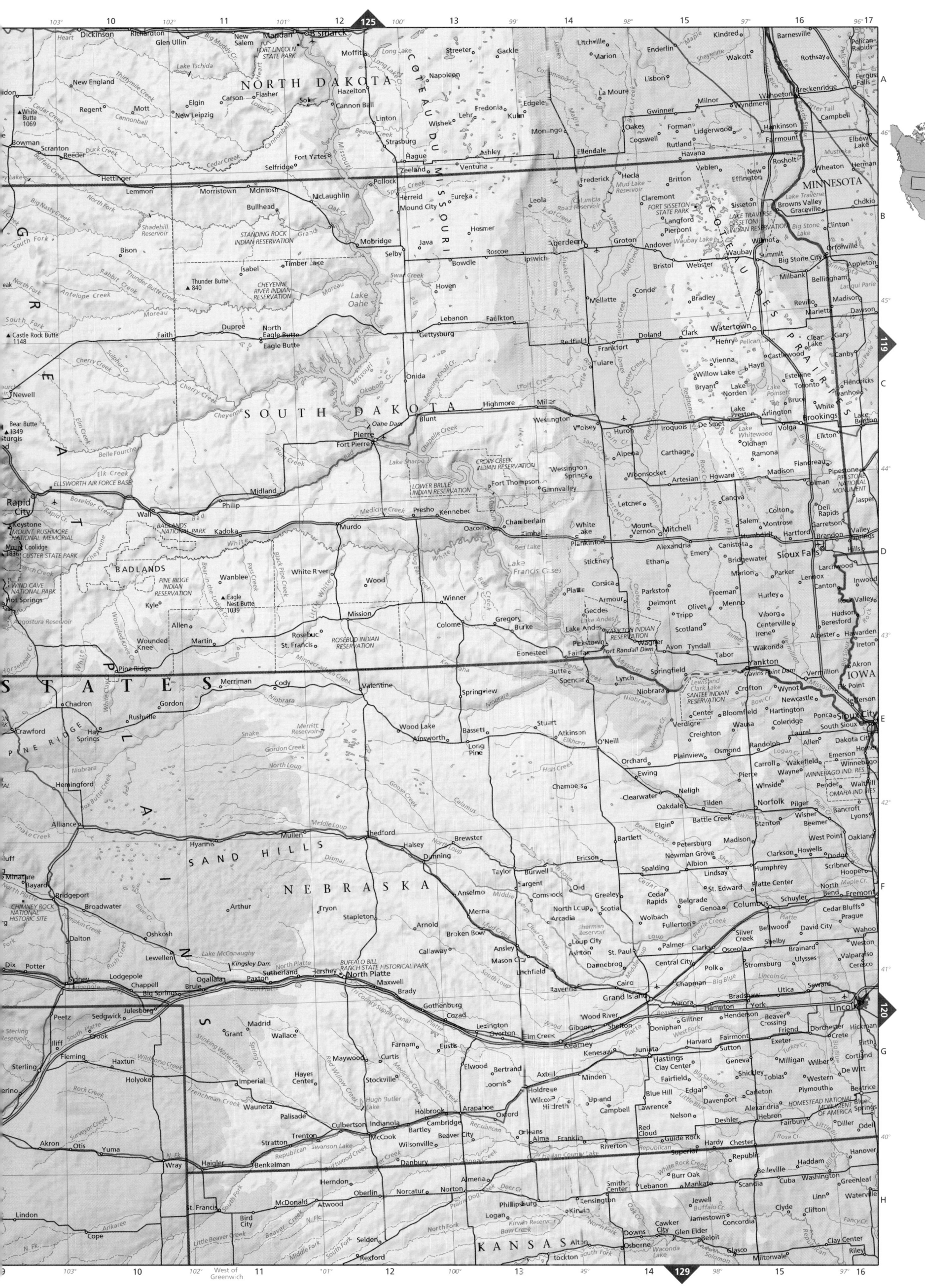

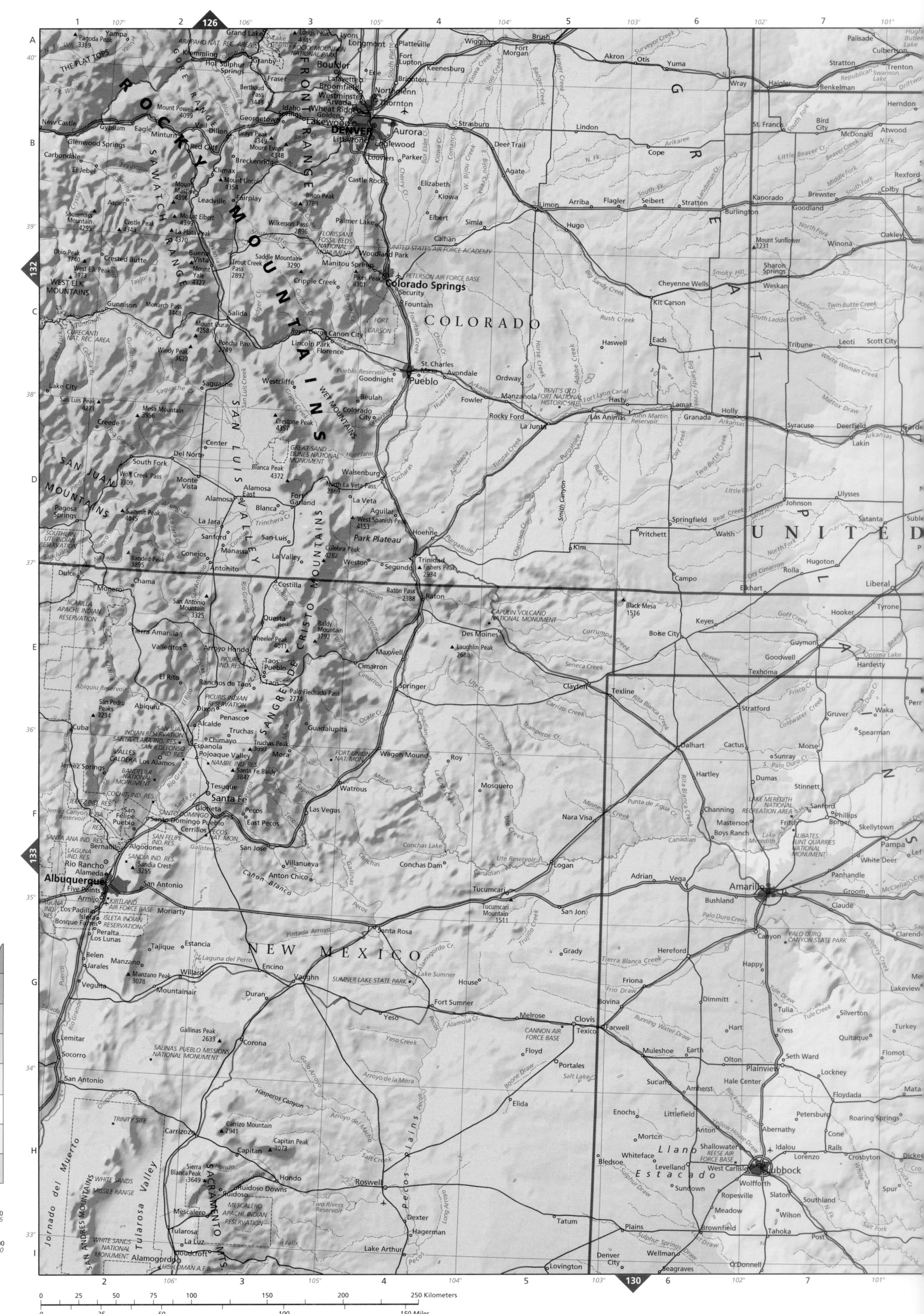

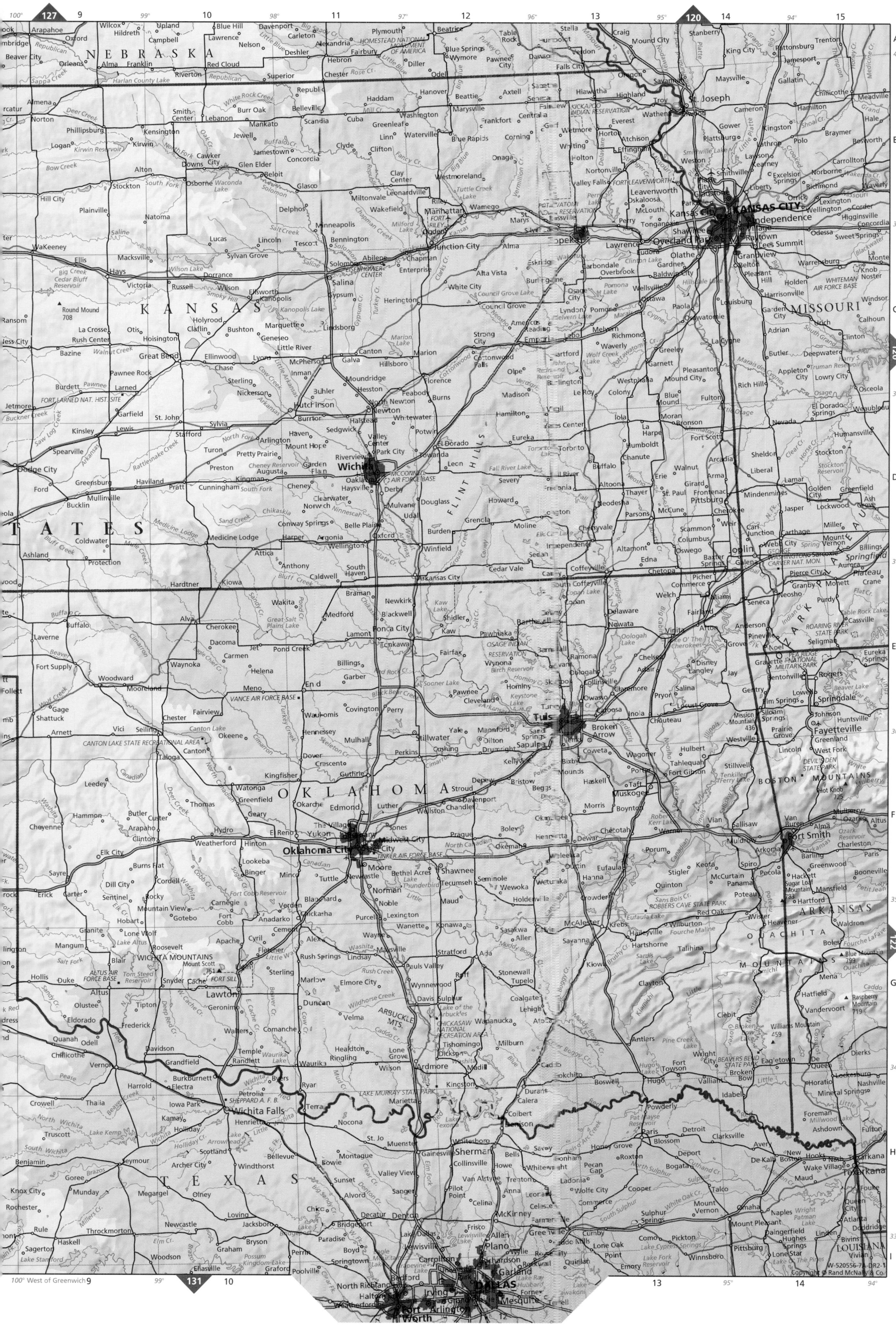

NEBRASKA

KANSAS

MISSOURI

OKLAHOMA

ARKANSAS

TEXAS

LOUISIANA

St. Joseph

KANSAS CITY

Independence

Overland Park

Topeka

Lawrence

Wichita

Tulsa

Broken Arrow

Oklahoma City

Norman

Fort Smith

Fayetteville

Springfield

Joplin

Lawton

Wichita Falls

Dallas

Fort Worth

Arlington

Plano

Garland

Mesquite

Irving

FLINT HILLS

OSAGE INDIAN RESERVATION

WICHITA MOUNTAINS

ARBUCKLE MTS.

OUACHITA MOUNTAINS

BOSTON MOUNTAINS

OZARK

FORT SILL

ALTUS AIR FORCE BASE

SHEPPARD A.F.B.

VANCE AIR FORCE BASE

McCONNELL AIR FORCE BASE

TINKER AIR FORCE BASE

WHITEMAN AIR FORCE BASE

FORT RILEY

FORT LEAVENWORTH

EISENHOWER CENTER

FORT LARNED NAT. HIST. SITE

HOMESTEAD NATIONAL MONUMENT OF AMERICA

CHICKASAW NATIONAL RECREATION AREA

LAKE MURRAY STATE PARK

ROBBERS CAVE STATE PARK

BEAVERS BEND STATE PARK

ROARING RIVER STATE PARK

DEVIL'S DEN STATE PARK

PEA RIDGE NATIONAL MILITARY PARK

GEORGE WASHINGTON CARVER NAT. MON.

CANTON LAKE STATE RECREATIONAL AREA

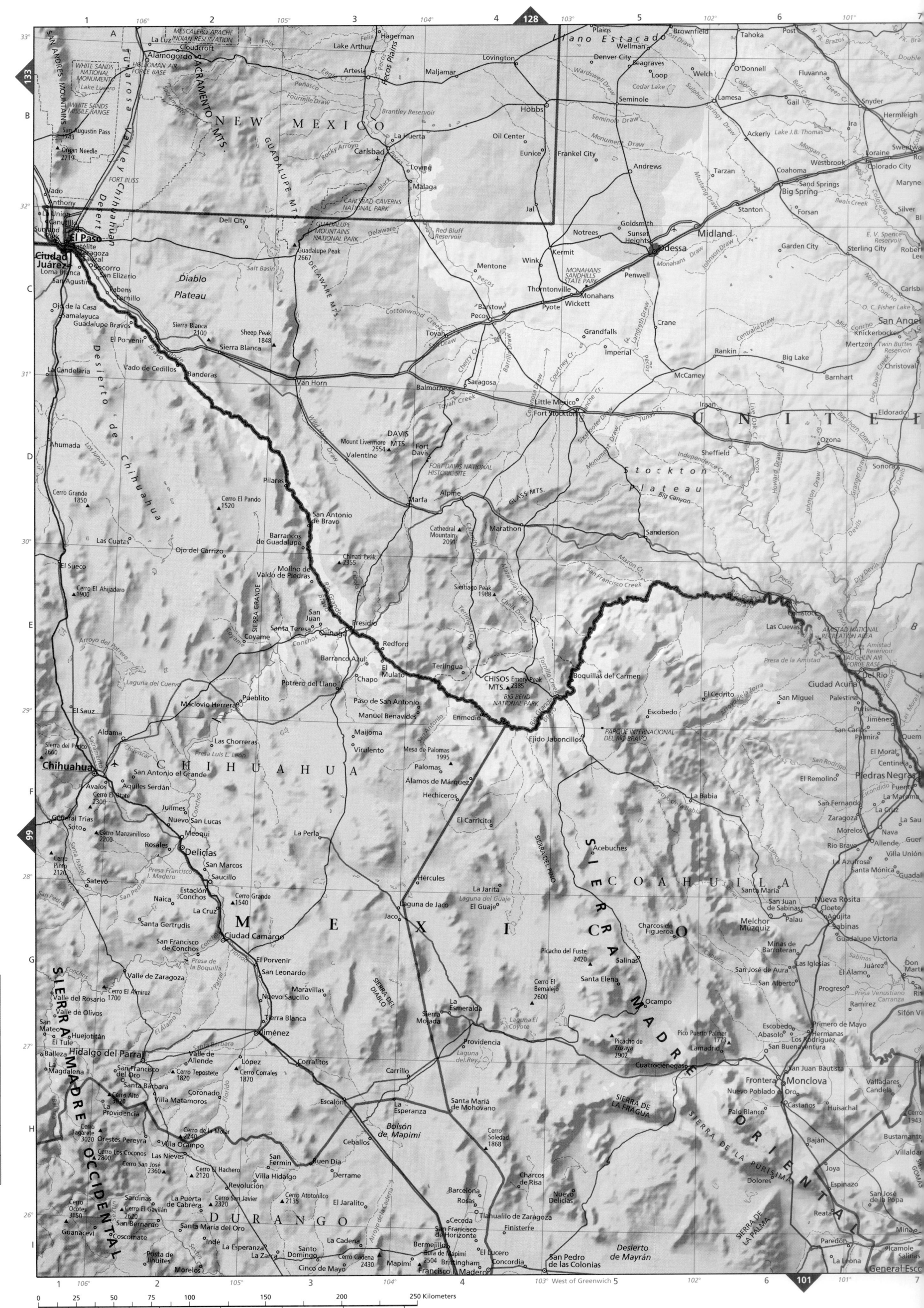

Scale 1 : 2,500,000   Lambert Conformal Conic Projection

Gulf of Mexico

LOUISIANA

TEXAS

TAMAULIPAS

EDWARDS PLATEAU

NUECES PLAINS

W-520564-7A-DR2-1
Copyright © Rand McNally & Co.

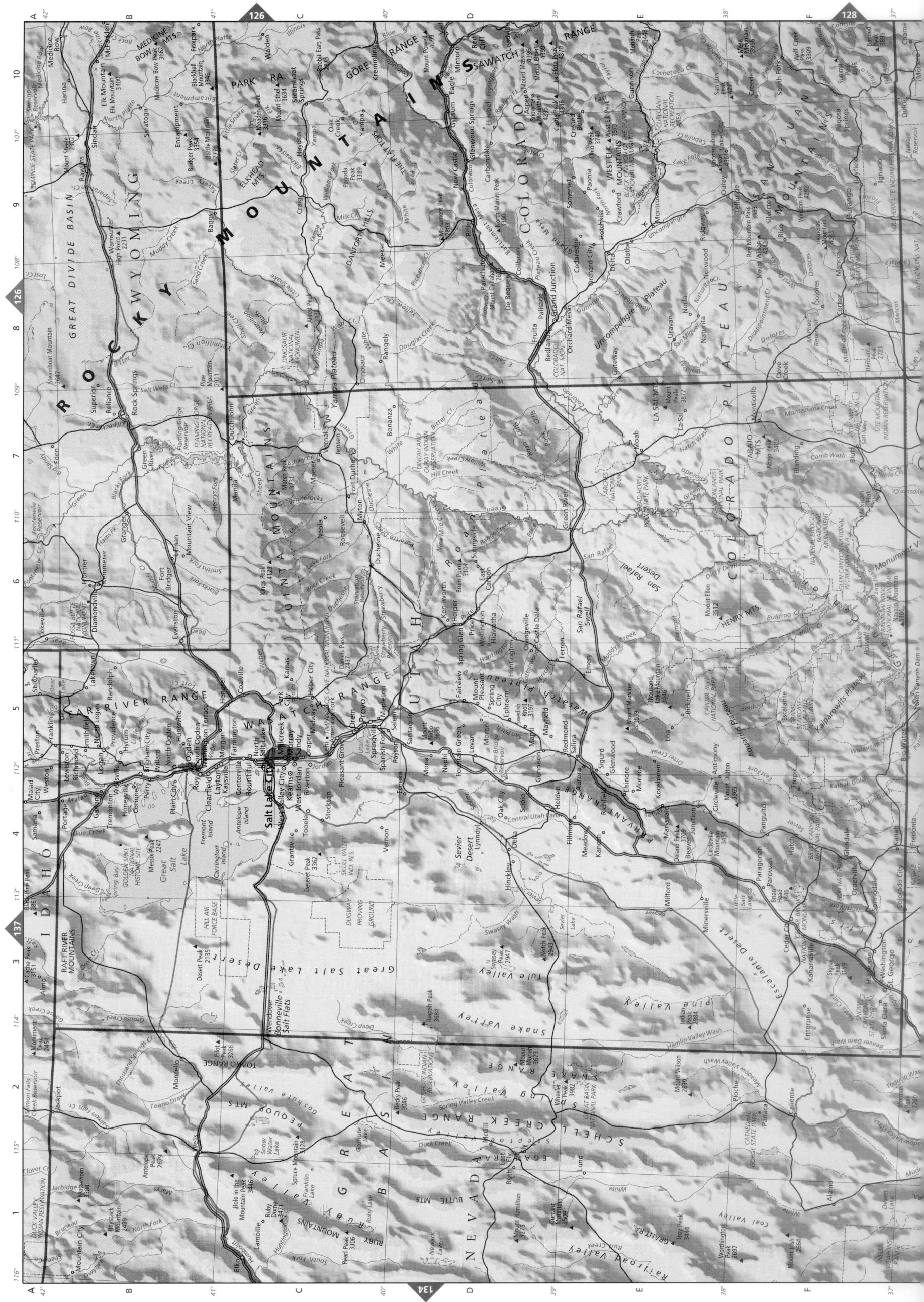

Scale 1 : 2,500,000

Lambert Conformal Conic Projection

W32h0557 A0R1 1
Copyright Rand McNally & Co.

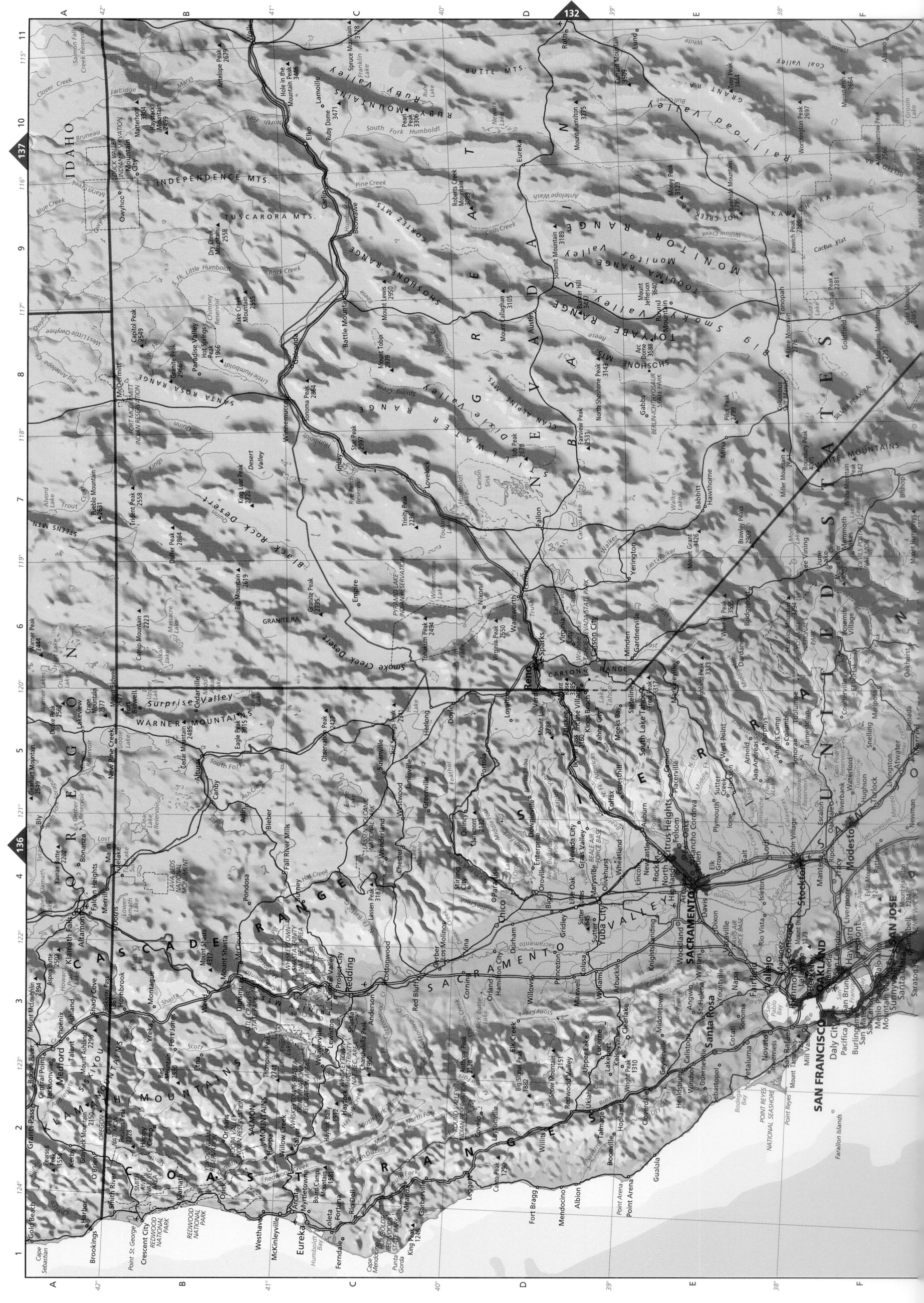

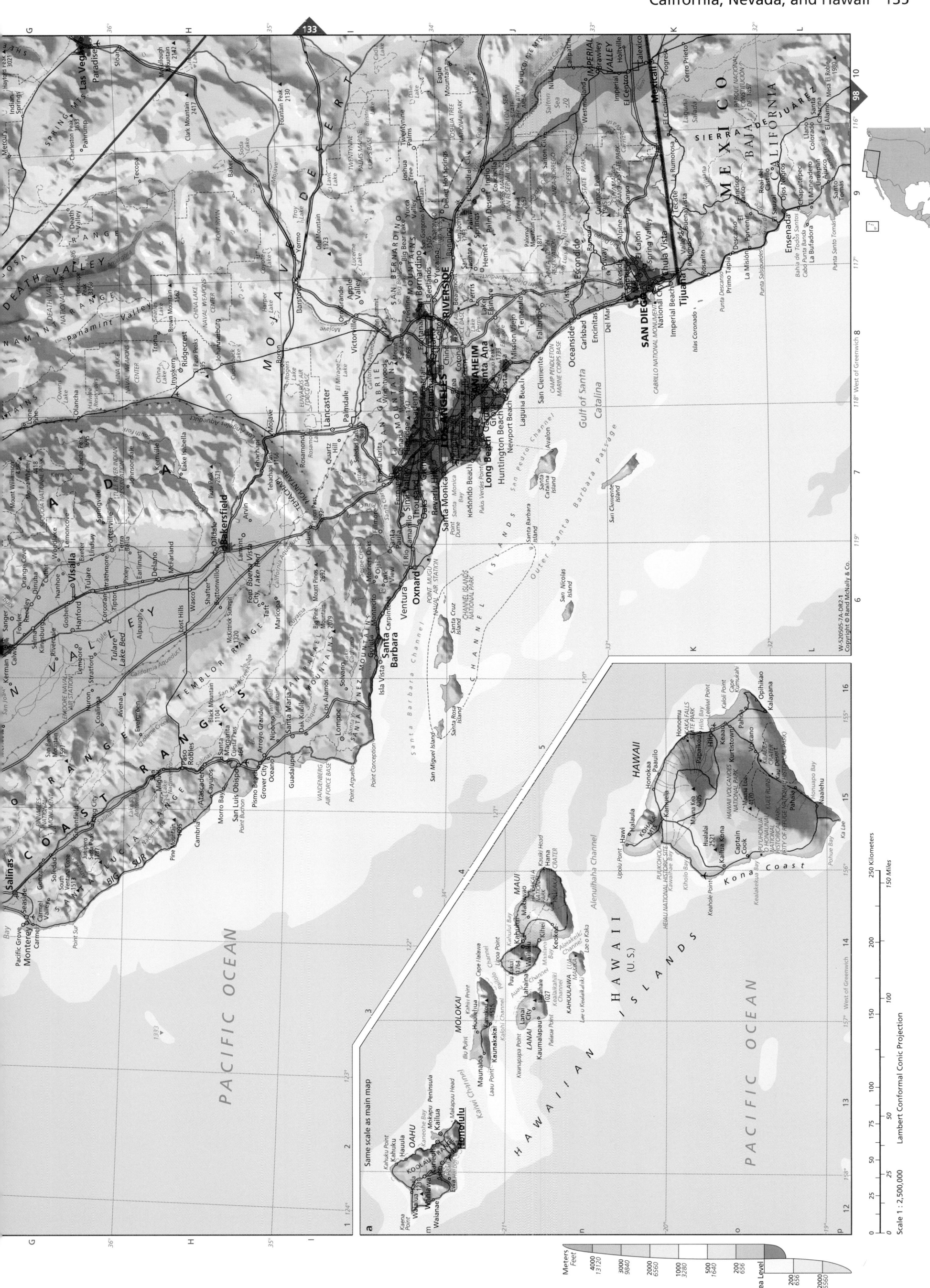

Meters Feet
4000 13120
3000 9840
2000 6560
1000 3280
500 1640
200 656
Sea Level
200 656
2000 6560

Scale 1 : 2,500,000
Lambert Conformal Conic Projection

250 Kilometers
150 Miles

W-520505-7A-DR2,1
Copyright © Rand McNally & Co.

Same scale as main map

PACIFIC OCEAN

BRITISH COLUMBIA

VANCOUVER ISLAND

VANCOUVER

Meters Feet
4000 13120
3000 9840
2000 6560
1000 3280
500 1640
200 656
Sea Level
200 656
2000 6560

0 25 50 75 100 150 200 250 Kilometers
0 25 50 100 150 Miles

Scale 1 : 2,500,000   Lambert Conformal Conic Projection

W-520299-7A-DR2-1
Copyright © Rand McNally & Co.

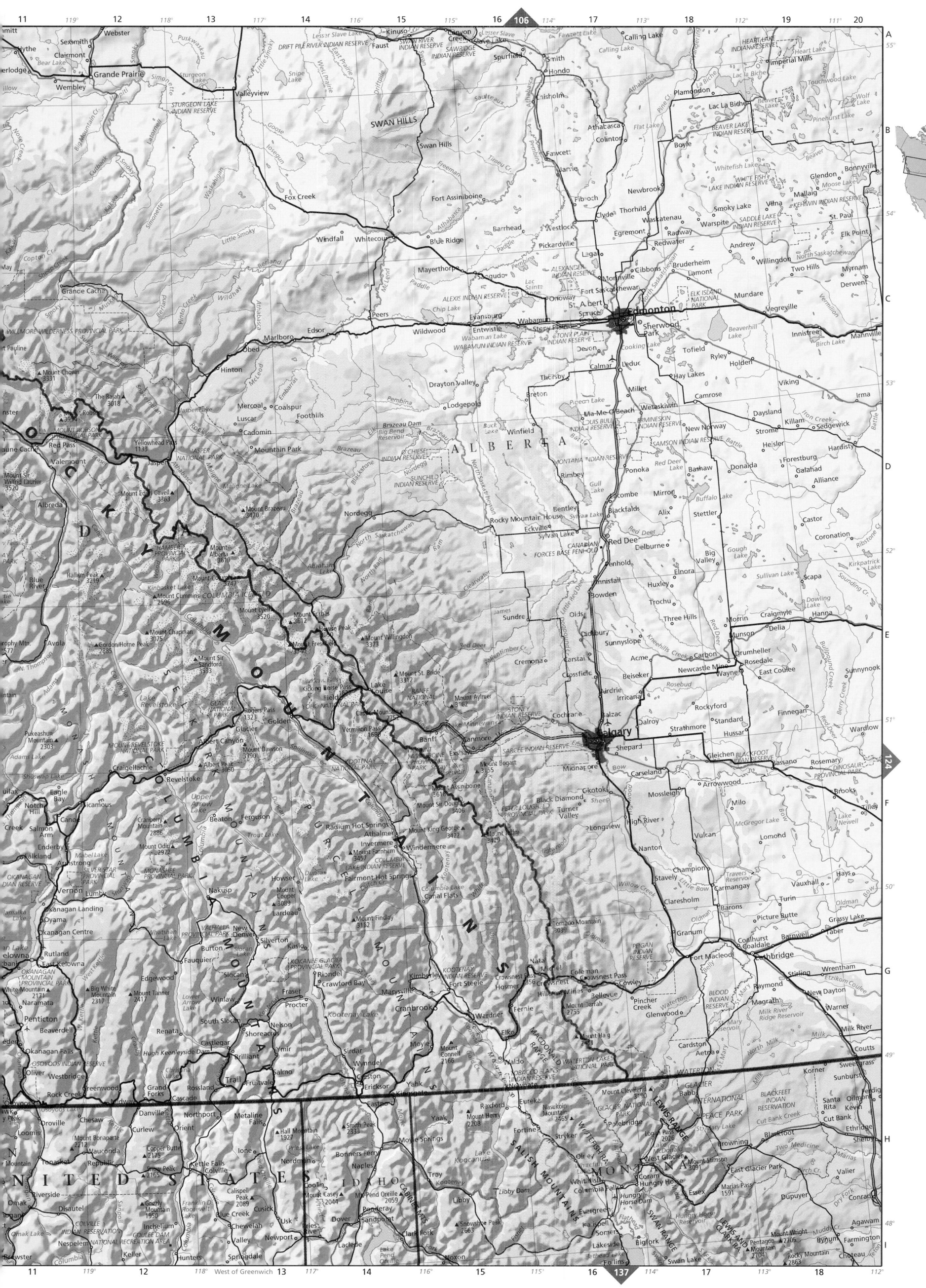

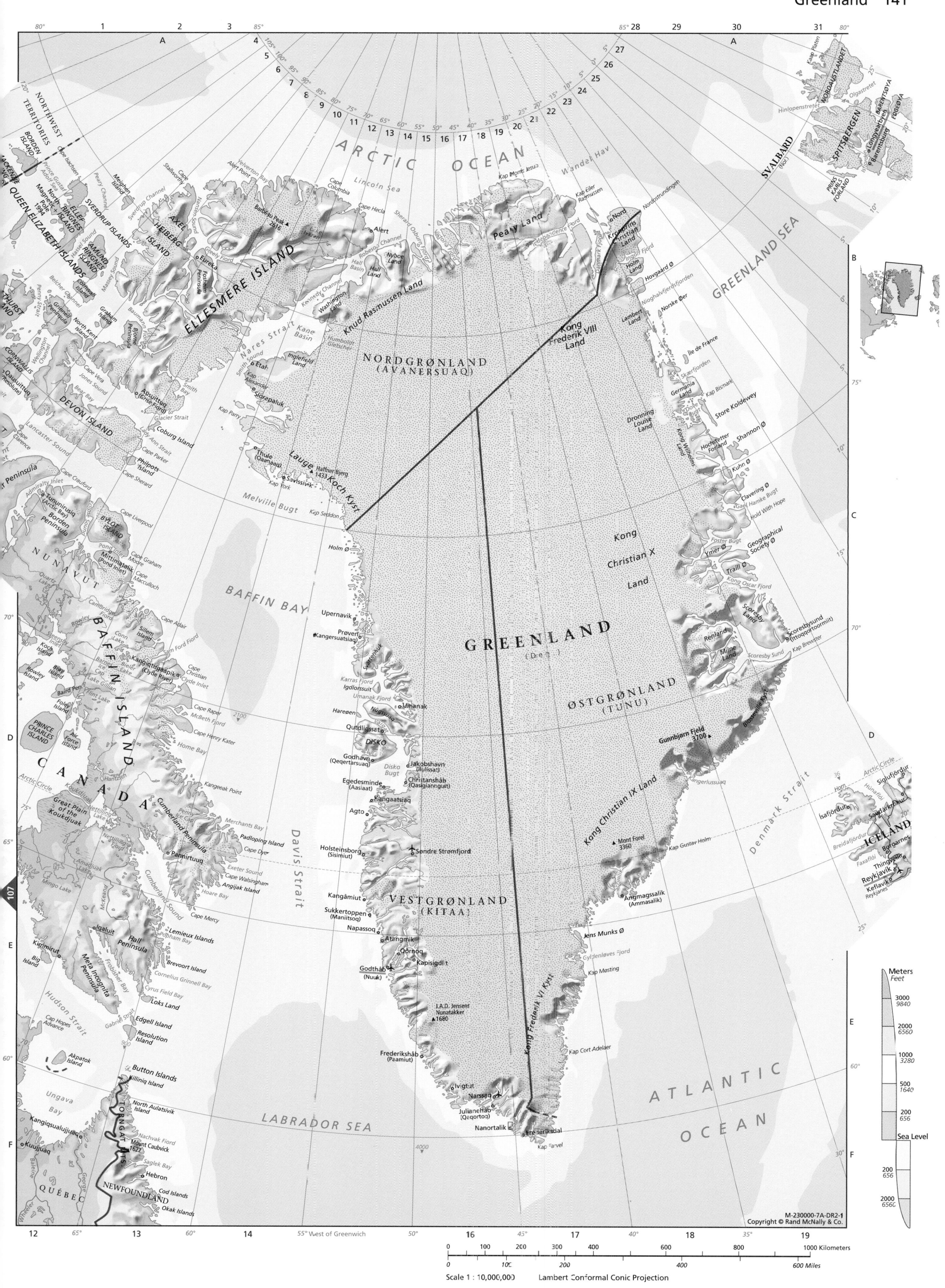

ARCTIC OCEAN

NORTHWEST
TERRITORIES

QUEEN ELIZABETH ISLANDS

ELLESMERE ISLAND

SVALBARD
(Nor.)

SPITSBERGEN

GREENLAND SEA

DEVON ISLAND

NORDGRØNLAND
(AVANERSUAQ)

Kong
Frederik VIII
Land

BAFFIN BAY

NUNAVUT

Kong
Christian X
Land

GREENLAND
(Den.)

BAFFIN ISLAND

CANADA

ØSTGRØNLAND
(TUNU)

Gunnbjørn Field 3700

Davis Strait

DISKO

Kong Christian IX Land

Mont Forel
3360

Denmark Strait

ICELAND

Reykjavik
Keflavik

VESTGRØNLAND
(KITAA)

Jens Munks Ø

Godthåb
(Nuuk)

J.A.D. Jensen
Nunatakker
1680

Kong Frederik VI Kyst

ATLANTIC

Frederikshåb
(Paamiut)

Ivigtut
Narssaq
Julianehåb
(Qeqortoq)
Nanortalik
Kap Farvel

OCEAN

LABRADOR SEA

HUDSON STRAIT

Ungava Bay

QUÉBEC

NEWFOUNDLAND

Meters
Feet

3000
9840

2000
6560

1000
3280

500
1640

200
656

Sea Level

200
656

2000
6560

M-230000-7A-DR2-1
Copyright © Rand McNally & Co.

0   100 200 300 400   600   800   1000 Kilometers
0   100   200   400   600 Miles
Scale 1 : 10,000,000   Lambert Conformal Conic Projection

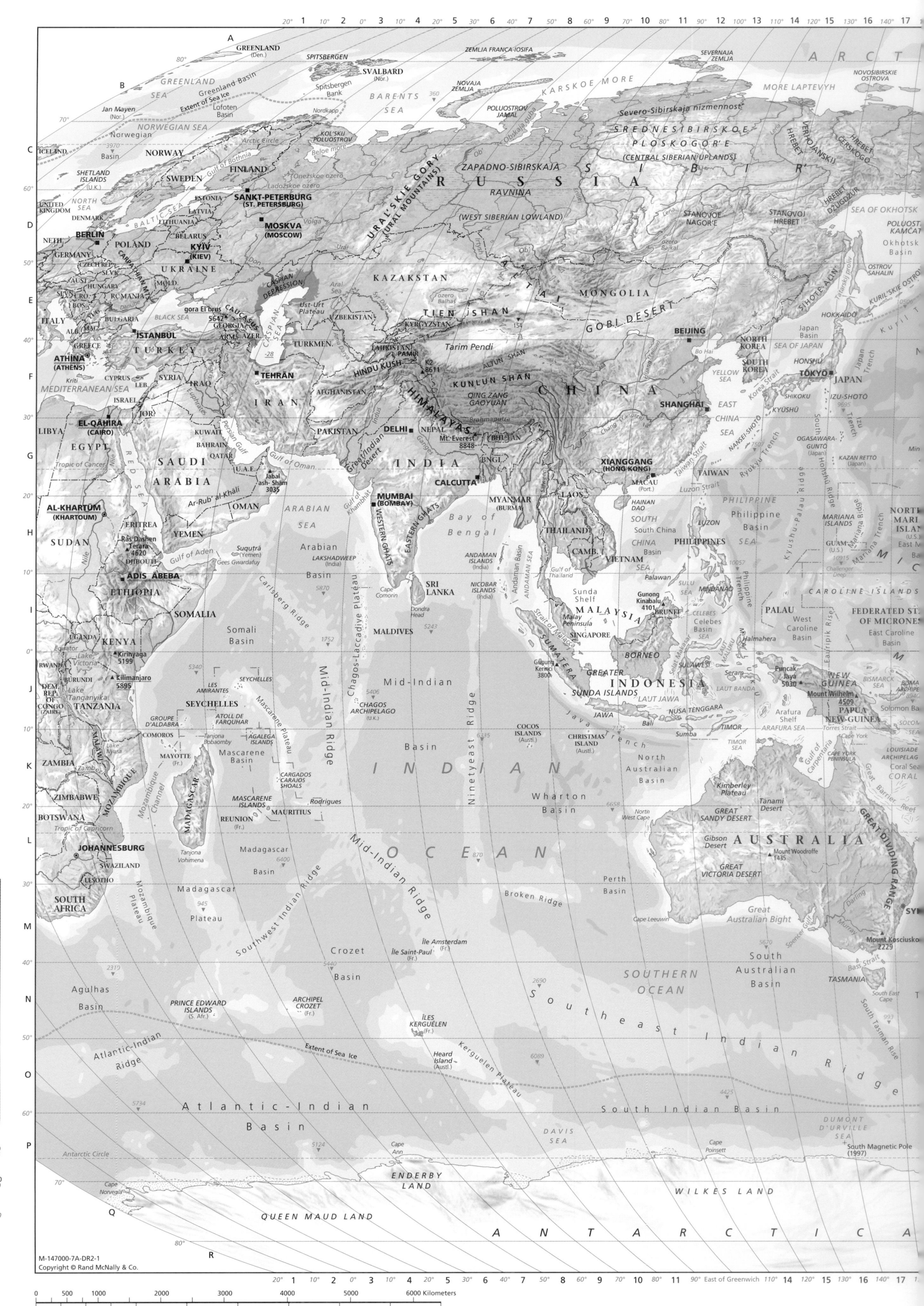

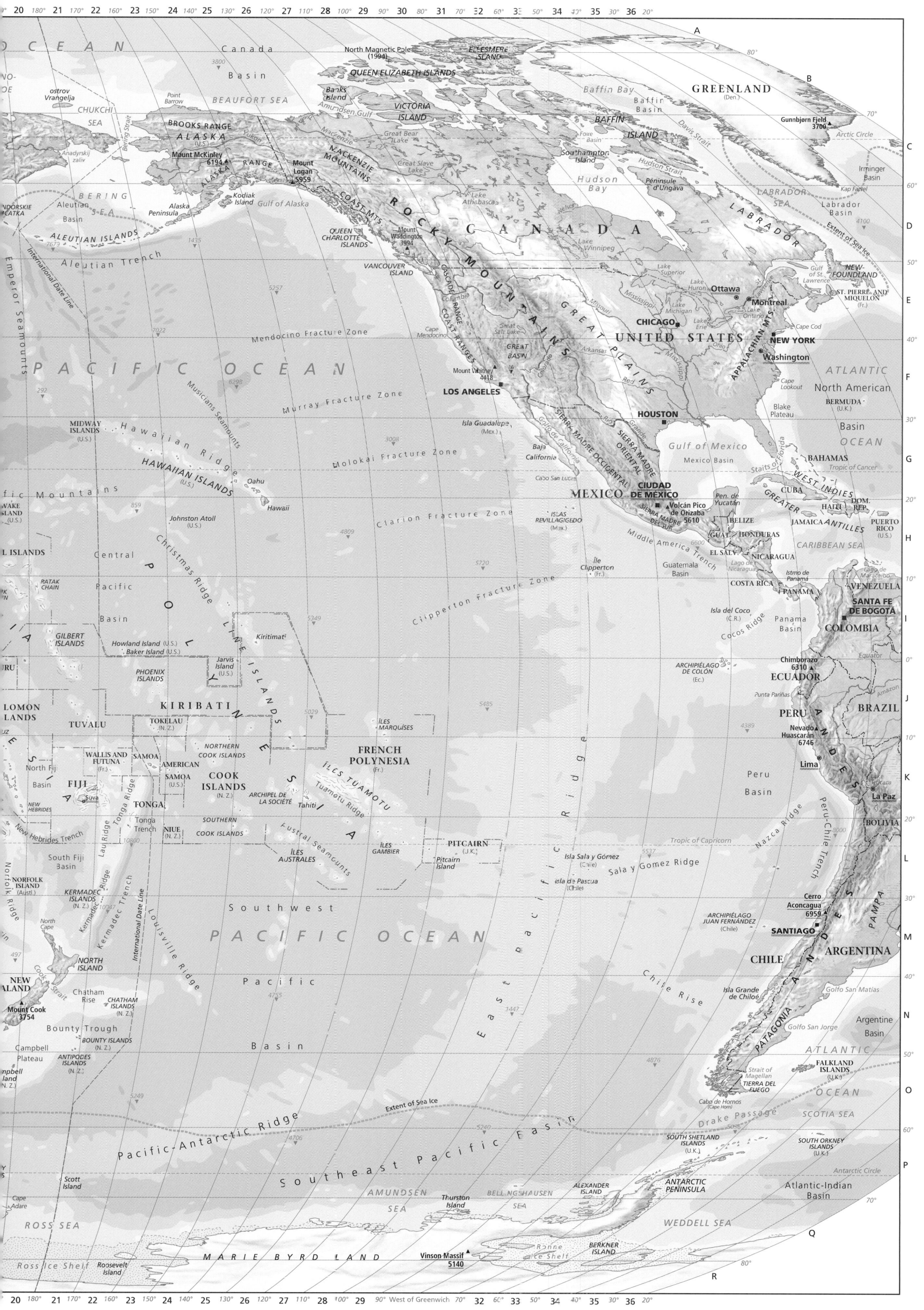

ATLANTIC OCEAN

North America / Greenland / Arctic

North Magnetic Pole (1994)
ELLESMERE ISLAND
QUEEN ELIZABETH ISLANDS
GREENLAND (Den.)
Baffin Bay
Baffin Basin
SPITSBERGEN
SVALBARD (Norway)
ZEMLJA FRANCA-IOSIFA
NOVAJA ZEMLJA
GREENLAND SEA
BARENTS SEA
VICTORIA ISLAND
Arctic Circle
Southampton Island
BAFFIN ISLAND
Foxe Basin
Davis Strait
Greenland Basin
Jan Mayen (Norway)
NORWEGIAN SEA
Extent of Sea Ice
Kol'skij poluostrov
360
Hudson Strait
Kap Farvel
Gunnbjørn Fjeld 3700
Kap Brewster
Denmark Strait
Norwegian Basin
3970
Nordkapp
Beloe More
Hudson Bay
Péninsule d'Ungava
Irminger Basin
ICELAND
3008
Reykjanes Ridge
FAROE ISLANDS (Den.)
SHETLAND ISLANDS (U.K.)
SWEDEN
FINLAND
SANKT-PETERBURG (ST. PETERSBURG)
RUSSIA
Nelson
CANADA
Lake Winnipeg
Labrador Sea
Iceland Basin
Rockall Rise
NORWAY
Gulf of Bothnia
Volga
MOSKVA (MOSCOW)
Lake Superior
Albany
Labrador Basin
Rockall Rise
NORTH SEA
DENMARK
ESTONIA
LATVIA
LITHUANIA
BELARUS
Ottawa
NEWFOUNDLAND
West European Basin
IRELAND
UNITED KINGDOM
LONDON
NETH.
GERMANY
BERLIN
POLAND
CZECH REP.
UKRAINE
Lake Huron
Lake Ontario
Montreal
ST. PIERRE AND MIQUELON (Fr.)
Mizen Head
Land's End
English Channel
PARIS
FRANCE
SWITZ.
AUS.
SLVK.
HUNGARY
MOLD.
ROMANIA
DON
CHICAGO
Lake Erie
Cape Cod
NEW YORK
Washington
Newfoundland Basin
6325
Bay of Biscay
Cabo de Fisterra
Mont Blanc 4807
PYRENEES
Corse
ITALY
YUG.
BULGARIA
BLACK SEA
GEORG.
UNITED STATES
APPALACHIAN MTS.
6309
ATLANTIC
Azores Plateau
AÇORES (AZORES) (Port.)
PORTUGAL
LISBOA
MADRID
SPAIN
ROMA
Sardegna
ISTANBUL
TURKEY
Cape Lookout
North American Basin
BERMUDA (U.K.)
Cabo de São Vicente
Strait of Gibraltar
EL DJAZAÏR (ALGIERS)
ATHINA (ATHENS)
CYPRUS
LEB.
ISRAEL
HOUSTON
Blake Plateau
Basin
4100
OCEAN
ARQUIPÉLAGO DA MADEIRA (MADEIRA ISLANDS) (Port.)
CASABLANCA
MOROCCO
Jebel Toubkal 4165
ATLAS MTS.
Tarābulus
MALTA
TUNISIA
MEDITERRANEAN SEA
Kriti
Khalij Surt
Tropic of Cancer
Mexico Basin
BAHAMAS
4689
ISLAS CANARIAS (CANARY ISLANDS) (Sp.)
WESTERN SAHARA
ALGERIA
LIBYA
EL-QÂHIRA (CAIRO)
EGYPT
CIUDAD DE MÉXICO
Straits of Florida
CUBA
DOM. REP.
6995
Canary Basin
AHAGGAR
MASSIF DE L'AIR
TIBESTI
Emi Koussi 3415
ENNEDI
AL-KHARTÛM (KHARTOUM)
MEXICO
PEN. DE YUCATÁN
BELIZE
JAMAICA
HAITI
PUERTO RICO (U.S.)
Puerto Rico Trench
8605
LESSER ANTILLES
SAHARA
MAURITANIA
MALI
NIGER
CHAD
Lake Chad
SUDAN

Central / South America / Africa

GUAT.
HONDURAS
GREATER ANTILLES
WEST INDIES
CAPE VERDE
DAKAR
Cap Vert
SENEGAL
THE GAMBIA
BURKINA FASO
NIGERIA
CENTRAL AFRICAN REPUBLIC
6600
EL SALV.
NICARAGUA
CARIBBEAN SEA
7292
GUINEA-BISSAU
GUINEA
CÔTE D'IVOIRE
GHANA
BENIN
COSTA RICA
Lago de Nicaragua
Venezuelan Basin
TRINIDAD AND TOBAGO
Cape Verde Basin
SIERRA LEONE
LIBERIA
LAGOS
ABIDJAN
CAMEROON
Ístmo de Panamá
CARACAS
Guiana Basin
6363
Gulf of Guinea
EQUAT. GUIN.
GABON
UGANDA
Isla del Coco (C.R.)
PANAMA
VENEZUELA
GUYANA
SURINAME
FRENCH GUIANA
SÃO TOMÉ AND PRINCIPE
DEM. REP. OF THE CONGO (ZAIRE)
RWANDA
BURUNDI
Cocos Ridge
SANTA FE DE BOGOTÁ
COLOMBIA
LLANOS
Lago de Maracaibo
7728
Romanche Gap
Guinea Basin
Congo
KINSHASA
Panama Basin
Equator
ECUADOR
Chimborazo 6310
SELVAS
BRAZIL
Negro
Amazon
5759
Cabo de São Roque
Ascension (St. Hel.)
84
ARCHIPIÉLAGO DE COLÓN (Ec.)
Punta Pariñas
Amazon
Madeira
RECIFE
ANGOLA
Nevado Huascarán 6746
PERU
Tapajós
Tocantins
São Francisco
Salvador
ATLANTIC
Angola Basin
ZAMBIA
4389
Lima
La Paz
PLANALTO DO MATO GROSSO
BRASÍLIA
ST. HELENA (U.K.)
Brazil Basin
6050
ZIMBABWE
Peru Basin
ANDES
BOLIVIA
Paraná
Paraguay
SÃO PAULO
RIO DE JANEIRO
Cabo Frio
Trindade (Brazil)
Ilhas Martin Vaz (Brazil)
Mid-Atlantic Ridge
NAMIBIA
NAMIB DESERT
BOTSWANA
Nazca Ridge
Asunción
Lagoa dos Patos
5764
OCEAN
JOHANNESBURG
SOUTH AFRICA
PERU-CHILE TRENCH
Tropic of Capricorn
Cerro Aconcagua 6959
PAMPA
URUGUAY
Río de la Plata
Bromley Plateau
Cape Basin
CAPE TOWN (KAAPSTAD)
LESOTHO
SWAZ.

Southern Ocean

ARCHIPIÉLAGO JUAN FERNÁNDEZ (Chile)
SANTIAGO
BUENOS AIRES
TRISTAN DA CUNHA GROUP (St. Hel.)
Cape of Good Hope
Agulhas Basin
2310
CHILE
ARGENTINA
Argentine Basin
Gough Island (St. Hel.)
411
1555
Chile Rise
Isla Grande de Chiloé
Golfo San Matías
Mid-Atlantic Ridge
PRINCE EDWARD ISLANDS (S. Afr.)
INDIAN OCEAN
4876
Golfo San Jorge
6212
Extent of Sea Ice
Atlantic-Indian Ridge
PACIFIC
PATAGONIA
Strait of Magellan
FALKLAND ISLANDS (U.K.)
South Georgia (U.K.)
8325
Bouvetøya (Norway)
5734
Southeast Pacific Basin
Cabo de Hornos (Cape Horn)
TIERRA DEL FUEGO
Scotia Ridge
SCOTIA SEA
SOUTH SANDWICH ISLANDS (U.K.)
South Sandwich Trench
Atlantic-Indian Basin
5124
5240
Drake Passage
SOUTH SHETLAND ISLANDS (U.K.)
SOUTH ORKNEY ISLANDS (U.K.)
5587
Pacific Basin
5036
BELLINGSHAUSEN
Antarctic Circle
ANTARCTIC PENINSULA
WEDDELL SEA
QUEEN MAUD LAND
MARIE BYRD LAND
AMUNDSEN SEA
Thurston Island
ALEXANDER ISLAND
Cape Norvegia
BERKNER ISLAND
Vinson Massif 5140
Ronne Ice Shelf
ANTARCTICA

Meters / Feet
6000 / 19680
4000 / 13120
3000 / 9840
2000 / 6560
1000 / 3280
500 / 1640
200 / 656
Sea Level
200 / 656
2000 / 6560
4000 / 13120
6000 / 19680

0 800 1600 3200 4800 6400 Kilometers
0 400 800 1200 1600 2400 3200 4000 Miles
Scale 1 : 60,000,000   Robinson Projection

Index to World Reference Maps

Introduction to the Index

This index includes in a single alphabetical list approximately 54,000 names of places and geographical features that appear on the reference maps. Each name is followed by the name of the country or continent in which it is located, an alpha-numeric map reference key, and a page reference.

Names The names of cities and towns appear in the index in regular type. The names of all other features appear in *italics*, followed by descriptive terms (hill, mtn., state) to indicate their nature.

Abbreviations of names on the maps have been standardized as much as possible. Names that are abbreviated on the maps are generally spelled out in full in the index.

Country names and names of features that extend beyond the boundaries of one country are followed by the name of the continent in which each is located. Country designations follow the names of all other places in the index. The locations of places in the United States, Canada, and the United Kingdom are further defined by abbreviations that indicate the state, province, or other political division in which each is located.

All abbreviations used in the index are defined in the List of Abbreviations to the right.

Alphabetization Names are alphabetized in the order of the letters of the English alphabet. Spanish *ll* and *ch*, for example, are not treated as distinct letters. Furthermore, diacritical marks are disregarded in alphabetization—German or Scandinavian *ä* or *ö* are treated as *a* or *o*.

The names of physical features may appear inverted, since they are always alphabetized under the proper, not the generic, part of the name, thus: "Gibraltar, Strait of". Otherwise every entry, whether consisting of one word or more, is alphabetized as a single continuous entity. "Lakeland", for example, appears after "La Crosse" and before "La Salle". Names beginning with articles (Le Havre, Den Helder, Al-Manāmah) are not inverted. Names beginning "St.", "Ste." and "Sainte" are alphabetized as though spelled "Saint".

In the case of identical names, towns are listed first, then political divisions, then physical features. Entries that are completely identical are listed alphabetically by country name.

Map Reference Keys and Page References The map reference keys and page references are found in the last two columns of each entry.

Each map reference key consists of a letter and number. The letters correspond to letters along the sides of the maps. Lowercase letters refer to inset maps. The numbers correspond to numbers that appear across the tops and bottoms of the maps.

Map reference keys for point features, such as cities and mountain peaks, indicate the locations of the symbols for these features. For other features, such as countries, mountain ranges, or rivers, the map reference keys indicate the locations of the names.

The page number generally refers to the main map for the country in which the feature is located. Page references for two-page maps always refer to the left-hand page.

List of Abbreviations

Ab., Can.	Alberta, Can.	Guad.	Guadeloupe	Ok., U.S.	Oklahoma, U.S.
Afg.	Afghanistan	Guat.	Guatemala	On., Can.	Ontario, Can.
Afr.	Africa	Guern.	Guernsey	Or., U.S.	Oregon, U.S.
Ak., U.S.	Alaska, U.S.	Gui.	Guinea	*p.*	pass
Al., U.S.	Alabama, U.S.	Gui.-B.	Guinea-Bissau	Pa., U.S.	Pennsylvania, U.S.
Alb.	Albania	Guy.	Guyana	Pak.	Pakistan
Alg.	Algeria	*gysr.*	geyser	Pan.	Panama
Am. Sam.	American Samoa	Hi., U.S.	Hawaii, U.S.	Pap. N. Gui.	Papua New Guinea
anch.	anchorage	*hist.*	historic site, ruins	Para.	Paraguay
And.	Andorra	*hist. reg.*	historic region	P.E., Can.	Prince Edward Island, Can.
Ang.	Angola	Hond.	Honduras		
Ant.	Antarctica	Hung.	Hungary	*pen.*	peninsula
Antig.	Antigua and Barbuda	*i.*	island	Phil.	Philippines
aq.	aqueduct	Ia., U.S.	Iowa, U.S.	Pit.	Pitcairn
Ar., U.S.	Arkansas, U.S.	Ice.	Iceland	*pl.*	plain, flat
Arg.	Argentina	*ice*	ice feature, glacier	*plat.*	plateau, highland
Arm.	Armenia	Id., U.S.	Idaho, U.S.	*p.o.i.*	point of interest
at.	atoll	Il., U.S.	Illinois, U.S.	Pol.	Poland
Aus.	Austria	In., U.S.	Indiana, U.S.	Port.	Portugal
Austl.	Australia	Indon.	Indonesia	P.R.	Puerto Rico
Az., U.S.	Arizona, U.S.	I. of Man	Isle of Man	Qc., Can.	Quebec, Can.
Azer.	Azerbaijan	Ire.	Ireland	*r.*	rock, rocks
b.	bay, gulf, inlet, lagoon	*is.*	islands	*reg.*	physical region
B.C., Can.	British Columbia, Can.	Isr.	Israel	*res.*	reservoir
Bah.	Bahamas	*isth.*	isthmus	Reu.	Reunion
Bahr.	Bahrain	Jam.	Jamaica	*rf.*	reef, shoal
Barb.	Barbados	Jer.	Jericho Area	R.I., U.S.	Rhode Island, U.S.
bas.	basin	Jord.	Jordan	Rom.	Romania
Bdi.	Burundi	Kaz.	Kazakhstan	Rw.	Rwanda
Bel.	Belgium	Kir.	Kiribati	S.A.	South America
Bela.	Belarus	Kor., N.	Korea, North	S. Afr.	South Africa
Ber.	Bermuda	Kor., S.	Korea, South	Samoa	Samoa
Bhu.	Bhutan	Ks., U.S.	Kansas, U.S.	*sand*	sand area
B.I.O.T.	British Indian Ocean Territory	Kuw.	Kuwait	Sau. Ar.	Saudi Arabia
		Ky., U.S.	Kentucky, U.S.	S.C., U.S.	South Carolina, U.S.
Blg.	Bulgaria	Kyrg.	Kyrgyzstan	*sci.*	scientific station
Bngl.	Bangladesh	*l.*	lake, pond	Scot., U.K.	Scotland, U.K.
Bol.	Bolivia	La., U.S.	Louisiana, U.S.	S.D., U.S.	South Dakota, U.S.
Bos.	Bosnia and Hercegovina	Lat.	Latvia	Sen.	Senegal
Bots.	Botswana	*lav.*	lava flow	Sey.	Seychelles
Braz.	Brazil	Leb.	Lebanon	S. Geor.	South Georgia
Bru.	Brunei	Leso.	Lesotho	Sing.	Singapore
Br. Vir. Is.	British Virgin Islands	Lib.	Liberia	Sk., Can.	Saskatchewan, Can.
Burkina	Burkina Faso	Liech.	Liechtenstein	S.L.	Sierra Leone
c.	cape, point	Lith.	Lithuania	Slov.	Slovakia
Ca., U.S.	California, U.S.	Lux.	Luxembourg	Slvn.	Slovenia
Cam.	Cameroon	Ma., U.S.	Massachusetts, U.S.	S. Mar.	San Marino
Camb.	Cambodia	Mac.	Macedonia	Sol. Is.	Solomon Islands
Can.	Canada	Madag.	Madagascar	Som.	Somalia
can.	canal	Malay.	Malaysia	Sp. N. Afr.	Spanish North Africa
C.A.R.	Central African Republic	Mald.	Maldives	Sri L.	Sri Lanka
Cay. Is.	Cayman Islands	Marsh. Is.	Marshall Islands	*state*	state, province, etc.
Christ. I.	Christmas Island	Mart.	Martinique	St. Hel.	St. Helena
C. Iv.	Cote d'Ivoire	Maur.	Mauritania	St. K./N.	St. Kitts and Nevis
clf.	cliff, escarpment	May.	Mayotte	St. Luc.	St. Lucia
Co., U.S.	Colorado, U.S.	Mb., Can.	Manitoba, Can.	*stm.*	stream (river, creek)
co.	county, district, etc.	Md., U.S.	Maryland, U.S.	S. Tom./P.	Sao Tome and Principe
Cocos Is.	Cocos (Keeling) Islands	Me., U.S.	Maine, U.S.	St. P./M.	St. Pierre and Miquelon
Col.	Colombia	Mex.	Mexico	*strt.*	strait, channel, etc.
Com.	Comoros	Mi., U.S.	Michigan, U.S.	St. Vin.	St. Vincent and the Grenadines
cont.	continent	Micron.	Micronesia, Federated States of		
Cook Is.	Cook Islands			Sur.	Suriname
C.R.	Costa Rica	Mid. Is.	Midway Islands	*sw.*	swamp, marsh
crat.	crater	*misc. cult.*	miscellaneous cultural	Swaz.	Swaziland
Cro.	Croatia	Mn., U.S.	Minnesota, U.S.	Swe.	Sweden
cst.	coast, beach	Mo., U.S.	Missouri, U.S.	Switz.	Switzerland
Ct., U.S.	Connecticut, U.S.	Mol.	Moldova	Tai.	Taiwan
ctry.	independent country	Mon.	Monaco	Taj.	Tajikistan
C.V.	Cape Verde	Mong.	Mongolia	Tan.	Tanzania
cv.	cave	Monts.	Montserrat	T./C. Is.	Turks and Caicos Islands
Cyp.	Cyprus	Mor.	Morocco		
Czech Rep.	Czech Republic	Moz.	Mozambique	Thai.	Thailand
D.C., U.S.	District of Columbia, U.S.	Mrts.	Mauritius	Tn., U.S.	Tennessee, U.S.
		Ms., U.S.	Mississippi, U.S.	Tok.	Tokelau
De., U.S.	Delaware, U.S.	Mt., U.S.	Montana, U.S.	Trin.	Trinidad and Tobago
Den.	Denmark	*mth.*	river mouth or channel	Tun.	Tunisia
dep.	dependency, colony	*mtn.*	mountain	Tur.	Turkey
depr.	depression	*mts.*	mountains	Turkmen.	Turkmenistan
des.	desert	Mwi.	Malawi	Tx., U.S.	Texas, U.S.
Dji.	Djibouti	Mya.	Myanmar	U.A.E.	United Arab Emirates
Dom.	Dominica	N.A.	North America	Ug.	Uganda
Dom. Rep.	Dominican Republic	N.B., Can.	New Brunswick, Can.	U.K.	United Kingdom
D.R.C.	Democratic Republic of the Congo	N.C., U.S.	North Carolina, U.S.	Ukr.	Ukraine
		N. Cal.	New Caledonia	*unds.*	undersea feature
Ec.	Ecuador	N. Cyp.	North Cyprus	Ur.	Uruguay
El Sal.	El Salvador	N.D., U.S.	North Dakota, U.S.	U.S.	United States
Eng., U.K.	England, U.K.	Ne., U.S.	Nebraska, U.S.	Ut., U.S.	Utah, U.S.
Eq. Gui.	Equatorial Guinea	Neth.	Netherlands	Uzb.	Uzbekistan
Erit.	Eritrea	Neth. Ant.	Netherlands Antilles	Va., U.S.	Virginia, U.S.
Est.	Estonia	Nf., Can.	Newfoundland, Can.	*val.*	valley, watercourse
est.	estuary	*ngh.*	neighborhood	Vat.	Vatican City
Eth.	Ethiopia	N.H., U.S.	New Hampshire, U.S.	Ven.	Venezuela
Eur.	Europe	N.J., U.S.	New Jersey, U.S.	Viet.	Vietnam
Falk. Is.	Falkland Islands	N.M., U.S.	New Mexico, U.S.	V.I.U.S.	Virgin Islands (U.S.)
Far. Is.	Faroe Islands	N. Mar. Is.	Northern Mariana Islands	*vol.*	volcano
Fin.	Finland			Vt., U.S.	Vermont, U.S.
Fl., U.S.	Florida, U.S.	Nmb.	Namibia	Wa., U.S.	Washington, U.S.
for.	forest, moor	Nor.	Norway	Wake I.	Wake Island
Fr.	France	Norf. I.	Norfolk Island	Wal./F.	Wallis and Futuna
Fr. Gu.	French Guiana	N.S., Can.	Nova Scotia, Can.	W.B.	West Bank
Fr. Poly.	French Polynesia	N.T., Can.	Northwest Territories, Can.	*well*	well, spring, oasis
Ga., U.S.	Georgia, U.S.			Wi., U.S.	Wisconsin, U.S.
Gam.	The Gambia	Nu., Can.	Nunavut, Can.	W. Sah.	Western Sahara
Gaza	Gaza Strip	Nv., U.S.	Nevada, U.S.	*wtfl.*	waterfall, rapids
Geor.	Georgia	N.Y., U.S.	New York, U.S.	W.V., U.S.	West Virginia, U.S.
Ger.	Germany	N.Z.	New Zealand	Wy., U.S.	Wyoming, U.S.
Gib.	Gibraltar	Oc.	Oceania	Yk., Can.	Yukon Territory, Can.
Golan	Golan Heights	Oh., U.S.	Ohio, U.S.	Yugo.	Yugoslavia
Grc.	Greece			Zam.	Zambia
Gren.	Grenada			Zimb.	Zimbabwe
Grnld.	Greenland				

Index

A

Name	Map Ref.	Page
Å, Nor.	C5	8
Aachen, Ger.	F1	16
Aalen, Ger.	H6	16
Aali, Sadd el- (Aswan High Dam), dam, Egypt	C6	62
Aalst (Alost), Bel.	D13	14
Äänekoski, Fin.	E11	8
Aarau, Switz.	C4	22
Aare, stm., Switz.	C5	22
Aarlen see Arlon, Bel.	E14	14
Aarschot, Bel.	D14	14
Aasiaat see Egedesminde, Grnld.	D15	141
Aat see Ath, Bel.	D12	14
Aba, China	E5	36
Aba, D.R.C.	D6	66
Aba, Nig.	H6	64
Abā al-Bawl, Qurayn, hill, Qatar	E7	56
Abacaxis, stm., Braz.	E6	84
Abaco, i., Bah.	B9	96
Abacou, Pointe, c., Haiti	D10	102
Abadab, Jabal, mtn., Sudan	D7	62
Ābādān, Iran	C6	56
Ābādeh, Iran	C7	56
Abadla, Alg.	C4	64
Abaeté, Braz.	J3	88
Abaeté, stm., Braz.	J3	88
Abaetetuba, Braz.	A1	88
Abag Qi, China	C7	36
Abaí, Para.	C10	92
Abaj, Kaz.	E12	32
Abakaliki, Nig.	H6	64
Abakan, Russia	D16	32
Abakan, stm., Russia	D15	32
Abakanovo, Russia	A20	10
Abakanskij hrebet, mts., Russia	D15	32
Abala, Niger	G5	64
Abalak, Niger	F6	64
Aban, Russia	C17	32
Abancay, Peru	F3	84
Abashiri, Japan	B16	38
Abasolo, Mex.	C6	100
Abasolo, Mex.	I7	130
Abasolo, Mex.	G6	130
Abau, Pap. N. Gui.	c4	79a
Abay see Abaj, Kaz.	E12	32
Ābay see Blue Nile, stm., Afr.	E6	62
Abaya, Lake see Ābaya Hāyk', l., Eth.	F7	62
Ābaya Hāyk', l., Eth.	F7	62
Abaza, Russia	D15	32
Abbadia San Salvatore, Italy	H8	22
Abbé, Lac see Abe, Lake, l., Afr.	E8	62
Abbeville, Fr.	D10	14
Abbeville, Ga., U.S.	D2	116
Abbeville, La., U.S.	H6	122
Abbeville, S.C., U.S.	B3	116
Abbey, Sk., Can.	D5	124
Abbeyfeale, Ire.	I3	12
Abbiategrasso, Italy	E5	22
Abbot, Mount, mtn., Austl.	B6	76
Abbot Ice Shelf, ice, Ant.	C31	81
Abbotsford, B.C., Can.	G8	138
Abbottābād, Pak.	A4	54
'Abd al-Kūrī, i., Yemen	G7	56
Ábdēra, hist., Grc.	B7	28
Abdulino, Russia	D8	32
Abe, Lake, l., Afr.	E8	62
Abéché, Chad	E4	62
Abel Tasman National Park, p.o.i., N.Z.	E5	80
Abemama, at., Kir.	C8	72
Abengourou, C. Iv.	H4	64
Abenójar, Spain	F6	20
Åbenrå, Den.	I3	8
Abensberg, Ger.	H7	16
Abeokuta, Nig.	H5	64
Aberdare, Wales, U.K.	J9	12
Aberdeen, S. Afr.	H6	70
Aberdeen, Scot., U.K.	D10	12
Aberdeen, Id., U.S.	H14	136
Aberdeen, Md., U.S.	E9	114
Aberdeen, Ms., U.S.	D10	122
Aberdeen, N.C., U.S.	A6	116
Aberdeen, S.D., U.S.	B14	126
Aberdeen, Wa., U.S.	D3	136
Aberdeen Lake, l., Nu., Can.	C10	106
Aberdeen Lake, res., Ms., U.S.	D10	122
Aberfeldy, Scot., U.K.	E9	12
Abergavenny, Wales, U.K.	J9	12
Abernant, Al., U.S.	D11	122
Abernathy, Tx., U.S.	H7	128
Abernethy, Sk., Can.	D10	124
Abert, Lake, l., Or., U.S.	H6	136
Aberystwyth, Wales, U.K.	I8	12
Abez', Russia	A10	32
Abhā, Sau. Ar.	F5	56
Abidjan, C. Iv.	H4	64
Abilene, Tx., U.S.	B8	130
Abingdon, Eng., U.K.	J11	12
Abingdon, Il., U.S.	D7	120
Abingdon, Va., U.S.	H4	114
Abiquiu, N.M., U.S.	E2	128
Abiquiu Reservoir, res., N.M., U.S.	E2	128
Abisko, Swe.	B8	8
Abitibi, stm., On., Can.	E14	106
Abitibi, Lake, l., Can.	F15	106
Abja-Paluoja, Est.	B8	10
Abnûb, Egypt	K2	58
Åbo see Turku, Fin.	F9	8
Abohar, India	C5	54
Abomey, Benin	H5	64
Abongabong, Gunung, mtn., Indon.	J3	48
Abong Mbang, Cam.	D2	66
Abony, Hung.	B6	26
Aborigen, pik, mtn., Russia	D18	34
Abou-Deïa, Chad	E3	62
Abou Simbel (Abu Simbel), hist., Egypt	C6	62
Abraham Lake, res., Ab., Can.	D14	138
Abra Pampa, Arg.	D3	90
Abre Campo, Braz.	K4	88
Abreu e Lima, Braz.	D8	88
Abring, India	B6	54
Abrud, Rom.	C10	26
Abruzzo, state, Italy	H10	22
Abruzzo, Parco Nazionale d', p.o.i., Italy	C7	24
Absaroka Range, mts., U.S.	C3	126
Absarokee, Mt., U.S.	E17	136
Absecon, N.J., U.S.	E11	114
Abū 'Alī, i., Sau. Ar.	D6	56
Abu Ballâs, mtn., Egypt	C5	62
Abu Dhabi see Abū Ẓaby, U.A.E.	E7	56
Abū Dulayq, Sudan	D6	62
Abū el-Hul (Sphinx), hist., Egypt	I1	58
Abufari, Braz.	E5	84
Abū Ḥamad, Sudan	D6	62
Abu Hammâd, Egypt	H2	58
Abuja, Nig.	H6	64
Abū Jabrah, Sudan	E5	62
Abū Jubayhah, Sudan	E6	62
Abū Kamāl, Syria	C5	56
Abukuma, stm., Japan	B13	40
Abukuma-kōchi, plat., Japan	B13	40
Abū Madd, Ra's, c., Sau. Ar.	E4	56
Abu Mendi, Eth.	E7	62
Abunã, Braz.	E4	84
Abu Qîr, Khalîg, b., Egypt	G1	58
Abu Qurqâs, Egypt	K1	58
Ābu Road, India	F4	54
Abū Rubayq, Sau. Ar.	E4	56
Abū Shajarah Ra's, c., Sudan	C7	62
Abu Shâma, Gebel, mtn., Egypt	I2	58
Abu Simbel see Abou Simbel, hist., Egypt	C6	62
Abu Tîg, Egypt	K2	58
Abū Zabad, Sudan	E5	62
Abū Ẓaby (Abu Dhabi), U.A.E.	E7	56
Abwong, Sudan	F6	62
Abyei, Sudan	F5	62
Abyssinia see Ethiopia, ctry., Afr.	F7	62
Acacías, Col.	E5	86
Acadia National Park, p.o.i., Me., U.S.	F8	110
Acadia Valley, Ab., Can.	C3	124
Açailândia, Braz.	C2	88
Acajutiba, Braz.	F7	88
Acámbaro, Mex.	E8	100
Acandí, Col.	C3	86
Acaponeta, Mex.	D6	100
Acaponeta, stm., Mex.	D6	100
Acapulco de Juárez, Mex.	G8	100
Acará, Braz.	A1	88
Acará, stm., Braz.	A1	88
Acarai Mountains, mts., S.A.	C6	84
Acará-Mirim, stm., Braz.	B1	88
Acaraú, Braz.	B5	88
Acaraú, stm., Braz.	B5	88
Acaray, stm., Para.	B10	92
Acarí, Peru	G3	84
Acari, stm., Braz.	H3	88
Acarigua, Ven.	C7	86
Acatlán de Osorio, Mex.	F9	100
Acay, Nevado de, mtn., Arg.	B4	92
Acayucan, Mex.	F11	100
Acceglio, Italy	F3	22
Accomac, Va., U.S.	G10	114
Accra, Ghana	H5	64
Acebuches, Mex.	A7	100
Aceguá, Braz.	E10	92
Aceh, state, Indon.	J3	48
Acerra, Italy	D8	24
Achacachi, Bol.	C3	90
Achaguas, Ven.	D7	86
Achalpur, India	H6	54
Achar, Ur.	F9	92
Acharnés, Grc.	E6	28
Achelóos, stm., Grc.	E4	28
Acheng, China	B7	38
Achern, Ger.	H4	16
Achill Head, c., Ire.	G2	12
Achill Island, i., Ire.	H2	12
Achiras, Arg.	F5	92
Achit nuur, l., Mong.	E16	32
Achwa, stm., Afr.	D6	66
Acı Göl, l., Tur.	F12	28
Ačinsk, Russia	C16	32
Acıpayam, Tur.	F12	28
Acireale, Italy	G9	24
Ačisaj, Kaz.	F11	32
Ackerly, Tx., U.S.	B6	130
Ackley, Ia., U.S.	B4	120
Acklins, i., Bah.	C10	96
Acklins, Bight of, b., Bah.	A10	102
Acme, Ab., Can.	E17	138
Aconcagua, Cerro, mtn., Arg.	F3	92
Aconchi, Mex.	G7	98
Acopiara, Braz.	D6	88
Açores (Azores), is., Port.	C3	60
Acorizal, Braz.	G6	84
A Coruña (Corunna), Spain	A2	20
A Coruña, co., Spain	A2	20
Acquasanta Terme, Italy	H10	22
Acqui Terme, Italy	F5	22
Acre see 'Akko, Isr.	F6	58
Acre, state, Braz.	E4	84
Acre, stm., S.A.	F4	84
Acri, Italy	E10	24
Acton Vale, Qc., Can.	E4	110
Actopan, Mex.	E9	100
Açucena, Braz.	J4	88
Acuña, Arg.	D8	92
Ada, Mn., U.S.	D2	118
Ada, Oh., U.S.	D2	114
Ada, Ok., U.S.	C2	122
Ādaba, Eth.	F7	62
Adair, Ia., U.S.	C3	120
Adair, Bahía de, b., Mex.	F6	98
Adair, Cape, c., Nu., Can.	A16	106
Adairsville, Ga., U.S.	C14	122
Adairville, Ky., U.S.	H11	120
Adaja, stm., Spain	C6	20
Adak Island, i., Ak., U.S.	g23	140a
Adam, Oman	E8	56
Adamantina, Braz.	D6	90
Adamaoua, mts., Afr.	C2	66
Adamclisi, Rom.	E14	26
Adamello, mts., Italy	D7	22
Adaminaby, Austl.	K7	76
Adams, Mn., U.S.	H6	118
Adams, Ne., U.S.	K2	118
Adams, N.Y., U.S.	E13	112
Adams, N.D., U.S.	F15	124
Adams, stm., B.C., Can.	E11	138
Adams, Mount, vol., Wa., U.S.	D5	136
Adam's Bridge, rf., Asia	G4	53
Adams Lake, l., B.C., Can.	E11	138
Adams Peak, mtn., Sri L.	H5	53
Adams Rock, r., Pit.	c28	78k
Adamstown, Pit.	c28	78k
Adamsville, Tn., U.S.	B10	122
'Adan (Aden), Yemen	G6	56
Adana, Tur.	A6	58
Adana, state, Tur.	A6	58
Adanero, Spain	D6	20
Adarama, Sudan	D6	62
Adare, Cape, c., Ant.	C22	81
Adavale, Austl.	E5	76
Adda, stm., Italy	E6	22
Ad-Dabbah, Sudan	D6	62
Ad-Dahnā', des., Sau. Ar.	D6	56
Ad-Dāmir, Sudan	D6	62
Ad-Dammām, Sau. Ar.	D7	56
Ad-Dānā, Syria	B7	58
Ad-Dawḥah (Doha), Qatar	D7	56
Ad-Dibdibah, reg., Sau. Ar.	D6	56
Addis, La., U.S.	G7	122
Addis Ababa see Ādīs Ābeba, Eth.	F7	62
Addis Abeba see Ādīs Ābeba, Eth.	F7	62
Addison, Mi., U.S.	F5	112
Ad-Dīwānīyah, Iraq	C6	56
Addo Elephant National Park, p.o.i., S. Afr.	H7	70
Addu Atoll, at., Mald.	j12	46a
Ad-Du'ayn, Sudan	E5	62
Ad-Duwayd, Sau. Ar.	C5	56
Ad-Duwaym, Sudan	E6	62
Adel, Ga., U.S.	E2	116
Adelaide, Austl.	J2	76
Adelaide, Bah.	n18	104f
Adelaide Island, i., Ant.	B33	81
Adelaide Peninsula, pen., Nu., Can.	B11	106
Adelaide River, Austl.	B6	74
Adèle Island, i., Austl.	C4	74
Adélie, Terre, cst., Ant.	B18	81
Adelie Coast see Adélie, Terre, cst., Ant.	B18	81
Adelong, Austl.	J6	76
Aden see 'Adan, Yemen	G6	56
Aden, Gulf of, b.	E9	62
Adendorp, S. Afr.	H7	70
Adi, Pulau, i., Indon.	F9	44
Adiaké, C. Iv.	H4	64
Adige (Etsch), stm., Italy	E8	22
Ādīgrat, Eth.	E7	62
Adıgüzel Barajı, res., Tur.	E12	28
Ādilābād, India	B4	53
Adimi, Russia	G16	34
Adin, Ca., U.S.	B5	134
Adirondack Mountains, mts., N.Y., U.S.	E15	112
Ādīs Ābeba (Addis Abeba), Eth.	F7	62
Adi Ugri, Erit.	E7	62
Adıyaman, Tur.	A9	58
Adıyaman, state, Tur.	A9	58
Adjuntas, Presa de las see Vicente Guerrero, Presa, res., Mex.	D9	100
Admiral, Sk., Can.	E5	124
Admiralty Gulf, b., Austl.	B5	74
Admiralty Inlet, b., Nu., Can.	A13	106
Admiralty Island, i., Nu., Can.	B10	106
Admiralty Island, i., Ak., U.S.	E13	140
Admiralty Islands, is., Pap. N. Gui.	a4	79a
Admiralty Mountains, mts., Ant.	C21	81
Ado, Nig.	H5	64
Ado-Ekiti, Nig.	H6	64
Adolfo Gonzales Chaves, Arg.	H7	92
Adolfo López Mateos, Mex.	A5	100
Adolfo López Mateos, Presa, res., Mex.	C5	100
Adolfo Rodriguez Sáa see Santa Rosa del Conlara, Arg.	F5	92
Ādoni, India	D3	53
Adour, stm., Fr.	F4	18
Ādra, India	G11	54
Adra, Spain	H7	20
Adrano, Italy	G8	24
Adrar, Alg.	D4	64
Adrâr, reg., Maur.	E2	64
Adria, Italy	E9	22
Adrian, Mi., U.S.	C1	114
Adrian, Mo., U.S.	F3	120
Adrian, Or., U.S.	G9	136
Adrian, Tx., U.S.	F6	128
Adrian, W.V., U.S.	F5	114
Adriatic Sea, Eur.	G11	22
A Dun, stm., Viet.	F9	48
Adutiškis, Lith.	E9	10
Advance, Mo., U.S.	G7	120
Advocate Harbour, N.S., Can.	E11	110
Ādwa, Eth.	E7	62
Adyča, stm., Russia	C16	34
Adygea see Adygeja, state, Russia	F6	32
Adygeja, state, Russia	F6	32
Adygheya see Adygeja, state, Russia	F6	32
Adzopé, C. Iv.	H4	64
Aegean Sea	E7	28
Aegina see Aígina, i., Grc.	F6	28
Aegviidu, Est.	A8	10
Aën, ostrov, i., Russia	B22	34
Aerku Hu, l., China	C9	54
Ærø, i., Den.	I4	8
Ærøskøbing, Den.	B6	16
A Estrada, Spain	B2	20
Aetna, Ab., Can.	G17	138
Afaahiti, Fr. Poly.	v22	78h
Afadjoto, mtn., Ghana	H5	64
Afareaitu, Fr. Poly.	v20	78h
Afars and Issas see Djibouti, ctry., Afr.	E8	62
Affton, Mo., U.S.	F7	120
Afghanistan, ctry., Asia	C9	56
Afgooye, Som.	D8	66
Afikpo, Nig.	H6	64
Aflou, Alg.	C5	64
Afmadow, Som.	D8	66
Afogados da Ingazeira, Braz.	D7	88
Afognak Island, i., Ak., U.S.	E9	140
Afoniha, Russia	B25	8
A Fonsagrada, Spain	A3	20
Africa, cont.	F14	4
'Afrīn, Syria	B7	58
Afton, N.Y., U.S.	B10	114
Afton, Ok., U.S.	H2	120
Afton, Wy., U.S.	H16	136
'Afula, Isr.	F6	58
Afyon, Tur.	E13	28
Afyon, state, Tur.	E13	28
Agadez, Niger	F6	64
Agadir, Mor.	C2	64
Agâdîr, Râs, c., Maur.	E1	64
Agadyr', Kaz.	E12	32
Agalak, Sudan	E6	62
Agalega Islands, is., Mrts.	K8	142
Agan, stm., Russia	B13	32
Agana, Guam	j10	78c
Agana Heights, Guam	j10	78c
Agano, stm., Japan	B12	40
Agapa, Russia	B6	34
Aga Point, c., Guam	k10	78c
Agar, India	G5	54
Agartala, India	G13	54
Agassiz, B.C., Can.	G9	138
Agassiz Pool, res., Mn., U.S.	C3	118
Agate, Co., U.S.	B5	128
Agate Fossil Beds National Monument, p.o.i., Ne., U.S.	E9	126
Agattu Island, i., Ak., U.S.	g21	140a
Agawa Bay, b., On., Can.	A5	112
Agawam, Mt., U.S.	B14	136
Agboville, C. Iv.	H4	64
Ağdam, Azer.	B6	56
Ageevo, Russia	F19	10
Agen, Fr.	E6	18
Agency, Ia., U.S.	D5	120
Agency Lake, l., Or., U.S.	H5	136
Aggeneys, S. Afr.	F4	70
Aggteleki Nemzeti Park, p.o.i., Hung.	A7	26
Āghā Jārī, Iran	C6	56
Agía Marína, Grc.	F9	28
Agiásos, Grc.	D9	28
Aginskoe, Russia	F11	34
Ágio Óros, state, Grc.	C7	28
Ágio Óros, pen., Grc.	C7	28
Ágios Nikólaos, Grc.	H8	28
Ağlasun, Tur.	F13	28
Agnes Lake, l., On., Can.	C7	118
Agnew, Austl.	E4	74
Agnibilékrou, C. Iv.	H4	64
Agno, Phil.	B2	52
Agno, stm., Phil.	C3	52
Ago, Japan	E9	40
Agogna, stm., Italy	E5	22
Agou, Mont, mtn., Togo	H5	64
Agout, stm., Fr.	F8	18
Āgra, India	E6	54
Agraciada, Ur.	F8	92
Agreda, Spain	C8	20
Ağrı, Tur.	B5	56
Agri, stm., Italy	D9	24
Ağrı Dağı (Ararat, Mount), mtn., Tur.	B5	56
Agrigento, Italy	G7	24
Agrihan, i., N. Mar. Is.	B5	72
Agrínio, Grc.	E4	28
Agrio, stm., Arg.	H2	92
Agrópoli, Italy	D9	24
Agro Pontino, reg., Italy	C6	24
Agto, Grnld.	D15	141
Água Branca, Braz.	C4	88
Agua Caliente, Mex.	B4	100
Agua Caliente Grande, Mex.	B4	100
Aguachica, Col.	C5	86
Água Clara, Braz.	D6	90
Aguada Cecilio, Arg.	H3	90
Aguada de Guerra, Arg.	H3	90
Aguada de Pasajeros, Cuba	A7	102
Aguadas, Col.	E4	86
Aguadilla, P.R.	B1	104a
Água Doce, Braz.	C12	92
Aguadulce, Pan.	H7	102
Agua Dulce, Tx., U.S.	G9	130
Agua Fria, stm., Az., U.S.	I4	132
Aguaí, Braz.	L2	88
Agualeguas, Mex.	H8	130
Aguán, stm., Hond.	E4	102
Aguanaval, stm., Mex.	C7	100
Aguapey, stm., Arg.	D9	92
Água Preta, Igarapé, stm., Braz.	H9	86
Agua Prieta, Mex.	F8	98
Aguaray Guazú, stm., Para.	A9	92
A Guardia, Spain	C1	20
Aguarico, stm., S.A.	H3	86
Aguaro-Guariquito, Parque Nacional, p.o.i., Ven.	C8	86
Aguaruto, Mex.	C5	100
Aguasabon, stm., On., Can.	C11	118
Águas Belas, Braz.	E7	88
Aguas Buenas, P.R.	B3	104a
Aguascalientes, Mex.	E7	100
Aguascalientes, state, Mex.	D7	100
Águas Formosas, Braz.	I5	88
Água Vermelha, Represa de, res., Braz.	C6	90
Aguayo, Arg.	E4	92
Agu Bay, b., Nu., Can.	A13	106
Agudos, Braz.	L1	88
Águeda, stm., Eur.	D4	20
Aguelhok, Mali	F5	64
Aguilar, Co., U.S.	D4	128
Aguilar de la Frontera, Spain	G6	20
Aguilares, Arg.	C5	92
Águilas, Spain	G9	20
Aguililla, Mex.	F7	100
Agujereada, Punta, c., P.R.	A1	104a
Agujita, Mex.	G6	130
Agulhas, Kaap, c., S. Afr.	I5	70
Agulhas Basin, unds.	M15	144
Agulhas Negras, Pico das, mtn., Braz.	L3	88
Agung, Gunung, vol., Indon.	G6	44
Agusan, stm., Phil.	F5	52
Agustín Codazzi, Col.	C5	86
Ağva, Tur.	B12	28
Ahaggar, mts., Alg.	E6	64
Ahaggar, Tassili ta-n-, plat., Alg.	E5	64
Ahalcihe, Geor.	F6	32
Ahar, Iran	B6	56
Ahaus, Ger.	D3	16
Ahipara Bay, b., N.Z.	B5	80
Ahlen, Ger.	E3	16
Ahmadābād, India	G4	54
Ahmadnagar, India	B2	53
Ahmadpur East, Pak.	D3	54
Ahmadpur Siāl, Pak.	C3	54
Ahmar Mountains, mts., Eth.	F8	62
Ahmetli, Tur.	E10	28
Ahmic Lake, l., On., Can.	C10	112
Ahoskie, N.C., U.S.	H9	114
Ahousat, B.C., Can.	G4	138
Ahraura, India	F9	54
Ahtuba, stm., Russia	E7	32
Ahtubinsk, Russia	E7	32
Ahuacatlán, Mex.	E6	100
Ahumada, Mex.	D1	130
Ahunui, at., Fr. Poly.	E12	72
Ahvāz, Iran	C6	56
Ahvenanmaa (Åland), state, Fin.	F9	8
Ahvenanmaa (Aland Islands), is., Fin.	F8	8
Aḥwar, Yemen	G6	56
Ahwa-ri, Kor., S.	D2	40
Å i Åfjord, Nor.	D4	8
Aibonito, P.R.	B3	104a
Aichi, state, Japan	D10	40
Aidong, China	I2	42
Aiea, Hi., U.S.	B3	78a
Aígina, Grc.	F6	28
Aígina, i., Grc.	F6	28
Aígio, Grc.	E5	28
Aigle, Switz.	D3	22
Aigle, stm., Qc., Can.	A1	110
Aiguá, Ur.	G10	92
Aigüestortes i Estany Sant Maurici, Parque Nacional d', p.o.i., Spain	B11	20
Aigüestortes i Llac de Sant Maurici, Parc Nacional d' see Aigüestortes i Esta, p.o.i., Spain	B11	20
Aikawa, Japan	A11	40
Aiken, S.C., U.S.	C4	116
Aikens Lake, l., Mb., Can.	C18	124
Ailao Shan, mts., China	G5	36
Aileron, Austl.	D6	74
Ailinglaplap, at., Marsh. Is.	C7	72
Ailsa Craig, On., Can.	E8	112
Ailsa Craig, i., Scot., U.K.	F7	12
Aim, Russia	E15	34
Aimorés, Braz.	J5	88
Ain, state, Fr.	D11	18
Ain, stm., Fr.	D11	18
Aïn Benian, Alg.	H13	20
Aïn Bessem, Alg.	H14	20
Aïn Defla, Alg.	H12	20
Aïn Draham, Tun.	H2	24
Aïn el Beïda, Alg.	B6	64
Ainslie Lake, l., N.S., Can.	D15	110
Aioi, Japan	E7	40
Aiora, Spain	E9	20
Aipe, Col.	F4	86
Aïr, Massif de l', mts., Niger	F6	64
Airai Airport, Palau	g8	78b
Airbangis, Indon.	C1	50
Airdrie, Ab., Can.	E16	138
Aire, stm., Fr.	F14	14
Aire, stm., Eng., U.K.	H11	12
Aire-sur-l'Adour, Fr.	F5	18
Air Force Island, i., Nu., Can.	B16	106
Airhaji, Indon.	D2	50
Airlie Beach, Austl.	C7	76
Airolo, Switz.	D5	22
Airuoca, Braz.	L3	88
Aishihik, Yk., Can.	C3	106
Aishihik Lake, l., Yk., Can.	C3	106
Aisne, state, Fr.	E12	14
Aisne, stm., Fr.	E12	14
Aïssa, Djebel, mtn., Alg.	C4	64
Aitape, Pap. N. Gui.	a3	79a
Aitkin, Mn., U.S.	E5	118
Aitolikó, Grc.	E4	28
Aitutaki, at., Cook Is.	E11	72
Aiuaba, Braz.	D5	88
Aiud, Rom.	C10	26
Aix, Île d', i., Fr.	C4	18
Aix, Mount, mtn., Wa., U.S.	D5	136
Aix-en-Provence, Fr.	F11	18
Aix-la-Chapelle see Aachen, Ger.	F1	16
Aix-les-Bains, Fr.	D11	18
Āīzawl, India	G14	54
Aizkraukle, Lat.	D8	10
Aizu-bange, Japan	B12	40
Aizu-wakamatsu, Japan	B12	40
Ajaccio, Fr.	H14	18
Ajaccio, Golfe d', b., Fr.	H14	18
Ajaguz, Kaz.	E13	32
Ajaguz, stm., Kaz.	E13	32
Ajajú, stm., Col.	G5	86
Ajan, Russia	E16	34
Ajan, stm., Russia	C7	34
Ajanta, India	H5	54
Ajanta Caves, hist., India	H5	54
Ajanta Range, mts., India	H5	54
Ajarani, stm., Braz.	F11	86
Ajax, On., Can.	E10	112
Ajdābiyā, Libya	A4	62
Ajdyrlinskij, Russia	D9	32
Ajjer, Tassili-n-, plat., Alg.	D6	64
Ajka, Hung.	B4	26
'Ajlūn, Jord.	F6	58
Ajmer, India	E5	54
Ajnāla, India	C5	54
Ajo, Az., U.S.	K4	132
Ajtos, Blg.	G14	26
Ajusco, Mex.	L9	134
Akabira, Japan	C15	38
Akabli, Alg.	D5	64
Akademii, zaliv, b., Russia	F16	34
Akagi-san, vol., Japan	C12	40
Akaishi-sammyaku, mts., Japan	D11	40
Āk'ak'ī Besek'a, Eth.	F7	62
Akalkot, India	C2	53
Akámas, Akrotírion, c., Cyp.	C3	58
Akan-kokuritsu-kōen, p.o.i., Japan	C16	38
'Akasha East, Sudan	C6	62
'Akāshāt, Iraq	C5	56
Akashi, Japan	E7	40
Akbarpur, India	E9	54
Akbulak, Russia	D9	32
Akçakale, Tur.	B9	58
Akçakoca, Tur.	B14	28
Akçakoyunlu, Tur.	B8	58
Akçaova, Tur.	F11	28
Akçay, Tur.	G12	28
Akçay, stm., Tur.	F11	28
Akchâr, reg., Maur.	E2	64
Akdoğan, N. Cyp.	C4	58
Ak-Dovurak, Russia	D15	32
Akeley, Mn., U.S.	D4	118
Aken, Ger.	E8	16
Akershus, state, Nor.	F4	8
Aketi, D.R.C.	D4	66
Akhaltsikhe see Ahalcihe, Geor.	F6	32
Akhḍar, Al-Jabal al-, mts., Libya	A4	62
Akhḍar, Al-Jabal al-, mts., Oman	E8	56
Akhḍar, Wādī al-, stm., Sau. Ar.	J7	58
Akhisar, Tur.	E10	28
Akhtarīn, Syria	B8	58
Akhtubinsk see Ahtubinsk, Russia	E7	32
Aki, Japan	F6	40
Akimiski Island, i., Nu., Can.	E14	106
Akıncı Burun, c., Tur.	B6	58
Akita, Japan	E13	38
Akjoujt, Maur.	F2	64
Akkeshi, Japan	C16	38
'Akko, Isr.	F6	58
Akkol', Kaz.	E13	32
Akkol', Kaz.	F12	32
Akköy, Tur.	F10	28
Aklavik, N.T., Can.	B4	106
'Aklé 'Aouâna, reg., Afr.	F3	64
Akmenrags, c., Lat.	D3	10
Akmola see Astana, Kaz.	D12	32
Akō, Japan	E7	40
Ākobo (Akūbū), stm., Afr.	F6	62
Akola, India	H6	54
Akonolinga, Cam.	D2	66
Akordat, Erit.	D7	62
Akören, Tur.	F15	28
Akot, India	H6	54
Akpatok Island, i., Nu., Can.	C17	106
Akpınar, Tur.	A9	58
Akrítas, Ákra, c., Grc.	G4	28
Akrokórinthos, hist., Grc.	F5	28
Akron, Co., U.S.	A5	128
Akron, In., U.S.	G4	112
Akron, N.Y., U.S.	E11	112
Akron, Oh., U.S.	C4	114
Akron, Pa., U.S.	H13	112
Akrotíri, Cyp.	D3	58
Akša, Russia	F11	34
Aksaj, Kaz.	D8	32
Aksaray, Tur.	B3	56
Aksayqin Hu, l., China	A7	54
Akşehir, Tur.	E14	28
Akşehir Gölü, l., Tur.	E14	28
Akseki, Tur.	F14	28
Aksu, China	F14	32
Aksu, Kaz.	D12	32
Aksu, stm., Kaz.	E13	32
Aksu, stm., Tur.	F13	28
Aksu, stm., Tur.	A8	58
Aksuat, Kaz.	E14	32
Aksuat, Kaz.	E14	32
Āksum, Eth.	E7	62
Aktau, Kaz.	F8	32
Aktau, Kaz.	D12	32
Aktjubinsk, Kaz.	D9	32
Akto, China	B12	56
Akūbū, Sudan	F6	62
Akūbū (Ākobo), stm., Afr.	F6	62
Akuliči Pervye, Russia	G16	10
Akune, Japan	G3	40
Akure, Nig.	H5	64
Akureyri, Ice.	k30	8a
Akutan Island, i., Ak., U.S.	F6	140
Akwanga, Nig.	H6	64
Akyazı, Tur.	C13	28
Ål, Nor.	F3	8
Alabama, state, U.S.	E12	122
Alabama, stm., Al., U.S.	F11	122
Alabaster, Al., U.S.	D12	122
Alacant (Alicante), Spain	F10	20
Alacant, co., Spain	F10	20
Alaçatı, Tur.	E9	28
Alachua, Fl., U.S.	G3	116
Alacrán, Arrecife, rf., Mex.	C7	96
Alacranes, Presa, res., Cuba	A7	102
Aladağ, mtn., Tur.	A6	58
Alagoa Grande, Braz.	D8	88
Alagoas, state, Braz.	E7	88
Alagoinhas, Braz.	G6	88
Alagón, Spain	C9	20
Alagón, stm., Spain	E4	20
Alahanpanjang, Indon.	D2	50
Alaior, Spain	E15	20
Alajku, Kyrg.	F12	32
Alajskij hrebet, mts., Asia	B11	56
Alajuela, C.R.	H5	102
Alajuela, Lago, res., Pan.	H8	102
Alakanuk, Ak., U.S.	D7	140
Alakol', ozero, l., Kaz.	E14	32
Alaköl Köli see Alakol', ozero, l., Kaz.	E14	32
Al-'Akrīshah, Egypt	G1	58
Alaktara, India	H9	54
Alakurtti, Russia	C13	8
Alalakeiki Channel, strt., Hi., U.S.	C5	78a
Alalaú, stm., Braz.	H11	86
Alamagan, i., N. Mar. Is.	B5	72
Al-'Amārah, Iraq	C6	56
Alameda, Ca., U.S.	F3	134
Alameda, N.M., U.S.	H10	132
Alamo, Ga., U.S.	D3	116
Alamo, Tn., U.S.	B9	122
Alamo, stm., Ca., U.S.	K1	132
Alamogordo, N.M., U.S.	B2	130
Alamo Heights, Tx., U.S.	E9	130
Alamo Lake, res., Az., U.S.	I3	132
Álamos, Mex.	B4	100
Álamos, stm., Mex.	A8	100
Alamosa, Co., U.S.	D3	128
Alamosa East, Co., U.S.	D3	128
Álamos de Márquez, Mex.	A7	100
Aland, India	C3	53
Åland see Ahvenanmaa, state, Fin.	F9	8
Åland see Ahvenanmaa, is., Fin.	F8	8
Aland Islands see Ahvenanmaa, is., Fin.	F8	8
Aland Sea, Eur.	G8	8
Alandur, India	E5	53
Alanya, Tur.	G15	28
Alaotra, Farihy, l., Madag.	D8	68
Alapaevsk, Russia	C10	32
Alapaha, Ga., U.S.	E2	116
Alapaha, stm., U.S.	F2	116
Alaplı, Tur.	B14	28
Alappuzha see Alleppey, India	G3	53
Al-'Aqabah, Jord.	I6	58
Alarcón, Spain	E8	20
Alarcón, Embalse de, res., Spain	E9	20
Alas, stm., Indon.	K3	48
Alas, Selat, strt., Indon.	H10	50
Alaşehir, Tur.	E11	28
Alashanyouqi, China	C5	36
Alaska, state, U.S.	D9	140
Alaska, Gulf of, b., Ak., U.S.	E10	140
Alaska Peninsula, pen., Ak., U.S.	E7	140
Alaska Range, mts., Ak., U.S.	D9	140
Alassio, Italy	F5	22
Alatan'aola see Xin Barag Youqi, China	B8	36
Alatri, Italy	I10	22
Alatyr', Russia	D7	32
Alausí, Ec.	I2	86
Alava see Arabako, co., Spain	B8	20
Alava, Cape, c., Wa., U.S.	B2	136
Al-'Ayn, U.A.E.	E8	56
Alayor see Alaior, Spain	E15	20
Alazeja, stm., Russia	B19	34
Al-'Azīzīyah, Libya	A2	62
Alba, Italy	F5	22
Alba, Mi., U.S.	D5	112
Alba, Tx., U.S.	E3	122
Alba, state, Rom.	C10	26
Al-Bāb, Syria	B8	58
Albacete, Spain	E9	20
Albacete, co., Spain	F9	20
Al-Bad', Sau. Ar.	J6	58
Alba de Tormes, Spain	D5	20
Albaida, Spain	F10	20
Alba Iulia, Rom.	C10	26
Al-Balqā', state, Jord.	F6	58
Al-Bālū'ah, l., Syria	C7	58
Albanel, Lac, l., Qc., Can.	E16	106
Albania, Col.	B5	86
Albania, ctry., Eur.	C14	24
Albano Laziale, Italy	I9	22
Albany, Ga., U.S.	E1	116
Albany, In., U.S.	H4	112
Albany, Ky., U.S.	H12	120
Albany, Mn., U.S.	F4	118
Albany, Mo., U.S.	D3	120
Albany, N.Y., U.S.	B12	114
Albany, Oh., U.S.	E3	114
Albany, Or., U.S.	F3	136
Albany, Tx., U.S.	B8	130
Albany, stm., On., Can.	E14	106
Albarracín, Spain	D9	20
Al-Baṣrah, Iraq	C6	56
Al-Batrā' (Petra), hist., Jord.	H6	58
Albatross Bay, b., Austl.	B8	74
Al-Bayḍā', Libya	A4	62
Albemarle, N.C., U.S.	A5	116
Albemarle Island see Isabela, Isla, i., Ec.	i11	84a
Albemarle Sound, strt., N.C., U.S.	H9	114
Albenga, Italy	F5	22
Alberche, stm., Spain	D6	20
Alberdi, Para.	C8	92
Alberga Creek, stm., Austl.	E6	74
Alberni Inlet, b., B.C., Can.	G6	138
Alberobello, Italy	D11	24
Albert, Fr.	E11	14
Albert, Lake, l., Afr.	D6	66
Albert, Lake, l., Austl.	J2	76
Alberta, Al., U.S.	E11	122
Alberta, state, Can.	E8	106
Alberta, Mount, mtn., Ab., Can.	D13	138
Albert Canyon, B.C., Can.	E13	138
Albert City, Ia., U.S.	I3	118
Albert Edward Bay, b., Nu., Can.	B10	106
Alberti, Arg.	G7	92
Albertirsa, Hung.	B6	26
Albertkanaal, can., Bel.	D14	14
Albert Lea, Mn., U.S.	H5	118
Albert Markham, Mount, mtn., Ant.	D21	81
Albert Nile, stm., Afr.	D6	66
Alberton, P.E., Can.	D12	110
Albertville, Fr.	D12	18
Albertville, Al., U.S.	C12	122
Albi, Fr.	F8	18
Albia, Ia., U.S.	C5	120
Albin, Wy., U.S.	F8	126
Albina, Sur.	B7	84
Albina, Ponta, c., Ang.	D1	68
Albion, Ca., U.S.	D2	134
Albion, Id., U.S.	H13	136
Albion, Il., U.S.	F9	120
Albion, In., U.S.	G4	112
Albion, Mi., U.S.	B1	114
Albion, N.Y., U.S.	E11	112
Albion, Pa., U.S.	C5	114
Albion, Wa., U.S.	D9	136
Al-Biqā', state, Leb.	D7	58
Al-Biqā' (Bekaa Valley), val., Leb.	D7	58
Al-Bi'r, Sau. Ar.	J7	58
Albocàsser, Spain	D10	20
Alboran Sea	B4	64
Ålborg, Den.	H4	8
Ålborg Bugt, b., Den.	H4	8
Alborz, Reshteh-ye Kūhhā-ye, mts., Iran	B7	56
Albuñol, Spain	H7	20
Albuquerque, N.M., U.S.	H10	132
Albuquerque, Cayos de, is., Col.	F6	102
Alburg, Vt., U.S.	E3	110
Alburquerque, Spain	E3	20
Albury, Austl.	J6	76
Alcains, Port.	E3	20
Alcalá de Guadaira, Spain	G5	20
Alcalá de Henares, Spain	D7	20
Alcalá la Real, Spain	G7	20
Alcalde, N.M., U.S.	E2	128
Alcamo, Italy	G6	24
Alcanar, Spain	D11	20
Alcañices, Spain	C4	20
Alcañiz, Spain	C10	20
Alcântara, Braz.	B3	88
Alcántara, Spain	E3	20
Alcantarilla, Spain	G9	20
Alcaraz, Spain	F8	20
Alcaudete, Spain	G6	20
Alcázar de San Juan, Spain	E7	20
Alcester, S.D., U.S.	A1	120
Alcira, Arg.	F5	92
Alcira see Alzira, Spain	E10	20
Alcobaça, Braz.	I6	88
Alcobendas, Spain	D7	20
Alcoi, Spain	F10	20
Alcolea del Pinar, Spain	C8	20
Alcolu, S.C., U.S.	C5	116

Name	Map Ref.	Page
Alcorn, Ms., U.S.	F7	122
Alcorta, Arg.	F7	92
Alcoutim, Port.	G3	20
Alcoy see Alcoi, Spain	F10	20
Alcúdia, Spain	E14	20
Alcúdia, Badia d', b., Spain	E14	20
Aldabra, Groupe d', is., Sey.	k11	69b
Aldama, Mex.	D9	100
Aldama, Mex.	A5	100
Aldan, Russia	E14	34
Aldan, stm., Russia	D15	34
Aldan Plateau see Aldanskoe nagor'e, plat., Russia	E14	34
Aldanskoe nagor'e (Aldan Plateau), plat., Russia	E14	34
Aldarchaan, Mong.	B4	36
Aldeia Nova de São Bento, Port.	G3	20
Alden, Mn., U.S.	H5	118
Alderney, i., Guern.	E6	14
Aldershot, Eng., U.K.	J12	12
Alderson, W.V., U.S.	G5	114
Aledo, Il., U.S.	C7	120
Aleg, Maur.	F2	64
Alegre, Braz.	K5	88
Alegrete, Braz.	D10	92
Alej, stm., Russia	D14	32
Alejandro Roca, Arg.	F5	92
Alejandro Selkirk, Isla, i., Chile	I6	82
Alejsk, Russia	D14	32
Aleksandrov, Russia	D21	10
Aleksandrovskij Zavod, Russia	F12	34
Aleksandrovskoe, Russia	B13	32
Aleksandrovsk-Sahalinskij, Russia	F17	34
Aleksandrów Kujawski, Pol.	D14	16
Alekseevka, Kaz.	D12	32
Alekseevka, Kaz.	E14	32
Alekseevka, Russia	D5	32
Alekseevsk, Russia	C19	32
Aleksejevka see Alekseevka, Kaz.	D12	32
Alekseyevka see Alekseevka, Kaz.	D12	32
Aleksin, Russia	F19	10
Aleksinac, Yugo.	F8	26
Alemania, Arg.	B5	92
Além Paraíba, Braz.	K4	88
Alençon, Fr.	F9	14
Alenquer, Braz.	D7	84
Alentejo, hist. reg., Port.	F3	20
Alenuihaha Channel, strt., Hi., U.S.	C5	78a
Aleppo see Ḥalab, Syria	B8	58
Aléria, Fr.	G15	18
Alert, Nu., Can.	A13	141
Alert Bay, B.C., Can.	F4	138
Alert Point, c., Nu., Can.	A8	141
Alès, Fr.	E10	18
Alëšnja, Russia	G16	10
Alessándria, Italy	F5	22
Ålesund, Nor.	E1	8
Aleutian Basin, unds.	D20	142
Aleutian Islands, is., Ak., U.S.	g22	140a
Aleutian Range, mts., Ak., U.S.	E8	140
Aleutian Trench, unds.	E21	142
Aleutka, Russia	G19	34
Alevina, mys, c., Russia	E19	34
Alex, Ok., U.S.	G11	128
Alexander, Mb., Can.	E13	124
Alexander, N.D., U.S.	G10	124
Alexander, Kap, c., Grnld.	B11	141
Alexander Archipelago, is., Ak., U.S.	E12	140
Alexander Bay, S. Afr.	F3	70
Alexander City, Al., U.S.	E12	122
Alexander Island, i., Ant.	B33	81
Alexandra, N.Z.	G3	80
Alexandra, stm., Austl.	B3	76
Alexandra Falls, wtfl, N.T., Can.	C7	106
Alexandretta see İskenderun, Tur.	B6	58
Alexandretta, Gulf of see İskenderun Körfezi, b., Tur.	B6	58
Alexandria, Braz.	D6	88
Alexandria, B.C., Can.	D8	138
Alexandria, On., Can.	E2	110
Alexandria see El-Iskandarīya, Egypt	A6	62
Alexandria, Rom.	F12	26
Alexandria, La., U.S.	F6	122
Alexandria, Mn., U.S.	F3	118
Alexandria, Mo., U.S.	D6	120
Alexandria, S.D., U.S.	D15	126
Alexandria, Tn., U.S.	H11	120
Alexandria, Va., U.S.	F8	114
Alexandria Bay, N.Y., U.S.	D14	112
Alexandrina, Lake, l., Austl.	J2	76
Alexandroúpoli, Grc.	C8	28
Alexis, Il., U.S.	C7	120
Alfambra, Spain	D9	20
Alfaro, Spain	B9	20
Alfarràs, Spain	C11	20
Alfarrás see Alfarràs, Spain	C11	20
Al-Fāshir, Sudan	E5	62
Alfeiós, stm., Grc.	F4	28
Alfeld, Ger.	D5	16
Alfenas, Braz.	K3	88
Alföld, pl., Hung.	C7	26
Alfonsine, Italy	F9	22
Alfred, On., Can.	E2	110
Alfred, Me., U.S.	G6	110
Alfred, N.Y., U.S.	B8	114
Al-Fujayrah, U.A.E.	D8	56
Al-Fuqahā', Libya	B3	62
Al-Furāt see Euphrates, stm., Asia	C6	56
Alga, Kaz.	E9	32
Ålgård, Nor.	G1	8
Algarrobal, Chile	D2	92
Algarrobo, Chile	F2	92
Algarrobo del Águila, Arg.	H4	92
Algarve, hist. reg., Port.	G2	20
Algeciras, Col.	F4	86
Algeciras, Spain	H5	20
Algemesí, Spain	E10	20
Algeria, ctry., Afr.	D5	64
Algérie see Algeria, ctry., Afr.	D5	64
Al-Ghāb, sw., Syria	C7	58
Al-Ghaydah, Yemen	F7	56
Al-Ghāzīyah, Leb.	E6	58
Alghero, Italy	D2	24
Algiers see El Djazaïr, Alg.	B5	64
Alginet, Spain	E10	20
Algoabaai, b., S. Afr.	H7	70
Algoa Bay see Algoabaai, b., S. Afr.	H7	70
Algodón, stm., Peru	I5	86
Algodones, N.M., U.S.	F2	128
Algoma Mills, On., Can.	B7	112
Algona, Ia., U.S.	A3	120
Algonac, Mi., U.S.	B3	114
Algonquin, Il., U.S.	B9	120
Algorta, Spain	A7	20
Algorta, Ur.	F9	92
Al-Ḥaffah, Syria	C7	58
Al-Ḥajarah, reg., Asia	C5	56
Al-Ḥamād, pl., Sau. Ar.	C4	56
Alhama de Murcia, Spain	G9	20
Alhandra, Braz.	D8	88
Al-Ḥarrah, lav., Sau. Ar.	C4	56
Al-Harūj al-Aswad, hills, Libya	B3	62
Al-Ḥasakah, Syria	B5	56
Alhaurín el Grande, Spain	H6	20
Al-Ḥawātah, Sudan	E7	62
Al-Ḥawrah, Yemen	G6	56
Al-Ḥijāz (Hejaz), reg., Sau. Ar.	D4	56
Al-Ḥillah, Iraq	C5	56
Al-Hirmil, Leb.	D7	58
Al-Hoceima, Mor.	B4	64
Al-Ḥudaydah (Hodeida), Yemen	G5	56
Al-Ḥufrah, reg., Sau. Ar.	J9	58
Al-Ḥufūf, Sau. Ar.	D6	56
Al Ḥūj, hills, Sau. Ar.	J9	58
Al-Ḥulwah, Sau. Ar.	E6	56
Alía, Spain	E5	20
Aliağa, Tur.	E9	28
Aliákmonas, stm., Grc.	C4	28
Aliança, Braz.	D8	88
Alībāg, India	B1	53
Alibates Flint Quarries National Monument, p.o.i., Tx., U.S.	F7	128
Äli Bayramlı, Azer.	B6	56
Alibei, ozero, l., Ukr.	D17	26
Alibey Adası, i., Tur.	D9	28
Alibunar, Yugo.	D7	26
Alicante see Alacant, Spain	F10	20
Alicante see Alacant, co., Spain	F10	20
Alice, S. Afr.	H8	70
Alice, Tx., U.S.	G9	130
Alice, stm., Austl.	D5	76
Alice, Punta, c., Italy	E11	24
Alice Springs, Austl.	D6	74
Alice Town, Bah.	K6	116
Aliceville, Al., U.S.	D10	122
Alick Creek, stm., Austl.	C4	76
Alīgarh, India	E6	54
Alignements de Carnac, hist., Fr.	G5	14
Alīgūdarz, Iran	C6	56
'Alī Kheyl, Afg.	B2	54
Al-Ikhṣāṣ al-Qiblīyah, Egypt	I2	58
Alima, stm., Congo	E3	66
Alim Island, i., Pap. N. Gui.	a4	79a
Alindao, C.A.R.	C4	66
Alingsås, Swe.	G5	8
Alīpur, Pak.	D3	54
Ālīpur Duār, India	E12	54
Aliquippa, Pa., U.S.	D5	114
Alīrājpur, India	G5	54
Aliseda, Spain	E4	20
Alitak, Cape, c., Ak., U.S.	E9	140
Alivéri, Grc.	E7	28
Aliwal North, S. Afr.	G8	70
Alix, Ab., Can.	D17	138
Al-Jabalayn, Sudan	E6	62
Al-Jafr, Jord.	H7	58
Al-Jaghbūb, Libya	B4	62
Al-Jahrah, Kuw.	D6	56
Al-Jawārah, Oman	F8	56
Al-Jawf, Libya	C4	62
Al-Jawf, Sau. Ar.	D4	56
Al-Jazaïr see El Djazaïr, Alg.	B5	64
Al-Jazīrah, reg., Sudan	E6	62
Al-Jifārah (Jeffara), pl., Afr.	C7	64
Al-Jubayl, Sau. Ar.	D6	56
Al-Junaynah, Sudan	E4	62
Aljustrel, Port.	G2	20
Al-Kafr, Syria	F7	58
Al-Karak, Jord.	G6	58
Al-Karak, state, Jord.	G6	58
Al-Khalīl (Hebron), W.B.	G5	58
Al-Khāliṣ, Iraq	C5	56
Al-Khandaq, Sudan	D6	62
Al-Kharṭām Baḥrī, Sudan	D6	62
Al-Kharṭūm (Khartoum), Sudan	D6	62
Al-Khaṣab, Oman	D8	56
Al-Khums, Libya	A2	62
Alkmaar, Neth.	B13	14
Al-Kufrah, Libya	C4	62
Al-Kūt, Iraq	C6	56
Al-Kuwayt (Kuwait), Kuw.	D6	56
Al-Labwah, Leb.	D7	58
Al-Lādhiqīyah (Latakia), Syria	C6	58
Al-Lādhiqīyah, state, Syria	C6	58
Allagash, stm., Me., U.S.	D7	110
Allahābād, India	F8	54
Allah-Jun', Russia	D16	34
Allakaket, Ak., U.S.	C9	140
Allan, Sk., Can.	C7	124
Allanmyo, Mya.	C2	48
Allanridge, S. Afr.	E8	70
Allatoona Lake, res., Ga., U.S.	C14	122
Alldays, S. Afr.	C9	70
Allegan, Mi., U.S.	F4	112
Allegany, N.Y., U.S.	B7	114
Allegheny, stm., U.S.	D6	114
Allegheny Mountains, mts., U.S.	E6	114
Allegheny Plateau, plat., U.S.	D5	114
Allegheny Reservoir, res., U.S.	C7	114
Allemands, Lac des, l., La., U.S.	H8	122
Allen, Ne., U.S.	I2	118
Allen, Ok., U.S.	C2	122
Allen, Tx., U.S.	D2	122
Allen, Lough, l., Ire.	G4	12
Allendale, Il., U.S.	F10	120
Allendale, S.C., U.S.	C4	116
Allende, Mex.	A8	100
Allenstein see Olsztyn, Pol.	C16	16
Allentown, Pa., U.S.	D10	114
Alleppey, India	G3	53
Aller, stm., Ger.	D5	16
Allevard, Fr.	D12	18
Allgäu see Kempten, Ger.	I6	16
Allgäu, reg., Ger.	I6	16
Alliance, Ab., Can.	D19	138
Alliance, Ne., U.S.	E10	126
Alliance, Oh., U.S.	D4	114
Al-Lidām, Sau. Ar.	E5	56
Allier, state, Fr.	C9	18
Allier, stm., Fr.	C9	18
Alligator Pond, Jam.	j13	104d
Allinagaram, India	F3	53
Allison, Ia., U.S.	B5	120
Al-Līth, Sau. Ar.	E5	56
Alloa, Scot., U.K.	E9	12
Allos, Fr.	E12	18
Allouez, Wi., U.S.	G11	118
Allred Peak, mtn., Co., U.S.	C8	132
All Saints, Antig.	f4	105b
Al-Luḥayyah, Yemen	F5	56
Allumette Lake, l., Can.	C12	112
Allumettes, Île aux, i., Qc., Can.	C12	112
Alma, N.B., Can.	E12	110
Alma, Qc., Can.	B5	110
Alma, Ar., U.S.	B4	122
Alma, Ga., U.S.	E3	116
Alma, Ks., U.S.	E1	120
Alma, Mi., U.S.	E5	112
Alma, Wi., U.S.	G7	118
Almada, Port.	F1	20
Almaden, Austl.	A5	76
Almadén, Spain	F6	20
Al-Madīnah (Medina), Sau. Ar.	E4	56
Al-Mafraq, Jord.	F7	58
Al-Mafraq, state, Jord.	F8	58
Almafuerte, Arg.	F5	92
Almagro, Spain	F7	20
Alma Hill, hill, N.Y., U.S.	B8	114
Al Māliḥah, Sudan	D5	62
Almalyk, Uzb.	F11	32
Al-Manāmah (Manama), Bahr.	D7	56
Almanor, Lake, res., Ca., U.S.	C4	134
Almansa, Spain	F9	20
Almanza, Spain	B5	20
Almanzor, mtn., Spain	D5	20
Al-Marj, Libya	A4	62
Almas, Braz.	F2	88
Almas, Pico das, mtn., Braz.	G4	88
Al-Mashrafah, Syria	D7	58
Almaty, Kaz.	F13	32
Al-Mawṣil, Iraq	B5	56
Almeida, Port.	D3	20
Almejas, Bahía, b., Mex.	C3	100
Almelo, Neth.	B15	14
Almena, Ks., U.S.	B9	128
Almenara, Braz.	I5	88
Almendra, Embalse de, res., Spain	C4	20
Almendralejo, Spain	F4	20
Almería, Spain	H8	20
Almería, co., Spain	G8	20
Almería, Golfo de, b., Spain	H8	20
Al'metevsk, Russia	D8	32
Al-Mijlad, Sudan	E5	62
Al-Mīnā', Leb.	D6	58
Almira, Wa., U.S.	C7	136
Almirante, Pan.	H6	102
Almirante Latorre, Chile	D2	92
Almirós, Grc.	D5	28
Almo, Id., U.S.	A3	132
Almodóvar del Campo, Spain	F6	20
Almont, Mi., U.S.	B2	114
Almonte, On., Can.	C13	112
Almonte, Spain	G4	20
Almonte, stm., Spain	E4	20
Almora, India	D7	54
Al-Mubarraz, Sau. Ar.	E6	56
Al-Mubarraz, Sau. Ar.	D6	56
Al-Mudawwarah, Jord.	I6	58
Almudévar, Spain	B10	20
Al-Muḥarraq, Bahr.	D7	56
Al-Mukallā, Yemen	G6	56
Al-Mukhā, Yemen	G5	56
Almuñécar, Spain	H7	20
Al-Muwayliḥ, Sau. Ar.	K6	58
Almyroú, Órmos, b., Grc.	H7	28
Alnwick, Eng., U.K.	F11	12
Alofi, Île, i., Wal./F.	E9	72
Alónnisos, Grc.	D6	28
Alónnisos, i., Grc.	D6	28
Alor, Pulau, i., Indon.	G7	44
Alor, Selat, strt., Indon.	G7	44
Alor Setar, Malay.	I5	48
Alosno, Spain	G3	20
Alost see Aalst, Bel.	D13	14
Alotau, Pap. N. Gui.	c5	79a
Aloysius, Mount, mtn., Austl.	E5	74
Alpachiri, Arg.	H5	92
Alpaugh, Ca., U.S.	H6	134
Alpena, Mi., U.S.	C6	112
Alpena, S.D., U.S.	C14	126
Alpercatas, stm., Braz.	D3	88
Alpes-de-Haute-Provence, state, Fr.	E12	18
Alpes-Maritimes, state, Fr.	F13	18
Alpha, Austl.	D6	76
Alpha, Il., U.S.	C7	120
Alpha, Mi., U.S.	B1	112
Alpharetta, Ga., U.S.	B1	116
Alphonse, i., Sey.	k12	69b
Alpine, Ca., U.S.	K9	134
Alpine, Tx., U.S.	D4	130
Alpine National Park, p.o.i., Austl.	K6	76
Alpinópolis, Braz.	K2	88
Alps, mts., Eur.	D6	22
Al-Qaḍārif, Sudan	E7	62
Al-Qaḍīmah, Sau. Ar.	E4	56
Al-Qāmishlī, Syria	B5	56
Al-Qaryah ash-Sharqīyah, Libya	A2	62
Al-Qaryatayn, Syria	D8	58
Al-Qaṭīf, Sau. Ar.	D6	56
Al-Qaṭrānah, Jord.	G7	58
Al-Qaṭrūn, Libya	C2	62
Al-Qayṣūmah, Sau. Ar.	D6	56
Al-Qunayṭirah, Syria	E6	58
Al-Qunayṭirah, state, Syria	E6	58
Al-Qunfudhah, Sau. Ar.	F5	56
Al-Quṭayfah, Syria	E7	58
Al-Quṭaynah, Sudan	E6	62
Als, i., Den.	I3	8
Alsace, hist. reg., Fr.	F16	14
Al'šany, Bela.	H10	10
Alsask, Sk., Can.	C4	124
Alsasua, Spain	B8	20
Alsea, Or., U.S.	F3	136
Alsek, stm., N.A.	D3	106
Alsen, N.D., U.S.	F15	124
Alsfeld, Ger.	F5	16
Alta, Nor.	B10	8
Altaelva, stm., Nor.	B10	8
Alta Gracia, Arg.	E5	92
Altagracia, Ven.	B6	86
Altagracia de Orituco, Ven.	C8	86
Altai, mts., Asia	E15	32
Altaj, state, Russia	D15	32
Altajskij, Russia	D14	32
Altamaha, stm., Ga., U.S.	E4	116
Altamira, Braz.	D7	84
Altamira, Chile	B3	92
Altamirano, Mex.	I10	130
Altamont, Ks., U.S.	G2	120
Altamont, Or., U.S.	A4	134
Altamont, Tn., U.S.	B13	122
Altamura, Italy	D10	24
Altamura, Isla, i., Mex.	C4	100
Altanbulag, Mong.	A6	36
Altar, Mex.	F7	98
Altar, stm., Mex.	F7	98
Altar, Desierto de, des., Mex.	F6	98
Altar de Los Sacrificios, hist., Guat.	D2	102
Altario, Ab., Can.	C3	124
Altata, Mex.	C4	100
Alta Vista, Ks., U.S.	C12	128
Altay, China	E15	32
Altay, Mong.	B4	36
Altay see Altaj, state, Russia	D15	32
Altay Mountains see Altai, mts., Asia	E15	32
Altdorf, Switz.	D5	22
Altenburg, Ger.	E8	16
Altentreptow, Ger.	C9	16
Alter do Chão, Port.	E3	20
Altevatnet, l., Nor.	B8	8
Altha, Fl., U.S.	G13	122
Altheimer, Ar., U.S.	C7	122
Altınekin, Tur.	E15	28
Altinho, Braz.	E7	88
Altınova, Tur.	D9	28
Altıntaş, Tur.	D13	28
Altiplano, plat., S.A.	G4	84
Altmark, reg., Ger.	D7	16
Altmühl, stm., Ger.	G6	16
Alto, Tx., U.S.	F3	122
Alto Araguaia, Braz.	G7	84
Alto Chicapa, Ang.	C2	68
Alto Garças, Braz.	G7	84
Alto Longá, Braz.	C4	88
Altomünster, Ger.	H7	16
Alton, Eng., U.K.	J11	12
Alton, Il., U.S.	F7	120
Alton, Ia., U.S.	B1	120
Alton, Ks., U.S.	B9	128
Alton, N.H., U.S.	G5	110
Altona, Mb., Can.	E16	124
Altoona, Al., U.S.	C12	122
Altoona, Ia., U.S.	C4	120
Altoona, Pa., U.S.	D7	114
Altoona, Wi., U.S.	G7	118
Alto Paraguai, Braz.	F6	84
Alto Paraíso de Goiás, Braz.	G2	88
Alto Paraná, state, Para.	B10	92
Alto Parnaíba, Braz.	E2	88
Alto Río Mayo, Arg.	I2	90
Alto Río Senguer, Arg.	I2	90
Altos, Braz.	C4	88
Alto Santo, Braz.	C6	88
Altötting, Ger.	H8	16
Altun Shan, mts., China	D2	36
Alturas, Ca., U.S.	B5	134
Altus, Ar., U.S.	B5	122
Altus, Ok., U.S.	G9	128
Alu see Shortland Island, i., Sol. Is.	d6	79b
Al-'Ubaylah, Sau. Ar.	E7	56
Al-Ubayyiḍ, Sudan	E6	62
Alubijid, Phil.	F5	52
Al-Udayyah, Sudan	E5	62
Alūksne, Lat.	C9	10
Al-'Ulā, Sau. Ar.	D4	56
Al-'Uqaylah, Libya	A3	62
Al-'Uwaynāt, Libya	B2	62
Alva, Ok., U.S.	E10	128
Alvaiázere, Port.	E2	20
Alvarado, Mex.	F11	100
Alvarado, Tx., U.S.	B10	130
Álvaro Obregón, Presa, res., Mex.	B4	100
Alvear, Arg.	D9	92
Alverca, Port.	F1	20
Alvernia, Mount, hill, Bah.	C10	96
Alvesta, Swe.	H6	8
Alvin, Tx., U.S.	H3	122
Alvinópolis, Braz.	K4	88
Älvkarleby, Swe.	F7	8
Alvord, Tx., U.S.	H11	128
Alvord Desert, des., Or., U.S.	H8	136
Al-Wajh, Sau. Ar.	D4	56
Alwar, India	E6	54
Alwaye, India	F3	53
Alxa Zuoqi, China	B1	42
Alytus, Lith.	F6	10
Alzey, Ger.	G4	16
Alzira, Spain	E10	20
Amacuro (Amakura), stm., S.A.	C11	86
Amadeus, Lake, l., Austl.	D6	74
Amadjuak Lake, l., Nu., Can.	B16	106
Amagasaki, Japan	E8	40
Amagi, Japan	F3	40
Amahai, Indon.	F8	44
Amaicha del Valle, Arg.	C4	92
Amaimon, Pap. N. Gui.	b4	79a
Amajac, stm., Mex.	E9	100
Amakura (Amacuro), stm., S.A.	D11	86
Amakusa-nada, Japan	G2	40
Amakusa-shotō, is., Japan	G2	40
Åmål, Swe.	G5	8
Amalāpuram, India	C6	53
Amalfi, Col.	B2	84
Amaliáda, Grc.	F4	28
Amalner, India	H5	54
Amambaí, Braz.	D5	90
Amami Islands see Amami-Ō-shima, i., Japan	k19	39a
Amami-Ō-shima, i., Japan	k19	39a
Amami-shotō, is., Japan	I19	39a
Amana, Ia., U.S.	C6	120
Amana, stm., Ven.	C10	86
Amanã, Lago, l., Braz.	I9	86
Amanda, Oh., U.S.	E3	114
Amantea, Italy	E9	24
Amapá, Braz.	C7	84
Amapá, state, Braz.	C7	84
Amarante, Braz.	D4	88
Amaranth, Mb., Can.	D15	124
Amarapura, Mya.	B3	48
Amărăștii de Jos, Rom.	F11	26
Amarāvati, stm., India	F3	53
Amares, Port.	C2	20
Amargosa, Braz.	G6	88
Amargosa, stm., U.S.	H9	134
Amarillo, Tx., U.S.	F7	128
Amarkantak, India	G8	54
Amaro, Monte, mtn., Italy	H11	22
Amasra, Tur.	B15	28
Amasya, Tur.	A4	56
aMatikulu, S. Afr.	F10	70
Amatsu-kominato, Japan	D13	40
Amawbia Awka, Nig.	H6	64
Amazar, Russia	F13	34
Amazon (Amazonas) (Solimões), stm., S.A.	D7	84
Amazonas, state, Braz.	D4	84
Amazonas, state, Col.	H6	86
Amazonas, state, Ven.	F8	86
Ambājogāi, India	B3	53
Ambāla, India	C6	54
Ambalangoda, Sri L.	H4	53
Ambalavao, Madag.	E8	68
Ambam, Cam.	D2	66
Ambanja, Madag.	C8	68
Ambarčik, Russia	C21	34
Ambargasta, Salinas de, pl., Arg.	D5	92
Ambato, Ec.	H2	86
Ambatolampy, Madag.	D8	68
Ambatondrazaka, Madag.	D8	68
Ambelau, Pulau, i., Indon.	F8	44
Amberg, Ger.	G7	16
Amberg, Wi., U.S.	C2	112
Ambergris Cay, i., Belize	C4	102
Ambérieu-en-Bugey, Fr.	D11	18
Ambert, Fr.	D9	18
Ambidédi, Mali	G2	64
Ambikāpur, India	G9	54
Ambilobe, Madag.	C8	68
Ambla, Est.	A8	10
Amble, Eng., U.K.	F11	12
Ambo, Peru	F2	84
Ambodifototra, Madag.	D8	68
Ambohimahasoa, Madag.	E8	68
Amboise, Fr.	G10	14
Ambon, Indon.	F8	44
Ambon, Pulau, i., Indon.	F8	44
Amboseli, Lake, l., Afr.	E7	66
Amboseli National Park, p.o.i., Kenya	E7	66
Ambositra, Madag.	E8	68
Ambovombe, Madag.	F8	68
Amboy, Il., U.S.	C8	120
Amboy, Mn., U.S.	H4	118
Ambridge, Pa., U.S.	D5	114
Ambriz, Ang.	B1	68
Ambrosia Lake, N.M., U.S.	H9	132
Ambrym, state, Vanuatu	k17	79d
Ambrym, i., Vanuatu	k17	79d
Ambuntentimur, Indon.	G8	50
Ambunti, Pap. N. Gui.	a3	79a
Āmbūr, India	E4	53
Amchitka Island, i., Ak., U.S.	g22	140a
Amchitka Pass, strt., Ak., U.S.	g22	140a
Am Dam, Chad	E4	62
Amdo, China	B13	54
Ameagle, W.V., U.S.	G4	114
Ameca, Mex.	E6	100
Ameca, stm., Mex.	E6	100
Ameghino, Arg.	G6	92
Ameland, i., Neth.	A14	14
Amelia Court House, Va., U.S.	G8	114
Amelia Island, i., Fl., U.S.	F4	116
Āmer, India	E5	54
American, North Fork, stm., Ca., U.S.	D5	134
American, South Fork, stm., Ca., U.S.	E5	134
Americana, Braz.	L2	88
American Falls Reservoir, res., Id., U.S.	H13	136
American Fork, Ut., U.S.	C5	132
American Highland, plat., Ant.	C12	81
Americanos, Barra de los, i., Mex.	C10	100
American Samoa, dep., Oc.	h12	79c
Americus, Ga., U.S.	D1	116
Americus, Ks., U.S.	F1	120
Amersfoort, Neth.	B14	14
Amery, Wi., U.S.	F6	118
Amery Ice Shelf, ice, Ant.	B12	81
Ames, Ia., U.S.	B4	120
Amesbury, Ma., U.S.	B14	114
Amfilochía, Grc.	E4	28
Ámfissa, Grc.	E5	28
Amga, Russia	D15	34
Amga, stm., Russia	D15	34
Amguema, stm., Russia	C24	34
Amguid, Alg.	D6	64
Amgun', stm., Russia	F16	34
Amherst, N.S., Can.	E12	110
Amherst, Ma., U.S.	B13	114
Amherst, N.Y., U.S.	A7	114
Amherst, Oh., U.S.	C3	114
Amherst, Tx., U.S.	G6	128
Amherst, Wi., U.S.	G9	118
Amherstburg, On., Can.	F6	112
Amherstdale, W.V., U.S.	G4	114
Amherst Island, i., On., Can.	D13	112
Amherstview, On., Can.	D13	112
Amiens, Austl.	G8	76
Amiens, Fr.	E11	14
Amīndīvi Islands, is., India	F3	46
Amino, Japan	D8	40
Aminuis, Nmb.	C4	70
Amirantes, Les, is., Sey.	k12	69b
Amisk, Ab., Can.	B2	124
Amisk Lake, l., Sk., Can.	E10	106
Amistad, Parque Internacional de la, p.o.i., C.R.	H6	102
Amistad, Presa de la (Amistad Reservoir), res., N.A.	E6	130
Amistad National Recreation Area, p.o.i., Tx., U.S.	E6	130
Amistad Reservoir (Amistad, Presa de la), res., N.A.	E6	130
Amite, La., U.S.	G8	122
Amite, stm., La., U.S.	G8	122
Amity, Ar., U.S.	C5	122
Āmla, India	H7	54
Åmli, Nor.	G3	8
'Ammān, Jord.	G6	58
'Ammān, state, Jord.	G7	58
Ämmänsaari, Fin.	D13	8
'Ammār, Tall, hill, Syria	F7	58
Ammasalik see Angmagssalik, Grnld.	D18	141
Ammon, Id., U.S.	G15	136
Amnat Charoen, Thai.	E7	48
Amnok-kang (Yalu), stm., Asia	D7	38
Amo (Torsa), stm., Asia	E12	54
Amo, stm., China	A5	48
Āmol, Iran	B7	56
Amorgós, i., Grc.	G8	28
Amory, Ms., U.S.	D10	122
Amos, Qc., Can.	F15	106
Åmot, Nor.	G2	8
Amoy see Xiamen, China	I7	42
Ampanihy, Madag.	E7	68
Amparo, Braz.	L2	88
Ampasimanolotra, Madag.	D8	68
Amposta, Spain	D11	20
Amqui, Qc., Can.	B9	110
Amrāvati, India	H6	54
Amreli, India	H3	54
Amritsar, India	C5	54
Amroha, India	D7	54
Amrum, i., Ger.	B4	16
Amsterdam, Neth.	B13	14
Amsterdam, S. Afr.	E10	70
Amsterdam, N.Y., U.S.	B11	114
Amsterdam, Île, i., Afr.	M10	142
Amstetten, Aus.	B11	22
Am Timan, Chad	E4	62
Amu Darya, stm., Asia	F10	32
Amugulang see Xin Barag Zuoqi, China	B8	36
Amund Ringnes Island, i., Nu., Can.	B6	141
Amundsen Gulf, b., Can.	B14	140
Amundsen-Scott, sci., Ant.	D19	81
Amundsen Sea, Ant.	P27	142
Amuntai, Indon.	E9	50
Amur (Heilong), stm., Asia	F16	34
Amursk, Russia	F16	34
Amuzhong, China	C10	54
Amvrakikós Kólpos, b., Grc.	E3	28
An, Mya.	C2	48
Ana, Parque Nacional dedo see Doñana, Parque Nacional de, p.o.i., Spain	H4	20
Anaa, at., Fr. Poly.	E12	72
Anabar, stm., Russia	B11	34
Anaco, Ven.	C9	86
Anaconda, Mt., U.S.	D14	136
Anaconda Range, mts., Mt., U.S.	E13	136
Anacortes, Wa., U.S.	B4	136
Anadarko, Ok., U.S.	F10	128
Anadolu (Anatolia), hist. reg., Tur.	H15	6
Anadyr', Russia	D24	34
Anadyr, stm., Russia	C23	34
Anadyr, Gulf of see Anadyrskij zaliv, b., Russia	C21	142
Anadyr Mountains see Anadyrskoe ploskogor'e, plat., Russia	C23	34
Anadyrskij liman, b., Russia	D24	34
Anadyrskij zaliv, b., Russia	C21	142
Anadyrskoe ploskogor'e, plat., Russia	C23	34
Anáfi, i., Grc.	G8	28
Anagni, Italy	C7	24
Anaheim, Ca., U.S.	J8	134
Anahim Lake, B.C., Can.	D5	138
Anáhuac, Mex.	I10	130
Ānai Mudi, mtn., India	F3	53
Anajás, Braz.	D8	84
Anakāpalle, India	C6	53
Anaktuvuk Pass, Ak., U.S.	C9	140
Analalava, Madag.	C8	68
Anamã, Braz.	D5	84
Anama Bay, Mb., Can.	C15	124
Ana María, Golfo de, b., Cuba	B8	102
Anambas, Kepulauan (Anambas Islands), is., Indon.	B5	50
Anambas Islands see Anambas, Kepulauan, is., Indon.	B5	50
Anamizu, Japan	B9	40
Anamoose, N.D., U.S.	G13	124
Anamur, Tur.	B3	58
Anamur Burnu, c., Tur.	B3	58
Anan, Japan	F7	40
Ānand, India	G4	54
Ānandapur, India	H11	54
Ananindeua, Braz.	A1	88
Anan'ïv, Ukr.	B16	26
Anantapur, India	D3	53
Anantnāg, India	B5	54
Anápolis, Braz.	I1	88
Anapurus, Braz.	B4	88
Añasco, P.R.	B1	104a
Anastasia Island, i., Fl., U.S.	G4	116
Anatahan, i., N. Mar. Is.	B5	72
Anatolia see Anadolu, hist. reg., Tur.	H15	6
Anatolikí Makedonía kai Thráki, state, Grc.	B8	28
Anatom, i., Vanuatu	m17	79d
Añatuya, Arg.	D6	92
Anauá, stm., Braz.	G11	86
Anavilhanas, Arquipélago das, is., Braz.	I11	86
Anbei, China	F17	32
Anbianbu, China	C2	42
Anbyŏn-ŭp, Kor., N.	E7	38
Ancaster, On., Can.	E9	112
Ancasti, Sierra de, mts., Arg.	D5	92
Anchiang see Qianyang, China	H3	42
Anch'ing see Anqing, China	F7	42
Anchorage, Ak., U.S.	D10	140
Anchuras, Spain	E6	20
Ancona, Italy	G10	22
Ancón de Sardinas, Bahía de, b., S.A.	G2	86
Ancuabe, Moz.	C6	68
Ancud, Chile	H2	90
Ancy-le-Franc, Fr.	G13	14
Anda, China	B10	36
Andacollo, Arg.	H2	92
Andahuaylas, Peru	F3	84
Andalgalá, Arg.	C4	92
Andalucía, state, Spain	G6	20
Andalusia see Jan Kempdorp, S. Afr.	E7	70
Andalusia, Al., U.S.	F12	122
Andalusia see Andalucía, state, Spain	G6	20
Andaman and Nicobar Islands, state, India	F7	46
Andaman Basin, unds.	H12	142
Andaman Islands, is., India	F7	46
Andaman Sea, Asia	G8	46
Andamook, Austl.	F7	74
Andapa, Madag.	C8	68
Andenes, Nor.	B6	8
Andéramboukane, Mali	F5	64
Andernach, Ger.	F3	16
Anderson, Ca., U.S.	C3	134
Anderson, In., U.S.	H4	112
Anderson, Mo., U.S.	H3	120
Anderson, S.C., U.S.	B3	116
Anderson, Tx., U.S.	G3	122
Anderson, stm., N.T., Can.	B5	106
Anderson, Mount, mtn., Wa., U.S.	C3	136
Anderson Dam, Id., U.S.	G11	136
Andes, Col.	E4	86
Andes, mts., S.A.	F7	82
Andfjorden, strt., Nor.	B7	8
Andhra Lake, res., India	B1	53
Andhra Pradesh, state, India	C4	53
Andilamena, Madag.	D8	68
Andingpu, China	B2	42
Andirlang, China	A5	46
Andižan, Uzb.	F12	32
Andkhvoy, Afg.	B10	56
Andoany, Madag.	C8	68
Andoga, stm., Russia	A19	10
Andong, Kor., S.	C1	40
Andong-chŏsuji, res., Kor., S.	C1	40
Andorra, ctry., Eur.	B12	20
Andorra, ctry., Eur.	B12	20
Andorra-la-Vella, And.	B12	20
Andover, Eng., U.K.	J11	12
Andover, Me., U.S.	F6	110
Andover, Ma., U.S.	H5	110
Andover, Oh., U.S.	C5	114
Andover, S.D., U.S.	B15	126
Andøya, i., Nor.	B6	8
Andradina, Braz.	D6	90
Andranopasy, Madag.	E7	68
Andreanof Islands, is., Ak., U.S.	g23	140a
Andreapol', Russia	D15	10
Andrews, In., U.S.	H4	112
Andrews, N.C., U.S.	A2	116
Andrews, S.C., U.S.	C6	116
Andrews, Tx., U.S.	B5	130
Andria, Italy	C10	24
Andriamena, Madag.	D8	68
Andriievo-Ivanivka, Ukr.	B17	26
Androka, Madag.	F7	68
Andronovskoe, Russia	F16	8
Andros, i., Bah.	C9	96
Ándros, i., Grc.	F7	28
Androscoggin, stm., Me., U.S.	F6	110
Āndrott Island, i., India	F1	53
Andrupene, Lat.	D10	10
Andudu, D.R.C.	D5	66
Andújar, Spain	F6	20
Andulo, Ang.	C2	68
Anduze, Fr.	E9	18
Anegada, Bahía, b., Arg.	H4	90
Anegada Passage, strt., N.A.	h15	96a
Anécho, Togo	H5	64
Añelo, Arg.	I3	92
Anemata, Passe d', strt., N. Cal.	m16	79d
Anenii Noi, Mol.	C16	26
Aneroid, Sk., Can.	E6	124
Aneta, N.D., U.S.	G16	124
Anétis, Mali	F5	64
Aneto, mtn., Spain	B11	20
Anfu, China	H6	42
Angamos, Punta, c., Chile	D2	90
Ang'angxi, China	B9	36
Angara, stm., Russia	E8	34
Angarsk, Russia	D18	32
Angas Downs, Austl.	D6	74
Angastaco, Arg.	B4	92
Angaul, Russia	D18	32
Ånge, Swe.	E6	8
Ángel, Salto (Angel Falls), wtfl, Ven.	E10	86
Ángel de la Guarda, Isla, i., Mex.	G6	98
Angeles, Phil.	C3	52
Angel Falls see Ángel, Salto, wtfl, Ven.	E10	86
Ängelholm, Swe.	H5	8
Angelina, stm., Tx., U.S.	F4	122
Angellala Creek, stm., Austl.	F6	76
Angels Camp, Ca., U.S.	E5	134
Angemuk, mtn., Indon.	F10	44
Ångermanälven, stm., Swe.	E7	8
Angermünde, Ger.	C9	16
Angers, Fr.	G8	14
Angical, Braz.	F3	88
Angical do Piauí, Braz.	D4	88
Angicos, Braz.	C7	88
Angijak Island, i., Nu., Can.	D13	141
Angikuni Lake, l., Nu., Can.	C11	106
Angkor Wat, hist., Camb.	F6	48
Ângk Tasaôm, Camb.	G7	48
Angle Inlet, Mn., U.S.	B3	118
Anglem, Mount, mtn., N.Z.	H2	80
Anglesey, i., Wales, U.K.	H8	12
Anglet, Fr.	F4	18
Angleton, Tx., U.S.	H3	122
Anglona, reg., Italy	D2	24
Angmagssalik (Ammasalik), Grnld.	D18	141
Angoche, Moz.	D6	68
Angol, Chile	H1	92
Angola, In., U.S.	G5	112
Angola, N.Y., U.S.	B6	114
Angola, ctry., Afr.	C2	68
Angola Basin, unds.	J14	144
Angora see Ankara, Tur.	D15	28
Angoram, Pap. N. Gui.	a3	79a
Angostura, Presa de la, res., Mex.	H12	100
Angoulême, Fr.	D6	18

Name	Map Ref.	Page
Angoumois, hist. reg., Fr.	D5	18
Angra dos Reis, Braz.	L3	88
Angren, Uzb.	F12	32
Angu, D.R.C.	D4	66
Angualasto, Arg.	D3	92
Anguilla, Ms., U.S.	E8	122
Anguilla, dep., N.A.	h15	96a
Anguille, Cape, c., Nf., Can.	C17	110
Angui Nur, l., China	A6	42
Anguo, China	B6	42
Angus, On., Can.	D10	112
Angusville, Mb., Can.	D13	124
Anhalt, hist. reg., Ger.	D7	16
Anholt, i., Den.	H4	8
Anhua, China	G4	42
Anhui, state, China	F7	42
Anhwei see Anhui, state, China	F7	42
Aniak, Ak., U.S.	D8	140
Anibare Bay, b., Nauru	q17	78f
Anie, Pic d', mtn., Fr.	F5	18
Anil, Braz.	B3	88
Animas, N.M., U.S.	L8	132
Animas, stm., U.S.	G9	132
Animas Valley, val., N.A.	L8	132
Anina, Rom.	D8	26
Anita, Ia., U.S.	C3	120
Anıtkaya, Tur.	E13	28
Aniva, mys, c., Russia	B13	36
Aniva, zaliv, b., Russia	G17	34
Aniwa, i., Vanuatu	I17	79d
Anjangaon, India	H6	54
Anjär, India	G2	54
'Anjar, Leb.	E6	58
Anjou, hist. reg., Fr.	G8	14
Anjouan see Nzwani, i., Com.	C7	68
Anjudin, Russia	B9	32
Anjujsk, Russia	C21	34
Anjujskij hrebet, mts., Russia	C21	34
Anju-Up, Kor., N.	E6	38
Anka, Nig.	G6	64
Ankaboa, Tanjona, c., Madag.	E7	68
Ankang, China	E3	42
Ankara, Tur.	D15	28
Ankara, state, Tur.	D15	28
Ankavandra, Madag.	D8	68
Ankazoabo, Madag.	E7	68
Ankazobe, Madag.	D8	68
Ankeny, Ia., U.S.	C4	120
Anking see Anqing, China	F7	42
Ankleshwar, India	H4	54
Ankoro, D.R.C.	F5	66
Anlong, China	F6	36
Ånlóng Vêng, Camb.	E6	48
Anlu, China	F5	42
An Muileann gCearr see Mullingar, Ire.	H5	12
Ann, I., Swe.	E5	8
Ann, Cape, c., Ant.	B10	81
Ann, Cape, pen., Ma., U.S.	H6	110
Anna, Il., U.S.	G8	120
Anna, Lake, res., Va., U.S.	F8	114
Annaba, Alg.	B6	64
An-Nabatīyah, state, Leb.	E6	58
An-Nabatīyah at-Tahtā, Leb.	E6	58
Annaberg-Buchholz, Ger.	F9	16
An-Nabk, Syria	D7	58
An-Nafūd, des., Sau. Ar.	D5	56
An-Najaf, Iraq	C5	56
Annam see Trung Phan, hist. reg., Viet.	D8	48
Annamitique, Chaîne, mts., Asia	D8	48
Annan, Scot., U.K.	G9	12
Annandale, Austl.	C7	76
Annandale, Mn., U.S.	F4	118
Annandale, val., Scot., U.K.	F9	12
Anna Plains, Austl.	C4	74
Annapolis, Md., U.S.	F9	114
Annapolis Royal, N.S., Can.	F11	110
Annapurna, mtn., Nepal	D9	54
Ann Arbor, Mi., U.S.	B2	114
An Nás see Naas, Ire.	H6	12
An-Nāsiriyah, Iraq	C6	56
An-Nāsiriyah, Syria	E7	58
An-Nawfaliyah, Libya	A3	62
Annecy, Fr.	D12	18
Annecy, Lac d', l., Fr.	D12	18
Annemasse, Fr.	C12	18
Annenkov Island, i., S. Geor.	J9	90
An Nhon, Viet.	F9	48
Anning, China	G5	36
Annobón, i., Eq. Gui.	J6	64
Annonay, Fr.	D10	18
An-Nuhūd, Sudan	E5	62
Annville, Ky., U.S.	G2	114
Annville, Pa., U.S.	D9	114
Anoka, Mn., U.S.	F5	118
Anori, Braz.	D5	84
Anpu, China	K3	42
Anqing, China	F7	42
Anqiu, China	C8	42
Anren, China	H5	42
Ansai, China	C3	42
Ansbach, Ger.	G6	16
Anse-d'Hainault, Haiti	C10	102
Anse La Raye, St. Luc.	m6	105c
Anselmo, Ne., U.S.	F13	126
Anserma, Col.	E4	86
Anshan, China	D5	38
Anshun, China	H1	42
Ansina, Ur.	E10	92
Ansley, Ne., U.S.	F13	126
Anson Bay, b., Austl.	B5	74
Anson Bay, b., Norf. I.	y24	78i
Ansongo, Mali	F5	64
Ansonville, N.C., U.S.	A5	116
Ansted, W.V., U.S.	F4	114
Antakya see Hatay, Tur.	B7	58
Antalaha, Madag.	C9	68
Antaliepté, Lith.	E8	10
Antalya, Tur.	G13	28
Antalya, state, Tur.	F14	28
Antalya, Gulf of see Antalya Körfezi, b., Tur.	G14	28
Antalya Körfezi (Antalya, Gulf of), b., Tur.	G14	28
Antananarivo, Madag.	D8	68
An tAonach see Nenagh, Ire.		
Antarctica, cont.	D11	81
Antarctic Peninsula, pen., Ant.	C35	81
Antas, Braz.	F7	88
Antas, stm., Braz.	D12	92
Antelope Island, i., Ut., U.S.	B4	132
Antelope Mine, Zimb.	B9	70
Antelope Peak, mtn., Nv., U.S.	B1	132
Antenor Navarro, Braz.	D6	88
Antequera, Para.	A9	92
Antequera, Spain	H6	20
Anthon, Ia., U.S.	B2	120
Anthony, Ks., U.S.	D10	128
Anthony, N.M., U.S.	K10	132
Anthony, Tx., U.S.	E9	98
Anti-Atlas, mts., Mor.	D3	64
Antibes, Fr.	F13	18
Anticosti, Île d', i., Can.	F18	106
Antifer, Cap d', c., Fr.	E8	14
Antigonish, N.S., Can.	E14	110
Antigua, i., Antig.	h15	105b
Antigua and Barbuda, ctry., N.A.	h15	96a
Antigua International Airport, Antig.	i4	105b
Antiguo Morelos, Mex.	D9	100
Antikythira, i., Grc.	H6	28
Anti-Lebanon (Sharqī, Al-Jabal ash-), mts., Asia	E7	58
Antilla, Cuba	B10	102
Antillen, Nederlandse see Netherlands Antilles, dep., N.A.	i14	96a
Antimony, Ut., U.S.	E5	132
Antioch see Hatay, Tur.	B7	58
Antioch, Il., U.S.	F1	112
Antioquia, Col.	D4	86
Antioquia, state, Col.	D4	86
Antipajuta, Russia	C4	34
Antipodes Islands, is., N.Z.	H9	72
Antisana, vol., Ec.	H2	86
Antler, stm., N.A.	E12	124
Antofagasta, Chile	A2	92
Antofagasta, state, Chile	B3	92
Antofagasta de la Sierra, Arg.	C4	92
Antofalla, Salar de, pl., Arg.	C3	92
Antofalla, Volcán, vol., Arg.	B3	92
Antón, Pan.	H7	102
Anton, Tx., U.S.	H6	128
Anton Chico, N.M., U.S.	F3	128
Antongila, Helodrano, b., Madag.	D8	68
Antonina, Braz.	B13	92
Antonina do Norte, Braz.	D5	88
Antônio Prado, Braz.	D12	92
Antonito, Co., U.S.	D2	128
Antón Lizardo, Punta, c., Mex.	F10	100
Antopal', Bela.	H7	10
Antrim, N. Ire., U.K.	G6	12
Antropovo, Russia	G20	8
Antsalova, Madag.	D7	68
Antsirabe, Madag.	D8	68
Antsirañana, Madag.	C8	68
Antsohihy, Madag.	C8	68
Antulai, Gunong, mtn., Malay.	A10	50
Antun', Russia	G16	34
Antung see Dandong, China	D5	38
Antwerp see Antwerpen, Bel.	C13	14
Antwerp, Oh., U.S.	C1	114
Antwerpen (Antwerp), Bel.	C13	14
An Uaimh see Navan, Ire.	H6	12
Anugul, India	H10	54
Anūpgarh, India	D4	54
Anuradhapura, Sri L.	G5	53
Anvers see Antwerpen, Bel.	C13	14
Anvers Island, i., Ant.	B34	81
Anvik, Ak., U.S.	D7	140
Anxi, China	C4	36
Anxi, China	I8	42
Anxiang, China	G5	42
Anxious Bay, b., Austl.	F6	74
Anyang, China	C6	42
A'nyêmaqên Shan, mts., China	D4	36
Anyer Kidul, Indon.	G4	50
Anykščiai, Lith.	E7	10
Anyuan, China	I6	42
Anyuanyi see Tianzhu, China	D5	36
Anyue, China	F1	42
Anze, China	C5	42
Anžero-Sudžensk, Russia	C15	32
Anzio, Italy	C6	24
Anzoátegui, state, Ven.	C9	86
Anžu, ostrova, is., Russia	A17	34
Aoba, i., Vanuatu	j16	79d
Aoba / Maéwo, state, Vanuatu	j17	79d
Aoga-shima, i., Japan	G12	40
Aohan Qi, China	C3	38
Aojiang, China	H9	42
Aoji-ri, Kor., N.	C9	38
Ao Luk, Thai.	H4	48
Aomar, Alg.	H14	20
Aomen see Macau, Macau	J5	42
Aomen see Macau, dep., Asia	J5	42
Aomori, Japan	D14	38
Aonla, India	D7	54
Aóós (Vjosës), stm., Eur.	D13	24
A'opo, Samoa	g11	79c
Aoral, Phnum, mtn., Camb.	F7	48
Aore, i., Vanuatu	j16	79d
Aoral, Alg.	D5	64
Aosta (Aoste), Italy	E4	22
Aoste see Aosta, Italy	E4	22
Aouderas, Niger	F6	64
Aouk, Bahr, stm., Afr.	F3	62
Aoukâr, reg., Maur.	F3	64
Aoya, Japan	D7	40
Aozou, Chad	C3	62
Apache Junction, Az., U.S.	J5	132
Apache Peak, mtn., Az., U.S.	L6	132
Apalachee, stm., Ga., U.S.	C2	116
Apalachicola, Fl., U.S.	H13	122
Apalachicola, stm., Fl., U.S.	H14	122
Apalachicola Bay, b., Fl., U.S.	H13	122
Apaporis, stm., S.A.	H7	86
Aparados da Serra, Parque Nacional da, p.o.i., Braz.	D12	92
Aparri, Phil.	A3	52
Apartadó, Col.	D3	86
Apatin, Yugo.	D5	26
Apatity, Russia	C15	8
Apatzingán de la Constitución, Mex.	F8	100
Apaxtla de Castrejón, Mex.	F8	100
Apeldoorn, Neth.	B15	14
Apennines see Appennino, mts., Italy	G11	6
Apex, N.C., U.S.	I7	114
Api, mtn., Nepal	D8	54
Apia, Samoa	g12	79c
Apiacás, Serra dos, plat., Braz.	E6	84
Apiaí, Braz.	B13	92
Apiaú, stm., Braz.	F11	86
Apishapa, stm., Co., U.S.	D4	128
Apizaco, Mex.	F9	100
Apo, Mount, mtn., Phil.	G5	52
Apodi, Braz.	C7	88
Apodi, stm., Braz.	C7	88
Apolakkiá, Grc.	H10	28
Apolda, Ger.	E7	16
Apolinario Saravia, Arg.	B5	92
Apolo, Bol.	B3	90
Apón, stm., Ven.	C5	86
Aponguao, stm., Ven.	E11	86
Apopka, Lake, l., Fl., U.S.	H4	116
Aporá, Braz.	F6	88
Aporé, Braz.	C6	90
Apostle Islands, is., Wi., U.S.	E8	118
Apostle Islands National Lakeshore, p.o.i., Wi., U.S.	D8	118
Apóstoles, Arg.	C10	92
Apostolove, Ukr.	E4	32
Appalaches, Les see Appalachian Mountains, mts., N.A.	D12	108
Appalachia, Va., U.S.	H3	114
Appalachian Mountains, mts., N.A.	D12	108
Appennino (Apennines), mts., Italy	G11	6
Appennino Abruzzese, mts., Italy	B7	24
Appennino Calabro, mts., Italy	E10	24
Appennino Ligure, mts., Italy	F6	22
Appennino Lucano, mts., Italy	D9	24
Appennino Tosco-Emiliano, mts., Italy	F8	22
Appennino Umbro-Marchigiano, mts., Italy	G9	22
Appenzell, Switz.	C6	22
Arc, stm., Fr.	D12	18
Apple Orchard Mountain, mtn., Va., U.S.	G6	114
Appleton, Mn., U.S.	F3	118
Appleton, Wi., U.S.	G10	118
Appleton City, Mo., U.S.	F3	120
Apple Valley, Ca., U.S.	I8	134
Appomattox, Va., U.S.	G7	114
Appomattox, stm., Va., U.S.	G7	114
Aprelevka, Russia	E20	10
Aprília, Italy	C6	24
Apšeronsk, Russia	F5	32
Apt, Fr.	F11	18
Apucarana, Braz.	A12	92
Apulia see Puglia, state, Italy	C10	24
Apure, state, Ven.	D7	86
Apure, stm., Ven.	D7	86
Apurímac, stm., Peru	F3	84
Apurito, Ven.	D7	86
Aqaba, Gulf of, b.	J5	58
Āqchah, Afg.	B10	56
'Aqīq, Sudan	D7	62
Aqtaū see Aktau, Kaz.	F8	32
Aqtöbe see Aktjubinsk, Kaz.	D9	32
Aquidabã, Braz.	F7	88
Aquidauana, Braz.	D5	90
Aquila, Mex.	F7	100
Aquiles Serdán, Mex.	A6	100
Aquiles Serdán, Mex.	C9	100
Aquin, Haiti	C11	102
Aquio, stm., Col.	F8	86
Ara, India	F10	54
Ara, stm., Japan	D12	40
Arab, Al., U.S.	C12	122
'Arab, Bahr al-, stm., Sudan	E5	62
'Araba, Wadi ('Arabah, Wādī), stm., Egypt	I3	58
'Arabah, Wādī al- (Ha'Arava), val., Asia	H6	58
Araban, Tur.	A8	58
Arabian Basin, unds.	H9	142
Arabian Desert (Eastern Desert), des., Egypt	B6	62
Arabian Gulf see Persian Gulf, b., Asia	D7	56
Arabian Peninsula, pen., Asia	E6	56
Arabian Sea	F9	56
Araçá, stm., Braz.	G10	86
Aracaju, Braz.	F7	88
Aracataca, Col.	B4	86
Aracati, Braz.	C7	88
Araçatuba, Braz.	D6	90
Aracena, Spain	G4	20
Araci, Braz.	F6	88
Aracides, Cape, c., Sol. Is.	e9	79b
Aracoiaba, Braz.	C6	88
Aracruz, Braz.	J5	88
Araçuaí, Braz.	I4	88
Araçuaí, stm., Braz.	I5	88
Arad, Rom.	C8	26
Arad, state, Rom.	C8	26
'Arad, Isr.	K2	58
Aradhippou, Cyp.	D4	58
Arafura Sea	J16	142
Arafura Shelf, unds.	K16	142
Aragarças, Braz.	G7	84
Aragats Lerr, mtn., Arm.	A5	56
Aragón, state, Spain	C10	20
Aragón, stm., Spain	B9	20
Aragua, state, Ven.	B8	86
Araguacema, Braz.	E8	84
Aragua de Barcelona, Ven.	C9	86
Araguaia, stm., Braz.	E8	84
Araguaína, Braz.	D1	88
Araguao, Caño, stm., Ven.	C11	86
Araguari, Braz.	J1	88
Araguari, stm., Braz.	J1	88
Araguatins, Braz.	C1	88
Arai, Japan	D10	40
Araioses, Braz.	B4	88
Árak, Alg.	D5	64
Arāk, Iran	C6	56
Arak see Rakhine, state, Mya.	C1	48
Arakan Yoma, mts., Mya.	C2	48
Arakkonam, India	E4	53
Araks see Aras, stm., Asia	B6	56
Araks see Araz, stm., Asia	B6	56
Aral Sea, l., Asia	E9	32
Aral'sk see Aral'sk, Kaz.	E10	32
Aramac, Austl.	D5	76
Aramac, stm., Austl.	D5	76
Arāmbāg, India	G11	54
Aramberri, Mex.	C8	100
Āran, Iran	C7	56
Aranda de Duero, Spain	C7	20
Arandas, Mex.	E7	100
Arandis, Nmb.	C2	70
Arang, India	H8	54
Āraṇi, India	E4	53
Aran Island, i., Ire.	G4	12
Aran Islands, is., Ire.	H3	12
Aranjuez, Spain	D7	20
Aranos, Nmb.	C4	70
Aransas, stm., Tx., U.S.	F10	130
Arantāngi, India	F4	53
Aranyaprathet, Thai.	F6	48
Arao, Japan	G3	40
Araouane, Mali	F4	64
Arapaho, Ok., U.S.	F9	128
Arapahoe, Ne., U.S.	A9	128
Arapey Grande, stm., Ur.	E9	92
Arapiraca, Braz.	E7	88
Arapongas, Braz.	D6	90
Arapoti, Braz.	B12	92
Araranguá, Braz.	D13	92
Araraquara, Braz.	K1	88
Araras, Braz.	L2	88
Araras, Açude, res., Braz.	C5	88
Ararat, Austl.	K4	76
Ararat, Mount see Ağrı Dağı, mtn., Tur.	B5	56
Arari, Braz.	B3	88
Araria, India	E11	54
Araripe, Braz.	D5	88
Araripe, Chapada do, plat., Braz.	D6	88
Araripina, Braz.	D5	88
Araruama, Lagoa de, b., Braz.	L4	88
Araruna, Braz.	D8	88
Aras (Araz), stm., Asia	B6	56
Aratuba, Braz.	C6	88
Arauca, Col.	D6	86
Arauca, state, Col.	D6	86
Arauca, stm., S.A.	D7	86
Araucária, Braz.	B13	92
Arauco, Chile	H1	92
Arauquita, Col.	D6	86
Araure, Ven.	C7	86
Araxá, Braz.	J2	88
Araya, Ven.	B9	86
Araya, Punta de, c., Ven.	B9	86
Araz (Aras), stm., Asia	B6	56
Árba Minch', Eth.	F7	62
Arbatax, Italy	E3	24
Arboga, Swe.	G6	8
Arboledas, Arg.	H7	92
Arbon, Switz.	C6	22
Arborea, reg., Italy	E2	24
Arborfield, Sk., Can.	A10	124
Arbroath, Scot., U.K.	E10	12
Arbuckle, Ca., U.S.	D3	134
Arcachon, Fr.	D12	18
Arcachon, Bassin d', b., Fr.	E4	18
Arcade, Ca., U.S.	E4	134
Arcade, N.Y., U.S.	B7	114
Arcadia, Ca., U.S.	I7	134
Arcadia, Fl., U.S.	I4	116
Arcadia, Ia., U.S.	B2	120
Arcadia, Ks., U.S.	G3	120
Arcadia, La., U.S.	E6	122
Arcadia, Mi., U.S.	D3	112
Arcadia, Wi., U.S.	G7	118
Arcanum, Oh., U.S.	D1	114
Arcas, Cayos, is., Mex.	E12	100
Arcata, Ca., U.S.	C1	134
Arc Dome, mtn., Nv., U.S.	E8	134
Arcelia, Mex.	F8	100
Arcevia, Italy	G9	22
Archangel see Arhangel'sk, Russia	D19	8
Archbold, Oh., U.S.	C1	114
Archer, Fl., U.S.	G3	116
Archer, stm., Austl.	B8	74
Archer, Mount, mtn., Austl.	D8	76
Archer City, Tx., U.S.	H10	128
Archer's Post, Kenya	D7	66
Arches National Park, p.o.i., Ut., U.S.	E7	132
Archiac, Fr.	D5	18
Archidona, Spain	G6	20
Arcis-sur-Aube, Fr.	F13	14
Arco, Id., U.S.	G13	136
Arcola, Il., U.S.	E9	120
Arcola, Ms., U.S.	D8	122
Arcos, Braz.	K3	88
Arcos de la Frontera, Spain	H5	20
Arcot, India	E4	53
Arcoverde, Braz.	E7	88
Arctic Bay, Nu., Can.	A14	106
Arctic Ocean	A21	4
Arctic Red, stm., N.T., Can.	B4	106
Arctic Village, Ak., U.S.	C10	140
Arda, stm., Eur.	H12	26
Ardabīl, Iran	B6	56
Ardahan, Tur.	A5	56
Ardakān, Iran	C7	56
Ardatov, Russia	I20	8
Ardèche, state, Fr.	E10	18
Ardee, Ire.	H6	12
Ardennes, state, Fr.	E13	14
Ardennes, reg., Eur.	D14	14
Ardennes, Canal des, can., Fr.	E13	14
Ardestān, Iran	C7	56
Ardill, Sk., Can.	E8	124
Ardlethan, Austl.	J6	76
Ardmore, Al., U.S.	B12	122
Ardmore, Ok., U.S.	G11	128
Ardmore, Pa., U.S.	D10	114
Åre, Swe.	E5	8
Areado, Braz.	K2	88
Arena, Point, c., Ca., U.S.	E2	134
Arena, Punta de, c., Mex.	D4	100
Arena de la Ventana, Punta, c., Mex.	C4	100
Arenal, P.R.	B2	104a
Arenápolis, Braz.	F6	84
Arenas, Cayo, i., Mex.	D13	100
Arenas, Punta de, c., Arg.	J3	90
Arenas de San Pedro, Spain	D5	20
Arendal, Nor.	G3	8
Arenys de Mar, Spain	C13	20
Arequipa, Peru	G3	84
Arequito, Arg.	F7	92
Arévalo, Spain	C6	20
Arezzo, Italy	G8	22
Arga, stm., Spain	B9	20
Argadargada, Austl.	D7	74
Argamasilla de Alba, Spain	E7	20
Arganda del Rey, Spain	D7	20
Arga-Sala, stm., Russia	C10	34
Argelès-Gazost, Fr.	F5	18
Argens, stm., Fr.	F12	18
Argent, Côte d', cst., Fr.	F4	18
Argenta, Italy	F8	22
Argentan, Fr.	F8	14
Argentat, Fr.	D7	18
Argenteuil, Fr.	F11	14
Argentina, ctry., S.A.	G3	90
Argentine Basin, unds.	L10	144
Argentino, Lago, l., Arg.	J2	90
Argenton-sur-Creuse, Fr.	H10	14
Argeș, state, Rom.	E11	26
Argeș, stm., Rom.	E13	26
Arghandāb, stm., Afg.	C10	56
Argolikós Kólpos (Argolis, Gulf of), b., Grc.	F6	28
Argolis, Gulf of see Argolikós Kólpos, b., Grc.	F6	28
Argonia, Ks., U.S.	D11	128
Argonne, reg., Fr.	E14	14
Argos, Grc.	F5	28
Argos, In., U.S.	G3	112
Argostóli, Grc.	E3	28
Arguello, Point, c., Ca., U.S.	I5	134
Argun' (Ergun), stm., Asia	F12	34
Argungu, Nig.	G5	64
Argyle, Lake, l., Austl.	C5	74
Arhangel'skaja oblast', co., Russia	E20	8
Arhangel'skoe, Russia	G20	10
Arhara see Arhara, Russia	G15	34
Arhipovka, Russia	C10	38
Árhus, Den.	H4	8
Ari Atoll, at., Mald.	i12	46a
Ari, stm., Braz.	D5	88
Ariano Irpino, Italy	C9	24
Ariari, stm., Col.	F5	86
Arias, Arg.	F6	92
Aripuanã, Braz.	E5	84
Arica, Chile	H10	88
Arichat, N.S., Can.	E16	110
Arichuna, Ven.	D8	86
Arid, Cape, c., Austl.	F4	74
Arida, Japan	E8	40
Aridaia, Grc.	C5	28
Ariège, state, Fr.	G7	18
Arifwāla, Pak.	C4	54
Ariguaní, stm., Col.	B4	86
Ariha (Jericho), Gaza	G6	58
Arīhā, Syria	B8	58
Aravalli Range, mts., India	F4	54
Arawa, Pap. N. Gui.	d6	79b
Araxá, stm., Braz.	J2	88
Araya, Ven.	B9	86
Araya, Punta de, c., Ven.	B9	86
Araz (Aras), stm., Asia	B6	56
Arba Minch', Eth.	F7	62
Arboga, Swe.	G6	8
Arborea, reg., Italy	E2	24
Ariano Irpino, Italy	C9	24
Ariari, stm., Col.	F5	86
Arinos, Braz.	F6	84
Arinos, stm., Braz.	F6	84
Ario de Rosáles, Mex.	F7	100
Ariporo, stm., Col.	D6	86
Aripuanã, stm., Braz.	E5	84
Ariquemes, Braz.	E5	84
Arisa, stm., Ven.	D9	86
Arish, Wadi al- ('Arish, Wādī al-), stm., Egypt	H4	58
Aristazabal Island, i., B.C., Can.	E5	106
Ariton, Al., U.S.	F13	122
Arivonimamo, Madag.	D8	68
Ariyalūr, India	F4	53
Arizaro, Salar de, pl., Arg.	B4	92
Arizgoiti, Spain	A8	20
Arizona, Arg.	G5	92
Arizona, state, U.S.	I5	132
Arizpe, Mex.	F7	98
Arja, Russia	H22	8
Arjasa, Indon.	G9	50
Arjona, Col.	B4	86
Arjona, Spain	G6	20
Arkadelphia, Ar., U.S.	C5	122
Arkansas, state, U.S.	B6	122
Arkansas, stm., U.S.	E9	108
Arkansas, Salt Fork, stm., U.S.	D7	122
Arkansas City, Ar., U.S.	D7	122
Arkansas City, Ks., U.S.	D11	128
Arkhara see Arhara, Russia	G15	34
Arklow, Ire.	I6	12
Arkoma, Ok., U.S.	B4	122
Arkona, Kap, c., Ger.	B9	16
Arkport, N.Y., U.S.	B8	114
Arktičeskogo instituta, ostrova, is., Russia	A5	34
Arlanza, stm., Spain	B7	20
Arlanzón, stm., Spain	B7	20
Arles, Fr.	F10	18
Arlington, S. Afr.	E8	70
Arlington, Ga., U.S.	F14	122
Arlington, Ks., U.S.	D10	128
Arlington, Ky., U.S.	H9	120
Arlington, Ne., U.S.	C1	120
Arlington, Oh., U.S.	D2	114
Arlington, Or., U.S.	E6	136
Arlington, Tn., U.S.	B10	130
Arlington, Tx., U.S.	B10	130
Arlington, Vt., U.S.	G3	110
Arlington, Va., U.S.	F8	114
Arlington, Wa., U.S.	B4	136
Arlington Heights, Il., U.S.	F2	112
Arlit, Niger	F6	64
Arlon, Bel.	E14	14
Arma, Ks., U.S.	G3	120
Arma, stm., Sk., Can.	D8	124
Armadale, Austl.	F3	74
Armageddon see Tel Megiddo, hist., Isr.	F6	58
Armagh, N. Ire., U.K.	G6	12
Armagnac, reg., Fr.	F6	18
Armavir, Russia	E6	32
Armavir, Arm.	A5	56
Armenia, Col.	E4	86
Armenia see Armenia, ctry., Asia	A5	56
Armenia, ctry., Asia	A5	56
Armenija see Armenia, ctry., Asia	A5	56
Armenistis, Grc.	F9	28
Armentières, Fr.	D11	14
Armería, Mex.	F6	100
Armero, Col.	E4	86
Armidale, Austl.	H8	76
Armijo, N.M., U.S.	H10	132
Armour, S.D., U.S.	D14	126
Armstrong, Arg.	F7	92
Armstrong, B.C., Can.	F11	138
Armstrong, On., Can.	A9	118
Armstrong, Mo., U.S.	E5	120
Armstrong, Mount, mtn., Yk., Can.	C4	106
Ārmūr, India	B4	53
Armutlu, Tur.	C11	28
Arnaoutis, Cape see Arnauti, Cape, c., Cyp.	C3	58
Arnauti, Cape, c., Cyp.	C3	58
Arnaud, stm., Qc., Can.	D16	106
Arnaudville, La., U.S.	G6	122
Arnay-le-Duc, Fr.	G13	14
Arnedo, Spain	B8	20
Arneiros, Braz.	D5	88
Arnett, Ok., U.S.	E8	128
Arnhem, Neth.	B14	14
Arnhem, Cape, c., Austl.	B7	74
Arnhem Bay, b., Austl.	B7	74
Arnhem Land, reg., Austl.	B6	74
Arno, at., Marsh. Is.	C8	72
Arno, stm., Italy	G7	22
Arnold, Ca., U.S.	E5	134
Arnold, Mn., U.S.	E6	118
Arnold, Mo., U.S.	F7	120
Arnold, Pa., U.S.	D6	114
Arnolds Park, Ia., U.S.	H3	118
Arnon, stm., Fr.	C8	18
Arnprior, On., Can.	C13	112
Arnsberg, Ger.	E4	16
Arnstadt, Ger.	F6	16
Aroa, stm., Ven.	B7	86
Aroa, Pointe, c., Fr. Poly.	u20	78h
Aroab, Nmb.	E4	70
Aroland, On., Can.	A12	118
Arolsen, Ger.	E5	16
Arona, Italy	E5	22
Arona, Pap. N. Gui.	b4	79a
Aroostook, stm., N.A.	D8	110
Arop Island (Long Island), i., Pap. N. Gui.	b4	79a
Arorae, i., Kir.	D8	72
Aroroy, Phil.	D4	52
Arosa, Ría de see Arousa, Ría de, est., Spain	B1	20
Arousa, Ría de (Arosa, Ría de), est., Spain	B1	20
Arp, Tx., U.S.	E3	122
Arpajon, Fr.	F11	14
Arqalyq see Arkalyk, Kaz.	D11	32
Arquata Scrivia, Italy	F5	22
Arraga, Arg.	D5	92
Arraias, Braz.	G2	88
Arraial do Cabo, Braz.	L4	88
Arraias, stm., Braz.	G8	84
Ar-Ramādī, Iraq	C5	56
Ar-Ramthā, Jord.	F7	58
Arran, Island of, i., Scot., U.K.	F7	12
Ar-Rank, Sudan	E6	62
Ar-Raqqah, Syria	B9	58
Ar-Raqqah, state, Syria	B9	58
Arras, Fr.	D11	14
Ar-Rastan, Syria	D7	58
Arrecifes, Arg.	G7	92
Arrey, N.M., U.S.	K9	132
Ar-Riyād (Riyadh), Sau. Ar.	E6	56
Arroio Grande, Braz.	F11	92
Arrojado, stm., Braz.	G3	88
Arronches, Port.	E3	20
Arroux, stm., Fr.	B10	18
Arrow, Lough, l., Ire.	G4	12
Arrowhead, Lake, l., U.S.	H10	128
Arrowrock Reservoir, res., Id., U.S.	G11	136
Arrowwood, Ab., Can.	F17	138
Arroyo, P.R.	C3	104a
Arroyo de la Luz, Spain	E4	20
Arroyo Grande, Ca., U.S.	H5	134
Arroyo Hondo, N.M., U.S.	E3	128
Arroyo Seco, Arg.	F7	92
Ar-Rub' al-Khālī, des., Asia	E6	56
Ar-Ruqayyah, hist., Syria	D7	58
Ar-Rusāfah, hist., Syria	C9	58
Ar-Rusayris, Sudan	E6	62
Ar-Rutbah, Iraq	C5	56
Arsenjev, Russia	B10	38
Arsikere, India	E3	53
Arsos, Cyp.	D4	58
Arta, Grc.	D3	28
Art, Île, i., N. Cal.	I14	79d
Artà see Artà, Spain	E14	20
Artĕmovsk, Russia	D16	34
Artĕmovskij, Russia	E12	34
Artĕmovskij, Russia	C10	36
Artesia, Ms., U.S.	D10	122
Artesia, N.M., U.S.	B3	130
Arthabaska, ngh., Qc., Can.	D5	110
Arthal, India	B6	54
Arthur, On., Can.	E9	112
Arthur, Il., U.S.	E9	120
Arthur, N.D., U.S.	D1	118
Arthur, Tn., U.S.	H2	114
Arthur's Pass National Park, p.o.i., N.Z.	F5	80
Arthur's Town, Bah.	C9	96
Artibonite, stm., Haiti	C11	102
Artigas, Ur.	E9	92
Artillery Lake, l., N.T., Can.	C9	106
Artois, hist. reg., Fr.	D11	14
Artsyz, Ukr.	D16	26
Artyk, Russia	D18	34
Aru, Kepulauan (Aru Islands), is., Indon.	G10	44
Aru, Tanjung, c., Indon.	E10	50
Aruanã, Braz.	F7	84
Aruba, dep., N.A.	F12	102
Aru Islands see Aru, Kepulauan, is., Indon.	G10	44
Arunāchal Pradesh, state, India	C7	46
Arun Qi, China	B9	36
Aruppukkottai, India	G4	53
Arurandeua, stm., Braz.	C1	88
Arusha, Tan.	E7	66
Aruvi, stm., Sri L.	G5	53
Aruwimi, stm., D.R.C.	D4	66
Arvada, Co., U.S.	B3	128
Arvayheer, Mong.	B5	36
Arvi, India	H7	54
Arviat, Nu., Can.	C12	106
Arvidsjaur, Swe.	D8	8
Arvika, Swe.	G5	8
Arvin, Ca., U.S.	H7	134
Arvon, Mount, mtn., Mi., U.S.	B1	112
Arvorezinha, Braz.	D11	92
Arxan, China	B8	36
Arys', Kaz.	F11	32
Arys, ozero, l., Kaz.	E11	32
Arzachena, Italy	C3	24
Arzamas, Russia	I20	8
Arzignano, Italy	E8	22
Arz Lubnān, for., Leb.	D7	58
Aš, Czech Rep.	F8	16
Aša, Russia	D9	32
Asa, stm., Nig.	H6	64
Asad, Buhayrat al- (Assad, Lake), res., Syria	B9	58
Asadābād, Afg.	A11	56
Asadābād, Iran	C6	56
Asahi, Japan	D13	40
Asahi, Japan	E6	40
Asahi-dake, vol., Japan	C15	38
Asahigawa see Asahikawa, Japan	C15	38
Asahikawa, Japan	C15	38
Asama-yama, vol., Japan	C11	40
Åsane, Nor.	F1	8
Āsansol, India	G11	54
Asarna, Swe.	E5	8
Asbe Teferī, Eth.	F8	62
Asbest, Russia	C10	32
Asbestos, Qc., Can.	E4	110
Asbestos Range National Park, p.o.i., Austl.	n13	77a
Asbury Park, N.J., U.S.	D12	114
Ascención, Bol.	B4	90
Ascención, Mex.	F9	98
Aschaffenburg, Ger.	G5	16
Aschersleben, Ger.	E7	16
Ascoli Piceno, Italy	H10	22
Ascoli Satriano, Italy	C9	24
Ascór (Oster), stm., Eur.	G14	10
Āseda, Swe.	H6	8
Åsele, Swe.	D7	8
Asenovgrad, Blg.	G11	26
Aseral, Nor.	G2	8
Aşgabat, Turkmen.	B9	56
Ashburton, N.Z.	F4	80
Ashburton, stm., Austl.	D3	74
Ashcroft, B.C., Can.	F9	138
Ashdod, Isr.	G5	58
Ashdod, Tel, hist., Isr.	G5	58
Ashdown, Ar., U.S.	D4	122
Asheboro, N.C., U.S.	I6	114
Ashern, Mb., Can.	C15	124
Asheville, N.C., U.S.	I3	114
Ash Flat, Ar., U.S.	H6	120
Ashford, Austl.	G8	76
Ashford, Eng., U.K.	J13	12
Ashford, Al., U.S.	F13	122
Ashford, Wa., U.S.	D4	136
Ash Fork, Az., U.S.	H4	132
Ashgabat see Aşgabat, Turkmen.	B8	56
Ashibe, Japan	F2	40
Ashikaga, Japan	C12	40
Ashington, Eng., U.K.	F11	12
Ashizuri-misaki, c., Japan	G5	40
Ashkhabad see Aşgabat, Turkmen.	B8	56
Ashland, Al., U.S.	D13	122
Ashland, Ks., U.S.	D9	128
Ashland, Ky., U.S.	F3	114
Ashland, Me., U.S.	D8	110
Ashland, Mt., U.S.	A5	126
Ashland, N.H., U.S.	G5	110
Ashland, Oh., U.S.	D3	114
Ashland, Or., U.S.	A2	134
Ashland, Va., U.S.	G8	114
Ashland, Wi., U.S.	E8	118
Ashland, Mount, mtn., Or., U.S.	A3	134
Ashland City, Tn., U.S.	H10	120
Ashley, Il., U.S.	F8	120
Ashley, In., U.S.	C1	114
Ashley, N.D., U.S.	A13	126
Ashley, Oh., U.S.	D2	114
Ashley, stm., Austl.	G7	76
Ashmore Islands, is., Austl.	B4	74
Ashqelon, Isr.	G5	58
Ash-Shaqrā' see Shaqrā', Sau. Ar.	D6	56
Ash-Shāriqah, U.A.E.	D8	56
Ash-Shawbak, Jord.	H6	58
Ash-Shiḥr, Yemen	G6	56
Ash-Shuqayq, Sau. Ar.	F5	56
Ashta, India	G6	54
Ashta, India	B3	53
Ashtabula, Oh., U.S.	C5	114
Ashtabula, Lake, res., N.D., U.S.	G16	124
Ashton, S. Afr.	H5	70
Ashton, Id., U.S.	F15	136
Ashton, Il., U.S.	C8	120
Ashton, St. Vin.	p11	105e
Ashuanipi Lake, l., Nf., Can.	E17	106
Ashuapmushuan, stm., Qc., Can.	B3	110
Ashville, Al., U.S.	D12	122
Ashwaubenon, Wi., U.S.	D1	112

Name	Map Ref.	Page
Asi see Orontes, stm., Asia.	B7	58
Asia, cont.	C19	4
Asia, Kepulauan, is., Indon.	E9	44
Asia Minor, hist. reg., Tur.	E13	28
Āsika, India	I10	54
Asinara, Golfo dell', b., Italy	D2	24
Asinara, Isola, i., Italy	C2	24
Asino, Russia	C15	32
Asintorf, Bela.	F13	10
Asipovičy, Bela.	G11	10
Askham, S. Afr.	E5	70
Askiz, Russia	D16	32
Askja, vol., Ice.	k31	8a
Aslanapa, Tur.	D12	28
Aslantaş Baraji, res., Tur.	A7	58
Asmara see Asmera, Erit.	D7	62
Asmera, Erit.	D7	62
Ašmjany, Bela.	F8	10
Asola, Italy	E7	22
Asomante, P.R.	B2	104a
Āsosa, Eth.	E6	62
Asoteriba, Jabal, mtn., Sudan	C7	62
Asotin, Wa., U.S.	D9	136
Asouf, Oued, stm., Alg.	D5	64
Asp, Spain	F10	20
Aspe see Asp, Spain	F10	20
Aspen, Co., U.S.	D10	132
Aspendos, hist., Tur.	G14	28
Aspermont, Tx., U.S.	A7	130
Aspiring, Mount, mtn., N.Z.	G3	80
Assad, Lake see Asad, Buhayrat al-, res., Syria.	B9	58
As-Saffirah, Syria	B8	58
As-Sāfiyah, Sudan	D6	62
As-Salt, Jord.	F6	58
Assam, state, India.	C7	46
As-Samāwah, Iraq	C6	56
As-Sanamayn, Syria	E7	58
As-Sarafand, Leb.	E6	58
Assaré, Braz.	D6	88
Assateague Island National Seashore, p.o.i., U.S.	G10	114
Assemini, Italy	E2	24
Assen, Neth.	A15	14
Asseria, hist., Cro.	F12	22
Assini, hist., Grc.	F5	28
Assiniboia, Sk., Can.	E8	124
Assiniboine, stm., Can.	E16	124
Assiniboine, Mount, mtn., Can.	F15	138
Assis, Braz.	D6	90
Assis Chateaubriand, Braz.	B11	92
Assisi, Italy	G9	22
Assomption, i., Sey.	k11	69b
Assu, Braz.	C7	88
As-Sudd, reg., Sudan	F6	62
As-Sufāl, Yemen	G6	56
As-Sulaymānīyah, Iraq	B6	56
As-Sulaymānīyah, Sau. Ar.	E6	56
As-Sulayyil, Sau. Ar.	E6	56
Assumption, Il., U.S.	E8	120
As-Suwaydā', Syria	E7	58
As-Suwayda', state, Syria	F7	58
Astakós, Grc.	E3	28
Astana (Akmola), Kaz.	D12	32
Astara, Azer.	B6	56
Asti, Italy	F5	22
Astica, Arg.	E4	92
Astola Island, i., Pak.	D9	56
Astorga, Spain	B4	20
Astoria, Il., U.S.	D7	120
Astoria, Or., U.S.	D3	136
Astove, i., Sey.	I11	69b
Astrahan', Russia	E7	32
Astrahan see Astrahan', Russia	E7	32
Astrašycki Haradok, Bela.	F10	10
Astrolabe, Cape, c., Sol. Is.	e9	79b
Astrolabe, Récifs de l', rf., N. Cal.	I15	79d
Astrolabe Reefs see Astrolabe, Récifs de l', rf., N. Cal.	I15	79d
Astryna, Bela.	E12	10
Astudillo, Spain	B6	20
Asturias, state, Spain	A5	20
Astypálaia, i., Grc.	G9	28
Asunción, Para.	B9	92
Asunción, Bahía la, b., Mex.	B1	100
Asunción Nochixtlán, Mex.	G10	100
Asunden, i., Swe.	H5	8
Asveja, Bela.	E11	10
Asvejskae, vozero, l., Bela.	D10	10
Aswān, Egypt	C6	62
Aswan High Dam see Aali, Sadd el-, dam, Egypt	C6	62
Asyūt, Egypt	K2	58
Asyūti, Wadi el- (Asyūţ, Wādī al-), stm., Egypt	K2	58
'Ata, i., Tonga	F9	72
Atabapo, stm., S.A.	F8	86
Atacama, state, Chile	C3	92
Atacama, Desierto de des., Chile	E2	90
Atacama, Puna de, plat., S.A.	B4	92
Atacama, Salar de, pl., Chile	D3	90
Atacama Desert see Atacama, Desierto de, des., Chile	E2	90
Ataco, Col.	F4	86
Atagaj, Russia	C17	32
Atakpamé, Togo	H5	64
Atalaia, Braz.	E7	88
Atambua, Indon.	G7	44
Atami, Japan	D12	40
Atangmik, Grnld.	E15	141
Atar, Maur.	E2	64
Atascadero, Ca., U.S.	H5	134
Atascosa, stm., Tx., U.S.	F9	130
Atasu, Kaz.	E12	32
Atata, i., Tonga	n14	78e
Atatürk Baraji, res., Tur.	A9	58
Atauro, Pulau, i., Indon.	G8	44
'Atbarah, stm., Afr.	D7	62
Atbasar, Kaz.	D11	32
Atchafalaya see Oudenaarde, Bel.	D12	14
Atchafalaya Bay, b., La., U.S.	H7	122
Atchison, Ks., U.S.	B1	120
Ateca, Spain	C9	20
Aterno, stm., Italy	H10	22
Atfih, Egypt	I2	58
Ath, Bel.	D12	14
Athabasca, Ab., Can.	B17	138
Athabasca, stm., Ab., Can.	D8	106
Athabasca, Lake, l., Can.	D9	106
Athalmer, B.C., Can.	F14	138
Athboy, Ire.	H6	12
Athena, Or., U.S.	E8	136
Athens, On., Can.	D14	112
Athens see Athína, Grc.	F6	28
Athens, Al., U.S.	C11	122
Athens, Ga., U.S.	C2	116
Athens, Il., U.S.	E8	120
Athens, La., U.S.	E5	122
Athens, Mi., U.S.	F4	112
Athens, Oh., U.S.	E3	114
Athens, Pa., U.S.	C9	114
Athens, Tn., U.S.	B14	122
Athens, Tx., U.S.	E3	122
Athens, W.V., U.S.	G5	114
Atherton, Austl.	A5	76
Athi, stm., Kenya	E7	66
Athíainou, Cyp.	C4	58
Athína (Athens), Grc.	F6	28
Athni, India	C2	53
Athok, Mya.	D2	48
Āthol, Ma., U.S.	B13	114
Athos, mtn., Grc.	C7	28
Athos, Mount see Áthos, mtn., Grc.	C7	28
Ati, Chad	E3	62
Atiak, Ug.	D6	66
Atienza, Spain	C8	20
Atikokan, On., Can.	C7	118
Atirāmpattinam, India	F4	53
Atka, Russia	D19	34
Atka Island, i., Ak., U.S.	g24	140a
Atkarsk, Russia	D6	32
Atkins, Ar., U.S.	B6	122
Atkinson, Il., U.S.	C8	120
Atkinson, N.C., U.S.	B7	116
Atlanta, Ga., U.S.	C1	116
Atlanta, Il., U.S.	D8	120
Atlanta, Mi., U.S.	C5	112
Atlanta, Mo., U.S.	E5	120
Atlanta, Tx., U.S.	C2	120
Atlantic, Ia., U.S.	C2	120
Atlantic, N.C., U.S.	B9	116
Atlantic Beach, Fl., U.S.	F4	116
Atlantic City, N.J., U.S.	E11	114
Atlantic-Indian Basin, unds.	O5	142
Atlantic-Indian Ridge, unds.	N15	144
Atlántico, state, Col.	B4	86
Atlantic Ocean	D9	144
Atlantic Peak, mtn., Wy., U.S.	E3	126
Atlas Mountains, mts., Afr.	C4	64
Atlasova, ostrov, i., Russia	F20	34
Atlas Saharien, mts., Alg.	C4	64
Atlin, B.C., Can.	D4	106
Atlin Lake, l., Can.	D4	106
'Atlit, Isr.	F5	58
Ātmakūr, India	D4	53
Atmore, Al., U.S.	F11	122
Atnarko, stm., B.C., Can.	D5	138
Atocha, Bol.	D3	90
Atoka, Ok., U.S.	C2	122
Atotonilco, Cerro, mtn., Mex.	H3	130
Atoyac, stm., Mex.	F9	100
Atoyac de Álvarez, Mex.	G8	100
Atrak (Atrek), stm., Asia	B7	56
Ātran, stm., Swe.	H5	8
Atran, stm., Col.	D3	86
Atrauli, India	D7	54
Atri, Italy	H10	22
Atsumi, Japan	E10	40
Atsumi-hantō, pen., Japan	E10	40
At-Tafīlah, Jord.	H6	58
At-Tafīlah, state, Jord.	H6	58
At-Tā'if, Sau. Ar.	E5	56
At-Tall, Syria	E7	58
Attalla, Al., U.S.	C12	122
Attapu, Laos	E8	48
Attawapiskat, On., Can.	E14	106
Attawapiskat, stm., On., Can.	E13	106
Attawapiskat Lake, l., On., Can.	E13	106
At-Tawīl, mts., Sau. Ar.	D4	56
At-Tayyibah, Syria	C9	58
Attendorn, Ger.	E3	16
Attersee, l., Aus.	C10	22
Attica, In., U.S.	H2	112
Attica, Ks., U.S.	D10	128
Attica, N.Y., U.S.	B7	114
Attica see Attikí, hist. reg., Grc.	E6	28
Attikí, state, Grc.	F6	28
Attikí, hist. reg., Grc.	E6	28
Attleboro, Ma., U.S.	C14	114
Attu, Ak., U.S.	g21	140a
Attu Island, i., Ak., U.S.	g21	140a
At-Tuwayshah, Sudan	E5	62
Atuel, stm., Arg.	G3	92
Atuel, Bañados del, sw., Arg.	H4	92
Atuntaqui, Ec.	G2	86
Atuona, Fr. Poly.	s18	78g
Atwater, Ca., U.S.	F5	134
Atwater, Mn., U.S.	F4	118
Atwood, Il., U.S.	E9	120
Atwood, Ks., U.S.	B7	128
Atwood, Tn., U.S.	I9	120
Atyrau, Kaz.	E8	32
Aua Island, i., Pap. N. Gui.	a3	79a
Auari, stm., Braz.	F9	86
Auau Channel, strt., Hi., U.S.	C5	78a
Aubagne, Fr.	F11	18
Aube, state, Fr.	F13	14
Aube, stm., Fr.	F13	14
Aubigny-sur-Nère, Fr.	G11	14
Aubinadong, stm., On., Can.	A6	112
Aubrey Cliffs, clf, Az., U.S.	H3	132
Aubrey Lake, l., N.T., Can.	B5	106
Aubry Lake, l., N.T., Can.	B5	106
Auburn, Al., U.S.	E13	122
Auburn, Ca., U.S.	E4	134
Auburn, Ia., U.S.	C2	120
Auburn, Il., U.S.	E8	120
Auburn, In., U.S.	G4	112
Auburn, Ky., U.S.	H11	120
Auburn, Me., U.S.	F6	110
Auburn, Ne., U.S.	B14	114
Auburn, N.Y., U.S.	B8	114
Auburn, Wa., U.S.	C4	136
Auburn, stm., Austl.	D8	76
Auca Mahuida, Cerro, mtn., Arg.	H3	92
Aucanquilcha, Co., Chile	C4	128
Auch, Fr.	F6	18
Auchi, Nig.	H6	64
Aucilla, stm., U.S.	F2	116
Auckland, N.Z.	C6	80
Auckland Islands, is., N.Z.	I7	72
Aude, state, Fr.	F8	18
Aude, stm., Fr.	G9	18
Auden, On., Can.	A11	118
Audenarde see Oudenaarde, Bel.	D12	14
Audierne, Fr.	F4	14
Audincourt, Fr.	G15	14
Audubon Lake, res., N.D., U.S.	G12	124
Aue, Ger.	F8	16
Aue, Ger.	F8	16
Augrabies, Austl.	F4	70
Augrabies Falls National Park, p.o.i., S. Afr.	F5	70
Augsburg, Ger.	H6	16
Augusta, Italy	G9	24
Augusta, Ga., U.S.	B7	122
Augusta, Il., U.S.	C3	116
Augusta, Ks., U.S.	D6	120
Augusta, Ky., U.S.	E1	114
Augusta, Mt., U.S.	C14	136
Augusta, Wi., U.S.	G7	118
Augusto, Japan	D8	40
Augusto Severo, Braz.	C7	88
Augustów, Pol.	C18	16
Augustowski, Kanał, can., Eur.	C19	16
Augustus, Mount, mtn., Austl.	D3	74
Auki, Sol. Is.	e9	79b
Aukštaitijos nacionalnis parkas, p.o.i., Lith.	E8	10
Aulander, N.C., U.S.	H8	114
Auld, Lake, l., Austl.	D4	74
Aulla, Italy	F6	22
Aulne, stm., Fr.	F5	14
Aulneau Peninsula, pen., On., Can.	B4	118
Aumale, Fr.	E10	14
Auna, Nig.	G5	64
Auob, stm., Afr.	E5	70
Auraiya, India	E7	54
Aurangābād, India	B2	53
Aurangābād, India	F10	54
Aure, Nor.	E3	8
Aurelia, Ia., U.S.	B12	120
Aurilândia, Braz.	G7	84
Aurillac, Fr.	E8	18
Aurine, Alpi (Zillertaler Alpen), mts., Eur.	C8	22
Aurora, On., Can.	D10	112
Aurora, Co., U.S.	B4	128
Aurora, Il., U.S.	C9	120
Aurora, In., U.S.	E13	120
Aurora, Me., U.S.	F8	110
Aurora, Mn., U.S.	D6	118
Aurora, N.Y., U.S.	B9	114
Aurora, N.C., U.S.	A9	116
Aurora, Ut., U.S.	E4	132
Aurora, W.V., U.S.	E6	114
Aurora do Norte, Braz.	G2	88
Aursunden, l., Nor.	E4	8
Aurukun, Austl.	B8	74
Aus, Nmb.	E3	70
Ausable, stm., Cn., Can.	E8	112
Au Sable, stm., Mi., U.S.	D6	112
Au Sable Forks, N.Y., U.S.	F3	110
Au Sable Point, c., Mi., U.S.	D6	112
Auschwitz see Oświęcim, Pol.	F15	16
Aust-Agder, state, Nor.	G3	8
Austin, In., U.S.	F12	120
Austin, Mn., U.S.	H6	118
Austin, Nv., U.S.	D8	134
Austin, Pa., U.S.	C7	114
Austin, Tx., U.S.	D10	130
Austin, Lake, l., Austl.	E3	74
Australes, îles, is., Fr. Poly.	F11	72
Australia, ctry., Oc.	D5	74
Australian Capital Territory, state, Austl.	J7	76
Austral Islands see Australes, îles, is., Fr. Poly.	F11	72
Austral Plateau, unds.	E5	144
Austral Seamounts, unds.	L24	142
Austria, ctry., Eur.	C11	22
Austvågøya, i., Nor.	B6	8
Autlán de Navarro, Mex.	F6	100
Autun, Fr.	H13	14
Auvergne, hist. reg., Fr.	D8	18
Auxerre, Fr.	G12	14
Auxi-le-Château, Fr.	D11	14
Auxvasse, Mo., U.S.	E6	120
Auyán Tepuy, mtn., Ven.	E10	86
Auzangate, Nevado, mtn., Peru	F3	84
Ava, Mo., U.S.	H5	120
Avaí, Braz.	L1	88
Avala, hist., Yugo.	E7	26
Avallon, Fr.	G12	14
Avalon, Ca., U.S.	J7	134
Avalos, Mex.	A5	100
Avanersuaq see Nordgrønland, state, Grnld.	B14	141
Avaré, Braz.	L1	88
Avarua, Cook Is.	a26	78j
Avarua Harbour, b., Cook Is.	a26	78j
Avatiu Harbour, b., Cook Is.	a26	78j
'Avedat, Horvot, hist., Isr.	H5	58
Aveiro, Port.	D2	20
Aveiro, state, Port.	D2	20
Aveiro, Ria de, mth., Port.	D1	20
Avellaneda, Arg.	G8	92
Avellaneda, Arg.	D8	92
Avellino, Italy	D8	24
Averøya, i., Nor.	E2	8
Aversa, Italy	D8	24
Avery, Id., U.S.	C11	136
Avery, Tx., U.S.	D4	122
Avery Island, La., U.S.	H8	122
Aves, Islas de, is., Ven.	B8	86
Avesnes-sur-Helpe, Fr.	D12	14
Avesta, Swe.	F6	8
Aveyron, state, Fr.	E8	18
Aveyron, stm., Fr.	E7	18
Avezzano, Italy	H10	22
Aviá Terai, Braz.	C7	92
Aviano, Italy	D9	22
Avigliano, Italy	D9	24
Avignon, Fr.	F10	18
Ávila, Spain	D6	20
Ávila, co., Spain	D6	20
Ávila, Sierra de, mts., Spain	D5	20
Avilés, Spain	A4	20
Aviño, Spain	A2	20
Avinurme, Est.	B10	10
Avola, Italy	H9	24
Avon, Mn., U.S.	F4	118
Avon, N.Y., U.S.	B8	114
Avon, N.C., U.S.	A9	116
Avon, stm., Eng., U.K.	K11	12
Avon, stm., Eng., U.K.	J10	12
Avon, stm., Austl.	F3	74
Avondale, Co., U.S.	C4	128
Avon Downs, Austl.	C7	74
Avonlea, Sk., Can.	E8	124
Avontuur, S. Afr.	H6	70
Avranches, Fr.	F7	14
Awaaso, Ghana	H4	64
Awaji, Japan	E8	40
Awaji-shima, i., Japan	E7	40
Awan, Pak.	B4	54
Āwarē, Eth.	F8	62
Awasa, Eth.	F7	62
Awash, Eth.	F8	62
Awash, stm., Eth.	E8	62
Awa-shima, i., Japan	A12	40
Awbārī, Libya	B2	62
Awbārī, Şahrā', reg., Libya	B2	62
Awe, Loch, l., Scot., U.K.	E7	12
Awjilah, Libya	B4	62
Awka, Nig.	H6	64
Awwal, Wādī, stm., Libya	B4	62
Axel Djellal, Alg.	D5	64
Axel Heiberg Island, i., Nu., Can.	A7	141
Axim, Ghana	I4	64
Axiós (Vardar), stm., Eur.	C5	28
Axis, Al., U.S.	G10	122
Axixá, Braz.	B3	88
Axtell, Ks., U.S.	L2	118
Axtell, Ne., U.S.	G13	126
Ayabaca, Peru	D2	84
Ayabe, Japan	D8	40
Ayacucho, Arg.	H8	92
Ayacucho, Peru	F3	84
Ayaguz, Kaz.	E14	32
Ayakkum Hu, l., China	D3	36
Ayamonte, Spain	G3	20
Ayapel, Col.	C4	86
Ayaviri, Peru	F3	84
Aydın, Tur.	F10	28
Aydın, state, Tur.	F11	28
Aydınkent, Tur.	A5	58
Ayer, Ma., U.S.	B14	114
Āyer, Iran	C7	56

B

Name	Map Ref.	Page
Ba, Fiji	p18	79e
Ba, stm., China	F6	42
Ba, stm., Viet.	F9	48
Baa, Indon.	H7	44
Baaba, Île, i., N. Cal.	l14	79d
Baao, Phil.	D4	52
Baardheere, Som.	D8	66
Baba Burnu, c., Tur.	D9	28
Babadag, Tur.	F11	28
Babaeski, Tur.	B10	28
Babahoyo, Ec.	H2	86
Babak, Phil.	G5	52
Babanango, S. Afr.	F10	70
Babanūsah, Sudan	E5	62
Babar, Kepulauan, is., Indon.	G8	44
Babayevo, Russia	A18	10
Babb, Mt., U.S.	B13	136
Babelthuap, i., Palau	g7	78b
Bab el Mandeb see Mandeb, Bab el, strt.	E8	62
Babia, Arroyo de la, stm., Mex.	F5	130
Babian, stm., China	A5	48
Babičy, Bela.	H12	10
Babina, Austl.	F7	54
Babine Lake, l., B.C., Can.	B5	138
Babine Range, mts., B.C., Can.	B4	138
Babo, Indon.	F9	44
Babol, Iran	B7	56
Baboquivari Peak, mtn., Az., U.S.	L5	132
Baborów, Pol.	F13	16
Babrujsk, Bela.	G12	10
Babuškin, Russia	F10	34
Babuyan Channel, strt., Phil.	A3	52
Babuyan Islands, is., Phil.	A3	52
Bacabal, Braz.	C3	88
Bacadéhuachi, Mex.	G8	98
Bacan, Pulau, i., Indon.	F8	44
Bacău, Rom.	C13	26
Bacău, state, Rom.	C13	26
Bac Giang, Viet.	B8	48
Bachiniva, Mex.	A5	100
Bach Ma, Viet.	D9	48
Bach Thong, Viet.	A7	48
Bachu, China	B12	56
Bac Lieu, Viet.	H8	48
Bac Ninh, Viet.	B8	48
Bacolod, Phil.	E4	52
Bacoor, Phil.	C3	52
Bács-Kiskun, state, Hung.	C6	26
Bacup, Eng., U.K.	H10	12
Bacuri, Lago do, l., Braz.	B4	88
Bād, Iran	C7	56
Bad, stm., Mi., U.S.	E5	112
Bad, stm., S.D., U.S.	C12	126
Badagara, India	F2	53
Badajós, Lago, l., Braz.	D5	84
Badajoz, Spain	F4	20
Badajoz, co., Spain	F4	20
Badalona, Spain	C13	20
Bādāmi, India	D2	53
Badanah, Sau. Ar.	C5	56
Badarīnāth, India	C7	54
Badas, Bru.	A9	50
Badas, Kepulauan, is., Indon.	C5	50
Bad Axe, Mi., U.S.	E7	112
Bad Bergzabern, Ger.	G3	16
Bad Bevensen, Ger.	C6	16
Bad Bramstedt, Ger.	C5	16
Baddeck, N.S., Can.	D16	110
Bad Doberan, Ger.	B7	16
Bad Dürrenberg, Ger.	E8	16
Bad Ems, Ger.	F3	16
Baden, Switz.	C5	22
Baden-Baden, Ger.	H4	16
Badenoch, hist. reg., Scot., U.K.	E8	12
Badenweiler, Ger.	I3	16
Baden-Württemberg, state, Ger.	H4	16
Badgastein, Aus.	C10	22
Badger, Mn., U.S.	C3	118
Bad Hall, Aus.	B11	22
Bad Harzburg, Ger.	E6	16
Bad Hersfeld, Ger.	F5	16
Bad Homburg vor der Höhe, Ger.	F4	16
Bad Honnef, Ger.	F3	16
Badin Lake, res., N.C., U.S.	A5	116
Bad Ischl, Aus.	C10	22
Bad Kissingen, Ger.	F6	16
Bad Kreuznach, Ger.	G3	16
Badlands, hills, U.S.	A9	126
Badlands, hills, S.D., U.S.	D10	126
Badlands National Park, p.o.i., S.D., U.S.	D10	126
Bad Langensalza, Ger.	E6	16
Bad Lauterberg im Harz, Ger.	E6	16
Bad Mergentheim, Ger.	G5	16
Bad Muskau, Ger.	E10	16
Bad Nauheim, Ger.	F4	16
Bad Neustadt an der Saale, Ger.	F6	16
Bad Oeynhausen, Ger.	D4	16
Bad Oldesloe, Ger.	C6	16
Bad Orb, Ger.	F5	16
Bad Pyrmont, Ger.	E5	16
Bad Reichenhall, Ger.	I8	16
Bad Salzuflen, Ger.	D4	16
Bad Salzungen, Ger.	F6	16
Bad Schwalbach, Ger.	F3	16
Bad Schwartau, Ger.	C6	16
Bad Segeberg, Ger.	C6	16
Bādshāhpur, India	F9	54
Bad Tölz, Ger.	I7	16
Bad Vöslau, Aus.	C13	22
Bad Waldsee, Ger.	I5	16
Bad Wildungen, Ger.	E4	16
Bad Wörishofen, Ger.	I6	16
Badžal'skij hrebet, mts., Russia	F15	34
Baena, Spain	G6	20
Baependi, Braz.	K3	88
Baer, Russia	C17	32
Baeza, Spain	G7	20
Baezaeko, stm., B.C., Can.	D7	138
Bafang, Cam.	D1	66
Baffin Basin, unds.	A7	144
Baffin Bay, b., N.A.	C12	141
Baffin Bay, b., Tx., U.S.	G10	130
Baffin Island, i., Nu., Can.	B16	106
Bafia, Cam.	D2	66
Bafing, stm., Afr.	G2	64
Bafoulabé, Mali	G2	64
Bafoussam, Cam.	C2	66
Bafra, Tur.	A4	56
Baft, Iran	D8	56
Bafwaboli, D.R.C.	D5	66
Bafwasende, D.R.C.	D5	66
Bagaces, C.R.	G5	102
Bagagem, stm., Braz.	H1	88
Bagalkot, India	C2	53
Bagamoyo, Tan.	F7	66
Bagan Datuk, Malay.	K5	48
Baganga, Phil.	G6	52
Bagansiapiapi, Indon.	C2	50
Bagasra, India	H3	54
Bagdad, Az., U.S.	I3	132
Bagdarin, Russia	F11	34
Bagé, Braz.	E10	92
Bagenkop, Den.	B6	16
Bāgerhāt, Bngl.	G12	54
Baggs, Wy., U.S.	B9	132
Bāgh, India	G5	54
Baghdād, Iraq	C5	56
Bāghlān, Afg.	B10	56
Bagley, Mn., U.S.	D3	118
Bagnères-de-Luchon, Fr.	G7	18
Bagni di Lucca, Italy	F7	22
Bagnols-sur-Cèze, Fr.	E10	18
Bago (Pegu), Mya.	D3	48
Bago, state, Mya.	C2	48
Bagodar, India	F10	54
Bagoé, stm., Afr.	G3	64
Bāgpat, India	D6	54
Bagrationovsk, Russia	F3	10
Baguio, Phil.	B3	52
Bāh, India	E7	54
Bahādurgarh, India	D6	54
Bahama, Canal Viejo de, strt., N.A.	A8	102
Bahamas, ctry., N.A.	C9	96
Baharampur, India	F11	54
Bahau, Malay.	K6	48
Bahawalnagar, Pak.	D4	54
Bahawalpur, Pak.	D3	54
Bahçe, Tur.	A7	58
Baheri, India	D7	54
Bahia see Salvador, Braz.	G6	88
Bahia, state, Braz.	G4	88
Bahía, Islas de la, is., Hond.	D4	102
Bahía Blanca, Arg.	I6	92
Bahía Bustamante, Arg.	I3	90
Bahía de Caráquez, Ec.	H1	86
Bahía Kino, Mex.	A2	100
Bahir Dar, Eth.	E7	62
Bahraich, India	E9	54
Bahrain, ctry., Asia	D7	56
Bahrīa, Russia	B15	32
Bahtīm, Egypt	H2	58
Bahušèwsk, Bela.	F13	10
Bai, stm., China	A7	42
Baia de Aramă, Rom.	E9	26
Baia Farta, Ang.	C1	68
Baía Mare, Rom.	B10	26
Baião, Braz.	B1	88
Baicheng, China	B9	36
Baicheng, China	C14	32
Baidoa see Baydhabo, Som.	D8	66
Baie-Comeau, Qc., Can.	A8	110
Baiersbronn, Ger.	H4	16
Baie-Saint-Paul, Qc., Can.	C6	110
Baie-Trinité, Qc., Can.	A9	110
Baie Verte, Nf., Can.	j22	107a
Baihe, China	B11	46
Baijnāth, India	D7	54
Baikal, Lake see Bajkal, ozero, l., Russia	F10	34
Baikal Mountains see Bajkal'skij hrebet, mts., Russia	F10	34
Baikonur see Bajkonur, Kaz.	E11	32
Bailadores, Ven.	C6	86
Baile Átha Cliath see Dublin, Ire.	H6	12
Baile Átha Luain see Athlone, Ire.	H4	12
Baile Govora, Rom.	D11	26
Bailén, Spain	F7	20
Bǎileşti, Rom.	F10	26
Bailey, N.C., U.S.	I7	114
Bail Hongal, India	D2	53
Bailicun, China	I4	42
Bailique, Ilha, i., Braz.	C8	84
Baillie Islands, is., N.T., Can.	B14	140
Baillif, Guad.	h5	105c
Bailong, stm., China	E1	42
Bailu Hu, l., China	G5	42
Bailundo, Ang.	C2	68
Baimamiao, China	C2	42
Baima Shan, mtn., China	H4	42
Baimuru, Pap. N. Gui.	b3	79a
Bainbridge, Ga., U.S.	G14	122
Bainbridge, N.Y., U.S.	B10	114
Bain-de-Bretagne, Fr.	G7	14
Baing, Indon.	H12	50
Bainville, Mt., U.S.	F9	124
Baio Grande, Spain	A2	20
Baiona, Spain	B2	20
Baipeng, China	I3	42
Baipu, China	E9	42
Baiquan, China	B10	36
Baird, Tx., U.S.	B8	130
Baird Mountains, mts., Ak., U.S.	C7	140
Baird Peninsula, pen., Nu., Can.	B15	106
Bairiki, Kir.	C8	72
Bairin Zuoqi, China	C8	36
Bairnsdale, Austl.	K6	76
Baïse, stm., Fr.	F6	18
Baisha, China	G2	42
Baisha, China	I8	42
Baishe, China	H7	42
Baishuijiang, China	E2	42
Baisogala, Lith.	E6	10
Baixingt, China	C4	38
Baixio, Braz.	D6	88
Baiyan Shan, mtn., China	H8	42
Baiyin, China	D5	36
Baiyü, China	E4	36
Baja, Hung.	C5	26
Baja, Punta, c., Chile	e29	78l
Baja California, state, Mex.	F5	98
Baja California, pen., Mex.	B2	96
Baja California Sur, state, Mex.	C2	100
Bajada del Agrio, Arg.	I2	92
Baján, Mex.	H6	130
Baján, Mong.	B7	36
Bajanaul, Kaz.	D13	32
Bajangol, Russia	F9	34
Bajánsenye, Hung.	C3	26
Bajdarackaja guba, b., Russia	C2	34
Bajestān, Iran	C8	56
Bajkal, Russia	F9	34
Bajkal, ozero (Baikal, Lake), l., Russia	F10	34
Bajkal'skij hrebet, mts., Russia	F10	34
Bajkit, Russia	B17	32
Bajkonur, Kaz.	E11	32
Bajmak, Russia	D9	32
Bajmok, Yugo.	D6	26
Bajo, Indon.	H11	50
Bajo Boquete, Pan.	H6	102
Bajool, Austl.	D8	76
Bajramaly, Turkmen.	B9	56
Bajsun, Uzb.	G11	32
Bakacak, Tur.	C10	28
Bakala, C.A.R.	C4	66
Bakanas, Kaz.	F13	32
Bake, Indon.	E2	50
Bakel, Sen.	G2	64
Baker, Ca., U.S.	H9	134
Baker, La., U.S.	G7	122
Baker, Mt., U.S.	A8	126
Baker, Or., U.S.	F9	136
Baker, Mount, vol., Wa., U.S.	B5	136
Baker Butte, mtn., Az., U.S.	I5	132
Baker Island, i., Oc.	C9	72
Baker Lake, Nu., Can.	C11	106
Baker Lake, l., Austl.	E5	74
Baker Lake, l., Can.	C11	106
Bakersfield, Ca., U.S.	H7	134
Bakhardok, Turkmen.	B8	56
Bakhtegān, Daryācheh-ye, l., Iran	D7	56
Bakı (Baku), Azer.	A6	56
Bakkafjördur, Ice.	j32	8a
Bakkaflói, b., Ice.	j32	8a
Baklan, Tur.	F12	28
Bako, C. Iv.	H3	64
Bako, Eth.	F7	62
Bakony, mts., Hung.	C4	26
Baksi see Baki, Azer.	A6	56
Bakumpai, Indon.	D9	50
Bakung, Pulau, i., Indon.	K3	43
Bakwanga see Mbuji-Mayi, D.R.C.	F4	66
Balā, Phil.	I1	52
Balabac, Phil.	G1	52
Balabac Island, i., Phil.	G1	52
Balabac Strait, strt., Asia	G1	52
Balabakk, Leb.	D7	58
Balabalagan, Kepulauan, is., Indon.	E10	50
Balabio, Île, i., N. Cal.	m15	79d
Balad, Iraq	C5	56
Balādēk, Russia	F15	34
Bālāghāt, India	H8	54
Bālāghāt Range, mts., India	B3	53
Balagne, Fr.	G14	18
Balaguer, Spain	C11	20
Balahna, Russia	H20	8
Balaikarangan, Indon.	C7	50
Balaipeuah, Indon.	D2	50
Balaklava, Austl.	J2	76
Balaklava, Russia	D7	32
Balakovo, Russia	D7	32
Balama, Moz.	C6	68
Balambangan, Pulau, i., Malay.	G1	52
Bālā Morghāb, Afg.	C9	56
Balancán, Mex.	D3	102
Balao, Ec.	I2	86
Balapulang, Indon.	G6	50
Balāngīr, India	H9	54
Balarāmpur, India	G11	54
Balašov, Russia	D6	32
Balassagyarmat, Hung.	A6	26
Balatina, Mol.	B14	26
Balaton, Mn., U.S.	G3	118

Name	Map Ref.	Page
Balaton, l., Hung.	C4	26
Balayan, Phil.	D3	52
Balbieriškis, Lith.	F6	10
Balbina, Represa, res., Braz.	H12	86
Balcanoona, Austl.	H2	76
Balcarce, Arg.	H8	92
Balcarres, Sk., Can.	D10	124
Bălcești, Rom.	E10	26
Balcones Escarpment, clf, Tx., U.S.	D9	130
Balde, Arg.	F4	92
Bald Knob, Ar., U.S.	B7	122
Bald Knob, mtn., Va., U.S.	G6	114
Bald Mountain, mtn., Or., U.S.	G5	136
Bald Mountain, mtn., Or., U.S.	F3	136
Baldock Lake, l., Mb., Can.	D11	106
Baldone, Lat.	D7	10
Baldwin, La., U.S.	H7	122
Baldwin, Mi., U.S.	E4	112
Baldwin, Wi., U.S.	G6	118
Baldwinsville, N.Y., U.S.	E13	112
Baldwyn, Ms., U.S.	C10	122
Baldy Mountain, mtn., Mb., Can.	C13	124
Baldy Mountain, mtn., N.M., U.S.	E3	128
Baldy Peak, mtn., Az., U.S.	J7	132
Bâle see Basel, Switz.	C4	22
Baleares see Balears, state, Spain	E13	20
Baleares, Islas see Balears, Illes, is., Spain	E12	20
Balearic Islands see Balears, state, Spain	E13	20
Balearic Islands see Balears, Illes, is., Spain	E12	20
Balears, state, Spain	E13	20
Balears, Illes (Balearic Islands), is., Spain	E12	20
Balease, Gunung, mtn., Indon.	E12	50
Baleh, stm., Malay.	C8	50
Baleia, Ponta da, c., Braz.	I6	88
Baleine, stm., Qc., Can.	D17	106
Baleine, Grande rivière de la, stm., Qc., Can.	D15	106
Baleine, Petite rivière de la, stm., Qc., Can.	D15	106
Balej, Russia	F12	34
Baler, Phil.	C3	52
Baler Bay, b., Phil.	C3	52
Bāleshwar, India	H11	54
Balezino, Russia	C8	32
Balfate, Hond.	E4	102
Balfour, N.C., U.S.	A3	116
Balgazyn, Russia	D17	32
Balhaš, ozero (Balkhash Lake), l., Kaz.	E13	32
Bāli, India	F4	54
Bali, state, Indon.	G9	50
Bali, i., Indon.	G9	50
Bali, Laut (Bali Sea), Indon.	G9	50
Bali, Selat, strt., Indon.	H9	50
Bali Barat National Park, p.o.i., Indon.	H9	50
Baliceaux, i., St. Vin.	p11	105e
Balige, Indon.	B1	50
Balıkesir, Tur.	D10	28
Balıkesir, state, Tur.	D10	28
Balīkh, stm., Syria	B10	58
Balikpapan, Indon.	D10	50
Balimbing, Indon.	F4	50
Balimbing, Phil.	H2	52
Balimo, Pap. N. Gui.	b3	79a
Balingen, Ger.	H4	16
Balingian, Malay.	B8	50
Balintang Channel, strt., Phil.	K9	42
Bali Sea see Bali, Laut, Indon.	G9	50
Bali Strait see Bali, Selat, strt., Indon.	H9	50
Baliza, Braz.	G7	84
Balkan Mountains, mts., Eur.	G11	26
Balkan Peninsula, pen., Eur.	B6	28
Balkaria see Kabardino-Balkarija, state, Russia	F6	32
Balkh, Afg.	B10	56
Balkhash, Lake see Balhaš, ozero, l., Kaz.	E13	32
Ballachulish, Scot., U.K.	E7	12
Balladonia, Austl.	F4	74
Ballālpur, India	B4	53
Ballangen, Nor.	B7	8
Ballantine, Mt., U.S.	B4	126
Ballarat, Austl.	K4	76
Ballard, Lake, l., Austl.	E4	74
Ballater, Scot., U.K.	D9	12
Ball Bay, b., Norf. I.	y25	78i
Ballenas, Bahía de, b., Mex.	B2	100
Ballenita, Punta, c., Chile	B2	92
Balleny Islands, is., Ant.	B21	81
Balleza, Mex.	B5	100
Balleza, stm., Mex.	B5	100
Ball Ground, Ga., U.S.	B1	116
Ballia, India	F10	54
Ballina, Austl.	G9	76
Ballina, Ire.	G3	12
Ballina, Ire.	I4	12
Ballinrobe, Ire.	H3	12
Ballston Spa, N.Y., U.S.	G2	110
Ballville, Oh., U.S.	C2	114
Ballybunnion, Ire.	I3	12
Ballyhaunis, Ire.	H4	12
Ballymena, N. Ire., U.K.	G6	12
Ballymoney, N. Ire., U.K.	F6	12
Ballyrogan, Lake, l., Austl.	I6	76
Balmaceda, Chile	I2	90
Balmoral, Austl.	K3	76
Balmorhea, Tx., U.S.	C4	130
Balnearia, Arg.	E6	92
Baloda Bāzār, India	H9	54
Balombo, Ang.	C1	68
Balong, Indon.	G7	50
Balonne, stm., Austl.	G7	76
Bālotra, India	F4	54
Balphakram National Park, p.o.i., India	F13	54
Balqash Köli see Balhaš, ozero, l., Kaz.	E13	32
Balrāmpur, India	E8	54
Balranald, Austl.	J4	76
Balș, Rom.	E11	26
Balsam Lake, Wi., U.S.	F6	118
Balsam Lake, l., On., Can.	D11	112
Balsas, Braz.	D2	88
Balsas, stm., Braz.	F2	88
Balsas, stm., Braz.	D3	88
Balsas, stm., Mex.	F8	100
Balsas, stm., Pan.	C3	86
Balsthal, Switz.	C4	22
Balta, Ukr.	B16	26
Baltasar Brum, Ur.	E9	92
Bălți, Mol.	B14	26
Baltic Sea, Eur.	D12	6
Baltijsk, Russia	F2	10
Baltijskaja kosa, spit, Eur.	F2	10
Baltijskoje more see Baltic Sea, Eur.	D12	6
Baltim, Egypt	G2	58
Baltimore, Ire.	J3	12
Baltimore, Md., U.S.	E9	114
Baltimore, Oh., U.S.	E3	114
Ba Lu, stm., Viet.	E9	48
Baluchistān, state, Pak.	C2	54
Baluchistan, hist. reg., Asia	D9	56
Balui, stm., Malay.	B8	50
Bālurghāt, India	F12	54
Balvi, Lat.	C10	10
Balygyčan, Russia	D19	34
Balykši, Kaz.	E8	32
Balzac, Ab., Can.	E16	138
Balzar, Ec.	H2	86
Bam, Iran	D8	56
Bama, China	I2	42
Bama, Nig.	G7	64
Bamaga, Austl.	B8	74
Bamako, Mali	G3	64
Bamba, Mali	F4	64
Bambamarca, Peru	E2	84
Bambana, stm., Nic.	F6	102
Bambari, C.A.R.	C4	66
Bambaroo, Austl.	B6	76
Bamberg, Ger.	G6	16
Bamberg, S.C., U.S.	C4	116
Bambio, C.A.R.	D3	66
Bambuí, Braz.	K2	88
Bam Co, l., China	C13	54
Bamenda, Cam.	C1	66
Bami, Turkmen.	B8	56
Bāmīān, Afg.	C10	56
Bamingui, C.A.R.	C4	66
Bampūr, Iran	D9	56
Bāmra Hills, hills, India	H10	54
Bamumo, China	B14	54
Banaba, i., Kir.	D7	72
Banabuiú, stm., Braz.	C6	88
Banabuiú, Açude, l., Braz.	C6	88
Banalia, D.R.C.	D5	66
Banamba, Mali	G3	64
Banana Islands, is., S.L.	H2	64
Bananal, stm., Braz.	E1	88
Bananal, Ilha do, i., Braz.	F7	84
Banarlı, Tur.	B10	28
Banās, stm., India	E6	54
Banâs, Râs, c., Egypt	C7	62
Banat, hist. reg., Eur.	D7	26
Banaz, Tur.	E12	28
Ban Ban, Laos	C6	48
Ban Bouang-nom, Laos	E8	48
Banbridge, N. Ire., U.K.	G6	12
Ban Bung Na Rang, Thai.	D5	48
Banbury, Eng., U.K.	I11	12
Ban Cha La, Laos	D7	48
Bancroft, On., Can.	C12	112
Bancroft, Id., U.S.	H15	136
Bancroft, Ia., U.S.	H4	118
Bancroft, Ne., U.S.	C1	120
Bānda, India	F8	54
Banda, Kepulauan, is., Indon.	F9	44
Banda, Laut (Banda Sea), Indon.	G8	44
Banda Aceh, Indon.	J2	48
Bānda Dāūd Shāh, Pak.	B3	54
Banda del Río Salí, Arg.	C5	92
Bandai-Asahi-kokuritsu-kōen, p.o.i., Japan	B12	40
Bandai-san, vol., Japan	B13	40
Bandama, stm., C. Iv.	H3	64
Bandama Blanc, stm., C. Iv.	H3	64
Ban Dan, Thai.	E7	48
Ban Dangtai, Laos	D7	48
Bandar Beheshtī, Iran	D9	56
Bandarbeyla, Som.	C10	66
Bandar-e 'Abbās, Iran	D8	56
Bandar-e Anzalī, Iran	B6	56
Bandar-e Būshehr, Iran	D7	56
Bandar-e Deylam, Iran	D7	56
Bandar-e Lengeh, Iran	D7	56
Bandar-e Māh Shahr, Iran	C6	56
Bandar-e Moghūyeh, Iran	D7	56
Bandar-e Torkeman, Iran	B7	56
Bandar Seri Begawan, Bru.	A9	50
Banda Sea see Banda, Laut, Indon.	G8	44
Bandeira, Pico da, mtn., Braz.	K5	88
Bandeirantes, Braz.	F7	84
Bandelier National Monument, p.o.i., N.M., U.S.	F2	128
Bandera, Arg.	D6	92
Bandera, Alto, mtn., Dom. Rep.	C12	102
Banderas, Mex.	C2	130
Banderas, Bahía de, b., Mex.	E6	100
Bandhavgarh National Park, p.o.i., India	G8	54
Bāndhi, Pak.	E2	54
Bandiagara, Mali	G4	64
Bandiantaolehai, China	C5	36
Bāndīkūi, India	E6	54
Bandipura, India	A5	54
Bandipur Tiger Reserve, India	F3	53
Bandırma, Tur.	C11	28
Bandon, Or., U.S.	G2	136
Ban Don, Ao, b., Thai.	H4	48
Ban Donhiang, Laos	C5	48
Bandundu, D.R.C.	E3	66
Bandung, Indon.	G5	50
Banes, Cuba	B10	102
Banff, Ab., Can.	E15	138
Banff, Scot., U.K.	D10	12
Banff National Park, p.o.i., Ab., Can.	E15	138
Banfora, Burkina	G4	64
Banga, D.R.C.	F4	66
Banga, India	C6	54
Banga, stm., Phil.	G5	52
Bangalore, India	E3	53
Bangaon, India	G12	54
Bangassou, C.A.R.	D4	66
Bangdag Co, l., China	A8	54
Banggai, Indon.	F7	44
Banggai, Kepulauan, is., Indon.	F7	44
Banggi, Pulau, i., Malay.	G1	52
Banggong Co, l., China	B7	54
Banghāzī (Bengasi), Libya	A3	62
Banghiang, stm., Laos	D7	48
Bangil, Indon.	G8	50
Bangka, Pulau, i., Indon.	E5	50
Bangka, Selat, strt., Indon.	E4	50
Bangkalan, Indon.	G8	50
Bangkaru, Pulau, i., Indon.	L3	48
Bangkinang, Indon.	C2	50
Bangkir, Indon.	C12	50
Bangko, Indon.	E3	50
Bangkog Co, l., China	C12	54
Bangkok see Krung Thep, Thai.	F5	48
Bangladesh, ctry., Asia	G13	54
Bang Lamung, Thai.	F5	48
Bang Mun Nak, Thai.	D5	48
Bangor, N. Ire., U.K.	G7	12
Bangor, Wales, U.K.	H8	12
Bangor, Me., U.S.	F8	110
Bangor, Pa., U.S.	D10	114
Bangriposi, India	G11	54
Bangs, Tx., U.S.	C8	130
Bangs, Mount, mtn., Az., U.S.	G3	132
Bang Saphan, Thai.	G4	48
Bangued, Phil.	B3	52
Bangui, C.A.R.	D3	66
Bangweulu, Lake, l., Zam.	C4	68
Bangweulu Swamps, sw., Zam.	C5	68
Bangxu, China	J2	42
Ban Hatgnao, Laos	E8	48
Ban Hèt, Laos	E8	48
Ban Hom, Thai.	E4	48
Ban Hong Muang, Laos	D7	48
Ban Houayxay, Laos	B5	48
Bani, C.A.R.	C4	66
Baní, Dom. Rep.	C12	102
Bani, Jbel, mts., Mor.	D3	64
Baniara, Pap. N. Gui.	b4	79a
Bani Bangou, Niger	F5	64
Banihāl Pass, p., India	B4	46
Banī Walīd, Libya	A2	62
Bāniyās, Golan	E6	58
Bāniyās, Syria	C6	58
Banja Luka, Bos.	E4	26
Banjarmasin, Indon.	E9	50
Banjul (Bathurst), Gam.	G1	64
Bānka, India	F11	54
Banka Banka, Austl.	C6	74
Ban Katèp, Laos	D7	48
Ban Kèngkabao, Laos	D7	48
Ban Kèngtangan, Laos	D7	48
Ban Kheun, Laos	B5	48
Ban Khuan Mao, Thai.	I4	48
Ban Kruat, Thai.	E6	48
Banks, Al., U.S.	F13	122
Banks, Îles (Banks Islands), is., Vanuatu	i16	79d
Banks Island, i., B.C., Can.	E4	106
Banks Island, i., N.T., Can.	B15	140
Banks Islands see Banks, Îles, is., Vanuatu	i16	79d
Banks Lake, res., Wa., U.S.	C7	136
Banks Peninsula, pen., N.Z.	F5	80
Banks Strait, strt., Austl.	n13	77a
Banks / Torres, state, Vanuatu	i16	79d
Bānkura, India	G11	54
Ban Mae La Luang, Thai.	C3	48
Ban Mit, Laos	C5	48
Ban Muangngat, Laos	C6	48
Bann, stm., N. Ire., U.K.	F6	12
Ban Nadou, Laos	E7	48
Ban Nahin, Laos	C7	48
Ban Nalan, Laos	E7	48
Ban Nam Chan, Thai.	C6	48
Ban Namnga, Laos	B6	48
Ban Nam Thaeng, Thai.	E7	48
Ban Naxouang, Laos	C7	48
Bannertown, N.C., U.S.	H5	114
Banning, Ca., U.S.	J9	134
Ban Nong Lumphuk, Thai.	E6	48
Bannu, Pak.	B3	54
Bañolas see Banyoles, Spain	B13	20
Baños, Ec.	H2	86
Banow, Afg.	B10	56
Ban Pak Bong, Thai.	C4	48
Ban Pakkhop, Laos	C5	48
Ban Pak Nam, Thai.	G4	48
Ban Phai, Thai.	D6	48
Ban Phai, Thai.	D6	48
Ban Pho, Thai.	F5	48
Ban Phông Pho, Laos	E7	48
Ban Pong, Thai.	F4	48
Ban Sa-ang, Laos	D7	48
Ban Salik, Thai.	C5	48
Ban Sam Pong, Laos	C6	48
Ban Samrong, Thai.	E6	48
Bānsda, India	H4	54
Banshadhāra, stm., India	B6	53
Banská Bystrica, Slov.	H15	16
Banská Štiavnica, Slov.	H14	16
Bansko, Blg.	H10	26
Ban Songkhon, Laos	C7	48
Bānswāra, India	G5	54
Bantaeng, Indon.	F11	50
Ban Takhlo, Thai.	E5	48
Bantarkawung, Indon.	G6	50
Bantayan, Phil.	E4	52
Ban Thabôk, Laos	C6	48
Ban Thapayi, Laos	D7	48
Ban Tian Sa, Laos	C6	48
Bantry, Ire.	J3	12
Bantry Bay, b., Ire.	J3	12
Ban Van Hom, Laos	C7	48
Ban Xènkhalôk, Laos	C5	48
Banya, Testa de la, c., Spain	D11	20
Banyak, Kepulauan, is., Indon.	K3	48
Ban Ya Plong, Thai.	H4	48
Banyo, Cam.	C2	66
Banyoles, Spain	B13	20
Banyuwangi, Indon.	H9	50
Banzare Coast, cst., Ant.	B17	81
Baode, China	B4	42
Baoding, China	B6	42
Baofeng, China	E5	42
Bao Ha, Viet.	A7	48
Baoji, China	D2	42
Baojing, China	G3	42
Bao Lac, Viet.	G8	48
Bao Lac, Viet.	A7	48
Baolunyuan, China	E1	42
Baoqing, China	B11	36
Baoshan, China	F4	36
Baoting, China	L3	42
Baotou, China	A4	42
Baoulé, stm., Mali	G3	64
Baowei, China	A8	48
Baoyi, China	E7	42
Baoying, China	E8	42
Bāpatla, India	D5	53
Bapaume, Fr.	D11	14
Baptiste Lake, res., On., Can.	C12	112
Bāqa el Gharbiyya, Isr.	F6	58
Baqing, China	B14	54
Ba'qūbah, Iraq	C5	56
Baquedano, Chile	A3	92
Bar, Yugo.	G6	26
Bara, Nig.	G7	64
Baraawe, Som.	D8	66
Barabinsk, Russia	C13	32
Barabinskaja step', pl., Russia	C13	32
Baraboo, Wi., U.S.	H9	118
Baraboo, stm., Wi., U.S.	H8	118
Baracaldo see Barakaldo, Spain	A8	20
Baracoa, Cuba	B10	102
Baradero, Arg.	F8	92
Baradine, Austl.	H7	76
Baraga, Mi., U.S.	B1	112
Bārah, Sudan	E6	62
Barahona, Dom. Rep.	C12	102
Barak, Tur.	B8	58
Barāk, stm., India	F14	54
Barakaldo, Spain	A8	20
Baraki, Afg.	B2	54
Barakula, Austl.	F8	76
Baralaba, Austl.	E7	76
Baram, stm., Malay.	A9	50
Barama, stm., Guy.	D12	86
Bārāmati, India	B2	53
Bārāmūla, India	A5	54
Baran', Bela.	F13	10
Bārān, India	F6	54
Baranagar, India	G12	54
Baranavičy, Bela.	G9	10
Barangbarang, Indon.	G12	50
Baranoa, Col.	B4	86
Baranof Island, i., Ak., U.S.	E12	140
Barany, Russia	C12	10
Baranya, state, Hung.	D5	26
Barão de Grajaú, Braz.	D4	88
Barão de Melgaço, Braz.	G6	84
Barão de Tromai, Braz.	A3	88
Baraški, Russia	D24	8
Barataria, La., U.S.	H8	122
Barataria Bay, b., La., U.S.	H8	122
Barat Daya, Kepulauan (Barat Daya Islands), is., Indon.	G8	44
Barat Daya Islands see Barat Daya, Kepulauan, is., Indon.	G8	44
Barauana, stm., Braz.	G11	86
Barauni, India	F10	54
Baraut, India	D6	54
Baraya, Col.	F4	86
Barbacena, Braz.	K4	88
Barbacoas, Col.	G2	86
Barbadillo del Mercado, Spain	B7	20
Barbados, ctry., N.A.	h16	96a
Barbalha, Braz.	D6	88
Barbar, Sudan	D6	62
Barbaria, Cap de, c., Spain	F12	20
Barbas, Cap, c., W. Sah.	E1	64
Barbaši, Russia	C11	10
Barbastro, Spain	B10	20
Barbate, Spain	H4	20
Barbeau Peak, mtn., Nu., Can.	A10	141
Barberena, Guat.	E2	102
Barberton, S. Afr.	D10	70
Barberton, Oh., U.S.	C4	114
Barbil, India	G10	54
Barbosa, Col.	E5	86
Barbuda, i., Antig.	e4	105b
Barby, Ger.	E7	16
Bârca, Rom.	F10	26
Barcaldine, Austl.	D5	76
Barcău (Berettyó), stm., Eur.	B8	26
Barcellona Pozzo di Gotto, Italy	F9	24
Barcelona, Mex.	B7	100
Barcelona, Spain	C13	20
Barcelona, Ven.	B9	86
Barcelona, co., Spain	C13	20
Barceloneta, P.R.	B2	104a
Barcelos, Braz.	H10	86
Barcelos, Port.	C2	20
Barcin, Pol.	D13	16
Barcoo, stm., Austl.	E4	76
Barczewo, Pol.	C16	16
Barda del Medio, Arg.	I3	92
Bardaï, Chad	C3	62
Bardawîl, Sabkhet el-, b., Egypt	G4	58
Barddhamān, India	G11	54
Bardejov, Slov.	G17	16
Bardeskan, Iran	B8	56
Bardīyah, Libya	A5	62
Bardo, Tun.	H4	24
Bārdoli, India	H4	54
Bardstown, Ky., U.S.	G12	120
Bardwell Lake, res., Tx., U.S.	E2	122
Bareilly, India	D7	54
Barentsburg, Nor.	B29	141
Barentsøya, i., Nor.	B30	141
Barents Sea, Eur.	B7	30
Bareta, India	D5	54
Barfleur, Fr.	E7	14
Bargaal, Som.	B10	66
Bargara, Austl.	E9	76
Bargarh, India	D5	46
Barguzin, stm., Russia	F11	34
Barguzinskij hrebet, mts., Russia	F11	34
Bar Harbor, Me., U.S.	F8	110
Barharwa, India	F11	54
Barhi, India	F10	54
Bāri, India	E6	54
Bari, Italy	C10	24
Baria, stm., Ven.	G8	86
Barī Gāv, Afg.	B1	54
Barigua, Salina de, pl., Ven.	p20	104g
Barillas, Guat.	E2	102
Barīm, i., Yemen	G5	56
Barima, stm., S.A.	C12	86
Barima-Waini, state, Guy.	D12	86
Barinas, P.R.	B2	104a
Barinas, Ven.	C6	86
Barinas, state, Ven.	C7	86
Baring, Cape, c., N.T., Can.	A7	106
Baringo, Lake, l., Kenya	D7	66
Bāripada, India	H11	54
Bariri, Braz.	L1	88
Bârîs, Egypt	C6	62
Bari Sādri, India	F5	54
Barisāl, Bngl.	G13	54
Barisāl, state, Bngl.	G13	54
Barisan, Pegunungan, mts., Indon.	E2	50
Barito, stm., Indon.	E9	50
Barjols, Fr.	F11	18
Barkam, China	E5	36
Barkava, Lat.	D9	10
Barkerville, B.C., Can.	C9	138
Bark Lake, l., On., Can.	C12	112
Barkley, Lake, res., U.S.	H10	120
Barkley Sound, strt., B.C., Can.	H5	138
Barkly East, S. Afr.	G8	70
Barkly Tableland, plat., Austl.	C7	74
Barkly West, S. Afr.	F7	70
Barkol, China	C3	36
Bârlad, Rom.	C14	26
Bârlad, stm., Rom.	D14	26
Bar-le-Duc, Fr.	F14	14
Barlee, Lake, l., Austl.	E3	74
Barletta, Italy	C10	24
Barlinek, Pol.	D11	16
Barling, Ar., U.S.	B4	122
Barlow, Ky., U.S.	G8	120
Barmedman, Austl.	J6	76
Bārmer, India	F3	54
Barmera, Austl.	J3	76
Barnagar, India	G5	54
Barnard Castle, Eng., U.K.	G11	12
Barnaul, Russia	D14	32
Barn Bluff, mtn., Austl.	n12	77a
Barnegat, N.J., U.S.	E11	114
Barnegat Bay, b., N.J., U.S.	E11	114
Barnes Ice Cap, ice, Nu., Can.	A16	106
Barnesville, Ga., U.S.	C1	116
Barnesville, Mn., U.S.	E2	118
Barnesville, Oh., U.S.	E4	114
Barneville-Carteret, Fr.	E7	14
Barnsdall, Ok., U.S.	E12	128
Barnsley, Eng., U.K.	H11	12
Barnstable, Ma., U.S.	C15	114
Barnstaple, Eng., U.K.	J8	12
Barnstaple Bay, b., Eng., U.K.	J8	12
Barnwell, Ab., Can.	G18	138
Barnwell, S.C., U.S.	C4	116
Baro, stm., Afr.	F7	62
Baron Bluff, clf, V.I.U.S.	g10	104c
Baron'ki, Bela.	G15	10
Barora Fa Island, i., Sol. Is.	d8	79b
Barora Ite Island, i., Sol. Is.	d8	79b
Baroua, Niger	G7	64
Barpeta, India	E13	54
Barqah (Cyrenaica), hist. reg., Libya	A4	62
Barques, Pointe aux, c., Mi., U.S.	D7	112
Barquisimeto, Ven.	B7	86
Barra, Braz.	F4	88
Barra, i., Scot., U.K.	D5	12
Barra, Ponta da, c., Moz.	C12	70
Barraba, Austl.	H8	76
Barra da Estiva, Braz.	G5	88
Barra del Colorado, C.R.	G6	102
Barra de Río Grande, Nic.	F6	102
Barra do Corda, Braz.	C3	88
Barra do Cuanza, Ang.	B1	68
Barra do Garças, Braz.	G7	84
Barra do Mendes, Braz.	F4	88
Barra do Piraí, Braz.	L3	88
Barra do Ribeiro, Braz.	E12	92
Barra Falsa, Ponta da, c., Moz.	C12	70
Barra Mansa, Braz.	L3	88
Barranca, Peru	F2	84
Barrancabermeja, Col.	D4	86
Barrancas, Ven.	C10	86
Barrancas, Ven.	C7	86
Barrancas, stm., Arg.	H2	92
Barranco Azul, Mex.	E3	130
Barranco do Velho, Port.	G3	20
Barranqueras, Arg.	C8	92
Barranquilla, Col.	B4	86
Barranquitas, P.R.	B3	104a
Barras, Braz.	C4	88
Barre, Vt., U.S.	F4	110
Barreal, Arg.	E3	92
Barreiras, Braz.	G3	88
Barreirinha, Braz.	D6	84
Barreiro, Port.	F1	20
Barreiros, Braz.	E8	88
Barren, stm., Ky., U.S.	H11	120
Barren, Nosy, is., Madag.	D7	68
Barren Islands, is., Ak., U.S.	E9	140
Barren River Lake, res., Ky., U.S.	H11	120
Barretos, Braz.	K1	88
Barrhead, Ab., Can.	B16	138
Barrie, On., Can.	D10	112
Barrie Island, i., On., Can.	C7	112
Barrière, B.C., Can.	E10	138
Barrier Range, mts., Austl.	H3	76
Barrigada, Guam	j10	78c
Barrington, N.S., Can.	G11	110
Barrington Tops National Park, p.o.i., Austl.	I8	76
Barringun, Austl.	G5	76
Barrouallie, St. Vin.	o11	105e
Barrow, Arg.	I7	92
Barrow, Ak., U.S.	B8	140
Barrow, stm., Ire.	I5	12
Barrow, Point, c., Ak., U.S.	B8	140
Barrow Creek, Austl.	D6	74
Barrow-in-Furness, Eng., U.K.	G9	12
Barrow Island, i., Austl.	D2	74
Barrows, Mb., Can.	B12	124
Barrow Strait, strt., Nu., Can.	C6	141
Barry, Wales, U.K.	J9	12
Barry, Il., U.S.	E6	120
Barryton, Mi., U.S.	E4	112
Barsalpur, India	D4	54
Bārsi, India	B2	53
Barsinghausen, Ger.	D5	16
Barstow, Ca., U.S.	I8	134
Barstow, Tx., U.S.	C4	130
Bar-sur-Seine, Fr.	F13	14
Bartang, Taj.	B11	56
Barth, Ger.	B8	16
Barthélemy, Deo, p., Viet.	C6	48
Bartholomew, Bayou, stm., U.S.	E7	122
Bartibougou, Burkina	G5	64
Bartica, Guy.	B6	84
Bartın, Tur.	B15	28
Bartle Frere, mtn., Austl.	A5	76
Bartlesville, Ok., U.S.	H2	120
Bartlett, N.H., U.S.	F5	110
Bartlett, Tn., U.S.	B9	122
Bartlett, Tx., U.S.	D10	130
Bartley, Ne., U.S.	A8	128
Barton, Vt., U.S.	F4	110
Bartoszyce, Pol.	B16	16
Bartow, Fl., U.S.	I4	116
Bartow, Ga., U.S.	D3	116
Barú, Volcán, vol., Pan.	H6	102
Bārūk, Jabal al-, mtn., Leb.	E6	58
Barumini, Italy	E2	24
Barumun, stm., Indon.	C2	50
Barung, Nusa, i., Indon.	H8	50
Barus, Indon.	L4	48
Baruun-Urt, Mong.	B7	36
Barvas, Scot., U.K.	C6	12
Barview, Or., U.S.	G2	136
Barwāh, India	G5	54
Barwāni, India	H5	54
Barwick, Ga., U.S.	F2	116
Barwon, stm., Austl.	H6	76
Barybino, Russia	E20	10
Barycz, stm., Pol.	E13	16
Barysau, Bela.	F11	10
Basail, Arg.	C8	92
Basalt, stm., Austl.	B5	76
Basankusu, D.R.C.	D3	66
Basarabeasca, Mol.	C15	26
Basatongwula Shan, mtn., China	B13	54
Basavakalyān, India	C3	53
Basavilbaso, Arg.	F8	92
Bascuñán, Cabo, c., Chile	D2	92
Basel (Bâle), Switz.	C4	22
Basella see Bassella, Spain	B12	20
Basey, Phil.	E5	52
Bashi Channel, strt., Asia	K9	42
Bashkortostan see Baškirija, state, Russia	D9	32
Basilan Island, i., Phil.	G4	52
Basilan Strait, strt., Phil.	G4	52
Basildon, Eng., U.K.	J13	12
Basile, La., U.S.	G6	122
Basilicata, state, Italy	D10	24
Basin, Mt., U.S.	D14	136
Basin, Wy., U.S.	C4	126
Basingstoke, Eng., U.K.	J11	12
Basin Lake, l., Sk., Can.	B8	124
Basīrhāt, India	G12	54
Baskahegan Lake, l., Me., U.S.	E8	110
Baskakovka, Russia	F17	10
Başkale, Tur.	B5	56
Baskatong, Réservoir, res., Qc., Can.	B13	112
Basket Lake, l., On., Can.	B6	118
Baškirija, state, Russia	D9	32
Baskomutan Milli Parkı, p.o.i., Tur.	E13	28
Basmat, India	B3	53
Bāsoda, India	G6	54
Basoko, D.R.C.	D4	66
Basora, Punt, c., Aruba	p20	104g
Basque Provinces see Euskal Herriko, state, Spain	A8	20
Basra see Al-Başrah, Iraq	C6	56
Bas-Rhin, state, Fr.	F16	14
Bassano, Ab., Can.	F18	138
Bassano del Grappa, Italy	E8	22
Bassari, Togo	H5	64
Bassas da India, rf., Reu.	E6	68
Bassein, stm., Mya.	D2	48
Bassella, Spain	B12	20
Basse Santa Su, Gam.	G2	64
Basse-Terre, Guad.	i5	105c
Basseterre, St. K./N.	C2	105a
Basse Terre, Trin.	s12	105f
Basse-Terre, i., Guad.	h5	105c
Bassett, Ne., U.S.	E13	126
Bassett, Va., U.S.	H6	114
Bassfield, Ms., U.S.	F9	122
Bassikounou, Maur.	F3	64
Bassila, Benin	H5	64
Bass River, N.S., Can.	E13	110
Bass Strait, strt., Austl.	L6	76
Basswood Lake, l., N.A.	C6	118
Båstad, Swe.	H5	8
Bastenaken see Bastogne, Bel.	D14	14
Bastersberge, hill, S. Afr.	G5	70
Basti, India	E9	54
Bastia, Fr.	G15	18
Bastogne, Bel.	D14	14
Bastrop, La., U.S.	E6	122
Bastrop, Tx., U.S.	D10	130
Basu, Pulau, i., Indon.	D3	50
Basutoland see Lesotho, ctry., Afr.	F9	70
Bata, Eq. Gui.	I6	64
Bataan Peninsula, pen., Phil.	C3	52
Batabanó, Golfo de, b., Cuba	A6	102
Batac, Phil.	A3	52
Batagaj, Russia	C15	34
Batagaj-Alyta, Russia	C15	34
Batak, Blg.	H11	26
Batala, India	C5	54
Batalha, Braz.	E7	88
Batalha, Port.	E2	20
Batam, Pulau, i., Indon.	C3	50
Batamaj, Russia	D14	34
Batang, China	E5	36
Batangafo, C.A.R.	C3	66
Batangas, Phil.	D3	52
Batangtoru, Indon.	C1	50
Batan Islands, is., Phil.	K9	42
Batanta, Pulau, i., Indon.	F9	44
Batatais, Braz.	K2	88
Batavia, Arg.	G5	92
Batavia see Jakarta, Indon.	G5	50
Batavia, Il., U.S.	C9	120
Batavia, Ia., U.S.	D5	120
Batavia, N.Y., U.S.	A7	114
Batchelor, Austl.	B6	74
Bătdâmbâng, Camb.	F6	48
Bateckij, Russia	B13	10
Batemans Bay, Austl.	J8	76
Bates, Mount, mtn., Norf. I.	y24	78i
Batesburg, S.C., U.S.	C4	116
Batesville, Ar., U.S.	B7	122
Batesville, Ms., U.S.	C9	122
Batesville, Tx., U.S.	F8	130
Bath, N.B., Can.	D9	110
Bath, Eng., U.K.	J10	12
Bath, Me., U.S.	G7	110
Bath, N.Y., U.S.	B8	114
Batha, stm., Chad	E3	62
Bathgate, N.D., U.S.	F16	124
Bathinda, India	C5	54
Bathsheba, Barb.	n8	105d
Bathurst, Austl.	I7	76
Bathurst, N.B., Can.	C11	110
Bathurst see Banjul, Gam.	G1	64
Bathurst, Cape, c., N.T., Can.	A5	106
Bathurst Inlet, Nu., Can.	B9	106
Bathurst Island, i., Austl.	B5	74
Bathurst Island, i., Nu., Can.	B5	141
Batlow, Austl.	J6	76
Batman, Tur.	B5	56
Batna, Alg.	B6	64
Ba To, Viet.	E9	48
Baton Rouge, La., U.S.	G7	122
Batouri, Cam.	D2	66
Batsawul, Afg.	A3	54
Batson, Tx., U.S.	G4	122
Batterie, Pointe de la, c., Mart.	k7	105c
Batticaloa, Sri L.	H5	53
Battipaglia, Italy	D8	24
Battle, stm., Can.	D19	138
Battle Creek, Mi., U.S.	F4	112
Battle Creek, Ne., U.S.	F15	126
Battle Creek, stm., N.A.	F4	124
Battle Ground, In., U.S.	H3	112
Battle Ground, Wa., U.S.	E4	136
Battle Harbour, Nf., Can.	i22	107a
Battle Mountain, Nv., U.S.	C8	134
Battle Mountain, mtn., Wy., U.S.	B9	132
Batu, mtn., Eth.	F7	62
Batu, Kepulauan, is., Indon.	F2	44
Batu-Batu, Indon.	F11	50
Batu Berincang, Gunong, mtn., Malay.	J5	48
Batubrok, Bukit, mtn., Indon.	C9	50
Batu Gajah, Malay.	J5	48
Batukelau, Indon.	C9	50
Batumi, Geor.	F6	32
Batu Pahat, Malay.	L6	48
Batupanjang, Indon.	C2	50
Baturaja, Indon.	F3	50
Baturino, Russia	C15	32
Baturité, Braz.	C6	88
Baturusa, Indon.	D5	50
Batusangkar, Indon.	D2	50
Batz, Île de, i., Fr.	F4	14
Bau, Malay.	C7	50
Baubau, Indon.	G7	44
Bauchi, Nig.	G6	64
Bauda, India	H10	54
Baudette, Mn., U.S.	C4	118
Baudó, stm., Col.	E3	86
Bauld, Cape, c., Nf., Can.	i22	107a
Bauman Fiord, b., Nu., Can.	B8	141
Baume-les-Dames, Fr.	G15	14
Baures, Bol.	B4	90
Bauru, Braz.	L1	88
Bauska, Lat.	D7	10
Bautzen, Ger.	E10	16
Bauxite, Ar., U.S.	C6	122
Bavaria see Bayern, state, Ger.	H7	16
Bavarian Alps, mts., Eur.	I7	16
Båven, l., Swe.	G7	8
Bavispe, Mex.	F8	98
Bavispe, stm., Mex.	F8	98
Bawang, Indon.	G6	50
Bawdwin, Mya.	A3	48
Bawean, Pulau, i., Indon.	F8	50
Bawiti, Egypt	B5	62
Bawmi, Mya.	D2	48
Baxaya, mtn., Som.	B9	66
Baxian, China	G2	42
Baxian, China	B7	42
Baxter, Ia., U.S.	C4	120
Baxter, Mn., U.S.	E4	118
Baxter, Tn., U.S.	H12	120
Baxterville, Ms., U.S.	F9	122
Bay, Ar., U.S.	B8	122
Bay, Laguna de, l., Phil.	C3	52
Bayamo, Cuba	B9	102
Bayamón, P.R.	B3	104a
Bayan, China	A7	38
Bayan, Indon.	H10	50
Bayāna, India	E6	54
Bayan Har Shan, mts., China	E4	36
Bayanhongor, Mong.	B5	36
Bayannaobao, China	B2	42
Bayano, Lago, res., Pan.	H8	102
Bayan Obo, China	C7	36
Bayard, Ia., U.S.	C3	120
Bayard, N.M., U.S.	K8	132
Bayard, W.V., U.S.	E6	114
Bayawan, Phil.	F4	52
Baybay, Phil.	E5	52
Bayboro, N.C., U.S.	A9	116
Bayburt, Tur.	A5	56
Bay City, Mi., U.S.	E6	112
Bay City, Or., U.S.	E3	136
Bay City, Tx., U.S.	F12	130
Baydhabo (Baidoa), Som.	D8	66
Baydrag, stm., Mong.	B4	36
Bayern (Bavaria), state, Ger.	H7	16
Bayeux, Braz.	D8	88
Bayeux, Fr.	E8	14
Bayfield, Co., U.S.	F9	132
Bayfield, Wi., U.S.	E8	118
Bayındır, Tur.	E10	28
Baykonur see Bajkonur, Kaz.	E11	32
Bay Minette, Al., U.S.	G11	122
Bayombong, Phil.	B3	52
Bayona see Baiona, Spain	B2	20
Bayonne, Fr.	F4	18
Bayou Bodcau Reservoir, res., La., U.S.	E5	122
Bayou Cane, La., U.S.	H8	122
Bayou D'Arbonne Lake, res., La., U.S.	E6	122
Bayovar, Peru	E1	84
Bay Port, Mi., U.S.	E6	112
Bayport, Mn., U.S.	F6	118
Bayramiç, Tur.	D9	28
Bayreuth, Ger.	G7	16

Name	Map Ref.	Page
Bayrūt (Beirut), Leb.	E6	58
Bays, Lake of, l., On., Can.	C10	112
Bay Saint Louis, Ms., U.S.	G9	122
Bay Shore, N.Y., U.S.	D12	114
Bayside, On., Can.	D12	112
Bay Springs Lake, res., Ms., U.S.	C10	122
Bayt ad-Dīn, Leb.	E6	58
Bayt al-Faqīh, Yemen	G5	56
Bayt Lahm (Bethlehem), W.B.	G6	58
Baytown, Tx., U.S.	H4	122
Bayyā'īyaḥ al-Kabīrah, Syria	C8	58
Baza, Spain	G8	20
Bazardüzü dağ, mtn., Azer.	A6	56
Bazaruto, Ilha do, i., Moz.	B12	70
Bazhong, China	F2	42
Bazière, Fr.	F7	18
Bazine, Ks., U.S.	C9	128
Be, stm., Viet.	G8	48
Be, Nosy, i., Madag.	C8	68
Beach Haven, N.J., U.S.	E11	114
Beachport, Austl.	K3	76
Beachville, On., Can.	E9	112
Beachy Head, c., Eng., U.K.	K13	12
Beacon, Austl.	F3	74
Beacon, N.Y., U.S.	C12	114
Beacon Hill, Wa., U.S.	D3	136
Beaconsfield, Austl.	n13	77a
Beagle Gulf, b., Austl.	B5	74
Bealanana, Madag.	C8	68
Bealdoaivi see Peäldoaivi, mtn., Fin.	B12	8
Beale, Cape, c., B.C., Can.	H5	138
Beals Creek, stm., Tx., U.S.	B7	130
Bear, stm., U.S.	I14	136
Bear, stm., Ca., U.S.	D4	134
Bear Bay, b., Nu., Can.	B8	141
Bear Creek, stm., U.S.	C10	122
Bear Creek, stm., U.S.	D6	122
Bearden, Ar., U.S.	D6	122
Beardmore, On., Can.	B11	118
Bear Island, i., Ant.	C29	81
Bear Island, i., Ire.	J3	12
Bear Island see Bjørnøya, i., Nor.	B5	30
Bear Lake, i., Ab., Can.	A11	138
Bear Lake, l., U.S.	A5	132
Bear Mountain, mtn., Or., U.S.	G3	136
Béarn, hist. reg., Fr.	F5	18
Bear River, N.S., Can.	F11	110
Bear River Range, mts., U.S.	B5	132
Beartooth Pass, p., Wy., U.S.	C3	126
Bear Town, Ms., U.S.	E8	122
Beās, stm., India	C6	54
Beasain, Spain	A8	20
Beata, Cabo, c., Dom. Rep.	D12	102
Beata, Isla, i., Dom. Rep.	D12	102
Beaton, B.C., Can.	F13	138
Beatrice, Al., U.S.	F11	122
Beatrice, Ne., U.S.	A12	128
Beatrice, Cape, c., Austl.	B7	74
Beattie, Ks., U.S.	L18	118
Beatton, stm., B.C., Can.	D6	106
Beatty, Nv., U.S.	G9	134
Beattyville, Ky., U.S.	G2	114
Beaucaire, Fr.	F10	18
Beauce, reg., Fr.	F10	14
Beauchêne, Lac, l., Qc., Can.	B11	112
Beauchêne Island, i., Falk. Is.	J5	90
Beaudesert, Austl.	F9	76
Beaufort, Malay.	A9	50
Beaufort, S.C., U.S.	D5	116
Beaufort Castle see Qal'at ash-Shaqīf, hist., Leb.	E6	58
Beaufort Sea, N.A.	B12	140
Beaufort West, S. Afr.	H6	70
Beaugency, Fr.	G10	14
Beauharnois, Qc., Can.	E2	110
Beaujolais, hist. reg., Fr.	C10	18
Beaumont, Fr.	E27	14
Beaumont, N.Z.	G3	80
Beaumont, Ca., U.S.	J8	134
Beaumont, Ms., U.S.	F9	122
Beaumont, Tx., U.S.	G5	122
Beaumont Hill, hill, Austl.	H5	76
Beaune, Fr.	G13	14
Beaupré, Qc., Can.	D5	110
Beaupré, Qc., Can.	C6	110
Beaurepaire, Fr.	D11	18
Beauséjour, Mb., Can.	D17	124
Beauséjour, Guad.	h6	105c
Beauvais, Fr.	E11	14
Beauvoir-sur-Mer, Fr.	H6	14
Beaver, Ok., U.S.	E8	128
Beaver, Pa., U.S.	D5	114
Beaver, Ut., U.S.	E4	132
Beaver, stm., Can.	D9	106
Beaver, stm., Can.	C6	108
Beaver, stm., Ut., U.S.	E3	132
Beaver Creek, stm., U.S.	G9	124
Beaver Creek, stm., U.S.	D9	126
Beaver Creek, stm., U.S.	A8	128
Beaver Creek, stm., Co., U.S.	G9	126
Beaver Creek, stm., Mt., U.S.	F6	124
Beaver Creek, stm., Ne., U.S.	F14	126
Beaver Creek, stm., Ne., U.S.	G14	126
Beaver Creek, stm., Ok., U.S.	G10	128
Beaver Creek, stm., Tx., U.S.	H9	128
Beaver Crossing, Ne., U.S.	G15	126
Beaver Dam, Ky., U.S.	G11	120
Beaver Dam, Wi., U.S.	H9	118
Beaverdell, B.C., Can.	G11	138
Beaver Falls, Pa., U.S.	D5	114
Beaverhead, stm., Mt., U.S.	E14	136
Beaverhead Mountains, mts., U.S.	E14	136
Beaverhill Lake, l., Ab., Can.	C18	138
Beaverhouse Lake, l., On., Can.	C6	118
Beaver Island, i., Mi., U.S.	C4	112
Beaver Lake, res., Ar., U.S.	B19	138
Bedford, S. Afr.	H8	70
Bedford, Eng., U.K.	I12	12
Bedford, In., U.S.	F11	120
Bedford, Ia., U.S.	D3	120
Bedford, Ky., U.S.	F12	120
Bedford, Pa., U.S.	D7	114
Bedford, Tx., U.S.	B10	130
Bedi, India	G3	54
Bedoba, Russia	C17	32
Bedourie, Austl.	E2	76
Bedworth, Eng., U.K.	I11	12
Beebe, Ar., U.S.	B7	122
Beechal Creek, stm., Austl.	F5	76
Beech Creek, Ky., U.S.	G10	120
Beech Fork, stm., Ky., U.S.	G12	120
Beech Grove, In., U.S.	I3	112
Beechworth, Austl.	K8	76
Beechy, Sk., Can.	D6	124
Beecroft Head, c., Austl.	J8	76
Beemer, Ne., U.S.	J2	118
Beenleigh, Austl.	F9	76
Bee Ridge, Fl., U.S.	I3	116
Beersheba see Be'ér Sheva', Isr.	G6	58
Beersheba Springs, Tn., U.S.	B13	122
Be'ér Sheva' (Beersheba), Isr.	G6	58
Beeskow, Ger.	D10	16
Beeville, Tx., U.S.	F10	130
Befale, D.R.C.	D4	66
Befandriana Avaratra, Madag.	E7	68
Bega, Austl.	K7	76
Bega, stm., Eur.	D9	26
Begamganj, India	G7	54
Begur, Cap de, c., Spain	C14	20
Begusarai, India	F11	54
Behbahān, Iran	C7	56
Behshahr, Iran	B7	56
Bei, stm., China	J5	42
Bei'an, China	B10	36
Beibei, China	G2	42
Beicheng, China	G5	36
Beigi, Eth.	F6	62
Beihai, China	K3	42
Beijing (Peking), China	B7	42
Beijing, state, China	B7	42
Beili, China	L3	42
Beiliu, China	J4	42
Beinamar, Chad	F3	62
Beipa, Pap. N. Gui.	b4	79a
Beipan, stm., China	I1	42
Beipiao, China	D4	38
Beira, Moz.	A12	70
Beira, hist. reg., Port.	E3	20
Beiru, stm., China	D5	42
Beirut see Bayrūt, Leb.	E6	58
Beiseker, Ab., Can.	E17	138
Beishan, China	I3	42
Bei Shan, mts., China	C4	36
Beitbridge, Zimb.	C10	70
Beizhen, China	D4	38
Beja, Port.	G3	20
Béja, Tun.	H3	24
Beja, state, Port.	G3	20
Bejaïa, Alg.	B6	64
Béjar, Spain	D5	20
Bejhi, stm., Pak.	D2	54
Bejneu, Kaz.	E8	32
Bejuco, Pan.	H8	102
Bekaa Valley see Al-Biqā', val., Leb.	D7	58
Bekabad, Uzb.	F11	32
Békés, state, Hung.	C8	26
Békéscsaba, Hung.	C7	26
Békilli, Tur.	E12	28
Bekily, Madag.	E8	68
Bekodoka, Madag.	D7	68
Bekopaka, Madag.	D7	68
Bela, India	F9	54
Bela, Pak.	D10	56
Belaazërsk, Bela.	H8	10
Bela Crkva, Yugo.	E8	26
Bel Air, Md., U.S.	E9	114
Belaja, stm., Russia	C8	32
Belaja Cerkov' see Bila Cerkva, Ukr.	E14	6
Belaja Holunica, Russia	C8	32
Belalcázar, Spain	F5	20
Belampalli, India	B4	53
Bela Palanka, Yugo.	F9	26
Belarus, ctry., Eur.	E14	6
Belaruskaja hrada, mts., Bela.	F10	10
Belau see Palau, ctry., Oc.	g8	78b
Bela Vista, Braz.	D5	90
Bela Vista, Moz.	E11	70
Belawan, Indon.	C10	50
Belayan, stm., Indon.	C10	50
Belcher, La., U.S.	E5	122
Belcherāgh, Afg.	B10	56
Belcher Channel, strt., Nu., Can.	B6	141
Belcher Islands, is., Nu., Can.	D14	106
Belding, Mi., U.S.	E4	112
Belebelka, Russia	D8	10
Belëm, Braz.	A1	88
Belém, Moz.	C6	68
Belém de São Francisco, Braz.	E6	88
Belén, Arg.	C4	92
Belén, Nic.	G4	102
Belén, Para.	D5	90
Belen, Tur.	B7	58
Belen, N.M., U.S.	I10	132
Belén, Ur.	E9	92
Belén, stm., Arg.	C4	92
Belep, Îles, is., N. Cal.	I14	79d
Belesar, Embalse de, res., Spain	B3	20
Belëv, Russia	G19	10
Belfast, N. Ire., U.K.	G6	12
Belfast, Me., U.S.	F7	110
Belfield, N.D., U.S.	H10	124
Belford, Eng., U.K.	F11	12
Belfort, Fr.	G15	14
Belfry, Mt., U.S.	B3	126
Belgaum, India	D2	53
Belgorod, Russia	D5	32
Belgrade, Mt., U.S.	E15	136
Belgrade, Ne., U.S.	F14	126
Belgrade see Beograd, Yugo.	E7	26
Belgrano II, sci., Ant.	C36	81
Belhaven, N.C., U.S.	A9	116
Belick, Bela.	H13	10
Beliliou, i., Palau	D9	44
Belin-Béliet see Belin, Fr.	E5	18
Belington, W.V., U.S.	E5	114
Belinyu, Indon.	D4	50
Belitung, i., Indon.	E5	50
Belize, ctry., N.A.	D3	102
Belize City, Belize	D3	102
Bel'kovskij, ostrov see Bel'kovskij, ostrov, i., Russia	A16	34
Bel'kovskij, ostrov, i., Russia	A16	34
Bella Bella, B.C., Can.	D2	138
Bella Coola, B.C., Can.	D4	138
Bella Coola, stm., B.C., Can.	D5	138
Bellaire, Fl., U.S.	F4	116
Bellaire, Oh., U.S.	D5	114
Bellaire, Tx., U.S.	H3	122
Bellamy, Al., U.S.	E10	122
Bellaria, Italy	F9	22
Bellary, India	D3	53
Beljęta, Austl.	G7	76
Bella Unión, Ur.	E9	92
Bella Vista, Arg.	C5	92
Bella Vista, Arg.	D8	92
Bellavista, Peru	E2	84
Bellbrook, Austl.	H9	76
Belle, W.V., U.S.	F4	114
Bellefontaine, Mart.	k6	105c
Bellefontaine, Oh., U.S.	D2	114
Bellefonte, Pa., U.S.	D8	114
Belle Fourche, S.D., U.S.	C9	126
Belle Fourche, stm., U.S.	C10	126
Bellegarde-sur-Valserine, Fr.	C11	18
Belle Glade, Fl., U.S.	J5	116
Belle Hôtesse, mtn., Guad.	h5	105c
Belle-Île, i., Fr.	G5	14
Belle Isle, i., Nf., Can.	i22	107a
Belle Isle, Strait of, strt., Nf., Can.	i22	107a
Bellenden Ker National Park, p.o.i., Austl.	A5	76
Belle Plaine, Ia., U.S.	C5	120
Belle Plaine, Ks., U.S.	D11	128
Belle Plaine, Mn., U.S.	G5	118
Belleterre, Qc., Can.	G11	122
Belleville, On., Can.	D12	112
Belleville, Il., U.S.	F8	120
Belleville, Ks., U.S.	B11	128
Belleville, Pa., U.S.	D8	114
Belleville-sur-Saône, Fr.	C10	18
Bellevue, Ab., Can.	G16	138
Bellevue, Id., U.S.	G12	136
Bellevue, Ia., U.S.	B7	120
Bellevue, Mi., U.S.	F4	112
Bellevue, Ne., U.S.	C2	120
Bellevue, Oh., U.S.	C3	114
Bellevue, Wa., U.S.	C4	136
Belley, Fr.	D11	18
Bellingham, Mn., U.S.	F2	118
Bellingham, Wa., U.S.	B4	136
Bellinghausen, sci., Ant.	B35	81
Bellingshausen Sea, Ant.	P29	142
Bellinzona, Switz.	D6	22
Bell Lake, l., On., Can.	B7	118
Bello, Col.	D4	86
Bellot Strait, strt., Nu., Can.	A12	106
Bell Peninsula, pen., Nu., Can.	C14	106
Bells, Tn., U.S.	B9	122
Bells, Tx., U.S.	D2	122
Bells Corners, On., Can.	C14	112
Belluno, Italy	D9	22
Bell Ville, Arg.	F6	92
Bellville, S. Afr.	H4	70
Bellwood, Pa., U.S.	D7	114
Belly, stm., N.A.	G17	138
Belmond, Ia., U.S.	B4	120
Belmont, N.S., Can.	E13	110
Belmont, S. Afr.	F7	70
Belmont, N.H., U.S.	G5	110
Belmont, Wi., U.S.	B7	120
Belmonte, Braz.	H6	88
Belmonte, Port.	D3	20
Belmonte, Spain	A4	20
Belmopan, Belize	D3	102
Beloe, Russia	B22	10
Beloe, ozero, l., Russia	F17	8
Beloe more (White Sea), Russia	D18	8
Belogorsk, Russia	F14	34
Belo Horizonte, Braz.	J3	88
Beloit, Ks., U.S.	B10	128
Beloit, Wi., U.S.	B8	120
Belo Jardim, Braz.	E7	88
Belomestnaja, Russia	H20	10
Belomorsk, Russia	D16	8
Belorečensk, Russia	F5	32
Belören, Tur.	F15	28
Belo sur Mer, Madag.	E7	68
Belot, Lac, l., N.T., Can.	B5	106
Belo Tsiribihina, Madag.	D7	68
Belousovo, Russia	E19	10
Belovo, Russia	D15	32
Belozërsk, Russia	F17	8
Belpre, Oh., U.S.	E4	114
Belt, Mt., U.S.	C16	136
Belt Creek, stm., Mt., U.S.	C16	136
Belton, Mo., U.S.	F3	120
Belton, Tx., U.S.	C10	130
Belton Lake, res., Tx., U.S.	C9	130
Beltrán, Arg.	C5	92
Belukha, Mount, mtn., Asia	E15	32
Belūr, India	E3	53
Beluran, Malay.	H1	52
Belvedere Marittimo, Italy	E9	24
Belvidere, Il., U.S.	B9	120
Belvidere, N.J., U.S.	D10	114
Belview, Mn., U.S.	G3	118
Belvoir see Kokhav HaYarden, hist., Isr.	F6	58
Belyando, stm., Austl.	D6	76
Belye Berega, Russia	G17	10
Belye Stolby, Russia	E20	10
Belyj Gorodok, Russia	C20	10
Belyj Jar, Russia	C15	32
Belzig, Ger.	D8	16
Belzoni, Ms., U.S.	E8	122
Bement, Il., U.S.	E9	120
Bemidji, Mn., U.S.	D4	118
Benaco see Garda, Lago di, l., Italy	E7	22
Bena-Dibele, D.R.C.	E4	66
Benagerie, Austl.	H3	76
Benalla, Austl.	K6	76
Benares see Vārānasi, India	F9	54
Ben Arous, Tun.	H4	24
Benavente, Spain	B5	20
Benavides, Tx., U.S.	F9	130
Benbecula, i., Scot., U.K.	D5	12
Ben Bolt, Tx., U.S.	G9	130
Ben Cat, Viet.	G8	48
Bencha, Khao Phanom, mtn., Thai.	H4	48
Ben-Chicao, Col de p., Alg.	H13	20
Bencubbin, Austl.	F3	74
Bend, Or., U.S.	F5	136
Bendemeer, Austl.	H8	76
Bender Cassim see Boosaaso, Som.	B9	66
Bendigo, Austl.	K5	76
Bône, Lat.	D6	10
Benedito Leite, Braz.	E3	88
Benepu', Rada, anch., Chile	f29	78l
Benevento, Italy	J4	22
Beng, stm., Laos	B5	48
Bengal, Bay of, b., Asia	F6	46
Bengara, Indon.	B10	50
Bengasi see Banghāzī, Libya	A7	62
Bengbu, China	E7	42
Benghazi see Banghāzī, Libya	A3	62
Bengkalis, Indon.	C3	50
Bengkalis, Pulau, i., Indon.	C3	50
Bengkayang, Indon.	C6	50
Bengkulu, Indon.	E3	50
Bengkulu, state, Indon.	E3	50
Benguela, Ang.	C1	68
Benguerua, Ilha, i., Moz.	B12	70
Banhā, Egypt	H2	58
Beni, D.R.C.	D5	66
Beni, stm., Bol.	B3	90
Beni Abbas, Alg.	C4	64
Beni Aïd el-Bahariya, Egypt	K1	58
Beni Ahmac, Egypt	J1	58
Benicarló, Spain	D11	20
Benidorm, Spain	F10	20
Beni Mazār, Egypt	I1	58
Beni Muhammadiyat, Egypt	K2	58
Benin, ctry., Afr.	G5	64
Benin, Bight of, b., Afr.	I5	64
Benin City, Nig.	H6	64
Benissa, Spain	F11	20
Beni Suef, Egypt	I2	58
Benito, Mb., Can.	C12	124
Benito Juárez, Arg.	H8	92
Benito Juárez, Presa, res., Mex.	G10	100
Benjamin, Tx., U.S.	H9	128
Benjamín, Isla, i., Chile	H2	90
Benjamin Constant, Braz.	D3	84
Benkelman, Ne., U.S.	A7	128
Benld, Il., U.S.	E8	120
Ben Lomond National Park, p.o.i., Austl.	n13	77a
Benndale, Ms., U.S.	G10	122
Bennett Island see Bennetta, ostrov, i., Russia	A18	34
Bennettsville, S.C., U.S.	B6	116
Bennington, Ks., U.S.	B11	128
Bennington, Vt., U.S.	B12	114
Benoît, Ms., U.S.	D7	122
Benoni, S. Afr.	E9	70
Ben Sakka, Raâs, c., Tun.	G3	24
Bensheim, Ger.	G4	16
Benson, Az., U.S.	L6	132
Benson, Mn., U.S.	F3	118
Benson, N.C., U.S.	A7	116
Benteng, Indon.	G12	50
Bentinck Island, i., Austl.	C7	74
Bentinck Island, i., Mya.	G4	48
Bento Gonçalves, Braz.	D12	92
Benton, Ar., U.S.	C6	122
Benton, Il., U.S.	F9	120
Benton, Ky., U.S.	H9	120
Benton, La., U.S.	E5	122
Benton, Mo., U.S.	G8	120
Benton, Wi., U.S.	B7	120
Benton Harbor, Mi., U.S.	F3	112
Bentonville, Ar., U.S.	H3	120
Benua, Pulau, i., Indon.	C5	50
Benue, stm., Afr.	H6	64
Ben Wheeler, Tx., U.S.	E3	122
Beočin, Yugo.	D5	38
Beograd (Belgrade), Yugo.	E7	26
Béoumi, C. Iv.	H3	64
Beowawe, Nv., U.S.	C9	134
Beppu, Japan	F4	40
Bequia, i., St. Vin.	o11	105e
Berat, Alb.	D13	24
Berati see Berat, Alb.	D13	24
Berău, stm., Indon.	B10	50
Berber, Som.	B9	66
Berbérati, C.A.R.	D3	66
Berchtesgaden, Ger.	I8	16
Berck, Fr.	D10	14
Berclair, Tx., U.S.	F10	130
Berdians'k, Ukr.	E5	32
Berdigestjah, Russia	D15	34
Berdsk, Russia	D14	32
Berea, Oh., U.S.	C4	114
Berea, S.C., U.S.	B3	116
Berehove, Ukr.	A9	26
Berekum, Ghana	H4	64
Berenice see Baranīs, Egypt	C7	62
Berens, stm., Mb., Can.	B17	124
Berens Island, i., Mb., Can.	B16	124
Berens River, Mb., Can.	B16	124
Beresford, S.D., U.S.	H2	118
Berettyó (Barcău), stm., Eur.	B8	26
Berettyóújfalu, Hung.	B8	26
Berëza, Bela.	H7	10
Berezivka, Ukr.	B17	26
Berëzovka, Russia	B10	32
Berëzovo, Russia	B10	32
Berëzovskij, Russia	C10	32
Berëzovskij Rjadok, Russia	B17	10
Berga, Spain	B12	20
Bergama, Tur.	D10	28
Bérgamo, Italy	E6	22
Bergantín, Ven.	C9	86
Bergby, Swe.	F7	8
Bergen auf Rügen, Ger.	B9	16
Bergen, N.Y., U.S.	A7	114
Bergen, Nor.	F1	8
Bergen op Zoom, Neth.	C13	14
Bergerac, Fr.	E6	18
Bergisch Gladbach, Ger.	F3	16
Bergsjö, Swe.	F7	8
Berhampore see Baharampur, India	F7	54
Berhampur see Brahmapur, India	I10	54
Bering Glacier, ice, Ak., U.S.	D11	140
Bering Sea	D21	142
Bering Strait, strt.	C6	140
Beringen, Bel.	C14	14
Berja, Spain	H8	20
Berkák, Nor.	E4	8
Berkeley, Ca., U.S.	F3	134
Berkeley Springs, W.V., U.S.	E7	114
Berkner Island, i., Ant.	C35	81
Berkovica, Blg.	F10	26
Berkshire Hills, hills, Ma., U.S.	B12	114
Berlevåg, Nor.	A13	8
Berlin, Ger.	D9	16
Berlin, Md., U.S.	F10	114
Berlin, N.H., U.S.	F5	110
Berlin, Pa., U.S.	E7	114
Berlin, Wi., U.S.	H9	118
Berlin, state, Ger.	D9	16
Bermejillo, Mex.	C7	100
Bermejo, stm., Arg.	B7	92
Bermejo, stm., Arg.	D4	90
Bermejo, Paso del p., S.A.	F2	92
Bermen, Lac, l., Qc., Can.	E17	106
Bermeo, Spain	A8	20
Bermuda, dep., N.A.	k16	104e
Bern (Berne), Switz.	D4	22
Bern, state, Switz.	D4	22
Bernalda, Italy	D10	24
Bernalillo, N.M., U.S.	G2	132
Bernasconi, Arg.	I6	92
Bernau bei Berlin, Ger.	D9	16
Bernay, Fr.	E9	14
Bernburg, Ger.	E7	16
Berndorf, Austria	C12	22
Berne, In., U.S.	H5	112
Berne see Bern, Switz.	D4	22
Bernese Alps see Berner Alpen, mts., Switz.	D4	22
Berneray, i., Scot., U.K.	D5	12
Bernice, La., U.S.	E6	122
Bernie, Mo., U.S.	H8	120
Bernier Bay, b., Nu., Can.	A12	106
Bernier Island, i., Austl.	D2	74
Bernina, Piz, mtn., Eur.	H18	14
Bernkastel-Kues, Ger.	G3	16
Berón de Astrada, Arg.	C9	92
Beroroha, Madag.	E8	68
Berounka, stm., Czech Rep.	F9	16
Berre, Étang de, l., Fr.	F11	18
Berri, Austl.	J3	76
Berriyane, Alg.	C5	64
Berry, hist. reg., Fr.	H11	14
Berry, Canal du, can., Fr.	G10	14
Berry Creek, stm., Ab., Can.	E19	138
Berryessa, Lake, res., Ca., U.S.	E3	134
Berry Islands, is., Bah.	B9	96
Bersenbrück, Ger.	D3	16
Bershad', Ukr.	A16	26
Berthold, N.D., U.S.	F12	124
Berthoud, Co., U.S.	G7	126
Berthoud Pass, p., Co., U.S.	B3	128
Bertoua, Cam.	D2	66
Bertrand, Mi., U.S.	G3	112
Bertrand, Ne., U.S.	G13	126
Beruri, Braz.	D5	84
Berwick, La., U.S.	H7	122
Berwick, Pa., U.S.	C9	114
Berwick-upon-Tweed, Eng., U.K.	F11	12
Besalampy, Madag.	D7	68
Besançon, Fr.	G14	14
Bešankovičy, Bela.	E12	10
Besar, Gunung, vol., Indon.	K6	48
Besar, Gunung, vol., Indon.	E9	50
Besedz', stm., Eur.	H14	10
Beskid Mountains see Beskids, mts., Eur.	G15	16
Beskids, mts., Eur.	G15	16
Beslan, Russia	F6	32
Besni, Tur.	A8	58
Bessarabia, hist. reg., Eur.	C15	26
Bessemer, Al., U.S.	D11	122
Bessemer, Mi., U.S.	E8	118
Bessemer City, N.C., U.S.	A4	116
Bestjah, Russia	D15	34
Bestobe, Kaz.	D12	32
Bétaré Oya, Cam.	C2	66
Betanzos, Spain	A2	20
Bétérou, Benin	H5	64
Bethal, S. Afr.	E9	70
Bethalto, Il., U.S.	F7	120
Bethany, Mo., U.S.	D3	120
Bethany, Ok., U.S.	F11	128
Bethel, Ak., U.S.	D7	140
Bethel, Me., U.S.	F6	110
Bethel, Mn., U.S.	F5	118
Bethel, N.C., U.S.	I8	114
Bethel Acres, Ok., U.S.	B2	122
Bethel Springs, Tn., U.S.	B10	122
Bethlehem, S. Afr.	F9	70
Bethlehem, Pa., U.S.	D10	114
Bethlehem, W.V., U.S.	H9	112
Bethlehem see Bayt Lahm, W.B.	G6	58
Bethune, Sk., Can.	D8	124
Béthune, Fr.	D11	14
Bethune, S.C., U.S.	B5	116
Betong, Malay.	C7	50
Betoota, Austl.	E3	76
Betpak-Dala, des., Kaz.	E11	32
Betroka, Madag.	E8	68
Betsiamites, stm., Qc., Can.	A8	110
Betsiamites, Pointe de, c., Qc., Can.	A7	110
Betsiboka, stm., Madag.	D8	68
Betsie, Point, c., Mi., U.S.	D3	112
Betsy Layne, Ky., U.S.	G3	114
Bettendorf, Ia., U.S.	C7	120
Bettiah, India	C10	54
Bettles Field, Ak., U.S.	C9	140
Bettola, Italy	F6	22
Bettül, India	H6	54
Betung, Indon.	E4	50
Betwa, stm., India	F7	54
Betzdorf, Ger.	F3	16
Beulah, Austl.	J4	76
Beulah, Mi., U.S.	D3	112
Beulah, N.D., U.S.	G12	124
Beulaville, N.C., U.S.	B8	116
Beverley, Eng., U.K.	H12	12
Beverly Hills, Ca., U.S.	I7	134
Beverly Lake, l., Nu., Can.	C10	106
Beverungen, Ger.	E5	16
Beverwijk, Neth.	B13	14
Bewani Mountains, mts., Pap. N. Gui.	a3	79a
Bexhill, Eng., U.K.	K13	12
Bexley, Oh., U.S.	D3	114
Bey Dağları, mts., Tur.	G13	28
Beyla, Gui.	H3	64
Beypazarı, Tur.	C14	28
Beypore, India	F2	53
Beyşehir, Tur.	F14	28
Beyşehir Gölü, l., Tur.	F14	28
Bežanickaja vozvyšennost', plat., Russia	D12	10
Bežanicy, Russia	C12	10
Bežeck, Russia	C19	10
Bezmein, Turkmen.	B8	56
Bhabhua, India	F9	54
Bhachau, India	G3	54
Bhadarwāh, India	B6	54
Bhādāsar, India	E4	54
Bhadaur, India	C5	54
Bhadgaon (Bhādgāon), Nepal	E10	54
Bhadra, India	E2	53
Bhadrakh, India	H11	54
Bhadra Reservoir, res., India	E2	53
Bhadrāvati, India	E3	53
Bhag, Pak.	D10	56
Bhāgalpur, India	F11	54
Bhāi Pheru, Pak.	C5	54
Bhairāb Bāzār, Bngl.	F13	54
Bhaironghāti, India	C8	54
Bhaktapur (Bhādgāon), Nepal	E10	54
Bhālki, India	B3	53
Bhalwāl, Pak.	B4	54
Bhamo, Mya.	D8	46
Bhandāra, India	H7	54
Bhānvad, India	H2	54
Bharatpur, Nepal	E10	54
Bharatpur, India	E6	54
Bharthana, India	E7	54
Bhārūch, India	H4	54
Bhatapāra, India	H8	54
Bhātghar Lake, res., India	B1	53
Bhatkal, India	E2	53
Bhātpāra, India	G12	54
Bhattiprolu, India	C5	53
Bhavāni, India	F3	53
Bhavāni, stm., India	F3	53
Bhavnagar, India	H4	54
Bhawāni Mandi, India	G6	54
Bhawānipatna, India	I9	54
Bhera, Pak.	B4	54
Bhilkangaon, India	H5	54
Bhilai, India	H8	54
Bhīlwāra, India	F5	54
Bhīmavaram, India	C5	53
Bhind, India	E7	54
Bhīnmāl, India	F4	54
Bhinga, India	B1	53
Bhiwandi, India	D6	53
Bhiwāni, India	D6	54
Bhojpur, Nepal	E11	54
Bhokardan, India	H5	54
Bhongīr, India	C4	53
Bhopāl, India	G6	54
Bhuban, India	H10	54
Bhubaneshwar, India	H10	54
Bhuj, India	G2	54
Bhusāwal, India	H5	54
Bhutan, ctry., Asia	E13	54
Bia, Phou, mtn., Laos	C6	48
Biafra, Bight of, b., Afr.	I6	64
Biak, i., Indon.	F10	44
Biała Piska, Pol.	C18	16
Biała Podlaska, Pol.	D19	16
Biała Podlaska, state, Pol.	E19	16
Białobrzegi, Pol.	E16	16
Białogard, Pol.	B12	16
Białowieski Park Narodowy, p.o.i., Pol.	D19	16
Białystok, Pol.	C19	16
Białystok, state, Pol.	C19	16
Bianco, Monte see Blanc, Mont, mtn., Eur.	D12	18
Biankouma, C. Iv.	H3	64
Biaora, India	F6	54
Biar, Pulau, i., Indon.	E8	44
Biarritz, Fr.	F4	18
Biasca, Switz.	D5	22
Biba, Egypt	I1	58
Bibala, Ang.	C1	68
Bibb City, Ga., U.S.	E14	122
Bibbiena, Italy	G8	22
Bibémi, Cam.	C2	66
Bicas, Braz.	K4	88
Bicaz, Rom.	C13	26
Biche, Lac la, l., Ab., Can.	B18	133
Bichiģt, Mong.	B4	36
Bicknell, In., U.S.	F10	120
Bicknell, Ut., U.S.	E5	132
Bicudo, stm., Braz.	J3	88
Bičura, Russia	F10	34
Bida, Nig.	H6	64
Bīdar, India	C3	53
Biddeford, Me., U.S.	G6	110
Bideford, Eng., U.K.	J8	12
Biebrza, stm., Pol.	C18	16
Biebrzański Park Narodowy, p.o.i., Pol.	C18	16
Biecz, Pol.	G17	16
Biedenkopf, Ger.	F4	16
Biel (Bienne), Switz.	C4	22
Bielawa, Pol.	F12	16
Bielefeld, Ger.	D4	16
Bieler Lake, l., Nu., Can.	A15	106
Biella, Italy	E4	22
Bielsko-Biała, Pol.	G14	16
Bielsko-Biała, state, Pol.	G15	16
Bielsk Podlaski, Pol.	D19	16
Bienfait, Sk., Can.	E11	124
Bien Hoa, Viet.	G8	48
Bienne see Biel, Switz.	C4	22
Bien Son, Viet.	B7	48
Bienville, La., U.S.	E5	122
Bienville, Lac, l., Qc., Can.	D16	106
Bierutów, Pol.	E13	16
Bieszczadzki Park Narodowy, p.o.i., Pol.	G18	16
Bifoun, Gabon	E2	66
Biga, Tur.	C10	28
Bigadiç, Tur.	D11	28
Big A Mountain, mtn., Va., U.S.	G3	114
Big Bald Mountain, mtn., Ga., U.S.	B1	116
Big Baldy Mountain, mtn., Mt., U.S.	D16	136
Big Bay, Mi., U.S.	B2	112
Big Bay, b., Vanuatu	j16	79d
Big Bay De Noc, b., Mi., U.S.	C3	112
Big Bear Lake, Ca., U.S.	I9	134
Big Beaver, Sk., Can.	E8	124
Big Belt Mountains, mts., U.S.	D15	136
Big Bend National Park, p.o.i., Tx., U.S.	E4	130
Big Black, stm., U.S.	E8	122
Big Blue, West Fork, stm., Ne., U.S.	G15	126
Big Bonito Creek, stm., Az., U.S.	J7	132
Big Canyon, val., Tx., U.S.	D5	130
Big Chino Wash, stm., Az., U.S.	H4	132
Big Creek, B.C., Can.	E6	138
Big Creek, stm., Ca., U.S.	E8	134
Big Creek, stm., Ks., U.S.	C9	128
Big Cypress National Preserve, Fl., U.S.	J4	116
Big Cypress Swamp, sw., Fl., U.S.	J4	116
Big Delta, Ak., U.S.	D10	140
Big Diomede Island see Ratmanova, ostrov, i., Russia	C27	34
Big Dry Creek, stm., U.S.	G7	124
Bigelow Bight, b., U.S.	G6	110
Bigfork, Mn., U.S.	D5	118
Big Fork, stm., Mn., U.S.	C5	118
Big Frog Mountain, mtn., U.S.	C14	122
Biggar, Sk., Can.	B6	124
Biggers, Ar., U.S.	H7	120
Biggs, Ca., U.S.	D4	134
Big Gull Lake, l., On., Can.	D12	112
Big Hole, stm., Mt., U.S.	E14	136
Bighorn, stm., U.S.	A5	126
Bighorn Canyon National Recreation Area, p.o.i., U.S.	B4	126
Bighorn Lake, res., U.S.	B4	126
Bighorn Mountains, mts., U.S.	C5	126
Bight, Head of, b., Austl.	F6	74
Big Island, i., Nu., Can.	C17	106
Big Lake, l., Me., U.S.	E9	110
Big Lookout Mountain, mtn., Or., U.S.	F9	136
Big Lost, stm., Id., U.S.	G13	136
Big Muddy, stm., Il., U.S.	G8	120

Name	Map Ref.	Page
Big Muddy Creek, stm., Mt., U.S.	F9	124
Big Nemaha, North Fork, stm., Ne., U.S.	K2	118
Bignona, Sen.	G1	64
Big Pine, Ca., U.S.	F7	134
Big Pine Mountain, mtn., Ca., U.S.	I6	134
Big Piney, Wy., U.S.	H16	136
Big Piney, stm., Mo., U.S.	G6	120
Bigpoint, Ms., U.S.	G10	122
Big Porcupine Creek, stm., Mt., U.S.	H6	124
Big Prairie Creek, stm., Al., U.S.	E11	122
Big Quill Lake, l., Sk., Can.	C9	124
Big Raccoon Creek, stm., In., U.S.	I2	112
Big Rapids, Mi., U.S.	E4	112
Big Rideau Lake, l., On., Can.	D13	112
Big River, Sk., Can.	E9	106
Big Sable Point, c., Mi., U.S.	D3	112
Big Sand Lake, l., Mb., Can.	D11	106
Big Sandy, Tn., U.S.	H9	120
Big Sandy, Tx., U.S.	E3	122
Big Sandy, stm., U.S.	F3	114
Big Sandy, stm., Wy., U.S.	F3	126
Big Sandy Creek, stm., Co., U.S.	C6	128
Bigsby Island, i., On., Can.	B4	118
Big Signal Peak, mtn., Ca., U.S.	D2	134
Big Sioux, stm., U.S.	E16	126
Big Sky, Mt., U.S.	E15	136
Big Smoky Valley, val., Nv., U.S.	E8	134
Big Spring, Tx., U.S.	B6	130
Big Spruce Knob, mtn., W.V., U.S.	F5	114
Big Stone City, S.D., U.S.	F2	118
Big Stone Gap, Va., U.S.	H3	114
Big Stone Lake, l., U.S.	F2	118
Big Sunflower, stm., Ms., U.S.	D8	122
Big Sur, reg., Ca., U.S.	H4	134
Big Timber, Mt., U.S.	E16	136
Big Trout Lake, l., On., Can.	E12	106
Biguaçu, Braz.	C13	92
Big Water, Ut., U.S.	F5	132
Big Wells, Tx., U.S.	F8	130
Big White Mountain, mtn., B.C., Can.	G12	138
Big Wood, stm., Id., U.S.	G12	136
Bihać, Bos.	E2	26
Bīhar, India	F10	54
Bihār, state, India	F10	54
Biharamulo, Tan.	E6	66
Bihor, state, Rom.	C9	26
Bihor, Vârful, mtn., Rom.	C9	26
Bihoro, Japan	C16	38
Bihosava, Bela.	E10	10
Bihu, China	G8	42
Bija, stm., Russia	D15	32
Bijagós, Arquipélago dos, is., Gui.-B.	G1	64
Bijainagar, India	F5	54
Bijaipur, India	E6	54
Bijāpur, India	C2	53
Bījāpur, India	B5	53
Bijeljina, Bos.	E6	26
Bijelo Polje, Yugo.	F6	26
Bijie, China	F6	36
Bijlikol', ozero, l., Kaz.	F12	32
Bijnor, India	D7	54
Bijsk, Russia	D15	32
Bīkāner, India	D4	54
Bikar, at., Marsh. Is.	B8	72
Bikeqi, China	A4	42
Bikin, Russia	B11	36
Bikini, at., Marsh. Is.	B7	72
Bīkkū Bīttī, mtn., Libya	C3	62
Bikoro, D.R.C.	E3	66
Bilāra, India	E4	54
Bilāri, India	D7	54
Bilāsipāra, India	E13	54
Bilāspur, India	C6	54
Bilāspur, India	G9	54
Bila Tserkva, Ukr.	F15	6
Bilauktaung Range, mts., Asia	F4	48
Bilbao, Spain	A7	20
Bilbeis, Egypt	H2	58
Bilbilis, hist., Spain	C9	20
Bileća, Bos.	G5	26
Bilecik, Tur.	C12	28
Bilecik, state, Tur.	C13	28
Biłgoraj, Pol.	F18	16
Bilgrām, India	E8	54
Bilhorod-Dnistrovs'kyi, Ukr.	C17	26
Bili, D.R.C.	D5	66
Biliaïvka, Ukr.	C17	26
Bīlīmora, India	H4	54
Bilin, Mya.	D3	48
Bilin, stm., Mya.	D3	48
Bílina, Czech Rep.	F9	16
Biliran Island, i., Phil.	E5	52
Billabong Creek, stm., Austl.	J5	76
Billings, Mo., U.S.	G4	120
Billings, Mt., U.S.	B4	126
Billings Heights, Mt., U.S.	B4	126
Billiton see Belitung, i., Indon.	E5	50
Bill Williams, stm., Az., U.S.	I3	132
Billy Chinook, Lake, res., Or., U.S.	F5	136
Bilma, Niger	F7	64
Biloela, Austl.	E8	76
Biloxi, Ms., U.S.	G10	122
Bilpa Morea Claypan, l., Austl.	E2	76
Bilqas Qism Awwal, Egypt	G2	58
Biltine, Chad	E4	62
Biltmore Forest, N.C., U.S.	A3	116
Bilugyun Island, i., Mya.	D3	48
Bimbo, C.A.R.	D3	66
Bimbowrie, Austl.	H3	76
Bimini Islands, is., Bah.	B9	96
Bīna-Etāwa, India	F7	54
Binaiya, Gunung, mtn., Indon.	F9	44
Binalbagan, Phil.	E4	52
Bin'an, China	B7	38
Bindki, India	E8	54
Bindloss, Ab., Can.	D3	124
Bindura, Zimb.	D5	68
Binéfar, Spain	C11	20
Binford, N.D., U.S.	G15	124
Binga, D.R.C.	D4	66
Binga, Monte, mtn., Afr.	D5	68
Bingara, Austl.	G8	76
Bingen, Ger.	G3	16
Binger, Ok., U.S.	F10	128
Binghamton, N.Y., U.S.	B10	114
Bin Ghunaymah, Jabal, mts., Libya	B3	62
Binhai, China	D8	42
Binh Gia, Viet.	B8	48
Binjai, Indon.	K4	48
Binnaway, Austl.	H7	76
Binongko, Pulau, i., Indon.	G7	44
Binscarth, Mb., Can.	D12	124
Bintan, Pulau, i., Indon.	C4	50
Bintimani, mtn., S.L.	H2	64
Bintuhan, Indon.	F3	50
Bintulu, Malay.	B8	50
Bintuni, Indon.	F9	44
Binxian, China	B7	38
Binxian, China	C7	42
Binxian, China	D3	42
Binyang, China	J3	42
Bin-Yauri, Nig.	G5	64
Biobío, state, Chile	H1	92
Biobío, stm., Chile	G2	90
Biogradska Gora Nacionalni Park, p.o.i., Yugo.	G6	26
Bioko, i., Eq. Gui.	I6	64
Bira, Russia	G15	34
Birac, Phil.	B3	52
Birāk, Libya	B2	62
Birakan, Russia	G15	34
Bi'r al Wa'r, Libya	C2	62
Birao, C.A.R.	B4	66
Birch, stm., Ab., Can.	D8	106
Birch Creek, stm., Mt., U.S.	B14	136
Birch Hills, Sk., Can.	B8	124
Birch Island, B.C., Can.	E10	138
Birch Island, i., Mb., Can.	B13	124
Birch Mountains, hills, Ab., Can.	D8	106
Birch Run, Mi., U.S.	E6	112
Birch Tree, Mo., U.S.	H6	120
Birchwood, Wi., U.S.	F7	118
Bird Creek, stm., Ok., U.S.	E13	128
Bird Island, Mn., U.S.	G4	118
Bird Island, sci., S. Geor.	J9	90
Birdsville, Austl.	E2	76
Birdtail Creek, stm., Mb., Can.	D13	124
Birdum, Austl.	C6	74
Birecik, Tur.	A9	58
Bireun, Indon.	J3	48
Bir Ghbalou, Alg.	H14	20
Birigui, Braz.	D6	90
Biriljussy, Russia	C16	32
Bīrjand, Iran	C8	56
Birjul'ka, Russia	D19	32
Birjusa, stm., Russia	C17	32
Birjusinsk, Russia	C17	32
Birken, B.C., Can.	F8	138
Birkenfeld, Ger.	G3	16
Birkenhead, Eng., U.K.	H9	12
Birmingham, Eng., U.K.	I10	12
Birmingham, Al., U.S.	D11	122
Birmingham, Ia., U.S.	D6	120
Birmingham, Mi., U.S.	B2	114
Birmitrapur, India	G10	54
Bîr Mogreïn, Maur.	D2	64
Birnin Gaouré, Niger	G5	64
Birnin-Kebbi, Nig.	G5	64
Birnin Konni, Niger	G5	64
Birnin Kudu, Nig.	G6	64
Birobidžan, Russia	G15	34
Birrie, stm., Austl.	G6	76
Birsk, Russia	C9	32
Birštonas, Lith.	F7	10
Birtle, Mb., Can.	D12	124
Birūr, India	E2	53
Biržai, Lith.	D7	10
Birżebbuġa, Malta	I8	24
Bisaccia, Italy	C9	24
Bīsalpur, India	D7	54
Bisbee, Az., U.S.	L7	132
Bisbee, N.D., U.S.	F14	124
Biscarrosse et de Parentis, Étang de, l., Fr.	E4	18
Biscay, Bay of, b., Eur.	E2	18
Biscayne Bay, b., Fl., U.S.	K5	116
Biscayne National Park, p.o.i., Fl., U.S.	K5	116
Bisceglie, Italy	C10	24
Bischofshofen, Aus.	C10	22
Bischofswerda, Ger.	E10	16
Biscoe, N.C., U.S.	A6	116
Bishnupur, India	G11	54
Bisho, S. Afr.	H8	70
Bishop, Ca., U.S.	F7	134
Bishop, Tx., U.S.	G10	130
Bishop Auckland, Eng., U.K.	G11	12
Bishop Rock, r., Eng., U.K.	L6	12
Bishop's Falls, Nf., Can.	j22	107a
Bishop's Stortford, Eng., U.K.	J13	12
Bishopville, S.C., U.S.	B5	116
Biškek, Kyrg.	F12	32
Biskupiec, Pol.	C16	16
Bislig, Phil.	F6	52
Bismarck, Mo., U.S.	G7	120
Bismarck, N.D., U.S.	A12	126
Bismarck Archipelago, is., Pap. N. Gui.	a4	79a
Bismarck Range, mts., Pap. N. Gui.	b3	79a
Bismarck Sea, Pap. N. Gui.	a4	79a
Bismark, Kap, c., Grnld.	B22	141
Bissa, Djebel, mtn., Alg.	H12	20
Bissau, Gui.-B.	G1	64
Bissett, Mb., Can.	C18	124
Bissikrima, Gui.	G2	64
Bistcho Lake, l., Ab., Can.	D7	106
Bistineau, Lake, res., La., U.S.	E5	122
Bistrica, Slvn.	D13	22
Bistriţa, Rom.	B11	26
Bistriţa, stm., Rom.	C13	26
Bistriţa-Năsăud, state, Rom.	B11	26
Biswān, India	E8	54
Bitam, Gabon	D2	66
Bitburg, Ger.	G2	16
Bitche, Fr.	E16	14
Bitlis, Tur.	B5	56
Bitola, Mac.	B4	28
Bitolj see Bitola, Mac.	B4	28
Bitonto, Italy	C10	24
Bitou, Burkina	G4	64
Bitter Creek, stm., Wy., U.S.	B8	132
Bitterfeld, Ger.	E8	16
Bitterfontein, S. Afr.	G4	70
Bitterroot, stm., Mt., U.S.	D13	136
Bitterroot, West Fork, stm., Mt., U.S.	E12	136
Bitterroot Range, mts., U.S.	C11	136
Bitung, Indon.	E8	44
Bitupitá, Braz.	B5	88
Biu, Nig.	G7	64
Bivins, Tx., U.S.	E4	122
Biwabik, Mn., U.S.	D6	118
Biwa-ko, l., Japan	D8	40
Bixby, Ok., U.S.	I2	120
Biyala, Egypt	G2	58
Biyang, China	E5	42
Bizana, S. Afr.	G9	70
Bizen, Japan	E7	40
Bizerte (Binzert), Tun.	G3	24
Bizerte, Lac de, l., Tun.	G3	24
Bizkaiko, co., Spain	A8	20
Bjahoml', Bela.	F10	10
Bjala, Blg.	G14	26
Bjala Slatina, Blg.	F10	26
Bjalyničy, Bela.	F12	10
Bjarèzina, stm., Bela.	H13	10
Bjarèzina, stm., Bela.	G9	10
Bjaroza, Bela.	H7	10
Bjarozauka, Bela.	G8	10
Bjelovar, Cro.	E13	22
Björna, Swe.	E8	8
Björneborg see Pori, Fin.	F9	8
Bjorne Peninsula, pen., Nu., Can.	B8	141
Bjørnøya, i., Nor.	B5	30
Bla, Mali	G3	64
Blace, Yugo.	F8	26
Black (Da, Song) (Lixian), stm., Asia	D9	46
Black, stm., Mb., Can.	D18	124
Black, stm., U.S.	I6	120
Black, stm., Ak., U.S.	C11	140
Black, stm., Az., U.S.	J6	132
Black, stm., La., U.S.	F7	122
Black, stm., Mi., U.S.	E7	112
Black, stm., N.Y., U.S.	E14	112
Black, stm., Wi., U.S.	G7	118
Blackall, Austl.	E5	76
Black Bay, b., On., Can.	C10	118
Black Bay Peninsula, pen., On., Can.	C10	118
Black Bear Creek, stm., Ok., U.S.	E11	128
Blackburn, Eng., U.K.	H10	12
Blackburn, Mount, mtn., Ak., U.S.	D11	140
Black Butte, mtn., Mt., U.S.	D15	136
Black Canyon of the Gunnison National Monument, p.o.i., Co., U.S.	E9	132
Black Creek, stm., Ms., U.S.	G9	122
Black Creek, stm., S.C., U.S.	B6	116
Black Diamond, Ab., Can.	F16	138
Black Diamond, Wa., U.S.	C5	136
Blackdown Tableland National Park, p.o.i., Austl.	D7	76
Blackduck, Mn., U.S.	D4	118
Black Eagle, Mt., U.S.	C15	136
Blackfoot, Id., U.S.	G14	136
Blackfoot, Mt., U.S.	B14	136
Blackfoot, stm., Id., U.S.	G15	136
Blackfoot, stm., Mt., U.S.	D13	136
Blackfoot Reservoir, res., Id., U.S.	H15	136
Black Forest see Schwarzwald, mts., Ger.	H4	16
Black Hills, mts., U.S.	C9	126
Black Island, i., Mb., Can.	C17	124
Black Lake, Qc., Can.	D5	110
Black Lake, l., Sk., Can.	D10	106
Black Lake, l., Mi., U.S.	C5	112
Black Lake, l., N.Y., U.S.	D14	112
Black Mesa, mtn., U.S.	E6	128
Blackmore, Mount, mtn., Mt., U.S.	E15	136
Black Mountain, N.C., U.S.	A3	116
Black Mountain, mtn., Az., U.S.	K5	132
Black Mountain, mtn., Ca., U.S.	H5	134
Black Mountain, mtn., Mt., U.S.	D14	136
Black Mountain, hill, Austl.	C2	76
Black Mountain, mts., U.S.	H2	114
Black Nossob, stm., Nmb.	C4	70
Black Pine Peak, mtn., Id., U.S.	A3	132
Blackpool, Eng., U.K.	H9	12
Black Range, mts., N.M., U.S.	J9	132
Black River, N.Y., U.S.	D14	112
Black River Falls, Wi., U.S.	G8	118
Black Rock, Ar., U.S.	H6	120
Black Rock, r., Ire.	G2	12
Black Rock, r., S. Geor.	J8	90
Black Rock Desert, des., Nv., U.S.	B7	134
Blacksburg, S.C., U.S.	A4	116
Blacksburg, Va., U.S.	G5	114
Black Sea	G15	6
Blacks Fork, stm., U.S.	B7	132
Blackshear, Lake, res., Ga., U.S.	D2	116
Blackstone, Va., U.S.	G8	114
Black Sturgeon Lake, l., On., Can.	B9	118
Blackville, S.C., U.S.	C4	116
Black Volta (Volta Noire) (Mouhoun), stm., Afr.	H4	64
Blackwater, Austl.	D7	76
Blackwater, stm., Ire.	I4	12
Blackwater, stm., Mo., U.S.	E4	120
Blackwater Creek, stm., Austl.	E5	76
Blackwater Draw, stm., Tx., U.S.	H7	128
Blackwater Lake, l., N.T., Can.	C6	106
Blackwell, Tx., U.S.	B7	130
Bladenboro, N.C., U.S.	B7	116
Bladensburg National Park, p.o.i., Austl.	D4	76
Bladgrond-Noord, S. Afr.	F4	70
Bladworth, Sk., Can.	C7	124
Bláfell, mtn., Ice.	k30	8a
Blagoevgrad, Blg.	G10	26
Blagoveščensk, Russia	D16	34
Blaine, Mn., U.S.	F5	118
Blaine, Wa., U.S.	B4	136
Blair, Ne., U.S.	C1	120
Blair, Ok., U.S.	G9	128
Blair, Wi., U.S.	G7	118
Blair Athol, Austl.	D6	76
Blairsville, Ga., U.S.	B2	116
Blairsville, Pa., U.S.	D6	114
Blaj, Rom.	C10	26
Blakely, Ga., U.S.	F13	122
Blake Plateau, unds.	E6	144
Blake Point, c., Mi., U.S.	C10	118
Blalock Island, i., Wa., U.S.	E7	136
Blanc, Mont, mtn., Eur.	D12	18
Blanca, Co., U.S.	D3	128
Blanca, Bahía, b., Arg.	G4	90
Blanca, Laguna, l., Chile	J2	90
Blanca, Punta, c., Chile	B2	92
Blanca, Sierra, mtn., Tx., U.S.	C2	130
Blanca Peak, mtn., Co., U.S.	D3	128
Blanchard, Ok., U.S.	F11	128
Blanchard, stm., Oh., U.S.	D2	114
Blanche, Lake, l., Austl.	G2	76
Blanche Channel, strt., Sol. Is.	e7	79b
Blanchester, Oh., U.S.	E1	114
Blanchisseuse, Trin.	s12	105f
Blanco, Tx., U.S.	D9	130
Blanco, stm., Arg.	D3	92
Blanco, stm., Ec.	G2	86
Blanco, stm., Tx., U.S.	E9	130
Blanco, Cabo, c., C.R.	H5	102
Blanco, Cañon, val., N.M., U.S.	F3	128
Blanco, Cape, c., Or., U.S.	H2	136
Blanco, Lago, l., Chile	J3	90
Blanc-Sablon, Qc., Can.	i22	107a
Bland, Va., U.S.	G4	114
Blanda, stm., Ice.	k30	8a
Blanding, Ut., U.S.	F7	132
Blandinsville, Il., U.S.	D7	120
Blanes, Spain	C13	20
Blangkejeren, Indon.	K3	48
Blangy-sur-Bresle, Fr.	E10	14
Blankenburg, Ger.	E6	16
Blanquilla, Isla, i., Ven.	B9	86
Blansko, Czech Rep.	G12	16
Blantyre, Mwi.	D6	68
Blarney Castle, hist., Ire.	J4	12
Błaszki, Pol.	E14	16
Blaubeuren, Ger.	H5	16
Blaufelden, Ger.	G5	16
Błażowa, Pol.	G18	16
Bledsoe, Tx., U.S.	H5	128
Blega, Indon.	G8	50
Bleik see Andenes, Nor.	B6	8
Blekinge, state, Swe.	H6	8
Blenheim, On., Can.	F8	112
Blenheim, N.Z.	E5	80
Blessing, Tx., U.S.	F11	130
Bletchley, Eng., U.K.	J12	12
Bligh Water, strt., Fiji	p18	79e
Blind River, On., Can.	B6	112
Blissfield, Mi., U.S.	C2	114
Blitar, Indon.	H8	50
Block Island, i., R.I., U.S.	C14	114
Blockton, Ia., U.S.	D3	120
Bloedel, B.C., Can.	F5	138
Bloemfontein, S. Afr.	F8	70
Bloemhof, S. Afr.	E7	70
Bloemhofdam, res., S. Afr.	E7	70
Blois, Fr.	G10	14
Blönduós, Ice.	k29	8a
Bloodvein, stm., Can.	E11	106
Bloody Foreland, c., Ire.	F4	12
Bloomer, Wi., U.S.	F7	118
Bloomfield, On., Can.	E12	112
Bloomfield, Ky., U.S.	G12	120
Bloomfield, Mo., U.S.	H8	120
Bloomfield, Ne., U.S.	E15	126
Bloomfield, N.M., U.S.	G9	132
Blooming Grove, Tx., U.S.	E2	122
Blooming Prairie, Mn., U.S.	H5	118
Bloomington, Il., U.S.	D9	120
Bloomington, In., U.S.	E11	120
Bloomington, Mn., U.S.	G5	118
Bloomington, Tx., U.S.	F11	130
Bloomington, Wi., U.S.	B7	120
Bloomsburg, Pa., U.S.	C9	114
Bloomsbury, Austl.	C7	76
Bloomville, Oh., U.S.	C2	114
Blora, Indon.	G7	50
Blosseville Kyst, cst., Grnld.	D20	141
Blossom, Tx., U.S.	D3	122
Blouberg, mtn., S. Afr.	C9	70
Blountstown, Fl., U.S.	G13	122
Blountsville, Al., U.S.	C12	122
Blowering Reservoir, res., Austl.	J6	76
Blowing Point Village, Anguilla	A1	105a
Blowing Rock, N.C., U.S.	H4	114
Bludenz, Aus.	C6	22
Blue, stm., Az., U.S.	J7	132
Blue, stm., Ok., U.S.	C2	122
Blue Creek, Wa., U.S.	B8	136
Blue Cypress Lake, l., Fl., U.S.	I5	116
Blue Earth, Mn., U.S.	H4	118
Blue Earth, stm., U.S.	H4	118
Bluefield, Va., U.S.	G4	114
Bluefield, W.V., U.S.	G4	114
Bluefields, Nic.	F6	102
Blue Hill, Ne., U.S.	A10	128
Blue Hill Bay, b., Me., U.S.	F8	110
Blue Island, Il., U.S.	G2	112
Blue Mound, Ks., U.S.	F3	120
Blue Mountain, Ms., U.S.	C9	122
Blue Mountain, mtn., Ar., U.S.	C4	122
Blue Mountain, mtn., Mt., U.S.	G9	124
Blue Mountain, mts., Pa., U.S.	D8	114
Blue Mountain Peak, mtn., Jam.	i14	104d
Blue Mountains, mts., Jam.	i14	104d
Blue Mountains, mts., U.S.	E8	136
Blue Mountains, mts., Me., U.S.	F6	110
Blue Mountains National Park, p.o.i., Austl.	J8	76
Blue Mud Bay, b., Austl.	B7	74
Blue Nile (Azraq, Al-Bahr al-) (Ābay), stm., Afr.	E6	62
Bluenose Lake, l., Nu., Can.	B6	106
Blue Ridge, Ab., Can.	B15	138
Blue Ridge, Ga., U.S.	B1	116
Blue Ridge, mts., U.S.	H4	114
Blue River, B.C., Can.	D11	138
Bluestone Dam, dam, W.V., U.S.	G5	114
Bluestone Lake, res., W.V., U.S.	G5	114
Bluewater, N.M., U.S.	H9	132
Bluff, N.Z.	H3	80
Bluff, Ut., U.S.	F7	132
Bluff Cape, c., Mya.	D2	48
Bluff Creek, stm., U.S.	D11	128
Bluff Dale, Tx., U.S.	B9	130
Bluff Park, Al., U.S.	D12	122
Bluffs, Il., U.S.	E7	120
Bluffton, In., U.S.	H4	112
Bluffton, S.C., U.S.	D5	116
Blumberg, Ger.	I4	16
Blumenau, Braz.	C13	92
Blumenhof, Sk., Can.	D6	124
Bly, Or., U.S.	A4	134
Blyth, On., Can.	E8	112
Blyth, Eng., U.K.	F11	12
Blythe, Ca., U.S.	J2	132
Blytheville, Ar., U.S.	I7	120
Bø, Nor.	G3	8
Bo, S.L.	H2	64
Boac, Phil.	D3	52
Boaco, Nic.	F5	102
Boa Esperança, Braz.	K3	88
Boa Esperança, Represa, res., Braz.	D3	88
Bo'ai, China	D5	42
Boane, Moz.	E11	70
Board Camp Mountain, mtn., Ca., U.S.	C2	134
Boardman, Oh., U.S.	C5	114
Boatman, Austl.	F6	76
Boa Viagem, Braz.	C5	88
Boa Vista, Braz.	F11	86
Boa Vista, i., C.V.	k10	65a
Boawai, Indon.	H12	50
Boaz, Al., U.S.	C12	122
Bobai, China	J3	42
Bobaomby, Tanjona, c., Madag.	C8	68
Bobbili, India	B6	53
Bobcaygeon, On., Can.	D11	112
Bobigny, Fr.	F11	14
Böblingen, Ger.	H4	16
Bobo-Dioulasso, Burkina	G4	64
Bobolice, Pol.	C12	16
Bobonaza, stm., Ec.	H3	86
Bobonong, Bots.	B9	70
Bobr, Bela.	F12	10
Bobtown, Pa., U.S.	E5	114
Bobures, Ven.	C6	86
Boby, mtn., Madag.	E8	68
Bôca da Mata, Braz.	E7	88
Boca do Acre, Braz.	E4	84
Boca do Jari, Braz.	D7	84
Bocage, Cap, c., N. Cal.	m15	79d
Boca Grande, Fl., U.S.	J3	116
Bocaiúva, Braz.	I3	88
Bocaranga, C.A.R.	C3	66
Boca Raton, Fl., U.S.	J5	116
Bocas del Toro, Pan.	H6	102
Bocay, Nic.	E5	102
Bochnia, Pol.	G16	16
Bocholt, Ger.	E2	16
Bochum, Ger.	E3	16
Bocón, Caño, stm., Col.	F7	86
Boconó, Ven.	C6	86
Bocşa, Rom.	D8	26
Boda, C.A.R.	D3	66
Bodajbo, Russia	E11	34
Bodalla, Austl.	K8	76
Bodcau Creek, stm., Ar., U.S.	D5	122
Bode, Ia., U.S.	I4	118
Bodélé, reg., Chad	D3	62
Boden, Swe.	D9	8
Bodensee see Constance, Lake, l., Eur.	I5	16
Bodhan, India	B3	53
Bodh Gaya, India	F10	54
Bodināyakkanūr, India	G3	53
Bodmin, Eng., U.K.	K8	12
Bodø, Nor.	C6	8
Bodoquena, Serra da, plat., Braz.	D5	90
Bodrum, Tur.	F10	28
Bodzentyn, Pol.	F16	16
Boende, D.R.C.	E4	66
Bœng Lvea, Camb.	F7	48
Boeo, Capo, c., Italy	G6	24
Boesmans, stm., S. Afr.	H7	70
Boeuf, stm., U.S.	E7	122
Boffa, Gui.	G2	64
Bogale, Mya.	D2	48
Bogalusa, La., U.S.	G9	122
Bogan, stm., Austl.	H6	76
Bogan Gate, Austl.	I6	76
Bogangolo, C.A.R.	C3	66
Bogata, Tx., U.S.	D3	122
Bogcang, stm., China	C11	54
Bogda Shan, mts., China	C2	36
Bogen, Ger.	H8	16
Boger City, N.C., U.S.	A4	116
Boggabilla, Austl.	G8	76
Boggabri, Austl.	H7	76
Boggy Peak, mtn., Antig.	f4	105b
Bogles, Gren.	p11	105e
Bognor Regis, Eng., U.K.	K12	12
Bogo, Phil.	E5	52
Bogoljubovo, Russia	E15	10
Bogong, Mount, mtn., Austl.	K6	76
Bogor, Indon.	G5	50
Bogorodick, Russia	G21	10
Bogorodsk, Russia	H20	8
Bogorodskoe, Russia	F17	34
Bogotá see Santa Fe de Bogotá, Col	E4	86
Bogotol, Russia	C15	32
Bogra, Bngl.	F12	54
Bogučany, Russia	C17	32
Bogué, Maur.	F2	64
Bogue Chitto, stm., U.S.	G8	122
Bogue Phalia, stm., Ms., U.S.	D8	122
Böğürtlen, Tur.	A8	58
Bo Hai (Chihli, Gulf of), b., China	B8	42
Bohai Haixia, strt., China	B9	42
Bohain-en-Vermandois, Fr.	D12	14
Bohai Wan, b., China	B8	42
Bohemian Forest, mts., Eur.	G8	16
Böhmer Wald see Bohemian Forest, mts., Eur.	G8	16
Bohol, i., Phil.	F4	52
Bohol Sea, Phil.	F5	52
Boiaçu, Braz.	H11	86
Boiano, Italy	C8	24
Boiestown, N.B., Can.	D10	110
Boipeba, Ilha de, i., Braz.	G6	88
Bois, stm., Braz.	C6	90
Bois, Lac des, l., N.T., Can.	B6	106
Bois Blanc Island, i., Mi., U.S.	C5	112
Bois de Sioux, stm., U.S.	F2	118
Boise, Id., U.S.	G10	136
Boise, stm., Id., U.S.	G10	136
Boise, Middle Fork, stm., Id., U.S.	G11	136
Boise, South Fork, stm., Id., U.S.	G11	136
Boise City, Ok., U.S.	E6	128
Boissevain, Mb., Can.	E13	124
Boistfort Peak, mtn., Wa., U.S.	D3	136
Boizenburg, Ger.	C6	16
Boja, Indon.	G7	50
Bojadła, Pol.	E11	16
Bojeador, Cape, c., Phil.	A3	52
Bojnūrd, Iran	B8	56
Bojonegoro, Indon.	G7	50
Bojuru, Braz.	E12	92
Bokāro Steel City, India	G10	54
Bokchito, Ok., U.S.	C2	122
Boké, Gui.	G2	64
Bokhara, stm., Austl.	G6	76
Bok Koŭ, Camb.	G6	48
Boknafjorden, strt., Nor.	G1	8
Boko, Congo	E2	66
Bokoro, Chad	E3	62
Bokote, D.R.C.	E4	66
Boksitogorsk, Russia	A16	10
Bokungu, D.R.C.	E4	66
Bol, Cro.	G13	22
Bolama, Gui.-B.	G1	64
Bolaños, stm., Mex.	E7	100
Bolaños de Calatrava, Spain	F7	20
Bolān Pass, p., Pak.	D10	56
Bolayır, Tur.	C9	28
Bolbec, Fr.	E9	14
Bole, China	F14	32
Bole, Ghana	H4	64
Boles, Ar., U.S.	C4	122
Bolesławiec, Pol.	E11	16
Boley, Ok., U.S.	B2	122
Bolgatanga, Ghana	G4	64
Bolhov, Russia	G18	10
Bolhrad, Ukr.	D15	26
Boli, China	B11	36
Boligee, Al., U.S.	E10	122
Bolingbrook, Il., U.S.	C9	120
Bolishan, China	C5	38
Bolívar, Col.	G3	86
Bolívar, Col.	G3	86
Bolivar, Mo., U.S.	G4	120
Bolivar, N.Y., U.S.	B7	114
Bolivar, Tn., U.S.	B9	122
Bolívar, state, Col.	C4	86
Bolívar, state, Ec.	H2	86
Bolívar, state, Ven.	D10	86
Bolívar, Cerro, mtn., Ven.	D10	86
Bolívar, Pico (La Columna), mtn., Ven.	C6	86
Bolivar Peninsula, pen., Tx., U.S.	H4	122
Bolivia, ctry., S.A.	G5	84
Bollnäs, Swe.	F7	8
Bollon, Austl.	G6	76
Bolmen, l., Swe.	H5	8
Bolobo, D.R.C.	E3	66
Bologna, Italy	F8	22
Bolognesi, Peru	F3	84
Bologoe, Russia	C17	10
Bologovo, Russia	D14	10
Bolohovo, Russia	F20	10
Bol'ŏj Anjuj, stm., Russia	C21	34
Bolomba, D.R.C.	D3	66
Bolon', ozero, l., Russia	G16	34
Bolotnoe, Russia	C14	32
Bolovens, Plateau des, plat., Laos	E8	48
Bol'šaja Balahnja, stm., Russia	B9	34
Bol'šaja Heta, stm., Russia	C5	34
Bol'šaja Kuonamka, stm., Russia	C10	34
Bol'šaja Murta, Russia	C16	32
Bol'šaja Ussurka, stm., Russia	B11	38
Bol'šaja Višera, Russia	B15	10
Bol'šakovo, Russia	F4	10
Bolsena, Italy	H8	22
Bolsena, Lago di, l., Italy	H9	22
Bol'šereče, Russia	C13	32
Bol'šereck, Russia	F20	34
Bol'ševik, Russia	D18	34
Bol'ševik, ostrov, i., Russia	A10	34
Bol'šezemel'skaja Tundra, reg., Russia	A9	32
Bolshevik see Bol'ševik, ostrov, i., Russia	A10	34
Bol'šie Uki, Russia	C12	32
Bol'šoe Mihajlovskoe, Russia	D20	10
Bol'šoe Polpino, Russia	G17	10
Bol'šoe Selo, Russia	C21	10
Bol'šoj Begičev, ostrov, i., Russia	B11	34
Bol'šoj Jugan, stm., Russia	B12	32
Bol'šoj Kamen', Russia	C10	38
Bol'šoj Ljahovskij, ostrov, i., Russia	B17	34
Bol'šoj Tal'cy, Russia	A15	10
Bolton, On., Can.	E10	112
Bolton, Eng., U.K.	H10	12
Bolton, Ms., U.S.	E8	122
Bolton, N.C., U.S.	B7	116
Bolu, Tur.	C14	28
Bolu, state, Tur.	C14	28
Bolva, stm., Russia	G17	10
Bolvadin, Tur.	E13	28
Bóly, Hung.	C5	26
Bolzano (Bozen), Italy	D8	22
Boma, D.R.C.	F2	66
Bomaderry, Austl.	J8	76
Bombala, Austl.	K7	76
Bombay see Mumbai, India	B1	53
Bomberai, Semenanjung, pen., Indon.	F9	44
Bomboma, D.R.C.	D3	66
Bom Conselho, Braz.	E7	88
Bom Despacho, Braz.	J3	88
Bomdila, India	E14	54
Bom Jesus, Braz.	E3	88
Bom Jesus da Lapa, Braz.	G4	88
Bomnak, Russia	F14	34
Bomokandi, stm., D.R.C.	D5	66
Bomongo, D.R.C.	D3	66
Bom Retiro, Braz.	C13	92
Bomu, stm., Afr.	D4	66
Bon, Cap, c., Tun.	G5	24
Bon Air, Va., U.S.	G8	114
Bonaire, i., Neth. Ant.	p23	104g
Bonampak, hist., Mex.	D2	102
Bonandolok, Indon.	C1	50
Bonanza, Or., U.S.	A4	134
Bonanza, Ut., U.S.	C7	132
Bonanza Peak, mtn., Wa., U.S.	B5	136
Bonao, Dom. Rep.	C12	102
Bonaparte, Ia., U.S.	D6	120
Bonaparte, stm., B.C., Can.	F9	138
Bonaparte, Mount, mtn., Wa., U.S.	B7	136
Bonaparte Lake, l., B.C., Can.	E10	138
Bonar Bridge, Scot., U.K.	D8	12
Bonasse, Trin.	s12	105f
Bonaventure, Qc., Can.	B11	110
Bonaventure, stm., Qc., Can.	B11	110
Bonaventure, Île, i., Qc., Can.	B12	110
Bonavista, Nf., Can.	j23	107a
Bonavista Bay, b., Nf., Can.	j23	107a
Bondeno, Italy	F8	22
Bondo, D.R.C.	E4	66
Bondo, D.R.C.	D4	66
Bondoc Peninsula, pen., Phil.	D4	52
Bondoukou, C. Iv.	H4	64
Bondowoso, Indon.	G8	50
Bonduel, Wi., U.S.	G10	118
Bone, Teluk, b., Indon.	F7	44
Bonebone, Indon.	E12	50
Boneogeh, Indon.	G12	50
Bonerate, Pulau, i., Indon.	G12	50
Bonesteel, S.D., U.S.	D13	126
Bonete Chico, Cerro, mtn., Arg.	D3	92
Bonete Grande, Cerro, mtn., Arg.	C3	92
Bongabong, Phil.	D3	52
Bongaigaon, India	E13	54
Bongandanga, D.R.C.	D4	66
Bongka, Indon.	F7	44
Bongo, Gabon	E2	66
Bongo, Massif des, mts., C.A.R.	C4	66
Bongor, Chad	E3	62
Bonham, Tx., U.S.	D2	122
Bonhomme, Morne, mtn., Haiti	C11	102
Bonifacio, Fr.	H15	18
Bonifacio, Strait of, strt., Eur.	H15	18
Bonifati, Capo, c., Italy	E9	24
Bonin Islands see Ogasawara-guntō, is., Japan	G18	30
Bonita, La., U.S.	E7	122
Bonita Springs, Fl., U.S.	J4	116
Bonito, Braz.	E8	88
Bonito, Braz.	D5	90
Bonito de Santa Fé, Braz.	D6	88
Bonn, Ger.	F2	16
Bonners Ferry, Id., U.S.	B10	136
Bonnet, Lac du, res., Mb., Can.	D17	124
Bonnétable, Fr.	F9	14
Bonne Terre, Mo., U.S.	G7	120
Bonnet Plume, stm., Yk., Can.	B3	106
Bonneville, Fr.	C12	18
Bonneville Peak, mtn., Id., U.S.	H14	136
Bonneville Salt Flats, pl., Ut., U.S.	C2	132
Bonney SE, Lake, l., Austl.	K3	76
Bonnie Rock, Austl.	F3	74
Bonny, Nig.	I6	64
Bonnyville, Ab., Can.	B20	138
Bono, Ar., U.S.	I7	120
Bonoi, Indon.	F10	44
Bonshaw, P.E., Can.	D13	110
Bontang, Indon.	C10	50
Bontebok National Park, p.o.i., S. Afr.	I5	70
Bonthe, S.L.	H2	64
Bontoc, Phil.	B3	52
Bon Wier, Tx., U.S.	G5	122
Booker, Tx., U.S.	E8	128
Booker T. Washington National Monument, p.o.i., Va., U.S.	H6	114
Boola, Gui.	H3	64
Boolaloo, Austl.	D3	74
Booleroo Centre, Austl.	I2	76
Boologooro, Austl.	D2	74
Boomarra, Austl.	B3	76
Boonah, Austl.	F9	76
Boone, Ia., U.S.	I5	118
Boone, N.C., U.S.	H4	114
Boone, stm., Ia., U.S.	B4	120
Booneville, Ar., U.S.	B5	122
Booneville, Ky., U.S.	G2	114
Booneville, Ms., U.S.	C10	122
Böön Tsagaan nuur, l., Mong.	B4	36
Boonville, Ca., U.S.	D2	134
Boonville, Mo., U.S.	F5	120
Boonville, N.Y., U.S.	E14	112
Boorindal, Austl.	H6	76
Booroorban, Austl.	J5	76
Boosaaso, Som.	B9	66
Booth, Al., U.S.	E12	122
Boothbay Harbor, Me., U.S.	G7	110
Boothia, Gulf of, b., Nu., Can.	A12	106
Boothia Peninsula, pen., Nu., Can.	A12	106
Boothville, La., U.S.	H9	122
Booué, Gabon	E2	66
Bophuthatswana, hist. reg., S. Afr.	E7	70
Boping Ling, mts., China	I7	42
Bopolu, Lib.	H2	64
Boqueirão, Serra do, hills, Braz.	F4	88
Boquilla, Presa de la, res., Mex.	B6	100
Boquim, Braz.	F7	88
Bor, Russia	H20	8
Bor, Russia	E20	8
Bor, Sudan	F6	62
Bor, Tur.	B3	56
Bor, Yugo.	E9	26
Bor, Lak, stm., Kenya	D7	66
Bora-Bora, i., Fr. Poly.	E11	72
Borabu, Thai.	E6	48
Borah Peak, mtn., Id., U.S.	F13	136

Name	Map Ref.	Page
Borås, Swe.	H5	8
Borba, Braz.	D6	84
Bordeaux, Fr.	E5	18
Bordeaux Mountain, hill, V.I.U.S.	e8	104b
Borden, Sk., Can.	B6	124
Borden Peninsula, pen., Nu., Can.	A14	106
Bordertown, Austl.	K3	76
Bordesholm, Ger.	B6	16
Bordighera, Italy	G4	22
Bordj Menaïel, Alg.	H14	20
Bordj Omar Idriss, Alg.	D6	64
Borðoy, i., Far. Is.	m34	8b
Borgå see Porvoo, Fin.	F11	8
Borgarnes, Ice.	k28	8a
Børgefjell Nasjonalpark, p.o.i., Nor.	D5	8
Borger, Tx., U.S.	F7	128
Borgholm, Swe.	H7	8
Borgne, Lake, b., La., U.S.	G9	122
Borgnesse, Pointe, c., Mart.	I7	105c
Borgomanero, Italy	E5	22
Borgo San Dalmazzo, Italy	F4	22
Borgosesia, Italy	E5	22
Borgo Val di Taro, Italy	F6	22
Borgworm see Waremme, Bel.	D14	14
Borikhan, Laos	C6	48
Borisoglebsk, Russia	D6	32
Borisoglebskij, Russia	C21	10
Borjas Blancas see Les Borges Blanques, Spain	C11	20
Borkavičy, Bela.	E11	10
Borken, Ger.	E2	16
Borkou, reg., Chad	D3	62
Borkum, i., Ger.	C2	16
Borlänge, Swe.	F6	8
Bormes, Fr.	F12	18
Borna, Ger.	E9	16
Borneo (Kalimantan), i., Asia	E5	44
Bornholm, state, Den.	I6	8
Bornholm, i., Den.	I6	8
Borocay Island, i., Phil.	E3	52
Borodino, Russia	C17	32
Borogoncy, Russia	D15	34
Borohoro Shan, mts., China	F14	32
Boromo, Burkina	G4	64
Boron, Ca., U.S.	H8	134
Boronga Islands, is., Mya.	I14	54
Borongan, Phil.	E5	52
Borovan, Blg.	F10	26
Boroviči, Russia	B16	10
Borovljanka, Russia	D14	32
Borovsk, Russia	E19	10
Borovskij, Russia	C11	32
Borovskoj, Kaz.	D10	32
Borrachudo, stm., Braz.	J3	88
Borrazópolis, Braz.	A12	92
Borriana, Spain	E10	20
Borroloola, Austl.	C7	74
Borș, Rom.	B8	26
Borșa, Rom.	B11	26
Borsad, India	G4	54
Borščovočnyj hrebet, mts., Russia	F12	34
Borsod-Abaúj-Zemplén, state, Hung.	A8	26
Bort-les-Orgues, Fr.	D8	18
Borūjerd, Iran	C6	56
Borzja, Russia	F12	34
Bosa, Italy	D2	24
Bosanska Dubica, Bos.	D3	26
Bosanska Gradiška, Bos.	D4	26
Bosanska Krupa, Bos.	E3	26
Bosanski Novi, Bos.	D3	26
Bosanski Šamac, Bos.	D5	26
Bosavi, Mount, mtn., Pap. N. Gui.	b3	79a
Boscobel, Wi., U.S.	A7	120
Bose, China	J2	42
Boshan, China	C7	42
Boshof, S. Afr.	F7	70
Bosilegrad, Yugo.	G9	26
Bosna, stm., Bos.	E5	26
Bosnia and Herzegovina, ctry., Eur.	E3	26
Bosnik, Indon.	F10	44
Bošnjakovo, Russia	G17	34
Bosobolo, D.R.C.	D3	66
Bōsō-hantō, pen., Japan	D13	40
Bosporus see İstanbul Boğazı, strt., Tur.	B12	28
Bossangoa, C.A.R.	C3	66
Bossembélé, C.A.R.	C3	66
Bossey Bangou, Niger	G5	64
Bossier City, La., U.S.	E5	122
Bosten Hu, l., China	C2	36
Boston, Eng., U.K.	H12	12
Boston, Ga., U.S.	F2	116
Boston, Ma., U.S.	B14	114
Boston Bar, B.C., Can.	G9	138
Boston Mountains, mts., Ar., U.S.	B5	122
Boswell, In., U.S.	H2	112
Boswell, Ok., U.S.	C3	122
Bosworth, Mo., U.S.	E4	120
Botād, India	G3	54
Botany Bay, b., Austl.	J8	76
Boteti, stm., Bots.	E3	68
Bothaville, S. Afr.	E8	70
Bothnia, Gulf of, b., Eur.	E9	8
Bothwell, On., Can.	F8	112
Boticas, Port.	C3	20
Botna, stm., Mol.	C15	26
Botoșani, Rom.	B13	26
Botoșani, state, Rom.	B13	26
Bo Trach, Viet.	D8	48
Botrange, mtn., Bel.	D15	14
Botswana, ctry., Afr.	E3	68
Botte Donato, Monte, mtn., Italy	E10	24
Bottineau, N.D., U.S.	F13	124
Botucatu, Braz.	L1	88
Botwood, Nf., Can.	j22	107a
Bouaflé, C. Iv.	H3	64
Bouaké, C. Iv.	H3	64
Bouar, C.A.R.	C3	66
Bouârfa, Mor.	C4	64
Bouca, C.A.R.	C3	66
Boucher, stm., Qc., Can.	A7	110
Bouches-du-Rhône, state, Fr.	F11	18
Bouctouche, N.B., Can.	D12	110
Boufarik, Alg.	H13	20
Bou Ficha, Tun.	H4	24
Bougainville, i., Pap. N. Gui.	d7	79b
Bougainville, Détroit de, strt., Vanuatu	j16	79d
Bougainville Strait, strt., Oc.	d7	79b
Bougouni, Mali	G3	64
Bouillante, Guad.	h5	105c
Bouillon, Bel.	E14	14
Bouïra, Alg.	B5	64
Boujdour, Cap, c., W. Sah.	D2	64
Boularderie Island, i., N.S., Can.	D16	110
Boulder, Co., U.S.	A3	128
Boulder, Mt., U.S.	D14	136
Boulder, stm., Mt., U.S.	D15	136
Boulder City, Nv., U.S.	H2	132
Boulia, Austl.	D2	76
Boulogne-sur-Mer, Fr.	D10	14
Bouloupari, N. Cal.	m15	79d
Boulsa, Burkina	G4	64
Bou Medfaa, Alg.	H13	20
Bouna, C. Iv.	H4	64
Boundary Peak, mtn., Nv., U.S.	F7	134
Boundiali, C. Iv.	H3	64
Boun Nua, Laos	B5	48
Bountiful, Ut., U.S.	C4	132
Bounty Bay, b., Pit.	c28	78k
Bounty Islands, is., N.Z.	H8	80
Bounty Trough, unds.	N20	142
Bourail, N. Cal.	m15	79d
Bourbeuse, stm., Mo., U.S.	F6	120
Bourbon, In., U.S.	G3	112
Bourbonnais, hist. reg., Fr.	C9	18
Bourbonne-les-Bains, Fr.	G14	14
Bourem, Mali	F4	64
Bourg, La., U.S.	H8	122
Bourg-en-Bresse, Fr.	C11	18
Bourges, Fr.	G11	14
Bourget, On., Can.	E1	110
Bourget, Lac du, l., Fr.	D11	18
Bourgogne (Burgundy), hist. reg., Fr.	B10	18
Bourgogne, Canal de, can., Fr.	G13	14
Bourgoin-Jallieu, Fr.	D11	18
Bourke, Austl.	H5	76
Bournemouth, Eng., U.K.	K11	12
Bou Saâda, Alg.	B5	64
Bou Salem, Tun.	H2	24
Bouse Wash, stm., Az., U.S.	J3	132
Bou Smail, Alg.	H13	20
Boussac, Fr.	C8	18
Bousso, Chad	E3	62
Boutilimit, Maur.	F2	64
Bouvetøya, i., Ant.	A5	81
Bouza, Niger	G6	64
Bøvågen, Nor.	F1	8
Bovec, Slvn.	D10	22
Bovey, Mn., U.S.	D5	118
Bovill, Id., U.S.	D10	136
Bovina, Tx., U.S.	G6	128
Bow, stm., Ab., Can.	G19	138
Bo-Wadrif, S. Afr.	H4	70
Bowbells, N.D., U.S.	F11	124
Bow Creek, stm., Ks., U.S.	B9	128
Bowden, Ab., Can.	E16	138
Bowdle, S.D., U.S.	B13	126
Bowdon, N.D., U.S.	G14	124
Bowen, Arg.	G4	92
Bowen, Austl.	C7	76
Bowen, Il., U.S.	D7	120
Bowen, stm., Austl.	C6	76
Bowie, Az., U.S.	K7	132
Bowie, Md., U.S.	F9	114
Bowling Green, Fl., U.S.	I4	116
Bowling Green, Ky., U.S.	H11	120
Bowling Green, Mo., U.S.	E6	120
Bowling Green, Oh., U.S.	C2	114
Bowling Green, Va., U.S.	F8	114
Bowling Green, Cape, c., Austl.	B6	76
Bowling Green Bay National Park, p.o.i., Austl.	B6	76
Bowman, N.D., U.S.	A9	126
Bowman, S.C., U.S.	C5	116
Bowman, Mount, mtn., B.C., Can.	E9	138
Bowmanville, On., Can.	E11	112
Bowral, Austl.	J8	76
Bowraville, Austl.	H9	76
Bowron, stm., B.C., Can.	C9	138
Bowsman, Mb., Can.	B12	124
Boxelder Creek, stm., U.S.	B8	126
Box Elder Creek, stm., Mt., U.S.	G5	124
Boxelder Creek, stm., S.D., U.S.	C10	126
Boxing, China	C8	42
Boyacá, state, Col.	E5	86
Boyang, China	G7	42
Boyce, La., U.S.	F6	122
Boyceville, Wi., U.S.	F6	118
Boyd, Tx., U.S.	A10	130
Boyd, stm., Austl.	G9	76
Boydton, Va., U.S.	H7	114
Boyer, stm., Ia., U.S.	C2	120
Boyertown, Pa., U.S.	D10	114
Boykins, Va., U.S.	H8	114
Boyle, Ms., U.S.	D8	122
Boylston, Al., U.S.	E12	122
Boyne, stm., Austl.	E8	76
Boyne, stm., Mb., Can.	E16	124
Boyne, stm., Ire.	H5	12
Boyne City, Mi., U.S.	C5	112
Boynton Beach, Fl., U.S.	J5	116
Boysen Reservoir, res., Wy., U.S.	D4	126
Boys Ranch, Tx., U.S.	F6	128
Bozburun, Tur.	G11	28
Bozburun Yarımadası, pen., Tur.	G11	28
Boz Dağ, mtn., Tur.	E11	28
Boz Dağlar, mts., Tur.	E10	28
Bozdoğan, Tur.	F11	28
Bozeman, Mt., U.S.	E15	136
Bozen see Bolzano, Italy	D8	22
Bozhen, China	B7	42
Bozhou, China	E6	42
Bozkurt, Tur.	F12	28
Bozoum, C.A.R.	C3	66
Bozova, Tur.	A9	58
Bozovici, Rom.	E9	26
Bozšakol', Kaz.	D12	32
Bozüyük, Tur.	D13	28
Bra, Italy	F4	22
Brač, Otok, i., Cro.	G13	22
Bracciano, Italy	H9	22
Bracciano, Lago di, l., Italy	H9	22
Bracebridge, On., Can.	C10	112
Brackendale, B.C., Can.	G7	138
Brackettville, Tx., U.S.	E7	130
Bracknell, Eng., U.K.	J12	12
Braço do Norte, Braz.	D13	92
Brad, Rom.	C9	26
Bradano, stm., Italy	D10	24
Bradenton, Fl., U.S.	I3	116
Bradford, Eng., U.K.	H11	12
Bradford, Ar., U.S.	B7	122
Bradford, Pa., U.S.	C7	114
Bradford, Tn., U.S.	H9	120
Bradford, Vt., U.S.	G4	110
Bradford West Gwillimbury, On., Can.	D10	112
Bradley, Ar., U.S.	D5	122
Bradley, Fl., U.S.	I3	116
Bradley, Il., U.S.	G2	112
Bradley, S.D., U.S.	B15	126
Brady, Mt., U.S.	B15	136
Brady, Ne., U.S.	F12	126
Brady, Tx., U.S.	C8	130
Brady Creek, stm., Tx., U.S.	C8	130
Braga, Port.	C2	20
Braga, state, Port.	C2	20
Bragado, Arg.	G7	92
Bragança, Braz.	D8	84
Bragança, Port.	C4	20
Bragança, state, Port.	C4	20
Bragança Paulista, Braz.	L2	88
Brāhmanbāria, Bngl.	F13	54
Brāhmani, stm., India	H10	54
Brahmapur, India	B7	53
Brahmaputra (Yarlung), stm., Asia	C7	46
Braich y Pwll, c., Wales, U.K.	I8	12
Braidwood, Austl.	J7	76
Braidwood, Il., U.S.	C9	120
Brăila, Rom.	D14	26
Brăila, state, Rom.	D14	26
Brainard, Ne., U.S.	F15	126
Brainerd, Mn., U.S.	E4	118
Braintree, Eng., U.K.	J13	12
Brak, stm., S. Afr.	G6	70
Brake, Ger.	C4	16
Bralorne, B.C., Can.	F8	138
Brampton, On., Can.	E10	112
Bramsche, Ger.	D3	16
Branchville, S.C., U.S.	C5	116
Branco, stm., Braz.	H11	86
Branco, stm., Braz.	F3	88
Brandaris, hill, Neth. Ant.	p23	104g
Brandberg, mtn., Nmb.	B2	70
Brandbu, Nor.	F4	8
Brandenburg, Ger.	D8	16
Brandenburg, Ky., U.S.	G11	120
Brandenburg, state, Ger.	D9	16
Brandfort, S. Afr.	F8	70
Brandon, Mb., Can.	E14	124
Brandon, Fl., U.S.	I3	116
Brandon, Ms., U.S.	E9	122
Brandon, S.D., U.S.	H2	118
Brandon, Vt., U.S.	G3	110
Brandsen, Arg.	G8	92
Brandvlei, S. Afr.	G5	70
Brandy Peak, mtn., Or., U.S.	H3	136
Brandýs nad Labem-Stará Boleslav, Czech Rep.	F10	16
Branford, Fl., U.S.	G2	116
Braniewo, Pol.	B15	16
Bransby, Austl.	G4	76
Bransby Point, c., Monts.	D3	105a
Bransfield Strait, strt., Ant.	B35	81
Branson, Mo., U.S.	H4	120
Brantford, On., Can.	E9	112
Brantley, Al., U.S.	F12	122
Brantley Tank, res., N.M., U.S.	B3	130
Brantôme, Fr.	D6	18
Brantville, N.B., Can.	C12	110
Bras d'Or Lake, l., N.S., Can.	E16	110
Brasiléia, Braz.	F4	84
Brasília, Braz.	H1	88
Brasília, Parque Nacional de, p.o.i., Braz.	H1	88
Brasília de Minas, Braz.	I3	88
Braslau, Bela.	E9	10
Brașov, Rom.	D12	26
Brașov, state, Rom.	D12	26
Brassey, Banjaran, mts., Malay.	A10	50
Brass Islands, is., V.I.U.S.	e7	104b
Brasstown Bald, mtn., Ga., U.S.	B2	116
Bratca, Rom.	C9	26
Bratislava, Slov.	H13	16
Bratislava, state, Slov.	H13	16
Bratsk, Russia	C18	32
Bratskoe vodohranilišče, res., Russia	C18	32
Bratsk Reservoir see Bratskoe vodohranilišče, res., Russia	C18	32
Brattleboro, Vt., U.S.	B13	114
Braulio Carrillo, Parque Nacional, p.o.i., C.R.	G5	102
Braúnas, Braz.	J4	88
Braunau am Inn, Aus.	B10	22
Braunschweig (Brunswick), Ger.	D6	16
Brava, i., C.V.	I10	65a
Brava, Costa, cst., Spain	C14	20
Brava, Laguna, l., Arg.	D3	92
Brava, Punta, c., Ur.	G9	92
Brave, Pa., U.S.	E5	114
Bravo (Rio Grande), stm., N.A.	H13	98
Bravo, Cerro, mtn., Peru	E2	84
Bravo del Norte see Bravo, stm., N.A.	H13	98
Brawley, Ca., U.S.	K10	134
Bray, Ire.	H6	12
Bray Island, i., Nu., Can.	B15	106
Brazeau, stm., Ab., Can.	D15	138
Brazeau, Mount, mtn., Ab., Can.	D13	138
Brazeau Dam, dam, Ab., Can.	C15	138
Brazil, In., U.S.	E10	120
Brazil, ctry., S.A.	F9	82
Brazil Basin, unds.	J11	144
Brazoria, Tx., U.S.	E12	130
Brazos, stm., Tx., U.S.	E8	108
Brazos, Clear Fork, stm., Tx., U.S.	B8	130
Brazos, Double Mountain Fork, stm., Tx., U.S.	H8	128
Brazos, North Fork, stm., Tx., U.S.	H3	122
Brazzaville, Congo	E2	66
Brčko, Bos.	E5	26
Brda, stm., Pol.	C13	16
Bré see Bray, Ire.	H6	12
Brea, Ca., U.S.	J8	134
Bream Bay, b., N.Z.	B6	80
Brea Pozo, Arg.	D6	92
Breaux Bridge, La., U.S.	G7	122
Brebes, Indon.	G6	50
Brechin, Scot., U.K.	E10	12
Breckenridge, Mi., U.S.	E5	112
Breckenridge, Mn., U.S.	E2	118
Breckenridge, Mo., U.S.	E4	120
Brecknock, Península, pen., Chile	J2	90
Břeclav, Czech Rep.	H12	16
Brecon, Wales, U.K.	J9	12
Brecon Beacons, hills, Wales, U.K.	J9	12
Brecon Beacons National Park, p.o.i., Wales, U.K.	J9	12
Breda, Neth.	C13	14
Breda, Ia., U.S.	B3	120
Bredasdorp, S. Afr.	I5	70
Bredenbury, Sk., Can.	D11	124
Bredy, Russia	D9	32
Breë, stm., S. Afr.	I5	70
Breese, Il., U.S.	F8	120
Bregalnica, stm., Mac.	A5	28
Bregenz, Aus.	C6	22
Bregovo, Blg.	E9	26
Bréhat, Île de, i., Fr.	F6	14
Breiðafjörður, b., Ice.	k28	8a
Brejinho de Nazaré, Braz.	F1	88
Brejo, Braz.	B4	88
Brejo Grande, Braz.	F7	88
Brejo Santo, Braz.	D6	88
Brekstad, Nor.	E3	8
Bremen, Ger.	C4	16
Bremen, Ga., U.S.	D13	122
Bremen, Oh., U.S.	E3	114
Bremen, state, Ger.	C4	16
Bremer Bay, Austl.	F3	74
Bremer Bay, b., Austl.	F3	74
Bremerhaven, Ger.	C4	16
Bremerton, Wa., U.S.	C4	136
Bremervörde, Ger.	C4	16
Bremond, Tx., U.S.	F2	122
Brenham, Tx., U.S.	G2	122
Brenner Pass, p., Eur.	C8	22
Brent, Fl., U.S.	G11	122
Brenta, stm., Italy	D8	22
Brentwood, Eng., U.K.	J13	12
Brentwood, N.Y., U.S.	D12	114
Brentwood, Tn., U.S.	H11	120
Breo, Italy	F4	22
Brescia, Italy	E7	22
Breslau see Wrocław, Pol.	E13	16
Bressanone, Italy	D8	22
Bressay, i., Scot., U.K.	n18	12a
Bresse, reg., Fr.	C11	18
Bressuire, Fr.	H8	14
Brèst, Bela.	H6	10
Brest, Fr.	F4	14
Brèst, state, Bela.	H8	10
Bretagne (Brittany), hist. reg., Fr.	F5	14
Bretenoux, Fr.	E7	18
Breton, Ab., Can.	C16	138
Breton Islands, is., La., U.S.	H9	122
Breton Sound, strt., La., U.S.	H9	122
Brett, Cape, c., N.Z.	B6	80
Bretten, Ger.	G4	16
Breueh, Pulau, i., Indon.	J2	48
Breuil-Cervinia, Italy	E4	22
Brevard, N.C., U.S.	A3	116
Breves, Braz.	D7	84
Brevoort Island, i., Nu., Can.	E13	141
Brewarrina, Austl.	G6	76
Brewer, Me., U.S.	F8	110
Brewster, Mn., U.S.	H3	118
Brewster, Ne., U.S.	F13	126
Brewster, Wa., U.S.	B7	136
Brewster, Kap, c., Grnld.	C21	141
Brewton, Al., U.S.	F11	122
Breyten, S. Afr.	E10	70
Březnice, Czech Rep.	G9	16
Brezno, Slov.	H15	16
Bria, C.A.R.	C4	66
Brian Boru Peak, mtn., B.C., Can.	A3	138
Briançon, Fr.	E12	18
Brian Head, mtn., Ut., U.S.	F4	132
Briare, Canal de, can., Fr.	G11	14
Bribie Island, i., Austl.	F9	76
Bricelyn, Mn., U.S.	H5	118
Briceni, Mol.	A14	26
Briceville, Tn., U.S.	A14	122
Bri Chuallan see Bray, Ire.	H6	12
Bridge, stm., B.C., Can.	F7	138
Bridge City, Tx., U.S.	G5	122
Bridge Lake, B.C., Can.	E10	138
Bridgend, Wales, U.K.	J9	12
Bridgeport, Ca., U.S.	E6	134
Bridgeport, Ct., U.S.	C12	114
Bridgeport, Mi., U.S.	E6	112
Bridgeport, Ne., U.S.	F9	126
Bridgeport, Tx., U.S.	H11	128
Bridgeport, Wa., U.S.	C7	136
Bridgeport, Lake, res., Tx., U.S.	H10	128
Bridger, Mt., U.S.	B4	126
Bridger Peak, mtn., Wy., U.S.	B9	132
Bridgeton, N.J., U.S.	E10	114
Bridgetown, Austl.	F3	74
Bridgetown, Barb.	n8	105d
Bridgetown, N.S., Can.	F11	110
Bridgeville, De., U.S.	F10	114
Bridgewater, N.S., Can.	F12	110
Bridgewater, Ma., U.S.	B15	114
Bridgewater, S.D., U.S.	D15	126
Bridgewater, Va., U.S.	F6	114
Bridgwater, Eng., U.K.	J9	12
Bridgwater Bay, b., Eng., U.K.	J9	12
Bridlington, Eng., U.K.	G12	12
Bridport, Eng., U.K.	K10	12
Brie, reg., Fr.	F12	14
Brier Creek, stm., Ga., U.S.	C4	116
Brig, Switz.	D5	22
Briggs, Tx., U.S.	D10	130
Brigham City, Ut., U.S.	B4	132
Bright, Austl.	K6	76
Brighton, On., Can.	D12	112
Brighton, Eng., U.K.	K12	12
Brighton, Co., U.S.	A4	128
Brighton, Ia., U.S.	C6	120
Brighton, Mi., U.S.	B2	114
Brighton, N.Y., U.S.	E12	112
Brighton Downs, Austl.	D3	76
Brignoles, Fr.	F11	18
Brijuni, i., Cro.	F10	22
Brilliant, B.C., Can.	G13	138
Brilliant, Al., U.S.	C11	122
Brillion, Wi., U.S.	D1	112
Brilon, Ger.	E4	16
Brindisi, Italy	D11	24
Brinkworth, Austl.	I2	76
Brion, Île, i., Qc., Can.	C15	110
Brioude, Fr.	D9	18
Brisbane, Austl.	F9	76
Brisighella, Italy	F8	22
Bristol, Eng., U.K.	J10	12
Bristol, Ct., U.S.	C12	114
Bristol, Fl., U.S.	G14	122
Bristol, N.H., U.S.	G5	110
Bristol, Pa., U.S.	D11	114
Bristol, R.I., U.S.	C14	114
Bristol, Tn., U.S.	H3	114
Bristol, Vt., U.S.	F3	110
Bristol Bay, b., Ak., U.S.	E7	140
Bristol Channel, strt., U.K.	J8	12
Bristol Island, i., S. Geor.	A2	81
Bristol Lake, l., Ca., U.S.	I10	134
Bristow, Ok., U.S.	B2	122
Britannia Beach, B.C., Can.	G7	138
British Columbia, state, Can.	E5	106
British Guiana see Guyana, ctry., S.A.	C6	84
British Honduras see Belize, ctry., N.A.	D3	102
British Indian Ocean Territory, dep., Afr.	G17	2
British Isles, is., Eur.	C12	4
British Mountains, mts., N.A.	C11	140
British Solomon Islands see Solomon Islands, ctry., Oc.	D7	72
British Virgin Islands, dep., N.A.	h15	96a
Brits, S. Afr.	D8	70
Britstown, S. Afr.	G6	70
Britt, Ia., U.S.	A4	120
Brittany see Bretagne, hist. reg., Fr.	F5	14
Britton, S.D., U.S.	B15	126
Brive-la-Gaillarde, Fr.	D7	18
Brixen see Bressanone, Italy	D8	22
Brixham, Eng., U.K.	K9	12
Brixton, Austl.	D5	76
Brjanka, Russia	C16	32
Brjansk, Russia	G17	10
Brjanskaja oblast', co., Russia	H16	10
Brno, Czech Rep.	G12	16
Broa, Ensenada de la, b., Cuba	A6	102
Broad, stm., U.S.	B4	116
Broad, stm., Ga., U.S.	B2	116
Broadalbin, N.Y., U.S.	G2	110
Broad Sound, b., Austl.	D7	76
Broad Sound Channel, strt., Austl.	C8	76
Broadus, Mt., U.S.	B7	126
Broadwater, Ne., U.S.	F10	126
Broadway, Va., U.S.	F7	114
Brocēni, Lat.	D5	10
Brochet, Mb., Can.	D10	106
Brock, Sk., Can.	C5	124
Brockman, Mount, mtn., Austl.	D3	74
Brockton, Ma., U.S.	B14	114
Brockton, Mt., U.S.	F9	124
Brockville, On., Can.	D14	112
Brockway, Pa., U.S.	C7	114
Brocton, N.Y., U.S.	B6	114
Brodeur Peninsula, pen., Nu., Can.	A13	106
Brodhead, Wi., U.S.	B8	120
Brodick, Scot., U.K.	F7	12
Brodnax, Va., U.S.	H7	114
Brodnica, Pol.	C15	16
Brogan, Or., U.S.	F9	136
Brok, Pol.	D17	16
Broken Arrow, Ok., U.S.	H2	120
Broken Bay, b., Austl.	I8	76
Broken Bow, Ok., U.S.	C4	122
Broken Bow Lake, res., Ok., U.S.	C4	122
Broken Hill, Austl.	H3	76
Broken Hill see Kabwe, Zam.	C4	68
Broken Ridge, unds.	M12	142
Brokopondo, Sur.	B6	84
Brokopondo Stuwmeer, res., Sur.	C6	84
Bromley Plateau, unds.	K10	144
Bromptonville, Qc., Can.	E4	110
Bromsgrove, Eng., U.K.	I10	12
Bronkhorstspruit, S. Afr.	D9	70
Bronlund Peak, mtn., B.C., Can.	D5	106
Bronnae, Bela.	H13	10
Bronnicy, Russia	E21	10
Bronson, Fl., U.S.	G3	116
Bronson, Ks., U.S.	G2	120
Bronson, Mi., U.S.	G4	112
Bronte, Italy	G8	24
Bronte, Tx., U.S.	C7	130
Brook, In., U.S.	H2	112
Brookeland, Tx., U.S.	F5	122
Brooker, Fl., U.S.	G3	116
Brookfield, N.S., Can.	E13	110
Brookfield, Wi., U.S.	E1	112
Brookford, N.C., U.S.	I4	114
Brookhaven, Ms., U.S.	F8	122
Brookings, Or., U.S.	A1	134
Brookings, S.D., U.S.	G2	118
Brookland, Ar., U.S.	B8	122
Brooklyn, N.S., Can.	F12	110
Brooklyn, Ia., U.S.	J6	118
Brooklyn, Mi., U.S.	B1	114
Brooklyn Center, Mn., U.S.	F5	118
Brookmere, B.C., Can.	G10	138
Brookneal, Va., U.S.	G7	114
Brookport, Il., U.S.	G9	120
Brooks, Ab., Can.	F19	138
Brooks Bay, b., B.C., Can.	F2	138
Brookshire, Tx., U.S.	H3	122
Brooks Range, mts., Ak., U.S.	C8	140
Brooksville, Fl., U.S.	H3	116
Brooksville, Ms., U.S.	D10	122
Brookville, In., U.S.	E12	120
Brookville, Pa., U.S.	C6	114
Brookville Lake, res., In., U.S.	E13	120
Broome, Austl.	C4	74
Broomfield, Co., U.S.	B3	128
Brooten, Mn., U.S.	F3	118
Brora, Scot., U.K.	C9	12
Brosna, stm., Ire.	H5	12
Brotas de Macaúbas, Braz.	G4	88
Brou, Fr.	F10	14
Broughton, Mount, mtn., Austl.	K5	76
Broughty Ferry, Scot., U.K.	E10	12
Browerville, Mn., U.S.	E4	118
Brown, Mount, mtn., Mt., U.S.	B15	136
Brown, Point, c., Wa., U.S.	D2	136
Brown Deer, Wi., U.S.	E2	112
Browne Bay, b., Nu., Can.	A11	106
Brownfield, Tx., U.S.	A5	130
Browning, Mo., U.S.	D4	120
Browning, Mt., U.S.	B13	136
Brownlee Reservoir, res., U.S.	F9	136
Brownsburg, Qc., Can.	E2	110
Brownsburg, In., U.S.	I3	112
Brownsdale, Mn., U.S.	H5	118
Browns Town, Jam.	i13	104d
Brownstown, In., U.S.	F11	120
Brownsville, Ky., U.S.	G11	120
Brownsville, La., U.S.	E6	122
Brownsville, Or., U.S.	F4	136
Brownsville, Tn., U.S.	B9	122
Brownsville, Tx., U.S.	I10	130
Brownton, Mn., U.S.	G4	118
Brownville, Me., U.S.	E7	110
Brownville, Ne., U.S.	D2	120
Brownville Junction, Me., U.S.	E7	110
Brownwood, Tx., U.S.	C8	130
Brownwood, Lake, res., Tx., U.S.	C9	130
Browse Island, i., Austl.	B4	74
Broxton, Ga., U.S.	E3	116
Broža, Bela.	H12	10
Bruay-en-Artois, Fr.	D11	14
Bruce, S.D., U.S.	G2	118
Bruce, Wi., U.S.	F7	118
Bruce, Mount, mtn., Austl.	D3	74
Bruce Mines, On., Can.	B6	112
Bruce Peninsula, pen., On., Can.	C8	112
Bruce Peninsula National Park, p.o.i., On., Can.	C8	112
Bruce Rock, Austl.	F3	74
Bruchsal, Ger.	G4	16
Bruck an der Leitha, Aus.	B13	22
Bruck an der Mur, Aus.	C12	22
Bruges see Brugge, Bel.	C12	14
Brugg, Switz.	C5	22
Brugge (Bruges), Bel.	C12	14
Brühl, Ger.	F2	16
Bruit, Pulau, i., Malay.	B7	50
Brule, Ne., U.S.	F11	126
Brumado, Braz.	H5	88
Brundidge, Al., U.S.	F13	122
Bruneau, Id., U.S.	H11	136
Bruneau, stm., U.S.	H11	136
Bruneck see Brunico, Italy	D8	22
Brunei, ctry., Asia	A9	50
Brunico, Italy	D8	22
Brunsbüttel, Ger.	C4	16
Brunson, S.C., U.S.	D4	116
Brunswick see Braunschweig, Ger.	D6	16
Brunswick, Ga., U.S.	E4	116
Brunswick, Me., U.S.	G6	110
Brunswick, Md., U.S.	E8	114
Brunswick, Mo., U.S.	E4	120
Brunswick, Oh., U.S.	C4	114
Brunswick, Península, pen., Chile	J2	90
Bruntál, Czech Rep.	F13	16
Brus, Laguna de, b., Hond.	E5	102
Brush, Co., U.S.	A5	128
Brusovo, Russia	C18	10
Brusque, Braz.	C13	92
Brussel see Bruxelles, Bel.	D13	14
Brussels see Bruxelles, Bel.	D13	14
Brussels, On., Can.	E8	112
Bruthen, Austl.	K6	76
Bruxelles (Brussels), Bel.	D13	14
Bruzual, Ven.	D7	86
Bryan, Oh., U.S.	C1	114
Bryan, Tx., U.S.	G2	122
Bryan, Mount, mtn., Austl.	I2	76
Bryant, Ar., U.S.	C6	122
Bryce Canyon National Park, p.o.i., Ut., U.S.	F4	132
Bryli, Bela.	G13	10
Bryson, Qc., Can.	C13	112
Bryson, Tx., U.S.	A9	130
Brzeg, Pol.	F13	16
Brześć Kujawski, Pol.	D14	16
Brzesko, Pol.	F16	16
Brzeziny, Pol.	E15	16
Bsharrī, Leb.	D6	58
Bua, Fiji	p19	79e
Bua Bay, b., Fiji	p19	79e
Buada Lagoon, b., Nauru	q17	78f
Buala, Sol. Is.	e8	79b
Bua Yai, Thai.	E6	48
Bubanza, Bdi.	E5	66
Bubaque, Gui.-B.	G1	64
Bubi, stm., Zimb.	B10	70
Būbiyān, i., Kuw.	D6	56
Bubuduo, China	C10	54
Bucak, Tur.	F13	28
Bucaramanga, Col.	D5	86
Buccaneer Archipelago, is., Austl.	C4	74
Buchanan, Sk., Can.	C11	124
Buchanan, Lib.	H2	64
Buchanan, Ga., U.S.	D13	122
Buchanan, Mi., U.S.	G3	112
Buchanan, Lake, l., Austl.	C5	76
Buchanan, Lake, l., Tx., U.S.	D9	130
Buchan Ness, c., Scot., U.K.	D11	12
Buchans, Nf., Can.	j22	107a
Bucharest see București, Rom.	E13	26
Buchen, Ger.	G5	16
Buchholz in der Nordheide, Ger.	C5	16
Buchloe, Ger.	H6	16
Buchon, Point, c., Ca., U.S.	H4	134
Buchs, Switz.	C6	22
Buckatunna, Ms., U.S.	F10	122
Buckatunna Creek, stm., Ms., U.S.	F10	122
Bückeburg, Ger.	D5	16
Buckeye, Az., U.S.	J4	132
Buckeye Lake, Oh., U.S.	I7	112
Buckhaven, Scot., U.K.	E9	12
Buckholts, Tx., U.S.	D10	130
Buckhorn Draw, stm., Tx., U.S.	D7	130
Buckie, Scot., U.K.	D10	12
Buckingham, Qc., Can.	C14	112
Buckingham, Va., U.S.	G7	114
Buckingham Bay, b., Austl.	B7	74
Buck Island, i., V.I.U.S.	g11	104c
Buck Island Reef National Monument, p.o.i., V.I.U.S.	g11	104c
Buck Lake, l., Ab., Can.	D16	138
Buckland, Ak., U.S.	C7	140
Buckley, Wa., U.S.	C4	136
Bucklin, Ks., U.S.	D9	128
Bucklin, Mo., U.S.	E5	120
Buck Mountain, mtn., Wa., U.S.	B7	136
Bucovăț, Mol.	B15	26
Buco Zau, Ang.	A1	68
București (Bucharest), Rom.	E13	26
București, state, Rom.	E13	26
Bucyrus, Oh., U.S.	D3	114
Buda, Il., U.S.	C8	120
Buda, Tx., U.S.	D10	130
Budalin, Mya.	A2	48
Budapest, Hung.	B6	26
Budapest, state, Hung.	B6	26
Budaun, India	D7	54
Budd Coast, cst., Ant.	B16	81
Buddh Gaya see Bodh Gaya, India	F10	54
Budduso, Italy	D3	24
Bude, Ms., U.S.	F8	122
Bude Bay, b., Eng., U.K.	K8	12
Budënnovsk, Russia	F6	32
Budești, Rom.	E13	26
Büdingen, Ger.	F5	16
Budišov nad Budišovkou, Czech Rep.	G13	16
Budjala, D.R.C.	D3	66
Budogovišči, Russia	G19	10
Budrio, Italy	F8	22
Budweis see České Budějovice, Czech Rep.	H10	16
Buea, Cam.	D1	66
Buena Esperanza, Arg.	G5	92
Buenaventura, Col.	F3	86
Buenaventura, Mex.	G9	98
Buena Vista, Bol.	C4	90
Buena Vista, Mex.	K9	134
Buenavista, Phil.	G4	52
Buena Vista, Co., U.S.	C2	128
Buena Vista, Ga., U.S.	E14	122
Buena Vista, Va., U.S.	G6	114
Buena Vista Lake Bed, reg., Ca., U.S.	H6	134
Buendía, Embalse de, res., Spain	D8	20
Buenópolis, Braz.	I3	88
Buenos Aires, Arg.	G8	92
Buenos Aires, Col.	F3	86
Buenos Aires, C.R.	H6	102
Buenos Aires, state, Arg.	G5	90
Buenos Aires, Lago see General Carrera, Lago, l., S.A.	I2	90
Buen Pasto, Arg.	I3	90
Buerarema, Braz.	H6	88
Buffalo, Ks., U.S.	G2	120
Buffalo, Mn., U.S.	F5	118
Buffalo, Mo., U.S.	G4	120
Buffalo, N.Y., U.S.	B7	114
Buffalo, Oh., U.S.	E4	114
Buffalo, S.C., U.S.	B4	116
Buffalo, S.D., U.S.	B9	126
Buffalo, Tx., U.S.	F2	122
Buffalo, stm., Can.	C8	106
Buffalo, stm., Ar., U.S.	H4	120
Buffalo, stm., Tn., U.S.	B11	122
Buffalo Creek, stm., Mn., U.S.	G4	118
Buffalo Lake, Mn., U.S.	G4	118
Buffalo Lake, l., Ab., Can.	D18	138
Buffalo Lake, l., N.T., Can.	C7	106
Buffalo Narrows, Sk., Can.	D8	106
Buffalo Pound Lake, l., Sk., Can.	D8	124
Buffels, stm., S. Afr.	F10	70
Buffels, stm., S. Afr.	F3	70
Buford, Ga., U.S.	B2	116
Buford Dam, dam, Ga., U.S.	B1	116
Buftea, Rom.	E12	26
Bug (Buh) (Zakhidnyy Buh), stm., Eur.	D17	16
Buga, Col.	F3	86
Bugala Island, i., Ug.	E6	66
Bugeat, Fr.	D7	18
Bugojno, Bos.	E4	26
Bugrino, Russia	B23	8
Bugsuk Island, i., Phil.	F1	52
Bugt, China	C4	38
Bugul'ma, Russia	D8	32
Buguruslan, Russia	D8	32
Buh, stm., China	D4	36
Buh (Bug) (Zakhidnyy Buh), stm., Eur.	D19	16
Buhara, Uzb.	G10	32
Buhl, Mn., U.S.	D6	118
Buhler, Ks., U.S.	C11	128
Buhuși, Rom.	C13	26
Buies Creek, N.C., U.S.	A7	116
Builth Wells, Wales, U.K.	I9	12
Buin, Chile	F2	92
Buin, Pap. N. Gui.	d6	79b
Buíque, Braz.	E7	88
Buitsivango (Rietfontein), stm., Afr.	B4	70
Buj, Russia	G19	8
Bujalance, Spain	G6	20
Buje, Cro.	E10	22
Bujnaksk, Russia	F7	32
Bujumbura, Bdi.	E5	66
Bukačača, Russia	F12	34
Bukama, D.R.C.	F5	66
Bukan', Russia	G17	10
Bukavu, D.R.C.	E5	66
Bukeya, D.R.C.	G5	66
Bukhara see Buhara, Uzb.	G10	32
Bukittinggi, Indon.	D2	50
Bükki Nemzeti Park, p.o.i., Hung.	A7	26
Bukoba, Tan.	E6	66
Bukovica, reg., Cro.	F12	22
Bukovina, hist. reg., Eur.	B12	26
Bukuru, Nig.	H6	64
Bula, Indon.	F9	44
Bulaevo, Kaz.	C12	32
Bulajevo see Bulaevo, Kaz.	C12	32
Bulan, Phil.	D4	52
Bulandshahr, India	D6	54
Bulawayo, Zimb.	B9	70
Bulbul, Syria	B7	58

Name | Map Ref. | Page

Buldan, Tur. — E11 28
Buldāna, India — H6 54
Buldir Island, i., Ak., U.S. — g22 140a
Bulgan, Mong. — B3 36
Bulgan, Mong. — B5 36
Bulgaria, ctry., Eur. — G12 26
Bulkley, stm., B.C., Can. — B3 138
Bullard, Tx., U.S. — E3 122
Bulla Regia, hist., Tun. — H2 24
Bullas, Spain — F9 20
Bullaxaar, Som. — B8 66
Bulle, Switz. — D4 22
Buller, stm., N.Z. — E5 80
Buller, Mount, mtn., Austl. — K6 76
Bullfinch, Austl. — F3 74
Bull Harbour, B.C., Can. — F2 138
Bullhead, S.D., U.S. — B11 126
Bullhead City, Az., U.S. — H2 132
Bullock, N.C., U.S. — H7 114
Bullock Creek, Austl. — A5 76
Bullock Creek, stm., Austl. — C5 76
Bulloo, stm., Austl. — G4 76
Bullpound Creek, stm., Ab., Can. — E19 138
Bulls Gap, Tn., U.S. — H2 114
Bull Shoals, Ar., U.S. — H5 120
Bull Shoals Lake, res., U.S. — H5 120
Bulnes, Chile — H1 92
Bulolo, Pap. N. Gui. — b4 79a
Bulsār, India — H4 54
Buluan, Phil. — G5 52
Bulukumba, Indon. — F12 50
Bululawang, Indon. — H8 50
Bumba, D.R.C. — D4 66
Bumpus, Mount, hill, Nu., Can. — B8 106
Bumu Hu, l., China — C13 54
Buna, Kenya — D7 66
Bunawan, Phil. — F5 52
Bunbury, Austl. — F3 74
Bunceton, Mo., U.S. — F5 120
Bundaberg, Austl. — E9 76
Bundarra, Austl. — H8 76
Bünde, Ger. — D4 16
Bündi, India — F5 54
Bundoran, Ire. — G4 12
Bündu, India — G10 54
Bungamas, Indon. — E3 50
Bungo-suidō, strt., Japan — G5 40
Bungo-takada, Japan — F4 40
Bungtlang, India — G14 54
Bunia, D.R.C. — D6 66
Bunker, Mo., U.S. — G6 120
Bunker Group, is., Austl. — D9 76
Bunker Hill, In., U.S. — H3 112
Bunker Hill, Or., U.S. — G2 136
Bunker Hill, mtn., Nv., U.S. — D8 134
Bunkie, La., U.S. — G6 122
Bunnell, Fl., U.S. — G4 116
Buñol see Bunyolo, Spain — E10 20
Buntok, Indon. — D9 50
Bunyolo, Spain — E10 20
Bunyu, Pulau, i., Indon. — B10 50
Buolkalah, Russia — B12 34
Buolkalakh see Buolkalah, Russia — B12 34
Buon Ma Thuot, Viet. — F9 48
Buor-Haja, guba, b., Russia — B15 34
Buor-Haja, mys, c., Russia — B15 34
Bupul, Indon. — G11 44
Buqayq, Sau. Ar. — D6 56
Bura, Kenya — E7 66
Burām, Sudan — E5 62
Burang, China — C8 54
Buranñem, stm., Braz. — I6 88
Buraq, Syria — E7 58
Burauen, Phil. — E5 52
Burbank, Wa., U.S. — D8 136
Burç, Tur. — A8 58
Burcher, Austl. — I6 76
Burco, Som. — C9 66
Burdekin, stm., Austl. — C6 76
Burdekin Falls, wtfl, Austl. — C6 76
Burden, Ks., U.S. — D12 128
Burdett, Ks., U.S. — C9 128
Burdur, Tur. — F13 28
Burdur, state, Tur. — F13 28
Burdur Gölü, l., Tur. — F12 28
Bureinskij hrebet, mts., Russia — G15 34
Bureja, Russia — G15 34
Bureja, stm., Russia — F15 34
Büren, Ger. — E4 16
Bürenhayrhan, Mong. — B3 36
Burford, On., Can. — E9 112
Burg, Ger. — D7 16
Burg, Den see Den Burg, Neth. — A13 14
Burgas, Blg. — G14 26
Burgas, state, Blg. — G13 26
Burgas, Gulf see Burgaski Zaliv, b., Blg. — G14 26
Burgaski Zaliv, b., Blg. — G14 26
Burg auf Fehmarn, Ger. — B7 16
Burgaw, N.C., U.S. — olis 118
Burgdorf, Switz. — C4 22
Burgenland, state, Aus. — C13 22
Burgeo, Nf. — j22 107a
Burgersdorp, S. Afr. — G8 70
Burghausen, Ger. — H8 16
Burghead, Scot., U.K. — D9 12
Burgin, Ky., U.S. — G13 120
Burgo de Osma, Spain — C7 20
Burgos, Mex. — C9 100
Burgos, Phil. — C3 52
Burgos, Spain — B7 20
Burgos, co., Spain — B7 20
Burgstädt, Ger. — F8 16
Burgundy see Bourgogne, hist. reg., Fr. — B10 18
Burhan Budai Shan, mts., China — D4 36
Burhaniye, Tur. — D9 28
Burhānpur, India — H5 54
Burias Island, i., Phil. — D4 52
Burica, Punta, c., N.A. — I6 102
Buri Ram, Thai. — E6 48
Buriti, Braz. — B4 88
Buriti Bravo, Braz. — C4 88
Buriticupu, stm., Braz. — C2 88
Buriti dos Lopes, Braz. — B4 88
Buritizeiro, Braz. — I3 88
Burjasot see Burjassot, Spain — E10 20
Burjassot, Spain — E10 20
Burjatija, state, Russia — F11 34
Burkburnett, Tx., U.S. — G10 128
Burke, S.D., U.S. — D13 126
Burketown, Austl. — A2 76
Burkina Faso, ctry., Afr. — G4 64
Burleson, Tx., U.S. — B10 130
Burley, Id., U.S. — H13 136
Burlingame, Ks., U.S. — F2 120
Burlington, On., Can. — E10 112
Burlington, Co., U.S. — B6 128
Burlington, Ia., U.S. — C6 120
Burlington, Ks., U.S. — F2 120
Burlington, Ky., U.S. — F3 110
Burlington, N.C., U.S. — H6 114
Burlington, Vt., U.S. — F3 110
Burlington, Wa., U.S. — B4 136
Burlington, Wi., U.S. — B9 120
Burlington, Wy., U.S. — C4 126
Burlington Junction, Mo., U.S. — D2 120
Burma see Myanmar, ctry., Asia — D8 46
Burnaby, B.C., Can. — G8 138
Burnet, Tx., U.S. — D9 130
Burnet, stm., Austl. — E8 76

Burnett Bay, b., N.T., Can. — B14 140
Burney, Ca., U.S. — C4 134
Burnie, Austl. — n12 77a
Burnley, Eng., U.K. — H10 12
Burns, Ks., U.S. — C12 128
Burns, Or., U.S. — G7 136
Burns, Tn., U.S. — H10 120
Burns, Wy., U.S. — F8 126
Burnside, Ky., U.S. — G13 120
Burnside, stm., Nu., Can. — B8 106
Burnside, Lake, l., Austl. — E4 74
Burnside, Lake, B.C., Can. — B5 138
Burnsville, Ms., U.S. — C10 122
Burnsville, N.C., U.S. — I3 114
Burnsville, W.V., U.S. — F5 114
Burnt, stm., Or., U.S. — F9 136
Burnt Pine, S.D., U.S. — y25 78i
Burntwood, stm., Mb., Can. — D11 106
Burqin, China — B2 36
Burra, Austl. — I2 76
Burragorang, Lake, res., Austl. — J7 76
Burrel, Alb. — C13 24
Burreli see Burrel, Alb. — C13 24
Burrendong, Lake, res., Austl. — I7 76
Burren Junction, Austl. — H7 76
Burriana see Borriana, Spain — E10 20
Burrinjuck Reservoir, res., Austl. — J7 76
Burr Oak, Ks., U.S. — B10 128
Burrton, Ks., U.S. — C11 128
Burruyacú, Arg. — E4 90
Bursa, Tur. — C11 28
Bursa, state, Tur. — C11 28
Bür Saʿīd (Port Said), Egypt — G3 58
Burstall, Sk., Can. — D4 124
Bür Sūdān (Port Sudan), Sudan — D7 62
Burton, Mi., U.S. — E6 112
Burton, Tx., U.S. — G2 122
Burton upon Trent, Eng., U.K. — I11 12
Buru, i., Indon. — F8 44
Burullus, Buheirat el-, l., Egypt — G1 58
Burundi, ctry., Afr. — E6 66
Burun-Sibertuj, gora, mtn., Russia — G10 34
Burwash, Bdi. — E5 66
Burwash Jct., On., Can. — B9 112
Burwell, Ne., U.S. — F13 126
Bury, Eng., U.K. — H10 12
Buryatia see Burjatija, state, Russia — F11 34
Bury Saint Edmunds, Eng., U.K. — I13 12
Burzil, Pak. — A5 54
Busa, Mount, mtn., Phil. — G5 52
Busan see Pusan-jikhalsi, state, Kor., S. — D2 40
Busanga, D.R.C. — E4 66
Busby, Mt., U.S. — B5 126
Büsh, Egypt — I2 58
Bushire see Bandar-e Büshehr, Iran — D7 56
Bushland, Tx., U.S. — F6 128
Bushman Land, reg., S. Afr. — F4 70
Bushnell, Fl., U.S. — H3 116
Bushnell, Il., U.S. — D7 120
Bushtyna, Ukr. — A10 26
Busia, Ug. — D6 66
Businga, D.R.C. — D4 66
Busira, stm., D.R.C. — E3 66
Buskerud, state, Nor. — F3 8
Busko-Zdrój, Pol. — F16 16
Busselton, Austl. — F3 74
Bussey, La., U.S. — C5 120
Bussum, Neth. — B14 14
Bustamante, Mex. — B8 100
Busto Arsizio, Italy — E5 22
Busuanga Island, i., Phil. — D2 52
Busu-Djanoa, D.R.C. — D4 66
Büsum, Ger. — B4 16
Buta, D.R.C. — D4 66
Buta Ranquil, Arg. — H2 92
Butare, Rw. — E5 66
Butaritari, atoll, Kir. — C8 72
Bute, Island of, i., Scot., U.K. — F7 12
Bute Inlet, b., B.C., Can. — F5 138
Butembo, D.R.C. — D5 66
Butera, Italy — G8 24
Butere, Kenya — D6 66
Butha-Buthe, Leso. — F9 70
Buthidaung, Mya. — D7 46
Butiá, Braz. — E11 92
Butler, Ga., U.S. — D1 116
Butler, In., U.S. — C1 114
Butler, Mo., U.S. — F3 120
Butler, Oh., U.S. — D3 114
Butler, Pa., U.S. — D6 114
Butler, N.C., U.S. — H7 114
Buto, hist., Egypt — G1 58
Buton, Pulau, i., Indon. — F7 44
Butrint, hist., Alb. — E14 24
Butru, Austl. — C2 76
Butte, Mt., U.S. — D14 136
Butte, Ne., U.S. — E14 126
Butte Creek, stm., Ca., U.S. — D4 134
Butte Falls, Or., U.S. — H4 136
Butternut, Wi., U.S. — E8 118
Butterworth, Malay. — J5 48
Butterworth, S. Afr. — H9 70
Buttle Lake, l., B.C., Can. — G5 138
Button Islands, is., Nu., Can. — C17 106
Buttonwillow, Ca., U.S. — H6 134
Butuan, Phil. — F5 52
Butung, Pulau, i., Indon. — F7 44
Buturlino, Russia — I21 8
Butwal, Nepal — E9 54
Butzbach, Ger. — F4 16
Bützow, Ger. — C7 16
Buulobarde, Som. — D9 66
Buur Gaabo, Som. — E8 66
Buurgplaatz, mtn., Lux. — D15 14
Buxtehude, Ger. — C5 16
Buxton, S. Afr. — E7 70
Buxton, Eng., U.K. — H11 12
Buxton, N.C., U.S. — A10 116
Buxton, Mount, mtn., B.C., Can. — E22 138
Buyr nuur, l., Asia — B8 36
Büyükada, Tur. — C12 28
Büyükçekmece, Tur. — B11 28
Büyükkarıştıran, Tur. — B10 28
Büyükkemikli Burnu, c., Tur. — C9 28
Büyükmenderes, stm., Tur. — F10 28
Buzau, Rom. — D13 26
Buzau, state, Rom. — D13 26
Buzau, stm., Rom. — D13 26
Buzen, Japan — F4 40
Búzi, stm., Moz. — A12 70
Buzias, Rom. — D8 26
Buzuluk, Russia — D8 32
Byādgi, India — D2 53
Byam Channel, strt., Nu., Can. — A19 140
Byam Martin Island, i., Nu., Can. — B19 140
Byaroza, Bela. — H8 10
Bychawa, Pol. — E18 16
Byczyna, Pol. — E14 16
Bydgoszcz, Pol. — C13 16
Bydgoszcz, state, Pol. — C13 16
Byelorussia see Belarus, ctry., Eur. — E14 6
Byerazino, Bela. — G10 10
Byesville, Oh., U.S. — E4 114
Bygdin, l., Nor. — F3 8

Byhalia, Ms., U.S. — C9 122
Byhaŭ, Bela. — G13 10
Bykle, Nor. — G2 8
Bylnice, Czech Rep. — G14 16
Bylot Island, i., Nu., Can. — A15 106
Byng Inlet, On., Can. — C9 112
Bynum, Mt., U.S. — C14 136
Bynum, N.C., U.S. — I6 114
Byrd, Lac, l., Qc., Can. — A13 112
Byrnedale, Pa., U.S. — C7 114
Byro, Austl. — E3 74
Byron, Ga., U.S. — D2 116
Byron, Il., U.S. — B8 120
Byron, Cape, c., Austl. — G9 76
Byron Bay, Austl. — G9 76
Byrranga, gory, mts., Russia — B8 34
Bystřice pod Hostýnem, Czech Rep. — G13 16
Bytantaj, stm., Russia — C15 34
Bytča, Slov. — G14 16
Bytom, Pol. — F14 16
Bytoš', Russia — G17 10
Bytów, Pol. — B13 16

C

Ca, stm., Asia — C7 48
Caacupé, Para. — B9 92
Caaguazú, Para. — B9 92
Caaguazú, state, Para. — B10 92
Caála, Ang. — C2 68
Caapiranga, Braz. — I11 86
Caatinga, Braz. — I3 88
Caazapá, Para. — C9 92
Caazapá, state, Para. — C9 92
Caibaiguán, Cuba — A8 102
Cabaliana, Lago, l., Braz. — I11 86
Caballococha, Peru — D3 84
Caballo Reservoir, res., N.M., U.S. — K9 132
Cabanatuan, Phil. — C3 52
Cabano, Qc., Can. — C8 110
Cabarroguis, Phil. — B3 52
Cabedelo, Braz. — D8 88
Cabeza del Buey, Spain — F5 20
Cabezas, Bol. — C4 90
Cabimas, Ven. — B6 86
Cabinda, Ang. — B1 68
Cabinda, state, Ang. — B1 68
Cabinet Mountains, mts., U.S. — B10 136
Cable, Wi., U.S. — E7 118
Cabo, Braz. — E8 88
Cabo Blanco, Arg. — I3 90
Cabo Frio, Braz. — L4 88
Cabonga, Réservoir, res., Qc., Can. — F15 106
Cabool, Mo., U.S. — G5 120
Caboolture, Austl. — F9 76
Caborca, Mex. — F6 98
Cabo Rojo, P.R. — B1 104a
Cabot, Ar., U.S. — C7 122
Cabot Head, c., On., Can. — C8 112
Cabot Strait, strt., Can. — j21 107a
Cabourg, Fr. — E8 14
Cabra Corral, Embalse, res., Arg. — B5 92
Cabramurra, Austl. — J7 76
Cabrera, stm., Col. — F4 86
Cabrera, Illa de, i., Spain — E13 20
Cabri, Sk., Can. — D5 124
Cabriel, stm., Spain — E9 20
Cabrillo National Monument, p.o.i., Ca., U.S. — K8 134
Cabruta, Ven. — D8 86
Cabudare, Ven. — B7 86
Cabuyaro, Col. — E5 86
Caçador, Braz. — C12 92
Čačak, Yugo. — F7 26
Caçapava, Braz. — L3 88
Caçapava do Sul, Braz. — E11 92
Cacapon, stm., W.V., U.S. — E7 114
Cacequi, Braz. — D10 92
Cáceres, Braz. — G6 84
Cáceres, Col. — D4 86
Cáceres, co., Spain — E4 20
Cačersk, Bela. — H13 10
Cache, stm., Ar., U.S. — B7 122
Cache, stm., Il., U.S. — G8 120
Cache Creek, B.C., Can. — F9 138
Cache Creek, stm., Ca., U.S. — E3 134
Cache la Poudre, stm., Co., U.S. — G7 126
Cache Peak, mtn., Id., U.S. — A3 132
Cachi, Arg. — B4 92
Cachimbo, Braz. — E7 84
Cachoeira Alta, Braz. — C6 90
Cachoeira de Manteiga, Braz. — I3 88
Cachoeiro de Itapemirim, Braz. — K5 88
Cachos, Punta, c., Chile — C2 92
Cacolo, Ang. — C2 68
Caconda, Ang. — C2 68
Cactus, Tx., U.S. — E6 128
Cactus Flat, pl., Nv., U.S. — F9 134
Cacuaco, Ang. — B1 68
Cacuié, Braz. — H4 88
Cacuri, Ven. — E9 86
Cadan, Russia — G14 16
Cadca, Slov. — G14 16
Caddo, stm., Ar., U.S. — C5 122
Caddo Lake, res., U.S. — E4 122
Caddo Mills, Tx., U.S. — D2 122
Cadell, stm., Austl. — D3 76
Cadena, Punta, c., P.R. — B1 104a
Cadillac, Sk., Can. — E6 124
Cadillac, Fr. — E5 18
Cadillac, Mi., U.S. — D4 112
Cádiz, Spain — H4 20
Cadiz, Ky., U.S. — H10 120
Cádiz, co., Spain — H5 20
Cádiz, Bahía de, b., Spain — H4 20
Cadiz Lake, l., Ca., U.S. — I10 134
Cadomin, Ab., Can. — C13 138
Cadore, reg., Italy — D9 22
Cadott, Wi., U.S. — G7 118
Cadwell, Ga., U.S. — D2 116
Caen, Fr. — E8 14
Caernarfon, Wales, U.K. — H8 12
Caernarfon Bay, b., Wales, U.K. — H8 12
Caerphilly, Wales, U.K. — J9 12
Caesarea see Qesari, Horbat, hist., Isr. — F5 58
Caetité, Braz. — H4 88
Cafayate, Arg. — C4 92
Cagayan, stm., Phil. — A3 52
Cagayan Islands, is., Phil. — F3 52
Cagayan de Oro, Phil. — F5 52
Cagayan Sulu Island, i., Phil. — G1 52
Cagda, Russia — E15 34
Cagli, Italy — G9 22
Cagliari, Italy — E3 24
Cagliari, Golfo di, b., Italy — E3 24

Cagliari, Stagno di, l., Italy — E2 24
Cagnes-sur-Mer, Fr. — F13 18
Cagoda, stm., Russia — A17 10
Cagodošča, stm., Russia — A18 10
Caguán, stm., Col. — G4 86
Caguas, P.R. — B3 104a
Cahaba, stm., Al., U.S. — E11 122
Cahama, Ang. — D1 68
Caher, Ire. — I4 12
Cahokia, Il., U.S. — F7 120
Cahora Bassa, Albufeira, res., Moz. — D5 68
Cahors, Fr. — E7 18
Cahto, stm., Ca., U.S. — D2 134
Cahuinari, stm., Col. — H6 86
Cahul, Mol. — D15 26
Cai, stm., Braz. — D12 92
Caianda, Ang. — C3 68
Caiapó, Serra do, mts., Braz. — G7 84
Caibarién, Cuba — A8 102
Caicara, Caño, stm., Ven. — D7 86
Caicara de Maturín, Ven. — C10 86
Caicara de Orinoco, Ven. — D8 86
Caicedonia, Col. — E4 86
Caicó, Braz. — D7 88
Caicos Islands, is., T./C. Is. — B11 102
Caicos Passage, strt., N.A. — B11 102
Caijiapo, China — D2 42
Caima Bay, b., Phil. — D4 52
Caimanera, Cuba — C10 102
Caimanero, Laguna del, l., Mex. — D5 100
Cain Creek, stm., S.D., U.S. — C14 126
Cairngorm, Scot., U.K. — G6 134
Cairns, Austl. — A5 76
Cairo see El-Qâhira, Egypt — H2 58
Cairo, Ga., U.S. — F1 116
Cairo, Il., U.S. — G8 120
Cairo, Ne., U.S. — F14 126
Cairo, W.V., U.S. — E4 114
Cairo Montenotte, Italy — F5 22
Caislean an Bharraigh see Castlebar, Ire. — H3 12
Caiundo, Ang. — D2 68
Caiwan, China — I4 42
Caizhi Hu, l., China — F7 42
Caja de Muertos, Isla, i., P.R. — C2 104a
Cajamarca, Peru — E2 84
Cajapió, Braz. — B3 88
Cajazeiras, Braz. — D6 88
Cajon Summit, p., Ca., U.S. — I8 134
Cajuru, Braz. — K2 88
Caka, China — D4 36
Cakmak, Tur. — A5 58
Cakovec, Cro. — D13 22
Calabar, Nig. — H6 64
Calabozo, Ven. — C8 86
Calabozo, Ensenada de, b., Ven. — B6 86
Calabria, state, Italy — F10 24
Calafat, Rom. — F9 26
Calagua Islands, is., Phil. — C4 52
Calahorra, Spain — B8 20
Calais, Fr. — C10 14
Calalaste, Sierra de, mts., Arg. — B4 92
Calama, Chile — D3 90
Calamar, Col. — B4 86
Calamar, Col. — F5 86
Calamian Group, is., Phil. — E3 52
Calamus, stm., Ne., U.S. — E13 126
Calañas, Spain — G4 20
Calang, Indon. — J2 48
Calapan, Mol. — D3 52
Calarași, Rom. — E14 26
Calarași, state, Rom. — E14 26
Calarcá, Col. — E4 86
Calatafimi, Italy — G6 24
Calatayud, Spain — C9 20
Calavite Passage, strt., Phil. — D3 52
Calayan Island, i., Phil. — A3 52
Calbayog, Phil. — D5 52
Calbe, Ger. — E7 16
Calbuco, Chile — H2 90
Calcasieu, stm., La., U.S. — G5 122
Calcasieu Lake, l., La., U.S. — G5 122
Calceta, Ec. — H1 86
Calchaquí, Arg. — D7 92
Calchaquí, stm., Arg. — B4 92
Calçoene, Braz. — C7 84
Calcutta, India — G12 54
Caldaro, Italy — D8 22
Caldas, Col. — D4 86
Caldas, state, Col. — E4 86
Caldas da Rainha, Port. — E1 20
Caldas de Reis, Spain — B2 20
Caldas de Reyes see Caldas de Reis, Spain — B2 20
Caldas Novas, Braz. — I1 88
Caldera, Chile — C2 92
Caldwell, Id., U.S. — G10 136
Caldwell, Ks., U.S. — D11 128
Caldwell, Oh., U.S. — E4 114
Caldwell, Tx., U.S. — G2 122
Caledon (Mohokare), stm., Afr. — F8 70
Caledonia, Belize — C3 102
Caledonia, Mn., U.S. — F11 110
Caledonia, Ms., U.S. — D10 122
Caledonia, N.Y., U.S. — A8 114
Caledonia, Oh., U.S. — D3 114
Calella, Spain — C13 20
Calen, Austl. — C7 76
Calera, Al., U.S. — D12 122
Caleta Olivia, Arg. — I3 90
Calexico, Ca., U.S. — K10 134
Calgary, Ab., Can. — E16 138
Calhan, Co., U.S. — B4 128
Calhoun, Al., U.S. — E12 122
Calhoun, Ga., U.S. — C14 122
Calhoun, Ky., U.S. — G10 120
Calhoun, Mo., U.S. — F4 120
Calhoun, Tn., U.S. — B14 122
Calhoun City, Ms., U.S. — D9 122
Cali, Col. — F3 86
Calico Rock, Ar., U.S. — H5 120
Calicut see Kozhikode, India — F2 53
Caliente, Nv., U.S. — F2 134
Caliente, Cerro, mtn., Mex. — F5 100
California, state, U.S. — D3 108
California, Golfo de (California, Gulf of), b., Mex. — B2 96
California, Gulf of see California, Golfo de, b., Mex. — B2 96
California Aqueduct, aq., U.S. — I8 134
Calilegua, Parque Nacional, p.o.i., Arg. — A5 92
Calimere, Point, c., India — F4 53
Calingasta, Arg. — E3 92
Calion, Ar., U.S. — D6 122
Calipatria, Ca., U.S. — J10 134
Calispell Peak, mtn., Wa., U.S. — B9 136
Calistoga, Ca., U.S. — E3 134
Calitri, Italy — D9 24
Callabonna, Lake, l., Austl. — H3 76
Callabonna Creek, stm., Austl. — G3 76

Callahan, Mount, mtn., Co., U.S. — D8 132
Callan, Ire. — I5 12
Callander, On., Can. — B10 112
Callao, Peru — F2 84
Callaquén, Volcán, vol., Chile — H2 92
Callaway, Ne., U.S. — F12 126
Calliaqua, St. Vin. — o11 105e
Calling Lake, Ab., Can. — A17 138
Calling Lake, l., Ab., Can. — A17 138
Callosa de Segura, Spain — F9 20
Calmar, Ab., Can. — C17 138
Calmar, Ia., U.S. — A6 120
Calne, Eng., U.K. — J11 12
Calobre, Pan. — H7 102
Caloundra, Austl. — F9 76
Calp, Spain — F11 20
Calpe see Calp, Spain — F11 20
Caltagirone, Italy — G8 24
Caltanissetta, Italy — G8 24
Calulo, Ang. — B2 68
Calumet, Mn., U.S. — D5 118
Calumet City, Il., U.S. — G2 112
Calunda, Ang. — C3 68
Caluula, Som. — B10 66
Calvados, state, Fr. — E8 14
Calvert, Al., U.S. — F10 122
Calvert, Tx., U.S. — G2 122
Calvert Island, i., B.C., Can. — E2 138
Calvillo, Mex. — E7 100
Calvin, Ok., U.S. — C2 122
Calvinia, S. Afr. — G4 70
Calw, Ger. — H4 16
Calwa, Ca., U.S. — G6 134
Calypso, N.C., U.S. — A7 116
Camabatela, Ang. — B2 68
Camacupa, Ang. — C2 68
Camaguán, Ven. — C8 86
Camagüey, Cuba — B9 102
Camaiore, Italy — G7 22
Camajuaní, Cuba — A8 102
Camaná, Peru — G3 84
Camanaú, stm., Braz. — H11 86
Camanche Reservoir, res., Ca., U.S. — E5 134
Camapuã, Braz. — D6 90
Camaquã, Braz. — E12 92
Camaquã, stm., Braz. — E11 92
Camará, Braz. — D5 84
Camarajibe, Braz. — D8 88
Camararé, stm., Braz. — F6 84
Camarat, Cap, c., Fr. — F12 18
Camarès, Fr. — F8 18
Camargo, Bol. — D3 90
Camargue, reg., Fr. — F10 18
Camarillo, Ca., U.S. — I6 134
Camarón, Arroyo, stm., Mex. — G7 130
Camarón, Cabo, c., Hond. — D5 102
Camarones, Arg. — H3 90
Camarones, Bahía, b., Arg. — H3 90
Camas Creek, stm., Id., U.S. — F14 136
Camatagua, Embalse de, l., Ven. — C8 86
Ca Mau, Viet. — H7 48
Ca Mau, Mui, c., Viet. — H7 48
Camba, Indon. — F11 50
Cambodia, ctry., Asia — E8 76
Cambooya, Austl. — F8 76
Camboriú, Braz. — C13 92
Camborne, Eng., U.K. — K7 12
Cambrai, Fr. — D12 14
Cambria, Ca., U.S. — H4 134
Cambrian Mountains, mts., Wales, U.K. — I9 12
Cambridge, On., Can. — E9 112
Cambridge, Jam. — i12 104d
Cambridge, Eng., U.K. — I12 12
Cambridge, Il., U.S. — C7 120
Cambridge, Ia., U.S. — C4 120
Cambridge, Md., U.S. — F9 114
Cambridge, Mn., U.S. — F5 118
Cambridge, Ne., U.S. — A8 128
Cambridge, N.Y., U.S. — G3 110
Cambridge, Oh., U.S. — D4 114
Cambridge Bay, Nu., Can. — B10 106
Cambridge Fiord, b., Nu., Can. — A15 106
Cambridge Springs, Pa., U.S. — C5 114
Cambrils, Spain — C11 20
Cambuí, Braz. — L2 88
Cambulo, Ang. — B3 68
Cambundi-Catembo, Ang. — C2 68
Camden, Austl. — J8 76
Camden, Al., U.S. — F11 122
Camden, Ar., U.S. — D6 122
Camden, Me., U.S. — F7 110
Camden, N.J., U.S. — E10 114
Camden, N.Y., U.S. — E14 112
Camden, N.C., U.S. — H9 114
Camden, Oh., U.S. — E1 114
Camden, S.C., U.S. — B5 116
Camden, Tn., U.S. — H9 120
Camden Bay, b., Ak., U.S. — B11 140
Camdenton, Mo., U.S. — G5 120
Camels Hump, mtn., Vt., U.S. — F3 110
Camenca, Mol. — A15 26
Camerino, Italy — G10 22
Cameron, Az., U.S. — H5 132
Cameron, La., U.S. — H5 122
Cameron, Mo., U.S. — E3 120
Cameron, Tx., U.S. — G2 122
Cameron, W.V., U.S. — E5 114
Cameron, Wi., U.S. — F7 118
Cameron, ctry., Afr. — C2 66
Cameron Hills, hills, Can. — D7 106
Cameroon, ctry., Afr. — C2 66
Cameroon Mountain, vol., Cam. — D1 66
Camerota, Italy — D9 24
Cametá, Braz. — A1 88
Camiguin Island, i., Phil. — A3 52
Camiguin Island, i., Phil. — F5 52
Camiling, Phil. — C3 52
Camilla, Ga., U.S. — E1 116
Camino, Ca., U.S. — E5 134
Camiranga, Braz. — A2 88
Camiri, Bol. — D4 90
Camissombo, Ang. — B3 68
Çamlıdere, Tur. — C15 28
Cam Lo, Viet. — D8 48
Camocim, Braz. — C5 88
Camooweal, Austl. — B2 76
Camorta Island, i., India — G7 46
Camotes Sea, Phil. — E5 52
Campagna di Roma, reg., Italy — C6 24
Campaign, Tn., U.S. — B13 122
Campana, Arg. — G8 92
Campana, Isla, i., Chile — I1 90
Campania, state, Italy — D8 24
Campania, Appennino, mts., Italy — C8 24
Campaspe, stm., Austl. — K5 76
Campbell, Ca., U.S. — F3 134
Campbell, Mo., U.S. — H7 120
Campbell, Ne., U.S. — A10 128
Campbell, Cape, c., N.Z. — E6 80
Campbell Hill, hill, Oh., U.S. — D2 114
Campbell Hills, hill, St. Vin. — o11 105e
Campbell Island, i., B.C., Can. — D2 138
Campbell Island, i., N.Z. — I7 72

Campbell Lake, l., B.C., Can. — G5 138
Campbell Plateau, unds. — O20 142
Campbellpore, Pak. — B4 54
Campbell River, B.C., Can. — F5 138
Campbell's Bay, Qc., Can. — C13 112
Campbellsport, Wi., U.S. — E1 112
Campbellton, N.B., Can. — C10 110
Campbellton, P.E., Can. — D12 110
Campbellton, Fl., U.S. — G13 122
Campbelltown, Austl. — J8 76
Campbell Town, Austl. — n13 77a
Campbeltown, Scot., U.K. — F7 12
Campeche, state, Mex. — C2 102
Campeche, Bahía de, b., Mex. — E13 100
Campeche, Gulf of see Campeche, Bahía de, b., Mex. — E13 100
Campechuela, Cuba — B9 102
Camperdown, Austl. — L4 76
Camperville, Mb., Can. — C13 124
Cam Pha, Viet. — B8 48
Camp Hill, Al., U.S. — E13 122
Campina, reg., Rom. — C10 26
Campina, reg., Spain — G5 20
Campina Grande, Braz. — D7 88
Campinas, Braz. — L2 88
Campina Verde, Braz. — J1 88
Campoalegre, Col. — F4 86
Campo, Braz. — I2 88
Campobasso, Italy — C8 24
Campo Belo, Braz. — K3 88
Campo de Criptana, Spain — E7 20
Campo Erê, Braz. — C11 92
Campo Florido, Braz. — J1 88
Campo Formoso, Braz. — F5 88
Campo Gallo, Arg. — C6 92
Campo Grande, Braz. — D6 90
Campo Largo, Braz. — B13 92
Campo Largo, Arg. — C7 92
Campo Maíor, Braz. — C4 88
Campo Maior, Port. — F3 20
Campo Mourão, Braz. — A11 92
Campo Novo, Braz. — C11 92
Campos, Braz. — K5 88
Campos Altos, Braz. — J2 88
Campo Santo, Arg. — B5 92
Campos Belos, Braz. — G2 88
Campos do Jordão, Braz. — L3 88
Campos Gerais, Braz. — K2 88
Campos Novos, Braz. — C12 92
Campos Sales, Braz. — D5 88
Camp Point, Il., U.S. — D6 120
Campti, La., U.S. — F5 122
Campton, Ky., U.S. — G2 114
Câmpulung, Rom. — D11 26
Câmpulung Moldovenesc, Rom. — B12 26
Cam Ranh, Viet. — G9 48
Cam Ranh Bay see Cam Ranh, Vinh, b., Viet. — G9 48
Camrose, Ab., Can. — C18 138
Camsell, stm., N.T., Can. — B7 106
Camuy, P.R. — B2 104a
Çan, Tur. — C10 28
Canaan, Vt., U.S. — E5 110
Cana-brava, stm., Braz. — G1 88
Canada, ctry., N.A. — D9 106
Canada Basin, unds. — A25 142
Cañada de Gómez, Arg. — F7 92
Cañada Honda, Arg. — F3 92
Canadian, Tx., U.S. — F8 128
Canadian, stm., U.S. — F13 128
Canadian, Deep Fork, stm., Ok., U.S. — F13 128
Canaguá, stm., Ven. — D7 86
Canaima, Parque Nacional, p.o.i., Ven. — E10 86
Canajoharie, N.Y., U.S. — B11 114
Canakkale, Tur. — C9 28
Çanakkale, state, Tur. — D9 28
Çanakkale Boğazı (Dardanelles), strt., Tur. — C9 28
Canala, N. Cal. — m15 79d
Canal Fulton, Oh., U.S. — D4 114
Canal Point, Fl., U.S. — J5 116
Canals, Arg. — F6 92
Canal Winchester, Oh., U.S. — E3 114
Canandaigua, N.Y., U.S. — B8 114
Canápolis, Mex. — ...
Cañar, state, Ec. — I2 86
Canarias, Islas (Canary Islands), is., Spain — D1 64
Canarreos, Archipiélago de los, is., Cuba — B6 102
Canary Basin, unds. — F11 142
Canary Islands see Canarias, Islas, is., Spain — D1 64
Cañas, C.R. — G5 102
Canaseraga, N.Y., U.S. — B8 114
Canatlán, Mex. — C6 100
Canaveral, Cape, c., Fl., U.S. — H5 116
Canaveral National Seashore, p.o.i., Fl., U.S. — H5 116
Cañaveras, Spain — D8 20
Canavieiras, Braz. — H6 88
Canavese, hist. reg., Italy — E4 22
Canberra, Austl. — J7 76
Canby, Mn., U.S. — G2 118
Canby, Or., U.S. — E4 136
Cancon, Fr. — E6 18
Cancún, Mex. — B4 102
Çandarlı Körfezi, b., Tur. — E9 28
Candé, Fr. — G7 14
Candeias, Braz. — G6 88
Candeias, stm., Braz. — E5 84
Candela, Mex. — B8 100
Candelaria, Arg. — C10 92
Candelaria, Mex. — C2 102
Candelo, Austl. — K7 76
Candia see Irákleio, Grc. — H8 28
Cándido Aguilar, Mex. — G6 100
Cândido de Abreu, Braz. — B12 92
Cândido Mendes, Braz. — A3 88
Candlemas Islands, is., S. Geor. — K12 82
Candlestick, Mesa, mtn., N.M., U.S. — E8 132
Cando, N.D., U.S. — F14 124
Candon, Phil. — B3 52
Canea see Chaniá, Grc. — H7 28
Canela, Braz. — C13 92
Canelones, Ur. — G9 92
Cañete, Chile — H1 92
Cañete, Spain — D9 20
Caney, Ks., U.S. — D13 128
Caney, stm., U.S. — F12 130
Caney Creek, stm., Tx., U.S. — B10 130
Cangas de Narcea, Spain — A4 20
Cangas de Onís, Spain — A5 20

Name	Map Ref.	Page
Cangkuang, Tanjung, c., Indon.	G4	50
Cangombe, Ang.	C2	68
Canguaretama, Braz.	D8	88
Canguçu, Braz.	E11	92
Cangumbe, Ang.	C2	68
Cangxi, China	F1	42
Cangzhou, China	B7	42
Caniapiscau, stm., Qc., Can.	D17	106
Caniapiscau, Lac, res., Qc., Can.	E17	106
Canicattì, Italy	G7	24
Canim Lake, B.C., Can.	E10	138
Canim Lake, l., B.C., Can.	E9	138
Canindé, Braz.	C6	88
Canindé, stm., Braz.	D4	88
Canindeyú, state, Para.	B10	92
Canisteo, N.Y., U.S.	B8	114
Canistota, S.D., U.S.	D15	126
Cañitas de Felipe Pescador, Mex.	D7	100
Canjáyar, Spain	G8	20
Çankırı, Tur.	A3	56
Çankırı, state, Tur.	C15	28
Canmore, Ab., Can.	E15	138
Cannanore, India	F2	53
Cannelton, In., U.S.	G11	120
Cannes, Fr.	F13	18
Canning, N.S., Can.	E12	110
Cannington, On., Can.	D10	112
Cannock, Eng., U.K.	I10	12
Cannon, stm., Mn., U.S.	G5	118
Cannonball, stm., N.D., U.S.	A11	126
Cannon Beach, Or., U.S.	E2	136
Cannon Falls, Mn., U.S.	G6	118
Cannonvale, Austl.	C7	76
Cann River, Austl.	K7	76
Canoas, Braz.	D12	92
Canoas, stm., Braz.	C12	92
Canoe, B.C., Can.	F11	138
Canoe, stm., B.C., Can.	D12	138
Canoinhas, Braz.	C12	92
Canon City, Co., U.S.	C3	128
Cañon de Río Blanco, Parque Nacional, p.o.i., Mex.	F10	100
Canonsburg, Pa., U.S.	D5	114
Canoochee, stm., Ga., U.S.	E4	116
Canora, Sk., Can.	C11	124
Canosa di Púglia, Italy	C10	24
Canossa, hist., Italy	F7	22
Canouan, i., St. Vin.	p11	105e
Canova, S.D., U.S.	D15	126
Canova Beach, Fl., U.S.	H5	116
Cañovanas, P.R.	B4	104a
Canowindra, Austl.	I7	76
Canso, N.S., Can.	E16	110
Cantábria, state, Spain	A6	20
Cantabrian Mountains see Cantábrica, Cordillera, mts., Spain	A5	20
Cantábrica, Cordillera, mts., Spain	A5	20
Cantagalo, Braz.	K4	88
Cantal, state, Fr.	D8	18
Cantalejo, Spain	C7	20
Cantanhede, Braz.	B3	88
Cantaura, Ven.	C9	86
Canterbury, Eng., U.K.	J14	12
Canterbury Bight, b., N.Z.	G4	80
Canterbury Plains, pl., N.Z.	G4	80
Can Tho, Viet.	G7	48
Canton see Guangzhou, China	J5	42
Canton, Il., U.S.	D7	120
Canton, Ks., U.S.	C11	128
Canton, Mn., U.S.	H7	118
Canton, Ms., U.S.	E8	122
Canton, Mo., U.S.	D6	120
Canton, N.Y., U.S.	D14	112
Canton, Oh., U.S.	D4	114
Canton, Ok., U.S.	E10	128
Canton, Pa., U.S.	C9	114
Canton, S.D., U.S.	H2	118
Canton, Tx., U.S.	E3	122
Canton see Kanton, i., Kir.	D9	72
Canton Lake, res., Ok., U.S.	E10	128
Cantonment, Fl., U.S.	G11	122
Cantù, Italy	E6	22
Cantu, stm., Braz.	B11	92
Cantwell, Ak., U.S.	D10	140
Cañuelas, Arg.	G8	92
Canumã, Braz.	D6	84
Canutama, Braz.	E5	84
Cany, Russia	C13	32
Cany, ozero, l., Russia	D13	32
Canyon, Tx., U.S.	G7	128
Canyon City, Or., U.S.	F8	136
Canyon Creek, Ab., Can.	A15	138
Canyon de Chelly National Monument, p.o.i., Az., U.S.	G7	132
Canyon Ferry Lake, res., Mt., U.S.	D15	136
Canyon Lake, res., Tx., U.S.	E9	130
Canyonlands National Park, p.o.i., Ut., U.S.	E6	132
Canyonville, Or., U.S.	H3	136
Cao, stm., China	D5	38
Cao Bang, Viet.	A7	48
Cao Lanh, Viet.	G8	48
Caombo, Ang.	B2	68
Caorle, Italy	E9	22
Caoxian, China	D6	42
Cap, Pointe du, c., St. Luc.	l7	105c
Capac, Mi., U.S.	E7	112
Capanaparo, stm., S.A.	D8	86
Capanema, Braz.	D8	84
Capão Bonito, Braz.	L1	88
Capão Doce, Morro do, mtn., Braz.	C12	92
Caparaó, Parque Nacional do, p.o.i., Braz.	K4	88
Caparo Viejo, stm., Ven.	D6	86
Capatárida, Ven.	B6	86
Cap aux Meules, Île du, i., Qc., Can.	C14	110
Cap-Chat, Qc., Can.	A10	110
Cap-de-la-Madeleine, Qc., Can.	D4	110
Cape, stm., Austl.	C5	76
Cape Barren Island, i., Austl.	n13	77a
Cape Basin, unds.	L14	144
Cape Breton Highlands National Park, p.o.i., N.S., Can.	D16	110
Cape Breton Island, i., N.S., Can.	D16	110
Cape Charles, Va., U.S.	G9	114
Cape Coast, Ghana	H4	64
Cape Cod Bay, b., Ma., U.S.	C15	114
Cape Cod National Seashore, p.o.i., Ma., U.S.	B16	114
Cape Coral, Fl., U.S.	J4	116
Cape Dorset, Nu., Can.	C15	106
Cape Elizabeth, Me., U.S.	G6	110
Cape Fear, stm., N.C., U.S.	B8	116
Cape Girardeau, Mo., U.S.	G8	120
Cape Hatteras National Seashore, p.o.i., N.C., U.S.	A10	116
Capelinha, Braz.	I4	88
Cape Lisburne, Ak., U.S.	C6	140
Capel'ka, Russia	B11	10
Capella, Austl.	D7	76
Capelongo, Ang.	C2	68
Cape Lookout National Seashore, p.o.i., N.C., U.S.	B9	116
Cape May, N.J., U.S.	F10	114
Cape May Court House, N.J., U.S.	E11	114
Cape Porpoise, Me., U.S.	G6	110
Capernaum see Kefar Nahum, hist., Isr.	F6	58
Cape Sable Island, i., N.S., Can.	G11	110
Capesterre, Guad.	i6	105c
Capesterre, Pointe de la, c., Guad.	h5	105c
Capesterre-Belle-Eau, Guad.	h5	105c
Cape Tormentine, N.B., Can.	D12	110
Cape Town (Kaapstad), S. Afr.	H4	70
Cape Verde, ctry., Afr.	k9	65a
Cape Verde Basin, unds.	G10	144
Cape Vincent, N.Y., U.S.	D13	112
Cape York Peninsula, pen., Austl.	B8	74
Cap-Haïtien, Haiti	C11	102
Capilla del Monte, Arg.	E5	92
Capim, stm., Braz.	A2	88
Capinota, Bol.	C3	90
Capira, Pan.	H8	102
Capitan, N.M., U.S.	H3	128
Capitán Arturo Prat, sci., Ant.	B34	81
Capitán Bado, Para.	D5	90
Capitán Bermúdez, Arg.	F7	92
Capitán Meza, Para.	C10	92
Capitão Enéas, Braz.	I4	88
Capitola, Ca., U.S.	G4	134
Capitol Peak, mtn., Nv., U.S.	B8	134
Capitol Reef National Park, p.o.i., Ut., U.S.	E5	132
Capivara, Represa de, res., Braz.	D6	90
Capivari, Braz.	L2	88
Capivari, stm., Braz.	G6	88
Cap-Pelé, N.B., Can.	D12	110
Cappella Islands, is., V.I.U.S.	e7	104b
Capraia, Italy	G2	22
Capraia, Isola di, i., Italy	G6	22
Caprara, Punta, c., Italy	C2	24
Caprarola, Italy	C3	24
Capreol, On., Can.	B9	112
Caprera, Isola, i., Italy	C3	24
Capri, Italy	D8	24
Capri, Isola di, i., Italy	D8	24
Capricorn Channel, strt., Austl.	D9	76
Capricorn Group, is., Austl.	D9	76
Caprivi Strip, hist. reg., Nmb.	D3	68
Capron, Il., U.S.	B9	120
Captain Cook, Hi., U.S.	D6	78a
Captain Cook Monument, hist., Norf. I.	x25	78i
Captains Flat, Austl.	J7	76
Capua, Italy	C8	24
Capucin, stm., Braz.	H12	86
Capucin, c., Dom.	i5	105c
Capulin Volcano National Monument, p.o.i., N.M., U.S.	E5	128
Caquetá, state, Col.	G4	86
Caquetá (Japurá), stm., S.A.	H7	86
Cara, stm., Russia	E12	34
Carabinani, stm., Braz.	I10	86
Carabobo, state, Ven.	B7	86
Caracal, Rom.	E11	26
Caracaraí, Braz.	G11	86
Caracas, Ven.	B8	86
Caracol, Braz.	E4	88
Caraguatatuba, Braz.	L3	88
Caraguatay, Para.	B9	92
Carajás, Braz.	E7	84
Carajás, Serra dos, hills, Braz.	E7	84
Carakol, hist., Belize	D3	102
Caranavi, Bol.	C3	90
Carandaí, Braz.	K4	88
Carangola, Braz.	K4	88
Caransebeş, Rom.	D9	26
Carapá, stm., Para.	B10	92
Carapina, Braz.	B1	88
Cara-Paraná, stm., Col.	H5	86
Caraquet, N.B., Can.	C11	110
Caraş-Severin, state, Rom.	D8	26
Caratasca, Laguna de, b., Hond.	E5	102
Caratinga, Braz.	J4	88
Carauari, Braz.	D4	84
Caraúbas, Braz.	C7	88
Caravaca de la Cruz, Spain	F8	20
Caravelas, Braz.	I6	88
Caravelí, Peru	G3	84
Caravelle, Presqu'île la, pen., Mart.	k7	105c
Caraway, Ar., U.S.	B8	122
Carazinho, Braz.	D11	92
Carballiño, Spain	B2	20
Carballo, Spain	A2	20
Carberry, Mb., Can.	E14	124
Carbon, Ab., Can.	E17	138
Carbon, Tx., U.S.	B9	130
Carbonara, Capo, c., Italy	E3	24
Carbondale, Co., U.S.	D9	132
Carbondale, Il., U.S.	G8	120
Carbondale, Pa., U.S.	C10	114
Carbonear, Nf., Can.	j23	107a
Carboneras de Guadazón, Spain	E9	20
Carbon Hill, Al., U.S.	D11	122
Carbonia, Italy	E2	24
Carcagente see Carcaixent, Spain	E10	20
Carcaixent, Spain	E10	20
Carcajou, stm., N.T., Can.	B5	106
Carcans, Lac de, l., Fr.	D4	18
Carcarañá, Arg.	F7	92
Carcarañá, stm., Arg.	F7	92
Carcassonne, Fr.	F8	18
Carchi, state, Ec.	G3	86
Carcross, Yk., Can.	C3	106
Çardak, Tur.	F12	28
Çardara, Kaz.	F11	32
Cardinskoye vodohranilišče, res., Asia	A10	56
Cárdenas, Cuba	A7	102
Cárdenas, Mex.	F12	100
Cárdenas, Mex.	D9	100
Cárdenas, Bahía de, b., Cuba	A7	102
Cardiel, Arg.	I2	90
Cardiff, Wales, U.K.	J9	12
Cardigan, P.E., Can.	D14	110
Cardigan, Wales, U.K.	I8	12
Cardigan Bay, b., Wales, U.K.	I8	12
Cardona, Ur.	F9	92
Cardonal, Punta, c., Mex.	A3	100
Cardoso, Braz.	D7	88
Cardston, Ab., Can.	G17	138
Cardwell, Austl.	B5	76
Cardwell, Mo., U.S.	H7	120
Cardwell Mountain, mtn., Tn., U.S.	B13	122
Çardžev, Turkmen.	B9	56
Carei, Rom.	B9	26
Careiro, Braz.	I12	86
Careiro, Ilha do, i., Braz.	I12	86
Carencro, La., U.S.	G6	122
Carey, Oh., U.S.	D2	114
Carey, Lake, l., Austl.	E4	74
Carey Downs, Austl.	E3	74
Cargados Carajos Shoals, is., Mrts.	K9	142
Carhaix-Plouguer, Fr.	F5	14
Carhué, Arg.	H6	92
Cariacica, Braz.	K5	88
Cariaco, Golfo de, b., Ven.	B9	86
Caribbean Sea	D7	82
Cariboo Mountains, mts., B.C., Can.	D10	138
Caribou, Me., U.S.	D8	110
Caribou Lake, l., On., Can.	A9	118
Caribou Mountain, mtn., Me., U.S.	E6	110
Caribou Mountains, mts., Ab., Can.	D7	106
Carichic, Mex.	B5	100
Caridade, Braz.	C6	88
Carigara, Phil.	E5	52
Carignan, Fr.	E14	14
Carinhanha, Braz.	H4	88
Carinhanha, stm., Braz.	H3	88
Carini, Italy	F7	24
Carinthia see Kärnten, state, Aus.	D10	22
Caripito, Ven.	B10	86
Carira, Braz.	F7	88
Cariré, Braz.	C5	88
Cariús, Braz.	D6	88
Carleton, Mi., U.S.	B2	114
Carleton, Mount, mtn., N.B., Can.	C10	110
Carleton Place, On., Can.	C13	112
Carletonville, S. Afr.	E8	70
Cârlibaba, Rom.	B12	26
Carlin, Nv., U.S.	C9	134
Carlingford Lough, b., Eur.	H7	12
Carlinville, Il., U.S.	E8	120
Carlisle, Eng., U.K.	G9	12
Carlisle, Ar., U.S.	C7	122
Carlisle, Ia., U.S.	C4	120
Carlisle, Ky., U.S.	F1	114
Carlisle, Pa., U.S.	D8	114
Carlos, Isla, i., Chile	J2	90
Carlos Casares, Arg.	G7	92
Carlos Chagas, Braz.	I5	88
Carlos Pellegrini, Arg.	E6	92
Carlow, Ire.	I5	12
Carlow, state, Ire.	I6	12
Carlsbad see Karlovy Vary, Czech Rep.	F8	16
Carlsbad, Ca., U.S.	J8	134
Carlsbad, N.M., U.S.	B3	130
Carlsbad, Tx., U.S.	C7	130
Carlsbad Caverns National Park, p.o.i., N.M., U.S.	B3	130
Carlsberg Ridge, unds.	I9	142
Carlton, Or., U.S.	E3	136
Carlton, Tx., U.S.	C9	130
Carlyle, Sk., Can.	E11	124
Carlyle Lake, res., Il., U.S.	F8	120
Carmacks, Yk., Can.	C3	106
Carmagnola, Italy	F4	22
Carman, Mb., Can.	E16	124
Carmangay, Ab., Can.	F17	138
Carmarthen, Wales, U.K.	J8	12
Carmarthen Bay, b., Wales, U.K.	J8	12
Carmel, Ca., U.S.	G3	134
Carmel, In., U.S.	I3	112
Carmel Head, c., Wales, U.K.	H8	12
Carmelo, Ur.	F8	92
Carmen see Ciudad del Carmen, Mex.	F12	100
Carmen, stm., Chile	D2	92
Carmen, Isla, i., Mex.	C3	100
Carmen, Isla del, i., Mex.	F13	100
Carmen de Areco, Arg.	G8	92
Carmen de Patagones, Arg.	H4	90
Carmi, Il., U.S.	F9	120
Carmila, Austl.	C7	76
Carmine, Tx., U.S.	D11	130
Carmo do Paranaíba, Braz.	J2	88
Carmona, Spain	G5	20
Carmópolis de Minas, Braz.	K3	88
Carnarvon, Austl.	D2	74
Carnarvon, S. Afr.	G5	70
Carnarvon National Park, p.o.i., Austl.	E6	76
Çarnaučycy, Bela.	H6	10
Carnduff, Sk., Can.	E12	124
Carnegie, Austl.	E4	74
Carnegie, Lake, l., Austl.	E4	74
Carney Island, i., Ant.	C29	81
Carnia, reg., Italy	D9	22
Carnic Alps, mts., Eur.	D9	22
Car Nicobar Island, i., India	G7	46
Carnot, C.A.R.	D3	66
Carnoustie, Scot., U.K.	E10	12
Carnsore Point, c., Ire.	I6	12
Carnwath, stm., N.T., Can.	B5	106
Caro, Mi., U.S.	E6	112
Carol City, Fl., U.S.	K5	116
Carolina, Braz.	D2	88
Carolina, P.R.	B4	104a
Carolina, S. Afr.	E10	70
Carolina Beach, N.C., U.S.	B8	116
Caroline, at., Kir.	D12	72
Caroline Islands, is., Oc.	C5	72
Caron, Sk., Can.	D8	124
Caroní, stm., Ven.	C10	86
Carora, Ven.	B6	86
Carpathian Mountains, mts., Eur.	B13	26
Carpați Meridionali (Transylvanian Alps), mts., Rom.	D11	26
Carpentaria, Gulf of, b., Austl.	B7	74
Carpenter, Wy., U.S.	F8	126
Carpenter Lake, res., B.C., Can.	F8	138
Carpentersville, Il., U.S.	B9	120
Carpentras, Fr.	E11	18
Carpi, Italy	F7	22
Carpina, Braz.	D8	88
Cărpineni, Mol.	C15	26
Carpio, N.D., U.S.	F12	124
Carp Lake, l., B.C., Can.	B7	138
Carpolac, Austl.	K3	76
Carrabelle, Fl., U.S.	H14	122
Carranza, Cabo, c., Chile	G1	92
Carrara, Italy	F7	22
Carrathool, Austl.	J5	76
Carriacou, i., Gren.	q11	105e
Carrick-on-Shannon, Ire.	H4	12
Carrick-on-Suir, Ire.	I5	12
Carrie, Mount, mtn., Wa., U.S.	C3	136
Carriers Mills, Il., U.S.	G9	120
Carrieton, Austl.	I2	76
Carrillo, Mex.	B6	100
Carrington, N.D., U.S.	G14	124
Carrión, stm., Spain	B6	20
Carrión de los Condes, Spain	B6	20
Carrizal Bajo, Chile	D2	92
Carrizo Creek, stm., U.S.	E5	128
Carrizo Mountain, mtn., N.M., U.S.	H3	128
Carrizo Springs, Tx., U.S.	F7	130
Carroll, Ne., U.S.	E15	126
Carrollton, Al., U.S.	D10	122
Carrollton, Ga., U.S.	D13	122
Carrollton, Il., U.S.	E7	120
Carrollton, Ky., U.S.	F12	120
Carrollton, Mi., U.S.	E5	112
Carrollton, Ms., U.S.	D8	122
Carrollton, Mo., U.S.	E4	120
Carrollton, Oh., U.S.	D4	114
Carrollton, Tx., U.S.	A10	130
Carrolltown, Pa., U.S.	D7	114
Carron, stm., Austl.	A3	76
Carrot, stm., Can.	E10	106
Carrot River, Sk., Can.	A10	124
Carry Falls Reservoir, res., N.Y., U.S.	F2	110
Carseland, Ab., Can.	F17	138
Carsk, Kaz.	E14	32
Carson, N.D., U.S.	A11	126
Carson, Wa., U.S.	E5	136
Carson, East Fork, stm., U.S.	E6	134
Carson City, Nv., U.S.	D6	134
Carson Lake, res., Nv., U.S.	D7	134
Carson Range, mts., U.S.	D6	134
Carson Sink, l., Nv., U.S.	D7	134
Carstairs, Ab., Can.	E16	138
Cartagena, Col.	B4	86
Cartagena, Spain	G9	20
Cartago, Col.	E3	86
Cartago, C.R.	H6	102
Cartaxo, Port.	E2	20
Cartaya, Spain	G3	20
Carter, Ok., U.S.	F9	128
Carter Lake, Ia., U.S.	C2	120
Cartersville, Ga., U.S.	C14	122
Carthage, Tun.	H4	24
Carthage, Ar., U.S.	C6	122
Carthage, Il., U.S.	D6	120
Carthage, Ms., U.S.	E9	122
Carthage, Mo., U.S.	G3	120
Carthage, N.C., U.S.	A6	116
Carthage, N.Y., U.S.	E14	112
Carthage, S.D., U.S.	C15	126
Carthage, Tn., U.S.	H11	120
Carthage, Tx., U.S.	E4	122
Carthage, hist., Tun.	H4	24
Cartier Islands, is., Austl.	B4	74
Cartwright, Mb., Can.	E14	124
Carúpano, Ven.	B10	86
Caruaru, Braz.	D8	88
Carutapera, Braz.	A3	88
Caruthersville, Mo., U.S.	H8	120
Carutu, stm., Ven.	E10	86
Carvoeiro, Braz.	H10	86
Carvoeiro, Cabo, c., Port.	E1	20
Cary, Ms., U.S.	E8	122
Cary, N.C., U.S.	I7	114
Čaryšskoje, Russia	D14	32
Caryville, Fl., U.S.	G13	122
Casablanca (Dar-el-Beida), Mor.	C3	64
Casa Branca, Braz.	K2	88
Casa de Piedra, Embalse, res., Arg.	I4	92
Casa Grande, Az., U.S.	K5	132
Casa Grande Ruins National Monument, p.o.i. Az., U.S.	K5	132
Casale Monferrato, Italy	E5	22
Casanare, state, Col.	D6	86
Casanare, stm., Col.	D6	86
Casa Nova, Braz.	E5	88
Casarano, Italy	D12	24
Casar de Cáceres, Spain	E4	20
Casas Adobes, Az., U.S.	K5	132
Casas Grandes, stm., Mex.	F9	98
Casavieja, Spain	D6	20
Casca, Braz.	D12	92
Cascade, B.C., Can.	G12	138
Cascade, Ia., U.S.	B6	120
Cascade, Mt., U.S.	C15	136
Cascade Bay, b., Norf. I.	y25	78i
Cascade Mountains see Cascade Range, mts., N.A.	C3	108
Cascade Range, mts., N.A.	C3	108
Cascade Reservoir, res., Id., U.S.	F10	136
Cascais, Port.	F1	20
Cascapédia, stm., Qc., Can.	B10	110
Cascavel, Braz.	C6	88
Cascavel, Braz.	B11	92
Cascina, Italy	G7	22
Case-Pilote, Mart.	k6	105c
Caserta, Italy	C8	24
Caseville, Mi., U.S.	E6	112
Casey, Il., U.S.	E9	120
Casey, sci., Ant.	B16	81
Casey, Mount, mtn., Id., U.S.	B10	136
Cashel, Ire.	I5	12
Cashiers, N.C., U.S.	A2	116
Cashmere, Wa., U.S.	C6	136
Cashton, Wi., U.S.	H8	118
Casigua, Ven.	C5	86
Casilda, Arg.	F7	92
Casino, Austl.	G9	76
Casiquiare, stm., Ven.	F8	86
Čáslav, Czech Rep.	G11	16
Casma, Peru	E2	84
Časniki, Bela.	F12	10
Casoli, Italy	H11	22
Caspe, Spain	C10	20
Casper, Wy., U.S.	E6	126
Caspian Depression (Prikaspijskaja nizmennost'), pl.	E7	32
Caspian Sea	F7	32
Cass, stm., Mi., U.S.	E6	112
Cass City, Mi., U.S.	E6	112
Casselman, On., Can.	C2	110
Casselton, N.D., U.S.	B11	114
Cassia, Braz.	K2	88
Cassiar, B.C., Can.	D5	106
Cassiar Mountains, mts., Can.	D5	106
Cassilândia, Braz.	C6	90
Cassinga, Ang.	D2	68
Cassino, Italy	C7	24
Cass Lake, Mn., U.S.	D4	118
Cass Lake, l., Mn., U.S.	D4	118
Cassongue, Ang.	C1	68
Cassopolis, Mi., U.S.	G3	112
Cassville, Mo., U.S.	H4	120
Cassville, Wi., U.S.	B7	120
Castagniccia, reg., Fr.	G15	18
Castanheira de Pêra, Port.	E3	20
Castanhal, Braz.	A1	88
Castaño, stm., Arg.	E3	92
Castaños, Mex.	H6	130
Castelbuono, Italy	G8	24
Castellabate, Italy	D8	24
Castellammare, Golfo di, b., Italy	F6	24
Castellammare del Golfo, Italy	F6	24
Castellammare di Stabia, Italy	D8	24
Castellana Grotte, Italy	D11	24
Castellane, Fr.	F12	18
Castellaneta, Italy	D10	24
Castelli, Arg.	H9	92
Castelló, Spain	D10	20
Castelló de la Plana see Castellón de la Plana, Spain	E11	20
Castellón de la Plana, Spain	E11	20
Castelnaudary, Fr.	F7	18
Castelnau-Montratier, Fr.	E7	18
Castelo, Braz.	K5	88
Castelo Branco, Port.	E3	20
Castelo Branco, state, Port.	E3	20
Castelo de Paiva, Port.	C2	20
Castel San Giovanni, Italy	E6	22
Castelsarrasin, Fr.	E6	18
Casteltermini, Italy	G7	24
Castelvetrano, Italy	G7	24
Casterton, Austl.	K3	76
Castets, Fr.	F4	18
Castile, N.Y., U.S.	B7	114
Castilla, Peru	E1	84
Castilla, Playa de, cst., Spain	G4	20
Castilla-La Mancha, state, Spain	E9	20
Castilla la Nueva, hist. reg., Spain	E7	20
Castilla la Vieja (Old Castille), hist. reg., Spain	C7	20
Castilla y León, state, Spain	C6	20
Castillo de San Marcos National Monument, p.o.i., Fl., U.S.	F5	116
Castillo Incaico de Ingapirca, hist., Ec.	I2	86
Castillon-la-Bataille, Fr.	E5	18
Castillos, Ur.	G11	92
Castillos, Laguna de, l., Ur.	G11	92
Castine, Me., U.S.	F8	110
Castlebar, Ire.	H3	12
Castle Bruce, Dom.	j6	105c
Castle Dome Peak, mtn., Az., U.S.	J2	132
Castleford, Eng., U.K.	H11	12
Castle Hills, Tx., U.S.	E9	130
Castleisland, Ire.	I3	12
Castlemaine, Austl.	K5	76
Castle Mountain, mtn., Yk., Can.	C3	106
Castle Peak, mtn., Co., U.S.	D10	132
Castlerea, Ire.	H4	12
Castlereagh, stm., Austl.	H7	76
Castle Rock, Co., U.S.	B3	128
Castle Rock, Wa., U.S.	D3	136
Castle Rock, mtn., Or., U.S.	F8	136
Castle Rock Butte, mtn., S.D., U.S.	B9	126
Castle Rock Lake, res., Wi., U.S.	H8	118
Castletown, I. of Man	G8	12
Castlewood, S.D., U.S.	C15	126
Castor, Ab., Can.	D19	138
Castor, stm., Mo., U.S.	G7	120
Castres, Fr.	F8	18
Castries, St. Luc.	l6	105c
Castro, Braz.	B13	92
Castro, Chile	H2	90
Castro Barros, Arg.	E5	92
Castro Daire, Port.	D3	20
Castro del Río, Spain	G6	20
Castronuño, Spain	C5	20
Castro Verde, Port.	G2	20
Castrovillari, Italy	E10	24
Castroville, Ca., U.S.	G4	134
Catacamas, Hond.	E5	102
Catacaos, Peru	E1	84
Catacocha, Ec.	D2	84
Cataguases, Braz.	K4	88
Catahoula Lake, l., La., U.S.	F6	122
Catalão, Braz.	J2	88
Çatalca, Tur.	B11	28
Catalina see Santa Catalina Island, i., Ca., U.S.	J7	134
Catalina, Punta, c., Chile	J3	90
Catalonia see Catalunya, state, Spain	C12	20
Cataluña see Catalunya, state, Spain	C12	20
Catalunya, state, Spain	C12	20
Catamarca, state, Arg.	C4	92
Catanauan, Phil.	D4	52
Catanduanes Island, i., Phil.	D5	52
Catanduva, Braz.	K1	88
Catania, Italy	G9	24
Catania, Golfo di, b., Italy	G9	24
Cataño, P.R.	B3	104a
Catanzaro, Italy	F10	24
Cataract Canyon, val., Az., U.S.	H4	132
Catarina, Braz.	D6	88
Catarino Rodríguez, Mex.	C8	100
Catarman, Phil.	D5	52
Catarroja, Spain	E10	20
Catatumbo, stm., Ven.	C5	86
Catawba, stm., U.S.	A4	116
Catawissa, Pa., U.S.	D9	114
Cat Ba, Dao, i., Viet.	B8	48
Catbalogan, Phil.	E5	52
Catete, Ang.	B1	68
Cathcart, S. Afr.	H8	70
Cathedral City, Ca., U.S.	J9	134
Catherine, Mount see Katherine, Gebel, mtn., Egypt	J4	58
Catherines Peak, mtn., Jam.	i14	104d
Cat Island, i., Bah.	C9	96
Cat Lake, l., On., Can.	E12	106
Catlettsburg, Ky., U.S.	F3	114
Catlin, Il., U.S.	H2	112
Catoche, Cabo, c., Mex.	B4	102
Catolé do Rocha, Braz.	D7	88
Catoosa, Ok., U.S.	H2	120
Catriló, Arg.	H6	92
Catrimani, stm., Braz.	G11	86
Catskill, N.Y., U.S.	B12	114
Catskill Mountains, mts., N.Y., U.S.	B11	114
Catt, Mount, mtn., Austl.	B6	74
Cattaraugus, N.Y., U.S.	B7	114
Cattolica, Italy	G9	22
Catu, Braz.	G6	88
Catuane, Moz.	E11	70
Catur, Moz.	C6	68
Catwick, Îles, is., Viet.	G9	48
Catyrtaš, Kyrg.	F13	32
Cau, stm., Viet.	B8	48
Cauaburi, stm., Braz.	G8	86
Caubvick, Mount see Iberville, Mont d', mtn., Can.	F13	141
Cauca, state, Col.	F3	86
Cauca, stm., Col.	D4	86
Caucaia, Braz.	B6	88
Caucasia, Col.	D4	86
Caucasus, mts.	F6	32
Caucete, Arg.	E3	92
Cauchari, Salar de, pl., Arg.	D3	90
Caudry, Fr.	D12	14
Caungula, Ang.	B2	68
Cauquenes, Chile	H1	92
Caura, stm., Ven.	D9	86
Caurés, stm., Braz.	H10	86
Căuşani, Mol.	C16	26
Causapscal, Qc., Can.	B9	110
Caussade, Fr.	E7	18
Cauto, stm., Cuba	B9	102
Caux, Pays de, reg., Fr.	E9	14
Cávado, stm., Port.	C2	20
Cavaillon, Fr.	F11	18
Cavalese, Italy	D8	22
Cavalier, N.D., U.S.	F16	124
Cavally (Cavally), stm., Afr.	H3	64
Cavan, Ire.	H5	12
Cavan, state, Ire.	H5	12
Cavarzere, Italy	E9	22
Çavdar, Tur.	F12	28
Çavdır, Tur.	F12	28
Cave City, Ky., U.S.	G11	120
Cave In Rock, Il., U.S.	G9	120
Caveiras, stm., Braz.	C12	92
Cavendish, Austl.	K4	76
Cave Run Lake, res., Ky., U.S.	F2	114
Cave Spring, Ga., U.S.	C13	122
Caviana de Fora, Ilha, i., Braz.	C8	84
Cavite, Phil.	C3	52
Cavour, Canale, can., Italy	E5	22
Çavuş, Tur.	A2	58
Çavuşy, Bela.	G14	10
Cawood, Ky., U.S.	H2	114
Cawston, B.C., Can.	G11	138
Caxambu, Braz.	K3	88
Caxias, Braz.	C4	88
Caxias do Sul, Braz.	D12	92
Cay, Tur.	E13	28
Cayambe, Ec.	G2	86
Cayambe, vol., Ec.	G3	86
Cayce, S.C., U.S.	C4	116
Caycuma, Tur.	B15	28
Çay Duong, Vinh, b., Viet.	G7	48
Cayenne, Fr. Gu.	C7	84
Cayey, P.R.	B3	104a
Caylus, Fr.	E7	18
Cayman Brac, i., Cay. Is.	C8	102
Cayman Islands, dep., N.A.	C7	102
Caynaba, Som.	C9	66
Cayon, St. K./N.	C2	105a
Cayuga, In., U.S.	I2	112
Cayuga, Tx., U.S.	F3	122
Cayuga Heights, N.Y., U.S.	B9	114
Cayuga Lake, res., N.Y., U.S.	B9	114
Cazalla de la Sierra, Spain	G5	20
Cazaux et de Sanguinet, Étang de, l., Fr.	E4	18
Cazères, Fr.	F6	18
Cazombo, Ang.	C3	68
Cazorla, Spain	G7	20
Cea, stm., Spain	C5	20
Ceanannus see Kells, Ire.	H6	12
Ceará, state, Braz.	C6	88
Ceará-Mirim, Braz.	C8	88
Ceará-Mirim, stm., Braz.	C8	88
Ceatharlach see Carlow, Ire.	I5	12
Cebaco, Isla de, i., Pan.	I7	102
Ceballos, Mex.	B6	100
Çeboksary, Russia	C7	32
Cebollar, Arg.	D4	92
Cebollas, Mex.	D6	100
Cebollatí, Ur.	F11	92
Cebollatí, stm., Ur.	F10	92
Cébonuco, Volcán, vol., Mex.	E6	100
Cebu, Phil.	E4	52
Cebu, i., Phil.	E4	52
Cebu Strait, strt., Phil.	F4	52
Ceceda, Mex.	H4	130
Cechtice, Czech Rep.	G11	16
Cechy, hist. reg., Czech Rep.	G10	16
Cecil, Ga., U.S.	E2	116
Cecilia, Ky., U.S.	G12	120
Cecina, Italy	G7	22
Cecina, stm., Italy	G7	22
Čečnja, state, Russia	F7	32
Cedar, stm., U.S.	J7	118
Cedar, stm., Ne., U.S.	F14	126
Cedar Bluffs, Ne., U.S.	J2	118
Cedar Breaks National Monument, p.o.i., Ut., U.S.	F3	132
Cedarburg, Wi., U.S.	E1	112
Cedar City, Ut., U.S.	F3	132
Cedar Creek, stm., Id., U.S.	B12	132
Cedar Creek, stm., N.D., U.S.	A11	126
Cedar Falls, Ia., U.S.	B5	120
Cedar Grove, Wi., U.S.	E2	112
Cedar Hill, Tn., U.S.	H10	120
Cedar Key, Fl., U.S.	G2	116
Cedar Lake, l., In., U.S.	G2	112
Cedar Lake, l., On., Can.	B5	112
Cedar Lake, res., Mb., Can.	E10	106
Cedar Mountain, mtn., Ca., U.S.	B5	134
Cedar Rapids, Ia., U.S.	C6	120
Cedars of Lebanon see Arz Lubnān, for., Leb.	D7	58
Cedar Springs, Mi., U.S.	E4	112
Cedartown, Ga., U.S.	C13	122
Cedar Tree Point, c., Antig.	e4	105b
Cedarvale, B.C., Can.	A1	138
Cedar Vale, Ks., U.S.	D12	128
Cedarville, Ca., U.S.	B5	134
Cedeira, Spain	A2	20
Cedillo, Embalse de, res., Eur.	E3	20
Cedral, Mex.	D8	100
Cedros, Isla, i., Mex.	A1	100
Ceduna, Austl.	F6	74
Ceelbuur, Som.	D9	66
Ceel Dheere, Som.	D9	66
Ceerigaabo, Som.	B9	66
Cefalonia see Kefallinía, i., Grc.	E3	28
Cefalù, Italy	F8	24
Cega, stm., Spain	C6	20
Cegdomyn, Russia	F15	34
Cegléd, Hung.	B6	26
Ceglie Messapico, Italy	D11	24
Čehov, Russia	E20	10
Čehov, Russia	G17	34
Çekerek, stm., Tur.	A4	58
Çekerek, Tur.	C15	28
Celâkovice, Czech Rep.	F10	16
Celano, Italy	H10	22
Celaya, Mex.	E8	100
Celebes see Sulawesi, i., Indon.	F7	44
Celebes Basin, unds.	I15	142
Celebes Sea, Asia	E7	44
Celeken, Turkmen.	B7	56
Celeste, Tx., U.S.	D2	122
Celestún, Mex.	B2	102
Čeljabinsk, Russia	C10	32
Çeljahany, Bela.	H8	10
Čeljuskin, Mys, c., Russia	A10	34
Celje, Slvn.	D12	22
Çelkar, Kaz.	E9	32
Celle, Ger.	D6	16
Celtic Sea, Eur.	J6	12
Çeltik, Tur.	D14	28
Çemal, Russia	D15	32
Cement, Ok., U.S.	G10	128
Cenajo, Embalse del, res., Spain	F9	20
Cenderawasih, Teluk, b., Indon.	F10	44
Cenovo, Blg.	F12	26
Centenario, Arg.	H3	92
Centenário do Sul, Braz.	D7	90
Center, N.D., U.S.	G12	124
Center, Ne., U.S.	E15	126
Center, Tx., U.S.	F4	122
Centerburg, Oh., U.S.	D3	114
Centerfield, Ut., U.S.	D5	132
Center Hill, Fl., U.S.	H3	116
Center Hill Lake, res., Tn., U.S.	H12	120
Center Moriches, N.Y., U.S.	D13	114
Center Point, Al., U.S.	D12	122
Center Point, Ia., U.S.	B6	120
Centerville, Ia., U.S.	D5	120
Centerville, Mo., U.S.	G7	120

Name	Map Ref.	Page
Centerville, Pa., U.S.	D5	114
Centerville, Tn., U.S.	B11	122
Centerville, Tx., U.S.	F2	122
Centerville, Ut., U.S.	C4	132
Central, Braz.	F4	88
Central, Phil.	D3	52
Central, Az., U.S.	K7	132
Central, N.M., U.S.	K8	132
Central, state, Bots.	C8	70
Central, state, Para.	B9	92
Central, state, Sol. Is.	e8	79b
Central, Cordillera, mts., Col.	E4	86
Central, Cordillera, mts., Peru	E2	84
Central, Cordillera, mts., Phil.	B3	52
Central, Cordillera, mts., P.R.	B2	104a
Central, Massif, mts., Fr.	D8	18
Central, Sistema, mts., Spain	D6	20
Central African Republic, ctry., Afr.	C4	66
Central Aguirre, P.R.	C3	104a
Central Arizona Project Aqueduct, aq., U.S.	J3	132
Central Bohemia see Středočeský, state, Czech Rep.	G10	16
Central Borneo see Kalimantan Tengah, state, Indon.	D8	50
Central Brāhui Range, mts., Pak.	D10	56
Central Celebes see Sulawesi Tengah, state, Indon.	D12	50
Central City, Il., U.S.	F8	120
Central City, Ia., U.S.	B6	120
Central City, Ky., U.S.	G10	120
Central City, Pa., U.S.	D7	114
Central Division, state, Fiji	q19	79e
Centralia, Il., U.S.	F8	120
Centralia, Ks., U.S.	E1	120
Centralia, Mo., U.S.	E5	120
Centralia, Wa., U.S.	D4	136
Centralina, Braz.	J1	88
Central Java see Jawa Tengah, state, Indon.	G7	50
Central Kalahari Game Reserve, Bots.	C6	70
Central Lake, Mi., U.S.	C4	112
Central Makrān Range, mts., Pak.	D9	56
Central'nyj, Russia	C15	32
Central Pacific Basin, unds.	I21	142
Central Point, Or., U.S.	A2	134
Central Range, mts., Pap. N. Gui.	a3	79a
Central Russian Upland see Srednerusskaja vozvyšennost', plat., Russia	H20	10
Central Siberian Plateau see Srednesibirskoe ploskogor'e, plat., Russia	C13	34
Central Siberian Uplands see Srednesibirskoe ploskogor'e, plat., Russia	C13	34
Central Slovakia see Stredoslovenský Kraj, state, Slov.	H15	16
Central Utah Canal, can., Ut., U.S.	D4	132
Central Valley, Ca., U.S.	C3	134
Central Valley see Longitudinal, Valle, val., Chile	H1	92
Centre, Canal du, can., Fr.	C10	18
Centreville, Al., U.S.	E11	122
Centreville, Md., U.S.	E9	114
Centreville, Ms., U.S.	F7	122
Centro Puntas, P.R.	B1	104a
Century, Fl., U.S.	G11	122
Ceos see Kéa, i., Grc.	F7	28
Čepelare, Blg.	H11	26
Cephalonia see Kefallinía, i., Grc.	E3	28
Cepu, Indon.	G7	50
Ceram see Seram, i., Indon.	F8	44
Ceram Sea see Seram, Laut, Indon.	F8	44
Čerčany, Czech Rep.	G10	16
Cerdas, Bol.	D3	90
Cereal, Ab., Can.	C3	124
Čereha, stm., Russia	C11	10
Čeremhovo, Russia	D18	32
Čeremšany, Russia	B11	38
Čerepanovo, Russia	D14	32
Čerepet', Russia	F19	10
Čerepovec, Russia	A20	10
Ceres, Arg.	D7	92
Ceres, Braz.	G8	84
Ceres, S. Afr.	H4	70
Ceresco, Ne., U.S.	J2	118
Ceresio see Lugano, Lago di, l., Eur.	D14	18
Cereté, Col.	C4	86
Čerevkovo, Russia	F21	8
Cerignola, Italy	C9	24
Cérilly, Fr.	H11	14
Çerkeş, Tur.	C15	28
Čerkessk, Russia	F6	32
Çerkezköy, Tur.	B10	28
Čerlak, Russia	D12	32
Cermei, Rom.	C8	26
Čermoz, Russia	C9	32
Cerna, Rom.	D15	26
Černá hora, mtn., Czech Rep.	G9	16
Cernavodă, Rom.	E15	26
Cernay, Fr.	G16	14
Černigovka, Russia	B10	38
Černjahovsk, Russia	F4	10
Černogorsk, Russia	D16	32
Černuška, Russia	C9	32
Černyševsk, Russia	F12	34
Černyševskij, Russia	D11	34
Cerralvo, Isla, i., Mex.	C4	100
Cërrik, Alb.	C14	24
Cërriku see Cërrik, Alb.	C14	24
Cerrillos, Arg.	B5	92
Cerrillos, N.M., U.S.	F2	128
Cerritos, Mex.	D8	100
Cerro Azul, Arg.	C10	92
Cerro Azul, Mex.	E9	100
Cerro Azul, Peru	F2	84
Cerro Chato, Ur.	F10	92
Cerro de las Mesas, hist., Mex.	F10	100
Cerro de Pasco, Peru	F2	84
Cerro Gordo, Il., U.S.	E9	120
Cerro Largo, Braz.	D10	92
Cerro Moreno, Chile	A2	92
Cerrón, Cerro, mtn., Ven.	B6	86
Cerrón Grande, Embalse, res., El Sal.	E3	102
Cerro Prieto, Mex.	K10	134
Cerros Colorados, Embalse, res., Arg.	I3	92
Cerro Tololo, Observatorio Astronómico, sci., Chile	E2	92
Čerskij, Russia	C21	34
Čerskogo, hrebet (Cherskiy Mountains), mts., Russia	C17	34
Čertolino, Russia	D16	10
Čèrven', Bela.	G11	10
Červen Brjag, Blg.	F11	26
Cervera, Spain	C12	20
Cervera de Pisuerga, Spain	B6	20
Cervia, Italy	F9	22
Cervialto, Monte, mtn., Italy	D9	24
Cervino see Matterhorn, mtn., Eur.	D13	18
Cervione, Fr.	G15	18
Cervo, Spain	A3	20
Cesar, state, Col.	C5	86
Cesar, stm., Col.	B5	86
Cesena, Italy	F9	22
Cesenatico, Italy	F9	22
Cēsis, Lat.	C8	10
Česká Kamenice, Czech Rep.	F10	16
Česká Lípa, Czech Rep.	F10	16
Česká Třebová, Czech Rep.	G12	16
České Budějovice, Czech Rep.	H10	16
Český Brod, Czech Rep.	F10	16
Çeşme, Tur.	E9	28
Češskaja guba (Chesha Bay), b., Russia	C21	8
Cessnock, Austl.	I8	76
Cesvaine, Lat.	D9	10
Cetina, stm., Cro.	G13	22
Cetinje, Yugo.	G5	26
Ceuta, Sp. N. Afr.	B3	64
Cévennes, reg., Fr.	E9	18
Cévennes, Parc National des, p.o.i., Fr.	E9	18
Cevizli, Tur.	F14	28
Ceyhan, Tur.	A6	58
Ceyhan, stm., Tur.	B6	58
Ceylon, Mn., U.S.	H4	118
Ceylon see Sri Lanka, ctry., Asia	G5	53
Cèze, stm., Fr.	E10	18
Cha-am, Thai.	F5	48
Chabanais, Fr.	D6	18
Chabás, Arg.	F7	92
Chabjuwardoo Bay, b., Austl.	D2	74
Chablais, reg., Fr.	C12	18
Chacabuco, Arg.	G7	92
Chachani, Nevado, vol., Peru	G3	84
Chachapoyas, Peru	E2	84
Chāchora, India	F6	54
Chāchro, Pak.	F3	54
Chaco, state, Arg.	C7	92
Chaco, stm., N.M., U.S.	G8	132
Chaco, Parque Nacional, p.o.i., Arg.	C8	92
Chaco Austral, reg., Arg.	C7	92
Chaco Boreal, reg., Para.	D4	90
Chaco Central, reg., Arg.	D4	90
Chaco Mesa, mtn., N.M., U.S.	H9	132
Chad, ctry., Afr.	E3	62
Chad, Lake, l., Afr.	G7	64
Chadbourn, N.C., U.S.	B7	116
Chadian, China	H1	42
Chadron, Ne., U.S.	E10	126
Chadwick, Il., U.S.	I9	118
Chaem, stm., Thai.	C4	48
Chāgai, Pak.	D9	56
Chāgai Hills, hills, Asia	D9	56
Chagos Archipelago, is., B.I.O.T.	J10	142
Chagos-Lacadive Plateau, unds.	J10	142
Chaguanas, Trin.	s12	105f
Chaguaramas, Ven.	C8	86
Chahal, Guat.	E3	102
Chahanwusu see Dulan, China	D4	36
Chahār Borjak, Afg.	C9	56
Chahe, China	E4	36
Chāībāsa, India	G10	54
Chaihe, China	B8	38
Chai Nat, Thai.	E4	48
Chaiya, Thai.	H4	48
Chaiyaphum, Thai.	E6	48
Chajarí, Arg.	E8	92
Chakaria, Bngl.	H14	54
Chākdaha, India	G12	54
Chake Chake, Tan.	F7	66
Chākia, India	E10	54
Chakkarat, Thai.	E6	48
Chakradharpur, India	G10	54
Chāksu, India	E5	54
Chakwāl, Pak.	B4	54
Chala, Peru	G3	84
Chalais, Fr.	D6	18
Chalatenango, El Sal.	F3	102
Chalaxung, China	E4	36
Chalbi Desert, des., Kenya	D7	66
Chalcidice see Chalkidikí, hist. reg., Grc.	C6	28
Chalcis see Chalkída, Grc.	E6	28
Chaleur Bay, b., Can.	C11	110
Chalía, stm., Arg.	I2	90
Chālisgaon, India	H5	54
Chalke see Chálki, i., Grc.	G10	28
Chálki, i., Grc.	G10	28
Chalkída, Grc.	E6	28
Chalkidikí, hist. reg., Grc.	C6	28
Chalk River, On., Can.	B12	112
Challakere, India	D3	53
Challapata, Bol.	C3	90
Challenger Deep, unds.	H17	142
Chalmette, La., U.S.	H9	122
Châlons-sur-Marne, Fr.	F13	14
Chalon-sur-Saône, Fr.	H13	14
Chalosse, reg., Fr.	F5	18
Chaltel, Cerro (Fitz Roy, Monte), mtn., S.A.	I2	90
Chaluhe, China	C6	38
Cham, Ger.	G8	16
Chama, N.M., U.S.	G10	132
Chama, stm., U.S.	E2	128
Chama, stm., Ven.	C6	86
Chamaicó, Arg.	G5	92
Chaman, Pak.	C10	56
Chamba, India	B6	54
Chambal, stm., India	E6	54
Chamberlain, Sk., Can.	D8	124
Chamberlain, S.D., U.S.	D13	126
Chamberlain, stm., Austl.	C5	74
Chamberlain Lake, l., Me., U.S.	D7	110
Chambers, Ne., U.S.	E14	126
Chambersburg, Pa., U.S.	E8	114
Chambers Island, i., Wi., U.S.	C2	112
Chambéry, Fr.	D11	18
Chambi, Jebel, mtn., Tun.	B6	64
Chamblee, Ga., U.S.	D14	122
Chambord, Qc., Can.	B4	110
Chamdo see Qamdo, China	E4	36
Chamical, Arg.	E4	92
Chamo, Lake see Ch'amo Hāyk', l., Eth.	F7	62
Ch'amo Hāyk', l., Eth.	F7	62
Chamois, Mo., U.S.	F6	120
Chamoli, India	C7	54
Chamonix-Mont-Blanc, Fr.	D12	18
Chāmpa, India	G9	54
Champagne, hist. reg., Fr.	F13	14
Champagne Castle, mtn., S. Afr.	F9	70
Champagnole, Fr.	H14	14
Champaign, Il., U.S.	D9	120
Champaquí, Cerro, mtn., Arg.	F5	92
Champasak, Laos	E7	48
Champdoré, Lac, l., Qc., Can.	D17	106
Champion, Ab., Can.	F17	138
Champion, Mi., U.S.	B1	112
Champion, Oh., U.S.	G9	112
Champlain, Lake, l., N.A.	D16	112
Champlitte-et-le-Prélot, Fr.	G14	14
Champotón, Mex.	C2	102
Chāmrājnagar Rāmasamudram, India	F3	53
Chana, Thai.	I5	48
Chañar, Arg.	E4	92
Chañaral, Chile	C2	92
Chañaral, Isla, i., Chile	D2	92
Chancay, Peru	F2	84
Chanchiang see Zhanjiang, China	K4	42
Chanco, Chile	G1	92
Chandalar, Ak., U.S.	C10	140
Chandalar, stm., Ak., U.S.	C10	140
Chandannagar, India	G11	54
Chandausi, India	D7	54
Chāndbāli, India	H11	54
Chandeleur Islands, is., La., U.S.	H10	122
Chandeleur Sound, strt., La., U.S.	H9	122
Chandīgarh, India	C6	54
Chandler, Qc., Can.	B12	110
Chandler, Az., U.S.	J5	132
Chandler, In., U.S.	F10	120
Chandler, Tx., U.S.	E3	122
Chandlerville, Il., U.S.	D7	120
Chāndpur, Bngl.	G13	54
Chāndpur, Bngl.	G14	54
Chāndpur, India	D7	54
Chandrapur, India	B4	53
Chāndvad, India	H5	54
Chang (Yangtze), stm., China	F8	36
Chang, stm., China	G1	42
Chang, Ko, i., Thai.	F6	48
Changan see Xi'an, China	D3	42
Changanācheri, India	G3	53
Changane, stm., Moz.	D11	70
Changcheng, China	L3	42
Chang Cheng (Great Wall), misc. cult., China	D6	36
Chang Chenmo, stm., Asia	A7	54
Changchiak'ou see Zhangjiakou, China	A6	42
Ch'angchih see Changzhi, China	C5	42
Changchou see Changzhou, China	F8	42
Changchou see Zhangzhou, China	I7	42
Changchow see Changzhou, China	F8	42
Changchow see Zhangzhou, China	I7	42
Changchun, China	C6	38
Changde, China	G4	42
Chang Hu, l., China	F5	42
Changhua, Tai.	I9	42
Changhŭng, Kor., S.	G7	38
Changji, China	C2	36
Changjiang, China	L3	42
Changkiakow see Zhangjiakou, China	A6	42
Changli, China	B8	42
Changling, China	B5	38
Changlun, Malay.	I5	48
Changmar, China	A7	54
Changning, China	G4	36
Changning, China	H5	42
Ch'angnyŏng, Kor., S.	D1	40
Changping, China	A7	42
Changsa, China	L4	42
Changsan-got, c., Kor., N.	E6	38
Changsha, China	G5	42
Changshan Qundao, is., China	B10	42
Changshou, China	G2	42
Changshu, China	F9	42
Ch'angte see Changde, China	G4	42
Changteh see Anyang, China	C6	42
Changtien see Zibo, China	C8	42
Changting, China	B8	38
Changting, China	I7	42
Changwŏn, Kor., S.	D1	40
Changwu, China	D2	42
Changxing, China	F8	42
Changxing Dao, i., China	B9	42
Changyi, China	C8	42
Changyŏn-ŭp, Kor., N.	E6	38
Changzhi, China	C5	42
Changzhou, China	F8	42
Chaniá, Grc.	H7	28
Chanión, Kólpos, b., Grc.	H6	28
Chankiang see Zhanjiang, China	K4	42
Channagiri, India	D2	53
Channapatna, India	E3	53
Channel Country, reg., Austl.	E3	76
Channel Islands, is., Eur.	L10	12
Channel Islands, is., Ca., U.S.	J6	134
Channel Islands National Park, p.o.i., Ca., U.S.	J6	134
Channel-Port aux Basques, Nf., Can.	j22	107a
Channelview, Tx., U.S.	H3	122
Channing, Mi., U.S.	B1	112
Channing, Tx., U.S.	F6	128
Chan-si see Shanxi, state, China	B5	42
Chantada, Spain	B3	20
Chanthaburi, Thai.	F6	48
Chantilly, Fr.	E11	14
Chan-tong see Shandong, state, China	C7	42
Chantrey Inlet, b., Nu., Can.	B11	106
Chanute, Ks., U.S.	G2	120
Chao, stm., China	A7	42
Chao'an, China	J7	42
Ch'aochou see Chao'an, China	J7	42
Chaochow see Chao'an, China	J7	42
Chao Hu, l., China	F7	42
Chao Phraya, stm., Thai.	E5	48
Chaor, stm., China	B9	36
Chaoxian, China	F7	42
Chaoyang, China	D4	38
Chaoyang, China	B7	38
Chaoyang, China	J7	42
Chaoyangshan, China	C6	38
Chapada dos Veadeiros, Parque Nacional da, p.o.i., Braz.	H2	88
Chapadinha, Braz.	B4	88
Chapala, Mex.	E7	100
Chapala, Laguna de, l., Mex.	E7	100
Chāparmukh, India	E14	54
Chaparral, Col.	F4	86
Chapecó, Braz.	C11	92
Chapel Hill, N.C., U.S.	I6	114
Chapelton, Jam.	i13	104d
Chapéu, Morro do, mtn., Braz.	H4	88
Chapicuy, Ur.	E9	92
Chapin, Il., U.S.	E7	120
Chapleau, On., Can.	F14	106
Chaplin, Sk., Can.	D7	124
Chaplin Lake, l., Sk., Can.	D7	124
Chapman, Ne., U.S.	F14	126
Chapman, Cape, c., Nu., Can.	B13	106
Chapmanville, W.V., U.S.	G3	114
Chapo, Mex.	E3	130
Chappal, Waddi, mtn., Afr.	H7	64
Chappell Hill, Tx., U.S.	G2	122
Chapultepec, Mex.	L9	134
Chaquiago, Arg.	C4	92
Charadai, Arg.	C8	92
Charalá, Col.	D5	86
Charata, Arg.	C7	92
Charcas, Mex.	D8	100
Charco Hondo, P.R.	B2	104a
Charcos de Risa, Mex.	B7	100
Charcot Island, i., Ant.	B33	81
Chard, Eng., U.K.	K10	12
Charente, state, Fr.	D6	18
Charente, stm., Fr.	C6	18
Charente-Maritime, state, Fr.	C5	18
Chari, stm., Afr.	E3	62
Chārīkār, Afg.	B10	56
Chariton, Ia., U.S.	C4	120
Chariton, stm., U.S.	E5	120
Chariton, Mussel Fork, stm., Mo., U.S.	E5	120
Charity, Guy.	B6	84
Charkhāri, India	F7	54
Charkhlik see Ruoqiang, China	D2	36
Charleroi, Bel.	D13	14
Charles, Cape, c., Va., U.S.	G10	114
Charles, Peak, mtn., Austl.	F4	74
Charles City, Ia., U.S.	A5	120
Charles City, Va., U.S.	G8	114
Charles Island, i., Nu., Can.	C16	106
Charles Mound, hill, Il., U.S.	B7	120
Charles Point, c., Austl.	B6	74
Charleston, Ar., U.S.	B4	122
Charleston, Il., U.S.	E9	120
Charleston, Ms., U.S.	C8	122
Charleston, Mo., U.S.	H8	120
Charleston, S.C., U.S.	D6	116
Charleston, W.V., U.S.	F4	114
Charleston Peak, mtn., Nv., U.S.	G10	134
Charlestown, St. K./N.	C2	105a
Charlestown, St. Vin.	p11	105e
Charlestown, S. Afr.	E9	70
Charlestown, In., U.S.	F12	120
Charleville, Austl.	F5	76
Charleville-Mézières, Fr.	E13	14
Charlevoix, Lake, l., Mi., U.S.	C5	112
Charlieu, Fr.	C10	18
Charlotte, Mi., U.S.	B1	114
Charlotte, N.C., U.S.	A5	116
Charlotte, Tn., U.S.	H10	120
Charlotte, Tx., U.S.	F9	130
Charlotte Amalie, V.I.U.S.	e7	104b
Charlotte Harbor, b., Fl., U.S.	J3	116
Charlotte Lake, l., B.C., Can.	D5	138
Charlottesville, Va., U.S.	F7	114
Charlottetown, P.E., Can.	D13	110
Charlotteville, Trin.	r13	105f
Charlton Island, i., Nu., Can.	E14	106
Charouine, Alg.	D4	64
Charron Lake, l., Mb., Can.	B18	124
Charroux, Fr.	C6	18
Chārsadda, Pak.	A3	54
Charter Oak, Ia., U.S.	I3	118
Charters Towers, Austl.	C6	76
Chartres, Fr.	F10	14
Chascomús, Arg.	G8	92
Chase, B.C., Can.	F11	138
Chase, Mount, mtn., Me., U.S.	D8	110
Chase City, Va., U.S.	H7	114
Chaska, Mn., U.S.	G5	118
Chateaubelair, St. Vin.	o11	105e
Châteaubriant, Fr.	G7	14
Château-du-Loir, Fr.	G9	14
Châteaudun, Fr.	F10	14
Chateaugay (Châteauguay), stm., N.A.	D15	112
Châteaulin, Fr.	F4	14
Châteauneuf-sur-Charente, Fr.	D5	18
Château-Renault, Fr.	G9	14
Château-Richer, Qc., Can.	C5	110
Châteauroux, Fr.	H10	14
Château-Thierry, Fr.	E12	14
Châtellerault, Fr.	H9	14
Chatfield, Mn., U.S.	H6	118
Chatham, N.B., Can.	C11	110
Chatham, On., Can.	F7	112
Chatham, Eng., U.K.	J13	12
Chatham, Il., U.S.	E8	120
Chatham, La., U.S.	E6	122
Chatham, Ma., U.S.	C15	114
Chatham, N.Y., U.S.	B12	114
Chatham, Isla, i., Chile	J2	90
Chatham Islands, is., N.Z.	H9	72
Chatham Rise, unds.	N20	142
Chatham Strait, strt., Ak., U.S.	E13	140
Châtillon-en-Bazois, Fr.	G12	14
Châtillon-sur-Seine, Fr.	G13	14
Chatkal Range, mts., Asia	F12	32
Chatom, Al., U.S.	F10	122
Chatra, India	F10	54
Chatsworth, Austl.	C3	76
Chatsworth, Ga., U.S.	C14	122
Chatsworth, Il., U.S.	D9	120
Chattahoochee, stm., U.S.	G14	122
Chattanooga, Tn., U.S.	B13	122
Chattaroy, W.V., U.S.	G3	114
Chaturat, Thai.	E5	48
Chaubourg, Mount, hill, St. Luc.	I7	105c
Chaudière, stm., Qc., Can.	D5	110
Chau Doc, Viet.	G7	48
Chauk, Mya.	B2	48
Chaumont, Fr.	F13	14
Chauncey, Oh., U.S.	E3	114
Chaungwabyin, Mya.	F4	48
Chauny, Fr.	E12	14
Chaupāran, India	F10	54
Chautauqua Lake, l., N.Y., U.S.	B6	114
Chauvin, La., U.S.	H8	122
Chavakkad, India	F2	53
Chavarría, Arg.	D8	92
Chaves, Port.	C3	20
Cháviva, Col.	E5	86
Chawa'nanake, China	C12	54
Chay, stm., Viet.	A7	48
Chayuan, China	G9	42
Chazy, N.Y., U.S.	F3	110
Chbar, stm., Camb.	F8	48
Cheaha Mountain, mtn., Al., U.S.	D13	122
Cheat, stm., U.S.	E6	114
Cheat, Shavers Fork, stm., W.V., U.S.	E6	114
Cheb, Czech Rep.	F8	16
Chebanse, Il., U.S.	G2	112
Cheboygan, Mi., U.S.	C5	112
Chech, 'Erg, des., Afr.	E4	64
Chechnya see Čečnja, state, Russia	F7	32
Chech'on, Kor., S.	B1	40
Chęciny, Pol.	F16	16
Checleset Bay, b., B.C., Can.	F3	138
Checotah, Ok., U.S.	B3	122
Chedabucto Bay, b., N.S., Can.	E15	110
Cheduba Island, i., Mya.	C1	48
Cheduba Strait, strt., Mya.	C1	48
Cheektowaga, N.Y., U.S.	B7	114
Cheepie, Austl.	F5	76
Chef-Boutonne, Fr.	C5	18
Chefoo see Yantai, China	C9	42
Chehalis, Wa., U.S.	D4	136
Chehalis, stm., Wa., U.S.	D3	136
Cheju, Kor., S.	H7	38
Cheju-do (Quelpart Island), i., Kor., S.	H7	38
Chekiang see Zhejiang, state, China	G8	42
Chela, Serra da, mts., Ang.	D1	68
Chelan, Lake, res., Wa., U.S.	B6	136
Chelif, Oued, stm., Alg.	B5	64
Chełm, Pol.	E19	16
Chełm, state, Pol.	E19	16
Chełmno, Pol.	C14	16
Chelmsford, On., Can.	B8	112
Chelmsford, Eng., U.K.	J13	12
Chełmża, Pol.	C14	16
Chelsea, Ia., U.S.	C5	120
Chelsea, Mi., U.S.	B1	114
Chelsea, Vt., U.S.	F4	110
Cheltenham, Eng., U.K.	J10	12
Chelva see Xelva, Spain	E9	20
Chelyuskin, Cape see Čeljuskin, mys, c., Russia	A9	34
Chemainus, B.C., Can.	H7	138
Chemba, Moz.	D5	68
Chemnitz, Ger.	F8	16
Chemult, Or., U.S.	G5	136
Chenāb, stm., Asia	D3	54
Chenango, stm., N.Y., U.S.	B10	114
Chenchiang see Zhenjiang, China	E8	42
Chenderoh, Tasik, l., Malay.	J5	48
Chénéville, Qc., Can.	E1	110
Cheney, Wa., U.S.	C9	136
Cheney Reservoir, res., Ks., U.S.	D10	128
Cheneyville, La., U.S.	F6	122
Chengbu, China	H4	42
Chengchou see Zhengzhou, China	D5	42
Chengchow see Zhengzhou, China	D5	42
Chengde, China	A7	42
Chengdu, China	E5	36
Chenggu, China	E2	42
Chenghai, China	J7	42
Chengmai, China	L3	42
Chengshan Jiao, c., China	C10	42
Chengteh see Chengde, China	A7	42
Chengtu see Chengdu, China	E5	36
Chengxian, China	E1	42
Chengyang, China	G8	42
Chengzitan, China	B10	42
Ch'enhsien see Chenzhou, China	I5	42
Chen Hu, l., China	F5	42
Chenliu, China	D6	42
Chennai (Madras), India	E5	53
Chenoa, Il., U.S.	D9	120
Chen-si see Shaanxi, state, China	E3	42
Chentang, China	J4	42
Chenxi, China	H3	42
Chenxiangtun, China	D5	38
Chenyang see Shenyang, China	D5	38
Chenzhou, China	I5	42
Cheonan see Ch'ŏnan, Kor., S.	F7	38
Cheongju see Ch'ŏngju, Kor., S.	F7	38
Chepén, Peru	E2	84
Chepes, Arg.	E4	92
Chepkotet, mtn., Kenya	D7	66
Chepo, Pan.	H8	102
Cher, state, Fr.	B8	18
Cher, stm., Fr.	B7	18
Cheradi, Isole, i., Italy	D11	24
Cherbourg, Fr.	E7	14
Cherchell, Alg.	H13	20
Chergui, Chott ech, l., Alg.	C5	64
Cheriton, Va., U.S.	G10	114
Cheriyam Island, i., India	F1	53
Cherkassy see Cherkasy, Ukr.	E4	32
Cherkasy, Ukr.	E4	32
Cherkessia see Karačaevo-Čerkesija, state, Russia	F6	32
Chernihiv, Ukr.	D4	32
Chernivtsi, Ukr.	A12	26
Chernivtsi, co., Ukr.	A13	26
Chernobyl see Chornobyl', Ukr.	D4	32
Cherokee, Ia., U.S.	B2	120
Cherokee, Ks., U.S.	G3	120
Cherokee, Ok., U.S.	E10	128
Cherokee, Tx., U.S.	C9	130
Cherokee Lake, res., Tn., U.S.	H2	114
Cherokee Point, c., Bah.	J8	116
Cherokees, Lake O' The, res., Ok., U.S.	H2	120
Cherokee Sound, Bah.	J8	116
Cherrapunji, India	F13	54
Cherry Creek, stm., S.D., U.S.	C11	126
Cherry Hill, N.J., U.S.	E10	114
Cherryvale, Ks., U.S.	G2	120
Cherry Valley, Ar., U.S.	B8	122
Cherryville, N.C., U.S.	A4	116
Cherskiy Mountains see Čerskogo, hrebet, mts., Russia	C17	34
Chesapeake, Va., U.S.	H9	114
Chesapeake Bay, b., U.S.	F9	114
Chesapeake Bay Bridge-Tunnel, Va., U.S.	G9	114
Chesapeake Beach, Md., U.S.	F9	114
Chesaw, Wa., U.S.	B7	136
Chesha Bay see Češskaja guba, b., Russia	C21	8
Cheshire, Ma., U.S.	B12	114
Cheslatta Lake, l., B.C., Can.	C5	138
Chesnee, S.C., U.S.	A4	116
Chest Creek, stm., Pa., U.S.	D7	114
Chester, Eng., U.K.	H10	12
Chester, Ca., U.S.	C4	134
Chester, Il., U.S.	G8	120
Chester, Mt., U.S.	B15	136
Chester, Ne., U.S.	A11	128
Chester, Ok., U.S.	E10	128
Chester, Pa., U.S.	E10	114
Chester, Va., U.S.	G8	114
Chester Basin, N.S., Can.	F12	110
Chesterfield, Eng., U.K.	H11	12
Chesterfield, S.C., U.S.	B5	116
Chesterfield, Îles, is., N. Cal.	E6	72
Chesterfield Inlet, Nu., Can.	C12	106
Chesterfield Inlet, b., Nu., Can.	C12	106
Chesterfield Islands see Chesterfield, Îles, is., N. Cal.	E6	72
Chesterhill, Oh., U.S.	E4	114
Chester-le-Street, Eng., U.K.	G11	12
Chestertown, Md., U.S.	E9	114
Chesterville, On., Can.	C14	112
Chesuncook Lake, l., Me., U.S.	E7	110
Chetek, Wi., U.S.	F7	118
Chéticamp, N.S., Can.	D16	110
Chetumal, Mex.	C3	102
Chetumal, Bahía, b., N.A.	C3	102
Chevelon Creek, stm., Az., U.S.	I6	132
Cheviot, Oh., U.S.	E13	120
Cheviot Hills, hills, U.K.	F10	12
Ch'ew Bahir see Stefanie, Lake, l., Afr.	G7	62
Chewelah, Wa., U.S.	B9	136
Cheyenne, Ok., U.S.	F9	128
Cheyenne, Wy., U.S.	F8	126
Cheyenne, stm., U.S.	C11	126
Cheyenne Wells, Co., U.S.	C6	128
Cheyne Bay, b., Austl.	F3	74
Chhabra, India	F6	54
Chhapra, India	F10	54
Chhātak, Bngl.	F13	54
Chhatarpur, India	F7	54
Chhatrapur, India	E6	46
Chhattīsgarh, pl., India	H9	54
Chhay Arêng, stm., Camb.	G6	48
Chhêb Kândal, Camb.	F7	48
Chhindwāra, India	H7	54
Chhlong, stm., Camb.	F8	48
Chhota-Chhindwāra, India	G7	54
Chhota Udepur Mhow, India	D3	46
Chi, stm., China	E7	42
Chi, stm., Thai.	E7	48
Chía, Col.	E4	86
Chiahsing see Jiaxing, China	F9	42
Chiai, Tai.	J9	42
Chiamussu see Jiamusi, China	B11	36
Chian see Ji'an, China	H6	42
Chiang Dao, Thai.	C4	48
Chiange, Ang.	D1	68
Chiang Kham, Thai.	C5	48
Chiang Khan, Thai.	D5	48
Chiang Mai, Thai.	C4	48
Chiangmen see Jiangmen, China	J5	42
Chiang Rai, Thai.	C4	48
Chiang Saen, Thai.	B4	48
Chiangtu see Yangzhou, China	E8	42
Chiangyin see Jiangyin, China	F9	42
Chiaohsien see Jiaoxian, China	C8	42
Chiaotso see Jiaozuo, China	D5	42
Chiapas, state, Mex.	D6	96
Chiavari, Italy	F6	22
Chiavenna, Italy	D6	22
Chiba, Japan	D13	40
Chiba, state, Japan	D13	40
Chibabava, Moz.	B11	70
Chibemba, Ang.	D1	68
Chibougamau, Qc., Can.	F15	106
Chibuto, Moz.	D11	70
Chibuzhangchu Hu, l., China	B13	54
Chicago, Il., U.S.	G2	112
Chicago Heights, Il., U.S.	C10	120
Chicapa, stm., Afr.	B3	68
Chichagof Island, i., Ak., U.S.	E12	140
Chīchāwatni, Pak.	C4	54
Chicheng, China	A6	42
Chichén Itzá, hist., Mex.	B3	102
Chichester, Eng., U.K.	K12	12
Chichibu, Japan	C11	40
Ch'ich'ihaerh see Qiqihar, China	B9	36
Chichiriviche, Ven.	B7	86
Chickamauga, Ga., U.S.	C13	122
Chickamauga Lake, res., Tn., U.S.	B14	122
Chickasaw, Al., U.S.	G10	122
Chickasawhay, stm., Ms., U.S.	F10	122
Chickasaw National Recreation Area, p.o.i., Ok., U.S.	G12	128
Chickasha, Ok., U.S.	F11	128
Chicken, Ak., U.S.	D11	140
Chiclana de la Frontera, Spain	H4	20
Chiclayo, Peru	E2	84
Chico, Ca., U.S.	D4	134
Chico, Tx., U.S.	H11	128
Chico, stm., Arg.	I2	90
Chico, stm., Arg.	I3	90
Chico, stm., Phil.	B3	52
Chicomba, Ang.	C2	68
Chicopee, Ga., U.S.	B2	116
Chicopee, Ma., U.S.	B13	114
Chicoutimi, Qc., Can.	B5	110
Chicoutimi, stm., Qc., Can.	B5	110
Chicuma, Ang.	C1	68
Chidambaram, India	F4	53
Chidenguele, Moz.	D12	70
Chiefland, Fl., U.S.	G3	116
Chiehyang see Jieyang, China	J7	42
Chiemsee, l., Ger.	I8	16
Chieo Lan Reservoir, res., Thai.	H4	48
Chieri, Italy	F4	22
Chiese, stm., Italy	E7	22
Chieti, Italy	H11	22
Chifeng, China	C3	38
Chigasaki, Japan	D12	40
Chignahuapan, Mex.	F9	100
Chignecto, Cape, c., N.S., Can.	E11	110
Chignecto Bay, b., Can.	E12	110
Chignik, Ak., U.S.	E8	140
Chigoubiche, Lac, l., Qc., Can.	A3	110
Chigubo, Moz.	C11	70
Chigu Co, l., China	D13	54
Ch'ihfeng see Chifeng, China	C3	38
Chihli, Gulf of see Bo Hai, b., China	B8	42
Chihsi see Jixi, China	B9	38
Chihuahua, Mex.	A5	100
Chihuahua, state, Mex.	B3	96
Chihuahua, Desierto de, des., N.A.	F6	108
Chihuahuan Desert see Chihuahua, Desierto de, des., N.A.	F6	108
Chii-san, mtn., Kor., S.	G7	38
Chikaskia, stm., U.S.	E11	128
Chik Ballāpur, India	E3	53
Chikhli, India	H6	54
Chikmagalūr, India	E2	53
Chiknāyakanhalli, India	E3	53
Chikodi, India	C2	53
Chikrêng, stm., Camb.	F7	48
Chikuma, stm., Japan	C11	40
Chi-kyaw, Mya.	B1	48
Chilakalūrupet, India	C4	53
Chilako, stm., B.C., Can.	C7	138
Chilanko Forks, B.C., Can.	D6	138
Chilapa de Álvarez, Mex.	G9	100
Chilās, Pak.	B11	56
Chilcotin, stm., B.C., Can.	E8	138
Childers, Austl.	E9	76
Childersburg, Al., U.S.	D12	122
Childress, Tx., U.S.	G8	128
Chile, ctry., S.A.	F2	90
Chile Chico, Chile	I2	90
Chilecito, Arg.	F3	92
Chilecito, Arg.	D4	92
Chile Rise, unds.	M5	144
Chilhowie, Va., U.S.	H4	114
Chilia, Braţul, stm., Eur.	D16	26
Chilika Lake, l., India	I10	54
Chililabombwe, Zam.	C4	68
Chilin see Jilin, China	C7	38
Chilko, stm., B.C., Can.	D7	138
Chilko Lake, l., B.C., Can.	E6	138
Chillagoe, Austl.	C8	74
Chillán, Chile	H1	92
Chillicothe, Mo., U.S.	E4	120
Chillicothe, Oh., U.S.	E3	114
Chillicothe, Tx., U.S.	G9	128
Chilliwack, B.C., Can.	G9	138
Chiloé, Isla Grande de, i., Chile	H2	90
Chilón, Mex.	G12	100
Chiloquin, Or., U.S.	H5	136
Chilpancingo de los Bravo, Mex.	G9	100
Chiluage, Ang.	B3	68
Chilumba, Mwi.	C5	68
Chilung, Tai.	I9	42
Chilwa, Lake, l., Afr.	D6	68
Chimaltenango, Guat.	E2	102
Chimán, Pan.	H8	102

Name	Map Ref.	Page
Chimayo, N.M., U.S.	E3	128
Chimbarongo, Chile	G2	92
Chimbas, Arg.	E3	92
Chimborazo, state, Ec.	H2	86
Chimborazo, vol., Ec.	H2	86
Chimbote, Peru	E2	84
Chimoio, Moz.	D5	68
Chimpay, Arg.	G3	90
Chin, state, Mya.	B1	48
China, Mex.	C9	100
China, ctry., Asia	B8	46
Chinan see Jinan, China	C7	42
Chinandega, Nic.	F4	102
Chinati Peak, mtn., Tx., U.S.	E3	130
Chincha Alta, Peru	F2	84
Chinchaga, stm., Can.	D7	106
Chinchilla, Austl.	F8	76
Chinchilla de Monte-Aragón, Spain	F9	20
Chinchiná, Col.	E4	86
Chinchou see Jinzhou, China	A9	42
Chinchow see Jinzhou, China	A9	42
Chincolco, Chile	F2	92
Chincoteague, Va., U.S.	G10	114
Chinde, Moz.	D6	68
Chindo, Kor., S.	G7	38
Chin-do, i., Kor., S.	G7	38
Chindong, Kor., S.	D1	40
Chindwinn, stm., Mya.	D7	46
Ch'ingchiang see Qingjiang, China	E8	42
Chingleput, India	E4	53
Chingola, Zam.	C4	68
Chingshih see Jinshi, China	G4	42
Ch'ingtao see Qingdao, China	C9	42
Chingtechen see Jingdezhen, China	G7	42
Chinguetti, Maur.	E2	64
Chinhae, Kor., S.	D1	40
Chin Hills, hills, Mya.	D7	46
Chinhoyi, Zimb.	D5	68
Chinhsien see Jinzhou, China	B9	42
Chinhua see Jinhua, China	G8	42
Ch'inhuangtao see Qinhuangdao, China	B8	42
Chining see Jining, China	D7	42
Chining see Jining, China	A5	42
Chiniot, Pak.	C4	54
Chinit, stm., Camb.	F7	48
Chinjan, Pak.	C1	54
Chinju, Kor., S.	G7	38
Chinkiang see Zhenjiang, China	E8	42
Chinko, stm., C.A.R.	C4	66
Chinle, Az., U.S.	G7	132
Chinle Wash, stm., Az., U.S.	G7	132
Chinmen Tao (Quemoy), i., Tai.	I8	42
Chino, Ca., U.S.	J8	134
Chinon, Fr.	G9	14
Chinook, Ab., Can.	C2	124
Chinook Cove, B.C., Can.	E10	138
Chino Valley, Az., U.S.	I4	132
Chinquapin, N.C., U.S.	B8	116
Chinsali, Zam.	C5	68
Chintāmani, India	E4	53
Chinú, Col.	C4	86
Chinwangtao see Qinhuangdao, China	B8	42
Chioco, Moz.	D5	68
Chioggia, Italy	E9	22
Chíos, Grc.	E9	28
Chíos, i., Grc.	E8	28
Chios see Chíos, i., Grc.	E8	28
Chipata, Zam.	C5	68
Chip Lake, l., Ab., Can.	C15	138
Chiplūn, India	C1	53
Chipman, N.B., Can.	D11	110
Chipola, stm., Fl., U.S.	G13	122
Chippenham, Eng., U.K.	J10	12
Chippewa, stm., Mn., U.S.	F3	118
Chippewa, stm., Wi., U.S.	G6	118
Chippewa, East Fork, stm., Wi., U.S.	F8	118
Chippewa Falls, Wi., U.S.	G7	118
Chiquimula, Guat.	E3	102
Chiquinquirá, Col.	E4	86
Chīrāla, India	D5	53
Chirāwa, India	D5	54
Chiredzi, Zimb.	B10	70
Chireno, Tx., U.S.	F4	122
Chirfa, Niger	E7	64
Chīrgaon, India	F7	54
Chiribiquete, Parque Nacional, p.o.i., Col.	G5	86
Chiricahua Mountains, mts., Az., U.S.	L7	132
Chiricahua National Monument, p.o.i., Az., U.S.	L7	132
Chiricahua Peak, mtn., Az., U.S.	L7	132
Chiriguaná, Col.	C5	86
Chirikof Island, i., Ak., U.S.	E8	140
Chiriquí, Golfo de, b., Pan.	H6	102
Chiriquí, Laguna de, b., Pan.	H6	102
Chiromo, Mwi.	D5	68
Chirpan see Čirpan, Blg.	G12	26
Chirripó, Cerro, mtn., C.R.	H6	102
Chirripó, Parque Nacional, p.o.i., C.R.	H6	102
Chisago City, Mn., U.S.	F5	118
Chisamba, Zam.	C4	68
Chisasibi, Qc., Can.	E15	106
Chisep'o, Kor., S.	E1	40
Ch'ishan, Tai.	J9	42
Chisholm, Ab., Can.	B16	138
Chisholm, Me., U.S.	F6	110
Chisholm, Mn., U.S.	D5	118
Chishtiān Mandi, Pak.	D4	54
Chishui, China	G1	42
Chishui, stm., China	F6	36
Chisimayu see Kismaayo, Som.	E8	66
Chişinău, Mol.	B15	26
Chişineu-Criş, Rom.	C8	26
Chita, Col.	D5	86
Chitado, Ang.	D1	68
Chitagá, Col.	D5	86
Chita-hantō, pen., Japan	E9	40
Chitato, Ang.	B3	68
Chitek Lake, l., Mb., Can.	B14	124
Chitembo, Ang.	C2	68
Chitina, Ak., U.S.	D11	140
Chitina, stm., Ak., U.S.	D11	140
Chitipa, Mwi.	B5	68
Chitokoloki, Zam.	C3	68
Chitose, Japan	C14	38
Chitradurga, India	D3	53
Chitrakūt Dham, India	F8	54
Chitrāl, Pak.	B11	56
Chitrāvati, stm., India	D3	53
Chitré, Pan.	H7	102
Chittagong, Bngl.	G13	54
Chittagong, state, Bngl.	G13	54
Chittāpur, India	C3	53
Chittaurgarh, India	F5	54
Chittoor, India	E4	53
Chittūr, India	F3	53
Chitungwiza, Zimb.	D5	68
Chiuchiang see Jiujiang, China	G6	42
Chiumbe (Tshumbe), stm., Afr.	B3	68
Chiume, Ang.	D3	68
Chiusi, Italy	G8	22
Chiva see Xiva, Spain	E10	20
Chivacoa, Ven.	B7	86
Chivasso, Italy	E4	22
Chivi, Zimb.	B10	70
Chivilcoy, Arg.	G7	92
Chivirira Falls, wtfl, Zimb.	B11	70
Chizu, Japan	D7	40
Chloride, Az., U.S.	H2	132
Chmielnik, Pol.	F16	16
Chŏâm Khsant, Camb.	E7	48
Choapa, stm., Chile	E2	92
Choceň, Czech Rep.	F12	16
Chochis, Cerro, mtn., Bol.	C5	90
Choch'iwŏn, Kor., S.	F7	38
Chociwel, Pol.	C11	16
Chocó, state, Col.	E3	86
Chocolate Mountains, mts., U.S.	J1	132
Chocontá, Col.	E5	86
Chocope, Peru	E2	84
Choctawhatchee, West Fork, stm., Al., U.S.	G13	122
Choctawhatchee Bay, b., Fl., U.S.	G12	122
Chodzież, Pol.	D12	16
Choele Choel, Arg.	G3	90
Choiseul, St. Luc.	m6	105c
Choiseul, state, Sol. Is.	d7	79b
Choiseul, i., Sol. Is.	d7	79b
Chojna, Pol.	D10	16
Chojnice, Pol.	C13	16
Chojnów, Pol.	E11	16
Ch'ok'ē, mts., Eth.	E7	62
Choke Canyon Reservoir, res., Tx., U.S.	F9	130
Chokio, Mn., U.S.	F2	118
Chókwe, Moz.	D11	70
Cholet, Fr.	G8	14
Choluteca, Hond.	F4	102
Choluteca, stm., Hond.	F4	102
Choma, Zam.	D4	68
Chomo Lhāri, mtn., Asia	E12	54
Chomūm, India	E5	54
Chomutov, Czech Rep.	F9	16
Ch'ŏnan, Kor., S.	F7	38
Chon Buri, Thai.	F5	48
Chon Daen, Thai.	D5	48
Chone, Ec.	H1	86
Chong'an, China	H8	42
Ch'ŏngdo, Kor., S.	D1	40
Ch'ŏngjin, Kor., N.	D8	38
Ch'ŏngju, Kor., S.	F7	38
Chŏng Kal, Camb.	E6	48
Chongming, China	I4	38
Chongming Dao, i., China	F9	42
Chongoroi, Ang.	C1	68
Chongqing (Chungking), China	G2	42
Chŏngsŏn, Kor., S.	B1	40
Chŏngŭp, Kor., S.	G7	38
Chongxin, China	D2	42
Chongzuo, China	A8	48
Chŏnju, Kor., S.	G7	38
Chonos, Archipiélago de los, is., Chile	I1	90
Ch'ŏnsu-ri, Kor., N.	D8	38
Chontaleña, Cordillera, mts., Nic.	G5	102
Cho Oyu see Chopu, mtn., Asia	D11	54
Cho Oyu see Qowowuyag, mtn., Asia	D11	54
Chop, Ukr.	A9	26
Chopda, India	H5	54
Chopim, stm., Braz.	C11	92
Chopinzinho, Braz.	B11	92
Chopu (Qowowuyag), mtn., Asia	D11	54
Chorna, Ukr.	B16	26
Chornobyl', Ukr.	D4	32
Choros, Isla, i., Chile	D2	92
Ch'ŏrwŏn, Kor., S.	E7	38
Chorzele, Pol.	C16	16
Chosen, Fl., U.S.	J5	116
Chōshi, Japan	D13	40
Chosica, Peru	F2	84
Chos Malal, Arg.	H2	92
Choszczno, Pol.	C11	16
Choteau, Mt., U.S.	C14	136
Chotila, India	G3	54
Chouchiak'ou see Shangshui, China	E6	42
Chouk'ou see Shangshui, China	E6	42
Choushan Islands see Zhoushan Qundao, is., China	F10	42
Chowchilla, Ca., U.S.	F5	134
Chown, Mount, mtn., Ab., Can.	C11	138
Choya, Arg.	D5	92
Choybalsan, Mong.	B7	36
Choyr, Mong.	B6	36
Chrisman, Il., U.S.	I2	112
Christanshåb (Qasigiannguit), Grnld.	D15	141
Christchurch, N.Z.	F5	80
Christian, Cape, c., Nu., Can.	A17	106
Christian, Point, c., Pit.	c28	78k
Christiana, Jam.	i13	104d
Christiana, S. Afr.	E7	70
Christian Island, i., On., Can.	D9	112
Christiansburg, Va., U.S.	G5	114
Christian Sound, strt., Ak., U.S.	E12	140
Christianstad, V.I.U.S.	h11	104c
Christmas Island, dep., Oc.	K13	142
Christmas Island, i., Christ. I.	E1	72
Christmas Island see Kiritimati, at., Kir.	C11	72
Christmas Ridge, unds.	I22	142
Christoval, Tx., U.S.	C7	130
Chrudim, Czech Rep.	G11	16
Chrzanów, Pol.	F15	16
Chu (Xam), stm., Asia	B7	48
Chuādanga, Bngl.	G12	54
Chuanchou see Quanzhou, China	I8	42
Chubbuck, Id., U.S.	H14	136
Chūbu-Sangaku-kokuritsu-kōen, p.o.i., Japan	C10	40
Chubut, state, Arg.	H3	90
Chubut, stm., Arg.	H3	90
Ch'üchiang see Shaoguan, China	I5	42
Chuchi Lake, l., B.C., Can.	A6	138
Chuchou see Zhuzhou, China	H5	42
Chuchow see Zhuzhou, China	H5	42
Chu Chua, B.C., Can.	E10	138
Chucunaque, stm., Pan.	H9	102
Chugach Mountains, mts., Ak., U.S.	D10	140
Chuginadak Island, i., Ak., U.S.	g25	140a
Chūgoku-sanchi, mts., Japan	D6	40
Chugwater Creek, stm., Wy., U.S.	F8	126
Chuhuichupa, Mex.	G8	98
Chuí, Braz.	F11	92
Chukchi Sea	C5	94
Chuke Hu, l., China	C11	54
Chukotsk Peninsula see Čukotskij poluostrov, pen., Russia	C26	34
Chula Vista, Ca., U.S.	K8	134
Chulucanas, Peru	E1	84
Chumbicha, Arg.	D4	92
Chum Phae, Thai.	D6	48
Chumphon, Thai.	G4	48
Chumphon Buri, Thai.	E6	48
Chum Saeng, Thai.	E5	48
Chumunjin, Kor., S.	B1	40
Chun'an, China	G8	42
Chunan, Tai.	I9	42
Chuncheon see Ch'unch'ŏn, Kor., S.	F7	38
Chunchi, Ec.	I2	86
Ch'unch'ŏn, Kor., S.	F7	38
Chunchula, Al., U.S.	G10	122
Ch'ungch'ŏng-bukto, state, Kor., S.	B1	40
Ch'ungju, Kor., S.	F7	38
Chungking see Chongqing, China	G2	42
Ch'ungmu, Kor., S.	E1	40
Chungshan see Zhongshan, China	J5	42
Chungyang Shanmo, mts., Tai.	J9	42
Chunhua, China	D3	42
Chunhuhux, Mex.	C3	102
Chuquibamba, Peru	G3	84
Chuquicamata, Chile	D3	90
Chur (Coire), Switz.	D6	22
Church Hill, Tn., U.S.	H3	114
Churchill, Mb., Can.	D12	106
Churchill, stm., Can.	D11	106
Churchill, stm., Nf., Can.	E18	106
Churchill, Mount, mtn., B.C., Can.	G7	138
Churchill, Mount, vol., Ak., U.S.	D11	140
Churchill Falls, wtfl, Nf., Can.	E17	106
Churchill Lake, l., Sk., Can.	D9	106
Church Point, La., U.S.	G6	122
Church Rock, N.M., U.S.	H8	132
Chūru, India	D5	54
Churubusco, In., U.S.	G4	112
Churuguara, Ven.	B7	86
Chushul, India	B7	54
Chute-Saint-Philippe, Qc., Can.	D1	110
Chutung, Tai.	I9	42
Chuuk, is., Micron.	C6	72
Chuvashia see Čuvašija, state, Russia	C7	32
Chuxian, China	E8	42
Chuxiong, China	F5	36
Ci, stm., China	B6	42
Ci, stm., China	E6	42
Ciadâr Lunga, Mol.	C15	26
Ciales, P.R.	B3	104a
Ciamis, Indon.	G6	50
Cianjur, Indon.	G5	50
Çianorte, Braz.	A11	92
Čiatura, Geor.	F6	32
Ciawi, Indon.	G5	50
Cibaliung, Indon.	G4	50
Cibatu, Indon.	G6	50
Cibinong, Indon.	G5	50
Cibolo Creek, stm., Tx., U.S.	E3	130
Cibolo Creek, stm., Tx., U.S.	E10	130
Cicero, Il., U.S.	G2	112
Cicero, In., U.S.	H3	112
Cícero Dantas, Braz.	F6	88
Cicurug, Indon.	G5	50
Cidra, P.R.	B3	104a
Ciechanów, Pol.	D16	16
Ciechanów, state, Pol.	C16	16
Ciechanowiec, Pol.	D18	16
Ciego de Ávila, Cuba	B8	102
Ciempozuelos, Spain	D7	20
Ciénaga, Col.	B4	86
Ciénega de Flores, Mex.	H7	130
Cienfuegos, Cuba	A7	102
Cíes, Illas, is., Spain	B1	20
Cies, Islas see Cíes, Illas, is., Spain	B1	20
Cieszanów, Pol.	F19	16
Cieszyn, Pol.	G14	16
Cieza, Spain	F9	20
Çifteler, Tur.	D13	28
Cifuentes, Spain	D8	20
Cigüela, stm., Spain	E7	20
Çihanbeyli, Tur.	E15	28
Čiili, Kaz.	F11	32
Cijara, Embalse de, res., Spain	E6	20
Cijulang, Indon.	G6	50
Cikampek, Indon.	G5	50
Çikobia, i., Fiji	o20	79e
Čikoj, Russia	F10	34
Cilacap, Indon.	G6	50
Cilamaya, Indon.	G5	50
Cilento, reg., Italy	D9	24
Cili, China	G4	42
Cilician Gates see Gülek Boğazı, p., Tur.	A5	58
Čilik, Kaz.	F13	32
Cill Chainnigh see Kilkenny, Ire.	I5	12
Cilleruelo de Bezana, Spain	B7	20
Cil'ma, stm., Russia	D24	8
Cimarron, N.M., U.S.	E4	128
Cimarron, stm., U.S.	F12	128
Cimarron, North Fork, stm., U.S.	D7	128
Čimbaj, Uzb.	F9	32
Cimişlia, Mol.	C15	26
Cimljanskoe vodohranilišče, res., Russia	E6	32
Cimone, Monte, mtn., Italy	F7	22
Cimpu, Indon.	E12	50
Cina, Tanjung, c., Indon.	G4	50
Cinaruco, stm., Ven.	D7	86
Cinaruco-Capanaparo Santos Luzardo, Parque Nacional, p.o.i., Ven.	D8	86
Cinca, stm., Spain	C11	20
Cincinnati, Ia., U.S.	D4	120
Cincinnati, Oh., U.S.	E1	114
Cinco, Canal Numero, can., Arg.	H9	92
Cinco de Mayo, Mex.	I3	130
Cinco Saltos, Arg.	I3	92
Çine, Tur.	F10	28
Ciney, Bel.	D14	14
Cinfães, Port.	C2	20
Cinişeuţi, Mol.	B15	26
Cintalapa, Mex.	G12	100
Cinto, Monte, mtn., Fr.	G14	18
Cintra, Golfe de, b., W. Sah.	E1	64
Ciociaria, reg., Italy	I10	22
Cipa, stm., Russia	F11	34
Cipatujah, Indon.	G5	50
Cipó, Braz.	F6	88
Cipó, stm., Braz.	J4	88
Cipolletti, Arg.	G3	90
Circeo, Parco Nazionale del, p.o.i., Italy	C6	24
Čirčik, Uzb.	F11	32
Circle, Ak., U.S.	C11	140
Circle, Mt., U.S.	G8	124
Circleville, Oh., U.S.	E3	114
Circleville, Ut., U.S.	E4	132
Circleville Mountain, mtn., Ut., U.S.	E4	132
Cirebon, Indon.	G6	50
Ciremay, Gunung, vol., Indon.	G6	50
Çirencester, Eng., U.K.	J11	12
Čirgalandy, Russia	D17	32
Ciriè, Italy	E4	22
Çirò Marina, Italy	E11	24
Čirpan, Blg.	G12	26
Ciskei, hist. reg., S. Afr.	H8	70
Cisnădie, Rom.	D11	26
Cisne, Il., U.S.	F9	120
Cisne, Islas del see Santanilla, Islas, is., Hond.	D6	102
Cisneros, Col.	D4	86
Cisolok, Indon.	G5	50
Çissna Park, Il., U.S.	H2	112
Čistoozërnoe, Russia	D13	32
Čistopol', Russia	C8	32
Čita, Russia	F11	34
Citlaltépetl, Volcán see Pico de Orizaba, Volcán, vol., Mex.	F10	100
Citra, Fl., U.S.	G3	116
Citrus Heights, Ca., U.S.	E4	134
Città di Castello, Italy	G9	22
Cittanova, Italy	F10	24
City of Sunrise see Sunrise, Fl., U.S.	J5	116
City Point, Fl., U.S.	H5	116
Ciudad Acuña, Mex.	A8	100
Ciudad Altamirano, Mex.	F8	100
Ciudad Anáhuac, Mex.	B8	100
Ciudad Bolívar, Ven.	C10	86
Ciudad Bolivia, Ven.	C6	86
Ciudad Camargo, Mex.	B6	100
Ciudad Camargo, Mex.	B9	100
Ciudad Constitución, Mex.	C3	100
Ciudad Cortés, C.R.	H6	102
Ciudad Darío, Nic.	F4	102
Ciudad del Carmen, Mex.	F12	100
Ciudad del Este, Para.	B10	92
Ciudad de Libertador General San Martín, Arg.	A5	92
Ciudad de México (Mexico City), Mex.	F9	100
Ciudad de Nutrias, Ven.	C7	86
Ciudadela see Ciutadella de Menorca, Spain	D14	20
Ciudad Guayana, Ven.	C10	86
Ciudad Hidalgo, Mex.	F8	100
Ciudad Jiménez see Jiménez, Mex.	B6	100
Ciudad Juárez, Mex.	C1	130
Ciudad Lerdo see Lerdo, Mex.	C7	100
Ciudad Madero, Mex.	D10	100
Ciudad Mante, Mex.	D9	100
Ciudad Miguel Alemán, Mex.	B9	100
Ciudad Morelos, Mex.	E5	98
Ciudad Netzahualcóyotl, Mex.	F9	100
Ciudad Obregón, Mex.	B4	100
Ciudad Ojeda, Ven.	B6	86
Ciudad Piar, Ven.	D10	86
Ciudad Real, Spain	F6	20
Ciudad Real, co., Spain	F6	20
Ciudad Rodrigo, Spain	D4	20
Ciudad Valles, Mex.	E9	100
Ciudad Victoria, Mex.	D9	100
Ciutadella de Menorca, Spain	D14	20
Civita Castellana, Italy	H9	22
Civitanova Marche, Italy	G10	22
Civitavecchia, Italy	H8	22
Çivril, Tur.	E12	28
Çixi, China	F9	42
Čiža, Russia	C21	8
Çjalūša, Bela.	G12	10
Čkalovsk, Russia	H20	8
Clackamas, stm., Or., U.S.	E4	136
Clacton-on-Sea, Eng., U.K.	J14	12
Claflin, Ks., U.S.	C10	128
Claiborne, Al., U.S.	F11	122
Clain, stm., Fr.	C6	18
Claire, Lake, l., Ab., Can.	D8	106
Clair Engle Lake, res., Ca., U.S.	C3	134
Clairton, Pa., U.S.	D6	114
Clallam Bay, Wa., U.S.	B2	136
Clanton, Al., U.S.	E12	122
Clanwilliam, S. Afr.	H4	70
Clapperton Island, i., On., Can.	B7	112
Clara, Ire.	H5	12
Clara, Ms., U.S.	F10	122
Clara, stm., Austl.	B4	76
Clara, Punta, c., Arg.	H4	90
Clare, Austl.	I4	76
Clare, Mi., U.S.	E5	112
Clare, state, Ire.	I3	12
Clare Island, i., Ire.	H2	12
Claremont, N.H., U.S.	G4	110
Claremont, S.D., U.S.	B15	126
Claremont, mtn., Ca., U.S.	D4	134
Claremore, Ok., U.S.	H2	120
Clarence, Mo., U.S.	E5	120
Clarence, stm., Austl.	G9	76
Clarence, stm., N.Z.	F5	80
Clarence, Cape, c., Nu., Can.	A13	106
Clarence, Isla, i., Chile	J2	90
Clarence Strait, strt., Austl.	B6	74
Clarence Strait, strt., Ak., U.S.	E13	140
Clarence Town, Bah.	C9	96
Clarendon, Ar., U.S.	C7	122
Clarendon, Tx., U.S.	G8	128
Clarenville, Nf., Can.	j23	107a
Claresholm, Ab., Can.	F17	138
Clarinda, Ia., U.S.	D2	120
Clarines, Ven.	C9	86
Clarington, On., Can.	E11	112
Clarion, Ia., U.S.	B4	120
Clarion, Pa., U.S.	C6	114
Clarion, stm., Pa., U.S.	C6	114
Clarion Fracture Zone, unds.	H25	142
Clarissa, Mn., U.S.	E3	118
Clark, Mount, mtn., N.T., Can.	C6	106
Clarke, stm., Austl.	B5	76
Clarke Island, i., Austl.	n14	77a
Clarkesville, Ga., U.S.	B2	116
Clarkfield, Mn., U.S.	G3	118
Clark Fork, Id., U.S.	B10	136
Clark Fork, stm., U.S.	C11	136
Clarks, La., U.S.	E6	122
Clarksburg, W.V., U.S.	E5	114
Clarksdale, Ms., U.S.	C8	122
Clark's Harbour, N.S., Can.	G11	110
Clarks Hill, In., U.S.	H3	112
Clarkson, Ky., U.S.	G11	120
Clarks Summit, Pa., U.S.	C10	114
Clarkston, Wa., U.S.	D9	136
Clark's Town, Jam.	i13	104d
Clarksville, Ar., U.S.	B5	122
Clarksville, Ia., U.S.	I6	118
Clarksville, Tn., U.S.	H10	120
Clarksville, Va., U.S.	H7	114
Clarkton, Mo., U.S.	H7	120
Clarkton, N.C., U.S.	B7	116
Claro, stm., Braz.	G7	84
Claude, Tx., U.S.	F7	128
Clausthal-Zellerfeld, Ger.	E5	16
Claveria, Phil.	B7	44
Clavering Ø, i., Grnld.	C22	141
Clavet, Sk., Can.	B7	124
Claxton, Ga., U.S.	D4	116
Clay, Ky., U.S.	G10	120
Clay, Tx., U.S.	G2	122
Clay Center, Ne., U.S.	G14	126
Clay City, Il., U.S.	F9	120
Clay City, In., U.S.	E10	120
Clay City, Ky., U.S.	G1	114
Claymont, De., U.S.	E10	114
Claypool, Az., U.S.	J6	132
Claysburg, Pa., U.S.	D7	114
Clayton, Al., U.S.	F13	122
Clayton, Ga., U.S.	B2	116
Clayton, Il., U.S.	D7	120
Clayton, La., U.S.	F7	122
Clayton, Mo., U.S.	F7	120
Clayton, N.M., U.S.	E5	128
Clayton, N.Y., U.S.	D13	112
Clayton, Ok., U.S.	C3	122
Clayton, Wa., U.S.	B9	136
Clear, Cape, c., Ire.	J3	12
Clear Boggy Creek, stm., Ok., U.S.	C2	122
Clearbrook, Mn., U.S.	D3	118
Clear Creek, stm., Wy., U.S.	C6	126
Clearfield, Pa., U.S.	C7	114
Clearfield, Ut., U.S.	B4	132
Clearlake, Ca., U.S.	E3	134
Clear Lake, Ia., U.S.	A4	120
Clear Lake, S.D., U.S.	G2	118
Clear Lake, Wi., U.S.	F6	118
Clear Lake, l., Mb., Can.	D14	124
Clear Lake, l., Ca., U.S.	D3	134
Clear Lake, res., La., U.S.	F5	122
Clear Lake Reservoir, res., Ca., U.S.	B4	134
Clearmont, Wy., U.S.	C6	126
Clearwater, B.C., Can.	E10	138
Clearwater, Mb., Can.	E14	124
Clearwater, Fl., U.S.	I3	116
Clearwater, Ne., U.S.	E14	126
Clearwater, stm., Can.	D8	106
Clearwater, stm., Ab., Can.	D15	138
Clearwater, stm., B.C., Can.	D10	138
Clearwater, stm., Id., U.S.	D10	136
Clearwater, stm., Mn., U.S.	D3	118
Clearwater, stm., Mt., U.S.	C13	136
Clearwater, Middle Fork, stm., Id., U.S.	D11	136
Clearwater, North Fork, stm., Id., U.S.	D11	136
Clearwater Lake, l., B.C., Can.	D10	138
Clearwater Mountains, mts., Id., U.S.	D11	136
Clebit, Ok., U.S.	C4	122
Cleburne, Tx., U.S.	B10	130
Cle Elum, stm., Wa., U.S.	C5	136
Cle Elum Lake, res., Wa., U.S.	C6	136
Cleethorpes, Eng., U.K.	H12	12
Clementsport, N.S., Can.	F11	110
Clemson, S.C., U.S.	B3	116
Clermont, Austl.	D6	76
Clermont, Qc., Can.	C6	110
Clermont, Fr.	E11	14
Clermont-Ferrand, Fr.	D9	18
Clevedon, Eng., U.K.	J10	12
Cleveland, Al., U.S.	D12	122
Cleveland, Ms., U.S.	D8	122
Cleveland, N.C., U.S.	A5	116
Cleveland, Oh., U.S.	C4	114
Cleveland, Ok., U.S.	A2	122
Cleveland, Tn., U.S.	B14	122
Cleveland, Tx., U.S.	G3	122
Cleveland, Va., U.S.	H3	114
Cleveland, Cape, c., Austl.	B6	76
Cleveland, Mount, mtn., Mt., U.S.	B13	136
Clevelândia, Braz.	C11	92
Cleves see Kleve, Ger.	E2	16
Clew Bay, b., Ire.	H3	12
Clewiston, Fl., U.S.	J4	116
Clifton, St. Vin.	p11	105e
Clifton, Az., U.S.	J7	132
Clifton, Tn., U.S.	B11	122
Clifton, Tx., U.S.	C10	130
Clifton Forge, Va., U.S.	G6	114
Clifton Hills, Austl.	F2	76
Climax, Sk., Can.	E5	124
Climax, Co., U.S.	B2	128
Clinch, stm., U.S.	I13	120
Clinchco, Va., U.S.	G15	120
Clingmans Dome, mtn., U.S.	I2	114
Clinton, B.C., Can.	E9	138
Clinton, On., Can.	E8	112
Clinton, Al., U.S.	E11	122
Clinton, Ar., U.S.	B6	122
Clinton, In., U.S.	I2	112
Clinton, Ia., U.S.	C7	120
Clinton, Ky., U.S.	H9	120
Clinton, La., U.S.	G7	122
Clinton, Mi., U.S.	B2	114
Clinton, Mn., U.S.	F2	118
Clinton, Ms., U.S.	E8	122
Clinton, N.C., U.S.	A7	116
Clinton, Ok., U.S.	F9	128
Clinton, S.C., U.S.	B4	116
Clinton, Wi., U.S.	B9	120
Clinton, Cape, c., Austl.	D8	76
Clinton, Lake, res., Il., U.S.	D9	120
Clinton-Colden Lake, l., N.T., Can.	C9	106
Clinton Lake, res., Ks., U.S.	F2	120
Clintonville, Wi., U.S.	G10	118
Clintwood, Va., U.S.	G3	114
Clio, Mi., U.S.	E6	112
Clio, S.C., U.S.	B6	116
Clipperton, Île, at., Oc.	H28	142
Clipperton Fracture Zone, unds.	I25	142
Clipperton Island see Clipperton, Île, at., Oc.	H28	142
Clisson, Fr.	G7	14
Clodomira, Arg.	C5	92
Cloete, Mex.	G6	130
Cloncurry, Austl.	C3	76
Cloncurry, stm., Austl.	B3	76
Clonmel, Ire.	I5	12
Clo-oose, B.C., Can.	H6	138
Cloppenburg, Ger.	D3	16
Cloquet, Mn., U.S.	E6	118
Clorinda, Arg.	B9	92
Cloud Peak, mtn., Wy., U.S.	C5	126
Clova, Qc., Can.	B1	110
Clover, S.C., U.S.	A4	116
Cloverdale, Ca., U.S.	E2	134
Cloverdale, In., U.S.	E11	120
Cloverport, Ky., U.S.	G11	120
Clovis, Ca., U.S.	G6	134
Clovis, N.M., U.S.	G5	128
Cluain Meala see Clonmel, Ire.	I5	12
Cluj, state, Rom.	C10	26
Cluj-Napoca, Rom.	C10	26
Clunes, Austl.	K4	76
Cluny, Austl.	E2	76
Cluny, Fr.	C10	18
Clusone, Italy	E7	22
Clute, Tx., U.S.	E12	130
Clutha, stm., N.Z.	H3	80
Clyde, Ks., U.S.	B11	128
Clyde, N.C., U.S.	A3	116
Clyde, Oh., U.S.	C3	114
Clyde, Tx., U.S.	B8	130
Clyde, stm., Scot., U.K.	F9	12
Clyde, Firth of, b., Scot., U.K.	F7	12
Clyde Inlet, b., Nu., Can.	A17	106
Clyde Park, Mt., U.S.	E16	136
Clyde River, Nu., Can.	A16	106
Çlymer, Pa., U.S.	D6	114
Ćmielów, Pol.	F17	16
Cna, stm., Russia	C17	10
Cna, stm., Russia	D6	32
Cnossus see Knosós, hist., Grc.	H8	28
Côa, stm., Port.	D3	20
Coachella, Ca., U.S.	J9	134
Coachella Canal, can., Ca., U.S.	K1	132
Coahoma, Tx., U.S.	B6	130
Coahuila, state, Mex.	B7	100
Coal City, Il., U.S.	J10	118
Coalcomán de Matamoros, Mex.	F7	100
Coal Creek, stm., Wa., U.S.	C8	136
Coaldale, Ab., Can.	G18	138
Coalgate, Ok., U.S.	C2	122
Coal Grove, Oh., U.S.	F3	114
Coal Hill, Ar., U.S.	B5	122
Coalinga, Ca., U.S.	G5	134
Coalmont, B.C., Can.	G10	138
Coalport, Pa., U.S.	D7	114
Coal River, B.C., Can.	D5	106
Coal Valley, val., Nv., U.S.	F1	132
Coalville, Eng., U.K.	I11	12
Coalville, Ut., U.S.	C5	132
Coamo, P.R.	B3	104a
Coaraci, Braz.	H6	88
Coari, Braz.	D5	84
Coari, stm., Braz.	D5	84
Coast Mountains, mts., N.A.	D4	106
Coast Ranges, mts., U.S.	C2	134
Coatbridge, Scot., U.K.	F9	12
Coatesville, Pa., U.S.	E10	114
Coaticook, Qc., Can.	E5	110
Coats Island, i., Nu., Can.	C14	106
Coats Land, reg., Ant.	C2	81
Coatzacoalcos, Mex.	F11	100
Cobá, hist., Mex.	B4	102
Cobalt, On., Can.	F14	106
Cobán, Guat.	E2	102
Cobar, Austl.	H5	76
Cobberas, Mount, mtn., Austl.	K6	76
Cobden, On., Can.	C13	112
Cobequid Bay, b., N.S., Can.	E13	110
Cobh, Ire.	J4	12
Cobham, stm., Can.	B18	124
Cobija, Bol.	B3	90
Coblence see Koblenz, Ger.	F3	16
Coblenz see Koblenz, Ger.	F3	16
Cobleskill, N.Y., U.S.	B11	114
Cobourg, On., Can.	E11	112
Cobquecura, Chile	H1	92
Cobram, Austl.	J5	76
Cobre, Barranca del (Copper Canyon), misc. cult., Mex.	B5	100
Cóbuè, Moz.	C5	68
Coburg, Ger.	F6	16
Coburg Island, i., Nu., Can.	B10	141
Coburg Peninsula, pen., Austl.	B6	74
Coca, stm., Ec.	H3	86
Cocal, Braz.	B5	88
Cocentaina, Spain	F10	20
Cöch, stm., Asia	B6	36
Cochabamba, Bol.	C3	90
Coche, Isla, i., Ven.	B10	86
Cochem, Ger.	F3	16
Cochin see Kochi, India	G3	53
Cochin China see Nam Phan, hist. reg., Viet.	G8	48
Cochinos, Bahía de (Pigs, Bay of), b., Cuba	B7	102
Cochise Head, mtn., Az., U.S.	K7	132
Cochrane, Ab., Can.	E16	138
Cochrane, On., Can.	F14	106
Cochrane, Wi., U.S.	G7	118
Cochrane, Lago (Pueyrredón, Lago), l., S.A.	I2	90
Cochranton, Pa., U.S.	C5	114
Cockburn, Austl.	I3	76
Cockburn, Mount, mtn., Austl.	E5	74
Cockburn, Mount, mtn., Austl.	D5	74
Cockburn Island, i., On., Can.	C6	112
Cockermouth, Eng., U.K.	G9	12
Cockpit Country, reg., Jam.	i13	104d
Côco, stm., Braz.	F1	88
Coco, stm., N.A.	E6	102
Coco, Cayo, i., Cuba	A8	102
Coco, Isla del, i., C.R.	F7	96
Cocoa, Fl., U.S.	H5	116
Cocoa Beach, Fl., U.S.	H5	116
Coco Channel, strt., Asia	F7	46
Cocodrie Lake, res., La., U.S.	G6	122
Coco Islands, is., Mya.	F7	46
Coconino Plateau, plat., Az., U.S.	H4	132
Cocos, Braz.	H3	88
Cocos Islands, dep., Oc.	K12	142
Cocos Lagoon, b., Guam	k9	78c
Cocos Ridge, unds.	H5	144
Cocula, Mex.	E7	100
Cod, Cape, pen., Ma., U.S.	C15	114
Codajás, Braz.	D5	84
Codera, Cabo, c., Ven.	B8	86
Coderre, Sk., Can.	D7	124
Codigoro, Italy	F9	22
Cod Island, i., Nf., Can.	F13	141
Codlea, Rom.	D12	26
Codó, Braz.	C3	88
Codogno, Italy	E6	22
Codòzinho, Braz.	C3	88
Codroy, Nf., Can.	C17	110
Cody, Ne., U.S.	E11	126
Cody, Wy., U.S.	C3	126
Coelho Neto, Braz.	C4	88
Coen, Austl.	B8	74
Coëtivy, i., Sey.	k13	69b
Coeur d'Alene, Id., U.S.	C10	136
Coeur d'Alene, stm., Id., U.S.	C10	136
Coeur d'Alene Lake, res., Id., U.S.	C10	136
Coffeeville, Ms., U.S.	D9	122
Coffeyville, Ks., U.S.	G2	120
Coffs Harbour, Austl.	H9	76
Cofre de Perote, Cerro, mtn., Mex.	F10	100
Cofre de Perote, Parque Nacional, p.o.i., Mex.	F10	100
Cofrentes see Cofrents, Spain	E9	20
Cofrents, Spain	E9	20
Cogâlnic (Kohyl'nyk), stm., Eur.	C15	26
Coggon, Ia., U.S.	B6	120
Cognac, Fr.	D5	18
Cogolludo, Spain	D7	20
Cogoon, stm., Austl.	F7	76
Cogswell, N.D., U.S.	A15	126
Cohocton, stm., N.Y., U.S.	F12	112
Cohoes, N.Y., U.S.	B12	114
Cohuna, Austl.	J5	76
Coiba, Isla de, i., Pan.	I6	102
Coig, stm., Arg.	J3	90
Coihaique, Chile	I2	90
Coimbatore (Koyambattur), India	F3	53
Coimbra, Braz.	K4	88
Coimbra, Port.	D2	20
Coimbra, state, Port.	D2	20
Coín, Spain	H6	20
Coipasa, Lago, l., Bol.	C3	90
Coipasa, Salar de, pl., S.A.	C3	90
Coire see Chur, Switz.	D6	22
Cojedes, state, Ven.	C7	86
Cojudo Blanco, Cerro, mtn., Arg.	I3	90
Cojutepeque, El Sal.	F3	102
Cokato, Mn., U.S.	F4	118
Çokeville, Wy., U.S.	A6	132
Çokpar, Kaz.	F12	32
Čokurdah, Russia	B18	34
Colac, Austl.	L4	76
Colatina, Braz.	J5	88
Colbeck, Cape, c., Ant.	C25	81
Colbert, Ok., U.S.	D2	122
Colbinabbin, Austl.	K5	76
Colbún, Chile	G2	92
Colbún, Embalse, res., Chile	G2	92
Colby, Ks., U.S.	B7	128
Colby, Wi., U.S.	G8	118
Colchester, Eng., U.K.	J13	12
Colchester, Il., U.S.	D7	120
Cold Bay, Ak., U.S.	E7	140
Cold Lake, Ab., Can.	E8	106
Cold Spring, Mn., U.S.	F4	118
Coldstream, Scot., U.K.	F10	12
Coldwater, Ks., U.S.	D9	128

Name	Map Ref.	Page
Coldwater, Mi., U.S.	G4	112
Coldwater, Oh., U.S.	H5	112
Coldwater, stm., Ms., U.S.	C8	122
Coldwater Creek, stm., U.S.	E7	128
Coleambally, Austl.	J5	76
Colebrook, N.H., U.S.	F5	110
Cole Camp, Mo., U.S.	F4	120
Coleman, Ab., Can.	G16	138
Coleman, Fl., U.S.	H3	116
Coleman, Mi., U.S.	E5	112
Coleman, Wi., U.S.	C1	112
Coleman, stm., Austl.	B8	74
Colenso, S. Afr.	F9	70
Coleraine, Austl.	K3	76
Coleraine, N. Ire., U.K.	F6	12
Coleridge, Ne., U.S.	E15	126
Coles, Ms., U.S.	F7	122
Colesberg, S. Afr.	G7	70
Coleville, Sk., Can.	C4	124
Colfax, In., U.S.	H3	112
Colfax, Ia., U.S.	C4	120
Colfax, La., U.S.	F6	122
Colfax, Wa., U.S.	D9	136
Colfax, Wi., U.S.	F7	118
Colgong, India	F11	54
Colhué Huapi, Lago, l., Arg.	I3	90
Colibris, Pointe des, c., Guad.	h6	105c
Colico, Italy	D6	22
Coligny, S. Afr.	E8	70
Colihaut, Dom.	j5	105c
Colima, Mex.	F7	100
Colima, state, Mex.	F7	100
Colima, Nevado de, vol., Mex.	F7	100
Colinas, Braz.	D3	88
Colinas, Braz.	H1	88
Colinton, Ab., Can.	B17	138
Coll, i., Scot., U.K.	E6	12
Collarenebri, Austl.	G7	76
College, Ak., U.S.	D10	140
Collegedale, Tn., U.S.	B13	122
College Park, Ga., U.S.	D14	122
College Place, Wa., U.S.	D8	136
College Station, Ar., U.S.	C6	122
College Station, Tx., U.S.	G2	122
Collerina, Austl.	G6	76
Colleymount, B.C., Can.	B4	138
Collie, Austl.	F3	74
Collier Bay, b., Austl.	C4	74
Collierville, Tn., U.S.	B9	122
Collingwood, On., Can.	D9	112
Collins, Ga., U.S.	D3	116
Collins, Ms., U.S.	F9	122
Collins Bay, On., Can.	D13	112
Collins Head, c., Norf. I.	y25	78i
Collinston, La., U.S.	E7	122
Collinsville, Austl.	C6	76
Collinsville, Al., U.S.	C13	122
Collinsville, Ok., U.S.	H2	120
Collinsville, Tx., U.S.	D2	122
Collinwood, Tn., U.S.	B11	122
Collipulli, Chile	H1	92
Colman, S.D., U.S.	H2	118
Colmar, Fr.	F16	14
Colmenar, Spain	H6	20
Colmenar Viejo, Spain	D7	20
Colmeneros, Mex.	F8	100
Colmesneil, Tx., U.S.	G4	122
Colnett, Punta, c., Mex.	F4	98
Cologne see Köln, Ger.	F2	16
Cologne, Mn., U.S.	G5	118
Coloma, Mi., U.S.	F3	112
Coloma, Wi., U.S.	G9	118
Colomb-Béchar see Béchar, Alg.	C4	64
Colombia, Col.	F4	86
Colombia, ctry., S.A.	C3	84
Colombie-Britannique see British Columbia, state, Can.	E5	106
Colombo, Braz.	B13	92
Colombo, Sri L.	H4	53
Colome, S.D., U.S.	D13	126
Colomiers, Fr.	F7	18
Colón, Arg.	F8	92
Colón, Arg.	F7	92
Colón, Cuba	A7	102
Colón, Pan.	H7	102
Colon, Mi., U.S.	G4	112
Colón, Ur.	F10	92
Colón, Archipiélago de (Galapagos Islands), is., Ec.	h12	84a
Colona, Austl.	F6	74
Colonelganj, India	E8	54
Colônia, stm., Braz.	H6	88
Colonia Alvear Norte see General Alvear, Arg.	G3	92
Colonia del Sacramento, Ur.	G9	92
Colonia Dora, Arg.	D6	92
Colonia Elisa, Arg.	C8	92
Colonia Lavalleja, Ur.	E9	92
Colonial Heights, Va., U.S.	G8	114
Colonia Providencia, P.R.	C4	104a
Colonia Suiza, Ur.	G9	92
Colonias Unidas, Arg.	C8	92
Colonne, Capo, c., Italy	E11	24
Colonsay, Sk., Can.	B8	124
Colonsay, i., Scot., U.K.	E6	12
Colony, Ks., U.S.	F2	120
Colorada Grande, Salina, pl., Arg.	I5	92
Coloradas, Lomas, hills, Arg.	H3	90
Colorado, Hond.	E4	102
Colorado, state, U.S.	D6	108
Colorado, stm., Arg.	G4	90
Colorado, stm., N.A.	E5	98
Colorado, stm., Tx., U.S.	F11	130
Colorado, Cerro, mtn., Arg.	H3	90
Colorado City, Co., U.S.	C4	128
Colorado City, Tx., U.S.	B7	130
Colorado Kolonie see Lago Kolonie, Aruba	p20	104g
Colorado National Monument, p.o.i., Co., U.S.	D8	132
Colorado Plateau, plat., U.S.	E7	132
Colorado River Aqueduct, aq., Ca., U.S.	E5	98
Colorado Springs, Co., U.S.	C4	128
Colotlán, Mex.	D7	100
Colquechaca, Bol.	C3	90
Colstrip, Mt., U.S.	B6	126
Colt, Ar., U.S.	B8	122
Coltauco, Chile	G2	92
Colton, Ca., U.S.	I8	134
Colton, S.D., U.S.	H2	118
Columbia, Ca., U.S.	E5	134
Columbia, Il., U.S.	F7	120
Columbia, Ky., U.S.	G12	120
Columbia, La., U.S.	E6	122
Columbia, Md., U.S.	E9	114
Columbia, Mo., U.S.	F5	120
Columbia, N.C., U.S.	I9	114
Columbia, Pa., U.S.	D9	114
Columbia, S.C., U.S.	C4	116
Columbia, Tn., U.S.	B11	122
Columbia, stm., N.A.	D3	136
Columbia, Cape, c., Nu., Can.	A11	141
Columbia, Mount, mtn., Ab., Can.	D13	138
Columbia Basin, bas., Wa., U.S.	C8	136
Columbia City, In., U.S.	G4	112
Columbia Falls, Me., U.S.	F9	110
Columbia Icefield, ice, Can.	D13	138
Columbia Mountains, mts., N.A.	G13	138
Columbiana, Al., U.S.	D12	122
Columbiana, Oh., U.S.	D5	114
Columbine, Cape, c., S. Afr.	H3	70
Columbrets, Illes, is., Spain	E11	20
Columbus, Ga., U.S.	E14	122
Columbus, In., U.S.	E12	120
Columbus, Ks., U.S.	G3	120
Columbus, Ms., U.S.	D10	122
Columbus, Ne., U.S.	F15	126
Columbus, N.M., U.S.	L9	132
Columbus, N.C., U.S.	A3	116
Columbus, N.D., U.S.	F11	124
Columbus, Oh., U.S.	E2	114
Columbus, Tx., U.S.	H2	122
Columbus, Wi., U.S.	H9	118
Columbus Point, c., Trin.	r13	105f
Columbus Salt Marsh, pl., Nv., U.S.	E8	134
Colusa, Ca., U.S.	D3	134
Colville, Wa., U.S.	B9	136
Colville, stm., Ak., U.S.	C9	140
Colville Lake, l., N.T., Can.	B5	106
Colwyn Bay, Wales, U.K.	H9	12
Comacchio, Italy	F9	22
Comacchio, Valli di, l., Italy	F9	22
Comala, Mex.	F7	100
Comalcalco, Mex.	F12	100
Comales, Mex.	H9	130
Coman, Mount, mtn., Ant.	C34	81
Comana, Rom.	F15	26
Comanche, Ok., U.S.	G10	128
Comandante Ferraz, sci., Ant.	B35	81
Comandante Fontana, Arg.	B7	92
Comandante Leal, Arg.	E5	92
Comandante Luis Piedra Buena, Arg.	I3	90
Comănești, Rom.	C13	26
Comayagua, Hond.	E4	102
Combarbalá, Chile	E2	92
Combermere Bay, b., Mya.	C1	48
Combourg, Fr.	F7	14
Comboyne, Austl.	H9	76
Comendador, Dom. Rep.	C12	102
Comer, Ga., U.S.	B2	116
Comercinho, Braz.	I5	88
Comet, stm., Austl.	E7	76
Cometela, Moz.	B12	70
Comfort, N.C., U.S.	B8	116
Comfort, Tx., U.S.	E8	130
Comfort, Cape, c., Nu., Can.	B14	106
Comfrey, Mn., U.S.	G4	118
Comilla, Bngl.	G13	54
Comino see Kemmuna, i., Malta	H8	24
Comiso, Italy	H8	24
Comitán de Domínguez, Mex.	G12	100
Commerce, Ga., U.S.	B2	116
Commerce, Ok., U.S.	H3	120
Commercy, Fr.	F14	14
Comminges, reg., Fr.	F6	18
Committee Bay, b., Nu., Can.	B13	106
Communism Peak see Kommunizma, pik, mtn., Taj.	B11	56
Como, Italy	E6	22
Como, Tx., U.S.	D3	122
Como, Lago di, l., Italy	D6	22
Comodoro Rivadavia, Arg.	I3	90
Comores, Archipel des, is., Afr.	C7	68
Comorin, Cape, c., India	G3	53
Comoros, ctry., Afr.	C7	68
Comox, B.C., Can.	G6	138
Compiègne, Fr.	E11	14
Compostela, Mex.	E6	100
Compton, Ca., U.S.	J7	134
Comrat, Mol.	C15	26
Comstock, Ne., U.S.	F13	126
Comstock, Tx., U.S.	E6	130
Comstock Park, Mi., U.S.	E4	112
Çon, stm., Viet.	C7	48
Čona, stm., Russia	B19	32
Co Nag, l., China	B13	54
Conakry, Gui.	H2	64
Conambo, stm., Ec.	H3	86
Cona Niyeo, Arg.	H3	90
Conasauga, stm., U.S.	C14	122
Concarán, Arg.	F5	92
Concarneau, Fr.	G5	14
Conceição, Braz.	D6	88
Conceição da Barra, Braz.	J6	88
Conceição das Alagoas, Braz.	J1	88
Conceição do Araguaia, Braz.	E1	88
Conceição do Canindé, Braz.	D5	88
Conceição do Coité, Braz.	F6	88
Conceição do Mato Dentro, Braz.	J4	88
Conceição do Norte, Braz.	G2	88
Concepción, Arg.	D9	92
Concepción, Arg.	C5	92
Concepción, Bol.	C4	90
Concepción, Chile	H1	92
Concepción, Col.	D5	86
Concepción, Para.	D5	90
Concepción, Bahía, b., Mex.	B2	100
Concepción, Canal, strt., Chile	J2	90
Concepción, Laguna, l., Bol.	C4	90
Concepción, Volcán, vol., Nic.	G5	102
Concepción de la Sierra, Arg.	D10	92
Concepción del Oro, Mex.	C8	100
Concepción del Uruguay, Arg.	F8	92
Conception, Point, c., Ca., U.S.	I5	134
Conception Bay, b., Nf., Can.	j23	107a
Conception Bay, b., Nmb.	C2	70
Conchas, stm., Arg.	B5	92
Conchas Dam, N.M., U.S.	F4	128
Conchas Lake, res., N.M., U.S.	F4	128
Concho, Az., U.S.	I7	132
Concho, stm., Tx., U.S.	C8	130
Conchos, stm., Mex.	A6	100
Conchos, stm., Mex.	C10	100
Conconully, Wa., U.S.	B7	136
Concord, Ca., U.S.	E4	134
Concord, Ga., U.S.	D14	122
Concord, N.H., U.S.	G5	110
Concord, N.C., U.S.	A5	116
Concordia, Arg.	E8	92
Concórdia, Braz.	C11	92
Concordia, Mex.	D5	100
Concordia, Mex.	I4	130
Concordia, Mo., U.S.	F4	120
Concrete, Wa., U.S.	B5	136
Con Cuong, Viet.	C7	48
Conda, Ang.	C1	68
Condamine, Austl.	F7	76
Condamine, stm., Austl.	F8	76
Condat, Fr.	D8	18
Conde, S.D., U.S.	B14	126
Condeúba, Braz.	H5	88
Condobolin, Austl.	I6	76
Condom, Fr.	F6	18
Condon, Or., U.S.	E6	136
Condoto, Col.	E3	86
Condroz, hist. reg., Bel.	D14	14
Cone, Tx., U.S.	H7	128
Conecuh, stm., U.S.	F12	122
Conegliano, Italy	E9	22
Conejos, Co., U.S.	D2	128
Conejos, stm., Co., U.S.	D3	128
Confuso, stm., Para.	B8	92
Congaree Swamp National Monument, p.o.i., S.C., U.S.	C5	116
Congaz, Mol.	C15	26
Conghua, China	J5	42
Congjiang, China	I3	42
Congleton, Eng., U.K.	H10	12
Congo, ctry., Afr.	E3	66
Congo (Zaïre), stm., Afr.	F2	66
Congo, Democratic Republic of the (Zaire), ctry., Afr.	E4	66
Congo, République démocratique du see Congo, Democratic Republic of the, ctry., Afr.	E4	66
Congo Basin, bas., Afr.	E4	66
Congonhinhas, Braz.	A12	92
Congress, Sk., Can.	E8	124
Conitaca, Mex.	C5	100
Conn, Lough, l., Ire.	G3	12
Connacht see Connaught, hist. reg., Ire.	H3	12
Connaught, hist. reg., Ire.	H3	12
Conneaut, Oh., U.S.	C5	114
Conneautville, Pa., U.S.	C5	114
Connecticut, state, U.S.	C13	114
Connecticut, stm., U.S.	H4	110
Connellsville, Pa., U.S.	D6	114
Connemara, reg., Ire.	H3	12
Connersville, In., U.S.	E12	120
Conn Lake, l., Nu., Can.	A15	106
Connors Range, mts., Austl.	C7	76
Cononaco, stm., Ec.	H3	86
Conorochite, stm., Ven.	F8	86
Conover, N.C., U.S.	I4	114
Conquest, Sk., Can.	C6	124
Conquista, Braz.	J2	88
Conrad, Ia., U.S.	B5	120
Conroe, Tx., U.S.	G3	122
Conroe, Lake, res., Tx., U.S.	G3	122
Consecon, On., Can.	D12	112
Conselheiro Lafaiete, Braz.	K4	88
Conselheiro Pena, Braz.	J5	88
Conselice, Italy	F8	22
Consett, Eng., U.K.	G10	12
Consolación del Sur, Cuba	A6	102
Con Son, is., Viet.	H8	48
Consort, Ab., Can.	B3	124
Constance see Konstanz, Ger.	I4	16
Constance, Lake (Bodensee), l., Eur.	I5	16
Constância, Port.	E2	20
Constanța, Rom.	E15	26
Constanța, state, Rom.	E15	26
Constantina, Spain	G5	20
Constantine see Qacentina, Alg.	B6	64
Constantine, Mi., U.S.	G4	112
Constantine, Cape, c., Ak., U.S.	E8	140
Constantinople see İstanbul, Tur.	B12	28
Constitución, Chile	G1	92
Constitución, Ur.	E9	92
Constitución de 1857, Parque Nacional, p.o.i., Mex.	K10	134
Consuegra, Spain	E7	20
Contai, India	H11	54
Contas, stm., Braz.	H6	88
Contentnea Creek, stm., N.C., U.S.	A8	116
Continental Peak, mtn., Wy., U.S.	E4	126
Contratación, Col.	D5	86
Contreras, Embalse de, res., Spain	E9	20
Contreras, Isla, i., Chile	J1	90
Contursi, Italy	D9	24
Contwoyto Lake, l., Can.	B8	106
Convent, La., U.S.	G8	122
Conversano, Italy	D10	24
Converse, In., U.S.	H4	112
Conway, Ar., U.S.	B6	122
Conway, Mo., U.S.	G5	120
Conway, N.H., U.S.	F5	110
Conway, N.C., U.S.	H8	114
Conway, S.C., U.S.	C6	116
Conway, Lake, res., Ar., U.S.	C6	122
Conway National Park, p.o.i., Austl.	C7	76
Conway Springs, Ks., U.S.	D11	128
Conwy, Wales, U.K.	H9	12
Coober Pedy, Austl.	E6	74
Cook, Austl.	F6	74
Cook, Mn., U.S.	D6	118
Cook, Ne., U.S.	D1	120
Cook, Cape, c., B.C., Can.	F2	138
Cook, Mount, mtn., N.Z.	F4	80
Cook, Récif de, rf., N. Cal.	I14	79d
Cookeville, Tn., U.S.	H12	120
Cooking Lake, l., Ab., Can.	C17	138
Cook Inlet, b., Ak., U.S.	D9	140
Cook Islands, dep., Oc.	E10	72
Cook Strait, strt., N.Z.	E6	80
Cooktown, Austl.	C9	74
Coolabah, Austl.	H6	76
Cooladdi, Austl.	F5	76
Coolamon, Austl.	J6	76
Coolangatta, Austl.	G9	76
Cooleemee, N.C., U.S.	I5	114
Coolgardie, Austl.	F4	74
Coolidge, Ga., U.S.	E2	116
Coolidge, Tx., U.S.	F2	122
Coolidge, Mount, mtn., S.D., U.S.	D9	126
Coolidge Dam, dam, Az., U.S.	J6	132
Coolin, Id., U.S.	B10	136
Cooloola National Park, p.o.i., Austl.	F9	76
Cooma, Austl.	K7	76
Coonabarabran, Austl.	H7	76
Coonalpyn, Austl.	J2	76
Coonamble, Austl.	H7	76
Coonoor, India	F3	53
Coon Rapids, Mn., U.S.	F5	118
Coon Valley, Wi., U.S.	H8	118
Cooper, Tx., U.S.	D3	122
Cooper Creek, stm., Austl.	G2	76
Cooper Road, La., U.S.	E5	122
Coopers, Al., U.S.	E12	122
Cooperstown, N.Y., U.S.	B11	114
Coopersville, Mi., U.S.	E4	112
Coopracambra National Park, p.o.i., Austl.	K7	76
Coorong National Park, p.o.i., Austl.	K2	76
Coorow, Austl.	E3	74
Cooroy, Austl.	F9	76
Coosa, stm., U.S.	E12	122
Coos Bay, Or., U.S.	G2	136
Cootamundra, Austl.	J7	76
Cootehill, Ire.	G5	12
Copacabana, Arg.	D4	92
Copacabana, Col.	D4	86
Copainalá, Mex.	G12	100
Copan, Ok., U.S.	H2	120
Copán, hist., Hond.	E3	102
Copatana, Braz.	I8	86
Copeland, Fl., U.S.	K4	116
Copenhagen see København, Den.	I4	8
Copenhagen, N.Y., U.S.	E14	112
Copertino, Italy	D11	24
Copiapó, Chile	C2	92
Copiapó, stm., Chile	C2	92
Copley, Austl.	H2	76
Copparo, Italy	F8	22
Copper, stm., Ak., U.S.	D11	140
Copperas Cove, Tx., U.S.	C9	130
Copper Butte, mtn., Wa., U.S.	B8	136
Copper Canyon see Cobre, Barranca del, misc. cult., Mex.	B5	100
Copper Center, Ak., U.S.	D10	140
Copper Harbor, Mi., U.S.	D10	118
Coppermine, stm., Can.	B7	106
Copper Mine Point, c., Br. Vir. Is.	e9	104b
Copper Mountain, B.C., Can.	G10	138
Coquí, P.R.	C3	104a
Coquilhatville see Mbandaka, D.R.C.	D3	66
Coquimbo, Chile	E2	92
Coquimbo, state, Chile	E2	92
Corabia, Rom.	F11	26
Coração de Jesus, Braz.	I3	88
Coradi, Isole see Cheradi, Isole, i., Italy	D11	24
Coral Gables, Fl., U.S.	K5	116
Coral Harbour, Bah.	n18	104f
Coral Harbour, Nu., Can.	C14	106
Coral Sea, Oc.	E6	72
Coral Sea Basin, unds.	K18	142
Coral Sea Islands Territory, dep., Oc.	B9	76
Coralville, Ia., U.S.	C6	120
Coram, Mt., U.S.	B12	136
Corangamite, Lake, l., Austl.	K4	76
Corato, Italy	C10	24
Corbeil-Essonnes, Fr.	F11	14
Corbett National Park, p.o.i., India	D7	54
Corbigny, Fr.	G12	14
Corbin, Ky., U.S.	H1	114
Corbones, stm., Spain	G5	20
Corby, Eng., U.K.	I12	12
Corcaigh see Cork, Ire.	J4	12
Córcega, P.R.	B1	104a
Corcoran, Ca., U.S.	G6	134
Corcovado, Golfo, b., Chile	H2	90
Corcovado, Parque Nacional, p.o.i., C.R.	H6	102
Corcovado, Volcán, vol., Chile	H2	90
Corcubión, Spain	B1	20
Cordeiro, Braz.	L4	88
Cordele, Ga., U.S.	E2	116
Cordell Hull Reservoir, res., Tn., U.S.	H12	120
Corder, Mo., U.S.	E4	120
Cordillera, state, Para.	B9	92
Cordillo Downs, Austl.	F3	76
Córdoba, Arg.	E5	92
Córdoba, Mex.	F10	100
Córdoba (Cordova), Spain	G6	20
Córdoba, state, Arg.	E5	92
Córdoba, state, Col.	C4	86
Córdoba, co., Spain	F6	20
Córdova, Peru	F2	84
Cordova see Córdoba, Spain	G6	20
Cordova, Al., U.S.	D11	122
Cordova, Ak., U.S.	D10	140
Cordova, Il., U.S.	C7	120
Cordova Peak, mtn., Ak., U.S.	D10	140
Coreaú, Braz.	B5	88
Coreaú, stm., Braz.	B5	88
Corentyne, stm., S.A.	C6	84
Corfield, Austl.	C4	76
Corfu see Kérkyra, Grc.	D2	28
Corfu see Kérkyra, i., Grc.	D2	28
Coria, Spain	D4	20
Coria del Río, Spain	G4	20
Coribe, Braz.	G3	88
Coricudgy, Mount, mtn., Austl.	I8	76
Corigliano Calabro, Italy	E10	24
Corinne, Ut., U.S.	B4	132
Corinne, W.V., U.S.	G4	114
Corinth see Kórinthos, Grc.	F5	28
Corinth, Ms., U.S.	C10	122
Corinth, N.Y., U.S.	G3	110
Corinth, Gulf of see Korinthiakós Kólpos, b., Grc.	E5	28
Corinto, Braz.	J3	88
Corisco, Isla de, i., Eq. Gui.	I6	64
Corjeuți, Mol.	A14	26
Cork, Ire.	J4	12
Cork, state, Ire.	I4	12
Corleone, Italy	G7	24
Çorlu, Tur.	B10	28
Cornelia, Ga., U.S.	B2	116
Cornélio Procópio, Braz.	D6	90
Cornelius, N.C., U.S.	A5	116
Cornelius Grinnell Bay, b., Nu., Can.	E13	141
Cornell, Wi., U.S.	F7	118
Corner Brook, Nf., Can.	j22	107a
Cornești, Mol.	B14	26
Corneta, Punta, c., Mex.	H10	100
Corning, Ar., U.S.	H7	120
Corning, Ca., U.S.	D3	134
Corning, Ia., U.S.	D3	120
Corning, Ks., U.S.	B12	128
Corning, N.Y., U.S.	B8	114
Cornish, Me., U.S.	G6	110
Černoe more see Black Sea	G15	6
Corno Grande, mtn., Italy	H10	22
Cornwall, On., Can.	E2	110
Cornwallis Island, i., Nu., Can.	B7	141
Cornwall Island, i., Nu., Can.	B6	141
Coro, Ven.	B7	86
Coro, Golfete de, b., Ven.	B6	86
Coroaci, Braz.	J4	88
Coroatá, Braz.	C3	88
Corocoro, Bol.	C3	90
Corocoro, Isla, i., S.A.	C11	86
Coroico, Bol.	C3	90
Coromandel, Braz.	J2	88
Coromandel Coast, cst., India	E5	53
Coromandel Peninsula, pen., N.Z.	C6	80
Corona, Ca., U.S.	J8	134
Corona, N.M., U.S.	G3	128
Coronado, Mex.	D8	100
Coronado, Bahía de, b., C.R.	H6	102
Coronado, Islas, is., Mex.	K8	134
Coronation, Ab., Can.	D19	138
Coronation Gulf, b., Nu., Can.	B8	106
Coronation Island, i., Ant.	B36	81
Coronda, Arg.	E7	92
Coronel, Chile	H1	92
Coronel Bogado, Para.	C9	92
Coronel Dorrego, Arg.	I7	92
Coronel Fabriciano, Braz.	J4	88
Coronel Moldes, Arg.	B5	92
Coronel Moldes, Arg.	F5	92
Coronel Oviedo, Para.	B9	92
Coronel Pringles, Arg.	H7	92
Coronel Suárez, Arg.	H6	92
Coronel Vidal, Arg.	H9	92
Coronel Vivida, Braz.	C11	92
Corongo, Peru	E2	84
Coropuna, Nevado, vol., Peru	G3	84
Corossol, Guad.	B2	105a
Çorovodë, Alb.	D14	24
Corowa, Austl.	J6	76
Corozal, Belize	C3	102
Corozal, Col.	C4	86
Corozal, P.R.	B3	104a
Corpus Christi, Tx., U.S.	G10	130
Corpus Christi, Lake, res., Tx., U.S.	F9	130
Corpus Christi Bay, b., Tx., U.S.	G10	130
Corral, Chile	H2	90
Corral de Almaguer, Spain	E7	20
Corral de Bustos, Arg.	F6	92
Corrales, Cerro, mtn., Mex.	H2	130
Corralito, Arg.	F5	92
Correctionville, Ia., U.S.	B2	120
Corregidor Island, i., Phil.	C3	52
Corrente, Braz.	F3	88
Corrente, stm., Braz.	G4	88
Correntes, Cabo das, c., Moz.	D12	70
Correntina, Braz.	G3	88
Corrèze, state, Fr.	D7	18
Corrib, Lough, l., Ire.	H3	12
Corrientes, Arg.	C8	92
Corrientes, state, Arg.	D9	92
Corrientes, stm., Arg.	D8	92
Corrientes, stm., S.A.	D2	84
Corrientes, Bahía de, b., Cuba	B5	102
Corrientes, Cabo, c., Arg.	I9	92
Corrientes, Cabo, c., Col.	E3	86
Corrientes, Cabo, c., Mex.	E6	100
Corrigan, Tx., U.S.	F4	122
Corrigin, Austl.	F3	74
Corriverton, Guy.	B6	84
Corrumpa Creek, stm., U.S.	E5	128
Corry, Pa., U.S.	C6	114
Corse (Corsica), i., Fr.	G15	18
Corse, Cap, c., Fr.	F15	18
Corse-du-Sud, state, Fr.	H15	18
Corsica see Corse, i., Fr.	G15	18
Corsicana, Tx., U.S.	E2	122
Cort Adelaer, Kap, c., Grnld.	E17	141
Cortazar, Mex.	E8	100
Corte, Fr.	G15	18
Cortés, Mar de see California, Golfo de, b., Mex.	B2	96
Cortez, Co., U.S.	F8	132
Cortez, Sea of see California, Golfo de, b., Mex.	B2	96
Cortina d'Ampezzo, Italy	D8	22
Cortland, Ne., U.S.	K2	118
Cortland, N.Y., U.S.	B9	114
Cortland, Oh., U.S.	C5	114
Cortona, Italy	G8	22
Corubal, stm., Afr.	G2	64
Coruche, Port.	F2	20
Çorum, Tur.	A4	56
Corumbá, Braz.	C5	90
Corumbá, stm., Braz.	I1	88
Corumbaíba, Braz.	J1	88
Corumbataí, stm., Braz.	B11	92
Corumo, stm., Ven.	D11	86
Corunna see A Coruña, Spain	A2	20
Corunna, Mi., U.S.	F5	112
Coruripe, Braz.	F7	88
Corvallis, Mt., U.S.	D12	136
Corvallis, Or., U.S.	F3	136
Corwith, Ia., U.S.	B3	120
Corydon, In., U.S.	F11	120
Corydon, Ky., U.S.	G10	120
Corzu, Rom.	E10	26
Corzuela, Arg.	C7	92
Cos see Kos, i., Grc.	G10	28
Cosamaloapan de Carpio, Mex.	F10	100
Coscomate, Mex.	I2	130
Cosenza, Italy	E10	24
Coshocton, Oh., U.S.	D4	114
Cosigüina, Punta, c., Nic.	F4	102
Cosigüina, Volcán, vol., Nic.	F4	102
Cosmoledo, Atoll de, i., Sey.	k11	69b
Cosmos, Mn., U.S.	G4	118
Cosne-sur-Loire, Fr.	G11	14
Cosquín, Arg.	E5	92
Cossato, Italy	E5	22
Cossatot, stm., Ar., U.S.	C4	122
Costa Mesa, Ca., U.S.	J8	134
Costa Rica, Mex.	C5	100
Costa Rica, ctry., N.A.	H5	102
Coswig, Ger.	E9	16
Coswig, Ger.	E8	16
Cotabato, Phil.	G4	52
Cotahuasi, Peru	G3	84
Cotati, Ca., U.S.	E3	134
Coteaux, Haiti	C10	102
Cote d'Ivoire, ctry., Afr.	H3	64
Côte-d'Or, state, Fr.	G13	14
Cotegipe, Braz.	F3	88
Cotentin, pen., Fr.	E7	14
Côtes-d'Armor, state, Fr.	F6	14
Cotingo, stm., Braz.	E11	86
Cotiujeni, Mol.	B15	26
Cotonou, Benin	H5	64
Cotopaxi, state, Ec.	H2	86
Cotopaxi, vol., Ec.	H2	86
Cotopaxi, Parque Nacional, p.o.i., Ec.	H2	86
Cotswold Hills, hills, Eng., U.K.	J10	12
Cottage Grove, Or., U.S.	G3	136
Cottbus, Ger.	E10	16
Cotter, Ar., U.S.	H5	120
Cottian Alps, mts., Eur.	E12	18
Cottondale, Fl., U.S.	G13	122
Cotton Plant, Ar., U.S.	C7	122
Cottonport, La., U.S.	G6	122
Cotton Valley, La., U.S.	E5	122
Cottonwood, Az., U.S.	I5	132
Cottonwood, Ca., U.S.	C3	134
Cottonwood, Mn., U.S.	G3	118
Cottonwood, stm., Ks., U.S.	C12	128
Cottonwood, stm., Mn., U.S.	G3	118
Cottonwood Creek, stm., Mt., U.S.	F5	124
Cottonwood Falls, Ks., U.S.	C12	128
Coubre, Pointe de la, c., Fr.	D4	18
Couchiching, Lake, l., On., Can.	D10	112
Coudersport, Pa., U.S.	C8	114
Coudres, Île aux, i., Qc., Can.	C6	110
Coulee City, Wa., U.S.	C7	136
Coulee Dam, Wa., U.S.	B8	136
Coulommiers, Fr.	F12	14
Coulonge, stm., Qc., Can.	C13	112
Coulterville, Il., U.S.	F8	120
Counce, Tn., U.S.	B10	122
Council, Id., U.S.	F10	136
Council Bluffs, Ia., U.S.	C2	120
Council Grove, Ks., U.S.	C12	128
Coupeville, Wa., U.S.	B4	136
Courantyne see Corentyne, stm., S.A.	C6	84
Courland (Kurzeme), hist. reg., Lat.	C5	10
Courland Lagoon, b., Eur.	E3	10
Courmayeur, Italy	E3	22
Courtenay, B.C., Can.	G5	138
Courtland, Al., U.S.	C11	122
Courtland, Va., U.S.	H8	114
Courtrai see Kortrijk, Bel.	D12	14
Coutras, Fr.	D5	18
Coutts, Ab., Can.	G19	138
Couture, Lac, l., Qc., Can.	C16	106
Covasna, state, Rom.	C12	26
Cove, Or., U.S.	E9	136
Cove Island, i., On., Can.	C8	112
Covelo, Ca., U.S.	D2	134
Coventry, Eng., U.K.	I11	12
Covert, Mi., U.S.	F3	112
Covilhã, Port.	D3	20
Covington, Ga., U.S.	C2	116
Covington, In., U.S.	H2	112
Covington, Ky., U.S.	E1	114
Covington, La., U.S.	G8	122
Covington, Oh., U.S.	H5	112
Covington, Ok., U.S.	E11	128
Covington, Tn., U.S.	B9	122
Covington, Va., U.S.	G5	114
Cowal, pen., Scot., U.K.	E7	12
Cowal, Lake, l., Austl.	I6	76
Cowan, Tn., U.S.	B13	122
Cowan, Lake, l., Austl.	F4	74
Cowansville, Qc., Can.	E4	110
Cowarie, Austl.	E7	74
Cow Creek, stm., Ks., U.S.	C10	128
Cow Creek, stm., Or., U.S.	H3	136
Cowdenbeath, Scot., U.K.	E9	12
Cowell, Austl.	F7	74
Cowen, W.V., U.S.	F5	114
Coweta, Ok., U.S.	I2	120
Cowhouse Creek, stm., Tx., U.S.	C10	130
Cowichan Bay, B.C., Can.	H7	138
Cowichan Lake, l., B.C., Can.	H6	138
Cowley, Austl.	F5	76
Cowley, Wy., U.S.	C4	126
Cowlic, Az., U.S.	L4	132
Cowlitz, stm., Wa., U.S.	D4	136
Cowpasture, stm., Va., U.S.	F6	114
Cowpens, S.C., U.S.	A4	116
Cowra, Austl.	I7	76
Coxá, stm., Braz.	H3	88
Coxim, Braz.	C6	90
Cox's Bāzār, Bngl.	H13	54
Coyaguaima, Cerro, mtn., Arg.	D3	90
Coyame, Mex.	A6	100
Coyle see Coig, stm., Arg.	J3	90
Coyote, stm., Mex.	F6	98
Coyote Wash, stm., N.M., U.S.	G8	132
Coyuca de Benítez, Mex.	G8	100
Coyuca de Catalán, Mex.	F8	100
Cozad, Ne., U.S.	G13	126
Cozumel, Mex.	B4	102
Cozumel, Isla, i., Mex.	B4	102
Crab Orchard, Tn., U.S.	I13	120
Crab Orchard Lake, res., Il., U.S.	G9	120
Cradle Mountain-Lake Saint Clair National Park, p.o.i., Austl.	n12	77a
Cradock, S. Afr.	H7	70
Craig, Co., U.S.	C9	132
Craig, Mo., U.S.	D2	120
Craig, Ne., U.S.	J2	118
Craigellachie, B.C., Can.	E12	138
Craigmont, Id., U.S.	D10	136
Craigsville, Va., U.S.	F6	114
Craik, Sk., Can.	C8	124
Crailsheim, Ger.	G6	16
Craiova, Rom.	E10	26
Cranberry Lake, l., N.Y., U.S.	F1	110
Cranbrook, Austl.	F3	74
Cranbrook, B.C., Can.	G15	138
Crandon, Wi., U.S.	F9	118
Crane, Az., U.S.	K2	132
Crane, In., U.S.	F11	120
Crane, Tx., U.S.	C5	130
Crane Lake, l., Sk., Can.	D4	124
Crane Mountain, mtn., Or., U.S.	A5	134
Crângeni, Rom.	E11	26
Cranston, R.I., U.S.	C14	114
Crasna, Rom.	D13	26
Crasna, stm., Eur.	I18	16
Crasnoe, Mol.	C16	26
Crater Lake, l., Or., U.S.	H4	136
Crater Lake National Park, p.o.i., Or., U.S.	H5	136
Craters of the Moon National Monument, p.o.i., Id., U.S.	G13	136
Crateús, Braz.	C5	88
Crato, Braz.	D6	88
Crauford, Cape, c., Nu., Can.	A14	106
Cravo Norte, Col.	D6	86
Cravo Norte, stm., Col.	D6	86
Cravo Sur, stm., Col.	E6	86
Crawford, Co., U.S.	E9	132
Crawford, Ms., U.S.	D10	122
Crawford, Tx., U.S.	C10	130
Crawford Bay, B.C., Can.	G14	138
Crawfordsville, Ar., U.S.	B8	122
Crawfordsville, In., U.S.	H2	112
Crawfordville, Ga., U.S.	C3	116
Crawley, Eng., U.K.	J12	12
Crazy Woman Creek, stm., Wy., U.S.	C6	126
Creal Springs, Il., U.S.	G9	120
Cree, stm., Sk., Can.	D9	106
Creede, Co., U.S.	F10	132
Creedmoor, N.C., U.S.	H7	114
Cree Lake, l., Sk., Can.	D9	106
Creemore, On., Can.	D9	112
Creighton, Ne., U.S.	E15	126
Creighton Mine, On., Can.	B8	112
Creil, Fr.	E11	14
Crema, Italy	E6	22
Cremona, Italy	E7	22
Crenshaw, Ms., U.S.	C8	122
Crepori, stm., Braz.	E6	84
Crépy-en-Valois, Fr.	E11	14
Cres, Cro.	E11	22
Cres, Otok, i., Cro.	F11	22
Cresaptown, Md., U.S.	E7	114
Crescent, Or., U.S.	G5	136
Crescent City, Ca., U.S.	B1	134
Crescent City, Fl., U.S.	G4	116
Crescent Spur, B.C., Can.	C10	138
Cresco, Ia., U.S.	H6	118
Crespo, Arg.	F7	92
Cresson, Tx., U.S.	B10	130
Cressy, Austl.	K4	76
Crested Butte, Co., U.S.	E9	132
Crestline, Ca., U.S.	I8	134
Creston, B.C., Can.	G14	138
Creston, Ia., U.S.	C3	120
Crestone Peak, mtn., Co., U.S.	D3	128
Crestview, Fl., U.S.	G12	122
Crestwood Hills, Tn., U.S.	I1	114
Creswell, Or., U.S.	G3	136
Creswell Bay, b., Nu., Can.	A12	106
Crete, Il., U.S.	G2	112
Crete, Ne., U.S.	G16	126
Crete see Kríti, i., Grc.	H7	28
Crete, Sea of see Kritikón Pélagos, Grc.	H8	28
Créteil, Fr.	F11	14
Cretin, Cape, c., Pap. N. Gui.	b4	79a
Creus, Cap de, c., Spain	B14	20
Creuse, state, Fr.	C8	18
Creuse, stm., Fr.	C6	18
Creussen, Ger.	G7	16
Creve Coeur, Il., U.S.	K9	118
Crevillent, Spain	F10	20
Crevillente see Crevillent, Spain	F10	20
Crewe, Eng., U.K.	H10	12
Crewe, Va., U.S.	G7	114
Cricaré, stm., Braz.	J5	88
Criciúma, Braz.	D13	92
Crikvenica, Cro.	E11	22
Crimea see Krymsʹkyi pivostriv, pen., Ukr.	E4	32
Crimean Peninsula see Krymsʹkyi pivostriv, pen., Ukr.	E4	32
Crimmitschau, Ger.	F8	16
Cripple Creek, Co., U.S.	C3	128
Crisfield, Md., U.S.	F10	114
Criss Creek, B.C., Can.	E10	138
Crissiumal, Braz.	C10	92
Cristal, Monts de, mts., Afr.	I7	64
Cristalândia, Braz.	F1	88

Name	Map Ref.	Page

Cristália, Braz. — I4 88
Cristalina, Braz. — I2 88
Cristinápolis, Braz. — F7 88
Cristino Castro, Braz. — E3 88
Cristóbal Colón, Pico, mtn., Col. — B5 86
Crişul Alb, stm., Eur. — C8 26
Crişul Negru, stm., Eur. — C8 26
Crişul Repede (Sebes Körös), stm., Eur. — B8 26
Crivitz, Wi., U.S. — C1 112
Crna, stm., Mac. — B4 28
Crna Gora (Montenegro), state, Yugo. — G6 26
Crni Drim (Drinit të Zi), stm., Eur. — C14 24
Cmomeli, Slvn. — E12 22
Croajingolong National Park, p.o.i., Austl. — K7 76
Croatia, ctry., Eur. — E13 22
Croche, stm., Qc., Can. — C4 110
Crocker, Mo., U.S. — G5 120
Crocker, Banjaran, mts., Malay. — H1 52
Crockett, Tx., U.S. — F3 122
Crocodilopolis, hist., Egypt — I1 58
Crocus Hill, hill, Anguilla — A1 105a
Crofton, Ky., U.S. — G10 120
Croghan, N.Y., U.S. — E14 112
Croix, Lac la, l., N.A. — C6 118
Croker, Cape, c., Austl. — B6 74
Croker, Cape, c., On., Can. — D9 112
Croker Island, i., Austl. — B6 74
Cromer, Eng., U.K. — I14 12
Cromínia, Braz. — I1 88
Crompton Point, c., Dom. — i6 105c
Cromwell, N.Z. — G3 80
Cromwell, Al., U.S. — E10 122
Crooked, stm., Or., U.S. — F5 136
Crooked Creek, Ak., U.S. — D8 140
Crooked Creek, stm., U.S. — D8 128
Crooked Island, i., Bah. — A10 102
Crooked Island Passage, strt., Bah. — A10 102
Crooked River, Sk., Can. — B10 124
Crookston, Mn., U.S. — D2 118
Crooksville, Oh., U.S. — E3 114
Crosby, Mn., U.S. — E5 118
Crosby, N.D., U.S. — F10 124
Crosby, Mount, mtn., Wy., U.S. — D3 126
Crosbyton, Tx., U.S. — H7 128
Cross, stm., Afr. — H6 64
Crossett, Ar., U.S. — D7 122
Cross Lake, res., Mb., Can. — E11 106
Crossman Peak, mtn., Az., U.S. — I2 132
Cross Plains, Tx., U.S. — B8 130
Cross Plains, Wi., U.S. — H9 118
Cross Sound, strt., Ak., U.S. — E12 140
Crossville, Il., U.S. — F9 120
Crossville, Tn., U.S. — I12 120
Croswell, Mi., U.S. — E7 112
Crotone, Italy — E11 24
Crow, North Fork, stm., Mn., U.S. — F5 118
Crow, South Fork, stm., Mn., U.S. — G4 118
Crow Agency, Mt., U.S. — B5 126
Crow Creek, stm., U.S. — G8 126
Crowder, Ms., U.S. — C8 122
Crowduck Lake, l., Mb., Can. — A3 118
Crowdy Head, c., Austl. — H9 76
Crowell, Tx., U.S. — H9 128
Crow Lake, On., Can. — B5 118
Crowley, La., U.S. — G6 122
Crowleys Ridge, mts., U.S. — B8 122
Crown Mountain, mtn., V.I.U.S. — e7 104b
Crown Point, In., U.S. — G2 112
Crownpoint, N.M., U.S. — H8 132
Crown Point, N.Y., U.S. — G3 110
Crown Prince Frederik Island, i., Nu., Can. — A13 106
Crowsnest Pass, p., Can. — G16 138
Crowsnest Pass, p., Can. — G16 138
Crows Nest Peak, mtn., S.D., U.S. — C8 126
Crow Wing, stm., Mn., U.S. — E4 118
Croydon, Austl. — B4 76
Croydon Station, B.C., Can. — C11 138
Crozet, Va., U.S. — F7 114
Crozet, Îles, is., Afr. — J16 4
Crozet Basin, unds. — M9 142
Crucea, Rom. — E15 26
Cruces, Cuba — A7 102
Cruger, Ms., U.S. — D8 122
Crump Lake, l., Or., U.S. — A6 134
Cruz, Cabo, c., Cuba — C9 102
Cruz Alta, Arg. — F6 92
Cruz Alta, Braz. — D11 92
Cruz Bay, V.I.U.S. — e7 104b
Cruz del Eje, Arg. — E5 92
Cruzeiro, Braz. — L3 88
Cruzeiro do Oeste, Braz. — A11 92
Cruzeta, Braz. — E3 84
Cruzeiro do Sul, Braz. — D7 88
Cruz Grande, Chile — D2 92
Crysler, On., Can. — C14 112
Crystal, Mn., U.S. — F5 118
Crystal, N.D., U.S. — F16 124
Crystal Brook, Austl. — I2 76
Crystal City, Mb., U.S. — E15 124
Crystal City, Mo., U.S. — F7 120
Crystal City, Tx., U.S. — F8 130
Crystal Falls, Mi., U.S. — B1 112
Crystal Lake, l., U.S. — B9 120
Crystal Lake, l., Mi., U.S. — D3 112
Crystal Lake, l., Vt., U.S. — E8 122
Crystal Springs, Ms., U.S. — C7 26
Csongrád, Hung. — C7 26
Csongrád, state, Hung. — C7 26
Csorna, Hung. — B4 26
Cu, U.S., Asia — F11 32
Cúa, Ven. — B8 86
Cuajinicuilapa, Mex. — G9 100
Cuamba, Moz. — C6 68
Cuando (Kwando), stm., Afr. — D3 68
Cuangar, Ang. — D2 68
Cuango, Ang. — B2 68
Cuango see Kwango, stm., Afr. — F3 66
Cuanza, stm., Ang. — C2 68
Cuao, stm., Ven. — E8 86
Cuareim (Quaraí), stm., S.A. — E9 92
Cuaró, stm., Ur. — E9 92
Cuarto, stm., Arg. — F6 92
Cuatrociénegas, Mex. — B7 100
Cuauhtémoc, Mex. — A5 100
Cuautitlán, Mex. — F6 100
Cuba, Port. — F3 20
Cuba, Il., U.S. — D7 120
Cuba, Mo., U.S. — F6 120
Cuba, N.M., U.S. — G10 132
Cuba, ctry., N.A. — C9 96
Cubagua, Isla, i., Ven. — B9 86
Cubal, Ang. — C1 68
Cubango (Okavango), stm., Afr. — D2 68
Cubati, Braz. — D7 88
Cublas, Russia — D21 8
Çubuk, Tur. — C15 28
Cuchi, stm., Ang. — C2 68
Cuchivero, stm., Ven. — D9 86
Cuchí Co, Arg. — I5 92
Cucurpe, Mex. — F7 98
Cúcuta, Col. — D5 86
Cucuy, Piedra de, hill, Ven. — G8 86
Cudalore, India — F4 53
Cuddapah, India — D4 53

Čudovo, Russia — A14 10
Cudworth, Sk., Can. — B8 124
Çudzin, Bela. — H9 10
Cue, Austl. — E3 74
Cuemba, Ang. — C2 68
Cuenca, Ec. — I2 86
Cuenca, Spain — D8 20
Cuenca, co., Spain — E9 20
Cuenca, co., Spain — E9 20
Cuencamé de Ceniceros, Mex. — C7 100
Cuernavaca, Mex. — F9 100
Cuero, Tx., U.S. — E10 130
Cuers, Fr. — F12 18
Cuervo, Laguna del, l., Mex. — A6 100
Cuesta Pass, p., Ca., U.S. — H5 134
Cueto, Cuba — B9 102
Cugir, Rom. — D10 26
Cugueuka, Russia — B10 38
Çuhlomskoe, ozero, l., Russia — G19 8
Cuiabá, Braz. — G6 84
Cuiabá, stm., Braz. — G6 84
Cuiari, Braz. — G7 86
Cuicatlán, Mex. — G10 100
Cuilapa, Guat. — E2 102
Cuilco see Grijalva, stm., N.A. — G12 100
Cuité, Braz. — D7 88
Cuito, stm., Ang. — D2 68
Cuito Cuanavale, Ang. — D2 68
Cuitzeo, Lago de, l., Mex. — F8 100
Cuiuni, stm., Braz. — H10 86
Cukai, Malay. — J6 48
Čukas, Indon. — D4 50
Čukotskij, mys, c., Russia — D26 34
Čukotskij poluostrov (Chukotsk Peninsula), pen., Russia — C26 34
Çukurca, Tur. — B6 56
Çukurkuy, Kaz. — F11 32
Culasi, Phil. — F9 124
Cul de Sac, Guad. — A1 105a
Cul de Sac, Neth. Ant. — A1 105a
Culebra, P.R. — B5 104a
Culebra, Isla de, i., P.R. — B5 104a
Culebra Peak, mtn., Co., U.S. — D3 128
Culfa, Azer. — B6 56
Culgoa, stm., Austl. — G6 76
Culiacán, Mex. — C5 100
Culiacán, stm., Mex. — C5 100
Culion, Phil. — J9 134
Culion Island, i., Phil. — E2 52
Cúlar, Spain — G8 20
Culberson, Mt., U.S. — E5 22
Culebra, stm. — ES 122
Culleoka, Tn., U.S. — B12 122
Cullera, Spain — E10 20
Cullman, Al., U.S. — C12 122
Cullman, Al., U.S. — D9 120
Cul'man, Russia — E13 34
Culpeper, Va., U.S. — F7 114
Culpina, Bol. — D4 90
Culuene, stm., Braz. — F7 84
Culver, In., U.S. — G3 112
Culver, Or., U.S. — F5 136
Culverden, N.Z. — F5 80
Culym, Russia — C14 32
Čulym, stm., Russia — C14 32
Cum, Russia — C1 34
Cumaná, Ven. — B9 86
Cumare, Cerro, hill, Col. — G5 86
Cumari, Braz. — J1 88
Cumbal, Nevado, vol., Col. — G2 86
Cumbe, Braz. — F7 88
Cumberland, B.C., Can. — G5 138
Cumberland, Ky., U.S. — G3 114
Cumberland, Md., U.S. — E7 114
Cumberland, Wi., U.S. — G7 114
Cumberland, Wi., U.S. — F6 118
Cumberland, stm., U.S. — H2 114
Cumberland, Lake, res., Ky., U.S. — H13 120
Cumberland, South Fork, stm., U.S. — H13 120
Cumberland Gap, p., U.S. — H2 114
Cumberland Island National Seashore, p.o.i., Ga., U.S. — F4 116
Cumberland Islands, is., Austl. — C7 76
Cumberland Lake, l., Sk., Can. — E10 106
Cumberland Peninsula, pen., Nu., Can. — B17 106
Cumberland Plateau, plat., U.S. — G14 110
Cumberland Sound, strt., Nu., Can. — B17 106
Cumbernauld, Scot., U.K. — F9 12
Cumbrian Mountains, mts., Eng., U.K. — G9 12
Cumby, Tx., U.S. — D3 122
Cumikan, Russia — F16 34
Cumming, Ga., U.S. — B1 116
Cummings, Austl. — F7 74
Cummins, Austl. — F7 74
Cumnock, Scot., U.K. — F8 12
Cumpas, Mex. — F8 98
Cumra, Tur. — F15 28
Cunani, Braz. — C7 84
CunawIche, Ven. — D8 86
Cunco, Chile — G2 90
Cundinamarca, state, Col. — E4 86
Cunduá, Braz. — C11 92
Cunene (Kunene), stm., Afr. — D1 68
Cuneo (Coni), Italy — F4 22
Cunha Porã, Braz. — C11 92
Cunja, stm., Russia — B17 32
Cunnamulla, Austl. — G5 76
Cunningham, N.S., U.S. — D10 128
Cunskij, Russia — C17 32
Cunucunuma, stm., Ven. — F9 86
Cuny, Russia — C7 8
Cuorgnè, Italy — E4 22
Cupar, Sk., Can. — D9 124
Cupar, Scot., U.K. — E9 12
Cupica, Golfo de, b., Col. — E3 86
Cuprovo, Russia — D22 8
Cuquenán, stm., Ven. — E11 86
Çuruçá, Braz. — E8 88
Curaçao, i., Neth. Ant. — p21 104g
Curanilahue, Chile — H1 92
Curanipe, Chile — G1 92
Curapça, Russia — D15 34
Curaray, stm., S.A. — H3 86
Curepipe, Mrts. — i10 69a
Curicó, Chile — G2 92
Curicuriari, stm., Braz. — H8 86
Curimatá, Braz. — E3 88
Curimatá, stm., Braz. — E3 88
Curitiba, Braz. — B13 92
Curitibanos, Braz. — C12 92
Curiúau, stm., Braz. — H11 86
Curlewa, Braz. — D8 84
Curlewis, Austl. — H2 76
Çurovici, Russia — H15 10
Currais Novos, Braz. — D7 88
Curralinho, Braz. — D8 84
Current, stm., Mo., U.S. — E1 134
Current Mountain, mtn., Nv., U.S. — H7 120
Dagö see Hiiumaa, i., Est. — C5 10
Curitis, Austl. — m12 77a
Currituck, N.C., U.S. — H9 114
Currituck Sound, strt., N.C., U.S. — H10 114
Curtea de Argeş, Rom. — D11 26
Curtina, Ur. — F9 92
Curtis, Ar., U.S. — D5 122
Curtis, Ne., U.S. — G12 126
Curtis, Port b., Austl. — D8 76
Curtis Channel, strt., Austl. — D8 76
Curtis Island, i., Austl. — D8 76

Curtis Island, i., N.Z. — G9 72
Curu, stm., Braz. — B6 88
Curuá, stm., Braz. — D7 84
Curuá, stm., Braz. — E7 84
Curuá, Ilha do, i., Braz. — C7 84
Curuá-Una, stm., Braz. — D7 84
Curuçá, Braz. — D8 84
Curumu, Braz. — D7 84
Curup, Indon. — E3 50
Curupá, Braz. — E2 88
Cururupu, Braz. — A3 88
Curuzú Cuatiá, Arg. — D8 92
Curvelo, Braz. — J3 88
Cusco, Peru — F3 84
Cushing, Ok., U.S. — B2 122
Cushing, Tx., U.S. — F4 122
Cushing, Tx., U.S. — I6 120
Cusiana, stm., Col. — E5 86
Cusihuiriachic, Mex. — A5 100
Çusovaja, stm., Russia — C9 32
Çusovoj, Russia — C9 32
Cusset, Fr. — C9 18
Cusseta, Ga., U.S. — E14 122
Cust, Uzb. — F12 32
Custer, Mt., U.S. — E3 112
Custer, Mt., U.S. — A5 126
Custer, S.D., U.S. — D9 126
Custódia, Braz. — D7 88
Cut Bank, Mt., U.S. — B14 136
Cutbank, stm., Ab., Can. — B12 138
Cut Bank Creek, stm., U.S. — F12 124
Cut Bank Creek, stm., Mt., U.S. — B14 136
Cutervo, Peru — E2 84
Cuthbert, Ga., U.S. — F14 122
Cutler, Ca., U.S. — G6 134
Cutler, Me., U.S. — F9 110
Cutlerville, Mi., U.S. — F4 112
Cutral-Có, Arg. — I3 90
Cutro, Italy — E10 24
Cuttack, India — H10 54
Cuttaink, stm., Ab., Can. — F8 100
Čuvašija, state, Russia — C7 32
Cuvier, Cape, c., Austl. — D2 74
Cuvo, stm., Ang. — C1 68
Cuxhaven, Ger. — C4 16
Cuyahoga Falls, Oh., U.S. — C4 114
Cuyapa, stm., Ca., U.S. — I6 134
Cuyamaca Peak, mtn., Ca., U.S. — J9 134
Cuyari, stm., S.A. — G7 86
Cuyo, Phil. — B1 48
Cuyo East Pass, strt., Phil. — E3 52
Cuyo Islands, is., Phil. — E3 52
Cuyo West Pass, strt., Phil. — E3 52
Cuyubini, stm., Ven. — D11 86
Cuyuni-Mazaruni, state, Guy. — D11 86
Cwmbran, Wales, U.K. — J10 12
Cyclades see Kikládhes, is., Grc. — F7 28
Cypress, La., U.S. — F5 122
Cypress Hills, hills, Can. — E14 124
Cypress River, Mb., Can. — E14 124
Cypress Springs, Lake, res., Tx., U.S. — D3 122
Cyprus, ctry., Asia — C4 58
Cyprus, North, ctry., Asia — C4 58
Cyrenaica see Barqah, hist. reg., Libya — A4 62
Cyril, Ok., U.S. — G10 128
Cyril E. King Airport, V.I.U.S. — e7 104b
Cyrus Field Bay, b., Nu., Can. — E13 141
Çyrvonae, vozero, l., Bela. — H10 10
Cythera see Kýthira, i., Grc. — G5 28
Czaplinek, Pol. — C12 16
Czarna Woda, Pol. — C14 16
Czarnków, Pol. — D12 16
Czechoslovakia see Czech Republic, ctry., Eur. — G11 16
Czechowice-Dziedzice, Pol. — G15 16
Czech Republic, ctry., Eur. — G11 16
Czernjejewo, Pol. — D13 16
Czerwieńsk, Pol. — D11 16
Czersk, Czech Rep. — F15 16
Częstochowa, Pol. — F15 16
Częstochowa, state, Pol. — F15 16
Człuchów, Pol. — C13 16

D
Da, stm., China — G8 42
Da, Song see Black, stm., Asia — D9 46
Da'an, China — J4 42
Dabajuro, Ven. — B6 86
Daba Shan, mts., China — E3 42
Dabat, Eth. — E7 62
Dabeiba, Col. — D3 86
Dabhoi, India — G4 54
Dabie, Pol. — D14 16
Dabie Shan, mts., China — F6 42
Dabola, Gui. — G2 64
Dabou, C. Iv. — H4 64
Daboya, Ghana — H4 64
Dabrowa, Pol. — I7 42
Dąbrowa Białostocka, Pol. — C19 16
Dabrowa Tarnowska, Pol. — G16 16
Dabu, China — I7 42
Dac Glei, Viet. — E8 48
Dachau, Ger. — H7 16
Dacice, Czech Rep. — G11 16
Dacoma, Ok., U.S. — E10 128
Dadanawa, Guy. — F12 86
Dade City, Fl., U.S. — H3 116
Dadeldhurā, Nepal — D8 54
Dac Doi, Viet. — E13 122
Dādra and Nagar Haveli, state, India — I4 54
Dādu, Pak. — D10 56
Daegu see Taegu, Kor., S. — D1 40
Daejeon see Taejón, Kor., S. — F7 38
Daet, Phil. — C4 52
Dafang, China — F6 36
Dafeng, China — E9 42
Dáfni, Grc. — F5 28
Dafoe, Sk., Can. — C9 124
Dafu, stm., China — F5 42
Dagã, stm., Mya. — D2 53
Dagana, Sen. — F1 64
Dagda, Lat. — D10 10
Dagda, stm., Russia — B7 42
Dagestan, state, Russia — F7 32
Daglung, China — D13 54
Dagupan, Pap. N. Gui. — a3 79a
Daguao, P.R. — B4 104a
Dagupan, Phil. — C6 38
Dagzê Co, l., China — B11 54

Dāhod, India — G5 54
Dahomey see Benin, ctry., Afr. — G5 64
Dahra, Libya — B3 62
Dahra, mts., Alg. — H11 20
Dahshur, Pyramides de (Dashur, Pyramids of), hist., Egypt — I1 58
Dai, i., Sol. Is. — d9 79b
Dai Hai, l., China — A5 42
Daik-u, Mya. — D3 48
Dā'il, Syria — F7 58
Daimiel, Spain — E7 20
Daingean, Ire. — H5 12
Daingerfield, Tx., U.S. — D4 122
Dainkog, China — E5 36
Daireaux, Arg. — H7 92
Dairen see Dalian, China — B9 42
Daïrût, Egypt — K1 58
Dai-sen, vol., Japan — D6 40
Daisetta, Tx., U.S. — G4 122
Daning, China — D4 42
Daiyun Shan, mts., China — I8 42
Dajarra, Austl. — C2 76
Dajian Shan, mtn., China — F5 36
Dakar, Sen. — G1 64
Dakeng, China — H6 42
Dakhin Shāhbāzpur Island, i., Bngl. — G13 54
Dakhla, W. Sah. — E1 64
Dākoānk, India — G7 46
Dakoro, Niger — G6 64
Dakota City, Ia., U.S. — B3 120
Dakota City, Ne., U.S. — B1 120
Dakovica, Yugo. — G7 26
Dakovo, Cro. — E15 22
Dala, Sol. Is. — e9 79b
Dalaba, Gui. — G2 64
Dalad Qi, China — A4 42
Dälälven, stm., Swe. — F7 8
Dalaman, Tur. — G11 28
Dalándzadgad, Mong. — C5 36
Dalarna, state, Swe. — F6 8
Da Lat, Viet. — F9 48
Dālbandīn, Pak. — D9 56
Dalby, Austl. — F8 76
Dalby, Nor. — F1 8
Dale, Nor. — F1 8
Dale Hollow Lake, res., U.S. — H12 120
Dalet, Mya. — B1 48
Daleville, In., U.S. — H4 112
Dalgan, Egypt — K1 58
Dalhart, Tx., U.S. — E6 128
Dalhousie, N.B., Can. — B10 110
Dalhousie, India — B5 54
Dalhousie, Cape, c., N.T., Can. — B14 140
Dali, China — F5 36
Dálkola, India — F11 54
Dallas, Ga., U.S. — D14 122
Dallas, Or., U.S. — F3 136
Dallas, Tx., U.S. — B11 130
Dallas, Wi., U.S. — F7 118
Dallas Center, Ia., U.S. — J4 118
Dalli Rājhara, India — H8 54
Dall Lake, l., Ak., U.S. — D7 140
Dalmacija (Dalmatia, hist. reg., Eur. — G12 22
Dalmatia, hist. reg., Eur. — G12 22
Dalmau, India — E8 54
Dal'negorsk, Russia — B11 38
Dal'nyk, Ukr. — C17 26
Daloa, C. Iv. — H3 64
Dalqū, Sudan — C6 62
Dalroy, Ab., Can. — E17 138
Dalrymple, Mount, mtn., Austl. — C7 76
Dalsingh Sarai, India — F10 54
Dāltenganj, India — F10 54
Dalton, Ga., U.S. — C13 122
Dalton, Ma., U.S. — B12 114
Dalton, Ne., U.S. — F10 126
Daludalu, Indon. — C2 50
Dalupiri Island, i., Phil. — A3 52
Dalwallinu, Austl. — E3 74
Daly, stm., Austl. — B6 74
Daly Bay, b., Nu., Can. — C13 106
Daly City, Ca., U.S. — F3 134
Daly Lake, l., Sk., Can. — D9 106
Daly Waters, Austl. — C6 74
Dam, stm., China — B14 54
Damaia, Port. — F1 20
Damai, Indon. — H4 54
Damanhūr, Egypt — G1 58
Damān and Diu, state, India — H4 54
Damar, Pulau, i., Indon. — G8 44
Damara, C.A.R. — C3 66
Damaraland, hist. reg., Nmb. — E2 68
Damascus see Dimashq, Syria — E7 58
Damascus, Ar., U.S. — B6 122
Damascus, Ga., U.S. — F14 122
Damascus, Va., U.S. — H3 114
Damaturu, Nig. — G7 64
Damāvand, Qolleh-ye, vol., Iran — B7 56
Damba, Ang. — B2 68
Dambarta, Nig. — G6 64
Damboa, Nig. — G7 64
Dâmbovita, stm., Rom. — E12 26
Damen Dao, i., China — H9 42
Dāmghān, Iran — B7 56
Damiao, China — C1 42
Damietta Mouth see Dumyāt, Masabb, mth., Egypt — G3 58
Daming, China — C6 42
Dāmodar, stm., India — G11 54
Damoh, India — G7 54
Damongo, Ghana — H4 64
Dampier, Austl. — D3 74
Dampier, Selat, strt., Indon. — F9 44
Dampier Land, pen., Austl. — C4 74
Dâmrei, Chuŏr Phnum, mts., Camb. — G7 48
Damxung, China — C13 54
Damwald, China — B7 36
Dana, Indon. — C3 50
Danakil, reg., Afr. — E8 62
Danané, C. Iv. — H3 64
Danao, Phil. — D9 48
Dang, stm., China — F16 32
Danba, China — E5 36
Danbury, Ct., U.S. — C12 114
Danbury, Ne., U.S. — A8 128
Danby Lake, l., Ca., U.S. — I1 132
Dandeldhurā see Dadeldhurā, Nepal — D2 53
Dandeli, India — D2 53
Dandong, Austl. — D5 38
Dandridge, Tn., U.S. — H2 114
Danfeng, China — E4 42
Dantian Ding, mtn., China — J4 42
Danforth, Me., U.S. — E9 110

Dang, stm., China — F16 32
Dangan Liedao, is., China — K6 42
Dangara, Taj. — B10 56
Danger Point, c., S. Afr. — I5 70
Danggali Conservation Park, p.o.i., Austl. — I3 76
Dangila, Eth. — E7 62
Dangriga, Belize — D3 102
Dangshan, China — D7 42
Dangtu, China — F8 42
Dan-Gulbi, Nig. — G6 64
Daniel, Wy., U.S. — H16 136
Daniel-Johnson, Barrage, dam, Qc., Can. — E17 106
Daniëlskuil, S. Afr. — F6 70
Danielson, Ct., U.S. — C13 114
Daniels Pass, p., Ut., U.S. — C5 132
Danielsville, Ga., U.S. — B2 116
Danilov, Russia — G18 8
Danilovka, Kaz. — D12 32
Daning, China — I4 42
Danjiangkou Shuiku, res., China — E4 42
Danjo-guntō, is., Japan — G1 40
Danli, Hond. — F4 102
Danmark Fjord, b., Grnld. — A22 141
Dannebrog, Ne., U.S. — F14 126
Dannenberg, Ger. — C6 16
Dannevirke, N.Z. — E7 80
Danshui, China — J6 42
Danville, N.Y., U.S. — B8 114
Dante, Va., U.S. — H3 114
Dantewāra, India — B5 53
Danube, stm., Eur. — F11 6
Danube, Mouths of the, mth., Eur. — E16 26
Danvers, Il., U.S. — D8 120
Danville, Ca., U.S. — E4 134
Danville, Il., U.S. — D2 116
Danville, Ky., U.S. — G13 120
Danville, Pa., U.S. — D9 114
Danville, Vt., U.S. — F4 110
Danville, Vt., U.S. — F4 110
Danville, Va., U.S. — H6 114
Danyang, China — F8 42
Danzig see Gdansk, Pol. — B14 16
Danzig, Gulf of see Gdansk, Gulf of, b., Eur. — B15 16
Daocheng, China — F5 36
Daokou, China — B8 42
Daohu, China — G7 42
Daosa, India — E6 54
Daotiandi, China — B10 36
Daoukro, C. Iv. — H4 64
Daoxian, China — I4 42
Daozhen, China — G2 42
Dapaong, Togo — G5 64
Dapchi, Nig. — G7 64
Daphne, Al., U.S. — G11 122
Daqing, China — B9 42
Daqin, China — D4 36
Daqu, stm., China — E5 36
Dara, Sen. — F1 64
Darā', Syria — F7 58
Dar'ā, state, Syria — F7 58
Dārāb, Iran — D7 56
Dārāban, Pak. — C3 54
Darabani, Rom. — A13 26
Darasun, Russia — F11 34
Daravica, mtn., Yugo. — G7 26
Dārayyā, Syria — E7 58
Darb al-Hajj, Jabal, mtn., Jord. — H6 58
Darbhanga, India — E10 54
D'Arbonne, Bayou, stm., La., U.S. — E6 122
Darby, Mt., U.S. — D12 136
Dardanelle, Ar., U.S. — B5 122
Dardanelle Lake, res., Ar., U.S. — B5 122
Dardanelles see Çanakkale Boğazı, strt., Tur. — C9 28
Dar-el-Beida see Casablanca, Mor. — C3 64
Dar es Salaam, Tan. — F7 66
Darfo, Italy — E7 22
Dargai, India — A3 54
Dargan-Ata, Turkmen. — A9 56
Dargaville, N.Z. — B5 80
Dargol, Niger — G5 64
Darhan, Mong. — B6 36
Darién, Col. — F3 86
Darién, Tur. — C12 28
Darién, Parque Nacional, p.o.i., Pan. — D2 86
Darién, Serranía del, mts., Col. — C3 86
Dārjiling, India — E12 54
Dark Head, c., St. Vin. — o11 105e
Darlag, China — E4 36
Darling, Ms., U.S. — H4 70
Darling, stm., Austl. — I4 76
Darling Downs, reg., Austl. — F8 76
Darling Range, mts., Austl. — F3 74
Darlington, Eng., U.K. — G11 12
Darlington, Wi., U.S. — B8 120
Darlington Dam, res., S. Afr. — H7 70
Darlot, Lake, l., Austl. — E4 74
Darłowo, Pol. — B12 16
Darmstadt, Ger. — G4 16
Darnah, Libya — A4 62
Darnall, S. Afr. — F10 70
Darney, Fr. — F15 14
Darnley, Cape, c., Ant. — B11 81
Darnley Bay, b., N.T., Can. — B6 106
Darr, stm., Austl. — D4 76
Darregueira, Arg. — H6 92
Darreh Gaz, Iran — B8 56
Darrington, Wa., U.S. — B5 136
Darrouzett, Tx., U.S. — E8 128
Dart, Cape, c., Ant. — C27 81
Dartmoor, Austl. — K3 76
Dartmoor National Park, p.o.i., Eng., U.K. — K9 12
Dartmouth, N.S., Can. — F13 110
Dartmouth, Eng., U.K. — K9 12
Dartmouth, Lake, l., Austl. — E5 76
Dartmouth Reservoir, res., Austl. — K6 76
Daru, Pap. N. Gui. — b3 79a
Daruvar, Cro. — E14 22
Darvaza, Turkmen. — A8 56
Dārwha, India — H6 54
Darwin, Austl. — B6 74
Darwin, Bahía, b., Chile — I2 90
Darya Khan, Pak. — C3 54
Dashbalbar, Mong. — B7 36
Dashitou, China — C8 38
Dashoguz, Turkmen. — A8 56
Dasht, stm., Pak. — D9 56
Dashte Kavir, des., Iran — C7 56
Dashur, Pyramids of see Dahshur, Pyramides de, hist., Egypt — I1 58
Dashutang, China — A6 48
Dasol Bay, b., Phil. — C2 52
Dastgardān, Iran — C8 56
Datang, China — I3 42
Datça, Tur. — G10 28
Date, Japan — C14 38
Datia, India — F7 54
Datian, China — I7 42
Datian Ding, mtn., China — J4 42
Datong, China — D5 36

Datong, China — B9 36
Datong, China — A5 42
Datong Shan, mts., China — D4 36
Datu, Cape, c., Asia — E4 44
Datumakuta, Indon. — B10 50
Datu Piang, Phil. — G5 52
Daua (Dawa), stm., Afr. — G8 62
Daudnagar, India — F10 54
Daugai, Lith. — F7 10
Daugavpils, Lat. — E9 10
Dauhinava, Bela. — F10 10
Daule, Ec. — H2 86
Daule, stm., Ec. — H1 86
Daund, India — B2 53
Daung Kyun, i., Mya. — F3 48
Dauphin, Mb., Can. — C13 124
Dauphin, Mb., Can. — C15 124
Dauphiné, hist. reg., Fr. — E11 18
Dauphin Island, Al., U.S. — G10 122
Dauphin Lake, l., Mb., Can. — C13 124
Daura, Nig. — G6 64
Dāvangere, India — D2 53
Davant, La., U.S. — H9 122
Davao, Phil. — G5 52
Davao Gulf, b., Phil. — G5 52
Dāvarzan, Iran — B8 56
Davenport, Fl., U.S. — H4 116
Davenport, Ia., U.S. — C7 120
Davenport, Ok., U.S. — B2 122
Davenport, Wa., U.S. — C8 136
Davenport Downs, Austl. — D4 76
Davey, Port, b., Austl. — o12 77a
David, Pan. — H6 102
David City, Ne., U.S. — F15 126
Davidson, Sk., Can. — C7 124
Davidson Mountains, mts., Ak., U.S. — C11 140
Davie, Fl., U.S. — J5 116
Davis, Ca., U.S. — E4 134
Davis, N.C., U.S. — B9 116
Davis, Ok., U.S. — G11 128
Davis, W.V., U.S. — E6 114
Davis, stm., Austl. — D4 74
Davis, sci., Ant. — B12 81
Davis, Mount, mtn., Pa., U.S. — E6 114
Davisboro, Ga., U.S. — C3 116
Davis Dam, dam, U.S. — H2 132
Davis Inlet, Nf., Can. — D18 106
Davis Mountains, mts., Tx., U.S. — D3 130
Davis Sea, Ant. — P11 142
Davis Strait, strt., N.A. — D14 141
Davos, Switz. — D6 22
Davy, W.V., U.S. — G4 114
Davyd-Haradok, Bela. — H9 10
Dawa (Daua), stm., Afr. — G7 62
Dawei (Tavoy), Mya. — E4 48
Dawen, stm., China — D7 42
Dawlan, Mya. — D4 48
Dawna Range, mts., Mya. — D4 48
Dawson, Yk., Can. — C3 106
Dawson, Ga., U.S. — F14 122
Dawson, Mn., U.S. — G2 118
Dawson, N.D., U.S. — A14 126
Dawson, Ne., U.S. — D2 120
Dawson, Tx., U.S. — F2 122
Dawson, Isla, i., Chile — J2 90
Dawson, Mount, mtn., B.C., Can. — D7 76
Dawson Bay, b., Mb., Can. — B13 124
Dawson Creek, B.C., Can. — D7 106
Dawson Inlet, b., Nu., Can. — C12 106
Dawson Range, mts., Yk., Can. — C3 106
Dawsonville, Ga., U.S. — B1 116
Dax, Fr. — F4 18
Daxian, China — F2 42
Daxing, China — B7 42
Daxu, China — I4 42
Daxue Shan, mts., China — F5 36
Dayang, stm., China — F5 36
Dayangshu, China — F5 36
Dayao, China — F5 36
Daye, China — F6 42
Daylesford, Austl. — K5 76
Dayong, China — E9 32
Dayong, China — G4 42
Dayr az-Zawr, Syria — B4 56
Dayr Ḥāfir, Syria — B8 58
Daysland, Ab., Can. — D18 138
Dayton, Oh., U.S. — E1 114
Dayton, Or., U.S. — E3 136
Dayton, Tn., U.S. — B13 122
Dayton, Tx., U.S. — G4 122
Dayton, Wa., U.S. — D9 136
Dayton, Wy., U.S. — C5 126
Daytona Beach, Fl., U.S. — G5 116
Dayu, China — I6 42
Dayu Ling, mts., China — I6 42
Da Yunhe (Grand Canal), can., China — E8 42
Dayville, Or., U.S. — F7 136
Dazhu, China — F2 42
Dazkin, Tur. — F12 28
De Aar, S. Afr. — G7 70
Deadhorse, Ak., U.S. — B10 140
Deadman's Cay, Bah. — A10 102
Dead Sea, l., Asia — G6 58
Deadwood, S.D., U.S. — C9 126
Deakin, Austl. — F6 74
Deal, Eng., U.K. — J14 12
Dealesville, S. Afr. — F7 70
Deal Island, Md., U.S. — F10 114
De'an, China — G6 42
Dean, stm., B.C., Can. — D4 138
Deán Funes, Arg. — E5 92
Deans Dundas Bay, b., N.T., Can. — B16 140
Dearborn, Mi., U.S. — B2 114
Dearg, Beinn, mtn., Scot., U.K. — D8 12
Dease, stm., B.C., Can. — D5 106
Dease, stm., B.C., Can. — B6 106
Dease Strait, strt., Nu., Can. — B9 106
Death Valley, val., Ca., U.S. — G9 134
Death Valley National Park, p.o.i., Ca., U.S. — G8 134
Deauville, Fr. — E12 102
Deba, Nig. — G7 64
Debao, China — J2 42
Debar, Mac. — B3 28
De Bary, Fl., U.S. — H4 116
Debica, Pol. — F17 16
Débo, Lac, l., Mali — F4 64
Deborah West, Lake, l., Austl. — F3 74
Deboyne Islands, is., Pap. N. Gui. — B10 74
Debre Birhan, Eth. — F7 62
Debrecen, Hung. — B8 26
Debre Mark'os, Eth. — E7 62
Debre Tabor, Eth. — E7 62
Debre Zeyit, Eth. — F7 62
Debrznio, Pol. — C13 16
Decatur, Al., U.S. — C11 122
Decatur, Ga., U.S. — D14 122
Decatur, In., U.S. — H4 112
Decatur, Mi., U.S. — F3 112
Decatur, Mi., U.S. — C1 120
Decatur, Tx., U.S. — B10 130
Decatur, Tn., U.S. — B14 122
Decazeville, Fr. — E8 18
Deccan, plat., India — B4 53
Decelles, Réservoir, res., Qc., Can. — F15 106
Deception, stm., Bots. — B6 70

Name	Map Ref.	Page
Deception, Mount, mtn., Wa., U.S.	C3	136
Decherd, Tn., U.S.	B12	122
Dechhu, India	E4	54
Děčín, Czech Rep.	F10	16
Decize, Fr.	H12	14
Decker Lake, B.C., Can.	B5	138
Decorah, Ia., U.S.	H7	118
Dedaye, Mya.	D2	48
Dededo, Guam	i10	78c
Dedegöl Tepesi, mtn., Tur.	F14	28
De Doorns, S. Afr.	H4	70
Dédougou, Burkina	G4	64
Dedoviči, Russia	C12	10
Dedovsk, Russia	E20	10
Deduru, stm., Sri L.	H5	53
Dee, stm., U.K.	I9	12
Dee, stm., Scot., U.K.	D10	12
Deenwood, Ga., U.S.	E3	116
Deep, stm., N.C., U.S.	A6	116
Deep Creek, stm., U.S.	H14	136
Deep River, On., Can.	B12	112
Deep River, Ia., U.S.	C5	120
Deepwater, Mo., U.S.	F4	120
Deep Well, Austl.	D6	74
Deer Creek, stm., Ms., U.S.	D8	122
Deerfield, Il., U.S.	F2	112
Deerfield, Ks., U.S.	C7	128
Deerfield Beach, Fl., U.S.	J5	116
Deering, Ak., U.S.	C7	140
Deer Island, i., N.B., Can.	F10	110
Deer Isle, Me., U.S.	F8	110
Deer Lake, Nf., Can.	j22	107a
Deer Lodge, Mt., U.S.	D14	136
Deer Park, Al., U.S.	F10	122
Deer Park, Wa., U.S.	C9	136
Deerpass Bay, b., N.T., Can.	B6	106
Deer Trail, Co., U.S.	B4	128
Defiance, Ia., U.S.	C2	120
Defiance, Oh., U.S.	C1	114
Defiance, Mount, mtn., Or., U.S.	E5	136
De Forest, Wi., U.S.	H9	118
De Funiak Springs, Fl., U.S.	G12	122
Dêgê, China	E4	36
Degeh Bur, Eth.	F8	62
Dégelis, Qc., Can.	C8	110
Degerfors, Swe.	G6	8
Deggendorf, Ger.	H8	16
Degh, stm., Asia	B5	54
Değirmendere, Tur.	E10	28
De Gray Lake, res., Ar., U.S.	C5	122
De Grey, stm., Austl.	D3	74
Dehalak' Desēt, i., Erit.	D8	62
Dehiwala-Mount Lavinia, Sri L.	H4	53
Dehlorān, Iran	C6	56
Dehra Dūn, India	C7	54
Dehra Dūn Cantonment, India	C6	54
Dehri, India	F10	54
Dehu, India	B1	53
Dehua, China	I8	42
Dehui, China	B6	38
Deinze, Bel.	D12	14
Deir Mawâs, Egypt	K1	58
Dej, Rom.	B10	26
Dejnau, Turkmen.	B9	56
De Kalb, Il., U.S.	C9	120
De Kalb, Ms., U.S.	E10	122
De Kalb, Tx., U.S.	D4	122
Dekese, D.R.C.	E4	66
Deke Sokehs, i., Micron.	m11	78d
Dékoa, C.A.R.	C3	66
De Land, Fl., U.S.	G4	116
Delanggu, Indon.	G7	50
Delano, Ca., U.S.	H6	134
Delano, Mn., U.S.	F5	118
Delaport Point, c., Bah.	m18	104f
Delapu, China	C13	54
Delarof Islands, is., Ak., U.S.	g23	140a
Delaware, Oh., U.S.	D2	114
Delaware, Ok., U.S.	H2	120
Delaware, state, U.S.	F10	114
Delaware, stm., U.S.	D10	114
Delaware, stm., Ks., U.S.	E2	120
Delaware, East Branch, stm., N.Y., U.S.	B10	114
Delaware, West Branch, stm., U.S.	B11	114
Delaware Bay, b., U.S.	E10	114
Delaware City, De., U.S.	E10	114
Delburne, Ab., Can.	D17	138
Del Campillo, Arg.	G5	92
Del City, Ok., U.S.	F11	128
Delegate, Austl.	K7	76
Delémont, Switz.	C4	22
De Leon, Tx., U.S.	B9	130
Delfinópolis, Braz.	K2	88
Délfoi, hist., Grc.	E5	28
Delft, Neth.	B13	14
Delft Island, i., Sri L.	G4	53
Delfzijl, Neth.	A15	14
Delgado, Cabo, c., Moz.	C7	68
Delger, stm., Mong.	G8	34
Delgerhet, Mong.	B7	36
Delhi, On., Can.	F9	112
Delhi, India	D6	54
Delhi, Ia., U.S.	B6	120
Delhi, La., U.S.	E7	122
Delhi, N.Y., U.S.	B11	114
Delhi, state, India	D6	54
Delia, Ab., Can.	E18	138
Deliblato, Yugo.	E8	26
Delicias, Mex.	A6	100
Delight, Ar., U.S.	C5	122
Delījān, Iran	C7	56
Deline, N.T., Can.	B6	106
Delingde, Russia	B11	34
Delingha, China	D4	36
Dēliņkalns, hill, Lat.	C9	10
Delisle, Sk., Can.	C6	124
Delitzsch, Ger.	E8	16
Dell City, Tx., U.S.	C2	130
Delle, Fr.	G16	14
Dellys, Alg.	H14	20
Del Mar, Ca., U.S.	K8	134
Delmar, Ia., U.S.	C7	120
Delmar, Md., U.S.	F10	114
Delmarva Peninsula, pen., U.S.	F10	114
Delmas, Sk., Can.	B5	124
Delmenhorst, Ger.	C4	16
Delmiro Gouveia, Braz.	E7	88
Delnice, Cro.	E11	22
Del Norte, Co., U.S.	D2	128
De-Longa, ostrova, is., Russia	A19	34
De Long Mountains, mts., Ak., U.S.	C7	140
Deloraine, Mb., Can.	E13	124
Delorme, Lac, l., Qc., Can.	E16	106
Delos see Dílos, hist., Grc.	F8	28
Delphi, In., U.S.	H3	112
Delphi see Délfoi, hist., Grc.	E5	28
Delphos, Ks., U.S.	B11	128
Delportshoop, S. Afr.	F7	70
Delray Beach, Fl., U.S.	J5	116
Del Rio, Tx., U.S.	E7	130
Delta, Co., U.S.	E8	132
Delta, Mo., U.S.	G8	120
Delta, Ut., U.S.	D4	132
Delta Amacuro, state, Ven.	C11	86
Delta Beach, Mb., Can.	D15	124
Delta City, Ms., U.S.	D8	122
Delta Downs, Austl.	C8	74
Delta Junction, Ak., U.S.	D10	140
Delta Peak, mtn., B.C., Can.	D4	106
Del Valle, Tx., U.S.	D10	130
Del Verme Falls, wtfl, Eth.	F8	62
Delvinë, Alb.	E14	24
Demak, Indon.	G7	50
Demarcation Point, c., Ak., U.S.	C11	140
Demavend, Mount see Damāvand, Qolleh-ye, vol., Iran	B7	56
Demba, D.R.C.	F4	66
Dembī, Eth.	F7	62
Dembia, C.A.R.	C4	66
Dembī Dolo, Eth.	F6	62
Demidov, Russia	E14	10
Deming, N.M., U.S.	K9	132
Demini, stm., Braz.	H10	86
Demirci, Tur.	D11	28
Demirköprü Barajı, res., Tur.	E11	28
Demirköy, Tur.	B10	28
Demjanka, stm., Russia	C12	32
Demjanovo, Russia	F22	8
Demjanskoe, Russia	C11	32
Demmin, Ger.	C8	16
Demmitt, Ab., Can.	A11	138
Demopolis, Al., U.S.	E11	122
Demorest, Ga., U.S.	B2	116
Dempo, Gunung, vol., Indon.	F3	50
Demta, Indon.	F11	44
Denain, Fr.	D12	14
Denali, Ak., U.S.	D10	140
Denali National Park, Ak., U.S.	D10	140
Denan, Eth.	F8	62
Denau, Uzb.	G11	32
Den Burg, Neth.	A13	14
Dendang, Indon.	E5	50
Dendermonde (Termonde), Bel.	C12	14
Deng Deng, Cam.	C2	66
Dengkou, China	A2	42
Dêngqên, China	E4	36
Dengxian, China	E5	42
Denham, Austl.	E2	74
Denham, Mount, mtn., Jam.	i13	104d
Denham Range, mts., Austl.	C6	76
Denham Springs, La., U.S.	G8	122
Den Helder (Helder), Neth.	B13	14
Dénia, Spain	F11	20
Deniliquin, Austl.	J5	76
Deniskoviči, Russia	H14	10
Denison, Tx., U.S.	D2	122
Denison, Mount, vol., Ak., U.S.	E9	140
Denizli, Tur.	F12	28
Denizli, state, Tur.	F12	28
Denkanikota, India	E3	53
Denmark, Austl.	F3	74
Denmark, S.C., U.S.	C4	116
Denmark, Wi., U.S.	D2	112
Denmark, ctry., Eur.	D10	6
Denmark Strait, strt.	C20	94
Dennery, St. Luc.	m7	105c
Denpasar, Indon.	H9	50
Denton, Md., U.S.	F10	114
Denton, Mt., U.S.	C17	136
Denton, N.C., U.S.	A5	116
Denton, Tx., U.S.	H11	128
Denton Creek, stm., Tx., U.S.	H11	128
D'Entrecasteaux, Point, c., Austl.	F3	74
D'Entrecasteaux Islands, is., Pap. N. Gui.	D6	72
Denver, Co., U.S.	B3	128
Denver, Pa., U.S.	D9	114
Denver City, Tx., U.S.	A5	130
Deoband, India	D6	54
Deogarh, India	F4	54
Deogarh, India	F7	54
Deogarh, mtn., India	G9	54
Deogarh Hills, hills, India	G9	54
Deoghar, India	F11	54
Deori, India	G7	54
Deoria, India	E9	54
De Pere, Wi., U.S.	D1	112
Depew, Ok., U.S.	B2	122
Depoe Bay, Or., U.S.	F2	136
Depok, Indon.	G5	50
Deposit, N.Y., U.S.	B10	114
Depue, Il., U.S.	C8	120
Dêqên, China	F4	36
Deqing, China	J4	42
De Queen, Ar., U.S.	C4	122
De Quincy, La., U.S.	G5	122
Dera, Lach, stm., Afr.	D8	66
Dera Bugti, Pak.	D2	54
Dera Ghāzi Khān, Pak.	C3	54
Dera Ismāīl Khān, Pak.	C3	54
Derāwar Fort, Pak.	D3	54
Derbent, Russia	F7	32
Derby, Austl.	C4	74
Derby, Austl.	n13	77a
Derby, Eng., U.K.	I11	12
Derby, Ks., U.S.	D11	128
Derby, N.Y., U.S.	B6	114
Dereköy, Tur.	B10	28
Derg, Lough, l., Ire.	I4	12
Dergači, Russia	D7	32
De Ridder, La., U.S.	G5	122
Dermott, Ar., U.S.	D7	122
Dernieres, Isles, is., La., U.S.	H8	122
Dêrong, China	F4	36
Derrame, Mex.	H3	130
Derry see Londonderry, N. Ire., U.K.	F6	12
Derry, N.H., U.S.	B14	114
Derudeb, Sudan	D7	62
Derventa, Bos.	E4	26
Derwent, Ab., Can.	C19	138
Derwent, stm., Austl.	o13	77a
Derwent, stm., Eng., U.K.	G12	12
Derwent Water, l., Eng., U.K.	G9	12
Deržavinsk, Kaz.	D11	32
Desaguadero, stm., Arg.	F4	92
Desaguadero, stm., S.A.	G4	84
Désappointement, Îles du, is., Fr. Poly.	E12	72
Des Arc, Ar., U.S.	C7	122
Descabezado Grande, Volcán, vol., Chile	G2	92
Descanso, Braz.	C11	92
Descanso, Ca., U.S.	K9	134
Descanso, Punta, c., Mex.	K8	134
Descartes, Fr.	G9	14
Deschambault Lake, l., Sk., Can.	E10	106
Deschutes, stm., Or., U.S.	E6	136
Desdunes, Haiti	C11	102
Desē, Eth.	E7	62
Deseado, stm., Arg.	I3	90
Desengaño, Punta, c., Arg.	I3	90
Desenzano del Garda, Italy	E7	22
Deseret Peak, mtn., Ut., U.S.	C4	132
Deseronto, On., Can.	D12	112
Désert, stm., Qc., Can.	B13	112
Désert, Lac, l., Qc., Can.	B13	112
Desert Hot Springs, Ca., U.S.	J9	134
Desert Lake, l., Nv., U.S.	F1	132
Desert Peak, mtn., Ut., U.S.	B3	132
Desert Valley, val., Nv., U.S.	B7	134
Desha, Ar., U.S.	B7	122
Deshaies, Guad.	h5	105c
Deshler, Oh., U.S.	C1	114
Deshnok, India	E4	54
Desiderio Tello, Arg.	E4	92
Deskáti, Grc.	D4	28
Desloge, Mo., U.S.	G7	120
Des Moines, Ia., U.S.	C4	120
Des Moines, N.M., U.S.	E5	128
Des Moines, stm., U.S.	K7	118
Des Moines, East Fork, stm., U.S.	H4	118
Desna, stm., Eur.	D4	32
Desolación, Isla, i., Chile	J2	90
De Soto, Il., U.S.	G8	120
De Soto, Mo., U.S.	F7	120
Despatch, S. Afr.	H7	70
Despeñaperros, Desfiladero de, p., Spain	F7	20
Des Plaines, Il., U.S.	F1	112
Des Plaines, stm., U.S.	C9	120
Desroches, i., Sey.	k12	69b
Desruisseaux, St. Luc.	m7	105c
Dessau, Ger.	E8	16
Destruction Bay, Yk., Can.	C3	106
Desvres, Fr.	D10	14
Detčino, Russia	F19	10
Dete, Zimb.	D4	68
Detmold, Ger.	E4	16
Detour, Point, c., Mi., U.S.	C3	112
De Tour Village, Mi., U.S.	C5	112
Detrital Wash, stm., Az., U.S.	H2	132
Detroit, Mi., U.S.	B2	114
Detroit, Or., U.S.	F4	136
Detroit, Tx., U.S.	D3	122
Detroit Beach, Mi., U.S.	C2	114
Dettifoss, wtfl, Ice.	k31	8a
Det Udom, Thai.	E7	48
Detva, Slov.	H15	16
Deua National Park, p.o.i., Austl.	J7	76
Deūlgaon Rāja, India	H5	54
Deutsche Bucht, b., Ger.	C4	16
Deutschlandsberg, Aus.	D12	22
Deux-Sèvres, state, Fr.	C5	18
Deva, Rom.	D9	26
Devakottai, India	G4	53
Dévaványa, Hung.	B7	26
Deventer, Neth.	B15	14
Deveron, stm., Scot., U.K.	D10	12
Devgadh Bāriva, India	G4	54
De View, Bayou, stm., Ar., U.S.	B8	122
Devīkot, India	E3	54
Devils, stm., Tx., U.S.	E6	130
Devils Island see Diable, Île du, i., Fr. Gu.	B7	84
Devils Lake, N.D., U.S.	F15	124
Devils Lake, l., N.D., U.S.	F14	124
Devils Postpile National Monument, p.o.i., Ca., U.S.	F6	134
Devils Tower National Monument, p.o.i., Wy., U.S.	C8	126
Devine, B.C., Can.	F8	138
Devine, Tx., U.S.	E9	130
Devjatiny, Russia	F17	8
Devli, India	F5	54
Devoll, stm., Alb.	D14	24
Devon, Ab., Can.	C17	138
Devon Island, i., Nu., Can.	B8	141
Devonport, Austl.	n13	77a
Devoto, Arg.	E6	92
Devrek, Tur.	B14	28
Dewakang-lompo, Pulau, i., Indon.	F11	50
Dewar, Ok., U.S.	B3	122
Dewās, India	G5	54
Dewey, Ok., U.S.	H1	120
Deweyville, Tx., U.S.	G5	122
De Witt, Ar., U.S.	C7	122
De Witt, Ia., U.S.	C7	120
De Witt, Ne., U.S.	G16	126
De Witt, N.Y., U.S.	A9	114
Dexing, China	G7	42
Dexter, Me., U.S.	E7	110
Dexter, Mi., U.S.	B2	114
Dexter, N.M., U.S.	H4	128
Dexter, N.Y., U.S.	D13	112
Dexterity Fiord, b., Nu., Can.	A16	106
Deyang, China	E5	36
Dey-Dey, Lake, l., Austl.	E6	74
Dezfūl, Iran	C6	56
Dezhou, China	C7	42
Dežneva, mys, c., Russia	C27	34
Dezong, China	B13	54
Dhahran see Aẓ-Ẓahrān, Sau. Ar.	D6	56
Dhaka (Dacca), Bngl.	G13	54
Dhaka, state, Bngl.	F13	54
Dhamār, Yemen	G5	56
Dhāmpur, India	D7	54
Dhamtari, India	H8	54
Dhanbād, India	G11	54
Dhandhuka, India	G3	54
Dhangaḍhī, Nepal	D8	54
D'Hanis, Tx., U.S.	E8	130
Dhankuṭa, Nepal	E11	54
Dhār, India	G5	54
Dharān, Nepal	E11	54
Dhārāpuram, India	F3	53
Dharmābād, India	B3	53
Dharmapuri, India	E4	53
Dharmavaram, India	D3	53
Dharmjaygarh, India	G9	54
Dharmshāla, India	B6	54
Dhaulpur, India	E6	54
Dhawalāgiri, mtn., Nepal	D9	54
Dhenkānāl, India	H10	54
Dherínia, Cyp.	C4	58
Dhodhekánisos (Dodecanese), is., Grc.	G10	28
Dhodhóni, hist., Grc.	D3	28
Dhofar see Ẓufar, reg., Oman	F7	56
Dholka, India	G4	54
Dhone, India	D3	53
Dhoomadheere, Som.	D8	66
Dhorāji, India	H3	54
Dhrāngadhra, India	G3	54
Dhrol, India	G3	54
Dhuburi, India	E13	54
Dhule, India	H5	54
Dhuliān, India	F12	54
Dhupgāri, India	E12	54
Dhuusamarreeb, Som.	C9	66
Diable, Île du (Devils Island), i., Fr. Gu.	B7	84
Diable, Pointe du, c., Mart.	k7	105c
Diables, Morne aux, vol., Dom.	i5	105c
Diablo, Canyon, val., Az., U.S.	H5	132
Diablo, Mount, mtn., Ca., U.S.	F4	134
Diablo, Pico del, mtn., Mex.	F4	98
Diablo Range, mts., Ca., U.S.	G4	134
Diablotins, Morne, vol., Dom.	j6	105c
Diaca, Moz.	C6	68
Dialakoto, Sen.	G2	64
Diamante, Arg.	F7	92
Diamante, stm., Arg.	G4	92
Diamantina, Braz.	J4	88
Diamantina, stm., Austl.	E2	76
Diamantina Lakes, Austl.	D3	76
Diamantino, Braz.	F6	84
Diamond, Mo., U.S.	G3	120
Diamond Harbour, India	G12	54
Diamond Islets, is., Austl.	A8	76
Diamond Peak, mtn., Id., U.S.	F13	136
Diamond Peak, mtn., Wa., U.S.	D9	136
Diamondville, Wy., U.S.	B6	132
Diana Bay, b., Can.	C16	106
Dianbai, China	K4	42
Dian Chi, l., China	G5	36
Dianjiang, China	F2	42
Dianópolis, Braz.	F2	88
Diapaga, Burkina	G5	64
Diaz, Ar., U.S.	B7	122
Diaz Point, c., Nmb.	E2	70
Dibai, India	D7	54
Dibaya, D.R.C.	F4	66
Dibeng, S. Afr.	E6	70
D'Iberville, Ms., U.S.	G9	122
Dibete, Bots.	C8	70
Dibrugarh, India	C7	46
Dickens, Tx., U.S.	H8	128
Dickinson, N.D., U.S.	A10	126
Dickinson, Tx., U.S.	H3	122
Dickson, Tn., U.S.	H10	120
Didao, China	B9	38
Didsbury, Ab., Can.	E16	138
Dīdwāna, India	E5	54
Didymóteicho, Grc.	B9	28
Dieburg, Ger.	G4	16
Dieciocho de Julio, Ur.	F11	92
Diefenbaker, Lake, res., Sk., Can.	C7	124
Diego de Almagro, Chile	C2	92
Diego de Almagro, Isla, i., Chile	J1	90
Diego de Ocampo, Pico, mtn., Dom. Rep.	C12	102
Diégo-Suarez see Antsiraṅana, Madag.	C8	68
Diemuchuoke, China	B7	54
Dien Bien, Viet.	B6	48
Dien Bien Phu see Dien Bien, Viet.	B6	48
Diepholz, Ger.	D4	16
Dieppe, N.B., Can.	D12	110
Dieppe, Fr.	E9	14
Dieppe Bay Town, St. K./N.	C2	105a
Dierks, Ar., U.S.	C4	122
Di'er Songhua, stm., China	B6	38
Diest, Bel.	D14	14
Dieulefit, Fr.	E10	18
Dieveniškės, Lith.	F8	10
Diez de Octubre, Mex.	C6	100
Dif, Kenya	D8	66
Diffa, Niger	G7	64
Differdange, Lux.	E14	14
Dīg, India	E6	54
Digba, D.R.C.	D5	66
Digboi, India	C8	46
Digby, N.S., Can.	F11	110
Digby Neck, pen., N.S., Can.	F10	110
Digges Islands, is., Nu., Can.	C15	106
Dighton, Ks., U.S.	C8	128
Dīglūr, India	B3	53
Digne-les-Bains, Fr.	E12	18
Digoin, Fr.	C9	18
Digos, Phil.	G5	52
Digras, India	H6	54
Digul, stm., Indon.	G10	44
Diinsor, Som.	D8	66
Dijon, Fr.	G14	14
Dikaja, Russia	A22	10
Dike, Ia., U.S.	B5	120
Dikhil, Dji.	E8	62
Dikili, Tur.	D9	28
Dikirnis, Egypt	G2	58
Dikodougou, C. Iv.	H3	64
Diksmuide, Bel.	C11	14
Dikson, Russia	B5	34
Dikwa, Nig.	G7	64
Dīla, Eth.	F7	62
Dilek Yarımdası Milli Parkı, p.o.i., Tur.	F10	28
Dili, Indon.	G8	44
Dillenburg, Ger.	F4	16
Diller, Ne., U.S.	A12	128
Dilley, Tx., U.S.	F8	130
Dilling, Sudan	E5	62
Dillingen an der Donau, Ger.	H6	16
Dillingham, Ak., U.S.	E8	140
Dillon, Mt., U.S.	E14	136
Dillon, S.C., U.S.	B6	116
Dillon Mountain, mtn., N.M., U.S.	J8	132
Dillwyn, Va., U.S.	G7	114
Dilolo, D.R.C.	G4	66
Dílos, hist., Grc.	F8	28
Dilworth, Mn., U.S.	H17	124
Dimāpur, India	C7	46
Dimashq (Damascus), Syria	E7	58
Dimashq, state, Syria	E7	58
Dimbelenge, D.R.C.	F4	66
Dimbokro, C. Iv.	H4	64
Dimbulah, Austl.	A5	76
Dimitrovgrad, Blg.	G12	26
Dimitrovgrad, Russia	D8	32
Dimitsána, Grc.	F4	28
Dimlang, mtn., Nig.	H7	64
Dimmitt, Tx., U.S.	G6	128
Dimona, Isr.	G6	58
Dinagat, Phil.	E5	52
Dinagat Island, i., Phil.	E5	52
Dinājpur, Bngl.	F12	54
Dinan, Fr.	F6	14
Dinant, Bel.	D13	14
Dinar, Tur.	E13	28
Dinard, Fr.	F6	14
Dinaric Alps (Dinara), mts., Eur.	G13	22
Dindi, stm., India	C4	53
Dindigul, India	F4	53
Dindori, India	G8	54
Dingalan Bay, b., Phil.	C3	52
Ding'an, China	L4	42
Dingbian, China	C2	42
Dingbianji, China	C3	42
Dinggyê, China	D11	54
Dinghai, China	F9	42
Dingle, Ire.	I2	12
Dingle Bay, b., Ire.	I2	12
Dingnan, China	I6	42
Dingo, Austl.	D7	76
Dingolfing, Ger.	H8	16
Dingshuzhen, China	F8	42
Dingtao, China	D6	42
Dinguiraye, Gui.	G2	64
Dingwall, N.S., Can.	D16	110
Dingxian, China	B6	42
Dingxiang, China	B5	42
Dingyuan, China	E7	42
Dinhāta, India	E12	54
Dinh Hoa, Viet.	B7	48
Dinh Lap, Viet.	B8	48
Dinkelsbühl, Ger.	G6	16
Dinnebito Wash, stm., Az., U.S.	H5	132
Dinorwic, On., Can.	B6	118
Dinorwic Lake, l., On., Can.	B6	118
Dinosaur National Monument, p.o.i., U.S.	C8	132
Dinsmore, Sk., Can.	C6	124
Dinuba, Ca., U.S.	G6	134
Dinwiddie, Va., U.S.	G8	114
Dionísio Cerqueira, Braz.	C11	92
Diouloulou, Sen.	G1	64
Diourbel, Sen.	G1	64
Dīpālpur, Pak.	C4	54
Diplo, Pak.	F2	54
Dipolog, Phil.	F4	52
Dippoldiswalde, Ger.	F9	16
Dīr, Pak.	B11	56
Diré, Mali	F4	64
Dirē Dawa, Eth.	F8	62
Dirico, Ang.	D3	68
Dirj, Libya	A2	62
Dirk Hartog Island, i., Austl.	E2	74
Dirkou, Niger	F7	64
Dirranbandi, Austl.	G7	76
Dīsa, India	F4	54
Disappointment, Cape, c., S. Geor.	J9	90
Disappointment, Cape, c., Wa., U.S.	D2	136
Disappointment, Lake, l., Austl.	D4	74
Disaster Bay, b., Austl.	K8	76
Disautel, Wa., U.S.	B7	136
Discovery Bay, b., Austl.	L3	76
Dishman, Wa., U.S.	C9	136
Disko, i., Grnld.	D15	141
Disko Bugt, b., Grnld.	D15	141
Dismal, stm., Ne., U.S.	F12	126
Dispur, India	E13	54
Disraëli, Qc., Can.	E5	110
Distrito Capital, state, Col.	E4	86
Distrito Federal, state, Braz.	H2	88
Distrito Federal, state, Mex.	F9	100
Distrito Federal, state, Ven.	B8	86
Dis Ûq, Egypt	G1	58
Dithmarschen, reg., Ger.	B5	16
Diu, India	H3	54
Dive, can., Fr.	B5	18
Divenskaja, Russia	A12	10
Divernon, Il., U.S.	E8	120
Divinhe, Moz.	B12	70
Divinópolis, Braz.	K3	88
Divi Point, c., India	D5	53
Divisor, Serra do, plat., S.A.	E3	84
Divnoe, Russia	E6	32
Divnogorsk, Russia	C16	32
Divo, C. Iv.	H3	64
Dīwāl Qol, Afg.	A1	54
Dix, Ne., U.S.	F9	126
Dixie Valley, val., Nv., U.S.	D8	134
Dixon, Ca., U.S.	E4	134
Dixon, Il., U.S.	C8	120
Dixon, Ky., U.S.	G10	120
Dixon, Mo., U.S.	G5	120
Dixon, N.M., U.S.	E3	128
Dixon Entrance, strt., N.A.	E4	106
Diyarbakır, Tur.	B4	56
Dizhou, China	J2	42
Djado, Niger	E7	64
Djado, Plateau du, plat., Niger	E7	64
Djakarta see Jakarta, Indon.	G5	50
Djamâa, Alg.	C6	64
Djambala, Congo	E2	66
Djanet, Alg.	E6	64
Djaret, Oued, stm., Alg.	D5	64
Djat'kovo, Russia	G17	10
Djedi, Oued, stm., Alg.	C5	64
Djéma, C.A.R.	C5	66
Djenné, Mali	G4	64
Djenoun, Garet el, mtn., Alg.	D6	64
Djérem, stm., Cam.	C2	66
Djibo, Burkina	G4	64
Djibouti, Dji.	E8	62
Djibouti, ctry., Afr.	E8	62
Djoku-Punda, D.R.C.	F4	66
Djolu, D.R.C.	D4	66
Djougou, Benin	H5	64
Djourab, Erg du, sand, Chad	D3	62
Djugu, D.R.C.	D6	66
Djurås, Swe.	F6	8
Djurtjuli, Russia	C8	32
Dmitrija Lapteva, proliv, strt., Russia	B16	34
Dmitrov, Russia	D20	10
Dneprovskoe, Russia	E16	10
Dnieper, stm., Eur.	F15	6
Dniester (Dnister), stm., Eur.	G19	16
Dniprodzerzhyns'k, Ukr.	E5	32
Dnipropetrovs'k, Ukr.	E4	32
Dnistrovs'kyi lyman, l., Ukr.	C17	26
Dnjaprouska Buhski, kanal, can., Bela.	I8	10
Dno, Russia	C12	10
Do, Lac, l., Mali	F4	64
Dôa, Moz.	D5	68
Doaktown, N.B., Can.	D10	110
Doangdoangan-Besar, Pulau, i., Indon.	F10	50
Doba, Chad	F3	62
Dobczyce, Pol.	G15	16
Dobele, Lat.	D6	10
Döbeln, Ger.	E8	16
Doberai, Jazirah (Doberai Peninsula), pen., Indon.	F9	44
Doberai Peninsula see Doberai, Jazirah, pen., Indon.	F9	44
Dobo, Indon.	G9	44
Doboj, Bos.	E4	26
Dobra, Pol.	E14	16
Dobre Miasto, Pol.	C16	16
Dobrič, Blg.	F14	26
Dobříš, Czech Rep.	G10	16
Dobrjanka, Russia	C9	32
Dobroe, Russia	C15	10
Dobroteasa, Rom.	E11	26
Dobruja, hist. reg., Eur.	E15	26
Dobruš, Bela.	H14	10
Dobruška, Czech Rep.	F12	16
Dobrzyń nad Wisłą, Pol.	D15	16
Dobson, N.C., U.S.	H5	114
Dobzha, China	D12	54
Doce, stm., Braz.	J6	88
Dock Junction, Ga., U.S.	E4	116
Doctor Cecilio Báez, Para.	B9	92
Doctor Coss, Mex.	I8	130
Doctor González, Mex.	I8	130
Dod Ballāpur, India	E3	53
Doddridge, Ar., U.S.	D4	122
Dodecanese see Dhodhekánisos, is., Grc.	G10	28
Dodge Center, Mn., U.S.	G5	118
Dodge City, Ks., U.S.	D9	128
Dodgeville, Wi., U.S.	B7	120
Dodoma, Tan.	F7	66
Dodsland, Sk., Can.	C5	124
Dodson, Mt., U.S.	F5	124
Dodson, Tx., U.S.	G8	128
Doerun, Ga., U.S.	E1	116
Doetinchem, Neth.	C15	14
Dogai Coring, l., China	A12	54
Doğanbey, Tur.	E9	28
Doğanhisar, Tur.	E14	28
Dog Island, i., Fl., U.S.	H14	122
Dog Islands, is., Br. Vir. Is.	e9	104b
Dog Lake, l., Mb., Can.	C15	124
Dog Lake, l., On., Can.	C9	118
Dogliani, Italy	F4	22
Dōgo, i., Japan	C6	40
Do Gonbadān, Iran	C7	56
Dogondoutchi, Niger	G5	64
Doğu Karadeniz Dağları, mts., Tur.	A5	56
Doha see Ad-Dawḥah, Qatar	D7	56
Dohrīghāt, India	E9	54
Doiran, Lake, l., Eur.	B5	28
Dois Irmãos de Goiás, Braz.	E1	88
Doi Suthep-Pui National Park, p.o.i., Thai.	C4	48
Doka, Indon.	G9	44
Dokkum, Neth.	A14	14
Doksy, Czech Rep.	F10	16
Doland, S.D., U.S.	C14	126
Dolbeau, Qc., Can.	B4	110
Dol-de-Bretagne, Fr.	F7	14
Dole, Fr.	G14	14
Dolega, Pan.	H6	102
Dolgeville, N.Y., U.S.	E15	112
Dolgij Most, Russia	C17	32
Dolgoščele, Russia	C20	8
Dolinsk, Russia	G17	34
Dolj, state, Rom.	E10	26
Dolni Dăbnik, Blg.	F11	26
Dolný Kubín, Slov.	G15	16
Dolomites see Dolomiti, mts., Italy	D8	22
Dolomiti, mts., Italy	D8	22
Dolores, Arg.	H9	92
Dolores, Col.	F4	86
Dolores, Guat.	D3	102
Dolores, Mex.	H6	130
Dolores, Ur.	F8	92
Dolores, stm., U.S.	E7	132
Dolores Hidalgo, Mex.	E8	100
Dolphin, Cape, c., Falk. Is.	J5	90
Dolphin and Union Strait, strt., Nu., Can.	B7	106
Dolphin Head, mtn., Jam.	i12	104d
Dolsk, Pol.	D13	16
Dolžicy, Russia	C12	10
Domaniči, Russia	G16	10
Domažlice, Czech Rep.	G8	16
Dombås, Nor.	E3	8
Dombes, reg., Fr.	D11	18
Dombóvár, Hung.	C4	26
Dom Cavati, Braz.	J4	88
Dôme, Puy de, mtn., Fr.	D8	18
Dome Creek, B.C., Can.	C9	138
Domeyko, Chile	D2	92
Domeyko, Cordillera, mts., Chile	D3	90
Domfront, Fr.	F8	14
Domiciano Ribeiro, Braz.	I2	88
Domingo M. Irala, Para.	B10	92
Dominica, ctry., N.A.	j5	105c
Dominica Channel see Martinique Passage, strt., N.A.	k6	105c
Dominicana, República see Dominican Republic, ctry., N.A.	D10	96
Dominican Republic, ctry., N.A.	D10	96
Dominica Passage, strt., N.A.	i6	105c
Dominion, Cape, c., Nu., Can.	B15	106
Dominion City, Mb., Can.	E16	124
Dom Joaquim, Braz.	J4	88
Domo, Eth.	F9	62
Domodedovo, Russia	E20	10
Domodossola, Italy	D5	22
Dom Pedrito, Braz.	E10	92
Dom Pedro, Braz.	C3	88
Dompu, Indon.	H11	50
Domremy, Sk., Can.	B8	124
Domuyo, Volcán, vol., Arg.	H2	92
Dom Yai, stm., Thai.	E7	48
Don, stm., India	C2	53
Don, stm., Laos	E7	48
Don, stm., Russia	E6	32
Don, stm., Scot., U.K.	D10	12
Donadeu, Arg.	C6	92
Donaghadee, N. Ire., U.K.	G7	12
Donald, Austl.	K4	76
Donalda, Ab., Can.	D18	138
Donaldson, Ar., U.S.	C6	122
Donaldsonville, La., U.S.	G7	122
Doñana, Parque Nacional de, p.o.i., Spain	H4	20
Donau, stm., Eur.	F11	6
Donaueschingen, Ger.	I4	16
Donauwörth, Ger.	H6	16
Don Benito, Spain	F5	20
Doncaster, Eng., U.K.	H11	12
Dondaicha, India	H5	54
Dondo, Ang.	B1	68
Dondo, Moz.	A12	70
Dondo, Teluk, b., Indon.	C12	50
Dondra Head, c., Sri L.	I5	53
Dondușeni, Mol.	A14	26
Donegal, Ire.	G4	12
Donegal, state, Ire.	G5	12
Donegal Bay, b., Ire.	G4	12
Doneraile, S.C., U.S.	B6	116
Donets'k, Ukr.	E5	32
Dong, stm., China	J6	42
Dong'an, China	B11	36
Dong'an, China	H4	42
Dongara, Austl.	E3	74
Dongchuan, China	F5	36
Dongfang, China	L3	42
Dongfeng, China	C6	38
Donggala, Indon.	D11	50
Donggi Cona, l., China	D4	36
Donggong Shan, mts., China	H8	42
Dongguan, China	J5	42
Dongguang, China	C7	42
Dong Ha, Viet.	D8	48
Donghai Dao, i., China	K4	42
Dong Hoi, Viet.	D8	48
Dong Hu, l., China	B10	54
Dongjielang, China	F6	42
Dongjingcheng, China	B8	38
Donglan, China	I2	42
Dongliao, stm., China	C5	38
Dong Nai, stm., Viet.	G8	48
Dongning, China	B9	38
Dongo, D.R.C.	D3	66
Dongou, Congo	D3	66
Dongping, China	K5	42
Dongping, China	D7	42
Dong San Shen (Manchuria), hist. reg., China	B5	38
Dongshan, China	L4	42
Dongshan Dao, i., China	J7	42
Dongsheng, China	B4	42
Dongtai, China	E9	42
Dongting Hu, l., China	G5	42
Dong Trieu, Viet.	B8	48
Dongwe, stm., Zam.	C3	68
Dongxi, China	G2	42
Dongxiang, China	G7	42
Dongyang, China	G9	42
Dongzhi, China	F7	42
Donie, Tx., U.S.	F2	122
Doniphan, Ne., U.S.	G14	126
Donja Stubica, Cro.	E12	22
Donjek, stm., Yk., Can.	C3	106
Don Martín, Mex.	G7	130
Donna, Tx., U.S.	H9	130
Donnacona, Qc., Can.	D5	110
Donnelly, Id., U.S.	F10	136
Donner, La., U.S.	H7	122
Donner Pass, p., Ca., U.S.	D5	134
Donner und Blitzen, stm., Or., U.S.	G8	136
Donnybrook, Austl.	F3	74
Donora, Pa., U.S.	D6	114
Donostia (San Sebastián), Spain	A9	20
Donostia-San Sebastián see Donostia, Spain	A9	20
Don Pedro Reservoir, res., Ca., U.S.	F5	134
Don Peninsula, pen., B.C., Can.	D2	138
Donskoj, Russia	G21	10
Doolow, Som.	D8	66
Doonerak, Mount, mtn., Ak., U.S.	C9	140
Doornik see Tournai, Bel.	D12	14
Door Peninsula, pen., Wi., U.S.	D2	112
Dor, Isr.	F5	58
Dora, Al., U.S.	D11	122
Dora, Lake, l., Austl.	D4	74
Dora Baltea, stm., Italy	E4	22
Dorado, P.R.	B3	104a
Doraville, Ga., U.S.	D14	122
Dorcheat, Bayou, stm., U.S.	D5	122
Dorchester, N.B., Can.	E12	110
Dorchester, On., Can.	F8	112
Dorchester, Eng., U.K.	K10	12
Dorchester, Ne., U.S.	G15	126
Dorchester, Cape, c., Nu., Can.	B15	106
Dordabis, Nmb.	C3	70
Dordogne, state, Fr.	D6	18
Dordogne, stm., Fr.	D8	18
Dordrecht, Neth.	C13	14
Dordrecht, S. Afr.	G8	70
Dore Lake, l., Sk., Can.	E9	106
Dorena, Or., U.S.	G4	136
Dores do Indaiá, Braz.	J3	88
Dorfen, Ger.	H8	16
Dorgali, Italy	D3	24

Name | Map Ref. | Page

Dörgön nuur, l., Mong. B3 36
Dori, Burkina G4 64
Doring, stm., S. Afr. G4 70
Dornbirn, Aus. C6 22
Dornoch, Scot., U.K. D8 12
Dorog, Hung. B5 26
Dorogobuž, Russia F16 10
Dorohoi, Rom. A13 26
Dorokempo, Indon. H11 50
Dorre Island, i., Austl. E2 74
Dorrigo, Austl. H9 76
Dorris, Ca., U.S. B4 134
Dorsale, mts., Tun. I3 24
Dort see Dordrecht, Neth. C13 14
Dortmund, Ger. E3 16
Dorton, Ky., U.S. G3 114
Dörtyol, Tur. B7 58
Doruma, D.R.C. D5 66
Dos, Canal Numero, can., Arg. H9 92
Dosatuj, Russia A8 36
Dos Bahías, Cabo, c., Arg. H3 90
Dos Bocas, P.R. B2 104a
Döşemealtı, Tur. F13 28
Dos Hermanas, Spain G4 20
Do Son, Viet. B8 48
Dos Pos, Neth. Ant. p23 104g
Dos Quebradas, Col. E4 86
Dosso, Niger G5 64
Dossor, Kaz. E8 32
Dothan, Al., U.S. F13 122
Dotnuva, Lith. E6 10
Dou, stm., China B8 42
Douai, Fr. D11 14
Douala, Cam. D1 66
Douarnenez, Fr. F4 14
Doublé, Pointe, c., Guad. h7 105c
Double Island Point, c., Austl. E9 76
Double Springs, Al., U.S. C11 122
Doubletop Peak, mtn., Wy., U.S. G16 136
Doubs, state, Fr. G15 14
Doubs, stm., Eur. H14 14
Doubtful Sound, strt., N.Z. G2 80
Doubtless Bay, b., N.Z. B5 80
Douentza, Mali F4 64
Dougga, hist., Tun. H3 24
Douglas, Mb., Can. E14 124
Douglas, I. of Man G8 12
Douglas, S. Afr. F6 70
Douglas, Ak., U.S. E13 140
Douglas, Az., U.S. L7 132
Douglas, Ga., U.S. E3 116
Douglas, Wy., U.S. E7 126
Douglas Channel, strt., B.C., Can. C1 138
Douglas Lake, B.C., Can. F10 138
Douglas Lake, res., Tn., U.S. H2 114
Douglasville, Ga., U.S. D14 122
Doullens, Fr. D11 14
Dourada, Serra, plat., Braz. G1 88
Dourados, Braz. D6 90
Dourbali, Chad E3 62
Douro (Duero), stm., Eur. C2 20
Dousk, Bela. G13 10
Douz, Tun. C6 64
Dove Bugt, strt., Grnld. B21 141
Dove Creek, Co., U.S. F7 132
Dover, Austl. o13 77a
Dover, Eng., U.K. J14 12
Dover, De., U.S. E10 114
Dover, Id., U.S. B10 136
Dover, N.H., U.S. G6 110
Dover, N.J., U.S. D11 114
Dover, N.C., U.S. A8 116
Dover, Oh., U.S. D4 114
Dover, Ok., U.S. E11 128
Dover, Tn., U.S. H10 120
Dover, Strait of, strt., Eur. K14 12
Dover-Foxcroft, Me., U.S. E7 110
Dovrefjell Nasjonalpark, p.o.i., Nor. E3 8
Dow City, Ia., U.S. C2 120
Dowlatābād, Iran D8 56
Downey, Id., U.S. H14 136
Downieville, Ca., U.S. D5 134
Downing, Mo., U.S. D5 120
Downingtown, Pa., U.S. D10 114
Downpatrick, N. Ire., U.K. G7 12
Downs, Ks., U.S. B10 128
Downton, Mount, mtn., B.C., Can. D6 138
Dows, Ia., U.S. B4 120
Dowshī, Afg. B10 56
Doyle, Ca., U.S. C5 134
Doyles, Nf., Can. C17 110
Doylestown, Pa., U.S. D10 114
Doyline, La., U.S. E5 122
Dōzen, is., Japan C5 40
Dozier, Al., U.S. F12 122
Dra, Cap, c., Mor. D2 64
Dra'a, Hamada du, des., Alg. D3 64
Drâa, Oued, stm., Afr. D2 64
Drac, stm., Fr. E2 22
Dracena, Braz. D6 90
Drachten, Neth. A15 14
Dracut, Ma., U.S. B14 114
Dragalina, Rom. E14 26
Drăgănești-Vlașca, Rom. E12 26
Drăgășani, Rom. E11 26
Dragonera, Sa, i., Spain E13 20
Dragons Mouths, strt. s12 105f
Dragoon, Az., U.S. K6 132
Draguignan, Fr. F12 18
Drahičyn, Bela. H8 10
Drake, N.D., U.S. G13 124
Drakensberg, mts., Afr. F9 70
Drake Passage, strt. K8 82
Drakesboro, Ky., U.S. G10 120
Drakes Branch, Va., U.S. H7 114
Dráma, Grc. B7 28
Drammen, Nor. G3 8
Drang, stm., Asia F8 48
Drangajökull, ice, Ice. j28 8a
Dranov, Ostrovul, i., Rom. E16 26
Drau (Dráva), stm., Eur. D11 22
Dráva (Drau), stm., Eur. D14 22
Dravograd, Slvn. D12 22
Drawsko Pomorskie, Pol. C11 16
Drayton, N.D., U.S. C1 118
Drayton, S.C., U.S. B4 116
Drayton Valley, Ab., Can. C15 138
Dresden, On., Can. F7 112
Dresden, Ger. E9 16
Dresden, Oh., U.S. D3 114
Drètun', Bela. E12 10
Dreux, Fr. F10 14
Drew, Ms., U.S. D8 122
Drienov, Slov. H17 16
Driftwood, B.C., Can. D5 106
Driftwood, stm., In., U.S. E12 120
Driggs, Id., U.S. G15 136
Drin, stm., Alb. C13 24
Drina, stm., Eur. F16 22
Drinit, Gjiri i, b., Alb. C13 24
Drinit të Zi (Crni Drim), stm., Eur. C14 24
Driskill Mountain, hill, La., U.S. E6 122
Drissa (Drysa), stm., Eur. E11 10
Drniš, Cro. G13 22
Drobeta-Turnu Severin, Rom. E9 26
Drochia, Mol. A14 26
Drogheda, Ire. H6 12
Droichead Átha see Drogheda, Ire. H6 12
Droichead Nua, Ire. H6 12
Drôme, state, Fr. E11 18
Dronero, Italy F4 22
Dronne, stm., Fr. D6 18
Dronning Louise Land, reg., Grnld. B20 141
Druc', stm., Bela. G12 10
Druif, Aruba o19 104g
Druja, Bela. E10 10
Drūkšiai, l., Eur. E9 10
Drumheller, Ab., Can. E18 138
Drummond, Mt., U.S. D13 136
Drummond, Wi., U.S. E7 118
Drummond Island, i., Mi., U.S. C6 112
Drummondville, Qc., Can. E4 110
Druskininkai, Lith. F7 10
Družba, Kaz. E14 32
Druzhba see Družba, Kaz. E14 32
Družina, Russia C18 34
Drvar, Bos. E3 26
Dry Arm, b., Mt., U.S. G7 124
Dry Bay, b., Ak., U.S. E12 140
Dryberry Lake, l., On., Can. B4 118
Dry Cimarron, stm., U.S. B2 122
Dry Creek Mountain, mtn., Nv., U.S. B9 134
Dryden, On., Can. B6 118
Dry Devils, stm., Tx., U.S. D7 130
Dry Prong, La., U.S. F6 122
Dry Ridge, Ky., U.S. F1 114
Drysdale, stm., Austl. C5 74
Dry Tortugas, is., Fl., U.S. G11 108
Dry Tortugas National Park, p.o.i., Fl., U.S. L3 116
Drzewica, Pol. E16 16
Dschang, Cam. C1 66
Du, stm., China E4 42
Du'an, China I3 42
Duaringa, Austl. D7 76
Duarte, Pico, mtn., Dom. Rep. C12 102
Duartina, Braz. L1 88
Dubā, Sau. Ar. K6 58
Dubach, La., U.S. E6 122
Dubai see Dubayy, U.A.E. D8 56
Dubăsari, Mol. B16 26
Dubăsari, Lacul, res., Mol. B15 26
Dubawnt, stm., Can. C10 106
Dubawnt Lake, l., Can. C10 106
Dubayy (Dubai), U.A.E. D8 56
Dubbo, Austl. I7 76
Dubh Artach, r., Scot., U.K. E6 12
Dublin (Baile Átha Cliath), Ire. H6 12
Dublin, Ga., U.S. D3 116
Dublin, Tx., U.S. B9 130
Dublin, Va., U.S. G5 114
Dublin, state, Ire. H6 12
Dubna, Russia F19 10
Dubna, Russia D20 10
Dubna, stm., Russia D21 10
Dubnica nad Váhom, Slov. H14 16
Dubois, In., U.S. F11 120
Du Bois, Ne., U.S. D1 120
Du Bois, Pa., U.S. C7 114
Dubois, Wy., U.S. D3 126
Dubossary Reservoir see Dubăsari, Lacul, res., Mol. B15 26
Dubovka, Russia E6 32
Dubrājpur, India G11 54
Dubréka, Gui. H2 64
Dubrouna, Bela. F13 10
Dubrovka, Russia G16 10
Dubrovnik, Cro. H15 22
Dubrovnoe, Russia C11 32
Dubuque, Ia., U.S. B7 120
Dubysa, stm., Lith. E6 10
Duchang, China G7 42
Duchesne, Ut., U.S. C6 132
Duchesne, stm., Ut., U.S. C7 132
Duchess, Austl. C2 76
Duck, stm., Tn., U.S. B11 122
Duck Creek, stm., Nv., U.S. D2 132
Duck Hill, Ms., U.S. D9 122
Duck Lake, Sk., Can. B7 124
Ducktown, Tn., U.S. B14 122
Duda, stm., Col. F4 86
Dudačkino, Russia A15 10
Duderstadt, Ger. E6 16
Dudinka, Russia C6 34
Dudley, Eng., U.K. I10 12
Dudleyville, Az., U.S. K6 132
Dudna, stm., India B2 53
Dudorovskij, Russia G18 10
Dudwa National Park, p.o.i., India D8 54
Dueré, stm., Braz. F1 88
Duero (Douro), stm., Eur. C2 20
Due West, S.C., U.S. B3 116
Dufourspitze, mtn., Eur. D13 18
Dufur, Or., U.S. E5 136
Duga-Zapadnaja, mys, c., Russia E18 34
Dugdemona, stm., La., U.S. F6 122
Dugi Otok, i., Cro. F11 22
Dugna, Russia F19 10
Du Gué, stm., Qc., Can. D16 106
Duhovščina, Russia E15 10
Duida, Cerro, mtn., Ven. F9 86
Duisburg, Ger. E2 16
Duitama, Col. E5 86
Duiwelskloof, S. Afr. C10 70
Dujuuma, Som. D8 66
Duke, Ok., U.S. G9 128
Duke of York Bay, b., Nu., Can. B13 106
Duk Fadiat, Sudan F6 62
Dukhān, Qatar D7 56
Duki, Pak. C2 54
Dukla Pass, p., Eur. G17 16
Dukou, China F5 36
Dūkštas, Lith. E9 10
Dulan, China D4 36
Dulce, N.M., U.S. G9 132
Dulce, stm., Arg. D6 92
Dulce, Golfo, b., C.R. H6 102
Dul'durga, Russia F11 34
Dulgalah, stm., Russia C15 34
Dullstroom, S. Afr. D10 70
Dulovka, Russia C11 10
Dulq Maghār, Syria B9 58
Duluth, Ga., U.S. C14 122
Duluth, Mn., U.S. E6 118
Dūmā, Syria E7 58
Dumaguete, Phil. F4 52
Dumai, Indon. C2 50
Dumalag, Phil. E4 52
Dumali Point, c., Phil. D3 52
Dumaran Island, i., Phil. E2 52
Dumaresq, stm., Austl. G8 76
Dumaring, Indon. C11 50
Dumas, Tx., U.S. F7 128
Dumbarton, Scot., U.K. F8 12
Dumbrăveni, Rom. C11 26
Dume, Point, c., Ca., U.S. J7 134
Dumfries, Scot., U.K. F9 12
Dumka, India F11 54
Dumlupınar, Tur. E12 28
Dummar, Syria E7 58
Dumoine, Lac, l., Qc., Can. B12 112
Dumont, Ia., U.S. B4 120
Dumont d'Urville, sci., Ant. B18 81
Dumpu, Pap. N. Gui. b4 79a
Dumraon, India F10 54
Dumyât, Masabb (Damietta Mouth), mth., Egypt G3 58
Duna see Danube, stm., Eur. F11 6
Dunaharaszti, Hung. B6 26
Dunaj see Danube, stm., Eur. F11 6
Dunajec, stm., Eur. F16 16
Dunajská Streda, Slov. H13 16
Dunakeszi, Hung. B6 26
Dunărea Veche, Brațul, stm., Rom. E15 26
Dunaújváros, Hung. C5 26
Dunavățu de Sus, Rom. E16 26
Duna-völgyi-főcsatorna, can., Hung. C6 26
Dunav-Tisa-Dunav, Kanal, can., Yugo. D6 26
Dunbar, Scot., U.K. E10 12
Dunblane, Sk., Can. C6 124
Duncan, B.C., Can. H7 138
Duncan, Az., U.S. K7 132
Duncan, Ok., U.S. G11 128
Duncan, stm., B.C., Can. F13 138
Duncan Lake, res., B.C., Can. F14 138
Duncannon, Pa., U.S. D8 114
Duncan Passage, strt., India F7 46
Duncans, Jam. i13 104d
Duncansby Head, c., Scot., U.K. C9 12
Dundaga, Lat. C5 10
Dundalk, On., Can. D9 112
Dundalk (Dún Dealgan), Ire. G6 12
Dundalk, Md., U.S. E9 114
Dundalk Bay, b., Ire. H6 12
Dundas, On., Can. E9 112
Dundas, Lake, l., Austl. F4 74
Dundas Peninsula, pen., Can. B17 140
Dundas Strait, strt., Austl. B6 74
Dún Dealgan see Dundalk, Ire. G6 12
Dundee, S. Afr. F10 70
Dundee, Scot., U.K. E10 12
Dundee, Fl., U.S. H4 116
Dundee, Mi., U.S. C2 114
Dundurn, Sk., Can. C7 124
Dunedin, N.Z. G4 80
Dunedin, Fl., U.S. H3 116
Dunedoo, Austl. I7 76
Dunfermline, Scot., U.K. E9 12
Dungannon, N. Ire., U.K. G6 12
Dūngarpur, India G4 54
Dungarvan, Ire. I5 12
Dungeness, c., Eng., U.K. K13 12
Dungog, Austl. I8 76
Dungu, D.R.C. D5 66
Dungun, Malay. J6 48
Dunhua, China C8 38
Dunhuang, China C3 36
Dunilovo, Russia C21 10
Dunkerque (Dunkirk), Fr. C11 14
Dunkirk see Dunkerque, Fr. C11 14
Dunkirk, In., U.S. H4 112
Dunkirk, N.Y., U.S. B6 114
Dunkirk, Oh., U.S. D2 114
Dunkwa, Ghana H4 64
Dún Laoghaire, Ire. H6 12
Dunlap, Tn., U.S. B13 122
Dunmore, Pa., U.S. C10 114
Dunmore Town, Bah. K9 116
Dunn, N.C., U.S. A7 116
Dunnellon, Fl., U.S. G3 116
Dunnet Head, c., Scot., U.K. C9 12
Dunning, Ne., U.S. F12 126
Dunnville, On., Can. F10 112
Dunoon, Scot., U.K. F8 12
Dunqulah, Sudan D5 62
Dunqunāb, Sudan C7 62
Duns, Scot., U.K. F10 12
Dunseith, N.D., U.S. F13 124
Dunsmuir, Ca., U.S. B3 134
Dunstable, Eng., U.K. J12 12
Dunster, B.C., Can. C11 138
Dunyāpur, Pak. D3 54
Duolun, China C2 38
Duolundabohuer, China B14 54
Duomula, China A9 54
Duozhu, China J6 42
Dupang Ling, mts., China I4 42
Dupnica, Blg. G10 26
Dupnitsa see Dupnica, Blg. G10 26
Dupuyer, Mt., U.S. B14 136
Duque Bacelar, Braz. C4 88
Duque de Caxias, Braz. L4 88
Duque de York, Isla, i., Chile J1 90
Duran, N.M., U.S. G3 128
Durance, stm., Fr. F11 18
Durand, Il., U.S. B8 120
Durand, Wi., U.S. G7 118
Durand, Récif, rf., N. Cal. n17 79d
Durand Reef see Durand, Récif, rf., N. Cal. n17 79d
Durango, Mex. C6 100
Durango, Spain A8 20
Durango, Co., U.S. F9 132
Durango, state, Mex. C6 100
Durant, Ia., U.S. C6 120
Durant, Ms., U.S. D9 122
Durant, Ok., U.S. D2 122
Duras, Fr. E6 18
Durazno, Ur. F9 92
Durban, S. Afr. F10 70
Đurđevac, Cro. D14 22
Düren, Ger. F2 16
Durg, India H8 54
Durgāpur, India G11 54
Durham, On., Can. D9 112
Durham, Eng., U.K. G11 12
Durham, Ca., U.S. D4 134
Durham, N.H., U.S. G5 110
Durham, N.C., U.S. H6 114
Durham Downs, Austl. F3 76
Durham Heights, mtn., N.T., Can. A6 106
Durlas éile see Thurles, Ire. I5 12
Durlești, Mol. B15 26
Durmitor, mtn., Yugo. F5 26
Durmitor Nacionalni Park, p.o.i., Yugo. F6 26
Dürnkrut, Aus. B13 22
Durrës, Alb. C13 24
Durrësi see Durrës, Alb. C13 24
Durrie, Austl. E3 76
Dursunbey, Tur. D11 28
Duru Gölü, l., Tur. B11 28
Durūz, Jabal ad-, mtn., Syria F7 58
D'Urville, Tanjung, c., Indon. F10 44
D'Urville Island, i., N.Z. E5 80
Dušak, Turkmen. B9 56
Dusa Marreb see Dhuusamarreeb, Som. C9 66
Dušanbe, Taj. B10 56
Dušekan, Russia B19 32
Dusetos, Lith. E8 10
Dushan, China I2 42
Du Shan, mtn., China A8 42
Dushanzi, China C1 36
Duson, La., U.S. G6 122
Düsseldorf, Ger. E2 16
Dustin, Ok., U.S. B2 122
Dutch John, Ut., U.S. C7 132
Dutton, Mt., U.S. C15 136
Dutton, stm., Austl. C4 76
Duvno, Bos. F4 26
Duxun, China J7 42
Duyfken Point, c., Austl. B8 74
Duyun, China H2 42
Düzce, Tur. C14 28
Dve Mogili, Blg. F12 26
Dvine, ozero, l., Russia D14 10
Dvinskaja guba, b., Russia D17 8
Dvuh Cirkov, gora, mtn., Russia C22 34
Dvůr Králové nad Labem, Czech Rep. F11 16
Dwārka, India G2 54
Dwight, Il., U.S. C9 120
Dworshak Reservoir, res., Id., U.S. D11 136
Dwyka, stm., S. Afr. H5 70
Dyer, Tn., U.S. H8 120
Dyer, Cape, c., Nu., Can. D13 141
Dyer Bay, b., On., Can. C8 112
Dyersburg, Tn., U.S. H8 120
Dyje (Thaya), stm., Eur. H12 16
Dyment, On., Can. B6 118
Dynów, Pol. G18 16
Dysart, Sk., Can. D9 124
Dysart, Ia., U.S. B5 120
Dysna (Dzisna), stm., Eur. E9 10
Dytikí Eláda, state, Grc. E4 28
Dytikí Makedonía, state, Grc. C4 28
Džagdy, hrebet, mts., Russia F15 34
Džala-Abad, Kyrg. F12 32
Džalinda, Russia F13 34
Džambejty, Kaz. D8 32
Džanybek, Kaz. E7 32
Dzaoudzi, May. C8 68
Džardžan, Russia C13 34
Dzavhan, stm., Mong. B3 36
Dzeržinsk, Russia H20 8
Dzeržinskoe, Russia C16 32
Džetygara, Kaz. D10 32
Dzhankoi, Ukr. E4 32
Dzhugdzhur Mountains see Džugdžur, hrebet, mts., Russia E16 34
Dzhungarian Alatau Mountains, mts., Asia E14 32
Działoszyce, Pol. F16 16
Dzibilchaltún, hist., Mex. B3 102
Dzierżoniów, Pol. F12 16
Dzilam González, Mex. B3 102
Dzisna, Bela. E11 10
Dzisna (Dysna), stm., Eur. E9 10
Dzitbalché, Mex. B2 102
Dziwnów, Pol. B10 16
Džizak, Uzb. F11 32
Dzjarečyn, Bela. G7 10
Dzjaržynskaja, hara, hill, Bela. G9 10
Dzjaržynsk, Bela. G9 10
Dzjatlavičy, Bela. H9 10
Dzöölön, Mong. F8 34
Džugdžur, hrebet, mts., Russia E16 34
Dzūkijos nacionalinis parkas, p.o.i., Lith. F7 10
Dzungarian Basin see Junggar Pendi, bas., China B2 36
Dzungarian Gate, p., Asia E14 32
Džusaly, Kaz. E10 32
Dzüünharaa, Mong. B6 36
Dzuunmod, Mong. B6 36
Dzyhivka, Ukr. A15 26

E

Eads, Co., U.S. C6 128
Eagle, Ak., U.S. D11 140
Eagle, Co., U.S. D10 132
Eagle, stm., Co., U.S. B2 128
Eagle Bay, B.C., Can. F11 138
Eagle Butte, S.D., U.S. C11 126
Eagle Creek, stm., Sk., Can. B6 124
Eagle Grove, Ia., U.S. B4 120
Eaglehawk, Austl. K4 76
Eagle Lake, Tx., U.S. H2 122
Eagle Lake, l., On., Can. B5 118
Eagle Lake, l., Ca., U.S. C5 134
Eagle Lake, l., Me., U.S. D7 110
Eagle Mountain, Ca., U.S. J1 132
Eagle Mountain, mtn., Id., U.S. D11 136
Eagle Mountain, mtn., Mn., U.S. D8 118
Eagle Mountain Lake, res., Tx., U.S. A10 130
Eagle Pass, Tx., U.S. F7 130
Eagle Peak, mtn., Ca., U.S. B5 134
Eagle River, Mi., U.S. D10 118
Eagle River, Wi., U.S. F9 118
Eagletown, Ok., U.S. C4 122
Ear Falls, On., Can. A5 118
Earle, Ar., U.S. B8 122
Earl Grey, Sk., Can. D9 124
Earlham, Ia., U.S. C3 120
Earlimart, Ca., U.S. H6 134
Earlville, Il., U.S. C8 120
Early, Ia., U.S. B2 120
Early, Tx., U.S. C9 130
Eas, Vanuatu k17 79d
Easley, S.C., U.S. B3 116
East Alton, Il., U.S. F7 120
East Angus, Qc., Can. E5 110
East Antarctica, reg., Ant. C8 81
East Aurora, N.Y., U.S. B7 114
East Bay, b., Tx., U.S. H4 122
East Bend, N.C., U.S. H5 114
East Bernard, Tx., U.S. H2 122
East Bernstadt, Ky., U.S. G1 114
East Borneo see Kalimantan Timur, state, Indon. C10 50
Eastbourne, Eng., U.K. K13 12
East Brady, Pa., U.S. D6 114
East Brewton, Al., U.S. F11 122
East Cache Creek, stm., Ok., U.S. G10 128
East Caicos, i., T./C. Is. B12 102
East Cape, c., N.Z. C8 80
East Cape, c., Fl., U.S. K4 116
East Carbon, Ut., U.S. D6 132
East Caroline Basin, unds. I17 142
East Chicago, In., U.S. G2 112
East China Sea, Asia F9 36
East Cote Blanche Bay, b., La., U.S. H7 122
East Coulee, Ab., Can. E18 138
East Dereham, Eng., U.K. I13 12
East Dismal Swamp, sw., N.C., U.S. A9 116
East Dubuque, Il., U.S. B7 120
East Ely, Nv., U.S. D2 132
East End, V.I.U.S. e8 104b
Easter Island see Pascua, Isla de, i., Chile f30 78l
Eastern Cape, state, S. Afr. G8 70
Eastern Channel see Tsushima-kaikyō, strt., Japan F2 40
Eastern Creek, stm., Austl. C3 76
Eastern Desert see Arabian Desert, des., Egypt B6 62
Eastern Division, state, Fiji q20 79e
Eastern Ghāts, mts., India E4 53
Eastern Point, c., Guad. A1 105a
Eastern Sayans see Vostočnyj Sajan, mts., Russia D17 32
East Falkland, i., Falk. Is. J5 90
East Fayetteville, N.C., U.S. A7 116
East Frisian Islands see Ostfriesische Inseln, is., Ger. C3 16
East Gaffney, S.C., U.S. A4 116
East Germany see Germany, ctry., Eur. E6 16
East Glacier Park, Mt., U.S. B13 136
East Grand Forks, Mn., U.S. D2 118
East Grand Rapids, Mi., U.S. F4 112
East Grinstead, Eng., U.K. J12 12
Easthampton, Ma., U.S. B13 114
East Java see Jawa Timur, state, Indon. G8 50
East Jordan, Mi., U.S. C4 112
East Kelowna, B.C., Can. G11 138
East Kilbride, Scot., U.K. F8 12
Eastlake, Mi., U.S. D3 112
Eastlake, Oh., U.S. C4 114
Eastland, Tx., U.S. B9 130
East Lansing, Mi., U.S. B1 114
East Laurinburg, N.C., U.S. B6 116
Eastleigh, Eng., U.K. K11 12
East Liverpool, Oh., U.S. D5 114
East London (Oos-Londen), S. Afr. H9 70
Eastmain, Qc., Can. E15 106
Eastmain, stm., Qc., Can. E15 106
Eastmain-Opinaca, Réservoir, res., Qc., Can. E15 106
Eastman, Ga., U.S. D2 116
East Mariana Basin, unds. H18 142
East Matagorda Bay, b., Tx., U.S. F11 130
East Missoula, Mt., U.S. D13 136
East Moline, Il., U.S. C7 120
East Naples, Fl., U.S. J4 116
East Nishnabotna, stm., Ia., U.S. C2 120
East Nusa Tenggara see Nusa Tenggara Timur, state, Indon. H12 50
East Olympia, Wa., U.S. D3 136
Easton, Md., U.S. F9 114
Easton, Pa., U.S. D10 114
East Pacific Rise, unds. N27 142
East Palatka, Fl., U.S. G4 116
East Pecos, N.M., U.S. F3 128
East Peoria, Il., U.S. D8 120
Eastpoint, Fl., U.S. H14 122
East Point, Ga., U.S. D14 122
East Point, c., P.E., Can. D15 110
East Point, c., V.I.U.S. g11 104c
Eastport, Id., U.S. B10 136
Eastport, Me., U.S. F9 110
East Prairie, Mo., U.S. H8 120
East Prairie, stm., Ab., Can. A14 138
East Pryor Mountain, mtn., Mt., U.S. B4 126
East Retford, Eng., U.K. H12 12
East Saint Louis, Il., U.S. F7 120
East Sea (Japan, Sea of), Asia D11 38
East Shoal Lake, l., Mb., Can. D16 124
East Siberian Sea see Vostočno-Sibirskoe more, Russia B20 34
East Sister Island, i., Austl. L6 76
East Slovakia see Východoslovenský Kraj, state, Slov. H17 16
East Stroudsburg, Pa., U.S. D11 114
East Troy, Wi., U.S. B9 120
Eastville, Va., U.S. G10 114
East Wenatchee, Wa., U.S. C6 136
East Wilmington, N.C., U.S. B8 116
Eaton, In., U.S. H4 112
Eaton, Oh., U.S. E1 114
Eaton Rapids, Mi., U.S. B1 114
Eatonton, Ga., U.S. C2 116
Eatonville, Wa., U.S. D4 136
Eau Claire, Wi., U.S. G7 118
Eau Claire, Lac à l', l., Qc., Can. D16 106
Eauripik, at., Micron. C5 72
Eauripik Rise, unds. I17 142
Eauze, Fr. F6 18
Ebano, Mex. D9 100
Ebb and Flow Lake, l., Mb., Can. D14 124
Ebbw Vale, Wales, U.K. J9 12
Ebebiyín, Eq. Gui. I7 64
Eben Junction, Mi., U.S. B2 112
Ebensee, Aus. C10 22
Eberbach, Ger. G4 16
Eber Gölü, l., Tur. E14 28
Ebern, Ger. F6 16
Ebersbach, Ger. E10 16
Eberswalde-Finow, Ger. D9 16
Ebetsu, Japan C14 38
Ebino, Japan G3 40
Ebinur Hu, l., China F14 32
Eboli, Italy D9 24
Ebolowa, Cam. D2 66
Ebon, at., Marsh. Is. C7 72
Ebre see Ebro, stm., Spain C11 20
Ebre, Delta de l', Spain D11 20
Ebro (Ebre), stm., Spain C11 20
Ebro, Delta del see Ebre, Delta de l', Spain D11 20
Ebro, Embalse del, res., Spain B7 20
Eceabat, Tur. C9 28
Ech Cheliff, Alg. B5 64
Echeng, China E7 36
Echínos, Grc. B7 28
Echt, Neth. E1 16
Echuca, Austl. K5 76
Écija, Spain G5 20
Eckernförde, Ger. B5 16
Eckerö, i., Fin. F8 8
Eckville, Ab., Can. D16 138
Eclectic, Al., U.S. E12 122
Eclipse Sound, strt., Nu., Can. A14 106
Ecoporanga, Braz. J5 88
Écorce, Lac de l', res., Qc., Can. B13 112
Écrins, Barre des, mtn., Fr. E12 18
Écrins, Massif des, plat., Fr. E12 18
Ecru, Ms., U.S. C9 122
Ecuador, ctry., S.A. D2 84
Ed, Swe. G4 8
Edam, Sk., Can. A5 124
Eddrachillis Bay, b., Scot., U.K. C7 12
Eddystone Rocks, r., Eng., U.K. K8 12
Eddyville, Ia., U.S. C5 120
Eddyville, Ky., U.S. G9 120
Ede, Neth. B14 14
Ede, Nig. H5 64
Edéa, Cam. D2 66
Edehon Lake, l., Nu., Can. C11 106
Edelény, Hung. A7 26
Eden, Austl. K7 76
Eden, Ms., U.S. D8 122
Eden, N.C., U.S. H6 114
Eden, Wy., U.S. A7 132
Eden, stm., Eng., U.K. G10 12
Edendale, S. Afr. F10 70
Eden Valley, Mn., U.S. F4 118
Edenville, S. Afr. E8 70
Eder, stm., Ger. E4 16
Édessa, Grc. C4 28
Edfu, Egypt C6 62
Edgar, Ne., U.S. G14 126
Edgar, Wi., U.S. G8 118
Edgard, La., U.S. H8 122
Edgartown, Ma., U.S. C15 114
Edgeley, N.D., U.S. A14 126
Edgell Island, i., Grnld. E13 141
Edgemont, S.D., U.S. D9 126
Edgeøya, i., Nor. B30 141
Edgeroi, Austl. H7 76
Edgerton, Ab., Can. B3 124
Edgerton, Mn., U.S. H2 118
Edgerton, Oh., U.S. C1 114
Edgerton, Wi., U.S. B8 120
Edgewater, Fl., U.S. H5 116
Edgewood, Il., U.S. F9 120
Edgewood, Ia., U.S. B6 120
Edgewood, Md., U.S. E9 114
Edgewood, Tx., U.S. E3 122
Edina, Mn., U.S. G5 118
Edina, Mo., U.S. D5 120
Edinburg, Il., U.S. E8 120
Edinburg, In., U.S. E11 120
Edinburg, Ms., U.S. E9 122
Edinburg, Tx., U.S. H9 130
Edinburg, Va., U.S. F7 114
Edinburgh, Scot., U.K. F9 12
Edincik, Tur. C10 28
Edineț, Mol. A14 26
Edirne, Tur. B9 28
Edirne, state, Tur. B9 28
Edison, Ga., U.S. F14 122
Edisto, stm., S.C., U.S. D5 116
Edisto, North Fork, stm., S.C., U.S. C4 116
Edisto Island, i., S.C., U.S. D5 116
Edith, Mount, mtn., Mt., U.S. D15 136
Edith Cavell, Mount, mtn., Ab., Can. D12 138
Edjeleh, Alg. D6 64
Edmond, Ok., U.S. F11 128
Edmonds, Wa., U.S. C4 136
Edmonton, Austl. A5 76
Edmonton, Ab., Can. C17 138
Edmonton, Ky., U.S. G12 120
Edmore, N.D., U.S. F15 124
Edmundston, N.B., Can. C8 110
Edna, Ks., U.S. G2 120
Edna, Tx., U.S. E11 130
Edremit, Tur. D10 28
Edremit Körfezi, b., Tur. D9 28
Edrovo, Russia C16 10
Edson, Ab., Can. C14 138
Eduardo Castex, Arg. G5 92
Eduni, Mount, mtn., N.T., Can. C5 106
Edward, stm., Austl. J5 76
Edward, Lake, l., Afr. E5 66
Edward Island, i., On., Can. C10 118
Edwards, Ms., U.S. E8 122
Edwards Air Force Base, Ca., U.S. I8 134
Edwards Plateau, plat., Tx., U.S. D7 130
Edwardsville, Il., U.S. F8 120
Edward VII Peninsula, pen., Ant. C25 81
Eek, Ak., U.S. D7 140
Eeklo, Bel. C12 14
Eel, stm., Ca., U.S. D2 134
Eel, stm., In., U.S. G4 112
Eel, stm., In., U.S. E10 120
Eems (Ems), stm., Eur. A16 14
Éfaté, state, Vanuatu k17 79d
Éfaté, i., Vanuatu k17 79d
Eferding, Aus. B10 22
Efes (Ephesus), hist., Tur. F10 28
Effigy Mounds National Monument, p.o.i., Ia., U.S. A6 120
Effingham, Il., U.S. E9 120
Effingham, Ks., U.S. E2 120
Eflâni, Tur. B15 28
Eforie Nord, Rom. E15 26
Eforie Sud, Rom. F15 26
Efremov, Russia G20 10
Eg, stm., Mong. F9 34
Egadi, Isole, is., Italy G5 24
Egaña, Arg. H8 92
Egan Range, mts., Nv., U.S. D2 132
Egedesminde (Aasiaat), Grnld. D15 141
Egegik, Ak., U.S. E8 140
Eger, Hung. B7 26
Egersund, Nor. G1 8
Eggenfelden, Ger. H8 16
Egg Harbor City, N.J., U.S. E11 114
Égletons, Fr. D7 18
Egmont, Cape, c., N.Z. D5 80
Egmont, Mount see Taranaki, Mount, vol., N.Z. D6 80
Egmont Bay, b., P.E., Can. D12 110
Egmont National Park, p.o.i., N.Z. D5 80
Egorevsk, Russia E22 10
Egremont, Ab., Can. B17 138
Eğridir, Tur. F13 28
Eğridir Gölü, l., Tur. E13 28
Éguas, stm., Braz. G3 88
Egvekinot, Russia C25 34
Egypt, ctry., Afr. B5 62
Eha-Amufu, Nig. H6 64
Ehime, state, Japan F5 40
Ehingen, Ger. H5 16
Ehrhardt, S.C., U.S. C4 116
Eibar, Spain A8 20
Eibiswald, Aus. D12 22
Eichstätt, Ger. H7 16
Eidsvold, Austl. E8 76
Eifel, mts., Ger. F2 16
Eigg, i., Scot., U.K. E6 12
Eight Degree Channel, strt., Asia h12 46a
Eights Coast, cst., Ant. C31 81
Eighty Mile Beach, cst., Austl. C4 74
Eildon, Austl. K5 76
Eildon, Lake, res., Austl. K5 76
Eilenburg, Ger. E8 16
Eiler Rasmussen, Kap, c., Grnld. A21 141
Einasleigh, Austl. B5 76
Einasleigh, stm., Austl. A4 76
Einbeck, Ger. E5 16
Eindhoven, Neth. C14 14
Einme, Mya. D2 48
Eirunepé, Braz. E4 84
Eiseb, stm., Afr. B4 70
Eisenach, Ger. E6 16
Eisenberg, Ger. F7 16
Eisenerz, Aus. C11 22
Eisenhüttenstadt, Ger. D10 16
Eisenstadt, Aus. C13 22
Eisfeld, Ger. F6 16
Eišiškės, Lith. F7 10
Eislingen, Ger. H5 16
Eitorf, Ger. F3 16
Eivissa (Iviza), Spain F12 20
Eivissa (Ibiza), i., Spain F12 20
Ejea de los Caballeros, Spain B9 20
Ejeda, Madag. E7 68
Ejido Jaboncillos, Mex. A7 100
Ejin Horo Qi, China B3 42
Ejin Qi, China C5 36
Ejsk, Russia E5 32
Ejura, Ghana H4 64
Ejutla de Crespo, Mex. G10 100
Ekaterinburg, Russia C10 32
Ekaterinino, Russia E16 10
Ekateriny, proliv, strt., Russia B17 38
Ekenäs see Tammisaari, Fin. G10 8
Ekibastuz, Kaz. D13 32
Ekimčan, Russia F15 34
Ekonda, Russia C10 34
Ekwan, stm., On., Can. E14 106
Ela, Mya. C3 48
El Aaiún (Laayoune), W. Sah. D2 64
El 'Açâba, plat., Maur. F2 64
El Affroun, Alg. H13 20
El Agreb, Alg. C6 64
El Ahijadero, Cerro, mtn., Mex. E1 130
Elaine, Ar., U.S. C8 122
El-'Aiyât, Egypt I2 58
El-Alamein, Egypt A5 62
El Álamo, Mex. G7 130
El Álamo, Mex. H8 130
El Álamo, Mex. L9 134
El Alto, Arg. D5 92
Elan', Russia D6 32
Elancy, Russia F10 34
El Ángel, Ec. G2 86
El-Arish, Egypt G4 58
Elat, Isr. I5 58

Name	Map Ref.	Page
Elat, Gulf of see Aqaba, Gulf of, b.	J5	58
El Ávila, Parque Nacional, p.o.i., Ven.	B8	86
Elazig, Tur.	B4	56
Elba, Isola d', i., Italy	H7	22
El-Badâri, Egypt	K2	58
El-Bahnasa, Egypt	J1	58
El-Balyana, Egypt	B6	62
El'ban, Russia	F16	34
El Banco, Col.	C4	86
El Barco de Ávila, Spain	D5	20
Elbasan, Alb.	C13	24
Elbasani see Elbasan, Alb.	C13	24
El Baúl, Ven.	C7	86
El Baúl, Cerro, mtn., Mex.	G11	100
Elbe (Labe), stm., Eur.	C5	16
Elbe-Havel-Kanal, can., Ger.	C7	16
Elbert, Co., U.S.	B4	128
Elbert, Mount, mtn., Co., U.S.	D10	132
Elberta, Mi., U.S.	D3	112
Elberton, Ga., U.S.	B3	116
Elbeuf, Fr.	E10	14
Elbeyli, Tur.	B8	58
El Beyyadh, Alg.	C5	64
Elblag, Pol.	B15	16
Elblag, state, Pol.	B15	16
El Bluff, Nic.	G6	102
El Bonillo, Spain	F8	20
El Boulaïda, Alg.	B5	64
Elbow, stm., Ab., Can.	E16	138
Elbow Lake, Mn., U.S.	E3	118
El'brus, gora, mtn., Russia	F6	32
Elbrus, Mount see El'brus, gora, mtn., Russia		
El-Burg, Egypt	G1	58
El-Burgâya, Egypt	J1	58
Elburs see Alborz, Reshteh-ye Kühhä-ye, mts., Iran	B7	56
Elburz Mountains see Alborz, Reshteh-ye Kühhä-ye, mts., Iran	B7	56
El Cadilla, Embalse, res., Arg.	C5	92
El Cajon, Ca., U.S.	K9	134
El Calafate, Arg.	J2	90
El Callao, Ven.	D11	86
El Calvario, Ven.	C8	86
El Campamento, P.R.	B3	104a
El Campo, Tx., U.S.	H2	122
El Capitan, mtn., Mt., U.S.	D12	136
El Carmen, Arg.	B5	92
El Carmen, Col.	C3	86
El Carmen, stm., Mex.	F9	98
El Carmen de Bolívar, Col.	C4	86
El Carricito, Mex.	A7	100
El Carril, Arg.	B5	92
El Centinela, Mex.	K10	134
El Centro, Ca., U.S.	K10	134
El Cerrito, Col.	F3	86
El Cerro Del Aripo, mtn., Trin.	s12	105f
Elche see Elx, Spain	F10	20
El Chile, Montaña, mtn., Nic.	E4	102
Elcho, Wi., U.S.	F9	118
Elcho Island, i., Austl.	B7	74
El Cocuy, Col.	D5	86
El Colorado, Arg.	C8	92
El Cóndor, Cerro, vol., Arg.	C3	92
El Corazón, Ec.	H2	86
El Corpus, Hond.	F4	102
El Coto, P.R.	B2	104a
El'cy, Russia	D16	10
Elda, Spain	F10	20
El Desemboque, Mex.	G6	98
El Desemboque, Mex.	F6	98
El'dikan, Russia	D16	34
El-Dilingât, Egypt	H1	58
El Diviso, Col.	G2	86
El Djazaïr (Algiers), Alg.	B5	64
El Djelfa, Alg.	C5	64
Eldon, Ia., U.S.	D5	120
Eldora, Ia., U.S.	B4	120
Eldorado, Arg.	C10	92
Eldorado, Braz.	B13	92
El Dorado, Ar., U.S.	D6	122
Eldorado, Il., U.S.	G9	120
El Dorado, Ks., U.S.	D12	128
Eldorado, Ok., U.S.	G9	128
El Dorado, Ven.	D11	86
El Dorado Springs, Mo., U.S.	G3	120
Eldoret, Kenya	D7	66
Eldred, Pa., U.S.	C7	114
Eldridge, Al., U.S.	D11	122
Eleanor, W.V., U.S.	F3	114
Elec, Russia	H21	10
Electric City, Wa., U.S.	C7	136
Elefantes (Olifants), stm., Afr.	D10	70
Elefsína, Grc.	E6	28
Eleftheroúpoli, Grc.	C7	28
Elektrostal', Russia	E21	10
Elena, Blg.	G12	26
El Encanto, Col.	H5	86
Elephant Butte Reservoir, res., N.M., U.S.	J9	132
Elephant Mountain, mtn., Me., U.S.	F6	110
Elesbão Veloso, Braz.	D4	88
El Estor, Guat.	E3	102
Eleuthera, i., Bah.	B9	96
Eleva, Wi., U.S.	G7	118
Eleven Point, stm., U.S.	H6	120
El Fahs, Tun.	H3	24
El Faro, P.R.	B2	104a
El-Fashn, Egypt	J1	58
El-Fayoum, Egypt	I1	58
El Ferrol del Caudillo see Ferrol, Spain	A2	20
El-Fiqriya, Egypt	K1	58
Elfrida, Az., U.S.	L7	132
El Fuerte, Mex.	B4	100
El Galpón, Arg.	B5	92
Elgin, Scot., U.K.	D9	12
Elgin, Il., U.S.	B9	120
Elgin, Ia., U.S.	B6	120
Elgin, Mn., U.S.	G6	118
Elgin, Ne., U.S.	F14	126
Elgin, N.D., U.S.	A11	126
Elgin, Ok., U.S.	G10	128
Elgin, Or., U.S.	E8	136
El-Gindîya, Egypt	J1	58
El-Gîza (Giza), Egypt	I1	58
Elgon, Mount, mtn., Afr.	D6	66
El Grove see O Grove, Spain	B2	20
El Guaje, Mex.	A7	100
El Guamo, Col.	B4	86
El Guapo, Ven.	B9	86
El Hachero, Cerro, mtn., Mex.	H2	130
El-Hammâmi, reg., Maur.	E2	64
El-Hamûl, Egypt	G2	58
El Hank, clf., Afr.	E3	64
El-Hawâmdîya, Egypt	I2	58
Elhovo, Blg.	G13	26
El Huisache, Mex.	D8	100
Eliase, Indon.	G9	44
Elida, N.M., U.S.	H5	128
Elila, stm., D.R.C.	E5	66
Elim, Ak., U.S.	D7	140
Elisenvaara, Russia	F13	8
Eliseu Martins, Braz.	E4	88
El-Iskandarîya (Alexandria), Egypt	A6	62
Elizabeth, Austl.	E6	32
Elizabeth, Co., U.S.	J2	58
Elizabeth, Il., U.S.	B4	120
Elizabeth, N.J., U.S.	D11	114
Elizabeth, W.V., U.S.	E4	114
Elizabeth City, N.C., U.S.	H9	114
Elizabethton, Tn., U.S.	H3	114
Elizabethtown, Ky., U.S.	G11	120
Elizabethtown, N.Y., U.S.	F3	110
Elizabethtown, Pa., U.S.	D9	114
Elizavety, mys, c., Russia	F17	34
Elizovo, Russia	F20	34
El-Jadida, Mor.	C3	64
El Jaralito, Mex.	B6	100
El Jebel, Co., U.S.	D9	132
Efk, Pol.	C18	16
Elk, stm., B.C., Can.	F16	138
Elk, stm., U.S.	G9	120
Elk, stm., W.V., U.S.	F4	114
Elkader, Ia., U.S.	B6	120
Elk City, Ok., U.S.	F9	128
Elk Creek, Ca., U.S.	D3	134
Elk Creek, stm., S.D., U.S.	C10	126
El Kef, Tun.	H2	24
El-Kelaa-Srarhna, Mor.	C3	64
El Kerê, Eth.	F8	62
Elk Grove, Ca., U.S.	E4	134
El-Khânka, Egypt	H2	58
El-Khârga, Egypt	B6	62
Elkhart, In., U.S.	G4	112
Elkhart, Ks., U.S.	D7	128
Elkhart, Tx., U.S.	F3	122
El Khnâchîch, clf, Mali	E4	64
Elkhorn, Mb., Can.	D12	124
Elkhorn, Wi., U.S.	B2	120
Elkhorn, stm., Ne., U.S.	F16	126
Elkhorn City, Ky., U.S.	G3	114
Elkhorn Mountain, mtn., B.C., Can.	G4	138
Elkhovo see Elhovo, Blg.	G13	26
Elkins, W.V., U.S.	F6	114
Elk Island, i., Mb., Can.	D17	124
Elk Island National Park, p.o.i., Ab., Can.	C18	138
Elkland, Pa., U.S.	C8	114
Elk Mountain, mtn., Wy., U.S.	B10	132
Elko, B.C., Can.	G15	138
Elko, Nv., U.S.	C1	132
Elk Point, Ab., Can.	C19	138
Elk Point, S.D., U.S.	B1	120
Elk Rapids, Mi., U.S.	D4	112
Elk River, Mn., U.S.	F5	118
Elkton, Md., U.S.	E10	114
Elkton, Mi., U.S.	E6	112
Elkton, S.D., U.S.	G2	118
Elkton, Va., U.S.	F7	114
Ellaville, Ga., U.S.	D1	116
Ellef Ringnes Island, i., Nu., Can.	B5	141
Ellen, Mount, mtn., Ut., U.S.	E6	132
Ellendale, Mn., U.S.	H5	118
Ellendale, N.D., U.S.	A14	126
Ellensburg, Wa., U.S.	C6	136
Ellenton, Ga., U.S.	E2	116
Ellesmere, Lake, l., N.Z.	F5	80
Ellesmere Island, i., Nu., Can.	B9	141
Ellettsville, In., U.S.	E11	120
Ellice, stm., Nu., Can.	B10	106
Ellice Islands see Tuvalu, ctry., Oc.	D8	72
Ellicottville, N.Y., U.S.	B7	114
Ellijay, Ga., U.S.	B1	116
Ellinwood, Ks., U.S.	C10	128
Elliot, S. Afr.	G8	70
Elliot, Mount, mtn., Austl.	B6	76
Elliot Lake, On., Can.	B7	112
Elliott Lake, l., Mb., Can.	B18	124
Elliott, Ia., U.S.	C2	120
Elliott, Ms., U.S.	D9	122
Ellisras, S. Afr.	C8	70
Elliston, Austl.	F6	74
Elliston, Mt., U.S.	D14	136
Ellisville, Ms., U.S.	F9	122
Ellon, Scot., U.K.	D10	12
Ellora Caves, hist., India	A2	53
Elloree, S.C., U.S.	C5	116
Ellsworth, Ks., U.S.	C10	128
Ellsworth, Me., U.S.	F8	110
Ellsworth, Mi., U.S.	C4	112
Ellsworth, Mn., U.S.	H3	118
Ellsworth, Wi., U.S.	G6	118
Ellsworth Land, reg., Ant.	C32	81
Ellsworth Mountains, mts., Ant.	C32	81
El Lucero, Mex.	I4	130
Ellwangen, Ger.	H5	16
Ellwood City, Pa., U.S.	D5	114
Elm, stm., U.S.	B14	126
Elma, Wa., U.S.	D3	136
El-Mahalla el-Kubra, Egypt	I2	58
El-Maimûn, Egypt	I2	58
Elmali, Tur.	G12	28
El Maneadero, Mex.	L9	134
El-Mansûra, Egypt	G2	58
El Manteco, Ven.	D10	86
El-Manzala, Egypt	G3	58
El-Matariya, Egypt	G3	58
Elm Creek, Mb., Can.	E16	124
Elm Creek, Ne., U.S.	G13	126
El Médano, Mex.	C3	100
El Menia, Alg.	C5	64
Elmer, N.J., U.S.	E10	114
Elmhurst, Il., U.S.	G2	112
El-Minya (Minya), Egypt	J1	58
Elmira, On., Can.	E9	112
Elmira, P.E., Can.	D14	110
Elmira, N.Y., U.S.	B9	114
El Moral, Mex.	F7	130
Elmore, Austl.	K5	76
Elmore, Mn., U.S.	H4	118
Elmore, Oh., U.S.	C2	114
Elmore City, Ok., U.S.	G11	128
El Morro, hist., P.R.	B3	104a
El Morro National Monument, p.o.i., N.M., U.S.	H8	132
El Mreyyé, reg., Maur.	F3	64
Elmshorn, Ger.	C5	16
Elm Springs, Ar., U.S.	H3	120
El Mulato, Mex.	E3	130
El Muñâ, Egypt	K2	58
Elmvale, On., Can.	D10	112
Elmwood, Il., U.S.	K8	118
Elmwood, On., Can.	D8	112
Elmwood, Ne., U.S.	B15	14
Elmwood, Wi., U.S.	H2	16
El Negrito, Hond.	E4	102
Elnora, Ab., Can.	D17	138
Elnora, In., U.S.	F10	120
Elorza, Ven.	D7	86
El Otate, Cerro, mtn., Mex.	F1	130
Eloten, Turkmen.	B9	56
Eloy, Az., U.S.	K5	132
Eloy Alfaro, Ec.	I2	86
El Palmar de los Sepúlveda, Mex.	C5	100
El Palmito, Mex.	I8	130
El Palqui, Chile	E2	92
El Pao, Ven.	C7	86
El Paso, Il., U.S.	D8	120
El Paso, Tx., U.S.	C1	130
El Paso de Robles see Paso Robles, Ca., U.S.	H5	134
El Paso Peaks, mtn., Ca., U.S.	H8	134
El Perú, Ven.	D11	86
El Pintado, Arg.	B7	92
El Pital, Cerro, mtn., N.A.	E3	102
El Planchón, Volcán (Planchón, Cerro del), vol., S.A.	G2	92
El Polvorín, P.R.	B3	104a
El Portal, Ca., U.S.	F6	134
El Porvenir, Mex.	G3	130
El Porvenir, Mex.	G3	128
El Porvenir, Pan.	H8	102
El Potrero, Mex.	H7	130
El Potro, Cerro (Potro, Cerro del), mtn., S.A.	D3	92
El Prat de Llobregat, Spain	C12	20
El Progreso, Hond.	E4	102
El Puerto de Santa María, Spain	H4	20
El Puesto, Arg.	C4	92
El-Qâhira (Cairo), Egypt	H2	58
El-Qantara el-Sharqîya, Egypt	H3	58
El-Qasr, Egypt	B5	62
El Quebrachal, Arg.	B5	92
El Quelite, Mex.	D5	100
Elqui, stm., Chile	D2	92
El-Qûsîya, Egypt	K1	58
El Real de Santa María, Pan.	H9	102
El Remolino, Mex.	F6	130
El Reno, Ok., U.S.	F10	128
El Rio, Ca., U.S.	I6	134
El Roble, Mesa, mtn., Mex.	L10	134
Elroy, Wi., U.S.	H8	118
Elsa, Yk., Can.	C3	106
Elsa, Tx., U.S.	H9	130
El-Saff, Egypt	I2	58
El-Sa'îd (Upper Egypt), hist. reg., Egypt	J2	58
El Salado, Chile	C2	92
El Salado, Parque Nacional, p.o.i., Ec.	I1	86
El Salto, Mex.	D6	100
El Salvador, Chile	C3	92
El Salvador, ctry., N.A.	F3	102
El Samán de Apure, Ven.	D7	86
El Sauz, Mex.	A5	100
El Sauzal, Mex.	L9	134
Elsberry, Mo., U.S.	E7	120
El Seibo, Dom. Rep.	C13	102
Elsen Nur, l., China	D3	36
El-Simbillawein, Egypt	H2	58
Elsinore see Helsingør, Den.	H5	8
Elsinore, Ut., U.S.	E4	132
El Sombrero, Ven.	C8	86
Elsterwerda, Ger.	E9	16
El Sueco, Mex.	H1	130
El-Suweis (Suez), Egypt	I3	58
El Tajín, hist., Mex.	E10	100
El Tala, Arg.	C5	92
El Tanque, Mex.	H8	130
El Tecuán, Mex.	C5	100
El-Thamad, Egypt	I5	58
El Tigre, Ven.	C9	86
Eltmann, Ger.	G6	16
El Toco, Chile	D3	90
El Tocuyo, Ven.	C7	86
Elton, La., U.S.	G6	122
El Tránsito, Chile	D2	92
El Trébol, Arg.	F7	92
El Tule, Mex.	G1	130
El Tuparro, Parque Nacional, p.o.i., Col.	E7	86
El-Tûr, Egypt	J4	58
El Turbio, Arg.	J2	90
El-Uqsor (Luxor), Egypt	B6	62
Eluru, India	C5	53
El Valle, Pan.	H7	102
Elvas, Port.	F3	20
El Vendrell, Spain	C12	20
Elverum, Nor.	F4	8
El Viejo, Nic.	F4	102
El Vigia, Ven.	C6	86
Elvira, Arg.	G8	92
El Volcán, Chile	F2	92
El Wad, Alg.	C6	64
El-Wâsta, Egypt	I2	58
Elwell, Lake, res., Mt., U.S.	B15	136
Elwood, In., U.S.	H4	112
Elwood, Ne., U.S.	G13	126
Elx, Spain	F10	20
Ely, Eng., U.K.	I13	12
Ely, Mn., U.S.	D7	118
Ely, Nv., U.S.	D2	132
El Yagual, Ven.	D7	86
Elyria, Oh., U.S.	C3	114
El Yunque, mtn., P.R.	B4	104a
El-Zarqa, Egypt	G3	58
Encampment, Wy., U.S.	B10	132
Encantado, Braz.	D11	92
Encarnación, Para.	C9	92
Enchi, Ghana	H4	64
Enchilayas, Mex.	F6	98
Encinal, Tx., U.S.	F8	130
Encinitas, Ca., U.S.	J8	134
Encino, N.M., U.S.	G3	128
Encontrados, Ven.	C5	86
Encounter Bay, b., Austl.	J2	76
Encruzilhada, Braz.	H5	88
Encruzilhada do Sul, Braz.	E11	92
Encs, Hung.	A8	26
Endako, B.C., Can.	B5	138
Ende, Indon.	G7	44
Endeavor, Wi., U.S.	H9	118
Endeavour Strait, strt., Austl.	B8	74
Enderby, B.C., Can.	F11	138
Enderby Land, reg., Ant.	B10	81
Enderlin, N.D., U.S.	A15	126
Endicott, N.Y., U.S.	B9	114
Endicott Mountains, mts., Ak., U.S.	C9	140
Ene, stm., Peru	F3	84
Enewetak, at., Marsh. Is.	B7	72
Enez, Tur.	C9	28
Enfield, N.C., U.S.	H8	114
Engaño, Cabo, c., Dom. Rep.	C13	102
Engcobo, S. Afr.	G9	70
Engelhard, N.C., U.S.	A10	116
Engel's, Russia	D7	32
Engen, B.C., Can.	B6	138
Engenheiro Navarro, Braz.	I3	88
Enggano, Pulau, i., Indon.	F2	50
England, state, U.K.	I12	12
Englefield, Cape, c., Nu., Can.	B13	106
Englehart, On., Can.	F15	106
Englewood, B.C., Can.	F3	138
Englewood, Co., U.S.	B4	128
Englewood, Fl., U.S.	J3	116
Englewood, Ks., U.S.	D8	128
Englewood, Tn., U.S.	A1	116
English, stm., On., Can.	A4	118
English Channel, strt., Eur.	D7	14
English Coast, cst., Ant.	C33	81
Engure, Lat.	C6	10
Engures ezers, l., Lat.	C6	10
Enid, Ok., U.S.	E11	128
Enid Lake, res., Ms., U.S.	C9	122
Enis Head, c., Ire.	G2	12
Enisej, stm., Russia	C6	34
Enisejsk, Russia	C16	32
Enisejskij krjaž, mts., Russia	C16	32
Enisejskij zaliv, b., Russia	B5	34
Eniwetok see Enewetak, at., Marsh. Is.	B7	72
Enka, N.C., U.S.	A3	116
Enkhuizen, Neth.	B14	14
Enmedio, Mex.	E4	130
Enmedio, Cerro de, mtn., Mex.	F8	100
Enna, Italy	G8	24
Ennadai Lake, l., Nu., Can.	C10	106
Ennedi, plat., Chad	D4	62
Ennis, Ire.	I3	12
Ennis, Mt., U.S.	E15	136
Ennis, Tx., U.S.	E2	122
Enniscorthy, Ire.	I6	12
Enniskillen, N. Ire., U.K.	G5	12
Enns, Aus.	B11	22
Enns, stm., Aus.	B11	22
Enon, Oh., U.S.	E2	114
Enontekiö, Fin.	B10	8
Enoree, stm., S.C., U.S.	B3	116
Enosburg Falls, Vt., U.S.	F4	110
Enping, China	J5	42
Enrekang, Indon.	E11	50
Enrile, Phil.	p20	104g
Enriquillo, Dom. Rep.	D12	102
Enriquillo, Lago, l., Dom. Rep.	C12	102
Enschede, Neth.	B15	14
Ensenada, Arg.	G9	92
Ensenada, Mex.	L9	134
Enshi, China	F3	42
Enshū-nada, Japan	E10	40
Ensley, Fl., U.S.	G11	122
Enstone, Eng., U.K.	J11	12
Entebbe, Ug.	D6	66
Enterprise, N.T., Can.	C7	106
Enterprise, Al., U.S.	F13	122
Enterprise, Ca., U.S.	D4	134
Enterprise, Ms., U.S.	E10	122
Enterprise, Or., U.S.	E9	136
Enterprise, Ut., U.S.	F3	132
Entrepenas, Embalse de, res., Spain	D8	20
Entre Ríos, Bol.	D4	90
Entre Ríos, Braz.	G7	88
Entre Ríos, state, Arg.	F8	92
Entrevaux, Fr.	E12	18
Entroncamento, Port.	E2	20
Entwistle, Ab., Can.	C16	138
Enugu, Nig.	H6	64
Enurmino, Russia	C26	34
Envalira, Port d', p., And.	B12	20
Envigado, Col.	D4	86
Enviken, Swe.	F6	8
Enyamba, D.R.C.	E5	66
Enyellé, Congo	D3	66
Eolie, Isole (Lipari, Isole), is., Italy	F8	24
Epecuén, Lago, l., Arg.	H6	92
Épernay, Fr.	E12	14
Épernon, Fr.	F10	14
Ephesus see Efes, hist., Tur.	F10	28
Ephrata, Pa., U.S.	D9	114
Ephrata, Wa., U.S.	C7	136
Épi, state, Vanuatu	k17	79d
Epidavros, hist., Grc.	F6	28
Epila, Spain	C9	20
Épinal, Fr.	F15	14
Epirus see Ipeiros, hist. reg., Grc.	D3	28
Epsom, Eng., U.K.	J12	12
Epukiro, Nmb.	B4	70
Epukiro, stm., Nmb.	B4	70
Eqlid, Iran	C7	56
Equatorial Guinea, ctry., Afr.	I6	64
Erap, Pap. N. Gui.	b4	79a
Erath, La., U.S.	H6	122
Erave, Pap. N. Gui.	b3	79a
Erawan National Park, p.o.i., Thai.	E4	48
Erbaa, Tur.	A4	58
Erbeskopf, mtn., Ger.	G3	16
Erbil see Arbil, Iraq	B5	56
Ercek, Tur.	B5	56
Erçek, Gölü, l., Tur.	B5	56
Erciş, Tur.	B5	56
Erciyeş Daği, vol., Tur.	B3	56
Érd, Hung.	B5	26
Erdao, stm., China	C7	38
Erdaobaihe, China	C8	38
Erdaohezi, Mong.	B9	36
Erdek, Tur.	C10	28
Erdemli, Tur.	B4	58
Erding, Ger.	H7	16
Erdinger Moos, reg., Ger.	H7	16
Erebus, Mount, mtn., Ant.	C21	81
Erechim, Braz.	C11	92
Erech, hist., Iraq	C5	56
Ereğli, Tur.	B4	58
Ereğli, Tur.	C14	28
Erenhot, China	C7	36
Ereymentaü, Kaz.	D12	32
Erfoud, Mor.	C4	64
Erft, stm., Ger.	E2	16
Erfurt, Ger.	F7	16
Ergene, stm., Tur.	B10	28
Ergeni, hills, Russia	E6	32
Érgli, Lat.	D8	10
Erguig, Arg.	D5	92
Ergun Youqi, China	A9	36
Ergun Zuoqi, China	F13	34
Er Hai, l., China	F5	36
Erice, Italy	F6	24
Ericeira, Port.	F1	20
Erichsen Lake, l., Nu., Can.	A14	106
Erick, Ok., U.S.	F9	128
Erickson, Mb., Can.	D14	124
Ericson, Ne., U.S.	F14	126
Erie, Co., U.S.	A3	128
Erie, Il., U.S.	C7	120
Erie, Pa., U.S.	B5	114
Erie, Lake, l., N.A.	B4	114
Erie Canal see New York State Barge Canal, can., N.Y., U.S.	E12	112
Eriksdale, Mb., Can.	D15	124
Erimo-misaki, c., Japan	D15	38
Erin, On., Can.	E9	112
Erin, Tn., U.S.	H10	120
Eriskay, i., Scot., U.K.	D5	12
Eritrea, ctry., Afr.	D7	62
Erkelenz, Ger.	E2	16
Erkner, Ger.	D9	16
Erlangen, Ger.	G7	16
Ermak, Kaz.	D13	32
Ermelo, S. Afr.	E10	70
Ermenek, stm., Tur.	B3	58
Ermenek, Tur.	B3	58
Ermentau, Kaz.	D12	32
Ermica, Russia	C25	8
Ermolaevo, Russia	D9	32
Ermoúpoli, Grc.	F7	28
Erne, Lower Lough, l., Ire., U.K.	G4	12
Erne, Upper Lough, l., Eur.	G5	12
Ernée, Fr.	F8	14
Erode, India	F3	53
Erofej Pavlovič, Russia	F13	34
Eromanga, Austl.	F4	76
Erongo, state, Nmb.	C2	70
Erongo, mtn., Nmb.	B2	70
Eropol, Russia	C22	34
Erota, Erit.	D7	62
Er-Rachidia, Mor.	C4	64
Errego, Moz.	D6	68
Errigal Mountain, mtn., Ire.	F4	12
Errinundra National Park, p.o.i., Austl.	K7	76
Erris Head, c., Ire.	G2	12
Errol Heights, Or., U.S.	E4	136
Erromango, i., Vanuatu	I17	79d
Erši, Russia	F17	10
Eršov, Russia	D7	32
Erstein, Fr.	F16	14
Erval, Braz.	F11	92
Ervy-le-Châtel, Fr.	F12	14
Erwin, N.C., U.S.	A7	116
Erwin, Tn., U.S.	H3	114
Erwood, Sk., Can.	B11	124
Eryuan, China	F4	36
Erzhan, China	B8	38
Erzin, Russia	D17	32
Erzincan, Tur.	B4	56
Erzurum, Tur.	B5	56
Esa'ala, Pap. N. Gui.	b5	79a
Esashi, Japan	D13	38
Esbjerg, Den.	I3	8
Esbo see Espoo, Fin.	F11	8
Escalante, stm., Ut., U.S.	F6	132
Escalón, Mex.	B6	100
Escambia, stm., Fl., U.S.	G11	122
Escanaba, Mi., U.S.	C2	112
Escanaba, stm., Mi., U.S.	B2	112
Escandón, Puerto, p., Spain	D10	20
Escárcega, Mex.	C2	102
Escarpada Point, c., Phil.	A4	52
Escatawpa, stm., U.S.	G10	122
Esch-sur-Alzette, Lux.	E15	14
Escobedo, Mex.	G6	130
Escocesa, Bahía, b., Dom. Rep.	C13	102
Escondido, Ca., U.S.	J8	134
Escondido, stm., Mex.	F6	102
Escondido, stm., Nic.	F6	102
Escuinapa de Hidalgo, Mex.	D5	100
Escuintla, Guat.	E2	102
Escuintla, Mex.	H12	100
Eşen, Tur.	G12	28
Eşen, stm., Tur.	G12	28
Eṣfahān, Iran	C7	56
Esgueva, stm., Spain	C6	20
Eshowe, S. Afr.	F10	70
Esil see Ishim, stm., Asia	C12	32
Esil, Kaz.	D11	32
Esk, Austl.	F9	76
Eskdale, W.V., U.S.	F4	114
Es'ki, Russia	C19	10
Eskilstrup, Den.	B7	16
Eskilstuna, Swe.	G7	8
Eskimo Lakes, l., N.T., Can.	B4	106
Eskimo Point see Arviat, Nu., Can.	C12	106
Eskişehir, Tur.	D13	28
Eskişehir, state, Tur.	D13	28
Eskridge, Ks., U.S.	F1	120
Esla, stm., Spain	C5	20
Eslāmābād, Iran	C6	56
Eslöv, Swe.	I5	8
Esme, Tur.	E11	28
Esmeralda, Austl.	A4	76
Esmeralda, Cuba	B8	102
Esmeralda, Isla, i., Chile	I1	90
Esmeraldas, Ec.	G2	86
Esmeraldas, state, Ec.	G2	86
Esmeraldas, stm., Ec.	G2	86
Esnagami Lake, l., On., Can.	A11	118
Espada, Punta, c., Col.	A6	86
Espalion, Fr.	E8	18
Espanola, On., Can.	B8	112
Espanola, N.M., U.S.	F2	128
Espejo, Spain	G6	20
Espelkamp, Ger.	D4	16
Esperança, Braz.	D8	88
Esperance, Austl.	F4	74
Esperanza, Arg.	E7	92
Esperanza, Mex.	B4	100
Esperanza, P.R.	B5	104a
Esperanza, sci., Ant.	B35	81
Espichel, Cabo, c., Port.	F1	20
Espinal, Col.	E4	86
Espinho, Port.	D2	20
Espírito Santo, state, Braz.	J5	88
Espíritu Santo, i., Vanuatu	j16	79d
Espíritu Santo, Isla, i., Mex.	C3	100
Espoo, Fin.	F11	8
Espungabera, Moz.	B11	70
Esquel, Arg.	H2	90
Esquimalt, B.C., Can.	H7	138
Esquina, Arg.	D8	92
Esquiú, Arg.	D5	92
Essaouira, Mor.	C3	64
Essej, Russia	C9	34
Essen, Ger.	E3	16
Essendon, Mount, mtn., Austl.	D3	74
Essequibo, stm., Guy.	C6	84
Es Sers, Tun.	H2	24
Essex, On., Can.	F7	112
Essex, Md., U.S.	E9	114
Essex Junction, Vt., U.S.	F3	110
Essexville, Mi., U.S.	E6	112
Esslingen am Neckar, Ger.	H5	16
Essonne, state, Fr.	F11	14
Est, Pointe de l', c., Qc., Can.	A15	110
Estaca de Bares, Punta da, c., Spain	A3	20
Estaca de Bares, Punta de la see Estaca de Bares, Punta da, c., Spain	A3	20
Estacado, Llano, pl., U.S.	H6	128
Estación Adolfo Rodríguez Sáa see Santa Rosa del Conlara, Arg.	F5	92
Estación Colonia Alvear Norte see General Alvear, Arg.	G3	92
Estación Foguista J. F. Juárez see El Galpón, Arg.	B5	92
Estación Gobernador Vera see Vera, Arg.	D7	92
Estación J. J. Castelli see Castelli, Arg.	B7	92
Estación Justino Solari see Mariano I. Loza, Arg.	D8	92
Estación Manuel F. Mantilla see Pedro R. Fernández, Arg.	D8	92
Estación Vela see María Ignacia, Arg.	H8	92
Estados, Isla de los, i., Arg.	J4	90
Eṣtahbān, Iran	D7	56
Estância, Braz.	F7	88
Estanislao del Campo, Arg.	B7	92
Estarreja, Port.	D2	20
Estats, Pic d' (Estats, Pique d'), mtn., Eur.	G7	18
Estats, Pico de see Estats, Pic d', mtn., Eur.	G7	18
Estats, Pique d' (Estats, Pic d'), mtn., Eur.	G7	18
Este, Italy	E8	22
Esteio, Braz.	D12	92
Esteli, Nic.	F4	102
Estella, Spain	B8	20
Estelline, S.D., U.S.	G2	118
Estelline, Tx., U.S.	G8	128
Estepa, Spain	G6	20
Estepona, Spain	H5	20
Esterhazy, Sk., Can.	C11	124
Estes Park, Co., U.S.	G7	126
Este Sudeste, Cayos del, is., Col.	F7	102
Estevan, Sk., Can.	E10	124
Estevan Point, B.C., Can.	G4	138
Estherville, Ia., U.S.	A3	120
Estill, S.C., U.S.	D4	116
Estiva, stm., Braz.	G3	88
Eston, Sk., Can.	C5	124
Estonia, ctry., Eur.	G11	8
Estrela, Braz.	D11	92
Estrela, mtn., Port.	D3	20
Estrela do Sul, Braz.	J2	88
Estremadura, hist. reg., Port.	E1	20
Estremoz, Port.	F3	20
Estrondo, Serra do, plat., Braz.	E1	88
Esztergom, Hung.	B5	26
Etadunna, Austl.	G2	76
Etah, Grnld.	B11	141
Etah, India	E7	54
Étain, Fr.	E14	14
Étampes, Fr.	F11	14
Etamunbanie, Lake, l., Austl.	F2	76
Étaples, Fr.	D10	14
Etâwah, India	E7	54
Etchojoa, Mex.	B4	100
Ethan, S.D., U.S.	D14	126
Ethel, Ms., U.S.	D9	122
Ethel, Mount, mtn., Co., U.S.	C10	132
Ethiopia, ctry., Afr.	F7	62
Ethiopian Plateau, plat., Eth.	E7	62
Ethridge, Mt., U.S.	B14	136
Ethridge, Tn., U.S.	B11	122
Etigo-heiya, pl., Japan	B12	40
Etive, Loch, l., Scot., U.K.	E7	12
E. T. Joshua Airport, St. Vin.	o11	105e
Etna, Monte, vol., Italy	G8	24
Etna, Pa., U.S.	B14	114
Etobicoke, ngh., On., Can.	E10	112
Etolin Island, i., Ak., U.S.	E13	140
Etolin Strait, strt., Ak., U.S.	D6	140
Etomi, stm., Sk., Can.	B11	124
Eton, Austl.	C7	76
Étorofu-tō (Iturup, ostrov), i., Russia	B17	38
Etosha Pan, pl., Nmb.	D2	68
Etoumbi, Congo	D2	66
Etowah, Tn., U.S.	B14	122
Etowah, stm., Ga., U.S.	C14	122
Étréchy, Fr.	F11	14
Étretat, Fr.	E9	14
Etsch see Adige, stm., Italy	E8	22
Et Tidra, i., Maur.	F1	64
Ettlingen, Ger.	H4	16
Etzikom Coulee, stm., Ab., Can.	E2	124
Eu, Fr.	D10	14
Eua, i., Tonga	o8	78e
Eua Iki, i., Tonga	n15	78e
Euboea see Évvoia, i., Grc.	E6	28
Euboea, Gulf of see Vórios Evvoïkós Kólpos, b., Grc.	E5	28
Eucla, Austl.	F5	74
Euclid, Oh., U.S.	C4	114
Euclides da Cunha, Braz.	F6	88
Eucumbene, Lake, res., Austl.	K7	76
Eudora, Ar., U.S.	D7	122
Eudora, Ks., U.S.	F2	120
Eudunda, Austl.	J2	76
Eufaula, Al., U.S.	E13	122
Eufaula, Ok., U.S.	B3	122
Eufaula Lake, res., Ok., U.S.	B3	122
Eugene, Or., U.S.	F3	136
Eugenia, Punta, c., Mex.	B1	100
Eugenio Bustos, Arg.	F3	92
Eugowra, Austl.	I7	76
Eumungerie, Austl.	H7	76
Eunápolis, Braz.	I6	88
Eungella National Park, p.o.i., Austl.	C7	76
Eunice, La., U.S.	G6	122
Eunice, N.M., U.S.	B5	130
Euphrates (Al-Furāt), stm., Asia	C5	56
Eupora, Ms., U.S.	D9	122
Eura, Fin.	F9	8
Eure, state, Fr.	E10	14
Eure, stm., Fr.	E9	14
Eure-et-Loir, state, Fr.	F10	14
Eureka, Ca., U.S.	C1	134
Eureka, Ks., U.S.	D12	128
Eureka, Mt., U.S.	B12	136
Eureka, Nv., U.S.	D10	134

Name	Map Ref.	Page
Eureka, S.C., U.S.	B4	116
Eureka Springs, Ar., U.S.	H4	120
Eurinilla Creek, stm., Austl.	H3	76
Euroa, Austl.	K5	76
Europa, Île, i., Reu.	E7	68
Europa Island see Europa, Île, i., Reu.	E7	68
Europa Point, c., Gib.	H5	20
Europe, cont.	C13	4
Euskal Herriko, state, Spain	A8	20
Euskirchen, Ger.	F2	16
Eustace, Tx., U.S.	E2	122
Eustis, Fl., U.S.	H4	116
Eustis, Lake, l., Fl., U.S.	H4	116
Euston, Austl.	J4	76
Eutaw, Al., U.S.	E11	122
Eutin, Ger.	B6	16
Eutsuk Lake, l., B.C., Can.	C4	138
Eva, Al., U.S.	C12	122
Evadale, Tx., U.S.	G4	122
Evandale, Austl.	n13	77a
Evans, Lac, l., Qc., Can.	E15	106
Evans, Mount, mtn., Co., U.S.	B3	128
Evansburg, Ab., Can.	B16	138
Evans City, Pa., U.S.	D5	114
Evansdale, Ia., U.S.	I6	118
Evans Strait, strt., Nu., Can.	C14	106
Evanston, Il., U.S.	F2	112
Evanston, Wy., U.S.	B6	132
Evansville, In., U.S.	F10	120
Evansville, Mn., U.S.	E3	118
Evansville, Wi., U.S.	B8	120
Evansville, Wy., U.S.	E6	126
Evart, Mi., U.S.	E4	112
Eveleth, Mn., U.S.	D6	118
Evening Shade, Ar., U.S.	H6	120
Evensk, Russia	D20	34
Everard, Lake, l., Austl.	F6	74
Everest, Mount (Qomolangma Feng), mtn., Asia	D11	54
Everett, Pa., U.S.	E7	114
Everett, Wa., U.S.	C4	136
Everett, Mount, mtn., Ma., U.S.	B12	114
Everglades, The, sw., Fl., U.S.	K4	116
Everglades City, Fl., U.S.	K4	116
Everglades National Park, p.o.i., Fl., U.S.	K5	116
Evergreen, Al., U.S.	F12	122
Evergreen, Mt., U.S.	B12	136
Evermann, Cerro, vol., Mex.	F3	100
Evesham, Sk., Can.	B4	124
Evesham, Eng., U.K.	I11	12
Évian-les-Bains, Fr.	C12	18
Evje, Nor.	G2	8
Évora, Port.	F3	20
Évora, state, Port.	F3	20
Évoron, ozero, l., Russia	F16	34
Évreux, Fr.	E10	14
Évry, Fr.	F11	14
E. V. Spence Reservoir, res., Tx., U.S.	C7	130
Évvoia, i., Grc.	E6	28
Ewa, Hi., U.S.	B3	78a
Ewing, Ne., U.S.	E14	126
Ewing, Va., U.S.	H2	114
Ewo, Congo	E2	66
Exaltación, Bol.	B3	90
Excelsior Mountain, mtn., Ca., U.S.	E6	134
Excelsior Springs, Mo., U.S.	E3	120
Exeter, On., Can.	E8	112
Exeter, Eng., U.K.	K9	12
Exeter, Ca., U.S.	G6	134
Exeter, N.H., U.S.	G6	110
Exeter Sound, strt., Nu., Can.	D13	141
Exira, Ia., U.S.	C3	120
Exmoor, plat., Eng., U.K.	J9	12
Exmoor National Park, p.o.i., Eng., U.K.	J9	12
Exmore, Va., U.S.	G10	114
Exmouth, Austl.	D2	74
Exmouth, Eng., U.K.	K9	12
Exmouth Gulf, b., Austl.	D2	74
Exshaw, Ab., Can.	E15	138
Extremadura, state, Spain	E4	20
Exuma Cays, is., Bah.	C9	96
Exuma Sound, strt., Bah.	C9	96
Eyasi, Lake, l., Tan.	E6	66
Eyebrow, Sk., Can.	D7	124
Eyemouth, Scot., U.K.	F10	12
Eye Peninsula, pen., Scot., U.K.	C6	12
Eyjafjörður, b., Ice.	j30	8a
Eyl, Som.	C9	66
Eyl, val., Som.	C9	66
Eylar Mountain, mtn., Ca., U.S.	F4	134
Eyota, Mn., U.S.	H6	118
Eyrarbakki, Ice.	I29	8a
Eyre, Austl.	F5	74
Eyre Creek, stm., Austl.	F2	76
Eyre North, Lake, l., Austl.	E7	74
Eyre Peninsula, pen., Austl.	F7	74
Eyre South, Lake, l., Austl.	E7	74
Ezequiel Ramos Mexía, Embalse, res., Arg.	G3	90
Ežerelis, Lith.	F6	10
Ezine, Tur.	D9	28

F

Name	Map Ref.	Page
Faaone, Fr. Poly.	v22	78h
Faber Lake, l., N.T., Can.	C7	106
Fabriano, Italy	G9	22
Facatativá, Col.	E4	86
Fachi, Niger	F7	64
Facpi Point, c., Guam	j9	78c
Factoryville, Pa., U.S.	C10	114
Fada, Chad	D4	62
Fada-Ngourma, Burkina	G5	64
Faddeevskij, ostrov, i., Russia	A18	34
Fadejobja, zaliv, b., Russia	A10	34
Fadiffolu Atoll at., Mald.	h12	46a
Faenza, Italy	F8	22
Faer, Port.	C2	20
Făgăraş, Rom.	D11	26
Fagersta, Swe.	F6	8
Faguibine, Lac, l., Mali	F4	64
Fagurhólsmýri, Ice.	I31	8a
Fairbank, Az., U.S.	B5	120
Fairbanks, Ak., U.S.	D10	140
Fairbanks, La., U.S.	E6	122
Fair Bluff, N.C., U.S.	B6	116
Fairborn, Oh., U.S.	E1	114
Fairbury, Il., U.S.	K10	118
Fairbury, Ne., U.S.	A11	128
Fairchance, Pa., U.S.	E6	114
Fairchild, Wi., U.S.	G8	118
Fairdale, N.D., U.S.	F15	124
Fairfax, Mn., U.S.	G4	118
Fairfax, Mo., U.S.	D2	120
Fairfax, S.D., U.S.	D14	126
Fairfax, Vt., U.S.	F3	110
Fairfax, Va., U.S.	F8	114
Fairfield, Al., U.S.	D11	122
Fairfield, Ia., U.S.	E3	120
Fairfield, Id., U.S.	G12	136
Fairfield, Il., U.S.	F9	120
Fairfield, Me., U.S.	F7	110
Fairfield, Oh., U.S.	E1	114
Fairfield, Tx., U.S.	F2	122
Fairgrove, Mi., U.S.	E6	112
Fairhaven, Ma., U.S.	C15	114
Fair Haven, N.Y., U.S.	E13	112
Fair Head, c., N. Ire., U.K.	F6	12
Fairhope, Al., U.S.	G11	122
Fair Isle, i., Scot., U.K.	B11	12
Fairland, In., U.S.	E12	120
Fairlie, N.Z.	G4	80
Fairmont, Mn., U.S.	H4	118
Fairmont, Ne., U.S.	G15	126
Fairmont, N.C., U.S.	B6	116
Fairmont, W.V., U.S.	E5	114
Fairmont Hot Springs, B.C., Can.	F14	138
Fairmount, Il., U.S.	H2	114
Fairmount, In., U.S.	H4	112
Fairmount, N.D., U.S.	E2	118
Fair Ness, c., Nu., Can.	C16	106
Fair Oaks, Ca., U.S.	E4	134
Fair Plain, Mi., U.S.	F3	112
Fairplay, Co., U.S.	B3	128
Fairview, Ab., Can.	C13	122
Fairview, Il., U.S.	D7	120
Fairview, Mi., U.S.	D5	112
Fairview, Mt., U.S.	G9	124
Fairview, Tn., U.S.	I10	120
Fairview, Ut., U.S.	D5	132
Fairview Park, In., U.S.	I2	112
Fairview Peak, mtn., Nv., U.S.	D7	134
Fairweather Mountain, mtn., N.A.	D3	106
Faisalabad (Lyallpur), Pak.	C4	54
Faison, N.C., U.S.	A7	116
Faistós, hist., Grc.	H7	28
Faith, S.D., U.S.	B10	126
Faizābād, India	E9	54
Fajardo, P.R.	B4	104a
Fajou, Îlet à, i., Guad.	h5	105c
Fajr, Bi'r, well, Sau. Ar.	J8	58
Fajr, Wādī, stm., Sau. Ar.	H9	58
Fajr, Wādī, stm., Sau. Ar.	J8	58
Fakse Bugt, b., Den.	A8	16
Faku, China	C5	38
Falaba, S.L.	H2	64
Falaise, Fr.	F8	14
Fālākāta, India	E12	54
Falam, Mya.	A1	48
Falcón, state, Ven.	B7	86
Falcón, Presa (Falcon Reservoir), res., N.A.	H8	130
Falconara Marittima, Italy	G10	22
Falcon Reservoir (Falcón, Presa), res., N.A.	H8	130
Faleālupo, Samoa	g11	79c
Falémé, stm., Afr.	G2	64
Faleşti, Mol.	B14	26
Falfurrias, Tx., U.S.	G9	130
Falher, Ab., Can.	A14	138
Falkenberg, Ger.	E9	16
Falkenberg, Swe.	H5	8
Falkensee, Ger.	D9	16
Falkenstein, Ger.	F8	16
Falkirk, Scot., U.K.	E9	12
Falkland Islands, dep., S.A.	J4	90
Falkland Sound, strt., Falk. Is.	J5	90
Falköping, Swe.	G5	8
Falkville, Al., U.S.	C11	122
Fall, stm., Ks., U.S.	D13	128
Fallbrook, Ca., U.S.	J8	134
Fallon, Nv., U.S.	D7	134
Fall River, Ks., U.S.	G12	120
Fall River, Ma., U.S.	C14	114
Fall River, Wi., U.S.	H9	118
Fall River Mills, Ca., U.S.	C4	134
Falls City, Ne., U.S.	D2	120
Falls City, Or., U.S.	F3	136
Falls City, Tx., U.S.	E9	130
Falls Lake, res., N.C., U.S.	I7	114
Falmouth, Jam.	i13	104d
Falmouth, Eng., U.K.	K7	12
Falmouth, Me., U.S.	G6	110
Falmouth, Ma., U.S.	C15	114
False Bay, b., S. Afr.	I4	70
False Divi Point, c., India	D5	53
False Pass, Ak., U.S.	F7	140
Falset, Spain	C11	20
Falso, Cabo, c., Dom. Rep.	D12	102
Fălticeni, Rom.	B13	26
Falun, Swe.	F6	8
Famagusta see Gazimağusa, N. Cyp.	C4	58
Famaillá, Arg.	C5	92
Famatina, Sierra de, mts., Arg.	D4	92
Famenne, reg., Bel.	D14	14
Family Lake, l., Mb., Can.	B18	124
Fanchang, China	F8	42
Fanch'eng see Xiangfan, China	F4	42
Fanchon, Pointe, c., Haiti	C10	102
Fancy, St. Vin.	o11	105e
Fang, Thai.	C4	48
Fangak, Sudan	F6	62
Fangcheng, China	D6	38
Fangcheng, China	E5	42
Fangxian, China	E4	42
Fangshan, China	B10	36
Fangshan, Tai.	B34	81
Fangzheng, China	A6	48
Fan Si Pan, mtn., Viet.	A6	48
Fanjiatun, China	C6	38
Fanny Bay, B.C., Can.	G6	138
Fano, Italy	G10	22
Fanø, i., Den.	I2	8
Faradje, D.R.C.	D5	66
Farafangana, Madag.	E8	68
Farāh, Afg.	C9	56
Faranah, Gui.	G2	64
Farasān, Jazā'ir, is., Sau. Ar.	F5	56
Fareham, Eng., U.K.	K11	12
Farewell, Ak., U.S.	D9	140
Farewell, Cape, c., N.Z.	E5	80
Fargo, N.D., U.S.	G5	118
Faribault, Mn., U.S.	G5	118
Faribault, Lac, l., Qc., Can.	D16	106
Farīdābād, India	D6	54
Farīdkot, India	C5	54
Farīdpur, India	D7	54
Farilhões, is., Port.	E1	20
Farīm, Gui.-B.	G1	64
Farit, Amba, mtn., Eth.	E7	62
Farley, Ia., U.S.	B7	120
Farmer City, Il., U.S.	D9	120
Farmersville, Tx., U.S.	E2	122
Farmington, Il., U.S.	D7	120
Farmington, Me., U.S.	F6	110
Farmington, Mn., U.S.	G5	118
Farmington, Mo., U.S.	G7	120
Farmington, N.H., U.S.	G5	110
Farmington, N.M., U.S.	G8	132
Farmington, Ut., U.S.	C5	132
Far Mountain, mtn., B.C., Can.	D5	138
Farmville, N.C., U.S.	A8	116
Farmville, Va., U.S.	G7	114
Farne Islands, is., Eng., U.K.	F11	12
Farnham, Qc., Can.	E3	110
Faro, Braz.	D6	84
Faro, Yk., Can.	C4	106
Faro, Port.	H3	20
Faro, state, Port.	G3	20
Faroe Islands, dep., Eur.	n34	8b
Fårön, i., Swe.	H8	8
Farquhar, Atoll de, i., Sey.	l12	69b
Farquhar, Cape, c., Austl.	D2	74
Farragut, Ia., U.S.	D2	120
Farrars Creek, stm., Austl.	E3	76
Farrell, Pa., U.S.	C5	114
Farrukhābād, India	E7	54
Fársala, Grc.	D5	28
Fartak, Ra's, c., Yemen	F7	56
Farvel, Kap, c., Grnld.	F17	141
Farwell, Mi., U.S.	E5	112
Fern Park, Fl., U.S.	H4	116
Fasā, Iran	D7	56
Fasano, Italy	D11	24
Fastnet Rock, r., Ire.	J3	12
Fatehābād, India	D5	54
Fatehjang, Pak.	B3	54
Fatehpur, India	F8	54
Fatehpur, India	E5	54
Fatehpur Sīkri, India	E6	54
Fathom Five National Marine Park, p.o.i., On., Can.	C8	112
Fatick, Sen.	G1	64
Fátima, Port.	E2	20
Fatu Hiva, i., Fr. Poly.	E13	72
Fatumu, Tonga	n14	78e
Fatwā, India	F10	54
Fauabu, Sol. Is.	e9	79b
Faucilles, Monts, mts., Fr.	F15	14
Faulkton, S.D., U.S.	B13	126
Fauquier, B.C., Can.	G12	138
Fáurei, Rom.	D14	26
Fauresmith, S. Afr.	F7	70
Fauske, Nor.	C6	8
Faust, Ab., Can.	A15	138
Favara, Italy	G7	24
Fawcett Lake, l., Ab., Can.	A17	138
Fawnie Nose, mtn., B.C., Can.	C5	138
Faxaflói, b., Ice.	k28	8a
Faxinal do Soturno, Braz.	D11	92
Faya-Largeau, Chad	D3	62
Fayette, Al., U.S.	D11	122
Fayette, Ia., U.S.	B6	120
Fayette, Ms., U.S.	F7	122
Fayette, Mo., U.S.	E5	120
Fayette, Lake, res., Tx., U.S.	E2	122
Fayetteville, Ar., U.S.	H3	120
Fayetteville, Ga., U.S.	D14	122
Fayetteville, N.C., U.S.	A7	116
Fayetteville, Tn., U.S.	B12	122
Fayetteville, W.V., U.S.	F4	114
Fāyid, Egypt	H3	58
Fāzilka, India	C5	54
Fāzilpur, Pak.	D3	54
Fazzān, hist. reg., Libya	B2	62
Fdérik, Maur.	E2	64
Fear, Cape, c., N.C., U.S.	C8	116
Feather, Middle Fork, stm., Ca., U.S.	D5	134
Feather, North Fork, East Branch, stm., Ca., U.S.	C5	134
Fécamp, Fr.	E9	14
Federación, Arg.	E8	92
Federal, Arg.	E8	92
Federally Administered Tribal Areas, state, Pak.	B2	54
Federal Republic of Germany see Germany, ctry., Eur.	E6	16
Federalsburg, Md., U.S.	F10	114
Federated States of Micronesia see Micronesia, Federated States of, ctry., Oc.	C6	72
Fehérgyarmat, Hung.	A9	26
Fehmarn, i., Ger.	B7	16
Feia, Lagoa, b., Braz.	L5	88
Fei Huang, stm., China	D8	42
Feijó, Braz.	E3	84
Feira de Santana, Braz.	G6	88
Feixi, China	F7	42
Feixian, China	D7	42
Fejér, state, Hung.	B5	26
Felanitx, Spain	E14	20
Felda, Fl., U.S.	J4	116
Feldbach, Aus.	D12	22
Feldberg, mtn., Ger.	I4	16
Feldkirch, Aus.	C6	22
Feliciano, P.R.	B1	104a
Feliciano, Arroyo, stm., Arg.	E8	92
Felipe Carrillo Puerto, Mex.	C4	102
Félix, Cape, c., Nu., Can.	B11	106
Felixlândia, Braz.	J3	88
Felixstowe, Eng., U.K.	I14	12
Felletin, Fr.	D8	18
Fellsmere, Fl., U.S.	I5	116
Feltre, Italy	E8	22
Femund, l., Nor.	E4	8
Femundsmarka Nasjonalpark, p.o.i., Nor.	E4	8
Fen, stm., China	D4	42
Fenelon Falls, On., Can.	D11	112
Fengcheng, China	D6	38
Fengcheng, China	G6	42
Fengqing, China	G4	36
Fengdu, China	G2	42
Fengfeng, China	C6	42
Fenggang, China	H2	42
Fenghuang, China	H3	42
Fengjiabao, China	C1	42
Fengjie, China	F3	42
Fengning, China	A7	42
Fengqing, China	G4	36
Fengqiu, China	D6	42
Fengtai, China	e9	42
Fengtai, China	E7	42
Fengtien see Shenyang, China	D5	38
Fengxi, China	J7	42
Fengxian, China	D7	42
Fengxiang, China	D2	42
Fengyang, China	E7	42
Fengzhen, China	A5	42
Feni, Bngl.	G13	54
Fennimore, Wi., U.S.	B7	120
Fenoarivo Atsinanana, Madag.	D8	68
Fenton, Mi., U.S.	B2	114
Fentress, Tx., U.S.	E10	130
Fenwick, W.V., U.S.	F5	114
Fenyang, China	C4	42
Fenyi, China	H6	42
Feodosija, Ukr.	F14	6
Fer, Cap de, c., Alg.	B6	64
Ferdinand, In., U.S.	F10	120
Ferdows, Iran	C8	56
Ferentino, Italy	I10	22
Fergana Mountains see Ferganskij hrebet, mts., Kyrg.	F12	32
Ferganskij hrebet, mts., Kyrg.	F12	32
Fergus, On., Can.	E9	112
Fergus Falls, Mn., U.S.	E2	118
Ferguson, B.C., Can.	F13	138
Ferguson, Ky., U.S.	G13	120
Fergusson Island, i., Pap. N. Gui.	b5	79a
Ferkéssédougou, C. Iv.	H4	64
Ferland, Qc., Can.		
Ferlo, reg., Sen.	F2	64
Ferme-Neuve, Qc., Can.	B14	112
Fermo, Italy	G10	22
Fermont, Qc., Can.	E17	106
Fermoselle, Spain	C4	20
Fermoy, Ire.	I4	12
Fernández, Arg.	C6	92
Fernandina, isla, i., Ec.	i11	84a
Fernandina Beach, Fl., U.S.	F4	116
Fernando de la Mora, Para.	B9	92
Fernando de Noronha, ilha, i., Braz.	F11	82
Fernandópolis, Braz.	D6	90
Fernando Póo see Bioko, i., Eq. Gui.	I6	64
Fernán-Núñez, Spain	G6	20
Ferndale, Ca., U.S.	C1	134
Ferndale, Wa., U.S.	B4	136
Fernie, B.C., Can.	G15	138
Ferney, Nv., U.S.	D6	134
Fern Park, Fl., U.S.	H4	116
Fern Ridge Lake, res., Or., U.S.	F3	136
Fernwood, Id., U.S.	C10	136
Fernwood, Ms., U.S.	F8	118
Ferrandina, Italy	D10	24
Ferrara, Italy	F8	22
Ferrato, Capo, c., Italy	E3	24
Ferreira Gomes, Braz.	C7	84
Ferreñafe, Peru	E2	84
Ferret, Cap, c., Fr.	E4	18
Ferrières, Fr.	F11	14
Ferris, Tx., U.S.	E2	122
Ferrol, Spain	A2	20
Ferron, Ut., U.S.	D5	132
Ferrysburg, Mi., U.S.	E3	112
Fès (Fez), Mor.	C3	64
Feshi, D.R.C.	F3	66
Fessenden, N.D., U.S.	G14	124
Festus, Mo., U.S.	F7	120
Fetești, Rom.	E14	26
Fethiye, Tur.	G12	28
Fetisovo, Kaz.	F8	32
Fetlar, i., Scot., U.K.	n19	12a
Feucht, Ger.	G7	16
Feuchtwangen, Ger.	G6	16
Feuilles, stm., Qc., Can.	D16	106
Feuilles, Baie aux, b., Qc., Can.	D16	106
Fevzıabad, Afg.	B11	56
Fez see Fès, Mor.	C3	64
Fezzan see Fazzān, hist. reg., Libya	B2	62
Ffestiniog, Wales, U.K.	I9	12
Fianarantsoa, Madag.	E8	68
Fianga, Chad	F3	62
Fiche, Eth.	F7	62
Fichtelgebirge, mts., Eur.	F7	16
Ficksburg, S. Afr.	F8	70
Fidalgo, stm., Braz.	E5	88
Fidenza, Italy	F7	22
Fier, Alb.	D13	24
Fier, stm., Fr.	D11	18
Fiery Creek, stm., Austl.	B2	76
Fierzës, Liqeni i, res., Alb.	B14	24
Fife Lake, Mi., U.S.	D4	112
Fife Lake, Sk., Can.	E8	124
Fife Ness, c., Scot., U.K.	E10	12
Fifield, Wi., U.S.	F8	118
Fifth Cataract see Khamis, Ash-Shallāl al-, wtfl, Sudan	D6	62
Figeac, Fr.	E7	18
Figtree, Zimb.	B9	70
Figueira da Foz, Port.	D1	20
Figueiras see Figueres, Spain	B13	20
Figueres, Spain	B13	20
Figuig, Mor.	C4	64
Fiji, i., Kir.	E11	72
Filabusi, Zimb.	B9	70
Filadelfia, Italy	F10	24
Filchner Ice Shelf, ice, Ant.	C1	81
Filey, Eng., U.K.	G12	12
Filiaşi, Rom.	E10	26
Filiatrá, Grc.	F4	28
Filingué, Niger	G5	64
Filippi, hist., Grc.	B7	28
Filipstad, Swe.	G6	8
Fillmore, Sk., Can.	E10	124
Fillmore, Ca., U.S.	I7	134
Fillmore, Ut., U.S.	E4	132
Filtu, Eth.	F8	62
Fimi, stm., D.R.C.	E3	66
Finale Emilia, Italy	F8	22
Finale Ligure, Italy	F5	22
Finca El Rey, Parque Nacional, p.o.i., Arg.	B5	92
Findlay, Oh., U.S.	E2	114
Findlay, Mount, mtn., B.C., Can.	F14	138
Fingal, N.D., U.S.	H16	124
Fingoè, Moz.	D5	68
Finisterre, state, Fr.	F5	14
Finisterre, Cabo de, c., Spain	B1	20
Finke, Austl.	E6	74
Finland, ctry., Eur.	C12	8
Finland, Gulf of, b., Eur.	G11	8
Finlay, stm., B.C., Can.	D5	106
Finley, Austl.	J5	76
Finley, N.D., U.S.	G16	124
Finnegan, Ab., Can.	E18	138
Finnis, stm., Austl.	B6	74
Finnmark, state, Nor.	B11	8
Finnsnes, Nor.	B8	8
Finschhafen, Pap. N. Gui.	b4	79a
Finse, Nor.	F2	8
Finspång, Swe.	G6	8
Finsterwalde, Ger.	E9	16
Fiordland National Park, p.o.i., N.Z.	G2	80
Fiorenzuola d'Arda, Italy	F6	22
Fire Island National Seashore, p.c.i., N.Y., U.S.	D12	114
Firenze (Florence), Italy	G8	22
Firmat, Arg.	F7	92
Firminy, Fr.	D10	18
Firovo, Russia	C16	10
Fīrozābād, India	E7	54
Fīrozpur, India	C5	54
Fīrozpur Jhirka, India	E6	54
First Cataract, wtfl, Egypt	C6	62
Firth, stm., N.A.	C11	140
Firth, N.Z.		
Fīrūzābād, Iran	D7	56
Fisher, Il., U.S.	D9	120
Fisher Branch, Mb., U.S.	C16	124
Fisher Peak, mtn., U.S.	H5	114
Fisher Strait, strt., Nu., Can.	C14	106
Fishing Creek, Md., U.S.	F9	114
Fishing Creek, stm., N.C., U.S.	H8	114
Fishing Lake, l., Mb., Can.	B18	124
Fisk, Mo., U.S.	H7	120
Fiskárdo, Grc.	E3	28
Fismes, Fr.	E12	14
Fitchburg, Ma., U.S.	B13	114
Fito, Mount, vol., Samoa	g12	79c
Fitri, Lac, l., Chad	E3	62
Fitz Roy, Arg.	I3	90
Fitzroy, stm., Austl.	C4	74
Fitzroy, stm., Austl.	D8	76
Fitz Roy, Monte (Chaltel Cerro), mtn., S.A.	I2	90
Fitzroy Crossing, Austl.	C5	74
Fitzwilliam Island, i., On., Can.	C8	112
Fiuggi, Italy	I10	22
Fiume see Rijeka, Cro.	E11	22
Fiumicino, Italy	I9	22
Five Islands, N.S., Can.	E12	110
Five Islands Harbour, b., Antig.	f4	105b
Five Points, N.M., U.S.	H10	132
Fivemile Creek, stm., Wy., U.S.	D4	126
Fizi, D.R.C.	E5	66
Fivizzano, Italy	F7	22
Fjällbacka, Swe.	C8	8
Flagler, Co., U.S.	B5	128
Flagstaff, Az., U.S.	H5	132
Flagstaff Lake, res., Me., U.S.	E6	110
Flamands, Anse des, Guad.	B2	105a
Flambeau, stm., Wi., U.S.	F8	118
Flamborough, On., Can.	E9	112
Flamborough Head, c., Eng., U.K.	G12	12
Fläming, reg., Ger.	E8	16
Flaming Gorge National Recreation Area, p.o.i., U.S.	B7	132
Flaming Gorge Reservoir, res., U.S.	B7	132
Flanagan, Il., U.S.	D9	120
Flanders, On., Can.	C6	118
Flasher, N.D., U.S.	A11	126
Flåsjön, l., Swe.	D6	8
Flat, Ak., U.S.	D8	140
Flat, Tx., U.S.	C10	130
Flat, stm., Mi., U.S.	E4	112
Flatey, Ice.	k28	8a
Flathead (Flathead, North Fork), stm., N.A.	B16	138
Flathead, stm., Mt., U.S.	C12	136
Flathead, Middle Fork, stm., Mt., U.S.	B13	136
Flathead, North Fork (Flathead), stm., N.A.	B16	138
Flathead, South Fork, stm., Mt., U.S.	B13	136
Flathead Lake, l., Mt., U.S.	C12	136
Flat Lake, l., Ab., Can.	B17	138
Flatonia, Tx., U.S.	E10	130
Flat River, P.E., Can.	D13	110
Flat Rock, Al., U.S.	C13	122
Flattery, Cape, c., Wa., U.S.	B2	136
Flatts, Ber.	k15	104e
Flatwillow Creek, stm., Mt., U.S.	H5	124
Flatwood, Al., U.S.	E11	122
Flatwoods, Ky., U.S.	F3	114
Flaxton, N.D., U.S.	F11	124
Flaxville, Mt., U.S.	F8	124
Fleetwood, Eng., U.K.	H10	12
Fleetwood, Pa., U.S.	D10	114
Flekkefjord, Nor.	G2	8
Fleming-Neon, Ky., U.S.	G3	114
Flemingsburg, Ky., U.S.	F2	114
Flen, Swe.	G7	8
Flensburg, Ger.	B5	16
Fletcher, N.C., U.S.	A3	116
Fletcher Pond, l., Mi., U.S.	D5	112
Fleurance, Fr.	F6	18
Flinders, stm., Austl.	A3	76
Flinders Island, i., Austl.	m14	77a
Flinders Ranges National Park, p.o.i., Austl.	H2	76
Flinders Reefs, rf., Austl.	A7	76
Flin Flon, Mb., Can.	E10	106
Flint, Wales, U.K.	H9	12
Flint, i., Kir.	E11	72
Flint, Mi., U.S.	E6	112
Flint, stm., Ga., U.S.	G14	122
Flint, stm., Mi., U.S.	C12	122
Flint Hills, Ks., U.S.	B16	136
Flint Lake, l., Nu., Can.	B16	106
Flinton, Austl.	F7	76
Flintville, Tn., U.S.	B12	122
Flippin, Ar., U.S.	H5	120
Flirey, Pantá de, res., Spain	C11	20
Flomaton, Al., U.S.	G11	122
Floodwood, Mn., U.S.	E6	118
Flora, Il., U.S.	F9	120
Flora, In., U.S.	H3	112
Florac, Fr.	E9	18
Floral City, Fl., U.S.	H3	116
Floral Park, Ms., U.S.	E14	136
Flora Vista, N.M., U.S.	G8	132
Florence, Piton, mtn., St. Luc.	m7	105c
Florence, Al., U.S.	C11	122
Florence, Az., U.S.	J5	132
Florence, Co., U.S.	C3	128
Florence, Ks., U.S.	C12	128
Florence, S.C., U.S.	B6	116
Florence, Tx., U.S.	C10	130
Florence, Wi., U.S.	C1	112
Florencia, Col.	G4	86
Florentino Ameghino, Embalse, res., Arg.	H3	90
Flores, Braz.	D7	88
Flores, i., Indon.	G7	44
Flores, Laut (Flores Sea), Indon.	G11	50
Flores, Selat, strt., Indon.	G7	44
Flores de Goiás, Braz.	H2	88
Flores Sea see Flores, Laut, Indon.	G11	50
Floresta, Braz.	E6	88
Floresville, Tx., U.S.	E9	130
Floriano, Braz.	D4	88
Floriano Peixoto, Braz.	E4	84
Florianópolis, Braz.	C13	92
Florida, Col.	B8	102
Florida, Cuba		
Florida, P.R.		
Florida, state, U.S.	G3	116
Florida, Straits of, strt., N.A.	G11	108
Florida Bay, b., Fl., U.S.	L4	116
Floridablanca, Col.	D5	86
Florida City, Fl., U.S.	K5	116
Florida Islands, is., Sol. Is.	e9	79b
Florida Keys, is., Fl., U.S.	L4	116
Floridia, Italy	G9	24
Florido, stm., Mex.	B6	100
Florien, La., U.S.	F5	122
Flórina, Grc.	C4	28
Florissant Fossil Beds National Monument, p.o.i., Co., U.S.	B3	128
Florø, Nor.	F1	8
Flotte, Cap de, c., N. Cal.	m16	79d
Floyd, N.M., U.S.	G5	128
Floyd, Va., U.S.	H5	114
Floyd, stm., Ia., U.S.	B2	120
Floydada, Tx., U.S.	G7	128
Flumendosa, stm., Italy	E3	24
Fluminimaggiore, Italy	E2	24
Flushing see Vlissingen, Neth.	C12	14
Fluvanna, Tx., U.S.	B6	130
Foam Lake, Sk., Can.	C10	124
Foça, Tur.	E9	28
Focşani, Rom.	D14	26
Fogang, China	J5	42
Foggaret ez Zoua, Alg.	D5	64
Foggia, Italy	C9	24
Fogo, i., C.V.	k10	65a
Fogo Island, i., Nf., Can.	j23	107a
Foguista J. F. Juárez see El Galpón, Arg.	B5	92
Föhr, i., Ger.	B4	16
Fóia, mtn., Port.	G2	20
Foix, Fr.	G7	18
Foix, hist. reg., Fr.	F7	18
Fokina, Bos.	F4	26
Fokino, Russia	G17	10
Folda, b., Nor.	C6	8
Foley, Al., U.S.	G11	122
Foleyet, On., Can.	F14	106
Foley Island, i., Nu., Can.	B15	106
Folgefonni, ice, Nor.	G2	8
Foligno, Italy	H9	22
Folkestone, Eng., U.K.	J14	12
Folkston, Ga., U.S.	F3	116
Follett, Tx., U.S.	E8	128
Föllinge, Swe.	E6	8
Follonica, Italy	H7	22
Follonica, Golfo di, b., Italy	H7	22
Folsom, Ca., U.S.	E4	134
Folsom Lake, res., Ca., U.S.	E4	134
Fomboni, Com.	C7	68
Fominiči, Russia	F17	10
Fominskoe, Russia	A22	10
Fonda, N.Y., U.S.	B11	114
Fond du Lac, Wi., U.S.	H10	118
Fond du Lac, stm., Sk., Can.	D9	106
Fondi, Italy	C7	24
Fonni, Italy	D3	24
Fonseca, Col.	B5	86
Fonseca, Golfo de b., N.A.	F11	14
Fontainebleau, Fr.	F11	14
Fontana, Arg.	C8	92
Fontana, Ca., U.S.	I8	134
Fontana Lake, res., N.C., U.S.	A2	116
Fontanelle, Ia., U.S.	A2	116
Fontas, stm., Can.	D6	106
Fonte Boa, Braz.	I8	86
Fontenay-le-Comte, Fr.	C5	18
Fontenelle, Qc., Can.	B12	110
Fontenelle Reservoir, res., Wy., U.S.	A6	132
Fontur, c., Ice.	j32	8a
Fonyód, Hung.	C4	26
Foochow see Fuzhou, China	I8	42
Foothills, Ab., Can.	C14	138
Forari, Vanuatu	k17	79d
Forbach, Fr.	E15	14
Forbach, Ger.	H4	16
Forbes, Austl.	I7	76
Forbes, Mount, mtn., Ab., Can.	E14	138
Forbesganj, India	E11	54
Forchheim, Ger.	G7	16
Ford, Ks., U.S.	D9	128
Ford, stm., Mi., U.S.	B2	112
Ford City, Ca., U.S.	H6	134
Ford City, Pa., U.S.	D6	114
Førde, Nor.	F1	8
Ford Ranges, mts., Ant.	C26	81
Fords Bridge, Austl.	G5	76
Fordville, N.D., U.S.	F16	124
Fordyce, Ar., U.S.	D6	122
Forecariah, Gui.	H2	64
Forel, Mont, mtn., Grnld.	D18	141
Foreman, Ar., U.S.	D4	122
Forest, On., Can.	E8	112
Forest, Ms., U.S.	E9	122
Forest Acres, S.C., U.S.	B4	116
Forestburg, Ab., Can.	D18	138
Forest City, N.C., U.S.	A4	116
Forest City, Pa., U.S.	C10	114
Forest Grove, B.C., Can.	E9	138
Foresthill, Ca., U.S.	D5	134
Forestier Peninsula, pen., Austl.	o14	77a
Forest Lake, Mn., U.S.	F5	118
Forest Park, Ga., U.S.	D14	122
Forestville, Qc., Can.	B7	110
Forgan, Ok., U.S.	E8	128
Forges-les-Eaux, Fr.	E10	14
Forillon, Parc national de, p.o.i., Qc., Can.	B12	110
Forked Deer, stm., Tn., U.S.	C8	120
Forks, Wa., U.S.	C2	136
Forlì, Italy	F9	22
Formby Point, c., Eng., U.K.	H9	12
Formentera, i., Spain	F12	20
Formentor, Cap de, c., Spain	E14	20
Formia, Italy	C7	24
Formiga, Braz.	K3	88
Formosa, Arg.	C8	92
Formosa, Braz.	H2	88
Formosa, state, Arg.	B8	92
Formosa see Taiwan, ctry., Asia	J9	42
Formosa, stm., Braz.	G3	88
Formosa Strait see Taiwan Strait, strt., Asia	I8	42
Formoso, stm., Braz.	G3	88
Forney, Tx., U.S.	E2	122
Fornosovo, Russia	A13	10
Forres, Scot., U.K.	D9	12
Forrest, Austl.		
Forrest, Il., U.S.	D9	120
Forrest City, Ar., U.S.	B8	122
Forreston, Il., U.S.	B8	120
Forsayth, Austl.	B4	76
Forst, Ger.	E10	16
Forster, Austl.	I9	76
Forsyth, Ga., U.S.	C2	116
Forsyth, Mo., U.S.	H4	120
Forsyth, Mt., U.S.	A5	126
Fort Abbās, Pak.	D4	54
Fort Albany, On., Can.	E14	106
Fortaleza, Bol.	B3	90
Fortaleza, Braz.	C7	88
Fortaleza de Ituxi, Braz.	E4	84
Fort Assiniboine, Ab., Can.	B15	138
Fort Atkinson, Wi., U.S.	B9	120
Fort Bayard see Zhanjiang, China	K4	42
Fort Beaufort, S. Afr.	H8	70
Fort Benton, Mt., U.S.	C16	136
Fort Bragg, Ca., U.S.	D2	134
Fort Bragg, La., U.S.		
Fort Branch, In., U.S.	F10	120
Fort Bridger, Wy., U.S.	B7	132
Fort Calhoun, Ne., U.S.	C1	120
Fort Chipewyan, Ab., Can.	D8	106
Fort Collins, Co., U.S.	G7	126
Fort-Coulonge, Qc., Can.	C13	112
Fort Covington, N.Y., U.S.	E15	112
Fort Davis, Al., U.S.	E13	122
Fort-de-France, Mart.	k6	105c
Fort-de-France, Baie de, b., Mart.	k6	105c
Fort Deposit, Al., U.S.	F12	122
Fort Dodge, Ia., U.S.	B3	120
Fort Duchesne, Ut., U.S.	C7	132
Forte dei Marmi, Italy	G7	22
Fort Edward, N.Y., U.S.	G3	110
Fort Erie, On., Can.	F10	112
Fortescue, stm., Austl.	D3	74
Fortezza, Italy	D8	22
Fort Frances, On., Can.	C5	118
Fort Franklin see Déline, N.T., Can.	B6	106
Fort Frederica National Monument, p.o.i., Ga., U.S.	E4	116
Fort Gaines, Ga., U.S.	F13	122
Fort Garland, Co., U.S.	D3	128
Fort Gibson, Ok., U.S.	I2	120
Fort Good Hope, N.T., Can.	B5	106
Forth, Firth of, b., Scot., U.K.	E10	12

Name	Map Ref.	Page
Fort Hall, Id., U.S.	G14	136
Fortine, Mt., U.S.	B12	136
Fortín Uno, Arg.	I5	92
Fort Jones, Ca., U.S.	B3	134
Fort Klamath, Or., U.S.	H4	136
Fort Knox, Ky., U.S.	G12	120
Fort-Lamy see N'Djamena, Chad	E3	62
Fort Laramie, Wy., U.S.	E8	126
Fort Lauderdale, Fl., U.S.	J5	116
Fort Liard, N.T., Can.	C6	106
Fort Loramie, Oh., U.S.	D1	114
Fort Loudoun Lake, res., Tn., U.S.	B15	122
Fort Lyon Canal, can., Co., U.S.	C5	128
Fort MacKay, Ab., Can.	D8	106
Fort Macleod, Ab., Can.	G17	138
Fort Madison, Ia., U.S.	D6	120
Fort Matanzas National Monument, p.o.i., Fl., U.S.	G4	116
Fort McMurray, Ab., Can.	D8	106
Fort McPherson, N.T., Can.	B4	106
Fort Meade, Fl., U.S.	I4	116
Fort Mill, S.C., U.S.	A5	116
Fort Morgan, Co., U.S.	A5	128
Fort Myers, Fl., U.S.	J3	116
Fort Myers Beach, Fl., U.S.	J3	116
Fort Nelson, B.C., U.S.	D6	106
Fort Nelson, stm., B.C., Can.	D6	106
Fort Ogden, Fl., U.S.	I4	116
Fort Payne, Al., U.S.	C13	122
Fort Peck, Mt., U.S.	F7	124
Fort Peck Dam, dam, Mt., U.S.	G7	124
Fort Peck Lake, res., Mt., U.S.	G7	124
Fort Pierce, Fl., U.S.	I5	116
Fort Plain, N.Y., U.S.	B11	114
Fort Portal, Ug.	D6	66
Fort Providence, N.T., Can.	C7	106
Fort Pulaski National Monument, p.o.i., Ga., U.S.	E5	116
Fort Qu'Appelle, Sk., Can.	D10	124
Fort Randall Dam, dam, S.D., U.S.	D14	126
Fort Recovery, Oh., U.S.	D1	114
Fort Resolution, N.T., Can.	C8	106
Fort Rixon, Zimb.	B9	70
Fort Saint James, B.C., Can.	B6	138
Fort Saint John, B.C., Can.	D6	106
Fort Saskatchewan, Ab., Can.	C17	138
Fort Scott, Ks., U.S.	G3	120
Fort-Ševčenko, Kaz.	F7	32
Fort Severn, On., Can.	D13	106
Fort Simpson, N.T., Can.	C6	106
Fort Smith, N.T., Can.	C8	106
Fort Smith, Ar., U.S.	B4	122
Fort Stockton, Tx., U.S.	D4	130
Fort Sumner, N.M., U.S.	G4	128
Fort Sumter National Monument, p.o.i., S.C., U.S.	D6	116
Fort Supply, Ok., U.S.	E9	128
Fort Thomas, Az., U.S.	J7	132
Fort Totten, N.D., U.S.	G14	124
Fort Towson, Ok., U.S.	D3	122
Fortuna, Arg.	G5	92
Fortuna, C.R.	G5	102
Fortuna, Ca., U.S.	C1	134
Fortuna, V.I.U.S.	e6	104b
Fortune Bay, b., Nf., Can.	j22	107a
Fortuneswell, Eng., U.K.	K10	12
Fort Union National Monument, p.o.i., N.M., U.S.	F3	128
Fort Valley, Ga., U.S.	D2	116
Fort Vermilion, Ab., Can.	D7	106
Fort Victoria, hist., Ber.	k16	104e
Fort Walton Beach, Fl., U.S.	G12	122
Fort Wayne, In., U.S.	G4	112
Fort White, Fl., U.S.	G3	116
Fort William, Scot., U.K.	E7	12
Fort Worth, Tx., U.S.	B10	130
Fort Yates, N.D., U.S.	A12	126
Fort Yukon, Ak., U.S.	C10	140
Fosheim Peninsula, pen., Nu., Can.	B9	141
Foso, Ghana	H4	64
Fossano, Italy	F4	22
Fossil, Or., U.S.	F6	136
Fossil Butte National Monument, p.o.i., Wy., U.S.	B6	126
Fossil Lake, l., Or., U.S.	G6	136
Fossombrone, Italy	G9	22
Fosston, Mn., U.S.	D3	118
Foster, Austl.	L6	76
Foster Bugt, strt., Grnld.	C21	141
Fosters, Al., U.S.	D11	122
Fostoria, Oh., U.S.	C2	114
Fougamou, Gabon	E2	66
Fougères, Fr.	F7	14
Fouhsin see Fuxin, China	C4	38
Fou-kien see Fujian, state, China	I7	42
Foula, i., Scot., U.K.	n17	12a
Fouling see Fuling, China	G2	42
Foulwind, Cape, c., N.Z.	E4	80
Foumban, Cam.	C2	66
Foum-el-Hassan, Mor.	D3	64
Foum-Zguid, Mor.	C3	64
Foundiougne, Sen.	G1	64
Fountain, Co., U.S.	C3	128
Fountain, Fl., U.S.	G13	122
Fountain City, Wi., U.S.	G7	118
Fountain Green, Ut., U.S.	D5	132
Fountain Peak, mtn., Ca., U.S.	I1	132
Fountain Place, La., U.S.	G7	122
Fourche LaFave, stm., Ar., U.S.	C6	122
Fourchu, N.S., Can.	E16	110
Four Corners, Or., U.S.	F4	136
Fourmies, Fr.	D13	14
Four Mountains, Islands of, is., Ak., U.S.	g24	140a
Four Oaks, N.C., U.S.	A7	116
Fourth Cataract see Rābi', Ash-Shallāl ar-, wtfl, Sudan	D6	62
Fous, Pointe des, c., Dom.	j6	105c
Fouta Djalon, reg., Gui.	G2	64
Foux, Cap à, c., Haiti	C11	102
Fouyang see Fuyang, China	E6	42
Foveaux Strait, strt., N.Z.	H3	80
Fowler, Co., U.S.	C4	128
Fowler, In., U.S.	H2	112
Fowler, Mi., U.S.	E5	112
Fowlers Bay, Austl.	F6	74
Fowlerville, Mi., U.S.	B1	114
Fox, stm., U.S.	C9	120
Fox, stm., U.S.	D5	120
Fox, stm., Wi., U.S.	H10	118
Fox Creek, Ab., Can.	B14	138
Foxe Basin, b., Nu., Can.	B15	106
Foxe Channel, strt., Nu., Can.	C15	106
Foxe Peninsula, pen., Nu., Can.	C15	106
Foxford, Ire.	H3	12
Fox Islands, is., Ak., U.S.	g25	140a
Fox Lake, Il., U.S.	B9	120
Foxpark, Wy., U.S.	B10	132
Fox Valley, Sk., Can.	D4	124
Foxworth, Ms., U.S.	F9	122
Foyle, Lough, b., Eur.	F5	12
Foz do Areia, Represa de, res., Braz.	B12	92
Foz do Cunene, Ang.	D1	68
Foz do Iguaçu, Braz.	B10	92
Foz do Jordão, Braz.	E3	84
Foz Giraldo, Port.	E3	20
Fraga, Spain	C11	20
Fraile Muerto, Ur.	F10	92
Framingham, Ma., U.S.	B14	114
França, Braz.	F5	88
Franca, Braz.	K2	88
Franca-Iosifa, Zemlja, is., Russia	B9	30
Francavilla al Mare, Italy	H11	22
Francavilla Fontana, Italy	D11	24
France, ctry., Eur.	C8	18
Frances, stm., Yk., Can.	C5	106
Frances Lake, l., Yk., Can.	C4	106
Francés Viejo, Cabo, c., Dom. Rep.	C13	102
Franceville, Gabon	E2	66
Franche-Comté, hist. reg., Fr.	B12	18
Francis, Sk., Can.	D10	124
Francis Case, Lake, res., S.D., U.S.	D13	126
Francisco Beltrão, Braz.	B11	92
Francisco I. Madero, Mex.	C6	100
Francisco I. Madero, Mex.	I4	130
Francisco Murguía, Mex.	C7	100
Francisco Sá, Braz.	I4	88
Francistown, Bots.	B8	70
Francofonte, Italy	G8	24
François Lake, B.C., Can.	B5	138
François Lake, l., B.C., Can.	C5	138
Francs Peak, mtn., Wy., U.S.	C3	126
Frankel City, Tx., U.S.	B5	130
Franken, hist. reg., Ger.	G6	16
Frankenberg, Ger.	F9	16
Frankenberg, Ger.	E4	16
Frankenmuth, Mi., U.S.	E6	112
Frankford, On., Can.	D12	112
Frankfort, Mo., U.S.	E6	120
Frankfort, S. Afr.	E9	70
Frankfort, In., U.S.	H3	112
Frankfort, Ks., U.S.	B12	128
Frankfort, Ky., U.S.	F13	120
Frankfort, N.Y., U.S.	A10	114
Frankfort, Oh., U.S.	E2	114
Frankfort, S.D., U.S.	C14	126
Frankfurt, Ger.	D10	16
Frankfurt am Main, Ger.	F4	16
Franklin, Ga., U.S.	D13	122
Franklin, Ga., U.S.	D13	122
Franklin, Id., U.S.	A5	132
Franklin, Il., U.S.	E7	120
Franklin, In., U.S.	E11	120
Franklin, Ma., U.S.	B14	114
Franklin, Ne., U.S.	A9	128
Franklin, N.H., U.S.	G5	110
Franklin, N.J., U.S.	C11	114
Franklin, N.C., U.S.	A2	116
Franklin, Oh., U.S.	E1	114
Franklin, Pa., U.S.	C6	114
Franklin, Tn., U.S.	I11	120
Franklin, Tx., U.S.	F2	122
Franklin, Va., U.S.	H9	114
Franklin, Wi., U.S.	F1	112
Franklin Bay, b., N.T., Can.	B5	106
Franklin D. Roosevelt Lake, res., Wa., U.S.	B4	108
Franklin Gordon Wild Rivers National Park, p.o.i., Austl.	o12	77a
Franklin Grove, Il., U.S.	C8	120
Franklin Lake, l., Nu., Can.	B12	106
Franklin Mountains, mts., N.T., Can.	B5	106
Franklin Strait, strt., Nu., Can.	A11	106
Franklinton, La., U.S.	G8	122
Franklinville, N.Y., U.S.	B7	114
Frankston, Tx., U.S.	E3	122
Frankton, In., U.S.	H4	112
Fransfontein, Nmb.	B2	70
Franzensfeste see Fortezza, Italy	D8	22
Franz Josef Land see Franca-Iosifa, Zemlja, is., Russia	B9	30
Frascati, Italy	I9	22
Fraser, B.C., Can.	G13	138
Fraser, Co., U.S.	B3	128
Fruges, Fr.	D11	14
Fruita, Co., U.S.	D8	132
Fruitdale, Or., U.S.	H3	136
Fruithurst, Al., U.S.	D13	122
Fruitland, Id., U.S.	F10	136
Fruitport, Mi., U.S.	E3	112
Fruitvale, B.C., Can.	G13	138
Fruitvale, Wa., U.S.	D6	136
Frunzivka, Ukr.	B16	26
Frutal, Braz.	J1	88
Frutigen, Switz.	D4	22
Frýdek-Místek, Czech Rep.	G14	16
Fryeburg, Me., U.S.	G6	110
Fú, stm., China	G7	42
Fu, stm., China	F2	42
Fu, stm., China	G6	42
Fua'amotu International Airport, Tonga	n14	78e
Fu'an, China	H8	42
Fuchou see Fuzhou, China	H8	42
Fuchow see Fuzhou, China	G7	42
Fuchū, Japan	E6	40
Fuding, China	H9	42
Fuego, Volcán de, vol., Guat.	E2	102
Fuencaliente, Spain	F6	20
Fuengirola, Spain	H6	20
Fuensalida, Spain	D6	20
Fuente, Mex.	F7	130
Fuente de Cantos, Spain	F4	20
Fuente de Oro, Col.	F5	86
Fuentes de Ebro, Spain	C10	20
Fuerte, stm., Mex.	B4	100
Fuerte Olimpo, Para.	D5	90
Fuga, Ok., U.S.	A3	52
Fugou, China	D6	42
Fuhai, China	B1	42
Fuhsien see Wafangdian, China	B9	42
Fuji, Japan	D11	40
Fuji, Mount see Fuji-san, vol., Japan	D11	40
Fujian, state, China	I7	42
Fujin, China	B11	36
Fujinomiya, Japan	D11	40
Fuji-san (Fuji, Mount), vol., Japan	D11	40
Fujisawa, Japan	D12	40
Fujiyama see Fuji-san, vol., Japan	D11	40
Fuji-yoshida, Japan	D11	40
Fukagawa, Japan	C14	38
Fukang, China	C2	36
Fukave, i., Tonga	n14	78e
Fukaya, Japan	C12	40
Fukien see Fujian, state, China	I7	42
Fukuchiyama, Japan	D8	40
Fukue, Japan	G1	40
Fukue-jima, i., Japan	G1	40
Fukui, Japan	C9	40
Fukui, state, Japan	D9	40
Fukuoka, Japan	F3	40
Fukuoka, state, Japan	F3	40
Fukuroi, Japan	E10	40
Fukushima, Japan	B13	40
Fukushima, state, Japan	B13	40
Fukuyama, Japan	E6	40
Fūlādī, Kūh-e, mtn., Afg.	C10	56
Fulaga Passage, strt., Fiji	q20	79e
Fulda, Ger.	F5	16
Fulda, Mn., U.S.	H3	118
Fulda, stm., Ger.	E5	16
Fuling, China	G2	42
Fullarton, stm., Austl.	C3	76
Fullerton, Ca., U.S.	J8	134
Fullerton Point, c., Antig.	I4	105b
Fulong, China	J2	42
Fulton, Al., U.S.	F11	122
Fulton, Il., U.S.	D5	122
Fulton, Il., U.S.	C7	120
Fulton, Ks., U.S.	F3	120
Fulton, Ky., U.S.	H9	120
Fulton, Mo., U.S.	F5	120
Fulton, N.Y., U.S.	E13	112
Fulton, Tx., U.S.	F10	130
Funabashi, Japan	D12	40
Funafuti, i., Tuvalu	D8	72
Funan, China	E6	42
Funchal, Port.	C1	64
Fundación, Col.	B4	86
Fundão, Port.	D3	20
Fundy National Park, p.o.i., N.B., Can.	E11	110
Funhalouro, Moz.	C12	70
Funiu Shan, mts., China	E5	42
Funsi, Ghana	G4	64
Funtua, Nig.	G6	64
Fuping, China	D3	42
Fuqing, China	I8	42
Fuquay-Varina, N.C., U.S.	A7	116
Furancungo, Moz.	C5	68
Furāt, Nahr al- (Euphrates), stm., Asia	C5	56
Furmanov, Russia	H19	8
Furnas, Represa de, res., Braz.	K2	88
Furneaux Group, is., Austl.	m13	77a
Furnes see Veurne, Bel.	C11	14
Fürstenberg / Havel, Ger.	C9	16
Fürstenfeld, Aus.	C12	22
Fürstenfeldbruck, Ger.	H7	16
Fürstenwalde, Ger.	D9	16
Fürth, Ger.	G6	16
Fürth im Wald, Ger.	G8	16
Furukawa, Japan	C10	40
Furukawa, Japan	A13	40
Fury and Hecla Strait, strt., Nu., Can.	B14	106
Fusagasugá, Col.	E4	86
Fusan see Pusan, Kor., S.	D2	40
Fushan, China	C9	42
Fushan, China	D4	42
Fushih see Yan'an, China	C3	42
Fushun, China	D5	38
Fushun, China	G1	42
Fusilier, Sk., Can.	C4	124
Fusong, China	C7	38
Füssen, Ger.	I6	16
Fuste, Picacho del, mtn., Mex.	G5	130
Fusui, China	J2	42
Futun, stm., China	H7	42
Futuna, Île, i., Wal./F.	E9	72
Futuyu, China	B6	42
Fuwa, Egypt	G1	58
Fuxian Hu, l., China	G5	36
Fuxin, China	C4	38
Fuyang, China	E6	42
Fuyang, stm., China	C6	42
Fuyu see Tongjiang, China	B9	36
Fuyuan, see Tongjiang, China	B11	36
Fuyuan, China	F5	36
Fuyun, China	B11	36
Fuzhou, China	G7	42
Fuzhou, China	H8	42
Fyn, state, Den.	I4	8
Fyn, i., Den.	I4	8
Fyne, Loch, b., Scot., U.K.	E7	12
Fyresvatnet, l., Nor.	G2	8

G

Name	Map Ref.	Page
Gaalkacyo, Som.	C9	66
Gabare, Blg.	F10	26
Gabarus, N.S., Can.	E16	110
Gabela, Ang.	C1	68
Gabes, Tun.	C7	64
Gabès, Golfe de, b., Tun.	C7	64
Gabiarra, Braz.	I6	88
Gabon, ctry., Afr.	E2	66
Gaborone, Bots.	D7	70
Gabras, Sudan	E5	62
Gabriel Strait, strt., Nu., Can.	C17	106
Gabriel y Galán, Embalse de, res., Spain	D4	20
Gabrovo, Blg.	G12	26
Gacko, N.D., U.S.	F9	14
Gadag, India	A13	126
Gadarwāra, India	D2	53
Gado Bravo, Ilha do, i., Braz.	G7	54
Gádor, Spain	F4	88
Gadsden, Al., U.S.	H8	20
Gadsden, Az., U.S.	C12	122
Gadwāl, India	K2	132
Gael Hamke Bugt, b., Grnld.	C3	53
Găeşti, Rom.	E12	141
Gaeta, Italy	D12	26
Gaeta, Golfo di, b., Italy	C7	24
Gaferut, i., Micron.	C7	24
Gaffney, S.C., U.S.	C5	72
Gafour, Tun.	A4	116
Gafsa, Tun.	H3	24
Gag, Pulau, i., Indon.	C6	64
Gagarin, Russia	F8	44
Gagnoa, Gk., U.S.	E18	8
Gagnon, Braz.	H4	128
Gagnoa, Geor.	G6	88
Gaibandha, Bngl.	F5	32
Gail, Tx., U.S.	F12	54
Gaillac, Fr.	B6	130
Gaillimh see Galway, Ire.	F7	18
Gaimán, Arg.	H3	12
Gaīnīānagar, India	H3	90
Gaināpur, India	H12	54
Gainesville, Fl., U.S.	F5	54
Gainesville, Ga., U.S.	G3	116
Gainesville, Mo., U.S.	B2	116
Gainesville, Tx., U.S.	H5	120
Gainsborough Creek, stm., Can.	H11	128
Gairdner, Lake, l., Austl.	E12	124
Gaithersburg, Md., U.S.	F7	74
Gaixian, China	A10	114
Gaizina Kalns, hill, Lat.	D8	42
Gajapatinagaram, India	C9	10
Gajendragarh, India	B2	53
Gajny, Russia	C22	32
Gakona, Ak., U.S.	D10	140
Gakuch, India, Afr.	B11	54
Galāl el Bahariya, Gebel el-, mts., Egypt	I3	58
Galāl el-Qiblīya, Gebel el-, mts., Egypt	J3	58
Galán, Cerro, mtn., Arg.	C4	92
Galápagos Islands see Colón, Archipiélago de, is., Ec.	h12	84a
Galashiels, Scot., U.K.	F9	12
Galați, Rom.	D14	26
Galați, state, Rom.	D14	26
Galatia, Il., U.S.	G9	120
Galatina, Italy	D12	24
Galaxídi, Grc.	E5	28
Galdhøpiggen, mtn., Nor.	F2	8
Galeana, Mex.	F9	98
Galeana, Mex.	C8	100
Galela, Indon.	E8	44
Galena, Ak., U.S.	D8	140
Galena, Il., U.S.	B7	120
Galena, Mo., U.S.	H4	120
Galena Park, Tx., U.S.	E12	130
Galeota Point, c., Trin.	s13	105f
Galera, Punta, c., Chile	G2	90
Galera, Punta, c., Ec.	G1	86
Galera Point, c., Trin.	s13	105f
Galeras, Volcán, vol., Col.	G3	86
Galesburg, Il., U.S.	D7	120
Galesville, Wi., U.S.	G7	118
Galeton, Pa., U.S.	C8	114
Galiano Island, i., B.C., Can.	H7	138
Galič, Russia	G20	8
Galicia, hist. reg., Eur.	G18	16
Galičica Nacionalni Park, p.o.i., Russia	C3	28
Galičskaja vozvyšennost', hills, Russia	G20	8
Galičskoe, ozero, l., Russia	G20	8
Galilee, Lake, l., Austl.	D5	76
Galilee, Sea of see Kinneret, Yam, l., Isr.	F6	58
Galiléia, Braz.	J5	88
Galina Point, c., Jam.	i14	104d
Galion, Oh., U.S.	D3	114
Galite, Canal de la, strt., Tun.	G3	24
Gallarate, Italy	E5	22
Gallatin, Tn., U.S.	H11	120
Gallatin, stm., U.S.	E15	136
Galle, Sri L.	H5	53
Gállego, stm., Spain	B10	20
Gallegos, stm., Arg.	J3	90
Galliano, La., U.S.	H8	122
Gallinas, stm., N.M., U.S.	F4	128
Gallinas, Punta, c., Col.	A6	86
Gallipoli, Italy	D11	24
Gallipoli see Gelibolu, Tur.	C9	28
Gallipoli Peninsula see Gelibolu Yarımadası, pen., Tur.	C9	28
Gallipolis, Oh., U.S.	F3	114
Gällivare, Swe.	C9	8
Gallo, Capo, c., Italy	F7	24
Gallo Arroyo, stm., N.M., U.S.	G3	128
Galloo Island, i., N.Y., U.S.	E13	112
Galloway, hist. reg., Scot., U.K.	G8	12
Galloway, Mull of, c., Scot., U.K.	G8	12
Gallup, N.M., U.S.	H8	132
Gallura, reg., Italy	D3	24
Galoa Harbour, b., Fiji	q19	79e
Galt, Ca., U.S.	E4	134
Galtat Zemmour, W. Sah.	D2	64
Galty Mountains, mts., Ire.	I4	12
Galva, Il., U.S.	C7	120
Galva, Ks., U.S.	C11	128
Galveston, In., U.S.	H3	112
Galveston, Tx., U.S.	H4	122
Galveston Bay, b., Tx., U.S.	H4	122
Galveston Island, i., Tx., U.S.	E13	130
Gálvez, Arg.	F7	92
Galway, state, Ire.	H4	12
Galway, Ire.	H3	12
Galway Bay, b., Ire.	H3	12
Gam (Jin), stm., Asia	A7	48
Gama, Isla, i., Arg.	H4	90
Gamagōri, Japan	E10	40
Gambaga, Col.	S5	86
Gamay, Phil.	D5	52
Gamba, China	D12	54
Gambaga, Ghana	G4	64
Gambēla, Eth.	F6	62
Gambell, Ak., U.S.	D5	140
Gambia (Gambie), stm., Afr.	G1	64
Gambia, The, ctry., Afr.	G1	64
Gambie (Gambia), stm., Afr.	G2	64
Gambier, Îles, is., Fr. Poly.	F13	72
Gamboa, Pan.	H8	102
Gamboma, Congo	E3	66
Gamboula, C.A.R.	D2	66
Gamka, stm., S. Afr.	H5	70
Gamlakarleby see Kokkola, Fin.	E10	8
Gamleby, Swe.	H7	8
Gammon Ranges National Park, p.o.i., Austl.	H2	76
Ga-Mogara, stm., S. Afr.	E6	70
Gan, stm., China	B10	38
Gan, stm., China	G6	42
Ganado, Az., U.S.	H7	132
Ganado, Tx., U.S.	E11	130
Gananoque, On., Can.	D13	112
Gäncä, Azer.	A6	56
Gand see Gent, Bel.	C12	14
Gandadiwata, Bulu, mtn., Indon.	E11	50
Gandajika, D.R.C.	F4	66
Gandak (Nārāyani), stm., Asia	E10	54
Gander, Nf., Can.	j23	107a
Ganderkesee, Ger.	C4	16
Gandesa, Spain	C11	20
Gandevi, India	H4	54
Gāndhidhām, India	G3	54
Gandhinagar, India	G4	54
Gandhi Reservoir see Gāndhi Sāgar, res., India	F5	54
Gāndhi Sāgar, res., India	F10	20
Gandia, Braz.	G6	88
Gandia, Spain	F10	20
Gandu, Braz.	G6	88
Ganga (Ganges) (Padma), stm., Asia	F11	54
Gangānagar, India	D4	54
Gangāpur, India	E6	54
Gangāpur, India	F5	54
Gangaw, Mya.	A2	48
Gangdisê Shan, mts., China	C9	54
Ganges (Ganga) (Padma), stm., Asia	G13	54
Ganges, Mouths of the, mth., Asia	H7	54
Ganghu, China	B11	54
Gangmar Co, l., China	B10	54
Gangneung see Kangnŭng, Kor., S.	D1	40
Gangtok, India	E12	54
Gangu, China	D1	42
Gangwŏn see Kangwŏn-do, state, Kor., S.	B1	40
Gannan, China	B9	36
Gannett Peak, mtn., Wy., U.S.	D3	126
Gannvalley, S.D., U.S.	C14	126
Ganquan, China	C3	42
Gansbaai, S. Afr.	I4	70
Gansu, state, China	D5	36
Gantang, China	H8	42
Gantt, Al., U.S.	F12	122
Gantung, Indon.	E6	50
Ganyanchi, China	C1	42
Ganyesa, S. Afr.	E7	70
Ganzê, China	E4	36
Ganzhou, China	I6	42
Gao, Mali	F4	64
Gao'an, China	G6	42
Gaochun, China	F8	42
Gaohebu, China	F7	42
Gaojian, China	F9	36
Gaolan, China	D5	36
Gaolong, China	H5	42
Gaotan, China	C1	42
Gaotang, China	C7	42
Gaoua, Burkina	G4	64
Gaoual, Gui.	G2	64
Gaoxian, China	F5	36
Gaoyi, China	E8	42
Gaoyou, China	E8	42
Gaoyou Hu, l., China	K4	42
Gaozhou, China	K4	42
Gap, Fr.	E12	18
Gar, stm., China	B8	54
Gar, China	C8	54
Gara, Lough, l., Ire.	H4	12
Garagumskij kanal (Kara-Kum Canal), can., Turkmen.	B9	56
Garagumy (Kara-Kum), des., Turkmen.	A8	56
Garaina, Pap. N. Gui.	b4	79a
Garanhuns, Braz.	E7	88
Garapan, N. Mar. Is.	B5	72
Garara, Pap. N. Gui.	b4	79a
Garber, Ok., U.S.	E11	128
Garberville, Ca., U.S.	C2	134
Gårdbovo, Rom.	E10	26
Garça, Braz.	L1	88
García, Mex.	G8	98
García de Sola, Embalse de, res., Spain	E5	20
Garda, Italy	E7	22
Garda, Lago di, l., Italy	E7	22
Gardelegen, Ger.	D7	16
Garden City, Ks., U.S.	C8	128
Garden City, Mo., U.S.	F3	120
Garden City, Tx., U.S.	C6	130
Gardendale, Al., U.S.	D12	122
Garden Grove, Ca., U.S.	J7	134
Garden Grove, Ia., U.S.	D4	120
Garden Peninsula, pen., Mi., U.S.	C3	112
Garden Reach, India	G11	54
Gardenton, Mb., Can.	E17	124
Gardey, Arg.	H8	92
Gardiner, Mt., U.S.	E16	136
Gardiner, Or., U.S.	G2	136
Gardiner Dam, dam, Sk., Can.	C6	124
Gardner, Ks., U.S.	F2	120
Gardner, Ma., U.S.	B13	114
Gardner Canal, b., B.C., Can.	C2	138
Gardnerville, Nv., U.S.	E6	134
Garessio, Italy	F5	22
Garet, Mont, vol., Vanuatu	j16	79d
Garfield, Ks., U.S.	C9	128
Garfield, N.M., U.S.	K9	132
Garfield Mountain, mtn., Mt., U.S.	F14	136
Gargano, Promontorio del, mts., Italy	I12	22
Gargaliáni, Grc.	F4	28
Gargano, Testa del, c., Italy	I13	22
Gargždai, Lith.	E4	10
Garhākota, India	G7	54
Garibaldi, Braz.	D12	92
Garibaldi, Or., U.S.	E3	136
Garibaldi, Mount, vol., B.C., Can.	G8	138
Gariep Dam, res., S. Afr.	G7	70
Garies, S. Afr.	G4	70
Garigliano, stm., Italy	C7	24
Gariglione, Monte, mtn., Italy	E10	24
Garissa, Kenya	E7	66
Garland, Tx., U.S.	E2	122
Garland, Ut., U.S.	B4	132
Garlasco, Italy	E5	22
Garlin, Fr.	F5	18
Garmen, Blg.	H11	26
Garmisch-Partenkirchen, Ger.	I7	16
Garnavillo, Ia., U.S.	B6	120
Garner, Ia., U.S.	A4	120
Garner, N.C., U.S.	I7	114
Garnpung Lake, l., Austl.	I4	76
Garonne (Garona), stm., Eur.	E5	18
Garonne (Garona), stm., Eur.	E5	18
Garoowe, Som.	C9	66
Garoua, Cam.	C2	66
Garoua Boulaï, Cam.	C2	66
Garqu Yan, China	A14	54
Garrel, Ger.	D3	16
Garretson, S.D., U.S.	H2	118
Garrett, In., U.S.	G4	112
Garrett, Ky., U.S.	G3	114
Garrison, Tx., U.S.	G12	124
Garrison, Tx., U.S.	F4	122
Garrison Dam, dam, N.D., U.S.	G12	124
Garry Bay, b., Nu., Can.	B13	106
Garry Lake, l., Nu., Can.	B10	106
Garsen, Kenya	E8	66
Garson, On., Can.	B9	112
Garut, Indon.	G5	50
Garwolin, Pol.	E17	16
Gary, In., U.S.	H2	112
Gary, Tx., U.S.	G12	124
Gary, W.V., U.S.	G4	114
Garyarsa, China	C9	54
Garza, Arg.	C6	92
Garza García, Mex.	H7	130
Garzón, Col.	F3	86
Gasan-Kuli, Turkmen.	B7	56
Gas City, In., U.S.	H4	112
Gasconade, stm., Mo., U.S.	F6	120
Gasconade, Osage Fork, stm., Mo., U.S.	G5	120
Gascogne (Gascony), hist. reg., Fr.	F6	18
Gascony see Gascogne, hist. reg., Fr.	F6	18
Gascoyne, stm., Austl.	D2	74
Gasherbrum, mtn., Asia	H7	54
Gashua, Nig.	G7	64
Gaspar, Braz.	C13	92
Gasparilla Island, i., Fl., U.S.	J3	116
Gaspé, Qc., Can.	B12	110
Gaspé, Baie de, b., Qc., Can.	B12	110
Gaspé, Cap, c., Qc., Can.	B12	110
Gaspe Peninsula see Gaspésie, Péninsule de la, pen., Qc., Can.	B11	110
Gaspésie, Péninsule de la (Gaspe Peninsula), pen., Qc., Can.	B11	110
Gassaway, W.V., U.S.	F5	114
Gasteiz (Vitoria), Spain	B8	20
Gaston, Lake, res., U.S.	H7	114
Gastonia, N.C., U.S.	A4	116
Gastre, Arg.	H3	90
Gata, Cabo de, c., Spain	H9	20

Name	Map Ref.	Page

Gata, Sierra de, mts., Spain — D4 20
Gătaia, Rom. — D8 26
Gátas, Akrotírion, c., Cyp. — D4 58
Gatčina, Russia — A12 10
Gate City, Va., U.S. — H3 114
Gateshead, Eng., U.K. — G11 12
Gateshead Island, i., Nu., Can. — A11 106
Gatesville, N.C., U.S. — H9 114
Gatesville, Tx., U.S. — C10 130
Gateway, Co., U.S. — E8 132
Gatineau, Qc., Can. — C14 112
Gatineau, stm., Qc., Can. — C14 112
Gatineau, Parc de la, p.o.i., Qc., Can. — C13 112
Gatlinburg, Tn., U.S. — I2 114
Gattinara, Italy — E5 22
Gatton, Austl. — F9 76
Gatún, Lago, res., Pan. — H7 102
Gatun Lake see Gatún, Lago, res., Pan. — H7 102
Gauer Lake, l., Mb., Can. — D11 106
Gauja (Koiva), stm., Eur. — C7 10
Gaujiena, Lat. — C9 10
Gauley, stm., W.V., U.S. — F4 114
Gauley Bridge, W.V., U.S. — F4 114
Gaurela, India — C9 54
Gauribidanūr, India — E3 53
Gause, Tx., U.S. — G2 122
Gaustatoppen, mtn., Nor. — G3 8
Gauteng, state, S. Afr. — D9 70
Gavà, Spain — C12 20
Gávdos, i., Grc. — I7 28
Gavião, stm., Braz. — H5 88
Gavins Point Dam, dam, U.S. — E15 126
Gävle, Swe. — F7 8
Gävleborg, state, Swe. — F7 8
Gavorrano, Italy — H7 22
Gavrilov-Jam, Russia — H18 8
Gawachab, Nmb. — E3 70
Gāwān, India — F10 54
Gawler, Austl. — J2 76
Gawler Ranges, mts., Austl. — F7 74
Gaya, India — F10 54
Gaya, Niger — G5 64
Gaya, Nig. — G6 64
Gaylord, Mn., U.S. — G4 118
Gayndah, Austl. — E8 76
Gays Mills, Wi., U.S. — H8 118
Gaza see Ghazzah, Gaza — G5 58
Gaza, state, Moz. — C11 70
Gazandzhik see Gazandzhyk, Turkmen. — B8 56
Gazandzyk, Turkmen. — B8 56
Gazaoua, Niger — G6 64
Gaza Strip, dep., Asia — G5 58
Gazelle Peninsula, pen., Pap. N. Gui. — a5 79a
Gaziantep, Tur. — A8 58
Gaziantep, state, Tur. — B8 58
Gazimağusa (Famagusta), N. Cyp. — C4 58
Gazimağusa Körfezi, b., N. Cyp. — C4 58
Gazipaşa, Tur. — G15 28
Gazivoda Jezero, res., Yugo. — G7 26
Gbanga, Lib. — H3 64
Gboko, Nig. — H6 64
Gdańsk (Danzig), Pol. — B14 16
Gdańsk, state, Pol. — B14 16
Gdansk, Gulf of, b., Eur. — B15 16
Gdov, Russia — B10 10
Gdynia, Pol. — B14 16
Gearhart Mountain, mtn., Or., U.S. — A5 134
Geary, N.B., Can. — E10 110
Geary, Ok., U.S. — F10 128
Gebe, Pulau, i., Indon. — E8 44
Gebze, Tur. — C12 28
Geçitkale, N. Cyp. — C4 58
Gediz, Tur. — D12 28
Gediz (Hermus), stm., Tur. — B7 16
Gedser, Den. — B7 16
Geel, Bel. — C13 14
Geelong, Austl. — L5 76
Geelvink Channel, strt., Austl. — E2 74
Geeshacht, Ger. — C6 16
Geeveston, Austl. — o13 77a
Ge Hu, l., China — F8 42
Geiger, Al., U.S. — E10 122
Geikie, stm., Sk., Can. — D9 106
Geisenfeld, Ger. — H7 16
Geislingen an der Steige, Ger. — H5 16
Geistown, Pa., U.S. — D7 114
Geita, Tan. — E6 66
Geiyu, China — G5 36
Gela, Italy — G8 24
Gela, Golfo di, b., Italy — H7 24
Gelādī, Eth. — F9 62
Gelang, Tanjong, c., Malay. — K6 48
Gelasa, Selat, strt., Indon. — E5 50
Geleen, Neth. — D14 14
Gelembe, Tur. — D10 28
Gelendžik, Russia — F5 32
Gelgaudiškis, Lith. — E6 10
Gelibolu, Tur. — C9 28
Gelibolu Yarımadası (Gallipoli Peninsula), pen., Tur. — C9 28
Gellibrand River, Austl. — L4 76
Gelsenkirchen, Ger. — E2 16
Gemas, Malay. — K6 48
Gemena, D.R.C. — D3 66
Gemert, Neth. — E1 16
Gemlik, Tur. — C12 28
Gemlik Körfezi, b., Tur. — C11 28
Gemona del Friuli, Italy — D10 22
Gemsa, Egypt — K4 58
Gemsbok National Park, p.o.i., Bots. — D5 70
Gemünden, Ger. — F5 16
Gen, stm., China — A9 36
Genalē (Jubba), stm., Afr. — C8 66
Gending, Indon. — G8 50
General Acha, Arg. — H5 92
General Alvear, Arg. — G3 92
General Alvear, Arg. — H8 92
General Belgrano, Arg. — G8 92
General Bernardo O'Higgins, sci., Ant. — B35 81
General Bravo, Mex. — C9 100
General Cabrera, Arg. — F6 92
General Campos, Arg. — E8 92
General Carrera, Lago, l., S.A. — I2 90
General Conesa, Arg. — H4 92
General Conesa, Arg. — H9 92
General Daniel Cerri, Arg. — I6 92
General Elizardo Aquino, Para. — C9 92
General Enrique Martínez, Ur. — F10 92
General Escobedo, Mex. — I7 130
General Eugenio A. Garay, Para. — D4 90
General Galarza, Arg. — F8 92
General Güemes, Arg. — B5 92
General Guido, Arg. — H8 92
General José de San Martín, Arg. — C8 92
General Juan José Ríos, Mex. — C4 100
General Juan Madariaga, Arg. — H9 92
General La Madrid, Arg. — H7 92
General Lavalle, Arg. — G9 92
General Levalle, Arg. — G5 92
General Manuel Belgrano, Cerro, mtn., Arg. — D4 92
General Pico, Arg. — G6 92

General Pinedo, Arg. — C7 92
General Pizarro, Arg. — B6 92
General Ramírez, Arg. — F7 92
General Roca, Arg. — G3 90
General San Martín, Arg. — G8 92
General Santos, Phil. — G5 52
General Terán, Mex. — C9 100
General Toševo, Blg. — F14 26
General Toshevo see General Toševo, Blg. — F14 26
General Treviño, Mex. — H8 130
General Trias, Mex. — F1 130
General Viamonte, Arg. — G7 92
General Villegas, Arg. — G6 92
Genesee, Id., U.S. — D9 136
Genesee, stm., U.S. — F12 112
Geneseo, Il., U.S. — C7 120
Geneseo, Ks., U.S. — C10 128
Geneseo, N.Y., U.S. — B8 114
Geneva see Genève, Switz. — D3 22
Geneva, Il., U.S. — J10 118
Geneva, In., U.S. — H5 112
Geneva, Ne., U.S. — G15 126
Geneva, N.Y., U.S. — B8 114
Geneva, Oh., U.S. — C4 114
Geneva, Lake, l., Eur. — C12 18
Genève (Geneva), Switz. — D3 22
Genève, Lac de see Geneva, Lake, l., Eur. — C12 18
Genf see Genève, Switz. — D3 22
Gengma, China — G4 36
Genil, stm., Spain — G5 20
Genk, Bel. — C14 14
Genkai-nada, Japan — F2 40
Genoa see Genova, Italy — F5 22
Genoa, Ne., U.S. — F15 126
Genoa, Oh., U.S. — C2 114
Genoa, Wi., U.S. — H7 118
Genoa (Genova), Italy — F5 22
Genova, Golfo di, b., Italy — G5 22
Genova (Genoa), Italy — F5 22
Genrietty, ostrov, i., Russia — A20 34
Gens de Terre, stm., Qc., Can. — B13 112
Genshiryoku-kenkyūsho, sci., Japan — C13 40
Gent (Ghent), Bel. — C12 14
Genteng, Gili, i., Indon. — G8 50
Genthin, Ger. — D8 16
Gentio do Ouro, Braz. — F4 88
Genzano di Roma, Italy — I9 22
Geographe Bay, b., Austl. — F3 74
Geographical Society Ø, i., Grnld. — C21 141
Geok-Tepe, Turkmen. — B8 56
George, S. Afr. — H6 70
George, Ia., U.S. — H2 118
George, stm., Qc., Can. — D17 106
George, Lake, l., Austl. — D4 74
George, Lake, l., Austl. — J7 76
George, Lake, l., Ug. — E6 66
George, Lake, l., Fl., U.S. — G4 116
George, Lake, res., N.Y., U.S. — G3 110
Georgetown, Austl. — B4 76
George Town, Austl. — n13 77a
Georgetown, On., Can. — E9 112
Georgetown, P.E.I., Can. — D14 110
George Town, Cay. Is. — C7 102
Georgetown, Gam. — G2 64
Georgetown, Guy. — B6 84
George Town (Penang), Malay. — J4 48
Georgetown, St. Vin. — o11 105e
Georgetown, Co., U.S. — B3 128
Georgetown, De., U.S. — F10 114
Georgetown, Fl., U.S. — G4 116
Georgetown, Id., U.S. — H15 136
Georgetown, Ky., U.S. — F1 114
Georgetown, Ms., U.S. — F8 122
Georgetown, Oh., U.S. — F2 114
Georgetown, S.C., U.S. — C6 116
Georgetown, Tx., U.S. — D10 130
George V Coast, cst., Ant. — B19 81
George Washington Birthplace National Monument, p.o.i., Va., U.S. — F9 114
George Washington Carver National Monument, p.o.i., Mo., U.S. — H3 120
George West, Tx., U.S. — F9 130
Georgia, ctry., Asia — F6 32
Georgia, state, U.S. — E11 108
Georgia, Strait of, strt., N.A. — G7 138
Georgian Bay, b., Can. — C8 112
Georgian Bay Islands National Park, p.o.i., On., Can. — D9 112
Georgievka, Kaz. — E14 32
Georg von Neumayer, sci., Ant. — B3 81
Gera, Ger. — F7 16
Geral, Serra, mts., Braz. — C12 92
Geral, Serra, clf, Braz. — F2 88
Gerald, Mo., U.S. — F6 120
Geral de Goiás, Serra, clf, Braz. — G2 88
Geraldine, B.C., Can. — C16 136
Geraldton, Austl. — E2 74
Geraldton, On., Can. — B11 118
Gérardmer, Fr. — F15 14
Gerber, Ca., U.S. — C3 134
Gerdine, Mount, mtn., Ak., U.S. — D9 140
Gerede, Tur. — C15 28
Gereshk, Afg. — C9 56
Gérgal, Spain — G8 20
Gerik, Malay. — J5 48
Gerlachovský štít, mtn., Slov. — G16 16
German Democratic Republic see Germany, ctry., Eur. — E6 16
Germania Land, reg., Grnld. — B21 141
Germantown, Il., U.S. — F8 120
Germantown, Tn., U.S. — B9 122
Germantown, Wi., U.S. — E1 112
Germany, ctry., Eur. — E6 16
Germany, Federal Republic of see Germany, ctry., Eur. — E6 16
Germencik, Tur. — F10 28
Germfask, Mi., U.S. — B4 112
Germiston, S. Afr. — E9 70
Gernika, Spain — A8 20
Gero, Japan — D10 40
Geroliménas, Grc. — H5 28
Gerona see Girona, Spain — B13 20
Geronimo, Ok., U.S. — G10 128
Gers, stm., Fr. — F6 18
Gers, state, Fr. — F6 18
Geseke, Ger. — E4 16
Geser, Indon. — F9 44
Getafe, Spain — D7 20
Gettysburg, Pa., U.S. — E8 114
Getúlio Vargas, Braz. — C11 92
Geumpang, Indon. — J2 48
Gevgelija, Mac. — B5 28
Geyikli, Tur. — D9 28
Geyser, Mt., U.S. — C16 136
Geyserville, Ca., U.S. — E3 134
Geyve, Tur. — C13 28
Ghaapplato, plat., S. Afr. — E7 70
Ghadāmis, Libya — B1 62
Ghaggar, stm., India — D5 54
Ghāghara (Kauriālā), stm., Asia — E9 54
Ghāghara see Ghāghara, stm., Asia — E9 54
Ghakhar, Pak. — B4 54

Ghana, ctry., Afr. — H4 64
Ghanzi, Bots. — B5 70
Ghanzi, state, Bots. — C6 70
Gharandal, hist., Jord. — H6 58
Gharaunda, India — D6 54
Ghardaïa, Alg. — C5 64
Ghardimaou, Tun. — H2 24
Gharyān, Libya — A2 62
Ghāt, Libya — F12 26
Ghatere, Mount, mtn., Sol. Is. — d8 79b
Ghātprabha, stm., India — C2 53
Ghātsīla, India — G11 54
Ghazāl, Bahr al-, stm., Sudan — F6 62
Ghāziābād, India — D6 54
Ghāzīpur, India — F9 54
Ghazlūna, Pak. — C1 54
Ghaznī, Afg. — C10 56
Ghaznī, state, Afg. — B2 54
Ghazzah (Gaza), Gaza — G5 58
Ghazzah, Leb. — E6 58
Ghent see Gent, Bel. — C12 14
Gheorgheni, Rom. — C12 26
Gherla, Rom. — C10 26
Gheroo, Geziret, i., Egypt — G1 58
Ghinah, Wādī al-, stm., Sau. Ar. — H9 58
Ghisonaccia, Fr. — H15 18
Ghizo see Gizo Island, i., Sol. Is. — e7 79b
Ghizunabeana Islands, is., Sol. Is. — d8 79b
Ghotki, Pak. — E2 54
Ghubaysh, Sudan — E5 62
Ghūrīān, Afg. — C9 56
Gianh, stm., Viet. — C7 48
Giannitsá, Grc. — C5 28
Giant Mountain, mtn., N.Y., U.S. — F3 110
Giant's Castle, mtn., S. Afr. — F9 70
Giant's Castle Game Reserve, S. Afr. — F9 70
Gia Rai, Viet. — H7 48
Giarre, Italy — G9 24
Gibara, Cuba — B9 102
Gibbon, Mn., U.S. — G4 118
Gibbons, Ab., Can. — C17 138
Gibbonsville, Id., U.S. — E13 136
Gibb River, Austl. — C5 74
Gibeon, Nmb. — D3 70
Gibraléon, Spain — G3 20
Gibraltar, Gib. — H5 20
Gibraltar, dep., Eur. — H5 20
Gibraltar, Strait of, strt., Eur. — B3 64
Gibraltar Point, c., Eng., U.K. — H13 12
Gibsland, La., U.S. — E5 122
Gibson City, Il., U.S. — D9 120
Gibson Desert, des., Austl. — D4 74
Gibsons, B.C., Can. — G7 138
Giddalūr, India — D4 53
Giddings, Tx., U.S. — D11 130
Gidgī, Lake, l., Austl. — E5 74
Giedraičiai, Lith. — E8 10
Giessen, Ger. — F4 16
Gifatin, Geziret, is., Egypt — K4 58
Gifford, Fl., U.S. — I5 116
Gifford, stm., Nu., Can. — A14 106
Gifford Creek, Austl. — D4 74
Gifhorn, Ger. — D6 16
Gifu, Japan — D9 40
Gifu, state, Japan — D10 40
Giganta, Sierra de la, mts., Mex. — C3 100
Gigena see Alcira, Arg. — F5 92
Gigha Island, i., Scot., U.K. — F7 12
Giglio, Isola del, i., Italy — H7 22
Gihu see Gifu, Japan — D9 40
Gijón, Spain — A5 20
Gila, stm., U.S. — K2 132
Gila Bend, Az., U.S. — K4 132
Gila Cliff Dwellings National Monument, p.o.i., N.M., U.S. — J8 132
Gilbert, La., U.S. — E7 122
Gilbert, stm., Austl. — C8 74
Gilbert Islands see Kiribati, ctry., Oc. — D9 72
Gilbert Islands, is. Kir. — D8 72
Gilbert Peak, mtn., Wa., U.S. — D5 136
Gilbert Plains, Mb., Can. — C13 124
Gilbués, Braz. — E3 88
Gildford, Mt., U.S. — B16 136
Gilford Island, i., B.C., Can. — F4 138
Gilgandra, Austl. — H7 76
Gilgil, Kenya — E7 66
Gil Gil Creek, stm., Austl. — G7 76
Gilgit, Pak. — B11 56
Giliraing, Indon. — E12 50
Gil Island, i., B.C., Can. — C1 138
Giljuj, stm., Russia — F14 34
Gillam, Mb., Can. — D12 106
Gillespie, Il., U.S. — E8 120
Gillett, Ar., U.S. — C7 122
Gillette, Wy., U.S. — C7 126
Gillett, Lake, l., Nu., Can. — B16 106
Gillingham, Eng., U.K. — J13 12
Gills Rock, Wi., U.S. — C3 112
Gilman, Il., U.S. — D10 120
Gilman, Wi., U.S. — F8 118
Gilmer, Tx., U.S. — E4 122
Gilroy, Ca., U.S. — F4 134
Giltner, Ne., U.S. — G14 126
Giluwe, Mount, mtn., Pap. N. Gui. — b3 79a
Gimbī, Eth. — F7 62
Gimcheon see Kimch'ŏn, Kor., S. — F8 38
Gimie, Mount, vol., St. Luc. — m6 105c
Gimli, Mb., Can. — D16 124
Gimpu, Indon. — D12 50
Gīneina, Rās el-, mtn., Egypt — I4 58
Gin Gin, Austl. — E8 76
Gingoog, Phil. — F5 52
Ginīr, Eth. — F8 62
Ginosa, Italy — D10 24
Gioia, Golfo di, b., Italy — F9 24
Gioia del Colle, Italy — D10 24
Gioia Tauro, Italy — F9 24
Giong Rieng, Viet. — H7 48
Giovinazzo, Italy — C10 24
Gīr National Park, p.o.i., India — H3 54
Girard, Ks., U.S. — G3 120
Girard, Oh., U.S. — C5 114
Girardot, Col. — E4 86
Giraud, Pointe, c., Dom. — j6 105c
Girgarre, Austl. — K5 76
Girīdīh, India — F11 54
Girna, stm., India — H5 54
Girne (Kyrenia), N. Cyp. — C4 58
Girón, Ec. — D2 84
Girona, Spain — B13 20
Gironde, state, Fr. — E5 18
Gironde, est., Fr. — D4 18
Gīr Range, mts., India — H3 54
Giru, Austl. — B6 76
Giruá, Braz. — D10 92
Girvan, Scot., U.K. — F8 12

Gisborne, N.Z. — D8 80
Giscome, B.C., Can. — B8 138
Gislaved, Swe. — H5 8
Gisors, Fr. — E10 14
Gitarama, Rw. — E5 66
Gitega, Bdi. — E5 66
Giulianova, Italy — H11 22
Giurgiu, Rom. — F12 26
Giurgiulești, Rom. — E13 26
Giuvala, Pasul, p., Rom. — D12 26
Givet, Fr. — D13 14
Givors, Fr. — D10 18
Giyon, Eth. — F7 62
Giza see El-Gîza, Egypt — H1 58
Gizduvan, Uzb. — F10 32
Gižiga, Russia — D21 34
Gizo, Sol. Is. — e7 79b
Gizo Island, i., Sol. Is. — e7 79b
Giżycko, Pol. — B17 16
Gjirokastër, Alb. — D14 24
Gjirokastra see Gjirokastër, Alb. — D14 24
Gjoa Haven, Nu., Can. — B11 106
Gjøvik, Nor. — F4 8
Glace Bay, N.S., Can. — D17 110
Glacier, B.C., Can. — E13 138
Glacier Bay, b., Ak., U.S. — E12 140
Glacier National Park, p.o.i., B.C., Can. — E13 138
Glacier National Park, p.o.i., Mt., U.S. — B12 136
Glacier Peak, vol., Wa., U.S. — B5 136
Glacier Strait, strt., Nu., — B10 141
Gladbrook, Ia., U.S. — B5 120
Gladewater, Tx., U.S. — E4 122
Gladstone, Austl. — D8 76
Gladstone, Mb., Can. — D14 124
Gladstone, Mi., U.S. — C2 112
Gladstone, Mo., U.S. — E3 120
Gladwin, Mi., U.S. — E5 112
Gláma, stm., Nor. — F4 8
Glan, Phil. — H5 52
Glaris see Glarus, Switz. — C5 22
Glarner Alpen, mts., Switz. — D6 22
Glarus, Switz. — C5 22
Glärnisch see Glarner Alpen, mts., Switz. — D6 22
Glasco, Ks., U.S. — B11 128
Glasgow, Scot., U.K. — F8 12
Glasgow, Ky., U.S. — G12 120
Glasgow, Mo., U.S. — E5 120
Glasgow, Mt., U.S. — F7 124
Glasgow, Va., U.S. — G6 114
Glassboro, N.J., U.S. — E10 114
Glastonbury, Eng., U.K. — J10 12
Glauchau, Ger. — F8 16
Glazov, Russia — C8 32
Glazunovka, Russia — H19 10
Gleichen, Ab., Can. — F17 138
Glen Alpine, N.C., U.S. — A4 116
Glenavon, Sk., Can. — D10 124
Glenboro, Mb., Can. — E14 124
Glenburn, N.D., U.S. — F12 124
Glen Burnie, Md., U.S. — E9 114
Glen Canyon, val., U.S. — F6 132
Glen Canyon Dam, dam, Az., U.S. — G5 132
Glen Canyon National Recreation Area, p.o.i., U.S. — F6 132
Glencoe, On., Can. — F8 112
Glencoe, S. Afr. — F9 70
Glencoe, Mn., U.S. — G4 118
Glendale, Az., U.S. — J4 132
Glendale, Ca., U.S. — I7 134
Glendale, Ms., U.S. — C8 134
Glendale, Ut., U.S. — F4 132
Glendale, Wi., U.S. — A10 120
Glendive, Mt., U.S. — G9 124
Glendo, Wy., U.S. — E7 126
Glendo Reservoir, res., Wy., U.S. — E8 126
Glen Elder, Ks., U.S. — B10 128
Glengarriff, Ire. — J3 12
Glengyle, Austl. — E2 76
Glen Innes, Austl. — G8 76
Glenmora, La., U.S. — G6 122
Glennallen, Ak., U.S. — D10 140
Glennville, Ga., U.S. — E4 116
Glenns Ferry, Id., U.S. — H11 136
Glenoma, Wa., U.S. — D4 136
Glenormiston, Austl. — D7 74
Glen Robertson, On., Can. — E2 110
Glenrock, Wy., U.S. — E7 126
Glenrothes, Scot., U.K. — E9 12
Glens Falls, N.Y., U.S. — G3 110
Glenville, Mn., U.S. — H5 118
Glenville, W.V., U.S. — F5 114
Glenwood, Ab., Can. — G17 138
Glenwood, Al., U.S. — F12 122
Glenwood, Ia., U.S. — C2 120
Glenwood, Mn., U.S. — F3 118
Glenwood, N.M., U.S. — J7 132
Glenwood City, Wi., U.S. — F6 118
Glenwood Springs, Co., U.S. — D9 132
Glidden, Wi., U.S. — E8 118
Glide, Or., U.S. — G3 136
Glina, Cro. — E13 22
Glittertind see Glittertinden, mtn., Nor. — F3 8
Glittertinden, mtn., Nor. — F3 8
Gliwice, Pol. — F14 16
Gljadjanskoe, Russia — D10 32
Globe, Az., U.S. — J6 132
Gloceni, Mol. — B14 26
Glodeanu-Sărat, Rom. — D13 26
Głogów Małopolski, Pol. — F17 16
Głogów, Pol. — E11 16
Glomma see Gláma, stm., Nor. — F4 8
Glorieta, N.M., U.S. — F3 128
Glorieuses, Îles, is., Reu. — C8 68
Glorioso Islands see Glorieuses, Îles, is., Reu. — C8 68
Glossop, Eng., U.K. — H11 12
Gloucester, Eng., U.K. — J10 12
Gloucester, Ma., U.S. — B15 114
Gloucester, Va., U.S. — G9 114
Gloucester Island, i., Austl. — B7 76
Glouster, Oh., U.S. — E3 114
Glovertown, Nf., Can. — j23 107a
Głowno, Pol. — E15 16
Głubczyce, Pol. — F13 16
Glubokoe see Hlybokae, Bela. — E9 10
Głuchołazy, Pol. — F13 16
Glücksburg, Ger. — B5 16
Glückstadt, Ger. — C5 16
Gluchiv see Hluchiv, Ukr. — D4 32
Glubokoe, Kaz. — D14 32
Gmelinka, Russia — D7 32
Gmünd, Aus. — B12 22
Gmunden, Aus. — C10 22
Gnarp, Swe. — E7 8
Gnesta, Swe. — G7 8
Gniew, Pol. — C14 16
Gniezno, Pol. — D13 16
Gnjilane, Yugo. — G8 26
Gnowangerup, Austl. — F3 74
Gō, stm., Japan — E5 40

Goa, state, India — D2 53
Goālpāra, India — E13 54
Goaso, Ghana — H4 64
Goat Island, i., Antig. — e4 105b
Goat Point, c., Antig. — e4 105b
Goba, Eth. — F8 62
Gobabis, Nmb. — C4 70
Göbel, Tur. — D11 28
Gobernador Gregores, Arg. — I2 90
Gobernador Ingeniero Valentín Virasoro, Arg. — D9 92
Gobernador Juan E. Martínez, Arg. — D8 92
Gobernador Vera see Vera, Arg. — D7 92
Gobi Desert, des., Asia — C5 36
Gobō, Japan — F8 40
Goce Delčev, Blg. — H10 26
Goch, Ger. — E2 16
Godafoss, wtfl, Ice. — k31 8a
Godāvari, stm., India — C5 53
Godāvari, Mouths of the, mth., India — C5 53
Godbout, Qc., Can. — A9 110
Goderich, On., Can. — E8 112
Godfrey, Il., U.S. — F7 120
Godhavn (Qeqertarsuaq), Grnld. — D15 141
Godhra, India — G4 54
Gödöllő, Hung. — B6 26
Godoy Cruz, Arg. — F3 92
Gods, stm., Mb., Can. — D12 106
Gods Lake, l., Mb., Can. — E12 106
Gods Mercy, Bay of, b., Nu., Can. — C13 106
Godthåb (Nuuk), Grnld. — E15 141
Godwin Austen see K2, mtn., Asia — B12 56
Goeie Hoop, Kaap die see Good Hope, Cape of, c., S. Afr. — I4 70
Goéland, Lac au, l., Qc., Can. — E15 106
Goes, Neth. — C12 14
Goffstown, N.H., U.S. — G5 110
Gogebic, Lake, res., Mi., U.S. — E9 118
Gogol, Moz. — B11 70
Gogrial, Sudan — F5 62
Gohad, India — E7 54
Gohpur, India — E14 54
Goiana, Braz. — D8 88
Goianésia, Braz. — H1 88
Goiânia, Braz. — I1 88
Goianinha, Braz. — D8 88
Goiás, Braz. — G7 84
Goiás, state, Braz. — C7 90
Goio-Erê, Braz. — B11 92
Góio-Erê, stm., Braz. — B11 92
Góis, Port. — D2 20
Gojō, Japan — E8 40
Gojra, Pak. — C4 54
Gokāk, India — C2 53
Gökçeada, i., Tur. — C8 28
Gökova Körfezi (Kerme, Gulf of), b., Tur. — G10 28
Göksu, stm., Tur. — B4 58
Göksun, Tur. — A4 58
Göktepe, Tur. — F11 28
Gokwe, Zimb. — D4 68
Golāghāt, India — C7 46
Gola Gokarannāth, India — D8 54
Golańcz, Pol. — D13 16
Gölbaşı, Tur. — D15 28
Gölbaşı, Tur. — A8 58
Golconda, hist., India — C4 53
Golconda, Il., U.S. — G9 120
Golconda, Nv., U.S. — C8 134
Gold Bridge, B.C., Can. — F8 138
Gold Coast see Southport, Austl. — F9 76
Gold Coast, cst., Ghana — I4 64
Golden, B.C., Can. — E13 138
Golden, Co., U.S. — B3 128
Golden, Il., U.S. — D7 120
Golden Bay, b., N.Z. — E5 80
Golden City, Mo., U.S. — G3 120
Goldendale, Wa., U.S. — E6 136
Golden Gate Highlands National Park, p.o.i., S. Afr. — F9 70
Golden Hinde, mtn., B.C., Can. — G5 138
Golden Meadow, La., U.S. — H8 122
Golden Lake, l., On., Can. — C12 112
Goldfield, Ia., U.S. — B3 120
Goldfield, Nv., U.S. — F8 134
Gold Mountain, mtn., Nv., U.S. — B10 130
Gold River, B.C., Can. — G4 138
Goldsboro, N.C., U.S. — A7 116
Goldsmith, Tx., U.S. — B5 130
Goldsworthy, Austl. — D3 74
Goldthwaite, Tx., U.S. — C9 130
Goleniów, Pol. — C10 16
Goleta, Ca., U.S. — I6 134
Golfito, C.R. — H6 102
Golfo de Santa Clara, Mex. — F5 98
Gölhisar, Tur. — F12 28
Goliad, Tx., U.S. — E10 130
Golicyno, Russia — E19 10
Golina, Pol. — D13 16
Golin Baixing, China — B4 38
Gölmarmara, Tur. — E10 28
Golmud, China — A7 46
Golmud, stm., China — A7 46
Golovin, Ak., U.S. — D7 140
Golpāyegān, Iran — C7 56
Golpazarı, Tur. — C13 28
Golub-Dobrzyń, Pol. — C14 16
Golva, N.D., U.S. — A8 126
Golyšmanovo, Russia — C11 32
Goma, D.R.C. — E5 66
Gomang Co, l., China — C12 54
Gomati, stm., India — E8 54
Gombe, Nig. — G7 64
Gombi, Nig. — G7 64
Gómez Farías, Mex. — A5 100
Gómez Palacio, Mex. — C7 100
Gómez Plata, Col. — D4 86
Gomo Co, l., China — B12 54
Gomogomo, Indon. — b1 79a
Gonābād, Iran — B8 56
Gonaïves, Haiti — C11 102
Gonam, Russia — E15 34
Gonarezhou National Park, p.o.i., Zimb. — B10 70
Gonâve, Golfe de la, b., Haiti — C11 102
Gonâve, Île de la, i., Haiti — C11 102
Gonbad-e Qābūs, Iran — B8 56
Gonda, India — E8 54
Gondal, India — H3 54
Gonder see Gonder, Eth. — E7 62
Gondia, India — H7 54
Gönen, Tur. — D10 28
Gong'an, China — F4 42
Gongchangqiao, China — I4 42
Gonggar, China — D13 54

Gonghe, China — D5 36
Gongliu, China — F14 32
Gongola, stm., Nig. — G7 64
Gongshiya, China — C10 54
Gongxi, China — H6 42
Gongxian, China — D5 42
Gongzhuling, China — C6 38
Goñi, Ur. — F9 92
Goniądz, Pol. — C18 16
Gonohe, Japan — F2 40
Gonzales, Ca., U.S. — G4 134
Gonzales, La., U.S. — G8 122
González, Mex. — D9 100
González Moreno, Arg. — G6 92
Goochland, Va., U.S. — G6 114
Goodenough Island, i., Pap. N. Gui. — b5 79a
Gooderham, On., Can. — D11 112
Goodeve, Sk., Can. — C10 124
Good Hope, Cape of (Goeie Hoop, Kaap die), c., S. Afr. — I4 70
Good Hope Mountain, mtn., B.C., Can. — E6 138
Goodhue, Mn., U.S. — G6 118
Goodland, Fl., U.S. — K4 116
Goodland, In., U.S. — K11 118
Goodland, Ks., U.S. — B7 128
Goodlands, Mb., Can. — E13 124
Goodman, Wi., U.S. — C1 112
Goodnews Bay, Ak., U.S. — E7 140
Goodnight, Co., U.S. — C4 128
Goodooga, Austl. — G6 76
Goodrich, N.D., U.S. — G13 124
Good Spirit Lake, l., Sk., Can. — C11 124
Goodwater, Al., U.S. — D12 122
Goodyear, Az., U.S. — J4 132
Goole, Eng., U.K. — H12 12
Goolgowi, Austl. — I5 76
Goonda, Moz. — A11 70
Goondiwindi, Austl. — G8 76
Goongarrie, Austl. — F4 74
Goose, stm., N.D., U.S. — G17 124
Goose Creek, S.C., U.S. — C6 116
Goose Island, i., B.C., Can. — E2 138
Goose Lake, l., U.S. — B5 134
Gooty, India — C3 53
Gopālganj, Bngl. — G12 54
Gopālganj, India — E10 54
Gopichettipālaiyam, India — F3 53
Göppingen, Ger. — H5 16
Goqên, China — F4 36
Go Quao, Viet. — H7 48
Góra Kalwaria, Pol. — E17 16
Gorakhpur, India — E9 54
Goražde, Bos. — F5 26
Gorda, Punta, c., Cuba — A6 102
Gorda, Punta, c., Nic. — F6 102
Gordeevka, Russia — H14 10
Gordil, C.A.R. — C4 66
Gordo, Al., U.S. — D11 122
Gordon, Ga., U.S. — D2 116
Gordon, Ne., U.S. — E11 126
Gordon, Wi., U.S. — E7 118
Gordon, Lake, res., Austl. — o13 77a
Gordon Creek, stm., Ne., U.S. — E11 126
Gordon Downs, Austl. — C5 74
Gordon Horne Peak, mtn., B.C., Can. — E12 138
Gordonsville, Va., U.S. — F7 114
Gordonvale, Austl. — A5 76
Gore, N.S., Can. — E13 110
Goré, Chad — F3 62
Gorē, Eth. — F7 62
Gore, N.Z. — H3 80
Goreda, Indon. — F9 44
Goree, Tx., U.S. — H9 128
Gore Range, mts., U.S. — H6 126
Goreville, Il., U.S. — G8 120
Gorgān, Iran — B7 56
Gorgona, Isla, i., Col. — F2 86
Gorgota, Rom. — E13 26
Gorham, Me., U.S. — G6 110
Gori, Geor. — F6 32
Gorica see Gorizia, Italy — E10 22
Goricy, Russia — C19 10
Gorinchem, Neth. — C14 14
Gorizia (Gorica), Italy — E10 22
Gorj, state, Rom. — E10 26
Gorkhā, Nepal — E10 54
Gorki see Nižnij Novgorod, Russia — H21 8
Gorki, Russia — A11 32
Gorkiy Reservoir see Gor'kovskoe vodohranilišče, Russia — H20 8
Gor'kovskoe vodohranilišče (Gorkiy Reservoir), res., Russia — H20 8
Gorlice, Pol. — G17 16
Görlitz, Ger. — E10 16
Gorman, Tx., U.S. — B9 130
Gorna Orjahovica, Blg. — F12 26
Gornjak, Russia — D14 32
Gornji Vakuf, Bos. — F4 26
Gorno-Altajsk, Russia — D15 32
Gornozavodsk, Russia — B13 36
Gornye Ključi, Russia — B10 38
Gorodec, Russia — B12 10
Gorodenka see Horodenka, Ukr. — A12 26
Gorong, Pulau, i., Indon. — F9 44
Gorongosa, stm., Moz. — B12 70
Gorongosa, Serra da, mtn., Moz. — D5 68
Gorontalo, Indon. — E7 44
Górowo Iławeckie, Pol. — B16 16
Gor'kovo, Russia — F20 10
Görükle, Tur. — D11 28
Gorutuba, stm., Braz. — H4 88
Gorzno, Pol. — C15 16
Gorzów Śląski, Pol. — E14 16
Gorzów Wielkopolski (Landsberg), Pol. — D11 16
Goschen Strait, strt., Pap. N. Gui. — c5 79a
Gosen, Japan — B12 40
Gosford, Austl. — I8 76
Goshen, N.S., Can. — E15 110
Goshen, Ca., U.S. — G6 134
Goshen, In., U.S. — G4 112
Goshen, N.Y., U.S. — C11 114
Goshen, Ut., U.S. — D5 132
Goshogawara, Japan — F2 40
Goshute Lake, l., Nv., U.S. — C2 132
Goshute Valley, Nv., U.S. — C2 132
Goslar, Ger. — E6 16
Gosnells, Austl. — F3 74
Gospić, Cro. — F12 22
Gosport, Eng., U.K. — K11 12
Gossas, Sen. — G1 64
Gostivar, Mac. — B3 28
Gostyń, Pol. — E13 16
Gostynin, Pol. — D15 16
Göta, stm., Swe. — G5 8
Gotebo, Ok., U.S. — F10 128
Göteborg (Gothenburg), Swe. — H4 8
Gotemba, Japan — D11 40
Gotești, Mol. — C15 26
Gotha, Ger. — F6 16
Gothenburg see Göteborg, Swe. — H4 8
Gothenburg, Ne., U.S. — G12 126
Gotland, i., Swe. — H8 8
Gotland, state, Swe. — H8 8
Gotō-rettō, is., Japan — G1 40
Gotska Sandön, i., Swe. — G8 8
Göttingen, Ger. — E5 16
Goubangzi, China — D4 38

Name	Map Ref.	Page
Gouda, Neth.	B13	14
Goudge, Arg.	G3	92
Goudiri, Sen.	G2	64
Gough Island, i., St. Hel.	K5	60
Gough Lake, l., Ab., Can.	D18	138
Gouin, Réservoir, res., Qc., Can.	B1	110
Goulais, stm., On., Can.	B6	112
Goulburn, Austl.	J7	76
Goulburn Islands, is., Austl.	B6	74
Goulburn River National Park, p.o.i., Austl.	I7	76
Gould, Ar., U.S.	D7	122
Goulds, Fl., U.S.	K5	116
Goumbou, Mali	G3	64
Goundam, Mali	F4	64
Goundi, Chad	F3	62
Gourbeyre, Guad.	h5	105c
Gourdon, Fr.	E7	18
Gouré, Niger	G7	64
Gourma-Rharous, Mali	F4	64
Gournay-en-Bray, Fr.	E10	14
Gouro, Chad	D3	62
Gouverneur, N.Y., U.S.	D14	112
Govan, Sk., Can.	C9	124
Gove, Ks., U.S.	C8	128
Govena, mys, c., Russia	E22	34
Govenlock, Sk., Can.	E4	124
Governador Valadares, Braz.	J5	88
Govind Ballabh Pant Reservoir see Govind Ballabh Pant Sägar, res., India	F9	54
Govind Ballabh Pant Sägar, res., India	F9	54
Govind Reservoir see Govind Sägar, res., India	C6	54
Govind Sägar, res., India	C6	54
Gowanda, N.Y., U.S.	B7	114
Gower, Mo., U.S.	E3	120
Gowmal (Gumal), stm., Asia	B2	54
Gowmal Kalay, Afg.	B2	54
Gowrie, Ia., U.S.	B3	120
Goya, Arg.	D8	92
Goyaves, Îlets à, is., Guad.	h5	105c
Göyçay, Azer.	A6	56
Goz Beïda, Chad	E4	62
Gozdnica, Pol.	E11	16
Gozha Co, l., China	A5	46
Gozo see Ghawdex, i., Malta	H8	24
Graaff-Reinet, S. Afr.	H7	70
Grabo, C. Iv.	I3	64
Grabow, Ger.	C7	16
Grabów nad Prosną, Pol.	E13	16
Gračac, Cro.	F12	22
Gračanica, Bos.	E5	26
Grace, Id., U.S.	H15	136
Gracefield, Qc., Can.	B13	112
Graceville, Fl., U.S.	G13	122
Gracias a Dios, Cabo, c., N.A.	E6	102
Gracaús, Braz.	E7	84
Grado, Italy	E10	22
Grado, Spain	A4	20
Grad Sofija, state, Blg.	G10	26
Grady, Ar., U.S.	C7	122
Grady, N.M., U.S.	G5	128
Graettinger, Ia., U.S.	H4	118
Grafenau, Ger.	H9	16
Gräfenhainichen, Ger.	E8	16
Grafing bei München, Ger.	H7	16
Grafton, Austl.	G9	76
Grafton, Il., U.S.	F7	120
Grafton, N.D., U.S.	F16	124
Grafton, W.V., U.S.	E5	114
Grafton, Wi., U.S.	E2	112
Grafton, Cape, c., Austl.	A5	76
Graham, N.C., U.S.	H6	114
Graham, Mount, mtn., Az., U.S.	K7	132
Graham Island, i., B.C., Can.	E4	106
Graham Island, i., Nu., Can.	B7	141
Graham Lake, res., Me., U.S.	F8	110
Graham Land, reg., Ant.	B34	81
Graham Moore, Cape, c., Nu., Can.	A15	106
Grahamstad see Grahamstown, S. Afr.	H8	70
Grahamstown, S. Afr.	H8	70
Grain Coast, cst., Lib.	I3	64
Grainfield, Ks., U.S.	B8	128
Grajaú, Braz.	C2	88
Grajaú, stm., Braz.	B3	88
Grajewo, Pol.	C18	16
Gramada, Blg.	F9	26
Grambling, La., U.S.	E6	122
Gramilla, Arg.	C5	92
Grammichele, Italy	G8	24
Grampian Mountains, mts., Scot., U.K.	E9	12
Grampians National Park, p.o.i., Austl.	K3	76
Gramsh, Alb.	D14	24
Granada, Col.	F5	86
Granada, Nic.	G5	102
Granada, Spain	G7	20
Granada, co., Spain	G7	20
Granadella see La Granadella, Spain	C11	20
Granbury, Tx., U.S.	B10	130
Granbury, Lake, res., Tx., U.S.	B10	130
Granby, Qc., Can.	E4	110
Granby, Co., U.S.	A3	128
Granby, Mo., U.S.	H3	120
Granby, B.C., Can.	G12	138
Granby, Lake, res., Co., U.S.	A2	128
Gran Chaco, reg., S.A.	D5	90
Grand, stm., On., Can.	E9	112
Grand, stm., Mi., U.S.	E4	112
Grand, stm., Mi., U.S.	E3	112
Grand, stm., Oh., U.S.	C4	114
Grand, stm., S.D., U.S.	B12	126
Grand, East Fork, stm., U.S.	D3	120
Grand, Lac, l., Qc., Can.	A12	112
Grand, North Fork, stm., U.S.	B10	126
Grand, South Fork, stm., S.D., U.S.	B9	126
Grandas, Spain	A4	20
Gran Bahama, i., Bah.	B9	96
Grand Ballon, mtn., Fr.	G16	14
Grand Bank, Nf., Can.	j22	107a
Grand-Bassam, C. Iv.	H4	64
Grand Bay, Al., U.S.	G10	122
Grand Beach, Mb., Can.	D17	124
Grand Bend, On., Can.	E8	112
Grand-Bourg, Guad.	i6	105c
Grand Caille Point, c., St. Luc.	m6	105c
Grand Calumet, Île du, i., Qc., Can.	C13	112
Grand Canal see Da Yunhe, can., China	E8	42
Grand Canal, can., Ire.	H6	12
Grand Cane, La., U.S.	E5	122
Grand Canyon, Az., U.S.	G4	132
Grand Canyon, val., U.S.	G4	132
Grand Canyon National Park, p.o.i., Az., U.S.	G4	132
Grand Case, Guad.	A1	105a
Grand Cayman, i., Cay. Is.	C7	102
Grand Cess, Lib.	I3	64
Grand Chenier, La., U.S.	H6	122
Grand Coulee Dam, dam, Wa., U.S.	C7	136
Grand Cul de Sac, Guad.	B2	105a
Grande, stm., Arg.	H3	92
Grande, stm., Arg.	A5	92
Grande, stm., Bol.	C4	90
Grande, stm., Braz.	F4	88
Grande, stm., Braz.	C7	90
Grande, stm., S.A.	J3	90
Grande, stm., Ven.	C11	86
Grande, Arroyo, stm., Ur.	F9	92
Grande, Bahía, b., Arg.	J3	90
Grande, Boca, mth., Ven.	C11	86
Grande, Cerro, mtn., Mex.	F7	100
Grande, Cerro, mtn., Mex.	G2	130
Grande, Ilha, i., Braz.	L3	88
Grande, Ilha, i., Braz.	A11	92
Grande, Ponta, c., Braz.	I6	88
Grande, Rio see Rio Grande, stm., N.A.	H13	98
Grande, Serra, mts., Braz.	D5	88
Grande-Anse, Qc., Can.	C4	110
Grande Cache, Ab., Can.	C11	138
Grande Cayemite, i., Haiti	C11	102
Grande de Manacapuru, Lago, l., Braz.	I11	86
Grande de Matagalpa, stm., Nic.	F6	102
Grande de Santiago, stm., Mex.	E6	100
Grande do Gurupá, Ilha, i., Braz.	D7	84
Grande-Entrée, Qc., Can.	C15	110
Grande Prairie, Ab., Can.	A12	138
Grand Erg de Bilma, des., Niger	F7	64
Grand Erg Occidental, des., Alg.	C5	64
Grand Erg Oriental, des., Alg.	C6	64
Grande-Rivière, Qc., Can.	B12	110
Grande Rivière, La, stm., Qc., Can.	E15	106
Grande Ronde, stm., U.S.	E9	136
Grandes, Salinas, pl., Arg.	A4	92
Grandes, Salinas, pl., Arg.	D5	92
Grand-Étang, N.S., Can.	D15	110
Grande-Terre, i., Guad.	h6	105c
Grande Vigie, Pointe de la, c., Guad.	g6	105c
Grand Falls, N.B., Can.	C9	110
Grandfather Mountain, mtn., N.C., U.S.	H4	114
Grandfield, Ok., U.S.	G10	128
Grand Forks, B.C., Can.	G12	138
Grand Forks, N.D., U.S.	D1	118
Grand Haven, Mi., U.S.	E3	112
Grand Island, Ne., U.S.	G14	126
Grand Island, i., Mi., U.S.	B3	112
Grand Isle, La., U.S.	H9	122
Grand Junction, Co., U.S.	D8	132
Grand Junction, Ia., U.S.	B3	120
Grand Lake, l., N.A.	E9	110
Grand Lake, l., La., U.S.	H6	122
Grand Lake, l., La., U.S.	C6	122
Grand Lake, res., Oh., U.S.	D1	114
Grand Ledge, Mi., U.S.	B1	114
Grand Manan, N.B., Can.	F10	110
Grand Manan Island, i., N.B., Can.	F10	110
Grand Marais, Mi., U.S.	B4	112
Grand Meadow, Mn., U.S.	H6	118
Grand-Mère, Qc., Can.	D4	110
Grand Morin, stm., Fr.	F12	14
Grand Portage, Mn., U.S.	D9	118
Grand Portage National Monument, p.o.i., Mn., U.S.	C9	118
Grand Prairie, Tx., U.S.	B11	130
Grand Rapids, Mb., Can.	A14	124
Grand Rapids, Mi., U.S.	F4	112
Grand Rapids, Mn., U.S.	D5	118
Grand Rhône, stm., Fr.	F10	18
Grand Saline, Tx., U.S.	E3	122
Grand Staircase–Escalante National Monument, p.o.i., Ut., U.S.	F5	132
Grand Teton, mtn., Wy., U.S.	G16	136
Grand Teton National Park, p.o.i., Wy., U.S.	F16	136
Grand Tower, Il., U.S.	G8	120
Grand Traverse Bay, b., Mi., U.S.	C4	112
Grand Turk, T./C. Is.	B12	102
Grandview, Mb., Can.	C13	124
Grandview, Mo., U.S.	F3	120
Grandview, Tx., U.S.	B10	130
Grandview, Wa., U.S.	D6	136
Grand View, Wi., U.S.	E7	118
Grand Wash Cliffs, clf, Az., U.S.	H3	132
Grañén, Spain	C10	20
Graneros, Chile	G2	92
Granger, Wa., U.S.	D6	136
Granger, Wy., U.S.	B6	132
Granger Draw, stm., Tx., U.S.	D7	130
Granger Lake, res., Tx., U.S.	D10	130
Granges see Grenchen, Switz.	C4	22
Grangeville, Id., U.S.	E10	136
Granite City, Il., U.S.	F7	120
Granite Falls, Mn., U.S.	G3	118
Granite Falls, N.C., U.S.	I4	114
Granite Falls, Wa., U.S.	B5	136
Granite Pass, p., Wy., U.S.	C5	126
Granite Peak, Austl.	E4	74
Granite Peak, mtn., Mt., U.S.	E14	136
Granite Peak, mtn., Nv., U.S.	C6	134
Granite Peak, mtn., Mt., U.S.	E17	136
Graniteville, S.C., U.S.	C4	116
Granitola, Capo, c., Italy	G6	24
Granja, Braz.	B5	88
Gran Laguna Salada, l., Arg.	H3	90
Gränna, Swe.	G6	8
Granollers, Spain	C13	20
Gran Paradiso, mtn., Italy	E4	22
Gran Paradiso, Parco Nazionale del, p.o.i., Italy	E4	22
Gran Rio, stm., Sur.	C6	84
Gran Sasso d'Italia, mtn., Italy	H10	22
Gransee, Ger.	C9	16
Grant, Fl., U.S.	I5	116
Grant, Mi., U.S.	E4	112
Grant City, Mo., U.S.	D3	120
Grantham, Eng., U.K.	I12	12
Grantley Adams International Airport, Barb.	n9	105d
Grant Park, Il., U.S.	C10	120
Grant Point, c., Nu., Can.	B11	106
Grants, N.M., U.S.	H9	132
Grantsburg, Wi., U.S.	F6	118
Grants Pass, Or., U.S.	A2	134
Grantsville, W.V., U.S.	F4	114
Granum, Ab., Can.	G17	138
Granville, Fr.	F7	14
Granville, Il., U.S.	C9	118
Granville, N.D., U.S.	F13	124
Granville, N.Y., U.S.	G3	110
Granville, W.V., U.S.	E5	114
Granville Lake, l., Mb., Can.	D10	106
Grão Mogol, Braz.	I4	88
Grapeland, Tx., U.S.	F3	122
Grapevine Lake, res., Tx., U.S.	B10	130
Grapevine Peak, mtn., Nv., U.S.	G8	134
Gras, Lac de, l., N.T., Can.	C8	106
Gräsö, i., Swe.	F8	8
Grass, stm., N.Y., U.S.	D15	112
Grass Creek, Wy., U.S.	D4	126
Grasse, Fr.	F12	18
Grassflat, Pa., U.S.	D7	114
Grasslands National Park, p.o.i., Sk., Can.	E6	124
Grass Valley, Ca., U.S.	D4	134
Grass Valley, Or., U.S.	E6	136
Grassy, Austl.	n12	77a
Grassy Plains, B.C., Can.	C4	138
Graulhet, Fr.	F7	18
Gravelbourg, Sk., Can.	E7	124
Gravelines, Fr.	D11	14
Gravelotte, S. Afr.	C10	70
Gravenhage, 's- see 's-Gravenhage, Neth.	B12	14
Gravenhurst, On., Can.	D10	112
Gravesend, Eng., U.K.	J13	12
Gravette, Ar., U.S.	H3	120
Gravina in Puglia, Italy	D10	24
Gray, Fr.	G14	14
Gray, Ga., U.S.	D2	116
Grayback Mountain, mtn., Or., U.S.	A2	134
Grayling, Mi., U.S.	D5	112
Grays, Eng., U.K.	J13	12
Grays Harbor, b., Wa., U.S.	D2	136
Grays Lake, sw., Id., U.S.	G15	136
Grayson, Sk., Can.	D11	124
Grayson, Al., U.S.	C11	122
Grayson, La., U.S.	E6	122
Grays Peak, mtn., Co., U.S.	B3	128
Graysville, Tn., U.S.	B13	122
Grayville, Il., U.S.	F9	120
Graz, Aus.	C12	22
Grdelica, Yugo.	G9	26
Great Artesian Basin, bas., Austl.	E3	76
Great Australian Bight, b., Austl.	F5	74
Great Barrier Island, i., N.Z.	C6	80
Great Barrier Reef, rf., Austl.	C9	74
Great Basin, bas., U.S.	C4	108
Great Basin National Park, p.o.i., Nv., U.S.	E2	132
Great Bear, stm., N.T., Can.	B6	106
Great Bear Lake, l., N.T., Can.	B6	106
Great Beaver Lake, l., B.C., Can.	B7	138
Great Belt see Storebælt, strt., Den.	I4	8
Great Bend, Ks., U.S.	C10	128
Great Bitter Lake see Murrat el-Kubra, Buheirat, l., Egypt	H3	58
Great Britain see United Kingdom, ctry., Eur.	D8	6
Great Camanoe, i., Br. Vir. Is.	e8	104b
Great Central, B.C., Can.	G6	138
Great Channel, strt., Asia	G7	46
Great Dismal Swamp, sw., U.S.	H9	114
Great Divide Basin, bas., Wy., U.S.	F4	126
Great Dividing Range, mts., Austl.	C8	74
Great Driffield, Eng., U.K.	G12	12
Greater Antilles, is., N.A.	H15	94
Greater Khingan Range see Da Hinggan Ling, mts., China	B9	36
Greater Sunda Islands, is., Asia	F4	44
Great Exuma, i., Bah.	C9	96
Great Falls, Mb., Can.	D18	124
Great Falls, Mt., U.S.	C15	136
Great Falls, S.C., U.S.	B4	116
Great Himalayan National Park, p.o.i., India	C6	54
Great Inagua, i., Bah.	B11	102
Great Indian Desert (Thar Desert), des., Asia	D3	54
Great Karroo (Groot Karroo), plat., S. Afr.	H6	70
Great La Cloche Island, i., On., Can.	B8	112
Great Lake, res., Austl.	n13	77a
Great Malvern, Eng., U.K.	I10	12
Great Miami, stm., U.S.	E13	120
Great Namaqualand (Groot Namaland), hist. reg., Nmb.	D3	70
Great Nicobar, i., India	G7	46
Great Ouse, stm., Eng., U.K.	I13	12
Great Palm Island, i., Austl.	B6	76
Great Pee Dee, stm., S.C., U.S.	C6	116
Great Plain of the Koukdjuak, pl., Nu., Can.	B16	106
Great Plains, pl., N.A.	C4	108
Great Point, c., Ma., U.S.	C15	114
Great Ruaha, stm., Tan.	F7	66
Great Sacandaga Lake, res., N.Y., U.S.	G2	110
Great Sale Cay, i., Bah.	I7	116
Great Salt Lake, l., Ut., U.S.	B4	132
Great Salt Lake Desert, des., Ut., U.S.	C3	132
Great Salt Plains Lake, res., Ok., U.S.	E10	128
Great Sand Dunes National Monument, p.o.i., Co., U.S.	D3	128
Great Sand hills, hills, Sk., Can.	D4	124
Great Sandy Desert, des., Austl.	D4	74
Great Sandy National Park, p.o.i., Austl.	E9	76
Great Scarcies, stm., Afr.	H2	64
Great Sea Reef, rf., Fiji	p19	79e
Great Slave Lake, l., N.T., Can.	C8	106
Great Smoky Mountains, mts., U.S.	A2	116
Great Smoky Mountains National Park, p.o.i., U.S.	A2	116
Great Tenasserim, stm., Mya.	F4	48
Great Thatch Island, i., Br. Vir. Is.	e7	104b
Great Tobago, i., Br. Vir. Is.	e7	104b
Great Victoria Desert, des., Austl.	E5	74
Great Wall see Chang Cheng, misc. cult., China	D6	36
Great Yarmouth, Eng., U.K.	I14	12
Gréboun, mtn., Niger	F6	64
Grecco, Ur.	F9	92
Gredos, Sierra de, mts., Spain	D5	20
Greece, N.Y., U.S.	E12	112
Greece, ctry., Eur.	H13	6
Greeley, Co., U.S.	G2	126
Greeley, Ne., U.S.	F14	126
Greeleyville, S.C., U.S.	C6	116
Greely Fiord, b., Nu., Can.	A8	141
Green, stm., Wa., U.S.	C4	136
Green, stm., U.S.	E7	132
Green, stm., Ky., U.S.	G10	120
Green, stm., N.Y., U.S.	G17	136
Green, stm., N.D., U.S.	C5	136
Green Bay, Wi., U.S.	D1	112
Green Bay, b., U.S.	D2	112
Green Brier, Ar., U.S.	B6	122
Green Brier, Tn., U.S.	H11	120
Greenbrier, stm., W.V., U.S.	F5	114
Greenburg, La., U.S.	G8	122
Greenbush, Mn., U.S.	C2	118
Greencastle, In., U.S.	E10	120
Greencastle, Pa., U.S.	E8	114
Green Cove Springs, Fl., U.S.	G4	116
Gris-Nez, Cap, c., Fr.	D10	14
Greendale, In., U.S.	E13	120
Greene, Ia., U.S.	B5	120
Greeneville, Tn., U.S.	H3	114
Greenfield, Ca., U.S.	B13	114
Greenfield, Il., U.S.	E7	120
Greenfield, Ia., U.S.	C3	120
Greenfield, Ma., U.S.	H4	110
Greenfield, Mo., U.S.	G4	120
Greenfield, Oh., U.S.	E2	114
Greenfield, Ok., U.S.	F10	128
Green Forest, Ar., U.S.	H4	120
Green Island Bay, b., Phil.	E2	52
Green Islands, is., Pap. N. Gui.	a3	79a
Gui.	D6	72
Green Lake, Wi., U.S.	H10	118
Green Lake, l., Sk., Can.	E9	138
Green Lake, l., B.C., Can.	E9	138
Green Lake, l., Wi., U.S.	H9	118
Greenland, Ar., U.S.	I3	120
Greenland, dep., N.A.	B19	94
Greenland Basin, unds.	A14	144
Greenland Sea	B21	94
Greenleaf, Ks., U.S.	B11	128
Green Lookout Mountain, mtn., Wa., U.S.	D4	136
Green Mountains, mts., N.A.	G4	110
Greenock, Scot., U.K.	F8	12
Greenore Point, c., Ire.	I6	12
Greenport, N.Y., U.S.	C13	114
Green River, Pap. N. Gui.	a3	79a
Green River, Ut., U.S.	D7	132
Green River, Wy., U.S.	B7	132
Green River Lake, res., Ky., U.S.	G12	120
Greensboro, Fl., U.S.	G14	122
Greensboro, Ga., U.S.	C2	116
Greensboro, N.C., U.S.	H6	114
Greensburg, In., U.S.	E12	120
Greensburg, Ks., U.S.	D9	128
Greensburg, Pa., U.S.	D6	114
Green Springs, Oh., U.S.	C2	114
Green Swamp, sw., N.C., U.S.	B7	116
Greentown, In., U.S.	H4	112
Greenup, Il., U.S.	E9	120
Greenup, Ky., U.S.	F3	114
Greenvale, Austl.	B5	76
Green Valley, Az., U.S.	L6	132
Greenville, Lib.	H3	64
Greenville, Al., U.S.	F12	122
Greenville, Ga., U.S.	D14	122
Greenville, Il., U.S.	E8	120
Greenville, Ky., U.S.	G10	120
Greenville, Me., U.S.	E7	110
Greenville, Mi., U.S.	E4	112
Greenville, Ms., U.S.	D7	122
Greenville, Mo., U.S.	G7	120
Greenville, N.C., U.S.	A8	116
Greenville, Oh., U.S.	D1	114
Greenville, Pa., U.S.	C5	114
Greenville, S.C., U.S.	B3	116
Greenville, Tx., U.S.	D2	122
Greenwater Lake, l., On., Can.	C8	118
Greenwich, Ct., U.S.	C12	114
Greenwich, Oh., U.S.	C3	114
Greenwood, Ar., U.S.	B4	122
Greenwood, In., U.S.	E11	120
Greenwood, Ms., U.S.	D8	122
Greenwood, S.C., U.S.	B3	116
Greenwood, Wi., U.S.	G8	118
Greenwood, Lake, res., S.C., U.S.	B4	116
Greers Ferry Lake, res., Ar., U.S.	B6	122
Greeson, Lake, res., Ar., U.S.	C5	122
Gregório, stm., Braz.	E3	84
Gregory, Mi., U.S.	B1	114
Gregory, S.D., U.S.	D13	126
Gregory, Tx., U.S.	G10	130
Gregory, stm., Austl.	C7	74
Gregory, Lake, l., Austl.	E3	74
Gregory, Lake, l., Austl.	D5	74
Gregory, Lake, l., Austl.	H2	74
Gregory Range, mts., Austl.	B4	76
Greifswald, Ger.	B9	16
Greifswalder Bodden, b., Ger.	B9	16
Greiz, Ger.	F8	16
Gremiha, Russia	B18	8
Grenå, Den.	H4	8
Grenada, Ms., U.S.	D9	122
Grenada, ctry., N.A.	q11	105e
Grenada Lake, res., Ms., U.S.	D9	122
Grenchen, Switz.	C4	22
Grenen, c., Den.	H4	8
Grenfell, Austl.	I7	76
Grenfell, Sk., Can.	D11	124
Grenoble, Fr.	D11	18
Grenora, N.D., U.S.	F10	124
Grenville, Gren.	q10	105e
Gresham, Or., U.S.	E4	136
Gresik, Indon.	G8	50
Gresik, Indon.	E3	50
Gressåmoen Nasjonalpark, p.o.i., Nor.	D5	8
Gretna, Mb., Can.	E16	124
Gretna, La., U.S.	H8	122
Gretna, Va., U.S.	H6	114
Gretna Green, Scot., U.K.	F9	12
Greven, Ger.	D3	16
Grevená, Grc.	C4	28
Grevenbroich, Ger.	E2	16
Grevesmühlen, Ger.	C7	16
Greybull, Wy., U.S.	C4	126
Grey Eagle, Mn., U.S.	F4	118
Grey Islands, is., Nf., Can.	i22	107a
Greylock, Mount, mtn., Ma., U.S.	B12	114
Greymouth, N.Z.	F4	80
Grey Range, mts., Austl.	F4	76
Greytown, S. Afr.	F10	70
Gribbell Island, i., B.C., Can.	C1	138
Gribingui, stm., C.A.R.	C3	66
Gridley, Ca., U.S.	D4	134
Gridley, Il., U.S.	D9	120
Griesheim, Ger.	G4	16
Griffin, Ga., U.S.	C1	116
Griffin, Lake, l., Fl., U.S.	H4	116
Griffith, Austl.	J6	76
Griggsville, Il., U.S.	E7	120
Grignols, Fr.	E5	18
Grigoriopol, Mol.	B16	26
Grijalva (Culco), stm., N.A.	G12	100
Grim, Cape, c., Austl.	n12	77a
Grimari, C.A.R.	C4	66
Grimaud, Fr.	F12	18
Grimma, Ger.	E8	16
Grimmen, Ger.	B9	16
Grimsby, On., Can.	E10	112
Grimsby, Eng., U.K.	H12	12
Grimsel Pass, p., Switz.	D5	22
Grimsey, i., Ice.	j30	8a
Grimshaw, Ab., Can.	D7	106
Grimstad, Nor.	G3	8
Grímsvötn, vol., Ice.	k31	8a
Grindelwald, Switz.	D5	22
Grinnell, Ia., U.S.	C5	120
Grinnell Peninsula, pen., Nu., Can.	B7	141
Grintavec, mtn., Slvn.	D11	22
Griqualand East, hist. reg., S. Afr.	G9	70
Griqualand West, hist. reg., S. Afr.	F6	70
Grise Fiord, Nu., Can.	B9	141
Griswold, Mb., Can.	E13	124
Griswold, Ia., U.S.	C2	120
Grizzly Bear Mountain, mtn., N.T., Can.	B6	106
Grizzly Mountain, mtn., Id., U.S.	C10	136
Grjadcy, Russia	D14	10
Grjazovec, Russia	G18	8
Groais, Braz.	B5	88
Groblersdal, S. Afr.	D9	70
Grodekov, Pol.	F13	16
Grodzisk Mazowiecki, Pol.	D16	16
Groen, stm., S. Afr.	G6	70
Groesbeck, Tx., U.S.	F2	122
Grofa, hora, mtn., Ukr.	A10	26
Groix, Fr.	G5	14
Groix, Île de, i., Fr.	G5	14
Grójec, Pol.	E16	16
Grombalia, Tun.	H4	24
Gronau, Ger.	D3	16
Grong, Nor.	D5	8
Groningen, Neth.	A15	14
Groningen, Sur.	B6	84
Groom, Tx., U.S.	F7	128
Groot, stm., S. Afr.	H7	70
Groot-Berg, stm., S. Afr.	H4	70
Groot-Brakrivier, S. Afr.	H7	70
Grootdraaidam, res., S. Afr.	E9	70
Groote Eylandt, i., Austl.	B7	74
Grootfontein, Nmb.	D2	68
Grootgeluk, S. Afr.	C8	70
Groot Karasberge, mts., Nmb.	E4	70
Groot Karroo see Great Karroo, plat., S. Afr.	H7	70
Groot-Kei, stm., S. Afr.	H9	70
Groot Laagte, stm., Afr.	B5	70
Groot Nameland see Great Namaqualand, hist. reg., Nmb.	D3	70
Groot-Swartberge, mts., S. Afr.	H5	70
Groot-Vis, stm., S. Afr.	H8	70
Grootvloer, pl., S. Afr.	F5	70
Gros Islet, St. Luc.	l7	105c
Gros-Morne, Mart.	k6	105c
Gros Morne, mtn., Nf., Can.	j22	107a
Gros Piton, vol., St. Luc.	m6	105c
Grossenhain, Ger.	E9	16
Grosse Pointe, Mi., U.S.	B3	114
Grosse Pointe, c., Guad.	h6	105c
Grosser Beerberg, mtn., Ger.	F6	16
Grosseto, Italy	H7	22
Gross-Gerau, Ger.	G4	16
Grossglockner, mtn., Aus.	C9	22
Grossos, Braz.	C7	88
Grossvenediger, mtn., Aus.	C9	22
Groton, N.Y., U.S.	F13	112
Groton, S.D., U.S.	B14	126
Grottaglie, Italy	D11	24
Grottammare, Italy	G11	22
Grottoes, Va., U.S.	F7	114
Grouard Mission, Ab., Can.	D7	106
Groundhog, stm., On., Can.	F14	106
Grove City, Mn., U.S.	F4	118
Grove City, Oh., U.S.	E2	114
Grove City, Pa., U.S.	C5	114
Grove Hill, Al., U.S.	F11	122
Grove Mountains, mts., Ant.	C12	81
Grover City, Ca., U.S.	H5	134
Groves, Tx., U.S.	H5	122
Groveton, N.H., U.S.	F5	110
Groveton, Tx., U.S.	F3	122
Grovetown, Ga., U.S.	C3	116
Growa Point, c., Lib.	I3	64
Growler Peak, mtn., Az., U.S.	K3	132
Groznyj, Russia	F7	32
Grubišno Polje, Cro.	E14	22
Grudziądz, Pol.	C14	16
Grulla, Tx., U.S.	H9	130
Grumo Appula, Italy	D10	24
Grundy, Va., U.S.	G3	114
Grundy Center, Ia., U.S.	B5	120
Grušino, Russia	G21	8
Gruver, Tx., U.S.	E7	128
Gruzovka, Russia	E10	34
Gryfice, Pol.	C11	16
Gryfino, Pol.	C10	16
Grytviken, S. Geor.	J9	90
Guacanayabo, Golfo de, b., Cuba	B9	102
Guacara, Ven.	B7	86
Guacarí, Col.	F3	86
Gu Achi, Az., U.S.	K4	132
Guachiria, stm., Col.	E6	86
Guachochi, Mex.	B5	100
Guadajoz, stm., Spain	G6	20
Guadalajara, Mex.	E7	100
Guadalajara, Spain	D8	20
Guadalajara, co., Spain	D8	20
Guadalcanal, state, Sol. Is.	f8	79b
Guadalcanal, i., Sol. Is.	e9	79b
Guadalcázar, Mex.	D8	100
Guadalhorce, stm., Spain	H6	20
Guadalimar, stm., Spain	F7	20
Guadalmena, stm., Spain	F8	20
Guadalope, stm., Spain	D10	20
Guadalquivir, stm., Spain	H5	20
Guadalquivir, Marismas del, sw., Spain	H4	20
Guadalupe, Mex.	D7	100
Guadalupe, Mex.	H8	130
Guadalupe, Ca., U.S.	H5	134
Guadalupe, stm., Ca., U.S.	I5	134
Guadalupe, Isla, i., Mex.	D2	100
Guadalupe, stm., Tx., U.S.	E9	130
Guadalupe Bravos, Mex.	C1	130
Guadalupe Mountains, mts., U.S.	B3	130
Guadalupe Mountains National Park, p.o.i., Tx., U.S.	C3	130
Guadalupe Peak, mtn., Tx., U.S.	C3	130
Guadalupe Victoria, Mex.	C6	100
Guadalupe Victoria, Mex.	C6	100
Guadarrama, Puerto de, p., Spain	D6	20
Guadarrama, Sierra de, mts., Spain	D7	20
Guadeloupe, dep., N.A.	h15	96a
Guadeloupe Passage, strt., N.A.	g5	105c
Guadiana, Eur.	G3	20
Guadiana Menor, stm., Spain	G7	20
Guadiato, stm., Spain	G5	20
Guadiela, stm., Spain	D8	20
Guadix, Spain	G7	20
Guafo, Isla, i., Chile	H1	90
Guaíba, Braz.	E12	92
Guaíba, est., Braz.	E12	92
Guaimaca, Hond.	E4	102
Guainía, state, Col.	F8	86
Guainía, stm., S.A.	F8	86
Guaiquinima, Cerro, mtn., Ven.	E10	86
Guaíra, Braz.	K1	90
Guaíra, state, Para.	B9	92
Guaíra, Salto del (Sete Quedas, Salto do), wtfl, S.A.	B10	92
Guaítara, stm., Col.	G3	86
Guaitecas, Islas, is., Chile	H2	90
Guajaba, Cayo, i., Cuba	B9	102
Guajará-Açu, Braz.	A1	88
Guajará-Mirim, Braz.	F4	84
Guaje, Laguna del, l., Mex.	B7	100
Gualaca, Pan.	H6	102
Gualaceo, Ec.	I2	86
Gualala, Ca., U.S.	E2	134
Gualdo Tadino, Italy	G9	22
Gualeguay, Arg.	F8	92
Gualeguay, stm., Arg.	F8	92
Gualeguaychú, Arg.	F8	92
Gualicho, Salina del, pl., Arg.	H4	90
Guam, dep., Oc.	j10	78c
Guamá, stm., Braz.	A1	88
Guamal, Col.	F5	86
Guamal, Col.	C4	86
Guamini, Arg.	H6	92
Guam International Airport, Guam	i10	78c
Guamote, Ec.	H2	86
Guamúchil, Mex.	C4	100
Guamúes, stm., Col.	G3	86
Gua Musang, Malay.	J5	48
Guanacaste, Cordillera de, mts., C.R.	G5	102
Guanacevi, Mex.	C6	100
Guanahacabibes, Golfo de, b., Cuba	A5	102
Guana Island, i., Br. Vir. Is.	e8	104b
Guanaja, Hond.	D5	102
Guanaja, Isla de, i., Hond.	D5	102
Guanajuato, Mex.	E8	100
Guanajuato, state, Mex.	E8	100
Guanambi, Braz.	H4	88
Guanare, Ven.	C7	86
Guanare, stm., Ven.	C7	86
Guanarito, Ven.	C7	86
Guandacol, Arg.	D3	92
Guandu, China	I5	42
Guane, Cuba	A5	102
Guang'an, China	F1	42
Guangchang, China	H7	42
Guangde, China	F8	42
Guangdong, state, China	J5	42
Guangfeng, China	H8	42
Guanghua see Laohekou, China	E4	42
Guangling, China	B6	42
Guangming Ding, mtn., China	F7	42
Guangnan, China	F5	36
Guangning, China	J5	42
Guangrao, China	C8	42
Guangshan, China	E6	42
Guangshui, China	F5	42
Guangxi, state, China	J3	42
Guangxi Zhuangzu Zizhiqu see Guangxi, state, China	G6	36
Guangyuan, China	E1	42
Guangze, China	H7	42
Guangzhou (Canton), China	J5	42
Guanhães, Braz.	J4	88
Guánica, P.R.	C2	104a
Guanipa, stm., Ven.	C10	86
Guanta, Ven.	B9	86
Guantánamo, Cuba	B10	102
Guantao, China	C6	42
Guanting Shuiku, res., China	A6	42
Guanxian, China	E5	36
Guanxian, China	D8	42
Guapi, Col.	F3	86
Guápiles, C.R.	G6	102
Guaporé, Braz.	D11	92
Guaporé (Iténez), stm., S.A.	F5	84
Guará, stm., Braz.	G3	88
Guarabira, Braz.	D8	88
Guaraciaba do Norte, Braz.	C5	88
Guaraciaba, Braz.	I4	88
Guaranda, Ec.	H2	86
Guarapari, Braz.	K5	88
Guarapava, Braz.	B12	92
Guarapuava, Braz.	B12	92
Guararapes, Braz.	D6	90
Guaratinga, Braz.	I6	88
Guaratinguetá, Braz.	L3	88
Guaratuba, Braz.	B13	92
Guarda, Port.	D3	20
Guarda, state, Port.	D3	20
Guardafui, Cape see Gwardafuy, Gees, c., Som.	B10	66
Guarda Escolta, Braz.	D6	92
Guardiagrele, Italy	H11	22
Guardia Mitre, Arg.	H4	90
Guardo, Spain	B6	20
Guareña, Spain	F4	20
Guarenas, Ven.	B8	86
Guárico, state, Ven.	C8	86
Guárico, stm., Ven.	C8	86
Guárico, Embalse del, l., Ven.	C8	86
Guasare, stm., Ven.	B5	86
Guasave, Mex.	C4	100
Guasdualito, Ven.	D6	86
Guaspati, Ven.	D11	86
Guastalla, Italy	F7	22
Guatemala, Guat.	E2	102
Guatemala, ctry., N.A.	H29	142
Guatemala Basin, unds.	H29	142
Guatimozin, Arg.	F6	92
Guatopo, Parque Nacional, p.o.i., Ven.	B8	86
Guatuaro Point, c., Trin.	s13	105f
Guaviare, state, Col.	G6	86
Guaviare, stm., Col.	F8	86
Guaxupé, Braz.	K2	88
Guayabal, Cuba	B9	102
Guayabal, Mex.	D7	100
Guayama, P.R.	C3	104a
Guayana see Guyana, ctry., S.A.	C6	84
Guayana, Macizo de (Guiana Highlands), plat., S.A.	E10	86
Guayaneco, Archipiélago, is., Chile	I1	90
Guayanilla, P.R.	C2	104a
Guayapa, stm., Hond.	E4	102
Guayape, stm., Hond.	E5	102
Guayaquil, Ec.	I1	86
Guayaquil, Golfo de, b., S.A.	D1	84
Guayaramerín, Bol.	B3	90
Guayas, state, Ec.	H1	86
Guayas, stm., Ec.	I1	86
Guaymallén, Arg.	F3	92
Guaymas, Mex.	B3	100
Guaynabo, P.R.	B3	104a
Guazapares, Mex.	B4	100
Guazárachi, Mex.	B5	100
Guba, D.R.C.	G5	66
Gûbâ, Madîq (Jubal, Strait of), strt., Egypt	K4	58
Gubakha, Russia	C9	32
Gubat, Phil.	D5	52
Gúbbio, Italy	G9	22
Gubin, Pol.	E10	16
Gucheng, China	E4	42
Gūdalūr, India	F3	53
Gudar, Sierra de, mts., Spain	D10	20
Gudata, Geor.	F6	32
Gudermes, Russia	F7	32
Gudivāda, India	C5	53

Name	Map Ref.	Page
Gudiyāttam, India	E4	53
Güdül, Tur.	C15	28
Gūdūr, India	D4	53
Guebwiller, Fr.	G16	14
Güejar, stm., Col.	F5	86
Guékédou, Gui.	H2	64
Guélengdeng, Chad	E3	62
Guelma, Alg.	B6	64
Guelmime, Mor.	D2	64
Guelph, On., Can.	E9	112
Guérande, Fr.	G6	14
Guercif, Mor.	C4	64
Guerdjoumane, Djebel, mtn., Alg.	H13	20
Güere, stm., Ven.	C9	86
Guéréda, Chad	E4	62
Guéret, Fr.	C7	18
Guerla Mandata Shan, mtn., China	C8	54
Guernesey see Guernsey, dep., Eur.	L10	12
Guerneville, Ca., U.S.	E3	134
Guernica see Gernika, Spain	A8	20
Guernica y Luno see Gernika, Spain	A8	20
Guernsey, dep., Eur.	E6	14
Guernsey, i., Guern.	E6	14
Guerrero, Mex.	A5	100
Guerrero, Mex.	F7	130
Guerrero, state, Mex.	G8	100
Guerrero Negro, Mex.	B1	100
Gueydan, La., U.S.	G6	122
Guga, Russia	F16	34
Gugē, mtn., Eth.	F7	62
Guguan, i., N. Mar. Is.	B5	72
Gui, stm., China	I4	42
Guiana Basin, unds.	G9	144
Guiana Highlands (Guayana, Macizo de), mts., S.A.	E10	86
Güicán, Col.	D5	86
Guichi, China	F7	42
Guide, China	D5	36
Guidimouni, Niger	G6	64
Guiding, China	H2	42
Guier, Lac de, l., Sen.	F1	64
Guijuelo, Spain	D5	20
Guilarte, Monte, mtn., P.R.	B2	104a
Guildford, Eng., U.K.	J12	12
Guildhall, Vt., U.S.	F5	110
Guilford, Me., U.S.	E7	110
Guilin, China	I4	42
Guillaume-Delisle, Lac, l., Qc., Can.	D15	106
Guillestre, Fr.	E12	18
Guimarães, Braz.	B3	88
Guimaras Island, i., Phil.	E4	52
Guimba, Phil.	C3	52
Guin, Al., U.S.	D11	122
Guinan, China	D5	36
Guindulman, Phil.	F5	52
Guinea, ctry., Afr.	G2	64
Guinea, Gulf of, b., Afr.	I6	64
Guinea Basin, unds.	H13	144
Guinea-Bissau, ctry., Afr.	G1	64
Güines, Cuba	A7	102
Guingamp, Fr.	F5	14
Güinope, Hond.	F4	102
Guiping, China	J4	42
Guipúzcoa see Gipuzkoako, co., Spain	A8	20
Guiratinga, Braz.	G7	84
Güiria, Ven.	B10	86
Guitry, C. Iv.	H3	64
Guiuan, Phil.	E5	52
Guixian, China	J3	42
Guiyang, China	I5	42
Guiyang, China	H2	42
Güiza, stm., Col.	G2	86
Guizhou, state, China	F6	36
Gujarāt, state, India	G3	54
Gūjar Khān, Pak.	B4	54
Gujrānwāla, Pak.	B4	54
Gujrāt, Pak.	B4	54
Gukou, China	H8	42
Gulargambone, Austl.	H7	76
Gulbarga, India	C3	53
Gulbene, Lat.	C9	10
Güldüzü, Tur.	B8	58
Guledagudda, India	C2	53
Gülek Boğazı, p., Tur.	A5	58
Gulf Islands National Seashore, p.o.i., U.S.	G10	122
Gulfport, Ms., U.S.	G9	122
Gulf Shores, Al., U.S.	G11	122
Gulgong, Austl.	I7	76
Gulian, China	F13	34
Gulistan, Uzb.	F11	32
Gulkana, Ak., U.S.	D10	140
Gull, stm., On., Can.	B9	118
Gullfoss, wtfl, Ice.	k29	8a
Gull Lake, Sk., Can.	D5	124
Gull Lake, l., Ab., Can.	D17	138
Gull Lake, l., Mn., U.S.	E4	118
Güllük, Tur.	F10	28
Güllük Körfezi, b., Tur.	F10	28
Gülpınar, Tur.	D9	28
Gulu, Ug.	D6	66
Guluogongba, China	A10	54
Gumaca, Phil.	D4	52
Gumal (Gowmal), stm., Asia	B2	54
Gumbalie, Austl.	G5	76
Gumdag, Turkmen.	B7	56
Gumel, Nig.	G6	64
Gumla, India	G10	54
Gumma, state, Japan	C11	40
Gummersbach, Ger.	E3	16
Gümüşhane, Tur.	A4	56
Gümüşsü, Tur.	E12	28
Guna, India	F6	54
Gundagai, Austl.	J7	76
Gundji, D.R.C.	D4	66
Gundlupet, India	F3	53
Gündoğdu, Tur.	C9	28
Güney, Tur.	E12	28
Gungu, D.R.C.	F3	66
Gunmi, Nig.	G6	64
Gunnar, Sk., Can.	D9	106
Gunnarn, Swe.	D7	8
Gunnbjørn Fjeld, mtn., Grnld.	D19	141
Gunnedah, Austl.	H7	76
Gunnison, Ut., U.S.	D5	132
Gunnison, stm., Co., U.S.	E8	132
Gunong Mulu National Park, p.o.i., Malay.	A9	50
Gun Point, c., Gren.	p11	105e
Gunpowder Creek, stm., Austl.	B2	76
Gunsan see Kunsan, Kor., S.	F7	38
Guntakal, India	D3	53
Guntersville, Al., U.S.	C12	122
Guntersville Dam, dam, Al., U.S.	C12	122
Guntersville Lake, res., Al., U.S.	C12	122
Guntūr, India	C5	53
Gunungkencana, Indon.	G4	50
Gunungsahilan, Indon.	C2	50
Gunungsitoli, Indon.	L3	48
Gunupur, India	B6	53
Günzburg, Ger.	H6	16
Gunzenhausen, Ger.	G6	16
Guo, stm., China	E7	42
Guoyang, China	E7	42
Guoyangzhen, China	B5	42
Gupis, Pak.	B11	56
Gurabo, P.R.	B4	104a
Gura Humorului, Rom.	B12	26
Gurais, India	A5	54
Gurdāspur, India	B5	54
Gurdon, Ar., U.S.	D5	122
Güre, Tur.	E12	28
Gurevsk, Russia	D15	32
Gurgueia, stm., Braz.	D4	88
Gurha, India	F3	54
Guri, Embalse de, res., Ven.	D10	86
Gurskoe, Russia	F16	34
Gurskøya, i., Nor.	E1	8
Gürsu, Tur.	C12	28
Gurupá, Braz.	D7	84
Gurupi, Braz.	F1	88
Gurupi, stm., Braz.	D8	84
Guru Sikhar, mtn., India	F4	54
Gurvan Sayhan uul, mts., Mong.	C5	36
Gusau, Nig.	G6	64
Gusev, Russia	F5	10
Gušgy, Turkmen.	B9	56
Gushan, China	B10	42
Gushi, China	E6	42
Gus'-Hrustal'nyj, Russia	I19	8
Gusino, Russia	F14	10
Gusinoozersk, Russia	F10	34
Gus'-Khrustal'nyy see Gus'-Hrustal'nyj, Russia	I19	8
Guspini, Italy	E2	24
Güssing, Aus.	C13	22
Gustav Holm, Kap, c., Grnld.	D19	141
Gustavus, Ak., U.S.	E12	140
Gustine, Ca., U.S.	F5	134
Gustine, Tx., U.S.	C9	130
Güstrow, Ger.	C8	16
Gütersloh, Ger.	E4	16
Guthrie, Ok., U.S.	F11	128
Guthrie, Tx., U.S.	H8	128
Guthrie Center, Ia., U.S.	C3	120
Gutian, China	H8	42
Gutiérrez Zamora, Mex.	E10	100
Guttenberg, Ia., U.S.	B6	120
Guwāhāti, India	E13	54
Guxian, China	E5	42
Guyana, ctry., S.A.	C6	84
Guyang, China	A4	42
Guye, China	B8	42
Guy Fawkes River National Park, p.o.i., Austl.	H9	76
Guymon, Ok., U.S.	E7	128
Guyot, Mount, mtn., U.S.	I2	114
Guyra, Austl.	H8	76
Guyton, Ga., U.S.	D4	116
Guyuan, China	D2	42
Guzar, Uzb.	G11	32
Güzelyurt, N. Cyp.	C3	58
Güzelyurt Körfezi, b., N. Cyp.	C3	58
Guzhen, China	E7	42
Guzmán, Mex.	F9	98
Guzmán, Mex.	F7	100
Gvardejsk, Russia	F4	10
Gwa, Mya.	D2	48
Gwaai, Zimb.	D4	68
Gwādar, Pak.	D9	56
Gwalia, Austl.	E4	74
Gwalior (Lashkar), India	E7	54
Gwanda, Zimb.	B9	70
Gwane, D.R.C.	D5	66
Gwangju see Kwangju, Kor., S.	G7	38
Gwardafuy, Gees, c., Som.	B10	66
Gwātar Bay, b., Asia	E9	56
Gwayi, stm., Zimb.	D4	68
Gwda, stm., Pol.	C12	16
Gweedore, Ire.	F4	12
Gweru, Zimb.	D4	68
Gwinn, Mi., U.S.	B2	112
Gwydir, stm., Austl.	G7	76
Gyangtse see Gyangzê, China	D12	54
Gyangzê, China	D12	54
Gyaring Co, l., China	C12	54
Gyaring Hu, l., China	E4	36
Gyda, Russia	B4	34
Gydanskaja guba, b., Russia	B4	34
Gydanskij poluostrov, pen., Russia	B4	34
Gyeongju see Kyŏngju, Kor., S.	D2	40
Gyirong, China	D10	54
Gyldenløves Fjord, b., Grnld.	E17	141
Gym Peak, mtn., N.M., U.S.	K9	132
Gympie, Austl.	F9	76
Gyobingauk, Mya.	C2	48
Gyoma, Hung.	C7	26
Gyöngyös, Hung.	B6	26
Győr (Raab), Hung.	B4	26
Győr-Moson-Sopron, state, Hung.	B4	26
Gypsum, Co., U.S.	D10	132
Gypsum, Ks., U.S.	C11	128
Gypsumville, Mb., Can.	C15	124
Gyula, Hung.	C8	26
Gyulafehérvár see Alba Iulia, Rom.	C10	26
Gyzylarbat, Turkmen.	B8	56

H

Haag in Oberbayern, Ger.	H8	16
Haaksbergen, Neth.	D2	16
Haapiti, Fr. Poly.	v20	78h
Haapsalu, Est.	G10	8
Haar, Ger.	H7	16
Ha'Arava ('Arabah, Wādī al-), val., Asia	H6	58
Ha'Arava (Jayb, Wādī al-), stm., Asia	H6	58
Haarlem, Neth.	B13	14
Habaqila, China	C6	36
Habarovsk, Russia	G16	34
Habary, Russia	D13	32
Ḥabashīyah, Jabal, mts., Yemen	F7	56
Habbān, Yemen	G6	56
Habermehl Peak, mtn., Ant.	C6	81
Habiganj, Bngl.	F13	54
Habomai Islands see Malaja Kuril'skaja Grjada, is., Russia	C17	38
Hachijō-jima, i., Japan	F12	40
Hachiman, Japan	D9	40
Hachinohe, Japan	D14	38
Hachiōji, Japan	D12	40
Hackberry, La., U.S.	H5	122
Hackberry Creek, stm., Ks., U.S.	C8	128
Hackett, Ar., U.S.	B4	122
Hackettstown, N.J., U.S.	D11	114
Hadāli, Pak.	B4	54
HaDarom, state, Isr.	H5	58
Ḥadd, Ra's al-, c., Oman	E8	56
Haddam, Ks., U.S.	B11	128
Haddington, Scot., U.K.	F10	12
Haddock, Ga., U.S.	C2	116
Haddon Downs, Austl.	F3	76
Hadejia, Nig.	G7	64
Hadejia, stm., Nig.	G6	64
Haden, Austl.	F8	76
Ḥadera, Isr.	F5	58
Haderslev, Den.	I3	8
Hadībū, Yemen	G7	56
Ḥadīthah, Iraq	C5	56
Hadley Bay, b., Nu., Can.	A9	106
Hadlock, Wa., U.S.	B4	136
Ha Dong, Viet.	B7	48
Ḥaḍramawt, reg., Yemen	F6	56
Hadrian's Wall, misc. cult., Eng., U.K.	G10	12
Hadzilavičy, Bela.	G13	10
Haeju, Kor., N.	E6	38
Haenam, Kor., S.	G7	38
Haerhpin see Harbin, China	B7	38
Haffner Bjerg, mtn., Grnld.	B13	141
Hafford, Sk., Can.	B6	124
Haffouz, Tun.	I3	24
Hāfizābād, Pak.	B4	54
Hāflong, India	F14	54
Hafnarfjörður, Ice	k28	8a
Haft Gel, Iran	C6	56
Hagan, Ga., U.S.	D3	116
Hagari, stm., India	D3	53
Hagemeister Island, i., Ak., U.S.	E7	140
Hagen, Ger.	E3	16
Hagenow, Ger.	C7	16
Hagensborg, B.C., Can.	D4	138
Hagerman, N.M., U.S.	A3	130
Hagerstown, In., U.S.	I4	112
Hagerstown, Md., U.S.	E8	114
Hagersville, On., Can.	F9	112
Hagfors, Swe.	F5	8
Haggin, Mount, mtn., Mt., U.S.	D13	136
Hagi, Japan	E4	40
Ha Giang, Viet.	A7	48
Hagondange, Fr.	E15	14
Hags Head, c., Ire.	I3	12
Hague, Sk., Can.	B7	124
Hague, Cap de la, c., Fr.	E7	14
Haguenau, Fr.	F16	14
Hagues Peak, mtn., Co., U.S.	G7	126
Hahira, Ga., U.S.	F2	116
Hai'an, China	E9	42
Haibei, China	B10	36
Haicheng, China	A10	42
Haichow Bay see Haizhou Wan, b., China	D8	42
Haidargarh, India	E8	54
Hai Duong, Viet.	B8	48
Haifa see Ḥefa, Isr.	F5	58
Haifa see Ḥefa, state, Isr.	F5	58
Haifeng, China	J6	42
Haig, Austl.	F5	74
Haigler, Ne., U.S.	A7	128
Haikang, China	K3	42
Haikou, China	K4	42
Haikou, China	G9	42
Ḥā'il, Sau. Ar.	D5	56
Hailākāndi, India	F14	54
Hailar, China	B8	36
Hailar, stm., China	B8	36
Haileyville, Ok., U.S.	C3	122
Hailin, China	B8	38
Hailun, China	B10	36
Hailuoto, i., Fin.	D11	8
Haimen, China	J7	42
Haimen, China	G9	42
Hainan, state, China	L3	42
Hainan Dao (Hainan Island), i., China	L4	42
Hainan Island see Hainan Dao, i., China	L4	42
Hainan Strait see Qiongzhou Haixia, strt., China	K4	42
Haines, Ak., U.S.	E12	140
Haines, Or., U.S.	F8	136
Haines City, Fl., U.S.	H4	116
Haines Junction, Yk., Can.	C3	106
Haining, China	F9	42
Hai Ninh, Viet.	B8	48
Hai Phong, Viet.	B8	48
Haiphong see Hai Phong, Viet.	B8	48
Haiti, ctry., N.A.	C11	102
Haitun, China	D4	36
Haivoron, Ukr.	A16	26
Haiyuan, China	C1	42
Haizhou, China	D8	42
Haizhou Wan, b., China	D8	42
Hajdú-Bihar, state, Hung.	B8	26
Hajdúböszörmény, Hung.	B8	26
Hajdúnánás, Hung.	B8	26
Hajdúszoboszló, Hung.	B8	26
Hājīpur, India	F10	54
Hajnówka, Pol.	D19	16
Hakasija, state, Russia	D16	32
Hakha, Mya.	A1	48
Hakken-san, mtn., Japan	E8	40
Hakodate, Japan	D14	38
Hakone-yama, vol., Japan	D12	40
Hakui, Japan	C9	40
Haku-san, vol., Japan	C9	40
Haku-san-kokuritsu-kōen, p.o.i., Japan	C9	40
Hal see Halle, Bel.	D13	14
Halab (Aleppo), Syria	B8	58
Halab, state, Syria	B8	58
Halachó, Mex.	B2	102
Halahai, China	B6	38
Halā'ib, Sudan	C7	62
Halawa, Cape, c., Hi., U.S.	B5	78a
Halberstadt, Ger.	E7	16
Halbrite, Sk., Can.	E10	124
Halcon, Mount, mtn., Phil.	D3	52
Halden, Nor.	G4	8
Haldensleben, Ger.	D7	16
Haldimand, On., Can.	F10	112
Haldwāni, India	D7	54
Hale, Mo., U.S.	E4	120
Haleakala Crater, crat., Hi., U.S.	C5	78a
Haleakala National Park, p.o.i., Hi., U.S.	C5	78a
Hale Center, Tx., U.S.	G7	128
Halenkov, Czech Rep.	G14	16
Halfmoon Bay, B.C., Can.	G6	138
Halfway, Md., U.S.	E8	114
Halfway, Or., U.S.	F9	136
Halicarnassus, hist., Tur.	F10	28
Halifax, Austl.	B6	76
Halifax, N.S., Can.	F13	110
Halifax, Eng., U.K.	H11	12
Halifax, N.C., U.S.	H8	114
Halifax, Va., U.S.	H6	114
Halifax Bay, b., Austl.	B6	76
Haliyāl, India	D2	53
Haljala, Est.	A9	10
Halkapınar, Tur.	A5	58
Halland, state, Swe.	H5	8
Hallandale, Fl., U.S.	K5	116
Hallānīyah, Juzur al- (Kuria Muria Islands), is., Oman	F8	56
Halla-san, mtn., Kor., S.	H7	38
Hall Basin, b., N.A.	A13	141
Halle, Bel.	D13	14
Halle, Ger.	E7	16
Hällefors, Swe.	G6	8
Hallein, Aus.	C10	22
Hallettsville, Tx., U.S.	E11	130
Halley, sci., Ant.	C2	81
Halligen, is., Ger.	B4	16
Hall in Tirol, Aus.	C8	22
Hall Islands, is., Micron.	C6	72
Hall Lake, l., Nu., Can.	B14	106
Hall Land, reg., Grnld.	A14	141
Hall Mountain, mtn., Wa., U.S.	B9	136
Hallock, Mn., U.S.	C2	118
Hallowell, Me., U.S.	F7	110
Hall Peninsula, pen., Nu., Can.	C17	106
Halls, Tn., U.S.	I8	120
Hallsberg, Swe.	G6	8
Halls Creek, Austl.	C5	74
Hallstahammar, Swe.	G7	8
Hallstavik, Swe.	F8	8
Hallstead, Pa., U.S.	C10	114
Hallsville, Mo., U.S.	E5	120
Halmahera, i., Indon.	E8	44
Halmahera, Laut (Halmahera Sea), Indon.	F8	44
Halmahera Sea see Halmahera, Laut, Indon.	F8	44
Hal'mer-Ju, Russia	A10	32
Halmstad, Swe.	H5	8
Haloučyn, Bela.	F12	10
Hal'šany, Bela.	F8	10
Halsey, Ne., U.S.	F12	126
Halsey, Or., U.S.	F3	136
Halstead, Ks., U.S.	D11	128
Haltern, Ger.	E3	16
Haltiatunturi, mtn., Eur.	B9	8
Haltom City, Tx., U.S.	B10	130
Halton Hills see Georgetown, On., Can.	E9	112
Halvorson, Mount, mtn., B.C., Can.	C10	138
Ham, stm., Nmb.	F4	70
Hamada, Japan	E4	40
Hamadān, Iran	C6	56
Hamāh, Syria	C7	58
Hamāh, state, Syria	C8	58
Hamamatsu, Japan	E10	40
Haman, Kor., S.	D1	40
Hamana-ko, l., Japan	E10	40
Hamar, Nor.	F4	8
Ha Marakabei, Leso.	F9	70
Hamar-Daban, hrebet, mts., Russia	F9	34
Hamburg, Ger.	C6	16
Hamburg, Ar., U.S.	D7	122
Hamburg, Ia., U.S.	D2	120
Hamburg, N.J., U.S.	C11	114
Hamburg, N.Y., U.S.	B7	114
Hamburg, state, Ger.	C6	16
Hamden, Ct., U.S.	C13	114
Hamden, Oh., U.S.	E3	114
Häme, state, Fin.	F11	8
Hämeenlinna (Tavastehus), Fin.	F10	8
Hamelin, Austl.	E2	74
Hameln, Ger.	D5	16
HaMerkaz, state, Isr.	F5	58
Hamersley Range, mts., Austl.	D3	74
Hamgyŏng-sanjulgi, mts., Kor., N.	D8	38
Hamhŭng, Kor., N.	E7	38
Hami, China	C3	36
Hamilton, Austl.	K4	76
Hamilton, Ber.	k15	104e
Hamilton, On., Can.	E10	112
Hamilton, N.Z.	C6	80
Hamilton, Scot., U.K.	F8	12
Hamilton, Al., U.S.	C11	122
Hamilton, Ga., U.S.	E14	122
Hamilton, Il., U.S.	D6	120
Hamilton, Mi., U.S.	F4	112
Hamilton, Mo., U.S.	E3	120
Hamilton, Mt., U.S.	D12	136
Hamilton, N.Y., U.S.	B10	114
Hamilton, Oh., U.S.	E1	114
Hamilton, stm., Austl.	D3	76
Hamilton, Lake, res., Ar., U.S.	C5	122
Hamilton, Mount, mtn., Ca., U.S.	F4	134
Hamilton City, Ca., U.S.	D3	134
Hamilton Dome, Wy., U.S.	D4	126
Hamilton Hotel, Austl.	D3	76
Hamilton Mountain, mtn., N.Y., U.S.	G2	110
Hamina, Fin.	F12	8
Hamiota, Mb., Can.	D13	124
Hamīrpur, India	F7	54
Hamlin, Tx., U.S.	B7	130
Hamlin, W.V., U.S.	F3	114
Hamlin Valley Wash, stm., U.S.	E3	132
Hamm, Ger.	E3	16
Hammamet, Tun.	H4	24
Hammamet, Golfe de, b., Tun.	H4	24
Hammam Lif, Tun.	H4	24
Hammelburg, Ger.	F5	16
Hammerdal, Swe.	E6	8
Hammerfest, Nor.	A10	8
Hammon, Ok., U.S.	F9	128
Hammond, In., U.S.	G2	112
Hammond, La., U.S.	G8	122
Hammondsport, N.Y., U.S.	F12	112
Hampden, Me., U.S.	F8	110
Hampden, N.D., U.S.	F15	124
Hampi, India	D3	53
Hampshire, Il., U.S.	I10	118
Hampstead, N.C., U.S.	B8	116
Hampton, N.B., Can.	E11	110
Hampton, Ar., U.S.	D6	122
Hampton, Fl., U.S.	G3	116
Hampton, Ga., U.S.	C1	116
Hampton, Ne., U.S.	G15	126
Hampton, N.H., U.S.	H6	110
Hampton, Tn., U.S.	H3	114
Hampton, Va., U.S.	G9	114
Hampton Butte, mtn., Or., U.S.	G6	136
Hampton Tableland, plat., Austl.	F5	74
Hamra, Swe.	F6	8
Ḥamrā', Al-Ḥamādah al-, des., Libya	B2	62
Hamra, As Saquia al, stm., W. Sah.	D2	64
Hamsara, stm., Russia	D16	32
Hams Fork, stm., Wy., U.S.	F2	126
Hamīṭa, Gebel (Ḥamāṭah, Jabal), mtn., Egypt	C6	62
Ham Tan, Viet.	G8	48
Hāmūn, Daryācheh-ye, l., Iran	C9	56
Han, stm., China	I7	42
Han, stm., China	F6	42
Han, Nong, l., Thai.	D7	48
Hana, Hi., U.S.	C6	78a
Hanahan, S.C., U.S.	D5	116
Hanamaki, Japan	E14	38
Hananui see Anglem, Mount, mtn., N.Z.	H2	80
Hanapepe, Hi., U.S.	B2	78a
Hanateio, Fr. Poly.	s18	78g
Hanatetena, Fr. Poly.	s18	78g
Hanau am Main, Ger.	F4	16
Hanbury, stm., N.T., Can.	C9	106
Hancavičy, Bela.	H9	10
Hâncești, Mol.	C15	26
Hanceville, Al., U.S.	C12	122
Hancheng, China	D7	36
Hancheng, China	D4	42
Hanchung see Hanzhong, China	E2	42
Hancock, Md., U.S.	E7	114
Hancock, Mi., U.S.	D10	118
Hancock, Mn., U.S.	F3	118
Hancock, N.Y., U.S.	C10	114
Handa, Japan	E9	40
Handan, China	C6	42
Handlová, Slov.	H14	16
Handsworth, Sk., Can.	E10	124
Handyga, Russia	D16	34
HaNegev (Negev Desert), reg., Isr.	H5	58
Hanford, Ca., U.S.	G6	134
Hanga Roa, Chile	e29	78l
Hangayn nuruu, mts., Mong.	B4	36
Hangchou see Hangzhou, China	F9	42
Hangchow see Hangzhou, China	F9	42
Hangchow Bay see Hangzhou Wan, b., China	F9	42
Hanggin Houqi, China	A2	42
Hanggin Qi, China	B3	42
Hangman Creek, stm., U.S.	C9	136
Hangö see Hanko, Fin.	G10	8
Hangokurt, Russia	B10	32
Hangu, China	B7	42
Hangu, Pak.	B3	54
Hanguang, China	I5	42
Hangzhou, China	F9	42
Hangzhou Wan, b., China	F9	42
Hanino, Russia	F19	10
Ḥanīsh, is., Yemen	G5	56
Hanish Islands see Ḥanīsh, is., Yemen	G5	56
Hanjiang, China	I8	42
Hankinson, N.D., U.S.	E2	118
Hanko, Fin.	G10	8
Hankow see Wuhan, China	F6	42
Hanku see Hangu, China	B7	42
Hānle, India	B7	54
Hanley, Sk., Can.	C7	124
Hanna, Ab., Can.	E19	138
Hanna, Ok., U.S.	B3	122
Hanna, Wy., U.S.	B10	132
Hanna City, Il., U.S.	D8	120
Hannah, N.D., U.S.	F15	124
Hannah Bay, b., On., Can.	E14	106
Hannibal, Mo., U.S.	E6	120
Hannover, Ger.	D5	16
Ha Noi (Hanoi), Viet.	B7	48
Hanoi see Ha Noi, Viet.	B7	48
Hanover, On., Can.	D8	112
Hanover see Hannover, Ger.	D5	16
Hanover, S. Afr.	G7	70
Hanover, Il., U.S.	B7	120
Hanover, In., U.S.	F12	120
Hanover, N.H., U.S.	G4	110
Hanover, N.M., U.S.	K8	132
Hanover, Pa., U.S.	E9	114
Hanover, Va., U.S.	G8	114
Hanover, Isla, i., Chile	J2	90
Hansdiha, India	F11	54
Hānsi, India	D5	54
Hanska, Mn., U.S.	G4	118
Hantajskoe, ozero, l., Russia	C6	34
Hantan see Handan, China	C6	42
Hantau, Kaz.	F12	32
Hantsport, N.S., Can.	E12	110
Hanty-Mansijsk, Russia	B11	32
Hantzsch, stm., Nu., Can.	B16	106
Hanumāngarh, India	C3	46
Hanumangarh, India	D4	54
Hanuy, stm., Mong.	B5	36
Hanyin, China	E3	42
Hanzhong, China	E2	42
Hanzhuang, China	D7	42
Haojiadian, China	F5	42
Haoli see Hegang, China	B11	36
Hāora, India	G12	54
Haparanda, Swe.	D10	8
Hapčeranga, Russia	G11	34
Happy, Tx., U.S.	G7	128
Happy Jack, Az., U.S.	I5	132
Happy Valley-Goose Bay, Nf., Can.	E18	106
Hāpur, India	D6	54
Ḥaql, Sau. Ar.	I5	58
Ḥaraḍ, Sau. Ar.	E6	56
Haradok, Bela.	E13	10
Haradzec, Bela.	H7	10
Haradzec, Bela.	G13	10
Haradziščа, Bela.	G9	10
Haramachi, Japan	B13	40
Haranor, Russia	A8	36
Harar see Hārer, Eth.	F8	62
Harare, Zimb.	D5	68
Harazé Mangueigne, Chad	E4	62
Harbala, Russia	D13	34
Harbavičy, Bela.	G13	10
Harbin, China	B7	38
Harbiye, Tur.	B7	58
Harbor, Or., U.S.	A1	134
Harbor Beach, Mi., U.S.	E7	112
Harbour Breton, Nf., Can.	j22	107a
Harbourville, N.S., Can.	E12	110
Harda, India	G6	54
Hardangerfjorden, b., Nor.	F2	8
Hardangerjøkulen, ice, Nor.	F2	8
Hardangervidda Nasjonalpark, p.o.i., Nor.	F2	8
Hardap, state, Nmb.	D3	70
Hardeeville, S.C., U.S.	D4	116
Harderwijk, Neth.	B14	14
Hardin, Il., U.S.	E7	120
Hardin, Mt., U.S.	B5	126
Harding, S. Afr.	G9	70
Harding, Lake, res., U.S.	E13	122
Hardinsburg, Ky., U.S.	G11	120
Hardisty Lake, l., N.T., Can.	C7	106
Hardoi, India	E7	54
Hardtner, Ks., U.S.	D10	128
Hardwick, Ga., U.S.	C2	116
Hardwick, Vt., U.S.	F4	110
Hardy, Ar., U.S.	H6	120
Hardy, Ne., U.S.	G15	126
Hardy Bay, b., N.T., Can.	B16	140
Hare Bay, b., Nf., Can.	i22	107a
Hare Indian, stm., N.T., Can.	B5	106
Hareøen, i., Grnld.	C14	141
Hārer, Eth.	F8	62
Hargeysa, Som.	C8	66
Harghita, state, Rom.	C12	26
Har Hu, l., China	D4	36
Hari, stm., Indon.	D3	50
Ḥarīb, Yemen	G6	56
Haridwār, India	D7	54
Harihar, India	D2	53
Ḥārim, Syria	B7	58
Harīpur, Pak.	B4	54
Harīrūd (Tedžen), stm., Asia	C9	56
Harischandra Range, mts., India	B1	53
Haritonovo, Russia	F22	8
Harkers Island, N.C., U.S.	B9	116
Harlan, Ky., U.S.	H2	114
Harlan County Lake, res., Ne., U.S.	A9	128
Harlem, Fl., U.S.	J5	116
Harlem, Ga., U.S.	C3	116
Harleton, Tx., U.S.	E4	122
Harlingen, Neth.	A14	14
Harlingen, Tx., U.S.	H10	130
Harlovka, Russia	B17	8
Harlow, Eng., U.K.	J13	12
Harlowton, Mt., U.S.	D17	136
Harman, W.V., U.S.	F6	114
Harmancık, Tur.	D12	28
Harmanli, Blg.	H12	26
Harmony, In., U.S.	E10	120
Harnai, India	C1	53
Harney Basin, bas., Or., U.S.	G8	136
Harney Lake, l., Or., U.S.	G7	136
Harney Peak, mtn., S.D., U.S.	D9	126
Härnösand, Swe.	E8	8
Har nuur, l., Mong.	B3	36
Haro, Spain	B8	20
Haro, Cabo, c., Mex.	B3	100
Harovsk, Russia	F18	8
Harpanahalli, India	D3	53
Harper, Lib.	I3	64
Harper, Ks., U.S.	D10	128
Harper, Tx., U.S.	D8	130
Harper, Mount, mtn., Ak., U.S.	D11	140
Harqin Qi, China	D3	38
Harrai, India	G7	54
Harricana, stm., Can.	E15	106
Harriman, Tn., U.S.	I13	120
Harrington, De., U.S.	F10	114
Harrington, Me., U.S.	F9	110
Harris, Sk., Can.	C6	124
Harris, Monts.	D3	105a
Harris, Mn., U.S.	F5	118
Harris, reg., Scot., U.K.	D6	12
Harris, Lake, l., Fl., U.S.	H4	116
Harrisburg, Ar., U.S.	B8	122
Harrisburg, Ne., U.S.	F9	126
Harrisburg, Or., U.S.	F3	136
Harrisburg, Pa., U.S.	D8	114
Harrismith, S. Afr.	F9	70
Harrison, Ar., U.S.	H4	120
Harrison, Mi., U.S.	D5	112
Harrison, Ne., U.S.	E9	126
Harrison Bay, b., Ak., U.S.	B9	140
Harrisonburg, La., U.S.	F7	122
Harrisonburg, Va., U.S.	F6	114
Harrison Islands, is., Nu., Can.	B13	106
Harrison Lake, l., B.C., Can.	G9	138
Harriston, On., Can.	E9	112
Harriston, Ms., U.S.	F7	122
Harrisville, N.Y., U.S.	D14	112
Harrisville, W.V., U.S.	E4	114
Harrodsburg, Ky., U.S.	G13	120
Harrogate, Eng., U.K.	H11	12
Harrold, Tx., U.S.	G9	128
Harrowsmith, On., Can.	D13	112
Harry S. Truman Reservoir, res., Mo., U.S.	F4	120
Har Sai Shan, mtn., China	D4	36
Harsīn, Iran	C6	56
Hârșova, Rom.	E14	26
Harstad, Nor.	B7	8
Harsūd, India	G6	54
Hart, Mi., U.S.	E3	112
Hart, Tx., U.S.	G6	128
Hart, stm., Yk., Can.	B3	106
Hartbees, stm., S. Afr.	F5	70
Hartberg, Aus.	C12	22
Hartford, Ar., U.S.	C4	122
Hartford, Ct., U.S.	C13	114
Hartford, Ks., U.S.	F2	120
Hartford, Mi., U.S.	F3	112
Hartford, S.D., U.S.	H2	118
Hartford, Wi., U.S.	H10	118
Hartford City, In., U.S.	H4	112
Hartland, N.B., Can.	D9	110
Hartland, Me., U.S.	F7	110
Hartlepool, Eng., U.K.	G11	12
Hartley, Ia., U.S.	H3	118
Hartley Bay, B.C., Can.	C1	138
Hart Mountain, mtn., Mb., Can.	B12	124
Hartney, Mb., Can.	E13	124
Harts, stm., S. Afr.	E7	70
Hartselle, Al., U.S.	C12	122
Hartshorne, Ok., U.S.	C3	122
Hartsville, S.C., U.S.	B5	116
Hartville, Mo., U.S.	G5	120
Hartwell, Ga., U.S.	B3	116
Hartwell Lake, res., U.S.	B2	116
Hartz Mountains National Park, p.o.i., Austl.	o13	77a
Hārūnābād, Pak.	D4	54
Haruniye, Tur.	A7	58
Harūr, India	E4	53
Har-Us nuur, l., Mong.	B3	36
Hārūt, stm., Afg.	C9	56
Harvard, Ne., U.S.	G14	126
Harvey, N.B., Can.	E12	110
Harvey, Il., U.S.	G2	112
Harvey, N.D., U.S.	G14	124
Harwich, Eng., U.K.	J14	12
Haryāna, state, India	D6	54
Haryn', stm., Eur.	H10	10
Harz, mts., Ger.	E6	16
Hasavjurt, Russia	F7	32
Hasdo, stm., India	G9	54
Hase, stm., Ger.	D3	16
Hasenkamp, Arg.	E8	92
Hashima, Japan	D9	40
Hashimoto, Japan	E8	40
Hāsilpur, Pak.	D4	54
Haskell, Ok., U.S.	I2	120
Haskell, Tx., U.S.	A8	130
Haskovo, Blg.	H12	26
Haskovo, state, Blg.	G12	26
Haslemere, Eng., U.K.	J12	12
Hasperos Canyon, val., N.M., U.S.	H3	128
Ḥaṣṣ, Jabal al-, hill, Syria	C8	58
Hassa, Tur.	B7	58
Hassan, India	E3	53
Hassayampa, stm., Az., U.S.	J4	132
Hassel Sound, strt., Nu., Can.	B6	141
Hasselt, Bel.	D14	14
Hassfurt, Ger.	F6	16
Hassi Messaoud, Alg.	C6	64
Hässleholm, Swe.	H5	8
Hastings, Barb.	n8	105d
Hastings, On., Can.	D11	112
Hastings, N.Z.	D7	80
Hastings, Eng., U.K.	K13	12
Hastings, Mi., U.S.	F4	112
Hastings, Mn., U.S.	G6	118
Hastings, Ne., U.S.	G14	126
Haswell, Co., U.S.	C5	128
Hatanga, Russia	B9	34
Hatanga, stm., Russia	B9	34
Hatangskij zaliv, b., Russia	B10	34
Hatay (Antioch), Tur.	B7	58
Hatay, state, Tur.	B7	58
Hatch, N.M., U.S.	K9	132
Hatch, Ut., U.S.	F4	132
Hat Chao Mai National Park, p.o.i., Thai.	I4	48
Hatchie, stm., U.S.	B9	122
Hatfield, Austl.	I4	76
Hatfield, Ar., U.S.	C4	122
Hatfield, Ma., U.S.	B13	114
Hatgal, Mong.	F9	34
Hāthras, India	E7	54
Ha Tien, Viet.	G7	48
Hatillo, P.R.	A2	104a
Ha Tinh, Viet.	C7	48
Hatip, Tur.	F15	28
Hato, Bocht van, b., Neth. Ant.	p21	104g
Hato Mayor del Rey, Dom. Rep.	C13	102
Hāt Pīplia, India	G6	54
Hatta, India	F7	54
Hatteras, N.C., U.S.	A10	116
Hatteras, Cape, c., N.C., U.S.	A10	116
Hatteras Island, i., N.C., U.S.	A10	116
Hattiesburg, Ms., U.S.	F9	122
Hatton, Al., U.S.	C11	122
Hatton, N.D., U.S.	G16	124
Hatunsaray, Tur.	A3	58
Hatvan, Hung.	B6	26
Hat Yai, Thai.	I5	48
Hatyrka, Russia	D24	34
Haugesund, Nor.	G1	8
Haukeligrend, Nor.	G2	8
Haukivesi, l., Fin.	E12	8
Hauraki Gulf, b., N.Z.	C6	80
Hausach, Ger.	H4	16
Haut, Isle au, i., Me., U.S.	F8	110
Haut Atlas, mts., Mor.	C3	64
Haute-Corse, state, Fr.	G15	18
Haute-Garonne, state, Fr.	F7	18
Haute-Loire, state, Fr.	D9	18
Haute-Marne, state, Fr.	F14	14
Hautes-Alpes, state, Fr.	E12	18
Haute-Saône, state, Fr.	G14	14
Haute-Savoie, state, Fr.	C12	18
Hautes-Pyrénées, state, Fr.	F6	18
Haute-Vienne, state, Fr.	D7	18
Haut-Rhin, state, Fr.	G16	14
Haut Sheila, N.B., Can.	C11	110
Hauts Plateaux, reg., Afr.	C5	64
Hauula, Hi., U.S.	B4	78a
Hauwâret el-Maqta', Egypt	I1	58
Havana see La Habana, Cuba	A6	102
Havana, Fl., U.S.	G14	122
Havana, Il., U.S.	D7	120
Havana, N.D., U.S.	B15	126
Havannah, Canal de la, strt., N. Cal.	n16	79d
Havant, Eng., U.K.	K12	12

Name	Map Ref.	Page

Havast, Uzb. — F11 32
Havasu, Lake, res., U.S. — I2 132
Havasu Creek, stm., Az., U.S. — H4 132
Havel, stm., Ger. — D8 16
Havelberg, Ger. — D8 16
Haveli, Pak. — C4 54
Havelland, reg., Ger. — D8 16
Havelock, N.C., U.S. — B8 116
Havelock, On., Can. — D12 112
Haverfordwest, Wales, U.K. — J7 12
Haverhill, Eng., U.K. — I13 12
Haverhill, Ma., U.S. — B14 114
Haviland, Ks., U.S. — D2 53
Haviland, Ks., U.S. — D9 128
Havlíčkův Brod, Czech Rep. — G14 16
Havlíčkův Brod, Czech Rep. — G11 16
Havre see Le Havre, Fr. — E8 14
Havre, Mt., U.S. — B17 136
Havre-Aubert, Qc., Can. — C15 110
Havre Aubert, Île du, i., Qc., Can. — C14 110
Havre de Grace, Md., U.S. — E9 114
Havre North, Mt., U.S. — B17 136
Havsa, Tur. — B9 28
Haw, stm., N.C., U.S. — A7 116
Hawaii, state, U.S. — B5 78a
Hawaii, i., Hi., U.S. — C6 78a
Hawaiian Islands, is., Hi., U.S. — C4 78a
Hawaiian Ridge, unds. — G21 142
Hawaii Volcanoes National Park, p.o.i., Hi., U.S. — D6 78a
Hawarden, Sk., Can. — C7 124
Hawea, Lake, l., N.Z. — G3 80
Hawera, N.Z. — D6 80
Hawesville, Ky., U.S. — G11 120
Hawi, Hi., U.S. — C6 78a
Hawick, Scot., U.K. — F10 12
Hawke, Cape, c., Austl. — I9 76
Hawke Bay, b., N.Z. — D7 80
Hawker, Austl. — H2 76
Hawkes, Mount, mtn., Ant. — D36 81
Hawkesbury, On., Can. — E2 110
Hawkesbury Island, i., B.C., Can. — C1 138
Hawkeye, Ia., U.S. — B6 120
Hawkins, Tx., U.S. — E3 122
Hawkins, Wi., U.S. — F8 118
Haw Knob, mtn., U.S. — A1 116
Hawksbill Creek, b., Bah. — J7 116
Hawkwood, Austl. — E8 76
Hawley, Mn., U.S. — E2 118
Hawley, Pa., U.S. — C10 114
Hawthorne, Fl., U.S. — G3 116
Hawthorne, Nv., U.S. — E7 134
Hawwāret'Adlan, Egypt — I1 58
Hay, Austl. — J5 76
Hay, stm., Austl. — D7 74
Hay, stm., Can. — D7 106
Hay, Cape, c., N.T., Can. — B17 140
Hayang, Kor., S. — E14 14
Hayange, Fr. — E14 14
Haybān, Jabal, mtn., Sudan — E6 62
Haydarlı, Tur. — E13 28
Hayden, Co., U.S. — C9 132
Haydenville, Oh., U.S. — E3 114
Hayes, La., U.S. — G6 122
Hayes, stm., Mb., Can. — D12 106
Hayes, stm., Nu., Can. — B11 106
Hayes, Mount, mtn., Ak., U.S. — D10 140
Hayes Center, Ne., U.S. — G11 126
Hayesville, Or., U.S. — F4 136
Hayfield, Mn., U.S. — H6 118
Hayford Peak, mtn., Nv., U.S. — G1 132
Hayfork, Ca., U.S. — C2 134
Hay Lakes, Ab., Can. — C17 138
Haynes, Ar., U.S. — C8 122
Hayneville, Al., U.S. — E12 122
Hayrabolu, Tur. — B10 28
Hay River, N.T., Can. — C7 106
Hays, Ab., Can. — F19 138
Hays, Ks., U.S. — C9 128
Hays, Mt., U.S. — F5 124
Hay Springs, Ne., U.S. — E10 126
Haystack Mountain, mtn., Nv., U.S. — B1 132
Hayti, Mo., U.S. — H8 120
Hayti, S.D., U.S. — C15 126
Hayward, Ca., U.S. — F3 134
Hayward, Wi., U.S. — E7 118
Haywards Heath, Eng., U.K. — J13 12
HaZafon, state, Isr. — F6 58
Hazard, Ky., U.S. — G2 114
Hazārībāg, India — G10 54
Hazawzā', Sabkhat, l., Sau. Ar. — H9 58
Hazebrouck, Fr. — D11 14
Hazel Green, Wi., U.S. — I8 118
Hazelton, B.C., Can. — A3 138
Hazelton, N.D., U.S. — A12 126
Hazelton Mountains, mts., B.C., Can. — B3 138
Hazelwood, N.C., U.S. — A2 116
Hazen, Ar., U.S. — C7 122
Hazen, N.D., U.S. — G12 124
Hazen, Lake, l., Nu., Can. — A11 141
Hazlehurst, Ms., U.S. — F8 122
Hazlet, Sk., Can. — D5 124
Hazleton, Ia., U.S. — B6 120
Hazleton, Pa., U.S. — D9 114
Hazlett, Lake, l., Austl. — D5 74
He, stm., China — E8 58
He, stm., China — I4 42
Healdsburg, Ca., U.S. — E2 134
Healdton, Ok., U.S. — G11 128
Healesville, Austl. — K5 76
Healy, Ks., U.S. — C8 128
Heard Island, i., Austl. — O10 142
Hearst, On., Can. — F14 106
Heart, stm., N.D., U.S. — H12 124
Heart Lake, l., Ab., Can. — A19 138
Heathcote, Austl. — K5 76
Heathcote, Pc., Qc., Can. — D5 110
Heath Springs, S.C., U.S. — B5 116
Heathsville, Va., U.S. — G9 114
Heavener, Ok., U.S. — C4 122
Hebei, state, China — D8 36
Hebel, Austl. — G6 76
Heber, Az., U.S. — I6 132
Heber City, Ut., U.S. — C5 132
Heber Springs, Ar., U.S. — B6 122
Hebgen Lake, res., Mt., U.S. — F15 136
Hebi, China — D6 42
Hebrides, is., Scot., U.K. — D5 12
Hebrides, Sea of the, Scot., U.K. — D6 12
Hebron, Nf., Can. — F13 141
Hebron, Il., U.S. — B9 120
Hebron, Ne., U.S. — A11 128
Hebron, N.D., U.S. — H11 124
Hebron see Al-Khalīl, W.B. — G5 58
Hecate Strait, strt., B.C., Can. — E4 106
Hecelchakán, Mex. — B2 102
Hechi, China — I3 42
Hechuan, Mex. — F4 130
Hechuan, China — H4 42
Hecla, Mb., Can. — C17 124
Hecla, Cape, c., Nu., Can. — A13 141
Hecla Island, i., Mb., Can. — D17 124
Hectanooga, N.S., Can. — F10 110
Hector, Mn., U.S. — G4 118
Hede, Swe. — E5 8
Hedemora, Swe. — F6 8
He Devil, mtn., Id., U.S. — E10 136
Hedley, Tx., U.S. — G8 128
Hedmark, state, Nor. — F4 8
Hedrick, Ia., U.S. — C5 120

Heerenveen, Neth. — B14 14
Heerlen, Neth. — D15 14
Hefa (Haifa), Isr. — F5 58
Hefa, state, Isr. — F5 58
Hefei, China — F7 42
Heflin, Al., U.S. — D13 122
Hegang, China — B11 36
Heho, Mya. — B3 48
Heide, Ger. — B5 16
Heidelberg, Ger. — G4 16
Heidelberg, S. Afr. — E9 70
Heidelberg, Ms., U.S. — F10 122
Heidenheim, Ger. — G6 16
Heihe, China — A10 36
Heilbad Heiligenstadt, Ger. — E6 16
Heilbron, S. Afr. — E8 70
Heilbronn, Ger. — G5 16
Heiligenhafen, Ger. — B6 16
Heiligonguan, China — C4 42
Heilong (Amur), stm., Asia — F14 34
Heilongjiang, state, China — B10 36
Heilungkiang see Heilongjiang, state, China — B8 38
Heimaey, i., Ice. — I29 8a
Heinola, Fin. — F12 8
Heishan, China — D4 38
Heishuisi, China — C3 42
Hejaz see Al-Ḥijāz, reg., Sau. Ar. — D4 56
Hejian, China — B7 42
Hejiang, China — G1 42
Hejing, China — C2 36
Hekou, China — G4 42
Hekou, China — A6 48
Helagsfjället, mtn., Swe. — E5 8
Helan Mountains see Helan Shan, mts., China — B1 42
Helan Shan, mts., China — B1 42
Helbra, Ger. — E7 16
Helder see Den Helder, Neth. — B13 14
Helen, Mount, hill, Austl. — C3 76
Helena, Ar., U.S. — C8 122
Helena, Mt., U.S. — D14 136
Helena, Ok., U.S. — E10 128
Helendale, Ca., U.S. — E8 12 → H13 134?
Helendale, Ca., U.S. — H13 120
Helensburgh, Scot., U.K. — E8 12
Helgoland, i., Ger. — B3 16
Helgoländer Bucht, b., Ger. — C4 16
Heli, China — B11 36
Heliopolis, hist., Egypt — H2 58
Helix, China — F8 42
Hellesylt, Nor. — E2 8
Hellin, Spain — F9 20
Hells Canyon, val., U.S. — E10 136
Hells Canyon National Recreation Area, p.o.i., Or., U.S. — E10 136
Hells Gate, val., B.C., Can. — G9 138
Hervey Bay, b., Austl. — E9 76
Helmand, stm., Asia — C9 56
Helmcken Falls, wtfl, B.C., Can. — E10 138
Helmond, Neth. — C14 14
Helmstedt, Ger. — D6 16
Helong, China — C8 38
Helper, Ut., U.S. — D6 132
Helsingborg, Swe. — H5 8
Helsingfors see Helsinki, Fin. — F11 8
Helsingor, Den. — H5 8
Helsinki (Helsingfors), Fin. — F11 8
Helska, Mierzeja, pen., Pol. — B14 16
Helston, Eng., U.K. — K7 12
Helvecia, Arg. — E7 92
Helwan, Egypt — I2 58
Helwan Observatory, sci., Egypt — I2 58
Hemau, Ger. — G7 16
Hemāvati, stm., India — E2 53
Hemel Hempstead, Eng., U.K. — J12 12
Hemet, Ca., U.S. — J9 134
Hemingford, Ne., U.S. — E9 126
Hemingway, S.C., U.S. — C6 116
Hemphill, Tx., U.S. — F5 122
Hemsön, i., Swe. — E8 8
Henan, state, China — E5 42
Henares, stm., Spain — D7 20
Henbury, Austl. — D6 74
Hendek, Tur. — C13 28
Henderson, Ky., U.S. — G10 120
Henderson, Mn., U.S. — G5 118
Henderson, Ne., U.S. — G15 126
Henderson, Nv., U.S. — G1 132
Henderson, N.C., U.S. — H7 114
Henderson, Tn., U.S. — B10 122
Henderson, Tx., U.S. — E4 122
Hendersonville, Tn., U.S. — H11 120
Hendricks, Mn., U.S. — G2 118
Hendricks, W.V., U.S. — E6 114
Hengchun, Pap. N. Gui. — b4 79a
Hengchow see Hengyang, China — H5 42
Hengdaozi, China — C7 38
Hengelo, Neth. — B15 14
Hengfeng, China — G7 42
Henglu, China — D7 38
Hengshan, China — C3 42
Hengshan, China — H5 42
Heng Shan, mts., China — C6 42
Hengshui, China — J3 42
Hengxian, China — H5 42
Hengyang, China — H5 42
Hénin-Beaumont, Fr. — D11 14
Henlopen, Cape, c., De., U.S. — F10 114
Hennebont, Fr. — G5 14
Hennef, Ger. — F3 16
Hennessey, Ok., U.S. — E11 128
Henniker, N.H., U.S. — E5 114
Henning, Mn., U.S. — E3 118
Henrietta, N.Y., U.S. — A8 114
Henrietta, Tx., U.S. — H10 128
Henrietta Island see Genrietty, ostrov, i., Russia — A20 34
Henrietta Maria, Cape, c., On., Can. — D14 106
Henri Pittier, Parque Nacional, p.o.i., Ven. — B8 86
Henry, Il., U.S. — C8 120
Henry, Cape, c., Va., U.S. — H10 114
Henry, Mount, mtn., Mt., U.S. — B11 136
Henryetta, Ok., U.S. — B2 122
Henry Kater, Cape, c., Nu., Can. — B17 106
Henrys Fork, stm., Id., U.S. — F15 136
Hensall, On., Can. — E8 112
Henslow, Cape, c., Sol. Is. — e9 79b
Hentiesbaai, Nmb. — B2 70
Hentiyn nuruu, mts., Mong. — G10 34
Henzada, Mya. — D2 48
Heppignies, Ger. — E7 16
Hepu, China — K3 42
Hequ, China — B4 42
Hér	adsflói, b., Ice. — k32 8a
Herāt, Afg. — C9 56
Hérault, state, Fr. — F9 18
Hérault, stm., Fr. — F9 18
Herbert, Ut., U.S. — B5 76
Herberton, Austl. — A5 76
Herbertsdale, S. Afr. — H5 70
Herborn, Ger. — F4 16
Herceg-Novi, Yugo. — G5 26

Hércules, Mex. — A7 100
Herdubreid, vol., Ice. — k31 8a
Heredia, C.R. — G5 102
Hereford, Eng., U.K. — I10 12
Hereford, Az., U.S. — L6 132
Hereford, Tx., U.S. — G6 128
Herencia, Spain — E7 20
Herford, Ger. — D4 16
Herkimer, N.Y., U.S. — E15 112
Herlong, Ca., U.S. — C5 134
Herma Ness, c., Scot., U.K. — n18 12a
Hermann, Mo., U.S. — F7 120
Hermannsburg, Ger. — D6 16
Hermansverk, Nor. — F2 8
Hermanus, S. Afr. — I4 70
Hermanville, Ms., U.S. — F8 122
Hermiston, Or., U.S. — E7 136
Hermitage, Ar., U.S. — D6 122
Hermit Islands, is., Pap. N. Gui. — a4 79a
Hermon, Mount (Shaykh, Jabal ash-), mtn., Asia — E6 58
Hermosillo, Mex. — A3 100
Hermyingyi, Mya. — E4 48
Hernád (Hornad), stm., Eur. — H17 16
Hernandarias, Arg. — E8 92
Hernandarias, Para. — B10 92
Hernando, Arg. — F6 92
Hernando, Fl., U.S. — H3 116
Hernando, Ms., U.S. — C9 122
Herndon, Pa., U.S. — D9 114
Herne, Ger. — E3 16
Herne Bay, Eng., U.K. — J14 12
Herning, Den. — H3 8
Heroica Zitácuaro, Mex. — F8 100
Heron Lake, Mn., U.S. — H3 118
Heron Island, i., Austl. — D8 76
Hérouville-Saint-Clair, Fr. — E8 14
Herradura, Arg. — C8 92
Herreid, S.D., U.S. — B12 126
Herrera de Pisuerga, Spain — B6 20
Herrick, Austl. — n13 77a
Herrin, Il., U.S. — G8 120
Hersbruck, Ger. — G7 16
Herschel, Sk., Can. — C5 124
Herschel, S. Afr. — G8 70
Herschel Island, i., Yk., Can. — C12 140
Hershey, Ne., U.S. — F11 126
Hershey, Pa., U.S. — D9 114
Herstal, Bel. — D14 14
Herten, Ger. — J12 12
Hertogenbosch, 's- see 's-Hertogenbosch, Neth. — C14 14
Herval d'Oeste, Braz. — C12 92
Hervás, Spain — D5 20
Hervey Bay, b., Austl. — E9 76
Hervey-Jonction, Qc., Can. — D4 110
Herzberg, Ger. — E9 16
Herzberg am Harz, Ger. — E6 16
Heshan, China — J3 42
Heshui, China — J4 42
Heshui, China — C5 42
Hesperia, Mi., U.S. — E3 112
Hesperus Mountain, mtn., Co., U.S. — F8 132
Hess, stm., Yk., Can. — C4 106
Hessen, state, Ger. — F5 16
Hesston, Ks., U.S. — C11 128
Het, stm., Laos — B6 48
Heta, stm., Russia — B8 34
Hetang, China — H8 42
Hetauṇḍā, Nepal — E10 54
Hetch Hetchy Aqueduct, aq., Ca., U.S. — F4 134
Hettinger, N.D., U.S. — D6 8? → Hettinger, N.D., U.S. — A10 126
Hettstedt, Ger. — E7 16
Heuvelton, N.Y., U.S. — D14 112
Heves, Hung. — B7 26
Heves, state, Hung. — A7 26
Hewanorra International Airport, St. Luc. — m6 105c
Hewu, China — H5 42
Hexham, Eng., U.K. — F11 12
Hexian, China — D3 42
Heyang, China — D3 42
Heyburn, Id., U.S. — H13 136
Heysham, Eng., U.K. — G10 12
Heyuan, China — J6 42
Heyworth, Il., U.S. — D9 120
Heze, China — D6 42
Hezheng, China — D5 36
Hialeah, Fl., U.S. — K5 116
Hiawatha, Ks., U.S. — E2 120
Hiawatha, Ut., U.S. — D6 132
Hibbard, Qc., Can. — C4 110
Hibbing, Mn., U.S. — D5 118
Hickman, Ky., U.S. — H8 120
Hickory, N.C., U.S. — A4 116
Hickory, N.C., U.S. — I4 114
Hickory Flat, Ms., U.S. — C9 122
Hicks, Point, c., Austl. — K7 76
Hico, Tx., U.S. — C9 130
Hida see Hita, Japan — F3 40
Hidalgo, Mex. — B8 100
Hidalgo, Mex. — H5 42 → Hidalgo, Mex. — C9 100
Hidalgo, Mex. — B9 100
Hidalgo, state, Mex. — E9 100
Hidalgo del Parral, Mex. — B6 100
Hida-sammyaku, mts., Japan — C10 40
Hidrolândia, Braz. — I1 88
Hieflau, Aus. — C11 22
Hienghène, N. Cal. — m15 79d
Hierapolis see Pamukkale, hist., Tur. — F12 28
Higashihiroshima, Japan — E5 40
Higashiichiki, Japan — H3 40
Higashine, Japan — A13 40
Higashiōsaka, Japan — E8 40
Higgins, Tx., U.S. — E8 128
Higgins Lake, l., Mi., U.S. — D5 112
Higginsville, Mo., U.S. — E4 120
Highbury, Austl. — C8 74
Highland, Il., U.S. — F8 120
Highland, In., U.S. — G2 112
Highland, Ks., U.S. — E2 120
Highland Park, Il., U.S. — F2 112
Highlands, N.C., U.S. — A2 116
Highlands, Tx., U.S. — H3 122
High Level, Ab., Can. — D7 106
High Point, mtn., N.J., U.S. — C11 114
High Point, mtn., Wy., U.S. — B9 132
High Point, c., Ber. — I15 104e
High River, Ab., Can. — F17 138
Highrock Lake, l., Mb., Can. — D10 106
Highrock Lake, l., Sk., Can. — D9 106
High Rock Lake, res., N.C., U.S. — A5 116
High Springs, Fl., U.S. — G3 116
Hightstown, N.J., U.S. — D11 114
Highwood, Mt., U.S. — C16 136
Highwood, stm., Ab., Can. — F17 138
Highwood Baldy, mtn., Mt., U.S. — C16 136
High Wycombe, Eng., U.K. — J11 12
Higuera de Abuya, Mex. — C5 100
Higuera de Zaragoza, Mex. — B4 100
Higüero, Punta, c., P.R. — B1 104a
Higüey, Dom. Rep. — C13 102
Hiiumaa, i., Est. — G10 8
Hikari, Japan — F4 40

Hikone, Japan — D9 40
Hoch'uan see Hechuan, China — G2 42
Hocimsk, Bela. — G15 10
Hockenheim, Ger. — G4 16
Hocking, stm., Oh., U.S. — E15 120
Hodal, India — E6 54
Hodeida see Al-Ḥudaydah, Yemen — G5 56
Hodge, La., U.S. — E6 122
Hodgenville, Ky., U.S. — G12 120
Hodgeville, Sk., Can. — D7 124
Hódmezővásárhely, Hung. — C7 26
Hodna, Chott el, l., Alg. — B6 64
Hodonín, Czech Rep. — H12 16
Hoek van Holland, Neth. — C12 14
Hoensbroek, Ger. — F6 16
Hofei see Hefei, China — F7 42
Hoffman, Mn., U.S. — F3 118
Hofgeismar, Ger. — E5 16
Hofheim am Taunus, Ger. — F4 16
Hofheim in Unterfranken, Ger. — F6 16
Hofors, Swe. — F7 8
Hofsjökull, ice, Ice. — k30 8a
Höfu, Japan — E4 40
Hofuf see Al-Hufūf, Sau. Ar. — D6 56
Hogansville, Ga., U.S. — D14 122
Hogback Mountain, mtn., Ne., U.S. — F9 126
Hogback Mountain, mtn., S.C., U.S. — A3 116
Högsby, Swe. — H6 8
Hohenwald, Tn., U.S. — B11 122
Hoher Dachstein, mtn., Aus. — C10 22
Hohe Tauern, mts., Aus. — C9 22
Hohhot, China — A4 42
Hohoe, Ghana — H5 64
Hōhoku, Japan — E3 40
Hoh Xil Hu, l., China — D3 36
Hoh Xil Shan, mts., China — D2 36
Hoi An, Viet. — E9 48
Hoihong see Haikang, China — K3 42
Hoihow see Haikou, China — K4 42
Hoima, Ug. — D6 66
Hoisington, Ks., U.S. — C10 128
Hōjai, India — E14 54
Højer, Den. — B4 16
Hōjō, Japan — F5 40
Hokah, Mn., U.S. — H7 118
Hokang see Hegang, China — B11 36
Hokitika, N.Z. — F4 80
Hokkaidō, i., Japan — C15 38
Hokksund, Nor. — G3 8
Hola Prystan', Ukr. — F4 32 → E4 32
Holalkere, India — D3 53
Holberg, B.C., Can. — F2 138
Holbrook, Austl. — J6 76
Holbrook, Az., U.S. — I6 132
Holbrook, Ne., U.S. — A8 128
Holden, Ab., Can. — C18 138
Holden, Mo., U.S. — F4 120
Holden, W.V., U.S. — G3 114
Holden Village, Wa., U.S. — B6 136
Holder, Fl., U.S. — H3 116
Holderness, pen., Eng., U.K. — H12 12
Holdfast, Sk., Can. — D8 124
Holdingford, Mn., U.S. — F4 118
Hole in the Mountain Peak, mtn., Nv., U.S. — C1 132
Hole Narsipur, India — E2 53
Holetown, Barb. — n8 105d
Holgate, Oh., U.S. — C1 114
Holguín, Cuba — B9 102
Holíč, Slov. — H13 16
Hollabrunn, Aus. — B13 22
Holland, Mi., U.S. — F3 112
Holland, Tx., U.S. — D10 130
Holland, hist. reg., Neth. — B13 14
Holland see Netherlands, ctry., Eur. — B15 14
Hollandale see Jayapura, Indon. — F11 44
Hollandsbird Island, i., Nmb. — D2 70
Holley, N.Y., U.S. — E11 112
Holliday, Tx., U.S. — H10 128
Hollins, Va., U.S. — G6 114
Hollister, Ca., U.S. — G4 134
Hollow Rock, Tn., U.S. — H9 120
Holly, Co., U.S. — C6 128
Holly Grove, Ar., U.S. — C7 122
Holly Hill, Fl., U.S. — G4 116
Holly Springs, Ms., U.S. — C9 122
Hollywood, Fl., U.S. — J5 116
Holm, Russia — C14 10
Holman, N.T., Can. — A7 106
Hólmavík, Ice. — k28 8a
Holmen, Wi., U.S. — H7 118
Holmes, Mount, mtn., Wy., U.S. — F16 136
Holm Land, pen., Grnld. — A22 141
Holm Ø, i., Grnld. — C14 141
Holmogorskaja, Russia — E19 8
Holmsk, Russia — G17 34
Holmsund, Swe. — E9 8
Holon, Israel — F5 58
Holoog, Nmb. — E4 70
Holovanivs'k, Ukr. — A17 26
Holstebro, Den. — H3 8
Holsteinsborg (Sisimiut), Grnld. — D15 141
Holston, stm., Tn., U.S. — H2 114
Holston, North Fork, stm., U.S. — H3 114
Holsworthy, Eng., U.K. — K8 12
Holt, Fl., U.S. — G12 122
Holt, Mi., U.S. — B1 114
Holton, Ks., U.S. — E2 120
Holts Summit, Mo., U.S. — F5 120
Holy Cross, Ak., U.S. — D8 140
Holy Cross Mountain, mtn., B.C., Can. — C10 138
Holyhead, Wales, U.K. — H8 12
Holy Island, i., Eng., U.K. — F11 12
Holyoke, Co., U.S. — G10 126
Holyoke, Ma., U.S. — B13 114
Holyrood, Ks., U.S. — C10 128
Holzkirchen, Ger. — I7 16
Holzminden, Ger. — E5 16
Homalin, Mya. — D7 46
Homathko, stm., B.C., Can. — E6 138
Homberg, Ger. — E6 16
Hombori Tondo, mtn., Mali — F4 64
Hombre Muerto, Salar del, pl., Arg. — B4 92
Homburg, Ger. — G3 16
Home Bay, b., Nu., Can. — B17 106
Home Hill, Austl. — B6 76
Homedale, Id., U.S. — G10 136
Homel', Bela. — H13 10
Homel', state, Bela. — H12 10
Homer, Ga., U.S. — B2 116
Homer, La., U.S. — E5 122
Homer, Mi., U.S. — B1 114
Homer, Ne., U.S. — I2 118
Homer, N.Y., U.S. — B9 114
Homer City, Pa., U.S. — D6 114
Homerville, Ga., U.S. — K5 116
Homestead, Fl., U.S. — K5 116

Homestead National Monument of America, p.o.i., Ne., U.S. — A11 128
Homewood, Al., U.S. — D12 122
Hommura, Japan — E12 40
Honbān̄ād, India — C3 53
Hōd, reg., Maur. — F3 64
Homoine, Moz. — C12 70
Homosassa, Fl., U.S. — H3 116
Homs see Al-Khums, Libya — A2 62
Homs see Hims, Syria — D7 58
Honan see Henan, state, China — E5 42
Honan see Luoyang, China — D5 42
China — E5 42
Honāvar, India — D2 53
Hon Chong, Viet. — G7 48
Honda, Col. — E4 86
Honda, Bahía, b., Col. — A5 86
Honda Bay, b., Phil. — F2 52
Hondeklipbaai, S. Afr. — G3 70
Hon Dien, Nui, mtn., Viet. — A16 138 → A16 48?
Hondo, Japan — H3 40
Hondo, N.M., U.S. — H3 128
Hondo, stm., N.A. — C3 102
Honduras, ctry., N.A. — E4 102
Honduras, Cabo de, c., Hond. — D5 102
Honduras, Gulf of, b., N.A. — D4 102
Honea Path, S.C., U.S. — B3 116
Hønefoss, Nor. — F4 8
Honesdale, Pa., U.S. — C10 114
Honey Grove, Tx., U.S. — D3 122
Honey Lake, l., Ca., U.S. — C5 134
Honeyville, Ut., U.S. — B4 132
Honfleur, Fr. — E9 14
Hong, stm., China — E6 42
Hong, Song see Red, stm., Asia — D9 46
Hon Gai, Viet. — B8 48
Hong Hu, l., China — F5 42
Hongjiang, China — H4 42
Hong Kong see Xianggang, China — J6 42
Hongliuyuan, China — F17 32
Hong Ngu, Viet. — G7 48
Hongqi, China — B7 38
Hongshi, China — C7 38
Hongshui, stm., China — J3 42
Hongtong, China — C4 42
Hongueedo, Détroit d', strt., Qc., Can. — A12 110
Hongze, China — E8 42
Hongze Hu, l., China — E8 42
Honiara, Sol. Is. — e8 79b
Honjō, Japan — E13 38
Honningsvåg, Nor. — A11 8
Honokaa, Hi., U.S. — C6 78a
Honokohau, Hi., U.S. — b3 78a
Honolulu, Hi., U.S. — B4 78a
Honomu, Hi., U.S. — D6 78a
Hon Quan, Viet. — G8 48
Honshū, i., Japan — G12 38
Honuu, Russia — C17 34
Hood, stm., Nu., Can. — B9 106
Hood, Mount, vol., Or., U.S. — E5 136
Hood Canal, b., Wa., U.S. — C4 136
Hoodoo Peak, mtn., Wa., U.S. — B6 136
Hood Point, c., Austl. — F3 74
Hoodsport, Wa., U.S. — C3 136
Hoogeveen, Neth. — B15 14
Hoogeveense Vaart, can., Neth. — B15 14
Hooker, Ok., U.S. — E7 128
Hook Head, c., Ire. — I6 12
Hook Point, c., Austl. — E9 76
Hooks, Tx., U.S. — D4 122
Hoonah, Ak., U.S. — E12 140
Hoopa, Ca., U.S. — B2 134
Hooper, Ne., U.S. — C1 120
Hooper Bay, Ak., U.S. — D6 140
Hoople, N.D., U.S. — F16 124
Hoopstad, S. Afr. — E7 70
Hoorn, Neth. — B14 14
Hoosick Falls, N.Y., U.S. — H3 110? → B13?
Hoover Dam, dam, U.S. — D2 132
Hooversville, Pa., U.S. — H11 112
Hopatcong, N.J., U.S. — D11 114
Hope, B.C., Can. — G9 138
Hope, Ar., U.S. — D5 122
Hope, In., U.S. — E12 120
Hope, Ben, mtn., Scot., U.K. — C8 12
Hope, Point, c., Ak., U.S. — H9 122
Hopedale, La., U.S. — H9 122
Hopeh see Hebei, state, China — D8 36
Hopelchén, Mex. — C3 102
Hope Mills, N.C., U.S. — B7 116
Hopër, stm., Russia — E17 6
Hopes Advance, Cap, c., Qc., Can. — C17 106
Hopetoun, Austl. — J4 76
Hopetown, S. Afr. — F6 70
Hope Valley, R.I., U.S. — C14 114
Hopewell, Va., U.S. — G8 114
Hopewell Culture National Historic Park, p.o.i., Oh., U.S. — E2 114
Hopewell Islands, is., Nu., Can. — D14 106
Hopi see Hebi, China — D6 42
Hopkins, Mo., U.S. — D3 120
Hopkins, stm., Austl. — K4 76
Hopkinsville, Ky., U.S. — H10 120
Hopkinton, Ia., U.S. — B6 120
Hoppo see Beihai, China — K3 42
Hoppo see Hepu, China — K3 42
Hopwood, Mount, hill, Austl. — C5 76
Hoquiam, Wa., U.S. — D3 136
Hor, Russia — G16 34
Hor, stm., Russia — B12 36
Horatio, Ar., U.S. — D4 122
Hordaland, state, Nor. — F2 8
Horgen, Switz. — D10 26
Horicon, Wi., U.S. — H10 118
Horinsk, Russia — F10 34
Horizon Deep, unds. — G10 142
Horizontina, Braz. — C10 92
Horlick Mountains, mts., Ant. — D29 81
Horlivka, Ukr. — E5 32
Horlovo, Russia — E21 10
Hormigueros, P.R. — B1 104a
Hormuz, Strait of, strt., Asia — D8 56
Horn, c., Ice. — j28 8a
Horn, stm., N.T., Can. — C7 106
Horn see Cape see Hornos, Cabo de, c., Chile — K3 90
Hornád (Hornad), stm., Eur. — H17 16
Hornavan, l., Swe. — C7 8
Hornby Bay, b., N.T., Can. — B8 106
Hornbrook, Ca., U.S. — B3 134
Horneburg, Ger. — C5 16
Horn Island, i., Ms., U.S. — G10 122
Hornell, N.Y., U.S. — B8 114
Hornepayne, On., Can. — F14 106
Horn Lake, Ms., U.S. — C8 122
Hornos, Cabo de (Horn, Cape), c., Chile — K3 90
Horn Plateau, plat., N.T., Can. — C6 106

Name	Map Ref.	Page
Hornsea, Eng., U.K.	H12	12
Horodkivka, Ukr.	A15	26
Horodok, Ukr.	G19	16
Horog, Taj.	B11	56
Horol´, Russia	B10	38
Horqin Youyi Qianqi, China	B9	36
Horqin Youyi Zhongqi, China	B4	38
Horqin Zuoyi Houqi, China	C4	38
Horqin Zuoyi Zhongqi, China	B5	38
Horqueta, Para.	D5	90
Horse Cave, Ky., U.S.	G12	120
Horse Creek, stm., U.S.	F8	126
Horse Creek, stm., Co., U.S.	C5	128
Horsefly, B.C., Can.	D9	138
Horsefly Lake, l., B.C., Can.	D10	138
Horseheads, N.Y., U.S.	B9	114
Horse Islands, is., Nf., Can.	i22	107a
Horsens, Den.	I3	8
Horseshoe Bend, Id., U.S.	G10	136
Horsham, Austl.	K4	76
Horsham, Eng., U.K.	J12	12
Horšovský Týn, Czech Rep.	G8	16
Horten, Nor.	G4	8
Hortobágy, reg., Hung.	B8	26
Hortobágyi Nemzeti Park, p.o.i., Hung.	B8	26
Horton, Ks., U.S.	E2	120
Horton, stm., N.T., Can.	B6	106
Horton Lake, l., N.T., Can.	B6	106
Hortonville, Wi., U.S.	G10	118
Hory, Bela.	F14	10
Hosa´ina, Eth.	F7	62
Hösbach, Ger.	F5	16
Hosedahard, Russia	A9	32
Hosford, Fl., U.S.	G14	122
Hoshāb, Pak.	D9	56
Hoshangābād, India	G6	54
Hoshiārpur, India	C5	54
Hosh Isa, Egypt	H1	58
Hosmer, B.C., Can.	G15	138
Hospers, Ia., U.S.	A2	120
Hospet, India	D3	53
Hospitalet see L'Hospitalet de Llobregat, Spain	C13	20
Hossegor, Fr.	F4	18
Hosston, La., U.S.	E5	122
Hosta Butte, mtn., N.M., U.S.	H8	132
Hoste, Isla, i., Chile	K3	90
Hosūr, India	E3	53
Hotagen, l., Swe.	E5	8
Hotaka-dake, mtn., Japan	C10	40
Hotamiş, Tur.	A4	58
Hotan, China	A5	46
Hotazel, S. Afr.	E6	70
Hotevilla, Az., U.S.	H6	132
Hotlovo, Russia	C17	10
Hot'kovo, Russia	G18	10
Hot'kovo, Russia	D21	10
Hot Springs, Ar., U.S.	C5	122
Hot Springs, N.C., U.S.	I3	114
Hot Springs, S.D., U.S.	D9	126
Hot Springs, Va., U.S.	F6	114
Hot Springs National Park see Hot Springs, Ar., U.S.	C5	122
Hot Springs Peak, mtn., Nv., U.S.	B8	134
Hot Sulphur Springs, Co., U.S.	A2	128
Hottah Lake, l., N.T., Can.	B7	106
Hottentotsbaai, b., Nmb.	E2	70
Hotynec, Russia	G18	10
Houaïlou, N. Cal.	m15	79d
Houat, Île de, i., Fr.	G6	14
Houdan, Fr.	F10	14
Houghton, Mi., U.S.	D10	118
Houghton, N.Y., U.S.	B7	114
Houghton Lake, l., Mi., U.S.	D4	112
Houlka, Ms., U.S.	C10	122
Houlton, Me., U.S.	D9	110
Houma, China	D4	42
Houma, Tonga	n13	78e
Houma, La., U.S.	H8	122
Hou-pei see Hubei, state, China	F5	42
Hourtin, Étang d´, l., Fr.	D4	18
Housatonic, Ma., U.S.	B12	114
House, N.M., U.S.	G5	128
Houston, B.C., Can.	B4	138
Houston, Mn., U.S.	H7	118
Houston, Mo., U.S.	G6	120
Houston, Tx., U.S.	H3	122
Houston, Lake, res., Tx., U.S.	H3	122
Hout, stm., S. Afr.	C9	70
Houtman Abrolhos, is., Austl.	E2	74
Houxinqiu, China	C5	38
Hovd, Mong.	B3	36
Hovd, Mong.	C5	36
Hovd, stm., Mong.	E16	32
Hove, Eng., U.K.	K12	12
Hoven, S.D., U.S.	B13	126
Hovenweep National Monument, p.o.i., U.S.	F7	132
Hoverla, hora, mtn., Ukr.	A11	26
Hovgaard Ø, i., Grnld.	A22	141
Hövsgöl nuur, l., Mong.	F9	34
Hovu-Aksy, Russia	D16	32
Howar, Wādī, val., Afr.	D5	62
Howard, Austl.	E9	76
Howard, Ks., U.S.	D12	128
Howard, Pa., U.S.	D8	114
Howard, S.D., U.S.	C15	126
Howard City, Mi., U.S.	E4	112
Howard Draw, Tx., U.S.	D6	130
Howard Lake, Mn., U.S.	F4	118
Howe, In., U.S.	G4	112
Howe, Cape, c., Austl.	K7	76
Howe Island, i., On., Can.	D13	112
Howells, Ne., U.S.	J15	126
Howell, Mi., U.S.	B2	114
Howick, S. Afr.	F10	70
Howitt, Mount, mtn., Austl.	K6	76
Howland Island, i., Oc.	C9	72
Howser, B.C., Can.	F13	138
Howson Peak, mtn., B.C., Can.	B3	138
Hoxie, Ar., U.S.	H6	120
Hoxie, Ks., U.S.	B8	128
Höxter, Ger.	E5	16
Hoxtolgay, China	B2	36
Hoy, i., Scot., U.K.	C9	12
Hoyerswerda, Ger.	E10	16
Hoyos, Spain	D4	20
Höytiäinen, l., Fin.	E13	8
Hoyt Lakes, Mn., U.S.	D6	118
Hradec Králové, Czech Rep.	F11	16
Hradzjanka, Bela.	G11	10
Hranice, Czech Rep.	G13	16
Hřesk, Bela.	H10	10
Hristoforovo, Russia	F22	8
Hrodna, Bela.	G6	10
Hrodna, state, Bela.	G7	10
Hroma, stm., Russia	B17	34
Hron, stm., Slov.	H14	16
Hronov, Czech Rep.	F12	16
Hrubieszów, Pol.	F19	16
Hrustal'nyj, Russia	B11	38
Hsiakuan see Dali, China	F5	36
Hsiamen see Xiamen, China	I7	42
Hsian see Xi'an, China	D3	42
Hsiang'an see Xiangtan, China		
Hsianyang see Xianyang, China	H5	42
Hsinchu, Tai.	I9	42
Hsin-hseng, Mya.	B3	48
Hsilo, Tai.	J9	42
Hsim, stm., Mya.	B4	48
Hsinchu, Tai.	I9	42
Hsinghua see Xinghua, China	E8	42
Hsing'ai see Xingtai, China	C6	42
Hsinhailien see Lianyungang, China	D8	42
Hsinhsiang see Xinxiang, China	D5	42
Hsining see Xining, China	D5	36
Hsinking see Changchun, China	C6	38
Hsinp'u see Lianyungang, China	D8	42
Hsintien, Tai.	I9	42
Hsinyang see Xinyang, China	E6	42
Hsipaw, Mya.	A3	48
Hsüanhua see Xuanhua, China	A6	42
Hsüch'ang see Xuchang, China	D5	42
Hsüchou see Xuzhou, China	D7	42
Hua'an, China	I7	42
Huab, stm., Nmb.	B2	70
Huachi, Bol.	B4	90
Huacho, Peru	F2	84
Huachuca City, Az., U.S.	L6	132
Huadian, China	C7	38
Huading Shan, mtn., China	G9	42
Hua Hin, Thai.	F4	48
Huai, stm., China	C6	42
Huai'an, China	E8	42
Huai'an, China	A6	42
Huaibin, China	E6	42
Huaicheng see Huai'an, China	E8	42
Huaidezhen, China	C6	38
Huailai, China	A6	42
Huainan, China	E7	42
Huairou, China	A7	42
Huaite see Gongzhuling, China	C6	38
Huaiyang, China	E6	42
Huai Yot, Thai.	I4	48
Huaiyuan, China	E7	42
Huajuapan de León, Mex.	G10	100
Hualahuises, Mex.	C9	100
Hualalai, vol., Hi., U.S.	D6	78a
Hualañé, Chile	G2	92
Hualfín, Arg.	C4	92
Hualien, Tai.	J9	42
Huallaga, stm., Peru	E2	84
Huallanca, Peru	E2	84
Huambo, Ang.	C2	68
Huamei Shan, mtn., China	I5	42
Huan, stm., China	B11	38
Huanan, China	B8	38
Huancabamba, Peru	E2	84
Huancané, Peru	G4	84
Huancavelica, Peru	F2	84
Huancayo, Peru	F2	84
Huang (Yellow), stm., China	D8	36
Huanghua, China	B7	42
Huangchuan, China	E6	42
Huanggang Hu, l., China	G5	42
Huanggang, China	F6	42
Huanggangliang, mtn., China	B7	42
Huanghua, China	B7	42
Huangjinbu, China	G7	42
Huangling, China	D3	42
Huanglong, China	D3	42
Huangnihe, China	C7	38
Huangpi, China	F6	42
Huangqi, China	H4	42
Huangshahe, China	H4	42
Huangshan see Guangming Ding, mtn., China	F7	42
Huangshi, China	F6	42
Huangtang Hu, l., China	G6	42
Huangtuliangzi, China	A8	42
Huanguelén, Arg.	H6	92
Huangxian, China	C9	42
Huangyan, China	G9	42
Huangzhong, China	D5	36
Huangzhu, China	L4	42
Huanjiang, China	I3	42
Huanren, China	D6	38
Huánuco, Peru	E2	84
Huanni, Bol.	C3	90
Huanxian, China	C2	42
Huara, Chile	C3	90
Huaral, Peru	F2	84
Huaráz, Peru	E2	84
Huarmey, Peru	F2	84
Huarong, China	G5	42
Huasaga, stm., S.A.	I3	86
Hua Sai, Thai.	H5	48
Huascarán, Nevado, mtn., Peru	E2	84
Huasco, Chile	D2	92
Huasco, stm., Chile	D2	92
Huatabampo, Mex.	B4	100
Huating, China	D2	42
Huatong, China	A9	42
Huauchinango, Mex.	E9	100
Huautla, Mex.	C5	96
Huaxian, China	G5	42
Huaxian, China	D4	42
Huayamota, stm., Mex.	D6	100
Huazamota, Mex.	D6	100
Huazhou, China	K4	42
Hubbard, Ia., U.S.	B4	120
Hubbard Creek Reservoir, l., Tx., U.S.	B8	130
Hubbard Lake, l., Mi., U.S.	D6	112
Hubbards, N.S., Can.	F12	110
Hubbell, Mi., U.S.	D10	118
Hubei, state, China	F5	42
Huberdeau, Qc., Can.	E2	110
Hubli-Dhārwār, India	D2	53
Hubuleng, China	A4	42
Huchow see Huzhou, China	F9	42
Huckleberry Mountain, mtn., U.S.	B11	136
Hucknall, Eng., U.K.	H11	12
Huddersfield, Eng., U.K.	H11	12
Huddinge, Swe.	G8	8
Huder, China	A9	36
Hudiksvall, Swe.	F8	8
Hudson, Fl., U.S.	H3	116
Hudson, Ma., U.S.	B14	114
Hudson, N.Y., U.S.	B12	114
Hudson, N.Y., U.S.	H3	110
Hudson, Oh., U.S.	C4	114
Hudson, S.D., U.S.	H2	118
Hudson, Wy., U.S.	E4	126
Hudson, stm., U.S.	G16	112
Hudson, Baie d' see Hudson Bay, b., Can.	C13	106
Hudson Bay, Sk., Can.	E10	106
Hudson Bay, b., Can.	C13	106
Hudson Falls, N.Y., U.S.	B12	114
Hudson's Hope, B.C., Can.	D6	106
Hudson Strait, strt., Can.	C16	106
Hudžand, Taj.	A10	56
Hue, Viet.	D8	48
Huebra, stm., Spain	D4	20
Huehuetenango, Guat.	E2	102
Huejotzingo, Mex.	F9	100
Huejúcar, Mex.	D7	100
Huejuquilla el Alto, Mex.	D6	100
Huelgoat, Fr.	F5	14
Huelva, Spain	H4	20
Huelva, co., Spain	G3	20
Huelva, stm., Spain	G4	20
Huentelauquén, Chile	E2	92
Huércal-Overa, Spain	G8	20
Huerfano, stm., Co., U.S.	C4	128
Huerlumada, China	B13	54
Huérva, stm., Spain	C9	20
Huesca, Spain	B10	20
Huesca, co., Spain	B10	20
Huéscar, Spain	G8	20
Huetamo de Núñez, Mex.	F8	100
Hueytown, Al., U.S.	D11	122
Hufrat an-Nahās, Sudan	F4	62
Hughenden, Austl.	C4	76
Hughes, Ak., U.S.	C9	140
Hughes, Ar., U.S.	C8	122
Hughes Springs, Tx., U.S.	E4	122
Hugh Keenleyside Dam, dam, B.C., Can.	G12	138
Hughson, Ca., U.S.	F5	134
Hugh Town, Eng., U.K.	L6	12
Hugli, India	G12	54
Hugli, stm., India	G12	54
Hugo, Co., U.S.	B5	128
Hugo, Ok., U.S.	C3	122
Hugoton, Ks., U.S.	D7	128
Huhar, stm., China	B4	38
Huhehaote see Hohhot, China	A4	42
Huhhot see Hohhot, China	A4	42
Huichang, China	I6	42
Huicheng see Huilai, China	J7	42
Huichol, Far. Is.	n34	8b
Huichou see Huizhou, China	J6	42
Huila, state, Col.	F4	86
Huila, Nevado del, vol., Col.	F3	86
Huilai, China	J7	42
Huili, China	F5	36
Huillapima, Arg.	D4	92
Huimin, China	C7	42
Huinan, China	C7	38
Huisachal, Mex.	H6	130
Huishui, China	H2	42
Huisne, stm., Fr.	F9	14
Huitong, China	H3	42
Huitzo, Mex.	G10	100
Huitzuco de los Figueroa, Mex.	F9	100
Huixian, China	E2	42
Huixian, China	D5	42
Huixtla, Mex.	H12	100
Huize, China	F5	36
Huizhou, China	J6	42
Hūksan-chedo, is., Kor., S.	D5	70
Hukuntsi, Bots.	D5	70
Hulan, China	B7	38
Hulan Ergi, China	B9	36
Hulbert, Mi., U.S.	B4	112
Hulett, Wy., U.S.	C8	126
Hulga, stm., Russia	B10	32
Hulin, China	B11	36
Hulin, stm., China	B4	38
Huliu, stm., China	A6	42
Hull, Qc., Can.	C14	112
Hull, Il., U.S.	E6	120
Hull, Ia., U.S.	H2	118
Hulun see Hailar, China	B8	36
Hulun Nur, l., China	B8	36
Huma, China	F14	34
Huma, Tonga	o15	78e
Humacao, P.R.	B4	104a
Humahuaca, Arg.	D3	90
Humaitá, Braz.	E5	84
Humaitá, Para.	C8	92
Humansdorp, S. Afr.	I7	70
Humansville, Mo., U.S.	G4	120
Humara, Jabal al-, hill, Sudan	D6	62
Humbe, Ang.	D1	68
Humber, stm., Eng., U.K.	H12	12
Humbird, Wi., U.S.	G8	118
Humboldt, Sk., Can.	B8	124
Humboldt, Az., U.S.	I4	132
Humboldt, Il., U.S.	E9	120
Humboldt, Ia., U.S.	B3	120
Humboldt, Ne., U.S.	D2	120
Humboldt, S.D., U.S.	D15	126
Humboldt, stm., Nv., U.S.	C7	134
Humboldt, North Fork, stm., Nv., U.S.	B1	132
Humboldt, South Fork, stm., Nv., U.S.	C1	132
Humboldt Gletscher, ice, Grnld.	B13	141
Humboldt Lake, l., Nv., U.S.	D7	134
Hume, Ca., U.S.	G7	134
Hume, Lake, res., Austl.	J6	76
Humenné, Slov.	H17	16
Humeston, Ia., U.S.	D4	120
Humphrey, Ne., U.S.	F15	126
Humphreys, Mount, mtn., U.S.	F7	134
Humphreys Peak, mtn., Az., U.S.	H5	132
Humpolec, Czech Rep.	G11	16
Humpty Doo, Austl.	B6	74
Hūn, Libya	B3	62
Hun, stm., China	D5	38
Hun, stm., China	D6	38
Húnaflói, b., Ice.	j29	8a
Hunan, state, China	H4	42
Hunchun, China	C9	38
Hundred, W.V., U.S.	E5	114
Hunedoara, Rom.	D10	26
Hunedoara, state, Rom.	C10	26
Hünfeld, Ger.	F5	16
Hungary, ctry., Eur.	B5	26
Hungchiang see Hongjiang, China	H4	42
Hŭngnae-dong, Kor., N.	E7	38
Hungerford, Austl.	G5	76
Hungerford, Tx., U.S.	H2	122
Hungry Horse Dam, dam, Mt., U.S.	B13	136
Hungry Horse Reservoir, res., Mt., U.S.	B13	136
Hung Yen, Viet.	B8	48
Hunsrück, mts., Ger.	G3	16
Hunsūr, India	E3	53
Hunte, stm., Ger.	D4	16
Hunter, N.D., U.S.	D1	118
Hunter, stm., Austl.	I8	76
Hunter Island, i., Austl.	n12	77a
Hunter Island, i., B.C., Can.	E2	138
Hunter River, P.E., Can.	D13	110
Hunters, Wa., U.S.	B8	136
Hunters Bay, b., Mya.	C1	48
Huntingdon, Qc., Can.	E2	110
Huntingdon, Eng., U.K.	I12	12
Huntingdon, Pa., U.S.	D7	114
Huntingdon, Tn., U.S.	I9	120
Huntington, In., U.S.	H4	112
Huntington, Tx., U.S.	F4	122
Huntington, Ut., U.S.	D5	132
Huntington, W.V., U.S.	F3	114
Huntington Beach, Ca., U.S.	J7	134
Huntly, N.Z.	C6	80
Huntly, Scot., U.K.	D10	12
Huntsville, On., Can.	C10	112
Huntsville, Al., U.S.	C12	122
Huntsville, Mo., U.S.	E5	120
Huntsville, Tn., U.S.	H13	120
Huntsville, Tx., U.S.	G3	122
Huntsville, Ut., U.S.	B5	132
Hunyuan, China	B5	42
Huong Hoa, Viet.	D8	48
Huon Gulf, b., Pap. N. Gui.	b4	79a
Huon Peninsula, pen., Pap. N. Gui.	b4	79a
Huonville, Austl.	o13	77a
Huoqiu, China	E7	42
Huoshan, China	F7	42
Huoxian, China	C4	42
Hurd, Cape, c., On. Can.	C8	112
Hüren Tovon uul, mtn., Mong.	C4	36
Hurg Qi, China	C4	36
Hurghada, Egypt	K4	58
Hurley, N.M., U.S.	K8	132
Hurley, S.D., U.S.	D15	126
Hurley, Wi., U.S.	E8	118
Huron, Ca., U.S.	G5	134
Huron, Oh., U.S.	C3	114
Huron, S.D., U.S.	C14	126
Huron, stm., Mi., U.S.	B2	114
Huron, Lake, l., N.A.	D7	112
Huron Mountains, hills, Mi., U.S.	B2	112
Hurricane, Ut., U.S.	F3	132
Hurstbridge, Austl.	K5	76
Hurtado, stm., Chile	E2	92
Hurtsboro, Al., U.S.	E13	122
Hurunui, stm., N.Z.	F5	80
Húsavík, Far. Is.	n34	8b
Húsavík, Ice.	j31	8a
Hushitai, China	C5	38
Husi, Rom.	C15	26
Huslia, Ak., U.S.	C3	140
Husum, Ger.	B4	16
Hutag, Mong.	B5	36
Hutanopan, Indon.	C1	50
Hutchinson, S. Afr.	G5	70
Hutchinson, Ks., U.S.	C11	128
Hutchinson, Mn., U.S.	G4	118
Hutch Mountain, mtn., Az., U.S.	I5	132
Hutto, Tx., U.S.	D10	130
Hutuo, stm., China	B5	42
Huwei, Tai.	J9	42
Huxi, China	H6	42
Huxian, China	D3	42
Huxley, Ab., Can.	E17	138
Huy, Bel.	D14	14
Huzhou, China	G8	42
Huzhou, China	F9	42
Hvannadalshnúkur, mtn., Ice.	k31	8a
Hvar, Cro.	G13	22
Hvar, Otok, i., Cro.	G13	22
Hveragerdi, Ice.	k29	8a
Hvolsvöllur, Ice.	l29	8a
Hwainan see Huainan, China	E7	42
Hwange, Zimb.	D4	68
Hwang Ho see Huang, stm., China	D8	36
Hwangju-ŭp, Kor., N.	E6	38
Hwangshih see Huangshi, China	F6	42
Hyannis, Ma., U.S.	C15	114
Hyannis, Ne., U.S.	F11	126
Hyargas nuur, l., Mong.	B3	36
Hyattville, Wy., U.S.	C5	126
Hydaburg, Ak., U.S.	E13	140
Hyde Park, Guy.	B6	84
Hyde Park, N.Y., U.S.	C12	114
Hyde Park, Vt., U.S.	F4	110
Hyderābād, India	C5	53
Hyderābād, Pak.	F2	54
Hydra see Ýdra, i., Grc.	F6	28
Hydraulic, B.C., Can.	D9	138
Hydro, Ok., U.S.	F10	128
Hyères, Fr.	F12	18
Hyères, Îles d', is., Fr.	G12	18
Hyesan, Kor., N.	D8	38
Hyland, stm., Can.	C5	106
Hyndman, Pa., U.S.	E7	114
Hyndman Peak, mtn., Id., U.S.	G12	136
Hyōgo, state, Japan	D7	40
Hyrum, Ut., U.S.	B5	132
Hysham, Mt., U.S.	A5	126
Hythe, Eng., U.K.	J13	12
Hyūga, Japan	G4	40
Hyūga-nada, Japan	G4	40
Hyvinkää, Fin.	F11	8

I

Name	Map Ref.	Page
Iaciara, Braz.	H2	88
Iaco (Yaco), stm., S.A.	F4	84
Iaçu, Braz.	G5	88
Iaeger, W.V., U.S.	G4	114
Ialomiţa, state, Rom.	E14	26
Ialomiţa, stm., Rom.	E13	26
Ialoveni, Mol.	C15	26
Iamonia, Lake, l., Fl., U.S.	F1	116
Iapu, Braz.	J4	88
Iargara, Mol.	C15	26
Iaşi, Rom.	B14	26
Iaşi, state, Rom.	B14	26
Iatt, Lake, res., La., U.S.	F6	122
Ib, stm., India	G10	54
Iba, Phil.	C2	52
Ibagué, Col.	E4	86
Ibaiti, Braz.	A12	92
Ibâneşti, Rom.	C12	26
Ibar, stm., Yugo.	F7	26
Ibaraki, state, Japan	C13	40
Ibarra, Ec.	G2	86
Ibarreta, Arg.	B8	92
Ibb, Yemen	G5	56
Ibbenbüren, Ger.	D3	16
Ibembo, D.R.C.	D4	66
Ibera, Esteros del, sw., Arg.	D8	92
Iberia, Mo., U.S.	F5	120
Iberian Peninsula, pen., Eur.	D12	4
Ibérico, Sistema (Iberian Mountains), mts., Spain	D8	20
Ibiá, Braz.	J2	88
Ibiapaba, Serra da, plat., Braz.	B5	88
Ibicaraí, Braz.	H6	88
Ibicuí, stm., Braz.	D9	92
Ibicuy, Arg.	F8	92
Ibiracu, Braz.	J5	88
Ibirama, Braz.	C13	92
Ibirapuitã, stm., Braz.	D10	92
Ibirataia, Braz.	H6	88
Ibitiara, Braz.	G4	88
Ibiúna, Braz.	L2	88
Ibiza see Eivissa, Spain	F12	20
Ibiza see Eivissa, i., Spain	F12	20
Ibo, Moz.	C7	68
Ibotirama, Braz.	G4	88
Ibrīktepe, Tur.	B9	28
Ibshawāi, Egypt	I1	58
Ibusuki, Japan	H3	40
Ica, Peru	F2	84
Icá (Putumayo), stm., S.A.	E10	86
Icabarú, stm., Ven.	E10	86
Içana, Braz.	G7	86
Içana (Isana), stm., S.A.	G7	86
Icaño, Arg.	D5	92
Iceberg Pass, p., Co., U.S.	G7	126
İçel (Mersin), Tur.	B5	58
İçel, state, Tur.	B4	58
Iceland, ctry., Eur.	k30	8a
Iceland Basin, unds.	C11	144
Ice Mountain, mtn., B.C., Can.	B9	138
Ichalkaranji, India	C2	53
Ichchāpuram, India	B7	53
Ichikawa, Japan	D12	40
Ichinomiya, Japan	D9	40
Ichkeul, Lac, l., Tun.	G3	24
Ich'ŏn, Kor., S.	F7	38
Ich'un see Yichun, China	B10	36
Iĉinskaja Sopka, vulkan, vol., Russia	E20	34
Iĉinskoe, Russia	D19	10
Icó, Braz.	D6	88
Icy Cape, c., Ak., U.S.	B7	140
Ida, Mount see Ídhi Óros, mtn., Grc.	H7	28
Idabel, Ok., U.S.	D4	122
Ida Grove, Ia., U.S.	B2	120
Idah, Nig.	H6	64
Idaho, state, U.S.	G12	136
Idaho City, Id., U.S.	G11	136
Idaho Falls, Id., U.S.	G14	136
Idaho National Engineering Laboratory, sci., Id., U.S.	G14	136
Idalou, Tx., U.S.	H7	128
Idanha-a-Nova, Port.	E3	20
Idāppādi, India	F3	53
Idar, India	G4	54
Idar-Oberstein, Ger.	G3	16
Idelès, Alg.	E6	64
Ídhi Óros, mtn., Grc.	H7	28
Idiofa, D.R.C.	F3	66
Idku, Bahra el-, l., Egypt	G1	58
Idlib, Syria	C7	58
Idlib, state, Syria	C7	58
Idolo, Isla del, i., Mex.	E10	100
Idoûkâl-en-Taghès, mtn., Niger	F6	64
Idre, Swe.	F5	8
Idrija, Slvn.	D11	22
Idutywa, S. Afr.	H9	70
Iecava, stm., Lat.	D7	10
Ieper, Bel.	D11	14
Ierápetra, Grc.	H8	28
Iermak, Tan.	F7	66
Ierzu, Italy	E3	24
Iesi, Italy	G10	22
Iesolo, Italy	E9	22
Ifakara, Tan.	F7	66
Ife, Nig.	H5	64
Iferouâne, Niger	F6	64
Iferten see Yverdon-les-Bains, Switz.	D3	22
Ifôghas, Adrar des, mts., Afr.	F5	64
Igan, Malay.	B7	50
Iganga, Ug.	D6	66
Igaporã, Braz.	G4	88
Igara, Braz.	F5	88
Igara Paraná, stm., Col.	H5	86
Igarapava, Braz.	K2	88
Igarapé, Braz.	K3	88
Igarapé-Açu, Braz.	D8	84
Igarapé-Miri, Braz.	B1	88
Igarka, Russia	A15	32
Igatpuri, India	B1	53
Igboho, Nig.	H5	64
Igharghar, Oued, stm., Alg.	D6	64
Igiugig, Ak., U.S.	E8	140
Iglesias, Italy	E2	24
Iglesias, Cerro las, mtr., Mex.	B5	100
Igiesiente, reg., Italy	E2	24
Igloolik, Nu., Can.	B14	106
Ignacio, Co., U.S.	F9	132
Ignalina, Lith.	E9	10
Ignatei, Mol.	B15	26
Igoumenítsa, Grc.	D3	28
Igra, Russia	C8	32
Iguaçu (Iguazú), stm., S.A.	B10	92
Iguaçu, Parque Nacional do, p.o.i., Braz.	B11	92
Igual, Braz.	H5	88
Iguala, Mex.	F9	100
Igualada, Spain	C12	20
Iguana, stm., Ven.	D9	86
Iguape, Braz.	B14	92
Iguatama, Braz.	K3	88
Iguazú (Iguaçu), stm., S.A.	B10	92
Iguazú, Parque Nacional, p.o.i., S.A.	B10	92
Iguéla, Lagune, b., Gabon	E1	66
Igunga, Ug.	E6	66
Igwŏn, Kor., N.	D8	38
Igžej, Russia	D18	32
Iharaña, Madag.	C9	68
Iheya-shima, i., Japan	I18	39a
Ihnâsiya el-Madina, Egypt	I1	58
Ihosy, Madag.	E8	68
Ihtiman, Blg.	G10	26
Ii, Fin.	D11	8
Iida, Japan	D10	40
Iijoki, stm., Fin.	D12	8
Iisalmi, Fin.	E12	8
Iiyama, Japan	C11	40
Iizuka, Japan	F3	40
Ijebu-Ode, Nig.	H5	64
IJmuiden, Neth.	B13	14
IJssel, stm., Neth.	B15	14
IJsselmeer, l., Neth.	B14	14
Ijuí, Braz.	D10	92
Ijuí, stm., Braz.	C10	92
Ikali, D.R.C.	E4	66
Ikaría, i., Grc.	F9	28
Ikatskij hrebet, mts., Russia	F11	34
Ikeda, Japan	E6	40
Ikej, Russia	D17	32
Ikeja, Nig.	H5	64
Ikela, D.R.C.	E4	66
Ikere, Nig.	H6	64
Iki, i., Japan	F2	40
Ikizce, Tur.	D15	28
Ikom, Nig.	H6	64
Ikot-Ekpene, Nig.	H6	64
Ikuno, Japan	D7	40
Ikurangi, hill, Cook Is.	a26	78j
Ila, Nig.	H5	64
Ilagan, Phil.	B3	52
Ilaiyānkudi, India	G4	53
Ilām, Iran	C6	56
Ilam, Nepal	E11	54
Ilan, Tai.	I9	42
Ilanskij, Russia	C16	32
Ilaro, Nig.	H5	64
Iława, Pol.	C15	16
Ilbenge, Russia	D13	34
Ilebo, D.R.C.	E4	66
Île-de-France, hist. reg., Fr.	F11	14
Île-de-France, i., Grnld.	B22	141
Île-à-la-Crosse, Sk., Can.	D9	106
Ilek, Russia	D8	32
Ilero, Nig.	H5	64
Ilesha, Nig.	H5	64
Iles Loyauté, state, N. Cal.	m16	79d
Île Tintamarre, i., Anguilla	A2	105a
Ileza, Russia	F20	8
Ilford, Mb., Can.	D12	106
Ilfracombe, Austl.	D5	76
Ilfracombe, Eng., U.K.	J8	12
Ilha Grande, Baía da, b., Braz.	L3	88
Ilha Solteira, Represa de, res., Braz.	D6	90
Ilha Point, c., Nmb.	C2	70
Ilhéus, Braz.	H6	88
Ilia, Rom.	D9	26
Iliamna, Ak., U.S.	E8	140
Iliamna Lake, l., Ak., U.S.	D9	140
Iliĉ, il´, Kaz.	F11	32
Iliff, Co., U.S.	G9	126
Iligan, Phil.	F5	52
Iligan Bay, b., Phil.	F4	52
Iliniza, vol., Ec.	H2	86
Ilion, N.Y., U.S.	A10	114
Ilir, Russia	C18	32
Ilizi, Alg.	D6	64
Il'ja, Bela.	F10	10
Iljino, Russia	E14	10
Iljinskaja Sopka, vulkan, vol., Russia	G17	34
Iljinskij, Russia	D19	10
Iljinsko-Podomskoe, Russia	F23	8
Il'jnij gory, hills, Russia	D17	10
Ilkal, India	D2	53
Ilkley, Eng., U.K.	H11	12
Illampu, Nevado, mtn., Bol.	C3	90
Illana Bay, b., Phil.	G4	52
Ille-et-Vilaine, state, Fr.	F7	14
Illéla, Niger	G6	64
Illertissen, Ger.	H6	16
Illescas, Mex.	D7	100
Illichivs'k, Ukr.	C17	26
Illimani, Nevado, mtn., Bol.	C3	90
Illinois, state, U.S.	D8	120
Illinois, stm., Il., U.S.	E7	120
Illinois, stm., Or., U.S.	H3	136
Il'men', ozero, l., Russia	B14	10
Ilo, Peru	G3	84
Iloilo, Phil.	E4	52
Ilomantsi, Fin.	E14	8
Ilorin, Nig.	H5	64
Il pyrskij, Russia	D21	34
Ilûkste, Lat.	E9	10
Iulissat see Jakobshavn, Grnld.	D15	141
Ilwaki, Indon.	G8	44
Iŵól-san, mtn., Kor., S.	C1	40
Imabari, Japan	E5	40
Imaichi, Japan	C12	40
Imandra, ozero, l., Russia	C14	8
Imari, Japan	F2	40
Imarui, Braz.	D13	92
Imaruí, Lagoa do, l., Braz.	D13	92
Imatra, Fin.	F13	8
Imavere, Est.	B8	10
Imbabura, state, Ec.	G2	86
Imbituba, Braz.	D13	92
Imeni Cjurupy, Russia	E21	10
Imeni Kirova, Russia	E14	34
Imeni Poliny Osipenko, Russia	F16	34
Imeni Stepana Razina, Russia	I21	8
Imeni Željabova, Russia	A19	10
Imil, Eth.	F8	62
Imías, Cuba	B10	102
Imilac, Chile	B3	92
Imlay, Nv., U.S.	C7	134
Imlay City, Mi., U.S.	E6	112
Immenstadt, Ger.	I6	16
Immokalee, Fl., U.S.	J4	116
Imnaha, stm., Or., U.S.	E10	136
Imola, Italy	F8	22
Imonda, Pap. N. Gui.	a3	79a
Impasugong, Phil.	F5	52
Imperatriz, Braz.	C2	88
Imperia, Italy	G5	22
Imperial, Sk., Can.	C8	124
Imperial, Ca., U.S.	K10	134
Imperial, Tx., U.S.	C5	130
Imperial Beach, Ca., U.S.	K8	134
Imperial Dam, dam, U.S.	K2	132
Imperial de Aragón, Canal, can., Spain	C9	20
Imperial Valley, val., Ca., U.S.	E5	98
Impfondo, Congo	D3	66
Imphal, India	D7	46
Imroz, Tur.	C8	28
Imst, Aus.	C7	22
Imuris, Mex.	F7	98
Ina, Japan	D10	40
Ina, Il., U.S.	F9	120
Inajá, Braz.	E7	88
I-n-Amenas, Alg.	D6	64
Inambari, stm., Peru	F4	84
Inari, Fin.	B12	8
Inarigda, Russia	C19	34
Inarijärvi, l., Fin.	B12	8
Inawashiro-ko, l., Japan	B12	40
Inca, Spain	E13	20
Inca de Oro, Chile	C3	92
Incahuasi, Cerro de, mtn., S.A.	C3	92
Ince Burun, c., Tur.	C10	28
Íncekum Burnu, c., Tur.	B4	58
Inchelium, Wa., U.S.	B8	136
Inch'ŏn, Kor., S.	F7	38
Incirliova, Tur.	F10	28
Incomati (Komati), stm., Afr.	E10	70
Incudine, Monte, mtn., Fr.	H15	18
Incy, Russia	D19	8
Indaiá, stm., Braz.	J3	88
Indalsälven, stm., Swe.	E7	8
Inde, Mex.	C6	100
Independence, Ca., U.S.	G7	134
Independence, Ia., U.S.	B6	120
Independence, Ks., U.S.	D12	128
Independence, Ky., U.S.	F13	120
Independence, Mo., U.S.	E3	120
Independence, Va., U.S.	H4	114
Independence, Wi., U.S.	G7	118
Independence Fjord, b., Grnld.	A20	141
Independência, Bol.	C3	90
Independencia, Braz.	C5	88
Inderborskij, Kaz.	E8	32
Indi, India	C3	53
India, ctry., Asia	D4	46
Indialantic, Fl., U.S.	H5	116
Indian, stm., On., Can.	C8	112
Indiana, state, U.S.	D11	120
Indiana Dunes National Lakeshore, p.o.i., In., U.S.	G2	112
Indianapolis, In., U.S.	I3	112
Indian Bayou, stm., Ar., U.S.	C7	122
Indian Head, Sk., Can.	D10	124
Indian Head, Md., U.S.	F8	114
Indian Lake, l., N.Y., U.S.	A10	114
Indian Lake, l., Mi., U.S.	B3	112
Indian Ocean	K11	142
Indianola, Ia., U.S.	C4	120
Indianola, Ms., U.S.	D8	122
Indianola, Ne., U.S.	A8	128
Indianópolis, Braz.	J1	88
Indian Peak, mtn., Ut., U.S.	E3	132
Indian Prairie Canal, can., Fl., U.S.	J4	116
Indian River, Mi., U.S.	C5	112
Indian Rock, mtn., Wa., U.S.	D6	136
Indiara, Braz.	I1	88
Indiga, Russia	C23	8
Indiera Alta, P.R.	B2	104a
Indigirka, stm., Russia	C18	34
Indin, Mya.	A2	48
Indira Gandhi Canal, can., India	E4	54
Indispensable Strait, strt., Sol. Is.	e9	79b
Indochina, reg., Asia	D7	48
Indonesia, ctry., Asia	J16	30
Indore, India	G5	54
Indragiri, stm., Indon.	D2	50
Indramayu, Indon.	G6	50
Indrāvati, stm., India	B5	53

Name — Map Ref. — Page

Indravati Tiger Reserve, p.o.i., India B5 53
Indre, state, Fr. C7 18
Indre, stm., Fr. G10 14
Indre-et-Loire, state, Fr. G9 14
Indus, stm., Asia D2 46
Industry, Tx., U.S. H2 122
İnece, Tur. B10 28
In Ecker, Alg. E6 64
İnegöl, Tur. C12 28
Ineu, Rom. C8 26
Inez, Ky., U.S. G3 114
Inez, Tx., U.S. F11 130
Inferior, Laguna, b., Mex. G11 100
Infiernillo, Canal del, strt., Mex. G6 98
Infiernillo, Presa del, res., Mex. F7 100
Ing, stm., Thai. C5 48
Ingá, Braz. D8 88
Ingabu, Mya. D2 48
Ingal, Niger F6 64
Ingall Point, c., On., Can. B10 118
Ingelheim, Ger. G4 16
Ingende, D.R.C. E3 66
Ingeniero Jacobacci, Arg. H3 90
Ingeniero Luiggi, Arg. G5 92
Ingham, Austl. B6 76
Inglefield Land, reg., Grnld. B12 141
Ingleside, Tx., U.S. G10 130
Inglewood, Austl. G8 76
Inglewood, Austl. K4 76
Inglewood, Ca., U.S. J7 134
Inglis, Mb., Can. D12 124
Ingolf Fjord, b., Grnld. A22 141
Ingolstadt, Ger. H7 16
Ingonish, N.S., Can. D16 110
Ingrāj Bāzār, India F12 54
Ingrid Christensen Coast, cst., Ant. B12 81
In Guezzam, Alg. F6 64
Ingušetija, state, Russia F6 32
Ingushetia see Ingušetija, state, Russia F6 32
Inhaca, Ilha da, i., Moz. E11 70
Inhambane, Moz. C12 70
Inhambane, state, Moz. C12 70
Inhambane, Baía de, b., Moz. C12 70
Inhambupe, Braz. F6 88
Inhaminga, Moz. D5 68
Inhapim, Braz. J4 88
Inharrime, Moz. D12 70
Inhassoro, Moz. B12 70
Inhuma, Braz. D5 88
Inhumas, Braz. I1 88
Inimutaba, Braz. J3 88
Ining see Yining, China F14 32
Inírida, stm., Col. F7 86
Inis see Ennis, Ire. I3 12
Inis Córthaidh see Enniscorthy, Ire. I6 12
Inishbofin, i., Ire. H2 12
Inishmore, i., Ire. H3 12
Inishowen, pen., Ire. F5 12
Inishturk, i., Ire. H2 12
Inja, Russia E17 34
Inja, stm., Russia D18 34
Injune, Austl. E7 76
Inkom, Id., U.S. H14 136
Inkster, N.D., U.S. F16 124
Inland Lake, l., Mb., Can. B14 124
Inland Sea see Seto-naikai, Japan E5 40
Inle Lake, l., Mya. B3 48
Inman, Ks., U.S. C11 128
Inman Mills, S.C., U.S. A3 116
Inn, stm., Eur. B10 22
Innamincka, Austl. F3 76
Inner Channel, strt., Belize D3 102
Inner Hebrides, is., Scot., U.K. E6 12
Inner Mongolia see Nei Monggol, state, China C7 36
Inner Sister Island, i., Austl. m13 77a
Innisfail, Austl. A6 76
Innisfail, Ab., Can. D17 138
Innisfree, Ab., Can. C19 138
Innokentevka, Russia G16 34
Innoko, stm., Ak., U.S. D8 140
Innoshima, Japan E6 40
Innsbruck, Aus. C8 22
Innviertel, reg., Aus. B10 22
Inola, Ok., U.S. H2 120
Inongo, D.R.C. E3 66
İnönü, Tur. D13 28
Inowrocław, Pol. D14 16
In Salah, Alg. D5 64
Instow, Sk., Can. E5 124
Inta, Russia A10 32
Intendente Alvear, Arg. G6 92
İntepe, Tur. D9 28
Interlaken, Switz. D4 22
Interlândia, Braz. I1 88
International Falls, Mn., U.S. C5 118
Inthanon, Doi, mtn., Thai. C4 48
Intiyaco, Arg. D7 92
Intracoastal Waterway, strt., U.S. L5 116
Intracoastal Waterway, strt., U.S. H10 130
Intu, Indon. D9 50
Inubō-saki, c., Japan D13 40
Inukjuak, Qc., Can. D15 106
Inuvik, N.T., Can. B4 106
Inverbervie, Scot., U.K. E10 12
Invercargill, N.Z. H3 80
Inverell, Austl. G8 76
Inverloch, Austl. L5 76
Invermay, Sk., Can. C10 124
Invermere, B.C., Can. F14 138
Inverness, N.S., Can. D15 110
Inverness, Scot., U.K. D8 12
Inverness, Ca., U.S. E3 134
Inverness, Fl., U.S. H3 116
Inverurie, Scot., U.K. D10 12
Inverway, Austl. C5 74
Investigator Strait, strt., Austl. G7 74
Inwood, Mb., Can. D16 124
Inyangani, mtn., Zimb. D5 68
Inyathi, Zimb. D4 68
Inyo, Mount, mtn., Ca., U.S. G8 134
Inyokern, Ca., U.S. H8 134
Inyo Mountains, mts., Ca., U.S. G7 134
Inzana Lake, l., B.C., Can. B6 138
Ioánnina, Grc. D3 28
Iokanga, stm., Russia C18 8
Iola, Ks., U.S. G2 120
Ioma, Pap. N. Gui. b4 79a
Iona, Ang. D1 68
Iona, N.S., Can. D16 110
Iona, Id., U.S. G15 136
Iona, i., Scot., U.K. E6 12
Ione, Ca., U.S. E5 134
Ione, Wa., U.S. B9 136
Ionia, Mi., U.S. E4 112
Ionian Islands see Iónioi Nísoi, is., Grc. E3 28
Ionian Sea, Eur. F11 24
Iónioi Nísoi, state, Grc. E3 28
Iónioi Nísoi (Ionian Islands), is., Grc. E3 28
Iony, ostrov, i., Russia E17 34
Íos, i., Grc. G8 28
Iosegun Lake see Fox Creek, Ab., Can. B14 138
Iowa, La., U.S. G5 122
Iowa, state, U.S. I5 118
Iowa, stm., Ia., U.S. C6 120
Iowa City, Ia., U.S. C6 120
Iowa Falls, Ia., U.S. B4 120
Iowa Park, Tx., U.S. H10 128
Ipameri, Braz. I1 88
Ipanema, stm., Braz. E7 88
Ipanguaçu, Braz. C7 88
Ipatinga, Braz. J4 88
Ipatovo, Russia E6 32
Ipaumirim, Braz. D6 88
Ipeiros, state, Grc. D3 28
Ipeiros, hist. reg., Grc. D3 28
Ipel' (Ipoly), stm., Eur. I14 16
Ipiales, Col. G3 86
Ipiaú, Braz. H6 88
Ipin see Yibin, China F5 36
Ipirá, Braz. G6 88
Ipixuna, Braz. C3 88
Ipoh, Malay. J5 48
Ipojuca, stm., Braz. E7 88
Ipoly (Ipel'), stm., Eur. I14 16
Iporã, Braz. G7 84
Iporã, Braz. A11 92
Ipota, Vanuatu I17 79d
İpsala, Tur. C9 28
Ipswich, Austl. F9 76
Ipswich, Eng., U.K. I14 12
Ipswich, Ma., U.S. B15 114
Ipswich, S.D., U.S. B13 126
Ipu, Braz. C5 88
Ipubi, Braz. D5 88
Ipuc' (Iput'), stm., Eur. H14 10
Ipueiras, Braz. C5 88
Iput' (Ipuc'), stm., Eur. H14 10
Iqaluit, Nu., Can. C17 106
Iqfahs, Egypt J1 58
Iquique, Chile D2 90
Iquitos, Peru D3 84
Ira, Tx., U.S. B7 130
Iracema, Braz. C6 88
Irákleia, i., Grc. G8 28
Irákleio, Grc. H8 28
Iran, ctry., Asia C7 56
Iran Mountains, mts., Asia C9 50
Īrānshahr, Iran D9 56
Irapa, Ven. B10 86
Irapuato, Mex. E8 100
Iraq, ctry., Asia C5 56
Irará, Braz. F6 88
Irati, Braz. B12 92
Irazú, Volcán, vol., C.R. G6 102
Irbejskoe, Russia C17 32
Irbid, Jord. F6 58
Irbid, state, Jord. F6 58
Irbīl, Iraq B5 56
Irbit, Russia C10 32
Irdning, Aus. C11 22
Irebu, D.R.C. E3 66
Irecê, Braz. F5 88
Ireland, ctry., Eur. H4 12
Ireland Island North, i., Ber. k15 104e
Irene, S.D., U.S. D15 126
Ireng (Maú), stm., S.A. F12 86
Ireton, Ia., U.S. B1 120
Irgiz, Kaz. E10 32
Iri, Kor., S. G7 38
Iriba, Chad E4 62
Iriga, Phil. D4 52
Iríqui, reg., Afr. F3 64
Iringa, Tan. F7 66
Irinjālakuda, India F3 53
Iriomote-jima, i., Japan G9 36
Iriri, stm., Braz. D7 84
Irish, Mount, mtn., Nv., U.S. F1 132
Irish Sea, Eur. H7 12
Irituia, Braz. A2 88
Irkutsk, Russia D18 32
Irma, Ab., Can. D19 138
Irminger Basin, unds. B10 144
Irnijärvi, l., Fin. D13 8
Iroise, b., Fr. F4 14
Iron Bottom Sound, strt., Sol. Is. e8 79b
Iron Bridge, On., Can. B6 112
Iron City, Tn., U.S. B11 122
Irondale, Al., U.S. D12 122
Irondale, Mo., U.S. G7 120
Irondequoit, N.Y., U.S. E12 112
Iron Gate, val., Eur. E9 26
Iron Knob, Austl. F7 74
Iron Mountain, Mi., U.S. C1 112
Iron Range, Austl. B8 74
Iron River, Mi., U.S. E10 118
Ironton, Mn., U.S. E4 118
Ironton, Mo., U.S. G7 120
Ironton, Oh., U.S. F3 114
Ironwood, Mi., U.S. E8 118
Iroquois, On., Can. D14 112
Iroquois, stm., U.S. H2 112
Iroquois Falls, On., Can. F14 106
Irō-zaki, c., Japan E11 40
Irrawaddy see Ayeyarwady, stm., Mya. E8 46
Irricana, Ab., Can. E17 138
Irrigon, Or., U.S. E7 136
Irshava, Ukr. A10 26
Irsina, Italy D10 24
Irtyš see Irtysh, stm., Asia C11 32
Irtysh (Irtyš) (Ertix), stm., Asia C11 32
Irtyšsk, Kaz. D12 32
Irún, Spain A9 20
Iruña see Pamplona, Spain B9 20
Irurzun, Spain B9 20
Irú Tepuy, mtn., Ven. E11 86
Irvine, Ab., Can. E3 124
Irvine, Scot., U.K. F8 12
Irvines Landing, B.C., Can. G6 138
Irving, Tx., U.S. B10 130
Irvington, Ky., U.S. G11 120
Isa, Nig. G6 64
Isaac, stm., Austl. D7 76
Isaac Lake, l., B.C., Can. C10 138
Isabel, state, Sol. Is. d8 79b
Isabela, Phil. G3 52
Isabela, P.R. A1 104a
Isabela, Cabo, c., Dom. Rep. C12 102
Isabela, Isla, i., Ec. i11 84a
Isabelia, Cordillera, mts., Nic. F5 102
Isaccea, Rom. D15 26
Isachsen, Nu., Can. B5 141
Isachsen, Cape, c., Nu., Can. B4 141
Ísafjarðardjúp, b., Ice. j28 8a
Ísafjörður, Ice. j28 8a
Isahaya, Japan G3 40
Isak, Indon. J3 48
Isaka, Tan. E6 66
Īsa Khel, Pak. B3 54
Işalniţa, Rom. E10 26
Isana (Içana), stm., S.A. G7 86
Isangel, Vanuatu I17 79d
Isanti, Mn., U.S. F5 118
Isar, stm., Eur. H8 16
Isarog, Mount, vol., Phil. D4 52
İscehisar, Tur. E13 28
Ischia, Italy D7 24
Ischia, Isola d', i., Italy D7 24
Ise, Japan E9 40
Iseo, Lago d', l., Italy E6 22
Isère, state, Fr. D11 18
Isère, stm., Fr. D11 18
Iserlohn, Ger. E3 16
Isernia, Italy C8 24
Isesaki, Japan C12 40
Ise-shima-kokuritsu-kōen, p.o.i., Japan E9 40
Ise-wan, b., Japan E9 40
Iseyin, Nig. H5 64
Isezaki see Isesaki, Japan C12 40
Isfahan see Eşfahān, Iran C7 56
Isfara, Taj. A11 56
Isherton, Guy. F12 86
Ishigaki, Japan G9 36
Ishikari, stm., Japan C14 38
Ishikari-wan, b., Japan C14 38
Ishikawa, state, Japan C9 40
Ishim (Išim), stm., Asia C12 32
Ishinomaki, Japan A14 40
Ishioka, Japan C13 40
Ishizuchi-san, mtn., Japan F5 40
Ishpeming, Mi., U.S. B2 112
Ishurdi, Bngl. F12 54
Isigny-sur-Mer, Fr. E7 14
Işıklı, Tur. E12 28
Isil'kul', Russia C12 32
Išim, Russia C11 32
Išimskaja ravnina, pl., Asia C11 32
Isiolo, Kenya D7 66
Isipingo, ngh., S. Afr. G10 70
Isiro, D.R.C. D5 66
Isis, Austl. E9 76
Iskăr, stm., Blg. F11 26
Iskăr, Jazovir, res., Blg. G10 26
İskenderun (Alexandretta), Tur. B6 58
İskenderun Körfezi, b., Tur. B6 58
Iskitim, Russia D14 32
Iskut, stm., B.C., Can. D4 106
Isla, Mex. G11 100
Isla, Salar de la, pl., Chile B3 92
İslâhiye, Tur. A7 58
Islāmābād, Pak. B4 54
Islāmkot, Pak. F3 54
Islāmpur, India C2 53
Islāmpur, India F10 54
Islāmpur, India E12 54
Island, Ky., U.S. G10 120
Island Falls, Me., U.S. E8 110
Island Harbour, Anguilla A1 105a
Island Lake, l., Mb., Can. E12 106
Island Park, Id., U.S. F15 136
Island Pond, Vt., U.S. F5 110
Islands, Bay of, b., Nf., Can. j22 107a
Isla Patrulla, Ur. F10 92
Isla Vista, Ca., U.S. I5 134
Islay, i., Scot., U.K. F6 12
Isle, Mn., U.S. E5 118
Isle, stm., Fr. E5 18
Isle of Man, dep., Eur. G8 12
Isle of Wight, Va., U.S. H9 114
Isle Royale National Park, p.o.i., Mi., U.S. C10 118
Islesboro Island, i., Me., U.S. F8 110
Isleta, N.M., U.S. I10 132
Isleton, Ca., U.S. E4 134
Islón, Chile D2 92
Ismailia (Al-Ismā'īlīyah), Egypt H3 58
Isna, Egypt B6 62
Isny, Ger. I5 16
Isoka, Zam. C5 68
Isola del Liri, Italy I10 22
Isola di Capo Rizzuto, Italy F11 24
Isonzo, stm., Eur. E10 22
Isparta, Tur. F13 28
Isparta, state, Tur. F13 28
Ispica, Italy H8 24
Israel, ctry., Asia G5 58
Isrā'īl see Israel, ctry., Asia G5 58
Issa, stm., Russia D11 10
Isser, Oued, stm., Alg. H14 20
Issia, C. Iv. H3 64
Issoire, Fr. D9 18
Issoudun, Fr. H10 14
Issuna, Tan. F6 66
Issyk-Kul', Kyrg. F13 32
Issyk-Kul, Lake see Issyk-Kul', ozero, l., Kyrg. F13 32
Issyk-Kul', ozero, l., Kyrg. F13 32
Īstādeh-ye Moqor, Āb-e, l., Afg. B2 54
İstanbul, Tur. B12 28
İstanbul, state, Tur. B11 28
İstanbul Boğazı (Bosporus), strt., Tur. B12 28
Istiaía, Grc. E6 28
Istmina, Col. E3 86
Isto, Mount, mtn., Ak., U.S. C11 140
Istra, Russia E19 10
Istria, pen., Eur. E10 22
Itá, Para. B9 92
Itabaiana, Braz. D8 88
Itabaiana, Braz. F7 88
Itabaianinha, Braz. F7 88
Itabapoana, Braz. K5 88
Itaberaba, Braz. G5 88
Itaberaí, Braz. G8 84
Itabi, Braz. F7 88
Itabira, Braz. J4 88
Itabuna, Braz. H6 88
Itacajá, Braz. E2 88
Itacambiruçu, stm., Braz. I4 88
Itacoatiara, Braz. D6 84
Itacurubí del Rosario, Para. B9 92
Itaeté, Braz. G5 88
Itaguajé, Braz. D6 90
Itaguara, Braz. K3 88
Itaguari, stm., Braz. H3 88
Itagüí, Col. D4 86
Itaí, Braz. A13 92
Itaiçaba, Braz. C7 88
Itaim, stm., Braz. D5 88
Itainópolis, Braz. D5 88
Itaipu Reservoir, res., S.A. B10 92
Itäisen Suomenlahden kansallispuisto, p.o.i., Fin. F12 8
Itaituba, Braz. D6 84
Itajaí, Braz. C13 92
Itajubá, Braz. L3 88
Itaju do Colônia, Braz. H6 88
Itajuípe, Braz. H6 88
Itala Game Reserve, S. Afr. E10 70
Itálica, hist., Spain G4 20
Italy, Tx., U.S. B11 130
Italy, ctry., Eur. G11 6
Itamaraju, Braz. I6 88
Itamarandiba, Braz. I4 88
Itamarandiba, stm., Braz. I4 88
Itamari, Braz. G6 88
Itambacuri, Braz. I5 88
Itambé, Braz. H5 88
Itami, Japan E8 40
Itampolo, Madag. E7 68
Itānagar, India E14 54
Itanhaém, Braz. B14 92
Itanhém, Braz. I5 88
Itaobim, Braz. I5 88
Itapagipe, Braz. J1 88
Itapajé, Braz. B6 88
Itaparica, Ilha de, i., Braz. G6 88
Itaparica, Represa de, res., Braz. E6 88
Itapebi, Braz. H6 88
Itapecerica, Braz. K3 88
Itapecuru-Mirim, Braz. B3 88
Itapemirim, Braz. K5 88
Itaperuna, Braz. K5 88
Itapetim, Braz. D7 88
Itapetinga, Braz. H5 88
Itapetininga, Braz. L1 88
Itapetininga, stm., Braz. A14 92
Itapeva, Braz. L1 88
Itapicuru, Braz. F6 88
Itapicuru, stm., Braz. B3 88
Itapicuru, stm., Braz. F6 88
Itapipoca, Braz. B6 88
Itapiranga, Braz. D6 84
Itapirapuã, Braz. G7 84
Itapiúna, Braz. C6 88
Itápolis, Braz. K1 88
Itaporã de Goiás, Braz. D1 88
Itaporanga, Braz. D6 88
Itaporanga d'Ajuda, Braz. F7 88
Itapúa, state, Para. C10 92
Itaquara, Braz. G6 88
Itaquari, Braz. K5 88
Itaqui, Braz. D9 92
Itarantim, Braz. H5 88
Itararé, Braz. B13 92
Itararé, stm., Braz. A13 92
Itārsi, India G6 54
Itarumã, Braz. C6 90
Itasca, Tx., U.S. B10 130
Itasca, Lake, l., Mn., U.S. D3 118
Itata, stm., Chile H1 92
Itatinga, Braz. L1 88
Itatira, Braz. C6 88
Itatupã, Braz. D7 84
Itaueira, Braz. D4 88
Itaueira, stm., Braz. D4 88
Itaúna, Braz. K3 88
Itbayat Island, i., Phil. K9 42
Itéa, Grc. E5 28
Iténez (Guaporé), stm., S.A. F5 84
Ithaca, Mi., U.S. E5 112
Ithaca, N.Y., U.S. B9 114
Ithaca see Itháki, i., Grc. E3 28
Itháki, i., Grc. E3 28
Itimbiri, stm., D.R.C. D4 66
Itinga, Braz. I5 88
Itiquira, stm., Braz. G6 84
Itiruçu, Braz. G5 88
Itiúba, Braz. F5 88
Itla el-Bâsha, hill, Egypt K3 58
Itō, Japan E12 40
Itoigawa, Japan B10 40
Iton, stm., Fr. F9 14
Itororó, Braz. H5 88
Itsuki, Japan G3 40
Ittiri, Italy D2 24
Ittoqqortoormiit see Scoresbysund, Grnld. C21 141
Itu, Braz. L2 88
Itu, stm., Braz. D10 92
Ituaçu, Braz. G5 88
Ituango, Col. D4 86
Ituberá, Braz. G6 88
Itueta, Braz. J5 88
Ituí, stm., Braz. E3 84
Ituiutaba, Braz. J1 88
Itumbiara, Braz. J1 88
Ituna, Sk., Can. C10 124
Itupiranga, Braz. E8 84
Ituporanga, Braz. C13 92
Iturama, Braz. C6 90
Iturbide, Mex. C3 102
Iturup, ostrov (Etorofu-tō), i., Russia B17 38
Ituverava, Braz. K2 88
Ituxi, stm., Braz. E4 84
Ituzaingó, Arg. C9 92
Itzehoe, Ger. C5 16
Iuka, Ms., U.S. C10 122
Iul'tin, Russia C25 34
Iúna, Braz. K5 88
Ivacėvičy, Bela. H8 10
Ivačovo, Russia F17 8
Ivaí, stm., Braz. D6 90
Ivaiporã, Braz. B12 92
Ivalo, Fin. B12 8
Ivalojoki, stm., Fin. B12 8
Ivanava, Bela. H8 10
Ivančice, Czech Rep. G12 16
Ivangorod, Russia A11 10
Ivangrad, Yugo. G6 26
Ivanhoe, Austl. I5 76
Ivanhoe, Ca., U.S. G6 134
Ivanhoe, Mn., U.S. G2 118
Ivanhoe, Va., U.S. H4 114
Ivanišči, Russia D18 10
Ivanjica, Yugo. F7 26
Ivan'kovo, Russia F20 10
Ivan'kovskoe vodohranilišče, res., Russia D19 10
Ivano-Frankivs'k, Ukr. F13 6
Ivano-Frankivs'k, co., Ukr. A11 26
Ivanovka, Russia F14 34
Ivanovo, Russia H19 8
Ivanovskaja oblast', co., Russia H19 8
Ivanovskoe, Russia A11 10
Ivanpah Lake, l., Ca., U.S. H1 132
Ivdel', Russia B9 32
Ivigtut, Grnld. E16 141
Ivindo, stm., Gabon D2 66
Ivinheíma, stm., Braz. D6 90
Iviza see Eivissa, Spain F12 20
Ivjanec, Bela. G9 10
Ivohibe, Madag. E8 68
Ivory Coast see Cote d'Ivoire, ctry., Afr. H3 64
Ivory Coast, cst., C. Iv. I3 64
Ivrea, Italy E4 22
İvrindi, Tur. D10 28
Ivujivik, Qc., Can. C15 106
Iwaki, Japan B13 40
Iwaki-san, vol., Japan D14 38
Iwakuni, Japan E5 40
Iwami, Japan D7 40
Iwanuma, Japan A13 40
Iwata, Japan E10 40
Iwate, state, Japan A14 40
Iwate-san, vol., Japan E14 38
'Iweibid, Gebel, mtn., Egypt H3 58
Iwo, Nig. H5 64
Ixmiquilpan, Mex. E9 100
Ixopo, S. Afr. G10 70
Ixtapa, Mex. G8 100
Ixtepec, Mex. G11 100
Ixtlán del Río, Mex. E6 100
Iyang see Yiyang, China G5 42
Iyo, Japan F5 40
Iyo-mishima, Japan F6 40
Iyo-nada, Japan F5 40
Izabal, Lago de, l., Guat. E3 102
Izamal, Mex. B3 102
Izapa, hist., Mex. H12 100
Izberbaš, Russia F7 32
Izbica, Pol. F19 16
Izegem, Bel. D12 14
Iževsk, Russia C8 32
Izium, Ukr. E5 32
Ižma, stm., Russia B8 32
Izmaïl, Ukr. D15 26
Izmalkovo, Russia H21 10
Izmayil see Izmaïl, Ukr. D15 26
İzmir (Smyrna), Tur. E10 28
İzmir, state, Tur. E10 28
İzmir Körfezi, b., Tur. E9 28
İzmit (Kocaeli), Tur. C12 28
İzmit Körfezi, b., Tur. C12 28
İznik, Tur. C12 28
İznik Gölü, l., Tur. C12 28
Iznoski, Russia E18 10
Izozog, Bañados del, sw., Bol. C4 90
Izra', Syria F7 58
Izsák, Hung. C6 26
Iztaccíhuatl, Volcán, vol., Mex. F9 100
Iztaccíhuatl y Popocatéptl, Parques Nacionales, p.o.i., Mex. F9 100
Izucar de Matamoros, Mex. F9 100
Izu-hantō, pen., Japan E11 40
Izuhara, Japan E2 40
Izu Islands see Izu-shotō, is., Japan E12 40
Izumi, Japan G3 40
Izumi, Japan A13 40
Izumi, Japan E8 40
Izumo, Japan D5 40
Izu-shotō (Izu Islands), is., Japan E12 40
Izu Trench, unds. G17 142
Izvestij CIK, ostrova, is., Russia A5 34
Izvorul Muntelui, Lacul, l., Rom. C12 26

J

Jabal, Bahr al- see Mountain Nile, stm., Afr. F6 62
Jabal al-Awliyā', Sudan D6 62
Jabal Lubnān, state, Leb. D6 58
Jabalón, stm., Spain F7 20
Jabalpur, India G7 54
Jabālyah, Gaza G5 58
Jabbūl, Sabkhat al-, l., Syria C8 58
Jabiru, Austl. B6 74
Jablah, Syria C6 58
Jablanica, Bos. F4 26
Jablaničko jezero, res., Bos. F4 26
Jablonec nad Nisou, Czech Rep. F11 16
Jabłonka, Pol. G15 16
Jablonovyj hrebet, mts., Russia F11 34
Jablunkov, Czech Rep. G14 16
Jaboticabal, Braz. K1 88
Jaca, Spain B10 20
Jacala, Mex. E9 100
Jacaré, stm., Braz. F5 88
Jacareí, Braz. L2 88
Jacarezinho, Braz. D7 90
Jáchal, stm., Arg. E4 92
Jaciara, Braz. G6 84
Jacinto, Braz. I5 88
Jacinto Aráuz, Arg. I6 92
Jacinto City, Tx., U.S. H3 122
Jackfish Lake, l., Sk., Can. A5 124
Jackhead Harbour, Mb., Can. C16 124
Jack Mountain, mtn., Mt., U.S. D14 136
Jackpot, Nv., U.S. B2 132
Jacksboro, Tn., U.S. H1 114
Jacksboro, Tx., U.S. H10 128
Jackson, Ca., U.S. E5 134
Jackson, Ky., U.S. G2 114
Jackson, La., U.S. G7 122
Jackson, Mi., U.S. B1 114
Jackson, Mn., U.S. H4 118
Jackson, Ms., U.S. E8 122
Jackson, N.C., U.S. H8 114
Jackson, Oh., U.S. E3 114
Jackson, S.C., U.S. C4 116
Jackson, Tn., U.S. B10 122
Jackson, Wy., U.S. G16 136
Jackson, stm., Va., U.S. G6 114
Jackson, Mount, mtn., Ant. C34 81
Jackson, Mount, mtn., Austl. F3 74
Jackson Creek, stm., Can. E12 124
Jackson Lake, l., Wy., U.S. G16 136
Jacksonville, Al., U.S. D13 122
Jacksonville, Ar., U.S. C6 122
Jacksonville, Fl., U.S. F4 116
Jacksonville, Il., U.S. E7 120
Jacksonville, N.C., U.S. B8 116
Jacksonville, Or., U.S. A2 134
Jacksonville, Tx., U.S. F3 122
Jacksonville Beach, Fl., U.S. F4 116
Jacmel, Haiti C11 102
Jaco, Mex. B6 100
Jacobābād, Pak. D2 54
Jacobina, Braz. F5 88
Jacobsdal, S. Afr. F7 70
Jacques-Cartier, Mont, mtn., Qc., Can. A11 110
Jacu, stm., Braz. D8 88
Jacuí, stm., Braz. D11 92
Jacuípe, stm., Braz. F5 88
Jacumba, Ca., U.S. K9 134
Jacundá, Braz. D8 84
Jacupiranga, Braz. B13 92
Jacuriaí, stm., Braz. F6 88
Jadebusen, b., Ger. C4 16
J.A.D. Jensens Nunatakker, mtn., Grnld. E16 141
Jadraque, Spain D8 20
Jādū, Libya A2 62
Jaén, Peru E2 84
Jaén, Spain G7 20
Jaén, co., Spain G7 20
Jāfarābād, India H3 54
Jaffa, Cape, c., Austl. K2 76
Jaffna, Sri L. G4 53
Jaffna Lagoon, b., Sri L. G4 53
Jaffrey, N.H., U.S. B13 114
Jafr, Qā' al-, depr., Jord. H7 58
Jagalūr, India D3 53
Jagannāthganj Ghāt, Bngl. F12 54
Jagatsingpur, India H11 54
Jagdalpur, India B6 53
Jageljurta, gora, hill, Russia C17 8
Jagersfontein, S. Afr. F7 70
Jaggayyapeta, India C5 53
Jagodnoe, Russia D18 34
Jagraon, India C5 54
Jagtiāl, India B4 53
Jaguaquara, Braz. G6 88
Jaguarão, Braz. F11 92
Jaguarão (Yaguarón), stm., S.A. F11 92
Jaguarari, Braz. F5 88
Jaguari, Braz. D10 92
Jaguariaíva, Braz. B13 92
Jaguaribara, Braz. C6 88
Jaguaribe, Braz. C6 88
Jaguaribe, stm., Braz. C7 88
Jaguaruna, Braz. D13 92
Jagüey Grande, Cuba A7 102
Jahānābād, India F10 54
Jahrom, Iran D7 56
Jahroma, Russia D20 10
Jaicós, Braz. D5 88
Jailolo, Indon. E8 44
Jaintiāpur, Bngl. F14 54
Jaipur, India E5 54
Jaipur Hāt, Bngl. F12 54
Jais, India E8 54
Jaisalmer, India E3 54
Jaito, India C5 54
Jaja, Russia C15 32
Jājapur, India H11 54
Jajce, Bos. E4 26
Jakarta, Indon. G5 50
Jakarta, Teluk, b., Indon. F5 50
Jakaulevičy, Bela. F13 10
Jakhāu, India G2 54
Jakobshavn (Ilulissat), Grnld. D15 141
Jakobstad see Pietarsaari, Fin. E10 8
Jakovlevka, Russia B10 38
Jakša, Russia B9 32
Jakutija, state, Russia C14 34
Jakutsk, Russia D14 34
Jal, N.M., U.S. B4 130
Jalaid Qi, China B9 36
Jalālābād, Afg. C11 56
Jalālpur, India E9 54
Jalandhar, India C5 54
Jalapa, Guat. E3 102
Jalapa see Xalapa, Mex. F10 100
Jālaun, India E7 54
Jales, Braz. D6 90
Jalesar, India E7 54
Jaleshwar, India H11 54
Jālgaon, India H5 54
Jālgaon, India H6 54
Jalingo, Nig. H7 64
Jalisco, state, Mex. E6 100
Jālna, India B2 53
Jalón, stm., Spain C9 20
Jālor, India F4 54
Jalostotitlán, Mex. E7 100
Jalpa, Mex. E7 100
Jalpāiguri, India E12 54
Jaluit, at., Marsh. Is. C7 72
Jalutorovsk, Russia C11 32
Jamaame, Som. E8 66
Jamaica, ctry., N.A. D8 102
Jamaica Channel, strt., N.A. D9 102
Jamal, poluostrov, pen., Russia B2 34
Jam-Alin', hrebet, mts., Russia F15 34
Jamālpur, Bngl. F12 54
Jamālpur, India F11 54
Jamanota, hill, Aruba o20 104g
Jamantau, gora, mtn., Russia D9 32
Jamanxim, stm., Braz. E6 84
Jamari, stm., Braz. E5 84
Jamarovka, Russia F11 34
Jambelí, Canal de, strt., Ec. I2 86
Jambi, Indon. D3 50
Jambi, state, Indon. D3 50
Jamboaye, stm., Indon. J3 48
Jambol, Blg. G13 26
Jambongan, Pulau, i., Malay. G1 52
Jambuair, Tanjung, c., Indon. J3 48
Jambusar, India G4 54
James, stm., U.S. C8 108
James, stm., Mo., U.S. H4 120
James, stm., Va., U.S. G8 114
James, Isla, i., Chile H2 90
James Bay, b., Can. E14 106
James City, N.C., U.S. A8 116
James Craik, Arg. F6 92
James Island, S.C., U.S. D5 116
James Point, c., Bah. K9 116
Jamesport, Mo., U.S. E4 120
James Ross, Cape, c., N.T., Can. B17 140
James Ross Island, i., Ant. B35 81
James Ross Strait, strt., Nu., Can. A11 106
Jamestown, Austl. I2 76
Jamestown, S. Afr. G8 70
Jamestown, Ca., U.S. F5 134
Jamestown, Ky., U.S. H12 120
Jamestown, N.Y., U.S. B6 114
Jamestown, N.C., U.S. I6 114
Jamestown, N.D., U.S. H15 124
Jamestown, Tn., U.S. H13 120
Jamestown, misc. cult., Va., U.S. G9 114
Jām Jodhpur, India H3 54
Jamkhandi, India C2 53
Jamm, Russia B10 10
Jammerbugten, b., Den. H3 8
Jammu, India B5 54
Jammu and Kashmir see Kashmir, hist. reg., Asia B4 46
Jamnagar (Navanagar), India G3 54
Jampang-kulon, Indon. G5 50
Jāmpur, Pak. D3 54
Jämsä, Fin. F11 8
Jamshedpur, India G10 54
Jamsk, Russia E19 34
Jämtland, state, Swe. E6 8
Jamūi, India F11 54
Jamuna, stm., Bngl. F12 54
Jana, stm., Russia C16 34
Janaúba, Braz. H4 88
Janaucu, Ilha, i., Braz. C7 84
Jand, Pak. B4 54
Jandaia, Braz. G7 84
Jandiāla, India C5 54
Jandowae, Austl. F8 76
Jándula, stm., Spain F7 20
Janeiro, stm., Braz. F3 88
Janesville, Ca., U.S. C5 134
Janesville, Mn., U.S. G5 118
Janesville, Wi., U.S. B9 120
Jangamo, Moz. D12 70
Jangeru, Indon. E10 50
Jangijul', Uzb. F11 32
Jangīpur, India F11 54
Jangoon, India C4 53
Janīn, W.B. F6 58
Janisjarvi, ozero, l., Russia E14 8
Janiuay, Phil. E4 52
Jankan, hrebet, mts., Russia E12 34
Jan Kempdorp, S. Afr. E7 70
Janlohong, Indon. B10 50
Jan Mayen, i., Nor. B22 94
Janos, Mex. F8 98
Jánosháza, Hung. B4 26
Janowiec Wielkopolski, Pol. D13 16
Janskij, Russia C15 34
Janskij zaliv, b., Russia B16 34
Jantra, stm., Blg. F12 26
Januária, Braz. H3 88
Januário Cicco, Braz. D8 88
Jaora, India G5 54
Japan, ctry., Asia E12 38
Japan, Sea of (East Sea), Asia D11 38
Japan Basin, unds. E16 142
Japan Trench, unds. F17 142
Japaratinga, Braz. E8 88
Japi, Braz. D7 88
Japonskoje more see East Sea, Asia D11 38
Japonskoje more see Japan, Sea of, Asia D11 38
Japtiksalja, Russia C3 34
Japurá, Braz. H8 86
Japurá (Caquetá), stm., S.A. D5 84
Jaqué, Pan. D2 86
Jarābulus, Syria B9 58
Jaraguá, Braz. H1 88
Jaraguá do Sul, Braz. C13 92
Jaraíz de la Vera, Spain D5 20
Jarales, N.M., U.S. I10 132
Jarama, stm., Spain D7 20
Jaramānah, Syria E7 58
Jaransk, Russia C7 32
Jarānwāla, Pak. C4 54
Jarash, Jord. F6 58
Jarash, hist., Jord. F6 58
Jarcevo, Russia E15 10
Jardim, Braz. D6 88
Jardim, Braz. D5 90
Jardim de Piranhas, Braz. D7 88
Jardín América, Arg. C10 92
Jardines de la Reina, Archipiélago de los, is., Cuba B8 102
Jardinópolis, Braz. K1 88
Jarej-Uliga-Delap, Marsh. Is. C8 72
Jarenga, Russia E23 8
Jarensk, Russia E23 8
Jargalant, Mong. B4 36
Jari, stm., Braz. C7 84
Jaridih, India G11 54
Jarkand see Shache, China B12 56
Jarkino, Russia C17 32
Jarocin, Pol. D13 16
Jarohta, Russia C17 32
Jaroměř, Czech Rep. F11 16
Jaroslavl', Russia H19 8
Jaroslavskaja oblast', co., Russia H18 8
Jarosław, Pol. F18 16
Jarratt, Va., U.S. H8 114
Jar-Sale, Russia A12 32
Jartai Yanchi, l., China B1 42
Jarud Qi, China B4 38
Järvakandi, Est. G11 8
Järvenpää, Fin. F11 8
Jarvie, Ab., Can. B17 138
Jarvis, On., Can. F9 112
Jarvisburg, N.C., U.S. H10 114
Jarvis Island, i., Oc. D10 72
Jasdan, India G3 54
Jasel'da, stm., Bela. H8 10
Jashpurnagar, India D5 46
Jasień, Pol. E11 16
Jāsk, Iran D8 56
Jaškul', Russia E7 32

Name | Map Ref. | Page

Jasło, Pol. G17 16
Jasnogorsk, Russia F20 10
Jasnyj, Russia F14 34
Jason Islands, is., Falk. Is. J4 90
Jasper, Ab., Can. D12 138
Jasper, Al., U.S. D11 122
Jasper, Ar., U.S. I4 120
Jasper, Fl., U.S. F3 116
Jasper, Ga., U.S. B1 116
Jasper, In., U.S. F10 120
Jasper, Mn., U.S. H2 118
Jasper, Mo., U.S. G3 120
Jasper, Tn., U.S. B13 122
Jasper Lake, l., Ab., Can. C13 138
Jasper National Park, p.o.i., Ab., Can. D13 138
Jastarnia, Pol. B14 16
Jászapáti, Hung. B7 26
Jászberény, Hung. B6 26
Jász-Nagykun-Szolnok, state, Hung. B7 26
Jataí, Braz. G7 84
Jatapu, stm., Braz. D6 84
Jatate, stm., Mex. G13 100
Jati, Braz. D6 88
Jāti, Pak. F2 54
Játiva see Xàtiva, Spain F10 20
Jatni, India H10 54
Jaú, Braz. L1 88
Jaú, stm., Braz. H11 86
Jaú, Parque Nacional do, p.o.i., Braz. I10 86
Jauaperi, stm., Braz. H11 86
Jauá Sarisariñama, Parque Nacional, p.o.i., Ven. E9 86
Jauja, Peru F2 84
Jaunjelgava, Lat. D7 10
Jaunpiebalga, Lat. C9 10
Jaunpur, India F9 54
Java see Jawa, i., Indon. H6 50
Javalambre, mtn., Spain D9 20
Java Sea see Jawa, Laut, Indon. F6 50
Java Trench, unds. J13 142
Jávea see Xàbia, Spain F11 20
Javorník, Czech Rep. F13 16
Javorová skála, mtn., Czech Rep. G10 16
Jawa (Java), i., Indon. H6 50
Jawa, Laut (Java Sea), Indon. F6 50
Jawa Barat, state, Indon. G5 50
Jawa Tengah, state, Indon. G7 50
Jawa Timur, state, Indon. G8 50
Jawhar, Som. D9 66
Jawi, Indon. D6 50
Jawor, Pol. E12 16
Jaworzno, Pol. F15 16
Jay, Fl., U.S. G11 122
Jay, Ok., U.S. H3 120
Jaya, Puncak (Jaya Peak), mtn., Indon. F10 44
Jaya Peak see Jaya, Puncak, mtn., Indon. F10 44
Jayapura, Indon. F11 44
Jayb, Wādī al- (Ha'Arava), stm., Asia H6 58
Jaynes, Az., U.S. K5 132
Jaypur, India B6 53
Jayuya, P.R. B2 104a
Jažełbicy, Russia B15 10
Jažma, Russia C21 8
Jeanerette, La., U.S. H7 122
Jeannette Island see Žannetty, ostrov, i., Russia A20 34
Jebba, Nig. H5 64
Jebel, Rom. D8 26
Jedburgh, Scot., U.K. F10 12
Jeddah see Jiddah, Sau. Ar. E4 56
Jędrzejów, Pol. F16 16
Jeffara (Al-Jifārah), pl., Afr. C7 64
Jeffers, Mn., U.S. G3 118
Jefferson, Ga., U.S. B2 116
Jefferson, Oh., U.S. C5 114
Jefferson, Or., U.S. F3 136
Jefferson, S.C., U.S. B5 116
Jefferson, S.D., U.S. B1 120
Jefferson, Wi., U.S. A9 120
Jefferson, Mount, mtn., U.S. F15 136
Jefferson, Mount, mtn., Nv., U.S. E8 134
Jefferson, Mount, vol., Or., U.S. F5 136
Jefferson City, Mo., U.S. F5 120
Jefferson City, Tn., U.S. H2 114
Jeffersontown, Ky., U.S. F12 120
Jeffersonville, Ga., U.S. D2 116
Jeffersonville, In., U.S. F12 120
Jeffrey City, Wy., U.S. E5 126
Jega, Nig. G5 64
Jehol see Chengde, China A7 42
Jejsk see Ejsk, Russia E5 32
Jeju see Cheju, Kor., S. H7 38
Jēkabpils, Lat. D8 10
Jekyll Island, i., Ga., U.S. E4 116
Jelai, stm., Indon. E7 50
Jelenia Góra, Pol. F11 16
Jelenia Góra, state, Pol. E11 16
Jelgava, Lat. D6 10
Jelgavkrasti, Lat. C7 10
Jellicoe, On., Can. B11 118
Jelm Mountain, mtn., Wy., U.S. F7 126
Jemaja, Pulau, i., Indon. B4 50
Jember, Indon. H8 50
Jemez Canyon Reservoir, res., N.M., U.S. H9 132
Jemez Springs, N.M., U.S. H10 132
Jemnice, Czech Rep. H11 16
Jempang, Kenohan, l., Indon. D9 50
Jena, Ger. F7 16
Jena, La., U.S. F6 122
Jendouba, Tun. H2 24
Jeneponto, Indon. F11 50
Jenks, Ok., U.S. H2 120
Jennings, Fl., U.S. F2 116
Jennings, La., U.S. G6 122
Jensen, Ut., U.S. C7 132
Jens Munk Island, i., Nu., Can. B14 106
Jens Munks Ø, i., Grnld. E17 141
Jenu, Indon. D6 50
Jeonju see Chŏnju, Kor., S. G7 38
Jepara, Indon. G7 50
Jeparit, Austl. K4 76
Jeptha Knob, hill, Ky., U.S. F12 120
Jequié, Braz. G5 88
Jequitinhonha, Braz. I5 88
Jequitinhonha, stm., Braz. H5 88
Jerada, Mor. C4 64
Jerba, Île de, i., Tun. C7 64
Jerécuaro, Mex. E8 100
Jérémie, Haiti C10 102
Jeremoabo, Braz. F6 88
Jerevan see Yerevan, Arm. A5 56
Jerez de García Salinas, Mex. D7 100
Jerez de la Frontera, Spain H4 20
Jerez de los Caballeros, Spain F4 20
Jericho, Austl. D5 76
Jericho see Arīḥā, Gaza G6 58
Jericó, Braz. D7 88
Jerid, Chott, l., Tun. C6 64
Jerimoth Hill, hill, R.I., U.S. C14 114
Jeroaquara, Braz. G7 84
Jerome, Az., U.S. I4 132
Jerome, Id., U.S. H12 136
Jersey, dep., Eur. E6 14
Jersey, i., Jersey E6 14
Jersey City, N.J., U.S. D11 114
Jerseyville, Il., U.S. E7 120
Jerumenha, Braz. D4 88
Jerusalem see Yerushalayim, Isr. G6 58
Jervis, Cape, c., Austl. J1 76
Jervis Bay, b., Austl. J8 76
Jervis Bay Territory, co., Austl. J8 76
Jervis Inlet, b., B.C., Can. F7 138
Jesenice, Czech Rep. F9 16
Jeseník, Czech Rep. F13 16
Jesi (Iesi), Italy G10 22
Jessen, Ger. E9 16
Jessore, Bngl. G12 54
Jesup, Ga., U.S. E4 116
Jesup, Ia., U.S. B5 120
Jesús Carranza, Mex. G11 100
Jesús María, Arg. E5 92
Jesús Menéndez, Cuba B9 102
Jet, Ok., U.S. E10 128
Jetmore, Ks., U.S. C9 128
Jetpur, India H3 54
Jeune Landing, B.C., Can. F3 138
Jever, Ger. C3 16
Jewel Cave National Monument, p.o.i., S.D., U.S. D8 126
Jewell, Ks., U.S. B10 128
Jewell Ridge, Va., U.S. G4 114
Jewett, Il., U.S. E9 120
Jewett City, Ct., U.S. C13 114
Jezercës, maja e, mtn., Alb. B13 24
Jeziorany, Pol. B16 16
Jhābua, India G5 54
Jha Jha, India F11 54
Jhālakāti, Bngl. G13 54
Jhālāwār, India F6 54
Jhang Sadar, Pak. C4 54
Jhānsi, India F7 54
Jhārgrām, India G11 54
Jharia, India G11 54
Jhārsuguda, India H10 54
Jhelum, Pak. B4 54
Jhelum, stm., Asia C4 54
Jhinkpāni, India G10 54
Jhok Rind, Pak. C3 54
Jhunjhunūn, India D5 54
Jiaban, China I2 42
Jiading, China F9 42
Jiāganj, India F12 54
Jiahe, China I5 42
Jiali, China C14 54
Jialing, stm., China G2 42
Jialu, stm., China E5 42
Jiamusi, China B11 36
Ji'an, China D7 38
Ji'an, China H6 42
Jian, stm., China H8 42
Jianchang, China A8 42
Jianchang, China B10 42
Jianchuan, China F4 36
Jiande, China G8 42
Jiang'an, China G1 42
Jiangcheng, China A5 48
Jiangdu, China E8 42
Jiange, China E1 42
Jianghua, China I4 42
Jiangjin, China G2 42
Jiangkou, China J4 42
Jiangkou, China H3 42
Jiangkou, China F4 42
Jiangle, China H7 42
Jiangling, China F4 42
Jiangmen, China J5 42
Jiangmifeng, China B7 38
Jiangshan, China G8 42
Jiangsu, state, China E8 42
Jiangtun, China J5 42
Jiangxi, state, China H6 42
Jiangya, China G4 42
Jiangyin, China F9 42
Jiangyou, China F1 42
Jiangzhong, China D14 54
Jianli, China G5 42
Jianning, China H7 42
Jian'ou, China H8 42
Jianping, China D3 38
Jianshi, China F3 42
Jianshui, China G5 36
Jianyang, China E5 36
Jianyang, China H8 42
Jiaocheng, China C4 42
Jiaohe, China C7 38
Jiaolai, stm., China C4 38
Jiaonan, China D8 42
Jiaoxian, China C8 42
Jiaozhou Wan, b., China C9 42
Jiaozuo, China D5 42
Jiashan, China E7 42
Jiashi, China B12 56
Jiashun Hu, l., China A10 54
Jiawang, China D7 42
Jiaxian, China D5 42
Jiaxian, China B4 42
Jiaxing, China F9 42
Jiazi, China J6 42
Jibuti see Djibouti, Dji. E8 62
Jicarón, Isla, i., Pan. I7 102
Jičín, Czech Rep. F11 16
Jiddah (Jeddah), Sau. Ar. E4 56
Jidingxilin, China B14 54
Jieshi Wan, b., China J6 42
Jieshou, China E6 42
Jiexi, China J6 42
Jiexiu, China C4 42
Jieyang, China J7 42
Jieznas, Lith. F7 10
Jiguaní, Cuba B9 102
Jigüey, Bahía de, strt., Cuba A8 102
Jigzhi, China E5 36
Jihlava, Czech Rep. G11 16
Jihlava, stm., Czech Rep. G12 16
Jihočeský kraj, state, Czech Rep. G10 16
Jihomoravský kraj, state, Czech Rep. G12 16
Jijia, stm., Rom. B14 26
Jijiga, Eth. F8 62
Jilantai, China B1 42
Jilib, Som. D8 66
Jili Hu, l., China B2 36
Jilin, China C7 38
Jilin, state, China C10 36
Jill, Kediet ej, mtn., Maur. E2 64
Jiloca, stm., Spain C9 20
Jīma, Eth. F7 62
Jimbolia, Rom. D7 26
Jimena de la Frontera, Spain H5 20
Jiménez, Mex. B6 100
Jiménez, Mex. A8 100
Jiménez del Téul, Mex. D7 100
Jimeta, Nig. H7 64
Jim Ned Creek, stm., Tx., U.S. C8 130
Jimo, China C9 42
Jimsar, China C2 36
Jim Thorpe, Pa., U.S. D10 114
Jin (Gam), stm., Asia A7 48
Jin, stm., China H7 42
Jinan (Tsinan), China C7 42
Jincang, China C9 38
Jincheng, China D5 42
Jīnd, India D6 54
Jindabyne, Austl. K7 76
Jindřichův Hradec, Czech Rep. G11 16
Jing, stm., China D3 42
Jing'an, China G6 42
Jingbian, China C3 42
Jingbohu, res., China C8 38
Jingde, China F8 42
Jingdezhen, China G7 42
Jinggangshan, China H6 42
Jinghai, China B7 42
Jinghe, China F14 32
Jinghong, China B5 48
Jingle, China B4 42
Jingmen, China F5 42
Jingning, China D1 42
Jingxi, China J2 42
Jingxian, China F8 42
Jingxian, China C7 42
Jingxian, China H3 42
Jingxin, China I6 42
Jingyu, China C7 38
Jingzhi, China C8 42
Jinhae see Chinhae, Kor., S. D1 40
Jinhua, China G8 42
Jining, China D7 42
Jining, China A5 42
Jinja, Ug. D6 66
Jinjiazhen, China C5 38
Jinju see Chinju, Kor., S. G7 38
Jinmu Jiao, c., China L3 42
Jinning, China G5 36
Jinotega, Nic. F5 102
Jinotepe, Nic. G4 102
Jinping, China H3 42
Jinqian, stm., China E3 42
Jinsha, China H1 42
Jinsha (Yangtze), stm., China F5 36
Jinshi, China G4 42
Jintian, China H6 42
Jintotolo Channel, strt., Phil. E4 52
Jinxi, China A9 42
Jinxi, China H7 42
Jinxian, China G7 42
Jinxian, China B6 42
Jinzhou, China B9 42
Jinzhou, China A9 42
Ji-Paraná, Braz. F5 84
Jipijapa, Ec. H1 86
Jiquiriçá, stm., Braz. G6 88
Jiri, stm., India F14 54
Jirkov, Czech Rep. F9 16
Jishou, China G3 42
Jisr ash-Shughūr, Syria C7 58
Jitaúna, Braz. G6 88
Jiu, stm., Rom. F10 26
Jiudaoliang, China F4 42
Jiufeng, China I7 42
Jiujiang, China G6 42
Jiulian Shan, mts., China I6 42
Jiuliguan, China F6 42
Jiuling Shan, mts., China G6 42
Jiulong, China J5 42
Jiulong, stm., China I7 42
Jiuquan, China D4 36
Jiutai, China B6 38
Jiuyuanqu, China D4 42
Jiuzhan, China C7 38
Jiuzhen, China I7 42
Jiwen, China A9 36
Jixi, China B9 38
Jixi, China F8 42
Jixian, China A7 42
Jixian, China D6 42
Jiyi, China D4 42
Jiyuan, China D5 42
Jiyun, stm., China B7 42
Jīzān, Sau. Ar. F5 56
Jizl, Wādī al-, stm., Sau. Ar. K8 58
J. J. Castelli see Castelli, Arg. B7 92
J.M. Lencinas see Las Catitas, Arg. F3 92
Joaçaba, Braz. C12 92
Joana Coeli, Braz. A1 88
Joanes, Braz. D8 84
João Câmara, Braz. C8 88
João Monlevade, Braz. J4 88
João Pessoa, Braz. D8 88
João Pinheiro, Braz. I2 88
Joaquim Távora, Braz. A12 92
Joaquin, Tx., U.S. F4 122
Joaquín V. González, Arg. B5 92
Jobos, P.R. C3 104a
Job Peak, mtn., Nv., U.S. D7 134
Jocolí, Arg. F3 92
Jódar, Spain G7 20
Jodhpur, India E4 54
Jodiya, India G3 54
Joensuu, Fin. E13 8
Joetsu, Japan B11 40
Jõgeva, Est. G12 8
Jog Falls, wtfl, India D2 53
Joggins, N.S., Can. E12 110
Jogjakarta see Yogyakarta, Indon. G7 50
Jōhana, Japan C9 40
Johannesburg, S. Afr. E8 70
John Day, Or., U.S. F8 136
John Day, stm., Or., U.S. E6 136
John Day, Middle Fork, stm., Or., U.S. F8 136
John Day, North Fork, stm., Or., U.S. F8 136
John Day Fossil Beds National Monument, p.o.i., Or., U.S. F7 136
John F. Kennedy Space Center, sci., Fl., U.S. H5 116
John H. Kerr Reservoir, res., U.S. H7 114
John Martin Reservoir, res., Co., U.S. C6 128
John o' Groats, Scot., U.K. C9 12
John Redmond Reservoir, res., Ks., U.S. F1 120
Johns Island, i., S.C., U.S. D5 116
Johnson, Ar., U.S. H3 120
Johnson, Ks., U.S. D7 128
Johnsonburg, Pa., U.S. C7 114
Johnson City, N.Y., U.S. B10 114
Johnson City, Tn., U.S. H3 114
Johnson City, Tx., U.S. D9 130
Johnsondale, Ca., U.S. H7 134
Johnson Draw, stm., Tx., U.S. D6 130
Johnson Point, c., St. Vin. o11 105e
Johnsonville, S.C., U.S. C6 116
Johnston, Ia., U.S. C4 120
Johnston, S.C., U.S. C4 116
Johnston, Lake, l., Austl. F4 74
Johnston Atoll, at., Oc. B10 72
Johnstown, Co., U.S. G8 126
Johnstown, N.Y., U.S. G2 110
Johnstown, Oh., U.S. D3 114
Johnstown, Pa., U.S. D7 114
Johor, state, Malay. L6 48
Johor Bahru, Malay. L6 48
Joigny, Fr. G12 14
Joiner, Ar., U.S. B8 122
Joinville, Braz. C13 92
Joinville Island, i., Ant. B35 81
Jojogan, Indon. G7 50
Jokkmokk, Swe. C8 8
Jökulsá á Brú, stm., Ice. k32 8a
Jökulsårgljúfur Nasjonalpark, p.o.i., Ice. k32 8a
Joliet, Il., U.S. C9 120
Joliette, Qc., Can. D3 110
Jolo, Phil. G3 52
Jolo Group, is., Phil. G3 52
Jolo Island, i., Phil. H3 52
Jombang, Indon. G8 50
Jomda, China E4 36
Jonava, Lith. E7 10
Jones, Ok., U.S. F11 128
Jonesboro, Ar., U.S. I7 120
Jonesboro, Ga., U.S. C1 116
Jonesboro, Il., U.S. G8 120
Jonesboro, La., U.S. E6 122
Jonesborough, Tn., U.S. H3 114
Jones Mill, Ar., U.S. C6 122
Jonesport, Me., U.S. F9 110
Jones Sound, strt., Nu., Can. B8 141
Jonestown, Ms., U.S. C8 122
Jonesville, La., U.S. F7 122
Jonesville, Mi., U.S. B1 114
Jonglei Canal, can., Sudan F6 62
Joniškėlis, Lith. D6 10
Joniškis, Lith. D6 10
Jönköping, Swe. H6 8
Jönköping, state, Swe. H6 8
Jonquière, Qc., Can. B5 110
Jonuta, Mex. F12 100
Jonzac, Fr. D5 18
Joplin, Mo., U.S. G3 120
Joplin, Mt., U.S. B16 136
Joppa, Il., U.S. G9 120
Jora, India E6 54
Jordan, Mn., U.S. G5 118
Jordan, Mt., U.S. G6 124
Jordan, ctry., Asia H7 58
Jordan (Al-Urdunn) (HaYarden), stm., Asia F6 58
Jordan, stm., Ut., U.S. C5 132
Jordan Creek, stm., U.S. H10 136
Jordânia, Braz. H5 88
Jordan Valley, Or., U.S. G10 136
Jordão, stm., Braz. B12 92
Jorge Montt, Isla, i., Chile J2 90
Jorhāt, India C7 46
Jornado del Muerto, des., N.M., U.S. J10 132
Joroinen, Fin. E12 8
Jos, Nig. G6 64
Jose Abad Santos, Phil. H5 52
José Batlle y Ordóñez, Ur. F10 92
José Bonifácio, Braz. K1 88
José de Freitas, Braz. C4 88
José de San Martín, Arg. H2 90
José Pedro Varela, Ur. F10 92
Joseph, Or., U.S. E9 136
Joseph, Lac, l., Nf., Can. E17 106
Joseph Bonaparte Gulf, b., Austl. B5 74
Joshīmath, India C7 54
Jōshin-Etsu-kōgen-kokuritsu-kōen, p.o.i., Japan C11 40
Joshua, Tx., U.S. B10 130
Joshua Tree, Ca., U.S. I9 134
Joshua Tree National Park, p.o.i., Ca., U.S. J10 134
Jostedalsbreen, ice, Nor. F2 8
Jostedalsbreen Nasjonalpark, p.o.i., Nor. F2 8
Jotunheimen Nasjonalpark, p.o.i., Nor. F2 8
Joubertina, S. Afr. H6 70
Jourdanton, Tx., U.S. F9 130
Joutsijärvi, Fin. C13 8
Joviânia, Braz. I1 88
Jowai, India F14 54
Joya, Mex. H6 130
Joyce, La., U.S. F6 122
Joyuda, P.R. B1 104a
J. Percy Priest Lake, res., Tn., U.S. H11 120
J. Strom Thurmond Reservoir, res., U.S. C3 116
Juami, stm., Braz. I7 86
Juana Díaz, P.R. B2 104a
Juan Aldama, Mex. C7 100
Juan Bautista Alberdi, Arg. C5 92
Juan de Fuca, Strait of, strt., N.A. B2 136
Juan de Garay, Arg. I5 92
Juan de Nova, Île, i., Reu. D7 68
Juan E. Barra, Arg. H7 92
Juan Fernández, Archipiélago, is., Chile I6 82
Juanjuí, Peru E2 84
Juan N. Fernández, Arg. I8 92
Juan Viñas, C.R. H6 102
Juárez see Benito Juárez, Arg. H8 92
Juárez, Mex. F8 98
Juárez, Mex. B8 100
Juatinga, Ponta de, c., Braz. L3 88
Juazeirinho, Braz. D7 88
Juazeiro, Braz. E5 88
Juazeiro do Norte, Braz. D6 88
Juba, Sudan G6 62
Juba see Genalē, stm., Afr. C8 66
Juba see Jubba, stm., Afr. D8 66
Jubal, Strait of see Gûbâl, Madîq, strt., Egypt K4 58
Jubayl, Leb. D6 58
Jubba (Genalē), stm., Afr. D8 66
Juby, Cap, c., Mor. D2 64
Júcar (Xúquer), stm., Spain E10 20
Juchipila, Mex. E7 100
Juchitán de Zaragoza, Mex. G11 100
Jucurucu, stm., Braz. I5 88
Jucurutu, Braz. C7 88
Judenburg, Aus. C11 22
Judino, Russia B22 10
Judique, N.S., Can. E15 110
Judith, stm., Mt., U.S. C17 136
Judith Gap, Mt., U.S. D17 136
Judith Peak, mtn., Mt., U.S. C17 136
Judoma, stm., Russia E16 34
Jufari, stm., Braz. H10 86
Jug, stm., Russia G21 8
Jugorskij poluostrov, pen., Russia A10 32
Juhnov, Russia F18 10
Juidongshan, China J7 42
Juigalpa, Nic. F5 102
Juist, i., Ger. C2 16
Juiz de Fora, Braz. K4 88
Jujuy, state, Arg. D3 90
Jukagirskoe ploskogor'e, plat., Russia C19 34
Jukta, Russia B19 32
Jula, stm., Russia E21 8
Julesburg, Co., U.S. G10 126
Juliaca, Peru G3 84
Julia Creek, Austl. C3 76
Julia Creek, stm., Austl. C3 76
Julianadorp, Neth. Ant. p22 104g
Julian Alps, mts., Eur. D10 22
Juliana Top, mtn., Sur. C6 84
Julianehåb (Qaqortoq), Grnld. E16 141
Jülich, Ger. F2 16
Juliette, Lake, res., Ga., U.S. D2 116
Julimes, Mex. A6 100
Júlio de Castilhos, Braz. D11 92
Juma, Russia D15 8
Juma, stm., China B6 42
Jumba, Som. E8 66
Jumilla, Spain F9 20
Jumlā, Nepal D9 54
Jūnāgadh, India H3 54
Juncos, P.R. B4 104a
Junction, Tx., U.S. D8 130
Junction City, Ar., U.S. E6 122
Junction City, Ks., U.S. B12 128
Junction City, Ky., U.S. G13 120
Jundah, Austl. E4 76
Jundiaí, Braz. L2 88
Juneau, Ak., U.S. E13 140
Juneau, Wi., U.S. H10 118
Junee, Austl. J6 76
June Lake, Ca., U.S. F6 134
Jungar Qi, China B4 42
Jungfrau, mtn., Switz. D4 22
Junggar Pendi, bas., China B2 36
Juniata, Ne., U.S. G14 126
Juniata, stm., Pa., U.S. D8 114
Junín, Arg. G7 92
Junín, Ec. H1 86
Junín de los Andes, Arg. G2 90
Juniper, N.B., Can. D9 110
Junipero Serra Peak, mtn., Ca., U.S. G4 134
Jūniyah, Leb. E6 58
Junlian, China F5 36
Junnar, India B1 53
Junqueiro, Braz. E7 88
Junxian, China E4 42
Juodkrantė, Lith. E3 10
Juozapinės kalnas, hill, Lith. F8 10
Juparanã, Lagoa, l., Braz. J5 88
Jupiter, Fl., U.S. J5 116
Juquiá, Braz. B14 92
Juquiá, Ponta do, c., Braz. B14 92
Jur, Russia E16 34
Jur, stm., Sudan F5 62
Jura, Mol. B16 26
Jura, state, Fr. C11 18
Jura, mts., Eur. B12 18
Jura, i., Scot., U.K. F7 12
Jūra, stm., Lith. E5 10
Jurbarkas, Lith. E5 10
Jurenino, Russia G20 8
Jurevec, Russia H20 8
Jurga, Russia C15 32
Juriti, Braz. D6 84
Jūrmala, Lat. C6 10
Jurong, China F8 42
Juruá, stm., S.A. D4 84
Juruena, stm., Braz. E6 84
Jurumirim, Represa de, res., Braz. L1 88
Jusepín, Ven. C10 86
Juškovo, Russia G21 8
Justiniano Posse, Arg. F6 92
Justino Solari see Mariano I. Loza, Arg. D8 92
Justo Daract, Arg. F5 92
Jutaí, stm., Braz. D4 84
Jüterbog, Ger. D9 16
Jutiapa, Guat. E3 102
Juticalpa, Hond. E4 102
Jutland see Jylland, reg., Den. H3 8
Jutrosin, Pol. E13 16
Juventud, Isla de la (Pines, Isle of), i., Cuba B6 102
Juxian, China D8 42
Juye, China D6 42
Juža, Russia H20 8
Južna Morava, stm., Yugo. F8 26
Južno-Enisejskij, Russia C17 32
Južno-Sahalinsk, Russia G17 34
Južno-Ural'sk, Russia D10 32
Južnyj, mys, c., Russia E20 34
Južnyj Ural, mts., Russia D9 32
Jwayyā, Leb. E6 58
Jyekundo see Yushu, China E4 36
Jylland (Jutland), reg., Den. H3 8
Jyväskylä, Fin. E11 8

K

K2, mtn., Asia B12 56
Kaabong, Ug. D6 66
Kaahka, Turkmen. B8 56
Kaala, mtn., Hi., U.S. B3 78a
Kaala-Gomen, N. Cal. m15 79d
Kaapstad see Cape Town, S. Afr. H4 70
Kaarli, Est. A9 10
Kaatoan, Mount, mtn., Phil. F5 52
Kabacan, Phil. G5 52
Kabaena, Pulau, i., Indon. G7 44
Kabah, hist., Mex. B3 102
Kabala, S.L. H2 64
Kabale, Ug. E5 66
Kabalega Falls, wtfl, Ug. D6 66
Kabalo, D.R.C. F5 66
Kabambare, D.R.C. E5 66
Kabanjahe, Indon. K4 48
Kabankalan, Phil. F4 52
Kabardin-Balkaria see Kabardino-Balkarija, state, Russia F6 32
Kabardino-Balkarija, state, Russia F6 32
Kabba, Nig. H6 64
Kabbani, stm., India F3 53
Kåbdalis, Swe. C8 8
Kabetogama Lake, l., Mn., U.S. C5 118
Kab-hegy, mtn., Hung. B4 26
Kabinda, D.R.C. F4 66
Kabinu, Indon. A9 50
Kabīr Kūh, mts., Iran C6 56
Kabna, Sudan D6 62
Kābol, Afg. C10 56
Kābol, state, Afg. A2 54
Kabompo, Zam. C3 68
Kabompo, stm., Zam. C3 68
Kabongo, D.R.C. F5 66
Kābul see Kābol, Afg. C10 56
Kabul (Kābol), stm., Asia A4 54
Kabwe, Zam. C4 68
Kabylie, reg., Alg. H14 20
Kačanik, Yugo. G8 26
Kačerginė, Lith. F6 10
Kachchh, Gulf of, b., India G2 54
Kačiry, Kaz. D13 32
Kačkanar, Russia C10 32
Kačug, Russia D19 32
Kadaiyanallūr, India G3 53
Kadaň, Czech Rep. F9 16
Kadan Kyun, i., Mya. F4 48
Kadapongan, Pulau, i., Indon. F9 50
Kaddam, res., India B4 53
Kade, Ghana H4 64
Kadéï, stm., Afr. G2 62
Kadi, India G4 54
Kadina, Austl. F7 74
Kading, stm., Laos C7 48
Kadınhanı, Tur. E15 28
Kadiolo, Mali G3 64
Kādīpur, India E9 54
Kadiri, India D4 53
Kadirli, Tur. A7 58
Kadoka, S.D., U.S. D11 126
Kadoma, Zimb. D4 68
Kaduj, Russia A20 10
Kaduna, Nig. G6 64
Kaduna, stm., Nig. G6 64
Kāduqlī, Sudan E5 62
Kadūr, India E3 53
Kaduvu, i., Fiji q19 79e
Kaduvu Passage, strt., Fiji q18 79e
Kadyj, Russia H20 8
Kadžerom, Russia B9 32
Kaédi, Maur. F2 64
Kaélé, Cam. B2 66
Kaena Point, c., Hi., U.S. B3 78a
Kaesŏng, Kor., N. F7 38
Kafanchan, Nig. H6 64
Kaffrine, Sen. G1 64
Kafia Kingi, Sudan F4 62
Kafr el-Dauwar, Egypt G1 58
Kafr el-Sheikh, Egypt G1 58
Kafr el-Zaiyât, Egypt H1 58
Kafr Sa'd, Egypt G2 58
Kafue, Zam. D4 68
Kafue, stm., Zam. D4 68
Kaga, Japan C9 40
Kaga Bandoro, C.A.R. C3 66
Kāgān, Pak. A4 54
Kagan, Uzb. G10 32
Kagawa, state, Japan E6 40
Kagawong, Lake, l., On., Can. C7 112
Kagaznagar, India B4 53
Kagera, stm., Afr. E6 66
Kagmar, Sudan E6 62
Kagoshima, Japan H3 40
Kagoshima, state, Japan H3 40
Kagoshima-wan, b., Japan H3 40
Kahama, Tan. E6 66
Kahayan, stm., Indon. D8 50
Ka-Hem see Malyj Enisej, stm., Russia F8 34
Kahemba, D.R.C. F3 66
Kahiu Point, c., Hi., U.S. B5 78a
Kahoka, Mo., U.S. D6 120
Kahoolawe, i., Hi., U.S. C5 78a
Kahouanne, Îlet à, i., Guad. h5 105c
Kahramanmaraş (Maraş), Tur. A7 58
Kahraman Maraş, state, Tur. A7 58
Kahuku Point, c., Hi., U.S. B4 78a
Kahului, Hi., U.S. C5 78a
Kai, Kepulauan (Kai Islands), is., Indon. G9 44
Kaiapoi, N.Z. F5 80
Kaibab Plateau, plat., Az., U.S. G4 132
Kaidu, stm., China F15 32
Kaieteur Fall, wtfl, Guy. E12 86
Kaieteur National Park, p.o.i., Guy. E12 86
Kaifeng, China D6 42
Kaihua, China G8 42
Kai Islands see Kai, Kepulauan, is., Indon. G9 44
Kaijian, China J4 42
Kaijiang, China F2 42
Kai Kecil, i., Indon. G9 44
Kaikoura, N.Z. F5 80
Kailahun, S.L. H2 64
Kailas see Kangrinboqê Feng, mtn., China C8 54
Kailāshahar, India F14 54
Kailas Range see Gangdisê Shan, mts., China C9 54
Kaili, China H2 42
Kailu, China C4 38
Kailua, Hi., U.S. B4 78a
Kailua Kona, Hi., U.S. D6 78a
Kaïmaktsalán (Kajmakčalan), mtn., Eur. C15 24
Kaimana, Indon. F9 44
Kaimon-dake, vol., Japan H3 40
Kainabrivier, stm., Nmb. E4 70
Kainan, Japan E8 40
Kainantu, Pap. N. Gui. b4 79a
Kainji Reservoir, res., Nig. G5 64
Kaipara Harbour, b., N.Z. C5 80
Kaiparowits Plateau, plat., Ut., U.S. F5 132
Kaiping, China J5 42
Kairouan, Tun. I3 24
Kairuku, Pap. N. Gui. b4 79a
Kaiserslautern, Ger. G3 16
Kaišiadorys, Lith. F7 10
Kait, Tanjung, c., Indon. E5 50
Kaitangata, N.Z. H3 80
Kaithal, India D6 54
Kaituma, stm., Guy. D12 86
Kaiwi Channel, strt., Hi., U.S. B4 78a
Kaixian, China F3 42
Kaiyang, China H2 42
Kaiyuan, China G5 36
Kaiyuan, China C6 38
Kaiyuancheng, China C6 38
Kaiyuh Mountains, mts., Ak., U.S. D8 140
Kajaani, Fin. D12 8
Kajabbi, Austl. B2 76
Kajakī, Band-e, res., Afg. C10 56
Kajang, Malay. K5 48
Kajga, Kaz. D10 32
Kajmysovy, Russia C13 32
Kajo Kaji, Sudan G6 62
Kaka, Sudan E6 62
Kakabeka Falls, wtfl, On., Can. C9 118
Kakagi Lake, l., On., Can. B5 118
Kakamas, S. Afr. F5 70
Kakamega, Kenya D6 66
Kakamigahara, Japan D9 40
Kakata, Lib. H2 64
Kākdwīp, India H12 54
Kakegawa, Japan E10 40
Kakhonak, Ak., U.S. E9 140
Kakhovka Reservoir see Kakhovs'ke vodoskhovyshche, res., Ukr. E4 32
Kakhovs'ke vodoskhovyshche, res., Ukr. E4 32
Kākināda (Cocanada), India C6 53
Kakisa Lake, l., N.T., Can. C7 106
Kakizaki, Japan B11 40
Kakogawa, Japan E7 40
Kakšaal-Too, hrebet, mts., Asia F13 32
Kaktovik, Ak., U.S. B11 140
Kakuda, Japan B13 40
Kakus, stm., Malay. B8 50
Kakwa, stm., Ab., Can. B12 138
Kala, stm., Sri L. G4 53
Kalaa Kebira, Tun. I4 24
Kalabahi, Indon. G7 44
Kalabakan, Malay. A10 50
Kalabo, Zam. D3 68
Kalač, Russia D6 32
Kalačinsk, Russia D12 32
Kalač-na-Donu, Russia E6 32
Kaladan, stm., Asia G14 54
Ka Lae, c., Hi., U.S. E6 78a
Kalahari Desert, des., Afr. C5 70
Kalahari Gemsbok National Park, p.o.i., S. Afr. D5 70
Kalajoki, Fin. D10 8
Kalakan, Russia E12 34
Kalām, Pak. B11 56
Kalama, Wa., U.S. D4 136
Kalamalka Lake, l., B.C., Can. F11 138
Kalamáta, Grc. F5 28
Kalamazoo, Mi., U.S. F4 112
Kalamazoo, stm., Mi., U.S. F4 112
Kalamb, India B1 53
Kalampising, Indon. B10 50
Kalao, Pulau, i., Indon. G12 50
Kalaotoa, Pulau, i., Indon. G7 44
Kalar, stm., Russia E12 34
Kalasin, Thai. D6 48
Kalašnikovo, Russia C18 10
Kalāt, Pak. D10 56
Kalávryta, Grc. E5 28
Kalaw, Mya. B3 48
Kalbarri, Austl. E2 74
Kale, Tur. F11 28
Kale, Tur. G12 28
Kaleden, B.C., Can. G11 138
Kalegauk Island, i., Mya. E3 48
Kalehe, D.R.C. E5 66
Kalemie, D.R.C. F5 66
Kalemyo, Mya. D7 46
Kaletwa, Mya. H14 54
Kalevala, Russia D14 8
Kalewa, Mya. D7 46
Kálfafell, Ice. k31 8a
Kalgan see Zhangjiakou, China A6 42
Kalgoorlie-Boulder, Austl. F4 74
Kaliakra, nos, c., Blg. F15 26
Kalianda, Indon. F4 50
Kalibo, Phil. E4 52
Kalima, D.R.C. E5 66
Kalimantan (Borneo), i., Asia F5 44

Name	Map Ref.	Page
Kalimantan Barat, state, Indon.	D7	50
Kalimantan Selatan, state, Indon.	E9	50
Kalimantan Tengah, state, Indon.	D8	50
Kalimantan Timur, state, Indon.	C10	50
Kālimpang, India	E12	54
Kállinadi, stm., India	D2	53
Kalinin see Tver', Russia	D18	10
Kaliningrad (Königsberg), Russia	F3	10
Kaliningradskaja oblast', co., Russia	F4	10
Kalinpuvičy, Bela.	H12	10
Kaliro, Ug.	D6	66
Kalisat, Indon.	H8	50
Kāli Sindh, stm., India	F4	66
Kalispell, Mt., U.S.	B12	136
Kalisz, Pol.	E14	16
Kalisz, state, Pol.	E13	16
Kalisz Pomorski, Pol.	C11	16
Kaliua, Tan.	E6	66
Kaliveli Tank, l., India	E4	53
Kalixälven, stm., Swe.	C9	8
Kaljazin, Russia	C20	10
Kālka, India	C6	54
Kalkaska, Mi., U.S.	D4	112
Kalkfonteindam, res., S. Afr.	F7	70
Kalkim, Tur.	D10	28
Kalkrand, Nmb.	D3	70
Kallar Kahār, Pak.	B4	54
Kallavesi, l., Fin.	E12	8
Kallsjön, l., Swe.	E5	8
Kalmar, Swe.	H6	8
Kalmar, state, Swe.	H7	8
Kalmarsund, strt., Swe.	H7	8
Kalmykia see Kalmykija, state, Russia	E7	32
Kalmykija, state, Russia	E7	32
Kalmykovo, Kaz.	E8	32
Kālna, India	G12	54
Kalocsa, Hung.	C5	26
Kalofer, Blg.	G12	26
Kalohi Channel, strt., Hi., U.S.	B4	78a
Kalol, India	G4	54
Kālol, India	G4	54
Kalomo, Zam.	D4	68
Kalona, Ia., U.S.	J7	118
Kalone Peak, mtn., B.C., Can.	D4	138
Kalpeni Island, i., India	F1	53
Kālpi, India	E7	54
Kalpin, China	A12	56
Kalsūbai, mtn., India	B1	53
Kaltag, Ak., U.S.	D8	140
Kaluga, Russia	F19	10
Kalukalukuang, Pulau, i., Indon.	F10	50
Kalumburu, Austl.	B5	74
Kalusyn, Pol.	D17	16
Kalutara, Sri L.	H4	53
Kalužskaja oblast', co., Russia	F18	10
Kalyān, India	B1	53
Kalyāndurg, India	D3	53
Kálymnos, Grc.	G9	28
Kálymnos, i., Grc.	F9	28
Kama, stm., Russia	C8	32
Kamae, Japan	G4	40
Kamaishi, Japan	E14	38
Kamakou, mtn., Hi., U.S.	B5	78a
Kamakura, Japan	D12	40
Kamālia, Pak.	C4	54
Kamamaung, Mya.	D3	48
Kaman, stm., Laos	E8	48
Kamanjab, Nmb.	D1	68
Kamarān, i., Yemen	F5	56
Kāmāreddi, India	B4	53
Kama Reservoir see Kamskoe vodohranilišče, res., Russia	C9	32
Kamas, Ut., U.S.	C5	132
Kamay, Tx., U.S.	H10	128
Kambalda, Austl.	F4	74
Kambam, India	G3	53
Kambarka, Russia	C8	32
Kambja, Est.	B9	10
Kambove, D.R.C.	G5	66
Kamčatka, stm., Russia	E21	34
Kamčatka, poluostrov, pen., Russia	E19	34
Kamčatskij poluostrov, pen., Russia	E21	34
Kamčatskij zaliv, b., Russia	E21	34
Kamchatka Peninsula see Kamčatka, poluostrov, pen., Russia	E20	34
Kameda, Japan	B12	40
Kamen', gora, mtn., Russia	C8	34
Kameng, stm., India	E14	54
Kamenjak, Rt, c., Cro.	F10	22
Kamenka, Kaz.	D11	32
Kamenka, Russia	D21	8
Kamenka, Russia	D6	32
Kamenka, Russia	D14	32
Kameno, Blg.	G14	26
Kamen-Rybolov, Russia	B9	38
Kamenskoe, Russia	D22	34
Kamensk-Ural'skij, Russia	C10	32
Kamenz, Ger.	E10	16
Kāmet, mtn., Asia	C7	54
Kam'ians'ke, Ukr.	D16	26
Kamień Krajeński, Pol.	C13	16
Kamienna Góra, Pol.	F12	16
Kamieńsk, Pol.	E15	16
Kamieskroon, S. Afr.	G3	70
Kamiiso, Japan	D14	38
Kamilukuak Lake, l., Can.	C10	106
Kamina, D.R.C.	F4	66
Kaminak Lake, l., Nu., Can.	C12	106
Kaminoyama, Japan	A13	40
Kaminuriak Lake, l., Nu., Can.	C12	106
Kamioka, Japan	C10	40
Kāmiros, hist., Grc.	G10	28
Kamjanec, Bela.	H6	10
Kamkhat Muhaywir, hill, Jord.	G7	58
Kamloops, B.C., Can.	F10	138
Kamnik, Slvn.	D11	22
Kamo, Japan	B12	40
Kamoa Mountains, mts., Guy.	C6	84
Kamojima, Japan	E7	40
Kāmoke, Pak.	C5	54
Kampala, Ug.	D6	66
Kampar, Malay.	J5	48
Kampar, stm., Indon.	C3	50
Kamparkalns, hill, Lat.	C5	10
Kampar Kanan, stm., Indon.	C2	50
Kampen, Neth.	B14	14
Kamphaeng Phet, Thai.	D4	48
Kampinoski Park Narodowy, p.o.i., Pol.	D16	16
Kâmpóng Cham, Camb.	F7	48
Kâmpóng Chhnăng, Camb.	F7	48
Kâmpóng Saôm, Camb.	G6	48
Kâmpóng Saôm, Chhâk, b., Camb.	G6	48
Kâmpóng Thum, Camb.	F7	48
Kâmpóng Ulu, Malay.	K6	48
Kâmpôt, Camb.	G7	48
Kampsville, Il., U.S.	E7	120
Kampti, Burkina	G4	64
Kampuchea see Cambodia, ctry., Asia	F7	48
Kampungbaru, Indon.	D3	50
Kampung Litang, Malay.	A11	50
Kamrau, Teluk, b., Indon.	F9	44
Kamsack, Sk., Can.	C12	124
Kamskoe vodohranilišče, res., Russia	C9	32
Kāmthi, India	H7	54
Kamuela, Hi., U.S.	D6	78a
Kámuk, Cerro, mtn., C.R.	H6	102
Kamundan, stm., Indon.	F9	44
Kamyšin, Russia	D7	32
Kamyšlov, Russia	C10	32
Kan, stm., Russia	C17	32
Kanaaupscow, stm., Qc., Can.	E15	106
Kanab, Ut., U.S.	F4	132
Kanab Creek, stm., U.S.	G4	132
Kanaga Island, i., Ak., U.S.	g23	140a
Kanagawa, state, Japan	D12	40
Kanakapura, India	E3	53
Kananga (Luluabourg), D.R.C.	F4	66
Kananggar, Indon.	I12	50
Kanawha, Ia., U.S.	B4	120
Kanawha, stm., W.V., U.S.	F4	114
Kanazawa, Japan	C9	40
Kanbauk, Mya.	E3	48
Kanchanaburi, Thai.	F4	48
Kānchenjunga (Kānchenjunga), mtn., Asia	E11	54
Kānchenjunga (Kānchanjanggā), mtn., Asia	E11	54
Kānchipuram, India	E4	53
Kanchow see Ganzhou, China	I6	42
Kańczuga, Pol.	F18	16
Kandahar, Sk., Can.	C9	124
Kandalakša, Russia	C15	8
Kandalakšskaja guba, b., Russia	C15	8
Kandale, D.R.C.	F3	66
Kandangan, Indon.	E9	50
Kandanghaur, Indon.	G6	50
Kandé, Togo	H5	64
Kandhkot, Pak.	D2	54
Kandi, India	G12	54
Kandi, Tanjung, c., Indon.	E7	44
Kandıra, Tur.	B13	28
Kandla, India	G3	54
Kandos, Austl.	I7	76
Kandreho, Madag.	D8	68
Kandy, Sri L.	H5	53
Kane, Pa., U.S.	C7	114
Kane Basin, b., N.A.	B12	141
Kanem, state, Chad	E3	62
Kaneohe, Hi., U.S.	B4	78a
Kaněvka, Russia	C18	8
Kang, Bots.	C6	70
Kangāba, Mali	G3	64
Kangalassy, Russia	D15	34
Kangalmiut, Grnld.	D15	141
Kangān, Iran	D7	56
Kangar, Malay.	I5	48
Kangaroo Island, i., Austl.	G7	74
Kangāvar, Iran	C6	56
Kangbao, China	C7	36
Kangding, China	C9	46
Kangean, Kepulauan (Kangean Islands), is., Indon.	G9	50
Kangean, Pulau, i., Indon.	G9	50
Kangean Islands see Kangean, Kepulauan, is., Indon.	G9	50
Kangeeak Point, c., Nu., Can.	B18	106
Kangerlussuaq, b., Grnld.	D19	141
Kangersuatsiaq see Prøven, Grnld.	C14	141
Kanger Valley National Park, p.o.i., India	B6	53
Kanggye, Kor., N.	D7	38
Kangiwa-do, i., Kor., S.	F7	38
Kangiqsualujjuaq, Qc., Can.	D17	106
Kangiqsujuaq, Qc., Can.	C16	106
Kangirsuk, Qc., Can.	C17	106
Kangmar, China	D12	54
Kangnŭng, Kor., S.	B1	40
Kango, Gabon	D2	66
Kangping, China	C5	38
Kangpu, China	F4	36
Kangrinboqê Feng, mtn., China	C8	54
Kangshan, Tai.	J9	42
Kangsŏ, Kor., N.	E6	38
Kangto, mtn., Asia	D14	54
Kangwŏn-do, state, Kor., S.	B1	40
Kanha National Park, p.o.i., India	G8	54
Kanhar, stm., India	F9	54
Kanhsien see Ganzhou, China	I6	42
Kani, Mya.	A2	48
Kaniama, D.R.C.	F4	66
Kanibadam, Taj.	A11	56
Kaniet Islands, is., Pap. N. Gui.	a4	79a
Kanigiri, India	C5	53
Kanin, poluostrov, pen., Russia	C21	8
Kanin-Kamen', mts., Russia	B21	8
Kanin Nos, Russia	B20	8
Kanin Nos, mys, c., Russia	B20	8
Kaniva, Austl.	K3	76
Kanjiža, Yugo.	C7	26
Kankaanpää, Fin.	F10	8
Kankakee, Il., U.S.	G2	112
Kankan, Gui.	G3	64
Kānker, India	H8	54
Kankunskij, Russia	E14	34
Kanmaw Kyun, i., Mya.	G4	48
Kannack, Viet.	E9	48
Kannad, India	H5	54
Kannapolis, N.C., U.S.	A5	116
Kanniyākumari, India	G3	53
Kannod, India	G6	54
Kannur see Cannanore, India	F2	53
Kanona, Fin.	F11	8
Kano, Nig.	G6	64
Kanoji, Japan	E6	40
Kanopolis, Ks., U.S.	C10	128
Kanorado, Ks., U.S.	B6	128
Kanosh, Ut., U.S.	E4	132
Kanoya, Japan	H3	40
Kānpetlet, Mya.	B1	48
Kānpur (Cawnpore), India	E7	54
Kansas, state, U.S.	C10	108
Kansas, stm., Ks., U.S.	B13	128
Kansas City, Ks., U.S.	E3	120
Kansas City, Mo., U.S.	E3	120
Kansk, Russia	C17	32
Kansŏng, Kor., S.	A1	40
Kansu see Gansu, state, China	D5	36
Kantang, Thai.	I4	48
Kantchari, Burkina	G5	64
Kānth, India	D7	54
Kantishna, stm., Ak., U.S.	D9	140a
Kantō-heiya, pl., Japan	D12	40
Kanton, i., Kir.	D9	72
Kantō-sanchi, mts., Japan	D11	40
Kantu-long, China	C3	48
Kantunilkin, Mex.	B4	102
Kanuku Mountains, mts., Guy.	F12	86
Kanuma, Japan	C12	40
Kanye, Bots.	D7	70
Kanyutkwin, Mya.	C3	48
Kaohlung see Kaohsiung, Tai.	J8	42
Kaohsiung, Tai.	J8	42
Kaohsiunghsien, Tai.	J9	42
Kaoka Bay, b., Sol. Is.	e9	79b
Kaoko Veld, plat., Nmb.	D1	68
Kaolack, Sen.	G1	64
Kaolinovo, Blg.	F14	26
Kaoma, Zam.	C3	68
Kaouar, reg., Niger	F7	64
Kapaa, Hi., U.S.	A2	78a
Kapadvanj, India	G4	54
Kapanga, D.R.C.	F4	66
Kapaonik, mts., Yugo.	G8	26
Kapatkevičy, Bela.	H11	10
Kapčagaj, Kaz.	F13	32
Kapčagajskoe vodohranilišče, res., Kaz.	F13	32
Kapčagajskoe Reservoir see Kapčagajskoe vodohranilišče, res., Kaz.	F13	32
Kapfenberg, Aus.	C12	22
Kapıdağ Yarımadası, pen., Tur.	C10	28
Kapingamarangi, at., Micron.	C6	72
Kapiri Mposhi, Zam.	C4	68
Kapisigdlit, Grnld.	E16	141
Kapiskau, stm., On., Can.	E14	106
Kapit, Malay.	C8	50
Kapoeta, Sudan	G6	62
Kapona, D.R.C.	F5	66
Kaposvár, Hung.	C4	26
Kaposvar Creek, stm., Sk., Can.	D11	124
Kappeln, Ger.	B5	16
Kapuas, stm., Indon.	D6	50
Kapuas, stm., Indon.	E9	50
Kapunda, Austl.	J2	76
Kapūrthala, India	C5	54
Kapuskasing, On., Can.	F14	106
Kapuvár, Hung.	B4	26
Kapyl', Bela.	G9	10
Kara, Russia	C1	34
Kara-Balta, Kyrg.	F12	32
Karabanovo, Russia	D21	10
Karabaš, Russia	C9	32
Kara-Bogaz-Gol, zaliv, b., Turkmen.	A7	56
Kara-Bogaz-Gol Gulf see Kara-Bogaz-Gol, zaliv, b., Turkmen.	A7	56
Karabük, Tur.	B15	28
Karabula, Russia	C17	32
Karaburun, Tur.	E9	28
Karabutak, Kaz.	D10	32
Karacabey, Tur.	C11	28
Karačaevo-Čerkesija, state, Russia	F6	32
Karačaevo-Čerkesija see Karačaevo-Čerkesija, state, Russia	F6	32
Karāchi, Pak.	E10	56
Karād, India	C2	53
Karaftit, Russia	F11	34
Karaganda, Kaz.	E12	32
Karagayly see Karkaralinsk, Kaz.	E13	32
Karaginskij, ostrov, i., Russia	E21	34
Karaginskij zaliv, b., Russia	E21	34
Karagoš, gora, mtn., Russia	D15	32
Karahallı, Tur.	E12	28
Karaikkudi, India	F4	53
Karaisalı, Tur.	A6	58
Karaj, Iran	B7	56
Karakalong, Pulau, is., Indon.	E8	44
Karakax, stm., China	A7	54
Karakax, ozero, l., Kaz.	E11	32
Karakol, Kyrg.	F13	32
Karakoram Pass, p., Asia	A6	54
Karakoram Range, mts., Asia	A4	46
Karakul', Uzb.	G10	32
Karakum Canal see Garagum kanal, can., Turkmen.	B9	56
Karam, stm., Indon.	E11	50
Karamai see Karamay, China	B1	36
Karaman, Tur.	A4	58
Karaman, state, Tur.	A4	58
Karamanlı, Tur.	F12	28
Karamay, China	B1	36
Karamea Bight, b., N.Z.	E4	80
Karamürsel, Tur.	C12	28
Karamyševo, Russia	C18	32
Karanja, India	H5	54
Karanja, India	H10	54
Karapınar, Tur.	A4	58
Karas, state, Nmb.	E3	70
Karasburg, Nmb.	F4	70
Kara Sea see Karskoe more, Russia	B10	30
Karasjok, Nor.	B11	8
Karasu, stm., Tur.	B13	28
Karasu, Tur.	B4	58
Karasuk, Russia	D13	32
Karatal, Kaz.	E15	32
Karataş, Japan	B7	40
Karataş Burun, c., Tur.	B6	58
Karatau, Kaz.	F11	32
Karatau, hrebet, mts., Kaz.	F11	32
Karatau Range see Karatau, hrebet, mts., Kaz.	F11	32
Karatobe, Kaz.	E8	32
Karatsu, Japan	F2	40
Karaul, Russia	B5	34
Karauli, India	E6	54
Karawa, D.R.C.	D4	66
Karawang, Indon.	G5	50
Karawanken, mts., Eur.	D11	22
Karbalā', Iraq	C5	56
Karbole, Swe.	E6	8
Karcag, Hung.	B7	26
Kardámaina, Grc.	G9	28
Kardeljevo, Cro.	G14	22
Kárditsa, Grc.	D4	28
Kárdla, Est.	A6	10
Kŭrdžali, Blg.	H12	26
Karelia see Karelija, state, Russia	D15	8
Karelija, state, Russia	D15	8
Karema, Tan.	F6	66
Karen, India	F7	46
Karesuando, Swe.	B9	8
Kärevere, Est.	B9	10
Kargasok, Russia	C14	32
Kargat, Russia	C14	32
Kargil, India	A5	54
Kargopol', Russia	F18	8
Kari, Nig.	G7	64
Karibib, Nmb.	B2	70
Karibib, Lake, res., Afr.	D4	68
Karimata, Kepulauan, is., Indon.	D6	50
Karimata, Selat, strt., Indon.	E6	50
Karimganj, India	F14	54
Karīmnagar, India	B4	53
Karimunjawa, Kepulauan, is., Indon.	F7	50
Karimunjawa, Pulau, i., Indon.	F7	50
Karisimbi, vol., Afr.	E5	66
Káristos, Grc.	E7	28
Kariya, Japan	D10	40
Kārkal, India	E2	53
Karkar Island, i., Pap. N. Gui.	a4	79a
Karkonoski Park Narodowy, p.o.i.,	F11	16
Karksi-Nuia, Est.	B6	74
Karlby see Kökkola, Fin.	E10	8
Karlino, Pol.	B11	16
Karl-Marx-Stadt see Chemnitz, Ger.	F8	16
Karlovac, Cro.	E12	22
Karlovo, Blg.	G11	26
Karlovy Vary, Czech Rep.	F8	16
Karlsborg, Swe.	D10	8
Karlsburg see Alba Iulia, Rom.	C10	26
Karlshamn, Swe.	H6	8
Karlskoga, Swe.	G6	8
Karlskrona, Swe.	H6	8
Karlsruhe, Ger.	G4	16
Karlstad, Swe.	G5	8
Karluk, Ak., U.S.	E9	140
Karma, Bela.	H14	10
Karma, Niger	G5	64
Karmah an Nuzul, Sudan	D6	62
Karmāla, India	B2	53
Karmøy, i., Nor.	G1	8
Karnack, Tx., U.S.	E4	122
Karnāl, India	C6	54
Karnāli, stm., Asia	D8	54
Karnāli, stm., Nepal	E8	54
Karnaphuli Reservoir, res., Bngl.	G14	54
Karnātaka, state, India	D2	53
Karnobat, Blg.	G13	26
Kärnten, state, Aus.	D10	22
Karonga, Mwi.	B5	68
Karoo National Park, p.o.i., S. Afr.	H6	70
Karoonda, Austl.	J2	76
Kárpathos, Grc.	H10	28
Kárpathos, i., Grc.	H10	28
Karpats'kyi Pryrodnyi Natsional'nyi Park, p.o.i., Ukr.	A11	26
Karpenísi, Grc.	E4	28
Karpogory, Russia	D21	8
Karpuzlu, Tur.	F10	28
Karrats Fjord, b., Grnld.	C14	141
Kars, Tur.	A5	56
Karsakpaj, Kaz.	E11	32
Karsanti, Tur.	A6	58
Karši, Uzb.	G11	32
Karsin, Pol.	C13	16
Karskoe more (Kara Sea), Russia	B10	30
Kartala, vol., Com.	C7	68
Kartaly, Russia	D10	32
Kärthaus, Pa., U.S.	C7	114
Kartuzy, Pol.	B14	16
Karufa, Indon.	F9	44
Karumba, Austl.	A3	76
Karungi, Swe.	C10	8
Karunjie, Austl.	C5	74
Karūr, India	F4	53
Karvinà, Czech Rep.	G14	16
Karwār, India	D1	53
Karyés, Grc.	C7	28
Karymskoe, Russia	F11	34
Kasai (Cassai), stm., Afr.	E3	66
Kasaji, D.R.C.	G4	66
Kasama, Japan	C13	40
Kasama, Zam.	C5	68
Kasan, Bots.	D3	68
Kasanga, Tan.	F6	66
Kasangulu, D.R.C.	E3	66
Kasaoka, Japan	E6	40
Kasaragod, India	E2	53
Kasba, India	F11	54
Kasba Lake, l., Can.	C10	106
Kascjukoŭka, Bela.	H13	10
Kascjukovičy, Bela.	G14	10
Kaseda, Japan	H3	40
Kasempa, Zam.	C4	68
Kasenga, D.R.C.	G5	66
Kasenye, D.R.C.	D6	66
Kasese, Ug.	D6	66
Kaset Sombun, Thai.	D5	48
Kāshān, Iran	C7	56
Kashegelok, Ak., U.S.	D7	140a
Kashgar see Kashi, China	B12	56
Kashi, China	B12	56
Kashihara, Japan	E8	40
Kashima, Japan	C13	40
Kashima-nada, Japan	C13	40
Kashing see Jiaxing, China	F9	42
Kashiwa, Japan	D13	40
Kashiwazaki, Japan	B11	40
Kashmar, Iran	B8	56
Kashmir, hist. reg., Asia	A3	54
Kasia, India	E10	54
Kasimov, Russia	I19	8
Kasimbar, Indon.	D12	50
Kašin, Russia	C20	10
Kasiruta, Pulau, i., Indon.	F8	44
Kaskaskia, stm., Il., U.S.	E8	120
Kaskinen, Fin.	E9	8
Kaslo, B.C., Can.	G13	138
Kasongo, D.R.C.	E5	66
Kasongo-Lunda, D.R.C.	F3	66
Kásos, i., Grc.	H9	28
Kaspijsk, Russia	F7	32
Kaspijskoe more see Caspian Sea, l.	F7	32
Kasr, Ra's, c., Afr.	D7	62
Kassalā, Sudan	D7	62
Kassándra, Gulf see Kassándras, Kólpos, b., Grc.	C6	28
Kassándras, Kólpos, b., Grc.	C6	28
Kasserine, Tun.	B6	64
Kassel, Ger.	E5	16
Kastamonu, Tur.	A3	56
Kastamonu, state, Tur.	B16	28
Kastélli, Grc.	H6	28
Kastoría, Grc.	C4	28
Kastorías, Límni, l., Grc.	C4	28
Kastrakíou, Techniti Límni, res., Grc.	E4	28
Kasulu, Tan.	E6	66
Kasumiga-ura, l., Japan	C13	40
Kasungan, Indon.	E8	50
Kasūr, Pak.	C5	54
Kaszuby, hist. reg., Pol.	B13	16
Kataba, Zam.	D4	68
Katahdin, Mount, mtn., Me., U.S.	E7	110
Katako-Kombe, D.R.C.	E4	66
Katanga, hist. reg., D.R.C.	F4	66
Katanga, stm., Russia	C18	32
Katangli, India	G7	54
Katangli, Russia	F17	34
Katanning, Austl.	F3	74
Katchall Island, i., India	G7	46
Katepwa Beach, Sk., Can.	D10	124
Kateríni, Grc.	C5	28
Kates Needle, mtn., N.A.	D4	106
Katha, Mya.	D8	46
Katherína, Gebel, mtn., Egypt	J4	58
Katherine, Austl.	B6	74
Katherine, stm., Austl.	B6	74
Katherine Creek, stm., Austl.	D4	76
Kāthiāwār Peninsula, pen., India	H3	54
Kathla, India	C6	54
Kāthmāndau (Kathmandu), Nepal	E10	54
Kathmandu see Kāthmāndau, Nepal	E10	54
Kathor, India	H4	54
Kathua, India	B5	54
Kati, Mali	G3	64
Katibas, stm., Malay.	C8	50
Kathār, India	F11	54
Katimík Lake, l., Mb., Can.	B14	124
Katiola, C. Iv.	H4	64
Katipunan, Phil.	F4	52
Ka Tiriti o te Moana see Southern Alps, mts., N.Z.	F4	80
Katmai, Mount, vol., Ak., U.S.	E8	140a
Káto Achaḯa, Grc.	E4	28
Katoomba, Austl.	I8	76
Katowice, Pol.	F14	16
Katowice, state, Pol.	F15	16
Katrineholm, Swe.	G7	8
Katsina, Nig.	G6	64
Katsina Ala, stm., Afr.	H6	64
Katsuta, Japan	C13	40
Katsuura, Japan	D13	40
Katsuyama, Japan	C9	40
Katsuyama, Japan	D6	40
Kattakurgan, Uzb.	G11	32
Kattegat, strt., Eur.	H4	8
Katul, Jabal, mtn., Sudan	E5	62
Katun', stm., Russia	D15	32
Katunino, Russia	G21	8
Katwijk aan Zee, Neth.	B13	14
Katyn, Russia	F14	10
Katzenbuckel, mtn., Ger.	G5	16
Kauai, i., Hi., U.S.	B2	78a
Kauai Channel, strt., Hi., U.S.	B3	78a
Kaufbeuren, Ger.	I6	16
Kaufman, Tx., U.S.	E2	122
Kaukauna, Wi., U.S.	D1	112
Kaukau Veld, plat., Afr.	D3	68
Kaulakahi Channel, strt., Hi., U.S.	B2	78a
Kaumalapau, Hi., U.S.	C4	78a
Kauna-Namoda, Nig.	G6	64
Kaunas, Lith.	F6	10
Kauriālā (Ghāghara), stm., Asia	D8	54
Kautokeino, Nor.	B10	8
Kau-ye Kyun, i., Mya.	G4	48
Kavača, Russia	D23	34
Kavadarci, Mac.	B5	28
Kavajë, Alb.	C13	24
Kavali, India	C5	53
Kavalerovo, Russia	B11	38
Kavála, Grc.	C7	28
Kavaratti, India	F3	53
Kavaratti Island, i., India	D1	53
Kaveri (Cauvery), stm., India	F4	53
Kavieng, Pao. N. Gui.	a5	79a
Kavīr, Dasht-e, des., Iran	C8	56
Kävlinge, Swe.	I5	8
Kaw, Mya.	D3	48
Kawagama Lake, l., On., Can.	C10	112
Kawagoe, Japan	D12	40
Kawaguchi, Japan	D12	40
Kawaihoa, c., Hi., U.S.	B1	78a
Kawaikini, mtn., Hi., U.S.	A2	78a
Kawambwa, Zam.	B4	68
Kawanoe, Japan	E6	40
Kawardha, India	H8	54
Kawasaki, Japan	D12	40
Kawdut, Mya.	E3	48
Kawenawkamik Lake, l., Mb., Can.	B14	124
Kawhia Harbour, b., N.Z.	D6	80
Kawich Peak, mtn., Nv., U.S.	F9	134
Kawkareik, Mya.	D3	48
Kawlin, Mya.	D8	46
Kawm Umbū, Egypt	C6	62
Kawnipi Lake, l., On., Can.	C7	118
Kawthaung, Mya.	H4	48
Kaxgar, stm., China	A4	54
Kaya, Burkina	G4	64
Kayak Island, i., Ak., U.S.	E11	140a
Kayan, stm., Indon.	B10	50
Kayankulam, India	G3	53
Kaycee, Wy., U.S.	E6	126
Kayenta, Az., U.S.	G6	132
Kayes, Mali	G2	64
Kayin, state, Mya.	D3	48
Kaymaz, Tur.	D14	28
Kayseri, Tur.	B4	56
Kaysville, Ut., U.S.	B4	132
Kayuagung, Indon.	E4	50
Kazačje, Russia	B16	34
Kazakhskij melkosopočnik (Kazakh Hills), hills, Kaz.	D12	32
Kazakh Hills see Kazakhskij melkosopočnik, hills, Kaz.	D12	32
Kazaki, Russia	H21	10
Kazakstan, ctry., Asia	E10	32
Kazalinsk, Kaz.	E10	32
Kazan', stm., Can.	C11	106
Kazan-rettō, is., Japan	G18	30
Kazan', Russia	C7	32
Kazanlŭk, Blg.	G12	26
Kazanlı, Tur.	B5	58
Kazatin see Kozjatyn, Ukr.	B14	26
Kazerún, Iran	D7	56
Kazimierza Wielka, Pol.	F16	16
Kazincbarcika, Hung.	A7	26
Kaziranga National Park, p.o.i., India	E14	54
Kazlų Rūda, Lith.	F6	10
Kaztalovka, Kaz.	E7	32
Kazula, Moz.	D5	68
Kazym, Russia	B11	32
Kazym, stm., Russia	B11	32
Kazyr, stm., Russia	D16	32
Kbal Dâmrei, Camb.	E7	48
Kdyně, Czech Rep.	G9	16
Kéa, Grc.	F7	28
Kéa, i., Grc.	F7	28
Keahole Point, c., Hi., U.S.	D5	78a
Kealaikahiki Channel, strt., Hi., U.S.	C5	78a
Keams Canyon, Az., U.S.	H6	132
Keanapapa Point, c., Hi., U.S.	C4	78a
Kearney, Mo., U.S.	E3	120
Kearney, Ne., U.S.	G13	126
Kearns, Ut., U.S.	C4	132
Kearny, Az., U.S.	J6	132
Keban Baraji, res., Tur.	B4	56
Keban Reservoir see Keban Baraji, res., Tur.	B4	56
Kébémer, Sen.	F1	64
Kebnekaise, mtn., Swe.	B8	8
K'ebrī Dehar, Eth.	F8	62
Kechika, stm., B.C., Can.	D5	106
Kecskemét, Hung.	C6	26
Kedah, state, Malay.	J5	48
Kédainiai, Lith.	E6	10
Kediri, Indon.	G8	50
Kedon, Russia	D20	34
Kédougou, Sen.	G2	64
Kedzierzyn-Koźle, Pol.	F14	16
Keefers, B.C., Can.	F9	138
Keele, stm., N.T., Can.	C5	106
Keele Peak, mtn., Yk., Can.	C4	106
Keeling Islands see Cocos Islands, dep., Oc.	K12	142
Keene, Ky., U.S.	G13	120
Keene, N.H., U.S.	B13	114
Keeney Knob, mtn., W.V., U.S.	G5	114
Keer-Weer, Cape, c., Austl.	B8	74
Keeseville, N.Y., U.S.	F3	110
Keetmanshoop, Nmb.	E3	70
Keewatin, On., Can.	B4	118
Keewatin, Mn., U.S.	D5	118
Kefallinía, i., Grc.	E3	28
Kefamenanu, Indon.	G7	44
Kefar Nahum (Capernaum), hist., Isr.	F6	58
Kefar Sava, Isr.	F5	58
Keflavík, Ice.	k28	8a
Keffi, Nig.	H6	64
Ke Ga, Mui, c., Viet.	G9	48
Kegalla, Sri L.	H5	53
Kegen', Kaz.	F13	32
Kegums, Lat.	D7	10
Kegworth, Eng., U.K.	I11	12
Kehl, Ger.	H3	16
Kei-hsi Mänsäm, Mya.	B4	48
Keighley, Eng., U.K.	H10	12
Keila, Est.	G11	8
Keila, Est.	A8	10
Keimoes, S. Afr.	F5	70
Keith, Scot., U.K.	D9	12
Keith Arm, b., N.T., Can.	B6	106
Keithley Creek, B.C., Can.	D9	138
Keithsburg, Il., U.S.	J8	118
Keiyasi, Fiji	p18	79e
Kejsir, Or., U.S.	F3	136
Kekaha, Hi., U.S.	B1	78a
Kékes, mtn., Hung.	B7	26
Kekri, India	E5	54
K'elafo, Eth.	F8	62
Kelang, Indon.	C10	50
Kelantan, state, Malay.	J6	48
Kelantan, stm., Malay.	J6	48
Kelapa, Indon.	E4	50
Kelberg, Ger.	F2	16
Kelheim, Ger.	H7	16
Kelibia, Tun.	I4	24
Kéllé, Congo	E2	66
Kellerberrin, Austl.	F3	74
Keller Lake, l., N.T., Can.	C6	106
Kellett, Cape, c., N.T., Can.	B14	140
Kelleys Island, i., Oh., U.S.	C3	114
Kellogg, Id., U.S.	C10	136
Kellogg, Ia., U.S.	C5	120
Kellogg, Mn., U.S.	G6	118
Kelloselkä, Fin.	C13	8
Kells, Ire.	H6	12
Kélo, Chad	F3	62
Kelokolkan, Indon.	G11	138
Kelowna, B.C., Can.	G11	138
Kelsey Bay, B.C., Can.	F5	138
Kelseyville, Ca., U.S.	D3	134
Kelso, Scot., U.K.	F10	12
Kelso, Wa., U.S.	D4	136
Keluang, Malay.	K6	48
Kelvington, Sk., Can.	B9	124
Kelvin Island, i., On., Can.	C9	118
Kem', Russia	D16	8
Kem', stm., Russia	D15	8
Kemah, Tur.	B4	56
Kemano, B.C., Can.	C2	138
Kemena, stm., Malay.	B8	50
Kemer, Tur.	F13	28
Kemerovo, Russia	C15	32
Kemi, Fin.	D11	8
Kemijärvi, Fin.	C12	8
Kemijoki, stm., Fin.	C12	8
Kemmerer, Wy., U.S.	B6	132
Kemmuna (Comino), i., Malta	H8	24
Kemnath, Ger.	G7	16
Kemp, Tx., U.S.	E2	122
Kemp, Lake, res., Tx., U.S.	H9	128
Kempner, Tx., U.S.	C9	130
Kempsey, Austl.	H9	76
Kempston, Eng., U.K.	I12	12
Kempt, Lac, l., Qc., Can.	F16	106
Kempten, Ger.	I6	16
Kemptville, On., Can.	C14	112
Kemujan, Pulau, i., Indon.	F7	50
Ken, stm., India	G7	54
Kenai, Ak., U.S.	D9	140a
Kenai Mountains, mts., Ak., U.S.	E9	140a
Kenai Peninsula, pen., Ak., U.S.		
Kenansville, N.C., U.S.	B7	116
Kenbridge, Va., U.S.	H7	114
Kendal, Eng., U.K.	G10	12
Kendal, Austl.		
Kendall, Fl., U.S.	K5	116
Kendall, Cape, c., Nu., Can.	C13	106
Kendallville, In., U.S.	G4	112
Kendari, Indon.	F7	44
Kendawangan, Indon.	E7	50
Kendrāparha, India	H11	54
Kendrew, S. Afr.	H7	70
Kendrick, Fl., U.S.	G3	116
Kendujhargarh, India	H10	54
Keng Tung, Mya.	B4	48
Kenhardt, S. Afr.		

Name	Map Ref.	Page
Kenilworth, Ut., U.S.	D6	132
Kénitra, Mor.	C3	64
Kenly, N.C., U.S.	A7	116
Kenmare, Ire.	J3	12
Kenmare, N.D., U.S.	F11	124
Kennard, Tx., U.S.	F3	122
Kennebec, stm., Me., U.S.	F7	110
Kennebecasis Bay, b., N.B., Can.	E11	110
Kennebunk, Me., U.S.	G6	110
Kennedy, Al., U.S.	D11	122
Kennedy, Cape see Canaveral, Cape, c., Fl., U.S.	H5	116
Kennedy, Mount, mtn., B.C., Can.	F5	138
Kennedy, Mount, mtn., Yk., Can.	C3	106
Kennedy Lake, l., B.C., Can.	G5	138
Kenner, La., U.S.	G8	122
Kennetcook, N.S., Can.	E13	110
Kennett, Mo., U.S.	H7	120
Kennewick, Wa., U.S.	D7	136
Kenney Dam, dam, B.C., Can.	C6	138
Kenogami, stm., On., Can.	E13	106
Kénogami, Lac, res., Qc., Can.	B5	110
Keno Hill, Yk., Can.	C3	106
Kenora, On., Can.	B4	118
Kenosha, Wi., U.S.	F2	112
Kenozero, ozero, l., Russia	E18	8
Kensal, N.D., U.S.	G15	124
Kensett, Ar., U.S.	B7	122
Kensington, Ks., U.S.	B9	128
Kensington Park, Fl., U.S.	I3	116
Kent, Oh., U.S.	C4	114
Kent, Wa., U.S.	C4	136
Kentau, Kaz.	F11	32
Kent Group, is., Austl.	L6	76
Kentland, In., U.S.	H2	112
Kenton, Mi., U.S.	E10	118
Kenton, Tn., U.S.	H8	120
Kent Peninsula, pen., Nu., Can.	B9	106
Kentrikí Makedonía, state, Grc.	C6	28
Kentucky, state, U.S.	G12	120
Kentucky, stm., Ky., U.S.	F13	120
Kentucky, Middle Fork, stm., Ky., U.S.	G2	114
Kentucky, North Fork, stm., Ky., U.S.	G2	114
Kentucky Lake, res., U.S.	H9	120
Kentville, N.S., Can.	E12	110
Kentwood, La., U.S.	G8	122
Kenya, ctry., Afr.	D7	66
Kenya, Mount see Kirinyaga, mtn., Kenya	E7	66
Kenyon, Mn., U.S.	G6	118
Keokuk, Ia., U.S.	D6	120
Keoladeo National Park, p.o.i., India	E6	54
Keo Nua, Deo, p., Asia	C7	48
Keosauqua, Ia., U.S.	D5	120
Keota, Ia., U.S.	C6	120
Keota, Ok., U.S.	B4	122
Keowee, Lake, res., S.C., U.S.	B2	116
Kepi, Indon.	G10	44
Kepina, Russia	D19	8
Kępno, Pol.	E13	16
Keppel Bay, b., Austl.	D8	76
Kepsut, Tur.	D11	28
Kerala, state, India	F3	53
Keramadoo, mtn., Palau	f8	78b
Keramian, Pulau, i., Indon.	F9	50
Kerang, Austl.	J4	76
Keratéa, Grc.	F6	28
Keravat, Pap. N. Gui.	a5	79a
Kerch, Ukr.	E5	32
Kerec, mys, c., Russia	D18	8
Kerema, Pap. N. Gui.	b4	79a
Keremeos, B.C., Can.	G11	138
Keren, Erit.	D7	62
Kerens, Tx., U.S.	E2	122
Keret', Russia	C15	8
Keret', ozero, l., Russia	D15	8
Kerewan, Gam.	G1	64
Kerguelen, Îles, is., Afr.	J17	4
Kerguelen Plateau, unds.	O10	142
Kerí, Grc.	F3	28
Kericho, Kenya	E7	66
Kerinci, Gunung, vol., Indon.	D2	50
Kerkenna, Îles, is., Tun.	C7	64
Kerkhoven, Mn., U.S.	F3	118
Kerkiči, Turkmen.	B10	56
Kerkrade, Neth.	F2	16
Kérkyra (Corfu), Grc.	D2	28
Kérkyra (Corfu), i., Grc.	D2	28
Kermadec Islands, is., N.Z.	F9	72
Kermadec Ridge, unds.	M20	142
Kermadec Trench, unds.	M21	142
Kermān, Iran	C8	56
Kermānshāh (Bākhtarān), Iran	C6	56
Kerme, Gulf of see Gökova Körfezi, b., Tur.	G10	28
Kermit, Tx., U.S.	C4	130
Kern, stm., Ca., U.S.	H7	134
Kern, South Fork, stm., Ca., U.S.	H7	134
Kernersville, N.C., U.S.	H5	114
Kernville, Ca., U.S.	H7	134
Kérouané, Gui.	H3	64
Kerrobert, Sk., Can.	C4	124
Kerrville, Tx., U.S.	D8	130
Kerry, state, Ire.	I2	12
Kerry Head, c., Ire.	I2	12
Kershaw, S.C., U.S.	B5	116
Kersley, B.C., Can.	D8	138
Kertamulia, Indon.	D6	50
Kerulen, stm., Asia	B7	36
Kesagami Lake, l., On., Can.	E14	106
Keşan, Tur.	C9	28
Kesennuma, Japan	E14	38
Keshan, China	B10	36
Keshod, India	H3	54
Keski-Suomi, state, Fin.	E11	8
Kes'ma, Russia	B20	10
Kesova Gora, Russia	C20	10
Kestell, S. Afr.	F9	70
Keswick, Eng., U.K.	G9	12
Keszthely, Hung.	C4	26
Ket', stm., Russia	C14	32
Keta, Ghana	H5	64
Keta, ozero, l., Russia	C6	34
Ketapang, Indon.	F4	50
Ketapang, Indon.	D6	50
Ketchikan, Ak., U.S.	E13	140
Ketchum, Id., U.S.	G12	136
Kete-Krachi, Ghana	H4	64
Ketoj, ostrov, i., Russia	G19	34
Kętrzyn, Pol.	B17	16
Kettering, Eng., U.K.	I12	12
Kettering, Oh., U.S.	E1	114
Kettle, stm., N.A.	H12	138
Kettle Falls, Wa., U.S.	B8	136
Kęty, Pol.	G15	16
Keudeteunom, Indon.	J2	48
Keuka Lake, l., N.Y., U.S.	B8	114
Keukenhof, misc. cult., Neth.	B13	14
Keul', Russia	C18	32
Kevelaer, Ger.	E2	16
Kevin, Mt., U.S.	B14	136
Kew, T./C. Is.	A12	102
Kewanee, Il., U.S.	C7	120
Kewaunee, Wi., U.S.	D2	112
Keweenaw Bay, b., Mi., U.S.	E10	118
Keweenaw Peninsula, pen., Mi., U.S.	D11	118
Keweenaw Point, c., Mi., U.S.	D11	118
Key, Lough, l., Ire.	G4	12
Keya Paha, stm., U.S.	E13	126
Keyes, Ok., U.S.	E6	128
Keyhole Reservoir, res., Wy., U.S.	C8	126
Key Largo, Fl., U.S.	K5	116
Key Largo, i., Fl., U.S.	K5	116
Keyser, W.V., U.S.	E7	114
Keystone, S.D., U.S.	D9	126
Keystone, W.V., U.S.	G4	114
Keystone Lake, res., Ok., U.S.	A2	122
Keystone Peak, mtn., Az., U.S.	L5	132
Keysville, Va., U.S.	G7	114
Keytesville, Mo., U.S.	E5	120
Key West, Fl., U.S.	L4	116
Kezi, Zimb.	B9	70
Kežma, Russia	C18	32
Kežmarok, Slov.	G16	16
Kgalagadi, state, Bots.	D5	70
Kgatleng, state, Bots.	D8	70
Khadki, India	B1	53
Khadzhybeis'kyi lyman, l., Ukr.	C17	26
Khagaria, India	F11	54
Khairāgarh, India	H8	54
Khairpur, Pak.	E2	54
Khairpur, Pak.	D4	54
Khajrāho, India	F8	54
Khakassia see Hakasija, state, Russia	D16	32
Kha Khaeng, stm., Thai.	E4	48
Khakhea, Bots.	D6	70
Khalatse, India	A6	54
Khālidī, Khirbat al-, hist., Jord.	I6	58
Khalîya, Gebel, mtn., Egypt	I3	58
Khalūf, Oman	E8	56
Khambhāliya, India	G2	54
Khambhāt, India	G4	54
Khambhāt, Gulf of, b., India	H3	54
Khāmgaon, India	H6	54
Khāmis, Ash-Shallāl al- (Fifth Cataract), wtfl, Sudan	D6	62
Khamīs Mushayṭ, Sau. Ar.	F5	56
Khammam, India	C5	53
Khan, stm., Laos	C6	48
Khan, stm., Nmb.	C2	70
Khānābād, Afg.	B10	56
Khān Abū Shāmāt, Syria	E7	58
Khānaqīn, Iraq	C6	56
Khancoban, Austl.	K7	76
Khandela, India	E5	54
Khandwa, India	H6	54
Khānewāl, Pak.	C3	54
Khāngarh, Pak.	D3	54
Khangchendzonga National Park, p.o.i., India	E12	54
Khangkhai, Laos	C6	48
Khania, Gulf of see Chanión, Kólpos, b., Grc.	H6	28
Khanka, Lake, l., Asia	B10	38
Khanna, India	C6	54
Khānpur, Pak.	D3	54
Khansiir, Raas, c., Som.	B9	66
Khān Yūnus, Gaza	G5	58
Khao Laem Reservoir, res., Thai.	E4	48
Khao Sok National Park, p.o.i., Thai.	H4	48
Khao Yoi, Thai.	F4	48
Kharagpur, India	G11	54
Khārān, Pak.	D10	56
Kharāyij, Sabkhat al-, l., Syria	C8	58
Kharg Island see Khārk, Jazīreh-ye, i., Iran	D7	56
Khargon, India	H5	54
Khāriān Cantonment, Pak.	B4	54
Khārk, Jazīreh-ye, i., Iran	D7	56
Kharkiv, Ukr.	D5	32
Kharmanli see Harmanli, Blg.	H12	26
Khartoum see Al-Kharṭūm, Sudan	D6	62
Khartoum North see Al-Kharṭūm Baḥrī, Sudan	D6	62
Khasebake, Bots.	B7	70
Khāsh, Afg.	C9	56
Khāsh, Iran	D9	56
Khashm al-Qirbah, Sudan	D7	62
Khaskovo see Haskovo, Blg.	H12	26
Khatanga see Hatanga, Russia	B9	34
Khatanga see Hatanga, stm., Russia	B9	34
Khatauli, India	D6	54
Khatt, Oued al, stm., W. Sah.	D2	64
Khavast see Havast, Uzb.	F11	32
Khawsa, Mya.	E3	48
Khayung, stm., Thai.	E7	48
Khed, India	C1	53
Kheil, Katîb el-, sand, Egypt	H3	58
Khemis el Khechna, Alg.	H14	20
Khemis Melyana, Alg.	H13	20
Khemmarat, Thai.	D7	48
Khenchla, Alg.	B6	64
Khenifra, Mor.	C3	64
Kherson, Ukr.	F15	6
Kheta see Heta, stm., Russia	B8	34
Khetia, India	H5	54
Khimki see Himki, Russia	E20	10
Khipro, Pak.	F2	54
Khisfīn, Golan	F6	58
Khiva see Hiva, Uzb.	F10	32
Khlong Thom, Thai.	I4	48
Khlung, Thai.	F6	48
Khok Kloi, Thai.	H4	48
Khok Samrong, Thai.	E5	48
Kholm, Afg.	B10	56
Khomas, state, Nmb.	C3	70
Khomeynīshahr, Iran	C7	56
Khondmāl Hills, hills, India	H10	54
Khong see Mekong, stm., Asia	E10	46
Khon Kaen, Thai.	D6	48
Khordha, India	H10	54
Khorixas, Nmb.	B2	70
Khorog see Horog, Taj.	B11	56
Khorramābād, Iran	C6	56
Khorramshahr, Iran	C6	56
Khotyn, Ukr.	A13	26
Khouribga, Mor.	C3	64
Khowai, India	F13	54
Khowst, Afg.	C10	56
Khrisokhoús, Kólpos, b., Cyp.	C3	58
Khuis, Bots.	E5	70
Khuīyāla, India	E3	54
Khulna, Bngl.	G12	54
Khulna, state, Bngl.	G12	54
Khun Tan, Doi, mtn., Thai.	C4	48
Khunti, India	G10	54
Khurai, India	F7	54
Khurja, India	D6	54
Khushāb, Pak.	B4	54
Khust, Ukr.	A10	26
Khuzdār, Pak.	D10	56
Khvoy, Iran	B6	56
Khwae Noi, stm., Thai.	E4	48
Khyber Pass, p., Asia	A3	54
Khyriv, Ukr.	G18	16
Kiama, Austl.	J8	76
Kiama, D.R.C.	F3	66
Kiamba, Phil.	H5	52
Kiambi, D.R.C.	F5	66
Kiamichi, stm., Ok., U.S.	C3	122
Kiamusze see Jiamusi, China	B11	36
Kian see Ji'an, China	H6	42
Kiangarow, Mount, mtn., Austl.	F8	76
Kiang-si see Jiangxi, state, China	H6	42
Kiangsi see Jiangxi, state, China	H6	42
Kiang-sou see Jiangsu, state, China	E8	42
Kiangsu see Jiangsu, state, China	E8	42
Kiaohsien see Jiaoxian, China	C8	42
Kibangou, Congo	E2	66
Kibombo, D.R.C.	E5	66
Kibondo, Tan.	E6	66
Kibre Mengist, Eth.	F7	62
Kıbrıs see Cyprus, ctry., Asia	C4	58
Kıbrısçık, Tur.	C14	28
Kibuye, Rw.	E5	66
Kičevo, Mac.	B3	28
Kickapoo, stm., Wi., U.S.	H8	118
Kicking Horse Pass, p., Can.	E14	138
Kidal, Mali	F5	64
Kidapawan, Phil.	G5	52
Kidatu, Tan.	F7	66
Kidderminster, Eng., U.K.	I10	12
Kidira, Sen.	G2	64
Kidnappers, Cape, c., N.Z.	D7	80
Kidston, Austl.	B5	76
Kiefersfelden, Ger.	I8	16
Kiel, Ger.	B6	16
Kiel, Wi., U.S.	H10	118
Kiel Bay see Kieler Bucht, b., Ger.	B6	16
Kiel Canal see Nord-Ostsee-Kanal, can., Ger.	B5	16
Kielce, Pol.	F16	16
Kielce, state, Pol.	F16	16
Kieler Bucht, b., Ger.	B6	16
Kiester, Mn., U.S.	H5	118
Kiev see Kyïv, Ukr.	D4	32
Kievka, Kaz.	D12	32
Kiev Reservoir see Kyïvs'ke vodoskhovyshche, res., Ukr.	D4	32
Kiffa, Maur.	F2	64
Kifisiá, Grc.	E6	28
Kigali, Rw.	E6	66
Kigoma, Tan.	E5	66
Kihčik, Russia	F20	34
Kihei, Hi., U.S.	C5	78a
Kihniö, Fin.	E10	8
Kihnu, i., Est.	G10	8
Kii-hantō, pen., Japan	F8	40
Kiik, Kaz.	E12	32
Kii-suidō, strt., Japan	F7	40
Kikerino, Russia	A12	10
Kikinda, Yugo.	D7	26
Kikládhes (Cyclades), is., Grc.	F7	28
Kikori, Pap. N. Gui.	b3	79a
Kikori, stm., Pap. N. Gui.	b3	79a
Kikuchi, Japan	G3	40
Kikwit, D.R.C.	F3	66
Kīlakkarai, India	G4	53
Kilauea, Hi., U.S.	A2	78a
Kilauea Crater, crat., Hi., U.S.	D6	78a
Kılbasan, Tur.	A4	58
Kilbuck Mountains, mts., Ak., U.S.	D8	140
Kilchu-ŭp, Kor., N.	D8	38
Kilcoy, Austl.	F9	76
Kildare, state, Ire.	H6	12
Kildare, Cape, c., P.E., Can.	D13	110
Kildurk, Austl.	C5	74
Kilembe, D.R.C.	F3	66
Kilgore, Tx., U.S.	E4	122
Kilian Island, i., Nu., Can.	B18	140
Kılıç, Tur.	C12	28
Kiliia, Ukr.	D16	26
Kilikollūr, India	G3	53
Kilimanjaro, mtn., Tan.	E7	66
Kilimli, Tur.	B14	28
Kilindoni, Tan.	F7	66
Kilis, Tur.	B8	58
Kilkee, Ire.	I3	12
Kilkenny, Ire.	I5	12
Kilkenny, state, Ire.	I5	12
Kilkís, Grc.	C5	28
Killaloe, Ire.	I4	12
Killaloe Station, On., Can.	C12	112
Killam, Ab., Can.	D19	138
Killarney, Austl.	G9	76
Killarney, Mb., Can.	E14	124
Killarney, On., Can.	C8	112
Killarney, Ire.	I3	12
Killdeer, N.D., U.S.	G11	124
Killeen, Tx., U.S.	C10	130
Killen, Al., U.S.	C11	122
Killington Peak, mtn., Vt., U.S.	G4	110
Killiniq Island, i., Can.	E13	141
Killybegs, Ire.	G4	12
Kilmarnock, Scot., U.K.	F8	12
Kilmarnock, Va., U.S.	G9	114
Kilmore, Austl.	K5	76
Kilo, Indon.	H11	50
Kilombero, stm., Tan.	F7	66
Kilomines, D.R.C.	D5	66
Kilosa, Tan.	F7	66
Kilrush, Ire.	I3	12
Kilttān Island, i., India	F3	46
Kilwa, D.R.C.	F5	66
Kilwa Kivinje, Tan.	F7	66
Kim, Co., U.S.	D5	128
Kimba, Austl.	F7	74
Kimball, Ne., U.S.	F9	126
Kimball, S.D., U.S.	D13	126
Kimbe Bay, b., Pap. N. Gui.	b5	79a
Kimberley, B.C., Can.	G15	138
Kimberley, S. Afr.	F7	70
Kimberley Downs, Austl.	C4	74
Kimberley Plateau, plat., Austl.	C5	74
Kimberling City, Mo., U.S.	H4	120
Kimberly, Id., U.S.	H12	136
Kimberly, Wi., U.S.	G10	118
Kimch'aek, Kor., N.	D8	38
Kimch'ŏn, Kor., S.	F8	38
Kimhae, Kor., S.	D1	40
Kimito, Fin.	F10	8
Kim-me-ni-oli Wash, stm., N.M., U.S.	H8	132
Kimmirut, Nu., Can.	C17	106
Kímolos, i., Grc.	G7	28
Kimovsk, Russia	F21	10
Kimpō-zan, mtn., Japan	D11	40
Kimry, Russia	D20	10
Kinabalu, Gunong (Kinabalu, Mount), mtn., Malay.	G1	52
Kinabalu National Park, p.o.i., Malay.	H1	52
Kinabatangan, stm., Malay.	H2	52
Kinbasket Lake, res., B.C., Can.	D12	138
Kincaid, Sk., Can.	E6	124
Kincardine, On., Can.	D8	112
Kinchafoonee Creek, stm., Ga., U.S.	F14	122
Kinchega National Park, p.o.i., Austl.	I4	76
Kinda, D.R.C.	F4	66
Kinde, Mi., U.S.	E7	112
Kinder, La., U.S.	G6	122
Kindersley, Sk., Can.	C4	124
Kindia, Gui.	G2	64
Kindu, D.R.C.	E5	66
Kinešma, Russia	H19	8
King, N.C., U.S.	H5	114
King and Queen Court House, Va., U.S.	G9	114
Kingaroy, Austl.	F8	76
King City, On., Can.	E10	112
King City, Ca., U.S.	G4	134
Kingfield, Me., U.S.	F6	110
Kingfisher, Ok., U.S.	F10	128
King George, Va., U.S.	F8	114
King George, Mount, mtn., B.C., Can.	F15	138
King George Islands, is., Nu., Can.	D14	106
King George Sound, strt., Austl.	G3	74
King Hill, Id., U.S.	G11	136
Kingisepp, Russia	A11	10
King Island, i., Austl.	m12	77a
King Island, i., B.C., Can.	D3	138
King Leopold Ranges, mts., Austl.	C4	74
Kingman, Az., U.S.	H2	132
Kingman, Ks., U.S.	D10	128
Kingman Reef, rf., Oc.	C10	72
King Mountain, mtn., Or., U.S.	H3	136
Kingombe, D.R.C.	E5	66
Kingoonya, Austl.	F7	74
King Peak, mtn., Ca., U.S.	C1	134
Kings, stm., Ca., U.S.	G6	134
Kings Beach, Ca., U.S.	D5	134
Kingsbridge, Eng., U.K.	K9	12
Kingsburg, Ca., U.S.	G6	134
Kings Canyon National Park, p.o.i., Ca., U.S.	G7	134
Kingsford, Mi., U.S.	C1	112
Kingshill, V.I.U.S.	h10	104c
Kingsland, Ar., U.S.	D6	122
Kingsland, Ga., U.S.	F4	116
Kingsley, S. Afr.	E10	70
Kingsley, Ia., U.S.	B2	120
Kingsley, Mi., U.S.	D4	112
Kingsley Dam, dam, Ne., U.S.	F11	126
King's Lynn, Eng., U.K.	I13	12
Kings Mountain, N.C., U.S.	A4	116
King Solomon's Mines see Mikhrot Timna', hist., Isr.	I5	58
King Sound, strt., Austl.	C4	74
Kings Peak, mtn., Ut., U.S.	C6	132
Kingsport, Tn., U.S.	H3	114
Kingston, N.S., Can.	E11	110
Kingston, On., Can.	D13	112
Kingston, Jam.	i14	104d
Kingston, N.Z.	G3	80
Kingston, Norf. I.	y25	78i
Kingston, Ga., U.S.	C14	122
Kingston, Mo., U.S.	E3	120
Kingston, N.Y., U.S.	C11	114
Kingston, Ok., U.S.	C2	122
Kingston, Pa., U.S.	C9	114
Kingston, Tn., U.S.	I13	120
Kingston Southeast, Austl.	K2	76
Kingston upon Hull, Eng., U.K.	H12	12
Kingston upon Thames, Eng., U.K.	J12	12
Kingstown, St. Vin.	o11	105e
Kingstree, S.C., U.S.	C6	116
Kingsville, On., Can.	G7	112
Kingsville, Tx., U.S.	G10	130
Kingtechen see Jingdezhen, China	G7	42
King William Island, i., Nu., Can.	B11	106
King William's Town, S. Afr.	H8	70
Kinhwa see Jinhua, China	G8	42
Kınık, Tur.	D10	28
Kinira, stm., S. Afr.	G9	70
Kinistino, Sk., Can.	B9	124
Kinkala, Congo	E2	66
Kinlochleven, Scot., U.K.	E8	12
Kinnaird Head, c., Scot., U.K.	D10	12
Kinneret, Yam (Galilee, Sea of), l., Isr.	F6	58
Kinosaki, Japan	D7	40
Kinpoku-san, mtn., Japan	A11	40
Kinross, Scot., U.K.	E9	12
Kinsale, Monts.	D3	105a
Kinsale, Old Head of, c., Ire.	J4	12
Kinsarvik, Nor.	F2	8
Kinshasa (Léopoldville), D.R.C.	E3	66
Kinsley, Ks., U.S.	D9	128
Kinsman, Oh., U.S.	C5	114
Kinston, N.C., U.S.	A8	116
Kintampo, Ghana	H4	64
Kintyre, pen., Scot., U.K.	F7	12
Kintyre, Mull of, c., Scot., U.K.	F7	12
Kinuseo Falls, wtfl, B.C., Can.	B9	138
Kinuso, Ab., Can.	A15	138
Kinyangiri, Tan.	E6	66
Kinyeti, mtn., Sudan	G6	62
Kinzia, D.R.C.	E3	66
Kinzua, Or., U.S.	E7	136
Kinzua Dam, dam, Pa., U.S.	C6	114
Kiowa, Co., U.S.	B4	128
Kiowa, Ok., U.S.	C3	122
Kiowa Creek, stm., Co., U.S.	A4	128
Kipawa, stm., Qc., Can.	B11	112
Kipawa, Lac, res., Qc., Can.	A10	112
Kipembawe, Tan.	F6	66
Kipengere Range, mts., Tan.	F6	66
Kipili, Tan.	F6	66
Kipini, Kenya	E8	66
Kipling, Sk., Can.	D11	124
Kipnuk, Ak., U.S.	E7	140
Kipushi, D.R.C.	G5	66
Kirakira, Sol. Is.	f9	79b
Kirandul, India	B5	53
Kirausk, Bela.	G12	10
Kirazlı, Tur.	C9	28
Kirbla, Est.	B6	10
Kirchberg, Ger.	G5	16
Kirchmöser, Ger.	D8	16
Kireevsk, Russia	G20	10
Kirejkovo, Russia	G18	10
Kirenga, stm., Russia	C19	32
Kirensk, Russia	C19	32
Kirghizia see Kyrgyzstan, ctry., Asia	F12	32
Kirgiz Range, mts., Asia	F12	32
Kirgiz Soviet Socialist Republic see Kyrgyzstan, ctry., Asia	F12	32
Kiri, D.R.C.	E3	66
Kiribati, ctry., Oc.	D9	72
Kırıkhan, Tur.	B7	58
Kırıkkale, Tur.	B3	56
Kirillovo, Russia	H21	8
Kirin see Jilin, China	C7	38
Kirin see Jilin, state, China	C10	36
Kirinyaga (Kenya, Mount), mtn., Kenya	E7	66
Kirishima-Yaku-kokuritsu-kōen, p.o.i., Japan	H3	40
Kirishima-yama, vol., Japan	H3	40
Kiriši, Russia	A15	10
Kiritimati (Christmas Island), at., Kir.	C11	72
Kiriwina Islands (Trobriand Islands), is., Pap. N. Gui.	b5	79a
Kırka, Tur.	D13	28
Kırkağaç, Tur.	D10	28
Kirkcaldy, Scot., U.K.	E9	12
Kirkcudbright, Scot., U.K.	G8	12
Kirkenes, Nor.	B14	8
Kirkland, Il., U.S.	B9	120
Kirkland, Tx., U.S.	G8	128
Kirkland, Wa., U.S.	C4	136
Kirkland Lake, On., Can.	F14	106
Kırklareli, Tur.	B10	28
Kırklareli, state, Tur.	B10	28
Kirklin, In., U.S.	H3	112
Kirkpatrick, Mount, mtn., Ant.	D21	81
Kirksville, Mo., U.S.	D5	120
Kirkwall, Scot., U.K.	B9	12
Kirkwood, S. Afr.	H7	70
Kirkwood, Mo., U.S.	F7	120
Kirmir, stm., Tur.	C15	28
Kirn, Ger.	G3	16
Kirov, Russia	F17	10
Kirov, Russia	C7	32
Kirovakan see Vanadzor, Arm.	A5	56
Kirovohrad, Ukr.	E4	32
Kirovohrad, co., Ukr.	A17	26
Kirovsk, Russia	C15	8
Kirovsk, Turkmen.	B9	56
Kirovskaja oblast', co., Russia	F22	8
Kirovskij, Kaz.	F13	32
Kirovskij, Russia	F20	34
Kirovskij, Russia	B10	38
Kirriemuir, Scot., U.K.	E9	12
Kirs, Russia	C8	32
Kirsanov, Russia	D6	32
Kırşehir, Tur.	B3	56
Kīrthar Range, mts., Pak.	D10	56
Kirtland, N.M., U.S.	G8	132
Kiruna, Swe.	C8	8
Kirundu, D.R.C.	E5	66
Kirwin, Ks., U.S.	B9	128
Kiryū, Japan	C12	40
Kiržač, Russia	D21	10
Kisa, Swe.	G6	8
Kisangani (Stanleyville), D.R.C.	D5	66
Kisar, Pulau, i., Indon.	G8	44
Kisaran, Indon.	B1	50
Kisarazu, Japan	D12	40
Kisbey, Sk., Can.	E11	124
Kiselëvsk, Russia	D15	32
Kīsh, Jazīreh-ye, i., Iran	D7	56
Kishanganj, India	E11	54
Kishangarh, India	E3	54
Kishangarh Bās, India	E5	54
Kishi, Nig.	H5	64
Kishinev see Chişinău, Mol.	B15	26
Kishiwada, Japan	E8	40
Kishorganj, Bngl.	F13	54
Kisii, Kenya	E6	66
Kisiju, Tan.	F7	66
Kisiwada see Kishiwada, Japan	E8	40
Kiska Island, i., Ak., U.S.	g22	140a
Kiskatinaw, stm., B.C., Can.	A10	138
Kiska Volcano, vol., Ak., U.S.	g22	140a
Kiskörei-víztároló, res., Hung.	B7	26
Kiskőrös, Hung.	C6	26
Kiskunfélegyháza, Hung.	C6	26
Kiskunhalas, Hung.	C6	26
Kiskunmajsa, Hung.	C6	26
Kiskunsági Nemzeti Park, p.o.i., Hung.	C6	26
Kislovodsk, Russia	F6	32
Kismaayo, Som.	E8	66
Kiso, stm., Japan	D9	40
Kiso-sammyaku, mts., Japan	D10	40
Kissidougou, Gui.	H2	64
Kissimmee, Fl., U.S.	H4	116
Kissimmee, stm., Fl., U.S.	I4	116
Kissimmee, Lake, l., Fl., U.S.	I4	116
Kississing Lake, l., Mb., Can.	D10	106
Kisújszállás, Hung.	B7	26
Kisuki, Japan	D5	40
Kisumu, Kenya	E6	66
Kisvárda, Hung.	A9	26
Kita, Mali	G3	64
Kitaa see Vestgrønland, state, Grnld.	D16	141
Kitaibaraki, Japan	C13	40
Kitakami, stm., Japan	E14	38
Kitakata, Japan	B12	40
Kitakyūshū, Japan	F3	40
Kitale, Kenya	D7	66
Kitami, Japan	C15	38
Kitangiri, Lake, l., Tan.	E6	66
Kitchener, On., Can.	E9	112
Kithārah, Khirbat, hist., Jord.	I6	58
Kitimat, B.C., Can.	B2	138
Kitimat Ranges, mts., B.C., Can.	C2	138
Kitinen, stm., Fin.	C12	8
Kitíou, Akrotírion, c., Cyp.	D4	58
Kitridge Point, c., Barb.	n9	105d
Kitsuki, Japan	F4	40
Kittanning, Pa., U.S.	D6	114
Kittitas, Wa., U.S.	D6	136
Kitt Peak National Observatory, sci., Az., U.S.	K5	132
Kitui, Kenya	E7	66
Kitunda, Tan.	F6	66
Kitwanga, B.C., Can.	A2	138
Kitwe, Zam.	C4	68
Kityang see Jieyang, China	J7	42
Kitzbühel, Aus.	C9	22
Kitzingen, Ger.	G6	16
Kiukiang see Jiujiang, China	G6	42
Kiunga, Pap. N. Gui.	b3	79a
Kiuruvesi, Fin.	E12	8
Kivalina, Ak., U.S.	C7	140
Kivijärvi, l., Fin.	E11	8
Kiviõli, Est.	G12	8
Kivu, Lake, l., Afr.	E5	66
Kıyıköy, Tur.	B11	28
Kiyiu Lake, l., Sk., Can.	C5	124
Kızıl Adalar, is., Tur.	C11	28
Kızılcabölük, Tur.	F11	28
Kızılcahamam, Tur.	C15	28
Kızıldağ Milli Parkı, p.o.i., Tur.	F14	28
Kızılırmak, stm., Tur.	A4	56
Kızılören, Tur.	F15	28
Kizimkazi, Tan.	F7	66
Kızkalesi, hist., Tur.	B4	58
Kizljar, Russia	F7	32
Kizyl-Atrek, Turkmen.	B7	56
Kizyl-Su, Turkmen.	B7	56
Kjahta, Russia	F10	34
Kjungej-Ala-Too, hrebet, mts., Asia	F13	32
Kjusjur, Russia	B14	34
Kjustendil, Blg.	G9	26
Klabat, Gunung, vol., Indon.	E8	44
Kladno, Czech Rep.	F10	16
Kladovo, Yugo.	E9	26
Klagan, Malay.	G1	52
Klagenfurt, Aus.	D11	22
Klaipėda (Memel), Lith.	E3	10
Klakah, Indon.	G8	50
Klamath, stm., U.S.	B2	134
Klamath Falls, Or., U.S.	A3	134
Klamath Marsh, sw., Or., U.S.	H5	136
Klamath Mountains, mts., U.S.	B2	134
Klamono, Indon.	F9	44
Klang, Malay.	K5	48
Klangenan, Indon.	G6	50
Klangenang, Indon.	G6	50
Klangpi, Mya.	G14	54
Klatovy, Czech Rep.	G9	16
Klawer, S. Afr.	G4	70
Kleck, Bela.	G9	10
Kleczew, Pol.	D14	16
Kleena Kleene, B.C., Can.	E5	138
Klein Curaçao, i., Neth. Ant.	q22	104g
Klein Karroo see Little Karroo, plat., S. Afr.	H5	70
Klein Namaland see Little Namaqualand, hist. reg., S. Afr.	F3	70
Klekovača, mtn., Bos.	E3	26
Klemme, Ia., U.S.	A4	120
Klemtu, B.C., Can.	D2	138
Klerksdorp, S. Afr.	E8	70
Kletnja, Russia	G16	10
Kleve, Ger.	E2	16
Klickitat, stm., Wa., U.S.	E5	136
Klimavičy, Bela.	G14	10
Klimino, Russia	C17	32
Klimovo, Russia	H15	10
Klimovsk, Russia	E20	10
Klimpfjäll, Swe.	D6	8
Klin, Russia	D19	10
Klinaklini, stm., B.C., Can.	E5	138
Klincy, Russia	H15	10
Klingenthal, Ger.	F8	16
Klínovec, mtn., Czech Rep.	F8	16
Klintehamn, Swe.	H8	8
Klip, stm., S. Afr.	E9	70
Klipdale, S. Afr.	I4	70
Klipplaat, S. Afr.	H7	70
Klisura, Blg.	G11	26
Kljazma, stm., Russia	E21	10
Ključ, Bos.	E3	26
Ključevskaja Sopka, vulkan, vol., Russia	E21	34
Ključi, Russia	E21	34
Kljukvenka, Russia	C15	32
Kłobuck, Pol.	F14	16
Kłodawa, Pol.	D14	16
Kłodzko, Pol.	F12	16
Klondike, hist. reg., Yk., Can.	C3	106
Klooga, Est.	A7	10
Klosterneuburg, Aus.	B13	22
Kloten, Switz.	C5	22
Klotz, Lac, l., Qc., Can.	C16	106
Klötze, Ger.	D7	16
Kluane Lake, l., Yk., Can.	C3	106
Kluczbork, Pol.	F14	16
Klungkung, Indon.	H9	50
Knaddah, Syria	C7	58
Knapp, Wi., U.S.	G6	118
Kneehills Creek, stm., Ab., Can.	E17	138
Knee Lake, l., Mb., Can.	D12	106
Kneža, Blg.	F11	26
Knić, Yugo.	F7	26
Knickerbocker, Tx., U.S.	C7	130
Knife, stm., N.D., U.S.	G12	124
Knight Inlet, b., B.C., Can.	F4	138
Knights Landing, Ca., U.S.	E4	134
Knin, Cro.	F13	22
Knippa, Tx., U.S.	E8	130
Knittelfeld, Aus.	C11	22
Knjaževac, Yugo.	F9	26
Knob Noster, Mo., U.S.	F4	120
Knokke-Heist, Bel.	C12	14
Knosós, hist., Grc.	H8	28
Knox, Pa., U.S.	C6	114
Knox, Cape, c., B.C., Can.	E4	106
Knox City, Tx., U.S.	H9	128
Knox Coast, cst., Ant.	B15	81
Knoxville, Ga., U.S.	D2	116
Knoxville, Il., U.S.	D7	120
Knoxville, Tn., U.S.	I2	114
Knuckles, mtn., Sri L.	H5	53
Knud Rasmussen Land, reg., Grnld.	A14	141
Knysna, S. Afr.	I6	70
Knyszyn, Pol.	C18	16
Kob', Russia	C18	32
Kobar Sink, depr., Eth.	E8	62
Kobayashi, Japan	H3	40
Kōbe, Japan	E8	40
København (Copenhagen), Den.	I4	8
København, state, Den.	I5	8
Kobjaj, Russia	D14	34
Koblenz, Ger.	F3	16
K'obo, Eth.	E7	62
Koboža, Russia	B18	10
Koboža, stm., Russia	A18	10
Kobroor, Pulau, i., Indon.	G10	44
Kobryn, Bela.	H7	10
Kobuk, Ak., U.S.	C8	140
Kobuk, stm., Ak., U.S.	C8	140
Kobuleti, Geor.	F6	32
Kobylin, Pol.	E13	16
Kocaali, Tur.	B13	28
Kocaavşar, stm., Tur.	D10	28
Kocaeli, state, Tur.	C12	28
Kočani, Mac.	B5	28
Koçarlı, Tur.	F10	28
Kočečum, stm., Russia	C8	34
Kočevje, Slvn.	E11	22
Kočevo, Russia	C8	32
Kŏch'ang, Kor., S.	G7	38
Koch Bihār, India	E12	54
Kocher, stm., Ger.	G5	16
Kochi (Cochin), India	G3	53
Kōchi, Japan	F6	40
Kōchi, state, Japan	F6	40
Koch Island, i., Nu., Can.	B15	106
Kochiu see Gejiu, China	G5	36
Kodaikānal, India	F3	53
Kodar, hrebet, mts., Russia	E12	34
Kodāri, Nepal	E10	54
Kodarma, India	F10	54
Kodiak, Ak., U.S.	E9	140
Kodiak Island, i., Ak., U.S.	E9	140
Kodinār, India	H3	54
Kodok, Sudan	F6	62
Kodyma, Ukr.	A16	26
Kodyma, stm., Ukr.	B17	26
Koës, Nmb.	D4	70
Köflach, Aus.	C11	22
Koforidua, Ghana	H4	64
Kōfu, Japan	D11	40
Koga, Japan	C12	40
Kogaluc, stm., Qc., Can.	D15	106
Kogaluc, Baie, b., Qc., Can.	D15	106
Kogan, Austl.	F8	76
Køge, Den.	I5	8
Kogon, stm., Gui.	G2	64
Kohanava, Bela.	F12	10
Kohāt, Pak.	B3	54
Kohīma, India	C7	46
Kohler, Wi., U.S.	E2	112
Kohtla-Järve, Est.	G12	8
Kohyl'nyk (Cogâlnic), stm., Eur.	C15	26
Koide, Japan	B11	40
Koigi, Est.	B8	10
Koindu, S.L.	H2	64
Koiva (Gauja), stm., Eur.	C7	10
Kojda, Russia	C20	8
Kŏje-do, i., Kor., S.	E1	40
Kojgorodok, Russia	B8	32
Kojonup, Austl.	F3	74
Kok (Hkok), stm., Asia	B4	48
Kokalaat, Kaz.	E10	32
Kokand, Uzb.	F12	32
Kokas, Indon.	F9	44
Kokčetav, Kaz.	D12	32
Kokemäki, Fin.	F9	8
Kokenau, Indon.	F10	44
Kokhav HaYarden, hist., Isr.	F6	58
Kokiu see Gejiu, China	G5	36
Kokkilai Lagoon, b., Sri L.	G5	53
Kokkola, Fin.	E10	8
Kokoda, Pap. N. Gui.	b4	79a
Kokomo, In., U.S.	H3	112
Kokomo, Ms., U.S.	F8	122
Kokong, Bots.	D6	70
Kokopo, Pap. N. Gui.	a5	79a
Kokorevka, Russia	H17	10
Koksan-ŭp, Kor., N.	E7	38
Kökshetaū see Kokčetav, Kaz.	D12	32

Name	Map Ref.	Page
Koksoak, stm., Qc., Can.	D17	106
Kokstad, S. Afr.	G9	70
Kokubu, Japan	H3	40
Kola, Russia	B15	8
Kolachel, India	G3	53
Kolaka, Indon.	F7	44
Kolangār, Afg.	A2	54
Kola Peninsula see Kol'skij poluostrov, pen., Russia	C17	8
Kolār, India	E3	53
Kolāras, India	F6	54
Kolār Gold Fields, India	E4	53
Kolárovo, Slov.	I13	16
Kolašin, Yugo.	G6	26
Kolbio, Kenya	E8	66
Kolbuszowa, Pol.	F17	16
Kol'čugino, Russia	D22	10
Kolda, Sen.	G2	64
Kolding, Den.	I3	8
Kole, D.R.C.	E4	66
Kolea, Alg.	H13	20
Kolguev, ostrov, i., Russia	B18	6
Kolhāpur, India	C4	53
Kolhāpur, India	C1	53
Koli, Russia	A17	10
Kolín, Czech Rep.	F11	16
Koljubakino, Russia	E19	10
Kollam see Quilon, India	G3	53
Kollegāl, India	E3	53
Kolleru Lake, l., India	C5	53
Kolmogorovo, Russia	C16	32
Köln (Cologne), Ger.	E2	16
Kolno, Pol.	C17	16
Koło, Pol.	D14	16
Koloa, Hi., U.S.	B2	78a
Kołobrzeg, Pol.	B11	16
Kolodnja, Russia	F15	10
Kolokani, Mali	G3	64
Kolombangara Island, i., Sol. Is.	d7	79b
Kolomna, Russia	E21	10
Kolomyia, Ukr.	A12	26
Kolonga, Tonga	n14	78e
Kolonia, Micron.	m11	78d
Kolonodale, Indon.	F7	44
Kolosib, India	F14	54
Kolosovka, Russia	C12	32
Kolovai, Tonga	n13	78e
Kolozsvár see Cluj-Napoca, Rom.	C10	26
Kolp', stm., Russia	A19	10
Kolpaševo, Russia	C14	32
Kolpino, Russia	A13	10
Kolpny, Russia	H19	10
Kol'skij poluostrov (Kola Peninsula), pen., Russia	C17	8
Koluton, Kaz.	D11	32
Kolwezi, D.R.C.	G5	66
Kolyma, stm., Russia	C20	34
Kolyma Plain see Kolymskaja nizmennost', pl., Russia	C19	34
Kolymskaja, Russia	C20	34
Kolymskaja nizmennost' (Kolyma Plain), pl., Russia	C19	34
Kom, mtn., Blg.	F10	26
Koma, Mya.	E4	48
Komadugu Gana, stm., Nig.	G7	64
Komagane, Japan	D10	40
Komandorskie ostrova, is., Russia	D20	30
Komandorski Islands see Komandorskie ostrova, is., Russia	D20	30
Komárno, Slov.	I13	16
Komarnyky, Ukr.	G19	16
Komárom, Hung.	B5	26
Komárom-Esztergom, state, Hung.	B5	26
Komati (Incomati), stm., Afr.	E10	70
Komatipoort, S. Afr.	D10	70
Komatsu, Japan	C9	40
Komatsushima, Japan	E7	40
Kome Island, i., Ug.	E6	66
Komering, stm., Indon.	E4	50
Komfane, Indon.	G9	44
Komi, state, Russia	B8	32
Komissarovo, Russia	B9	38
Komló, Hung.	C5	26
Kommunizma, pik, mtn., Taj.	B11	56
Komodo, Pulau, i., Indon.	H11	50
Komodo National Park, p.o.i., Indon.	H11	50
Komoé, stm., Afr.	H4	64
Kom Ombo, Egypt	C6	62
Komoran, Pulau, i., Indon.	G10	44
Komoro, Japan	C11	40
Komotiní, Grc.	B8	28
Kompasberg, mtn., S. Afr.	G7	70
Komsomolec, Kaz.	D10	32
Komsomolec, zaliv, b., Kaz.	E8	32
Komsomol'sk, Russia	H18	8
Komsomol'sk, Russia	C15	32
Komsomol'sk-na-Amure, Russia	F16	34
Komsomol'skoj Pravdy, ostrova, is., Russia	A10	34
Konakovo, Russia	D19	10
Konakpınar, Tur.	D10	28
Konar, stm., Asia	A3	54
Konārak, India	I11	54
Konawa, Ok., U.S.	C2	122
Konch, India	F7	54
Konda, stm., Russia	B10	32
Kondagaon, India	B5	53
Kondega, Russia	F15	8
Kondinin, Austl.	F3	74
Kondoa, Tan.	E7	66
Kondopoga, Russia	E16	8
Kondrovo, Russia	F18	10
Kondukūr, India	D4	53
Kondūz, Afg.	B10	56
Koné, N. Cal.	m15	79d
Kong, stm., Asia	F8	48
Kŏng, Kaôh, i., Camb.	G6	48
Kongcheng, China	F7	42
Kong Christian IX Land, reg., Grnld.	D18	141
Kong Christian X Land, reg., Grnld.	C19	141
Kong Frederik VIII Land, reg., Grnld.	B19	141
Kong Frederik VI Kyst, cst., Grnld.	E17	141
Kongjiawopeng, China	B5	38
Kongju, Kor., S.	F7	38
Kongmoon see Jiangmen, China	J5	42
Kongolo, D.R.C.	F5	66
Kongor, Sudan	F6	62
Kong Oscar Fjord, strt., Grnld.	C21	141
Kongsvinger, Nor.	F5	8
Kongur Shan, mtn., China	G13	32
Kong Wilhelms Land, reg., Grnld.	B21	141
Konice, Czech Rep.	G12	16
Königsberg see Kaliningrad, Russia	F3	10
Königswinter, Ger.	F3	16
Konin, Pol.	D14	16
Konin, state, Pol.	D14	16
Konispol, Alb.	E14	24
Kónitsa, Grc.	C3	28
Konjic, Bos.	F4	26
Konkiep, stm., Nmb.	E3	70
Konkouré, stm., Gui.	G2	64
Konna, Mali	G4	64
Konnevesi, l., Fin.	E12	8
Konnur, India	C2	53
Konoša, Russia	F18	8
Kōnosu, Japan	C12	40
Konotop, Ukr.	E15	6
Końskie, Pol.	E16	16
Konstantinovskij, Russia	C22	10
Konstanz, Ger.	I4	16
Kontagora, Nig.	G5	64
Kontcha, Cam.	C2	66
Kontha, Mya.	C3	48
Kontseba, Ukr.	A16	26
Kon Tum, Viet.	E8	48
Konya, Tur.	F15	28
Konya, state, Tur.	E15	28
Konz, Ger.	G2	16
Konza, Kenya	E7	66
Konžakovskij Kamen', gora, mtn., Russia	C9	32
Koocanusa, Lake, res., N.A.	B11	136
Kookynie, Austl.	E4	74
Koolatah, Austl.	C8	74
Kooloonong, Austl.	J4	76
Koontz Lake, In., U.S.	G3	112
Koorawatha, Austl.	J7	76
Koosa, Est.	B9	10
Kooskia, Id., U.S.	D11	136
Kootenai (Kootenay), stm., N.A.	G13	138
Kootenay (Kootenai), stm., N.A.	G13	138
Kootenay Lake, l., B.C., Can.	G14	138
Kootenay National Park, p.o.i., B.C., Can.	F14	138
Kopāganj, India	E9	54
Kopargaon, India	B2	53
Kópavogur, Ice.	k29	8a
Kopejsk, Russia	C10	32
Koper, Slvn.	E10	22
Kopervik, Nor.	G1	8
Kopet Mountains, mts., Asia	B8	56
Köping, Swe.	G6	8
Koplik, Alb.	B13	24
Koppal, India	D3	53
Koppang, Nor.	F4	8
Koppies, S. Afr.	E8	70
Koprivnica, Cro.	D13	22
Köprü, stm., Tur.	F14	28
Köprülü Kanyon Milli Parkı, p.o.i., Tur.	F14	28
Kopylovo, Russia	F21	8
Korab (Korabit, Maja e), mtn., Eur.	C14	24
Korabit, Maja e (Korab), mtn., Eur.	C14	24
Korāput, India	B6	53
Korarou, Lac, l., Mali	F4	64
Koratla, India	B4	53
Korba, India	G9	54
Korba, Tun.	H4	24
Korbach, Ger.	E4	16
Korça see Korçë, Alb.	D14	24
Korçë, Alb.	D14	24
Korčula, Cro.	H14	22
Korčula, Otok, i., Cro.	H13	22
Korea, North, ctry., Asia	D7	38
Korea, South, ctry., Asia	G8	38
Korea Bay, b., Asia	E5	38
Korea Strait, strt., Asia	E2	40
Korelakša, Russia	D15	8
Korenovsk, Russia	E5	32
Korf, Russia	D22	34
Korhogo, C. Iv.	H3	64
Korientzé, Mali	F4	64
Korim, Indon.	F10	44
Korinthiakós Kólpos (Corinth, Gulf of), b., Grc.	E5	28
Kórinthos, Grc.	F5	28
Kōriyama, Japan	B13	40
Korjakskaja Sopka, vulkan, vol., Russia	F20	34
Korjakskoe nagor'e, mts., Russia	D22	34
Korjažma, Russia	F22	8
Korkino, Russia	D10	32
Korkuteli, Tur.	F13	28
Korla, China	C2	36
Korliki, Russia	B14	32
Körmend, Hung.	C3	26
Kornat, Otok, i., Cro.	G12	22
Kornati, Nacionalni Park, p.o.i., Cro.	G12	22
Korner, Mt., U.S.	A14	136
Korneuburg, Aus.	B13	22
Koro, i., Fiji	p19	79e
Köroğlu Tepesi, mtn., Tur.	C14	28
Korogwe, Tan.	F7	66
Koroleve, Ukr.	H19	16
Koromere see East Cape, c., N.Z.	C8	80
Koronadal, Phil.	G5	52
Koróni, Grc.	G4	28
Korónia, Límni, l., Grc.	C6	28
Korópi, Grc.	F6	28
Koror, Palau	g8	78b
Körös, stm., Hung.	C7	26
Koro Sea, Fiji	p20	79e
Korosten', Ukr.	E14	6
Koro Toro, Chad	D3	62
Korotyš, Russia	H20	10
Korovin Volcano, vol., Ak., U.S.	g24	140a
Korovou, Fiji	p19	79e
Koroyanitu, mtn., Fiji	p18	79e
Korsakov, Russia	G17	34
Korsakovo, Russia	G20	10
Korsør, Den.	I4	8
Koršunovo, Russia	C20	32
Kortrijk, Bel.	D12	14
Korucam, Cape see Koruçam Burnu, c., N. Cyp.	C3	58
Koruçam Burnu, c., N. Cyp.	C3	58
Korucu, Tur.	D10	28
Korumburra, Austl.	L5	76
Koryak Mountains see Korjakskoe nagor'e, mts., Russia	D22	34
Koryŏng, Kor., S.	D1	40
Kos (Cos), i., Grc.	G10	28
Kosa, Russia	C8	32
Kosa, Russia	F10	34
Kosai, Japan	E10	40
Kosaja Gora, Russia	F20	10
Koščagyl, Kaz.	E8	32
Kościan, Pol.	D12	16
Kościerzyna, Pol.	B14	16
Kosciusko, Ms., U.S.	D9	122
Kosciusko, Mount, mtn., Austl.	K6	76
Kosciusko National Park, p.o.i., Austl.	K6	76
Kose, Est.	A8	10
Koshikijima-rettō, is., Japan	H2	40
Koshkonong, Lake, l., Wi., U.S.	B9	120
Kōshoku, Japan	C11	40
Košice, Slov.	H17	16
Kosi Kalan, India	E6	54
Kosimeer, l., S. Afr.	E11	70
Kosiv, Ukr.	A12	26
Köşk, Tur.	F11	28
Koslan, Russia	E23	8
Kosŏng, Kor., S.	E1	40
Kosŏng-ŭp, Kor., N.	E8	38
Kosovo-Metohija, co., Yugo.	G7	26
Kosovska Mitrovica, Yugo.	G7	26
Kosrae, i., Micron.	C7	72
Kösreli, Tur.	A6	58
Kosse, Tx., U.S.	F2	122
Kossou, Lac de, res., C. Iv.	H3	64
Kostenec, Blg.	G10	26
Koster, S. Afr.	D8	70
Kostomukša, Russia	D14	8
Kostonjärvi, l., Fin.	D12	8
Kostroma, Russia	H19	8
Kostroma, stm., Russia	G19	8
Kostromskaja oblast', co., Russia	G20	8
Kostrzyn, Pol.	D10	16
Kosum Phisai, Thai.	D6	48
Koszalin, Pol.	B12	16
Koszalin, state, Pol.	C12	16
Kőszeg, Hung.	B3	26
Kota, India	G9	54
Kota, India	F5	54
Kotaagung, Indon.	F4	50
Kotabangun, Indon.	D10	50
Kotabaru, Indon.	E10	50
Kota Belud, Malay.	G1	52
Kota Bharu, Malay.	I6	48
Kotabumi, Indon.	F4	50
Kotadabok, Indon.	D4	50
Kot Addu, Pak.	C3	54
Kota Kinabalu, Malay.	G1	52
Kotamobagu, Indon.	E7	44
Kotapinang, Indon.	C1	50
Kota Tinggi, Malay.	L6	48
Kotawaringin, Indon.	E7	50
Kotcho Lake, l., B.C., Can.	D6	106
Kot Chutta, Pak.	D3	54
Kotel'nič, Russia	C7	32
Kotel'nikovo, Russia	E6	32
Kotel'nyj, ostrov, i., Russia	A16	34
Kotelnyj, ostrov, i., Russia	B3	34
Köthen, Ger.	E7	16
Kotikovo, Russia	G17	34
Kotka, Fin.	F12	8
Kot Kapūra, India	C5	54
Kotlas, Russia	F22	8
Kotli, Pak.	B4	54
Kotlik, Ak., U.S.	D7	140
Kôtomo, Île, i., N. Cal.	n16	79d
Kotor, Yugo.	G5	26
Kotoriba, Cro.	D13	22
Kotovs'k, Ukr.	B16	26
Kot Pūtli, India	E6	54
Kotri, Pak.	F2	54
Kottagūdem, India	C5	53
Kottayam, India	G3	53
Kotto, stm., C.A.R.	C4	66
Kottūru, India	D3	53
Kotuj, stm., Russia	B9	34
Kotzebue, Ak., U.S.	C7	140
Kotzebue Sound, strt., Ak., U.S.	C7	140
Kötzting, Ger.	G8	16
Kouang-si see Guangxi, state, China	G6	36
Kouang-tong see Guangdong, state, China	J6	42
Kouaoua, N. Cal.	m15	79d
Kouchibouguac National Park, p.o.i., N.B., Can.	D11	110
Koudougou, Burkina	G4	64
Kouei-tcheou see Guizhou, state, China	H2	42
Kouga, stm., S. Afr.	H7	70
Kougaberge, mts., S. Afr.	H6	70
Koukdjuak, stm., Nu., Can.	B16	106
Kouki, C.A.R.	C3	66
Koúklia, Cyp.	D3	58
Koulamoutou, Gabon	E2	66
Koulikoro, Mali	G3	64
Koumala, Austl.	C7	76
Koumbia, Gui.	G2	64
Koumpentoum, Sen.	G2	64
Koumra, Chad	F3	62
Koundâra, Gui.	G2	64
Kounradskij, Kaz.	E12	32
Kourou, Fr. Gu.	B7	84
Kouroussa, Gui.	G3	64
Kousséri, Cam.	B2	66
Koussi, Emi, mtn., Chad	D3	62
Koutiala, Mali	G3	64
Kouts, In., U.S.	G2	112
Kouvola, Fin.	F12	8
Kova, Russia	C18	32
Kovada Milli Parkı, p.o.i., Tur.	F13	28
Kovarskas, Lith.	E7	10
Kovdor, Russia	C14	8
Kovdozero, ozero, res., Russia	C14	8
Kovilpatti, India	G3	53
Kovrov, Russia	H19	8
Kovūr, India	D5	53
Kovža, Russia	F18	8
Kowalewo Pomorskie, Pol.	C14	16
Kowloon see Jiulong, China	J5	42
Kowŏn-ŭp, Kor., N.	E7	38
Kowt-e'Ashrow, Afg.	C10	56
Koxtag, China	A4	46
Köyceğiz Gölü, l., Tur.	G11	28
Koyna Reservoir, res., India	C1	53
Koyuk, Ak., U.S.	D7	140
Koyukuk, Ak., U.S.	D8	140
Koyukuk, stm., Ak., U.S.	C8	140
Kō-zaki, c., Japan	E2	40
Kozan, Tur.	A6	58
Kozáni, Grc.	C4	28
Kožany, Russia	H14	10
Kozel'sk, Russia	F18	10
Koževnikovo, Russia	C14	32
Kozhikode (Calicut), India	F2	53
Kozienice, Pol.	E17	16
Kozlov Bereg, Russia	B10	10
Kozlovo, Russia	D19	10
Kozlu, Tur.	B14	28
Koz'mino, Russia	F22	8
Kožposëlok, Russia	E17	8
Kōzu-shima, i., Japan	E12	40
Kpalimé, Togo	H5	64
Kra, Isthmus of, isth., Asia	H4	48
Kraai, stm., S. Afr.	G8	70
Krabi, Thai.	H4	48
Krâchéh, Camb.	F8	48
Kraeva, Russia	B9	38
Kragan, Indon.	G7	50
Kragujevac, Yugo.	F7	26
Krajenka, Pol.	C13	16
Krakatoa see Rakata, Pulau, i., Indon.	G4	50
Krakovets', Ukr.	G19	16
Kraków, Pol.	F15	16
Kraków, state, Pol.	G15	16
Kralendijk, Neth. Ant.	p23	104g
Kraljevo, Yugo.	F7	26
Kralovice, Czech Rep.	G9	16
Kralupy nad Vltavou, Czech Rep.	F10	16
Kramators'k, Ukr.	E5	32
Kramfors, Swe.	E7	8
Kranídi, Grc.	F6	28
Kranj (Krainburg), Slvn.	D11	22
Kranskop, S. Afr.	F10	70
Krapivna, Russia	G18	10
Krasavino, Russia	F22	8
Krasieo, stm., Thai.	E4	48
Krasivaja Meča, stm., Russia	G20	10
Krāslava, Lat.	E10	10
Krasnae, Bela.	F10	10
Krasnaja Gorbatka, Russia	I19	8
Krasnaja Slabada, Bela.	H9	10
Krasnaluki, Bela.	F11	10
Krasneno, Russia	D23	34
Kraśnik, Pol.	F18	16
Kraśnik Fabryczny, Pol.	F18	16
Krasni Okny, Ukr.	B16	26
Krasnoarmejsk, Russia	D21	10
Krasnoarmejskij, Russia	C23	34
Krasnobród, Pol.	F19	16
Krasnodar, Russia	E5	32
Krasnoe, ozero, l., Russia	D23	34
Krasnoe Selo, Russia	A12	10
Krasnoe Znamja, Russia	C18	10
Krasnogorodskoe, Russia	D11	10
Krasnogorsk, Russia	E20	10
Krasnogorsk, Russia	G17	34
Krasnojarovo, Russia	F14	34
Krasnojarsk, Russia	C16	32
Krasnojarskoe vodohranilišče, res., Russia	D16	32
Krasnokamsk, Russia	C8	32
Krasnomajskij, Russia	C17	10
Krasnoščele, Russia	C17	8
Krasnosel'kup, Russia	A14	32
Krasnoturjinsk, Russia	C10	32
Krasnoufimsk, Russia	C9	32
Krasnoural'sk, Russia	C10	32
Krasnovišersk, Russia	B9	32
Krasnovodskij poluostrov, pen., Turkmen.	A7	56
Krasnozavodsk, Russia	D20	10
Krasnozërskoe, Russia	D14	32
Krasnoznamensk, Russia	F5	10
Krasnoznamenskoe, Kaz.	D11	32
Krasnye Gory, Russia	B12	10
Krasnyj Čikoj, Russia	F10	34
Krasnyj Gorodok, Russia	C16	10
Krasnyj Jar, Russia	C12	32
Krasnyj Luč, Russia	C13	10
Krasnyj Oktjabr', Russia	D21	10
Krasnyj Tkač, Russia	E22	10
Krasnystaw, Pol.	E19	16
Kratovo, Mac.	A5	28
Krâvanh, Chuŏr Phnum, mts., Camb.	F6	48
Krbava, reg., Cro.	F12	22
Krečetovo, Russia	F18	8
Krefeld, Ger.	E2	16
Kremastón, Technití Límni, res., Grc.	E4	28
Kremenchug Reservoir see Kremenchuts'ke vodoskhovyshche, res., Ukr.	E4	32
Kremenchuk, Ukr.	E4	32
Kremenchuts'ke vodoskhovyshche, res., Ukr.	E4	32
Kremenskoe, Russia	E18	10
Kremmling, Co., U.S.	C10	132
Krems an der Donau, Aus.	B12	22
Kress, Tx., U.S.	G7	128
Kresta, zaliv, b., Russia	C25	34
Krestcy, Russia	B22	10
Krestcy, Russia	B15	10
Krest-Maër, Russia	C17	34
Kretinga, Lith.	E4	10
Kribi, Cam.	D1	66
Křimice, Czech Rep.	G9	16
Krishna, stm., India	C5	53
Krishna, Mouths of the, mth., India	D5	53
Krishnagiri, India	E4	53
Krishnanagar, India	G12	54
Krishnarāja Sāgara, res., India	E3	53
Krishnarājpet, India	E3	53
Kristiansand, Nor.	G3	8
Kristianstad, Swe.	I6	8
Kristiansund, Nor.	E2	8
Kristiinankaupunki (Kristinestad), Fin.	E9	8
Kristinehamn, Swe.	G6	8
Kristinestad see Kristiinankaupunki, Fin.	E9	8
Kríti, state, Grc.	H7	28
Kríti (Crete), i., Grc.	H7	28
Kritikón Pélagos (Crete, Sea of), Grc.	H8	28
Kriva Palanka, Mac.	A5	28
Krivodol, Blg.	F10	26
Križevci, Cro.	D13	22
Krjukovo, Russia	E20	10
Krjukovo, Russia	C20	34
Krk, Otok, i., Cro.	E11	22
Krnov, Czech Rep.	F13	16
Krobia, Pol.	E12	16
Krøderen, l., Nor.	F3	8
Krokodil, stm., S. Afr.	D8	70
Krom, stm., S. Afr.	G4	70
Kroměříž, Czech Rep.	G13	16
Kromy, Russia	H18	10
Kronach, Ger.	F7	16
Krŏng Kaôh Kŏng, Camb.	G6	48
Krŏng Kêb, Camb.	G7	48
Kronoberg, state, Swe.	H6	8
Kronockaja Sopka, vulkan, vol., Russia	F21	34
Kronockij zaliv, b., Russia	F21	34
Kronoki, Russia	F21	34
Kronprins Christian Land, reg., Grnld.	A22	141
Kronštadt, Russia	A12	10
Kroonstad, S. Afr.	E8	70
Kropotkin, Russia	E6	32
Kropotkin, Russia	E12	34
Krośniewice, Pol.	D14	16
Krosno, Pol.	G17	16
Krosno, state, Pol.	G17	16
Krotoszyn, Pol.	E13	16
Krotz Springs, La., U.S.	G7	122
Kroya, Indon.	G6	50
Krško, Slvn.	E12	22
Kruger National Park, p.o.i., S. Afr.	C10	70
Krugersdorp, S. Afr.	E8	70
Kruhlae, Bela.	F12	10
Krui, Indon.	F3	50
Kruisfontein, S. Afr.	H7	70
Kruja see Krujë, Alb.	C13	24
Krujë, Alb.	C13	24
Krumbach, Ger.	H6	16
Krumovgrad, Blg.	H12	26
Krung Thep (Bangkok), Thai.	F5	48
Kruså, Den.	B5	16
Kruševac, Yugo.	F8	26
Krušinovka, Bela.	G12	10
Krutcy, Russia	C12	10
Krutoe, Russia	H20	10
Kruzenšterna, proliv, strt., Russia	G19	34
Kruzof Island, i., Ak., U.S.	E12	140
Kryčau, Bela.	G14	10
Kryms'kyi pivostriv (Crimean Peninsula), pen., Ukr.	E4	32
Krynica, Pol.	G16	16
Krynychne, Ukr.	D15	26
Kryve Ozero, Ukr.	B17	26
Kryvošyn, Bela.	H8	10
Kryvyj Rih, Ukr.	E4	32
Kryzhopil', Ukr.	A15	26
Krzeszowice, Pol.	F15	16
Krzyż, Pol.	D11	16
Ksenevka, Russia	F12	34
Kstovo, Russia	H20	8
Kuah, Malay.	I4	48
Kuai, stm., China	E7	42
Kualacenako, Indon.	D3	50
Kuala Kangsar, Malay.	J5	48
Kualakapuas, Indon.	E9	50
Kuala Krai, Malay.	J6	48
Kuala Kubu Baharu, Malay.	K5	48
Kualakurun, Indon.	D8	50
Kualalangsa, Indon.	J4	48
Kuala Lipis, Malay.	J5	48
Kuala Lumpur, Malay.	K5	48
Kuala Nerang, Malay.	I5	48
Kualapesaguan, Indon.	E6	50
Kuala Pilah, Malay.	K6	48
Kuala Rompin, Malay.	K6	48
Kuala Sepetang, Malay.	J5	48
Kualasimpang, Indon.	J3	48
Kuala Terengganu, Malay.	J6	48
Kualu, stm., Indon.	B1	50
Kuamut, stm., Malay.	A10	50
Kuancheng, China	A8	42
Kuandian, China	D6	38
Kuan Shan, mtn., Tai.	J9	42
Kuantan, Malay.	K6	48
Kuanyün see Guanyun, China	D8	42
Kuban', stm., Russia	E6	32
Kubenskoe, ozero, l., Russia	G18	8
Kubokawa, Japan	F6	40
Kubrat, Blg.	F13	26
Kučema, Russia	D20	8
Kuchaiburi, India	G11	54
Kuchāman, India	E5	54
Kuching, Malay.	C7	50
Kūchnay Darweyshān, Afg.	C9	56
Kuchurhan, stm., Eur.	B16	26
Kuçova see Kuçovë, Alb.	D13	24
Kuçovë, Alb.	D13	24
Kūd, India	B5	54
Kudamatsu, Japan	F4	40
Kudat, Malay.	G1	52
Kudever', Russia	D12	10
Kudirkos Naumiestis, Lith.	F5	10
Kudus, Indon.	G7	50
Kudymkar, Russia	C8	32
Kuee Ruins, hist., Hi., U.S.	D6	78a
Kueisui see Hohhot, China	A4	42
Kueiyang see Guiyang, China	H2	42
K'uerhlo see Korla, China	C2	36
Kufstein, Aus.	C9	22
Kugluktuk, Nu., Can.	B8	106
Kugmallit Bay, b., N.T., Can.	C13	140
Kuhësi see Kukës, Alb.	B14	24
Kuhmoinen, Fin.	F11	8
Kuhn Ø, i., Grnld.	C22	141
Kuial'nyts'kyi lyman, l., Ukr.	C17	26
Kuiseb, stm., S. Afr.	C2	70
Kuitan, China	J7	42
Kuito, Ang.	C2	68
Kuiu Island, i., Ak., U.S.	E13	140
Kuivastu, Est.	G10	8
Kuja, Russia	D18	8
Kujang-ŭp, Kor., N.	E7	38
Kujawy, reg., Pol.	D14	16
Kujbyšev, Russia	C13	32
Kujbyševskoe vodohranilišče, res., Russia	D7	32
Kujgan, Kaz.	E12	32
Kujū-san, vol., Japan	F4	40
Kukalaya, stm., Nic.	F6	102
Kukawa, Nig.	G7	64
Kukës, Alb.	B14	24
Kukoboj, Russia	B22	10
Kükong see Shaoguan, China	I5	42
Kukshi, India	G5	54
Kukuj, Russia	A15	10
Kukukus Lake, l., On., Can.	B7	118
Kukurtli, Turkmen.	B8	56
Kula, Blg.	F9	26
Kula, Tur.	E11	28
Kula, Yugo.	D6	26
Kulagi, Russia	H15	10
Kula Gulf, strt., Sol. Is.	e7	79b
Kulai, Malay.	L6	48
Kula Kangri, mtn., Bhu.	E13	54
Kular, Russia	B15	34
Kulaura, Bngl.	F13	54
Kuldīga, Lat.	D5	10
Kuldja see Yining, China	F14	32
Kule, Bots.	C5	70
Kulebaki, Russia	I20	8
Kulen Vakuf, Bos.	E3	26
Kulim, Malay.	J5	48
Kuljab, Taj.	B10	56
Kulkyne Creek, stm., Austl.	H5	76
Kullu, India	B6	54
Kulm, N.D., U.S.	A13	126
Kulmbach, Ger.	F7	16
Kuloj, Russia	D20	8
Kuloj, Russia	F20	8
Kuloj, stm., Russia	D20	8
Kul'sary, Kaz.	E8	32
Kulti, India	G11	54
Kultuk, Russia	D18	32
Kulu, Tur.	D16	28
Kulunda, Russia	D13	32
Kulundinskaja ravnina, pl., Asia	D13	32
Kulundinskoe, ozero, l., Russia	D13	32
Kulwin, Austl.	J4	76
Kumagaya, Japan	C12	40
Kumai, Indon.	E8	50
Kumai, Teluk, b., Indon.	E7	50
Kumajri see Gjumri, Arm.	A5	56
Kumamoto, Japan	G3	40
Kumamoto, state, Japan	G3	40
Kumano, Japan	F9	40
Kumano-nada, Japan	F9	40
Kumanovo, Mac.	A4	28
Kumara, Russia	F14	34
Kumārghāt, India	F14	54
Kumasi, Ghana	H4	64
Kumba, Cam.	D1	66
Kumbakonam, India	F4	53
Kumbarilla, Austl.	F8	76
Kumdanlı, Tur.	E13	28
Kume-jima, i., Japan	I18	39a
Kŭm-gang, stm., Kor., S.	F7	38
Kumla, Swe.	G6	8
Kumluca, Tur.	B15	28
Kumluca, Tur.	G13	28
Kumo, Nig.	H7	64
Kumon Range, mts., Mya.	C8	46
Kumora, Russia	E11	34
Kumta, India	D2	53
Kumu, D.R.C.	D5	66
Kumukahi, Cape, c., Hi., U.S.	o16	135a
Kümüx, China	C2	36
Kŭmya-ŭp, Kor., N.	E7	38
Kuna, Id., U.S.	G10	136
Kunašir, ostrov (Kunashiri-tō), i., Russia	C16	38
Kunda, Est.	G12	8
Kunda Hills, hills, India	F3	53
Kundāpura, India	E2	53
Kundar, stm., Asia	C2	54
Kunderu, stm., India	D4	53
Kundiān, Pak.	B3	54
Kundiawa, Pap. N. Gui.	b3	79a
Kundla, India	H3	54
Kundur, Pulau, i., Indon.	C3	50
Kunene, state, Nmb.	B2	70
Kunene (Cunene), stm., Afr.	D1	68
Kunes, Nor.	A12	8
Kungchuling see Gongzhuling, China	C6	38
Kunggyü Yumco, l., China	C9	54
Kunghit Island, i., B.C., Can.	E4	106
Kungrad, Uzb.	F9	32
Kungsbacka, Swe.	H4	8
Kungur, Russia	C9	32
Kunhegyes, Hung.	B7	26
Kuningan, Indon.	G6	50
Kunisaki, Japan	F4	40
Kunisaki-hantō, pen., Japan	F4	40
Kunja, Russia	D13	10
Kunja, stm., Russia	D13	10
Kunlong, Mya.	D8	46
Kunlun Mountains see Kunlun Shan, mts., China	A5	46
Kunlun Shan, mts., China	A5	46
Kunming, China	F5	36
Kunnamkulam, India	F2	53
Kunsan, Kor., S.	F7	38
Kunshan, China	F9	42
Kunting, China	G9	42
Kununurra, Austl.	C5	74
Kunwi, Kor., S.	C1	40
Kunya, Nig.	G6	64
Künzelsau, Ger.	G5	16
Kuopio, Fin.	E12	8
Kuopio, state, Fin.	E12	8
Kupa, stm., Eur.	E12	22
Kupang, Indon.	H7	44
Kupanskoe, Russia	D21	10
Kup'ians'k, Ukr.	E5	32
Kupino, Russia	D13	32
Kupiškis, Lith.	E7	10
Kupreanof Island, i., Ak., U.S.	E13	140
Kuqa, China	F14	32
Kuqa, China	F14	32
Kuragino, Russia	D16	32
Kuranec, Bela.	F9	10
Kurashiki, Japan	E6	40
Kurasiki see Kurashiki, Japan	E6	40
Kurauli, India	E7	54
Kuraymah, Sudan	D6	62
Kurayoshi, Japan	D6	40
Kurčatov, Russia	D5	32
Kurčum, Kaz.	E14	32
Kurdistān, hist. reg., Asia	B5	56
Kurdistan see Kurdistān, hist. reg., Asia	B5	56
Kurdufān, state, Sudan	E6	62
Kurduvādi, India	B2	53
Kure, Japan	E5	40
Kurejka, stm., Russia	C7	34
Kuresaare, Est.	G10	8
Kurgal'džinskij, Kaz.	D12	32
Kurgan, Russia	C11	32
Kurgan-Tjube, Taj.	B10	56
Kuria, i., Kir.	C8	72
Kuria Muria Islands see Hallānīyah, Juzur al-, is., Oman	F8	56
Kuridala, Austl.	C3	76
Kurīgrām, Bngl.	F12	54
Kurikka, Fin.	E10	8
Kuril Islands see Kuril'skie ostrova, is., Russia	E19	30
Kuril'sk, Russia	B14	36
Kuril'skie ostrova (Kuril Islands), is., Russia	E19	30
Kuril Strait see Pervyj Kuril'skij proliv, strt., Russia	F20	34
Kuril Trench, unds.	E18	142
Kurinjippadi, India	F4	53
Kurinwás, stm., Nic.	F5	102
Kurjanovskaja, Russia	F19	8
Kurkliai, Lith.	E8	10
Kurmuk, Sudan	E6	62
Kurnool, India	D3	53
Kurobe, Japan	C10	40
Kurort Schmalkalden, Ger.	F6	16
Kurovskoe, Russia	E21	10
Kurow, N.Z.	G4	80
Kuršėnai, Lith.	D6	10
Kurseong, India	E12	54
Kuršiu nerija (Kuršskaja kosa), spit, Eur.	E3	10
Kursk, Russia	D5	32
Kurskaja oblast', co., Russia	H19	10
Kuršskaja kosa (Kuršiu nerija), spit, Eur.	E3	10
Kuršumlija, Yugo.	F8	26
Kurşunlu, Tur.	C16	28
Kūrtī, Sudan	D6	62
Kurtistown, Hi., U.S.	D6	78a
Kurtoğlu Burnu, c., Tur.	G11	28
Kuruktag, mts., China	C2	36
Kuruman, S. Afr.	E6	70
Kuruman, stm., S. Afr.	E5	70
Kurumanheuwels, mts., S. Afr.	E6	70
Kurume, Japan	F3	40
Kurumkan, Russia	F11	34
Kurunegala, Sri L.	H5	53
Kuruqi, China	B9	36
Kuryongp'o, Kor., S.	C2	40
Kuşadası, Tur.	F10	28
Kuşadası Körfezi, b., Tur.	F9	28
Kusan-ni, Kor., S.	B1	40
Kusawa Lake, l., Yk., Can.	D12	140
Kuş Gölü, l., Tur.	C10	28
Kuş Gölü Milli Parkı, p.o.i., Tur.	C10	28
Kushālgarh, India	G5	54
Kusheriki, Nig.	G6	64
Kushikino, Japan	H3	40
Kushima, Japan	H4	40
Kushiro, Japan	C16	38
Kushnytsia, Ukr.	A10	26
Kushtia, Bngl.	G12	54
Kushui, China	C3	36
Kusiro see Kushiro, Japan	C16	38
Kusiyāra, stm., Bngl.	F13	54
Kuskokwim, stm., Ak., U.S.	D7	140
Kuskokwim Bay, b., Ak., U.S.	E7	140
Kuskokwim Mountains, mts., Ak., U.S.	D8	140
Kuśmā, Nepal	D9	54
Kušmurun, Kaz.	D10	32
Kušmurun, ozero, l., Kaz.	D10	32
Kustanaj, Kaz.	D10	32
Kūstī, Sudan	E6	62
Kusu, Japan	F4	40
Kut, Ko, i., Thai.	G6	48
Kutabaru, Indon.	D3	50
Kutacane, Indon.	K3	48
Kütahya, Tur.	D13	28
Kütahya, state, Tur.	D12	28
Kutaisi, Geor.	F6	32
Kutch, Rann of (Kachchh, Rann of), reg., Asia	D2	46
Kutima, Russia	C19	32
Kutina, Cro.	E13	22
Kutiyāna, India	H3	54
Kutná Hora, Czech Rep.	G11	16
Kutno, Pol.	D15	16
Kutse Game Reserve, Bots.	C7	70
Kutu, D.R.C.	E3	66
Kutubdia Island, i., Bngl.	H13	54
Kutum, Sudan	E4	62
Kúty, Slov.	H13	16
Kuujjuaq, Qc., Can.	D17	106
Kuuli-Majak, Turkmen.	A7	56
Kuusamo, Fin.	D13	8
Kuusankoski, Fin.	F12	8
Kuvango, Ang.	C2	68
Kuvšinovo, Russia	C16	10
Kuwait see Al-Kuwayt, Kuw.	D6	56
Kuwait, ctry., Asia	D6	56
Kuwana, Japan	D9	40
Kuybyshev Reservoir see Kujbyševskoe vodohranilišče, res., Russia	D7	32
Kuye, stm., China	B4	42
Kuženkino, Russia	C16	10
Kuz'miniči, Russia	F16	10
Kuz'movka, Russia	B16	32
Kuzneck, Russia	D7	32
Kuzneckij Alatau, mts., Russia	D15	32
Kuznecovka, Russia	D11	10
Kuznetsk see Kuzneck, Russia	D7	32
Kuzomen', Russia	C17	8
Kvænangen, b., Nor.	A9	8
Kvaløya, i., Nor.	B8	8
Kvaløya, i., Nor.	A10	8
Kvam, Nor.	F3	8
Kvarnbergsvattnet, l., Swe.	D5	8
Kvarner, b., Cro.	F11	22
Kvarnerić, b., Cro.	F11	22
Kverkfjöll, vol., Ice.	k31	8a
Kvichak Bay, b., Ak., U.S.	E8	140
Kwa, stm., D.R.C.	E3	66
Kwai see Khwae Noi, stm., Thai.	E4	48

Name Map Ref. Page

Kwajalein, at., Marsh. Is. C7 72
Kwakoegron, Sur. B6 84
Kwamisa, mtn., Ghana H4 64
Kwamouth, D.R.C. E3 66
Kwando (Cuando), stm., Afr. D3 68
Kwangchow see Guangzhou, China J5 42
Kwangju, Kor., S. G7 38
Kwango (Cuango), stm., Afr. E3 66
Kwangsi Chuang see Guangxi, state, China G6 36
Kwangtung see Guangdong, state, China J6 42
KwaZulu-Natal, state, S. Afr. F10 70
Kweichow see Guizhou, state, China F6 36
Kweihwa see Hohhot, China A4 42
Kweilin see Guilin, China I4 42
Kweisui see Hohhot, China A4 42
Kweiyang see Guiyang, China H2 42
Kwekwe, Zimb. D4 68
Kweneng, state, Bots. C7 70
Kwenge (Caengo), stm., Afr. B2 68
Kwethluk, Ak., U.S. D7 140
Kwidzyn, Pol. C14 16
Kwigillingok, Ak., U.S. E7 140
Kwilu (Cuilo), stm., Afr. F3 66
Kyabra, Austl. F4 76
Kyabra Creek, stm., Austl. E4 76
Kyabram, Austl. K5 76
Kyaikkami, Mya. D3 48
Kyaiklat, Mya. D2 48
Kyaikto, Mya. D3 48
Kya-in, Mya. D4 48
Kyalite, Austl. J4 76
Kyancutta, Austl. F7 74
Ky Anh, Viet. C8 48
Kyaukhnyat, Mya. C3 48
Kyaukme, Mya. A3 48
Kyaukpa, Mya. F4 48
Kyaukpyu, Mya. C1 48
Kyaukse, Mya. B2 48
Kyauktaw, Mya. D7 46
Kyaunggon, Mya. D2 48
Kybartai, Lith. F5 10
Kyebang-san, mtn., Kor., S. B1 40
Kyeikdon, Mya. E4 48
Kyidaunggan, Mya. C3 48
Kyïv (Kiev), Ukr. D4 32
Kyïvs'ke vodoskhovyshche, res., Ukr. D4 32
Kyjov, Czech Rep. G13 16
Kykotsmovi Village, Az., U.S. H6 132
Kyle, Sk., Can. D5 124
Kyle, S.D., U.S. D10 126
Kyle, Lake, res., Zimb. B10 70
Kyllini, Grc. F4 28
Kymi, state, Fin. F12 8
Kyneton, Austl. K5 76
Kynšperk nad Ohří, Czech Rep. F8 16
Kyoga, Lake, l., Ug. D6 66
Kyogle, Austl. G9 76
Kyŏngju, Kor., S. D2 40
Kyŏngsan, Kor., S. D1 40
Kyŏngsang-bukto, state, Kor., S. C1 40
Kyŏngsang-namdo, state, Kor., S. D1 40
Kyŏngsŏng-ŭp, Kor., N. D8 38
Kyŏnkadun, Mya. D2 48
Kyonpyaw, Mya. D2 48
Kyōto, Japan D8 40
Kyōto, state, Japan D8 40
Kyparissia, Grc. F4 28
Kyparissiakós Kólpos, b., Grc. F4 28
Kyra, Russia G11 34
Kyren, Russia D18 32
Kyrgyzstan, ctry., Asia F12 32
Kyritz, Ger. D8 16
Kyrönjoki, stm., Fin. E10 8
Kyrösjärvi, l., Fin. F10 8
Kyštym, Russia C10 32
Kythira, Grc. G5 28
Kýthira, i., Grc. G5 28
Kýthnos, i., Grc. F7 28
Kyundon, Mya. B2 48
Kyungyi, i., Mya. E3 48
Kyuquot, B.C., Can. F3 138
Kyūshū, i., Japan G2 40
Kyushu-Palau Ridge, unds. H16 142
Kyūshū-sanchi, mts., Japan G4 40
Kywong, Austl. J6 76
Kyyjärvi, Fin. E11 8
Kyyvesi, l., Fin. E12 8
Kyzyl, Russia D16 32
Kyzylbair, Turkmen. B8 56
Kyzyl-Kija, Kyrg. F12 32
Kyzylkum, des., Asia F10 32
Kyzyluj, Kaz. E11 32
Kzyl-Orda, Kaz. F11 32
Kzyltu, Kaz. D12 32

L

La Aguja, Cabo de, c., Col. B4 86
La Albuera, Spain F4 20
La Alcarria, reg., Spain D8 20
La Algaba, Spain G4 20
La Almunia de Doña Godina, Spain C9 20
La Antigua, Salina, pl., Arg. D4 92
La Araucanía, state, Chile I1 92
Laascaanood, Som. C9 66
La Ascensión, hill, Mex. C8 100
La Asunción, Ven. B10 86
Laau Point, c., Hi., U.S. B4 78a
Laayoune see El Aaiún, W. Sah. D2 64
La Azufrosa, Mex. F7 130
La Babia, Mex. A7 100
Labadieville, La., U.S. H8 122
La Baie, Qc., Can. B6 110
La Banda, Arg. C5 92
La Bandera, Cerro, mtn., Mex. C6 100
La Bañeza, Spain B4 20
La Barca, Mex. E7 100
La Barge, Wy., U.S. H16 136
Labasa, Fiji p19 79e
La Baule-Escoublac, Fr. G6 14
Labé, Gui. G2 64
Labe (Elbe), stm., Eur. C5 16
Labelle, Qc., Can. D2 110
La Belle, Mo., U.S. D5 120
Laberge, Lake, l., Yk., Can. C4 106
Labi, Bru. A9 50
Labian, Tanjong, c., Malay. A11 50
La Biche, stm., Ab., Can. B18 138
Labis, Malay. K6 48
La Bisbal d'Empordà, Spain C13 20
Łabiszyn, Pol. D13 16
La Blanca Grande, Laguna, l., Arg. I5 92
Labná, hist., Mex. B3 102
Laboe, Ger. B6 16
Laborde, Arg. F6 92
Laborie, St. Luc. m7 105c
La Bostonnais, Qc., Can. C4 110
Laboulaye, Arg. G6 92
Labrador, reg., Nf., Can. E18 106
Labrador Basin, unds. C9 144
Labrador City, Nf., Can. E17 106
Labrador Sea, N.A. D17 94
Lábrea, Braz. E5 84
La Brea, Trin. s12 105f
Labuan, Malay. A9 50
Labuan, state, Malay. A9 50
Labuan, Pulau, i., Malay. A9 50
Labuchongshan, mts., China C10 54
La Bufadora, Mex. L9 134
Labuhan, Indon. G4 50
Labuhanbajo, Indon. H11 50
Labuhanbilik, Indon. B2 50
Labuhanpandan, Indon. H10 50
Labuhanruku, Indon. B1 50
Labuk, stm., Malay. H1 52
Labuk, Telukan, b., Malay. G1 52
Labu Kananga, Indon. H10 50
Labutta, Mya. D2 48
Labytnangi, Russia A11 32
Laç, Alb. C13 24
Lača, ozero, l., Russia F18 8
Lac-à-Beauce, Qc., Can. C4 110
La Cadena, Mex. I3 130
La Calera, Chile F2 92
La Campana, Spain G5 20
La Canada Flintridge, Ca., U.S. I7 134
La Candelaria, Arg. C5 92
La Candelaria, Mex. C1 130
Lacantum, stm., Mex. D2 102
La Capelle-en-Thiérache, Fr. D12 14
La Carlota, Arg. F6 92
La Carlota, Phil. E4 52
La Carolina, Spain F7 20
Lacaune, Fr. F8 18
Laccadive Islands see Lakshadweep, is., India F3 46
Lac-Édouard, Qc., Can. C4 110
La Ceiba, Hond. E4 102
Lacepede Bay, b., Austl. K2 76
Lac-Etchemin, Qc., Can. D6 110
Lacey, Wa., U.S. C4 136
Lac-Frontière, Qc., Can. D6 110
La Chapelle-d'Angillon, Fr. G11 14
La Châtaigneraie, Fr. C5 18
La Chaux-de-Fonds, Switz. C3 22
Lachhmangarh Sīkar, India E5 54
Lachine, Qc., Can. E3 110
Lachlan, stm., Austl. J5 76
La Chorrera, Col. H5 86
La Chorrera, Pan. H8 102
Lachute, Qc., Can. E2 110
Laçi see Laç, Alb. C13 24
La Ciénaga, Arg. C4 92
La Ciotat, Fr. F11 18
La Citadelle, hist., Haiti C11 102
La Ciudad, Mex. D6 100
Lackawanna, N.Y., U.S. B6 114
Lac La Biche, Ab., Can. B18 138
Lac la Hache, B.C., Can. E9 138
Laclede, Id., U.S. B10 136
Laclede, Mo., U.S. E4 120
La Clotilde, Arg. C7 92
Lac-Mégantic, Qc., Can. E6 110
La Colorada, Mex. A3 100
La Coma, Mex. C9 100
Lacombe, Ab., Can. D17 138
Lacombe, La., U.S. G9 122
Lacona, Ia., U.S. C4 120
La Concepción, Pan. H6 102
La Concepción, Ven. B5 86
Laconi, Italy E2 24
Laconia, N.H., U.S. G5 110
Laconia, Gulf of see Lakonikós Kólpos, b., Grc. G5 28
La Consulta, Arg. F3 92
Lacoochee, Fl., U.S. H3 116
La Coruña see A Coruña, Spain A2 20
La Coruña see A Coruña, co., Spain A2 20
La Coste, Tx., U.S. E9 130
La Courtine, Fr. D8 18
La Crescent, Mn., U.S. H7 118
La Crosse, Ks., U.S. C9 128
La Crosse, Va., U.S. H7 114
Lacrosse, Wa., U.S. D9 136
La Crosse, Wi., U.S. H7 118
La Cruz, Arg. D9 92
La Cruz, Col. G3 86
La Cruz, C.R. E7 96
La Cruz, Mex. G2 130
La Cruz de Río Grande, Nic. F5 102
Lac Seul, On., Can. A6 118
La Cuesta, P.R. B2 104a
La Cumbre, Arg. E5 92
La Cygne, Ks., U.S. F3 120
Ladākh, hist. reg., Pak. A6 54
Ladākh Range, mts., Asia A6 54
Ladder Creek, stm., Ks., U.S. C7 128
Laddonia, Mo., U.S. E6 120
La Désirade, i., Guad. h6 105c
La Digue, i., Sey. j13 69b
Ladismith, S. Afr. H5 70
Ladispoli, Italy I8 22
Lādīz, Iran D9 56
Ladner, B.C., Can. G7 138
Lādnūn, India E5 54
Ladoga, In., U.S. I3 112
Ladoga, Lake see Ladožskoe ozero, l., Russia F14 8
La Dorada, Col. E4 86
La Dormida, Arg. F4 92
Ladožskoe ozero (Ladoga, Lake), l., Russia F14 8
Ladushkin, Russia F3 10
Ladva-Vetka, Russia F15 8
Lady Ann Strait, strt., Nu., Can. B10 141
Lady Barron, Austl. n14 77a
Ladybrand, S. Afr. F8 70
Lady Elliot Island, i., Austl. E9 76
Ladysmith, B.C., Can. H7 138
Ladysmith, S. Afr. F9 70
Ladysmith, Wi., U.S. F8 118
Lae, Pap. N. Gui. b4 79a
La Encantada, Mex. C8 100
La Escondida, Mex. H8 130
La Esmeralda, Mex. B7 100
Læsø, i., Den. H4 8
La Esperanza, Cuba A5 102
La Esperanza, Hond. E3 102
La Esperanza, Mex. H4 130
La Esperanza, P.R. B3 104a
La Estrada see A Estrada, Spain B2 20
Lafa, China C7 38
La Falda, Arg. E5 92
La Farge, Wi., U.S. H8 118
Lafayette, Al., U.S. E13 122
Lafayette, Ca., U.S. F3 134
Lafayette, Co., U.S. A3 128
Lafayette, Ga., U.S. C13 122
Lafayette, In., U.S. H3 112
Lafayette, La., U.S. G6 122
Lafayette, Tn., U.S. H11 120
Lafayette, Mount, mtn., N.H., U.S. F5 110
La Feria, Tx., U.S. H10 130
La Ferté-Bernard, Fr. F9 14
La Ferté-Saint-Aubin, Fr. G10 14
Lafia, Nig. H6 64
Lafiagi, Nig. H6 64
Lafleche, Sk., Can. E7 124
La Flèche, Fr. G8 14
La Florida, Guat. D2 102
La Foa, N. Cal. m15 79d
La Follette, Tn., U.S. H1 114
Lafourche, Bayou, stm., La., U.S. H8 122
La Fragua, Arg. C5 92
La Fría, Ven. C5 86
La Fuente de San Esteban, Spain D4 20
La Galite, i., Tun. G2 24
La Gallareta, Arg. D7 92
Lagan, stm., Swe. E3 8
Lagarto, Braz. F7 88
Lagawe, Phil. B3 52
Lage, China D10 54
Lågen, stm., Nor. F4 8
Lages, Braz. C12 92
Laghmān, state, Afg. A3 54
Laghouat, Alg. C5 64
Lagkadás, Grc. C5 28
Lagoa da Prata, Braz. K3 88
Lagoa Vermelha, Braz. D12 92
Lagoa da Pedra, Braz. C3 88
Lago Kolonia, Aruba p20 104g
Lagolândia, Braz. H1 88
Lagonegro, Italy D9 24
Lagonoy Gulf, b., Phil. D4 52
Lago Posadas, Arg. I2 90
Lagos, Nig. H5 64
Lagos, Port. G2 20
Lagos de Moreno, Mex. E8 100
La Gouèra, W. Sah. E1 64
La Goulette, Tun. H4 24
Lago Viedma, Arg. I2 90
La Granadella, Spain C11 20
La Grande, Or., U.S. E8 136
La Grande Deux, Réservoir, res., Qc., Can. E15 106
La Grande Quatre, Réservoir, res., Qc., Can. E16 106
LaGrange, Austl. C4 74
La Grange, Ga., U.S. D13 122
La Grange, Ky., U.S. F12 120
La Grange, Mo., U.S. D6 120
La Grange, Tx., U.S. E11 130
Lagrange, Wy., U.S. F8 126
Lagrange Bay, b., Austl. C4 74
La Gran Sabana, pl., Ven. E10 86
La Guadeloupe, Qc., Can. E6 110
La Guajira, state, Col. G11 102
La Guajira, Península de, pen., S.A. A6 86
La Guardia, Arg. D5 92
La Guardia, Bol. C4 90
La Guardia see A Guardia, Spain C1 20
La Guerche-sur-l'Aubois, Fr. G11 14
Laguiole, Fr. E8 18
Laguna, Braz. D13 92
Laguna, N.M., U.S. H9 132
Laguna, Ilha da, i., Braz. D7 84
Laguna Beach, Ca., U.S. J8 134
Laguna Dam, dam, U.S. K2 132
Laguna de Jaco, Mex. G4 130
Laguna Larga, Arg. E6 92
Laguna Paiva, Arg. E7 92
Lagunas, Peru E2 84
Lagunas de Chacagua, Parque Nacional, p.o.i., Mex. H9 100
Lagunillas, Bol. C4 90
Laha, China B9 36
La Habana (Havana), Cuba A6 102
Lahad Datu, Malay. A11 50
Lahad Datu, Telukan, b., Malay. A11 50
La Harpe, Il., U.S. K7 118
La Harpe, Ks., U.S. G2 128
Lahat, Indon. E3 50
Lahdenpohja, Russia F14 8
Lahemaa rahvus, p.o.i., Est. G11 8
Lahewa, Indon. L3 48
Lahfān, Bi'r, well, Egypt G4 58
Lahij, Yemen G5 56
Lāhījān, Iran B7 56
Lahnstein, Ger. F3 16
Laholm, Swe. H5 8
Lahontan Reservoir, res., Nv., U.S. D6 134
Lahore, Pak. C5 54
La Horqueta, Col. F5 86
Lahr, Ger. H3 16
Lahti, Fin. F11 8
La Huerta, N.M., U.S. B3 130
Lahva, Bela. H10 10
Laï, Chad F3 62
Laiagam, Pap. N. Gui. b3 79a
Laibin, China J3 42
Lai Chau, Viet. A6 48
Laichow Bay see Laizhou Wan, b., China C8 42
Laifeng, China G3 42
L'Aigle, Fr. F9 14
Laihia, Fin. E9 8
Laimbélé, Mont, mtn., Vanuatu k16 79d
Laingsburg, S. Afr. H5 70
Laingsburg, Mi., U.S. B1 114
Lainioälven, stm., Swe. C10 8
Lainsitz see Lužnice, stm., Eur. G10 16
Laird Hill, Tx., U.S. E3 122
Lais, Indon. C12 50
Lais, Indon. E3 50
Lais, Phil. G5 52
Laitila, Fin. F9 8
Laiwu, China C7 42
Laixi, China C9 42
Laiyang, China C9 42
Laizhou Bay see Laizhou Wan, b., China C8 42
Laizhou Wan (Laizhou Bay), b., China C8 42
Laja, stm., Chile H2 92
Laja, Laguna de la, l., Chile H2 92
Laja, Salto del, wtfl, Chile H2 92
La Jara, Co., U.S. D2 128
La Jara, reg., Spain E5 20
La Jara Canyon, val., N.M., U.S. G9 132
La Jarita, Mex. F4 130
Lajas, P.R. B1 104a
Laje, Braz. G6 88
Lajeado, Braz. E7 88
Lajes, Braz. C7 88
Lajinha, Braz. K5 88
Laji Shan, mts., China D5 36
Lajosmizse, Hung. B6 26
Lajta (Leitha), stm., Eur. H12 16
La Junta, Co., U.S. D5 128
Lakar Kūh, mtn., Iran C8 56
Lakatoro, Vanuatu k16 79d
Lake, Ms., U.S. E9 122
Lake Alfred, Fl., U.S. H4 116
Lake Andes, S.D., U.S. D14 126
Lake Arthur, La., U.S. G6 122
Lakeba, i., Fiji q20 79e
Lakeba Passage, strt., Fiji q20 79e
Lake Benton, Mn., U.S. G2 118
Lake Brownwood, Tx., U.S. C8 130
Lake Cargelligo, Austl. I6 76
Lake Charles, La., U.S. G5 122
Lake Chelan National Recreation Area, p.o.i., Wa., U.S. B6 136
Lake City, Ar., U.S. B8 122
Lake City, Co., U.S. E9 132
Lake City, Fl., U.S. F3 116
Lake City, Ia., U.S. B3 120
Lake City, Mi., U.S. D4 112
Lake City, Mn., U.S. G6 118
Lake City, Pa., U.S. B5 114
Lake City, S.C., U.S. C6 116
Lake City, Tn., U.S. H1 114
Lake Cowichan, B.C., Can. H6 138
Lake Crystal, Mn., U.S. G4 118
Lake Dallas, Tx., U.S. A10 130
Lake Delton, Wi., U.S. H9 118
Lake District National Park, p.o.i., Eng., U.K. G9 12
Lake Elsinore, Ca., U.S. J8 134
Lakefield, On., Can. D11 112
Lakefield, Mn., U.S. H3 118
Lake Forest, Il., U.S. F2 112
Lake Fork Reservoir, res., Tx., U.S. E3 122
Lake Geneva, Wi., U.S. B9 120
Lake George, N.Y., U.S. G3 110
Lake Harbor, Fl., U.S. J5 116
Lake Havasu City, Az., U.S. I2 132
Lake Helen, Fl., U.S. H4 116
Lakehurst, N.J., U.S. D11 114
Lake Jackson, Tx., U.S. E12 130
Lake King, Austl. F3 74
Lakeland, Fl., U.S. H3 116
Lakeland, Ga., U.S. E2 116
Lake Linden, Mi., U.S. D10 118
Lake Louise, Ab., Can. E14 138
Lake Mead National Recreation Area, p.o.i., U.S. G2 132
Lake Mills, Wi., U.S. A8 120
Lake Minchumina, Ak., U.S. D9 140
Lake Mohawk see Sparta, N.J., U.S. C11 114
Lake Nash, Austl. D7 74
Lake Norden, S.D., U.S. C15 126
Lake Oswego, Or., U.S. E4 136
Lake Ozark, Mo., U.S. F5 120
Lake Park, Fl., U.S. J5 116
Lake Park, Ia., U.S. H3 118
Lake Placid, Fl., U.S. I4 116
Lake Placid, N.Y., U.S. F3 110
Lake Pleasant, N.Y., U.S. G2 110
Lakeport, Ca., U.S. D3 134
Lakeport, Mi., U.S. E7 112
Lake Preston, S.D., U.S. C15 126
Lakes Entrance, Austl. K7 76
Lakeshore, Ms., U.S. G9 122
Lakeside, Ca., U.S. K8 134
Lakeside, Mt., U.S. B12 136
Lake Stevens, Wa., U.S. B4 136
Laketown, Ut., U.S. B5 132
Lake View, Ar., U.S. C8 122
Lake View, Ia., U.S. B2 120
Lakeview, Mi., U.S. E4 112
Lakeview, Mi., U.S. F4 112
Lakeview, Oh., U.S. D2 114
Lakeview, Or., U.S. A5 134
Lake Village, Ar., U.S. D7 122
Lakeville, Mn., U.S. G5 118
Lake Wales, Fl., U.S. I4 116
Lake Wilson, Mn., U.S. G3 118
Lakewood, Co., U.S. B3 128
Lakewood, N.J., U.S. D11 114
Lakewood, Oh., U.S. C4 114
Lakewood, Wa., U.S. C4 136
Lakewood, Wi., U.S. C1 112
Lakewood Park, N.D., U.S. F15 124
Lake Worth, Fl., U.S. J5 116
Lakhdaria, Alg. H14 20
Lākheri, India F5 54
Lakhīmpur, India D8 54
Lakhīpur, India F14 54
Lakhnādon, India G7 54
Lakinsk, Russia H18 8
Lakonikós Kólpos (Laconia, Gulf of), b., Grc. G5 28
Lakota, N.D., U.S. F15 124
Laksefjorden, b., Nor. A12 8
Lakshadweep, state, India F3 46
Lakshadweep, is., India F3 46
Lakshadweep Sea, Asia F3 46
Lākshām, Bngl. G13 54
Lakshmeshwar, India D2 53
La Laja, Chile H1 92
Lāla Mūsa, Pak. B4 54
Lalapaşa, Tur. B9 28
L'Albufera, l., Spain E10 20
Laleham, Austl. D7 76
La Leona, Mex. I5 130
La Leonesa, Arg. C8 92
Lālganj, India F10 54
Lalibela, Eth. E7 62
La Libertad, Guat. D2 102
La Ligua, Chile F2 92
La Lima, Hond. E3 102
Lalin, stm., China B7 38
Lalindi, Indon. I12 50
La Línea de la Concepción, Spain H5 20
Lalitpur, India F7 54
Lalitpur, Nepal E10 54
Lalla Khedidja, Tamgout de, mtn., Alg. H14 20
Lalmanir Hat, Bngl. F12 54
La Loche, Sk., Can. D9 106
La Lora, plat., Spain B7 20
La Louvière, Bel. D13 14
L'Alpe-d'Huez, Fr. D12 18
Lālpur, India G2 54
Lālsot, India E6 54
La Luz, Mex. C10 100
La Luz, Mex. I10 130
Lama, ozero, l., Russia C7 34
La Macarena, Parque Nacional, p.o.i., Col. F5 86
La Macarena, Serranía de, mts., Col. F5 86
La Maddalena, Italy C3 24
La Madrid, Arg. C5 92
Lamadrid, Mex. G6 130
La Magdalena, Mex. H1 130
Lama-Kara, Togo H5 64
La Malbaie, Qc., Can. C6 110
La Mancha, reg., Spain E8 20
Lamandau, stm., Indon. E7 50
Lamap, Vanuatu k16 79d
Lamar, Co., U.S. C6 128
Lamar, Mo., U.S. G3 120
Lamarche, Fr. F14 14
La Marmora, Punta, mtn., Italy D3 24
La Maroma, Mex. F7 130
La Marque, Tx., U.S. H4 122
La Marsa, Tun. H4 24
La Martre, Qc., Can. A10 110
Lamas, Peru E2 84
Lamballe, Fr. F6 14
Lambaréné, Gabon E2 66
Lambari, stm., Braz. J3 88
Lambayeque, Peru E2 84
Lambay Island, i., Ire. H7 12
Lambert, Ms., U.S. C8 122
Lambert, Mt., U.S. G9 124
Lambert, Cape, c., Pap. N. Gui. a5 79a
Lambert Glacier, ice, Ant. C11 81
Lambert Land, reg., Grnld. B21 141
Lamberton, Mn., U.S. G3 118
Lambertsbaai see Lambert's Bay, S. Afr. H3 70
Lambert's Bay, S. Afr. H3 70
Lambton, Cape, c., N.T., Can. A6 106
Lame Deer, Mt., U.S. B6 126
La Media Luna, Arrecifes de, rf., Hond. E6 102
Lamentin, Guad. h5 105c
Lamèque, N.B., Can. C12 110
Lamèque, Île, i., N.B., Can. C12 110
La Merced, Arg. B5 92
La Merced, Arg. D5 92
Lameroo, Austl. J3 76
La Mesa, Ca., U.S. K8 134
Lamesa, Tx., U.S. B6 130
Lamía, Grc. E5 28
Lamine, stm., Mo., U.S. F5 120
Lamington National Park, p.o.i., Austl. G9 76
La Misión, Mex. K9 134
Lamitan, Phil. G4 52
Lamlam, Mount, hill, Guam j9 78c
Lammeulo, Indon. J2 48
La Moille, Il., U.S. C8 120
Lamoille, Nv., U.S. C1 132
Lamoille, stm., Vt., U.S. F4 110
Lamon Bay, b., Phil. C4 52
Lamone, stm., Italy F9 22
Lamongan, Indon. G8 50
Lamoni, Ia., U.S. D3 120
Lamont, Ca., U.S. H6 134
Lamont, Ia., U.S. I7 118
Lamont, Ok., U.S. E11 128
La Monte, Mo., U.S. F4 120
La Mothe, Lac, l., Qc., Can. B5 110
Lamothe-Achard, Fr. H7 14
Lamotrek, at., Micron. C5 72
Lamotte-Beuvron, Fr. G10 14
Lampang, Thai. C4 48
Lampasas, Tx., U.S. C9 130
Lampasas, stm., Tx., U.S. C9 130
Lampazos de Naranjo, Mex. B8 100
Lampedusa, Isola di, i., Italy I6 24
Lampertheim, Ger. G4 16
Lamphun, Thai. C4 48
Lampman, Sk., Can. E11 124
Lampung, state, Indon. F4 50
Lamskoe, Russia H21 10
Lamu, Kenya E8 66
La Mure, Fr. E11 18
Lan', stm., Bela. H10 10
Lana, Italy D8 22
Lanai, i., Hi., U.S. C4 78a
Lanai City, Hi., U.S. C4 78a
Lanaihale, mtn., Hi., U.S. C5 78a
Lanalhue, Lago, l., Chile I1 92
Lanark, On., Can. C13 112
Lanark, Scot., U.K. F9 12
Lanbi Kyun, i., Mya. G4 48
Lancang, China A4 48
Lancang see Mekong, stm., Asia D9 46
Lancaster, Eng., U.K. G10 12
Lancaster, Ca., U.S. I7 134
Lancaster, Mn., U.S. C2 118
Lancaster, Mo., U.S. D5 120
Lancaster, N.H., U.S. F5 110
Lancaster, Oh., U.S. E3 114
Lancaster, Pa., U.S. D9 114
Lancaster, S.C., U.S. B5 116
Lancaster, Tx., U.S. E2 122
Lancaster, Va., U.S. G9 114
Lancaster, Wi., U.S. B7 120
Lancaster Sound, strt., Nu., Can. C8 141
Lance Creek, Wy., U.S. D8 126
Lancelin, Austl. F2 74
Lanchou see Lanzhou, China D5 36
Lanchow see Lanzhou, China D5 36
Lanciano, Italy H11 22
Lancun, China C9 42
Łańcut, Pol. F18 16
Lândana, Ang. B1 68
Landau an der Isar, Ger. H8 16
Landau in der Pfalz, Ger. G4 16
Landeck, Aus. C7 22
Lander, Wy., U.S. E4 126
Landerneau, Fr. F4 14
Landes, state, Fr. F5 18
Landes, reg., Fr. E4 18
Landete, Spain E9 20
Landis, Sk., Can. B5 124
Lando, S.C., U.S. B4 116
Land O'Lakes, Wi., U.S. E9 118
Landösjön, l., Swe. E5 8
Landri Sales, Braz. D3 88
Landrum, S.C., U.S. A3 116
Landsborough Creek, stm., Austl. D5 76
Land's End, c., Eng., U.K. K7 12
Landshut, Ger. H7 16
Landskrona, Swe. I5 8
Lane, mth., Fr. G9 14
Lanesboro, Mn., U.S. H6 118
Lanett, Al., U.S. E13 122
Lanezi Lake, l., B.C., Can. C10 138
La'nga Co, l., China C8 54
Langa-Langa, D.R.C. E3 66
Langbank, Sk., Can. D11 124
Lang Bay, B.C., Can. G6 138
Langdale, Al., U.S. E13 122
Langdon, N.D., U.S. F15 124
Langeac, Fr. D9 18
Langeberg, mts., S. Afr. H5 70
Langeland, i., Den. I4 8
Langenhagen, Ger. D5 16
Langenthal, Switz. C4 22
Langfang, China B7 42
Langford, S.D., U.S. B15 126
Langgam, Indon. C2 50
Langham, Sk., Can. B6 124
Langhe, hist. reg., Italy F5 22
Langholm, Scot., U.K. F9 12
Langjökull, ice, Ice. k29 8a
Langkawi, Pulau, i., Malay. I4 48
Langley, B.C., Can. G8 138
Langley, Ok., U.S. A3 122
Langlo, stm., Austl. E5 76
Langnau im Emmental, Switz. C4 22
Langogne, Fr. E9 18
Langøya, i., Nor. B6 8
Langping, China F4 42
Langreo, Spain A5 20
Langres, Fr. G14 14
Langruth, Mb., Can. D15 124
Langsa, Indon. J3 48
Langsa, Teluk, b., Indon. J4 48
Langshan, China A2 42
Lang Son, Viet. B8 48
Lang Suan, Thai. H4 48
Languedoc, hist. reg., Fr. F8 18
L'Anguille, stm., Ar., U.S. C8 122
Langxi, China F8 42
Langzhong, China F1 42
Lanigan, Sk., Can. C8 124
Lanigan Creek, stm., Sk., Can. C9 124
Lanín, Volcán, vol., S.A. G2 90
Länkäran, Azer. B6 56
Länkipohja, Fin. F11 8
Lannemezan, Fr. F6 18
Lannion, Fr. F5 14
Lanping, China F4 36
Lansdowne, India D7 54
Lansdowne House, On., Can. E13 106
L'Anse, Mi., U.S. B1 112
Lansing, Ia., U.S. H7 118
Lansing, Mi., U.S. B1 114
Lantana, Fl., U.S. J5 116
Lantau Island, i., China J6 42
Lanta Yai, Ko, i., Thai. I4 48
Lantian, China D3 42
La Nurra, reg., Italy D2 24
Lanusei, Italy E3 24
Lanxi, China G8 42
Lan Yü, i., Tai. J9 42
Lanzhou, China D5 36
Lanzo Torinese, Italy E4 22
Lao, stm., Thai. C4 48
Laoag, Phil. A3 52
Laoang, Phil. D5 52
Lao Cai, Viet. A6 48
Laodao, stm., China G5 42
Laofu, China C3 38
Laoha, stm., China C4 38
Laohekou, China E4 42
Laohokow see Laohekou, China E4 42
Laois, state, Ire. I5 12
Lao Ling, mtn., China C9 38
Laon, Fr. E12 14
Laona, Wi., U.S. F10 118
La Orchila, Isla, i., Ven. B8 86
La Oroya, Peru F2 84
Laos, ctry., Asia C6 48
Laoshan Wan, b., China C9 42
Lapa, Braz. B13 92
Lapai, Nig. H6 64
Lapalisse, Fr. C9 18
La Palma, Col. E4 86
La Palma, Pan. H8 102
La Palma, Pan. I7 102
La Palma del Condado, Spain G4 20
La Paloma, Ur. G10 92
La Pampa, state, Arg. G3 90
La Paragua, Ven. D10 86
La Pasión, stm., Guat. D2 102
La Paya, Parque Nacional, p.o.i., Col. G4 86
La Paz, Arg. E8 92
La Paz, Arg. F4 92
La Paz, Bol. C3 90
La Paz, Col. B5 86
La Paz, Hond. E4 102
La Paz, Mex. C3 100
La Paz, Mex. D8 100
La Paz, Ur. G9 92
La Paz, Bahía de, b., Mex. C3 100
La Perla, Mex. A6 100
La Perouse, Bahía, b., Chile e30 78l
La Perouse Strait, strt., Asia B13 36
La Pesca, Mex. D10 100
La Piedad de Cabadas, Mex. E7 100
La Pine, Or., U.S. G5 136
La Place, La., U.S. G8 122
Lap Lae, Thai. D4 48
Lapland, hist. reg., Eur. C11 8
La Plata, Arg. G8 92
La Plata, Col. F4 86
La Plata, Md., U.S. F9 114
La Plata, Mo., U.S. D5 120
La Plata Peak, mtn., Co., U.S. D10 132
La Pobla de Segur, Spain B11 20
La Pocatière, Qc., Can. C6 110
Lapominka, Russia D19 8
Laporte, Co., U.S. G7 126
La Porte, In., U.S. G3 112
Laporte, Pa., U.S. C9 114
La Porte City, Ia., U.S. B5 120
La Potherie, Lac, l., Qc., Can. D16 106
La Poza Grande, Mex. C2 100
Lappajärvi, l., Fin. E10 8
Lappeenranta, Fin. F12 8
Lappi, state, Fin. C12 8
Laprida, Arg. D5 92
Laprida, Arg. H7 92
La Pryor, Tx., U.S. F8 130
Lapta, N. Cyp. C4 58
Laptev Sea see Laptevyh, more, Russia B4 32
Laptevyh, more, Russia B4 32
La Puebla de Montalbán, Spain E6 20
La Puerta, Arg. D5 92
La Puerta de Cabrera, Mex. H2 130
Lapu-Lapu, Phil. E4 52
La Purísima, Mex. B2 100
Lăpuş, Rom. B11 26
Lapwai, Id., U.S. D10 136
La Quiaca, Arg. D3 90
L'Aquila, Italy H10 22
Lār, Iran D7 56
Lara, state, Ven. B7 86
Laracha, Spain A2 20
Larache, Mor. B3 64
Laramie, Wy., U.S. F7 126
Laramie, stm., U.S. E8 126
Laramie Mountains, mts., Wy., U.S. F7 126
Laramie Peak, mtn., Wy., U.S. E7 126
Laranjal, Braz. K4 88
Laranjeiras, Braz. F7 88
Laranjeiras do Sul, Braz. B11 92
Larantuka, Indon. G7 44
Larap, Phil. C4 52
Larat, Indon. G9 44
Larat, Pulau, i., Indon. G9 44
Larche Pass, p., Eur. E12 18
Larchwood, Ia., U.S. H2 118
Larde, Moz. D6 68
L'Ardoise, N.S., Can. E16 110
Laredo, Spain A7 20
Laredo, Tx., U.S. G8 130
La Reforma, Mex. C4 100
Lares, P.R. B2 104a
Larga, Mol. A13 26
Larga, Laguna, l., Tx., U.S. G10 130
Largo, Fl., U.S. I3 116
Largo, Cañon, val., N.M., U.S. G9 132
Largo, Cayo, i., Cuba B7 102
Largs, Scot., U.K. F8 12
Lariang, stm., Indon. D11 50
Larimore, N.D., U.S. G16 124
Larino, Italy I11 22
Lario see Como, Lago di, l., Italy D6 22
La Rioja, Arg. D4 92
La Rioja, state, Arg. D4 92
La Rioja, state, Spain B8 20
Lárisa, Grc. D5 28
Lārkāna, Pak. D10 56
Lárnakos, Kólpos, b., Cyp. D4 58
Larne, N. Ire., U.K. G7 12
Larned, Ks., U.S. C9 128
La Robla, Spain B5 20
La Rochefoucauld, Fr. D6 18
La Rochelle, Fr. C4 18
La Roche-sur-Yon, Fr. H7 14
La Roda, Spain E8 20
La Romaine, Qc., Can. i21 107a
La Romana, Dom. Rep. C13 102
La Ronge, Sk., Can. D10 106
La Ronge, Lac, l., Sk., Can. D10 106
Laroquebrou, Fr. D8 18
Larose, Pointe, c., Mart. k7 105c
Larroque, Arg. F8 92
Larrys River, N.S., Can. E15 110
Larsen Ice Shelf, ice, Ant. B34 81
La Rubia, Arg. E7 92
La Rue, Oh., U.S. D2 114
Larvik, Nor. G3 8
Larzac, Causse du, plat., Fr. F9 18
La Sabanilla, Mex. C8 100
La Sal, Ut., U.S. E7 132
La Salle, Co., U.S. G8 126
La Salle, Il., U.S. C8 120
La Salle, stm., Mb., Can. E16 124
Lasan, Indon. C10 50
Las Animas, Co., U.S. C5 128
Las Arenas, P.R. B1 104a
La Sarre, Qc., Can. F15 106
Las Arrias, Arg. E6 92
Las Ballenas, Canal de, strt., Mex. G6 98
Las Breñas, Arg. C7 92
Las Cabezas de San Juan, Spain G5 20
Las Cabras, Chile G2 92
Lascano, Ur. F10 92
Las Casitas, mtn., Mex. D4 100
Las Catitas, Arg. F3 92
Las Choapas, Mex. G11 100
Las Chorreras, Mex. A6 100
Las Cruces, N.M., U.S. K10 132
Las Cuatas, Mex. D1 130
Las Cuevas, Mex. A8 100
Las Cumaraguas, Ven. p20 104g
La Selle, Morne, mtn., Haiti C11 102
La Serena, Chile D2 92
La Serena, reg., Spain F5 20
La Seu d'Urgell, Spain B12 20
La Seyne, Fr. F11 18
La Seyne, Fr. F11 18
Las Flores, Arg. G8 92

Name	Map Ref.	Page
Las Flores, P.R.	B3	104a
Las Flores, Arroyo, stm., Arg.	H7	92
Las Garcitas, Arg.	C7	92
Las Guayabas, Mex.	C10	100
Lashburn, Sk., Can.	A4	124
Las Heras, Arg.	I3	90
Las Heras, Arg.	F3	92
Lashio, Mya.	A3	48
Lashkar Gāh, Afg.	C9	56
Las Hormigas, Mex.	C9	100
Lasia, Pulau, i., Indon.	K3	48
Łasin, Pol.	C15	16
La Sirena, Ven.	p20	104g
Łaskarzew, Pol.	E17	16
Las Lajas, Arg.	I2	92
Las Lajas, Arg.	H7	102
Las Lajas, Pan.	H7	102
Las Lomitas, Arg.	B7	92
Las Malvinas, Arg.	G3	92
Las Mareas, P.R.	C3	104a
Las Margaritas, Mex.	G13	100
Las Marianas, Arg.	G8	92
Las Marías, P.R.	B1	104a
Las Minas, Cerro, mtn., Hond.	E3	102
Las Nopaleras, Cerro, mtn., Mex.	C7	100
La Solana, Spain	F7	20
Las Ovejas, Arg.	H2	92
Las Palmas, Arg.	C8	92
Las Palmas, P.R.	C3	104a
Las Palomas, Mex.	F9	98
La Spezia, Italy	F6	22
Las Piedras, P.R.	B4	104a
Las Piedras, Ur.	G9	92
Las Piedras, stm., Peru	F3	84
Las Plumas, Arg.	H3	90
Lasqueti Island, i., B.C., Can.	G6	138
Las Rosas, Arg.	F7	92
Las Rosas, Mex.	G12	100
Lassance, Braz.	I3	88
Lassen Peak, vol., Ca., U.S.	C4	134
Lassen Volcanic National Park, p.o.i., Ca., U.S.	C4	134
L'Assomption, stm., Qc., Can.	D3	110
Las Tablas, Pan.	I7	102
Las Tinajas, Arg.	C6	92
Last Mountain Lake, l., Sk., Can.	C8	124
Las Tórtolas, Cerro (Tórtolas, Cerro de las), mtn., S.A.	D2	92
Lastoursville, Gabon	E2	66
Las Tunas, Cuba	B9	102
Las Tunas Grandes, Laguna, l., Arg.	H6	92
Las Varas, Mex.	G8	98
Las Varas, Mex.	C6	100
Las Varillas, Arg.	E6	92
Las Vegas, P.R.	B1	104a
Las Vegas, Nv., U.S.	G1	132
Las Vegas, N.M., U.S.	F3	128
Las Vegas, Ven.	C7	86
Latacunga, Ec.	H2	86
La Tagua, Col.	H4	86
Latakia see Al-Lādhiqīyah, Syria	C6	58
Lata Mountain, vol., Am. Sam.	h13	79c
Latehar, India	G10	54
La Teste-de-Buch, Fr.	E4	18
Lāthi, India	H3	54
Lathrop, Mo., U.S.	E3	120
Latimer, Il., U.S.	I5	118
Latina, Italy	C6	24
Latisana, Italy	E10	22
Latium see Lazio, state, Italy	B6	24
Latjuga, Russia	D23	8
La Torrecilla, mtn., P.R.	B3	104a
La Tortuga, Isla, i., Ven.	B9	86
Latouche Treville, Cape, c., Austl.	C4	74
La Tour-d'Auvergne, Fr.	D8	18
La Trimouille, Fr.	C7	18
La Trinidad, Nic.	F4	102
La Trinidad, Phil.	B3	52
La Trinidad de Orichuna, Ven.	D7	86
La Trinité, Mart.	k6	105c
Latrobe, Pa., U.S.	D6	114
Latta, S.C., U.S.	B6	116
La Tuque, Qc., Can.	C4	110
Lātūr, India	B3	53
Latvia, ctry., Eur.	D7	10
Lau, Nig.	H7	64
Lauchhammer, Ger.	E9	16
Lauenburg, Ger.	C6	16
Lauf an der Pegnitz, Ger.	G7	16
Lauge Koch Kyst, cst., Grnld.	B13	141
Laughlin, Nv., U.S.	H2	132
Laughlin Peak, mtn., N.M., U.S.	E4	128
Lau Group, is., Fiji	p20	79e
Lauis see Lugano, Switz.	D5	22
Lauka, Fin.	E11	8
Laun, Thai.	G4	48
Launceston, Austl.	n13	77a
Launceston, Eng., U.K.	K8	12
La Unión, Chile	H2	90
La Unión, El Sal.	F4	102
La Unión, Mex.	G8	100
La Unión, Spain	G10	20
La Union, N.M., U.S.	L10	132
La Unión, Ven.	C8	86
La Urbana, Ven.	D8	86
Laupheim, Ger.	H5	16
Laura, Austl.	C8	74
Laurel, Fl., U.S.	I3	116
Laurel, In., U.S.	E12	120
Laurel, Md., U.S.	E9	114
Laurel, Ms., U.S.	F9	122
Laurel, Mt., U.S.	B4	126
Laurel, Ne., U.S.	E15	126
Laurel Bay, S.C., U.S.	D5	116
Laureldale, Pa., U.S.	D10	114
Laureles, Ur.	E9	92
Laurel River Lake, res., Ky., U.S.	G1	114
Laurelville, Oh., U.S.	E15	120
Laurencekirk, Scot., U.K.	E10	12
Laurens, S.C., U.S.	B3	116
Laurentides, Les, plat., Qc., Can.	F16	106
Lau Ridge, unds.	L21	142
Laurier, Mb., Can.	D14	124
Laurier-Station, Qc., Can.	D5	110
Laurinburg, N.C., U.S.	B6	116
Laurium, Mi., U.S.	D10	118
Lausanne, Switz.	D3	22
Lausitzer Neisse (Nysa Łużycka), stm., Eur.	F10	16
Laut, Pulau, i., Indon.	A5	50
Laut, Pulau, i., Indon.	E10	50
Laut, Selat, strt., Indon.	E9	50
Lauta, Ger.	E9	16
Lautaro, Chile	I1	92
Lauterbach, Ger.	F5	16
Lauter Sachsen, Ger.	F8	16
Laut Kecil, Kepulauan, is., Indon.	F9	50
Lautoka, Fiji	p18	79e
Lauzerte, Fr.	E7	18
Lava (Łyna), stm., Eur.	B16	16
Lava Beds National Monument, p.o.i., Ca., U.S.	B4	134
Lavaca, stm., Tx., U.S.	E11	130
Laval, Qc., Can.	E3	110
Laval, Fr.	F8	14
La Vall d'Uixó, Spain	E10	20
Lavalle, Arg.	D5	92
Lavalle, Arg.	D8	92
Lavapié, Punta, c., Chile	H1	92
Lavassaare, Est.	G11	8
'La Vega, Dom. Rep.	C12	102
La Vela de Coro, Ven.	B7	86
Lavelanet, Fr.	G7	18
Lavello, Italy	C9	24
La Venada, Mex.	I10	130
La Venta, hist., Mex.	F11	100
La Ventura, Mex.	C8	100
La Vera, reg., Spain	D5	20
La Vergne, Tn., U.S.	H11	120
Laverne, Ok., U.S.	E9	128
Laverton, Austl.	E4	74
La Veta, Co., U.S.	D4	128
Lavieille, Lake, l., On., Can.	C11	112
La Vila Joiosa, Spain	F10	20
Lavillette, N.B., Can.	C11	110
La Viña, Arg.	B5	92
Lavina, Mt., U.S.	A4	126
La Vista, Ne., U.S.	C1	120
La Voulte-sur-Rhône, Fr.	E10	18
Lavras, Braz.	K3	88
Lávrio, Grc.	F7	28
Lavumisa, Swaz.	E10	70
Lawang, Indon.	G8	50
Lawas, Malay.	A9	50
Lawdar, Yemen	G6	56
Lawers, Ben, mtn., Scot., U.K.	E8	12
Lawgi, Austl.	E8	76
Lawksawk, Mya.	B3	48
Lawler, Ia., U.S.	A5	120
Lawn, Tx., U.S.	B8	130
Lawndale, N.C., U.S.	A4	116
Lawn Hill, Austl.	C7	74
Lawn Hill Creek, stm., Austl.	C7	74
Lawrence, In., U.S.	I3	112
Lawrence, Ks., U.S.	F2	120
Lawrence, Ma., U.S.	B14	114
Lawrenceburg, In., U.S.	E12	120
Lawrenceburg, Ky., U.S.	F12	120
Lawrenceburg, Tn., U.S.	B11	122
Lawrenceville, Il., U.S.	F10	120
Lawrenceville, N.J., U.S.	D11	114
Lawson, Mo., U.S.	E3	120
Lawtey, Fl., U.S.	F3	116
Lawton, N.D., U.S.	F15	124
Lawton, Ok., U.S.	G10	128
Lawu, Gunung, vol., Indon.	G7	50
Lawz, Jabal al-, mtn., Sau. Ar.	J6	58
Laxå, Swe.	G6	8
Laxe, Spain	A1	20
Lay Lake, res., Al., U.S.	D12	122
Layou, St. Vin.	o11	105e
Layton, Ut., U.S.	B4	132
Laytonville, Ca., U.S.	D2	134
La Zarca, Mex.	C6	100
Lazarev, Russia	F17	34
Lázaro Cárdenas, Mex.	G7	100
Lázaro Cárdenas, Presa, res., Mex.	C6	100
Lazdijai, Lith.	F6	10
Lazio, state, Italy	B6	24
Ļbach, Camb.	F6	48
Leachville, Ar., U.S.	I7	120
Lead, S.D., U.S.	C9	126
Leadbetter Point, c., Wa., U.S.	D2	136
Leader, Sk., Can.	D4	124
Lead Hill, hill, Mo., U.S.	H4	120
Leadore, Id., U.S.	F13	136
Leadville, Co., U.S.	D10	132
Leaf, stm., Ms., U.S.	F10	122
Leaf Lake, l., Sk., Can.	A11	124
Leaghur Lake, l., Austl.	I4	76
League City, Tx., U.S.	H3	122
Leakey, Tx., U.S.	E8	130
Leaksville, N.C., U.S.	H5	114
Lealman, Fl., U.S.	I3	116
Leamington, On., Can.	F7	112
Le'an, China	H6	42
Leandro, Braz.	C3	88
Leandro N. Alem, Arg.	C10	92
Leary, Ga., U.S.	F14	122
Leatherman Peak, mtn., Id., U.S.	F13	136
Leavenworth, Ks., U.S.	E2	120
Leavenworth, Wa., U.S.	C5	136
Leawood, Ks., U.S.	F3	120
Lebak, Phil.	G5	52
Lebam, Wa., U.S.	D3	136
Lebanon, In., U.S.	H3	112
Lebanon, Ks., U.S.	B10	128
Lebanon, Ky., U.S.	G12	120
Lebanon, N.H., U.S.	G4	110
Lebanon, Oh., U.S.	E1	114
Lebanon, Or., U.S.	F3	136
Lebanon, Pa., U.S.	D9	114
Lebanon, S.D., U.S.	B13	126
Lebanon, Tn., U.S.	H11	120
Lebanon, Va., U.S.	H3	114
Lebanon, ctry., Asia	E6	58
Lebec, Ca., U.S.	I7	134
Lebesby, Nor.	A12	8
Le Bic, Qc., Can.	B8	110
Lebjaže, Kaz.	D13	32
Le Blanc, Fr.	H10	14
Lebo, D.R.C.	D4	66
Lebo, Ks., U.S.	F2	120
Ļebork, Pol.	B13	16
Lebrija, Spain	H4	20
Lebrija, stm., Col.	D5	86
Ļebsko, Jezioro, l., Pol.	B13	16
Lebu, Chile	H1	92
Le Carbet, Mart.	k6	105c
Lecce, Italy	D12	24
Lecco, Italy	E6	22
Le Center, Mn., U.S.	G5	118
Lech, stm., Eur.	H6	16
Lechainá, Grc.	F4	28
Lechang, China	I5	42
Le Chesne, Fr.	E13	14
Lechiguanas, Islas de las, is., Arg.	F8	92
Lechuguilla, Cerro, mtn., Mex.	D6	100
Lecompte, La., U.S.	F6	122
Le Creusot, Fr.	H13	14
Le Croisic, Fr.	G6	14
Ļęczyca, Pol.	D15	16
Ledesma, Spain	C4	20
Le Diamant, Mart.	l6	105c
Ledjanaja, gora, mtn., Russia	D23	8
Ledo, India	C8	46
Ledo, Indon.	C6	50
Ledong, China	L3	42
Leduc, Ab., Can.	C17	138
Leechburg, Pa., U.S.	D6	114
Leech Lake, l., Mn., U.S.	D4	118
Leedey, Ok., U.S.	F9	128
Leeds, Eng., U.K.	H11	12
Leeds, Al., U.S.	D12	122
Leek, Eng., U.K.	H10	12
Leelanau, Lake, l., Mi., U.S.	D4	112
Leelanau Peninsula, pen., Mi., U.S.	C4	112
Leer, Ger.	C3	16
Leesburg, Fl., U.S.	H4	116
Leesburg, Ga., U.S.	E1	116
Leesburg, Va., U.S.	E8	114
Lees Summit, Mo., U.S.	F3	120
Leesville, La., U.S.	F5	122
Leesville, S.C., U.S.	B4	116
Leeton, Austl.	J6	76
Leeton, Mo., U.S.	F4	120
Leeuwarden, Neth.	A14	14
Leeuwin, Cape, c., Austl.	F2	74
Lee Vining, Ca., U.S.	F6	134
Leeward Islands, is., N.A.	h15	96a
Lefkáda, Grc.	E3	28
Lefkáda, i., Grc.	E3	28
Lefke, N. Cyp.	C4	58
Lefkosía see Nicosia, Cyp.	C4	58
Lefors, Tx., U.S.	F8	128
Le François, Mart.	k7	105c
Lefroy, Lake, l., Austl.	F4	74
Legal, Ab., Can.	C17	138
Leganés, Spain	D7	20
Legaspi, Phil.	D4	52
Leggett, Ca., U.S.	D2	134
Leghorn see Livorno, Italy	G7	22
Legion, Zimb.	B9	70
Legionowo, Pol.	D16	16
Legnago, Italy	E8	22
Legnano, Italy	E5	22
Legnica, Pol.	E12	16
Legnica, state, Pol.	E12	16
Le Gosier, Guad.	h6	105c
Le Grand, Ca., U.S.	F5	134
La Guelta, Alg.	H11	20
Legume, Austl.	G9	76
Lehi, India	A6	54
Lehigh, Ia., U.S.	B3	120
Lehigh, Ok., U.S.	C2	122
Lehigh Acres, Fl., U.S.	J4	116
Lehighton, Pa., U.S.	D10	114
Lehrte, Ger.	D5	16
Lehtse, Est.	A8	10
Lehua, i., Hi., U.S.	A1	78a
Lehututu, Bots.	C5	70
Leiah, Pak.	C3	54
Leibnitz, Aus.	D12	22
Leicester, Eng., U.K.	I11	12
Leichhardt, stm., Austl.	A2	76
Leichhardt Falls, wtfl, Austl.	B2	76
Leiden (Leyden), Neth.	B13	14
Leigh Creek South, Austl.	H2	76
Leighton, Al., U.S.	C11	122
Leighton Buzzard, Eng., U.K.	J12	12
Leinan, Sk., Can.	D6	124
Leine, stm., Ger.	D5	16
Leinster, Eng., U.K.	I6	12
Leinster, state, Ire.	I6	12
Leinster, Mount, mtn., Ire.	I6	12
Leipalingis, Lith.	F6	10
Leipsic, Oh., U.S.	C2	114
Leipzig, Ger.	E8	16
Leiria, Port.	E2	20
Leiria, state, Port.	E2	20
Leirvik, Nor.	G1	8
Leishan, China	H2	42
Leisler, Mount, mtn., Austl.	D6	74
Leitariegos, Puerto de, p., Spain	A4	20
Leitha (Lajta), stm., Eur.	H12	16
Lesbos see Lésvos, i., Grc.	D9	28
Leitrim, state, Ire.	H5	12
Leivádia, Grc.	E5	28
Leiyang, China	H5	42
Leizhou, Col.	H5	42
Leizhou Bandao, pen., China	K3	42
Lejasciems, Lat.	C9	10
Lejasnieki, Lat.	D9	10
Lekitobi, Spain	A8	20
Lekoskozero, ozero, l., Russia	E14	8
Leksvik, Nor.	E4	8
Leland, Il., U.S.	C9	120
Leland, Mi., U.S.	C4	112
Leland, Ms., U.S.	D8	122
Leleiwi Point, c., Hi., U.S.	D7	78a
Leleque, Arg.	H2	90
Leles, Indon.	G5	50
Lesnoe, Russia	B18	10
Le Locle, Switz.	C3	22
Leli Shan, mtn., China	B8	54
Le Maire, Estrecho de, strt., Arg.	J4	90
Le Mans, Fr.	G9	14
Le Marin, Mart.	l7	105c
Lema Shilindi, Eth.	G8	62
Lembak, Indon.	C10	50
Lemdiyya, Alg.	H13	20
Le Mée, Braz.	L2	88
Lemesós (Limassol), Cyp.	D4	58
Lemhi, stm., Id., U.S.	F13	136
Lemhi Pass, p., U.S.	F13	136
Lemhi Range, mts., Id., U.S.	F13	136
Lemieux Islands, is., Nu., Can.	E13	141
Leming, Tx., U.S.	E9	130
Lemitar, N.M., U.S.	I10	132
Lemmatsi, Est.	B9	10
Lemmenjoen kansallispuisto, p.o.i., Fin.	B11	8
Lemmon, S.D., U.S.	B10	126
Lemmon, Mount, mtn., Az., U.S.	K6	132
Lemnos see Límnos, i., Grc.	D8	28
Lemoncove, Ca., U.S.	G7	134
Le Mont-Dore, N. Cal.	n16	79d
Lemoore, Ca., U.S.	G6	134
Le Moule, Guad.	h6	105c
Lempa, stm., N.A.	F3	102
Lempe, Indon.	D12	50
Lemro, stm., Mya.	B1	48
Le Murge, hills, Italy	D10	24
Le Muy, Fr.	F12	18
Lemyethna, Mya.	D2	48
Lena, Il., U.S.	B8	120
Lena, stm., Russia	B14	34
Lenart, Slvn.	D12	22
Lençóis, Braz.	G5	88
Lençóis Maranhenses, Parque Nacional dos, p.o.i., Braz.	B4	88
Lendery, Russia	E14	8
Lendinara, Italy	E8	22
Lenger, Kaz.	F12	32
Lenggong, stm., Malay.	K6	48
Lenghu, China	D3	36
Lenghuzhen, China	H4	42
Lenhovda, Swe.	H6	8
Leningrad see Sankt-Peterburg, Russia	A13	10
Leningradskaja oblast', co., Russia	G15	8
Leninogorsk see Leninogorsk, Kaz.	D14	32
Leninogorsk, Kaz.	D14	32
Lenin Peak, mtn., Asia	B10	32
Leninsk, Uzb.	F10	32
Leninskij, Russia	F20	10
Leninsk-Kuzneckij, Russia	D15	34
Leninskoe, Russia	G15	34
Lennox, Ga., U.S.	E2	116
Lennox, Isla, i., Chile	K3	90
Lennoxville, Qc., Can.	E5	110
Lenoir, N.C., U.S.	I4	114
Lenoir City, Tn., U.S.	I1	114
Lenora, Kansas	B9	128
Lenox, Ga., U.S.	E2	116
Lenox, Ia., U.S.	D3	120
Lens, Fr.	D11	14
Lensk, Russia	B20	34
Lent, Hung.	C3	26
Lentini, Italy	G9	24
Lenya, stm., Mya.	G4	48
Léo, Burkina	G4	64
Léogâne, Haiti	C11	102
Leola, Ar., U.S.	C6	122
Leola, S.D., U.S.	B14	126
Leominster, Eng., U.K.	I10	12
Leominster, Ma., U.S.	B14	114
León, Fr.	F4	18
León, Mex.	E8	100
León, Nic.	F4	102
León, Spain	B5	20
León, Ks., U.S.	D12	128
León, co., Spain	B5	20
León, Montes de, mts., Spain	B4	20
Leona, stm., Tx., U.S.	F8	130
Leonard, Tx., U.S.	D2	122
Leonardtown, Md., U.S.	F9	114
Leonardville, Ks., U.S.	B11	128
Leonberg, Ger.	H4	16
Leones, Arg.	F6	92
Leonforte, Italy	G8	24
Leongatha, Austl.	L5	76
Leonora, Austl.	E4	74
Leopold and Astrid Coast, cst., Ant.	B13	81
Leopoldina, Braz.	K4	88
Leopoldo de Bulhões, Braz.	I1	88
Léopoldville see Kinshasa, D.R.C.	E3	66
Leoti, Ks., U.S.	C7	128
Leova, Mol.	C15	26
Lepar, Pulau, i., Indon.	E5	50
Lepe, Spain	G3	20
Lepel', Bela.	F11	10
L'Épiphanie, Qc., Can.	E3	110
Lepontine Alps, mts., Eur.	C14	18
Lepreau, Point, c., N.B.,	E10	110
Leptis, hist., Phil.	E5	52
Lepsi see Lepsy, Kaz.	E13	32
Lepsy, Kaz.	E13	32
Le Puy, Fr.	D9	18
Lequeitio see Lekeitio, Spain	A8	20
Lercara Friddi, Italy	G7	24
Lerdo, Mex.	C7	100
Lerici, Italy	F6	22
Lérida, Col.	G6	86
Lérida see Lleida, Spain	C11	20
Lerma, stm., Mex.	E8	100
Le Roy, Il., U.S.	D9	120
Le Roy, Ks., U.S.	F2	120
Le Roy, N.Y., U.S.	B7	114
Lerum, Swe.	H5	8
Lerwick, Scot., U.K.	n18	12a
Les Abymes, Guad.	h6	105c
Le Saint-Esprit, Mart.	k7	105c
Les Andelys, Fr.	E10	14
Les Anses-d'Arlets, Mart.	l6	105c
Les Borges Blanques, Spain	C11	20
Les Cayes, Haiti	C11	102
Leshan, China	F5	36
Les Herbiers, Fr.	H7	14
Lesina, Lago di, b., Italy	I12	22
Leskovac, Pol.	G18	16
Leskovac, Yugo.	F8	26
Leskov Island, i., S. Geor.	K12	82
Les Laurentides see Laurentides, Les, plat., Qc., Can.	F16	106
Leslie, Ar., U.S.	I5	120
Leslie, Mi., U.S.	B1	114
Leslie, W.V., U.S.	F5	114
Lesnoe, Russia	B18	10
Lesogorsk, Russia	G7	34
Lesosibirsk, Russia	E7	34
Lesotho, ctry., Afr.	F9	70
Lesozavodsk, Russia	B10	38
Lesozavodskij, Russia	C15	8
Les Sables-d'Olonne, Fr.	H7	14
Les Saintes, is., Guad.	i5	105c
Lesser Antilles, is.	D8	82
Lesser Khingan Range see Xiao Hinggan Ling, mts., China	B10	36
Lesser Slave, stm., Ab., Can.	A16	138
Lesser Slave Lake, l., Ab., Can.	D8	106
Lesser Sunda Islands see Tenggara, Nusa, is., Indon.	G6	44
L'Esterre, Gren.	q10	105e
Lestock, Sk., Can.	C9	124
Le Sueur, Mn., U.S.	G4	118
Le Sueur, stm., Mn., U.S.	G5	118
Lešukonskoe, Russia	D21	8
Lésvos (Lesbos), i., Grc.	D9	28
Leszno, Pol.	E12	16
Leszno, state, Pol.	E12	16
Letaba, stm., S. Afr.	C10	70
Letcher, S.D., U.S.	D14	126
Letea, Ostrovul, i., Rom.	D16	26
Lethbridge, Ab., Can.	G18	138
Lethem, Guy.	F12	86
Le Thillot, Fr.	B12	18
Leti, Kepulauan, is., Indon.	G8	44
Leticia, Col.	D4	84
Letlhakane, Bots.	B7	70
Letlhakeng, Bots.	D7	70
Letnjaja Zolotica, Russia	D17	8
Letong, Indon.	B5	50
Le Tréport, Fr.	D10	14
Letsôk-aw Kyun, i., Mya.	G3	48
Letung, Indon.	B5	50
Leucate, Étang de, l., Fr.	G9	18
Leuk, Switz.	D4	22
Leuser, Gunung, mtn., Indon.	K3	48
Leutkirch, Ger.	I6	16
Leuven, Bel.	D13	14
Levack, On., Can.	B8	112
Levan, Ut., U.S.	D5	132
Levanger, Nor.	E4	8
Levant, Riviera du, cst., Italy	F6	22
Levanzo, Isola di, i., Italy	F6	24
Le Vauclin, Mart.	k7	105c
Levelland, Tx., U.S.	H6	128
Leveque, Cape, c., Austl.	C4	74
Leverkusen, Ger.	E2	16
Levice, Slov.	H14	16
Levin, N.Z.	E6	80
Levisa Fork, stm., U.S.	G3	114
Levittown, P.R.	B3	104a
Levittown, N.Y., U.S.	D12	114
Levkosia see Nicosia, Cyp.	C4	58
Levoča, Slov.	H16	16
Levski, Blg.	F12	26
Levuka, Fiji	p19	79e
L'vuo, stm., Lith.	E7	10
Lewe, Mya.	C2	48
Lewellen, Ne., U.S.	F10	126
Lewes, Eng., U.K.	J13	12
Lewes, De., U.S.	F10	114
Lewin Brzeski, Pol.	F13	16
Lewis, Ia., U.S.	J3	118
Lewis, Butt of, c., Scot., U.K.	C6	12
Lewis, Isle of, i., Scot., U.K.	C6	12
Lewis, Mount, mtn., Nv., U.S.	C8	134
Lewis and Clark Lake, res., U.S.	E15	126
Lewis and Clark Range, mts., Mt., U.S.	C13	136
Lewisburg, Ky., U.S.	H10	120
Lewisburg, Pa., U.S.	D8	114
Lewisburg, Tn., U.S.	B12	122
Lewis Range, mts., N.A.	B13	136
Lewis Run, Pa., U.S.	C7	114
Lewis Smith Lake, res., Al., U.S.	C11	122
Lewiston, Ca., U.S.	C3	134
Lewiston, Id., U.S.	D10	136
Lewiston, Me., U.S.	F6	110
Lewiston, Mi., U.S.	D5	112
Lewiston, Mn., U.S.	H7	118
Lewiston Orchards, Id., U.S.	D10	136
Lewistown, Il., U.S.	D7	120
Lewistown, Mt., U.S.	C17	136
Lewistown, Pa., U.S.	D8	114
Lewisville, N.B., Can.	D12	110
Lewisville, Tx., U.S.	D5	122
Lewisville Lake, res., Tx., U.S.	H12	128
Lewvan, Sk., Can.	D9	124
Lignite, N.D., U.S.	F11	124
Lexington, Ga., U.S.	C2	116
Lexington, Il., U.S.	D9	120
Lexington, Ky., U.S.	F1	114
Lexington, Ma., U.S.	B14	114
Lexington, Mi., U.S.	E7	112
Lexington, Ms., U.S.	D8	122
Lexington, N.C., U.S.	I5	114
Lexington, Ok., U.S.	F11	128
Lexington, S.C., U.S.	B4	116
Lexington, Tx., U.S.	D10	130
Lexington, Va., U.S.	G6	114
Lexington Park, Md., U.S.	F9	114
Leyden see Leiden, Neth.	B13	14
Leye, China	I2	42
Leyte, i., Phil.	E5	52
Leyte Gulf, b., Phil.	E5	52
Lezhë, Alb.	C13	24
Lezhi, China	F1	42
L'gov, Russia	D5	32
Lhasa, China	D13	54
Lhasa, stm., China	D13	54
Lhazê, China	D11	54
Lhoknga, Indon.	J2	48
Lhokseumawe, Indon.	J3	48
Lhoksukon, Indon.	J3	48
Lhorong, China	E4	36
L'Hospitalet de Llobregat, Spain	C13	20
Lhuntsi Dzong, Bhu.	E13	54
Li, Thai.	D4	48
Li, stm., China	I4	42
Li, stm., Thai.	D4	48
Liamuiga, Mount, vol., St. K./N.	C2	105a
Lian, stm., China	I5	42
Liancheng, China	I7	42
Lianga, Phil.	F6	52
Liangbao, China	D4	42
Liangbuaya, Indon.	C10	50
Liangdang, China	E1	42
Liangkeng, China	G3	42
Liangmentou, China	G9	42
Liangping, China	F2	42
Liangyuan, China	E7	42
Liangzi Hu, l., China	F6	42
Lianhe, China	H8	42
Lianhua Shan, mts., China	J6	42
Lianjiang, China	K4	42
Liannan, China	I5	42
Lianshui, China	E8	42
Lianxian, China	I5	42
Lianyuan, China	H4	42
Lianyungang, China	D8	42
Liao, stm., China	D5	38
Liaocheng, China	C7	42
Liaodong Bandao (Liaotung Peninsula), pen., China	D5	38
Liaodong Wan (Liaotung, Gulf of), b., China	A9	42
Liaoning, state, China	D5	38
Liaotung, Gulf of see Liaodong Wan, b., China	A9	42
Liaotung Peninsula see Liaodong Bandao, pen., China	E5	38
Liaoyang, China	D5	38
Liaozhong, China	D5	38
Liard, stm., Can.	C6	106
Liat, Pulau, i., Indon.	E5	50
Libano, Col.	E4	86
Libby, Mt., U.S.	B11	136
Libby Dam, dam, Mt., U.S.	B12	136
Libenge, D.R.C.	D3	66
Liberal, Ks., U.S.	D7	128
Liberal, Mo., U.S.	G3	120
Liberec, Czech Rep.	F11	16
Liberia, C.R.	G5	102
Liberia, ctry., Afr.	H3	64
Liberta, Antig.	f4	105b
Liberty, In., U.S.	E12	120
Liberty, Ky., U.S.	G13	120
Liberty, Mo., U.S.	E3	120
Liberty, N.Y., U.S.	C11	114
Liberty, N.C., U.S.	I6	114
Liberty, S.C., U.S.	B3	116
Liberty, Tx., U.S.	G4	122
Liberty Center, Oh., U.S.	C1	114
Libertyville, Il., U.S.	B9	120
Libjo, Phil.	E5	52
Libmod, Tanjung, c., Indon.	F8	44
Libode, S. Afr.	G9	70
Libourne, Fr.	E5	18
Librazhd, Alb.	C14	24
Libres, Mex.	F10	100
Libreville, Gabon	D1	66
Liburung, Indon.	F12	50
Libya, ctry., Afr.	B3	62
Libyan Desert, des., Afr.	C5	62
Libyan Plateau, plat., Afr.	A4	62
Licantén, Chile	G1	92
Licata, Italy	G7	24
Lich, Ger.	F4	16
Licheng see Liyang, China	F8	42
Lichfield, Eng., U.K.	I11	12
Lichinga, Moz.	C6	68
Lichtenau, Ger.	E4	16
Lichtenburg, S. Afr.	E7	70
Lichtenfels, Ger.	F7	16
Lichuan, China	F3	42
Lichuan, China	H7	42
Licking, Mo., U.S.	G6	120
Licking, stm., U.S.	F1	114
Ličko Polje, val., Cro.	F12	22
Lida, Bela.	G7	10
Lid Point, c., V.I.U.S.	e7	104b
Lidgerwood, N.D., U.S.	E1	118
Lidköping, Swe.	G5	8
Lido di Ostia, Italy	I9	22
Lidzbark, Pol.	C15	16
Lidzbark Warmiński, Pol.	B16	16
Liebenbergsvlei, stm., S. Afr.	E9	70
Liebig, Mount, mtn., Austl.	D6	74
Liège (Luik), Bel.	D14	14
Liepāja, Lat.	D4	10
Liepājas ezers, l., Lat.	D4	10
Lier, Bel.	C13	14
Lierre see Lier, Bel.	C13	14
Liestal, Switz.	C4	22
Liezen, Aus.	C11	22
Lièvre, stm., Qc., Can.	C14	112
Liezen, Aus.	C11	22
Liffey, stm., Ire.	H6	12
Lifford, Ire.	G5	12
Lifou, i., N. Cal.	m16	79d
Līgatne, Lat.	C7	10
Lighthouse Point, Fl., U.S.	J5	116
Lighthouse Point, c., Fl., U.S.	H14	122
Lighthouse Point, c., Fl.,	C4	112
Lightning Creek, stm., Wy., U.S.	D7	126
Lightning Ridge, Austl.	G6	76
Lignite, N.D., U.S.	F11	124
Ligny-en-Barrois, Fr.	F14	14
Ligonha, stm., Moz.	D6	68
Ligonier, In., U.S.	G4	112
Ligonier, Pa., U.S.	H10	112
Liguria, state, Italy	F5	22
Ligurian Sea, Eur.	G5	22
Lihir Island, i., Pap. N. Gui.	a5	79a
Lihou Reefs and Cays, rf., Austl.	A8	76
Lihue, Hi., U.S.	B2	78a
Lihuel Calel, Parque Nacional, p.o.i., Arg.	H5	92
Lihula, Est.	B6	10
Lijiang, China	F5	36
Lik, stm., Laos	C6	48
Likasi (Jadotville), D.R.C.	G5	66
Likati, D.R.C.	D4	66
Likely, B.C., Can.	D9	138
Liki, Indon.	D2	50
Likino-Dulevo, Russia	E21	10
Likoum, Mo., U.S.	H8	120
Lilibeo, Capo see Boeo, Capo, c., Italy	G6	24
Lilienfeld, Aus.	B12	22
Liling, China	H5	42
Lille, Fr.	D12	14
Lillebælt, strt., Den.	I3	8
Lillebonne, Fr.	E9	14
Lillers, Fr.	D11	14
Lillestrøm, Nor.	G4	8
Lillhärdal, Swe.	F6	8
Lillington, N.C., U.S.	A7	116
Lillooet, B.C., Can.	F9	138
Lillooet, stm., B.C., Can.	G8	138
Lillooet Lake, l., B.C., Can.	F8	138
Lilongwe, Mwi.	C5	68
Liloy, Phil.	F4	52
Lilydale, Austl.	n13	77a
Lim, stm., Eur.	G16	22
Lima, Para.	A9	92
Lima, Peru	F2	84
Lima, Mt., U.S.	F14	136
Lima, N.Y., U.S.	B8	114
Lima, Oh., U.S.	D1	114
Lima (Limia), stm., Eur.	C2	20
Liman, Russia	E7	32
Limanes, Chile	G1	92
Limas, Indon.	C4	50
Limassol see Lemesós, Cyp.	D4	58
Limavady, N. Ire., U.K.	F6	12
Limay, stm., Arg.	G3	90
Limay Mahuida, Arg.	H4	92
Limbang, stm., Malay.	A9	50
Limbani, India	G3	54
Limbe, Cam.	D1	66
Limbé, Haiti	C11	102
Limburg an der Lahn, Ger.	F4	16
Limbuhan see Pio V. Corpuz, Phil.	E5	52
Limeira, Braz.	L2	88
Limerick (Luimneach), Ire.	I4	12
Limerick, state, Ire.	I4	12
Limestone, Me., U.S.	D9	110
Limestone, Lake, res., Tx., U.S.	F2	122
Limfjorden, l., Den.	H3	8
Limia (Lima), stm., Eur.	C2	20
Limingen, l., Nor.	D5	8
Limmared, Swe.	H5	8
Limmen Bight, b., Austl.	B7	74
Limni, Grc.	E6	28
Limoeiro, Braz.	D8	88
Limoeiro do Norte, Braz.	C6	88
Limoges, Fr.	D7	18
Limón, Hond.	E5	102
Limón, C.R.	H6	102
Limone Piemonte, Italy	F4	22
Limoux, Fr.	G8	18
Limpopo, stm., Afr.	D10	70
Linahamari, Russia	B14	8
Lin'an, China	F8	42
Linapacan Island, i., Phil.	E2	52
Linares, Chile	G2	92
Linares, Mex.	C9	100
Linares, Spain	F7	20
Linch, Wy., U.S.	C6	126
Lincheng, China	C6	42
Linch'ing see Linqing, China	C6	42
Lincoln, Arg.	G7	92
Lincoln, Eng., U.K.	H12	12
Lincoln, Ca., U.S.	E4	134
Lincoln, Il., U.S.	D8	120
Lincoln, Ks., U.S.	B10	128
Lincoln, Me., U.S.	E8	110
Lincoln, Mt., U.S.	D14	136
Lincoln, N.H., U.S.	F5	110
Lincoln, Mount, mtn., Co., U.S.	B2	128
Lincoln City, Or., U.S.	F2	136
Lincoln Creek, stm., Ne., U.S.	F15	126
Lincoln Park, Co., U.S.	C3	128
Lincoln Park, Mi., U.S.	B2	114
Lincoln Sea, Arctic Ocean	A13	141
Lincolnton, Ga., U.S.	C3	116
Lincolnton, N.C., U.S.	A4	116
Lincoln Village, Ca., U.S.	E4	134
Lindale, Ga., U.S.	C13	122
Lindale, Tx., U.S.	E3	122
Linden, Guy.	B6	84
Linden, Al., U.S.	E11	122
Linden, Tn., U.S.	B10	122
Lindesnes, c., Nor.	H2	8
Lindi, Tan.	F7	66
Lindi, stm., D.R.C.	D5	66
Lindian, China	B10	38
Lindong see Bairin Zuoqi, China	C2	38
Lindsay, On., Can.	D11	112
Lindsay, Ca., U.S.	G7	134
Lindsay, Ok., U.S.	G11	128
Lindsborg, Ks., U.S.	C11	128
Lindsdal, Swe.	H7	8
Linde, stm., Russia	C13	34
Lingamakki Reservoir, res., India	D2	53
Lingao, China	L3	42
Lingayen, Phil.	B3	52
Lingayen Gulf, b., Phil.	B3	52
Lingbi, China	E7	42
Lingbo, Swe.	F7	8
Lingchuan, China	I3	42

Name	Map Ref.	Page

Lingen, Ger. — D3 16
Lingfengwei, China — I6 42
Lingga, Kepulauan, is., Indon. — C4 50
Lingga, Pulau, i., Indon. — C4 50
Linggo II, D.R.C. — D4 56
Lingqiu, China — B6 42
Lingshan, China — J3 42
Lingshi, China — C4 42
Lingshui, China — L4 42
Linguère, Sen. — F2 64
Lingwu, China — B2 42
Lingxian, China — H5 42
Lingyuan, China — A8 42
Linh, Ngoc, mtn., Viet. — E9 48
Linhai, China — G9 42
Linhares, Braz. — J5 88
Linhe, China — A2 42
Linhsia see Linxia, China — D5 36
Lini see Linyi, China — D8 42
Linjiang, China — D7 38
Linköping, Swe. — G6 8
Linkou, China — B9 38
Linksmakalnis, Lith. — F6 10
Linkuva, Lith. — D6 10
Linn, Ks., U.S. — B11 128
Linn, Mo., U.S. — F6 120
Linnansaaren kansallispuisto, p.o.i., Fin. — E13 8
Linnhe, Loch, b., Scot., U.K. — E7 12
Linqi, China — D5 42
Linqing, China — C6 42
Linqu, China — C8 42
Linquan, China — E6 42
Linru, China — D5 42
Lins, Braz. — K1 88
Linstead, Jam. — i13 104d
Lintan, China — E5 36
Linton, In., U.S. — E10 120
Linton, N.D., U.S. — A12 126
Lintong, China — D3 42
Linwu, China — I5 42
Linxi, China — C8 36
Linxi, China — C3 38
Linxia, China — D5 36
Linxian, China — C4 42
Linxian, China — C4 42
Linyi, China — D8 42
Linyi, China — C7 42
Linyü see Shanhaiguan, China — A8 42
Linz, Aus. — B11 22
Lio Matoh, Malay. — B9 50
Lion, Golfe du, b., Fr. — G10 18
Lion, Gulf of see Lion, Golfe du, g., Fr. — G10 18
Lionel Town, Jam. — j13 104d
Liouesso, Congo — D3 66
Lipa, Phil. — D3 52
Lipan, Tx., U.S. — B9 130
Lipari, Italy — F8 24
Lipari, Isola, i., Italy — F9 24
Lipari, Isole see Eolie, Isole, is., Italy — F8 24
Lipcani, Mol. — A13 26
Lipeck, Russia — D6 32
Lipez, Cerro, mtn., Bol. — D3 90
Lipicy, Russia — G20 10
Liping, China — H3 42
Lipki, Russia — G20 10
Lipník nad Bečvou, Czech Rep. — G13 16
Lipno, Pol. — D15 16
Lipno, údolní nádrž, res., Czech Rep. — H10 16
Lipova, Rom. — C8 26
Lipovcy, Russia — B9 38
Lippe, stm., Ger. — E2 16
Lippstadt, Ger. — E4 16
Lipscomb, Tx., U.S. — E8 128
Lipu, China — I3 42
Liuchew see Liuzhou, China — I3 42
Liucura, Chile — I2 92
Liufang, China — H7 42
Liuhe, China — C6 38
Liuhe Dao, i., China — G10 42
Liujiazi, China — A9 42
Liupan Shan, mts., China — D2 42
Liushuquan, China — F16 32
Liuxi, China — J5 42
Liuyang, China — G5 42
Liuyang, stm., China — G5 42
Liuzhou, China — I3 42
Livada, Rom. — B10 26
Livadija, Russia — C10 38
Livadija, Russia — D9 10
Livany, Lat. — D9 10
Livanjsko Polje, val., Bos. — F3 26
Lively, On., Can. — B8 112
Lively Island, i., Falk. Is. — J5 90
Live Oak, Ca., U.S. — D4 134
Live Oak, Fl., U.S. — F2 116
Liveringa, Austl. — C4 74
Livermore, Ca., U.S. — F4 134
Livermore, Ia., U.S. — B3 120
Livermore, Ky., U.S. — G10 120
Livermore, Mount, mtn., Tx., U.S. — D3 130
Livermore Falls, Me., U.S. — F6 110
Liverpool, N.S., Can. — F12 110
Liverpool, Eng., U.K. — H10 12
Liverpool, Cape, c., Nu., Can. — C10 141
Liverpool Bay, b., N.T., Can. — A5 106
Liverpool Bay, b., Eng., U.K. — H9 12
Livingston, Guat. — E3 102
Livingston, Al., U.S. — E10 122
Livingston, Il., U.S. — F8 120
Livingston, La., U.S. — G8 122
Livingston, Mt., U.S. — E16 136
Livingston, Tn., U.S. — H12 120
Livingston, Tx., U.S. — G4 122
Livingston, Lake, res., Tx., U.S. — G3 122
Livingston, Zam. — D4 68
Livingstone see Maramba, Zam. — D4 68
Livingstone Falls, wtfl, Afr. — A1 68
Livingstonia, Mwi. — C5 68
Livingston Manor, N.Y., U.S. — C11 114
Livny, Russia — H20 10
Livonia, La., U.S. — G7 122
Livonia, Mi., U.S. — B2 114
Livonia, N.Y., U.S. — B8 114
Livorno (Leghorn), Italy — G7 22
Livramento do Brumado, Braz. — G5 88
Liwale, Tan. — F7 66
Lixi, China — F5 36
Lixian, China — G4 42
Lixian see Black, stm., Asia — D9 56
Lixin, China — E7 42
Lixoúri, Grc. — E3 28
Liyang, China — F8 42
Lizarda, Braz. — E2 88
Lizard Point, c., Eng., U.K. — L7 12
Lizarra see Estella, Spain — B8 20
Ljady, Bela. — F14 10
Ljahavičy, Bela. — G9 10
Ljamca, Russia — D17 8
Ljaskavičy, Bela. — H11 10
Ljasnaja, Bela. — H8 10
Ljuban', Bela. — H10 10
Ljubercy, Russia — E20 10
Ljubešiv, Ukr. — C1 16
Ljubim, Russia — B18 8
Ljubinci, Russia — B17 34
Ljubljana, Slvn. — D11 22
Ljubno, Russia — C15 10
Ljubohna, Russia — G17 10
Ljubuški, Bos. — F3 26
Ljudinovo, Russia — G17 10
Ljudkovo, Russia — F17 10

Little Deep Creek, stm., N.D., U.S. — F12 124
Little Deschutes, stm., Or., U.S. — G5 136
Little Desert, des., Austl. — K3 76
Little Desert National Park, p.o.i., Austl. — K3 76
Little Dry Creek, stm., Mt., U.S. — G7 124
Little Falls, Mn., U.S. — E4 118
Little Falls, N.Y., U.S. — E15 112
Littlefork, Mn., U.S. — C5 118
Little Fork, stm., Mn., U.S. — C5 118
Little Hurricane Creek, stm., Ga., U.S. — E3 116
Little Inagua, i., Bah. — B11 102
Little Karroo (Klein Karroo), plat., S. Afr. — H5 70
Little Lake, i., La., U.S. — H8 122
Little London, Jam. — i12 104d
Little Lost, stm., Id., U.S. — F13 136
Little Mexico, Tx., U.S. — D4 130
Little Missouri, stm., U.S. — B7 108
Little Missouri, stm., Ar., U.S. — D5 122
Little Namaqualand (Klein Namaland), hist. reg., S. Afr. — F3 70
Little Nicobar, i., India — G7 46
Little Osage, stm., U.S. — G3 120
Little Pee Dee, stm., S.C., U.S. — B6 116
Little Pic, stm., On., Can. — C12 118
Little Powder, stm., U.S. — B7 126
Little Quill Lake, l., Sk., Can. — C10 124
Little Rann of Kachchh, reg., India — G3 54
Little Red, stm., Ar., U.S. — B7 122
Little Red, Middle Fork, stm., Ar., U.S. — B6 122
Little Red Deer, stm., Ab., Can. — E16 138
Little River, Ks., U.S. — C10 128
Little Rock, Ar., U.S. — C6 122
Little Rock, stm., U.S. — H2 118
Little Sable Point, c., Mi., U.S. — E3 112
Little Saint Bernard Pass, p., Eur. — D12 18
Little Sandy Creek, stm., Wy., U.S. — E3 126
Little Sioux, stm., U.S. — J3 118
Little Sioux, West Fork, stm., Ia., U.S. — B2 120
Little Smoky, stm., Ab., Can. — A14 138
Little Snake, stm., U.S. — C8 132
Littlestown, Pa., U.S. — E8 114
Little Tallapoosa, stm., U.S. — D13 122
Little Tennessee, stm., U.S. — A1 116
Little Tobago, i., Trin. — r13 105f
Littleton, Co., U.S. — B3 128
Littleton, N.H., U.S. — F5 110
Littleton, W.V., U.S. — E5 114
Little Valley, N.Y., U.S. — B7 114
Little Wabash, stm., U.S. — F9 120
Little White, stm., S.D., U.S. — D12 126
Little Wood, stm., Id., U.S. — G12 136
Litvínov, Czech Rep. — F9 16
Liu, stm., China — C6 38
Liu, stm., China — C5 38
Liu, stm., China — I3 42
Liuaniua see Ontong Java, at., Sol. Is. — D7 72
Liuba, China — E2 42
Liuboml', Ukr. — E20 16
Liuchew see Liuzhou, China — I3 42
Liucheng, China — I3 42
Liucura, Chile — I2 92
Liufang, China — H7 42
Liuhe, China — C6 38
Liuhe Dao, i., China — G10 42
Liujiazi, China — A9 42
Liupan Shan, mts., China — D2 42
Liushuquan, China — F16 32
Liuxi, China — J5 42
Liuyang, China — G5 42
Liuyang, stm., China — G5 42
Liuzhou, China — I3 42
Livada, Rom. — B10 26
Livadija, Russia — C10 38

Ljungan, stm., Swe. — E5 8
Ljungby, Swe. — H5 8
Ljusdal, Swe. — F7 8
Ljusina, Bela. — H9 10
Ljusnan, stm., Swe. — F6 8
Llancanelo, Laguna, l., Arg. — G3 92
Llandeilo, Wales, U.K. — J8 12
Llandindod Wells, Wales, U.K. — I9 12
Llandudno, Wales, U.K. — H9 12
Llanelli, Wales, U.K. — J8 12
Llanfairfechan, Wales, U.K. — H8 12
Llanidloes, Wales, U.K. — I9 12
Llano, Tx., U.S. — D8 130
Llano Colorado, Mex. — L9 134
Llanos, pl., S.A. — E7 86
Llanquihue, Lago, l., Chile — H2 90
Llata, Peru — C11 20
Lledr, stm., Wales, U.K. — H9 12
Lleida, Spain — C11 20
Lleida, co., Spain — B12 20
Llera de Canales, Mex. — D9 100
Llerena, Spain — F4 20
Lleulleu, Lago, l., Chile — I1 32
Llico, Chile — G1 32
Llíria, Spain — E10 20
Llivia, Spain — B12 20
Llobregat, stm., Spain — C12 20
Lloydminster, Sk., Can. — E9 106
Llucena, Spain — D10 20
Lluchmayor see Llucmajor, Spain — E13 20
Llucmajor, Spain — E13 20
Llullaillaco, Volcán, vol., S.A. — B3 92
Loa, Ut., U.S. — E5 132
Loa, stm., Chile — D3 90
Loanda, Braz. — A13 92
Loange (Luangue), stm., Afr. — F3 66
Lobamba, Swaz. — E10 70
Lobanovo, Russia — G21 10
Lobatse, Bots. — D7 70
Löbau, Ger. — E10 16
Lobaye, stm., C.A.R. — D3 66
Lobelville, Tn., U.S. — B11 122
Loberia, Arg. — I8 92
Lobnja, Russia — D20 10
Lobos, Arg. — G8 92
Lobos, Cay, i., Bah. — A9 102
Lobos, Isla, i., Mex. — B5 100
Lobskoe, Russia — E16 8
Łobżenica, Pol. — C13 16
Locarno, Switz. — D5 22
Loches, Fr. — G10 14
Loch Garman see Wexford, Ire. — I6 12
Lochinver, Scot., U.K. — C7 12
Lochsa, stm., Id., U.S. — D12 136
Lock, Austl. — F7 74
Lockeport, N.S., Can. — G11 110
Lockerbie, Scot., U.K. — F9 12
Lockesburg, Ar., U.S. — D4 122
Lockhart, Austl. — J6 76
Lock Haven, Pa., U.S. — C8 114
Lockney, Tx., U.S. — G7 128
Lockport, La., U.S. — H8 122
Lockport, N.Y., U.S. — C9 120
Locknock, stm., Austl. — K4 73
Lodève, Fr. — F9 13
Lodge Creek, stm., N.A. — F4 124
Lodge Grass, Mt., U.S. — B5 126
Lodgepole, Ab., Can. — C15 138
Lodgepole Creek, stm., U.S. — F10 126
Lodhrān, Pak. — D3 54
Lodi, Italy — E6 22
Lodi, Ca., U.S. — E4 134
Lodi, Wi., U.S. — H9 118
Lodja, D.R.C. — E4 66
Łodwar, Kenya — D7 66
Łódź, Pol. — E15 16
Łódź, state, Pol. — E15 16
Loei, Thai. — D5 48
Loeriesfontein, S. Afr. — G4 70
Lofer, Austl. — C8 22
Lofoten, is., Nor. — B5 8
Lofoten Basin, unds. — A14 144
Loga, Niger — G5 64
Logan, Ia., U.S. — C2 120
Logan, Ks., U.S. — B9 128
Logan, Oh., U.S. — E3 114
Logan, Ut., U.S. — B5 132
Logan, W.V., U.S. — G4 114
Logan, Mount, mtn., Yk., Can. — C2 106
Logan Creek, stm., Ne., U.S. — C15 126
Logan Island, i., On., Can. — A10 118
Logan Martin Lake, res., Al., U.S. — D12 122
Logan Mountains, mts., Yk., Can. — C5 106
Logan Pass, p., Mt., U.S. — B13 136
Logansport, In., U.S. — H3 112
Logansport, La., U.S. — F5 122
Loganville, Ga., U.S. — C2 116
Logone, stm., Afr. — F3 62
Logroño, Spain — B8 20
Logudoro, reg., Italy — D2 24
Lohārdaga, India — G10 54
Lohiniva, Fin. — C11 8
Lohne, Ger. — D4 16
Loho see Luohe, China — E6 42
Lohrville, Ia., U.S. — B3 120
Loi-Sault, On., Can. — E2 110
Loi (Nanlei), stm., Asia — A9 48
Loi, Phou, mtn., Laos — B6 48
Loikaw, Mya. — C3 48
Loi Mwe, Mya. — B4 48
Loing, stm., Fr. — F11 14
Loing, Canal du, can., Fr. — F11 14
Loir, stm., Fr. — G8 14
Loir-et-Cher, state, Fr. — G10 14
Loire, stm., Fr. — B4 18
Loire, Canal latéral à la, can., Fr. — G11 14
Loire-Atlantique, state, Fr. — G7 14
Loiret, state, Fr. — F11 14
Loja, Ec. — D2 84
Loja, Spain — G6 20
Loja, state, Ec. — D2 84
Lokan Reservoir see Lokan tekojärvi, res., Fin. — C12 8
Lokan tekojärvi, res., Fin. — C12 8
Lokeren, Bel. — C13 14
Loket, Czech Rep. — F8 16
Lokichokio, Kenya — D6 66
Lokja, Nig. — H6 64
Loknja, Russia — D13 10
Loknja, stm., Russia — D13 10
Lokolama, D.R.C. — E13 10
Lokot', Russia — H17 10
Loksa, Est. — A8 10
Lokshu, China — E13 10
Lol, stm., Sudan — F5 62
Lola, Gui. — H3 64
Loleta, Ca., U.S. — C1 134
Loliondo, Tan. — E7 66
Lolita, Tx., U.S. — F11 130
Lolland, i., Den. — I4 8
Lolo, Mt., U.S. — D12 136
Llodorf, Cam. — C2 66
Lolo Pass, p., U.S. — D12 136
Lolowai, Vanuatu — j16 79c

Loltong, Vanuatu — j16 79d
Loivavana, Passage, strt., Vanuatu — j16 79d
Lom, Blg. — F10 26
Lomami, stm., D.R.C. — C4 66
Lomax, I., U.S. — D6 120
Lomazy, Pol. — E19 16
Lombarda, state, Italy — E6 22
Lombardy see Lombardia, state, Italy — E6 22
Lomblen, Pulau, i., Indon. — G7 44
Lombok, Indon. — H10 50
Lombok, i., Indon. — H10 50
Lombok, Selat, strt., Indon. — H9 50
Lomé, Togo — H5 64
Lomela, D.R.C. — E4 66
Lomela, stm., D.R.C. — E4 66
Lometa, Tx., U.S. — C8 130
Lomié, Cam. — D2 66
Lomira, Wi., U.S. — H10 118
Lommel, Bel. — C14 14
Lomond, Loch, l., Scot., U.K. — E8 12
Lomonosov, Russia — A12 10
Lomonosovka, Kaz. — D11 32
Lomovoe, Russia — D13 8
Lompoc, Ca., U.S. — I5 134
Lomsak, Thai. — D5 48
Łomża, Pol. — C18 16
Łomża, state, Pol. — C18 16
Lonaconing, Md., U.S. — E7 114
Lonavale, India — B1 53
Loncoche, Chile — G2 90
Loncopué, Arg. — I2 92
London, On., Can. — F8 112
London, Eng., U.K. — J12 12
London, Ar., U.S. — B5 122
London, Ky., U.S. — G1 114
London, Tx., U.S. — D8 130
Londonderry, N.S., Can. — E13 110
Londonderry (Derry), N. Ire., U.K. — F6 12
Londonderry, Cape, c., Austl. — B5 74
Londonderry, N.B., Can. — C1 16
Londonderry, Isla, i., Chile — K2 90
Londrina, Braz. — D6 90
Lone Grove, Ok., U.S. — G11 128
Lone Oak, Ky., U.S. — G9 120
Lone Pine, Ca., U.S. — G7 134
Lone Rock, Wi., U.S. — A7 120
Lone Tree, Ia., U.S. — C6 120
Lone Wolf, Ok., U.S. — G9 128
Long, stm., China — I3 42
Longa, Arg. — G2 92
Longá, stm., Braz. — B6 88
Longa, proliv, strt., Russia — B24 34
Long Akah, Malay. — B9 50
Longana, Vanuatu — j17 79d
Longarone, Italy — D9 22
Longavi, Chile — G2 92
Longbangun, Indon. — C9 50
Long Bay, b., N.A. — J7 134
Long Beach, Ca., U.S. — J8 134
Long Beach, Ms., U.S. — G9 122
Long Beach, N.Y., U.S. — D12 114
Long Beach, Wa., U.S. — D2 136
Long Beach, cst., N.J., U.S. — E11 114
Longboat Key, Fl., U.S. — I3 116
Long Branch, N.J., U.S. — D12 114
Long Cay, i., Bah. — m18 104f
Long Cay, i., Ban. — C11 102
Longchuan, China — I6 42
Long Creek, stm., N.A. — E10 124
Long Eaton, Eng., U.K. — I11 12
Longford, Austl. — L6 76
Longford, Ire. — H5 12
Longford, state, Ire. — H5 12
Long Hu, i., China — A7 42
Longhua, China — H4 42
Longhui, China — H4 42
Longiram, Indon. — C9 50
Long Island, i., Antig. — f4 105b
Long Island, i., Austl. — C9 74
Long Island, i., Bah. — A10 102
Long Island, i., Nu., Can. — E14 106
Long Island, i., N.Y., U.S. — D12 114
Long Island Sound, strt., U.S. — D12 114
Longjiang, China — B9 36
Longkou, China — C9 42
Long Lake, N.Y., U.S. — G2 110
Long Lake, l., On., Can. — B11 118
Longleaf, La., U.S. — F6 122
Long Leaf Park, N.C., U.S. — B8 116
Longli, China — H2 42
Longli, China — G6 36
Longling, China — G4 36
Longlin, China — I1 42
Long Moc, Viet. — C7 48
Longmont, Co., U.S. — A3 128
Long Mountain, mtn., Mo., U.S. — H5 120
Long Pass, p., Mt., U.S. — B9 124
Longnawan, Indon. — C9 42
Long Pine, Ne., U.S. — E13 126
Long Point, c., Bah. — m18 104f
Long Point, c., N.S., Can. — D16 110
Long Point, c., Mb., Can. — A15 124
Long Point, pen., On., Can. — F9 112
Long Point Bay, b., On., Can. — F9 112
Longquan, China — G8 42
Long Range Mountains, mts., Nf., Can. — j22 107a
Longreach, Austl. — D5 76
Long-Sault, On., Can. — E2 110
Longsheng, China — I3 42
Longshan, China — G3 42
Longsheng, China — I3 42
Loué, stm., Fr. — H14 14
Long Swamp, Br. Vir. Is. — e8 104b
Long Thanh, Viet. — G8 48
Longtown, Eng., U.K. — F10 12
Longuyon, Fr. — E14 14
Longueau, Fr. — E11 14
Longueuil, Qc., Can. — E3 110
Long View, N.C., U.S. — I4 114
Long View, Tx., U.S. — E4 122
Longwai, Indon. — C10 50
Longxi, China — E5 36
Long Xuyen, Viet. — G7 48
Longyan, China — I7 42
Longyou, China — G8 42
Longzhou, China — J2 42

Lookout Ridge, mts., Ak., U.S. — C8 140
Loolmalassin, vol., Tan. — E7 66
Loomis, Ne., U.S. — G13 126
Loomis, Wa., U.S. — B7 136
Loon, China — A5 46
Loop, Tx., U.S. — B5 130
Loop Head, c., Ire. — I2 12
Lop, China — A5 46
Lop, stm., Viet. — F8 48
Lopatina, gora, mtn., Russia — F17 34
Lopatka, mys, c., Russia — F20 34
Lopatovo, Russia — D12 10
Lop Buri, Thai. — E5 48
Lopévi, i., Vanuatu — k17 79d
Lop Nur, l., China — C3 36
Lopez, Cap, c., Gabon — E1 66
Lopez, Cap, c., Gabon — E1 66
Lopon, China — A5 46
Loptjuga, Russia — E22 8
Lora del Río, Spain — G5 20
Lorain, Oh., U.S. — C3 114
Loraine, Tx., U.S. — B7 130
Loralai, Pak. — C2 54
Lorca, Spain — G9 20
Lord Howe Island, i., Austl. — G6 72
Lord Howe Rise, unds. — L19 142
Lord Mayor Bay, b., Nu., Can. — B12 106
Lordsburg, N.M., U.S. — K8 132
Lóvenice, Czech Rep. — F9 16
Lovozero, Russia — D13 8
Lovozero, ozero, l., Russia — C16 8
Lóvua, Ang. — B3 68
Low, Qc., Can. — C14 112
Low, Cape, c., Nu., Can. — C13 106
Lowa, D.R.C. — E5 66
Lowa, stm., D.R.C. — E5 66
Lowden, Ia., U.S. — C7 120
Lowell, Ar., U.S. — H3 120
Lowell, In., U.S. — G2 112
Lowell, Ma., U.S. — B14 114
Lowell, Or., U.S. — G4 136
Lowell, Vt., U.S. — F4 110
Lowell, Lake, res., Id., U.S. — G10 136
Löwen, stm., Nmb. — E3 70
Löwenberg, Ger. — D8 16
Lower Arrow Lake, res., B.C., Can. — G12 138
Lower Austria see Niederösterreich, state, Aus. — B12 22
Lower California see Baja California, pen., Mex. — B2 98
Lower Egypt see Misr el-Bahri, hist. reg., Fr. — G2 53
Lower Glenelg National Park, p.o.i., Austl. — L3 76
Lower Hutt, N.Z. — E6 80
Lower Lake, l., U.S. — B5 134
Lower Manitou Lake, l., On., Can. — B6 118
Lower Post, B.C., Can. — D5 106
Lower Red Lake, l., Mn., U.S. — D3 118
Lower Saxony see Niedersachsen, state, Ger. — D4 16
Lower Trajan's Wall, misc. cult., Eur. — D15 26
Lower West End Point, c., Anguilla — A1 105a
Lower Woods Harbour, N.S., Can. — G10 110
Lowestoft, Eng., U.K. — I14 12
Lowgar, state, Afg. — A2 54
Łowicz, Pol. — D15 16
Lowmoor, Va., U.S. — G6 114
Low Rocky Point, c., Austl. — o12 77a
Łowyn, Pol. — D18 16
Łosice, Pol. — D18 16
Lowry City, Mo., U.S. — F4 120
Lowville, N.Y., U.S. — E14 112
Loxton, Austl. — J3 76
Loyal, Wi., U.S. — G8 118
Loyalton, Ca., U.S. — D5 134
Loyalty Islands see Loyauté, Îles, is., N. Cal. — m16 79d
Loyang see Luoyang, China — D5 42
Loyauté, Îles (Loyalty Islands), is., N. Cal. — m16 79d
Loyoro, Ug. — D6 66
Lozère, state, Fr. — E9 18
Loznica, Yugo. — E6 26
Lualaba, stm., Afr. — E5 66
Lualaba, stm., Afr. — E5 66
Lu'an, China — F7 42
Luan, stm., China — E3 38
Luancheng, China — J3 42
Luanda, Ang. — B1 68
Luando, stm., Ang. — C2 68
Luang, Khao (Maw Taung), mtn., Asia — G4 48
Luang, Thale, l., Thai. — I5 48
Luang Chiang Dao, Doi, mtn., Thai. — C4 48
Luanginga, stm., Afr. — D3 68
Luang Prabang see Louangphrabang, Laos — C6 48
Luangue (Loange), stm., Afr. — F3 66
Luangwa, stm., Afr. — C5 68
Luanping, China — A7 42
Luanshya, Zam. — C4 68
Luan Toro, Arg. — H5 92
Luanxian, China — B8 42
Luapula, stm., Afr. — C4 68
Luar, Danau, l., Indon. — C8 50
Luarca, Spain — A4 20
Luba, Eq. Gui. — I6 64
Lubaantun, hist., Belize — D3 102
Lubań, Pol. — E11 16
Lubāna, Lat. — D9 10
Lubang Islands, is., Phil. — D2 52
Lubango, Ang. — C1 68
Lubanas, l., Lat. — D9 10
Lubartów, Pol. — E18 16
Lübben, Ger. — E9 16
Lübbenau, Ger. — E9 16
Lubbock, Tx., U.S. — H7 128
Lübeck, Ger. — C6 16
Lubefu, D.R.C. — E4 66
Lubefu, stm., D.R.C. — E4 66
Lubień Kujawski, Pol. — D15 16
Lubilash, stm., D.R.C. — F4 66
Lubin, Pol. — E12 16
Lublin, Pol. — E18 16
Lublin, state, Pol. — E18 16
Lubliniec, Pol. — F14 16
Lubny, Ukr. — D4 32
Lubon, D.R.C. — E10 12
Lubsko, Pol. — E10 16
Lübtheen, Ger. — C7 16
Lubuagan, Phil. — B3 52
Lubudi, D.R.C. — F5 66
Lubukbatang, Indon. — E3 50
Lubuklinggau, Indon. — E3 50
Lubuksikaping, Indon. — C1 50
Lubumbashi (Elisabethville), D.R.C. — G5 66
Lübz, Ger. — C7 16
Lucan, On., Can. — E8 112
Lucanas, Peru — F3 84
Lucania, hist. reg., Italy — D10 24
Lucania, Mount, mtn., Yk., Can. — C3 106
Lucapa, Ang. — B3 68
Lucas, Ky., U.S. — H11 120
Lucas, Ks., U.S. — B10 128
Lucban, Phil. — C3 52
Lucca, Italy — G7 22
Lucea, Jam. — i12 104d
Luce Bay, b., Scot., U.K. — G8 12
Lucedale, Ms., U.S. — G10 122
Lucélia, Braz. — D6 90
Lucena, Phil. — C3 52
Lucena del Cid see Llucena, Spain — D10 20
Lučenec, Slov. — H15 16
Lucera, Italy — C9 24

Name	Map Ref.	Page
Lucerne see Luzern, Switz.	C5	22
Lucerne, Ca., U.S.	D3	134
Lucerne, Lake of see Vierwaldstätter See, l., Switz.	D5	22
Luchou see Luzhou, China	G1	42
Luchow see Luzhou, China	G1	42
Lüchow, Ger.	C7	16
Luchuan, China	J4	42
Lucinda, Austl.	C6	76
Lucira, Ang.	C1	68
Luckau, Ger.	E9	16
Luckenwalde, Ger.	D9	16
Luckhoff, S. Afr.	F7	70
Luck Lake, l., Sk., Can.	C6	124
Lucknow, On., Can.	E8	112
Lucknow, India	E8	54
Lucky Lake, Sk., Can.	D6	124
Luçon, Fr.	C4	18
Lucusse, Ang.	C3	68
Luda Kamčija, stm., Blg.	G14	26
Ludao, China	C8	38
Lüdenscheid, Ger.	E3	16
Lüderitz, Nmb.	C5	64
Ludhiāna, India	E5	54
Ludian, China	F5	36
Ludington, Mi., U.S.	E3	112
Ludlow, Eng., U.K.	I10	12
Ludlow, Ma., U.S.	B13	114
Ludogorie, reg., Blg.	F13	26
Ludowici, Ga., U.S.	E4	116
Luduş, Rom.	C11	26
Ludvika, Swe.	F6	8
Ludwigsburg, Ger.	H4	16
Ludwigsfelde, Ger.	D9	16
Ludwigshafen am Rhein, Ger.	G4	16
Ludwigslust, Ger.	C7	16
Ludza, Lat.	D10	10
Luebo, D.R.C.	F4	66
Lueders, Tx., U.S.	B8	130
Luena, Ang.	C3	68
Luena, D.R.C.	F5	66
Luena, stm., Ang.	C3	68
Luepa, Ven.	E11	86
Lueyang, China	E2	42
Lufeng, China	J6	42
Lufico, Ang.	B1	68
Lufira, stm., D.R.C.	F5	66
Lufkin, Tx., U.S.	F4	122
Luga, Russia	B12	10
Luga, stm., Russia	A11	10
Lugano, Switz.	D5	22
Lugano, Lago di, l., Eur.	D14	18
Luganville, Vanuatu	j16	79d
Lugards Falls, wtfl, Kenya	E7	66
Lugenda, stm., Moz.	C6	68
Luggarus see Locarno, Switz.	D5	22
Lugnaquillia Mountain, mtn., Ire.	I6	12
Lugo, Italy	F8	22
Lugo, Spain	A3	20
Lugo, co., Spain	B3	20
Lugoj, Rom.	D8	26
Lugovoj, Kaz.	F12	32
Lugovskij, Russia	E11	34
Luhans'k, Ukr.	E5	32
Luhe, China	E8	42
Luhovicy, Russia	F21	10
Luhsien see Luzhou, China	G1	42
Luiana, Ang.	D3	68
Luido, Moz.	B12	70
Luik see Liège, Bel.	D14	14
Luimneach see Limerick, Ire.	I4	12
Luino, Italy	D5	22
Luishia, D.R.C.	G5	66
Luis L. León, Presa, res., Mex.	F2	130
Luis Muñoz Marin, Aeropuerto Internacional, P.R.	B3	104a
Luitpold Coast, cst., Ant.	C1	81
Luiza, D.R.C.	F4	66
Luján, Arg.	F4	92
Luján de Cuyo, Arg.	F3	92
Lujiang, China	F7	42
Lukang, Tai.	I9	42
Lukenie, stm., D.R.C.	E3	66
Lukeville, Az., U.S.	L4	132
Lukojanov, Russia	I21	8
Lukolela, D.R.C.	E3	66
Lukolela, D.R.C.	E4	66
Lukovit, Blg.	F11	26
Łukow, Pol.	E18	16
Lukuga, stm., D.R.C.	F5	66
Lukula, D.R.C.	F2	66
Lukulu, Zam.	C3	68
Lulaka, stm., D.R.C.	E4	66
Luleå, Swe.	D10	8
Luleälven, stm., Swe.	C8	8
Lüleburgaz, Tur.	B10	28
Lules, Arg.	C5	92
Lüliang, China	D5	42
Lüliang Shan, mts., China	C4	42
Luling, Tx., U.S.	E10	130
Lulonga, stm., D.R.C.	D3	66
Lulua, stm., D.R.C.	F4	66
Luluabourg see Kananga, D.R.C.	F4	66
Lumajang, Indon.	H8	50
Lumajangdong Co, l., China	B8	54
Lumaku, Gunong, mtn., Malay.	A9	50
Lumana, D.R.C.	E5	66
Lumbala Kaquengue, Ang.	C3	68
Lumbala N'guimbo, Ang.	C3	68
Lumber, stm., U.S.	B6	116
Lumber City, Ga., U.S.	E3	116
Lumberport, W.V., U.S.	E5	114
Lumberton, N.C., U.S.	B7	116
Lumberton, Tx., U.S.	G4	122
Lumbis, Indon.	A10	50
Lumbrales, Spain	D4	20
Lumby, B.C., Can.	F12	138
Lumding, India	E14	54
Lumpkin, Ga., U.S.	E14	122
Lumu, Indon.	E11	50
Lumut, Malay.	J5	48
Lumut, Tanjung, c., Indon.	E4	50
Luna Pier, Mi., U.S.	C2	114
Lūnāváda, India	G4	54
Lund, B.C., Can.	G6	138
Lund, Swe.	I5	8
Lund, Nv., U.S.	E2	132
Lundazi, Zam.	C5	68
Lundy, i., Eng., U.K.	J8	12
Lüneburg, Ger.	C6	16
Lüneburger Heide, reg., Ger.	C6	16
Lunel, Fr.	F10	18
Lünen, Ger.	E3	16
Lunenburg, N.S., Can.	F12	110
Lunenburg, Va., U.S.	H7	114
Lungch'i see Zhangzhou, China	I7	42
Lunge'nake, China	C10	54
Lunglei, India	G14	54
Lungtsin see Longzhou, China	J2	42
Lungué-Bungo (Lungwebungu), stm., Afr.	C3	68
Lungwebungu (Lungué-Bungo), stm., Afr.	C3	68
Lūni, India	E4	54
Lūni, stm., India	E4	54
Luninec, Bela.	H9	10
Luninets see Luninec, Bela.	H9	10
Lünkaransar, India	E4	54
Luntai, China	F14	32
Luo, stm., China	D4	42
Luo, stm., China	D4	42
Luobei, China	B11	36
Luobu, China	I3	42
Luocheng, China	I3	42
Luoding, China	J4	42
Luofu, D.R.C.	E5	66
Luohe, China	E6	42
Luoji, China	E7	42
Luonan, China	D4	42
Luoning, China	D4	42
Luoqi, China	G2	42
Luoshan, China	F6	42
Luotian, China	F6	42
Luowenba, China	F2	42
Luoxiao Shan, mts., China	H6	42
Luoyang, China	D5	42
Luoyuan, China	H8	42
Luozi, D.R.C.	F2	66
Lupanshui, China	F5	36
Lupar, stm., Malay.	C7	50
Łupawa, Pol.	B13	16
Lupeni, Rom.	D10	26
Lupin see Manzhouli, China	B8	36
Luputa, D.R.C.	F4	66
Luqiao, China	E7	42
Luqiao, China	G9	42
Luque, Spain	E5	36
Luque, Spain	G6	20
Luquillo, P.R.	B4	104a
Lure, Fr.	G15	14
Luremo, Ang.	B2	68
Lurgan, N. Ire., U.K.	G6	12
Luribay, Bol.	C3	90
Lurín, Peru	F2	84
Lúrio, Moz.	C7	68
Lúrio, stm., Moz.	C6	68
Lusaka, Zam.	D4	68
Lusambo, D.R.C.	E4	66
Lusanga, D.R.C.	E3	66
Lusangi, D.R.C.	E5	66
Luscar, Ab., Can.	C13	138
Luseland, Sk., Can.	B4	124
Lushan, China	E5	42
Lushnja see Lushnjë, Alb.	D13	24
Lushnjë, Alb.	D13	24
Lushoto, Tan.	E7	66
Lüshun (Port Arthur), China	E4	38
Lusk, Wy., U.S.	E8	126
Lussac-les-Châteaux, Fr.	C8	18
Lüt, Dasht-e, des., Iran	C8	56
Lü-ta see Dalian, China	B9	42
Lü Tao, i., Tai.	J9	42
Lutembo, Ang.	C3	68
Lutesville, Mo., U.S.	G7	120
Luther, Mi., U.S.	D4	112
Luther, Ok., U.S.	F11	128
Lutherstadt Eisleben, Ger.	E6	16
Lutherstadt Wittenberg, Ger.	E8	16
Luton, Eng., U.K.	J12	12
Lutong, Malay.	A8	50
Łutselk'e, N.T., Can.	C8	106
Lutz, Fl., U.S.	H3	116
Lützow, Ger.	C7	16
Lutzow-Holm Bay, b., Ant.	B8	81
Luuq, Som.	D8	66
Luverne, Al., U.S.	F12	122
Lu Verne, Ia., U.S.	I4	118
Luverne, Mn., U.S.	H2	118
Luvua, stm., D.R.C.	F5	66
Luvuvhu, stm., S. Afr.	C10	70
Luwegu, stm., Tan.	F7	66
Luwingu, Zam.	C4	68
Luwuk, Indon.	F7	44
Luxapallila Creek, stm., U.S.	D11	122
Luxembourg, Lux.	E14	14
Luxembourg, ctry., Eur.	E15	14
Luxemburg, Wi., U.S.	D2	112
Luxeuil-les-Bains, Fr.	G15	14
Luxi, China	G4	36
Luxor see El-Uqsor, Egypt	B6	62
Luz, Braz.	J3	88
Luza, Russia	F22	8
Luza, Russia	A14	10
Luzern (Lucerne), Switz.	C5	22
Luzhai, China	I3	42
Luzhou, China	G1	42
Luziânia, Braz.	I2	88
Luzilândia, Braz.	B4	88
Lużki, Bela.	E10	10
Luznice, stm., Eur.	G10	16
Luzon, i., Phil.	B3	52
Luzon Strait, strt., Asia	G16	30
L'viv, Ukr.	F13	6
L'viv, co., Ukr.	G19	16
L'vovskij, Russia	E20	10
Lwówek, Pol.	D12	16
Lyallpur see Faisalabad, Pak.	C4	54
Lyčkovo, Russia	C15	10
Lycksele, Swe.	D8	8
Lydenburg, S. Afr.	D10	70
Lydia Mills, S.C., U.S.	B3	116
Lyell, Mount, mtn., Can.	E13	138
Lyerly, Ga., U.S.	C13	122
Lyford, Tx., U.S.	H10	130
Lykošino, Russia	B16	10
Lyle, Mn., U.S.	H6	118
Lyman, Ne., U.S.	F8	126
Lyman, S.C., U.S.	B3	116
Lymans'ke, Ukr.	C16	26
Lyme Bay, b., Eng., U.K.	K9	12
Lyna (Łava), stm., Eur.	B16	16
Lynch, Ne., U.S.	E14	126
Lynchburg, Oh., U.S.	E2	114
Lynchburg, S.C., U.S.	B5	116
Lynchburg, Tn., U.S.	B12	122
Lynchburg, Va., U.S.	G6	114
Lynd, stm., Austl.	A4	76
Lynden, Wa., U.S.	B4	136
Lyndhurst, Austl.	B5	76
Lyndon, Ks., U.S.	F2	120
Lyndon, Ky., U.S.	F12	120
Lyndon, stm., Austl.	D2	74
Lyndon B. Johnson, Lake, res., Tx., U.S.	D9	130
Lyndon B. Johnson Space Center, sci., Tx., U.S.	H3	122
Lyngen, b., Nor.	B9	8
Lyngseidet, Nor.	B8	8
Lynn, Al., U.S.	C11	122
Lynn, Ma., U.S.	B14	114
Lyndyl, Ut., U.S.	D4	132
Lynn Haven, Fl., U.S.	G13	122
Lynn Lake, Mb., Can.	D10	106
Lyntupy, Bela.	E9	10
Lynx Lake, l., N.T., Can.	C9	106
Lyon, Fr.	D10	18
Lyon Inlet, b., Nu., Can.	B14	106
Lyon Mountain, N.Y., U.S.	F2	110
Lyonnais, hist. reg., Fr.	D10	18
Lyons, In., U.S.	E10	120
Lyons, Ks., U.S.	C10	128
Lyons, Mi., U.S.	F5	112
Lyons, Ne., U.S.	C1	120
Lyons, N.Y., U.S.	E13	112
Lyons, stm., Austl.	D3	74
Lysa Hora, Ukr.	A18	26
Łysica, mtn., Pol.	F16	16
Lyskovo, Russia	H21	8
Lys'va, Russia	C9	32
Lysychans'k, Ukr.	E5	32
Lytham Saint Anne's, Eng., U.K.	H9	12
Lytle, Tx., U.S.	E9	130

M

Name	Map Ref.	Page
Ma, stm., Asia	C7	48
Ma'ān, Jord.	H6	58
Ma'ān, state, Jord.	H7	58
Ma'anshan, China	F8	42
Maardu, Est.	G11	8
Maarianhamina (Mariehamn), Fin.	F9	8
Ma'arrat an-Nu'mān, Syria	C7	58
Maas (Meuse), stm., Eur.	D14	14
Maasin, Phil.	E5	52
Maastricht, Neth.	D14	14
Mabalane, Moz.	C11	70
Mabank, Tx., U.S.	E2	122
Mabaruma, Guy.	C12	86
Mabeleapodi, Bots.	B6	70
Mabel Lake, l., B.C., Can.	F12	138
Maben, Ms., U.S.	D9	122
Mablethorpe, Eng., U.K.	H13	12
Mableton, Ga., U.S.	D14	122
Mabton, Wa., U.S.	D6	136
Mabuasehube Game Reserve, Bots.	D6	70
Mača, Russia	E12	34
Maca, Cerro, vol., Chile	H2	90
Macachín, Arg.	H6	92
Macaé, Braz.	L5	88
Macaíba, Braz.	C8	88
Macajuba, Braz.	G5	88
Macalister, B.C., Can.	D8	138
Macalister, stm., Austl.	K6	76
Macalister, Mount, mtn., Austl.	J7	76
MacAlpine Lake, l., Nu., Can.	B10	106
Macan, Kepulauan, is., Indon.	G12	50
Macao see Macau, dep., Asia	J5	42
Macapá, Braz.	C7	84
Macará, Ec.	D2	84
Macareo, Caño, stm., Ven.	C11	86
MacArthur, Phil.	E5	52
Macas, Ec.	I2	86
Macau, Braz.	C7	88
Macau, Macau	J5	42
Macau, dep., Asia	J5	42
Macaúbas, Braz.	G4	88
MacClenny, Fl., U.S.	F3	116
Macclesfield, Eng., U.K.	H10	12
Macdonald, Lake, l., Austl.	D5	74
MacDonald Pass, p., Mt., U.S.	D14	136
MacDonnell Ranges, mts., Austl.	D6	74
Macdui, Ben, mtn., Scot., U.K.	D9	12
Macedonia, hist. reg., Eur.	H10	26
Macedonia, ctry., Eur.	B4	28
Maceió, Braz.	E8	88
Macenta, Gui.	H3	64
Macerata, Italy	G10	22
MacFarlane, stm., Sk., Can.	D9	106
Macgillycuddy's Reeks, mts., Ire.	J3	12
MacGregor, Mb., Can.	D15	124
Machado, Braz.	K3	88
Machado, stm., Braz.	F5	84
Machagai, Arg.	C7	92
Machakos, Kenya	E7	66
Machala, Ec.	D2	84
Machali, Chile	G2	92
Machalilla, Parque Nacional, p.o.i., Ec.	H1	86
Machanga, Moz.	B12	70
Machattie, Lake, l., Austl.	E2	76
Machaze, Moz.	B11	70
Macheng, China	F6	42
Macherla, India	C4	53
Machias, Me., U.S.	F9	110
Machilipatnam (Bandar), India	C5	53
Machiques, Ven.	B5	86
Machkund, res., India	B6	53
Macho, Arroyo del, stm., N.M., U.S.	H4	128
Machupicchu see Machupicchu, hist., Peru	F3	84
Machu Picchu see Machupicchu, hist., Peru	F3	84
Macia, Moz.	D11	70
Macin, Rom.	D15	26
Macintyre, stm., Austl.	G7	76
Mackay, Austl.	C7	76
Mackay, Id., U.S.	G13	136
Mackay, Lake, l., Austl.	D5	74
MacKay Lake, l., N.T., Can.	C8	106
Mackenzie, stm., Austl.	D7	76
Mackenzie, stm., N.T., Can.	B4	106
Mackenzie Bay, b.,	C12	140
Mackenzie King Island, i., Can.	B3	141
Mackenzie Mountains, mts., Can.	C4	106
Mackinac, Straits of, strt., Mi., U.S.	C4	112
Mackinac Bridge, Mi., U.S.	C5	112
Mackinac Island, Mi., U.S.	C5	112
Mackinaw, stm., Il., U.S.	D9	120
Mackinaw City, Mi., U.S.	C5	112
Mackinnon Road, Kenya	E7	66
Macklin, Sk., Can.	B4	124
Macksville, Austl.	H9	76
Macksville, Ks., U.S.	C9	128
Maclean, Austl.	G9	76
Maclear, S. Afr.	G9	70
Macleay, stm., Austl.	H9	76
Macleod, Lake, l., Austl.	D2	74
Macmillan, stm., Yk., Can.	C4	106
Macomb, Il., U.S.	D7	120
Macomer, Italy	D2	24
Mâcon, Fr.	C10	18
Macon, Ga., U.S.	D2	116
Macon, Il., U.S.	E9	120
Macon, Ms., U.S.	D10	122
Macon, Mo., U.S.	E5	120
Macon, Bayou, stm., U.S.	E7	122
Macondo, Ang.	C3	68
Macoris, Cabo, c., Dom. Rep.	C12	102
Macoupin Creek, stm., Il., U.S.	E8	120
Macovane, Moz.	B12	70
Macquarie, stm., Austl.	H6	76
Macquarie, stm., Austl.	n13	77a
Macquarie, Lake, l., Austl.	I8	76
Macquarie Harbour, b., Austl.	o12	77a
Macquarie Marshes, sw., Austl.	A20	81
Macquarie Ridge, unds.	O18	142
Mac. Robertson Land, reg., Ant.	B10	81
Macuacuau, Ven.	F9	86
Macugnaga, Italy	E4	22
Macumba, stm., Austl.	E7	74
Macuro, Ven.	B10	86
Macusani, Peru	F3	84
Macuspana, Mex.	G12	100
Mad, stm., Ca., U.S.	C2	134
Madaba, Jord.	G6	58
Madagascar, ctry., Afr.	D8	68
Madagascar Basin, unds.	L11	142
Madagascar Plateau, unds.	M7	142
Madan, Blg.	H11	26
Madanapalle, India	E4	53
Madang, Pap. N. Gui.	b4	79a
Madaoua, Niger	G6	64
Mādārīpur, Bngl.	G13	54
Madawaska, Me., U.S.	C9	110
Madawaska, stm., On., Can.	C13	112
Madawaska Highlands, plat., On., Can.	C12	112
Madaya, Mya.	A3	48
Maddalena, Isola, i., Italy	C3	24
Maddaloni, Italy	C8	24
Maddock, N.D., U.S.	G14	124
Madeira, i., Port.	C1	64
Madeira, Arquipélago da, is., Port.	C1	64
Madeira Islands see Madeira, Arquipélago da, is., Port.	C1	64
Madelegabel, mtn., Eur.	I6	16
Madeleine, Îles de la, is., Qc., Can.	C15	110
Madelia, Mn., U.S.	H4	118
Madeline Island, i., Wi., U.S.	E8	118
Madera, Mex.	A4	100
Madera, Ca., U.S.	G5	134
Madera see Madeira, stm., S.A.	E5	84
Madgaon, India	D1	53
Madhepura, India	F11	54
Madhubani, India	E10	54
Madhugiri, India	E3	53
Madhupur, India	F11	54
Madhya Pradesh, state, India	D4	46
Madibogo, S. Afr.	E7	70
Madida, China	C9	38
Madidi, stm., Bol.	B3	90
Madill, Ok., U.S.	C2	122
Madimba, D.R.C.	E3	66
Madīnat ash-Sha'b, Yemen	G5	56
Madingo-Kayes, Congo	E2	66
Madingou, Congo	E2	66
Madirovalo, Madag.	D8	68
Madison, Al., U.S.	C12	122
Madison, Fl., U.S.	F2	116
Madison, Ga., U.S.	C2	116
Madison, In., U.S.	F12	120
Madison, Me., U.S.	F6	110
Madison, Mn., U.S.	F2	118
Madison, Ne., U.S.	E15	126
Madison, N.C., U.S.	H5	114
Madison, S.D., U.S.	C15	126
Madison, Wi., U.S.	A8	120
Madison, stm., Mt., U.S.	E15	136
Madison Heights, Va., U.S.	G6	114
Madison Range, mts., Mt., U.S.	E15	136
Madisonville, Ky., U.S.	G10	120
Madisonville, La., U.S.	G8	122
Madisonville, Tn., U.S.	A1	116
Madisonville, Tx., U.S.	G2	122
Madiun, Indon.	G7	50
Madiyi, China	G4	42
Mado Gashi, Kenya	D7	66
Madoc, On., Can.	D11	112
Madona, Bela.	D9	10
Madora, Bela.	G13	10
Madras see Chennai, India	E5	53
Madras, Or., U.S.	F5	136
Madre, Laguna, b., Mex.	C10	100
Madre, Laguna, b., Tx., U.S.	H10	130
Madre, Sierra, mts., Phil.	B3	52
Madre de Chiapas, Sierra, mts., N.A.	G12	100
Madre de Dios, Isla, i., Chile	J1	90
Madre del Sur, Sierra, mts., Mex.	G9	100
Madre Occidental, Sierra, mts., Mex.	B3	96
Madre Oriental, Sierra, mts., Mex.	C8	100
Madrid, Spain	D7	20
Madrid, Al., U.S.	F13	122
Madrid, Ne., U.S.	G11	126
Madrid, stm., Spain	D7	20
Madridejos, Spain	E7	20
Madura, Selat, strt., Indon.	G8	50
Madurai, India	G4	53
Madurāntakam, India	E4	53
Maebashi, Japan	C11	40
Mae Hong Son, Thai.	C3	48
Mae Klong, stm., Thai.	E4	48
Mae Ping Mae Hat Mae Kor National Park, p.o.i., Thai.	D4	48
Mae Ramat, Thai.	D3	48
Mae Sariang, Thai.	C3	48
Mae Sot, Thai.	D4	48
Maesteg, U.K.	C7	132
Maestra, Sierra, mts., Cuba	B9	102
Maevatanana, Madag.	D8	68
Maéwo, i., Vanuatu	j17	79d
Mafeking, Mb., Can.	B12	124
Mafeking see Mafikeng, S. Afr.	D7	70
Mafeteng, Leso.	F8	70
Maffra, Austl.	K6	76
Mafia Island, i., Tan.	F8	66
Mafikeng, S. Afr.	D7	70
Mafra, Braz.	C13	92
Magadan, Russia	E19	34
Magadi, Kenya	E7	66
Magaguadavic Lake, l., N.B., Can.	E9	110
Magalhães de Almeida, Braz.	B4	88
Magallanes, Arg.	D4	52
Magangué, Col.	C4	86
Magaria, Niger	G6	64
Magazine Mountain, mtn., Ar., U.S.	B5	122
Magdagači, Russia	F14	34
Magdalena, Arg.	G9	92
Magdalena, Bol.	B4	90
Magdalena, Mex.	B4	100
Magdalena, N.M., U.S.	I9	132
Magdalena, state, Col.	B4	86
Magdalena, stm., Col.	C4	86
Magdalena, stm., Mex.	F7	98
Magdalena, Bahía, b., Mex.	C2	100
Magdalena, Isla, i., Chile	H2	90
Magdalena de Kino, Mex.	F7	98
Magdeburg, Ger.	D7	16
Magelang, Indon.	G7	50
Magellan, Strait of, strt., S.A.	J2	90
Magenta, Italy	E5	22
Māgha, Egypt	J1	58
Maghagha, Egypt	I1	58
Māgina, mtn., Spain	G7	20
Maglaj, Bos.	E5	26
Maglič, mtn., Bos.	F5	26
Maglie, Italy	D12	24
Magnet, Mb., Can.	C14	124
Magnetawan, On., Can.	C10	112
Magnetic Island, i., Austl.	B6	76
Magnitogorsk, Russia	D9	32
Magnolia, Ar., U.S.	D5	122
Magnolia, Ms., U.S.	F8	122
Mago, i., Fiji	p20	79e
Magog, Qc., Can.	E4	110
Magozal, Mex.	E10	100
Magrath, Ab., Can.	G18	138
Maguan, China	A7	48
Maguarinho, Cabo, c., Braz.	D8	84
Magumeri, Nig.	G7	64
Maguse Lake, l., Nu., Can.	C12	106
Magway, Mya.	B2	48
Magway, state, Mya.	B2	48
Mahābād, Iran	B6	56
Mahābaleshwar, India	C1	53
Mahabe, Madag.	D8	68
Mahabharat Lek, mts., Nepal	E11	54
Mahābhārat Range see Mahābhārat Lek, mts., Nepal	E11	54
Mahabo, Madag.	E7	68
Mahačkala, Russia	F7	32
Mahādeo Range, mts., India	C2	53
Mahagi, D.R.C.	D6	66
Mahajamba, stm., Madag.	D8	68
Mahajanga, Madag.	D8	68
Mahākāli (Sārda), stm., Asia	D8	54
Mahakam, stm., Indon.	D9	50
Mahalapye, Bots.	C8	70
Maham, India	D6	54
Mahānadi, stm., India	H10	54
Mahanoro, Madag.	D8	68
Mahanoy City, Pa., U.S.	D9	114
Maharagama, Sri L.	H4	53
Mahārājganj, India	E10	54
Mahārājpur, India	F7	54
Mahārāshtra, state, India	E4	46
Mahāsamund, India	H9	54
Maha Sarakham, Thai.	D6	48
Mahaut, Dom.	j6	105c
Mahaweli, stm., Sri L.	H5	53
Mahaxai, Laos	D7	48
Mahbūbābād, India	C4	53
Mahbūbnagar, India	C4	53
Mahd adh-Dhahab, Sau. Ar.	E5	56
Mahdia, Guy.	E12	86
Mahe, i., Sey.	j13	69b
Mahébourg, Mrts.	i10	69a
Mahendra Giri, mtn., India	B7	53
Mahendranagar, Nepal	D7	54
Mahenge, Tan.	F7	66
Mahesāna, India	G4	54
Maheshwar, India	G5	54
Mahia Peninsula, pen., N.Z.	D7	80
Mahilëŭ, Bela.	G13	10
Mahilëŭ, state, Bela.	G13	10
Mahina, Fr. Poly.	u21	78h
Mahlabatini, S. Afr.	F10	70
Mahmūdābād, India	D8	54
Mahmūdiye, Tur.	D14	28
Mahoba, India	F7	54
Mahogany Mountain, mtn., Or., U.S.	G9	136
Mahogany Tree, Anguilla	A1	105a
Mahomet, Il., U.S.	D9	120
Mahón see Maó, Spain	E15	20
Mahone Bay, N.S., Can.	F12	110
Mahood Lake, l., B.C., Can.	E10	138
Mahora, Spain	E9	20
Mahrāt, Jabal, plat., Yemen	F7	56
Mahrauni, India	F7	54
Mahuva, India	H3	54
Maiaky, Ukr.	C17	26
Maicao, Col.	B5	86
Maichen, China	K3	42
Maicuru, stm., Braz.	D7	84
Maiden, N.C., U.S.	A4	116
Maidenhead, Eng., U.K.	J12	12
Maidstone, Sk., Can.	A4	124
Maidstone, Eng., U.K.	J13	12
Maiduguri, Nig.	G7	64
Maihar, India	F8	54
Maijdi, India	F13	54
Maikala Range, mts., India	G8	54
Maikoor, Pulau, i., Indon.	G9	44
Mailāni, India	D8	54
Main, stm., Ger.	F4	16
Mainburg, Ger.	H7	16
Main Channel, strt., On., Can.	C8	112
Main-Donau-Kanal, can., Ger.	G7	16
Maine, state, U.S.	E7	110
Maine, hist. reg., Fr.	F8	14
Maine, Gulf of, b., N.A.	G8	110
Maine-et-Loire, state, Fr.	G7	14
Mainé-Soroa, Niger	G7	64
Mainhardt, Ger.	G5	16
Mainland, i., Scot., U.K.	B9	12
Mainland, i., Scot., U.K.	n18	12a
Mainpuri, India	E7	54
Maintirano, Madag.	D7	68
Mainz, Ger.	G4	16
Maio, i., C.V.	k10	65a
Maipo, stm., Chile	F2	92
Maipo, Volcán, vol., S.A.	G3	92
Maipú, Arg.	H9	92
Maipú, ngh., Chile	F2	92
Maiquetía, Ven.	B8	86
Maisí, Cabo, c., Cuba	B11	102
Maison Rouge, La., U.S.	E7	122
Maitland, Austl.	I8	76
Maitland, stm., On., Can.	E8	112
Maitri, sci., Ant.	C6	81
Maiz, Islas del, is., Nic.	F6	102
Maizuru, Japan	D8	40
Maja, stm., Russia	E15	34
Majari, stm., Braz.	F11	86
Majene, Indon.	E11	50
Maji, Eth.	F7	62
Majia, stm., China	A7	42
Majiang, China	H2	42
Majiangzong, China	C12	54
Majja, Russia	D15	34
Majkain, Kaz.	D13	32
Majkop, Russia	F6	32
Major, Puig, mtn., Spain	E13	20
Majorca see Mallorca, i., Spain	E13	20
Majskij, Russia	F7	32
Majuro, at., Marsh. Is.	C8	72
Maka, Sen.	G2	64
Makabana, Congo	E2	66
Makallé, Arg.	C8	92
Makālū, mtn., Asia	E11	54
Makanči, Kaz.	E14	32
Makapu'u Head, c., Hi., U.S.	b4	78a
Makarakomburu, Mount, mtn., Sol. Is.	e8	79b
Makarov, Russia	G17	34
Makarska, Cro.	G13	22
Makarьev, Russia	H20	8
Makasar, Selat (Makassar Strait), strt., Indon.	D11	50
Makassar Strait see Makasar, Selat, strt., Indon.	D11	50
Makat, Kaz.	E8	32
Makedonska Kamenica, Mac.	B6	28
Makeni, S.L.	H2	64
Makgadikgadi, pl., Bots.	B7	70
Makgadikgadi Pans Game Reserve, Bots.	B7	70
Makhaleng, stm., Afr.	F8	70
Makham, Thai.	F6	48
Maki, Indon.	F9	44
Makiivka, Ukr.	E5	32
Makinsk, Kaz.	D11	32
Makira, state, Sol. Is.	f10	79b
Makira Harbour, b., Sol. Is.	f9	79b
Makkovik, Nf., Can.	D19	106
Makó, Hung.	C7	26
Makokou, Gabon	D2	66
Makongolosi, Tan.	F6	66
Makoua, Congo	E3	66
Maków Mazowiecki, Pol.	D16	16
Makrai, India	G6	54
Makrāna, India	E5	54
Makrān Coast, cst., Asia	D9	56
Maksatiha, Russia	C18	10
Maksimkin Jar, Russia	C15	32
Maktar, Tun.	I3	24
Makumbi, D.R.C.	F4	66
Makung, Tai.	J8	42
Makurdi, Nig.	H6	64
Makushin Volcano, vol., Ak., U.S.	F6	140
Makwassie, S. Afr.	E8	70
Mala see Mallow, Ire.	I4	12
Mala, Punta, c., Pan.	I8	102
Malabang, Phil.	G5	52
Malabar Coast, cst., India	C1	53
Malabo, Eq. Gui.	I6	64
Malacacheta, Braz.	I4	88
Malacca see Melaka, Malay.	K6	48
Malacca, Strait of, strt., Asia	B2	50
Malacky, Slov.	H13	16
Malad, stm., U.S.	H14	136
Malad City, Id., U.S.	A4	132
Maladzečna, Bela.	D5	86
Málaga, Col.	D5	86
Málaga, Spain	H6	20
Málaga, co., Spain	H6	20
Malagarasi, Tan.	F6	66
Malagash, N.S., Can.	E13	110
Malagasy Republic see Madagascar, ctry., Afr.	D8	68
Malagón, Spain	E7	20
Malaimbandy, Madag.	E8	68
Malaita, state, Sol. Is.	d9	79b
Malaita, i., Sol. Is.	e9	79b
Malaja Kuril'skaja Grjada (Habomai-shotō), is., Russia	C17	38
Malaja Višera, Russia	B15	10
Malaka, Sempitan, strt., Indon.	J2	48
Malakāl, Sudan	F6	62
Malakand, Pak.	A3	54
Malakoff, Tx., U.S.	E3	122
Malakula, i., Vanuatu	k16	79d
Malamala, Indon.	E6	44
Malamyž, Russia	G16	34
Malang, Indon.	H8	50
Malanje, Ang.	B2	68
Malanville, Benin	G5	64
Malanzán, Arg.	E4	92
Mälaren, l., Swe.	G7	8
Malargüe, Arg.	G3	90
Malartic, Qc., Can.	F15	106
Malaspina Glacier, ice, Ak., U.S.	E11	140
Malatya, Tur.	B4	56
Malaut, India	C5	54
Malavalli, India	E3	53
Malawali, Pulau, i., Malay.	G1	52
Malawi, ctry., Afr.	C5	68
Malawi, Lake see Nyasa, Lake, l., Afr.	C5	68
Malaya see Semenanjung Malaysia, hist. reg., Malay.	K6	48
Malaybalay, Phil.	F5	52
Malāyer, Iran	H10	54
Malay Peninsula, pen., Asia	J5	48
Malay Reef, rf., Austl.	A8	76
Malaysia, ctry., Asia	E3	44
Malbon, Austl.	C3	76
Malbork, Pol.	B15	16
Malbrán, Arg.	D6	92
Malchin, Ger.	C8	16
Malchow, Ger.	C8	16
Malcolm Island, i., B.C., Can.	F4	138
Malcom, Ia., U.S.	C5	120
Malczyce, Pol.	E12	16
Malden, i., Kir.	D11	72
Mal di Ventre, Isola di, i., Italy	E2	24
Maldives, ctry., Asia	I11	30
Maldonado, Ur.	G10	92
Male', Mald.	i12	46a
Male, Myan.		
Male' Atoll, at., Mald.	i12	46a
Malé Karpaty (Little Carpathians), mts., Slov.	H13	16
Malema, Moz.	C6	68
Māler Kotla, India	C5	54
Malesherbes, Fr.	F11	14
Mali'hański hrebet, mts., Russia	F10	34
Malheur, stm., Or., U.S.	G8	136
Malheur, South Fork, stm., Or., U.S.	G8	136
Mali, Gui.	G2	64
Mali, ctry., Afr.	F4	64
Mali, stm., Mya.	C8	46
Malik, Wādī al-, val., Sudan	D5	62
Mali Kyun, i., Mya.	F4	48
Malili, Indon.	E12	50
Malin, Or., U.S.	A4	134
Malinau, Indon.	B10	50
Malindi, Kenya	E8	66
Malines see Mechelen, Bel.	C13	14
Malin Head, c., Ire.	F5	12
Malita, Phil.	G5	52
Malkara, Tur.	C9	28
Mallacoota, Austl.	K7	76
Mallaig, Scot., U.K.	D7	12
Mallan luonnonpuisto, p.o.i., Fin.	B9	8
Mallawī, Egypt	K1	58
Mallersdorf-Pfaffenberg, Ger.	H8	16
Mallery Lake, l., Nu., Can.	C11	106
Mallorca (Majorca), i., Spain	E13	20
Mallow, Ire.	I4	12
Malm, Nor.	D4	8
Malmberget, Swe.	C9	8
Malmesbury, S. Afr.	H4	70
Malmö, Swe.	I5	8
Malmok, c., Neth. Ant.	p23	104g
Malo, i., Vanuatu	j16	79d
Maloelap, at., Marsh. Is.	C8	72
Maloja Skuratovo, Russia	G19	10
Malojaroslavec, Russia	E19	10
Malolos, Phil.	C3	52
Malone, Fl., U.S.	G13	122
Malone, N.Y., U.S.	F2	110
Malonga, D.R.C.	G4	66
Małopolska, reg., Pol.	F17	16
Maloši, Russia	E17	34
Malošujka, Russia	E17	8
Malott, Wa., U.S.	B7	136

Name	Map Ref.	Page
Małowice, Pol.	E11	16
Måløy, Nor.	E1	8
Malozemel'skaja Tundra, reg., Russia	C24	8
Malpas, Austl.	J3	76
Malpe, India	E2	53
Malpeque Bay, b., P.E. Can.	D13	110
Malprabha, stm., India	D2	53
Mālpura, India	E5	54
Malta, Braz.	D7	88
Malta, Lat.	D10	10
Malta, Mt., U.S.	F6	124
Malta, ctry., Eur.	I8	24
Malta, i., Malta	I8	24
Malta Channel, strt., Eur.	H8	24
Maltahöhe, Nmb.	D3	70
Maluku (Moluccas), is., Indon.	F8	44
Maluku, Laut (Molucca Sea), Indon.	F8	44
Ma'lūlā, Syria	E7	58
Malu Mare, Rom.	E10	26
Malunda, Indon.	E11	50
Mälvan, India	C1	53
Malvern, Ar., U.S.	C6	122
Malvern, Ia., U.S.	K3	118
Malvern, Oh., U.S.	D4	114
Malvérnia, Moz.	C10	70
Malvinas Sur, Arg.	D8	72
Malý Dunaj, stm., Slov.	H13	16
Malyja Haradzjacičy, Bela.	H11	10
Malyj Anjuj, stm., Russia	C21	34
Malyj Enisej, stm., Russia	F8	34
Malyj Tajmyr, ostrov, i., Russia	A10	34
Mama, Russia	E11	34
Mamaia, Rom.	E15	26
Mamanguape, Braz.	D8	88
Mamasa, Indon.	E11	50
Mamasa, stm., Indon.	E11	50
Mambajao, Phil.	F5	52
Mambasa, D.R.C.	D5	66
Mamberamo, stm., Indon.	F10	44
Mamburao, Phil.	D3	52
Mamfe, Cam.	C1	66
Maml</table>

Name	Map Ref.	Page
Matagorda Island, i., Tx., U.S.	F11	130
Matagorda Peninsula, pen., Tx., U.S.	F11	130
Matahiae, Pointe, c., Fr. Poly.	w22	78h
Matâi, Egypt	J1	58
Mataiea, Fr. Poly.	w22	78h
Mataiva, at., Fr. Poly.	E12	72
Matak, Pulau, i., Indon.	B5	50
Matakana, Austl.	I5	76
Matale, Sri L.	H5	53
Matam, Sen.	F2	64
Matamoros, Mex.	C10	100
Matamoros, Mex.	C7	100
Matan, Indon.	D7	50
Matandu, stm., Tan.	F7	66
Matane, Qc., Can.	B9	110
Matanni, Pak.	B3	54
Matanzas, Cuba	A7	102
Matanzas, Mex.	E8	100
Matapan, Cape see Taínaro, Ákra, c., Grc.	G5	28
Matape, stm., Mex.	A3	100
Matapédia, Qc., Can.	C9	110
Matapédia, Lac, l., Qc., Can.	B9	110
Mataquito, stm., Chile	G2	92
Matara, Sri L.	I5	53
Mataram, Indon.	H9	50
Mataranka, Austl.	B6	74
Mataró, Spain	C13	20
Matasiri, Pulau, i., Indon.	F9	50
Matatiele, S. Afr.	G9	70
Matatula, Cape, c., Am. Sam.	h12	79c
Matâ'utu, Wal./F.	E9	72
Matavera, Cook Is.	a27	78j
Mataveri, Chile	e29	78l
Mataveri, Aeropuerto, Chile	f29	78l
Mataveri Airstrip see Mataveri, Aeropuerto, Chile	f29	78l
Matehuala, Mex.	D8	100
Mateke Hills, hills, Zimb.	B10	70
Matera, Italy	D10	24
Mateur, Tun.	G3	24
Matha, Fr.	D5	18
Mather, Mb., Can.	E14	124
Mather, Pa., U.S.	E5	114
Matheson, On., Can.	F14	106
Mathews, Va., U.S.	G9	114
Mathis, Tx., U.S.	F10	130
Mathura (Muttra), India	E6	54
Matias Barbosa, Braz.	K4	88
Matías Romero, Mex.	G11	100
Matícora, stm., Ven.	B6	86
Matinha, Braz.	B3	88
Matipó, Braz.	K4	88
Matiyure, stm., Ven.	D7	86
Mātli, Pak.	F2	54
Mato, Cerro, mtn., Ven.	D9	86
Mato Grosso, state, Braz.	F6	84
Mato Grosso, Planalto do, plat., Braz.	B5	90
Mato Grosso, Plateau of see Mato Grosso, Planalto do, plat., Braz.	B5	90
Mato Grosso do Sul, state, Braz.	C6	90
Matola Rio, Moz.	D11	70
Matopos, Zimb.	B9	70
Matosinhos, Port.	C2	20
Matouying, China	B8	42
Matozinhos, Braz.	J3	88
Maṭraḥ, Oman	E8	56
Matsudo, Japan	D12	40
Matsue, Japan	D6	40
Matsumoto, Japan	C10	40
Matsusaka, Japan	E9	40
Matsu Tao, i., Tai.	H8	42
Matsutō, Japan	C9	40
Matsuura, Japan	F2	40
Matsuyama, Japan	F5	40
Mattagami, stm., On., Can.	F14	106
Mattamuskeet, Lake, l., N.C., U.S.	A9	116
Mattaponi, stm., Va., U.S.	G8	114
Mattawa, On., Can.	B11	112
Mattawa, Wa., U.S.	D7	136
Mattawamkeag, stm., Me., U.S.	E8	110
Matterhorn, mtn., Eur.	D13	18
Matterhorn, mtn., Nv., U.S.	B1	132
Matthews Mountain, hill, Mo., U.S.	G7	120
Matthew Town, Bah.	C10	96
Mattighofen, Aus.	B10	22
Mattoon, Il., U.S.	E9	120
Mattoon, Wi., U.S.	F9	118
Mattydale, N.Y., U.S.	E13	112
Matua, Indon.	E7	50
Matudo see Matsudo, Japan	D12	40
Matue see Matsue, Japan	D6	40
Matuku, i., Fiji	q19	79e
Matumoto see Matsumoto, Japan	C10	40
Maturín, Ven.	C10	86
Matutina, Braz.	J2	88
Matuzaka see Matsusaka, Japan	E9	40
Maú (Ireng), stm., S.A.	F12	86
Maúa, Moz.	C6	68
Mau Aimma, India	F8	54
Maubeuge, Fr.	D12	14
Maud, Tx., U.S.	D4	122
Maudaha, India	F7	54
Maude, Austl.	J5	76
Maués, Braz.	D6	84
Maués, stm., Braz.	D6	84
Mauganj, India	F8	54
Maui, i., Hi., U.S.	C5	78a
Mauk, Indon.	F5	50
Mauldin, S.C., U.S.	B3	116
Maule, state, Chile	G2	92
Maule, stm., Chile	G1	92
Maule, Laguna del, l., Chile	G2	92
Mauléon-Licharre, Fr.	F5	18
Maumee, Oh., U.S.	G6	112
Maumee, stm., U.S.	G6	112
Maumelle, Lake, res., Ar., U.S.	C6	122
Maumere, Indon.	G7	44
Maun, Bots.	D3	68
Maunabo, P.R.	B4	104a
Mauna Kea, vol., Hi., U.S.	D6	78a
Maunaloa, Hi., U.S.	B4	78a
Mauna Loa, vol., Hi., U.S.	D6	78a
Maunath Bhanjan, India	F9	54
Maungdaw, Mya.	H14	54
Maungmagan, Mya.	E3	48
Maunoir, Lac, l., N.T., Can.	B6	106
Maupihaa, at., Fr. Poly.	E11	72
Mau Rānīpur, India	F7	54
Maurepas, Lake, l., La., U.S.	G8	122
Maurice, Lake, l., Austl.	E6	74
Mauricie, Parc national de la, p.o.i., Qc., Can.	D3	110
Mauritania, ctry., Afr.	F2	64
Mauritanie see Mauritania, ctry., Afr.	F2	64
Mauritius, ctry., Afr.	h10	69a
Mauron, Fr.	F6	14
Mauston, Wi., U.S.	H8	118
Mautau, c., Fr. Poly.	r19	78g
Mauterndorf, Aus.	C10	22
Mauthen, Aus.	D9	22
Mauvais Coulee, stm., N.D., U.S.	F14	124
Mava, Pap. N. Gui.	b3	79a
Maverick, Az., U.S.	J7	132
Mavinga, Ang.	D3	68
Mavrovo Nacionalni Park, p.o.i., Mac.	B3	28
Mavuradonha Mountains, mts., Zimb.	D5	68
Mawchi, Mya.	C3	48
Mawlaik, Mya.	D7	46
Mawlamyine (Moulmein), Mya.	D3	48
Mawson, sci., Ant.	B11	81
Maw Taung (Luang, Khao), mtn., Asia	G4	48
Max, N.D., U.S.	G12	124
Maxaranguape, Braz.	C8	88
Maxcanú, Mex.	B3	102
Maxixe, Moz.	C12	70
Maxville, On., Can.	E2	110
Maxwell, Ca., U.S.	D3	134
Maxwell, Ne., U.S.	F12	126
Maxwell, N.M., U.S.	E4	128
May, Tx., U.S.	B9	130
May, Cape, pen., N.J., U.S.	F11	114
May, Mount, mtn., Ab., Can.	B11	138
Maya, Pulau, i., Indon.	D6	50
Mayaguana, i., Bah.	A11	102
Mayaguana Passage, strt., Bah.	A11	102
Mayagüez, P.R.	B1	104a
Mayang, China	H3	42
Mayarí, Cuba	B10	102
Maybole, Scot., U.K.	F8	12
Maydena, Austl.	o13	77a
Maydh, Som.	B9	66
Mayen, Ger.	F3	16
Mayenne, Fr.	F8	14
Mayenne, state, Fr.	F8	14
Mayenne, stm., Fr.	F8	14
Mayer, Az., U.S.	I4	132
Mayerthorpe, Ab., Can.	C15	138
Mayfield, Ky., U.S.	H9	120
Mayfield, Ut., U.S.	D5	132
Mayflower, Ar., U.S.	C6	122
Māyir, Syria	B8	58
Maykain see Majkain, Kaz.	D13	32
Maymyo, Mya.	A3	48
Maynard, Ia., U.S.	B6	120
Maynardville, Tn., U.S.	H2	114
Mayne, stm., Austl.	D3	76
Mayo, Yk., Can.	C3	106
Mayo, Fl., U.S.	F2	116
Mayo, state, Ire.	H3	12
Mayo, stm., Arg.	I3	90
Mayo, stm., Mex.	B4	100
Mayon Volcano, vol., Phil.	D4	52
Mayor Buratovich, Arg.	G4	90
Mayotte, dep., Afr.	C8	68
Mayoyoque, Col.	G4	86
May Pen, Jam.	j13	104d
Mayreau, i., St. Vin.	p11	105e
Mays Landing, N.J., U.S.	E11	114
Maysville, Ky., U.S.	F2	114
Maysville, Mo., U.S.	E3	120
Maysville, N.C., U.S.	B8	116
Maysville, Ok., U.S.	G11	128
Mayumba, Gabon	E2	66
Māyūram, India	F4	53
Mayville, Mi., U.S.	E6	112
Mayville, N.Y., U.S.	B6	114
Mayville, N.D., U.S.	G16	124
Maywood, Ne., U.S.	G12	126
Maza, Arg.	H6	92
Mazabuka, Zam.	D4	68
Mazagão, Braz.	D7	84
Mazamet, Fr.	F8	18
Mazán, stm., Peru	I4	86
Mazara, Val di, reg., Italy	G7	24
Mazara del Vallo, Italy	G6	24
Mazār-e Sharīf, Afg.	B10	56
Mazarrón, Golfo de, b., Spain	G9	20
Mazaruni, stm., Guy.	D11	86
Mazatenango, Guat.	E2	102
Mazatlán, Mex.	D5	100
Mažeikiai, Lith.	D5	10
Mazenod, Sk., Can.	E7	124
Mazinga, mtn., Neth. Ant.	C2	105a
Mazirbe, Lat.	C5	10
Mazon, Il., U.S.	C9	120
Mazowe, stm., Afr.	D5	68
Mazury (Masuria), reg., Pol.	C16	16
Mazyr, Bela.	D3	32
Mbabane, Swaz.	E10	70
M'bahiakro, C. Iv.	H4	64
Mbaïki, C.A.R.	D3	66
Mbaké, Sen.	G1	64
Mbala, Zam.	B5	68
Mbalabala, Zimb.	B9	70
Mbale, Ug.	D6	66
Mbalmayo, Cam.	D2	66
Mbamba Bay, Tan.	G7	66
Mbandaka (Coquilhatville), D.R.C.	D3	66
Mbanga, Cam.	D1	66
Mbanika Island, i., Sol. Is.	e8	79b
M'banza Congo, Ang.	B1	68
Mbanza-Ngungu, D.R.C.	F3	66
Mbarara, Ug.	E6	66
Mbashe, stm., S. Afr.	H9	70
Mbava Island, i., Sol. Is.	d7	79b
Mbé, Cam.	C2	66
Mberengwa, Zimb.	B9	70
Mbeya, Tan.	F6	66
Mbigou, Gabon	E2	66
Mbinda, Congo	E2	66
Mbini, Eq. Gui.	I6	64
Mbini, stm., Afr.	I6	64
Mboi, D.R.C.	F4	66
Mboki, C.A.R.	C5	66
Mbola, Sol. Is.	e9	79b
Mborokua, i., Sol. Is.	e8	79b
Mborong, Indon.	H12	50
Mbouda, Cam.	C2	66
Mbour, Sen.	G1	64
Mbout, Maur.	F2	64
Mbuji-Mayi (Bakwanga), D.R.C.	F4	66
Mbuluzi, stm., Swaz.	E10	70
Mbwemkuru, stm., Tan.	F7	66
McAdam, N.B., Can.	E9	110
McAdoo, Pa., U.S.	D9	114
McAlester, Ok., U.S.	C3	122
McAllen, Tx., U.S.	H9	130
McArthur, Oh., U.S.	E3	114
McArthur, stm., Austl.	C7	74
McArthur River, Austl.	C7	74
McBain, Mi., U.S.	D4	112
McBee, S.C., U.S.	B5	116
McBeth Fjord, b., Nu., Can.	B17	106
McBride, B.C., Can.	C10	138
McCall Creek, Ms., U.S.	F8	122
McCamey, Tx., U.S.	C5	130
McCammon, Id., U.S.	H14	136
McCauley Island, i., B.C., Can.	E4	106
McCleary, Wa., U.S.	C3	136
McClellan Creek, stm., Tx., U.S.	F8	128
McClellanville, S.C., U.S.	C6	116
McClintock, Mount, mtn., Ant.	D21	81
McCloud, Ca., U.S.	B3	134
McCloud, stm., Ca., U.S.	B3	134
McClure, Il., U.S.	G8	120
Mcclusky, N.D., U.S.	G13	124
McColl, S.C., U.S.	B6	116
McComb, Ms., U.S.	F8	122
McConaughy, Lake, res., Ne., U.S.	F11	126
McConnellsburg, Pa., U.S.	E7	114
McConnelsville, Oh., U.S.	E4	114
McCook, Ne., U.S.	A8	128
McCormick, S.C., U.S.	C3	116
McCreary, Mb., Can.	D14	124
McCullough Mountain, mtn., Nv., U.S.	H1	132
McCune, Ks., U.S.	G2	120
McCurtain, Ok., U.S.	B4	122
McDade, Tx., U.S.	D10	130
McDermitt, Nv., U.S.	B8	134
McDermott, Oh., U.S.	F2	114
McDonald, Ks., U.S.	B7	128
McDonald, Lake, l., Mt., U.S.	B12	136
McDowell Peak, mtn., Az., U.S.	J4	132
Mcensk, Russia	G19	10
McEwen, Tn., U.S.	H10	120
McFadden, Wy., U.S.	B10	132
McFarland, Ca., U.S.	H6	134
McGehee, Ar., U.S.	D7	122
McGill, Nv., U.S.	D2	132
McGrath, Ak., U.S.	D8	140
McGraw, N.Y., U.S.	B9	114
McGregor, Tx., U.S.	C10	130
McGregor, stm., B.C., Can.	B9	138
McGregor Lake, l., Ab., Can.	F18	138
McHenry, Il., U.S.	B9	120
McHenry, Ms., U.S.	G9	122
Mchinji, Mwi.	C5	68
McIntosh, Al., U.S.	F10	122
McIntosh, Mn., U.S.	D3	118
McIntyre Bay, b., On., Can.	B10	118
McKeand, stm., Nu., Can.	C17	106
McKee, Ky., U.S.	G2	114
McKeesport, Pa., U.S.	D6	114
McKenzie, Tn., U.S.	H9	120
McKenzie, stm., Or., U.S.	F4	136
McKenzie Bridge, Or., U.S.	F4	136
McKenzie Island, On., Can.	E12	106
McKinlay, Austl.	C3	76
McKinlay, stm., Austl.	C3	76
McKinley, Mount, mtn., Ak., U.S.	D9	140
McKinleyville, Ca., U.S.	C1	134
McKinney, Tx., U.S.	D2	122
McKittrick Summit, mtn., Ca., U.S.	H6	134
McLain, Ms., U.S.	F10	122
McLaurin, Ms., U.S.	F9	122
McLean, Il., U.S.	D8	120
McLean, Tx., U.S.	F8	128
McLeansboro, Il., U.S.	F9	120
McLennan, Ab., Can.	D7	106
McLeod, stm., Ab., Can.	C15	138
McLeod Bay, b., N.T., Can.	C8	106
McLeod Lake, B.C., Can.	B7	138
M'Clintock Channel, strt., Nu., Can.	A10	106
McLoughlin, Mount, mtn., Or., U.S.	A3	134
McLouth, Ks., U.S.	E2	120
M'Clure Strait, strt., N.T., Can.	B16	140
McMahon, Sk., Can.	D6	124
McMinnville, Or., U.S.	E3	136
McMinnville, Tn., U.S.	B13	122
McMurdo, sci., Ant.	C22	81
McMurdo Sound, strt., Ant.	C22	81
McNary, Az., U.S.	I7	132
McNeil, Ar., U.S.	D5	122
McPherson, Ks., U.S.	C11	128
McQueeney, Tx., U.S.	E9	130
McRae, Ar., U.S.	B7	122
McRae, Ga., U.S.	D3	116
McVeigh, Ky., U.S.	G3	114
McVille, N.D., U.S.	G15	124
McWilliams, Al., U.S.	F11	122
Mdantsane, S. Afr.	H8	70
M'drak, Viet.	F9	48
Mead, Ne., U.S.	C1	120
Mead, Lake, res., U.S.	G2	132
Meade, Ks., U.S.	D8	128
Meaden Peak, mtn., Co., U.S.	C9	132
Meadow, Ut., U.S.	E4	132
Meadow Lake, Sk., Can.	E9	106
Meadow Valley Wash, stm., Nv., U.S.	F2	132
Meadowview, Va., U.S.	H3	114
Meadville, Ms., U.S.	F7	122
Meadville, Mo., U.S.	E4	120
Meadville, Pa., U.S.	C5	114
Meaford, On., Can.	D9	112
Mealhada, Port.	D2	20
Meandarra, Austl.	F7	76
Meander River, Ab., Can.	D7	106
Mearim, stm., Braz.	B3	88
Meath, state, Ire.	H6	12
Meath, hist. reg., Ire.	H6	12
Meaux, Fr.	F11	14
Mecaya, stm., Col.	G4	86
Mecca see Makkah, Sau. Ar.	E4	56
Mechanicsburg, Oh., U.S.	D2	114
Mechanicsville, Ia., U.S.	C6	120
Mechanicsville, Va., U.S.	G8	114
Mechanicville, N.Y., U.S.	B12	114
Mechelen (Malines), Bel.	C13	14
Mecklenburg, hist. reg., Ger.	C7	16
Mecklenburger Bucht, b., Ger.	B7	16
Mecklenburg-Vorpommern, state, Ger.	C8	16
Mecubúri, Moz.	C6	68
Mecula, Moz.	C6	68
Meda, Port.	D3	20
Medak, India	B4	53
Medan, Indon.	B1	50
Medanosa, Punta, c., Arg.	I3	90
Mede, Italy	E5	22
Medeiros Neto, Braz.	I5	88
Medellín, Col.	D4	86
Médenine, Tun.	C6	64
Mederdra, Maur.	F1	64
Medford, Ok., U.S.	E11	128
Medford, Or., U.S.	A2	134
Medford, Wi., U.S.	F8	118
Medgidia, Rom.	E15	26
Mediapolis, Ia., U.S.	C6	120
Mediaș, Rom.	C11	26
Medicine Bow, Wy., U.S.	B10	132
Medicine Bow, stm., Wy., U.S.	A10	132
Medicine Bow Mountains, mts., U.S.	F6	126
Medicine Creek, stm., Mo., U.S.	E4	120
Medicine Hat, Ab., Can.	D3	124
Medicine Lake, Mt., U.S.	F9	124
Medicine Lodge, Ks., U.S.	D10	128
Medicine Lodge, stm., U.S.	D10	128
Medina, Braz.	I5	88
Medina see Al-Madīnah, Sau. Ar.	E4	56
Medina, N.Y., U.S.	E11	112
Medina, Oh., U.S.	C4	114
Medina, Tx., U.S.	E8	130
Medina, stm., Tx., U.S.	E9	130
Medinaceli, Spain	C8	20
Medina del Campo, Spain	C6	20
Medina-Sidonia, Spain	H5	20
Medinīpur, India	G11	54
Medio, Punta, c., Chile	C2	92
Medio Creek, stm., Tx., U.S.	F10	130
Mediterranean Sea	A4	62
Medje, D.R.C.	D5	66
Medjez el Bab, Tun.	H3	24
Medkovec, Blg.	F10	26
Mednogorsk, Russia	D9	32
Médoc, reg., Fr.	D4	18
Medora, N.D., U.S.	H10	124
Médouneu, Gabon	D2	66
Meductic, N.B., Can.	E9	110
Medveđa, Yugo.	G8	26
Medvedica, stm., Russia	C19	10
Medvedica, stm., Russia	D6	32
Medvėgalis, hill, Lith.	E5	10
Medvežegorsk, Russia	E15	8
Medvežji ostrova, is., Russia	B21	34
Medyn', Russia	F18	10
Meekatharra, Austl.	E3	74
Meeker, Co., U.S.	C8	132
Meeks Bay, Ca., U.S.	D5	134
Meeladeen, Som.	B9	66
Meerane, Ger.	F8	16
Meersburg, Ger.	I5	16
Meerut, India	D6	54
Mēga, Eth.	G7	62
Mega, Pulau, i., Indon.	E2	50
Megalópoli, Grc.	F4	28
Mégantic, Lac, l., Qc., Can.	E5	110
Mégara, Grc.	E6	28
Megargel, Tx., U.S.	H9	128
Meghālaya, state, India	F13	54
Meghna, stm., Bngl.	G13	54
Megísti, i., Grc.	G12	28
Megra, Russia	C19	8
Mehakit, Indon.	E9	50
Meharry, Mount, mtn., Austl.	D3	74
Mehedinți, state, Rom.	E10	26
Mehekar, India	H6	54
Meherrin, stm., U.S.	H7	114
Mehidpur, India	G5	54
Mehikoorma, Est.	B10	10
Mehndāwal, India	E9	54
Mehren'ga, Russia	F19	8
Mehrenga, stm., Russia	E19	8
Mehtarlām, Afg.	C11	56
Mehun-sur-Yèvre, Fr.	G11	14
Mei, stm., China	I7	42
Mei, stm., China	H7	42
Meia Meia, Tan.	F7	66
Meia Ponte, stm., Braz.	I1	88
Meichuan, China	F6	42
Meiganga, Cam.	C2	66
Meighen Island, i., Nu., Can.	A5	141
Meigs, Ga., U.S.	E1	116
Meihekou, China	C6	38
Meihsien see Meizhou, China	I7	42
Meikeng, China	J6	42
Meiktila, Mya.	B2	48
Meiners Oaks, Ca., U.S.	I6	134
Meiningen, Ger.	F6	16
Meishan, China	E5	36
Meissen, Ger.	E9	16
Meitan, China	H2	42
Meizhou, China	I7	42
Mejillones, Chile	D2	90
Mejillones, Península, pen., Chile	A2	92
Mejnypil'gyno, Russia	D24	34
Mékambo, Gabon	D2	66
Mek'elē, Eth.	E7	62
Mékhé, Sen.	F1	64
Mekhtar, Pak.	C2	54
Mekka see Makkah, Sau. Ar.	E4	56
Meknès, Mor.	C3	64
Mekong (Mékôngk) (Khong) (Lancang), stm., Asia	F9	46
Mekongga, Gunung, mtn., Indon.	F7	44
Mékôngk see Mekong, stm., Asia	F10	46
Melado, stm., Chile	H2	92
Melaka, Malay.	K6	48
Melaka, state, Malay.	K6	48
Melanesia, is., Oc.	D7	72
Melawi, stm., Indon.	D8	50
Melbourne, Austl.	K5	76
Melbourne, Ar., U.S.	H6	120
Melbourne, Fl., U.S.	H5	116
Melbourne, Ia., U.S.	J5	118
Melbourne Island, i., Nu., Can.	B10	106
Melcher, Ia., U.S.	C4	120
Melchor, Isla, i., Chile	I2	90
Melchor Múzquiz, Mex.	B8	100
Meldorf, Ger.	B4	16
Meldrum Bay, On., Can.	C6	112
Meldrum Creek, B.C., Can.	D8	138
Mélé, Baie, b., Vanuatu	k17	79d
Melekeok, Palau	g8	78b
Melenki, Russia	I19	8
Meleuz, Russia	D9	32
Mélèzes, stm., Qc., Can.	D16	106
Melfi, Chad	E3	62
Melfi, Italy	C9	24
Melfort, Sk., Can.	B9	124
Meliane, Oued, stm., Tun.	H4	24
Meliau, Indon.	D7	50
Meligalás, Grc.	F4	28
Melilla, Sp. N. Afr.	B4	64
Melimoyu, Cerro, vol., Chile	H2	90
Melincué, Arg.	F7	92
Melita, Mb., Can.	E12	124
Melitopol', Ukr.	E5	32
Melívoia, Grc.	D5	28
Mellansel, Swe.	E7	8
Mellen, Wi., U.S.	E8	118
Mellerud, Swe.	G5	8
Mellish Reef, at., Austl.	C11	74
Mellit, Sudan	E5	62
Mělník, Czech Rep.	F10	16
Melo, Ur.	F10	92
Melolo, Indon.	H12	50
Melos see Mílos, i., Grc.	G7	28
Melrhir, Chott, l., Alg.	C6	64
Melrose, Austl.	E4	74
Melrose, Austl.	I6	76
Melrose, Mn., U.S.	F4	118
Melrose, N.M., U.S.	G5	128
Melrose, Wi., U.S.	G8	118
Melsungen, Ger.	E5	16
Meltaus, Fin.	C11	8
Melton Mowbray, Eng., U.K.	I12	12
Melun, Fr.	F11	14
Melūr, India	F4	53
Melvern, Ks., U.S.	F2	120
Melvern Lake, res., Ks., U.S.	F2	120
Melville, Sk., Can.	D11	124
Melville, La., U.S.	G7	122
Melville, Cape, c., Austl.	B9	74
Melville Bugt, b., Grnld.	B12	141
Melville Hall Airport, Dom.	i6	105c
Melville Hills, hills, Can.	B7	106
Melville Island, i., Austl.	B6	74
Melville Island, i., Can.	A17	140
Melville Peninsula, pen., Nu., Can.	B14	106
Melvin, Ky., U.S.	G3	114
Melvin, Tx., U.S.	C8	130
Melyana, Alg.	H13	20
Mélykút, Hung.	C6	26
Mêmar Co, l., China	A9	54
Memba, Moz.	C7	68
Membalong, Indon.	E5	50
Memboro, Indon.	H11	50
Memel see Klaipėda, Lith.	E3	10
Memel, S. Afr.	E9	70
Mēmele (Nemunėlis), stm., Eur.	D7	10
Memmingen, Ger.	I5	16
Mempawah, Indon.	C6	50
Memphis, Fl., U.S.	I3	116
Memphis, Mi., U.S.	B3	114
Memphis, Tn., U.S.	B8	122
Memphis, Tx., U.S.	G8	128
Memphrémagog, Lac (Memphremagog, Lake), l., N.A.	E4	110
Memphremagog, Lake (Memphrémagog, Lac), l., N.A.	E4	110
Memramcook, N.B., Can.	D12	110
Mena, Ar., U.S.	C4	122
Menado see Manado, Indon.	E7	44
Ménaka, Mali	F5	64
Menan, Id., U.S.	G15	136
Menard, Tx., U.S.	D8	130
Menasha, Wi., U.S.	G10	118
Menate, Indon.	D8	50
Mendawai, Indon.	E8	50
Mendawai, stm., Indon.	E8	50
Mende, Fr.	E9	18
Mendebo, mts., Eth.	F7	62
Mendenhall, Ms., U.S.	F9	122
Mendī, Eth.	F7	62
Mendi, Pap. N. Gui.	b3	79a
Mendocino, Ca., U.S.	D2	134
Mendocino, Cape, c., Ca., U.S.	C1	134
Mendocino Fracture Zone, unds.	E24	142
Mendon, Il., U.S.	D6	120
Mendota, Ca., U.S.	G5	134
Mendoza, Arg.	F3	92
Mendoza, state, Arg.	G3	92
Mendoza, stm., Arg.	F3	92
Mene de Mauroa, Ven.	B6	86
Mene Grande, Ven.	C6	86
Menemen, Tur.	E9	28
Menen, Bel.	D12	14
Menfi, Italy	G6	24
Mengban, China	A5	48
Mengcheng, China	E7	42
Mengellang, Palau	f8	78b
Menggala, Indon.	F4	50
Menggudai, China	B2	42
Menghai, China	B5	48
Mengjiawan, China	B3	42
Mengla, China	B5	48
Menglian, China	A4	48
Mengxian, China	D5	42
Mengyin, China	D7	42
Mengzi, China	A6	48
Menihek Lakes, l., Nf., Can.	E17	106
Menin see Menen, Bel.	D12	14
Menindee, Austl.	I4	76
Menjuša, Russia	B13	10
Menlo Park, Ca., U.S.	F3	134
Menno, S.D., U.S.	D15	126
Meno, Ok., U.S.	E10	128
Menominee, Mi., U.S.	C2	112
Menominee, stm., U.S.	C2	112
Menomonee Falls, Wi., U.S.	A9	120
Menomonie, Wi., U.S.	G7	118
Menongue, Ang.	C2	68
Menor, Mar, b., Spain	G10	20
Menorca (Minorca), i., Spain	D15	20
Mentasta Lake, Ak., U.S.	D11	140
Mentawai, Kepulauan, is., Indon.	E1	50
Mentawai, Selat, strt., Indon.	D2	50
Menton, Fr.	F13	18
Mentor, Oh., U.S.	C4	114
Menyapa, Gunung, mtn., Indon.	C9	50
Menzel Bourguiba, Tun.	G3	24
Menzel Bou Zelfa, Tun.	H4	24
Menzelinsk, Russia	C8	32
Menzel Temime, Tun.	H5	24
Menzies, Austl.	E4	74
Menzies, Mount, mtn., Ant.	C10	81
Meobbaai, b., Nmb.	D2	70
Meoqui, Mex.	A6	100
Meota, Sk., Can.	A5	124
Meppel, Neth.	B15	14
Meppen, Ger.	D3	16
Meqerghane, Sebkha, pl., Alg.	D5	64
Mequinenza, Embalse de, res., Spain	C10	20
Mequon, Wi., U.S.	E2	112
Merah, Indon.	C10	50
Meramec, stm., Mo., U.S.	F7	120
Meran see Merano, Italy	D8	22
Merangin, stm., Indon.	E3	50
Merano (Meran), Italy	D8	22
Meratus, Pegunungan, mts., Indon.	E9	50
Merauke, Indon.	G11	44
Merbau, Indon.	C3	50
Merbein, Austl.	J4	76
Mercaderes, Col.	G3	86
Mercāra, India	E2	53
Merced, Ca., U.S.	F5	134
Merced, stm., Ca., U.S.	F5	134
Mercedario, Cerro, mtn., Arg.	E2	92
Mercedes, Arg.	D8	92
Mercedes, Arg.	G8	92
Mercedes, Tx., U.S.	H10	130
Mercedes, Ur.	F8	92
Mercer, Mo., U.S.	D4	120
Mercer, Pa., U.S.	C5	114
Mercersburg, Pa., U.S.	E7	114
Merchants Bay, b., Nu., Can.	D13	141
Mercoal, Ab., Can.	C13	138
Mercury, Nv., U.S.	G10	134
Mercury Islands, is., N.Z.	C6	80
Mercy, Cape, c., Nu., Can.	E13	141
Mercy Bay, b., N.T., Can.	B16	140
Meredith, Lake, res., Tx., U.S.	F7	128
Meredosia, Il., U.S.	E7	120
Mereeg, Som.	D9	66
Méré Lava, i., Vanuatu	j17	79d
Merevari, stm., Ven.	E9	86
Merëža, Russia	A19	10
Mergui, Mya.	F4	48
Mergui Archipelago, is., Mya.	G3	48
Meribah, Austl.	J3	76
Mérida, Mex.	B3	102
Mérida, Spain	F4	20
Mérida, Ven.	C6	86
Mérida, state, Ven.	C6	86
Mérida, Cordillera de, mts., Ven.	C6	86
Meridian, Ga., U.S.	E4	116
Meridian, Ms., U.S.	E10	122
Meridian, Tx., U.S.	C10	130
Meridianville, Al., U.S.	C12	122
Mérignac, Fr.	E5	18
Merigold, Ms., U.S.	D8	122
Merikarvia, Fin.	F9	8
Merimbula, Austl.	K7	76
Merín, Laguna (Mirim, Lagoa), b., S.A.	F11	92
Merinda, Austl.	B6	76
Merino, Co., U.S.	G9	126
Merinos, Ur.	F9	92
Merizo, Guam	j9	78c
Merkinė, Lith.	F7	10
Merkys, stm., Lith.	F8	10
Merlin, On., Can.	F7	112
Merlin, Or., U.S.	H3	136
Merna, Ne., U.S.	F13	126
Meron, Har (Meron, Mount), mtn., Isr.	E6	58
Meron, Mount see Meron, Har, mtn., Isr.	E6	58
Merouane, Chott, l., Alg.	C6	64
Merredin, Austl.	F3	74
Merrick, mtn., Scot., U.K.	F8	12
Merrill, Ia., U.S.	B1	120
Merrill, Mi., U.S.	E5	112
Merrill, Or., U.S.	A4	134
Merrillan, Wi., U.S.	G8	118
Merrillville, In., U.S.	G2	112
Merrimack, stm., U.S.	H5	110
Merriman, Ne., U.S.	E11	126
Merritt, B.C., Can.	F10	138
Merritt Island, Fl., U.S.	H5	116
Merriwa, Austl.	I8	76
Mer Rouge, La., U.S.	E7	122
Merrygoen, Austl.	H7	76
Merryville, La., U.S.	G5	122
Mersa Matruh, Egypt	A5	62
Mersea Island, i., Eng., U.K.	J13	12
Merseburg, Ger.	E7	16
Mersey, stm., Austl.	n13	77a
Mersey, stm., N.S., Can.	F12	110
Mersing, Malay.	K6	48
Mērsrags, Lat.	C6	10
Merta, India	E5	54
Merthyr Tydfil, Wales, U.K.	J9	12
Mértola, Port.	G3	20
Mertz Glacier Tongue, ice, Ant.	B19	81
Méru, Fr.	E11	14
Meru, Kenya	D7	66
Meruoca, Braz.	B5	88
Merweville, S. Afr.	H5	70
Merzifon, Tur.	A4	56
Merzig, Ger.	G2	16
Mesa, Az., U.S.	J5	132
Mesabi Range, hills, Mn., U.S.	D6	118
Mesagne, Italy	D11	24
Mesáras, Órmos, b., Grc.	I7	28
Mesa Verde National Park, p.o.i., Co., U.S.	F8	132
Mescalero, N.M., U.S.	H3	128
Meščerino, Russia	G20	10
Meschede, Ger.	E4	16
Meščura, Russia	E24	8
Mesewa see Massawa, Erit.	D7	62
Mesgouez, Lac, l., Qc., Can.	E16	106
Mesick, Mi., U.S.	D4	112
Mesilla, N.M., U.S.	K10	132
Meškuičiai, Lith.	D6	10
Mesolóngi, Grc.	E4	28
Mesopotamia, hist. reg., Asia	C5	56
Mesquite, Tx., U.S.	E2	122
Messalo, stm., Moz.	C6	68
Messina, Italy	F9	24
Messina, S. Afr.	C9	70
Messina, Gulf of see Messiniakós Kólpos, b., Grc.	G5	28
Messina, Stretto di, strt., Italy	F9	24
Messini, Grc.	F4	28
Messíni, hist., Grc.	F4	28
Messiniakós Kólpos, b., Grc.	G5	28
Messix Peak, mtn., Ut., U.S.	B4	132
Messkirch, Ger.	H5	16
Messojaha, stm., Russia	C4	34
Mesta (Néstos), stm., Eur.	B6	28
Mestghanem, Alg.	B4	64
Mestre, ngh., Italy	E9	22
Mesuji, stm., Indon.	E4	50
Meta, state, Col.	F5	86
Meta, stm., S.A.	D7	86
Métabetchouan, Qc., Can.	B5	110
Métabetchouane, stm., Qc., Can.	B4	110
Meta Incognita Peninsula, pen., Nu., Can.	C17	106
Metairie, La., U.S.	H8	122
Metaline Falls, Wa., U.S.	B9	136
Metamora, Il., U.S.	D8	120
Metán, Arg.	B5	92
Metangula, Moz.	C5	68
Metapán, El Sal.	E3	102
Metaponto, hist., Italy	D10	24
Metapontum see Metaponto, hist., Italy	D10	24
Meteor Crater, crat., Az., U.S.	H6	132
Metharaw, Mya.	D4	48
Methow, Wa., U.S.	B7	136
Methow, stm., Wa., U.S.	B6	136
Methven, N.Z.	F4	80
Metica, stm., Col.	E5	86
Metiskow, Ab., Can.	B3	124
Metlakatla, Ak., U.S.	E13	140
Metlika, Slvn.	E12	22
Meto, Bayou, stm., Ar., U.S.	C7	122
Metropolis, Il., U.S.	G9	120
Metropolitan, Mi., U.S.	C2	112
Metter, Ga., U.S.	D3	116
Mettuppālaiyam, India	F3	53
Mettūr, India	F3	53
Metz, Fr.	E15	14
Metzingen, Ger.	H5	16
Meu, stm., Fr.	F7	14
Meulaboh, Indon.	J2	48
Meureudu, Indon.	J3	48
Meurthe, stm., Fr.	F15	14
Meurthe-et-Moselle, state, Fr.	F15	14
Meuse, state, Fr.	E14	14
Meuse (Maas), stm., Eur.	D14	14
Meuselwitz, Ger.	E8	16
Mexiana, Ilha, i., Braz.	C8	84
Mexicali, Mex.	K10	134
Mexican Hat, Ut., U.S.	F7	132
México see Ciudad de México, Mex.	F9	100
Mexico, Me., U.S.	F6	110
Mexico, Mo., U.S.	E6	120
Mexico, N.Y., U.S.	E13	112
México, state, Mex.	F9	100
Mexico, ctry., N.A.	C4	96
Mexico, Gulf of, b., N.A.	B6	96
Mexico Basin, unds.	F5	144
Mexico Bay, b., N.Y., U.S.	E13	112
Mexico City see Ciudad de México, Mex.	F9	100
Meycauayan, Phil.	C3	52
Meydān Khvolah, Afg.	B2	54
Meyersdale, Pa., U.S.	E6	114
Meymaneh, Afg.	B9	56
Meyronne, Sk., Can.	E7	124
Meyungs, Palau	g7	78b
Mëža (M'oža), stm., Eur.	E14	10
Meẓada, Ḥorvot (Masada), hist., Isr.	G6	58
Mezcala, Mex.	G9	100
Mezcalapa, stm., Mex.	G12	100
Meždurečensk, Russia	D15	32
Meždurečenskij, Russia	C10	32
Mèze, Fr.	F9	18
Mezen', Russia	D21	8
Mezen', stm., Russia	D21	8
Mezenskaja guba, b., Russia	C20	8
Mežica, Slvn.	D11	22
Mezőberény, Hung.	C8	26
Mezőcsát, Hung.	B7	26
Mezőkövesd, Hung.	B7	26
Mezőtúr, Hung.	B7	26
Mezquital, stm., Mex.	D6	100
Mfangano Island, i., Kenya	E6	66
Mgači, Russia	F17	34
M'Goun, Irhil, mtn., Mor.	C3	64
M'hai, B'nom, mtn., Viet.	G8	48
Mhasvād, India	C2	53
Mhow, India	G5	54
Mi, stm., China	H5	42
Mi, stm., China	C8	42
Mia, Oued, stm., Alg.	D5	64
Miahuatlán de Porfirio Díaz, Mex.	G10	100
Miajadas, Spain	E4	20
Miaméré, C.A.R.	C4	66
Miami, Mb., Can.	E15	124
Miami, Az., U.S.	J6	132
Miami, Fl., U.S.	K5	116
Miami, Ok., U.S.	H3	120
Miami, Tx., U.S.	F8	128
Miami Beach, Fl., U.S.	K5	116
Miami Canal, can., Fl., U.S.	J5	116
Miamisburg, Oh., U.S.	E1	114
Miami Springs, Fl., U.S.	K5	116
Miān Channūn, Pak.	C4	54
Mianchi, China	D4	42
Miandrivazo, Madag.	D8	68
Mianduhe, China	B9	36
Mīāneh, Iran	B6	56
Miang, Phu, mtn., Thai.	D5	48
Mianning, China	F5	36
Miānwāli, Pak.	B3	54

Name	Map Ref.	Page
Mianxian, China	E2	42
Mianyang, China	F1	42
Mianzhu, China	E5	36
Miaodao Qundao, is., China	B9	42
Miaoli, Tai.	I9	42
Miao Ling, mts., China	H2	42
Miass, Russia	C10	32
Miass, stm., Russia	C10	32
Miastko, Pol.	B12	16
Micang Shan, mts., China	E2	42
Michalovce, Slov.	H17	16
Michaud, Point, c., N.S., Can.	E16	110
Micheal Peak, mtn., B.C., Can.	C4	138
Michel, B.C., Can.	G16	138
Miches, Dom. Rep.	C13	102
Michigan, N.D., U.S.	F15	124
Michigan, state, U.S.	C10	108
Michigan, stm., Co., U.S.	G6	126
Michigan, Lake, l., U.S.	E2	112
Michigan City, In., U.S.	G3	112
Michipicoten Island, i., On., Can.	F13	106
Michoacán, state, Mex.	F8	100
Micoud, St. Luc.	m7	105c
Micronesia, is., Oc.	B6	72
Micronesia, Federated States of, ctry., Oc.	C6	72
Mičurinsk, Russia	D6	32
Midai, Pulau, i., Indon.	B5	50
Midale, Sk., Can.	E10	124
Mid-Atlantic Ridge, unds.	F9	144
Middelburg, Neth.	C12	14
Middelburg, S. Afr.	G7	70
Middelburg, S. Afr.	D9	70
Middle, stm., B.C., Can.	B5	138
Middle, stm., Ia., U.S.	C3	120
Middle, stm., Mn., U.S.	C2	118
Middle Alkali Lake, l., Ca., U.S.	B5	134
Middle America Trench, unds.	H29	142
Middle Andaman, i., India	F7	46
Middleboro, Ma., U.S.	C15	114
Middlebourne, W.V., U.S.	E5	114
Middleburg, N.Y., U.S.	B11	114
Middleburg, Pa., U.S.	D8	114
Middlebury, Vt., U.S.	F3	110
Middle Caicos, i., T./C. Is.	B12	102
Middle Fabius, stm., Mo., U.S.	D5	120
Middlefield, Oh., U.S.	C4	114
Middlegate, Norf. I.	y25	78i
Middle Loup, stm., Ne., U.S.	F14	126
Middlemount, Austl.	D7	76
Middle Musquodoboit, N.S., Can.	E13	110
Middleport, Oh., U.S.	E3	114
Middle Raccoon, stm., Ia., U.S.	J4	118
Middlesboro, Ky., U.S.	H2	114
Middlesbrough, Eng., U.K.	G11	12
Middlesex, Belize	D3	102
Middle Stewiacke, N.S., Can.	E13	110
Middleton, N.S., Can.	F11	110
Middleton, Mi., U.S.	E5	112
Middleton, Wi., U.S.	A8	120
Middleton Island, i., Ak., U.S.	E10	140
Middleton Reef, at., Austl.	E11	74
Middletown, Ca., U.S.	E3	134
Middletown, Ct., U.S.	C13	114
Middletown, Il., U.S.	K9	118
Middletown, In., U.S.	H4	112
Middletown, Ky., U.S.	F12	120
Middletown, Md., U.S.	E8	114
Middletown, N.Y., U.S.	C11	114
Middletown, Oh., U.S.	E1	114
Middletown, Pa., U.S.	D9	114
Middletown, R.I., U.S.	C14	114
Middleville, Mi., U.S.	F4	112
Midgic, N.B., Can.	E12	110
Midi, Canal du, can., Fr.	F9	18
Midi de Bigorre, Pic du, mtn., Fr.	G5	18
Mid-Indian Basin, unds.	J10	142
Mid-Indian Ridge, unds.	L10	142
Midland, On., Can.	D9	112
Midland, Ca., U.S.	J2	132
Midland, Mi., U.S.	E5	112
Midland, S.D., U.S.	C11	126
Midland, Tx., U.S.	C5	130
Midlands, state, Zimb.	B10	70
Midleton, Ire.	J4	12
Midlothian, Tx., U.S.	B11	130
Midnapore, Ab., Can.	F16	138
Midongy Atsimo, Madag.	E8	68
Mid-Pacific Mountains, unds.	G19	142
Midsayap, Phil.	G5	52
Midville, Ga., U.S.	D3	116
Midway, B.C., Can.	G12	138
Midway, Al., U.S.	E13	122
Midway, Ky., U.S.	F13	120
Midway, Tx., U.S.	F3	122
Midway Islands, dep., Oc.	G22	30
Midway Park, N.C., U.S.	B8	116
Midwest City, Ok., U.S.	F11	128
Midyan, reg., Sau. Ar.	J6	58
Midžur (Midžor), mtn., Eur.	F9	26
Mie, Japan	G4	40
Mie, state, Japan	E9	40
Międzybórz, Pol.	E13	16
Międzylesie, Pol.	F12	16
Międzyrzec Podlaski, Pol.	D18	16
Międzyrzecz, Pol.	D11	16
Miélan, Fr.	F6	18
Mielec, Pol.	F17	16
Mier, Mex.	B9	100
Miercurea-Ciuc, Rom.	C12	26
Mieres, Spain	A5	20
Mieroszów, Pol.	F12	16
Mier y Noriega, Mex.	D8	100
Miesbach, Ger.	I7	16
Mī'ēso, Eth.	F8	62
Mieszkowice, Pol.	D10	16
Mifflinburg, Pa., U.S.	H12	112
Miguel Alemán, Presa, res., Mex.	F10	100
Miguel Alves, Braz.	C4	88
Miguel Auza, Mex.	C7	100
Miguel Calmon, Braz.	F5	88
Miguel Hidalgo, Presa, res., Mex.	B4	100
Miguelópolis, Braz.	K1	88
Miguel Riglos, Arg.	H6	92
Mihăești, Rom.	D12	26
Mihajlovka, Russia	D6	32
Mihajlovka, Russia	D14	32
Mihajlovka, Russia	C10	38
Mihajlovskij, Russia	F20	8
Mihalgazi, Tur.	C13	28
Mihanavičy, Bela.	G10	10
Mihara, Japan	E5	40
Mihara-yama, vol., Japan	E12	40
Mihninskaja, Russia	F21	8
Mikame, Japan	F5	40
Mikasa, Japan	C14	38
Mikaševičy, Bela.	H10	10
Mikhrot Timna'(King Solomon's Mines), hist., Isr.	I5	58
Mikindani, Tan.	G8	66
Mikkeli (Sankt Michel), Fin.	F12	8
Mikkeli, state, Fin.	F12	8
Mikołajki, Pol.	C17	16
Mikołów, Pol.	F14	16
Mikrá Préspa, Límni, l., Eur.	D15	24
Mikšino, Russia	C18	10
Mikulino, Russia	E14	10
Mikumi, Tan.	F7	66
Mikun', Russia	E23	8
Mikuni, Japan	C9	40
Miladummadulu Atoll, at., Mald.	h12	46a
Milagro, Arg.	E5	92
Milagro, Ec.	I2	86
Milagros, Phil.	D4	52
Milan see Milano, Italy	E6	22
Milan, Ga., U.S.	D2	116
Milan, In., U.S.	E12	120
Milan, Mi., U.S.	B2	114
Milan, Mn., U.S.	F3	118
Milan, Mo., U.S.	D4	120
Milan, N.M., U.S.	H8	132
Milang, Austl.	J2	76
Milange, Moz.	D6	68
Milano (Milan), Italy	E6	22
Milâs, Tur.	F10	28
Milavidy, Bela.	H8	10
Milazzo, Italy	F9	24
Milazzo, Golfo di, b., Italy	F9	24
Milbank, S.D., U.S.	F2	118
Milburn, Ok., U.S.	C2	122
Milden, Sk., Can.	C6	124
Mildmay, On., Can.	D8	112
Mildura, Austl.	J4	76
Mile, China	G5	36
Miles, Austl.	F8	76
Miles, Tx., U.S.	C7	130
Miles City, Mt., U.S.	A7	126
Milestone, Sk., Can.	E9	124
Milet, hist., Tur.	F10	28
Milford, De., U.S.	F10	114
Milford, Ia., U.S.	H3	118
Milford, Me., U.S.	F8	110
Milford, Ma., U.S.	B14	114
Milford, Mi., U.S.	B2	114
Milford, N.H., U.S.	B14	114
Milford, Pa., U.S.	C11	114
Milford, Ut., U.S.	E4	132
Milford Center, Oh., U.S.	D2	114
Milford Haven, Wales, U.K.	J7	12
Milford Lake, res., Ks., U.S.	B11	128
Milford Sound, strt., N.Z.	G2	80
Mili, at., Marsh. Is.	C8	72
Milian, stm., Malay.	A10	50
Milicz, Pol.	E13	16
Miljatino, Russia	F17	10
Milk, stm., N.A.	B6	108
Milk, North Fork (North Milk), stm., N.A.	B13	136
Mil'kovo, Russia	F20	34
Milk River, Ab., Can.	G18	138
Millard, Ne., U.S.	C1	120
Millau, Fr.	E9	18
Millboro, Va., U.S.	F6	114
Millbrook, N.Y., U.S.	C12	114
Mill City, Or., U.S.	F4	136
Millcreek, Pa., U.S.	B5	114
Millcreek, Ut., U.S.	C5	132
Mill Creek, W.V., U.S.	F5	114
Milledgeville, Ga., U.S.	C2	116
Milledgeville, Il., U.S.	C8	120
Mille Lacs, Lac des, l., On., Can.	C8	118
Mille Lacs Lake, l., Mn., U.S.	E5	118
Millen, Ga., U.S.	D4	116
Miller, Mo., U.S.	G4	120
Miller, S.D., U.S.	C14	126
Miller Mountain, mtn., Nv., U.S.	E7	134
Millerovo, Russia	E6	32
Millersburg, Ky., U.S.	F1	114
Millersburg, Mi., U.S.	C5	112
Millersburg, Oh., U.S.	D4	114
Millersport, Oh., U.S.	I7	112
Millerton, N.Y., U.S.	C12	114
Millet, Ab., Can.	C17	138
Millevaches, Plateau de, plat., Fr.	D7	18
Millicent, Austl.	K3	76
Milligan, Fl., U.S.	G12	122
Milligan, Ne., U.S.	G15	126
Millington, Mi., U.S.	E6	112
Millington, Tn., U.S.	B9	122
Millinocket, Me., U.S.	E8	110
Mill Island, i., Ant.	B15	81
Mill Island, i., Nu., Can.	C15	106
Millry, Al., U.S.	F10	122
Mills, Wy., U.S.	E6	126
Mills Creek, stm., Austl.	D4	76
Mills Lake, l., N.T., Can.	C7	106
Millstream, Austl.	D3	74
Milltown, Mt., U.S.	D13	136
Milltown, Wi., U.S.	F6	118
Milltown Malbay, Ire.	I3	12
Mill Valley, Ca., U.S.	F3	134
Millville, N.J., U.S.	E10	114
Millwood, Va., U.S.	E7	114
Millwood Lake, res., Ar., U.S.	D4	122
Milne Land, i., Grnld.	C20	141
Milnor, N.D., U.S.	A15	126
Milo, Ab., Can.	F18	138
Mílos, i., Grc.	G7	28
Miłosław, Pol.	D13	16
Milparinka, Austl.	G3	76
Milroy, In., U.S.	E12	120
Milroy, Pa., U.S.	D8	114
Miltenberg, Ger.	G5	16
Milton, On., Can.	E10	112
Milton, N.Z.	H4	80
Milton, Fl., U.S.	G11	122
Milton, Ia., U.S.	D5	120
Milton, Pa., U.S.	G13	112
Milton, Wi., U.S.	B9	120
Milton-Freewater, Or., U.S.	E8	136
Milton Keynes, Eng., U.K.	I12	12
Miltonvale, Ks., U.S.	B11	128
Miltou, Chad	E3	62
Miluo, stm., China	G5	42
Milwaukee, Wi., U.S.	E2	112
Milwaukee, stm., Wi., U.S.	H11	118
Milwaukie, Or., U.S.	E4	136
Mimbres, stm., N.M., U.S.	K9	132
Mimizan-les-Bains, Fr.	E4	18
Mimoň, Czech Rep.	F10	16
Mimoso do Sul, Braz.	K5	88
Mims, Fl., U.S.	H5	116
Min, stm., China	F5	36
Min, stm., China	I8	42
Mina, Mex.	H7	130
Mina, Nv., U.S.	E7	134
Mīnā' al-Aḥmadī, Kuw.	D6	56
Mīnāb, Iran	D8	56
Minahasa, pen., Indon.	E7	44
Minakuchi, Japan	E9	40
Minamata, Japan	G3	40
Minami-Alps-kokuritsu-kōen, p.o.i., Japan	D11	40
Minami-Tori-shima, i., Japan	G19	30
Minas, Cuba	B9	102
Minas, Indon.	C2	50
Minas, Ur.	G10	92
Minas Basin, b., N.S., Can.	E12	110
Minas de Barroterán, Mex.	B8	100
Minas de Corrales, Ur.	E10	92
Minas de Matahambre, Cuba	A5	102
Minas Gerais, state, Braz.	C8	90
Minas Novas, Braz.	I4	88
Minatare, Ne., U.S.	F9	126
Minatitlán, Mex.	F11	100
Minbu, Mya.	B2	48
Minbya, Mya.	B1	48
Minbyin, Mya.	C1	48
Mincio, stm., Italy	E7	22
Minco, Ok., U.S.	F10	128
Minčol, mtn., Slov.	G17	16
Mindanao, i., Phil.	G5	52
Mindanao, stm., Phil.	G5	52
Mindelheim, Ger.	H6	16
Mindelo, C.V.	k10	65a
Mindemoya, On., Can.	C7	112
Minden, On., Can.	D11	112
Minden, Ger.	D4	16
Minden, La., U.S.	E5	122
Minden, Ne., U.S.	G14	126
Minden, Nv., U.S.	E6	134
Minden City, Mi., U.S.	E7	112
Mindoro, i., Phil.	D3	52
Mindoro Strait, strt., Phil.	D3	52
Mine, Japan	E4	40
Mine Centre, On., Can.	C6	118
Minehead, Eng., U.K.	J9	12
Mineiros, Braz.	G7	84
Mineola, Tx., U.S.	E3	122
Mineral, Wa., U.S.	D4	136
Mineral Point, Wi., U.S.	B7	120
Mineral Springs, Ar., U.S.	D5	122
Mineral Wells, Tx., U.S.	B9	130
Minersville, Pa., U.S.	H13	112
Minerva, Oh., U.S.	D4	114
Minervino Murge, Italy	C9	24
Mineville, N.Y., U.S.	F3	110
Minfeng, China	A5	46
Minga, D.R.C.	G5	66
Mingäçevir, Azer.	A6	56
Mingāora, Pak.	C11	56
Mingary, Austl.	I3	76
Mingene, Austl.	E3	74
Mingin, Mya.	A2	48
Minglanilla, Spain	E9	20
Mingo Junction, Oh., U.S.	D5	114
Mingo Lake, l., Nu., Can.	C16	106
Mingshui, China	B10	36
Mingulay, i., Scot., U.K.	E5	12
Mingyuegou, China	C8	38
Minhang, China	F9	42
Minh Hai, Viet.	H7	48
Minhla, Mya.	B2	48
Minhla, Mya.	C2	48
Minho, hist. reg., Port.	C2	20
Minho (Miño), stm., Eur.	B2	20
Minićevo, Yugo.	F9	26
Minicoy Island, i., India	G3	46
Minigwal, Lake, l., Austl.	E4	74
Minija, stm., Lith.	E4	10
Minilya, Austl.	D2	74
Minilya, stm., Austl.	D2	74
Miniota, Mb., Can.	D12	124
Minitonas, Mb., Can.	B12	124
Minle, China	D5	36
Minna, Nig.	H6	64
Minneapolis, Ks., U.S.	B11	128
Minneapolis, Mn., U.S.	G5	118
Minnedosa, Mb., Can.	D13	124
Minneola, Ks., U.S.	D8	128
Minneota, Mn., U.S.	G2	118
Minnesota, state, U.S.	E4	118
Minnesota, stm., Mn., U.S.	G5	118
Minnesota Lake, Mn., U.S.	H5	118
Minnewanka, Lake, res., Ab., Can.	E15	138
Minnitaki Lake, l., On., Can.	B6	118
Mino, Japan	D9	40
Miño (Minho), stm., Eur.	B2	20
Minocqua, Wi., U.S.	F9	118
Minong, Wi., U.S.	E7	118
Minonk, Il., U.S.	D8	120
Minorca see Menorca, i., Spain	D15	20
Minot, N.D., U.S.	F12	124
Minqing, China	H8	42
Minquan, China	D6	42
Minquiers, Plateau des, is., Jersey	E6	14
Min Shan, mts., China	E5	36
Minsk, Bela.	G10	10
Minsk, state, Bela.	G10	10
Minskae uzvyšša, plat., Bela.	G10	10
Mińsk Mazowiecki, Pol.	D17	16
Minta, Cam.	D2	66
Minto, Mb., Can.	E13	124
Minto, Yk., Can.	C3	106
Minto, N.D., U.S.	C1	118
Minto, Lac, l., Qc., Can.	D16	106
Minto, Mount, mtn., Ant.	C22	81
Minto Inlet, b., N.T., Can.	A7	106
Minton, Sk., Can.	E9	124
Minturn, Co., U.S.	D10	132
Minûf, Egypt	H1	58
Minusinsk, Russia	D16	32
Minvoul, Gabon	D2	66
Minxian, China	E5	36
Minya see El-Minya, Egypt	J1	58
Minya el-Qamh, Egypt	H2	58
Mio, Mi., U.S.	D5	112
Miquan, China	F15	32
Mir, Bela.	G9	10
Mira, stm., Col.	G2	86
Mīrābād, Afg.	C9	56
Mirabella, Gulf of see Mirampéllou, Kólpos, b., Grc.	H8	28
Miracema do Tocantins, Braz.	E1	88
Mirador, Braz.	D3	88
Miradouro, Braz.	K4	88
Miraflores, Col.	E5	86
Miraflores, Col.	G5	86
Miraj, India	C2	53
Miramar, Arg.	I9	92
Miramar, Moz.	C12	70
Miramas, Fr.	F10	18
Miramichi Bay, b., N.B., Can.	C11	110
Mirampéllou, Kólpos, b., Grc.	H8	28
Mīrān, Pak.	C3	54
Miranda, Braz.	D5	90
Miranda, Col.	F3	86
Miranda, state, Ven.	B8	86
Miranda, stm., Braz.	D5	90
Miranda de Ebro, Spain	B7	20
Mirande, Fr.	F6	18
Mirando City, Tx., U.S.	G8	130
Mirandola, Italy	F8	22
Mira Táglio, Italy	E9	22
Miravalles, Volcán, vol., C.R.	G5	102
Miravete, Puerto de, p., Spain	E5	20
Mirbāṭ, Oman	F7	56
Mirecourt, Fr.	F14	14
Miri, Malay.	A9	50
Miria, Niger	G6	64
Miriam Vale, Austl.	E8	76
Mirim, Lagoa (Merín, Laguna), b., S.A.	F11	92
Miriñay, stm., Arg.	D9	92
Miritiparaná, stm., Col.	H6	86
Miriyama, Pap. N. Gui.	a3	79a
Mirnoe Ozero, Russia	C13	32
Mirny, sci., Ant.	B14	81
Mirnyj, Russia	D11	34
Mirnyy, sci., Ant.	B14	81
Miroslav, Czech Rep.	H12	16
Mirow, Ger.	C8	16
Mīrpur, Bngl.	G13	54
Mīrpur, Pak.	B4	54
Mīrpur Batoro, Pak.	F2	54
Mīrpur Khās, Pak.	F2	54
Mirror, Ab., Can.	D17	138
Mirtóon Pélagos, Grc.	G6	28
Miryang, Kor., S.	D1	40
Mirzāpur, India	F9	54
Misantla, Mex.	F10	100
Misawa, Japan	D14	38
Miscou Centre, N.B., Can.	C12	110
Miscou Island, i., N.B., Can.	C12	110
Miscou Point, c., N.B., Can.	B12	110
Mishan, China	B9	38
Mishawaka, In., U.S.	G3	112
Mishicot, Wi., U.S.	D2	112
Misima Island, i., Pap. N. Gui.	B10	74
Misiones, state, Arg.	C10	92
Misiones, state, Para.	C9	92
Misión Santa Rosa, Para.	D4	90
Misión San Vicente, Mex.	F4	98
Miskitos, Cayos, is., Nic.	E6	102
Miskolc, Hung.	A7	26
Mišnëvo, Russia	G19	10
Misool, Pulau, i., Indon.	F9	44
Miṣrātah, Libya	A3	62
Misr el-Bahrî (Lower Egypt), hist. reg., Egypt	G2	58
Misrikh, India	E8	54
Missinaibi, stm., On., Can.	E14	106
Missinaibi Lake, l., On., Can.	F14	106
Mission, B.C., Can.	G8	138
Mission, S.D., U.S.	D12	126
Mission, Tx., U.S.	H9	130
Mission Mountain, hill, Ok., U.S.	H3	120
Mission Viejo, Ca., U.S.	J8	134
Mississagi, stm., On., Can.	B6	112
Mississauga, On., Can.	E10	112
Mississinewa, stm., U.S.	H4	112
Mississippi, state, U.S.	D9	122
Mississippi, stm., On., Can.	C13	112
Mississippi, stm., U.S.	E9	108
Mississippi Lake, l., On., Can.	C13	112
Mississippi River Delta, La., U.S.	H9	122
Mississippi Sound, strt., U.S.	G10	122
Mississippi State, Ms., U.S.	D10	122
Missoula, Mt., U.S.	D12	136
Missouri, state, U.S.	F5	120
Missouri, stm., U.S.	D9	108
Missouri City, Tx., U.S.	H3	122
Mistake Creek, stm., Austl.	D6	76
Mistassibi, stm., Qc., Can.	A4	110
Mistassini, Qc., Can.	E16	106
Mistassini, Qc., Can.	B4	110
Mistassini, stm., Qc., Can.	B4	110
Mistassini, Lac, l., Qc., Can.	E16	106
Mistatim, Sk., Can.	B10	124
Mistelbach an der Zaya, Aus.	B13	22
Misterbianco, Italy	G9	24
Misti, Volcán, vol., Peru	G3	84
Misumi, Japan	E4	40
Mišutino, Russia	A19	10
Mita, Punta de, c., Mex.	E6	100
Mitchell, Austl.	F6	76
Mitchell, On., Can.	E8	112
Mitchell, In., U.S.	F11	120
Mitchell, Or., U.S.	F6	136
Mitchell, S.D., U.S.	D14	126
Mitchell, stm., Austl.	C8	74
Mitchell, stm., Austl.	K6	76
Mitchell, Mount, mtn., N.C., U.S.	I3	114
Mitchinamecus, stm., Qc., Can.	C2	110
Mitchinamecus, Réservoir, res., Qc., Can.	C1	110
Mīt Ghamr, Egypt	H2	58
Mithapur, India	G2	54
Mithi, Pak.	F2	54
Mitidja, Plaine de la, pl., Alg.	H14	20
Mitiškovo, Russia	F16	10
Mitla, hist., Mex.	G10	100
Mito, Japan	C13	40
Mitsio, Nosy, i., Madag.	C8	68
Mitsukaidō, Japan	C13	40
Mitsuke, Japan	B11	40
Mittellandkanal, can., Ger.	D5	16
Mittenwald, Ger.	I7	16
Mittersill, Aus.	C9	22
Mittweida, Ger.	E9	16
Mitú, Col.	G6	86
Mitumba, Monts, mts., D.R.C.	F5	66
Mitwaba, D.R.C.	F5	66
Mitzic, Gabon	D2	66
Miura, Japan	D12	40
Miura-hantō, pen., Japan	D12	40
Mixian, China	D5	42
Miyagi, state, Japan	A13	40
Miyake-jima, i., Japan	E12	40
Miyako, Japan	E14	38
Miyako-jima, i., Japan	G10	36
Miyakonojō, Japan	H4	40
Miyama, Japan	E9	40
Miyanojō, Japan	H3	40
Miyazaki, Japan	H4	40
Miyazaki, state, Japan	G4	40
Miyazu, Japan	D8	40
Miyoshi, Japan	E5	40
Miyun, China	A7	42
Miyun Shuiku, res., China	A7	42
Mīzan Teferī, Eth.	F7	62
Mizdah, Libya	A2	62
Mize, Ms., U.S.	F9	122
Mizen Head, c., Ire.	I6	12
Mizen Head, c., Ire.	J3	12
Mizhhir'ia, Ukr.	A10	26
Mizhi, China	C4	42
Mizil, Rom.	E13	26
Mizoram, state, India	G14	54
Mizpah Creek, stm., Mt., U.S.	A7	126
Mizque, Bol.	C3	90
Mizukaidō see Mitsukaidō, Japan	C13	40
Mizusawa, Japan	E14	38
Mjadzel, Bela.	F9	10
Mjakit, Russia	D19	34
Mjaksa, Russia	B21	10
Mjölby, Swe.	G6	8
Mjøsa, l., Nor.	F4	8
Mkalama, Tan.	E6	66
Mkhondvo, stm., Afr.	E10	70
Mkokotoni, Tan.	F7	66
Mkomazi, stm., S. Afr.	G10	70
Mkulwe, Tan.	F6	66
Mkuze, S. Afr.	E10	70
Mkuze, stm., S. Afr.	E11	70
Mkuze Game Reserve, S. Afr.	E11	70
Mladá Boleslav, Czech Rep.	F11	16
Mladenovac, Yugo.	E7	26
Mlava, stm., Yugo.	E8	26
Mława, Pol.	C16	16
Mljet, Otok, i., Cro.	H14	22
Mljet Nacionalni Park, p.o.i., Cro.	H14	22
Mmabatho, S. Afr.	D7	70
Mmadinare, Bots.	B8	70
Moa, stm., Afr.	H2	64
Moab, Ut., U.S.	E7	132
Moala, i., Fiji	q18	79e
Moama, Austl.	K5	76
Moamba, Moz.	D11	70
Moanda, Gabon	E2	66
Moar Lake, l., Can.	C18	124
Moate, Ire.	H5	12
Moba, D.R.C.	F5	66
Mobara, Japan	D13	40
Mobaye, C.A.R.	D4	66
Mobeetie, Tx., U.S.	F8	128
Moberly, Mo., U.S.	E5	120
Mobile, Al., U.S.	G10	122
Mobile, Az., U.S.	J4	132
Mobile, stm., Al., U.S.	G11	122
Mobile Bay, b., Al., U.S.	G10	122
Mobridge, S.D., U.S.	B12	126
Moca, Dom. Rep.	C12	102
Mocajuba, Braz.	B1	88
Mo Cay, Viet.	G8	48
Mocha see Al-Mukhā, Yemen	G5	56
Mochudi, Bots.	D8	70
Mocksville, N.C., U.S.	I5	114
Moclips, Wa., U.S.	C2	136
Môco, Morro de, mtn., Ang.	C2	68
Mocoa, Col.	G3	86
Mococa, Braz.	K2	88
Mocodoene, Moz.	C12	70
Mocoretá, Arg.	E8	92
Moctezuma, Mex.	G8	98
Moctezuma, stm., Mex.	G8	98
Moctezuma, stm., Mex.	E9	100
Mocuba, Moz.	D6	68
Modane, Fr.	D12	18
Modāsa, India	G4	54
Modder, stm., S. Afr.	F7	70
Módena, Italy	F7	22
Modeste, Mount, mtn., B.C., Can.	H6	138
Modesto, Ca., U.S.	F4	134
Modica, Italy	H8	24
Mödling, Aus.	B13	22
Modowi, Indon.	F9	44
Modra, Slov.	H13	16
Moe, Austl.	L6	76
Moeda, Braz.	K3	88
Moei (Thaungyin), stm., Asia	D3	48
Moema, Braz.	J3	88
Moengo, Sur.	B7	84
Moen-jo-Daro, hist., Pak.	D10	56
Moenkopi, Az., U.S.	G5	132
Moenkopi Wash, stm., Az., U.S.	G6	132
Moeris, Lake see Qârûn, Birket, l., Egypt	I1	58
Moeskroen see Mouscron, Bel.	D12	14
Moffat, Scot., U.K.	F9	12
Moga, India	C5	54
Mogadiscio see Muqdisho, Som.	D9	66
Mogadishu see Muqdisho, Som.	D9	66
Mogalakwena, stm., S. Afr.	C9	70
Mogami, stm., Japan	A13	40
Mogaung, Mya.	C8	46
Mogdy, Russia	F15	34
Mogilno, Pol.	D13	16
Mogincual, Moz.	D7	68
Mogoča, Russia	F12	34
Mogočin, Russia	C14	32
Mogogh, Sudan	F6	62
Mogok, Mya.	A3	48
Mogollon Rim, clf, Az., U.S.	I6	132
Mogor, Afg.	B1	54
Mogotes, Col.	D5	86
Mogotón, mtn., N.A.	F4	102
Moguer, Spain	G4	20
Mogzon, Russia	F11	34
Mohács, Hung.	C5	26
Mohall, N.D., U.S.	F12	124
Mohammed, Râs, c., Egypt	K5	58
Mohammedia, Mor.	C3	64
Mohania, India	F9	54
Mohawk, Mi., U.S.	D10	118
Mohawk, stm., N.Y., U.S.	B11	114
Mohe, China	F13	34
Mohéli see Mwali, i., Com.	C7	68
Mohnyin, Mya.	D8	46
Mohokare (Caledon), stm., Afr.	F8	70
Mohyliv-Podil's'kyi, Ukr.	A14	26
Moi, Nor.	G2	8
Moinești, Rom.	C13	26
Moira, stm., On., Can.	D12	112
Moiraba, Braz.	B1	88
Mo i Rana, Nor.	C5	8
Moiseevka, Russia	C13	32
Moisés Ville, Arg.	E7	92
Moisie, Qc., Can.	E17	106
Moisie, stm., Qc., Can.	E17	106
Moitaco, Ven.	C9	86
Mojácar, Spain	G9	20
Mojave, Ca., U.S.	H7	134
Mojave, stm., Ca., U.S.	H9	134
Mojave Desert, des., Ca., U.S.	D4	98
Mojero, stm., Russia	C9	34
Mojiguaçu, stm., Braz.	K2	88
Mojikit Lake, res., On., Can.	A10	118
Moji-Mirim, Braz.	L2	88
Mojo, Eth.	F7	62
Moju, Braz.	A1	88
Moju, stm., Braz.	D8	84
Mōka, Japan	C12	40
Mokāma, India	F10	54
Mokapu Peninsula, pen., Hi., U.S.	B4	78a
Mokau, stm., N.Z.	D6	80
Mokelumne, stm., Ca., U.S.	E5	134
Moknine, Tun.	B7	64
Mokochu, Khao, mtn., Thai.	E4	48
Mokokchūng, India	C7	46
Mokolo, Cam.	B2	66
Mokolo, stm., S. Afr.	C8	70
Mokpalin, Mya.	D3	48
Mokp'o, Kor., S.	G7	38
Mokša, stm., Russia	D6	32
Mokwa, Nig.	H5	64
Mol, Bel.	C14	14
Mola di Bari, Italy	C11	24
Molat, Otok, i., Cro.	F11	22
Moldary, Kaz.	D13	32
Moldau see Vltava, stm., Czech Rep.	F10	16
Moldavia, hist. reg., Rom.	C13	26
Molde, Nor.	E2	8
Moldova, ctry., Eur.	B15	26
Moldova, stm., Rom.	C13	26
Moldoveanu, Vârful, mtn., Rom.	D11	26
Môle, Cap du, c., Haiti	C11	102
Mole Creek, Austl.	n13	77a
Molega Lake, l., N.S., Can.	F12	110
Molène, Île de, i., Fr.	F3	14
Molepolole, Bots.	D7	70
Molėtai, Lith.	E8	10
Molfetta, Italy	C10	24
Molina, Chile	G2	92
Molina de Aragón, Spain	D9	20
Molina de Segura, Spain	F9	20
Moline, Il., U.S.	C7	120
Moline, Ks., U.S.	D12	128
Molino, Fl., U.S.	G11	122
Molino de Valdo de Piedras, Mex.	E3	130
Molinos, Arg.	B4	92
Molise, state, Italy	C8	24
Mollendo, Peru	G3	84
Mölln, Ger.	C6	16
Mölndal, Swe.	H4	8
Molodežnaja, sci., Ant.	B9	81
Molodogvardejskoe, Kaz.	D11	32
Mologa, stm., Russia	B19	10
Molokai, i., Hi., U.S.	B5	78a
Molokai Fracture Zone, unds.	G24	142
Molokovo, Russia	B19	10
Molong, Austl.	I7	76
Molopo, stm., Afr.	E5	70
Moloundou, Cam.	D3	66
Molson Lake, l., Mb., Can.	E11	106
Molu, Pulau, i., Indon.	G9	44
Moluccas see Maluku, is., Indon.	F8	44
Molucca Sea see Maluku, Laut, Indon.	F8	44
Molvoticy, Russia	C15	10
Moma, Moz.	D6	68
Moma, stm., Russia	C17	34
Mombaça, Braz.	C6	88
Mombasa, Kenya	E7	66
Mombetsu, Japan	B15	38
Momčilgrad, Blg.	H12	26
Momi, Fiji	p18	79e
Momotombo, Volcán, vol., Nic.	F4	102
Mompono, D.R.C.	D4	66
Mompós, Col.	C4	86
Momskij hrebet, mts., Russia	C18	34
Mon, state, Mya.	E3	48
Møn, i., Den.	I5	8
Mona, Ut., U.S.	D5	132
Mona, Isla de, i., P.R.	h14	96a
Mona, Punta, c., C.R.	H6	102
Monaca, Pa., U.S.	D5	114
Monach Islands, is., Scot., U.K.	D5	12
Monaco, Mon.	G4	22
Monaco, ctry., Eur.	F13	18
Monadnock Mountain, mtn., N.H., U.S.	B13	114
Monagas, state, Ven.	C10	86
Monaghan, Ire.	G6	12
Monaghan, state, Ire.	G6	12
Monahans, Tx., U.S.	C5	130
Monakino, Russia	C10	38
Mona Passage, strt., N.A.	C13	102
Monapo, Moz.	C7	68
Monarch, S.C., U.S.	B4	116
Monarch Mountain, mtn., B.C., Can.	E5	138
Monarch Pass, p., Co., U.S.	E10	132
Monashee Mountains, mts., B.C., Can.	F12	138
Monastir, Tun.	I4	24
Moncalieri, Italy	F4	22
Moncalvo, Italy	E5	22
Monção, Braz.	B3	88
Mončegorsk, Russia	B15	8
Mönchengladbach, Ger.	E2	16
Monchique, Port.	G2	20
Moncks Corner, S.C., U.S.	C5	116
Monclova, Mex.	B8	100
Moncton, N.B., Can.	D12	110
Monday, stm., Para.	B10	92
Mondego, stm., Port.	D3	20
Mondjamboli, D.R.C.	D4	66
Mondoubleau, Fr.	F9	14
Mondovi, Wi., U.S.	G7	118
Mondragone, Italy	C7	24
Monemvasía, Grc.	G6	28
Monessen, Pa., U.S.	D5	114
Monesterio, Spain	F4	20
Monett, Mo., U.S.	H4	120
Monette, Ar., U.S.	I7	120
Monfalcone, Italy	E10	22
Monferrato, hist. reg., Italy	F5	22
Monforte de Lemos, Spain	B3	20
Monga, D.R.C.	D4	66
Mongaguá, Braz.	B14	92
Mongalla, Sudan	F6	62
Mongers Lake, l., Austl.	E3	74
Monggon Qulu, China	B8	36
Möng Hai, Mya.	B4	48
Möng Hsat, Mya.	B4	48
Mongibello see Etna, Monte, vol., Italy	G8	24
Möng Küng, Mya.	B3	48
Möng Ma, Mya.	B4	48
Möng Nai, Mya.	B3	48
Mongo, Chad	E3	62
Mongol Altayn nuruu, mts., Asia	E16	32
Mongolia, ctry., Asia	E14	30
Mongonu, Nig.	G7	64
Möng Pai, Mya.	C3	48
Möng Pawn, Mya.	B3	48
Mongu, Zam.	D3	68
Möng Yai, Mya.	A4	48
Monico, Wi., U.S.	F9	118
Monida Pass, p., U.S.	F14	136
Monino, Russia	E21	10
Moniquirá, Col.	E5	86
Mõniste, Est.	H12	8
Monitor Valley, val., Nv., U.S.	E9	134
Mońki, Pol.	C18	16
Monkira, Austl.	E3	76
Monmouth, Wales, U.K.	J10	12
Monmouth, Or., U.S.	F3	136
Monmouth Mountain, mtn., B.C., Can.	E7	138
Mono, stm., Afr.	H5	64
Mono, Caño, stm., Col.	E7	86
Mono Island, i., Sol. Is.	d6	79b
Mono Lake, l., Ca., U.S.	E7	134
Monon, In., U.S.	H3	112
Monona, Ia., U.S.	H7	118
Monona, Wi., U.S.	A8	120
Monongahela, stm., U.S.	E6	114
Monopoli, Italy	D11	24
Monor, Hung.	B6	26
Monreal del Campo, Spain	D9	20
Monreale, Italy	F7	24
Monroe, La., U.S.	E6	122
Monroe, Mi., U.S.	C2	114
Monroe, N.Y., U.S.	C11	114
Monroe, N.C., U.S.	B5	116
Monroe, Or., U.S.	F3	136
Monroe, Ut., U.S.	E4	132
Monroe, Va., U.S.	G6	114
Monroe, Wa., U.S.	C4	136
Monroe, Wi., U.S.	B8	120
Monroe City, In., U.S.	F10	120
Monroe Lake, res., In., U.S.	E11	120
Monroeville, Al., U.S.	F11	122
Monroeville, In., U.S.	D1	114
Monroeville, Oh., U.S.	C3	114
Monroeville, Pa., U.S.	D6	114
Monrovia, Lib.	H2	64
Mons, Bel.	D12	14
Monsefú, Peru	E2	84
Monselice, Italy	E8	22
Monsenhor Hipólito, Braz.	D5	88
Monsenhor Tabosa, Braz.	C5	88
Mönsterås, Swe.	H7	8
Montabaur, Ger.	F3	16
Montagne, Neth. Ant.	p23	104g
Montagu, S. Afr.	H5	70
Montague, P.E., Can.	D14	110
Montague, Mi., U.S.	E3	112
Montague, Tx., U.S.	H11	128
Montague, Isla, i., Mex.	F5	98
Montague Island, i., Ak., U.S.	E10	140
Montagu Island, i., S. Geor.	K12	82
Montaigu, Fr.	H7	14
Montalbano Ionico, Italy	D10	24
Montalegre, Port.	C3	20
Montana, Blg.	F10	26
Montana, state, Blg.	F10	26
Montana, state, U.S.	B6	108
Montaña de Covadonga, Parque Nacional de la, p.o.i., Spain	A5	20
Montánchez, Spain	E4	20
Montanha, Braz.	J5	88
Montargis, Fr.	G11	14
Montauban, Fr.	E7	18
Montauk Point, c., N.Y., U.S.	C14	114
Montbard, Fr.	G13	14
Montbéliard, Fr.	G15	14
Mont Belvieu, Tx., U.S.	H3	122
Montblanc, Spain	C11	20
Montblanch see Montblanc, Spain	C11	20
Montbrison, Fr.	D9	18
Montbron, Fr.	D6	18
Montceau-les-Mines, Fr.	H13	14
Montclair, Ca., U.S.	I8	134
Mont-de-Marsan, Fr.	F5	18
Montdidier, Fr.	E11	14
Monte, Laguna del, l., Arg.	H6	92
Monteagudo, Bol.	C4	90
Monte Albán, hist., Mex.	G10	100
Monte Alegre, Braz.	D7	84
Monte Alegre de Goiás, Braz.	G2	88

Name | Map Ref. | Page

Monte Alegre de Minas, Braz. J1 88
Monte Alegre de Sergipe, Braz. F7 88
Monte Azul, Braz. H4 88
Montebello, Qc., Can. C14 112
Montebello, P.R. B2 104a
Montecarlo, Arg. C10 92
Monte Carmelo, Braz. J2 88
Monte Caseros, Arg. E8 92
Montecassino, Abbazia di, Italy C7 24
Montecatini Terme, Italy G7 22
Montecito, Ca., U.S. I6 134
Monte Comán, Arg. G4 92
Monte Creek, B.C., Can. F11 138
Monte Cristi, Dom. Rep. C12 102
Monte Cristo, Bol. B4 90
Montecristo, Isola di, i., Italy H7 22
Monte do Carmo, Braz. F1 88
Monte Escobedo, Mex. D7 100
Montefalco, Italy H9 22
Montefiascone, Italy H8 22
Montego Bay, Jam. i12 104d
Monteiro, Braz. D7 88
Montejicar, Spain G7 20
Montejinni, Austl. C6 74
Montelíbano, Col. C4 86
Montélimar, Fr. E10 18
Monte Lindo, stm., Para. A9 92
Montellano, Spain H5 20
Montello, Nv., U.S. B2 132
Montello, Wi., U.S. H9 118
Monte Maíz, Arg. F6 92
Montemayor, Meseta de, plat., Arg. H3 90
Montemorelos, Mex. C9 100
Montemor-o-Velho, Port. D2 20
Montemuro, mtn., Port. C2 20
Montenegro, Braz. D12 92
Montenegro see Crna Gora, state, Yugo. G6 26
Monte Pascoal, Parque Nacional de, p.o.i., Braz. I5 88
Monte Patria, Chile E2 92
Montepuez, Moz. C6 68
Montepulciano, Italy G8 22
Monte Quemado, Arg. B6 92
Montereau-Faut-Yonne, Fr. F11 14
Monterey, Ca., U.S. G3 134
Monterey, Va., U.S. F6 114
Monterey Bay, b., Ca., U.S. G3 134
Montería, Col. C3 86
Monteros, Arg. C5 92
Monterotondo, Italy H9 22
Monterrey, Mex. C8 100
Montesano, Wa., U.S. C3 136
Monte Sant'Angelo, Italy I12 22
Monte Santu, Capo di, c., Italy D3 24
Montes Claros, Braz. I3 88
Montesilvano Marina, Italy H11 22
Montevallo, Al., U.S. D12 122
Montevarchi, Italy G8 22
Montevideo, Mn., U.S. G3 118
Montevideo, Ur. G9 92
Monte Vista, Co., U.S. D2 128
Montezuma, Ga., U.S. D1 116
Montezuma, In., U.S. I2 112
Montezuma, Ks., U.S. D8 128
Montezuma Castle National Monument, p.o.i., Az., U.S. I4 132
Montgenèvre, Col de, p., Fr. E12 18
Montgomery, Al., U.S. E12 122
Montgomery, La., U.S. F6 122
Montgomery, Mn., U.S. G5 118
Montgomery, Pa., U.S. C8 114
Montgomery, Tx., U.S. G3 122
Montgomery City, Mo., U.S. E6 120
Montguyon, Fr. D5 18
Monthey, Switz. D3 22
Monticello, Ar., U.S. D7 122
Monticello, Fl., U.S. F2 116
Monticello, Il., U.S. D9 120
Monticello, In., U.S. H3 112
Monticello, Ky., U.S. H13 120
Monticello, Mn., U.S. F5 118
Monticello, Ms., U.S. F8 122
Monticello, Mo., U.S. D6 120
Monticello, N.Y., U.S. C11 114
Monticello, Ut., U.S. F7 132
Monticello, hist., Va., U.S. G7 114
Montigny-le-Roi, Fr. G14 14
Montigny-lès-Metz, Fr. E15 14
Montijo, Pan. I7 102
Montijo, Port. F2 20
Montijo, Spain F4 20
Montijo, Golfo de, b., Pan. I7 102
Montilla, Spain G6 20
Montivilliers, Fr. E9 14
Mont-Joli, Qc., Can. B8 110
Mont-Laurier, Qc., Can. B14 112
Montluçon, Fr. C8 18
Montmagny, Qc., Can. D6 110
Montmédy, Fr. E14 14
Montmorillon, Fr. C6 18
Monto, Austl. E8 76
Montoro, Spain F6 20
Montour Falls, N.Y., U.S. B9 114
Montpelier, Jam. i13 104d
Montpelier, Id., U.S. H15 136
Montpelier, In., U.S. H4 112
Montpelier, Oh., U.S. C1 114
Montpelier, Vt., U.S. F4 110
Montpellier, Fr. F9 18
Montréal, Qc., Can. E3 110
Montreal, Wi., U.S. E8 118
Montreal, stm., On., Can. A10 112
Montreal Lake, l., Sk., Can. E9 106
Montreuil-sur-Mer, Fr. D10 14
Montreux, Switz. D3 22
Montrose, Scot., U.K. E10 12
Montrose, Co., U.S. E9 132
Montrose, Mi., U.S. E6 112
Montrose, Pa., U.S. C9 114
Montrose, S.D., U.S. D15 126
Montross, Va., U.S. F9 114
Monts, Pointe des, c., Qc., Can. A9 110
Mont-Saint-Michel, Qc., Can. D1 110
Mont-Saint-Michel, Baie du, b., Fr. F7 14
Mont-Saint-Michel, Le, Fr. F7 14
Montserrat, dep., N.A. h15 96a
Mont-Tremblant, Parc de récréation du, p.o.i., Qc., Can. D2 110
Monument, Or., U.S. F7 136
Monument Draw, stm., U.S. B5 130
Monument Peak, mtn., Co., U.S. D9 132
Monument Valley, val., U.S. F6 132
Monviso, mtn., Italy F4 22
Monyo, Mya. C2 48
Monywa, Mya. A2 48
Monza, Italy E6 22
Monze, Zam. D4 68
Monzen, Japan B9 40
Monzón, Spain C11 20
Mooi, stm., S. Afr. F10 70
Moolawatana, Austl. G2 76
Moon, Mountains of the see Ruwenzori, mts., Afr. D6 66
Moonie, Austl. F8 76
Moonie, stm., Austl. G7 76
Moora, Austl. F3 74
Moorcroft, Wy., U.S. C8 126
Moore, Id., U.S. G13 136
Moore, Ok., U.S. F11 128
Moore, Tx., U.S. E8 130
Moore, Lake, l., Austl. E3 74
Moorea, i., Fr. Poly. v20 78h
Moorefield, W.V., U.S. E7 114
Moore Haven, Fl., U.S. J4 116
Mooreland, Ok., U.S. E9 128
Mooresville, N.C., U.S. A5 116
Moorhead, Mn., U.S. E2 118
Moorhead, Ms., U.S. D8 122
Mooringsport, La., U.S. E5 122
Moornanyah Lake, l., Austl. I4 76
Moorreesburg, S. Afr. H4 70
Moosburg an der Isar, Ger. H7 16
Moosehead Lake, l., Me., U.S. E7 110
Moose Island, i., Mb., Can. C16 124
Moose Jaw, Sk., Can. D8 124
Moose Jaw, stm., Sk., Can. D8 124
Moose Lake, Mn., U.S. E6 118
Moose Lake, l., Ab., Can. B19 138
Mooselookmeguntic Lake, l., Me., U.S. F5 110
Moose Mountain, mtn., Sk., Can. E11 124
Moose Mountain Creek, stm., Sk., Can. E11 124
Moose Pass, Ak., U.S. D10 140
Moosomin, Sk., Can. D12 124
Moosonee, On., Can. E14 106
Mootwingee National Park, p.o.i., Austl. H4 76
Mopane, S. Afr. C9 70
Mopipi, Bots. B7 70
Moppo see Mokp'o, Kor., S. G7 38
Mopti, Mali G4 64
Moquegua, Peru G3 84
Mór, Hung. B5 26
Mòr, Glen, val., Scot., U.K. D8 12
Mora, Cam. B2 66
Mora, Port. F2 20
Mora, Swe. F6 8
Mora, Mn., U.S. F5 118
Mora, stm., N.M., U.S. F4 128
Morač, stm., Bela. H10 10
Morādābād, India D7 54
Morada Nova, Braz. C6 88
Morada Nova de Minas, Braz. J3 88
Morąg, Pol. C15 16
Moral de Calatrava, Spain F7 20
Moraleda, Canal, strt., Chile H2 90
Morales, Laguna de, b., Mex. D10 100
Moramanga, Madag. D8 68
Moran, Ks., U.S. G2 120
Moran, Mi., U.S. B5 112
Moran, Tx., U.S. B8 130
Morant Bay, Jam. j14 104d
Morant Cays, is., Jam. D10 102
Morant Point, c., Jam. j14 104d
Morar, Loch, l., Scot., U.K. E7 12
Moratalla, Spain F9 20
Moratuwa, Sri L. H4 53
Morava, hist. reg., Czech Rep. G13 16
Morava (March), stm., Eur. H12 16
Moravia, N.Y., U.S. B9 114
Moravské Budějovice, Czech Rep. G11 16
Morawa, Austl. E3 74
Morawhanna, Guy. C12 86
Moray Firth, b., Scot., U.K. D9 12
Morbi, India G3 54
Morbihan, state, Fr. G6 14
Morcenx, Fr. E5 18
Morden, Mb., Can. E15 124
Mordovia see Mordovija, state, Russia D6 32
Mordovija, state, Russia D6 32
Mordves, Russia F21 10
Mordvinia see Mordovija, state, Russia D6 32
Mordy, Pol. D18 16
More, Ben, mtn., Scot., U.K. E7 12
Moreau, stm., S.D., U.S. B12 126
Moreau, North Fork, stm., S.D., U.S. B9 126
Moreau, South Fork, stm., S.D., U.S. B9 126
Moreau Peak, mtn., S.D., U.S. B9 126
Moreauville, La., U.S. F7 122
Morecambe, Eng., U.K. G9 12
Morecambe Bay, b., Eng., U.K. H9 12
Moree, Austl. G7 76
Morehead, Ky., U.S. F2 114
Morehead City, N.C., U.S. B9 116
Moreland, Ga., U.S. D14 122
Moreland, Ky., U.S. G13 120
Morelia, Mex. F8 100
Morell, P.E., Can. D14 110
Morella, Austl. D4 76
Morelos, Mex. B5 100
Morelos, Mex. I2 130
Morelos, state, Mex. F9 100
Morena, India E6 54
Morena, Sierra, mts., Spain F5 20
Morenci, Az., U.S. J7 132
Moreni, Rom. D12 26
Moreno, Bahía, b., Chile A2 92
Møre og Romsdal, state, Nor. E2 8
Moresby Island, i., B.C., Can. E4 106
Moreton, Austl. B8 74
Moreton Island, i., Austl. F9 76
Moreuil, Fr. E11 14
Morez, Fr. H14 14
Morgan, Mn., U.S. G3 118
Morgan, Mt., U.S. F6 124
Morgan, Tx., U.S. B10 130
Morgan, Ut., U.S. B5 132
Morgan City, Al., U.S. C12 122
Morgan City, La., U.S. H7 122
Morganfield, Ky., U.S. G10 120
Morgan Hill, Ca., U.S. F4 134
Morganito, Ven. E8 86
Morganton, N.C., U.S. I4 114
Morgantown, In., U.S. E11 120
Morgantown, Ms., U.S. F8 122
Morgantown, Ms., U.S. F7 122
Morgantown, W.V., U.S. E6 114
Morgenzon, S. Afr. E9 70
Morghāb (Murgab), stm., Asia B9 56
Moriah, Mount, mtn., Nv., U.S. D2 132
Moriarty, N.M., U.S. G2 128
Morice, stm., B.C., Can. B4 138
Morice Lake, l., B.C., Can. B3 138
Morichal Largo, stm., Ven. C10 86
Moricsala rezervāts, Lat. C5 10
Moriki, Nig. G6 64
Morino, Russia C13 10
Morinville, Ab., Can. C17 138
Morioka, Japan E14 38
Morīri, Tso, l., India B6 54
Morisset, Austl. I8 76
Morjakovskij Zaton, Russia C14 32
Morkoka, stm., Russia D11 34
Morlaix, Fr. F5 14
Morley, Mi., U.S. E4 112
Mormal', Bela. H12 10
Mormugao, India D1 53
Morne-à-l'Eau, Guad. h5 105c
Morne du Vitet, hill, Guad. B2 105a
Morne Trois Pitons National Park, p.o.i., Dom. j6 105c
Morney, Austl. E3 76
Morning Sun, Ia., U.S. C6 120
Mornington, Austl. L5 76
Mornington, Isla, i., Chile I1 90
Mornington Island, i., Austl. C7 74
Morobe, Pap. N. Gui. b4 79a
Morocco, In., U.S. H2 112
Morocco, ctry., Afr. C3 64
Moro Creek, stm., Ar., U.S. D6 122
Morogoro, Tan. F7 66
Moro Gulf, b., Phil. G4 52
Moroleón, Mex. E8 100
Morombe, Madag. E7 68
Morón, Arg. G8 92
Morón, Cuba A8 102
Mörön, Mong. B5 36
Morón, Ven. B7 86
Morona, stm., S.A. I3 86
Morona Santiago, state, Ec. I3 86
Morondava, Madag. E7 68
Morón de Almazán, Spain C8 20
Morón de la Frontera, Spain G5 20
Moroni, Com. C7 68
Moroni, Ut., U.S. D5 132
Moron Us, stm., China E3 36
Morošečnoe, Russia E20 34
Morotai, i., Indon. E8 44
Moroto, Ug. D6 66
Moroto, mtn., Ug. D6 66
Morovis, P.R. B3 104a
Morozovsk, Russia E6 32
Morpeth, Eng., U.K. F11 12
Morrilton, Ar., U.S. B6 122
Morrin, Ab., Can. E18 138
Morrinhos, Braz. B5 88
Morrinhos, Braz. I1 88
Morrinsville, N.Z. C6 80
Morris, Mb., Can. E16 124
Morris, Il., U.S. C9 120
Morris, Mn., U.S. F2 118
Morrisburg, On., Can. D14 112
Morris Jesup, Kap, c., Grnld. A19 141
Morrison, Arg. F6 92
Morrison, Il., U.S. C8 120
Morrisonville, Il., U.S. E8 120
Morristown, Az., U.S. J4 132
Morristown, In., U.S. E12 120
Morristown, S.D., U.S. B11 126
Morristown, Tn., U.S. H2 114
Morrisville, Pa., U.S. H15 112
Morro, Punta, c., Mex. C2 102
Morro Bay, Ca., U.S. H5 134
Morro do Chapéu, Braz. F5 88
Morros, Braz. B3 88
Morrosquillo, Golfo de, b., Col. C3 86
Morrow, La., U.S. G6 122
Morrumbala, Moz. D6 68
Morrumbene, Moz. C12 70
Morse, La., U.S. G6 122
Morse, Tx., U.S. E7 128
Morsi, India H6 54
Mörskom see Myrskylä, Fin. F11 8
Morson, On., Can. B4 118
Mortagne-sur-Sèvre, Fr. H8 14
Mortara, Italy E5 22
Morteau, Fr. G15 14
Morteros, Arg. E6 92
Mortes, stm., Braz. F7 84
Mortlach, Sk., Can. D7 124
Mortlock Islands, is., Micron. C6 72
Morton, Il., U.S. D8 120
Morton, Mn., U.S. G4 118
Morton, Tx., U.S. H6 128
Morton, Wa., U.S. D4 136
Morton National Park, p.o.i., Austl. J7 76
Morua, Vanuatu k17 79d
Moruya, Austl. J7 76
Morvan, mts., Fr. G13 14
Morvant, Trin. s12 105f
Morven, Austl. F6 76
Morven, Ga., U.S. F2 116
Morven, N.C., U.S. B5 116
Morwell, Austl. L6 76
Moryń, Pol. D10 16
Moržovec, ostrov, i., Russia C20 8
Mosal'sk, Russia F17 10
Mosbach, Ger. G5 16
Moscos Islands, is., Mya. E3 48
Moscow see Moskva, Russia E20 10
Moscow, Id., U.S. D10 136
Moscow see Moskva, stm., Russia E21 10
Mosel (Moselle), stm., Eur. G2 16
Moselebe, stm., Bots. D7 70
Moselle, Ms., U.S. F9 122
Moselle, state, Fr. F15 14
Moselle (Mosel), stm., Eur. G2 16
Moses Lake, Wa., U.S. C7 136
Moses Point, Ak., U.S. D7 140
Moshaweng, stm., S. Afr. E6 70
Mosheim, Tn., U.S. H3 114
Moshi, Tan. E7 66
Mosinee, Wi., U.S. G9 118
Mosjøen, Nor. D5 8
Moskalvo, Russia F17 34
Moskenesøya, i., Nor. C5 8
Moskovskaja oblast', co., Russia D19 10
Moskovskaja vozvyšennost', plat., Russia E19 10
Moskva (Moscow), Russia E20 10
Moskva, stm., Russia E21 10
Moskvy, kanal imeni, can., Russia D20 10
Mosomane, Bots. C8 70
Mosonmagyaróvár, Hung. B4 26
Mosopa, Bots. D7 70
Mosqueiro, Braz. D8 84
Mosquera, Col. F2 86
Mosquito Coast see Mosquitos, Costa de, hist. reg., Nic. F6 102
Mosquitos, Costa de, hist. reg., Nic. F6 102
Mosquitos, Golfo de los, b., Pan. H7 102
Moss, Nor. G4 8
Mossaka, Congo E3 66
Mossbank, Sk., Can. E7 124
Mossburn, N.Z. G2 80
Mosselbaai (Mossel Bay), S. Afr. I6 70
Mossel Bay see Mosselbaai, S. Afr. I6 70
Mossleigh, Ab., Can. F17 138
Mossman, Austl. C9 74
Moss Mountain, mtn., Ar., U.S. C6 122
Mossoró, Braz. C7 88
Moss Point, Ms., U.S. G10 122
Moss Vale, Austl. J8 76
Mossy, stm., Mb., Can. C13 124
Most, Czech Rep. F9 16
Mostar, Bos. F4 26
Mostardas, Braz. E12 92
Møsting, Kap, c., Grnld. E17 141
Mostovaja, Russia D16 10
Mostyn, Malay. A11 50
Mosul see Al-Mawṣil, Iraq B5 56
Møsvatnet, l., Nor. G2 8
Mot'a, Eth. E7 62
Mota del Cuervo, Spain E8 20
Mota del Marqués, Spain C5 20
Motagua, stm., N.A. E3 102
Motal', Bela. H8 10
Motala, Swe. G6 8
Mota Lava, i., Vanuatu i16 79d
Motaze, Moz. D11 70
Moteve, Cap, c., Fr. Poly. s18 78g
Motherwell, Scot., U.K. F9 12
Motihāri, India E10 54
Motloutse, stm., Bots. B9 70
Motopu, Fr. Poly. s18 78g
Motozintla de Mendoza, Mex. H12 100
Motril, Spain H7 20
Motru, Rom. E10 26
Mott, N.D., U.S. A10 126
Motu, stm., N.Z. C7 80
Motueka, N.Z. E5 80
Motul de Felipe Carrillo Puerto, Mex. B3 102
Motutapu, i., Cook Is. a27 78j
Motygino, Russia C17 32
Motyklejka, Russia E18 34
Mouaskar, Alg. B5 64
Mouchoir Passage, strt., N.A. B12 102
Moudjéria, Maur. F2 64
Moúdros, Grc. D8 28
Mouila, Gabon E2 66
Mould Bay, N.T., Can. A16 140
Moule à Chique, Cap, c., St. Luc. m7 105c
Moulins, Fr. H12 14
Moulmein see Mawlamyine, Mya. D3 48
Moulmeingyun, Mya. D2 48
Moulouya, Oued, stm., Mor. C4 64
Moulton, Al., U.S. C11 122
Moulton, Ia., U.S. D5 120
Moulton, Tx., U.S. E10 130
Moultrie, Ga., U.S. E2 116
Moultrie, Lake, res., S.C., U.S. C5 116
Mouly, N. Cal. m16 79d
Mounana, Gabon E2 66
Mound City, Ks., U.S. F3 120
Mound City, Mo., U.S. D2 120
Mound City, S.D., U.S. B12 126
Moundou, Chad F3 62
Moundridge, Ks., U.S. C11 128
Mounds, Ok., U.S. B2 122
Moundsville, W.V., U.S. E5 114
Moundville, Al., U.S. E11 122
Mounlapamôk, Laos E7 48
Mountain, Wi., U.S. C1 112
Mountain, stm., N.T., Can. C5 106
Mountainair, N.M., U.S. G2 128
Mountainaire, Az., U.S. H5 132
Mountain Brook, Al., U.S. D12 122
Mountain City, Ga., U.S. B2 116
Mountain City, Nv., U.S. B1 132
Mountain Creek, Al., U.S. E12 122
Mountain Grove, Mo., U.S. G5 120
Mountain Home, Ar., U.S. H5 120
Mountain Home, Id., U.S. G11 136
Mountain Iron, Mn., U.S. D6 118
Mountain Lake, Mn., U.S. H3 118
Mountain Nile, stm., Afr. F6 62
Mountain Park, Ab., Can. D13 138
Mountain Pine, Ar., U.S. C5 122
Mountain View, Ar., U.S. I5 120
Mountain View, Ca., U.S. F3 134
Mountain View, Ok., U.S. F10 128
Mountain View, Wy., U.S. E6 126
Mountain Village, Ak., U.S. D7 140
Mountain Zebra National Park, p.o.i., S. Afr. H7 70
Mount Airy, N.C., U.S. H5 114
Mount Alida, S. Afr. F10 70
Mount Angel, Or., U.S. E4 136
Mount Aspiring National Park, p.o.i., N.Z. G3 80
Mount Athos see Ágio Óros, state, Grc. C7 28
Mount Ayliff, S. Afr. G9 70
Mount Ayr, Ia., U.S. D3 120
Mount Barker, Austl. F3 74
Mount Barker, Austl. J2 76
Mount Berry, Ga., U.S. C13 122
Mount Buffalo National Park, p.o.i., Austl. K5 76
Mount Calm, Tx., U.S. C11 130
Mount Carmel, Il., U.S. F10 120
Mount Carmel, Pa., U.S. D9 114
Mount Carroll, Il., U.S. B7 120
Mount Clemens, Mi., U.S. B3 114
Mount Cook National Park, p.o.i., N.Z. F4 80
Mount Dora, Fl., U.S. H4 116
Mount Enterprise, Tx., U.S. F4 122
Mount Field National Park, p.o.i., Austl. o13 77a
Mount Forest, On., Can. D9 112
Mount Frere, S. Afr. G9 70
Mount Gambier, Austl. K3 76
Mount Garnet, Austl. A5 76
Mount Gay, W.V., U.S. G3 114
Mount Hagen, Pap. N. Gui. b3 79a
Mount Holly, N.C., U.S. A4 116
Mount Holly Springs, Pa., U.S. H12 112
Mount Hope, Austl. F7 74
Mount Hope, Ks., U.S. D11 128
Mount Horeb, Wi., U.S. B8 120
Mount Ida, Ar., U.S. C5 122
Mount Isa, Austl. C2 76
Mount Jackson, Va., U.S. F7 114
Mount Juliet, Tn., U.S. H11 120
Mount Kaputar National Park, p.o.i., Austl. H8 76
Mount Lebanon, Pa., U.S. D6 114
Mount Lofty Ranges, mts., Austl. I2 76
Mount Magnet, Austl. E3 74
Mount Manara, Austl. I4 76
Mount Margaret, Austl. F4 76
Mount Morgan, Austl. D8 76
Mount Morris, Il., U.S. I9 118
Mount Morris, Mi., U.S. E6 112
Mount Olive, Il., U.S. E8 120
Mount Olive, Ms., U.S. F9 122
Mount Olive, N.C., U.S. A7 116
Mount Orab, Oh., U.S. E2 114
Mount Perry, Austl. E8 76
Mount Pleasant, On., Can. E9 112
Mount Pleasant, Ia., U.S. D6 120
Mount Pleasant, Mi., U.S. E5 112
Mount Pleasant, Pa., U.S. D6 114
Mount Pleasant, S.C., U.S. D6 116
Mount Pleasant, Tn., U.S. B11 122
Mount Pleasant, Tx., U.S. D4 122
Mount Pleasant, Ut., U.S. D5 132
Mount Pulaski, Il., U.S. D8 120
Mount Rainier National Park, p.o.i., Wa., U.S. D5 136
Mount Revelstoke National Park, p.o.i., B.C., Can. E12 138
Mount Riddock, Austl. D6 74
Mount Saint Helens National Volcanic Monument, p.o.i., Wa., U.S. D5 136
Mount Selinda, Zimb. B11 70
Mount Somers, N.Z. F4 80
Mount Sterling, Il., U.S. E7 120
Mount Sterling, Ky., U.S. F2 114
Mount Sterling, Oh., U.S. E2 114
Mount Uniacke, N.S., Can. F12 110
Mount Union, Pa., U.S. D8 114
Mount Vernon, Austl. D3 74
Mount Vernon, Al., U.S. F10 122
Mount Vernon, Ga., U.S. D3 116
Mount Vernon, Il., U.S. F8 120
Mount Vernon, Ia., U.S. C6 120
Mount Vernon, Ky., U.S. G1 114
Mount Vernon, Mo., U.S. G4 120
Mount Vernon, Oh., U.S. D3 114
Mount Vernon, Or., U.S. F7 136
Mount Vernon, S.D., U.S. D14 126
Mount Vernon, Wa., U.S. B4 136
Mount Vernon, hist., Va., U.S. F8 114
Mount William National Park, p.o.i., Austl. n13 77a
Mount Willoughby, Austl. E6 74
Mount Wolf, Pa., U.S. H13 112
Moura, Braz. H11 86
Moura, Port. F3 20
Mourdi, Dépression du, depr., Chad D4 62
Mourdiah, Mali G3 64
Mourne Mountains, mts., N. Ire., U.K. G6 12
Mouscron, Bel. D12 14
Moussa 'Ali, mtn., Afr. B8 66
Moussoro, Chad E3 62
Moutier, Switz. C4 22
Moutong, Indon. E7 44
Mouzáki, Grc. D4 28
Movenda, D.R.C. D4 66
Moweaqua, Il., U.S. E8 120
Moxotó, stm., Braz. E7 88
Moyahua, Mex. E7 100
Moyale, Kenya D7 66
Moyamba, S.L. H2 64
Moyen Atlas, mts., Mor. C4 64
Moyeuvre-Grande, Fr. E14 14
Moyie, B.C., Can. G15 138
Moyie, stm., N.A. H14 138
Moyo, Pulau, i., Indon. H10 50
Moyobamba, Peru E2 84
Moyu, China A4 46
M'oža (Mëža), stm., Eur. E14 10
Možajsk, Russia E18 10
Mozambique, ctry., Afr. D5 68
Mozambique Channel, strt., Afr. D7 68
Mozambique Plateau, unds. M6 142
Mozdok, Russia F6 32
Mozolevo, Russia A16 10
Mpala, D.R.C. F5 66
Mpanda, Tan. F6 66
Mphoengs, Zimb. B8 70
Mpika, Zam. C5 68
Mporokoso, Zam. B5 68
Mpui, Tan. F6 66
Mpumalanga, state, S. Afr. E9 70
Mpwapwa, Tan. F7 66
Mqanduli, S. Afr. G9 70
Mrągowo, Pol. C17 16
Mrkonjić Grad, Bos. E3 26
M'Saken, Tun. I4 24
Mscislau, Bela. F14 10
Msciž, Bela. F11 10
Msta, Russia C17 10
Msta, stm., Russia B15 10
Mszczonów, Pol. E16 16
Mtama, Tan. G7 66
Mtamvuna, stm., S. Afr. G9 70
Mtwara, Tan. G8 66
Mu, N. Cal. m16 79d
Mu, stm., Mya. A2 48
Mu, Cerro, mtn., S.A. C5 86
Mu'a, Tonga n14 78e
Mualang, Indon. C7 50
Muanda, D.R.C. F2 66
Muang Hay, Laos B5 48
Muang Hôngsa, Laos C5 48
Muang Hounxianghoung, Laos B6 48
Muang Khammouan, Laos D7 48
Muang Khao, Laos C6 48
Muang Không, Laos E7 48
Muang Khôngxédôn, Laos E7 48
Muang La, Laos B6 48
Muang Long, Laos B5 48
Muang Ngoy, Laos B6 48
Muang Nong, Laos D8 48
Muang Ou Tai, Laos A5 48
Muang Pak-Lay, Laos C5 48
Muang Paktha, Laos B5 48
Muang Pakxan, Laos C6 48
Muang Phalan, Laos D7 48
Muang Phônthong, Laos E7 48
Muang Sam Sip, Thai. E7 48
Muang Sing, Laos B5 48
Muang Souvannakhili, Laos E7 48
Muang Sung, Laos B6 48
Muang Thatèng, Laos E8 48
Muang Va, Laos B6 48
Muang Vangviang, Laos C6 48
Muang Xaignabouri, Laos C5 48
Muang Xamtong, Laos C6 48
Muang Xépôn, Laos D7 48
Muang Yo, Laos B5 48
Muar, Malay. L6 48
Muar, stm., Malay. K6 48
Muara, Bru. A9 50
Muaraancalung, Indon. C10 50
Muarabenangin, Indon. D9 50
Muarabungo, Indon. D2 50
Muaradua, Indon. F4 50
Muaraenim, Indon. E3 50
Muarajuloi, Indon. D8 50
Muarakelingi, Indon. E3 50
Muaralabuh, Indon. D2 50
Muaralakitan, Indon. E3 50
Muaralembu, Indon. D2 50
Muarapangean, Indon. B10 50
Muarapayang, Indon. D9 50
Muarasabak, Indon. D3 50
Muarasiberut, Indon. D1 50
Muaratebo, Indon. D3 50
Muarateladang, Indon. E4 50
Muaratembesi, Indon. D3 50
Muaratewe, Indon. D9 50
Muaratunan, Indon. D10 50
Mubārakpur, India E9 54
Mubende, Ug. D6 66
Mubi, Nig. G7 64
Mubur, Pulau, i., Indon. B4 50
Mucaitá, stm., Braz. D4 88
Mucajaí, stm., Braz. F11 86
Muchinga Escarpment, clf, Zam. C4 68
Muchinga Mountains, mts., Zam. C5 68
Muckadilla, Austl. F7 76
Mučkas, Russia D23 8
Mucojo, Moz. C7 68
Muconda, Ang. C3 68
Mucujê, Braz. G5 88
Muçum, Braz. D11 92
Mucuri, Braz. J6 88
Mucuri, stm., Braz. J6 88
Muda, stm., Malay. J5 48
Mudan, stm., China B10 36
Mudanjiang, China B8 38
Mudanya, Tur. C11 28
Mud Creek, stm., Ne., U.S. F13 126
Mud Creek, stm., Tx., U.S. E3 122
Muddus Nationalpark, p.o.i., Swe. C9 8
Muddy, stm., Nv., U.S. G2 132
Muddy Boggy Creek, stm., Ok., U.S. C3 122
Muddy Creek, stm., Ut., U.S. E6 132
Mudgee, Austl. I7 76
Mudhol, India C2 53
Mudjuga, Russia E18 8
Mud Lake, l., Nv., U.S. F8 134
Mudon, Mya. D3 48
Mudurnu, Tur. C14 28
Muelle de los Bueyes, Nic. G5 102
Muenster, Tx., U.S. H11 128
Muerto, Mar, l., Mex. G11 100
Mufulira, Zam. C4 68
Mufu Shan, mtn., China G5 42
Mufu Shan, mts., China G6 42
Mughal Sarāi, India F9 54
Mugi, Japan F7 40
Mu Gia, Deo, p., Asia D7 48
Muğla, Tur. F11 28
Muğla, state, Tur. F11 28
Muḥammad Qawl, Sudan C7 62
Muhanovo, Russia D21 10
Muhavec, stm., Bela. H7 10
Muhino, Russia F14 34
Mühlacker, Ger. H4 16
Mühldorf am Inn, Ger. H8 16
Mühlhausen, Ger. E6 16
Muhlig-Hofmann Mountains, mts., Ant. C5 81
Mühlviertel, reg., Aus. B11 22
Muhradah, Syria C7 58
Muhu, i., Est. G10 8
Muié, Ang. C3 68
Mui Hopohoponga Point, c., Tonga n14 78e
Muineachán see Monaghan, Ire. G6 12
Muine Bheag, Ire. I6 12
Muite, Moz. C6 68
Muja, Russia E12 34
Mujnak, Uzb. F9 32
Mukah, Malay. B8 50
Mukalla see Al-Mukallā, Yemen G6 56
Mukatsjeve, Ukr. A9 26
Mukāwir, hist., Jord. G6 58
Mukdahan, Thai. D7 48
Mukden see Shenyang, China D5 38
Mukeriān, India C5 54
Mukharram al-Fawqānī, Syria D7 58
Mukilteo, Wa., U.S. C4 136
Mukinbudin, Austl. F3 74
Mukomuko, Indon. E2 50
Mukry, Turkmen. B10 56
Muktsar, India C5 54
Mūl, India A4 53
Mula, China F5 36
Mula, Spain F9 20
Mula, stm., India B2 53
Mula, stm., India B1 53
Mulaku Atoll, at., Mald. i12 46a
Mulan, China B10 36
Mulas, Punta de, c., Cuba B10 102
Mulatos, Mex. A4 100
Mulbāgal, India E4 53
Mulberry, Ar., U.S. B4 122
Mulberry, Fl., U.S. I4 116
Mulberry Fork, stm., Al., U.S. D12 122
Mulberry Mountain, mtn., Ar., U.S. I5 120
Mulchatna, stm., Ak., U.S. D8 140
Mulchén, Chile H1 92
Mulde, stm., Ger. E8 16
Muldoon, Tx., U.S. E10 130
Muldraugh, Ky., U.S. G12 120
Muldrow, Ok., U.S. B4 122
Muleshoe, Tx., U.S. G6 128
Mulgowie, Austl. F9 76
Mulgrave, N.S., Can. E15 110
Mulhacén, mtn., Spain G7 20
Mulhall, Ok., U.S. E11 128
Mulhouse, Fr. G16 14
Muling, China B9 38
Muling, China B9 38
Muling, stm., China B9 38
Mulinu'u, Cape, c., Samoa g11 79c
Mūlki, India E2 53
Mull, Island of, i., Scot., U.K. E6 12
Mullengudgery, Austl. H6 76
Muller, Pegunungan, mts., Indon. C8 50
Mullet Peninsula, pen., Ire. G2 12
Mullet Pond Bay, Neth. Ant. A1 105a
Mullett Lake, l., Mi., U.S. C5 112
Mullewa, Austl. E3 74
Müllheim, Ger. I3 16
Mullin, Tx., U.S. C9 130
Mullingar, Ire. H5 12
Mullins, S.C., U.S. B6 116
Mulobezi, Zam. D4 68
Mulongo, D.R.C. F5 66
Mulshi Lake, res., India B1 53
Multai, India H7 54
Multān, Pak. C3 54
Multé, Mex. D2 102
Mulumbe, Monts, mts., D.R.C. F5 66
Mulvane, Ks., U.S. D11 128
Mumbai (Bombay), India B1 53
Mumbwa, Zam. D4 68
Mumen, China E2 42
Mumeng, Pap. N. Gui. b4 79a
Mumford, Tx., U.S. G2 122
Mun, stm., Thai. E7 48
Muna, stm., Russia C13 34
Muna, Pulau, i., Indon. F7 44
Muncar, Indon. H9 50
Münchberg, Ger. F7 16
München (Munich), Ger. H7 16
Munchique, Cerro, mtn., Col. F3 86
Munchique, Parque Nacional, p.o.i., Col. F3 86
Muncie, In., U.S. H4 112
Muncy, Pa., U.S. C9 114
Mundare, Ab., Can. C18 138
Munday, Tx., U.S. H9 128
Mundelein, Il., U.S. B9 120
Münden, Ger. E5 16
Mundra, India G2 54
Mundrabilla, Austl. F5 74
Mundubbera, Austl. E8 76
Munfordville, Ky., U.S. G12 120
Mungallala Creek, stm., Austl. F6 76
Mungana, Austl. C8 74
Mungar Junction, Austl. E9 76
Mungbere, D.R.C. D5 66
Mungeli, India G8 54
Munger, India F11 54
Mungindi, Austl. G7 76
Mungo, Ang. C2 68
Mungo National Park, p.o.i., Austl. I4 76
Munhango, Ang. C2 68
Munich see München, Ger. H7 16
Muniesa, Spain C10 20
Munim, stm., Braz. B3 88
Munising, Mi., U.S. B3 112
Muniz Freire, Braz. K5 88
Munku-Sardyk, gora, mtn., Asia D17 32
Münsingen, Ger. H5 16
Munson, Ab., Can. E18 138
Münster, Ger. D3 16
Munster, Ger. C6 16
Munster, hist. reg., Ire. I3 12
Munte, Indon. C11 50
Muntok, Indon. E4 50
Munuscong Lake, l., N.A. B5 112
Muong Hinh, Viet. C7 48
Muong Saiapoun, Laos C5 48
Muonio, Fin. C10 8
Muping, China C9 42
Muqdisho (Mogadiscio), Som. D9 66
Muqui, Braz. K5 88
Mur (Mura), stm., Eur. D12 22
Mura (Mur), stm., Eur. D12 22
Murajá, Braz. D8 84
Murakami, Japan A12 40
Murana, Indon. F9 44
Muraši, Russia C7 32
Murat, Fr. D8 18
Murat, stm., Tur. H17 6
Murat Dağı, mtn., Tur. E12 28
Muratlı, Tur. B10 28
Muravera, Italy E3 24
Murayama, Japan A13 40
Murça, Port. C3 20
Murchison, Tx., U.S. E3 122
Murchison, stm., Austl. E2 74
Murchison, Mount, mtn., N.Z. F4 80
Murcia, Spain G9 20
Murcia, state, Spain G9 20
Mur-de-Barrez, Fr. E8 18

Name | Map Ref. | Page

Murdo, S.D., U.S. D12 126
Mürefte, Tur. C10 28
Mureş, state, Rom. C11 26
Mureş (Maros), stm., Eur. C7 26
Muret, Fr. F7 18
Murewa, Zimb. D5 68
Murfreesboro, Ar., U.S. C5 122
Murfreesboro, Tn., U.S. I11 120
Murgab, Taj. B11 56
Murgab (Morghāb), stm., Asia B9 56
Murgha Kibzai, Pak. C2 54
Murgon, Austl. F8 76
Muri, Cook Is. a27 78j
Muriaé, Braz. K4 88
Muriaé, stm., Braz. K5 88
Muribeca dos Guararapes, Braz. E8 88
Murici, Braz. E8 88
Muricizal, stm., Braz. D1 88
Murīdke, Pak. C5 54
Muriege, Ang. C3 68
Müritz, l., Ger. C8 16
Murmansk, Russia B15 8
Murmanskaja oblast', co., Russia C16 8
Murnau, Ger. I7 16
Muro Lucano, Italy D9 24
Murom, Russia I19 8
Muromcevo, Russia C13 32
Muroran, Japan C14 38
Muroto, Japan F7 40
Muroto-zaki, c., Japan F7 40
Murowana Goślina, Pol. D13 16
Murphy, Id., U.S. G10 136
Murphy, N.C., U.S. A1 116
Murphys, Ca., U.S. E5 134
Murra Murra, Austl. G6 76
Murrat el-Kubra, Buheirat (Great Bitter Lake), l., Egypt H3 58
Murray, Ia., U.S. C3 120
Murray, Ky., U.S. H9 120
Murray, Ut., U.S. C5 132
Murray, stm., Austl. J2 76
Murray, stm., B.C., Can. B9 138
Murray, Lake, l., Pap. N. Gui. b3 79a
Murray, Lake, res., S.C., U.S. B4 116
Murray Bridge, Austl. J2 76
Murray Fracture Zone, unds. F24 142
Murray Harbour, P.E., Can. E14 110
Murray Maxwell Bay, b., Nu., Can. A14 106
Murray River, P.E., Can. D14 110
Murraysburg, S. Afr. G6 70
Murree, Pak. B4 54
Murrhardt, Ger. H5 16
Murrumbidgee, stm., Austl. J4 76
Murrumburrah, Austl. J7 76
Murrupula, Moz. D6 68
Mursala, Pulau, i., Indon. L4 48
Murshidābād, India F12 54
Murska Sobota, Slvn. D13 22
Murtajāpur, India H6 54
Murtee, Austl. H4 76
Murter, Otok, i., Cro. G12 22
Murtle Lake, l., B.C., Can. D11 138
Murtoa, Austl. K4 76
Murtosa, Port. D2 20
Muru, Capu di, c., Fr. H14 18
Murud, India B1 53
Murud, Gunong, mtn., Malay. B9 50
Murukta, Russia C9 34
Murung, stm., Indon. C9 50
Mururoa, at., Fr. Poly. F13 72
Murwāra (Katni), India G8 54
Murwillumbah, Austl. G9 76
Murzuq, Libya B2 62
Murzūq, Idhān, des., Libya C2 62
Mürzzuschlag, Aus. C12 22
Muş, Tur. B5 56
Mūša (Mūša), stm., Eur. D6 10
Mūša (Mūsa), stm., Eur. D6 10
Mûsa, Gebel (Sinai, Mount), mtn., Egypt J5 58
Musadi, D.R.C. E4 66
Musā'id, Libya A4 62
Musala, mtn., Blg. G10 26
Musan-ŭp, Kor., N. C8 38
Muscat see Masqaṭ, Oman E8 56
Muscat and Oman see Oman, ctry., Asia F8 56
Muscatine, Ia., U.S. C6 120
Muscle Shoals, Al., U.S. C11 122
Musclow, Mount, mtn., B.C., Can. C3 138
Muscoda, Wi., U.S. A7 120
Musgrave, Austl. B8 74
Mus-Haja, gora, mtn., Russia D17 34
Mushie, D.R.C. E3 66
Mushin, Nig. H5 64
Mūsi, stm., India C4 53
Musi, stm., Indon. E4 50
Musicians Seamounts, unds. F22 142
Muskegon, Mi., U.S. E3 112
Muskegon, stm., Mi., U.S. E4 112
Muskingum, stm., Oh., U.S. E4 114
Muskogee, Ok., U.S. I2 120
Muskoka, Lake, l., On., Can. D10 112
Musoma, Tan. E6 66
Musquodoboit Harbour, N.S., Can. F13 110
Mussau Island, i., Pap. N. Gui. a4 79a
Musselshell, stm., Mt., U.S. G6 124
Mussende, Ang. C2 68
Mussidan, Fr. D6 18
Mussomeli, Italy G7 24
Mussuma, Ang. C3 68
Mustafakemalpaşa, Tur. C11 28
Mustafa Kemal Paşa, stm., Tur. D11 28
Mustahīl, Eth. F8 62
Mustāng, Nepal D9 54
Mustang Draw, stm., Tx., U.S. B5 130
Mustang Island, i., Tx., U.S. G10 130
Musters, Lago, l., Arg. I3 90
Mustla, Est. B8 10
Mustvee, Est. B9 10
Muswellbrook, Austl. I8 76
Mût, Egypt B5 62
Mut, Tur. B4 58
Mutá, Ponta do, c., Braz. G6 88
Mutanchiang see Mudanjiang, China B8 38
Mutankiang see Mudanjiang, China B8 38
Mutare, Zimb. D5 68
Mutlu (Rezovska), stm., Eur. G14 26
Mutoko, Zimb. D5 68
Mutoraj, Russia B17 32
Mutsamudu, Com. C7 68
Mutshatsha, D.R.C. G4 66
Mutsu, Japan D14 38
Mutsu-wan, b., Japan D14 38
Mutton Bay, Qc., Can. i22 107a
Mutuípe, Braz. G6 88
Mutum, Braz. J5 88
Mu Us Shamo (Ordos Desert), des., China B3 42
Mūvattupula, India F3 53
Muxima, Ang. B1 68
Muyinga, Bdi. E6 66
Muyumba, D.R.C. F5 66
Muzaffarābād, Pak. A4 54
Muzaffargarh, Pak. C3 54
Muzaffarnagar, India D6 54
Muzaffarpur, India E10 54
Muzat, stm., China C2 36
Muži, Russia A10 32
Muzillac, Fr. G6 14
Muztag, mtn., China D2 36
Muztag, mtn., China A5 46
Mvolo, Sudan F6 62
Mvoti, stm., S. Afr. F10 70
Mvuma, Zimb. D5 68
Mwadui, Tan. E6 66
Mwali, i., Com. C7 68
Mwanza, Tan. E6 66
Mweelrea, mtn., Ire. H3 12
Mweka, D.R.C. E4 66
Mwene-Ditu, D.R.C. F4 66
Mwenezi, Zimb. B10 70
Mwenezi, stm., Afr. B10 70
Mweru, Lake, l., Afr. B4 68
Mweru Wantipa, Lake, l., Zam. B4 68
Mwilitau Islands (Purdy Islands), is., Pap. N. Gui. a4 79a
Mwinilunga, Zam. C3 68
Myājlār, India E3 54
Myall Lakes National Park, p.o.i., Austl. I9 76
Myanaung, Mya. C2 48
Myanmar (Burma), ctry., Asia D8 46
Myaungmya, Mya. D2 48
Mycenae see Mykínes, hist., Grc. F5 28
Myebon, Mya. B1 48
Myingyan, Mya. B2 48
Myitkyinā, Mya. C8 46
Myitnge, stm., Mya. B3 48
Myitta, Mya. E4 48
Myittha, Mya. B2 48
Myittha, stm., Mya. B2 48
Myjava, Slov. H13 16
Mykines, i., Far. Is. m34 8b
Mykínes, hist., Grc. F5 28
Mykolaïv, Ukr. F15 6
Mykolaïv, co., Ukr. B17 26
Mykolaïvka, Ukr. C16 26
Mýkonos, i., Grc. F8 28
Myla, Russia D24 8
Mymensingh (Nasirābād), Bngl. F13 54
Mynaral, Kaz. E12 32
Mynfontein, S. Afr. G6 70
Myohaung, Mya. B1 48
Myohyang-san, mtn., Kor., N. D7 38
Myōkō-san, vol., Japan C11 40
Myra, hist., Tur. G12 28
Mýrdalsjökull, ice, Ice. I30 8a
Myrskylä, Fin. F11 8
Myrtle Beach, S.C., U.S. C7 116
Myrtle Creek, Or., U.S. G3 136
Myrtle Grove, Fl., U.S. G11 122
Myrtle Point, Or., U.S. G2 136
Myrtletowne, Ca., U.S. C1 134
Myškino, Russia C21 10
Myślenice, Pol. G15 16
Myślibórz, Pol. D10 16
Mysłowice, Pol. F15 16
Mysore, India E3 53
Mysore see Karnātaka, state, India F4 46
Mystic, Ct., U.S. C14 114
Mystrás, hist., Grc. F5 28
Mys Vhodnoj, Russia B6 34
Myszków, Pol. F15 16
Myt, Russia H20 8
My Tho, Viet. G8 48
Mytilíni, Grc. D9 28
Mytišči, Russia E20 10
Myton, Ut., U.S. C6 132
Mývatn, l., Ice. k31 8a
Mzimba, Mwi. C5 68
Mzimvubu, stm., S. Afr. G9 70
Mzintlava, stm., S. Afr. G9 70
Mzuzu, Mwi. C5 68

N

Na (Tengtiao), stm., Asia A6 48
Naab, stm., Ger. G7 16
Naalehu, Hi., U.S. D6 78a
Naas, Ire. H6 12
Nababeep, S. Afr. F3 70
Nabari, Japan E9 40
Nabberu, Lake, l., Austl. E4 74
Nabburg, Ger. G8 16
Naberežnye Čelny, Russia C8 32
Nabeul, Tun. H4 24
Nābha, India C6 54
Nabire, Indon. F10 44
Nabī Shu'ayb, Jabal an-, mtn., Yemen F5 56
Nabouwalu, Fiji p19 79e
Nabq, Egypt J5 58
Nabula, China C7 54
Nābulus, W.B. F6 58
Nacala-a-Velha, Moz. C7 68
Nachingwea, Tan. G7 66
Nāchna, India E3 54
Náchod, Czech Rep. F12 16
Nachvak Fiord, b., Nf., Can. F13 141
Nacimiento, Chile H1 92
Nacimiento, Lake, res., Ca., U.S. H5 134
Naco, Mex. F8 98
Naco, Az., U.S. L6 132
Nacogdoches, Tx., U.S. F4 122
Nácori Chico, Mex. G8 98
Nacozari de García, Mex. F8 98
Ñacunday, Para. B10 92
Nadarivatu, Fiji p18 79e
Nadela, Spain B3 20
Nadiād, India G4 54
Nadi Bay, b., Fiji p18 79e
Nădlac, Rom. C7 26
Naduri, Fiji p19 79e
Nadvoicy, Russia E16 8
Nadym, Russia A12 32
Nadym, stm., Russia A12 32
Naenwa, India F5 54
Nærbø, Nor. G1 8
Næstved, Den. I4 8
Nafada, Nig. G7 64
Nafī, Sau. Ar. D5 56
Náfpaktos, Grc. E4 28
Náfplio, Grc. F5 28
Nafūsah, Jabal, hills, Libya A2 62
Naga, Phil. D4 52
Nagahama, Japan D9 40
Nagahama, Japan F5 40
Naga Hills, mts., Asia C7 46
Nagai, Japan A12 40
Nagai Island, i., Ak., U.S. F7 140
Nāgāland, state, India C7 46
Nagano, Japan C11 40
Nagano, state, Japan C11 40
Nagaoka, Japan B11 40
Nagaon, India E14 54
Nāgappattinam, India F4 53
Nagara, stm., Japan D9 40
Nagarhole Tiger Reserve, India E2 53
Nāgārjuna Sāgar, res., India C4 53
Nagarote, Nic. F4 102
Nagasaki, Japan G2 40
Nagasaki, state, Japan G2 40
Nagato, Japan E4 40
Nāgaur, India E4 54
Nāgāvali, stm., India B6 53
Nagda, India G5 54
Nāgercoil, India G3 53
Nagīna, India D7 54
Nagłowice, Pol. F15 16
Nago, Japan I19 39a
Nagold, Ger. H4 16
Nagornyj, Russia E13 34
Nagoya, Japan D9 40
Nāgpur, India H7 54
Nagqu, China C14 54
Nagua, Dom. Rep. C12 102
Naguabo, P.R. B4 104a
Nagyatád, Hung. C4 26
Nagybánya see Baia Mare, Rom. B10 26
Nagyecsed, Hung. B9 26
Nagykanizsa, Hung. C4 26
Nagykáta, Hung. B6 26
Nagykőrös, Hung. B6 26
Naha, Japan I18 39a
Nahabuan, Indon. C9 50
Nāhan, India C6 54
Nahanni Butte, N.T., Can. C6 106
Nahariyya, Isr. E5 58
Nahāvand, Iran C6 56
Nahe, China B9 36
Nahe, stm., Ger. G3 16
Nahma, Mi., U.S. C3 112
Nahodka, Russia A13 32
Nahodka, Russia C10 38
Nahoe, Fr. Poly. r19 78g
Nahoï, Cap, c., Vanuatu j16 79d
Nahuel Huapi, Lago, l., Arg. H2 90
Nahuel Niyeu, Arg. H3 90
Naica, Mex. B6 100
Naicam, Sk., Can. B9 124
Naila, Ger. F7 16
Naiman Qi, China C4 38
Nā'īn, Iran C7 56
Naini Tāl, India D7 54
Nainpur, India G8 54
Nairai, i., Fiji p19 79e
Nairn, La., U.S. H9 122
Nairobi, Kenya E7 66
Naitauba, i., Fiji p20 79e
Naivasha, Kenya E7 66
Naizishan, China C7 38
Najac, Fr. E8 18
Najafābād, Iran C7 56
Najasa, stm., Cuba B9 102
Najd (Nejd), hist. reg., Sau. Ar. D5 56
Najībābād, India D7 54
Najin, Kor., N. C9 38
Naka, stm., Japan C13 40
Nakajō, Japan A12 40
Nakama, Japan F3 40
Nakaminato, Japan C13 40
Nakamura, Japan G5 40
Nakano, Japan C11 40
Nakano-shima, i., Japan k19 39a
Nakasongola, Ug. D6 66
Nakatsu, Japan F4 40
Nakatsugawa, Japan D10 40
Nakhl, Egypt I4 58
Nakhon Nayok, Thai. E5 48
Nakhon Pathom, Thai. F5 48
Nakhon Phanom, Thai. D7 48
Nakhon Ratchasima, Thai. E6 48
Nakhon Sawan, Thai. E4 48
Nakhon Si Thammarat, Thai. H5 48
Nakhon Thai, Thai. D5 48
Nakina, On., Can. A12 118
Nakło nad Notecią, Pol. C13 16
Nakodar, India C5 54
Nakonde, Zam. B5 68
Nakskov, Den. I4 8
Naktong-gang, stm., Kor., S. C1 40
Nakuru, Kenya E7 66
Nakusp, B.C., Can. F13 138
Nālanda, India F10 54
Nalayh, Mong. B6 36
Nalbāri, India E13 54
Nal'čik, Russia F6 32
Nałęczów, Pol. E18 16
Nalgonda, India C4 53
Nallamalla Hills, mts., India D4 53
Nallıhan, Tur. C14 28
Nalón, stm., Spain A5 20
Nalong, China J2 42
Nālūt, Libya A2 62
Nam (Nan'a), stm., Asia B4 48
Namaacha, Moz. D10 70
Namacurra, Moz. D6 68
Namadgi National Park, p.o.i., Austl. J7 76
Namak, Daryācheh-ye, l., Iran C7 56
Namakan Lake, l., N.A. C6 118
Nāmakkal, India F4 53
Namangan, Uzb. F12 32
Namanyere, Tan. F6 66
Namapa, Moz. C6 68
Namarrói, Moz. D6 68
Namatanai, Pap. N. Gui. a5 79a
Nambour, Austl. F9 76
Nam Co, l., China C13 54
Nam Dinh, Viet. B7 48
Nam Du, Quan Dao, is., Viet. H6 48
Nameh, Indon. B10 50
Namen see Namur, Bel. D13 14
Namerikawa, Japan C10 40
Nametil, Moz. D6 68
Nam-gang, stm., Kor., N. E7 38
Namhae-do, i., Kor., S. G8 38
Namhan-gang, stm., Kor., S. F7 38
Namhkam, Mya. D8 46
Namib Desert, des., Nmb. E1 68
Namibe, Ang. D1 68
Namibia, ctry., Afr. E2 68
Namib Naukluft Park, p.o.i., Nmb. D2 70
Namie, Japan B14 40
Namies, S. Afr. F4 70
Namji-ri, Kor., S. D1 40
Namlea, Indon. F8 44
Namling, China D12 54
Nam Nao National Park, p.o.i., Thai. D5 48
Nam Ngum Reservoir, res., Laos C6 48
Namnoi, Khao, mtn., Mya. G4 48
Namoi, stm., Austl. H7 76
Nampa, Id., U.S. G10 136
Nampala, Mali F3 64
Nam Pat, Thai. D5 48
Nampawng, Mya. A3 48
Nam Phan (Cochin China), hist. reg., Viet. G8 48
Namp'o, Kor., N. E6 38
Nampula, Moz. D6 68
Namsang, Mya. B3 48
Namsen, stm., Nor. D5 8
Namsos, Nor. D4 8
Nam Tok, Thai. E4 48
Nam Tok Mae Surin National Park, p.o.i., Thai. C4 48
Namtu, Mya. A3 48
Namu, B.C., Can. E3 138
Namuka-I-Lau, i., Fiji q20 79e
Namúli, Serra, mts., Moz. D6 68
Namur (Namen), Bel. D13 14
Namutoni, Nmb. D2 68
Namwala, Zam. D4 68
Namwŏn, Kor., S. G7 38
Namysłów, Pol. E13 16
Nan, Thai. C5 48
Nan, stm., Thai. D5 48
Nan'a (Nam), stm., Asia B4 48
Nanaimo, B.C., Can. G6 138
Nanam, Kor., N. D8 38
Nan'an, China I8 42
Nanango, Austl. F8 76
Nanao, Japan B9 40
Nanatsu-jima, is., Japan B9 40
Nanbu, China F1 42
Nancha, China B10 36
Nanchang, China G6 42
Nancheng, China H7 42
Nancheng see Hanzhong, China E2 42
Nanching see Nanjing, China E8 42
Nanchong, China F2 42
Nanchuan, China G2 42
Nanch'ung see Nanchong, China F2 42
Nancowry Island, i., India G7 46
Nancy, Fr. F15 14
Nanda Devi, mtn., India C8 54
Nandaime, Nic. G4 102
Nandan, Japan E7 40
Nānded, India B3 53
Nāndgaon, India H5 54
Nandi Drug, mtn., India E3 53
Nandikotkūr, India D4 53
Nandu, China F8 42
Nandu, stm., China L4 42
Nāndūra, India H6 54
Nandurbār, India H4 54
Nandyāl, India D4 53
Nanfen, China D5 38
Nanfeng, China H7 42
Nanga-Eboko, Cam. D2 66
Nangakelawit, Indon. C8 50
Nangamau, Indon. D7 50
Nangaobat, Indon. C8 50
Nanga Parbat, mtn., Pak. B11 56
Nangapinoh, Indon. D7 50
Nangarhār, state, Afg. A3 54
Nangatayap, Indon. D7 50
Nanggala Hill, mtn., Sol. Is. e7 79b
Nangin, Mya. G4 48
Nangnim-ŭp, Kor., N. D7 38
Nangong, China C6 42
Nang Rong, Thai. E6 48
Nanguan, China C5 42
Nanhua, China F5 36
Nan Hulsan Hu, l., China D4 36
Nanika Lake, l., B.C., Can. C3 138
Nanjangūd, India E3 53
Nanjiang, China E2 42
Nanjing, China I7 42
Nanjing (Nanking), China E8 42
Nankang, China I6 42
Nanking see Nanjing, China E8 42
Nankoku, Japan F6 40
Nankye, Mya. E3 48
Nanle, China C6 42
Nanlei (Loi), stm., Asia A4 48
Nanling, China F8 42
Nan Ling, mts., China I5 42
Nanliu, stm., China J3 42
Nanlou Shan, mtn., China C7 38
Nannine, Austl. E3 74
Nanning, China J3 42
Na Noi, Thai. C5 48
Nanortalik, Grnld. E16 141
Nanpan, stm., China G5 36
Nānpāra, India E8 54
Nanpiao, China A9 42
Nanping, China E5 36
Nanping, China H8 42
Nansei, Japan E9 40
Nansei-shotō (Ryukyu Islands), is., Japan k19 39a
Nan Shan see Qilian Shan, mts., China D4 36
Nanshan Island, i., Asia C6 44
Nantais, Lac, l., Qc., Can. C16 106
Nantai-zan, vol., Japan C12 40
Nanterre, Fr. F11 14
Nantes, Fr. G7 14
Nantes à Brest, Canal de, can., Fr. F5 14
Nanticoke, Pa., U.S. C9 114
Nanto, Japan E9 40
Nanton, Ab., Can. F17 138
Nantong, China E9 42
Nant'ou, Tai. J9 42
Nantucket, Ma., U.S. C15 114
Nantucket Island, i., Ma., U.S. C15 114
Nantucket Sound, strt., Ma., U.S. C15 114
Nantulo, Moz. C6 68
Nantung see Nantong, China E9 42
Nanty Glo, Pa., U.S. H11 112
Nanu, Pap. N. Gui. b3 79a
Nanuku Passage, strt., Fiji p20 79e
Nanumea, at., Tuvalu D8 72
Nanuque, Braz. I5 88
Nanusa, Kepulauan, is., Indon. E8 44
Nanxi, China G1 42
Nanxian, China G5 42
Nanxiang, China F9 42
Nanxiong, China I6 42
Nanyang, China E5 42
Nanyang Hu, l., China D7 42
Nanyi Hu, l., China F8 42
Nan-yō, Japan A13 40
Nanyuki, Kenya D7 66
Nanzamu, China C6 38
Nanzhao, China E5 42
Nao, Cabo de la see Nau, Cap de la, c., Spain F11 20
Naococane, Lac, l., Qc., Can. E16 106
Naogaon, Bngl. F12 54
Naokot, Pak. F2 54
Náousa, Grc. C5 28
Napa, Ca., U.S. E3 134
Napa, stm., Ca., U.S. E3 134
Napaku, Indon. B9 50
Napalkovo, Russia C3 34
Napanee, On., Can. D12 112
Napassoq, Grnld. D15 141
Naperville, Il., U.S. C9 120
Napido, Indon. F10 44
Napier, N.Z. D7 80
Napier, Mount, hill, Austl. C5 74
Napier Mountains, mts., Ant. B10 81
Naples see Napoli, Italy D8 24
Naples, Fl., U.S. J4 116
Naples, Id., U.S. B10 136
Naples, N.Y., U.S. B8 114
Naples, Tx., U.S. D4 122
Napo, state, Ec. H3 86
Napo, stm., S.A. D3 84
Napoleon, N.D., U.S. A13 126
Napoleonville, La., U.S. H7 122
Napoli (Naples), Italy D8 24
Napoli, Golfo di, b., Italy D8 24
Nappamerrie, Austl. F3 76
Nappanee, In., U.S. G4 112
Napu, Indon. H11 50
Nara, Japan E8 40
Nara, Mali F3 64
Nara, state, Japan E8 40
Nāra, stm., Pak. F2 54
Nara, stm., Russia E20 10
Narač, vozero, l., Bela. F9 10
Naracoorte, Austl. K3 76
Naradhan, Austl. I6 76
Naraini, India F8 54
Naramata, B.C., Can. G11 138
Naranjal, Ec. I2 86
Naranjito, P.R. B3 104a
Narasannapeta, India B7 53
Narasapur, India C5 53
Narasaraopet, India C4 53
Narasun, Russia A7 36
Narathiwat, Thai. I5 48
Narau (Narew), stm., Eur. D17 16
Nārāyanganj, Bngl. G13 54
Nārāyani (Gandak), stm., Asia E10 54
Nārāyanpet, India C3 53
Narbonne, Fr. F8 18
Nardò, Italy D11 24
Nares Strait, strt., N.A. B11 141
Narew (Narau), stm., Eur. D17 16
Nargund, India D2 53
Nariño, state, Col. G3 86
Narita, Japan D13 40
Nariva Swamp, sw., Trin. s12 105f
Nar'jan-Mar, Russia C25 8
Narkatiāganj, India E10 54
Narlı, Tur. A8 58
Narmada, stm., India H4 54
Nārnaul, India D6 54
Narodnaja, gora, mtn., Russia B10 32
Narodnaya, Mount see Narodnaja, gora, mtn., Russia B10 32
Naro-Fominsk, Russia E19 10
Narol, Pol. F19 16
Narooma, Austl. K8 76
Nārowāl, Pak. B5 54
Narrabri, Austl. H7 76
Narran, stm., Austl. G7 76
Narrandera, Austl. J6 76
Narraway, stm., Can. B11 138
Narrogin, Austl. F3 74
Narromine, Austl. I6 76
Narsaq see Narssaq, Grnld. E16 141
Narsimhapur, India G7 54
Narsinghgarh, India G6 54
Narsīpatnam, India C6 53
Narssaq, Grnld. E16 141
Naru, Japan G1 40
Naruto, Japan E7 40
Narva, Est. G13 8
Narva, Russia C16 32
Narva, stm., Eur. A11 10
Narvik, Nor. B7 8
Narvskij zaliv, b., Eur. A10 10
Narvskoe vodohranilišče, l., Eur. A10 10
Narwāna, India D6 54
Narwietooma, Austl. D6 74
Narym, Russia C14 32
Naryn, Kyrg. F13 32
Naryn, stm., Asia F13 32
Narynkol, Kaz. F13 32
Näsåker, Swe. E7 8
Na San, Thai. H4 48
Nasawa, Vanuatu j17 79d
Nasbinals, Fr. E9 18
Nasca, Peru F2 84
Nase see Naze, Japan k19 39a
Nash, Tx., U.S. D4 122
Nāshik, India H4 54
Nashua, Ia., U.S. B5 120
Nashua, N.H., U.S. B14 114
Nashville, Ar., U.S. D5 122
Nashville, Il., U.S. F8 120
Nashville, In., U.S. E11 120
Nashville, Mi., U.S. F4 112
Nashville, N.C., U.S. I8 114
Nashville, Tn., U.S. H11 120
Nashwaak, stm., N.B., Can. D10 110
Nashwauk, Mn., U.S. D5 118
Nasielsk, Pol. D16 16
Näsijärvi, l., Fin. F10 8
Nāṣir, Sudan F6 62
Nāṣir, Buheirat see Nasser, Lake, res., Afr. C6 62
Nasīrābād, India E5 54
Nasr, Egypt H1 58
Nass, stm., B.C., Can. E5 106
Nassarawa, Nig. H6 64
Nassau, Bah. m18 104f
Nassau, N.Y., U.S. B12 114
Nassau International Airport, Bah. m18 104f
Nassau Island, i., Cook Is. E10 72
Nassawadox, Va., U.S. G10 114
Nasser, Lake (Nâṣir, Buheirat), res., Afr. C6 62
Nässjö, Swe. H6 8
Nastapoka Islands, is., Nu., Can. D15 106
Nasu, Japan B13 40
Nasu-dake, vol., Japan B12 40
Nasukoin Mountain, mtn., Mt., U.S. B12 136
Nasva, Russia D13 10
Nata, Bots. E4 68
Nata, stm., Afr. B8 70
Natal, Braz. C8 88
Natal, B.C., Can. G16 138
Natal, Indon. C1 50
Natal see KwaZulu-Natal, state, S. Afr. F10 70
Natalia, Tx., U.S. E9 130
Natalkuz Lake, res., B.C., Can. C5 138
Natanes Plateau, plat., Az., U.S. J6 132
Natashquan, stm., Can. i21 107a
Natchez, Ms., U.S. F7 122
Natchez Trace Parkway, p.o.i., U.S. E9 122
Natchitoches, La., U.S. F5 122
Natewa Bay, b., Fiji p19 79e
Nāthdwāra, India F4 54
Natimuk, Austl. K3 76
Nation, stm., B.C., Can. A7 138
National City, Ca., U.S. K8 134
Natitingou, Benin G5 64
Native Bay, b., Nu., Can. C14 106
Natividade, Braz. F2 88
Natkyizin, Mya. E3 48
Natoma, Ks., U.S. B9 128
Nator, Bngl. F12 54
Natori, Japan A13 40
Natron, Lake, l., Afr. E7 66
Natrûn, Wadi el-, val., Egypt H1 58
Nattaung, mtn., Mya. C3 48
Natuna Besar, i., Indon. A6 50
Natuna Besar, Kepulauan, is., Indon. A5 50
Natuna Selatan, Kepulauan, is., Indon. B6 50
Natural Bridge, misc. cult., Va., U.S. G6 114
Natural Bridges National Monument, p.o.i., Ut., U.S. F6 132
Naturaliste, Cape, c., Austl. F2 74
Naturno, Italy D7 22
Nau, Cap de la, c., Spain F11 20
Naucelle, Fr. E8 18
Naucratis, hist., Egypt H1 58
Nauen, Ger. D8 16
Naugatuck, Ct., U.S. C12 114
Naughton, On., Can. B8 112
Naujamiestis, Lith. E6 10
Naujan, Lake, l., Phil. D3 52
Naujoji Akmenė, Lith. D5 10
Naumburg, Ger. E7 16
Naunglon, Mya. D3 48
Nā'ūr, Jord. G6 58
Nauru, state, Oc. p17 78f
Nauru International Airport, Nauru q17 78f
Nauški, Russia F10 34
Nausori, Fiji p19 79e
Nauta, Peru D3 84
Nautanwa, India E9 54
Nautla, Mex. E10 100
Nauvoo, Il., U.S. D6 120
Nava, Mex. A8 100
Navadwip, India G12 54
Navael'nja, Bela. G8 10
Navahrudak, Bela. G8 10
Navajo, N.M., U.S. H7 132
Navajo Mountain, mtn., Ut., U.S. F6 132
Navajo National Monument, p.o.i., Az., U.S. G6 132
Navajo Reservoir, res., U.S. G9 132
Naval, Phil. C7 44
Navalmoral de la Mata, Spain E5 20
Navan, Ire. H6 12
Navapolack, Bela. E11 10
Navāpur, India H4 54
Navarin, mys, c., Russia D24 34
Navarino, Isla, i., Chile K3 90
Navarra, state, Spain B9 20
Navarro Mills Lake, res., Tx., U.S. F2 122
Navasëlki, Bela. H7 10
Navasota, Tx., U.S. G2 122
Navasota, stm., Tx., U.S. D11 130
Navassa, N.C., U.S. B7 116
Navassa Island, i., N.A. C10 102
Navesnoe, Russia H20 10
Navia, Arg. G4 92
Navia, stm., Spain A4 20
Navidad, Chile F1 92
Navidad, stm., Tx., U.S. E11 130
Navio, Riacho do, stm., Braz. E6 88
Naviti, i., Fiji p18 79e
Navlja, Russia H17 10
Năvodari, Rom. E15 26
Navoi, Uzb. F11 32
Navojoa, Mex. B4 100
Navolato, Mex. C5 100
Navsāri, India H4 54
Nawa see Naha, Japan I18 39a
Nawābganj, Bngl. F12 54
Nawābganj, India E8 54
Nawābshāh, Pak. E2 54
Nawāda, India F10 54
Nāwah, Afg. B1 54
Nawalgarh, India E5 54
Nawāpāra, India H8 54
Naxçıvan, Azer. B6 56
Naxi, China G1 42
Náxos, i., Grc. F8 28
Nayāgarh, India H10 54
Nayarit, state, Mex. E6 100
Nāy Band, Kūh-e, mtn., Iran C8 56
Naylor, Mo., U.S. H7 120
Nayoro, Japan B15 38
Nazaré, Braz. D2 88
Nazaré, Port. E1 20
Nazaré da Mata, Braz. D8 88
Nazaré do Piauí, Braz. D4 88
Nazareth see Nazerat, Isr. F6 58
Nazarovo, Russia C16 32
Nazas, Mex. C6 100
Nazas, stm., Mex. C6 100
Nazca Ridge, unds. K5 144
Naze, Japan k19 39a
Naze, The see Lindesnes, c., Nor. H2 8
Nazerat (Nazareth), Isr. F6 58
Nazerat'Illit, Isr. F6 58
Nazija, Russia A14 10
Nazilli, Tur. F11 28
Nazina, Russia B13 32
Nazko, stm., B.C., Can. D7 138
Nazlet el-'Amûdein, Egypt J1 58
Nazran', Russia F7 32
Nazrēt, Eth. F7 62
Nazwá, Oman E8 56
Nazyvaevsk, Russia C12 32
N'dalatando, Ang. B1 68
Ndali, Benin H5 64
Ndélé, C.A.R. C4 66
Ndendé, Gabon E2 66
N'Djamena (Fort-Lamy), Chad E3 62
Ndjolé, Gabon E2 66
Ndogo, Lagune, l., Gabon E2 66
Ndola, Zam. C4 68
Ndumu Game Reserve, S. Afr. E11 70
Neabul Creek, stm., Austl. F6 76
Neagh, Lough, l., N. Ire., U.K. G6 12
Neah Bay, Wa., U.S. B2 136
Neale, Lake, l., Austl. D6 74
Neamt, state, Rom. B13 26
Néa Páfos (Paphos), Cyp. D3 58
Neápoli, Grc. G6 28
Near Islands, is., Ak., U.S. g21 140a
Neath, Wales, U.K. J9 12
Nebine Creek, stm., Austl. G6 76
Nebitdag, Turkmen. B7 56
Neblina, Cerro de la see Neblina, Pico da, mtn., S.A. G9 86
Neblina, Pico da, mtn., S.A. G9 86
Nebo, Il., U.S. E7 120
Nebo, Mount, mtn., Ut., U.S. D5 132
Nebolči, Russia A16 10
Nebraska, state, U.S. C7 108
Nebraska City, Ne., U.S. D1 120
Necedah, Wi., U.S. G8 118
Nechako, stm., B.C., Can. C7 138
Nechako Reservoir, res., B.C., Can. C5 138
Neches, Tx., U.S. F3 122
Neches, stm., Tx., U.S. G4 122
Nechí, Col. C4 86
Nechí, stm., Col. D4 86
Nechranice, vodní nádrź, res., Czech Rep. F9 16
Neckarsulm, Ger. G5 16
Necker Island, i., Br. Vir. Is. d9 104b
Necochea, Arg. I8 92
Nederland, Tx., U.S. H4 122
Nêdong, China D13 54
Needhams Point, c., Barb. n8 105d
Needle Mountain, mtn., Wy., U.S. F17 136
Needles, Ca., U.S. I2 132
Needville, Tx., U.S. H3 122
Neegro, Qooriga, b., Som. C10 66
Ñeembucú, state, Para. C8 92
Neenah, Wi., U.S. G10 118
Neepawa, Mb., Can. D14 124
Nefëdovo, Russia C12 32
Nefta, Tun. C6 64
Neftçala, Azer. B6 56
Neftejugansk, Russia B12 32
Nefza, Tun. H3 24
Negage, Ang. B2 68
Negara, Indon. H9 50
Negara, stm., Indon. E9 50
Negaunee, Mi., U.S. B2 112
Negēlē, Eth. F7 62
Negeribatin, Indon. F4 50
Negeri Sembilan, state, Malay. K6 48
Negev Desert see HaNegev, reg., Isr. H5 58
Negombo, Sri L. H4 53
Negra, Laguna, l., Ur. G11 92
Negreira, Spain B2 20
Nègres, Pointe des, c., Mart. k6 105c
Negreşti-Oaş, Rom. B10 26
Negritos, Peru D1 84
Negro, stm., Arg. H4 90
Negro, stm., Braz. C13 92
Negro, stm., Col. E4 86
Negro, stm., Para. B9 92
Negro, stm., S.A. I11 86
Negro, stm., S.A. F9 92
Negros, i., Phil. F4 52
Nehalem, stm., Or., U.S. E3 136
Neharèlae, Bela. G9 10
Nehawka, Ne., U.S. D1 120
Nehbandān, Iran C8 56
Nehe see Nahe, China B9 36
Néhoué, Baie de, b., N. Cal. m14 79d
Neiba, Dom. Rep. C12 102

Name	Map Ref.	Page
Neichiang see Neijiang, China	G1	42
Neidpath, Sk., Can.	D6	124
Neiges, Piton des, mtn., Reu.	i10	69a
Neijiang, China	G1	42
Neikiang see Neijiang, China	G1	42
Neilburg, Sk., Can.	B4	124
Neillsville, Wi., U.S.	G8	118
Nei Monggol, state, China.	C7	36
Nei Monggol see Nei Monggol, state, China	C7	36
Neiqiu, China	C6	42
Neira, Col.	E4	86
Neisse see Lausitzer Neisse, stm., Eur.	F10	16
Neisse see Nysa Łużycka, stm., Eur.	E10	16
Neiva, Col.	F4	86
Neixiang, China	E4	42
Neja, Russia	D12	10
Nejapa de Madero, Mex.	G11	100
Nejd see Najd, hist. reg., Sau. Ar.	D5	56
Nejdek, Czech Rep.	F8	16
Nek'emtē, Eth.	F7	62
Nelichu, mtn., Sudan	F6	62
Nelidovo, Russia	D15	10
Neligh, Ne., U.S.	E14	126
Neljaty, Russia	E12	34
Nel'kan, Russia	E16	34
Nellikuppam, India	F4	53
Nellore, India	D4	53
Nel'ma, Russia	G16	34
Nelson, B.C., Can.	G13	138
Nelson, N.Z.	E5	80
Nelson, Ne., U.S.	A10	128
Nelson, stm., Mb., Can.	D12	106
Nelson, Cape, c., Austl.	L3	76
Nelson, Estrecho, strt., Chile	J2	90
Nelson Lakes National Park, p.o.i., N.Z.	E5	80
Nelson's Dockyard, hist., Antig.	f4	105b
Nelsonville, Oh., U.S.	E3	114
Nelspoort, S. Afr.	H6	70
Nelspruit, S. Afr.	D10	70
Néma, Maur.	F3	64
Nemadji, stm., U.S.	E6	118
Neman, Russia	E4	10
Neman (Nemunas), stm., Eur.	E4	10
Nembe, Nig.	I6	64
Nemenčinė, Lith.	F8	10
Nemeriči, Russia	G16	10
Nemours, Fr.	F11	14
Nemunas (Neman), stm., Eur.	E4	10
Nemunėlis (Mēmele), stm., Eur.	D7	10
Nemuro, Japan	C16	38
Nemuro Strait, strt., Asia	C16	38
Nen, stm., China	B9	36
Nenagh, Ire.	I4	12
Nenana, Ak., U.S.	D10	140
Nenana, stm., Ak., U.S.	D10	140
Nendo, i., Sol. Is.	E7	72
Nene, stm., Eng., U.K.	I13	12
Neneckij avtonomnyj okrug, Russia	C23	8
Nenets see Neneckij avtonomnyj okrug, Russia	C23	8
Nenetsia see Neneckij avtonomnyj okrug, Russia	C23	8
Nenggiri, stm., Malay.	J5	48
Neodesha, Ks., U.S.	G2	120
Neoga, Il., U.S.	E9	120
Néo Karlovási, Grc.	F9	28
Neola, Ia., U.S.	C6	132
Neopit, Wi., U.S.	G10	118
Neosho, Mo., U.S.	H3	120
Neosho, stm., U.S.	H2	120
Nepa, stm., Russia	C19	32
Nepal, ctry., Asia	E9	54
Nepālgañj, Nepal	D8	54
Nepa Nagar, India	H6	54
Nepeña, Peru	E2	84
Nephi, Ut., U.S.	D5	132
Nephin, mtn., Ire.	G3	12
Nepisiguit, stm., N.B., Can.	C10	110
Nepisiguit Bay, b., N.B., Can.	C11	110
Neptune, N.J., U.S.	D11	114
Neptune Beach, Fl., U.S.	F4	116
Nérac, Fr.	E6	18
Nerča, stm., Russia	F12	34
Nerčinsk, Russia	F12	34
Nerčinskij Zavod, Russia	F12	34
Nerehta, Russia	H19	8
Neretva, stm., Eur.	G15	22
Neriquinha, Ang.	D3	68
Neris (Vilija), stm., Eur.	F6	10
Nerja, Spain	H7	20
Nerjungri, Russia	E13	34
Nerl', Russia	C20	10
Nerl', stm., Russia	D22	10
Nerópolis, Braz.	I1	88
Nerussa, stm., Russia	H16	10
Nerva, Spain	G4	20
Nes, Neth.	C1	16
Nesbyen, Nor.	F3	8
Neščarda, vozero, l., Bela.	E11	10
Neskaupstaður, Ice.	k32	8a
Nesna, Nor.	C5	8
Nespelem, Wa., U.S.	B7	136
Ness, Loch, l., Scot., U.K.	D8	12
Ness City, Ks., U.S.	C8	128
Nesselrode, Mount, mtn., N.A.	D4	106
Nesterkovo, Russia	A13	10
Nestoíta, Ukr.	B16	26
Netanya, Isr.	F5	58
Netcher, Austl.	C7	76
Netherdale, Austl.	B14	14
Netherlands, ctry., Eur.	B14	14
Netherlands Antilles, dep., N.A.	i14	96a
Netherlands Guiana see Surinam, ctry., S.A.	C6	84
Netrakona, Bngl.	F13	54
Nettilling Fiord, b., Nu., Can.	B17	106
Nettilling Lake, l., Nu., Can.	B17	106
Nett Lake, l., Mn., U.S.	C5	118
Nettuno, Italy	C6	24
Neubrandenburg, Ger.	C9	16
Neuburg an der Donau, Ger.	H7	16
Neuchâtel, Switz.	D3	22
Neuchâtel, Lac de, l., Switz.	D3	22
Neudorf, Sk., Can.	D11	124
Neuenburg see Neuchâtel, Switz.	D3	22
Neuenhagen, Ger.	D9	16
Neuerburg, Ger.	F2	16
Neufchâteau, Fr.	F14	14
Neufchâtel-en-Bray, Fr.	E10	14
Neu-Isenburg, Ger.	F4	16
Neumarkt in der Oberpfalz, Ger.	G7	16
Neumünster, Ger.	B6	16
Neun, stm., Laos	C6	48
Neunkirchen, Aus.	C13	22
Neuquén, Arg.	G3	90
Neuquén, state, Arg.	G2	90
Neuquén, stm., Arg.	G3	90
Neurara, Chile	B3	92
Neuruppin, Ger.	D8	16
Neuse, stm., N.C., U.S.	A8	116
Neusiedl am See, Aus.	C13	22
Neuss, Ger.	E2	16
Neustadt, Ger.	F7	16
Neustadt an der Aisch, Ger.	G6	16
Neustadt an der Weinstrasse, Ger.	G3	16
Neustadt bei Coburg, Ger.	F6	16
Neustadt in Holstein, Ger.	B6	16

Name	Map Ref.	Page
Neustrelitz, Ger.	C9	16
Neutral Hills, hills, Ab., Can.	B3	124
Neu-Ulm, Ger.	H6	16
Neuvic, Fr.	D8	18
Neuwied, Ger.	F3	16
Neva, stm., Russia	A13	10
Nevada, Ia., U.S.	B4	120
Nevada, Mo., U.S.	G3	120
Nevada, state, U.S.	D4	108
Nevada, Sierra, mts., Spain	G7	20
Nevada, Sierra, mts., Ca., U.S.	F6	134
Nevada City, Ca., U.S.	D4	134
Nevado, Cerro, mtn., Arg.	G3	92
Nevado, Cerro, mtn., Col.	E4	86
Nevado de Colima, Parque Nacional del, p.o.i., Mex.	F7	100
Nevado de Toluca, Parque Nacional, p.o.i., Mex.	F8	100
Neve, Serra da, mts., Ang.	C1	68
Nevel', Russia	D12	10
Nevel'sk, Russia	G17	34
Nevel'skogo, proliv, strt., Russia	F17	34
Never, Russia	F13	34
Nevers, Fr.	G12	14
Nevesinje, Bos.	F5	26
Nevis, i., St. K./N.	C2	105a
Nevis, Ben, mtn., Scot., U.K.	E7	12
Nevis Peak, vol., St. K./N...	C2	105a
Nevjansk, Russia	C10	32
Nevşehir, Tur.	B3	56
New, stm., Belize	D3	102
New, stm., Guy.	C6	84
New, stm., U.S.	F4	114
New, stm., S.C., U.S.	D4	116
Newala, Tan.	G7	66
New Albany, In., U.S.	F12	120
New Albany, Ms., U.S.	C9	122
New Amsterdam, Guy.	B6	84
New Angledool, Austl.	G6	76
Newark, Ar., U.S.	B7	122
Newark, De., U.S.	E10	114
Newark, N.J., U.S.	D11	114
Newark, N.Y., U.S.	A8	114
Newark, Oh., U.S.	D3	114
Newark Lake, l., Nv., U.S.	D1	132
Newark-on-Trent, Eng., U.K.	H12	12
Newark Valley, N.Y., U.S.	B9	114
New Athens, Il., U.S.	F8	120
New Augusta, Ms., U.S.	F9	122
New Baden, Il., U.S.	F8	120
New Bedford, Ma., U.S.	C15	114
Newberg, Or., U.S.	E4	136
New Berlin, Il., U.S.	E7	120
New Berlin, N.Y., U.S.	B10	114
New Berlin, Wi., U.S.	F1	112
Newbern, Al., U.S.	E11	122
New Bern, N.C., U.S.	A8	116
Newbern, Tn., U.S.	H8	120
Newberry, Mi., U.S.	G3	116
Newberry, S.C., U.S.	B4	116
Newberry National Volcanic Monument, p.o.i., Or., U.S.	G5	136
New Bloomfield, Pa., U.S.	H12	112
New Boston, Oh., U.S.	F3	114
New Boston, Tx., U.S.	D4	122
New Braunfels, Tx., U.S.	E9	130
New Britain, Ct., U.S.	C13	114
New Britain, i., Pap. N. Gui.	b5	79a
New Brockton, Al., U.S.	F12	122
Newbrook, Ab., Can.	B17	138
New Brunswick, N.J., U.S.	D11	114
New Brunswick, state, Can.	D10	110
Newburg, Mo., U.S.	G6	120
Newburgh, In., U.S.	G10	120
Newburgh, N.Y., U.S.	C11	114
Newbury, Eng., U.K.	J11	12
Newbury, Vt., U.S.	B15	114
Newcastle, Austl.	I8	76
Newcastle, N.B., Can.	C11	110
Newcastle, St. K./N.	C2	105a
Newcastle, N. Ire., U.K.	G7	12
Newcastle, Ok., U.S.	D9	132
New Castle, Co., U.S.	E10	114
New Castle, De., U.S.	I4	112
Newcastle, Ne., U.S.	I2	118
New Castle, In., U.S.	F11	128
New Castle, Pa., U.S.	D5	114
New Castle, Va., U.S.	A9	130
Newcastle, Wy., U.S.	D8	126
Newcastle Bay, b., Austl.	B8	74
Newcastle-under-Lyme, Eng., U.K.	I10	12
Newcastle upon Tyne, Eng., U.K.	G10	12
Newcastle Waters, Austl.	C6	74
Newcastle West, Ire.	I3	12
New City, N.Y., U.S.	C11	114
Newcomerstown, Oh., U.S.	D4	114
New Concord, Oh., U.S.	D4	114
New Cumberland, W.V., U.S.	D5	114
Newdegate, Austl.	F3	74
New Delhi, India	D6	54
New Denver, B.C., Can.	F13	138
New Edinburg, Ar., U.S.	D6	122
New Effington, S.D., U.S.	F1	118
Newell, Ia., U.S.	B2	120
Newell, W.V., U.S.	D5	114
Newell, Lake, l., Ab., Can.	F19	138
New Ellenton, S.C., U.S.	C4	116
Newellton, La., U.S.	E7	122
New England, N.D., U.S.	A10	126
New England National Park, p.o.i., Austl.	H9	76
Newfane, N.Y., U.S.	E11	112
Newfane, Vt., U.S.	A13	114
New Florence, Pa., U.S.	D6	114
Newfound Gap, p., U.S.	I2	114
Newfoundland, state, Can.	j22	107a
Newfoundland, i., Nf., Can.	D9	144
Newfoundland Basin, unds.	E5	120
New Franklin, Mo., U.S.	E5	120
New Freedom, Pa., U.S.	E9	114
New Galloway, Scot., U.K.	F8	12
Newgate, B.C., Can.	G15	138
New Georgia, i., Sol. Is.	e7	79b
New Georgia Group, is., Sol. Is.	d7	79b
New Georgia Sound, strt., Sol. Is.	e8	79b
New Germany, N.S., Can.	F12	110
New Glasgow, N.S., Can.	E14	110
New Guinea, i.	b3	79a
Newhalem, Wa., U.S.	B5	136
New Hamburg, On., Can.	E9	112
New Hampshire, state, U.S.	G5	110
New Hampton, Ia., U.S.	A5	120
New Hanover, i., Pap. N. Gui.	a4	79a
New Hanover, S. Afr.	F10	70
New Harmony, In., U.S.	F10	120
New Hartford, Ia., U.S.	I6	118
Newhaven, Eng., U.K.	K13	12
New Haven, Ct., U.S.	C13	114
New Haven, Il., U.S.	G9	120
New Haven, Ky., U.S.	G12	120
New Haven, Mo., U.S.	F6	120

Name	Map Ref.	Page
New Hazelton, B.C., Can.	A3	138
New Hebrides see Vanuatu, ctry., Oc.	k16	79d
New Hebrides, is., Vanuatu	k16	79d
New Hebrides Trench, unds.	L20	142
Newhebron, Ms., U.S.	F9	122
New Holland, Oh., U.S.	E2	114
New Holland, Pa., U.S.	D9	114
New Hope, Al., U.S.	C12	122
New Iberia, La., U.S.	G7	122
New Ireland, i., Pap. N. Gui.	a5	79a
New Jersey, state, U.S.	D11	114
New Johnsonville, Tn., U.S.	H10	120
New Kensington, Pa., U.S.	D6	114
New Kent, Va., U.S.	G9	114
Newkirk, Ok., U.S.	E11	128
New Kowloon see Xinjiulong, China	J6	42
Newlands, Austl.	C6	76
New Lexington, Oh., U.S.	E3	114
New Lisbon, Wi., U.S.	H8	118
New Liskeard, On., Can.	F14	106
New Llano, La., U.S.	F5	122
New London, Ct., U.S.	C13	114
New London, Mo., U.S.	E6	120
New London, Oh., U.S.	C3	114
New London, Tx., U.S.	E4	122
New London, Wi., U.S.	G10	118
New Madrid, Mo., U.S.	H8	120
Newman, Austl.	D3	74
Newman, Ca., U.S.	F4	134
Newman Grove, Ne., U.S.	F15	126
Newmarket, On., Can.	D10	112
Newmarket, Eng., U.K.	I13	12
New Market, Al., U.S.	C12	122
New Market, Ia., U.S.	D3	120
New Market, Va., U.S.	F7	114
Newmarket, N.H., U.S.	G5	110
New Martinsville, W.V., U.S.	E4	114
New Mexico, state, U.S.	D9	98
New Milford, Ct., U.S.	C12	114
New Milford, Pa., U.S.	C10	114
Newnan, Ga., U.S.	D14	122
New Norfolk, Austl.	o13	77a
New Norway, Ab., Can.	D18	138
New Orleans, La., U.S.	G8	122
New Paris, Oh., U.S.	I5	112
New Philadelphia, Oh., U.S.	D4	114
New Plymouth, N.Z.	D5	80
New Plymouth, Id., U.S.	G10	136
Newport, Eng., U.K.	K11	12
Newport, Wales, U.K.	J10	12
Newport, Ar., U.S.	B7	122
Newport, Ky., U.S.	E1	114
Newport, Me., U.S.	F7	110
Newport, N.C., U.S.	B8	116
Newport, N.H., U.S.	G4	110
Newport, Or., U.S.	F2	136
Newport, Pa., U.S.	D8	114
Newport, R.I., U.S.	C14	114
Newport, Tn., U.S.	I2	114
Newport, Vt., U.S.	F4	110
Newport Beach, Ca., U.S.	J7	134
Newport News, Va., U.S.	G9	114
New Port Richey, Fl., U.S.	H3	116
New Providence, i., Bah.	C9	96
Newquay, Eng., U.K.	K7	12
New Richland, Mn., U.S.	H5	118
New Richmond, Qc., Can.	B10	110
New Richmond, Wi., U.S.	F8	118
New River, St. K./N.	C2	105a
New Road, N.S., Can.	F13	110
New Roads, La., U.S.	G7	122
New Rochelle, N.Y., U.S.	D12	114
New Ross, N.S., Can.	F12	110
New Ross, Ire.	I6	12
Newry, N. Ire., U.K.	G6	12
Newry, S.C., U.S.	B3	116
New Salem, N.D., U.S.	A11	126
New Schwabenland, reg., Ant.	C5	81
New Sharon, Ia., U.S.	C5	120
New Siberian Islands see Novosibirskie ostrova, is., Russia	A18	34
New Smyrna Beach, Fl., U.S.	G5	116
New South Wales, state, Austl.	I6	76
New Tazewell, Tn., U.S.	H2	114
New Tecumseth, On., Can.	D9	112
Newton, Ga., U.S.	F14	122
Newton, Il., U.S.	F9	120
Newton, Ia., U.S.	C4	120
Newton, Ks., U.S.	C11	128
Newton, Ma., U.S.	B14	114
Newton, Ms., U.S.	E9	122
Newton, N.J., U.S.	C11	114
Newton, Tx., U.S.	G5	122
Newton Falls, N.Y., U.S.	D7	110
Newton Stewart, Scot., U.K.	G8	12
New Town, N.D., U.S.	F11	124
Newtownabbey, N. Ire., U.K.	G6	12
Newtownards, N. Ire., U.K.	G7	12
Newtownhamilton, N. Ire., U.K.	B12	114
New Ulm, Mn., U.S.	G4	118
New Ulm, Tx., U.S.	H2	122
New Washington, Oh., U.S.	D3	114
New Waterford, N.S., Can.	D16	110
New Waverly, Tx., U.S.	G3	122
New Westminster, B.C., Can.	G8	138
New Whiteland, In., U.S.	E11	120
New York, N.Y., U.S.	D12	114
New York, state, U.S.	C12	108
New York Mills, Mn., U.S.	E3	118
New York State Barge Canal, can., N.Y., U.S.	E12	112
New Zealand, ctry., Oc.	D4	80
Neyrīz, Iran	D7	56
Neyshābūr, Iran	B8	56
Neyveli, India	F4	53
Neyyāttinkara, India	G3	53
Nezahualcóyotl, Presa, res., Mex.	G12	100
Nezperce, Id., U.S.	D10	136
Ngabang, Indon.	C6	50
Ngabé, Congo	E3	66
Ngamli, Lake, l., Bots.	B6	70
Ngamiland, state, Bots.	B6	70
Ngan-chouei see Anhui, state, China	F7	42
Nganglong Kangri, mts., China	B9	54
Nganjuk, Indon.	G7	50
Ngangué Co, l., China	C11	54
Ngangué Co, l., China	C11	54
Ngaoui, Mont, mtn., Afr.	F3	62
Ngaoundéré, Cam.	C2	66
Ngape, Mya.	B2	48
Ngapitaw, Mya.	D2	48
Ngara, Tan.	E6	66
Ngatangiia, Cook Is.	a27	78j
Ngatangiia Harbour, b., Cook Is.	a27	78j
Ngawi, Indon.	G7	50
Ngay Nua, Laos	B5	48
Ngcheangel, i., Palau	D9	44
Ngchemiangel, i., Palau	g8	78b
Ngerkeai, Palau	g8	78b
Ngeremlengui, Palau	g7	78b
Ngeruktabel, i., Palau	h7	78b
Ngetbong, Palau	f8	78b
Nggatokae Island, i., Sol. Is.	e8	79b
Nggela Pile, i., Sol. Is.	e9	79b
Nghia Hanh, Viet.	E9	48
Ngiap, stm., Laos	C6	48

Name	Map Ref.	Page
Ngidinga, D.R.C.	F3	66
Ng'iro, mtn., Kenya	D7	66
Ngiro, Ewaso, stm., Kenya	D7	66
Ngo, Congo	E3	66
Ngoko, stm., Afr.	D3	66
Ngom, stm., China	B8	46
Ngong, Kenya	E7	66
Ngomeni, Ras, c., Kenya	E8	66
Ngoring Hu, l., China	E4	36
Ngouri, Chad	E3	62
Ngourti, Niger	G7	64
Ngqeleni, S. Afr.	H9	70
Ngudu, stm., Laos	C6	48
Nguigmi, Niger	G7	64
Ngum, stm., Laos	C6	48
Nguna, Île, i., Vanuatu	k17	79d
Ngunu, Nig.	G7	64
Nhacoongo, Moz.	D12	70
Nhamundá, stm., Braz.	D6	84
Nha Trang, Viet.	F9	48
Nhill, Austl.	K3	76
Nhoma, stm., Afr.	D2	68
Niafounké, Mali	F4	64
Niagara, Wi., U.S.	C1	112
Niagara Falls, On., Can.	E10	112
Niagara Falls, N.Y., U.S.	A6	114
Niagara Falls, wtfl, N.A.	E10	112
Niagara-on-the-Lake, On., Can.	E10	112
Niagassola, Gui.	G3	64
Niah, Malay.	B8	50
Niamey, Niger	G5	64
Niangara, D.R.C.	D5	66
Niangay, Lac, l., Mali	F4	64
Niangoloko, Burkina	G4	64
Niangua, stm., Mo., U.S.	G5	120
Nia-Nia, D.R.C.	D5	66
Niantic, Il., U.S.	E8	120
Nianyushan, China	G7	42
Nianzishan, China	B9	36
Niari, stm., Congo	E2	66
Nias, Pulau, i., Indon.	L3	48
Nicaragua, ctry., N.A.	F5	102
Nicaragua, Lago de, l., Nic.	G5	102
Nicaragua, Lake see Nicaragua, Lago de, l., Nic.	G5	102
Nicastro, Italy	F10	24
Nice, Fr.	F13	18
Niceville, Fl., U.S.	G12	122
Nichinan, Japan	H4	40
Nicholas Channel (San Nicolás, Canal de), strt., N.A.	A5	—
Nicholasville, Ky., U.S.	G13	120
Nicholls, Ga., U.S.	E3	116
Nicholl's Town, Bah.	B9	96
Nicholson, Pa., U.S.	C10	114
Nickel Centre, On., Can.	B8	112
Nickerson, Ks., U.S.	C10	128
Nicobar Islands, is., India	G7	46
Nicola, B.C., Can.	F10	138
Nicola, stm., B.C., Can.	F9	138
Nicolae Bălcescu, Rom.	B13	26
Nicolet, Qc., Can.	D4	110
Nicolet, Lake, l., Mi., U.S.	B5	112
Nicolet Sud-Ouest, stm., Qc., Can.	E5	110
Nicollet, Mn., U.S.	G4	118
Nicosia (Levkosía), Cyp.	C4	58
Nicosia, Italy	G8	24
Nicoya, Golfo de, b., C.R.	H5	102
Nicoya, Península de, pen., C.R.	H5	102
Nida, stm., Pol.	F16	16
Nidadavole, India	C5	53
Nidzica, Pol.	C16	16
Niebüll, Ger.	B4	16
Niedere Tauern, mts., Aus.	C10	22
Niederösterreich, state, Aus.	B12	22
Niedersachsen, state, Ger.	D4	16
Nieekerkshoop, S. Afr.	F6	70
Niemba, D.R.C.	F5	66
Niemodlin, Pol.	F13	16
Nienburg, Ger.	D5	16
Niers, stm., Eur.	C15	14
Niesky, Ger.	E10	16
Niese, stm., Eur.	C15	14
Nieszawa, Pol.	D14	16
Nieu-Bethesda, S. Afr.	G7	70
Nieuport see Nieuwpoort, Bel.	C11	14
Nieuw Amsterdam, Sur.	B6	84
Nieuw Nickerie, Sur.	B6	84
Nieuwpoort, Bel.	C11	14
Nieuwpoort, Neth. Ant.	p22	104g
Nièvre, state, Fr.	G12	14
Nifisha, Egypt	H3	58
Niğde, Tur.	A5	58
Niğde, state, Tur.	F3	138
Nigel, S. Afr.	E9	70
Niger, ctry., Afr.	F6	64
Niger, state, Nig.	H6	64
Niger, stm., Afr.	H6	64
Niger Delta, Nig.	I6	64
Nigeria, ctry., Afr.	H7	64
Nightcaps, N.Z.	G3	80
Nighthawk, Wa., U.S.	B7	136
Nigríta, Grc.	C6	28
Nihiki, Indon.	—	—
Niheidei el-Sûd, Gebel el-, mtn., Egypt	J3	58
Nihommatsu, Japan	B13	40
Nihuil, Embalse del, res., Arg.	G3	92
Niigata, Japan	B11	40
Niigata, state, Japan	B11	40
Niihau, i., Hi., U.S.	a2	78a
Niihau, i., Hi., U.S.	B1	78a
Nii-jima, i., Japan	E12	40
Niitsu, Japan	B12	40
Nijar, Spain	H8	20
Nijmegen, Neth.	C14	14
Nijvel see Nivelles, Bel.	D13	14
Nikel', Russia	B14	8
Niki, Benin	G5	64
Nikkō, Japan	C12	40
Nikkō-kokuritsu-kōen, p.o.i., Japan	B12	40
Nikolaevo, Russia	B12	10
Nikolaevsk-na-Amure, Russia	F17	34
Nikol'sk, Russia	C6	32
Nikol'sk, Russia	D8	32
Nikolski, Ak., U.S.	F6	140
Nikol'skij, Russia	F15	34
Nikol'skoe, Russia	E22	32
Nikopol', Ukr.	E4	32
Nikšić, Yugo.	G5	26
Nikšić, Yugo.	G5	26
Nikumaroro, at., Kir.	D8	72
Nikunau, i., Kir.	D8	72
Nīl, Bahr el- see Nile, stm., Afr.	B6	62
Nīl, Nahr an- see Nile, stm., Afr.	D6	62
Nila, i., Indon.	G8	44
Niland, Ca., U.S.	J10	134
Nile, stm., Afr.	B6	62
Nile Delta, Egypt	H1	58
Niles, Mi., U.S.	G3	112
Niles, Oh., U.S.	C5	114
Nilgiri, India	H11	54
Nilka, China	F14	32
Nilsiä, Fin.	E12	8
Nīmach, India	F5	54
Nimba, Mont, mtn., Afr.	H3	64
Nîmes, Fr.	F10	18
Nimmitabel, Austl.	K7	76
Nimpkish Lake, l., B.C., Can.	F3	138
Nimule, Sudan	G6	62
Ninda, Ang.	C3	68

Name	Map Ref.	Page
Nindigully, Austl.	G7	76
Nine Degree Channel, strt., India	G3	46
Ninetta, Mb., Can.	E14	124
Ninetyeast Ridge, unds.	K11	142
Ninety Mile Beach, cst., Austl.	L6	76
Ninety Six, S.C., U.S.	B3	116
Ninfas, Punta, c., Arg.	H4	90
Ning'an, China	B8	38
Ningbo, China	G9	42
Ningcheng, China	D3	38
Ningde, China	H8	42
Ningdu, China	H6	42
Ningguo, China	F8	42
Ninghai, China	G9	42
Ning-hia see Ningxia, state, China	D6	36
Ninghua, China	H7	42
Ningi, Nig.	G6	64
Ningjing Shan, mts., China	F4	36
Ningming, China	J2	42
Ningnan, China	F5	36
Ningpo see Ningbo, China	G9	42
Ningqiang, China	E2	42
Ningshan, China	E3	42
Ningsia see Yinchuan, China	B2	42
Ningsia Hui see Ningxia, state, China	D6	36
Ningsia Hui Autonomous Region see Ningxia, state, China	D6	36
Ningwu, China	B4	42
Ningxia, state, China	D6	36
Ningxiang, China	G5	42
Ningyuan, China	I4	42
Ninh Binh, Viet.	B7	48
Ninh Hoa, Viet.	F9	48
Ninigo Group, is., Pap. N. Gui.	a3	79a
Ninnescah, North Fork, stm., Ks., U.S.	D10	128
Ninnescah, South Fork, stm., Ks., U.S.	D10	128
Ninohe, Japan	D14	38
Nioaque, Braz.	D5	90
Niobrara, stm., U.S.	E14	126
Niobrara, stm., U.S.	E14	126
Niokolo-Koba, Parc National du, p.o.i., Sen.	G2	64
Nioki, D.R.C.	E3	66
Nioro, Mali	G3	64
Nioro, Mali	F3	64
Niort, Fr.	C5	18
Nipāni, India	C2	53
Nipawin, Sk., Can.	E10	106
Nipe, Bahía de, b., Cuba	B10	102
Nipigon, On., Can.	B10	118
Nipigon, Lake, res., On.	B10	118
Nipigon Bay, b., On., Can.	C10	118
Nipissing, Lake, l., On., Can.	B10	112
Nipomo, Ca., U.S.	H5	134
Niquelândia, Braz.	H1	88
Niquero, Cuba	B9	102
Niquivil, Arg.	E3	92
Nīra, stm., India	B2	53
Nirasaki, Japan	D11	40
Nirgua, Ven.	B7	86
Nirmal, India	B4	53
Nirmali, India	E11	54
Niš, Yugo.	F8	26
Nisāb, Yemen	G6	56
Niscemi, Italy	G8	24
Nishio, Japan	E10	40
Nishiwaki, Japan	E7	40
Nisporeni, Mol.	B15	26
Nisqually, stm., Wa., U.S.	D4	136
Nissan, stm., Swe.	H4	8
Nisswa, Mn., U.S.	E4	118
Ntaure, Lat.	C8	10
Niterói, Braz.	L4	88
Nith, stm., On., Can.	E9	112
Nitinat Lake, l., B.C., Can.	H6	138
Nitra, Slov.	H14	16
Nitra, stm., Slov.	H14	16
Niuafo'ou, i., Tonga	E9	72
Niuatoputapu, i., Tonga	E10	72
Niue, dep., Oc.	E10	72
Niulakita, i., Tuvalu	E8	72
Niut, Gunung, mtn., Indon.	C6	50
Niutao, i., Tuvalu	D8	72
Niutoushan, China	B7	38
Niuzhuang, China	A10	42
Nive, stm., Austl.	E6	76
Nivelles, Bel.	D13	14
Nivernais, hist. reg., Fr.	G12	14
Niverville, Mb., Can.	E16	124
Nixa, Mo., U.S.	G4	120
Nixon, Nv., U.S.	D6	134
Nixon, Tx., U.S.	E10	130
Nizāmābād, India	B4	53
Nizāna Sāgar, res., India	C3	53
Nizhniy Novgorod see Nižnij Novgorod (Gorki), Russia	H21	8
Nizina, N.C., U.S.	H7	114
Nizip, Tur.	A8	58
Nízke Tatry, Národny Park, p.o.i., Slov.	H15	16
Nizza Monferrato, Italy	F5	22
Njandoma, Russia	F19	8
Njazvidž, Bela.	G9	10
Njegoš, i., Com.	F7	66
Njesuthi, mtn., Afr.	F9	70
Njombe, stm., Tan.	F7	66
Njuhča, Russia	D19	8
Njuja, Russia	D12	34
Njuja, stm., Russia	D12	34
Njuk, ozero, l., Russia	D14	8
Njukša, Russia	D14	8
Njurba, Russia	D12	34
Nkambe, Cam.	C2	66
Nkawkaw, Ghana	H4	64
Nkayi, Zimb.	A9	70
Nkhata Bay, Mwi.	C5	68
Nkhotakota, Mwi.	C5	68
Nkomi, Lagune, l., Gabon	E1	66
Nkongsamba, Cam.	D1	66
Nkurenkuru, Nmb.	D2	68
Nkwalini, S. Afr.	F10	70
Nmai, stm., Mya.	C8	46
Noākhāli, Bngl.	G13	54
Noatak, Ak., U.S.	C7	140
Noatak, stm., Ak., U.S.	C8	140
Noble, Il., U.S.	F9	120
Noble, La., U.S.	F5	122
Noblesville, In., U.S.	H3	112
Nobres, Braz.	F6	84
Nocatee, Fl., U.S.	I4	116
Noce, stm., Italy	D8	22

Name	Map Ref.	Page
Nocera Inferiore, Italy	D8	24
Nockatunga, Austl.	F4	76
Nocona, Tx., U.S.	H11	128
Nocupétaro, Mex.	F8	100
Noetinger, Arg.	F6	92
Nogales, Mex.	F7	98
Nogales, Az., U.S.	L5	132
Nogent-le-Rotrou, Fr.	F9	14
Nogent-sur-Seine, Fr.	F12	14
Noginsk, Russia	E21	10
Nogliki, Russia	F17	34
Nogoa, stm., Austl.	E6	76
Nogoyá, Arg.	F7	92
Nógrád, state, Hung.	B6	26
Noguera Pallaresa, stm., Spain	B12	20
Noguera Ribagorçana, stm., Spain	B11	20
Nohar, India	D5	54
Noia, Spain	B2	20
Noir, Causse, plat., Fr.	E9	18
Noir, Isla, i., Chile	J2	90
Noire, stm., Qc., Can.	B13	112
Noirmoutier, Île de, i., Fr.	H6	14
Noirmoutier-en-l'Île, Fr.	H6	14
Nojima-zaki, c., Japan	E12	40
Nokha Mandi, India	E4	54
Nokomis, Fl., U.S.	I3	116
Nokomis, Il., U.S.	E8	120
Nokou, Chad	E2	62
Nokuku, Vanuatu	j16	79d
Nola, C.A.R.	D3	66
Nola, Italy	D8	24
Nolichucky, stm., U.S.	H2	114
Nolin, Ky., U.S.	G11	120
Nolin Lake, res., Ky., U.S.	G11	120
Nolinsk, Russia	C7	32
Nólsoy, i., Far. Is.	n34	8b
Nombre de Dios, Pan.	H8	102
Nome, Ak., U.S.	D6	140
Nomozaki, Japan	G2	40
Nomtsas, Nmb.	D3	70
Nonacho Lake, l., N.T., Can.	C8	106
Nonburg, Russia	D24	8
Nondalton, Ak., U.S.	D8	140
Nong'an, China	B6	38
Nong Han, Thai.	D6	48
Nong Khai, Thai.	D6	48
Nongpoh, India	F13	54
Nongstoin, India	F13	54
Nonoava, Mex.	B5	100
Nonogasta, Arg.	D3	92
Nonouti, at., Kir.	D8	72
Nonsuch Bay, b., Antig.	f4	105b
Nonthaburi, Thai.	F5	48
Nooksack, Wa., U.S.	B4	136
Noonkanbah, Austl.	C4	74
Noordoostpolder, reg., Neth.	B14	14
Noordwijk aan Zee, Neth.	p21	104g
Noorvik, Ak., U.S.	C7	140
Nootka Island, i., B.C., Can.	G4	138
Nóqui, Ang.	B1	68
Norah, is., Erit.	D7	62
Nora Islands see Norah, is., Erit.	D7	62
Noralee, B.C., Can.	B4	138
Nora Springs, Ia., U.S.	A5	120
Norcatur, Ks., U.S.	B8	128
Norcia, Italy	H10	22
Norcross, Ga., U.S.	D14	122
Nord, Grnld.	A22	141
Nord, state, N. Cal.	m15	79d
Nord, Canal du, can., Fr.	D12	14
Nordborg, Den.	A5	16
Norddeg, Ab., Can.	D14	138
Nordegg, stm., Ab., Can.	D15	138
Norden, Ger.	C3	16
Nordenham, Ger.	C4	16
Nordenšeľ'da, arhipelag, is., Russia	A8	34
Nordenskiold Archipelago see Nordenšeľ'da, arhipelag, is., Russia	A8	34
Norderstedt, Ger.	C6	16
Nordfjord, b., Nor.	F1	8
Nordfold, Nor.	C6	8
Nordgrønland (Avanersuaq), state, Grnld.	B15	141
Nordhausen, Ger.	E6	16
Nordhorn, Ger.	D2	16
Nordjylland, state, Den.	H4	8
Nordkapp (North Cape), c., Nor.	A11	8
Nordkinnhalvøya, pen., Nor.	A12	8
Nordland, state, Nor.	H6	8
Nördlingen, Ger.	H6	16
Nordmaling, Swe.	E8	8
Nordman, Id., U.S.	B9	136
Nordostrundingen, c., Grnld.	A23	141
Nord-Ostsee-Kanal (Kiel Canal), can., Ger.	B5	16
Nordrhein-Westfalen, state, Ger.	E4	16
Nordstrand, i., Ger.	B4	16
Nord-Trøndelag, state, Nor.	D5	8
Nordvik, Russia	E15	128
Norfolk, Ne., U.S.	E15	128
Norfolk, Va., U.S.	H9	114
Norfolk Island, dep., Norf. I.	x25	78i
Norfolk Island National Park, p.o.i., Norf. I.	y25	78i
Norfolk Ridge, unds.	L19	142
Norfork Lake, res., U.S.	H5	120
Norikura-dake, vol., Japan	C10	40
Noril'sk, Russia	C6	34
Norlina, N.C., U.S.	H7	114
Normal, Il., U.S.	D9	120
Norman, Ok., U.S.	C5	122
Norman, stm., Austl.	B3	76
Norman, Lake, res., N.C., U.S.	A4	116
Normanby Island, i., Pap. N. Gui.	c5	79a
Normandes, Îles see Channel Islands, is., Eur.	L10	12
Normandie, hist. reg., Fr.	E7	14
Normandie, Collines de, hills, Fr.	F7	14
Normandin, Qc., Can.	B4	110
Normandy see Normandie, hist. reg., Fr.	E7	14
Normandy, Hills of see Normandie, Collines de, hills, Fr.	F7	14
Normangee, Tx., U.S.	F2	122
Norman Island, i., Br. Vir. Is.	e8	104d
Normanton, Austl.	B3	76
Norman Wells, N.T., Can.	B5	106
Norquay, Sk., Can.	C11	124
Norquinco, Arg.	H2	90
Norra Storfjället, mtn., Swe.	D6	8
Norrbotten, state, Swe.	C9	8
Nørresundby, Den.	H3	8
Norridgewock, Me., U.S.	F6	110
Norris Lake, res., Tn., U.S.	H1	114
Norris Point, Nf., Can.	D10	110
Norristown, Pa., U.S.	D10	114
Norrköping, Swe.	G7	8
Norrtälje, Swe.	G8	8
Norseman, Austl.	F4	74
Norsjö, Swe.	D8	8
Norsk, Russia	F15	34
Norske Øer, is., Grnld.	B22	141

Name	Map Ref.	Page
Norsup, Vanuatu	k16	79d
Norte, Cabo, c., Braz.	C8	84
Norte, Serra do, plat., Braz.	F6	84
Norte de Santander, state, Col.	C5	86
Nortelândia, Braz.	F6	84
North, S.C., U.S.	C4	116
North, stm., Ia., U.S.	C3	120
North, Cape, c., N.S., Can.	C16	110
North Adams, Ma., U.S.	B12	114
North Adams, Mi., U.S.	C1	114
North Albany, Or., U.S.	F3	136
Northallerton, Eng., U.K.	G11	12
Northam, Austl.	F3	74
North America, cont.	C5	4
North American Basin, unds.	E7	144
Northampton, Austl.	E2	74
Northampton, Eng., U.K.	I12	12
Northampton, Ma., U.S.	B13	114
North Andaman, i., India	F7	46
North Atlanta, Ga., U.S.	C1	116
North Augusta, S.C., U.S.	C4	116
North Aulatsivik Island, i., Nf., Can.	F13	141
North Australian Basin, unds.	K14	142
North Baltimore, Oh., U.S.	C2	114
North Battleford, Sk., Can.	B5	124
North Bay, On., Can.	B10	112
North Bend, B.C., Can.	G9	138
North Bend, Ne., U.S.	J2	118
North Bennington, Vt., U.S.	B12	114
North Berwick, Scot., U.K.	E10	12
North Berwick, Me., U.S.	G6	110
North Borneo see Sabah, state, Malay.	H1	52
North Bourke, Austl.	H5	76
North Branch, Mi., U.S.	E6	112
North Caicos, i., T./C. Is.	B11	102
North Canadian, stm., Ok., U.S.	F12	128
North Canton, Ga., U.S.	C14	122
North Canton, Oh., U.S.	D4	114
North Cape, c., P.E., Can.	C13	110
North Cape, c., N.Z.	B5	80
North Cape see Nordkapp, c., Nor.	A11	8
North Caribou Lake, l., On., Can.	E12	106
North Carolina, state, U.S.	D11	108
North Cascades National Park, p.o.i., Wa., U.S.	B5	136
North Channel, strt., On., Can.	B7	112
North Channel, strt., U.K.	F7	12
North Charleston, S.C., U.S.	D5	116
North Chicago, Il., U.S.	F2	112
North Chungcheong see Ch'ungch'ŏng-bukto, state, Kor., S.	B1	40
Northcliffe, Austl.	F3	74
North College Hill, Oh., U.S.	E13	120
North Collins, N.Y., U.S.	F11	112
North Concho, stm., Tx., U.S.	C7	130
North Conway, N.H., U.S.	F5	110
North Crossett, Ar., U.S.	D6	122
North Cyprus see Cyprus, North, ctry., Asia	C4	58
North Dakota, state, U.S.	G13	124
North Downs, hills, Eng., U.K.	J13	12
North Eagle Butte, S.D., U.S.	B11	126
North East, Md., U.S.	E9	114
North-East, state, Bots.	B8	70
Northeast Cape, Ak., U.S.	D6	140
Northeast Cape Fear, stm., N.C., U.S.	B8	116
North East Point, c., Bah.	A11	102
Northeast Providence Channel, strt., Bah.	B9	96
Northeim, Ger.	E6	16
North English, Ia., U.S.	C5	120
Northern see HaZafon, state, Isr.	F6	58
Northern, state, S. Afr.	C9	70
Northern Cape, state, S. Afr.	G5	70
Northern Cook Islands, is., Cook Is.	E10	72
Northern Division, state, Fiji	p20	79e
Northern Donets, stm., Eur.	F16	6
Northern Dvina see Severnaja Dvina, stm., Russia	E19	8
Northern Indian Lake, l., Mb., Can.	D11	106
Northern Ireland, state, U.K.	G6	12
Northern Marianas, dep., Oc.	B6	72
Northern Sporades see Vórioi Sporádhes, is., Grc.	D6	28
Northern Territory, state, Austl.	D6	74
North Fabius, stm., U.S.	D6	120
Northfield, Ma., U.S.	B13	114
Northfield, Mn., U.S.	G5	118
Northfield, Vt., U.S.	F4	110
North Fiji Basin, unds.	K20	142
North Flinders Range, mts., Austl.	H2	76
North Fond du Lac, Wi., U.S.	H10	118
North Foreland, c., Eng., U.K.	J14	12
North Fork, Ca., U.S.	F6	134
North Fork, stm., U.S.	H5	120
North Fort Myers, Fl., U.S.	J4	116
North Frisian Islands, is., Eur.	B3	16
Northglenn, Co., U.S.	B4	128
North Gulfport, Ms., U.S.	G9	122
North Gyeongsang see Kyŏngsang-bukto, state, Kor., S.	C1	40
North Henik Lake, l., Nu., Can.	C11	106
North Hero, Vt., U.S.	F3	110
North Highlands, Ca., U.S.	E4	134
North Horr, Kenya	D7	66
North Island, i., N.Z.	C5	80
North Judson, In., U.S.	G3	112
North Kent Island, i., Nu., Can.	B7	141
North Kingsville, Oh., U.S.	C5	114
North Knife Lake, l., Mb., Can.	D11	106
North Korea see Korea, North, ctry., Asia	D7	38
North Lakhimpur, India	C7	46
North Las Vegas, Nv., U.S.	G1	132
North La Veta Pass, p., Co., U.S.	D3	128
North Little Rock, Ar., U.S.	C6	122
North Llano, stm., Tx., U.S.	D8	130
North Logan, Ut., U.S.	B5	132
North Loup, Ne., U.S.	F14	126
North Loup, stm., Ne., U.S.	F14	126
North Magnetic Pole, misc. cult.	B4	141
North Mamm Peak, mtn., Co., U.S.	D9	132
North Manchester, In., U.S.	H4	112
North Manitou Island, i., Mi., U.S.	C3	112
North Mankato, Mn., U.S.	G4	118
North Miami, Fl., U.S.	K5	116
North Miami Beach, Fl., U.S.	K5	116
North Milk (Milk, North Fork), stm., N.A.	B13	136
North Myrtle Beach, S.C., U.S.	C7	116
North New River Canal, can., Fl., U.S.	J5	116
North Newton, Ks., U.S.	C11	128
North Ogden, Ut., U.S.	B5	132
North Ossetia see Severnaja Osetija, state, Russia	F6	32
North Palisade, mtn., Ca., U.S.	F7	134
North Palm Beach, Fl., U.S.	J5	116
North Park, Il., U.S.	B8	120
North Peninsula, pen., On., Can.	A10	118
North Plains, pl., N.M., U.S.	I8	132
North Platte, Ne., U.S.	F12	126
North Platte, stm., U.S.	F11	126
North Point, c., Barb.	n8	105c
North Pole, misc. cult.	A4	94
Northport, Al., U.S.	D11	122
Northport, Mi., U.S.	C4	112
Northport, Wa., U.S.	B9	136
North Portal, Sk., Can.	E11	124
North Raccoon, stm., Ia., U.S.	C3	120
North Rhine-Westphalia see Nordrhein-Westfalen, state, Ger.	E4	16
North Richland Hills, Tx., U.S.	B10	130
North Rim, Az., U.S.	G4	132
North Ronaldsay, i., Scot., U.K.	B10	12
North Rustico, P.E., Can.	D13	110
North Salt Lake, Ut., U.S.	C5	132
North Saskatchewan, stm., Can.	E9	106
North Sea, Eur.	D9	6
North Shoal Lake, l., Mb., Can.	D16	124
North Shore City, N.Z.	C6	80
North Shoshone Peak, mtn., Nv., U.S.	D8	134
North Siberain Lowland see Severo-Sibirskaja nizmennost', pl., Russia	B6	34
North Skunk, stm., Ia., U.S.	C5	120
North Solitary Island, i., Austl.	G9	76
North Solomons, state, Pap. N. Gui.	d7	79b
North Spicer Island, i., Nu., Can.	B15	106
North Stradbroke Island, i., Austl.	F9	76
North Sumatra see Sumatera Utara, state, Indon.	K4	48
North Sydney, N.S., Can.	D16	110
North Taranaki Bight, b., N.Z.	D5	80
North Terre Haute, In., U.S.	E10	120
North Thompson, stm., B.C., Can.	F10	138
North Troy, Vt., U.S.	F4	110
North Tunica, Ms., U.S.	C8	122
North Uist, i., Scot., U.K.	D5	12
Northumberland Isles, is., Austl.	C7	76
Northumberland National Park, p.o.i., Eng., U.K.	F10	12
Northumberland Strait, strt., Can.	D12	110
North Umpqua, stm., Or., U.S.	G4	136
North Vancouver, B.C., Can.	G7	138
North Vietnam see Vietnam, ctry., Asia	E9	48
Northville, N.Y., U.S.	G2	110
North-West, state, S. Afr.	E7	70
North West Bluff, c., Monts.	D3	105a
North West Cape, c., Austl.	D2	74
North-West Frontier, state, Pak.	A4	54
Northwest Miramichi, stm., N.B., Can.	C10	110
Northwest Pacific Basin, unds.	F18	142
Northwest Providence Channel, strt., Bah.	m17	104f
Northwest Territories, state, Can.	B10	106
North Wichita, stm., Tx., U.S.	H9	128
North Wilkesboro, N.C., U.S.	H4	114
North Windham, Me., U.S.	G6	110
Northwood, Ia., U.S.	H5	118
Northwood, N.D., U.S.	G16	124
North York, ngh., On., Can.	E10	112
North York Moors National Park, p.o.i., Eng., U.K.	G12	12
North Zulch, Tx., U.S.	G2	122
Norton, Ks., U.S.	B9	128
Norton, Va., U.S.	H3	114
Norton Shores, Mi., U.S.	E3	112
Norton Sound, strt., Ak., U.S.	D6	140
Nortonville, Ks., U.S.	E2	120
Norvegia, Cape, c., Ant.	C3	81
Norwalk, Ct., U.S.	C12	114
Norwalk, Ia., U.S.	C4	120
Norwalk, Oh., U.S.	C3	114
Norway, Ia., U.S.	C6	120
Norway, Me., U.S.	F6	110
Norway, ctry., Eur.	E3	8
Norway Bay, b., Nu., Can.	A10	106
Norway House, Mb., Can.	E11	106
Norwegian Basin, unds.	B13	144
Norwegian Sea, Eur.	C3	30
Norwich, On., Can.	E9	112
Norwich, Eng., U.K.	I14	12
Norwich, Ct., U.S.	C13	114
Norwich, N.Y., U.S.	B10	114
Norwood, On., Can.	D11	112
Norwood, Co., U.S.	E8	132
Norwood, Ma., U.S.	B14	114
Norwood, Mn., U.S.	G5	118
Norwood, N.C., U.S.	A5	116
Norwood, Oh., U.S.	E1	114
Noshiro, Japan	D13	38
Nosop (Nossob), stm., Afr.	D5	70
Nosovaja, Russia	B26	8
Nosovščina, Russia	E17	8
Nossa Senhora das Dores, Braz.	F7	88
Nossob (Nosop), stm., Afr.	D5	70
Nosy-Varika, Madag.	E8	68
Notasulga, Al., U.S.	E13	122
Notch Hill, B.C., Can.	F11	138
Noteć, stm., Pol.	D11	16
Nótio Aigaío, state, Grc.	G9	28
Noto, Italy	H9	24
Noto, Japan	B10	40
Noto, Golfo di, b., Italy	H9	24
Noto-hantō, pen., Japan	B10	40
Notozero, ozero, l., Russia	C14	8
Notre-Dame, N.B., Can.	D12	110
Notre-Dame, Monts, mts., Qc., Can.	B9	110
Notre Dame Bay, b., Nf., Can.	j22	107a
Notre-Dame-du-Laus, Qc., Can.	B14	112
Notrees, Tx., U.S.	C5	130
Nottawasaga, stm., On., Can.	D10	112
Nottawasaga Bay, b., On., Can.	D9	112
Nottaway, stm., Qc., Can.	E15	106
Nottingham, Eng., U.K.	I11	12
Nottingham Island, i., Nu., Can.	C15	106
Nottoway, stm., Va., U.S.	H8	114
Notukeu Creek, stm., Sk., Can.	E6	124
Notwane, stm., Afr.	D8	70
Nouâdhibou, Maur.	E1	64
Nouâdhibou, Râs, c., Afr.	E1	64
Nouakchott, Maur.	F1	64
Nouâmghâr, Maur.	F1	64
Nouméa, N. Cal.	n16	79d
Noupoort, S. Afr.	G7	70
Nouveau-Québec, Cratère du, crat., Qc., Can.	C16	106
Nouvelle, Qc., Can.	B10	110
Nouvelle-Calédonie (New Caledonia), i., N. Cal.	m15	79d
Nouvelle-Écosse see Nova Scotia, state, Can.	G18	106
Nouvelle-France, Cap de, c., Qc., Can.	C16	106
Nova Andradina, Braz.	D6	90
Nová Baňa, Slov.	H14	16
Nova Caipemba, Ang.	B1	68
Nova Era, Braz.	J4	88
Nova Friburgo, Braz.	L4	88
Nova Gorica, Slvn.	D10	22
Nova Gradiška, Cro.	E14	22
Nova Granada, Braz.	K1	88
Nova Iguaçu, Braz.	L4	88
Novaja Kazanka, Kaz.	E7	32
Novaja Ladoga, Russia	F14	8
Novaja Maluksa, Russia	A14	10
Novaja Sibir', ostrov, i., Russia	B19	34
Novaja Zemlja, is., Russia	B8	30
Nova Kakhovka, Ukr.	E4	32
Nova Lamego, Gui.-B.	G2	64
Nova Lima, Braz.	K4	88
Novalukoml', Bela.	F11	10
Nova Mambone, Moz.	B12	70
Nova Olinda, Braz.	D6	88
Nová Paka, Czech Rep.	F11	16
Nova Ponte, Braz.	J2	88
Nova Prata, Braz.	D12	92
Novara, Italy	E5	22
Nova Roma, Braz.	G2	88
Nova Russas, Braz.	C5	88
Nova Scotia, state, Can.	G18	106
Nova Soure, Braz.	F6	88
Novato, Ca., U.S.	E3	134
Nova Venécia, Braz.	J5	88
Nova Vida, Braz.	F5	84
Novaya Zemlya see Novaja Zemlja, is., Russia	B8	30
Nova Zagora, Blg.	G13	26
Nové Hrady, Czech Rep.	H10	16
Novelda, Spain	F10	20
Nové Město nad Váhom, Slov.	H13	16
Nové Město na Moravě, Czech Rep.	G12	16
Nové Zámky, Slov.	I14	16
Novgorod, Russia	B14	10
Novgorodskaja oblast', co., Russia	B15	10
Novi Bečej, Yugo.	D7	26
Novi Beograd, Yugo.	E7	26
Novice, Tx., U.S.	C8	130
Novigrad, Cro.	E10	22
Novikovo, Russia	G17	34
Novi Ligure, Italy	F5	22
Novinger, Mo., U.S.	D5	120
Novi Pazar, Blg.	F14	26
Novi Pazar, Yugo.	F7	26
Novi Sad, Yugo.	D6	26
Novo, Lago, l., Braz.	C7	84
Novo Airão, Braz.	H11	86
Novoaltajsk, Russia	D14	32
Novo Aripuanã, Braz.	E5	84
Novočerkassk, Russia	E6	32
Novodvinsk, Russia	D19	8
Novoe, Russia	C11	32
Novoenisejsk, Russia	C16	32
Novo Hamburgo, Braz.	D12	92
Novo Horizonte, Braz.	K1	88
Novoizborsk, Russia	C10	10
Novokačalinsk, Russia	B10	38
Novokaširsk, Russia	F21	10
Novokazalinsk, Kaz.	F10	32
Novokujbyševsk, Russia	D7	32
Novokuzneck, Russia	D15	32
Novolazarevskaja, sci., Ant.	C6	81
Novo Mesto, Slvn.	E12	22
Novomoskovsk (Stalinogorsk), Russia	F21	10
Novo Oriente, Braz.	C5	88
Novopetrovskoe, Russia	E19	10
Novorossijsk, Russia	F5	32
Novorybnoe, Russia	B10	34
Novoržev, Russia	C12	10
Novošahtinsk, Russia	E6	32
Novošelovo, Russia	E7	34
Novoselytsia, Ukr.	A13	26
Novosergievka, Russia	D8	32
Novosibirsk, Russia	C14	32
Novosibirskie ostrova, is., Russia	A18	34
Novosibirskoe vodohranilišče, res., Russia	D14	32
Novosil's'ke, Ukr.	D15	26
Novosokol'niki, Russia	D12	10
Novotroick, Russia	D9	32
Novotroickoe, Kaz.	F12	32
Novouzensk, Russia	D7	32
Novovjatsk, Russia	C7	32
Novozavidovskij, Russia	D19	10
Novozybkov, Russia	H14	10
Novska, Cro.	E13	22
Nový Bohumín, Czech Rep.	G14	16
Nový Bor, Czech Rep.	F10	16
Novyja Valosavičy, Bela.	F11	10
Nový Jičín, Czech Rep.	G13	16
Novyj Nekouz, Russia	C20	10
Novyj Port, Russia	A12	32
Novyj Uzen', Kaz.	F8	32
Novyj Vasjugan, Russia	C13	32
Novy Pahost, Bela.	E10	10
Nowa Ruda, Pol.	F12	16
Nowa Sól, Pol.	E11	16
Nowe, Pol.	C14	16
Nowe Miasto nad Pilicą, Pol.	E16	16
Nowendoc, Austl.	H8	76
Nowgong, India	F7	54
Nowitna, stm., Ak., U.S.	D9	140
Nowogard, Pol.	C11	16
Nowogrodziec, Pol.	E11	16
Nowood, stm., Wy., U.S.	C5	126
Nowra, Austl.	J8	76
Nowrangapur, India	B6	53
Nowshāk, mtn., Asia	B11	56
Nowshera, Pak.	B4	54
Nowshera, Pak.	C11	56
Nowy Dwór Mazowiecki, Pol.	D16	16
Nowy Sącz, Pol.	G16	16
Nowy Sącz, state, Pol.	G16	16
Nowy Staw, Pol.	B15	16
Nowy Targ, Pol.	G15	16
Noxapater, Ms., U.S.	E9	122
Noxen, Pa., U.S.	C9	114
Noxon, Mt., U.S.	B11	136
Noxubee, stm., U.S.	D10	122
Noy, stm., Laos	D7	48
Noya see Noia, Spain	B2	20
Noyant, Fr.	G9	14
Noyon, Fr.	E11	14
Nsanje, Mwi.	D6	68
Nsawam, Ghana	H4	64
Nsok, Eq. Gui.	I7	64
Nsukka, Nig.	H6	64
Nsuta, Ghana	H4	64
Ntwetwe Pan, pl., Bots.	B7	70
Nu see Salween, stm., Asia	C8	46
Nūbah, Jibāl an-, mts., Sudan	E6	62
Nubian Desert, des., Sudan	C6	62
Ñuble, stm., Chile	H2	92
Nucet, Rom.	C9	26
Nudol'-Šarino, Russia	D19	10
Nueces, stm., Tx., U.S.	G10	130
Nueces Plains, pl., Tx., U.S.	F8	130
Nueltin Lake, l., Can.	C11	106
Nuestra Señora de Talavera, Arg.	B6	92
Nueva, Isla, i., Chile	K3	90
Nueva Antioquia, Col.	D7	86
Nueva Ciudad Guerrero, Mex.	B9	100
Nueva Esparta, state, Ven.	B9	86
Nueva Galia, Arg.	G5	92
Nueva Germania, Para.	A9	92
Nueva Gerona, Cuba	B6	102
Nueva Imperial, Chile	G2	90
Nueva Italia de Ruiz, Mex.	F7	100
Nueva Loja, Ec.	G3	86
Nueva Palmira, Ur.	F8	92
Nueva Rosita, Mex.	A8	100
Nueva San Salvador, El Sal.	F3	102
Nueva Toltén, Chile	G2	90
Nueve, Canal Numero, can., Arg.	H8	92
Nueve de Julio, Arg.	G7	92
Nuevitas, Cuba	B9	102
Nuevo, Bajo, unds., Col.	E8	102
Nuevo, Cayo, i., Mex.	E12	100
Nuevo, Golfo, b., Arg.	H4	90
Nuevo Camarón, Mex.	G8	130
Nuevo Casas Grandes, Mex.	F9	98
Nuevo Delicias, Mex.	B7	100
Nuevo Laredo, Mex.	B9	100
Nuevo León, state, Mex.	B8	100
Nuevo Primero de Mayo, Mex.	H9	130
Nuevo Progreso, Mex.	F12	100
Nuevo Rocafuerte, Ec.	H4	86
Nuevo San Lucas, Mex.	F2	130
Nûgssuaq, pen., Grnld.	C15	141
Nugu, res., India	F3	53
Nui, at., Tuvalu	D8	72
Nuku'alofa, Tonga	n14	78e
Nukuhu, Pap. N. Gui.	b4	79a
Nukus, Uzb.	F9	32
Nul, Vanuatu	k17	79d
Nulato, Ak., U.S.	D8	140
Nullagine, Austl.	D4	74
Nullarbor, Austl.	F6	74
Nullarbor Plain, pl., Austl.	F5	74
Numan, Nig.	H7	64
Numancia (Numantia), hist., Spain	C8	20
Numantia see Numancia, hist., Spain	C8	20
Numata, Japan	C12	40
Numazu, Japan	D11	40
Numfoor, Pulau, i., Indon.	F10	44
Nunavut, state, Canada	B11	106
Nunda, N.Y., U.S.	B7	114
Nuneaton, Eng., U.K.	I11	12
Nuñez, Cape, c., S. Geor.	J9	90
Nunivak Island, i., Ak., U.S.	D6	140
Nunjiang, China	B10	36
Nunkun, mtn., India	A6	54
Nunnelly, Tn., U.S.	I10	120
Nuomin, stm., China	B10	36
Nuoro, Italy	D3	24
Nuquí, Col.	E3	86
Nura, Kaz.	E12	32
Nura, stm., Kaz.	E12	32
Nur Dağlari, mts., Tur.	B7	58
Nuremberg see Nürnberg, Ger.	G6	16
Nuremburg see Nürnberg, Ger.	G6	16
Nuriootpa, Austl.	J2	76
Nürnberg (Nuremberg), Ger.	G6	16
Nūrpur, India	B5	54
Nürtingen, Ger.	H5	16
Nusa Tenggara Barat, state, Indon.	G10	50
Nusa Tenggara Timur, state Indon.	H12	50
Nuşayrīyah, Jabal an-, mts., Syria	C7	58
Nu Shan, mts., China	F4	36
Nüshan Hu, l., China	E8	42
Nushki, Pak.	D10	56
Nutrioso, Az., U.S.	J7	132
Nutter Fort, W.V., U.S.	E5	114
Nuuk see Godthåb, Grnld.	E15	141
Nuwerus, S. Afr.	G4	70
Nuweveldberge, mts., S. Afr.	H5	70
Nūzvīd, India	C5	53
Nyabéssan, Cam.	D2	66
Nyabing, Austl.	F3	74
Nyack, N.Y., U.S.	C12	114
Nyahanga, Tan.	E6	66
Nyainqêntanglha Feng, mtn., China	C13	54
Nyainqêntanglha Shan, mts., China	C6	46
Nyainrong, China	B14	54
Nyakanazi, Tan.	E6	66
Nyala, Sudan	E5	62
Nyalam, China	D10	54
Nyamlell, Sudan	F5	62
Nyamtumbo, Tan.	G7	66
Nyang, stm., China	D14	54
Nyanga, stm., Afr.	J7	64
Nyasa, Lake, l., Afr.	C5	68
Nyaunglebin, Mya.	C3	48
Nyboe Land, reg., Grnld.	A14	141
Nyborg, Den.	I4	8
Nybro, Swe.	H6	8
Nyda, Russia	A12	32
Nyêmo, China	C7	46
Nyeri, Kenya	E7	66
Nyerol, Sudan	F6	62
Nyimba, Zam.	C5	68
Nyingchi, China	F3	36
Nyírbátor, Hung.	B9	26
Nyíregyháza, Hung.	B8	26
Nykøbing, Den.	I4	8
Nyköping, Swe.	G7	8
Nyland see Uusimaa, state, Fin.	F11	8
Nylstroom, S. Afr.	D9	70
Nymboida, stm., Austl.	G9	76
Nymburk, Czech Rep.	F11	16
Nynäshamn, Swe.	G7	8
Nyngan, Austl.	H6	76
Nyon, Switz.	D3	22
Nyons, Fr.	E11	18
Nýrsko, Czech Rep.	G9	16
Nyš, Russia	F17	34
Nysa, Pol.	F13	16
Nysa Kłodzka, stm., Pol.	F12	16
Nysa Łużycka (Lausitzer Neisse), stm., Eur.	E10	16
Nyslott see Savonlinna, Fin.	F13	8
Nysted, Den.	B7	16
Nyunzu, D.R.C.	F5	66
Nyūzen, Japan	C10	40
Nyvrovo, Russia	F17	34
Nzébéla, Gui.	H3	64
Nzérékoré, Gui.	H3	64
N'zeto, Ang.	B1	68
Nzwani, i., Com.	C7	68

O

Name	Map Ref.	Page
Oahe, Lake, res., U.S.	A12	126
Oahe Dam, dam, S.D., U.S.	C12	126
Oahu, i., Hi., U.S.	B4	78a
Oakbank, Austl.	I3	76
Oak Bay, B.C., Can.	H7	138
Oak Bluffs, Ma., U.S.	C15	114
Oakburn, Mb., Can.	D13	124
Oak City, N.C., U.S.	I8	114
Oak City, Ut., U.S.	D4	132
Oakdale, Ca., U.S.	F5	134
Oakdale, La., U.S.	G6	122
Oakdale, Ne., U.S.	E14	126
Oakes, N.D., U.S.	A14	126
Oakesdale, Wa., U.S.	C9	136
Oakey, Austl.	F8	76
Oakfield, Me., U.S.	D8	110
Oakfield, Wi., U.S.	H10	118
Oak Grove, La., U.S.	E7	122
Oak Harbor, Wa., U.S.	B4	136
Oak Hill, Fl., U.S.	H5	116
Oak Hill, Oh., U.S.	F3	114
Oak Hill, W.V., U.S.	G4	114
Oakhurst, Ca., U.S.	F6	134
Oak Knolls, Ca., U.S.	I5	134
Oak Lake, Mb., Can.	E13	124
Oak Lake, l., Mb., Can.	E13	124
Oak Lake, l., On., Can.	A5	118
Oakland, Ca., U.S.	F3	134
Oakland, Ia., U.S.	C2	120
Oakland, Me., U.S.	F7	110
Oakland, Md., U.S.	E6	114
Oakland, Ms., U.S.	C9	122
Oakland, Ne., U.S.	C1	120
Oakland, Or., U.S.	G3	136
Oakland City, In., U.S.	F10	120
Oakland Park, Fl., U.S.	J5	116
Oak Lawn, Il., U.S.	G2	112
Oakley, Id., U.S.	H13	136
Oakley, Ks., U.S.	B8	128
Oakman, Al., U.S.	D11	122
Oakohay Creek, stm., Ms., U.S.	F9	122
Oakover, stm., Austl.	D4	74
Oak Park, Il., U.S.	G2	112
Oak Ridge, Tn., U.S.	H1	114
Oak Ridge National Laboratory, sci., Tn., U.S.	H1	114
Oaktown, In., U.S.	F10	120
Oak View, Ca., U.S.	I6	134
Oakville, Mb., Can.	E15	124
Oakville, On., Can.	E10	112
Oakwood, Oh., U.S.	C1	114
Oamaru, N.Z.	G4	80
Oancea, Rom.	D14	26
Ōarai, Japan	C13	40
Oatman, Az., U.S.	H2	132
Oaxaca, state, Mex.	G10	100
Oaxaca de Juárez, Mex.	G10	100
Ob', stm., Russia	A11	32
Obabika Lake, l., On., Can.	A9	112
Obal', stm., Bela.	E12	10
Obala, Cam.	D2	66
Obama, Japan	D8	40
Obama, Japan	G3	40
Oban, Austl.	C2	76
Oban, Scot., U.K.	E7	12
Obanazawa, Japan	A13	40
O Barco de Valdeorras, Spain	B3	20
Ob Bay see Obskaja guba, b., Russia	A12	32
Obed, Ab., Can.	C13	138
Obeliai, Lith.	E8	10
Oberá, Arg.	C10	92
Oberhausen, Ger.	E2	16
Oberlin, La., U.S.	G6	122
Oberlin, Oh., U.S.	C3	114
Oberösterreich, state, Aus.	B10	22
Oberpullendorf, Aus.	C13	22
Oberursel, Ger.	F4	16
Oberviechtach, Ger.	G8	16
Ob Gulf see Obskaja guba, b., Russia	A12	32
Obi, Kepulauan, is., Indon.	F8	44
Obi, Pulau, i., Indon.	F8	44
Obi, Selat, strt., Indon.	F8	44
Óbidos, Braz.	D6	84
Obihiro, Japan	C15	38
Obi Islands see Obi, Kepulauan, is., Indon.	F8	44
Obion, Tn., U.S.	H8	120
Obion, stm., Tn., U.S.	H8	120
Obion, Middle Fork, stm., Tn., U.S.	H9	120
Oblačnaja, gora, mtn., Russia	C11	38
Oblong, Il., U.S.	F9	120
Obluče, Russia	G15	34
Obninsk, Russia	E19	10
Obnova, Blg.	F12	26
Obo, C.A.R.	C5	66
Obock, Dji.	E8	62
Obokote, D.R.C.	E5	66
Obozërskij, Russia	E19	8
O'Brien, Or., U.S.	A2	134
Obrovac, Cro.	F12	22
Obša, stm., Russia	E16	10
Obščij syrt, mts., Eur.	D8	32
Obskaja guba, b., Russia	A12	32
Obuasi, Ghana	H4	64
Obudu, Nig.	H6	64
Ocala, Fl., U.S.	G3	116
Ocamo, stm., Ven.	F9	86
Ocampo, Mex.	A4	100
Ocaña, Col.	C5	86
Ocaña, Spain	E7	20
Occhito, Lago di, res., Italy	C8	24
Occidental, Cordillera, mts., Col.	E3	86
Oceana, W.V., U.S.	G4	114
Ocean Cape, c., Ak., U.S.	E12	140
Ocean City, Md., U.S.	F10	114
Ocean City, N.J., U.S.	E11	114
Ocean Falls, B.C., Can.	D3	138
Ocean Island see Banaba, i., Kir.	D7	72
Ocean Park, Wa., U.S.	D2	136
Oceanside, Ca., U.S.	J8	134
Ocean Springs, Ms., U.S.	G10	122
Ocheyedan, Ia., U.S.	H3	118
Ōchi, Japan	E7	40
Ochlocknee, Ga., U.S.	F1	116
Ochlockonee, stm., U.S.	G14	122
Ocho Rios, Jam.	i13	104d
Ochsenfurt, Ger.	G5	16
Ocilla, Ga., U.S.	E2	116
Ockelbo, Swe.	F7	8
Ocmulgee National Monument, p.o.i., Ga., U.S.	D2	116
Ocnița, Mol.	A14	26
Ocoa, Bahía de, b., Dom. Rep.	C12	102
Ocoee, Fl., U.S.	H4	116
Ocoña, stm., Peru	G3	84
Oconee, stm., Ga., U.S.	D3	116
Oconee, Lake, res., Ga., U.S.	C2	116
Oconomowoc, Wi., U.S.	A9	120
Oconto, Wi., U.S.	D2	112
Oconto Falls, Wi., U.S.	D1	112
Ocosingo, Mex.	G12	100
Ocotal, Nic.	F4	102
Ocotes, Cerro, mtn., Mex.	B5	100
Ocotlán, Mex.	E7	100
Ocotlán de Morelos, Mex.	G10	100
Ocozocuautla, Mex.	G12	100
Ocracoke Island, i., N.C., U.S.	A10	116
Ocumare del Tuy, Ven.	B8	86
Oda, Ghana	H4	64
Ōda, Japan	D5	40
Oda, Jabal, mtn., Sudan	C7	62
Odaka, Japan	B14	40
Ōdate, Japan	D14	38
Odawara, Japan	D12	40
Odebolt, Ia., U.S.	B2	120
Odell, Il., U.S.	D9	120
Odell, Tx., U.S.	G9	128
Odem, Tx., U.S.	G10	130
Odemira, Port.	G2	20
Ödemiş, Tur.	E10	28
Odendaalsrus, S. Afr.	E8	70
Odense, Den.	I3	8
Odenwald, mts., Ger.	G4	16
Oder (Odra), stm., Eur.	D10	16
Oderzo, Italy	E9	22
Odesa, Ukr.	C17	26
Odesa, co., Ukr.	C16	26
Odessa see Odesa, Ukr.	C17	26
Odessa, Mo., U.S.	F3	120
Odessa, Tx., U.S.	C5	130
Odessa, Wa., U.S.	C8	136
Odesskoe, Russia	D12	32
Odiel, stm., Spain	G4	20
Odienné, C. Iv.	H3	64
Odin, Mount, mtn., B.C., Can.	F12	138
Odincovo, Russia	E20	10
Odobești, Rom.	D13	26
Odolanów, Pol.	E13	16
Odon, In., U.S.	F11	120
O'Donnell, Tx., U.S.	B6	130
Odorheiu Secuiesc, Rom.	C12	26
Odra (Oder), stm., Eur.	D10	16
Odrzywół, Pol.	E16	16
Odum, Ga., U.S.	E3	116
Odžaci, Yugo.	D6	26
Oebisfelde, Ger.	D6	16
Oeiras, Braz.	D4	88
Oelsnitz, Ger.	F8	16
Oelwein, Ia., U.S.	B6	120
Oenpelli, Austl.	B6	74
Oetz, Aus.	C7	22
O'Fallon, Mo., U.S.	F7	120
Ofanto, stm., Italy	D9	24
Ofaqim, Isr.	G5	58
Offa, Nig.	H5	64
Offaly, state, Ire.	H5	12
Offenbach am Main, Ger.	F4	16
Offenburg, Ger.	H3	16
Oficina Alemania, Chile	B3	92
Ofu, i., Am. Sam.	h13	79c
Ogaden, reg., Afr.	F8	62
Ōgaki, Japan	D9	40
Ogallala, Ne., U.S.	F11	126
Ogan, stm., Indon.	E4	50
Ogasawara-guntō, is., Japan	G18	30
Ogatsu, Japan	A14	40
Ogawa, Japan	G3	40
Ogbomosho, Nig.	H5	64
Ogden, Ks., U.S.	B12	128
Ogden, Ut., U.S.	B5	132
Ogdensburg, N.Y., U.S.	D14	112
Ogeechee, stm., Ga., U.S.	D4	116
Ogema, Sk., Can.	E8	124
Ogidaki Mountain, hill, On., Can.	A6	112
Ogilvie, Mn., U.S.	F5	118
Ogilvie Mountains, mts., Yk., Can.	C3	106
Oglesby, Il., U.S.	C8	120
Oglethorpe, Ga., U.S.	D1	116
Ogliastra, reg., Italy	E3	24
Oglio, stm., Italy	E6	22
Ogmore, Austl.	D7	76
Ognon, stm., Fr.	G15	14
Ogoja, Nig.	H6	64
Ogoki, stm., On., Can.	E13	106
Ogooué, stm., Afr.	I7	64
Ogōri, Japan	E4	40
Ogosta, stm., Blg.	F10	26
Ogre, Lat.	D7	10
Ogre, stm., Lat.	D8	10
O Grove, Spain	B2	20
Ogulin, Cro.	E12	22
Ogunquit, Me., U.S.	G6	110
Ogurdžaly, ostrov, i., Turkmen.	B7	56
Oğuzeli, Tur.	B8	58
Oha, Russia	F17	34
Ohanet, Alg.	D6	64
Ōhara, Japan	D13	40
O'Higgins, Cabo, c., Chile	e30	78l
O'Higgins, Lago (San Martín, Lago), l., S.A.	I2	90
Ohio, state, U.S.	D3	114
Ohio, stm., U.S.	G9	120
Ohio Peak, mtn., Co., U.S.	E9	132
'Ohonua, Tonga	o15	78e
Ohoopee, stm., Ga., U.S.	D3	116
Ohota, stm., Russia	E17	34
Ohotsk, Russia	E17	34
Ohře, stm., Eur.	F9	16
Ohrid, Mac.	B3	28
Ohrid, Lake, l., Eur.	D14	24
Ohrigstad, S. Afr.	D10	70
Öhringen, Ger.	G5	16
Ohuira, Bahía de, l., Mex.	C4	100
Ōi, stm., Japan	E11	40
Oiapoque, Braz.	C7	84
Oiapoque (Oyapok), stm., S.A.	C7	84
Oies, Île aux, i., Qc., Can.	C6	110
Oil Center, N.M., U.S.	B4	130
Oil City, La., U.S.	E4	122
Oil City, Pa., U.S.	C6	114
Oildale, Ca., U.S.	H7	134
Oilton, Ok., U.S.	A2	122
Oilton, Tx., U.S.	G9	130
Oil Trough, Ar., U.S.	B7	122
Oise, state, Fr.	E11	14
Oise, stm., Eur.	E11	14
Oistins, Barb.	n8	105d
Ōita, Japan	F4	40
Ōita, state, Japan	F4	40
Oituz, Pasul, p., Rom.	C13	26
Ojat', stm., Russia	F16	8
Öje, Swe.	F5	8
Ojinaga, Mex.	A6	100
Ojiya, Japan	B11	40
Ojmjakon, Russia	D17	34
Ojocaliente, Mex.	D7	100
Ojo de la Casa, Mex.	C1	130
Ojo del Carrizo, Mex.	E2	130
Ojo de Liebre, Laguna, b., Mex.	B1	100
Ojos del Salado, Nevado, mtn., S.A.	C3	92
Ojos Negros, Mex.	L9	134
Oka, stm., Russia	D6	32
Oka, stm., Russia	D18	32
Okaba, Indon.	G10	44
Okahandja, Nmb.	B3	70
Okaihau, N.Z.	B5	80
Okak Islands, is., Nf., Can.	F13	141
Okanagan (Okanogan), stm., N.A.	G11	138
Okanagan Falls, B.C., Can.	G11	138
Okanagan Lake, l., B.C., Can.	G10	138
Okanagan Landing, B.C., Can.	F11	138
Okanogan, Wa., U.S.	B7	136
Okanogan (Okanagan), stm., N.A.	G11	138
Okanogan Range, mts., Can.	A6	136
Okāra, Pak.	C4	54
Okaukuejo, Nmb.	D2	68
Okavango (Cubango), stm., Afr.	D2	68
Okavango Delta, Bots.	D3	68
Ōkawa, Japan	F3	40
Okawville, Il., U.S.	F8	120
Okaya, Japan	C11	40
Okayama, Japan	E6	40
Okayama, state, Japan	E6	40
Okazaki, Japan	E10	40
Okeechobee, Fl., U.S.	I5	116
Okeechobee, Lake, l., Fl., U.S.	J5	116

Name	Map Ref.	Page
Okeene, Ok., U.S.	E10	128
Okefenokee Swamp, sw., U.S.	F3	116
Okemos, Mi., U.S.	B1	114
Okene, Nig.	H6	64
Okhaldunggã, Nepal	E11	54
Okhotsk, Sea of, Asia	D18	30
Okhotsk Basin, unds.	D17	142
Okhtyrka, Ukr.	D4	32
Okiep, S. Afr.	F3	70
Okinawa, Japan	I18	39a
Okinawa Island see Okinawa-jima, i., Japan	I19	39a
Okinawa-jima, i., Japan	I19	39a
Okinawa-shotō, is., Japan	I18	39a
Okino-Erabu-shima, i., Japan	I19	39a
Oki-shotō, is., Japan	C6	40
Okitipupa, Nig.	H5	64
Oklahoma, state, U.S.	F11	128
Oklahoma City, Ok., U.S.	F11	128
Oklawaha, Fl., U.S.	G4	116
Oklee, Mn., U.S.	D3	118
Okmulgee, Ok., U.S.	D6	66
Okollo, Ug.	D6	66
Okolona, Ms., U.S.	D5	122
Okolona, Ky., U.S.	F12	120
Okondja, Gabon	E2	66
Okonek, Pol.	C12	16
Okotoks, Ab., Can.	F16	138
Okoyo, Congo	E2	66
Oktjabr', Russia	C20	10
Oktjabr'sk, Kaz.	E9	32
Oktjabr'skij, Russia	F20	8
Oktjabr'skij, Russia	G21	8
Oktjabr'skij, Russia	D8	32
Oktjabr'skij, Russia	F14	34
Oktjabr'skoe, Russia	D11	32
Oktjabr'skoe, Russia	B10	32
Okuchi, Japan	G3	40
Okulovka, Russia	B16	10
Okunëv Nos, Russia	C25	8
Okushiri-tō, i., Japan	C13	38
Okuta, Nig.	H5	64
Okwa, stm., Afr.	C6	70
Ola, Russia	E19	34
Ola, Ar., U.S.	B5	122
Ólafsfjördur, Ice.	j30	8a
Olancha, Ca., U.S.	G8	134
Olancha Peak, mtn., Ca., U.S.	G7	134
Olanchito, Hond.	E4	102
Öland, i., Swe.	H7	8
Olanta, S.C., U.S.	C6	116
Olary, Austl.	I3	76
Olathe, Co., U.S.	E8	132
Olathe, Ks., U.S.	F3	120
Olavarría, Arg.	H7	92
Oława (Ohlau), Pol.	F13	16
Olbia, Italy	D3	24
Olcott, N.Y., U.S.	E11	112
Old Castile see Castilla la Vieja, hist. reg., Spain	C7	20
Old Cork, Austl.	D3	76
Old Crow, Yk., Can.	C12	140
Old Crow, stm., N.A.	C11	140
Olden, Tx., U.S.	B9	130
Oldenburg, Ger.	C3	16
Oldenburg, hist. reg., Ger.	C3	16
Oldenburg in Holstein, Ger.	B6	16
Oldenzaal, Neth.	B15	14
Old Faithful Geyser, gysr., Wy., U.S.	F16	136
Old Forge, Pa., U.S.	C10	114
Old Fort Bay see Vieux-Fort, Qc., Can.	i22	107a
Oldham, Eng., U.K.	H10	12
Oldham, S.D., U.S.	C15	126
Old Harbor, Ak., U.S.	E9	140
Old Harbour, Jam.	j13	104d
Old Hickory Lake, res., Tn., U.S.	H11	120
Oldman, stm., Ab., Can.	G19	138
Old Mkushi, Zam.	C4	68
Old Norwood, Monts.	D3	105a
Old Road, Antig.	f4	105b
Old Road Bluff, c., Antig.	f4	105b
Old Road Town, St. K./N.	C2	105a
Olds, Ab., Can.	E16	138
Old Saybrook, Ct., U.S.	C13	114
Old Speck Mountain, mtn., Me., U.S.	F5	110
Old Tate, Bots.	B8	70
Old Town, Me., U.S.	F8	110
Olduvai Gorge, val., Tan.	E7	66
Old Wives Lake, l., Sk., Can.	D8	124
Olean, N.Y., U.S.	B7	114
O'Leary, P.E., Can.	D12	110
Olecko, Pol.	B18	16
Olëkma, stm., Russia	E13	34
Olëkminsk, Russia	D13	34
Olëkminskij Stanovik, mts., Russia	F12	34
Ølen, Nor.	G1	8
Olenegorsk, Russia	B15	8
Olenëk, Russia	C11	34
Olenëk, stm., Russia	C12	34
Olenëkskij zaliv, b., Russia	B4	34
Olenino, Russia	D16	10
Oléron, Île d', i., Fr.	D4	18
Oleśnica, Pol.	E13	16
Olesno, Pol.	F14	16
Ol'ga, Russia	C11	38
Olga, Mount, mtn., Austl.	D6	74
Olgastretet, strt., Nor.	B30	141
Olgiy, Mong.	E16	32
Olhão, Port.	G3	20
Olho d'Água das Flores, Braz.	E7	88
Ol'hon, ostrov, i., Russia	F10	34
Olib, Otok, i., Cro.	F11	22
Olifants (Elefantes), stm., Afr.	D10	70
Olifants, stm., S. Afr.	H6	70
Olifants, stm., S. Afr.	H4	70
Olifantshoek, S. Afr.	E6	70
Olimbos (Olympus), mtn., Cyp.	C3	58
Olimpia, Braz.	K1	88
Olin, Ia., U.S.	B6	120
Olinda, Braz.	D8	88
Olio, Austl.	C4	76
Oliva, Arg.	F6	92
Oliva, Spain	F10	20
Oliva de la Frontera, Spain	F3	20
Olivares, Cerro de, mtn., S.A.	E2	92
Olive Branch, Ms., U.S.	C9	122
Olivees Mountain, mtn., St. K./N.	C2	105a
Olive Hill, Ky., U.S.	F2	114
Olivehurst, Ca., U.S.	E4	134
Oliveira, Braz.	K3	88
Oliveira dos Brejinhos, Braz.	G4	88
Olivenza, Spain	F3	20
Oliver Springs, Tn., U.S.	H13	120
Olivet, Mi., U.S.	B1	114
Olivet, S.D., U.S.	D15	126
Olji Moron, stm., China	B4	38
Oljutorskij, mys, c., Russia	E23	34
Oljutorskij zaliv, b., Russia	D22	34
Olla, La., U.S.	F6	122
Ollagüe, Volcán, vol., S.A.	D3	90
Ollei, Palau	f8	78b
Olmedo, Spain	C6	20
Olmos, Peru	E2	84
Olney, Mt., U.S.	B12	136
Olney, Il., U.S.	E9	120
Olney, Tx., U.S.	H10	128
Olomouc, Czech Rep.	G13	16
Olonec, Russia	F15	8
Olongapo, Phil.	C2	52
Oloron-Sainte-Marie, Fr.	F5	18
Olot, Spain	B13	20
Olovjannaja, Russia	F12	34
Olpe, Ger.	E3	16
Olpe, Ks., U.S.	F1	120
Olsufevo, Russia	G16	10
Olsztyn, Pol.	C16	16
Olsztyn, state, Pol.	C16	16
Olt, state, Rom.	E11	26
Olt, stm., Rom.	D11	26
Olta, Arg.	E4	92
Olten, Switz.	C4	22
Olteni, Rom.	E12	26
Olteniţa, Rom.	E13	26
Olteţ, stm., Rom.	E10	26
Olton, Tx., U.S.	G6	128
Oluan Pi, c., Tai.	K9	42
Olustee, Fl., U.S.	F3	116
Olutanga Island, i., Phil.	G4	52
Olvera, Spain	H5	20
Olympia, Wa., U.S.	C3	136
Olympía, hist. Grc.	F4	28
Olympia see Olympía, hist., Grc.	F4	28
Olympic Mountains, mts., Wa., U.S.	C3	136
Olympic National Park, p.o.i., Wa., U.S.	C3	136
Ólympos (Olympus, Mount), mtn., Grc.	C5	28
Olympus see Ólimbos, mtn., Cyp.	C3	58
Olympus, Mount see Ólympos, mtn., Grc.	C5	28
Olympus, Mount, mtn., Wa., U.S.	C3	136
Om', stm., Russia	D13	32
Ōmachi, Japan	C10	40
Omae-zaki, c., Japan	E11	40
Ōmagari, Japan	E14	38
Omagh, N. Ire., U.K.	G5	12
Omaha, Ne., U.S.	C2	120
Omaha, Tx., U.S.	D4	122
Omaheke, state, Nmb.	C4	70
Omak, Wa., U.S.	B7	136
Oman, ctry., Asia	F8	56
Oman, Gulf of, b., Asia	E8	56
Omaruru, Nmb.	B2	70
Omaruru, stm., Nmb.	B2	70
Omatako, mtn., Nmb.	B3	70
Omatako, stm., Nmb.	B3	70
Omate, Peru	G3	84
Omboué, Gabon	E1	66
Ombrone, stm., Italy	H8	22
Omčak, Russia	D18	34
Omdurman see Umm Durmān, Sudan	D6	62
Ōme, Japan	D12	40
Omega, Ga., U.S.	E2	116
Omega, Italy	E5	22
Omemee, On., Can.	D11	112
Omeo, Austl.	K6	76
Ōmerköy, Tur.	D10	28
Omerli Baraji, res., Tur.	C12	28
Ometepe, Isla de, i., Nic.	G5	102
Ometepec, Mex.	G9	100
Ōmi-hachiman, Japan	D8	40
Omineca, stm., B.C., Can.	D6	106
Omineca Mountains, mts., B.C., Can.	D5	106
Ōmiya, Japan	D12	40
Ommaney, Cape, c., Ak., U.S.	E13	140
Ommanney Bay, b., Nu., Can.	A10	106
Omo, stm., Eth.	F7	62
Omoloj, stm., Russia	B15	34
Omolon, stm., Russia	C20	34
Omoa, stm., Russia	C12	32
Omsk, Russia	C12	32
Omsukčan, Russia	D20	34
Omul, Vârful, mtn., Rom.	D12	26
Omura, Japan	G2	40
Ōmurtag, Blg.	F13	26
Ōmuta, Japan	F3	40
Omutinskij, Russia	C11	32
Omutninsk, Russia	C8	32
Onabas, Mex.	A4	100
Onaga, Ks., U.S.	E1	120
Onaman Lake, l., On., Can.	A11	118
Onamia, Mn., U.S.	E5	118
Onancock, Va., U.S.	G9	114
Onaping Lake, l., On., Can.	A8	112
Onarga, Il., U.S.	D10	120
Onatchiway, Lac, res., Qc., Can.	A5	110
Onawa, Ia., U.S.	B1	120
Onaway, Mi., U.S.	C5	112
Oncativo, Arg.	E6	92
Once, Canal Numero, can., Arg.	H8	92
Oncócua, Ang.	D1	68
Onda, Spain	E10	20
Ondangwa, Nmb.	D2	68
Ondas, stm., Braz.	G3	88
Ondava, stm., Slov.	H17	16
Ondjiva, Ang.	D2	68
Ondo, Japan	E5	40
Ondo, Nig.	H5	64
Öndörhaan, Mong.	B7	36
Öndörxaan see Öndörhaan, Mong.	B7	36
Onega, Russia	E17	8
Onega, stm., Russia	E18	8
Onega, Lake see Onežskoe ozero, l., Russia	F16	8
Onega Bay see Onežskaja guba, b., Russia	D17	8
One Hundred and Two, stm., Mo., U.S.	D3	120
One Hundred Fifty Mile House, B.C., Can.	D9	138
One Hundred Mile House, B.C., Can.	E9	138
Oneida, Il., U.S.	C7	120
Oneida, N.Y., U.S.	E14	112
Oneida, Tn., U.S.	H13	120
Oneida Lake, l., N.Y., U.S.	E14	112
O'Neill, Ne., U.S.	E14	126
Onekama, Mi., U.S.	D3	112
Onekotan, ostrov, i., Russia	G20	34
Oneonta, Al., U.S.	D12	122
Oneonta, N.Y., U.S.	B10	114
Oneşti, Rom.	C13	26
Oneval, i., Tonga	n14	78e
Onežskaja guba (Onega Bay), b., Russia	D17	8
Onežskij poluostrov, pen., Russia	D17	8
Onežskoe ozero (Onega, l.), l., Russia	F16	8
Ongin-ûp, Kor., N.	F6	38
Ongniud Qi, China	C3	38
Ongole, India	D5	53
Onilahy, stm., Madag.	F7	68
Onion Creek, stm., Tx., U.S.	D10	130
Onitsha, Nig.	H6	64
Ōno, Japan	D9	40
Onoda, Japan	F4	40
Onomichi, Japan	E6	40
Onon, Mong.	B7	36
Onon Gol, stm., Asia	G11	34
Onoto, Ven.	C9	86
Onotoa, at., Kir.	D8	72
Onset, Ma., U.S.	C15	114
Onslow, Austl.	D3	74
Onslow Bay, b., N.C., U.S.	B8	116
On-take, vol., Japan	H3	40
Ontake-san, vol., Japan	D10	40
Ontario, Ca., U.S.	I8	134
Ontario, Or., U.S.	F10	136
Ontario, state, Can.	E13	106
Ontario, Lake, l., N.A.	E11	112
Ontinyent, Spain	F10	20
Ontojärvi, l., Fin.	D13	8
Ontonagon, Mi., U.S.	E9	118
Ontong Java, at., Sol. Is.	D7	72
Onverwacht, Sur.	B6	84
Oodnadatta, Austl.	E7	74
Ooldea, Austl.	F6	74
Oologah, Ok., U.S.	H2	120
Oologah Lake, res., Ok., U.S.	H2	120
Oorlogskloof, stm., S. Afr.	G4	70
Oos-Londen see East London, S. Afr.	H8	70
Oostburg, Wi., U.S.	E2	112
Oostelijk Flevoland, reg., Neth.	B14	14
Oostende, Bel.	C11	14
Oosterhout, Neth.	C13	14
Oosterschelde, est., Neth.	C12	14
Ootsa Lake, B.C., Can.	C4	138
Ootsa Lake, res., B.C., Can.	C4	138
Opaka, Blg.	F13	26
Opala, D.R.C.	E4	66
Oparino, Russia	G22	8
Opatija, Cro.	E11	22
Opava, Czech Rep.	G13	16
Opawica, stm., Qc., Can.	A2	110
Opečenskij Posad, Russia	B17	10
Opelika, Al., U.S.	E13	122
Opelousas, La., U.S.	G6	122
Opeongo, stm., On., Can.	C12	112
Opeongo Lake, l., On., Can.	C11	112
Ophir, Ak., U.S.	D8	140
Ophir, Or., U.S.	H2	136
Opihikao, Hi., U.S.	D7	78a
Opinaca, stm., Qc., Can.	E15	106
Opinaca, stm., Qc., Can.	E17	106
Opobo, Nig.	I6	64
Opočka, Russia	D11	10
Opoczno, Pol.	E16	16
Opole, Pol.	F13	16
Opole, state, Pol.	F13	16
Opotiki, N.Z.	D7	80
Oppdal, Nor.	E3	8
Oppland, state, Nor.	F2	8
Opportunity, Mt., U.S.	D14	136
Opportunity, Wa., U.S.	C9	136
Optima Lake, res., Ok., U.S.	E7	128
Opua, N.Z.	B6	80
Opunake, N.Z.	D5	80
Opuwo, Nmb.	D1	68
Oquawka, Il., U.S.	K7	118
Or, Côte d', mts., Fr.	G13	14
Oracle, Az., U.S.	K6	132
Oradea, Rom.	B8	26
Orahovica, Cro.	E14	22
Orai, India	F7	54
Oraibi Wash, stm., Az., U.S.	H6	132
Oral see Ural'sk, Kaz.	E8	32
Oran see Wahran, Alg.	B4	64
Orange, Austl.	I7	76
Orange, Fr.	E10	18
Orange, Ma., U.S.	B13	114
Orange, Tx., U.S.	G5	122
Orange (Oranje) (Senqu), stm., Afr.	F3	70
Orange, Cabo o, Braz.	C7	84
Orangeburg, S.C., U.S.	C4	116
Orange City, la., U.S.	A1	120
Orange Cove, Ca., U.S.	G6	134
Orange Free State see Free State, state, S. Afr.	F8	70
Orange Grove, Tx., U.S.	G9	130
Orange Lake, Fl., U.S.	G3	116
Orange Lake, l., Fl., U.S.	G3	116
Orangeville, On., Can.	D9	112
Orangeville, Ut., U.S.	D5	132
Orange Walk, Belize	C3	102
Orango, Ilha de, i., Gui.-B.	G1	64
Orani, Phil.	C3	52
Oranienburg, Ger.	D8	16
Oranje see Orange, stm., Afr.	F3	70
Oranje Gebergte, mts., Sur.	C6	84
Oranjemund, Nmb.	F3	70
Oranjestad, Aruba	o19	104g
Oranjestad, Neth. Ant.	C1	105a
Oranje Vrijstaat see Free State, state, S. Afr.	F8	70
Orăştie, Rom.	D10	26
Orba Co, l., China	A8	54
Orbetello, Italy	H8	22
Orbigo, stm., Spain	B5	20
Orbisonia, Pa., U.S.	D8	114
Orbost, Austl.	K7	76
Orbyhus, Swe.	F7	8
Orcadas, sci., Ant.	B36	81
Orchard City, Co., U.S.	E8	132
Orchard Homes, Mt., U.S.	D12	136
Orchard Mesa, Co., U.S.	E8	132
Orchard Park, N.Y., U.S.	B7	114
Ord, Ne., U.S.	F14	126
Ord, stm., Austl.	C5	74
Ord, Mount, mtn., Austl.	C5	74
Ordenes see Ordes, Spain	A2	20
Orderville, Ut., U.S.	F4	132
Ordes, Spain	A2	20
Ordesa y Monte Perdido, Parque Nacional de, p.o.i., Spain	B10	20
Ord Mountain, mtn., Ca., U.S.	I9	134
Ordos Desert see Mu Us Shamo, des., China	B3	42
Ord River, Austl.	C4	74
Ordu, Tur.	A4	56
Ordway, Co., U.S.	C5	128
Ordžonikidzeabad, Taj.	B10	56
Örebro, Swe.	G6	8
Örebro, state, Swe.	G6	8
Oredež, Russia	B13	10
Oredež, stm., Russia	B13	10
Oregon, Il., U.S.	B8	120
Oregon, Mo., U.S.	D2	120
Oregon, Oh., U.S.	C2	114
Oregon, state, U.S.	G6	136
Oregon Caves National Monument, p.o.i., Or., U.S.	A2	134
Oregon City, Or., U.S.	E4	136
Oregon Dunes National Recreation Area, p.o.i., Or., U.S.	G2	136
Orehovo-Zuevo, Russia	E21	10
Orel, Russia	G18	10
Orel', ozero, l., Russia	F16	34
Orem, Ut., U.S.	C5	132
Ore Mountains, mts., Eur.	F8	16
Orenburg, Russia	D8	32
Örencik, Tur.	D12	28
Orense, Arg.	I8	92
Orense see Ourense, Spain	B3	20
Orense see Ourense, co., Spain	B3	20
Oreor, i., Palau	g8	78b
Orestes Pereyra, Mex.	B6	100
Orestiáda, Grc.	B9	28
Øresund, strt., Eur.	I5	8
Orford Ness, c., Eng., U.K.	I14	12
Organ Pipe Cactus National Monument, p.o.i., Az., U.S.	K4	132
Orgaz, Spain	E7	20
Orgelet, Fr.	H14	14
Orgosolo, Italy	D3	24
Orgῧn, Afg.	C10	56
Orhangazi, Tur.	C12	28
Orhei, Mol.	B15	26
Orhon, stm., Mong.	B5	36
Orichuna, stm., Ven.	D7	86
Orick, Ca., U.S.	B1	134
Orient, Ia., U.S.	C3	120
Orient, Wa., U.S.	B8	136
Oriental, Cordillera, mts., Col.	E5	86
Oriental, Cordillera, mts., Peru	F3	84
Orientos, Austl.	G3	76
Orihuela see Oriola, Spain	F10	20
Orihuela, Spain	F10	20
Orillia, On., Can.	D10	112
Orinduik, Guy.	E11	86
Orinoco, stm., S.A.	C10	86
Orinoco, Delta del, Ven.	C11	86
Oriola, Spain	F10	20
Orion, Il., U.S.	C7	120
Oriskany, N.Y., U.S.	E14	112
Orissa, state, India	D5	46
Orissaare, Est.	B5	10
Oristano, Italy	E2	24
Oristano, Golfo di, b., Italy	E2	24
Orituco, stm., Ven.	C8	86
Orivesi, l., Fin.	E13	8
Oriximiná, Braz.	D6	84
Orizaba, Mex.	F10	100
Orjen, mtn., Yugo.	G5	26
Orjahovo, Blg.	F10	26
Orkney, Sk., Can.	E5	124
Orkney, S. Afr.	E8	70
Orkney Islands, is., Scot., U.K.	C10	12
Orlândia, Braz.	K1	88
Orléanais, hist. reg., Fr.	F11	14
Orléans, On., Can.	C14	112
Orléans, Fr.	G10	14
Orleans, Ca., U.S.	B2	134
Orleans, Ma., U.S.	C15	114
Orleans, Ne., U.S.	A9	128
Orleans, Vt., U.S.	F4	110
Orléans, Canal d', can., Fr.	G11	14
Orléans, Île d', i., Qc., Can.	D6	110
Orlik, Russia	D18	32
Orlovskaja oblast', co., Russia	H19	10
Orly, Fr.	F11	14
Ormāra, Pak.	D9	56
Ormiston, Sk., Can.	E8	124
Ormoc, Phil.	E5	52
Ormond Beach, Fl., U.S.	G4	116
Ormont, stm., Fr.	F14	14
Ormans, Fr.	G15	14
Orne, state, Fr.	F8	14
Orne, stm., Fr.	E14	14
Ørnes, Nor.	F8	8
Oro, Nig.	I6	64
Oro, stm., Kir.	D9	72
Orob, Braz.	D6	88
Orós, Açude, res., Braz.	D6	88
Orosei, Italy	D3	24
Orosei, Golfo di, b., Italy	D3	24
Orosháza, Hung.	C7	26
Oroszlány, Hung.	B5	26
Orote Peninsula, pen., Guam	j9	78c
Oroville, Ca., U.S.	D4	134
Oroville, Lake, res., Ca., U.S.	E4	134
Orpheus Island, i., Austl.	B6	76
Orrick, Mo., U.S.	E3	120
Orrin, N.D., U.S.	F13	124
Orrono, Austl.	I2	76
Orrs Island, Me., U.S.	G7	110
Orša, Bela.	F13	10
Orsa, Swe.	F6	8
Orsha see Orša, Bela.	F13	10
Orsk, Russia	D9	32
Orşova, Rom.	E9	26
Ortaca, Tur.	G11	28
Ortakent, Tur.	F10	28
Ortaklar, Tur.	F10	28
Orta Nova, Italy	C9	24
Ortega, Col.	F4	86
Ortegal, Cabo, c., Spain	A2	20
Orteguaza, stm., Col.	G4	86
Orthon, stm., Bol.	B3	90
Ortigueira, Braz.	B12	92
Ortigueira, Spain	A3	20
Orting, Wa., U.S.	C4	136
Ortiz, Mex.	A3	100
Ortiz, Ven.	C8	86
Ortona, Italy	H11	22
Ortonville, Mn., U.S.	F2	118
Orūmīyeh, Iran	B6	56
Orūmīyeh, Daryācheh-ye (Urmia, Lake), l., Iran	B6	56
Orust, i., Swe.	G4	8
Orvieto, Italy	H9	22
Orwell, Oh., U.S.	C5	114
Orxon, stm., China	B8	36
Oryahovo see Orjahovo, Blg.	F10	26
Orzinuovi, Italy	E6	22
Orzyc, stm., Pol.	D17	16
Os, Nor.	F3	8
Oš, Kyrg.	F12	32
Osa, Península de, pen., C.R.	H6	102
Osage, Wy., U.S.	D8	126
Osage, stm., Mo., U.S.	F5	120
Osage Beach, Mo., U.S.	F5	120
Osage City, Ks., U.S.	F2	120
Ōsaka, Japan	E8	40
Ōsaka, state, Japan	E8	40
Osakarovka, Kaz.	D12	32
Ōsaka-wan, b., Japan	E8	40
Osăm, stm., Blg.	F11	26
Osawatomie, Ks., U.S.	F3	120
Osborne, Ks., U.S.	B10	128
Osburn, Id., U.S.	C11	136
Osceola, Ar., U.S.	B8	122
Osceola, Ia., U.S.	C4	120
Osceola, Mo., U.S.	F4	120
Osceola, Ne., U.S.	F15	126
Osceola, Wi., U.S.	F6	118
Oschatz, Ger.	E8	16
Oschersleben, Ger.	D7	16
Osečina, Yugo.	E6	26
Osëtr, stm., Russia	F21	10
Osgood, In., U.S.	E12	120
Osh see Oš, Kyrg.	F12	32
Oshamambe, Japan	C14	38
Oshawa, On., Can.	E11	112
Ō-shima, i., Japan	E12	40
Oshima-hantō, pen., Japan	C14	38
Oshkosh, Ne., U.S.	F10	126
Oshkosh, Wi., U.S.	H10	118
Oshogbo, Nig.	H5	64
Oshwe, D.R.C.	E3	66
Osica de Jos, Rom.	E11	26
Osijek, Cro.	E15	22
Osimo, Italy	G10	22
Osipovo Selo, Russia	D13	10
Oskaloosa, Ia., U.S.	C5	120
Oskaloosa, Ks., U.S.	E2	120
Oskarshamn, Swe.	H7	8
Oslo, Nor.	G4	8
Oslo, state, Nor.	F4	8
Oslofjorden, b., Nor.	G4	8
Osmānābād, India	B3	53
Osmaneli, Tur.	C12	28
Osmānīye, Tur.	A7	58
Osmino, Russia	A11	10
Osmussaar, i., Est.	A6	10
Osnabrück, Ger.	D4	16
Osorno, Chile	H2	90
Osorno, Spain	B6	20
Osoyoos, B.C., Can.	G11	138
Ossa, Mount, mtn., Austl.	n13	77a
Ossabaw Island, i., Ga., U.S.	E4	116
Osseo, Wi., U.S.	G7	118
Ossian, In., U.S.	A6	120
Ossining, N.Y., U.S.	C12	114
Ossipee, N.H., U.S.	G5	110
Ossjøen, l., Nor.	F4	8
Ossora, Russia	E21	34
Ostashkov see Ostaškov, Russia	C16	10
Ostaškov, Russia	D15	10
Ostende see Oostende, Bel.	C11	14
Osterburg, Ger.	D7	16
Östergötland, state, Swe.	G7	8
Osterholz-Scharmbeck, Ger.	C4	16
Osterode am Harz, Ger.	E6	16
Østerøyni, i., Nor.	F1	8
Osterwieck, Ger.	E6	16
Østfold, state, Nor.	G4	8
Ostfriesische Inseln (East Frisian Islands), is., Ger.	C3	16
Ostfriesland, nist. reg., Ger.	C3	16
Østgrønland (Tunu), state, Grnld.	C18	141
Östhammar, Swe.	F8	8
Ostpreussen, hist. reg., Eur.	F4	10
Ostrava, Czech Rep.	G14	16
Ostróda, Pol.	C15	16
Ostrogožsk, Russia	D5	32
Ostrołeka, Pol.	C17	16
Ostrołeka, state, Pol.	D17	16
Ostrorόg, Pol.	D12	16
Ostrov, Czech Rep.	F8	16
Ostrov, Russia	C11	10
Ostrov, i., Slov.	I13	16
Ostrov-Zalit, Russia	B11	10
Ostrowiec Świętokrzyski, Pol.	F17	16
Ostrów Mazowiecka, Pol.	D17	16
Ostrów Wielkopolski, Pol.	E13	16
Ostrzeszów, Pol.	E13	16
Osŧuni, Italy	D11	24
Osum, stm., Alb.	D14	24
Osumi-hantō, pen., Japan	H3	40
Ōsumi Islands see Ōsumi-shotō, is., Japan	I9	38
Ōsumi-kaikyō, strt., Japan	I9	38
Ōsumi-shotō, is., Japan	I9	38
Osuna, Spain	G5	20
Oswegatchie, stm., N.Y., U.S.	C9	120
Oswego, Ks., U.S.	G2	120
Oswego, N.Y., U.S.	E13	112
Oswestry, Eng., U.K.	I9	12
Oświęcim (Auschwitz), Pol.	F15	16
Osyka, Ms., U.S.	F8	122
Ōta, Japan	C12	40
Otaci, Mol.	A14	26
Ōtake, Japan	E5	40
Otaki, N.Z.	E6	80
Otaru, Japan	C14	38
Otava, Fin.	F12	8
Otava, stm., Czech Rep.	G9	16
Otavi, Nmb.	D2	68
Otawara, Japan	C12	40
Otego Creek, stm., N.Y., U.S.	B10	114
Oteotea, Sol. Is.	e9	79b
Oteros, stm., Mex.	C6	100
Othello, Wa., U.S.	C7	136
Otish, Monts, mts., Qc., Can.	E16	106
Otjinene, Nmb.	B4	70
Otjiwarongo, Nmb.	B3	70
Otjozondjou, stm., Nmb.	B5	70
Otjozondjupa, state, Nmb.	B3	70
Otočac, Cro.	F12	22
Otoskwin, stm., On., Can.	E13	106
Otra, stm., Nor.	G2	8
Otradnyj, Russia	D8	32
Otranto, Italy	D12	24
Otranto, Strait of, strt., Eur.	D12	24
Otrokovice, Czech Rep.	G13	16
Otrøya, i., Nor.	E2	8
Ōtscher, mtn., Aus.	C12	22
Ōtsu, Japan	D8	40
Otta, Nor.	F3	8
Ottawa (Outaouais), stm., Can.	C14	112
Ottawa, Il., U.S.	C9	120
Ottawa, Ks., U.S.	F2	120
Ottawa, Oh., U.S.	C1	114
Ottawa Islands, is., Nu., Can.	D14	106
Otterburne, Mb., Can.	E16	124
Otter Creek, Fl., U.S.	G3	116
Otter Creek, stm., Vt., U.S.	F3	110
Otterøya, see Otrøya, i., Nor.	E2	8
Otter Tail, stm., Mn., U.S.	E2	118
Otter Tail Lake, l., Mn., U.S.	E2	118
Otterville, On., Can.	F9	112
Ottoville, Oh., U.S.	C1	114
Ottoshoop, S. Afr.	D8	70
Ottumwa, Ia., U.S.	C5	120
Otukpo, Nig.	H6	64
Otway, Cape, c., Austl.	L4	76
Otwock, Pol.	D17	16
Ōtztaler Alpen (Venoste, Alpi), mts., Eur.	D17	22
Ou, stm., China	G9	42
Ou, stm., Laos	B6	48
Ouachita, stm., U.S.	E7	122
Ouachita, Lake, res., Ar., U.S.	C5	122
Ouachita Mountains, mts., U.S.	C4	122
Ouaco, N. Cal.	m15	79d
Ouadda, C.A.R.	C4	66
Ouagadougou, Burkina	G4	64
Ouahigouya, Burkina	G4	64
Ouahran see Wahran, Alg.	B4	64
Ouaka, stm., C.A.R.	C4	66
Oualâta, Maur.	F3	64
Ouallene, Alg.	E5	64
Ouanda Djallé, C.A.R.	C4	66
Ouango, C.A.R.	D4	66
Ouanne, stm., Fr.	G12	14
Ouarâne, reg., Maur.	E3	64
Ouargla, Alg.	C6	64
Ouarzazate, Mor.	C3	64
Oubangui (Ubangi), stm., Afr.	D3	66
Oued Fodda, Alg.	H12	20
Oued-Zem, Mor.	C3	64
Ouémé, stm., Benin	H5	64
Ouen, Île, i., N. Cal.	n16	79d
Ouessant, Île d' (Ushant), i., Fr.	F3	14
Ouesso, Congo	D3	66
Ouezzane, Mor.	C3	64
Ouham, stm., Afr.	F3	62
Ouidah, Benin	H5	64
Ouimet Canyon, misc. cult., On., Can.	C10	118
Ouistreham, Fr.	E8	14
Oujda, Mor.	C4	64
Oulangan kansallispuisto, p.o.i., Fin.	C13	8
Oulu (Uleåborg), Fin.	D11	8
Oulu, stm., Fin.	D12	8
Oulujärvi, l., Fin.	D12	8
Oum-Chalouba, Chad	D4	62
Oumé, C. Iv.	H3	64
Oum-Hadjer, Chad	E3	62
Ounasjoki, stm., Fin.	C11	8
Ounianga Kébir, Chad	D3	62
Ourém, Braz.	A2	88
Ourense, Spain	B3	20
Ourense, co., Spain	B3	20
Ouricuri, Braz.	D5	88
Ourinhos, Braz.	D7	90
Ouro Branco, Braz.	D7	88
Ouro Fino, Braz.	L2	88
Ouro Preto, Braz.	K4	88
Ours, Grande chute à l', wtfl, Qc., Can.	B4	110
Ourthe, stm., Bel.	D14	14
Ōu-sammyaku, mts., Japan	E14	38
Oust, can., Fr.	F6	14
Outaouais (Ottawa), stm., Can.	C15	112
Outardes, stm., Qc., Can.	E17	106
Outer Hebrides, is., Scot., U.K.	D5	12
Outer Island, i., Wi., U.S.	D8	118
Outer Santa Barbara Passage, strt., Ca., U.S.	J7	134
Outjo, Nmb.	B3	70
Outlook, Sk., Can.	C6	124
Outlook, Mt., U.S.	F9	124
Out Skerries, is., Scot., U.K.	n19	12a
Ouvéa, i., N. Cal.	m16	79d
Ouyen, Austl.	J4	76
Ovacık, Tur.	B15	28
Ovada, Italy	F5	22
Ovalle, Chile	E2	92
Ovana, Cerro, mtn., Ven.	D2	86
Ovar, Port.	D2	20
Ovejas, Col.	C4	86
Overbrook, Ks., U.S.	F2	120
Overflowing, stm., Can.	A12	124
Overland Park, Ks., U.S.	F3	120
Overton, Ne., U.S.	G13	126
Overton, Tx., U.S.	E4	122
Overton Arm, b., Nv., U.S.	G2	132
Övertorneå, Swe.	C10	8
Ovid, Mi., U.S.	B9	114
Ovidiopol', Ukr.	C17	26
Oviedo, Spain	A5	20
Ovinišče, Russia	B20	10
Oviš, Lat.	C4	10
Ovoot, Mong.	B7	36
Øvre Anárjohka Nasjonalpark, p.o.i., Nor.	B13	8
Øvre Dividal Nasjonalpark, p.o.i., Nor.	B8	8
Ovstug, Russia	G16	10
Owando, Congo	E3	66
Owase, Japan	E9	40
Owasso, Ok., U.S.	H2	120
Owatonna, Mn., U.S.	G5	118
Owbeh, Afg.	C9	56
Owego, N.Y., U.S.	B9	114
Owen, Wi., U.S.	G8	118
Owendo, Gabon	D1	66
Owens, stm., Ca., U.S.	F7	134
Owensboro, Ky., U.S.	G10	120
Owens Lake, l., Ca., U.S.	G8	134
Owen Sound, On., Can.	D9	112
Owen Sound, b., On., Can.	D9	112
Owen Stanley Range, mts., Pap. N. Gui.	b4	79a
Owensville, In., U.S.	F10	120
Owensville, Mo., U.S.	F6	120
Owerri, Nig.	H6	64
Owikeno Lake, l., B.C., Can.	E2	138
Owingsville, Ky., U.S.	F2	114
Owl, stm., Ab., Can.	A19	138
Owo, Nig.	H6	64
Owosso, Mi., U.S.	E5	112
Owyhee, Nv., U.S.	B9	134
Owyhee, stm., U.S.	G9	136
Owyhee, Lake, res., Or., U.S.	G9	136
Owyhee, South Fork, stm., U.S.	H10	136
Öxarfjördur, b., Ice.	j31	8a
Oxelösund, Swe.	G7	8
Oxford, N.Z.	F5	80
Oxford, Eng., U.K.	J11	12
Oxford, Al., U.S.	D13	122
Oxford, In., U.S.	H2	112
Oxford, Ks., U.S.	D11	128
Oxford, Me., U.S.	F6	110
Oxford, Ms., U.S.	C9	122
Oxford, N.Y., U.S.	B10	114
Oxford, N.C., U.S.	H7	114
Oxford, Oh., U.S.	E1	114
Oxford, Pa., U.S.	E9	114
Oxford Junction, Ia., U.S.	J8	118
Oxford Lake, l., Mb., Can.	E11	106
Oxford Peak, mtn., Id., U.S.	H14	136
Oxkutzcab, Mex.	B3	102
Oxley Downs, Austl.	J4	76
Oxley Wild Rivers National Park, p.o.i., Austl.	H8	76
Oxnard, Ca., U.S.	I6	134
Oxus see Amu Darya, stm., Asia	F10	32
Oya, stm., Malay.	C8	50
Oyabe, Japan	C9	40
Oyano, Japan	G3	40
Oyapock (Oiapoque), stm., S.A.	C7	84
Oyem, Gabon	D2	66
Oyen, Ab., Can.	D3	124
Oyo, Nig.	H5	64
Ozamis, Phil.	F4	52
Ozark, Al., U.S.	F13	122
Ozark, Ar., U.S.	B5	122
Ozark, Mo., U.S.	G4	120
Ozark Plateau, plat., U.S.	H4	120
Ozarks, Lake of the, res., Mo., U.S.	F5	120
Ozd, Hung.	A7	26
Ozërnovskij, Russia	F20	34
Ozërnyj, Russia	D10	32
Ozery, Russia	F21	10
Ozieri, Italy	D3	24
Ozinki, Russia	D7	32
Ozorków, Pol.	E15	16

Name	Map Ref.	Page
Ōzu, Japan	F5	40
Ozuluama, Mex.	E9	100
Ozurgeti, Geor.	F6	32

P

Name	Map Ref.	Page
Paagoumène, N. Cal.	m14	79d
Paama, state, Vanuatu	k17	79d
Paama, i., Vanuatu	k17	79d
Paamiut see Frederikshåb, Grnld.	E15	141
Paarl, S. Afr.	H4	70
Paauilo, Hi., U.S.	C6	78a
Pabbay, i., Scot., U.K.	D5	12
Pabbiring, Kepulauan, is., Indon.	F11	50
Pabean, Indon.	G9	50
Pabellón, Ensenada del, b., Mex.	C4	100
Pabianice, Pol.	E15	16
Pablo, Mt., U.S.	C12	136
Pābna, Bngl.	G12	54
Pabradė, Lith.	F8	10
Pacaás Novos, Serra dos, mts., Braz.	F5	84
Pacajus, Braz.	C6	88
Pacasmayo, Peru	E2	84
Pacatuba, Braz.	C6	88
Pachino, Italy	H9	24
Pachitea, stm., Peru	E3	84
Pachmarhi, India	G7	54
Pāchora, India	H5	54
Pachuca de Soto, Mex.	E9	100
Pacific, B.C., Can.	B2	138
Pacific, Mo., U.S.	F7	120
Pacifica, Ca., U.S.	F3	134
Pacific-Antarctic Ridge, unds.	P22	142
Pacific Grove, Ca., U.S.	G3	134
Pacific Ocean	F20	142
Pacific Ranges, mts., B.C., Can.	E5	138
Pacific Rim National Park, p.o.i., B.C., Can.	H5	138
Paciran, Indon.	G8	50
Pacitan, Indon.	H7	50
Pacora, Pan.	C2	86
Pacov, Czech Rep.	G11	16
Pacuí, stm., Braz.	I3	88
Padada, Phil.	G5	52
Padamo, stm., Ven.	F9	86
Padampur, India	H9	54
Padang, Indon.	D6	50
Padang, Indon.	G12	50
Padang, Indon.	D2	50
Padang, Pulau, i., Indon.	C3	50
Padang Endau, Malay.	K6	48
Padangpanjang, Indon.	D2	50
Padangsidempuan, Indon.	C1	50
Padany, Russia	E15	8
Padas, stm., Malay.	A9	50
Padauari, stm., Braz.	G9	86
Paddle, stm., Ab., Can.	B16	138
Paddle Prairie, Ab., Can.	D7	106
Paderborn, Ger.	E4	16
Padjelanta Nationalpark, p.o.i., Swe.	C7	8
Padloping Island, i., Nu., Can.	D13	141
Padma see Ganges, stm., Asia	G13	54
Pádova (Padua), Italy	E8	22
Pādra, India	G4	54
Padrauna, India	E9	54
Padre Bernardo, Braz.	H1	88
Padre Island, i., Tx., U.S.	G10	130
Padre Island National Seashore, p.o.i., Tx., U.S.	G10	130
Padre Paraíso, Braz.	I5	88
Padstow, Eng., U.K.	K8	12
Padua see Pádova, Italy	E8	22
Paducah, Ky., U.S.	G9	120
Paducah, Tx., U.S.	G8	128
Paea, Fr. Poly.	v21	78h
Paedun, Kor., S.	D1	40
Paektu-san, mtn., Asia	C10	36
Paestum, hist., Italy	D8	24
Páez, stm., Col.	F4	86
Pafúri, Moz.	C10	70
Pag, Otok, i., Cro.	F11	22
Pagadenbaru, Indon.	G5	50
Pagadian, Phil.	G4	52
Pagai Selatan, Pulau, i., Indon.	E2	50
Pagai Utara, Pulau, i., Indon.	E2	50
Pagan, Mya.	B2	48
Pagan, i., N. Mar. Is.	B5	72
Pagaralam, Indon.	E3	50
Pagasitikós Kólpos, b., Grc.	D5	28
Page, Az., U.S.	G5	132
Page, N.D., U.S.	G16	124
Pagėgiai, Lith.	E4	10
Pagerdewa, Indon.	E4	50
Paget, Mount, mtn., S. Geor.	J9	90
Pagoda Peak, mtn., Co., U.S.	C9	132
Pagoda Point, c., Mya.	E2	48
Pagon, Bukit, mtn., Asia	A9	50
Pago Pago, Am. Sam.	h12	79c
Pagosa Springs, Co., U.S.	F9	132
Paguate, N.M., U.S.	H9	132
Pagudpud, Phil.	A3	52
Pahača, Russia	D22	34
Pahala, Hi., U.S.	D6	78a
Pahang, state, Malay.	K6	48
Pahang, stm., Malay.	K6	48
Pahokee, Fl., U.S.	J5	116
Pahost, Bela.	G12	10
Pahrump, Nv., U.S.	G10	134
Pai, Thai.	C4	48
Pai, stm., Asia	C3	48
Paico, Peru	F3	84
Paide, Est.	B8	10
Paige, Tx., U.S.	D10	130
Paignton, Eng., U.K.	K9	12
Paiguano, Chile	E2	92
Päijänne, l., Fin.	F11	8
Paikü Co, l., China	D10	54
Pailolo Channel, strt., Hi., U.S.	B5	78a
Paimpol, Fr.	F5	14
Painan, Indon.	D2	50
Painesdale, Mi., U.S.	D10	118
Painesville, Oh., U.S.	C4	114
Paint, stm., Mi., U.S.	E10	118
Paint Creek, stm., Oh., U.S.	E14	120
Painted Desert, des., Az., U.S.	H5	132
Painted Rock Reservoir, res., Az., U.S.	K3	132
Paintsville, Ky., U.S.	G3	114
Paisley, Scot., U.K.	F8	12
Paisley, Or., U.S.	H6	136
Païta, N. Cal.	n16	79d
Paita, Peru	E1	84
Paitan, Telukan, b., Malay.	G1	52
Paiton, Indon.	G8	50
Pajala, Swe.	C10	8
Paján, Ec.	H1	86
Pajares, Puerto de, p., Spain	B5	20
Pajaros Point, c., Br. Vir. Is.	d9	104b
Pajęczno, Pol.	E14	16
Pajer, gora, mtn., Russia	C1	34
Pajeú, stm., Braz.	E6	88
Paj-Hoj, hills, Russia	A10	32
Paka, Malay.	J6	48
Pākāla, India	E4	53
Pakaraima Mountains, mts., S.A.	E11	86
Pakashkan Lake, l., On., Can.	B8	118
Pākaur, India	F11	54
Pak Chong, Thai.	E5	48
Pākhāl, l., India	C5	53
Pákhna, Cyp.	D3	58
Pakhoi see Beihai, China	K3	42
Pakistan, ctry., Asia	C2	46
Paklenica Nacionalni Park, p.o.i., Cro.	F12	22
Pakokku, Mya.	B2	48
Pakowki Lake, l., Ab., Can.	E2	124
Pākpattan, Pak.	C4	54
Pak Phanang, Thai.	H5	48
Pak Phayun, Thai.	I5	48
Pak Phraek, Thai.	H5	48
Pakrac, Cro.	E14	22
Pakruojis, Lith.	E6	10
Paks, Hung.	C5	26
Paktīā, state, Afg.	B2	54
Paktīkā, state, Afg.	B2	54
Pakwash Lake, l., On., Can.	A5	118
Pakxé, Laos	E7	48
Pala, Chad	F2	62
Pala, Mya.	F4	48
Palacios, Tx., U.S.	F11	130
Palagruža, Otoci, is., Cro.	H13	22
Palai, India	G3	53
Palaiochóra, Grc.	H6	28
Pālakodu, India	C5	53
Palamós, Spain	C14	20
Pālampur, India	B6	54
Palamu National Park, p.o.i., India	G10	54
Palamut, Tur.	D10	28
Palana, Russia	E20	34
Palanan Bay, b., Phil.	B4	52
Palanga, Lith.	E3	10
Palangkaraya, Indon.	E8	50
Palani, India	F3	53
Pālanpur, India	F4	54
Palaoa Point, c., Hi., U.S.	C4	78a
Palapye, Bots.	C8	70
Pālār, stm., India	E4	53
Palas de Rei, Spain	B3	20
Palatka, Russia	D19	34
Palatka, Fl., U.S.	G4	116
Palau, Italy	C3	24
Palau, ctry., Oc.	g8	78b
Palau Islands, is., Palau	D10	44
Palauk, Mya.	F4	48
Palaw, Mya.	F4	48
Palawan, i., Phil.	F2	52
Palawan Passage, strt., Phil.	F1	52
Palayan, Phil.	C3	52
Pālayankottai, India	G3	53
Palembang, Indon.	E4	50
Palena, Italy	I11	22
Palena, stm., S.A.	H2	90
Palencia, Spain	B6	20
Palencia, co., Spain	B6	20
Palen Lake, l., Ca., U.S.	J1	132
Palenque, Mex.	G13	100
Palenque, hist., Mex.	G12	100
Palermo, Col.	F4	86
Palermo, Italy	F7	24
Palermo, Ur.	F10	92
Palestina, Mex.	E6	130
Palestine, Ar., U.S.	B7	122
Palestine, Il., U.S.	E10	120
Palestine, Tx., U.S.	F3	122
Palestine, hist. reg., Asia	G6	58
Palestine, Lake, res., Tx., U.S.	E3	122
Palestrina, Italy	I9	22
Paletwa, Mya.	D7	46
Pālghāt, India	F3	53
Palgrave Point, c., Nmb.	E1	68
Palhano, stm., Braz.	C6	88
Pāli, India	F4	54
Palima, Indon.	F12	50
Palinuro, Capo, c., Italy	D9	24
Palisade, Ne., U.S.	A7	128
Palisades, Id., U.S.	G15	136
Palisades Reservoir, res., U.S.	G15	136
Pālitāna, India	H3	54
Palivere, Est.	A6	10
Palizada, Mex.	F12	100
Palk Bay, b., Asia	G4	53
Palkino, Russia	G20	8
Pālkonda, India	B6	53
Pālkonda Range, mts., India	D4	53
Palk Strait, strt., Asia	G4	53
Pallastunturi, mtn., Fin.	B11	8
Palliser, Cape, c., N.Z.	E6	80
Palma, Braz.	K4	88
Palma, Moz.	C7	68
Palma, stm., Braz.	G2	88
Palma, Badia de, b., Spain	E13	20
Palmácia, Braz.	C6	88
Palma del Río, Spain	G5	20
Palma de Mallorca, Spain	E13	20
Palma di Montechiaro, Italy	G7	24
Palmar, stm., Ven.	B6	86
Palmar, Lago Artificial del, res., Ur.	F9	92
Palmar Camp, Belize	D3	102
Palmarejo, P.R.	B1	104a
Palmares, Braz.	E8	88
Palmarito, Ven.	D6	86
Palmarola, Isola, i., Italy	D6	24
Palmas, Braz.	F1	88
Palmas, Braz.	C12	92
Palmas Bellas, Pan.	H7	102
Palmas de Monte Alto, Braz.	H4	88
Palma Soriano, Cuba	B9	102
Palm Bay, Fl., U.S.	H5	116
Palm Beach, Fl., U.S.	J5	116
Palmdale, Ca., U.S.	I7	134
Palm Desert, Ca., U.S.	J9	134
Palmeira, Braz.	B13	92
Palmeira das Missões, Braz.	C11	92
Palmeira dos Índios, Braz.	E7	88
Palmeiras, stm., Braz.	F2	88
Palmeirinhas, Ponta das, c., Ang.	B1	68
Palmelo, Braz.	I1	88
Palmer, P.R.	B4	104a
Palmer, Ak., U.S.	D10	140
Palmer, Ma., U.S.	B13	114
Palmer, Ne., U.S.	F14	126
Palmer, Tn., U.S.	B13	122
Palmer, sci., Ant.	B34	81
Palmer Lake, Co., U.S.	B3	128
Palmer Land, reg., Ant.	C34	81
Palmerston, N.Z.	G4	80
Palmerston, at., Cook Is.	E10	72
Palmerston, Cape, c., Austl.	C7	76
Palmerston North, N.Z.	E6	80
Palmerton, Pa., U.S.	D10	114
Palmetto, Ga., U.S.	D14	122
Palmetto, La., U.S.	G6	122
Palmetto Point, c., Antig.	e4	105b
Palmi, Italy	F9	24
Palmira, Col.	F3	86
Palmira, Cuba	A7	102
Palmira, Ec.	I2	86
Palmitas, Ur.	F9	92
Palm Springs, Ca., U.S.	J9	134
Palmyra see Tudmur, Syria	D9	58
Palmyra, Il., U.S.	E7	120
Palmyra, Mo., U.S.	E6	120
Palmyra, N.Y., U.S.	A8	114
Palmyra, Va., U.S.	G7	114
Palmyra, hist., Syria	D9	58
Palmyra Atoll, at., Oc.	C10	72
Palo Alto, Mex.	H8	130
Palo Alto, Ca., U.S.	F3	134
Palo Blanco, P.R.	B2	104a
Palo Flechado Pass, p., N.M., U.S.	E3	128
Paloh, Malay.	B7	50
Paloich, Sudan	E6	62
Palojoensuu, Fin.	B10	8
Palomar Mountain, mtn., Ca., U.S.	J9	134
Palomas, Mex.	F4	130
Palo Pinto, Tx., U.S.	B9	130
Palopo, Indon.	E12	50
Palos, Cabo de, c., Spain	G10	20
Palo Santo, Arg.	B8	92
Palos Verdes Point, c., Ca., U.S.	J7	134
Palouse, stm., U.S.	D8	136
Palo Verde, Ca., U.S.	J2	132
Palpa, Peru	F2	84
Palpalá, Arg.	B5	92
Palu, Indon.	D11	50
Palu, Teluk, b., Indon.	D11	50
Paluga, Russia	D21	8
Palwal, India	D6	54
Pama, Burkina	G5	64
Pamanukan, Indon.	G5	50
Pāmban Channel, strt., India	G4	53
Pāmban Island, i., India	G4	53
Pamekasan, Indon.	G8	50
Pamenang, Indon.	E3	50
Pameungpeuk, Indon.	G5	50
Pamiers, Fr.	F7	18
Pamir, mts., Asia	B11	56
Pamlico Sound, strt., N.C., U.S.	A10	116
Pampa, Tx., U.S.	F8	128
Pampã, stm., Braz.	I5	88
Pampa (Pampas), reg., Arg.	G4	90
Pampa Almirón, Arg.	C8	92
Pampa del Chañar, Arg.	E3	92
Pampa del Indio, Arg.	B7	92
Pampanga, stm., Phil.	C3	52
Pampanua, Indon.	F12	50
Pampas, Peru	F3	84
Pampas, stm., Peru	F3	84
Pampas see Pampa, reg., Arg.	F4	90
Pamplico, S.C., U.S.	B6	116
Pamplona, Col.	D5	86
Pamplona, Spain	B9	20
Pamukkale (Hierapolis), hist., Tur.	F12	28
Pamukova, Tur.	C13	28
Pana, Il., U.S.	E8	120
Panabá, Mex.	B3	102
Panabo, Phil.	G5	52
Panacea, Fl., U.S.	G14	122
Panadura, Sri L.	H4	53
Panagjurište, Blg.	G11	26
Panaitan, Pulau, i., Indon.	G4	50
Panaji, India	D1	53
Panamá, Pan.	H8	102
Panama, Ok., U.S.	B4	122
Panama, ctry., N.A.	F9	96
Panamá, Bahía de, b., Pan.	H8	102
Panamá, Canal de (Panama Canal), can., Pan.	H8	102
Panamá, Golfo de, b., Pan.	D2	86
Panama, Gulf of see Panamá, Golfo de, b., Pan.	D2	86
Panama, Isthmus of see Panamá, Istmo de, isth., Pan.	H8	102
Panamá, Istmo de (Panama, Isthmus of), isth., Pan.	H8	102
Panama Basin, unds.	H5	144
Panama Canal see Panamá, Canal de, can., Pan.	H8	102
Panama City, Fl., U.S.	G13	122
Panambi, Braz.	D11	92
Panamint Range, mts., Ca., U.S.	G8	134
Panamint Valley, val., Ca., U.S.	G8	134
Panao, Peru	E2	84
Panarea, Isola, i., Italy	F9	24
Panaro, stm., Italy	F8	22
Panay, i., Phil.	E4	52
Panay Gulf, b., Phil.	E4	52
Pančevo, Yugo.	E7	26
Panciu, Rom.	D14	26
Panda, Moz.	D12	70
Pandaria, India	G8	54
Pan de Azúcar, Ur.	G10	92
Pandėlys, Lith.	D8	10
Pāndharkawada, India	A4	53
Pandharpur, India	C2	53
Pāndhurna, India	H7	54
Pando, Ur.	G10	92
Panevėžys, Lith.	E7	10
Panfilov, Kaz.	F13	32
Pāng, stm., Mya.	B4	48
Panga, D.R.C.	D5	66
Pangala, Congo	E2	66
Pangandaran, Indon.	G6	50
Pangani, Tan.	F7	66
Pangani, stm., Tan.	E7	66
Pangburn, Ar., U.S.	B7	122
Pangfou see Bengbu, China	E7	42
Panghkam, Mya.	D8	46
Pangi, D.R.C.	E5	66
Pangkajene, Indon.	F11	50
Pangkalanbrandan, Indon.	J4	48
Pangkalanbuun, Indon.	E7	50
Pangkalpinang, Indon.	E5	50
Pangnirtung, Nu., Can.	B17	106
Pango Aluquem, Ang.	B1	68
Pangŏjin, Kor., S.	D2	40
Pangong Tso, l., Asia	B7	54
Panguiranan, Phil.	D4	52
Panguitch, Ut., U.S.	F4	132
Pangutaran, Phil.	G3	52
Pangutaran Group, is., Phil.	G3	52
Panhandle, Tx., U.S.	F7	128
Paniau, mtn., Hi., U.S.	B1	78a
Panié, Mont, mtn., N. Cal.	m15	79d
Panīpat, India	D6	54
Panitan, Phil.	E4	52
Panj (Pjandž), stm., Asia	B11	56
Panjang, Indon.	F4	50
Panjang, Selat, strt., Indon.	C3	50
Pankshin, Nig.	H6	64
Panlong (Lo), stm., Asia	A7	48
P'anmunjŏm-ni, Kor., N.	E7	38
Panna, India	F8	54
Panna National Park, p.o.i., India	F7	54
Pannawonica, Austl.	D3	74
Panola, U.S.	E10	122
Páno Lévkara, Cyp.	D4	58
Panopah, Indon.	D7	50
Panorama, Braz.	D6	90
Panovo, Russia	C18	32
Panruti, India	F4	53
Panshan, China	D4	38
Pantanal, reg., S.A.	C5	90
Pantanaw, Mya.	D2	48
Pantar, Pulau, i., Indon.	G7	44
Pantelleria, Isola di, i., Italy	H6	24
Pantonlabu, Indon.	J3	48
Pánuco, Mex.	E10	100
Pánuco, stm., Mex.	E9	100
Panxian, China	F5	36
Panyam, Nig.	H6	64
Panzós, Guat.	E3	102
Pao, stm., Thai.	D6	48
Pao, stm., Ven.	C8	86
Pao, stm., Ven.	C9	86
Paochi see Baoji, China	D2	42
Paoki see Baoji, China	D2	42
Paola, Italy	E9	24
Paola, Ks., U.S.	F3	120
Paoli, In., U.S.	F11	120
Paopao, Fr. Poly.	v20	78h
Paoting see Baoding, China	B6	42
Paotou see Baotou, China	A4	42
Paotow see Baotou, China	A4	42
Pápa, Hung.	B4	26
Papagaio, stm., Braz.	I10	86
Papagaios, Braz.	D3	88
Papagayo, Golfo de, b., C.R.	G4	102
Papaikou, Hi., U.S.	D6	78a
Papantla de Olarte, Mex.	E10	100
Papara, Fr. Poly.	v22	78h
Papa Stour, i., Scot., U.K.	n18	12a
Papeari, Fr. Poly.	w22	78h
Papeete, Fr. Poly.	v21	78h
Papenburg, Ger.	C3	16
Papetoai, Fr. Poly.	v20	78h
Paphos see Néa Páfos, Cyp.	D3	58
Papigochic, stm., Mex.	G8	98
Papillion, Ne., U.S.	C1	120
Paposo, Chile	B2	92
Papua, Gulf of, b., Pap. N. Gui.	D5	72
Papua New Guinea, ctry., Oc.	D5	72
Papulovo, Russia	F23	8
Papun, Mya.	C3	48
Papunáua, stm., Col.	G6	86
Papurí (Papurí), stm., S.A.	G6	86
Papuri (Papurí), stm., S.A.	G6	86
Pará, state, Braz.	D7	84
Pará, stm., Braz.	A1	88
Pará, stm., Braz.	J3	88
Parabel', Russia	C14	32
Paraburdoo, Austl.	D3	74
Paracatu, Braz.	I2	88
Paracatu, stm., Braz.	I3	88
Paracel Islands see Xisha Qundao, is., China	B5	50
Pārachinār, Pak.	B3	54
Paracho de Verduzco, Mex.	F7	100
Parachute, Co., U.S.	D8	132
Paraćin, Yugo.	F8	26
Paracuru, Braz.	B6	88
Parada, Punta, c., Peru	G2	84
Paradise, Ca., U.S.	D4	134
Paradise, Mt., U.S.	C12	136
Paradise, Nv., U.S.	G1	132
Paradise Island, i., Bah.	m18	104f
Paradise Valley, Az., U.S.	J5	132
Paradise Valley, Nv., U.S.	B8	134
Pāradwīp, India	H11	54
Paragonah, Ut., U.S.	F4	132
Paragould, Ar., U.S.	H7	120
Paraguá, stm., Bol.	B4	90
Paragua, stm., Ven.	D10	86
Paraguaçu, stm., Braz.	G6	88
Paraguai (Paraguay), stm., S.A.	D5	90
Paraguaipoa, Ven.	B6	86
Paraguaná, Península de, pen., Ven.	A6	86
Paraguarí, Para.	B9	92
Paraguarí, state, Para.	C9	92
Paraguay, ctry., S.A.	D5	90
Paraguay (Paraguai), stm., S.A.	E5	90
Paraíba, state, Braz.	D7	88
Paraíba do Sul, stm., Braz.	K5	88
Paraibano, Braz.	D3	88
Parainen, Fin.	F9	8
Paraíso, Mex.	F12	100
Paraiso, Pan.	H8	102
Parakou, Benin	H5	64
Paramakkudi, India	G4	53
Paramaribo, Sur.	B6	84
Parambu, Braz.	D5	88
Paramillo, Parque Nacional, p.o.i., Col.	D3	86
Paramirim, Braz.	G4	88
Paramirim, stm., Braz.	F4	88
Páramo de Masa, Puerto de, p., Spain	B7	20
Paramušir, ostrov, i., Russia	F20	34
Paramythiá, Grc.	D3	28
Paran, Naḥal (Girafi, Wadi), stm.	I5	58
Paraná, Arg.	E7	92
Paranã, Braz.	G1	88
Paraná, state, Braz.	D6	90
Paranã, stm., Braz.	G1	88
Paraná, stm., S.A.	F5	90
Paranaguá, Braz.	B13	92
Paranaguá, Baía de, b., Braz.	B13	92
Paranaíba, Braz.	C6	90
Paranaíba, stm., Braz.	C6	90
Paranaidji, Braz.	D2	88
Paranapanema, stm., Braz.	D6	90
Paranapiacaba, Serra do, mts., Braz.	B13	92
Paranavaí, Braz.	D6	90
Parang, Phil.	G5	52
Parang, Pulau, i., Indon.	F7	50
Parângu Mare, Vârful, mtn., Rom.	D10	26
Paranhos, Braz.	A10	92
Paranoá, Lago do, res., Braz.	H2	88
Paraopeba, Braz.	J3	88
Parapetí, stm., Bol.	C4	90
Parara, Indon.	E12	50
Paratinga, Braz.	G4	88
Paratoo, Austl.	I2	76
Paray-le-Monial, Fr.	C9	18
Pārbati, stm., India	F6	54
Pārbatipur, Bngl.	F12	54
Parbhani, India	B3	53
Parchim, Ger.	C7	16
Pardeeville, Wi., U.S.	H9	118
Pārdi, India	H4	54
Parding, China	B12	54
Pardo, stm., Braz.	K1	88
Pardo, stm., Braz.	H6	88
Pardo, stm., Braz.	L1	88
Pardo, stm., Braz.	D6	90
Pardo, stm., Braz.	D11	92
Pardubice, Czech Rep.	F11	16
Paredón, Mex.	C8	100
Parelhas, Braz.	D7	88
Paren', Russia	D21	34
Paren', stm., Russia	D21	34
Parent, Qc., Can.	C2	110
Parentis-en-Born, Fr.	E4	18
Parepare, Indon.	E11	50
Parera, Arg.	G5	92
Parfenevo, Russia	F20	8
Párga, Grc.	D3	28
Parham, Antig.	f4	105b
Paria, Gulf of, b.	B10	86
Paria, Península de, pen., Ven.	B10	86
Pariaguán, Ven.	C9	86
Pariaman, Indon.	D1	50
Paricutín, vol., Mex.	F7	100
Parigi, Indon.	D12	50
Parika, Guy.	B6	84
Parikkala, Fin.	F13	8
Parima, stm., Braz.	F10	86
Parima, Serra (Parima, Sierra), mts., S.A.	F9	86
Parima, Sierra (Parima, Serra), mts., S.A.	F9	86
Parima Tapirapecó, Parque Nacional, p.o.i., Ven.	F9	86
Parintins, Braz.	D6	84
Paris, On., Can.	E9	112
Paris, Fr.	F11	14
Paris, Ar., U.S.	B5	122
Paris, Il., U.S.	I2	112
Paris, Ky., U.S.	F1	114
Paris, Mo., U.S.	E5	120
Paris, Tn., U.S.	H9	120
Paris, Tx., U.S.	D3	122
Parisienne, Île, i., On., Can.	B5	112
Parita, Bahía de, b., Pan.	H7	102
Parit Buntar, Malay.	J5	48
Parkano, Fin.	E10	8
Park City, Mt., U.S.	B3	126
Park City, Ut., U.S.	C5	132
Parkdale, Or., U.S.	E5	136
Parker, Az., U.S.	I2	132
Parker, Co., U.S.	B4	128
Parker, Fl., U.S.	G13	122
Parker, Cape, c., Nu., Can.	B10	141
Parker City, In., U.S.	H4	112
Parker Dam, Ca., U.S.	I2	132
Parker Dam, dam, U.S.	I2	132
Parkersburg, Il., U.S.	F9	120
Parkersburg, Ia., U.S.	B5	120
Parkersburg, W.V., U.S.	E4	114
Parkes, Austl.	I7	76
Park Falls, Wi., U.S.	F8	118
Park Forest, Il., U.S.	G2	112
Parkhill, On., Can.	E8	112
Parkland, Wa., U.S.	C4	136
Park Range, mts., Co., U.S.	C10	132
Park Rapids, Mn., U.S.	E3	118
Parkrose, Or., U.S.	E4	136
Park Rynie, S. Afr.	G10	70
Parksley, Va., U.S.	G10	114
Parkston, S.D., U.S.	D14	126
Parksville, B.C., Can.	G6	138
Parkville, Md., U.S.	E9	114
Parkville, Mo., U.S.	E3	120
Parla, Spain	D7	20
Parlākimidi, India	B7	53
Parli, India	B3	53
Parma, Italy	F7	22
Parma, Mo., U.S.	H8	120
Parma, Oh., U.S.	C4	114
Parnaguá, Braz.	F3	88
Parnaíba, Braz.	B5	88
Parnaíba, stm., Braz.	B5	88
Parnaibinha, stm., Braz.	E2	88
Parnamirim, Braz.	E6	88
Parnassós, mtn., Grc.	E5	28
Párnitha, mtn., Grc.	E6	28
Pärnu, Est.	G11	8
Pärnu laht, b., Est.	G11	8
Paro, Bhu.	E12	54
Pārola, India	H5	54
Paromaj, Russia	F17	34
Paroo, stm., Austl.	G5	76
Páros, i., Grc.	F8	28
Parowan, Ut., U.S.	F4	132
Parque Nacional da Chapada da Diamantina, p.o.i., Braz.	G4	88
Parral, Chile	H2	92
Parral, stm., Mex.	B6	100
Parramatta, Austl.	I8	76
Parras de la Fuente, Mex.	C7	100
Parrish, Fl., U.S.	I3	116
Parrsboro, N.S., Can.	E12	110
Parry, Cape, c., N.T., Can.	A6	106
Parry Bay, b., Nu., Can.	B14	106
Parry Island, i., On., Can.	C9	112
Parry Peninsula, pen., N.T., Can.	B6	106
Parry Sound, On., Can.	C9	112
Parsberg, Ger.	G7	16
Parsęta, stm., Pol.	B11	16
Parshall, N.D., U.S.	G11	124
Paršino, Russia	C20	32
Parsnip, stm., B.C., Can.	A8	138
Parsons, Ks., U.S.	G2	120
Parsons, Tn., U.S.	B10	122
Pärsti, Est.	B8	10
Partanna, Italy	G6	24
Parthenay, Fr.	H8	14
Partinico, Italy	F7	24
Partizansk, Russia	C10	38
Partizánske, Slov.	H14	16
Paru, stm., Braz.	D7	84
Parú, stm., Ven.	E9	86
Paru de Oeste, stm., Braz.	C6	84
Parūr, India	F3	53
Pārvatīpuram, India	B6	53
Paryang, China	C9	54
Parys, S. Afr.	E8	70
Pasadena, Ca., U.S.	I7	134
Pasadena, Tx., U.S.	H3	122
Pasaje, Ec.	D2	84
Pa Sak, stm., Thai.	E5	48
Paşaköy, N. Cyp.	C4	58
Pasarbantal, Indon.	E2	50
Pasawng, Mya.	C3	48
Pascagoula, Ms., U.S.	G10	122
Pascagoula, stm., Ms., U.S.	G10	122
Paşcani, Rom.	B13	26
Pasco, Wa., U.S.	D7	136
Pascoag, R.I., U.S.	C14	114
Pascua, Isla de (Easter Island) (Rapa Nui), i., Chile	f30	78l
Pas-de-Calais, state, Fr.	D11	14
Pasewalk, Ger.	C10	16
Pasir Mas, Malay.	J6	48
Pasirpengarayan, Indon.	C2	50
Pasir Puteh, Malay.	J6	48
Paškovo, Russia	G15	34
Pasłęka, stm., Pol.	C16	16
Pasley Bay, b., Nu., Can.	A11	106
Pašman, Otok, i., Cro.	G12	22
Pasmore, stm., Austl.	H2	76
Pasni, Pak.	D9	56
Paso de Indios, Arg.	H3	90
Paso del Cerro, Ur.	E9	92
Paso de los Libres, Arg.	D9	92
Paso de los Toros, Ur.	F9	92
Paso de Patria, Para.	C8	92
Paso de San Antonio, Mex.	E3	130
Paso Hondo, Mex.	H13	100
Paso Robles, Ca., U.S.	H5	134
Pašozero, Russia	F16	8
Pasquia Hills, hills, Sk., Can.	A11	124
Pasrūr, Pak.	B5	54
Passadumkeag, Me., U.S.	E8	110
Passadumkeag Mountain, hill, Me., U.S.	E8	110
Passage Point, c., N.T., Can.	B16	140
Passaic, N.J., U.S.	H15	112
Passamaquoddy Bay, b., N.A.	E10	110
Passau, Ger.	H9	16
Passero, Capo, c., Italy	H9	24
Passo Fundo, Braz.	D11	92
Passo Real, Represa do, res., Braz.	D11	92
Passos, Braz.	K2	88
Pastavy, Bela.	E9	10
Pastaza, state, Ec.	H3	86
Pastaza, stm., S.A.	D2	84
Pastillo, P.R.	B3	104a
Pasto, Col.	G3	86
Pastos Bons, Braz.	D3	88
Pasuruan, Indon.	G8	50
Pasvalys, Lith.	D7	10
Pásztó, Hung.	B6	26
Patacamaya, Bol.	C3	90
Patadkal, hist., India	C3	53
Patagonia, Az., U.S.	L6	132
Patagonia, reg., Arg.	I2	90
Pātan, India	G3	54
Patchogue, N.Y., U.S.	D13	114
Patea, N.Z.	D6	80
Pategi, Nig.	H6	64
Pate Island, i., Kenya	E8	66
Patensie, S. Afr.	H7	70
Paterna, Spain	E10	20
Paternion, Aus.	D10	22
Paternò, Italy	G8	24
Paterson, N.J., U.S.	D11	114
Pathānkot, India	B5	54
Pathein, Mya.	D2	48
Pathfinder Reservoir, res., Wy., U.S.	E5	126
Pathiu, Thai.	G4	48
Pathum Thani, Thai.	E5	48
Pati, Indon.	G7	50
Patía, Col.	F3	86
Patía, stm., Col.	F2	86
Patiāla, India	C6	54
Patillas, P.R.	B3	104a
Pati Point, c., Guam	i10	78c
Pativilca, Peru	F2	84
Pātkai Range, mts., Asia	F4	36
Pat Mayse Lake, res., Tx., U.S.	D3	122
Pátmos, i., Grc.	F9	28
Patna, India	F10	54
Patna, India	H11	54
Patnāgarh, India	H9	54
Patnanongan Island, i., Phil.	C4	52
Pato Branco, Braz.	C11	92
Patoka, Il., U.S.	F8	120
Patoka, stm., In., U.S.	F10	120
Patoka Lake, res., In., U.S.	F11	120
Patomskoe nagor'e, plat., Russia	E12	34
Patonga, Ug.	D6	66
Patos, Braz.	D7	88
Patos, stm., Arg.	E3	92
Patos, Lagoa dos, b., Braz.	E12	92
Patos de Minas, Braz.	J2	88
Patquía, Arg.	D4	92
Pátra, Grc.	E4	28
Patrai, Gulf of see Patraikós Kólpos, b., Grc.	E4	28
Patraikós Kólpos, b., Grc.	E4	28
Patricio Lynch, Isla, i., Chile	I1	90
Patrocínio, Braz.	J2	88
Pattani, Thai.	I5	48
Pattaya, Thai.	F5	48
Patten, Me., U.S.	D8	110
Patterson, Ca., U.S.	F4	134
Patterson, Ga., U.S.	E3	116
Patterson, Mount, mtn., Yk., Can.	C4	106
Patti, Golfo di, b., Italy	F9	24
Pattison, Ms., U.S.	F8	122
Pattoki, Pak.	C4	54
Pattonsburg, Mo., U.S.	D3	120
Pattukkottai, India	F4	53
Pattullo, Mount, mtn., B.C., Can.	D5	106
Patuākhāli, Bngl.	G13	54
Patuca, stm., Hond.	E5	102
Pātūr, India	H6	54
Patusi, Pap. N. Gui.	a4	79a
Patuxent, stm., Md., U.S.	F9	114
Pátzcuaro, Mex.	F8	100
Pau, Fr.	F5	18
Pau, Gave de, stm., Fr.	F5	18
Pau Brasil, Braz.	H6	88
Pau dos Ferros, Braz.	D6	88
Pauh, Indon.	E3	50
Pauini, stm., Braz.	E4	84
Pauini, stm., Braz.	H10	86
Pauk, Mya.	B2	48
Pauksa Taung, mtn., Mya.	C2	48
Paul, Id., U.S.	H13	136
Paulding, Ms., U.S.	E9	122
Paulicéia, Braz.	D6	90
Paulina Peak, mtn., Or., U.S.	G5	136
Pauline, Mount, mtn., Can.	C11	138
Paulino Neves, Braz.	B4	88
Paulistana, Braz.	E5	88
Paulistas, Braz.	J4	88
Paullina, Ia., U.S.	B2	120
Paulo Afonso, Braz.	E6	88
Paulo Afonso, Cachoeira de, wtfl, Braz.	E6	88
Paulpietersburg, S. Afr.	E10	70
Pauls Valley, Ok., U.S.	G11	128
Paung, Mya.	D3	48
Paungde, Mya.	C2	48
Pauri, India	C7	54
Paute, Ec.	I2	86
Paute, stm., Ec.	I2	86
Pauto, stm., Col.	E6	86
Pavia, Italy	E6	22
Pavilion, B.C., Can.	F9	138
Pāvilosta, Lat.	D4	10
Pavlikeni, Blg.	F12	26
Pavlodar, Kaz.	D13	32
Pavlof Volcano, vol., Ak., U.S.	E7	140
Pavlovo, Russia	I20	8
Pavlovsk, Russia	A13	10
Pavlovsk, Russia	D14	32
Pavlovskij Posad, Russia	E21	10
Pavo, Ga., U.S.	F2	116
Pavullo nel Frignano, Italy	F7	22
Pavuvu Island, i., Sol. Is.	e8	79b
Pawan, stm., Indon.	D7	50
Pawhuska, Ok., U.S.	E12	128
Pawn, stm., Mya.	C3	48
Pawnee, Il., U.S.	E8	120
Pawnee, Ok., U.S.	A2	122
Pawnee, stm., Ks., U.S.	C9	128
Pawnee Rock, Ks., U.S.	C9	128
Pawni, India	H7	54
Pawota, Mya.	D3	48
Paw Paw, Il., U.S.	C8	120
Paw Paw, Mi., U.S.	F4	112
Pawtucket, R.I., U.S.	C14	114
Paxoí, i., Grc.	D3	28
Paxson, Ak., U.S.	D10	140
Paxton, Ne., U.S.	F11	126
Paya, Hond.	E5	102
Payakumbuh, Indon.	D2	50
Payamlı, Tur.	A9	58
Payerne, Switz.	D3	22
Payeti, Indon.	H12	50
Payette, Id., U.S.	F10	136
Payette, stm., Id., U.S.	G10	136
Payette, North Fork, stm., Id., U.S.	F11	136
Payette, South Fork, stm., Id., U.S.	F11	136
Payne, Oh., U.S.	C1	114
Payne, Lac, l., Can.	D16	106
Paynes Find, Austl.	E3	74
Paynton, Sk., Can.	A5	124
Paysandú, Ur.	F8	92
Payson, Az., U.S.	I5	132
Payson, Il., U.S.	E6	120
Payson, Ut., U.S.	C5	132
Payún, Cerro, mtn., Arg.	H3	92
Pazarbaşı Burnu, c., Tur.	B13	28
Pazarcık, Tur.	A8	58
Pazardžik, Blg.	G11	26
Pazaryeri, Tur.	D12	28
Paz de Ariporo, Col.	E6	86
Pčevža, Russia	A15	10
Pe, Mya.	F4	48
Pea, stm., U.S.	F12	122
Peabody, Ks., U.S.	C11	128
Peabody, Ma., U.S.	B14	114
Peace, stm., Can.	D8	106
Peace, stm., Fl., U.S.	I4	116
Peace River, Ab., Can.	D7	106
Peachland, B.C., Can.	G11	138
Peach Orchard, Ga., U.S.	C3	116
Peach Springs, Az., U.S.	H3	132
Peak District National Park, p.o.i., Eng., U.K.	H11	12
Peak Downs, Austl.	D7	76
Peak Hill, Austl.	E3	74
Peak Hill, Austl.	I7	76
Peäldoajvi, mtn., Fin.	B12	8
Peale, Mount, mtn., Ut., U.S.	E7	132
Pearisburg, Va., U.S.	G5	114
Pearl, Il., U.S.	E7	120
Pearl, Ms., U.S.	E8	122
Pearl, stm., U.S.	G9	122
Pearland, Tx., U.S.	H3	122
Pearl Harbor, b., Hi., U.S.	B3	78a
Pearl Peak, mtn., Nv., U.S.	C1	132
Pearl River, La., U.S.	G9	122
Pearson, Ga., U.S.	E3	116

Name | Map Ref. | Page

Name	Map Ref.	Page
Peary Land, reg., Grnld.	A18	141
Pease, stm., Tx., U.S.	G9	128
Pebane, Moz.	D6	68
Pebas, Peru	D3	84
Pebble Island, i., Falk. Is.	J5	90
Peć, Yugo.	G7	26
Pecan Gap, Tx., U.S.	D3	122
Peçanha, Braz.	J4	88
Peças, Ilha das, i., Braz.	B13	92
Pecatonica, Il., U.S.	B8	120
Pecatonica, stm., U.S.	B8	120
Pečenga, Russia	B14	8
Pechenizhyn, Ukr.	A11	26
Pechora see Pečora, stm., Russia	C25	8
Pechora Bay see Pečorskaja guba, b., Russia	A8	32
Pečora, Russia	A9	32
Pečora (Pechora), stm., Russia	A8	32
Pecoraro, Monte, mtn., Italy	F10	24
Pečorskaja guba, b., Russia	A8	32
Pečorskoe more, Russia	A8	32
Pečory, Russia	C10	10
Pecos, N.M., U.S.	F3	128
Pecos, Tx., U.S.	C4	130
Pecos, stm., U.S.	F12	98
Pecos National Monument, p.o.i., N.M., U.S.	F3	128
Pécs, Hung.	C5	26
Pedana, India	C5	53
Pedasí, Pan.	I7	102
Pedder, Lake, res., Austl.	o12	77a
Peddie, S. Afr.	H8	70
Pededze, stm., Eur.	C10	10
Pedernales, Dom. Rep.	C12	102
Pedernales, Ven.	C10	86
Pedernales, stm., Tx., U.S.	D9	130
Pedernales, Salar de, pl., Chile	C3	92
Pedra Azul, Braz.	I5	88
Pedra Branca, Braz.	C6	88
Pedra Lume, C.V.	k10	65a
Pedras de Fogo, Braz.	D8	88
Pedras Salgadas, Port.	C3	20
Pedraza, Col.	B4	86
Pedregal, Ven.	B6	86
Pedreiras, Braz.	C3	88
Pedriceña, Mex.	C6	100
Pedro, Point, c., Sri L.	G5	53
Pedro Afonso, Braz.	E1	88
Pedro Avelino, Braz.	C7	88
Pedro Cays, is., Jam.	D9	102
Pedro Gomes, Braz.	G7	84
Pedro II, Braz.	C5	88
Pedro II, Ilha, i., S.A.	G5	86
Pedro Juan Caballero, Para.	D5	90
Pedro Leopoldo, Braz.	J3	88
Pedro Osório, Braz.	E11	92
Pedro R. Fernández, Arg.	D8	92
Pedro Velho, Braz.	C7	88
Peebles, Scot., U.K.	F9	12
Peebles, Oh., U.S.	F2	114
Pee Dee, stm., U.S.	A6	116
Peekskill, N.Y., U.S.	C12	114
Peel, I. of Man	G8	12
Peel, stm., Can.	B4	106
Peel Point, c., N.T., Can.	B17	140
Peel Sound, strt., Nu., Can.	A11	106
Peene, stm., Ger.	C9	16
Peerless, Mt., U.S.	F8	124
Peesane, Sk., Can.	A9	124
Peetz, Co., U.S.	G9	126
Pegasus Bay, b., N.Z.	F5	80
Pegnitz, Ger.	G7	16
Pegu, stm., Mya.	D3	48
Pegu Yoma, mts., Mya.	C2	48
Pegyš, Russia	E24	8
Pehlivanköy, Tur.	B9	28
Pehuajó, Arg.	G7	92
Peian see Bei'an, China	B10	36
Peiching see Beijing, China	B7	42
Peihai see Beihai, China	K3	42
Peikang, Tai.	J9	42
Peine, Ger.	D6	16
Peine, Pointe à, c., Dom.	j6	105c
Peinnechaung, i., Mya.	I14	54
Peip'ing see Beijing, China	B7	42
Peipus, Lake, l., Eur.	B10	10
Peiraiás (Piraeus), Grc.	F6	28
Peissenberg, Ger.	I7	16
Peixe, Braz.	G1	88
Peixe, Braz.	D6	90
Peixian, China	D7	42
Peixoto, Represa de, res., Braz.	K2	88
Pekalongan, Indon.	G6	50
Pekan, Malay.	K6	48
Pekanbaru, Indon.	C2	50
Pekin, Il., U.S.	D8	120
Pekin, In., U.S.	F11	120
Peking see Beijing, China	B7	42
Peklino, Russia	G16	10
Pekul'nej, hrebet, mts., Russia	C24	34
Pelabohan Klang, Malay.	K5	48
Pelabuhanratu, Indon.	G5	50
Pelagie, Isole, is., Italy	I6	24
Pelaihari, Indon.	E9	50
Pelat, Mont, mtn., Fr.	E12	18
Petczyce, Pol.	C11	16
Peledui, Russia	C20	32
Pelée, Montagne, vol., Mart.	k6	105c
Pelee, Point, c., On., Can.	G7	112
Pelee Island, i., On., Can.	G7	112
Pelega, Vârful, mtn., Rom.	D9	26
Peleliu see Beliliou, i., Palau	D9	44
Peleng, Pulau, i., Indon.	F7	44
Pelham, In., U.S.	D12	122
Pelham, Ga., U.S.	E1	116
Pelhřimov, Czech Rep.	G11	16
Pelican, Ak., U.S.	E12	140
Pelican Bay, b., Mb., Can.	B13	124
Pelican Lake, Wi., U.S.	F9	118
Pelican Lake, l., Mn., U.S.	E14	124
Pelican Lake, l., Mn., U.S.	B3	124
Pelican Lake, l., Mn., U.S.	C5	118
Pelican Rapids, Mb., Can.	B13	124
Pelican Rapids, Mn., U.S.	E2	118
Pelister Nacionalni Park, p.o.i., Mac.	B4	28
Peljekaise Nationalpark see Pieljekaise Nationalpark, p.o.i., Swe.	C6	8
Pelješac, Poluotok, pen., Cro.	H14	22
Pella, Ia., U.S.	B15	10
Pella, la., U.S.	C5	120
Péla, hist., Grc.	C5	28
Pell City, Al., U.S.	D12	122
Pellegrini, Arg.	H6	92
Pellegrini, Lago, l., Arg.	I4	92
Pello, Fin.	C11	8
Pellworm, i., Ger.	B4	16
Pelly, Sk., Can.	C12	124
Pelly, stm., Yk., Can.	C4	106
Pelly Bay, b., Nu., Can.	B12	106
Pelly Crossing, Yk., Can.	C3	106
Pelly Lake, l., Nu., Can.	B10	106
Pelly Mountains, mts., Yk., Can.	C4	106
Pelón de Ñado, mtn., Mex.	E9	100
Peloponnesus see Pelopónnisos, pen., Grc.	F5	28
Pelopónnisos, state, Grc.	F5	28
Pelopónnisos (Peloponnesus), pen., Grc.	F5	28
Pelotas, Braz.	E11	92
Pelotas, stm., Braz.	C12	92
Pelusium Bay see Tîna, Khalîg et, b., Egypt	G3	58
Pemadumcook Lake, l., Me., U.S.	E7	110

Name	Map Ref.	Page
Pemalang, Indon.	G6	50
Pemangkat, Indon.	C6	50
Pematangsiantar, Indon.	B1	50
Pemba, Moz.	C7	68
Pemba, Zam.	D4	68
Pemba, i., Tan.	F7	66
Pemberton, Austl.	F3	74
Pemberton, B.C., Can.	F8	138
Pembina, N.D., U.S.	C1	118
Pembina, stm., Ab., Can.	B16	138
Pembina, stm., N.A.	F16	124
Pembina Hills, hills, N.A.	E15	124
Pembroke, On., Can.	C12	112
Pembroke, Wales, U.K.	J7	12
Pembroke, Ga., U.S.	D4	116
Pembroke, Ky., U.S.	H10	120
Pembroke, Me., U.S.	F9	110
Pembroke, N.C., U.S.	B6	116
Pembroke, Cape, c., Nu., Can.	C14	106
Pembroke Pines, Fl., U.S.	K5	116
Pembrokeshire Coast National Park, p.o.i., Wales, U.K.	J7	12
Pembuang, Indon.	E7	50
Pembuang, stm., Indon.	D8	50
Pemigewasset, stm., N.H., U.S.	G5	110
Pemuco, Chile	H1	92
Penafiel, Port.	C2	20
Peñalara, Pico de, mtn., Spain	D6	20
Penalva, Braz.	B3	88
Penang see George Town, Malay.	J4	48
Peñaranda de Bracamonte, Spain	D5	20
Pen Argyl, Pa., U.S.	D10	114
Perijá, Serranía de, mts., S.A.	C5	86
Peñarroya-Pueblonuevo, Spain	F5	20
Peñas, Cabo de, c., Spain	A5	20
Penas, Golfo de, b., Chile	I2	90
Penasco, N.M., U.S.	E3	128
Pench National Park, p.o.i., India	H7	54
Pendembu, S.L.	H2	64
Pendembu, S.L.	H2	64
Pendências, Braz.	C7	88
Pendleton, In., U.S.	H4	112
Pendleton, Or., U.S.	E8	136
Pendleton, S.C., U.S.	B3	116
Pendolo, Indon.	E12	50
Pend Oreille, stm., N.A.	B9	136
Pend Oreille, Lake, l., Id., U.S.	B10	136
Pendžikent, Taj.	B10	56
Penebel, Indon.	H9	50
Penedo, Braz.	F7	88
Penetanguishene, On., Can.	D9	112
Peneus see Pineiós, stm., Grc.	D5	28
Penfield, Pa., U.S.	C7	114
Penganga, stm., India	H6	54
Penghu, China	I8	42
P'enghu Ch'üntao (Pescadores), is., Tai.	J8	42
P'enghu Shuitao, strt., Tai.	J8	42
Pengkou, China	I7	42
Penglai, China	C9	42
Pengpu see Bengbu, China	E7	42
Pengshui, China	G2	42
Pengwaluote Shan, mtn., China	B11	54
Pengxi, China	F1	42
Pengxian, China	E5	36
Pengze, China	G7	42
Penha, Braz.	C13	92
Penhsi see Benxi, China	D5	38
Penibética, Cordillera, mts., Spain	G8	20
Peniche, Port.	E1	20
Penicuik, Scot., U.K.	F9	12
Peninsular Malaysia see Semenanjung Malaysia, hist. reg., Malay.	K6	48
Peníscola, Spain	D11	20
Penki see Benxi, China	D5	38
Pennant Station, Sk., Can.	D7	124
Penne, Italy	H10	22
Penneru, stm., India	D4	53
Penn Hills, Pa., U.S.	C13	18
Pennines, mts., Eng., U.K.	G10	12
Pennington Gap, Va., U.S.	H2	114
Pennsboro, W.V., U.S.	E4	114
Pennsylvania, state, U.S.	C8	114
Penn Yan, N.Y., U.S.	B8	114
Penny Ice Cap, ice, Nu., Can.	B17	106
Penny Strait, strt., Nu., Can.	B6	141
Peno, Russia	D15	10
Penobscot, stm., Me., U.S.	F8	110
Penobscot, East Branch, stm., Me., U.S.	D8	110
Penobscot, West Branch, stm., Me., U.S.	D7	110
Penobscot Bay, b., Me., U.S.	F7	110
Penola, Austl.	K3	76
Peñón de Ifac see Penyal d'Ifac, misc. cult., Spain	F11	20
Penonomé, Pan.	H7	102
Penrhyn, at., Cook Is.	D11	72
Penrith, Austl.	I8	76
Penrith, Eng., U.K.	G10	12
Pensacola, Fl., U.S.	G11	122
Pensacola Bay, b., Fl., U.S.	G11	122
Pensacola Mountains, mts., Ant.	D36	81
Pense, Sk., Can.	D9	124
Pensilvania, Col.	E4	86
Pentagon Mountain, mtn., Mt., U.S.	C13	136
Pentecostes, Braz.	C6	88
Pentecost Island see Pentecôte, i., Vanuatu	j17	79d
Pentecôte (Pentecost Island), i., Vanuatu	j17	79d
Penticton, B.C., Can.	G11	138
Pentland, Austl.	C5	76
Pentland Firth, strt., Scot., U.K.	C9	12
Pentwater, Mi., U.S.	E3	112
Penuba, Indon.	D4	50
Peñuelas, P.R.	B2	104a
Penugan, Indon.	E4	50
Penukonda, India	D3	53
Penyal d'Ifac, misc. cult., Spain	F11	20
Penza, Russia	D7	32
Penzance, Eng., U.K.	K7	12
Penzberg, Ger.	I7	16
Penžina, stm., Russia	D21	34
Penžinskaja guba, b., Russia	D21	34
Penžinskij hrebet, mts., Russia	D22	34
Peoples Creek, stm., Mt., U.S.	F5	124
People's Democratic Republic of Korea see Korea, North, ctry., Asia	D7	38
Peoria, Az., U.S.	J4	132
Peoria, Il., U.S.	D8	120
Peoria Heights, Il., U.S.	K9	118
Peotone, Il., U.S.	H2	64
Pepin, Wi., U.S.	G6	118
Pepin, Lake, l., U.S.	G7	118
Peqin, Alb.	C13	24
Perabumulih, Indon.	E4	50

Name	Map Ref.	Page
Perak, state, Malay.	J5	48
Perak, stm., Malay.	J5	48
Perak, Kuala, b., Malay.	J5	48
Perales de Alfambra, Spain	D9	20
Peralillo, Chile	G2	92
Peralta, N.M., U.S.	I10	132
Perambalur, India	F4	53
Percé, Qc., Can.	B12	110
Perchas, P.R.	B2	104a
Perche, Collines du, hills, Fr.	F9	14
Percival Lakes, l., Austl.	D4	74
Percy Isles, is., Austl.	C8	76
Perdida, stm., Braz.	E2	88
Perdido, Monte, mtn., Spain	B10	20
Perdizes, Braz.	J2	88
Perdue, Sk., Can.	B6	124
Perechyn, Ukr.	H18	16
Pereež'na, Russia	G22	8
Pereira, Col.	E4	86
Perelazy, Russia	G14	10
Peremyšl', Russia	F18	10
Pereslavl'-Zalesskij, Russia	D21	10
Pérez, Arg.	F7	92
Pergamino, Arg.	F7	92
Pergamon, hist., Tur.	D10	28
Pergine Valsugana, Italy	D8	22
Perham, Mn., U.S.	E3	118
Péribonka, Qc., Can.	B4	110
Péribonka, stm., Qc., Can.	B5	110
Péribonka, Lac, l., Qc., Can.	E16	106
Perico, Arg.	B5	92
Pericumã, stm., Braz.	B3	88
Peridot, Az., U.S.	J6	132
Perigiraja, Indon.	D3	50
Périgord, hist. reg., Fr.	D6	18
Périgueux, Fr.	D6	18
Perija see Barîm, i., Yemen	C5	56
Peri-Mirim, Braz.	B3	88
Perito Moreno, Arg.	I2	90
Peritoró, Braz.	C3	88
Periyar, stm., India	F3	53
Periyar Tiger Reserve, India	G3	53
Perkasie, Pa., U.S.	D10	114
Perkins, Ok., U.S.	A2	122
Perlas, Archipiélago de las, is., Pan.	H8	102
Perlas, Laguna de, b., Nic.	F6	102
Perleberg, Ger.	C7	16
Perlez, Yugo.	D7	26
Perlis, state, Malay.	I5	48
Perm', Russia	C9	32
Përmet, Alb.	D14	24
Pernambuco, state, Braz.	E6	88
Pernik, Blg.	G10	26
Péronne, Fr.	E11	14
Perote, Mex.	F10	100
Perow, B.C., Can.	B4	138
Perpignan, Fr.	F9	18
Perrault Falls, On., Can.	A5	118
Perrin, Tx., U.S.	A9	130
Perrine, Fl., U.S.	K5	116
Perris, Ca., U.S.	J8	134
Perro, Laguna del, l., N.M., U.S.	G3	128
Perro, Punta del, c., Spain	H4	20
Perros, Bahía de, strt., Cuba	A8	102
Perros-Guirec, Fr.	F5	14
Perry, Fl., U.S.	F2	116
Perry, Ga., U.S.	C2	120
Perry, Ks., U.S.	E2	120
Perry, Mi., U.S.	B1	114
Perry, Mo., U.S.	E6	120
Perry, N.Y., U.S.	B7	114
Perry, Kap, c., Grnld.	B11	141
Perry Lake, res., Ks., U.S.	E2	120
Perrysburg, Oh., U.S.	C2	114
Perryton, Tx., U.S.	E8	128
Perryville, Ak., U.S.	E8	140
Perryville, Ar., U.S.	B6	122
Perryville, Ky., U.S.	G12	120
Perseverancia, Bol.	B4	90
Persia, Ia., U.S.	C2	120
Persia see Iran, ctry., Asia	C7	56
Persian Gulf, b., Asia	D7	56
Perth, Austl.	F3	74
Perth, On., Can.	D13	112
Perth, Scot., U.K.	E9	12
Perth Amboy, N.J., U.S.	D11	114
Perth Basin, unds.	L13	142
Peru, Il., U.S.	C8	120
Peru, In., U.S.	H3	112
Peru, Ne., U.S.	D2	120
Peru, N.Y., U.S.	F3	110
Peru, ctry., S.A.	E2	84
Peru Basin, unds.	I5	144
Peru-Chile Trench, unds.	K6	144
Perugia, Italy	G9	22
Perugorría, Arg.	D8	92
Peruíbe, Braz.	B14	92
Perušić, Cro.	F12	22
Pervomais'k, Ukr.	A17	26
Pervomajsk, Russia	I20	8
Pervomajskij, Russia	F15	10
Pervoural'sk, Russia	C9	32
Peryj Kuril'skij proliv, strt., Russia	F20	34
Pes', Russia	B17	10
Pesaro, Italy	G9	22
Pescadores see P'enghu Ch'üntao, is., Tai.	J8	42
Pescadores Channel see P'enghu Shuitao, strt., Tai.	J8	42
Pescara, Italy	H11	22
Pescara, stm., Italy	H11	22
Pescasseroli, Italy	C7	24
Pescia, Italy	G7	22
Pesé, Pan.	D1	86
Peshāwar, Pak.	B3	54
Peshkopi, Alb.	C14	24
Peshkopija see Peshkopi, Alb.	C14	24
Peshtigo, Wi., U.S.	C2	112
Peshtigo, stm., Wi., U.S.	F10	118
Peski, Bela.	G7	10
Pesočnoe, Russia	B22	10
Peso da Régua, Port.	C3	20
Pessac, Fr.	E5	18
Pest, state, Hung.	B6	26
Peštera, Blg.	G11	26
Pestovo, Russia	B18	10
Pëstraja Dresva, Russia	D20	34
Petacalco, Bahía, b., Mex.	G7	100
Petah Tiqwa, Isr.	F5	58
Petal, Ms., U.S.	F9	122
Petalcingo, Mex.	G12	100
Petalión, Kólpos, b., Grc.	F7	28
Petaluma, Ca., U.S.	E3	134
Petano, Ven.	B8	86
Petatlán, Mex.	G8	100
Petawawa, On., Can.	C12	112
Petén Itzá, Lago, l., Guat.	D2	102
Petenwell Lake, l., Wi., U.S.	G8	118
Peterborough, On., Can.	D11	112
Peterborough, Eng., U.K.	I12	12
Peterhead, Scot., U.K.	D11	12
Peter I Øy, i., Br. Vir. Is.	B31	81
Peter Isay, i., Ant.	B31	81
Peter Lake, l., Nu., Can.	C12	106
Peterlee, Eng., U.K.	G11	12
Peterman, Al., U.S.	F11	122

Name	Map Ref.	Page
Peter Pond Lake, l., Sk., Can.	D9	106
Phra Chedi Sam Ong, p., Asia	E4	48
Petersburg, Ak., U.S.	E13	140
Petersburg, Il., U.S.	K9	118
Petersburg, In., U.S.	F10	120
Petersburg, Tn., U.S.	B12	122
Petersburg, Tx., U.S.	H7	128
Petersburg, Va., U.S.	G8	114
Petersburg, W.V., U.S.	F6	114
Petersfield, Eng., U.K.	J12	12
Peterson, Ia., U.S.	B2	120
Peter the Great Bay see Petra Velikogo, zaliv, b., Russia	C9	38
Petília Policastro, Italy	E10	24
Pétion-Ville, Haiti	C11	102
Petit-Bourg, Guad.	h5	105c
Petitcodiac, N.B., Can.	E11	110
Petit Jean, stm., Ar., U.S.	B5	122
Petitot, stm., Can.	D6	106
Petit Piton, vol., St. Luc.	m6	105c
Petitsikapau Lake, l., Nf., Jord.	E17	106
Petlād, India	G4	54
Peto, Mex.	B3	102
Petoskey, Mi., U.S.	C5	112
Petra see Al-Batrā', hist., Jord.	H6	58
Petra Velikogo, zaliv (Peter the Great Bay), b., Russia	C9	38
Petre, Point, c., On., Can.	E12	112
Petrič, Blg.	H10	26
Petrified Forest National Park, p.o.i., Az., U.S.	I7	132
Petrila, Rom.	D10	26
Petrinja, Cro.	E13	22
Petričevo, Russia	E19	10
Petrodvorec, Russia	A12	10
Petrolândia, Braz.	E6	88
Petrólea, Col.	C5	86
Petrolia, Tx., U.S.	G10	128
Petrolina, Braz.	E5	88
Petrolina de Goiás, Braz.	I1	88
Petrona, Punta, c., P.R.	C3	104a
Petropavlovsk, Kaz.	D11	32
Petropavlovsk, Russia	F10	34
Petropavlovsk-Kamčatskij, Russia	F20	34
Petrópolis, Braz.	L4	88
Petroșani, Rom.	D10	26
Petrovac, Yugo.	E8	26
Petrovsk, Russia	D6	32
Petrovskij, Russia	H18	8
Petrovsk-Zabajkal'skij, Russia	F10	34
Petrozavodsk, Russia	F15	8
Petrusburg, S. Afr.	F7	70
Petrusville, S. Afr.	G7	70
Petrykau, Bela.	H11	10
Pettus, Tx., U.S.	F10	130
Petuhovo, Russia	C11	32
Peuerulak, Indon.	J3	48
Peusangan, stm., Indon.	J3	48
Pevek, Russia	C23	34
Peza, stm., Russia	D23	8
Pézenas, Fr.	F9	18
Pezinok, Slov.	H13	16
Pfaffenhofen, Ger.	H6	16
Pforzheim, Ger.	H4	16
Pfronten, Ger.	I6	16
Pfullendorf, Ger.	D7	22
Phagatak, Ger.	G4	16
Pha-an, Mya.	D3	48
Phalaborwa, S. Afr.	C10	70
Phalodi, India	E4	54
Phaltan, India	C2	53
Phan, Thai.	C4	48
Phanat Nikhom, Thai.	F5	48
Phangan, Ko, i., Thai.	H5	48
Phangnga, Thai.	H4	48
Phaniang, stm., Thai.	D6	48
Phan Rang, Viet.	G9	48
Phan Thiet, Viet.	G9	48
Phan Thong, Thai.	F5	48
Pharenda, India	E9	54
Pharr, Tx., U.S.	H9	130
Phat Diem, Viet.	B8	48
Phatthalung, Thai.	I5	48
Phayao, Thai.	C4	48
Phelps, Ky., U.S.	G3	114
Phelps, Wi., U.S.	E9	118
Phelps Lake, l., N.C., U.S.	I9	114
Phenix City, Al., U.S.	E13	122
Phepane, stm., S. Afr.	E6	70
Phet Buri, stm., Thai.	F4	48
Phetchabun, Thai.	D5	48
Phetchabun, Thiu Khao, mts., Thai.	D5	48
Phetchaburi, Thai.	F4	48
Phibun Mangsahan, Thai.	E7	48
Phichai, Thai.	D5	48
Phichit, Thai.	D5	48
Philadelphia, Ms., U.S.	E9	122
Philadelphia, N.Y., U.S.	D14	112
Philadelphia, Pa., U.S.	E10	114
Phil Campbell, Al., U.S.	C11	122
Philip, S.D., U.S.	C11	126
Philippeville see Skikda, Alg.	B6	64
Philippeville, Bel.	D13	14
Philippi, W.V., U.S.	E5	114
Philippi see Filippoi, hist., Grc.	B7	28
Philippine Basin, unds.	H15	142
Philippine Sea	H15	142
Philippine Trench, unds.	I15	142
Philippolis, S. Afr.	G7	70
Philip Smith Mountains, mts., Ak., U.S.	C10	140
Philipsburg, Sint M.	A1	105a
Philippsburg, Ger.	G4	16
Philipstown, S. Afr.	G7	70
Phillaur, India	C5	54
Phillip Island, i., Austl.	L5	76
Phillips, Me., U.S.	F6	110
Phillips, Tx., U.S.	F7	128
Phillips, Wi., U.S.	F8	118
Phillipsburg, Ga., U.S.	E2	116
Phillipsburg, N.J., U.S.	D10	114
Philo, Il., U.S.	E9	120
Philo, Oh., U.S.	E4	114
Philpots Island, i., Nu., Can.	C10	141
Phippsburg, Co., U.S.	C10	132
Phitsanulok, Thai.	D5	48
Phnom Penh see Phnum Pénh, Camb.	G7	48
Phnum Pénh (Phnom Penh), Camb.	G7	48
Phoenix, Az., U.S.	J4	132
Phoenix, N.Y., U.S.	E13	112
Phoenix, Or., U.S.	A3	134
Phoenix Islands, is., Kir.	D9	72
Phoenixville, Pa., U.S.	D10	114
Phon, Thai.	E6	48
Phong, stm., Thai.	D6	48
Phôngsali, Laos	B6	48

Name	Map Ref.	Page
Phon Phisai, Thai.	D6	48
Phrae, Thai.	C5	48
Phra Nakhon Si Ayutthaya, Thai.	E5	48
Phran Kratai, Thai.	D4	48
Phrom Phiram, Thai.	D4	48
Phu Cat, Viet.	E9	48
Phuket, Thai.	I4	48
Phuket, Ko, i., Thai.	I4	48
Phu Ly, Viet.	B7	48
Phum Duang, stm., Thai.	H4	48
Phumi Bǎ Khâm, Camb.	F7	48
Phumi Béng, Camb.	F7	48
Phumi Châmbâk, Camb.	G7	48
Phumi Chhuk, Camb.	G7	48
Phumi Chruŏy Sléng, Camb.	F8	48
Phumi Kâmpóng Srălau, Camb.	E7	48
Phumi Kâmpóng Trâbâk, Camb.	F7	48
Phumi Kaôh Kért, Camb.	G7	48
Phumi Khpôb, Camb.	G7	48
Phumi Lvéa Kraôm, Camb.	F6	48
Phumi Narŭng, Camb.	F7	48
Phumi Prêk Kǎk, Camb.	F7	48
Phumi Puŏk Châs, Camb.	F6	48
Phumi Sâmraông, Camb.	E6	48
Phumi Srê Kôkir, Camb.	F8	48
Phumi Tbêng, Camb.	F7	48
Phumi Thmâ Pôk, Camb.	F6	48
Phumi Tœk Chou, Camb.	F6	48
Phu My, Viet.	E9	48
Phuoc Long, Viet.	G8	48
Phuoc Long, Viet.	G8	48
Phu Pan National Park, p.o.i., Thai.	D6	48
Phu Quoc, Dao, i., Viet.	G6	48
Phu Tho, Viet.	B7	48
Phu Vang, Viet.	D8	48
Pi, stm., China	F7	42
Piacabuçu, Braz.	F7	88
Piacenza, Italy	E6	22
Pialba, Austl.	E9	76
Piancó, Braz.	D7	88
Pianosa, Isola, i., Italy	H12	22
Pianosa, Isola, i., Italy	H6	22
Piapot, Sk., Can.	E4	124
Piaseczno, Pol.	D16	16
Piaski, Pol.	E18	16
Piatã, Braz.	G5	88
Piatra-Neamț, Rom.	B13	26
Piauí, state, Braz.	D4	88
Piauí, stm., Braz.	D4	88
Piave, stm., Italy	E9	22
Piaxtla, stm., Mex.	D5	100
Piazza Armerina, Italy	G8	24
Pibor, stm., Sudan	F6	62
Pibor Post, Sudan	B12	118
Pica, stm., Cuba	A5	102
Picacho, Az., U.S.	K5	132
Picardie, hist., Fr.	E11	14
Picardy see Picardie, hist. reg., Fr.	E11	14
Picayune, Ms., U.S.	G9	122
Pichanal, Arg.	D4	90
Picher, Ok., U.S.	H3	120
Pichilemu, Chile	G1	92
Pichimá, Col.	E3	86
Pichi Mahuida, Arg.	I5	92
Pichincha, state, Ec.	H2	86
Pichucalco, Mex.	G12	100
Pickardville, Ab., Can.	B16	138
Pickens, Ms., U.S.	E9	122
Pickens, W.V., U.S.	F5	114
Pickensville, Al., U.S.	D10	122
Pickerel Lake, l., Mb., Can.	B14	124
Pickering, Eng., U.K.	G12	12
Pickering, On., Can.	E10	112
Pickle Lake, On., Can.	E12	106
Pickstown, S.D., U.S.	D14	126
Pickton, Tx., U.S.	D3	122
Pickwick Lake, res., U.S.	B11	122
Pico, mtn., C.V.	l10	65a
Pico, i., Port.	C3	60
Pico da Neblina, Parque Nacional, p.c.i., Braz.	G9	86
Pico de Orizaba, Parque Nacional, p.c.i., Mex.	F10	100
Pico de Orizaba, Volcán (Citlaltépetl, Volcán), vol., Mex.	F10	100
Picos, Braz.	D5	88
Picquigny, Fr.	E11	14
Picton, On., Can.	D12	112
Picton, N.Z.	E6	80
Picton, Isla, i., Chile	K3	90
Pictou Island, i., N.S., Can.	E14	110
Picture Butte, Ab., Can.	G18	138
Pictured Rocks National Lakeshore, p.o.i., Mi., U.S.	B3	112
Picuí, Braz.	D7	88
Picún Leufú, Arg.	G3	90
Pidälion, Akrotírion, c., Cyp.	C5	58
Pidhorodna, Ukr.	A17	26
Pidurutalagala, mtn., Sri L.	H5	53
Piedecuesta, Col.	D5	86
Piedimonte Matese, Italy	C8	24
Piedmont, Mo., U.S.	G7	120
Piedmont see Piemonte, state, Italy	F5	22
Piedra, stm., Co., U.S.	F9	132
Piedra, Cerro, mtn., Chile	H2	90
Piedra de Águila, Arg.	H3	90
Piedrafita, Puerto de, p., Spain	B3	20
Piedrahita, Spain	D5	20
Piedras, Punta, c., Arg.	G9	92
Piedras Blancas, Arg.	E8	92
Piedras Negras, Guat.	D2	102
Piedras Negras, Mex.	A8	100
Pieksämäki, Fin.	E12	8
Pielinen, l., Fin.	E13	8
Pieljekaise Nationalpark, p.o.i., Swe.	C6	8
Pienaarsrivier, S. Afr.	D8	70
Pieniężno, Pol.	B16	16
Pienięźny Park Narodowy, p.o.i., Pol.	G16	16
Pienza, Italy	G8	22
Pierce, Ne., U.S.	E15	126
Pierce City, Mo., U.S.	E14	128
Pierpont, S.D., U.S.	B15	126
Pierre, S.D., U.S.	C12	126
Pierre, Bayou, stm., La., U.S.	F5	122
Pierre, Bayou, stm., Ms., U.S.	E8	122
Pierre Part, La., U.S.	G7	122
Pierreville, Trin.	s13	105f
Pierz, Mn., U.S.	F4	118
Piešťany, Slov.	H13	16
Piešt'any, Slov.	H13	16
Pietarsaari, Fin.	E10	8
Pietermaritzburg, S. Afr.	F10	70
Pietrasanta, Italy	G7	22
Piet Retief, S. Afr.	E10	70
Pietrosu, Vârful, mtn., Rom.	B12	26
Pigeon, Mi., U.S.	E6	112
Pigeon, stm., U.S.	I2	114
Pigeon Forge, Tn., U.S.	I2	114
Pigeon Lake, l., Ab., Can.	C16	138
Pigeon Lake, l., On., Can.	D11	112
Pigeon Point, c., Trin.	r12	105f
Pigg's Peak, Swaz.	E10	70
Pigs, Bay of see Cochinos, Bahía de, b., Cuba	B7	102
Pigüé, Arg.	H6	92
Pihāri, India	E8	54

Name	Map Ref.	Page
Pihlajavesi, l., Fin.	F13	8
Pihtipudas, Fin.	E11	8
Pijijiapan, Mex.	H12	100
Pikälevo, Russia	A17	10
Pikangikum, On., Can.	E12	106
Pikes Peak, mtn., Co., U.S.	C3	128
Pikes Rocks, hill, Pa., U.S.	C6	114
Pikesville, Md., U.S.	E9	114
Piketberg, S. Afr.	H4	70
Piketon, Oh., U.S.	E2	114
Pikeville, Tn., U.S.	B13	122
Pikou, China	B10	42
Pikounda, Congo	D3	66
Pila, Pol.	C12	16
Pita, state, Pol.	C12	16
Pilanesberg Game Reserve, p.o.i., S. Afr.	D8	70
Pilão Arcado, Braz.	E4	88
Pilar, Arg.	E5	92
Pilar, Braz.	E8	88
Pilar, Para.	C8	92
Pilar de Goiás, Braz.	H1	88
Pilar do Sul, Braz.	A14	92
Pilares, Mex.	D3	130
Pilas Group, is., Phil.	G3	52
Pilawa, Pol.	D17	16
Pilcomayo, Brazo Norte, stm., Para.	D4	90
Pilcomayo, Brazo Sur del, stm., S.A.	B8	92
Pilcomayo, Parque Nacional, p.o.i., Arg.	B8	92
Pilger, Ne., U.S.	E15	126
Pilgrim's Rest, S. Afr.	D10	70
Pili, Phil.	D4	52
Pilibhīt, India	D7	54
Pilica, stm., Pol.	E16	16
Pilliga, Austl.	H7	76
Pilot, the, mtn., Austl.	K7	76
Pilot Butte, Sk., Can.	D9	124
Pilot Knob, Mo., U.S.	G7	120
Pilot Knob, mtn., Id., U.S.	E11	136
Pilot Mound, Mb., Can.	E15	124
Pilot Mountain, N.C., U.S.	H5	114
Pilot Peak, mtn., Nv., U.S.	B8	134
Pilot Peak, mtn., Wy., U.S.	F16	136
Pilot Rock, Or., U.S.	E8	136
Pilsen see Plzeň, Czech Rep.	G9	16
Pilu, stm., Mya.	B3	48
Pilzno, Pol.	G17	16
Pima, Az., U.S.	K7	132
Pimba, Austl.	F7	74
Pimenteira, Vereda, stm., Braz.	F4	88
Pimental, Braz.	B3	88
Pinang, Pulau, i., Malay.	J4	48
Pinarbaşı, Tur.	B16	28
Pinar del Río, Cuba	A5	102
Pinarello, Fr.	H15	18
Pinarhisar, Tur.	B10	28
Pinas, Arg.	E5	92
Pinatubo, Mount, vol., Phil.	C3	52
Pincher Creek, Ab., Can.	G17	138
Pinchi Lake, l., B.C., Can.	B6	138
Pinckneyville, Il., U.S.	F8	120
Pinconning, Mi., U.S.	E5	112
Pindale, Mya.	B2	48
Pindamonhangaba, Braz.	L3	88
Pindaré, stm., Braz.	B3	88
Pindaré-Mirim, Braz.	B3	88
Píndhos Óros (Pindus Mountains), mts., Grc.	D4	28
Pindi Gheb, Pak.	B4	54
Pindobaçu, Braz.	F5	88
Pindus Mountains see Píndhos Óros, mts., Grc.	D4	28
Pindwāra, India	F4	54
Pine, Az., U.S.	I5	132
Pine, stm., Mi., U.S.	E5	112
Pine Apple, Al., U.S.	F11	122
Pine Barrens, reg., N.J., U.S.	E11	114
Pine Bluff, Ar., U.S.	C7	122
Pine Bush, N.Y., U.S.	C11	114
Pine Castle, Fl., U.S.	H4	116
Pine City, Mn., U.S.	F6	118
Pine Creek, Austl.	B6	74
Pine Creek, stm., Nv., U.S.	C9	134
Pine Creek, stm., Pa., U.S.	C8	114
Pinega, Russia	D20	8
Pinega, stm., Russia	D20	8
Pine Grove, W.V., U.S.	E5	114
Pine Hill, Austl.	D6	76
Pine Hills, Fl., U.S.	H4	116
Pinehouse Lake, l., Sk., Can.	D10	106
Pinehurst, Ga., U.S.	D2	116
Pinehurst, Id., U.S.	C10	136
Pinehurst, N.C., U.S.	A6	116
Pinehurst Lake, l., Ab., Can.	B19	138
Pineland, Tx., U.S.	F4	122
Pine Island, Mn., U.S.	G6	118
Pine Island, i., Fl., U.S.	J3	116
Pine Island Bay, b., Ant.	C30	81
Pine Mountain, Ca., U.S.		
Pine Mountain, mtn., Ca., U.S.	H4	134
Pine Pass, p., B.C., Can.	A8	138
Pine Point, N.T., Can.	C8	106
Pine Ridge, S.D., U.S.	D10	126
Pine River, Mb., Can.	E14	124
Pine River, Mn., U.S.	E4	118
Pinerolo, Italy	F4	22
Pines, Isle of see Juventud, Isla de la, i., Cuba	B6	102
Pines, Lake O' The, res., Tx., U.S.	E4	122
Pine Swamp Knob, mtn., W.V., U.S.	E6	114
Pinetop-Lakeside, Az., U.S.	I6	132
Pinetown, S. Afr.	F10	70
Pinetown, S. Afr.	F10	70
Pine Valley, val., Ut., U.S.	E3	132
Pineville, Ky., U.S.	H2	114
Pineville, La., U.S.	F6	122
Pineville, Mo., U.S.	H3	120
Pineville, W.V., U.S.	G4	114
Pinewood, Sk., Can.	C5	116
Ping, stm., Thai.	D4	48
Pingba, China	H2	42
Pingbian, China	A7	48
Pingding, China	C5	42
Pingdingshan, China	E5	42
Pingdu, China	C8	42
Pingelap, at., Micron.	C7	72
Pingelly, Austl.	F3	74
Pingguo, China	J2	42
Pinghu, China	F9	42
Pingjiang, China	G5	42
Pingli, China	E3	42
Pingliang, China	D2	42
Pingluo, China	B2	42
Pingnan, China	J4	42
Pingquan, China	A7	42
Pingree, N.D., U.S.	H5	124
Pingshan, China	C2	42
Pingtan Dao, i., China	I8	42
P'ingtung, Tai.	J9	42
Pingwu, China	E5	36
Pingxiang, China	H5	42
Pingxiang, China	J2	42
Pingyang, China	H9	42
Pingyao, China	C5	42
Pingyi, China	D7	42
Pingyin, China	C7	42
Pingyuan, China	C6	42

Name	Map Ref.	Page
Pinhão, Braz.	F7	88
Pinheiro, Braz.	B3	88
Pinheiros, Braz.	J5	88
Pinhel, Port.	D3	20
Pini, Pulau, i., Indon.	E2	44
Pinillos, Col.	C4	86
Pinjarra, Austl.	F3	74
Pinjug, Russia	F22	8
Pinkiang see Harbin, China	B7	38
Pink Mountain, B.C., Can.	D6	106
Pinnacle, mtn., Va., U.S.	E7	114
Pinnacle Buttes, mtn., Wy., U.S.	G17	136
Pinnacles National Monument, p.o.i., Ca., U.S.	G4	134
Pinnaroo, Austl.	J3	76
Pinneberg, Ger.	C5	16
Pinos, Mex.	D8	100
Pinos, Isla de see Juventud, Isla de la, i., Cuba	B6	102
Pinos, Mount, mtn., Ca., U.S.	I6	134
Pinos Puente, Spain	G7	20
Pinrang, Indon.	E11	50
Pins, Île des, i., N. Cal.	n16	79d
Pins, Pointe aux, c., On., U.S.	F8	112
Pinsk, Bela.	H9	10
Pinsk Marshes see Pripet Marshes, reg., Eur.	H12	10
Pinson, Al., U.S.	D12	122
Pinta, Isla, i., Ec.	h11	84a
Pintada Arroyo, stm., N.M., U.S.	G3	128
Pintados, Chile	D3	90
Pintasan, Malay.	A10	50
Pinto Butte, mtn., Sk., Can.	H3	86
Pintoyacu, stm., Ec.	H3	86
Pin Valley National Park, p.o.i., India	C6	54
Pioche, Nv., U.S.	F2	132
Piombino, Italy	H7	22
Pioneer Mine, B.C., Can.	F8	138
Pionerskij, Russia	F3	10
Pionki, Pol.	E17	16
Piorini, stm., Braz.	D5	84
Piorini, Lago, l., Braz.	D5	84
Piotrków, state, Pol.	E15	16
Piotrków Trybunalski, Pol.	E15	16
Piove di Sacco, Italy	E8	22
Pío XII, Braz.	B3	88
Pipanaco, Salar de, pl., Arg.	D4	92
Pīpār, India	E4	54
Piparia, India	G6	54
Pīpar Road, India	E4	54
Pipe Spring National Monument, p.o.i., Az., U.S.	G4	132
Pipestem Creek, stm., N.D., U.S.	G14	124
Pipestone, Mn., U.S.	H2	118
Pipestone, stm., On., Can.	E12	106
Pipestone Creek, stm., Can.	E12	124
Pipestone National Monument, p.o.i., Mn., U.S.	G2	118
Pipinas, Arg.	G9	92
Piplān, Pak.	B3	54
Pipmuacan, Réservoir, res., Qc., Can.	A6	110
Piqua, Oh., U.S.	D1	114
Piquet Carneiro, Braz.	C6	88
Piquiri, stm., Braz.	B11	92
Pira, stm., Braz.	I1	88
Piracanjuba, Braz.	I1	88
Piracanjuba, stm., Braz.	I1	88
Piracicaba, Braz.	L2	88
Piracicaba, stm., Braz.	L1	88
Piracuruca, Braz.	B5	88
Pirae, Fr. Poly.	v21	78h
Piraeus see Peiraiás, Grc.	F6	28
Piraí do Sul, Braz.	B12	92
Piraju, Braz.	L1	88
Pirajuí, Braz.	L1	88
Piram Island, i., India	H4	54
Piran, Slvn.	E10	22
Pirané, Arg.	B8	92
Piranga, Braz.	K4	88
Piranhas, Braz.	G7	84
Piranhas, stm., Braz.	E1	88
Piranhas, stm., Braz.	C7	88
Piranji, stm., Braz.	C6	88
Pirapora, Braz.	I3	88
Pirapemas, Braz.	B3	88
Pirapora, Braz.	B13	92
Pirassununga, Braz.	K2	88
Pirata, Monte, hill, P.R.	B4	104a
Piratinga, stm., Braz.	H2	88
Piratini, Braz.	E11	92
Piratini, stm., Braz.	D10	92
Piratuba, Braz.	C11	92
Pires do Rio, Braz.	I1	88
Piriápolis, Ur.	G10	92
Pirin, Parki Narodowe, p.o.i., Blg.	H10	26
Piripiri, Braz.	C5	88
Piritu, Ven.	C7	86
Pirmasens, Ger.	G3	16
Pirna, Ger.	F9	16
Pirojpur, Bngl.	G12	54
Pirot, Yugo.	F9	26
Pirovano, Arg.	H7	92
Pirovskoe, Russia	C16	32
Pīr Panjāl Range, mts., Asia	B5	54
Pirtleville, Fin.	L7	132
Pirttikylä, Fin.	E9	8
Piru, Indon.	F8	44
Pisa, Italy	G7	22
Pisagua, Chile	C2	90
Pisco, Peru	F2	84
Pişcolt, Rom.	B9	26
Písek, Czech Rep.	G10	16
Pishan, China	A4	46
Pishchanka, Ukr.	A15	26
Pisinemo, Az., U.S.	K4	132
Pismo Beach, Ca., U.S.	H5	134
Pisticci, Italy	D10	24
Pistoia, Italy	G7	22
Pisuerga, stm., Spain	C6	20
Pit, stm., Ca., U.S.	B4	134
Pit, North Fork, stm., Ca., U.S.	B5	134
Pita, Gui.	G2	64
Pitalito, Col.	G4	86
Pitanga, Braz.	B12	92
Pitangui, Braz.	J3	88
Pitcairn, dep., Pit.	c28	78k
Piteå, Swe.	D9	8
Piteälven, stm., Swe.	D8	8
Piteşti, Rom.	E11	26
Pithapuram, India	C6	53
Pithiviers, Fr.	F11	14
Pithom, hist., Egypt	H2	58
Pithorāgarh, India	D8	54
Pitinga, stm., Braz.	H12	86
Pitiquito, Mex.	F6	98
Pitkjaranta, Russia	F14	8
Pitlar, Russia	C2	34
Pitomača, Cro.	D14	22
Pitrufquén, Chile	G2	90
Pitt Island, i., B.C., Can.	E5	106
Pitt Lake, l., B.C., Can.	B7	138
Pittsboro, N.C., U.S.	I6	114
Pittsburg, Ks., U.S.	G4	120
Pittsburg, Tx., U.S.	E4	122
Pittsburgh, Pa., U.S.	D6	114
Pittsfield, Il., U.S.	E7	120
Pittsfield, Me., U.S.	F7	110
Pittsfield, Ma., U.S.	B12	114
Pittsford, Mi., U.S.	C1	114
Pittsview, Al., U.S.	E13	122
Pittsworth, Austl.	F8	76
Pituil, Arg.	D4	92
Pium, Braz.	F1	88
Piura, Peru	E1	84
Piute Peak, mtn., Ca., U.S.	H7	134
Pivan', Russia	F16	34
Pivdennyy Buh, stm., Ukr.	A17	26
Pizarro, Col.	E3	86
Pizzo, Italy	F10	24
Pjakupur, stm., Russia	B13	32
Pjalka, Russia	C19	8
Pjandž (Panj), stm., Asia	B11	56
Pjaozero, ozero, l., Russia	C14	8
Pjasina, stm., Russia	B6	34
Pjasino, ozero, l., Russia	B6	34
Pjasinskij zaliv, b., Russia	B5	34
Pjatigorsk, Russia	F6	32
Pjatovskij, Russia	F19	10
Pjažievaja Sal'ga, Russia	F19	10
Placentia Bay, b., Nf., Can.	j23	107a
Placerville, Ca., U.S.	E5	134
Placetas, Cuba	A8	102
Plácido Rosas, Ur.	F11	92
Plai Mat, stm., Thai.	E6	48
Plain City, Ut., U.S.	B4	132
Plain Dealing, La., U.S.	E5	122
Plainfield, Ct., U.S.	C13	114
Plainfield, In., U.S.	I3	112
Plainfield, N.J., U.S.	D11	114
Plains, Ga., U.S.	E14	122
Plains, Ks., U.S.	D8	128
Plains, Mt., U.S.	C12	136
Plainview, Mn., U.S.	G6	118
Plainview, Ne., U.S.	E15	126
Plainview, Tx., U.S.	G7	128
Plainville, In., U.S.	F10	120
Plainwell, Mi., U.S.	F4	112
Plakhtïvka, Ukr.	C16	26
Plamondon, Ab., Can.	B18	138
Plampang, Indon.	H10	50
Plana, Czech Rep.	G8	16
Plana, L'Illa, i., Spain	F10	20
Planada, Ca., U.S.	F5	134
Planalto, Braz.	C11	92
Planchón, Cerro del (El Planchón, Volcán), vol., S.A.	G2	92
Planeta Rica, Col.	C4	86
Plano, Il., U.S.	C9	120
Plano, Tx., U.S.	D2	122
Plantagenet, On., Can.	E2	110
Plantation, Fl., U.S.	J5	116
Plant City, Fl., U.S.	I3	116
Plantersville, Ms., U.S.	C10	122
Plantsite, Az., U.S.	J7	132
Plaquemine, La., U.S.	G7	122
Plasencia, Spain	D4	20
Plaster Rock, N.B., Can.	D9	110
Plasy, Czech Rep.	G9	16
Plata, Isla de la, i., Ec.	H1	86
Plata, Río de la, est., S.A.	G9	92
Plato, Col.	C4	86
Platte, stm., U.S.	E3	120
Platte, stm., Ne., U.S.	C7	108
Platte, Île, i., Sey.	k13	69b
Platte Center, Ne., U.S.	F15	126
Platte City, Mo., U.S.	E3	120
Platteville, Co., U.S.	A4	128
Platteville, Wi., U.S.	B7	120
Plattsburgh, N.Y., U.S.	F3	110
Plattsmouth, Ne., U.S.	D2	120
Plau, Ger.	C8	16
Plauen, Ger.	F8	16
Plav, Yugo.	G6	26
Plavsk, Russia	G20	10
Playa Azul, Mex.	G7	100
Playa de Fajardo, P.R.	B4	104a
Playa de Guayanilla, P.R.	B2	104a
Playa de Naguabo, P.R.	B4	104a
Playa de Ponce, P.R.	C2	104a
Playa Noriega, Laguna, l., Can.	A3	100
Playa Vicente, Mex.	G11	100
Playgreen Lake, l., Mb., Can.	E11	106
Play Ku, Viet.	F8	48
Plaza, N.D., U.S.	F12	124
Pleasant, Mount, hill, N.B., Can.	E9	110
Pleasant Bay, N.S., Can.	D16	110
Pleasantdale, Sk., Can.	B9	124
Pleasant Grove, Ut., U.S.	C5	132
Pleasant Hill, Il., U.S.	E7	120
Pleasant Hill, Mo., U.S.	F3	120
Pleasanton, Ks., U.S.	F3	120
Pleasanton, Tx., U.S.	E9	130
Pleasantville, N.J., U.S.	E11	114
Pleasantville, Pa., U.S.	C6	114
Pleaux, Fr.	D8	18
Plehanovo, Russia	F20	10
Plenty, Sk., Can.	C5	124
Plenty, Bay of, b., N.Z.	C7	80
Plentywood, Mt., U.S.	F9	124
Plešceevo, ozero, l., Russia	D21	10
Pleseck, Russia	E19	8
Plessisville, Qc., Can.	D5	110
Pleszew, Pol.	E13	16
Plétipi, Lac, l., Qc., Can.	E16	106
Plettenberg Bay, S. Afr.	I6	70
Pleven, Blg.	F11	26
Plevna, Mt., U.S.	A8	126
Plitvička Jezera Nacionalni Park, p.o.i., Cro.	F12	22
Pljevlja, Yugo.	F6	26
Pljusković, Russia	H16	8
Pljussa, stm., Russia	A11	10
Płock, Pol.	D15	16
Płock, state, Pol.	D15	16
Plöckenstein, Fr.	G2	18
Ploieşti, Rom.	E12	26
Plomb du Cantal, mtn., Fr.	D8	18
Plomer, Point, c., Austl.	H9	76
Plön, Ger.	B6	16
Płońsk, Pol.	D16	16
Ploskoe, Russia	H21	10
Plotnica, Bela.	H9	10
Plouhalménezeau, Fr.	F4	14
Plovdiv, Blg.	G11	26
Plovdiv, state, Blg.	G11	26
Plumerville, Ar., U.S.	B6	122
Plummer, Id., U.S.	C9	136
Plumridge Lakes, l., Austl.	E5	74
Plumtree, Zimb.	B8	70
Plunge, Lith.	E4	10
Plutarco Elias Calles, (Presa, res.), Mex.	G8	98
Plymouth, Monts.	D3	105a
Plymouth, Eng., U.K.	K8	12
Plymouth, Ca., U.S.	E5	134
Plymouth, In., U.S.	G3	112
Plymouth, Ma., U.S.	C15	114
Plymouth, Ne., U.S.	A11	128
Plymouth, N.H., U.S.	G5	110
Plymouth, N.C., U.S.	I9	114
Plymouth, Oh., U.S.	C3	114
Plymouth, Pa., U.S.	C10	114
Plymouth, Wi., U.S.	E1	112
Plymouth Bay, b., Ma., U.S.	B15	114
Plzeň, Czech Rep.	G9	16
Pô, Burkina	G4	64
Po, stm., Italy	F8	22
Po, Foci del, mth., Italy	F9	22
Po, Mouths of the see Po, Foci del, mth., Italy	F9	22
Poarta Orientală, Pasul, p., Rom.	D8	26
Pobè, Benin	H5	64
Pobeda, gora, mtn., Russia	C18	34
Pobedino, Russia	G17	34
Pobedino, Russia	C18	34
Pobedy, pik, mtn., Asia	F13	32
Poblado Cerro Gordo, P.R.	A3	104a
Poblado Jacaguas, P.R.	B2	104a
Poblado Mediania Alta, P.R.	B4	104a
Poblado Santana, P.R.	B2	104a
Pobra de Trives, Spain	B3	20
Pocahontas, Ar., U.S.	H6	120
Pocahontas, Ia., U.S.	B3	120
Poção, Braz.	E7	88
Pocatello, Id., U.S.	H14	136
Počep, Russia	H16	10
Pocitos, Russia	D4	32
Pocitos, Salar, pl., Arg.	B4	92
Poço da Cruz, Açude, res., Braz.	E7	88
Poções, Braz.	H5	88
Pocola, Ok., U.S.	B4	122
Pocomoke City, Md., U.S.	F10	114
Poconé, Braz.	G6	84
Pocono Mountains, hills, Pa., U.S.	C10	114
Pocono Summit, Pa., U.S.	C10	114
Poço Redondo, Braz.	E7	88
Poço de Caldas, Braz.	K2	88
Pocrane, Braz.	J5	88
Podbereze, Russia	D13	10
Podborov'e, Russia	A18	10
Podčerem, Russia	E14	16
Poddore, Russia	C13	10
Poddębice, Pol.	E14	16
Poděbrady, Czech Rep.	F11	16
Podgorica (Titograd), Yugo.	G6	26
Podjuga, Russia	F19	8
Podkamennaja Tunguska, Russia	B16	32
Podkamennaja Tunguska, stm., Russia	B16	32
Podlasie, reg., Pol.	D19	16
Podol'sk, Russia	E20	10
Podor, Sen.	F2	64
Podporože, Russia	F16	8
Podravska, reg., Cro.	E15	22
Podtësovo, Russia	C16	32
Podujevo, Yugo.	G7	26
Poel, i., Ger.	B7	16
Poelela, Lagoa, l., Moz.	D12	70
Pofadder, S. Afr.	F4	70
Pogar, Russia	H16	10
Poggibonsi, Italy	G8	22
Pogoanele, Rom.	E13	26
Pogorelec Gorodišče, Russia	D17	10
Pogradec, Alb.	D14	24
Pogradec see Pogradec, Alb.	D14	24
Pogranicnyj, Russia	B9	38
P'ohang, Kor., S.	C2	40
Pohjanmaa, reg., Fin.	D11	8
Pohjois-Karjala, state, Fin.	E14	8
Pohnpei, i., Micron.	l11	78d
Pohri, India	F6	54
Pohvistnevo, Russia	D8	32
Põide, Est.	B6	10
Poinsett, Cape, c., Ant.	B16	81
Poinsett, Lake, l., S.D., U.S.	C15	126
Point, Tx., U.S.	E3	122
Point Arena, Ca., U.S.	E2	134
Point Au Fer Island, i., La., U.S.	H7	122
Point Baker, Ak., U.S.	E13	140
Pointe-à-la-Garde, Qc., Can.	B10	110
Pointe a la Hache, La., U.S.	H9	122
Pointe-à-Pitre, Guad.	h5	105c
Pointe-à-Pitre-le Raizet, Aéroport de, Guad.	h5	105c
Pointe du Canonnier, c., Guad.	A1	105a
Point Edward, On., Can.	E7	112
Pointe-Noire, Congo	E2	66
Pointe-Noire, Guad.	h5	105c
Point Fortin, Trin.	s12	105f
Point Hope, Ak., U.S.	C6	140
Point Jupiter, c., St. Vin.	p11	105e
Point Lake, l., N.T., Can.	B8	106
Point Marion, Pa., U.S.	E5	114
Point Pelee National Park, p.o.i., On., Can.	G7	112
Point Pleasant, N.J., U.S.	D11	114
Point Reyes National Seashore, p.o.i., Ca., U.S.	E2	134
Point Roberts, Wa., U.S.	B3	136
Point Salines International Airport, Gren.	q10	105e
Point Sapin, N.B., Can.	D12	110
Poisson Blanc, Lac du, res., Qc., Can.	B14	112
Poissy, Fr.	F10	14
Poitiers, Fr.	H9	14
Poitou, hist. reg., Fr.	C5	18
Poivre Atoll, i., Sey.	k12	69b
Pojarkovo, Russia	G14	34
Pojoaque Valley, N.M., U.S.	F2	128
Pojuca, Braz.	G6	88
Pojuca, stm., Braz.	G6	88
Pokaran, India	E3	54
Pokataroo, Austl.	G7	76
Pokhara, Nepal	D10	54
Poko, D.R.C.	D5	66
Pokrovsk, Russia	D14	34
Pokrovskoe, Russia	E5	32
Pola, stm., Russia	C14	10
Polacca Wash, stm., Az., U.S.	H6	132
Polack, Bela.	E11	10
Pola de Lena, Spain	A5	20
Pola de Siero, Spain	A5	20
Polan, Iran	D9	56
Poland, ctry., Eur.	D15	16
Polanów, Pol.	B12	16
Polatlı, Tur.	D15	28
Polcura, Chile	H2	92
Poldnevica, Russia	H21	8
Polebridge, Mt., U.S.	B12	136
Pol-e Khomrī, Afg.	B10	56
Polese see Pripet Marshes, reg., Eur.	H12	10
Polesella, Italy	E8	22
Polewali, Indon.	E11	50
Polgár, Hung.	B8	26
Poli, Cam.	C2	66
Poli, China	D8	42
Policastro, Golfo di b., Italy	E9	24
Police (Pölitz), Pol.	C10	16
Polička, Czech Rep.	G12	16
Polillo Islands, is., Phil.	C3	52
Polis, Cyp.	C3	58
Polist', stm., Russia	C14	10
Polistena, Italy	F10	24
Poljarnyj, Russia	B15	8
Poljarnyj, Russia	C24	34
Poljarnyj Ural, mts., Russia	A10	32
Polk, Ne., U.S.	F15	126
Polk, Pa., U.S.	C5	114
Polkowice, Pol.	E12	16
Pollāchi, India	F3	53
Pollau, Aus.	C12	22
Pollino, Monte, mtn., Italy	E10	24
Pollock, La., U.S.	F6	122
Pollock, S.D., U.S.	B12	126
Polnovo-Seliger, Russia	C15	10
Polo, Il., U.S.	B8	120
Polomet', stm., Russia	C15	10
Polonnaruwa, Sri L.	H5	53
Polonnaruwa, hist., Sri L.	H5	53
Polonne-Rybnoe, Russia	A13	26
Polotnjanyj, Russia	E19	10
Polski Trâmbeš, Blg.	F12	26
Polson, Mt., U.S.	C12	136
Poltava, Ukr.	E4	32
Poltava, Russia	D9	32
Poltimore, Qc., Can.	C14	112
Põltsamaa, Est.	B8	10
Poluj, stm., Russia	A11	32
Polučnoe, Russia	C18	34
Polur, India	E4	53
Põlva, Est.	B9	10
Polynesia, is., Oc.	J22	142
Polysaevo, Russia	F6	34
Pomarkku, Fin.	F9	8
Pombal, Braz.	D7	88
Pomerania, hist. reg., Eur.	C11	16
Pomeranian Bay, b., Eur.	B10	16
Pomeroy, S. Afr.	F10	70
Pomerode, Braz.	C13	92
Pomeroy, Ia., U.S.	B3	120
Pomeroy, Wa., U.S.	D9	136
Pomfret, S. Afr.	D6	70
Pomi, Rom.	B10	26
Pomme de Terre, stm., Mn., U.S.	F3	118
Pomme de Terre, stm., Mo., U.S.	G4	120
Pomme de Terre Lake, res., Mo., U.S.	G4	120
Pomona, Ca., U.S.	I8	134
Pomona, Ks., U.S.	F2	120
Pomona Lake, res., Ks., U.S.	F2	120
Pompano Beach, Fl., U.S.	J5	116
Pompei, hist., Italy	D8	24
Pompejevka, Russia	G15	34
Pompéu, Braz.	J3	88
Ponass Lakes, l., Sk., Can.	B9	124
Ponazyrevo, Russia	G22	8
Ponca, Ne., U.S.	B1	120
Ponca City, Ok., U.S.	E11	128
Ponca Creek, stm., U.S.	E14	126
Ponce, P.R.	B2	104a
Ponce, Aeropuerto, P.R.	B2	104a
Ponce de Leon, Fl., U.S.	G12	122
Poncha Pass, p., Co., U.S.	C2	128
Pond Creek, Ok., U.S.	E11	128
Ponderay, Id., U.S.	B10	136
Pondicherry (Puducheri), India	F4	53
Pondicherry, state, India	E5	53
Pond Inlet, Nu., Can.	A15	106
Pond Inlet, b., Nu., Can.	A15	106
Ponferrada, Spain	B4	20
Pongola, stm., S. Afr.	E10	70
Poniatowa, Pol.	E17	16
Ponizove, Russia	E14	10
Ponnaiyār, stm., India	E4	53
Ponnāni, India	F2	53
Ponnūru Nidubrolu, India	C5	53
Ponoj, Russia	C19	8
Ponoj, stm., Russia	C18	8
Ponoka, Ab., Can.	D17	138
Ponorogo, Indon.	G7	50
Pons, Fr.	D5	18
Ponta Delgada, Port.	C3	60
Ponta Grossa, Braz.	B12	92
Ponta Porã, Braz.	D5	90
Pontarlier, Fr.	H15	14
Ponta de Pecra, Braz.	D8	88
Pontassieve, Italy	G8	22
Pontchartrain, Lake, l., La., U.S.	G8	122
Pontchâteau, Fr.	G6	14
Ponte-de-Vaux, Fr.	C10	18
Ponte Alta do Bom Jesus, Braz.	G2	88
Ponte-Caldelas, Spain	B2	20
Ponte de Lima, Port.	C2	20
Pontedera, Italy	G7	22
Pontedeume, Spain	A2	20
Ponte do Púngoe, Moz.	A12	70
Ponteix, Sk., Can.	E6	124
Ponte Nova, Braz.	K4	88
Ponte Serrada, Braz.	C12	92
Pontevedra, Spain	B2	20
Pontevedra, co., Spain	B2	20
Pontiac, Mi., U.S.	B2	114
Pontiac, Il., U.S.	D9	120
Pontianak, Indon.	C6	50
Pontine Islands see Ponziane, Isole, is., Italy	D6	24
Pontivy, Fr.	F5	14
Pontoise, Fr.	E11	14
Pontotoc, Ms., U.S.	C9	122
Pontotoc, Tx., U.S.	D9	130
Pontremoli, Italy	F6	22
Pontresina, Switz.	D6	22
Pont-Rouge, Qc., Can.	D5	110
Ponts, Spain	C12	20
Pont-sur-Yonne, Fr.	F12	14
Pontus Mountains see Doğu Karadeniz Dağları, mts., Tur.	A5	56
Pontypridd, Wales, U.K.	J9	12
Ponyri, Russia	H19	10
Ponziane, Isole (Pontine Islands), is., Italy	D6	24
Poole, Eng., U.K.	K11	12
Pooley Island, i., B.C., Can.	D2	138
Poolville, Tx., U.S.	B10	130
Poopó, Bol.	C3	90
Poopó, Lago, l., Bol.	C3	90
Popayán, Col.	F3	86
Pope, Ms., U.S.	C8	122
Popesti-Leordeni, Rom.	E13	26
Popham Bay, b., Nu., Can.	C17	106
Popigaj, stm., Russia	B10	34
Popiltah Lake, l., Austl.	I3	76
Poplar, Mt., U.S.	F8	124
Poplar, stm., Can.	F8	124
Poplar, stm., N.A.	F8	124
Poplar, West Fork (West Poplar), stm., N.A.	F8	124
Poplar Bluff, Mo., U.S.	H7	120
Poplar Hill, On., Can.	E12	106
Poplar Point, Mb., Can.	D16	124
Poplarville, Ms., U.S.	G9	122
Popocatépetl, Volcán, vol., Mex.	F9	100
Popoh, Indon.	H7	50
Popokabaka, D.R.C.	F3	66
Popoli, Italy	H10	22
Popondetta, Pap. N. Gui.	b4	79a
Popovo, Blg.	F13	26
Poprad, Slov.	G16	16
Poprad, stm., Eur.	G16	16
Popricani, Rom.	B14	26
Póptong-ŭp, Kor., N.	E7	38
Poquoson, Va., U.S.	G9	114
Porangatu, Braz.	G1	88
Porbandar, India	H2	54
Porcos, stm., Col.	D3	90
Porcher Island, i., B.C., Can.	C5	106
Porco, Bol.	C3	90
Porcos, stm., Braz.	G3	88
Porcuna, Spain	G6	20
Porcupine, stm., N.A.	C3	106
Pordenone, Italy	D9	22
Pordim, Blg.	F11	26
Poreče, Russia	E18	10
Poreče-Rybnoe, Russia	D21	10
Porhov, Russia	C12	10
Pori (Björneborg), Fin.	F9	8
Poriadjangka, Russia	C15	8
Porlamar, Ven.	B10	86
Porog, Russia	E18	8
Poronajsk, Russia	G17	34
Porpoise Bay, b., Ant.	B17	81
Porreta Terme, Italy	F7	22
Porsanger, b., Nor.	A11	8
Porsangerhalvøya, pen., Nor.	A11	8
Porsgrunn, Nor.	G3	8
Porsuk, stm., Tur.	D13	28
Portachuelo, Bol.	C4	90
Port Adelaide, Austl.	J2	76
Portadown, N. Ire., U.K.	G6	12
Portage, Mi., U.S.	F4	112
Portage, Ut., U.S.	B4	132
Portage Bay, b., Mb., Can.	C15	124
Portage Lake, l., Mi., U.S.	D10	118
Portage la Prairie, Mb., Can.	E15	124
Portageville, Mo., U.S.	H8	120
Portal, Ga., U.S.	D4	116
Portal, N.D., U.S.	F11	124
Port Alberni, B.C., Can.	G6	138
Portalegre, Port.	E3	20
Portalegre, state, Port.	E3	20
Portales, N.M., U.S.	G5	128
Port Alfred, S. Afr.	H8	70
Port Alice, B.C., Can.	F3	138
Port Allen, La., U.S.	G7	122
Port Alma, Austl.	D8	76
Port Angeles, Wa., U.S.	B3	136
Port Antonio, Jam.	i14	104d
Port Aransas, Tx., U.S.	G10	130
Portarlington, Ire	H5	12
Port Arthur, Austl.	o13	77a
Port Arthur see Lüshun, China	E4	38
Port Askaig, Scot., U.K.	F6	12
Port Augusta, Austl.	F7	74
Port au Port Peninsula, pen., Nf., Can.	B17	110
Port-au-Prince, Haiti	C11	102
Port-au-Prince, Baie de, b., Haiti	C11	102
Port Austin, Mi., U.S.	D6	112
Port Blair, India	F7	46
Port Borden, P.E., Can.	D13	110
Port Byron, Il., U.S.	J8	118
Port Canning, India	G12	54
Port-Cartier, Qc., Can.	E17	106
Port Chalmers, N.Z.	G4	80
Port Charlotte, Fl., U.S.	J3	116
Port Clinton, Oh., U.S.	C3	114
Port Clyde, Me., U.S.	G7	110
Port Colborne, On., Can.	F10	112
Port Coquitlam, B.C., Can.	G8	138
Port-de-Paix, Haiti	C11	102
Port Dickson, Malay.	K5	48
Port Edward, S. Afr.	G10	70
Port Edward see Weihai, China	C10	42
Port Edwards, Wi., U.S.	G9	118
Port Elgin, N.B., Can.	D12	110
Port Elgin, On., Can.	D8	112
Port Elizabeth, S. Afr.	H7	70
Port-en-Bessin, Fr.	E8	14
Port Erin, I. of Man	G8	12
Porter, Tx., U.S.	G3	122
Porter Point, c., St. Vin.	o11	105e
Porterville, S. Afr.	H4	70
Porterville, Ca., U.S.	G7	134
Portete, Bahía, b., Col.	A6	86
Port Fairy, Austl.	L4	76
Port Gamble, Wa., U.S.	C4	136
Port-Gentil, Gabon	E1	66
Port Gibson, Ms., U.S.	F8	122
Port Graham, Ak., U.S.	E9	140
Port-Harcourt, Nig.	I6	64
Port Hardy, B.C., Can.	F3	138
Port Hawkesbury, N.S., Can.	E15	110
Port Hedland, Austl.	D3	74
Port Heiden, Ak., U.S.	E8	140
Port Hill, P.E., Can.	D13	110
Porthmadog, Wales, U.K.	I8	12
Port Hood, N.S., Can.	D15	110
Port Hope, On., Can.	E11	112
Port Hope, Mi., U.S.	E7	112
Port Huron, Mi., U.S.	B3	114
Portimão, Port.	G2	20
Port Isabel, Tx., U.S.	H10	130
Port Jervis, N.Y., U.S.	C11	114
Port Kembla, Austl.	J8	76
Port Lairge see Waterford, Ire.	I5	12
Portland, Austl.	I7	76
Portland, Austl.	L3	76
Portland, Ar., U.S.	D7	122
Portland, In., U.S.	H5	112
Portland, Me., U.S.	G6	110
Portland, N.D., U.S.	G16	124
Portland, Or., U.S.	E4	136
Portland, Tn., U.S.	H11	120
Portland, Tx., U.S.	G10	130
Portland, Bill of, c., Eng., U.K.	K10	12
Portland, Cape, c., Austl.	n13	77a
Portland, Isle of, i., Eng., U.K.	K10	12
Portland Bay, b., Austl.	L3	76
Portland Bight, b., Jam.	j13	104d
Portland Point, c., Jam.	j13	104d
Portlaoise, Ire.	H5	12
Port Lavaca, Tx., U.S.	F11	130
Port Leyden, N.Y., U.S.	E14	112
Port Lincoln, Austl.	F7	74
Port Loko, S.L.	H2	64
Port-Louis, Guad.	h5	105c
Port-Louis, Mrts.	h10	69a
Port-Lyautey see Kénitra, Mor.	C3	64
Port MacDonnell, Austl.	L3	76
Port Macquarie, Austl.	H9	76
Port Maria, Jam.	i14	104d
Port McNeill, B.C., Can.	F3	138
Port McNicoll, On., Can.	D10	112
Port Moller, Ak., U.S.	E8	140
Port Morant, Jam.	j14	104d
Portmore, Jam.	j13	104d
Port Moresby, Pap. N. Gui.	b4	79a
Port Morien, N.S., Can.	D17	110
Port Neches, Tx., U.S.	H4	122
Port Nelson, Mb., Can.	D12	106
Port Neuf, Qc., Can.	C3	64
Port Nolloth, S. Afr.	F3	70
Port Norris, N.J., U.S.	E10	114
Porto, Port.	C2	20
Porto Acre, Braz.	E4	84
Porto Alegre, Braz.	E12	92
Porto Alegre, S. Tom./P.	I6	64
Porto Amboim, Ang.	C1	68
Porto Calvo, Braz.	E8	88
Porto de Moz, Braz.	D7	84
Porto de Pedras, Braz.	E8	88
Porto dos Gaúchos, Braz.	F7	84
Porto Esperança, Braz.	G6	84
Porto Esperidião, Braz.	G6	84
Porto Feliz, Braz.	L1	88
Portoferraio, Italy	H7	22
Porto Ferreira, Braz.	K2	88
Port of Ness, Scot., U.K.	C6	12
Port of Spain, Trin.	s12	105f
Portogruaro, Italy	E9	22
Portola, Ca., U.S.	D5	134
Portomaggiore, Italy	F8	22
Porto Mendes, Braz.	B10	92
Porto Murtinho, Braz.	D5	90
Porto Nacional, Braz.	F1	88
Porto-Novo, Benin	H5	64
Port Orange, Fl., U.S.	G5	116
Port Orchard, Wa., U.S.	C4	136
Port Orford, Or., U.S.	H2	136
Porto San Giorgio, Italy	G10	22
Porto Santana, Braz.	D7	84
Porto Santo, i., Port.	C1	64
Porto Santo Stefano, ngh., Italy	H7	22
Porto Seguro, Braz.	I6	88
Porto Tolle, Italy	F9	22
Porto Torres, Italy	D2	24
Porto União, Braz.	C12	92
Porto Válter, Braz.	E3	84
Porto-Vecchio, Fr.	H15	18
Porto Velho, Braz.	E5	84
Portoviejo, Ec.	H1	86
Port Patrick, Vanuatu	m17	79d
Port Perry, On., Can.	D11	112
Port Pirie, Austl.	F7	74
Portree, Scot., U.K.	D6	12
Port Renfrew, B.C., Can.	H6	138
Port Rowan, On., Can.	F9	112
Port Royal, Jam.	j14	104d
Port Royal, Pa., U.S.	D8	114
Port Royal, S.C., U.S.	D5	116
Port Said see Būr Sa‘īd, Egypt	G3	58
Port Saint Joe, Fl., U.S.	H13	122
Port Saint Johns, S. Afr.	G9	70
Port Sanilac, Mi., U.S.	E7	112
Port Saunders, Nf., Can.	i22	107a
Portsea, Austl.	L5	76
Portsmouth, Eng., U.K.	K11	12
Portsmouth, N.H., U.S.	G6	110
Portsmouth, Oh., U.S.	F2	114
Portsmouth, Va., U.S.	H9	114
Portsoy, Scot., U.K.	D10	12
Port Stanley, On., Can.	F8	112
Port Sudan see Būr Sūdān, Sudan	D7	62
Port Sulphur, La., U.S.	H9	122
Port Talbot, Wales, U.K.	J9	12
Porttipahdan tekojärvi, l., Fin.	B12	8
Port Townsend, Wa., U.S.	B4	136
Portugal, ctry., Eur.	D3	20
Portugalete, Spain	A7	20
Portuguesa, state, Ven.	C7	86
Portuguesa, stm., Ven.	C8	86
Portuguese Guinea see Guinea-Bissau, ctry., Afr.	G1	64
Port Vila, Vanuatu	k17	79d
Portville, N.Y., U.S.	B7	114
Port-Vladimir, Russia	B15	8
Port Wentworth, Ga., U.S.	D4	116
Port Wing, Wi., U.S.	E7	118
Porus, Jam.	i13	104d
Porvenir, Chile	J2	90
Porvoo, Fin.	F11	8
Porzuna, Spain	E6	20
Posadas, Arg.	C9	92
Posadas, Spain	G5	20
Posavina, val., Eur.	E14	22
Pošehon'e, Russia	B22	10
Poseidon, Temple of, hist., Grc.	F6	28
Posen, Mi., U.S.	C6	112
Poshan see Boshan, China	C7	42
Posio, Fin.	C12	8
Poso, Indon.	D12	50
Poso, Danau, l., Indon.	D12	50
Poso, Teluk, b., Indon.	D12	50
Pospelikha, Russia	D14	32
Posse, Braz.	H2	88
Possession Island, i., Nmb.	E2	70
Possneck, Ger.	F7	16
Possum Kingdom Lake, res., Tx., U.S.	B9	130
Post, Tx., U.S.	A6	130
Posta de Jihuites, Mex.	I2	130
Postelle, Tn., U.S.	A1	116
Postmasburg, S. Afr.	F6	70
Postojna, Slvn.	E11	22
Postrervalle, Bol.	C4	90
Postville, Ia., U.S.	A6	120
Potaro, stm., Guy.	E12	86
Potaro-Siparuni, state, Guy.	E12	86
Potchefstroom, S. Afr.	E8	70
Poteau, Ok., U.S.	B4	122
Poteet, Tx., U.S.	E9	130
Potenza, Italy	D9	24
Potgietersrus, S. Afr.	D9	70
Poth, Tx., U.S.	E9	130
Potholes Reservoir, res., Wa., U.S.	D7	136
Poti, Geor.	F6	32
Potiraguá, Braz.	H6	88
Potiskum, Nig.	G7	64
Potomac, Il., U.S.	H2	112
Potomac, stm., U.S.	F8	114
Potomac, North Fork South Branch, stm., U.S.	F6	114
Potomac, South Branch, stm., U.S.	E7	114
Potomac Heights, Md., U.S.	F8	114
Potosí, Bol.	C3	90
Potosí, state, Bol.	D3	90
Potosí, Mo., U.S.	G7	120
Potrerillos, Chile	C3	92
Potro, Cerro del (El Potro, Cerro), mtn., S.A.	D3	92
Potsdam, Ger.	D9	16
Potsdam, N.Y., U.S.	E16	112
Potter, Ne., U.S.	F9	126
Potterville, Mi., U.S.	B1	114
Potts Camp, Ms., U.S.	C9	122
Pottstown, Pa., U.S.	D10	114
Pottsville, Pa., U.S.	D9	114
Pouancé, Fr.	G7	14
Poughkeepsie, N.Y., U.S.	C11	114
Poulan, Ga., U.S.	E2	116
Poulsbo, Wa., U.S.	C4	136
Poultney, Vt., U.S.	G3	110
Poum, N. Cal.	m14	79d
Pouso Alegre, Braz.	L3	88
Poúthisat, Camb.	F6	48
Poúthisat, stm., Camb.	F6	48
Poutini see Westland National Park, p.o.i., N.Z.	F3	80
Poutrincourt, Lac, l., Qc., Can.	A2	110
Považská Bystrica, Slov.	G14	16
Povenec, Russia	E16	8
Póvoa de Varzim, Port.	C2	20
Povorino, Russia	D6	32
Povorotnyj, mys, c., Russia	C10	38
Povungnituk, Qc., Can.	C15	106
Powassan, On., Can.	B10	112
Poway, Ca., U.S.	K9	134
Powder, stm., Or., U.S.	F9	136
Powder, South Fork, stm., Wy., U.S.	D6	126
Powderly, Tx., U.S.	D3	122
Powell, Oh., U.S.	C2	114
Powell, Wy., U.S.	C5	126
Powell, Lake, res., U.S.	F6	132
Powell, Mount, mtn., Co., U.S.	D4	128
Powell Creek, stm., Austl.	C6	74
Powell Lake, l., B.C., Can.	F6	138
Powell River, B.C., Can.	G6	138
Powers, Or., U.S.	C2	134
Powers Lake, N.D., U.S.	F11	124
Powhatan, Va., U.S.	G7	114
Powhatan Point, Oh., U.S.	E4	114
Poxoréu, Braz.	G7	84

Name	Map Ref.	Page

Column 1

Poya, N. Cal. ... m15 79c
Poyang Hu, l., China ... G7 42
Poyen, Ar., U.S. ... C6 122
Poygan, Lake, l., Wi., U.S. ... G9 118
Poza Rica de Hidalgo, Mex. ... E10 100
Požarevac, Yugo. ... E8 26
Poza Rica de Hidalgo, Mex. ... E10 100
Požega, Cro. ... E14 22
Požega, Yugo. ... F7 26
Poznań, Pol. ... D12 16
Poznań, state, Pol. ... D12 16
Pozoblanco, Spain ... F6 20
Pozo-Cañada, Spain ... F9 20
Pozo del Molle, Arg. ... F6 92
Pozo del Tigre, Arg. ... B7 92
Pozuelos, Ven. ... B9 86
Pozzallo, Italy ... H8 24
Pozzuoli, Italy ... D8 24
Prachatice, Czech Rep. ... G10 16
Prachin Buri, Thai. ... E5 48
Prachuap Khiri Khan, Thai. ... G4 48
Pradera, Col. ... F3 86
Prado, Braz. ... I6 88
Prados, Braz. ... K3 88
Præstø, Den. ... A8 16
Prague see Praha, Czech Rep. ... F10 16
Prague, Ne., U.S. ... F16 126
Prague, Ok., U.S. ... B2 122
Praha (Prague), Czech Rep. ... F10 16
Praha, state, Czech Rep. ... F10 16
Praha, mtn., Czech Rep. ... G9 16
Prahova, state, Rom. ... D13 26
Prahova, stm., Rom. ... E13 26
Praia, C.V. ... I10 65a
Praia Grande, Braz. ... D13 92
Prainha Nova, Braz. ... E5 84
Prairie, Austl. ... C5 76
Prairie, stm., Mi., U.S. ... G4 112
Prairie City, Il., U.S. ... D7 120
Prairie City, Ia., U.S. ... C4 120
Prairie Creek, stm., Ne., U.S. ... F15 126
Prairie Dog Creek, stm., Ks., U.S. ... B8 128
Prairie du Chien, Wi., U.S. ... A6 120
Prairie du Sac, Wi., U.S. ... H9 118
Prairie River, Sk., Can. ... B11 124
Prairies, Coteau des, hills, U.S. ... C16 126
Prairies, Lake of the, res., Can. ... C12 124
Prairie View, Tx., U.S. ... G3 122
Prairie Village, Ks., U.S. ... B14 128
Pran Buri, Thai. ... F4 48
Pran Buri, stm., Thai. ... F4 48
Prānhita, stm., India ... B5 53
Praslin, i., Sey. ... j13 69b
Prasonísi, Akra, c., Grc. ... H10 28
Praszka, Pol. ... E14 16
Prata, Braz. ... J1 88
Prata, stm., Braz. ... J1 88
Prata, stm., Braz. ... I2 88
Pratāpgarh, India ... F5 54
Pratápolis, Braz. ... K2 88
Pratas Island see Tungsha Tao, i., Tai. ... K7 42
Prat de Llobregat see El Prat de Llobregat, Spain ... C12 20
Prato, Italy ... G8 22
Pratt, Ks., U.S. ... D10 128
Prattville, Al., U.S. ... E12 122
Pratudão, stm., Braz. ... H3 88
Pravdinskij, Russia ... D20 10
Pravia, Spain ... A4 20
Praya, Indon. ... H10 50
Preajba, Rom. ... E12 26
Prečistoe, Russia ... G19 8
Predeal, Rom. ... D12 26
Preeceville, Sk., Can. ... C11 124
Preetz, Ger. ... B6 16
Pregolja, stm., Russia ... F3 10
Pregonero, Ven. ... D6 86
Preguiças, stm., Braz. ... B4 88
Prêla, Lith. ... E4 10
Prêk Poûthi, Camb. ... G7 48
Prelate, Sk., Can. ... D4 124
Premnitz, Ger. ... D8 16
Premont, Tx., U.S. ... G9 130
Premuda, Otok, i., Cro. ... F11 22
Prenjasi see Prrenjas, Alb. ... C14 24
Prentiss, Ms., U.S. ... F9 122
Prenzlau, Ger. ... C9 16
Preobraženie, Russia ... C10 38
Preparis Island, i., Mya. ... F7 46
Preparis North Channel, strt., Mya. ... E7 46
Preparis South Channel, strt., Mya. ... F7 46
Přerov, Czech Rep. ... G13 16
Prescott, On., Can. ... D14 112
Prescott, Az., U.S. ... I4 132
Prescott, Ar., U.S. ... D5 122
Prescott, Wi., U.S. ... G6 118
Prescott Island, i., Nu., Can. ... A11 106
Presidencia de la Plaza, Arg. ... C7 92
Presidencia Roca, Arg. ... C8 92
Presidencia Roque Sáenz Peña, Arg. ... C7 92
Presidente Dutra, Braz. ... C3 88
Presidente Epitácio, Braz. ... D6 90
Presidente Hayes, state, Para. ... B8 92
Presidente Prudente, Braz. ... D6 90
Presidio, Tx., U.S. ... E5 130
Presidio, stm., Mex. ... D6 100
Presnogor'kovka, Kaz. ... D11 32
Prešov, Slov. ... H17 16
Prespa, lake, l., Eur. ... D14 24
Presque Isle, Me., U.S. ... D8 110
Presque Isle, pen., Pa., U.S. ... B5 114
Prestea, Ghana ... H4 64
Preston, Eng., U.K. ... H10 12
Preston, Id., U.S. ... A5 132
Preston, Ia., U.S. ... B7 120
Preston, Ks., U.S. ... D10 128
Preston, Mn., U.S. ... H6 118
Prestonsburg, Ky., U.S. ... G3 114
Prestwick, Scot., U.K. ... F8 12
Preto, stm., Braz. ... I9 86
Preto, stm., Braz. ... I2 88
Preto, stm., Braz. ... B4 88
Preto, stm., Braz. ... G1 88
Preto, stm., Braz. ... K1 88
Preto, stm., Braz. ... L4 88
Preto do Igapó-açu, stm., Braz. ... E5 84
Pretoria, S. Afr. ... E9 70
Pretty Prairie, Ks., U.S. ... D10 128
Préveza, Grc. ... E3 28
Prey Lvéa, Camb. ... G7 48
Prey Vêng, Camb. ... G8 48
Pribilof Islands, is., Ak., U.S. ... E5 140
Priboj, Yugo. ... F6 26
Příbram, Czech Rep. ... G10 16
Price, Ut., U.S. ... D6 132
Price, stm., Ut., U.S. ... D6 132
Price Island, i., B.C., Can. ... D2 138
Prichard, Al., U.S. ... G10 122
Prickly Pear Cays, is., Anguilla ... A1 105a
Priddy, Tx., U.S. ... C9 130
Priego de Córdoba, Spain ... G6 20
Priekule, Lat. ... D4 10
Priekule, Lith. ... E4 10
Prieska, S. Afr. ... F6 70
Priest, Lake, l., Id., U.S. ... B10 136
Priest Lake, res., Id., U.S. ... B9 136
Priest River, Id., U.S. ... B10 136
Prieta, Peña, mtn., Spain ... A6 20
Prieto Díaz, Phil. ... D5 52
Prievidza, Slov. ... H14 16
Prijedor, Bos. ... E3 26

Column 2

Prilep, Mac. ... B4 28
Priluki, Russia ... A22 10
Primeira Cruz, Braz. ... B4 88
Primera, Tx., U.S. ... H10 130
Primera, stm., Arg. ... E6 92
Primero, stm., Arg. ... E6 92
Primghar, Ia., U.S. ... A2 120
Primorsk, Russia ... F13 8
Primorskij, Russia ... C9 38
Primorskij hrebet, mts., Russia ... F10 34
Primorsko, Bul. ... G14 26
Primrose Lake, l., Can. ... E9 106
Prince Albert, Sk., Can. ... A8 124
Prince Albert, S. Afr. ... H6 70
Prince Albert Sound, strt., N.T., Can. ... A7 106
Prince Alfred, Cape, c., N.T., Can. ... B15 140
Prince Charles Island, i., Nu., Can. ... B15 106
Prince Charles Mountains, mts., Ant. ... C11 81
Prince Edward Island, state, Can. ... D13 110
Prince Edward Island, i., P.E., Can. ... F18 106
Prince Edward Island National Park, p.o.i., P.E., Can. ... D13 110
Prince Frederick, Md., U.S. ... F9 114
Prince George, B.C., Can. ... C8 138
Prince George, Va., U.S. ... G8 114
Prince Gustaf Adolf Sea, Can. ... B4 141
Prince of Wales Island, i., Austl. ... B8 74
Prince of Wales Island, i., Nu., Can. ... A11 106
Prince of Wales Island, i., Ak., U.S. ... E13 140
Prince of Wales Strait, strt., N.T., Can. ... B15 140
Prince Olav Coast, cst., Ant. ... B9 81
Prince Patrick Island, i., N.T., Can. ... A16 140
Prince Regent Inlet, b., Nu., Can. ... A12 106
Prince Rupert, B.C., Can. ... E4 106
Prince Rupert Bluff Point, c., Dom. ... i5 105c
Princes Islands see Kizil Adalar, is., Tur. ... C11 28
Princess Anne, Md., U.S. ... F10 114
Princess Astrid Coast, cst., Ant. ... C6 81
Princess Charlotte Bay, b., Austl. ... B8 74
Princess Martha Coast, cst., Ant. ... C4 81
Princess Ragnhild Coast, cst., Ant. ... C7 81
Princess Royal Island, i., B.C., Can. ... C1 138
Princeton Town, Trin. ... s12 105f
Princeton, B.C., Can. ... G10 138
Princeton, Ca., U.S. ... D3 134
Princeton, In., U.S. ... F10 120
Princeton, Ky., U.S. ... G9 120
Princeton, Me., U.S. ... E9 110
Princeton, N.C., U.S. ... A7 116
Princeton, N.J., U.S. ... D11 114
Princeton, W.V., U.S. ... G4 114
Princeton, Wi., U.S. ... H9 118
Princeville, Qc., Can. ... D4 110
Princeville, Il., U.S. ... D8 120
Prince William Sound, strt., Ak., U.S. ... D10 140
Príncipe, i., S. Tom./P. ... I6 64
Príncipe da Beira, Braz. ... F5 84
Pineville, Or., U.S. ... F6 136
Pringsewu, Indon. ... F4 50
Prinses Margrietkanaal, can., Neth. ... A14 14
Prins Karls Forland, i., Nor. ... B27 141
Prinzapolka, stm., Nic. ... F5 102
Priozërnyj, Kaz. ... E14 32
Priozersk, Russia ... F14 8
Priozersk, Russia ... F14 8
Pripet (Prypjac'), stm., Eur. ... H10 10
Pripet Marshes, reg., Eur. ... H12 10
Pripoljarnyj Ural, mts., Russia ... A9 32
Priština, Yugo. ... G8 26
Pritchett, Co., U.S. ... D6 128
Pritzwalk, Ger. ... C8 16
Privas, Fr. ... E10 18
Priverno, Italy ... C7 24
Privodino, Russia ... F22 8
Privolno, Russia ... G7 26
Prižala, Russia ... F15 8
Probolinggo, Indon. ... G8 50
Probstzella, Ger. ... F7 16
Procida, Isola di, i., Italy ... D7 24
Proctor, Mn., U.S. ... E6 118
Proctor Lake, res., Tx., U.S. ... C9 130
Prodatūr, India ... D4 53
Proença-a-Nova, Port. ... E2 20
Progreso, Mex. ... B8 100
Progreso, Mex. ... B3 102
Progreso, Ur. ... G9 92
Prohladnyj, Russia ... F6 32
Project City, Ca., U.S. ... C3 134
Prokopevsk, Russia ... D15 32
Prokuplje, Yugo. ... F8 26
Proletarskij, Russia ... E20 10
Prome (Pyè), Mya. ... C2 48
Pronja, stm., Bela. ... G14 10
Pronja, stm., Russia ... F21 10
Prony, Baie de, b., N. Cal. ... n16 79d
Prophet, stm., B.C., Can. ... D6 106
Prophetstown, Il., U.S. ... C8 120
Propriá, Braz. ... F7 88
Proserpine, Austl. ... C7 76
Prosna, stm., Pol. ... E14 16
Prospect, Oh., U.S. ... D2 114
Prosperidad, Phil. ... F5 52
Prosser, Wa., U.S. ... D7 136
Prostějov, Czech Rep. ... G12 16
Proston, Austl. ... F8 76
Protem, S. Afr. ... I5 70
Provadija, Blg. ... F14 26
Prøven (Kangersuatsiaq), Grnld. ... C14 141
Providence, hist. reg., Fr. ... F12 18
Providence, R.I., U.S. ... G10 120
Providence, Ut., U.S. ... B5 132
Providence, Atoll de, i., Sey. ... k12 69a
Providence, Cape, c., N.Z. ... H2 80
Providence, Mass. ... G4 130
Providence, Isla de, i., Col. ... F7 102
Providenciales, i., T./C. Is. ... B11 102
Provincetown, Ma., U.S. ... B15 114
Provins, Fr. ... F12 14
Provo, Ut., U.S. ... C5 132
Provost, Ab., Can. ... B3 124

Column 3

Pružany, Bela. ... H7 10
Prydz Bay, b., Ant. ... B12 81
Pryluky, Ukr. ... D4 32
Pryor, Ok., U.S. ... H2 120
Przasnysz, Pol. ... D16 16
Przedbórz, Pol. ... E15 16
Przemyśl, Pol. ... G18 16
Przemyśl, state, Pol. ... F18 16
Przeworsk, Pol. ... F18 16
Pszczná, Grc. ... E6 28
Pskov, Russia ... C11 10
Pskov, Lake, l., Eur. ... B11 10
Pskovskaja oblast', co., Russia ... C11 10
Pszczyna, Pol. ... G14 16
Ptolemaida, Grc. ... C4 28
Ptuj, Slvn. ... D12 22
Pualam, Cape, c., N.T., ... A7 106
Puakatike, Volcán, vol., Chile ... e30 78l
Puán, Arg. ... H6 92
Pucallpa, Peru ... E3 84
Pučeveem, stm., Russia ... C23 34
Pučež, Russia ... H20 8
Pucheng, China ... H8 42
Pucheng, China ... D3 42
Púchov, Slov. ... G14 16
Pučišča, Cro. ... G13 22
Pudasjärvi, Fin. ... D12 8
Pudož, Russia ... F17 8
Puduari, stm., Braz. ... I11 86
Puducheri see Pondicherry, India ... F4 53
Pudukkottai, India ... F4 53
Puebla, state, Mex. ... F10 100
Puebla de Don Fadrique, Spain ... G8 20
Puebla de Sanabria, Spain ... B4 20
Puebla de Zaragoza, Mex. ... F9 100
Pueblito, Mex. ... E2 130
Pueblito de Ponce, P.R. ... B1 104a
Pueblo, Co., U.S. ... C4 128
Pueblonuevo, Col. ... C4 86
Pueblo Nuevo, P.R. ... B2 104a
Pueblo Nuevo, Ven. ... B7 86
Pueblo Viejo, Laguna, l., Mex. ... D10 100
Pueblo Yaqui, Mex. ... B4 100
Pueblos Caldelas see Ponte-Caldelas, Spain ... B2 20
Puente del Arzobispo, Spain ... E5 20
Puentedeume see Pontedeume, Spain ... A2 20
Puente Genil, Spain ... G6 20
Puerca, Punta, c., P.R. ... B4 104a
Puerco, Punta, c., P.R. ... B4 104a
Puerco, stm., U.S. ... I7 132
Puerco, stm., N.M., U.S. ... I10 132
Puerto Acosta, Bol. ... C3 90
Puerto Adela, Para. ... B10 92
Puerto Aisén, Chile ... I2 90
Puerto Alegre, Bol. ... B4 90
Puerto Ángel, Mex. ... H10 100
Puerto Arista, Mex. ... H11 100
Puerto Armuelles, Pan. ... H6 102
Puerto Asís, Col. ... G3 86
Puerto Ayacucho, Ven. ... E8 86
Puerto Baquerizo Moreno, Ec. ... i12 84a
Puerto Barrios, Guat. ... E3 102
Puerto Bermúdez, Peru ... F3 84
Puerto Berrío, Col. ... D4 86
Puerto Bolívar, Ec. ... A5 86
Puerto Boyacá, Col. ... E4 86
Puerto Cabello, Ven. ... B7 86
Puerto Cabezas, Nic. ... F6 102
Puerto Carreño, Col. ... D8 86
Puerto Chicama, Peru ... E2 84
Puerto Colombia, Col. ... B4 86
Puerto Cortés, Hond. ... E3 102
Puerto Cumarebo, Ven. ... I3 90
Puerto Deseado, Arg. ... I3 90
Puerto Escondido, Mex. ... H10 100
Puerto Escondido, c., Ven. ... p20 104g
Puerto Esperanza, Arg. ... B10 92
Puerto Fonciere, Para. ... D5 90
Puerto Francisco de Orellana, Ec. ... H3 86
Puerto Heath, Bol. ... B3 90
Puerto Iguazú, Arg. ... B10 92
Puerto Ingeniero Ibáñez, Chile ... I2 90
Puerto Inírida, Col. ... F7 86
Puerto Juárez, Mex. ... B4 102
Puerto la Cruz, Ven. ... B9 86
Puerto Leguízamo, Col. ... H4 86
Puerto Libertad, Mex. ... G6 98
Puerto Limón, Col. ... F5 86
Puerto Limón, C.R. ... G6 102
Puertollano, Spain ... F6 20
Puerto Lobos, Arg. ... H4 90
Puerto López, Col. ... E5 86
Puerto Madero, Mex. ... H12 100
Puerto Madryn, Arg. ... H3 90
Puerto Maldonado, Peru ... F4 84
Puerto Montt, Chile ... H2 90
Puerto Morelos, Mex. ... B4 102
Puerto Natales, Chile ... J2 90
Puerto Padre, Cuba ... B9 102
Puerto Páez, Ven. ... D8 86
Puerto Palmer, Pico, mtn., Mex. ... G6 130
Puerto Peñasco, Mex. ... F6 98
Puerto Pinasco, Para. ... D5 90
Puerto Pirámides, Arg. ... H4 90
Puerto Piray, Arg. ... C10 92
Puerto Pírítu, Ven. ... B9 86
Puerto Plata, Dom. Rep. ... C12 102
Puerto Princesa, Phil. ... F2 52
Puerto Real, P.R. ... B1 104a
Puerto Real, Spain ... H4 20
Puerto Rico, Arg. ... C10 92
Puerto Rico, Bol. ... B3 90
Puerto Rico, Col. ... G4 86
Puerto Rico, dep., N.A. ... k3 104a
Puerto Rico Trench, unds. ... G7 144
Puerto Rondón, Col. ... D6 86
Puerto San Julián, Arg. ... I3 90
Puerto Santa Cruz, Arg. ... J3 90
Puerto Sastre, Para. ... D5 90
Puerto Suárez, Bol. ... C5 90
Puerto Tejada, Col. ... F3 86
Puerto Tolosa, Col. ... F3 86
Puerto Umbría, Col. ... G3 86
Puerto Vallarta, Mex. ... E6 100
Puerto Varas, Chile ... H2 90
Puerto Victoria, Arg. ... C10 92
Puerto Viejo, C.R. ... C7 34
Puerto Villamil, Ec. ... i11 84a
Puerto Villamizar, Col. ... C5 86
Puerto Wilches, Col. ... D5 86
Puerto Ybapobó, Para. ... D5 90
Pueyrredón, Lago (Cochrane, Lago), l., S.A. ... I2 90
Pugačov, Russia ... D7 32
Puget Sound, strt., Wa., U.S. ... C4 136
Puglia, state, Italy ... C10 24
Puhja, Est. ... B9 10
Puhi-waero see South West Cape, c., N.Z. ... H2 80
Puhuli, Tai. ... I9 42
Puigcerdà, Spain ... B12 20
Puigmal d'Err (Puigmal), mtn., Fr. ... G8 18
Pujiang, China ... G8 42
Pujili, Ec. ... H2 86
Puka see Pukë, Alb. ... B13 24
Pukaki, Lake, l., N.Z. ... F3 80
Pukch'ŏng-ŭp, Kor., N. ... D8 38

Column 4

Pukë, Alb. ... B13 24
Pukekohe, N.Z. ... C6 80
Pukhrāyān, India ... E7 54
Pukou, China ... H8 42
Puksoozero, Russia ... E19 8
Pula, Cro. ... F10 22
Pula, Italy ... F3 24
Pulacayo, Bol. ... D3 90
Pulantien see Xinjin, China ... B9 42
Pulaski, N.Y., U.S. ... E13 112
Pulaski, Tn., U.S. ... B11 122
Pulaski, Va., U.S. ... G5 114
Pulau, stm., Indon. ... G10 44
Pulau Pinang, state, Malay. ... J5 48
Pulaukida, Indon. ... E3 50
Puławy, Pol. ... E18 16
Pulgaon, India ... H7 54
Puli, Tai. ... J9 42
Pulicat, India ... E5 53
Pulicat Lake, l., India ... E4 53
Puliyangudi, India ... G3 53
Pullman, Wa., U.S. ... D9 136
Pulog, Mount, mtn., Phil. ... B3 52
Pulon'ga, Russia ... C18 8
Puttusk, Pol. ... D16 16
Puma Yumco, l., China ... D13 54
Pumei, China ... A7 48
Pumpkin Buttes, mtn., Wy., U.S. ... D7 126
Pumpkin Creek, stm., Mt., U.S. ... B7 126
Pumpkin Creek, stm., Ne., U.S. ... F10 126
Puná, Isla, i., Ec. ... I1 86
Punakha, Bhu. ... E12 54
Punan, Indon. ... B10 50
Punata, Bol. ... C3 90
Púnch, India ... B5 54
Punchaw, B.C., Can. ... C7 138
Pune (Poona), India ... B1 53
Pungangūru, India ... E4 53
P'ungsan-ŭp, Kor., N. ... D7 38
Punggol, Sing. ... L9 48
Punia, D.R.C. ... E5 66
Punilla, Sierra de la, mts., Arg. ... D3 92
Punjab, state, India ... C5 54
Punjab, state, Pak. ... C4 54
Punmich'ŏn, Kor., N. ... C9 124
Puno, Peru ... G3 84
Puno, state, Peru ... G3 84
Punta, Cerro de, mtn., P.R. ... B2 104a
Punta Alta, Arg. ... I6 92
Punta Arenas, Chile ... J2 90
Punta Banda, Cabo, c., Mex. ... L9 134
Punta Cardón, Ven. ... B6 86
Punta Colnett, Mex. ... F4 98
Punta de Agua Creek (Tramperos Creek), stm., U.S. ... E5 128
Punta de Díaz, Chile ... C2 92
Punta del Cobre, Chile ... C2 92
Punta del Este, Ur. ... G10 92
Punta Delgada, Arg. ... E4 92
Punta de Piedras, Ven. ... B9 86
Punta Gorda, Bel. ... G6 102
Punta Gorda, Fl., U.S. ... J3 116
Punta Gorda, Bahía de b., Nic. ... G6 102
Punta Negra, Salar de, pl., Chile ... B3 92
Punta Prieta, Mex. ... A1 100
Puntarenas, C.R. ... G5 102
Punta Santiago, P.R. ... B4 104a
Punto Fijo, Ven. ... B6 86
Punung, Indon. ... H7 50
Puppy's Point, c., Norf. I. ... y24 78i
Puqi, China ... G5 42
Puquan, Indon. ... L4 42
Puquio, Peru ... F3 84
Pur, stm., Russia ... A13 32
Puracé, Volcán, vol., Col. ... F3 86
Pūranpur, India ... D7 54
Purcell, Ok., U.S. ... F11 128
Purcell Mountains, mts., N.A. ... F14 138
Purcellville, Va., U.S. ... E8 114
Purdy, Mo., U.S. ... H3 120
Purê (Purui), stm., S.A. ... D5 128
Purgatoire, stm., Co., U.S. ... D5 128
Puri, India ... I10 54
Purificación, stm., Mex. ... C9 100
Purísima, Mex. ... E7 130
Purmerend, Neth. ... B13 14
Pūrna, stm., India ... H5 54
Pūrna, stm., India ... H6 54
Purnia, India ... F11 54
Puronga, Russia ... F19 8
Purui (Purê), stm., S.A. ... I6 84
Puruliya, India ... G11 54
Puruni, stm., Guy. ... D12 86
Purús, stm., S.A. ... E4 84
Purwakarta, Indon. ... G5 50
Purwodadi, Indon. ... G7 50
Purwodadi, Indon. ... G7 50
Purworejo, Indon. ... G7 50
Pusa, Malay. ... C7 50
Pusan (Fusan), Kor., S. ... D2 40
Pusan-jikhalsi, state, Kor., S. ... D2 40
Pusat Gayo, Pegunungan, mts., Indon. ... J3 48
Pushkar, India ... E5 54
Pushkin, Russia ... A13 10
Puškino, Russia ... D20 10
Püspökladány, Hung. ... B8 26
Püssi, Est. ... A10 10
Pustozersk, Russia ... C25 8
Putao, Mya. ... C8 46
Putian, China ... I8 42
Putian, China ... I8 42
Putignano, Italy ... D10 24
Puting, Tanjung, c., Indon. ... E7 50
Putla de Guerrero, Mex. ... G10 100
Putney, Ga., U.S. ... E1 116
Putney, Vt., U.S. ... B13 114
Putorana, plato, plat., Russia ... C7 34
Puttalam, Sri L. ... H4 53
Puttalam Lagoon, b., Sri L. ... G4 53
Puttür, India ... E3 53
Putumayo, state, Col. ... G3 86
Putumayo (Içá), stm., S.A. ... I9 86
Putuo, China ... F10 42
Putussibau, Indon. ... C8 50
Putyla, Ukr. ... B12 26
Puumala, Fin. ... F12 8
Puurmani, Est. ... B9 10
Puyallup, Wa., U.S. ... C4 136
Puyang, China ... D6 42
Puy-de-Dôme, state, Fr. ... D9 18
Puyo, Ec. ... H2 86
Puyuma, Mya. ... B3 48
Puyuma, C2 48
Pyapon, Mya. ... D2 48
Pyawbwe, Mya. ... B3 48
Pyhäjärvi, i., Fin. ... F3 80
Pyhäjärvi, l., Fin. ... E11 8

Column 5

Pyhäjoki, Fin. ... D10 8
Pyhäjoki, stm., Fin. ... D11 8
Pyhäselkä, l., Fin. ... E13 8
Pyhätunturi, mtn., Fin. ... C12 8
Pyinbongyi, Mya. ... D3 48
Pyin Oo Lwin see Maymyo, Mya. ... A3 48
Pyle, at., Micron. ... C5 72
Pymatuning Reservoir, res., U.S. ... C5 114
P'yŏngt'aek, Kor., N. ... D6 38
P'yŏngch'ang, Kor., S. ... B1 40
P'yŏnghae, Kor., S. ... C2 40
P'yŏng'aek, Kor., S. ... F7 38
P'yŏngyang, Kor., N. ... E6 38
Pyote, Tx., U.S. ... C4 130
Pyramid Lake, l., Nv., U.S. ... D6 134
Pyramid Peak, mtn., Wy., U.S. ... G16 136
Pyrenees, mts., Eur. ... G6 18
Pyrénées-Atlantiques, state, Fr. ... F5 18
Pyrénées Occident, Parc National des, p.o.i., Fr. ... G8 18
Pyrénées-Orientales, state, Fr. ... G8 18
Pýrgos, Grc. ... F4 28
Pytalovo, Russia ... C10 10
Pyu, Mya. ... C3 48
Pyŭthān, Nepal ... D9 54

Column 6 — Q

Qaanaaq see Thule, Grnld. ... B12 141
Qabbāsīn, Syria ... B8 58
Qacentina (Constantine), Alg. ... B6 64
Qā'en, Iran ... C8 56
Qagan Moron, stm., China ... C3 38
Qagan Nur, l., China ... C7 36
Qahar Youyi Zhongqi, China ... A5 42
Qaidam, stm., China ... D4 36
Qaidam Pendi, bas., China ... D3 36
Qal'ah, Afg. ... C10 56
Qal'at ash-Shaqīf (Beaufort Castle), hist., Leb. ... E6 58
Qal'at Bīshah, Sau. Ar. ... C6 56
Qal'eh-ye Now, Afg. ... C9 56
Qalābāt, Sudan ... E7 62
Qalyūb, Egypt ... H2 58
Qamar, Ghubbat al-, b., Yemen ... F7 56
Qamea, i., Fiji ... p20 79e
Qamīnis, Libya ... A3 62
Qāna, Leb. ... E6 58
Qandahār, Afg. ... C10 56
Qandala, Som. ... B9 66
Qaqortoq see Julianehåb, Grnld. ... E16 141
Qārah, Syria ... D7 58
Qarazhal see Karažal, Kaz. ... E12 32
Qardho, Som. ... C9 66
Qarqan, stm., China ... G15 32
Qārūn, Birket (Moeris, Lake), l., Egypt ... I1 58
Qarwāw, Ra's c., Oman ... F8 56
Qasigiannguit see Christianshåb, Grnld. ... D15 141
Qasr al-Azraq, hist., Jord. ... G7 58
Qasr al-Kharānah, hist., Jord. ... G7 58
Qasr al-Mushattá, hist., Jord. ... G7 58
Qasr at-Tūbah, hist., Jord. ... G7 58
Qasr Dab'ah, hist., Jord. ... G7 58
Qasr-e Shīrīn, Iran ... C6 56
Qasr Farāfra, Egypt ... B5 62
Qatana, Syria ... E6 58
Qatar, ctry., Asia ... D7 54
Qatrani, Gebel, hill, Egypt ... I1 58
Qattâra, Munkhafad el- (Qattara Depression), depr., Egypt ... B5 62
Qattara Depression see Qattâra, Munkhafad el-, depr., Egypt ... B5 62
Qātīnah, Buhayrat, res., Syria ... D7 58
Qāzigund, India ... B5 54
Qazmämmäd, Azer. ... B6 56
Qazvīn, Iran ... B6 56
Qena, Egypt ... B6 62
Qena, Wadi (Qinā, Wādī), stm., Egypt ... K3 58
Qeqertarsuaq see Godhavn, Grnld. ... D15 141
Qesari, Horbat (Caesarea), hist., Isr. ... F5 58
Qeshm, Jazīreh-ye, i., Iran ... D8 56
Qetura, Isr. ... H5 58
Qezel Owzan, stm., Iran ... B6 56
Qian, stm., China ... J3 42
Qian'an, China ... B6 38
Qian Gorlos, China ... B6 38
Qianning, China ... E5 36
Qianshan, China ... F7 42
Qianwei, China ... F5 36
Qianxi, China ... H1 42
Qiaomo, China ... C5 54
Qiaowan, China ... C4 36
Qidong, China ... H5 42
Qiemo, China ... A6 36
Qigong, China ... F5 36
Qijiang, China ... G1 42
Qijiaojing, China ... C3 36
Qijiaojing, China ... F9 42
Qikou, China ... C4 42
Qila Saifullāh, Pak. ... C2 54
Qilian Shan, mtn., China ... D4 36
Qilian Shan, mts., China ... D4 36
Qimen, China ... G7 42
Qin, stm., China ... D5 42
Qin'an, China ... D1 42
Qingchengzi, China ... D5 38
Qingdao (Tsingtao), China ... C9 42
Qingfeng, China ... D6 42
Qinghai, state, China ... D4 36
Qinghai Hu, l., China ... D5 36
Qingjian, China ... C3 42
Qingjiang, China ... F8 42
Qinglong, China ... F6 36
Qinglonggang, China ... F9 42
Qingshan, China ... D4 42
Qingshui, China ... D1 42
Qingshui, stm., China ... H3 42
Qingtang, China ... I6 42
Qingxian, China ... B6 42
Qingxu, China ... C4 42
Qingyang, China ... C2 42
Qingyang, China ... F7 42
Qingyuan, China ... C5 42
Qingzhou, China ... C8 42
Qing Zang Gaoyuan (Tibet, Plateau of), plat., China ... B6 46
Qinhuangdao, China ... B8 42
Qin Ling, mts., China ... E3 42
Qinshihuang Mausoleum (Terra Cotta Army), hist., China ... D3 42
Qinshui, China ... D5 42
Qinxian, China ... C5 42
Qinyang, China ... D5 42
Qinyuan, China ... C5 42
Qinzhou, China ... J3 42

Column 7

Qionghai, China ... L4 42
Qionglai, China ... E5 36
Qionglaishan, mts., China ... E5 36
Qiongzhong, China ... L3 42
Qiongzhou Haixia, strt., China ... K4 42
Qiqian, China ... F13 34
Qiqihar, China ... B9 36
Qira, China ... A5 46
Qiryat Ata, Isr. ... F6 58
Qiryat Gat, Isr. ... G5 58
Qiryat Shemona, Isr. ... E6 58
Qishn, Yemen ... F7 56
Qitai, China ... C2 36
Qitaihe, China ... B11 36
Qitamu, China ... B7 38
Qixia, China ... C8 42
Qixian, China ... D6 42
Qiyang, China ... H4 42
Qizhou, China ... F6 42
Qizil Jilga, China ... A7 54
Qizil Qala, China ... C7 56
Qonggyai, China ... D13 54
Qom, Iran ... C7 56
Qomsheh, Iran ... C7 56
Qonggyai, China ... D13 54
Qostanay see Kustanaj, Kaz. ... D10 32
Qowowuyag (Chopu), mtn., Asia ... D11 54
Qu, stm., China ... F2 42
Qu, stm., China ... G8 42
Quabbin Reservoir, res., Ma., U.S. ... B13 114
Quadra Island, i., B.C., Can. ... F5 138
Quadros, Lagoa dos, l., Braz. ... D12 92
Quakenbrück, Ger. ... D3 16
Qualicum Beach, B.C., Can. ... G6 138
Quambatook, Austl. ... J4 76
Quang Ngai, Viet. ... E9 48
Quang Trach, Viet. ... D8 48
Quantico, Va., U.S. ... F8 114
Quanyang, China ... C7 38
Quanzhou, China ... I8 42
Qu'Appelle, stm., Can. ... D10 124
Qu'Appelle, stm., Can. ... D12 124
Qu'Appelle Dam, dam, Sk., Can. ... D7 124
Quaraí, Braz. ... E9 92
Quaraí, stm., Braz. ... E9 92
Quaraí (Cuareim), stm., S.A. ... E9 92
Quareos, Pegunungan, mts., Indon. ... E11 50
Quarryville, Pa., U.S. ... E9 114
Quartier d'Orléans, Guad. ... A1 105a
Quartu Sant'Elena, Italy ... E3 24
Quartz Lake, l., N.T., Can. ... A14 106
Quartz Mountain, mtn., Or., U.S. ... G4 136
Quartzsite, Az., U.S. ... J2 132
Quba, Azer. ... A6 56
Québec, Qc., Can. ... D5 110
Québec, state, Can. ... E16 106
Quebeck, Tn., U.S. ... I12 120
Quebra-Anzol, stm., Braz. ... J2 88
Quebracho, Ur. ... E9 92
Quebrada Seca, P.R. ... B4 104a
Quedal, Cabo, c., Chile ... H2 90
Quedlinburg, Ger. ... E7 16
Queen Charlotte Islands, is., B.C., Can. ... E4 106
Queen Charlotte Sound, strt., B.C., Can. ... E2 138
Queen Charlotte Strait, strt., B.C., Can. ... F3 138
Queen City, Mo., U.S. ... D5 120
Queen City, Tx., U.S. ... D4 122
Queen Elizabeth Islands, is., Can. ... B13 94
Queen Mary Coast, cst., Ant. ... B14 81
Queen Maud Gulf, b., Nu., Can. ... B10 106
Queen Maud Land, reg., Ant. ... C4 81
Queen Maud Mountains, mts., Ant. ... D23 81
Queenscliff, Austl. ... L5 76
Queensland, state, Austl. ... D8 74
Queensport, N.S., Can. ... E15 110
Queenstown, Austl. ... o12 77a
Queenstown, N.Z. ... G3 80
Queenstown, S. Afr. ... H8 70
Queguay Grande, stm., Ur. ... E9 92
Queimada Nova, Braz. ... E5 88
Queimadas, Braz. ... F6 88
Queimadas, Braz. ... L4 89
Quela, Ang. ... B2 68
Quelelevu, i., Fiji ... p20 79e
Quelimane, Moz. ... D6 68
Quelpart Island see Cheju-do, i., Kor., S. ... H7 38
Quemado, Tx., U.S. ... F7 130
Quemado, Punta de, c., Cuba ... B10 102
Quemoy see Chinmen Tao, i., Tai. ... I8 42
Quemú Quemú, Arg. ... H6 92
Quequén, Arg. ... I8 92
Querary, stm., Col. ... G7 86
Quercy, hist. reg., Fr. ... E8 18
Querétaro, Mex. ... E8 100
Querétaro, state, Mex. ... E8 100
Querobabi, Mex. ... F7 98
Quesada, C.R. ... G5 102
Quesada, Spain ... G8 20
Queshan, China ... E6 42
Quesnel, B.C., Can. ... C8 138
Quesnel Lake, l., B.C., Can. ... D9 138
Que Son, Viet. ... E9 48
Questa, N.M., U.S. ... E3 128
Quetico Lake, l., On., Can. ... C7 118
Quezaltenango, Guat. ... E2 102
Quezon City, Phil. ... C3 52
Qufu, China ... D7 42
Quibala, Ang. ... C2 68
Quibdó, Col. ... E3 86
Quiberon, Fr. ... G5 14
Quiboro, Ang. ... B2 68
Quibala, Ang. ... C2 68
Quila, Mex. ... C5 100
Quilengues, Ang. ... C1 68
Quiliano, Italy ... F5 22
Quilcacolo, Bol. ... B3 90
Quill Lake, l., Sk., Can. ... B9 124
Quillota, Chile ... F2 92
Quilon, India ... G3 53
Quilpie, Austl. ... G5 76
Quilpué, Chile ... F2 92
Quimilí, Alto de, mtn., Col. ... B1 68
Quimilí, Arg. ... C6 92
Quimper (Kemper), Fr. ... F4 14
Quimperlé, Fr. ... G3 14
Quinault, Wa., U.S. ... C3 136
Quince Mil, Peru ... F3 84
Quincy, Ca., U.S. ... D5 134
Quincy, Fl., U.S. ... G14 122
Quincy, Il., U.S. ... E6 120
Quincy, Ma., U.S. ... B14 114
Quincy, Wa., U.S. ... C7 136
Quines, Arg. ... F4 92
Quinhagak, Ak., U.S. ... D7 140
Quinn, stm., Nv., U.S. ... B7 134

Name	Map Ref.	Page
Quintanar de la Orden, Spain	E7	20
Quintana Roo, state, Mex.	C3	102
Quinte, Bay of, b., On., Can.	D12	112
Quinto, Spain	C10	20
Quinto, stm., Arg.	G5	92
Quinton, Ok., U.S.	B3	122
Quipapá, Braz.	E7	88
Quirauk Mountain, mtn., Md., U.S.	E8	114
Quiriguá, hist., Guat.	E3	102
Quirihue, Chile	H1	92
Quirindi, Austl.	H8	76
Quirinópolis, Braz.	C6	90
Quiriquire, Ven.	C10	86
Quiroga, Mex.	F8	100
Quiros, Cap, c., Vanuatu	j16	79d
Quissanga, Moz.	C7	68
Quissico, Moz.	D12	70
Quitaque, Tx., U.S.	G7	128
Quitasueño, unds., Col.	E7	102
Quitasueño, Banco see Quitasueño, unds., Col.	E7	102
Quita Sueno Bank see Quitasueño, unds., Col.	E7	102
Quiterajo, Moz.	C7	68
Quitilipi, Arg.	C7	92
Quitman, Ga., U.S.	F2	116
Quitman, Tx., U.S.	E3	122
Quito, Ec.	H2	86
Quixadá, Braz.	C6	88
Quixeramobim, Braz.	C6	88
Qujiadian, China	C5	38
Qujing, China	F5	36
Qujiu, China	J2	42
Qulin, Mo., U.S.	H7	120
Qumarlêb, China	E4	36
Qumrān, Khirbat, hist., W.B.	G6	58
Quoich, stm., Nu., Can.	C12	106
Quorn, Austl.	F7	74
Quoxo, stm., Bots.	C7	70
Qurdūd, Sudan	E5	62
Qus, Egypt	B6	62
Quseir, Egypt	B6	62
Qutdligssat, Grnld.	C15	141
Quthing, Leso.	G8	70
Quweisna, Egypt	H2	58
Quxian, China	F2	42
Qüxü, China	D13	54
Quyang, China	B6	42
Quy Nhon, Viet.	F9	48
Quyon, Qc., Can.	C13	112
Quyquyó, Para.	C9	92
Quzhou, China	G8	42
Quzhou, China	C6	42
Qyzylorda see Kzyl-Orda, Kaz.	F11	32

R

Name	Map Ref.	Page
Raab (Rába), stm., Eur.	D12	22
Raalte, Neth.	B15	14
Ra'ananna, Isr.	F5	58
Raas, Pulau, i., Indon.	G9	50
Raasay, i., Scot., U.K.	D6	12
Raasiku, Est.	A8	10
Rab, Otok, i., Cro.	F11	22
Raba, Indon.	H11	50
Rába (Raab), stm., Eur.	D12	22
Rábade, Spain	A3	20
Rabak, Sudan	E6	62
Rabat, Malta	I8	24
Rabat, Malta	H8	24
Rabat, Mor.	C3	64
Rabaul, Pap. N. Gui.	a5	79a
Rabbit Creek, stm., S.D., U.S.	B10	126
Rabbit Ears Pass, p., Co., U.S.	C10	132
Rabi, i., Fiji	p20	79e
Rābi', Ash-Shallāl ar- (Fourth Cataract), wtfl, Sudan	D6	62
Rābigh, Sau. Ar.	E4	56
Rabka, Pol.	G15	16
Rabkavi Banhatti, India	C2	53
Râbnița, Mol.	B16	26
Rabočeostrovsk, Russia	D16	8
Rabwāh, Pak.	C4	54
Rabyānah, Ramlat, des., Libya	C4	62
Raccoon, stm., Ia., U.S.	C4	120
Raccoon Creek, stm., Oh., U.S.	E15	120
Race, Cape, c., Nf., Can.	j23	107a
Race Point, c., Ma., U.S.	B15	114
Rach Gia, Viet.	G7	48
Rach Gia, Vinh, b., Viet.	H7	48
Raciąż, Pol.	D16	16
Racibórz, Pol.	F14	16
Racine, Wi., U.S.	F2	112
Radaškovičy, Bela.	F10	10
Rădăuți, Rom.	B12	26
Radcliff, Ky., U.S.	G12	120
Radeberg, Ger.	E9	16
Radebeul, Ger.	E9	16
Radford, Va., U.S.	G5	114
Rādhanpur, India	G3	54
Rădinești, Rom.	E10	26
Radisson, Sk., Can.	B6	124
Radium Hot Springs, B.C., Can.	F14	138
Radnice, Czech Rep.	G9	16
Radofinnikovo, Russia	A13	10
Radom, Pol.	E17	16
Radom, state, Pol.	E16	16
Radomsko, Pol.	E15	16
Radomyśl Wielki, Pol.	F17	16
Radoviš, Mac.	B5	28
Radstadt, Aus.	C10	22
Radutino, Russia	H17	10
Radviliškis, Lith.	E6	10
Radville, Sk., Can.	E9	124
Radymno, Pol.	G18	16
Radzyń Chełmiński, Pol.	C14	16
Rae, N.T., Can.	C7	106
Rae, stm., Nu., Can.	B7	106
Rāe Bareli, India	E8	54
Raeford, N.C., U.S.	B6	116
Rae Isthmus, isth., Nu., Can.	B13	106
Rae Strait, strt., Nu., Can.	B12	106
Rafaela, Arg.	E7	92
Rafael Freyre, Cuba	B10	102
Rafah, Gaza	G5	58
Rafḩā', Sau. Ar.	D5	56
Rafsanjān, Iran	C8	56
Raft, stm., U.S.	H13	136
Raga, Sudan	F5	62
Ragay Gulf, b., Phil.	D4	52
Ragged Island, i., Bah.	A10	102
Ragged Island Range, is., Bah.	A10	102
Ragged Top Mountain, mtn., Wy., U.S.	F7	126
Ragland, Al., U.S.	D12	122
Raguva, Lith.	E7	10
Rahačou, Bela.	G12	10
Rahad al-Bardī, Sudan	E4	62
Rāhatgarh, India	G7	54
Rahimatpur, India	C1	53
Rahīm Ki Bāzār, Pak.	F2	54
Rahīmyār Khān, Pak.	D3	54
Rāichūr, India	C3	53
Raiganj, India	F12	54
Raigarh, India	H9	54
Rāikot, India	C5	54
Railroad Valley, val., Nv., U.S.	E10	134
Railton, Austl.	n13	77a
Rainbow Bridge National Monument, p.o.i., Ut., U.S.	F6	132
Rainbow Falls, wtfl, B.C., Can.	D11	138
Rainelle, W.V., U.S.	G5	114
Rainier, Mount, vol., Wa., U.S.	D5	136
Rainy, stm., N.A.	C4	118
Rainy Lake, l., N.A.	C5	118
Rainy River, On., Can.	C4	118
Raipur, India	H8	54
Raipur Uplands, plat., India	H9	54
Raisen, India	G6	54
Raisin, stm., Mi., U.S.	G6	112
Raivavae, i., Fr. Poly.	F12	72
Rajabasa, Indon.	F4	50
Rājahmundry, India	C5	53
Rājaldesar, India	E5	54
Rājampet, India	D4	53
Rajang, stm., Malay.	B7	50
Rājapālaiyam, India	G3	53
Rājāpur, India	C1	53
Rājasthān, state, India	E4	54
Rājbāri, Bngl.	G12	54
Rajčihinsk, Russia	G14	34
Rāj Gangpur, India	G10	54
Rājgarh, India	E6	54
Rājgarh, India	G6	54
Rājgarh, India	D5	54
Rajik, Indon.	E4	50
Rājkot, India	G3	54
Rāj Nāndgaon, India	H8	54
Rājpipla, India	H4	54
Rājpur, India	G5	54
Rājpura, India	C6	54
Rājshāhi, Bngl.	F12	54
Rājshāhi, state, Bngl.	F12	54
Rājula, India	H3	54
Raka, stm., China	D11	54
Rakamaz, Hung.	A8	26
Rakaposhi, mtn., Pak.	B11	56
Rakata, Pulau (Krakatoa), i., Indon.	G4	50
Rakhine, state, Mya.	C1	48
Rakhiv, Ukr.	A11	26
Rakitnoe, Russia	B11	36
Rakiura see Stewart Island, i., N.Z.	H3	80
Rakoniewice, Pol.	D12	16
Rakops, Bots.	B7	70
Rakovník, Czech Rep.	F9	16
Råkvåg see Råkvågen, Nor.	E4	8
Råkvågen, Nor.	E4	8
Rakvere, Est.	G12	8
Raleigh, Ms., U.S.	E9	122
Raleigh, N.C., U.S.	I7	114
Ralik Chain, is., Marsh. Is.	C7	72
Ralls, Tx., U.S.	H7	128
Ralston, Pa., U.S.	C9	114
Ramah, N.M., U.S.	H8	132
Rām Allāh, W.B.	G6	58
Rāmanagaram, India	E3	53
Rāmanāthapuram, India	G4	53
Rāmānuj Ganj, India	G9	54
Ramat Gan, Isr.	F5	58
Ramat HaSharon, Isr.	F5	58
Ramatlabama, Bots.	D7	70
Rambervillers, Fr.	F15	14
Rambouillet, Fr.	F10	14
Rambutyo Island, i., Pap. N. Gui.	a4	79a
Rām Dās, India	B5	54
Rāmdurg, India	C2	53
Ramea, Nf., Can.	j22	107a
Ramene, Russia	F20	8
Ramenskoe, Russia	E21	10
Rāmeswaram, India	G4	53
Rāmgarh, Bngl.	G13	54
Rāmgarh, India	E5	54
Rāmgarh, India	G10	54
Ram Head, c., V.I.U.S.	e8	104b
Rāmhormoz, Iran	C6	56
Ramírez, Mex.	I10	130
Ramírez, Mex.	G7	130
Ramla, Isr.	G5	58
Ramlu, mtn., Afr.	E8	62
Ramm, Jabal, mtn., Jord.	I6	58
Rāmnagar, India	F9	54
Rāmnagar, India	D7	54
Râmnicu Sărat, Rom.	D14	26
Râmnicu Vâlcea, Rom.	D11	26
Ramona, Ca., U.S.	J9	134
Ramona, S.D., U.S.	C15	126
Ramos, Mex.	D8	100
Ramos, stm., Mex.	C6	100
Ramotswa, Bots.	D7	70
Rampart, Ak., U.S.	C9	140
Ramparts, stm., N.T., Can.	B4	106
Rāmpur, India	D7	54
Rāmpur, India	C6	54
Rāmpura, India	F5	54
Rāmpur Hāt, India	F11	54
Ramree Island, i., Mya.	C1	48
Ramseur, N.C., U.S.	I6	114
Ramsey, I. of Man	G8	12
Ramsey Lake, l., On., Can.	A7	112
Ramsgate, Eng., U.K.	J14	12
Ramshorn Peak, mtn., Mt., U.S.	E15	136
Rāmtek, India	H7	54
Rāmu, Bngl.	H14	54
Ramu, stm., Pap. N. Gui.	a3	79a
Ramville, Îlet, i., Mart.	k7	105c
Ramygala, Lith.	E7	10
Rānāghāt, India	G12	54
Rana Kao, Volcán, vol., Chile	f29	78l
Rāna Pratāp Sāgar, res., India	F5	54
Ranau, Malay.	H1	52
Ranau, Danau, l., Indon.	F3	50
Ranburne, Al., U.S.	D13	122
Rancagua, Chile	G2	92
Rancah, Indon.	G6	50
Rancevo, Russia	D16	10
Rancharia, Braz.	D6	90
Ranchería, stm., Col.	B5	86
Ranchester, Wy., U.S.	C5	126
Rānchi, India	G10	54
Ranchillos, Arg.	C5	92
Ranch Lake, l., Sk., Can.	B9	124
Rancho Cordova, Ca., U.S.	E4	134
Rancho Nuevo, Mex.	H7	130
Ranchos, Arg.	G8	92
Ranco, Lago, l., Chile	H2	90
Rancul, Arg.	G5	92
Randazzo, Italy	G8	24
Randers, Den.	H4	8
Randleman, N.C., U.S.	I6	114
Randlett, Ok., U.S.	G10	128
Randolph, Az., U.S.	K5	132
Randolph, Me., U.S.	F7	110
Randolph, Ne., U.S.	E15	126
Randolph, N.Y., U.S.	B7	114
Randolph, Ut., U.S.	B5	132
Random Lake, Wi., U.S.	E2	112
Randsfjorden, l., Nor.	F3	8
Ranfurly, N.Z.	G4	80
Rāngāmāti, Bngl.	G13	54
Rangantemiang, Indon.	D8	50
Rangas, Tanjung, c., Indon.	E11	50
Rangasa, Tanjung, c., Indon.	E11	50
Rangaunu Bay, b., N.Z.	B5	80
Rangeley, Me., U.S.	E6	110
Ranger, Tx., U.S.	B9	130
Rangia, India	E13	54
Rangitaiki, stm., N.Z.	D7	80
Rangitata, stm., N.Z.	F4	80
Rangitikei, stm., N.Z.	D7	80
Rangkasbitung, Indon.	G4	50
Rangoon see Yangon, Mya.	D2	48
Rangoon, stm., Mya.	D3	48
Rangpur, Bngl.	F12	54
Rangpur, Pak.	C3	54
Rangsang, Pulau, i., Indon.	C3	50
Rānībennur, India	D2	53
Rānīganj, India	G11	54
Rānikhet, India	D7	54
Rankamhaeng National Park, p.o.i., Thai.	D4	48
Ranken, stm., Austl.	D7	74
Ranken Store, Austl.	C7	74
Rankin, Il., U.S.	H2	112
Rankin, Tx., U.S.	C6	130
Rankin Inlet, Nu., Can.	C12	106
Rankins Springs, Austl.	I6	76
Rann of Kutch see Kutch, Rann of, reg., Asia	D2	46
Ranong, Thai.	H4	48
Ranongga Island, i., Sol. Is.	e7	79b
Ranot, Thai.	I5	48
Ransiki, Indon.	F9	44
Ransom, Ks., U.S.	C8	128
Ranson, W.V., U.S.	E8	114
Rantabe, Madag.	D8	68
Rantaukampar, Indon.	C2	50
Rantaupanjang, Indon.	D2	50
Rantauprapat, Indon.	B1	50
Rantekombola, Bulu, mtn., Indon.	E12	50
Rantepao, Indon.	E11	50
Rantoul, Il., U.S.	D9	120
Raohe, China	B11	36
Raoping, China	J7	42
Raoul, Ga., U.S.	B2	116
Raoul-Blanchard, Mont, mtn., Qc., Can.	C6	110
Raoul Island, i., N.Z.	F9	72
Rapa, i., Fr. Poly.	F12	72
Rapallo, Italy	F6	22
Rapang, Indon.	E11	50
Rapa Nui see Pascua, Isla de, i., Chile	f30	78l
Rāpar, India	G3	54
Rapel, stm., Chile	F2	92
Rapel, Embalse, res., Chile	G2	92
Rapelli, Arg.	C5	92
Raper, Cape, c., Nu., Can.	B17	106
Rapidan, stm., Va., U.S.	F7	114
Rapid City, Mb., Can.	D13	124
Rapid City, S.D., U.S.	C9	126
Rapid Creek, stm., S.D., U.S.	D9	126
Rapide-Blanc, Qc., Can.	C4	110
Rapid River, Mi., U.S.	C2	112
Räpina, Est.	G12	8
Rappahannock, stm., Va., U.S.	G9	114
Rāpti, stm., Asia	E9	54
Rapu Rapu Island, i., Phil.	D5	52
Raraka, at., Fr. Poly.	E12	72
Rarotonga, i., Cook Is.	a26	78j
Rarotonga International Airport, Cook Is.	a26	78j
Rasa, Punta, c., Arg.	H9	92
Ra's al-Khaymah, U.A.E.	D8	56
Ra's Ba'labakk, Leb.	D7	58
Râșcani, Mol.	B14	26
Rașcov, Mol.	B15	26
Ras Dashen Terara, mtn., Eth.	E7	62
Ras Dejen see Ras Dashen Terara, mtn., Eth.	E7	62
Ras Djebel, Tun.	G4	24
Raseiniai, Lith.	E5	10
Râs el-Barr, Egypt	G2	58
Rashād, Sudan	E6	62
Rashid (Rosetta), Egypt	G1	58
Rashid, Masabb (Rosetta Mouth), mth., Egypt	G1	58
Rasht, Iran	B6	56
Raška, Yugo.	F7	26
Rās Koh, mtn., Pak.	D10	56
Rasm al-Arwām, Sabkhat, l., Syria	C8	58
Râșnov, Rom.	D12	26
Rasra, India	F9	54
Rasšua, ostrov, i., Russia	G19	34
Rast, Rom.	F10	26
Rastatt, Ger.	H4	16
Rastede, Ger.	C4	16
Rastenburg see Kętrzyn, Pol.	B17	16
Rásttigáisá, mtn., Nor.	A12	8
Ratak Chain, is., Marsh. Is.	C8	72
Ratamka, Bela.	G10	10
Ratangarh, India	D5	54
Rat Buri, Thai.	F4	48
Rāth, India	F7	54
Rathbun Lake, res., Ia., U.S.	D4	120
Rathdrum, Id., U.S.	C9	136
Rathenow, Ger.	D8	16
Rathkeale, Ire.	I3	12
Ráth Luirc, Ire.	I4	12
Rathwell, Mb., Can.	E15	124
Rat Island, i., Ak., U.S.	g22	140a
Rat Islands, is., Ak., U.S.	g22	140a
Ratlām, India	G5	54
Ratmanova, ostrov, i., Russia	C27	34
Ratnāgiri, India	C1	53
Ratnapura, Sri L.	H5	53
Raton, N.M., U.S.	E4	128
Raton Pass, p., N.M., U.S.	E4	128
Rats, stm., Qc., Can.	A4	110
Rattanaburi, Thai.	E6	48
Rattaphum, Thai.	I5	48
Rattlesnake, Mt., U.S.	D13	136
Rattlesnake Creek, stm., Ks., U.S.	D10	128
Ratz, Mount, mtn., B.C., Can.	D4	106
Ratzeburg, Ger.	C6	16
Rau, Indon.	C2	50
Raub, Malay.	K5	48
Rauch, Arg.	H8	92
Raul Soares, Braz.	K4	88
Rauma, Fin.	F9	8
Rauma, stm., Nor.	E2	8
Rauna, Lat.	C8	10
Raung, Gunung, vol., Indon.	H9	50
Raurkela, India	G10	54
Răut, stm., Mol.	B14	26
Ravalgaon, India	H5	54
Ravanusa, Italy	G7	24
Ravena, N.Y., U.S.	B12	114
Ravenna, Italy	F9	22
Ravenna, Ky., U.S.	G2	114
Ravenna, Ne., U.S.	F13	126
Ravenna, Oh., U.S.	G8	112
Ravensburg, Ger.	I5	16
Ravenscrag, Sk., Can.	E4	124
Ravenshoe, Austl.	A5	76
Ravensthorpe, Austl.	F4	74
Ravenswood, W.V., U.S.	F4	114
Rāvi, stm., Asia	C4	54
Ravnina, Turkmen.	B9	56
Rāwah, Iraq	C5	56
Rawaki, at., Kir.	D9	72
Rāwalpindi, Pak.	B4	54
Rawas, stm., Indon.	E3	50
Rawdon, Qc., Can.	D3	110
Rawicz, Pol.	E12	16
Rawlinna, Austl.	F4	74
Rawlins, Wy., U.S.	B9	132
Rawson, Arg.	H4	90
Rawson, Arg.	G7	92
Raxāul, India	E10	54
Ray, Cape, c., Nf., Can.	C17	110
Raya, Indon.	C11	50
Raya, Bukit, mtn., Indon.	D8	50
Rāyachoti, India	D4	53
Rāyadurg, India	D3	53
Rāyagarha, India	B6	53
Ray Hubbard, Lake, res., Tx., U.S.	E2	122
Raymond, Ab., Can.	G18	138
Raymond, Il., U.S.	E8	120
Raymond, Mn., U.S.	F3	118
Raymond, Wa., U.S.	D3	136
Raymond Terrace, Austl.	I8	76
Raymondville, Tx., U.S.	H10	130
Raymore, Sk., Can.	C9	124
Rayne, La., U.S.	G6	122
Rayones, Mex.	C8	100
Rayong, Thai.	F5	48
Rayside-Balfour, On., Can.	B8	112
Raytown, Mo., U.S.	E3	120
Rayville, La., U.S.	E7	122
Raz, Pointe du, c., Fr.	F4	14
Războieni, Rom.	B13	26
Razdolinsk, Russia	C16	32
Răzeni, Mol.	C15	26
Razgrad, Blg.	F13	26
Razim, Lacul, l., Rom.	E15	26
Rāznas ezers, l., Lat.	D10	10
Razorback Mountain, mtn., B.C., Can.	E6	138
Răzvani, Rom.	E13	26
Ré, Île de, i., Fr.	C4	18
Reading, Eng., U.K.	J11	12
Reading, Mi., U.S.	C1	114
Reading, Oh., U.S.	E1	114
Reading, Pa., U.S.	D9	114
Readlyn, Ia., U.S.	B5	120
Readstown, Wi., U.S.	H8	118
Real, stm., Braz.	F6	88
Real, Cordillera, mts., S.A.	G4	84
Real del Castillo, Mex.	L9	134
Real del Padre, Arg.	G4	92
Realicó, Arg.	G5	92
Reardan, Wa., U.S.	C8	136
Reata, Mex.	B8	100
Reay, Scot., U.K.	C9	12
Rebecca, Lake, l., Austl.	F4	74
Rebiana Sand Sea see Rabyānah, Ramlat, des., Libya	C4	62
Reboly, Russia	E14	8
Rebouças, Braz.	B12	92
Rebun-tō, i., Japan	B14	38
Recanati, Italy	G10	22
Recherche, Archipelago of the, is., Austl.	F4	74
Recife, Braz.	E8	88
Recinto, Chile	H2	92
Recklinghausen, Ger.	E2	16
Reconquista, Arg.	D8	92
Recreio, Braz.	K4	88
Recreo, Arg.	D5	92
Rector, Ar., U.S.	H7	120
Rècyča, Bela.	H13	10
Recz, Pol.	C11	16
Red (Hong, Song) (Yuan), stm., Asia	D9	46
Red, stm., N.A.	A2	118
Red, stm., U.S.	E9	108
Red, stm., U.S.	H10	120
Red, Elm Fork, stm., U.S.	F8	128
Red, North Fork, stm., U.S.	G9	128
Red, Prairie Dog Town Fork, stm., U.S.	H7	122
Red, Salt Fork, stm., U.S.	G9	128
Redang, Pulau, i., Malay.	J6	48
Red Bank, N.J., U.S.	D11	114
Red Bank, Tn., U.S.	B13	122
Red Bay, Nf., Can.	i22	107a
Red Bay, Al., U.S.	C10	122
Redbay, Fl., U.S.	G12	122
Redberry Lake, l., Sk., Can.	B6	124
Red Bluff, Ca., U.S.	C3	134
Red Bluff Reservoir, res., U.S.	C4	130
Red Boiling Springs, Tn., U.S.	H12	120
Red Canyon, val., S.D., U.S.	D9	126
Redcar, Eng., U.K.	G11	12
Red Cedar, stm., Mi., U.S.	F5	112
Red Cedar Lake, l., On., Can.	B9	112
Redcliff, Ab., Can.	D3	124
Red Cliff, Co., U.S.	D10	132
Redcliff see Red Cliff, Co., U.S.	D10	132
Redcliffe, Austl.	F9	76
Redcliffe, Mount, mtn., Austl.	E4	74
Red Cliffs, Austl.	J3	76
Red Cloud, Ne., U.S.	A10	128
Red Creek, stm., Ms., U.S.	G10	122
Red Deer, Ab., Can.	D17	138
Red Deer, stm., Can.	B12	124
Red Deer, stm., Can.	F19	138
Red Deer Lake, l., Mb., Can.	B12	124
Reddersburg, S. Afr.	F8	70
Red Devil, Ak., U.S.	D8	140
Redding, Ca., U.S.	C3	134
Redditch, Eng., U.K.	I10	12
Redenção, Braz.	C6	88
Redfield, S.D., U.S.	C14	126
Redford, Tx., U.S.	E3	130
Redhead, Trin.	s13	105f
Redja, stm., Russia	C14	10
Redkey, In., U.S.	H4	112
Redkino, Russia	D19	10
Red Lake, On., Can.	E12	106
Red Lake, l., On., Can.	E12	106
Red Lake, l., Az., U.S.	H2	132
Red Lake, stm., Mn., U.S.	D2	118
Red Lake Falls, Mn., U.S.	D2	118
Red Lake Road, On., Can.	B5	118
Redlands, Ca., U.S.	I8	134
Redlands, Co., U.S.	D8	132
Red Level, Al., U.S.	F12	122
Red Lion, Pa., U.S.	E9	114
Red Lodge, Mt., U.S.	B3	126
Redmond, Or., U.S.	F5	136
Redmond, Ut., U.S.	D5	132
Redmond, Wa., U.S.	C4	136
Red Mountain, mtn., Mt., U.S.	C14	136
Red Mountain Pass, p., Co., U.S.	F9	132
Red Oak, Ia., U.S.	D2	120
Redon, Fr.	G6	14
Redonda, Isla i., Ven.	t12	105f
Redonda Islands, is., B.C., Can.	F6	138
Redondela, Spain	B2	20
Redondo, Port.	F3	20
Redondo Beach, Ca., U.S.	J7	134
Redoubt Volcano, vol., Ak., U.S.	D9	140
Red Pass, B.C., Can.	D11	138
Red Rock, B.C., Can.	C8	138
Red Rock, On., Can.	C10	118
Red Rock, stm., Mt., U.S.	F14	136
Red Rock, Lake, res., Ia., U.S.	C4	120
Redruth, Eng., U.K.	K7	12
Red Sea	C7	62
Redvers, Sk., Can.	E12	124
Redwater, Ab., Can.	C17	138
Redwater, stm., Mt., U.S.	G8	124
Redwillow, stm., Can.	A11	138
Red Willow Creek, stm., Ne., U.S.	G12	126
Red Wing, Mn., U.S.	G6	118
Redwood, stm., Mn., U.S.	G3	118
Redwood Falls, Mn., U.S.	G3	118
Redwood National Park, p.o.i., Ca., U.S.	B1	134
Ree, Lough, l., Ire.	H5	12
Reed City, Mi., U.S.	E4	112
Reeder, N.D., U.S.	A10	126
Reed Lake, l., Sk., Can.	D6	124
Reedley, Ca., U.S.	G6	134
Reedsburg, Wi., U.S.	H8	118
Reedsville, Wi., U.S.	D2	112
Reefton, N.Z.	F4	80
Reelfoot Lake, l., Tn., U.S.	H8	120
Rees, Ger.	E2	16
Reese, Mi., U.S.	E6	112
Reese, stm., Nv., U.S.	C9	134
Reeseville, Wi., U.S.	H10	118
Refuge Cove, B.C., Can.	F6	138
Refugio, Tx., U.S.	F10	130
Rega, stm., Pol.	C11	16
Regência, Braz.	J6	88
Regeneração, Braz.	D4	88
Regensburg, Ger.	H8	16
Regent, N.D., U.S.	A10	126
Reggâne, Alg.	D5	64
Reggio di Calabria, Italy	F9	24
Reggio nell'Emilia, Italy	F7	22
Reghin, Rom.	C11	26
Regina, Sk., Can.	D9	124
Región Metropolitana, state, Chile	F2	92
Registan see Rīgestān, reg., Afg.	C9	56
Registro, Braz.	B14	92
Regozero, Russia	D14	8
Rehau, Ger.	F7	16
Rehoboth, Nmb.	C3	70
Rehoboth Beach, De., U.S.	F10	114
Rehovot, Isr.	G5	58
Reichenbach, Ger.	F8	16
Reidsville, Ga., U.S.	D3	116
Reidsville, N.C., U.S.	H6	114
Reigate, Eng., U.K.	J12	12
Reihoku, Japan	G2	40
Reims (Rheims), Fr.	E12	14
Rein Anteriur (Vorderrhein), stm., Switz.	D6	22
Reinbeck, Ia., U.S.	B5	120
Reindeer Lake, l., Can.	D10	106
Reinga, Cape, c., N.Z.	B5	80
Reinosa, Spain	A6	20
Reisa Nasjonalpark, p.o.i., Nor.	B10	8
Reisterstown, Md., U.S.	E9	114
Reitz, S. Afr.	E9	70
Reliance, N.T., Can.	C9	106
Remada, Tun.	C7	64
Remagen, Ger.	F3	16
Remanso, Braz.	E4	88
Rembang, Indon.	G7	50
Remedios, Col.	D4	86
Remedios, Pan.	H7	102
Remedios, Punta, c., El Sal.	F2	102
Remer, Mn., U.S.	D5	118
Remington, Va., U.S.	F8	114
Rémiré, Fr. Gu.	C7	84
Remiremont, Fr.	G15	14
Remoulins, Fr.	F10	18
Rempang, Pulau, i., Indon.	C3	50
Remscheid, Ger.	E3	16
Remsen, Ia., U.S.	B1	120
Remus, Mi., U.S.	E4	112
Renaix see Ronse, Bel.	D12	14
Renata, B.C., Can.	G12	138
Rencēni, Lat.	C8	10
Rende, Italy	E10	24
Rend Lake, res., Il., U.S.	F8	120
Rendova Island, i., Sol. Is.	e7	79b
Rendsburg, Ger.	B5	16
Renfrew, On., Can.	C13	112
Rengat, Indon.	D3	50
Rengel, Indon.	G8	50
Rengo, Chile	G2	92
Reng Tlāng, mtn., Asia	H14	54
Renheji, China	F6	42
Renhuai, China	H2	42
Reni, Ukr.	D15	26
Renland, reg., Grnld.	C20	141
Renmark, Austl.	J3	76
Rennell, i., Sol. Is.	E7	72
Rennell, Islas, is., Chile	J2	90
Rennell and Bellona, state, Sol. Is.	f9	79b
Rennes, Fr.	F7	14
Rennie, Mb., Can.	E18	124
Reno, Nv., U.S.	D6	134
Reno, stm., Italy	F8	22
Reno Hill, mtn., Wy., U.S.	E6	126
Renoster, stm., S. Afr.	G5	70
Renous, N.B., Can.	D11	110
Renovo, Pa., U.S.	C8	114
Rensjön, Swe.	B8	8
Rensselaer, In., U.S.	H2	112
Rensselaer, N.Y., U.S.	B12	114
Rentería, Spain	A9	20
Renton, Wa., U.S.	C4	136
Renville, Mn., U.S.	G3	118
Renwick, Ia., U.S.	B4	120
Reo, Indon.	H12	50
Repetek, Turkmen.	B9	56
Repton, Al., U.S.	F11	122
Republic, Mi., U.S.	B1	112
Republic, Mo., U.S.	G4	120
Republic, Wa., U.S.	B8	136
Republican, stm., U.S.	B11	128
Republican, North Fork, stm., U.S.	A6	128
Republican, South Fork, stm., U.S.	B7	128
Republic of Korea see Korea, South, ctry., Asia	G8	38
Repulse Bay, Nu., Can.	B13	106
Repulse Bay, b., Austl.	C7	76
Repvåg, Nor.	A11	8
Requena, Spain	E9	20
Reriutaba, Braz.	C5	88
Reşadiye Yarımadası, pen., Tur.	G10	28
Reschenpass (Resia, Passo di), p., Eur.	C16	18
Reschenscheideck see Reschenpass, p., Eur.	C16	18
Reschenscheideck see Resia, Passo di, p., Eur.	C16	18
Resen, Mac.	B4	28
Reserva, Braz.	B12	92
Reserve, La., U.S.	G8	122
Reserve, N.M., U.S.	J8	132
Resia, Passo di (Reschenpass), p., Eur.	C16	18
Resistencia, Arg.	C8	92
Reșița, Rom.	D8	26
Resko, Pol.	C11	16
Resolute (Kaujuitoq), Nu., Can.	C7	141
Resolution Island, i., Nu., Can.	E12	141
Resolution Island, i., N.Z.	G2	80
Resplendor, Braz.	J5	88
Restigouche, stm., Can.	C9	110
Restinga Seca, Braz.	D11	92
Reston, Mb., Can.	E12	124
Retalhuleu, Guat.	E2	102
Retamosa, Ur.	F10	92
Retezat, Parcul Național, p.o.i., Rom.	D9	26
Rethel, Fr.	E13	14
Réthymno, Grc.	H7	28
Rettihovka, Russia	B10	38
Reunion, dep., Afr.	I11	60
Reus, Spain	C12	20
Reuss, stm., Switz.	C5	22
Reuterstadt Stavenhagen, Ger.	C8	16
Reutlingen, Ger.	H5	16
Revda, Russia	C16	8
Revelstoke, B.C., Can.	F12	138
Revelstoke, Lake, res., B.C., Can.	E12	138
Reventazón, Peru	E1	84
Revilla del Campo, Spain	B7	20
Revillagigedo, Islas, is., Mex.	F2	100
Revillagigedo Island, i., Ak., U.S.	E13	140
Revillagigedo Islands see Revillagigedo, Islas, is., Mex.	F2	100
Revin, Fr.	E13	14
Revolución, Mex.	H2	130
Rewa, India	F8	54
Rewāri, India	D6	54
Rexburg, Id., U.S.	G15	136
Rexford, Ks., U.S.	B8	128
Rexford, Mt., U.S.	B11	136
Rey, Isla del, i., Pan.	H8	102
Rey, Laguna del, l., Mex.	B7	100
Reyes, Bol.	B3	90
Reyes, Point, c., Ca., U.S.	F2	134
Reyhanlı, Tur.	B7	58
Reykjanes Ridge, unds.	C10	144
Reykjavík, Ice.	k28	8a
Reyno, Ar., U.S.	H7	120
Reynolds, Ga., U.S.	D1	116
Reynolds, N.D., U.S.	G16	124
Reynosa, Mex.	B9	100
Rezé, Fr.	G7	14
Rēzekne, Lat.	D10	10
Rezina, Mol.	B15	26
Rezovo, Blg.	G15	26
Rezovska (Mutlu), stm., Eur.	G14	26
Rhaetian Alps, mts., Eur.	C15	18
Rhame, N.D., U.S.	A9	126
Rheda-Wiedenbrück, Ger.	E4	16
Rheims see Reims, Fr.	E12	14
Rhein, Sk., Can.	C11	124
Rhein see Rhine, stm., Eur.	C15	14
Rheine, Ger.	D3	16
Rheinland-Pfalz, state, Ger.	G3	16
Rhine, Ga., U.S.	E2	116
Rhine (Rhein) (Rhin), stm., Eur.	C15	14
Rhinelander, Wi., U.S.	F9	118
Rhineland-Palatinate see Rheinland-Pfalz, state, Ger.	G3	16
Rhinns Point, c., Scot., U.K.	F6	12
Rhir, Cap, c., Mor.	C2	64
Rho, Italy	E5	22
Rhode Island, state, U.S.	C14	114
Rhode Island Sound, strt., U.S.	C14	114
Rhodes see Ródos, Grc.	G11	28
Rhodes see Ródos, i., Grc.	G10	28
Rhodesia see Zimbabwe, ctry., Afr.	D4	68
Rhodes Matopos National Park, p.o.i., Zimb.	B8	70
Rhodes' Tomb, hist., Zimb.	B9	70
Rhodope Mountains, mts., Eur.	H11	26
Rhön, mts., Ger.	F5	16
Rhondda, Wales, U.K.	J9	12
Rhône, state, Fr.	D10	18
Rhône, stm., Eur.	F10	18
Rhyl, Wales, U.K.	H9	12
Riachão, Braz.	D2	88
Riachão do Jacuípe, Braz.	F6	88
Riacho de Santana, Braz.	G4	88
Riachos, Islas de los, is., Arg.	H4	90
Riamkanan, Waduk, res., Indon.	E9	50
Riaño, Spain	A6	20
Riau, state, Indon.	D2	50
Riau, Kepulauan, is., Indon.	C4	50
Riaza, Spain	C7	20
Ribadeo, Spain	A3	20
Ribas do Rio Pardo, Braz.	D6	90
Ribáuè, Moz.	C6	68
Ribe, Den.	I3	8
Ribe, state, Den.	I3	8
Ribeira, Braz.	B13	92
Ribeira do Pombal, Braz.	F6	88
Ribeirão, Braz.	E8	88
Ribeirão Preto, Braz.	K2	88
Ribeirão Vermelho, Braz.	K3	88
Ribeiro Gonçalves, Braz.	D3	88
Ribera, Italy	G7	24
Riberalta, Bol.	B3	90
Rib Lake, Wi., U.S.	F8	118
Ribnica, Slvn.	E11	22
Ribnitz-Damgarten, Ger.	B8	16
Ribstone Creek, stm., Ab., Can.	D19	138
Ricardo Flores Magón, Mex.	F9	98
Riccione, Italy	F9	22
Rice, Tx., U.S.	E2	122
Rice Lake, l., On., Can.	D11	112
Riceville, Ia., U.S.	H6	118
Riceville, Tn., U.S.	B14	122
Richan, On., Can.	B6	118
Richard B. Russell Lake, res., U.S.	B3	116
Richard Collinson Inlet, b., N.T., Can.	B17	140
Richards, Tx., U.S.	G3	122
Richards Bay, S. Afr.	F11	70
Richards Bay, b., S. Afr.	F11	70
Richards Island, i., N.T., Can.	C13	140
Richardson, Tx., U.S.	E2	122
Richardson, Wa., U.S.	B4	136
Richardson Mountains, mts., Can.	B3	106
Richard Toll, Sen.	F1	64
Riche, Pointe, c., Nf., Can.	i22	107a
Richelieu, Fr.	G9	14
Richelieu, stm., Qc., Can.	E3	110
Richer, Mb., Can.	E17	124
Richey, Mt., U.S.	G8	124
Richfield, Mn., U.S.	G5	118
Richfield, Pa., U.S.	D8	114
Richfield, Ut., U.S.	E4	132
Richfield Springs, N.Y., U.S.	B11	114
Richford, Vt., U.S.	F4	110
Rich Hill, Mo., U.S.	F3	120
Richibucto, N.B., Can.	D12	110
Richland, Ga., U.S.	E14	122
Richland, Mi., U.S.	F4	112
Richland, Mt., U.S.	F7	124
Richland, Wa., U.S.	D7	136
Richland Center, Wi., U.S.	H8	118
Richland Creek, stm., Tx., U.S.	C11	130
Richlands, Va., U.S.	G4	114
Richland Springs, Tx., U.S.	C9	130
Richmond, Austl.	C4	76
Richmond, Austl.	I8	76
Richmond, B.C., Can.	G7	138
Richmond, On., Can.	C14	112
Richmond, Qc., Can.	E4	110
Richmond, N.Z.	E5	80
Richmond, S. Afr.	G6	70
Richmond, S. Afr.	F10	70
Richmond, Eng., U.K.	G11	12
Richmond, Ca., U.S.	F3	134
Richmond, In., U.S.	I5	112
Richmond, Ky., U.S.	G1	114
Richmond, Me., U.S.	F7	110
Richmond, Mi., U.S.	B3	114
Richmond, Mn., U.S.	F4	118
Richmond, Mo., U.S.	E4	120
Richmond, Tx., U.S.	H3	122
Richmond, Ut., U.S.	B5	132
Richmond, Va., U.S.	G8	114
Richmond Heights, Fl., U.S.	K5	116
Richmond Highlands, Wa., U.S.	C4	136
Richmond Hill, On., Can.	E10	112
Richmond Hill, Ga., U.S.	E4	116
Richmond Peak, mtn., St. Vin.	o11	105e
Richton, Ms., U.S.	F9	122
Richwood, Oh., U.S.	D2	114
Richwood, W.V., U.S.	F5	114

Name	Map Ref.	Page
Ricobayo, Embalse de, res., Spain	C4	20
Riddle, Or., U.S.	H3	136
Rideau, stm., On., Can.	C14	112
Ridgecrest, Ca., U.S.	H8	134
Ridgedale, Sk., Can.	A9	124
Ridgeland, Ms., U.S.	E8	122
Ridgeland, S.C., U.S.	D4	116
Ridgetown, On., Can.	F8	112
Ridgeville, Mb., Can.	E16	124
Ridgeville, S.C., U.S.	C5	116
Ridgeway, Mo., U.S.	D4	120
Ridgway, Co., U.S.	E9	132
Ridgway, Il., U.S.	G9	120
Ridgway, Pa., U.S.	C7	114
Riding Mountain National Park, p.o.i., Mb., Can.	D13	124
Riegelwood, N.C., U.S.	B7	116
Riesa, Ger.	E9	16
Riesco, Isla, i., Chile	J2	90
Riesi, Italy	G8	24
Riet, stm., S. Afr.	F7	70
Riet, stm., S. Afr.	H5	70
Rietavas, Lith.	E4	10
Rietfontein (Buitsivango), stm., Afr.	B4	70
Rieti, Italy	H9	22
Rif, mts., Mor.	C4	64
Riffe Lake, res., Wa., U.S.	D4	136
Rifle, Co., U.S.	D9	132
Rifstangi, c., Ice.	j31	8a
Rift Valley, val., Afr.	F7	62
Rīga, Lat.	D7	10
Rīga, Gulf of, b., Eur.	C6	10
Rigaih, Indon.	J2	48
Rigby, Id., U.S.	G14	136
Rīgestān, reg., Afg.	C9	56
Riggins, Id., U.S.	E10	136
Rigi, mtn., Switz.	C5	22
Rigo, Pap. N. Gui.	b4	79a
Rig-Rig, Chad	E2	62
Riihimäki, Fin.	F11	8
Riiser-Larsen Peninsula, pen., Ant.	B8	81
Riječki Zaljev, b., Cro.	E11	22
Rijeka (Fiume), Cro.	E11	22
Rijssen, Neth.	C7	14
Rillito, r., U.S.	K5	132
Rimatara, i., Fr. Poly.	F11	72
Rimavská Sobota, Slov.	H15	16
Rimbey, Ab., Can.	D16	138
Rimersburg, Pa., U.S.	C6	114
Rimini, Italy	F9	22
Rimouski, Qc., Can.	B8	110
Rimouski, stm., Qc., Can.	B8	110
Rinbung, China	C7	46
Rinca, Pulau, i., Indon.	H11	50
Rincon, Ga., U.S.	D4	116
Rincon, N.M., U.S.	K9	132
Rinconada, Arg.	D3	90
Rincón del Bonete, Lago Artificial de, res., Ur.	F9	92
Rincón de Romos, Mex.	D7	100
Ringas, India	E5	54
Ringdove, Vanuatu	k16	79d
Ringebu, Nor.	F4	8
Ringgold, Ga., U.S.	C13	122
Ringim, Nig.	G6	64
Ringkøbing, Den.	H2	8
Ringkøbing Fjord, b., Den.	H2	8
Ringling, Ok., U.S.	G11	128
Ringsted, Ia., U.S.	H4	118
Ringvassøya, i., Nor.	A8	8
Rinjani, Gunung, vol., Indon.	H10	50
Rinteln, Ger.	D5	16
Rio, Wi., U.S.	H9	118
Riobamba, Ec.	H2	86
Río Blanco, Chile	F2	92
Río Branco, Braz.	E4	84
Río Branco, Braz.	F11	92
Río Bravo, Mex.	C9	100
Río Bravo, Parque Internacional del, p.o.i., Mex.	F5	130
Río Brilhante, Braz.	D6	90
Río Bueno, Chile	H2	90
Río Casca, Braz.	K4	88
Río Ceballos, Arg.	E5	92
Río Chico, Ven.	B9	86
Río Claro, Braz.	L2	88
Río Claro, Trin.	s12	105f
Río Colorado, Arg.	I5	92
Río Cuarto, Arg.	F5	92
Rio das Pedras, Moz.	C12	70
Rio de Janeiro, Braz.	L4	88
Rio de Janeiro, state, Braz.	L3	88
Rio Dell, Ca., U.S.	C1	134
Río de Oro, Col.	C5	86
Rio do Sul, Braz.	C13	92
Río Espera, Braz.	K4	88
Río Felix, stm., N.M., U.S.	H3	128
Rio Gallegos, Arg.	J3	90
Río Grande, Arg.	J3	90
Río Grande, Braz.	F11	92
Río Grande, Mex.	D7	100
Río Grande, Nic.	F4	102
Río Grande, P.R.	B4	104a
Rio Grande (Bravo), stm., N.A.	H13	98
Río Grande do Norte, state, Braz.	C7	88
Río Grande do Sul, state, Braz.	D11	92
Ríohacha, Col.	B5	86
Río Hato, Pan.	H7	102
Rio Hondo, Tx., U.S.	H10	130
Río Hondo, stm., N.M., U.S.	H3	128
Río Hondo, Embalse, res., Arg.	C5	92
Río Jueyes, P.R.	B3	104a
Riolândia, Braz.	D6	90
Río Largo, Braz.	E8	88
Riom, Fr.	D9	18
Río Mayo, Arg.	I2	90
Río Mulatos, Bol.	C3	90
Riondel, B.C., Can.	G14	138
Río Negro, Braz.	C13	92
Río Negro, Col.	D5	86
Río Negro, state, Arg.	G3	90
Río Negro, Pantanal do, sw., Braz.	C5	90
Rionero in Vulture, Italy	D9	24
Riópar, Spain	F8	20
Río Pardo, Braz.	E11	92
Río Pardo de Minas, Braz.	H4	88
Río Piedras, P.R.	B3	104a
Rio Piracicaba, Braz.	J4	88
Río Pomba, Braz.	K4	88
Río Preto, Braz.	L3	88
Rio Rancho, N.M., U.S.	H10	132
Río Real, Braz.	F6	88
Río Segundo, Arg.	E5	92
Riosucio, Col.	E4	86
Río Tercero, Arg.	F5	92
Rio Tinto, Braz.	D8	88
Rioverde, Mex.	E8	100
Rio Verde de Mato Grosso, Braz.	C6	90
Rio Vista, Ca., U.S.	E4	134
Riozinho, stm., Braz.	D4	84
Riozinho, stm., Braz.	E3	88
Ripley, N.Y., U.S.	B6	114
Ripley, Oh., U.S.	F2	114
Ripley, Tn., U.S.	B9	122
Ripoll, Spain	B13	20
Ripon, Qc., Can.	E1	110
Ripon, Eng., U.K.	G11	12
Ripon, Wi., U.S.	H10	118
Riposto, Italy	G9	24
Risaralda, state, Col.	E3	86
Risbäck, Swe.	D6	8
Rishīkesh, India	C7	54
Rishiri-suidō, strt., Japan	B14	38
Rishiri-tō, i., Japan	B14	38
Rishon LeZiyyon, Isr.	G5	58
Rising Star, Tx., U.S.	B9	130
Rising Sun, In., U.S.	F12	120
Rising Sun, Md., U.S.	E9	114
Risle, stm., Fr.	E9	14
Risnjak, mtn., Cro.	E11	22
Risti, Est.	A7	10
Ristna, Est.	G9	8
Rita Blanca Creek, stm., Tx., U.S.	F6	128
Ritchie, S. Afr.	F7	70
Ritidian Point, c., Guam	i10	78c
Ritter, Mount, mtn., Ca., U.S.	F6	134
Rittman, Oh., U.S.	D4	114
Ritzville, Wa., U.S.	C8	136
Rivadavia, Arg.	E3	92
Rivadavia, Arg.	G6	92
Rivadavia, Chile	D2	92
Riva del Garda, Italy	E7	22
Rivas, Nic.	G5	102
Rive-de-Gier, Fr.	D10	18
Rivera, Arg.	H6	92
Rivera, Ur.	E10	92
River Cess, Lib.	H3	64
Riverdale, Ca., U.S.	G6	134
Riverdale, N.D., U.S.	G12	124
River Falls, Al., U.S.	F12	122
River Falls, Wi., U.S.	G6	118
Riverhead, N.Y., U.S.	D13	114
Riverhurst, Sk., Can.	D7	124
Riverina, reg., Austl.	J5	76
River John, N.S., Can.	E13	110
River Jordan, B.C., Can.	H6	138
Rivers, Mb., Can.	D13	124
Riversdale, S. Afr.	I5	70
Riverside, Ca., U.S.	J8	134
Riverside, Ia., U.S.	C6	120
Riverside, Tx., U.S.	G3	122
Riverside, Wa., U.S.	B7	136
Rivers Inlet, B.C., Can.	E3	138
Riversleigh, Austl.	C7	74
Riverton, N.Z.	H2	80
Riverton, Il., U.S.	E8	120
Riverton, Ne., U.S.	A10	128
Riverton, Ut., U.S.	C4	132
Riverton, Va., U.S.	F7	114
Riverton, Wy., U.S.	D4	126
Riverton Heights, Wa., U.S.	C4	136
River View, Al., U.S.	E13	122
Rives, Fr.	H8	120
Rives, W.V., U.S.	E5	114
Riviera, Tx., U.S.	G10	130
Riviera Beach, Fl., U.S.	J5	116
Rivière-à-Pierre, Qc., Can.	C5	110
Rivière-Bleue, Qc., Can.	C7	110
Rivière-de-la-Chaloupe, Qc., Can.	A14	110
Rivière-du-Loup, Qc., Can.	C7	110
Rivière-Matawin, Qc., Can.	D3	110
Rivière-Pilote, Mart.	l7	105c
Rivière-Salée, Mart.	k7	105c
Rivne, Ukr.	E14	6
Rivoli, Italy	E4	22
Rivoli Bay, b., Austl.	K2	76
Riyadh see Ar-Riyāḍ, Sau. Ar.	E6	56
Rīyāq, Leb.	E7	58
Rize, Tur.	A5	56
Rizhao, China	D8	42
Rizzuto, Capo, c., Italy	F11	24
Rjád, Russia	C18	10
Rjazan', Russia	D5	32
Rjazancevo, Russia	D22	10
Rjazanskaja oblast', co., Russia	I19	8
Rjážsk, Russia	D6	32
Rjukan, Nor.	G3	8
Ro, N. Cal.	m16	79d
Roachdale, In., U.S.	I3	112
Road Town, Br. Vir. Is.	e8	104b
Roan Mountain, Tn., U.S.	H3	114
Roanne, Fr.	C9	18
Roanoke, Al., U.S.	D13	122
Roanoke, Va., U.S.	G6	114
Roanoke, stm., U.S.	H8	114
Roanoke Island, i., N.C., U.S.	I10	114
Roanoke Rapids, N.C., U.S.	H8	114
Roanoke Rapids Lake Dam, dam, N.C., U.S.	H8	114
Roan Plateau, plat., U.S.	D7	132
Roaring Spring, Pa., U.S.	D7	114
Roaring Springs, Tx., U.S.	H7	128
Roatán, Isla de, i., Hond.	D4	102
Robbins, Tn., U.S.	H13	120
Robbins Island, i., Austl.	n12	77a
Robbinsville, N.C., U.S.	A1	116
Robe, Austl.	K2	76
Robe, Mount, hill, Austl.	H3	76
Röbel, Ger.	C8	16
Robersonville, N.C., U.S.	I8	114
Roberta, Ga., U.S.	D1	116
Robert Louis Stevenson's Tomb, hist., Samoa	g12	79c
Roberts, Id., U.S.	G14	136
Robertsdale, Al., U.S.	G11	122
Robertsfors, Swe.	D9	8
Robert S. Kerr Lake, res., Ok., U.S.	B3	122
Robertson, S. Afr.	H4	70
Roberts Peak, mtn., B.C., Can.	D10	138
Roberts Port, Lib.	H2	64
Roberval, Qc., Can.	B4	110
Robinson, Il., U.S.	E10	120
Róbinson Crusoe, Isla, i., Chile	I7	82
Robinvale, Austl.	J4	76
Robledo, Spain	F8	20
Roblin, Mb., Can.	C12	124
Roblandillo, Col.	E3	86
Roboré, Bol.	C5	90
Rob Roy Island, i., Sol. Is.	d7	79b
Robson, Mount, mtn., B.C., Can.	C11	138
Robstown, Tx., U.S.	G10	130
Roby, Tx., U.S.	B7	130
Roca, Cabo da, c., Port.	F1	20
Roca Partida, Isla, i., Mex.	F2	100
Rocas, Atol das, at., Braz.	C8	88
Rocciamelone, mtn., Italy	E4	22
Rochechouart, Fr.	D6	18
Rochefort, Fr.	D5	18
Rochelle, Ga., U.S.	E2	116
Rochelle, Il., U.S.	C8	120
Roche-Percée, Sk., Can.	E10	124
Rochester, In., U.S.	G3	112
Rochester, Mi., U.S.	B2	114
Rochester, Mn., U.S.	G6	118
Rochester, N.H., U.S.	G5	110
Rochester, N.Y., U.S.	E12	112
Rochester, Tx., U.S.	H9	128
Rochlitz, Ger.	E8	16
Rock, stm., U.S.	H2	118
Rock, stm., U.S.	J8	118
Rockall, i., Scot., U.K.	C6	6
Rockall Rise, unds.	C12	144
Rock Bay, B.C., Can.	F5	138
Rock Creek, B.C., Can.	G11	138
Rock Creek, stm., N.A.	F7	124
Rock Creek, stm., Mt., U.S.	D13	136
Rock Creek, stm., Nv., U.S.	C9	134
Rock Creek Butte, mtn., Or., U.S.	F8	136
Rockdale, Il., U.S.	C9	120
Rockdale, Tx., U.S.	D11	130
Rockefeller Plateau, plat., Ant.	D27	81
Rockenhausen, Ger.	G3	16
Rock Falls, Il., U.S.	C8	120
Rockford, Il., U.S.	B8	120
Rockford, Ia., U.S.	A5	120
Rockford, Oh., U.S.	D1	114
Rockford, Tn., U.S.	B15	122
Rockglen, Sk., Can.	E8	124
Rockhampton, Austl.	D8	76
Rockhampton Downs, Austl.	C7	74
Rock Hill, S.C., U.S.	B4	116
Rockingham, N.C., U.S.	B6	116
Rockingham Bay, b., Austl.	B6	76
Rock Island, Il., U.S.	C7	120
Rockland, N.D., U.S.	F14	124
Rockland, On., Can.	C14	112
Rockland, Id., U.S.	H14	136
Rockland, Me., U.S.	F7	110
Rockland, Ma., U.S.	B15	114
Rocklands Reservoir, l., Austl.	K3	76
Rockledge, Fl., U.S.	H5	116
Rocklin, Ca., U.S.	E4	134
Rockmart, Ga., U.S.	D13	122
Rockport, In., U.S.	G10	120
Rockport, Ky., U.S.	G11	120
Rockport, Me., U.S.	F7	110
Rockport, Ma., U.S.	B15	114
Rock Port, Mo., U.S.	D2	120
Rock Rapids, Ia., U.S.	H2	118
Rock River, Wy., U.S.	F6	126
Rock Springs, Wy., U.S.	B7	132
Rocksprings, Tx., U.S.	E7	130
Rockstone, Guy.	B6	84
Rock Tombs see Speos, hist., Egypt	K1	58
Rockville, In., U.S.	I2	112
Rockville, Md., U.S.	E9	114
Rockwell, Ok., U.S.	G8	128
Rockwell, Ia., U.S.	B4	120
Rockwell, N.C., U.S.	A5	116
Rockwood, Me., U.S.	E7	110
Rockwood, Pa., U.S.	I10	112
Rockwood, Tn., U.S.	I13	120
Rocky Cape National Park, p.o.i., Austl.	n12	77a
Rockyford, Ab., Can.	E17	138
Rocky Ford, Co., U.S.	C5	128
Rocky Mount, N.C., U.S.	I8	114
Rocky Mount, Va., U.S.	H5	114
Rocky Mountain, mtn., Mt., U.S.	C14	136
Rocky Mountain House, Ab., Can.	D16	138
Rocky Mountain National Park, p.o.i., Co., U.S.	G7	126
Rocky Mountains, mts., N.A.	D6	106
Rocky Mountain Trench, val., N.A.	G15	138
Rocky Point, c., Bah.	B11	102
Rodalben, Ger.	G3	16
Rødbyhavn, Den.	I4	8
Rodeo, Arg.	E3	92
Rodeo, Mex.	C6	100
Rodeo, N.M., U.S.	L7	132
Roderick Island, i., B.C., Can.	D2	138
Rodewisch, Ger.	F8	16
Rodez, Fr.	E8	18
Roding, Ger.	G8	16
Rodinia, Russia	G21	8
Rodney, On., Can.	F8	112
Rodney, Cape, c., Ak., U.S.	D6	140
Rodniki, Russia	H19	8
Ródos (Rhodes), Grc.	G11	28
Ródos (Rhodes), i., Grc.	G11	28
Rodrigues, i., Mrts.	K9	142
Roebourne, Austl.	D4	74
Roebuck Bay, b., Austl.	C4	74
Roeland Park, Ks., U.S.	E3	120
Roermond, Neth.	C14	14
Roeselare, Bel.	D11	14
Roes Welcome Sound, strt., Nu., Can.	C13	106
Roff, Ok., U.S.	C2	122
Rogačevo, Russia	D20	10
Rogaguá, Laguna, l., Bol.	B3	90
Rogaguado, Laguna, l., Bol.	B3	90
Rogaland, state, Nor.	G2	8
Rogaška Slatina, Slvn.	D12	22
Rogers, Ar., U.S.	H3	120
Rogers, Tx., U.S.	D10	130
Rogers, Mount, mtn., Va., U.S.	H4	114
Rogers Lake, l., Ca., U.S.	I8	134
Rogers Pass, p., B.C., Can.	E13	138
Rogersville, N.B., Can.	D11	110
Rogersville, Al., U.S.	C11	122
Rogersville, Tn., U.S.	H3	114
Roggeveen, Cabo, c., Chile	e30	78l
Rogliano, Fr.	G15	18
Rognedino, Russia	G16	10
Rogue, stm., Or., U.S.	H2	136
Rohri, Pak.	E2	54
Rohtak, India	D6	54
Roi Et, Thai.	E6	48
Roi Georges, Îles du, is., Fr. Poly.	E12	72
Roilianka, Ukr.	C16	26
Rojas, Arg.	G7	92
Rojo, Cabo, c., Mex.	E10	100
Rojo, Cabo, c., P.R.	C1	104a
Rokan, Indon.	C2	50
Rokan, stm., Indon.	C2	50
Rokel, stm., S.L.	H2	64
Rokiškis, Lith.	E8	10
Rokycany, Czech Rep.	G9	16
Roland, Ar., U.S.	C6	122
Roland, Mb., Can.	E16	124
Roland, stm., Braz.	B4	90
Rolândia, Braz.	D6	90
Rolde, Neth.	B3	120
Rolfe, Ia., U.S.	B10	124
Rolla, Mo., U.S.	G6	120
Rolla, N.D., U.S.	F14	124
Rolling Fork, Ms., U.S.	E8	122
Rolling Fork, stm., Ky., U.S.	G12	120
Rollingstone, Austl.	B6	76
Rollins, Mt., U.S.	C12	136
Rolvsøya, i., Nor.	A10	8
Roma, Austl.	F7	76
Roma, (Rome), Italy	I9	22
Roma, Leso.	F9	70
Roma, Tx., U.S.	H8	130
Romain, Cape, c., S.C., U.S.	D6	116
Roman, Rom.	C13	26
Romanche Gap, unds.	I12	144
Romang, Pulau, i., Indon.	G8	44
Romania, ctry., Eur.	D11	26
Roman Nose Mountain, mtn., Or., U.S.	G3	136
Romano, Cape, c., Fl., U.S.	K4	116
Romanó, Cayo, i., Cuba	A9	102
Romans-sur-Isère, Fr.	D10	18
Romanzof Mountains, mts., Ak., U.S.	C11	140
Romblon, Phil.	D4	52
Rome see Roma, Italy	I9	22
Rome, Ga., U.S.	C13	122
Rome, N.Y., U.S.	E15	112
Romilly-sur-Seine, Fr.	F12	14
Romney, W.V., U.S.	E7	114
Romny, Ukr.	D4	32
Romont, Switz.	D3	22
Romorantin-Lanthenay, Fr.	G10	14
Rompin, stm., Malay.	K6	48
Romsey, Eng., U.K.	J11	12
Ron, Mui, c., Viet.	C8	48
Rona, i., Scot., U.K.	D7	12
Rona, i., Scot., U.K.	B7	12
Ronan, Mt., U.S.	C12	136
Roncador, Banco see Roncador, Cayos de, unds., Col.	F7	102
Roncador, Cayos de, unds., Col.	F7	102
Roncador, Serra do, plat., Braz.	F7	84
Roncador Bank see Roncador, Cayos de, unds., Col.	F7	102
Ronda, Spain	H5	20
Ronda, Serranía de, mts., Spain	H5	20
Rondane Nasjonalpark, p.o.i., Nor.	F3	8
Ronde, Pointe, c., Dom.	i5	105c
Rondônia, state, Braz.	F5	84
Rondonópolis, Braz.	G7	84
Rong'an, China	I3	42
Rongcheng, China	C10	42
Ronge, Lac la, l., Sk., Can.	D10	106
Rongelap, at., Marsh. Is.	B7	72
Rongjiang, China	I3	42
Rongkop, Indon.	H7	50
Rongqui, China	I3	42
Rongxian, China	J4	42
Rønne, Den.	I6	8
Ronneby, Swe.	H6	8
Ronne Ice Shelf, ice, Ant.	C34	81
Ronse, Bel.	D12	14
Ronuro, stm., Braz.	F7	84
Roodhouse, Il., U.S.	E7	120
Rooiboklaagte, stm., Nmb.	B5	70
Roorkee, India	D6	54
Roosendaal, Neth.	C13	14
Roosevelt, Mn., U.S.	C3	118
Roosevelt, Ok., U.S.	G9	128
Roosevelt, Ut., U.S.	C6	132
Roosevelt, stm., Braz.	E5	84
Roosevelt Campobello International Park, p.o.i., N.B., Can.	F10	110
Roosevelt Island, i., Ant.	C24	81
Root, stm., Mn., U.S.	H7	118
Ropaži, Lat.	C7	10
Roper, N.C., U.S.	I9	114
Roper, stm., Austl.	B6	74
Ropesville, Tx., U.S.	H6	128
Roper Valley, Austl.	B6	74
Roque, stm., Braz.	B3	88
Roquefort, Fr.	E5	18
Roraima, state, Braz.	C5	84
Roraima, Mount, mtn., S.A.	E11	86
Røros, Nor.	E4	8
Rosa, Lake, l., Bah.	B11	102
Rosalia, Wa., U.S.	C9	136
Rosamond, Ca., U.S.	I7	134
Rosamond Lake, l., Ca., U.S.	I7	134
Rosário, Braz.	B3	88
Rosario, Mex.	D5	100
Rosario, Para.	B9	92
Rosario, Ur.	G9	92
Rosario, Bahía del, b., Mex.	G4	98
Rosario, Islas del, is., Col.	B4	98
Rosario de Arriba, Mex.	F4	98
Rosario de la Frontera, Arg.	B5	92
Rosario de Lerma, Arg.	B5	92
Rosario del Tala, Arg.	F8	92
Rosário do Sul, Braz.	E10	92
Rosário Oeste, Braz.	F6	84
Rosarito, Mex.	A2	100
Rosarno, Italy	F9	24
Roscoe, S.D., U.S.	B13	126
Roscoe, Tx., U.S.	B7	130
Roscommon, Ire.	H4	12
Roscommon, state, Ire.	H4	12
Roscrea, Ire.	I5	12
Rose, Mount, mtn., Nv., U.S.	D5	134
Roseau, Dom.	j6	105c
Roseau, Mn., U.S.	C3	118
Roseau, stm., N.A.	E2	118
Roseberth, Austl.	E2	76
Rosebery, Austl.	n12	77a
Roseboro, N.C., U.S.	B7	116
Rosebud, Mt., U.S.	A6	126
Rosebud, S.D., U.S.	D12	126
Rosebud, Tx., U.S.	C11	130
Rosebud, stm., Ab., Can.	E17	138
Rosebud Creek, stm., Mt., U.S.	A6	126
Roseburg, Or., U.S.	G3	136
Rosebush, Mi., U.S.	E5	112
Rose City, Mi., U.S.	D5	112
Rosedale, Austl.	E8	76
Rosedale, Ab., Can.	E18	138
Rosedale, Ms., U.S.	D7	122
Rose Hill, N.C., U.S.	B7	116
Rose Hill, Va., U.S.	H2	114
Rose Island, i., Bah.	K8	116
Rosemary, Ab., Can.	E18	138
Rosenberg, Tx., U.S.	H3	122
Rosendal, S. Afr.	F8	70
Rosenheim, Ger.	I8	16
Roses, Golf de, b., Spain	B14	20
Roses, Golfo de see Roses, Golf de, b., Spain	B14	20
Roseto degli Abruzzi, Italy	H11	22
Rosetown, Sk., Can.	C6	124
Rosetta see Rashid, Egypt	G1	58
Rosetta Mouth see Rashid, Masabb, mth., Egypt	G1	58
Rose Valley, Sk., Can.	B10	124
Roseville, Ca., U.S.	E4	134
Roseville, Il., U.S.	D7	120
Roseville, Mi., U.S.	B2	114
Roseville, Mn., U.S.	F5	118
Rosholt, S.D., U.S.	E1	118
Rosholt, Wi., U.S.	G9	118
Rosica, stm., Blg.	F12	26
Rosiclare, Il., U.S.	G9	120
Roşiori de Vede, Rom.	E12	26
Roslavl', Russia	F15	10
Rosmead, S. Afr.	G7	70
Ros Mhic Thriúin see New Ross, Ire.	I6	12
Ross, Austl.	o13	77a
Ross, stm., Yk., Can.	C4	106
Ross, Ire.	I4	12
Rossano, Italy	E10	24
Rossan Point, c., Ire.	G4	12
Rossasna, Bela.	F13	10
Rossel Island, i., Pap. N. Gui.	C10	74
Rosseau, Lake, l., On., Can.	C10	112
Rossell y Rius, Ur.	F10	92
Rossford, Oh., U.S.	C2	114
Ross Ice Shelf, ice, Ant.	D23	81
Ross Island, i., Ant.	C22	81
Rossignol, Lake, l., N.S., Can.	F11	110
Rossland, B.C., Can.	G13	138
Rosslau, Ger.	E8	16
Rosso, Maur.	F1	64
Rossoš', Russia	D5	32
Ross R. Barnett Reservoir, res., Ms., U.S.	E9	122
Ross River, Yk., Can.	C4	106
Ross Sea, Ant.	C23	81
Rossvatnet, l., Nor.	D6	8
Rossville, Ga., U.S.	C13	122
Rossville, Il., U.S.	H2	112
Rossville, Ks., U.S.	E2	120
Røst, is., Nor.	C4	8
Rosthern, Sk., Can.	B7	124
Roštkala, Taj.	B11	56
Rostock, Ger.	B7	16
Rostov, Russia	C22	10
Rostov-na-Donu, Russia	E6	32
Rosvinskoe, Russia	C24	8
Roswell, Ga., U.S.	B1	116
Roswell, N.M., U.S.	H4	128
Rota, i., N. Mar. Is.	B7	72
Rotan, Tx., U.S.	B7	130
Rotenburg, Ger.	C5	16
Roth, Ger.	G7	16
Rothaar, sci., Ant.	B34	81
Rotherham, Eng., U.K.	H11	12
Rothesay, N.B., Can.	E11	110
Rothesay, Scot., U.K.	F7	12
Rothsay, Mn., U.S.	E2	118
Rothwell, N.B., Can.	D10	110
Roti, Pulau, i., Indon.	H7	44
Roto, Austl.	I5	76
Rotondella, Italy	D10	24
Rotorua, N.Z.	D7	80
Rottenburg, Ger.	H4	16
Rottenburg an der Laaber, Ger.	H8	16
Rotterdam, Neth.	C13	14
Rotterdam, N.Y., U.S.	B11	114
Rottweil, Ger.	H4	16
Rotuma, i., Fiji	E8	72
Roubaix, Fr.	D12	14
Roudnice nad Labem, Czech Rep.	F10	16
Rouen, Fr.	E10	14
Rouge, stm., Qc., Can.	E2	110
Rough, stm., Ky., U.S.	G11	120
Rough River Lake, res., Ky., U.S.	G11	120
Rouleau, Sk., Can.	D9	124
Roulers see Roeselare, Bel.	D11	14
Roulette, Pa., U.S.	C7	114
Round Hill Head, c., Austl.	E8	76
Round Lake, Mn., U.S.	H3	118
Round Lake, l., On., Can.	C12	112
Round Mountain, Nv., U.S.	E8	134
Round Mountain, mtn., Austl.	H9	76
Round Rock, Tx., U.S.	D10	130
Roundup, Mt., U.S.	A4	126
Rousay, i., Scot., U.K.	B9	12
Rouses Point, N.Y., U.S.	E3	110
Roussillon, hist. reg., Fr.	G8	18
Routhierville, Qc., Can.	B9	110
Rouyn-Noranda, Qc., Can.	F15	106
Rovaniemi, Fin.	C11	8
Rovenskaja Slabada, Bela.	H13	10
Rovereto, Italy	E8	22
Roversi, Arg.	C6	92
Rovigo, Italy	E8	22
Rovira, Col.	E4	86
Rovno see Rivne, Ukr.	E14	6
Rovuma (Ruvuma), stm., Afr.	C6	68
Rowan Lake, l., On., Can.	B5	118
Rowena, Austl.	G7	76
Rowland, N.C., U.S.	B6	116
Rowley, stm., Nu., Can.	A15	106
Rowley Island, i., Nu., Can.	B14	106
Roxas, Phil.	E4	52
Roxboro, N.C., U.S.	H7	114
Roxborough, Trin.	r13	105f
Roxburgh, N.Z.	G3	80
Roxton, Tx., U.S.	D3	122
Roy, N.M., U.S.	F4	128
Roy, Ut., U.S.	B4	132
Royal Bardiyā Wild Life Reserve, India	D8	54
Royal Canal, can., Ire.	H6	12
Royal Center, In., U.S.	H3	112
Royal Chitwan National Park, p.o.i., Nepal	E10	54
Royal City, Wa., U.S.	D7	136
Royal Gorge, val., Co., U.S.	C3	128
Royal Leamington Spa, Eng., U.K.	I11	12
Royal Natal National Park, p.o.i., S. Afr.	F9	70
Royal Oak, Mi., U.S.	B2	114
Royalton, Mn., U.S.	F4	118
Royal Tunbridge Wells, Eng., U.K.	J13	12
Royan, Fr.	D5	18
Royersford, Pa., U.S.	D10	114
Royston, Eng., U.K.	I12	12
Royston, Ga., U.S.	B2	116
Różan, Pol.	D17	16
Rozdil'na, Ukr.	C17	26
Rozewie, Przylądek, c., Pol.	B14	16
Rožňava, Slov.	H16	16
Roznov, Rom.	C13	26
Rożnów, Pol.	G16	16
Roztoky, Czech Rep.	F10	16
Rrogozhina see Rrogozhinë, Alb.	C13	24
Rrogozhinë, Alb.	C13	24
Rtishchevo, Russia	D6	32
Ru, stm., China	E6	42
Ruacana Falls, wtfl, Afr.	D1	68
Ruahine Range, mts., N.Z.	D7	80
Ruapehu, Mount, vol., N.Z.	D6	80
Ruapuke Island, i., N.Z.	H3	80
Rubbestadneset, Nor.	G1	8
Rubcovsk, Russia	D14	32
Rubi, stm., D.R.C.	D4	66
Rubio, Ven.	D5	86
Rubondo Island, i., Tan.	E6	66
Ruby, Ak., U.S.	D8	140
Ruby, stm., Mt., U.S.	E14	136
Ruby Dome, mtn., Nv., U.S.	C1	134
Ruby Lake, sw., Nv., U.S.	C1	134
Ruby Mountains, mts., Nv., U.S.	C1	132
Ruby Valley, val., Nv., U.S.	C1	132
Rucheng, China	I5	42
Ruciane-Nida, Pol.	C17	16
Ruda Śląska, Pol.	F14	16
Rudall, stm., Austl.	D4	74
Rudarpur, India	E9	54
Rüdersdorf, Ger.	D9	16
Rudnaja Pristan', Russia	B11	38
Rudnja, Russia	F14	10
Rudnyj, Kaz.	D10	32
Rūdnyy see Rudnyj, Kaz.	D10	32
Rudo, Bos.	F6	26
Rudol'f, Ostrov, i., Russia	A10	34
Rudolf, Lake see Turkana, Lake, l., Afr.	D7	66
Rudol'f Hākr' see Rudolf, Lake, l., Afr.	D7	66
Rudolstadt, Ger.	F8	16
Rudong, China	E9	42
Rudozem, Blg.	H11	26
Rudyard, Mi., U.S.	B5	112
Rue, Fr.	D10	14
Rufā'ah, Sudan	E6	62
Ruffin, S.C., U.S.	C5	116
Rufiji, stm., Tan.	F7	66
Rufino, Arg.	G6	92
Rufisque, Sen.	G1	64
Rufunsa, Zam.	D4	68
Rugao, China	E9	42
Rugby, N.D., U.S.	F14	124
Rugby, Eng., U.K.	I11	12
Rügen, i., Ger.	B9	16
Rugged Mountain, mtn., B.C., Can.	F4	138
Ruhan', Russia	G15	10
Ruhengeri, Rw.	E5	66
Ruhpolding, Ger.	I8	16
Ruhr, stm., Ger.	E3	16
Ruhuna National Park, p.o.i., Sri L.	H5	53
Rui'an, China	H9	42
Ruidoso, N.M., U.S.	H3	128
Ruidoso Downs, N.M., U.S.	H3	128
Ruijin, China	I6	42
Ruiz, Mex.	D6	100
Ruiz, Nevado del, vol., Col.	E4	86
Ruki, stm., D.R.C.	E3	66
Rukwa, Lake, l., Tan.	F6	66
Rule, Tx., U.S.	A8	130
Ruleville, Ms., U.S.	D8	122
Rúm, i., Scot., U.K.	D6	12
Rum, stm., Mn., U.S.	F5	118
Ruma, Yugo.	D6	26
Rumbek, Sudan	F5	62
Rum Cay, i., Bah.	C10	96
Rumia, Pol.	B14	16
Rumigny, Fr.	E13	14
Rum Jungle, Austl.	B6	74
Rumoi, Japan	B14	38
Runan, China	E6	42
Runanga, N.Z.	F4	80
Runde, stm., Zimb.	B10	70
Rundēni, Lat.	D10	10
Rundu, Nmb.	D2	68
Runge, Tx., U.S.	E10	130
Rungwa, Tan.	F6	66
Rungwa, stm., Tan.	F6	66
Running Water Draw, stm., U.S.	G6	128
Ruo, stm., China	C4	36
Ruoqiang, China	G3	36
Ruoxi, China	G6	42
Rupat, Pulau, i., Indon.	C2	50
Rupert, Id., U.S.	H13	136
Rupert, Qc., Can.	E15	106
Rupert, stm., Qc., Can.	E15	106
Rupert Creek, stm., Austl.	C4	76
Rupununi, stm., Guy.	F12	86
Rur, stm., Eur.	D15	14
Rural Retreat, Va., U.S.	H4	114
Rurrenabaque, Bol.	B3	90
Rurutu, i., Fr. Poly.	F11	72
Rusape, Zimb.	D5	68
Rusera, India	F11	54
Rushan, China	C9	42
Rush Center, Ks., U.S.	C9	128
Rush City, Mn., U.S.	F5	118
Rush Creek, stm., Co., U.S.	C5	128
Rushford, Mn., U.S.	H7	118
Rushmore, Mn., U.S.	H3	118
Rushville, Il., U.S.	D7	120
Rushville, In., U.S.	E12	120
Rushville, Ne., U.S.	E12	126
Rusizi, stm., Afr.	E5	66
Rusk, Tx., U.S.	F3	122
Rusné, Lith.	E4	10
Russas, Braz.	C6	88
Russell, Mb., Can.	D12	124
Russell, Ks., U.S.	C10	128
Russell, Cape, c., N.T., Can.	A16	140
Russell Cave National Monument, p.o.i., Al., U.S.	C13	122
Russell Islands, is., Sol. Is.	e8	79b
Russellkonda, India	I10	54
Russell Springs, Ky., U.S.	G12	120
Russellville, Al., U.S.	C11	122
Russellville, Ar., U.S.	B5	122
Russellville, Ky., U.S.	H11	120
Rüsselsheim, Ger.	B18	2
Russia, ctry., Eur.	E2	134
Russian, stm., Ca., U.S.	C9	38
Russkij, Russia	C13	22
Rust, Aus.	F7	32
Rustavi, Geor.	G6	114
Rustburg, Va., U.S.	E8	70
Rustenburg, S. Afr.	E6	122
Ruston, La., U.S.	E6	66
Rutana, Bdi.	G6	20
Rute, Spain	H12	50
Ruteng, Indon.	D1	134
Ruth, Nv., U.S.	H8	120
Rutherford, Tn., U.S.	A3	116
Rutherfordton, N.C., U.S.	H9	12
Ruthin, Wales, U.K.	A3	120
Ruthven, Ia., U.S.	G11	138
Rutland, B.C., Can.	A15	124
Rutland, N.D., U.S.	G4	110
Rutland, Vt., U.S.	C2	116
Rutledge, Ga., U.S.	B7	54
Rutog, China	E5	66
Rutshuru, D.R.C.	B9	112
Rutter, On., Can.	C6	68
Ruvuma (Rovuma), stm., Afr.	D6	66
Ruwenzori Range see Ruwenzori, mts., Afr.	D6	66
Ruwenzori, mts., Afr.	G5	88
Ruy Barbosa, Braz.	E19	10
Ruza, Russia	E18	10
Ruza, stm., Russia	H7	10
Ružany, Bela.	G15	16
Ružomberok, Slov.	E5	66
Rwanda, ctry., Afr.	G11	128
Ryan, Ok., U.S.	E14	32
Ryan Peak, mtn., Id., U.S.	G12	136
Rybače, Kaz.	B15	8
Rybačij, poluostrov, pen., Russia	B21	10
Rybinsk, Russia	B21	10
Rybinskoe vodohranilišče (Rybinsk Reservoir), res., Russia	B21	10
Rybnik, Pol.	F14	16
Rybnoje, Russia	D21	10
Ryde, Eng., U.K.	K11	12
Ryderwood, Wa., U.S.	D3	136
Rydzyna, Pol.	E12	16
Ryegate, Mt., U.S.	D17	136
Rye Patch Reservoir, res., Nv., U.S.	C7	134
Ryley, Ab., Can.	C18	138
Rylovici, Russia	H15	10
Ryl'sk, Russia	D4	32
Ryn, Pol.	C17	16
Ryōhaku-sanchi, mts., Japan	D9	38
Rymařov, Czech Rep.	G13	16
Ryōtsu, Japan	A11	40
Rysy, mtn., Eur.	G15	16

Name — Map Ref. — Page

Ryūgasaki, Japan D13 40
Ryukyu Islands see Nansei-shotō, is., Japan k19 39a
Ryukyu Trench, unds. G15 142
Ržanica, Russia G16 10
Rzeszów, Pol. F18 16
Rzeszów, state, Pol. F17 16
Ržev, Russia D17 10

S

Sa, Thai. C5 48
Saale, stm., Ger. E7 16
Saalfeld, Ger. F7 16
Saar see Saarland, state, Ger. G2 16
Saarbrücken, Ger. G2 16
Saarburg, Ger. G2 16
Saaremaa, i., Est. G9 8
Saarijärvi, Fin. E11 8
Saaristomeren kansallispuisto, p.o.i., Fin. G9 8
Saarland, state, Ger. G2 16
Saarlouis, Ger. G2 16
Saavedra, Arg. H6 92
Saba, i., Neth. Ant. B1 105a
Šabac, Yugo. E6 26
Sabadell, Spain C13 20
Sabae, Japan D9 40
Sabah, state, Malay. H1 52
Sabah, hist. reg., Malay. D6 44
Sabak, Malay. K5 48
Sabalana, Kepulauan, is., Indon. G11 50
Sabana, Archipiélago de, is., Cuba A7 102
Sabana de la Mar, Dom. Rep. C13 102
Sabana de Mendoza, Ven. C6 86
Sabanagrande, Hond. F4 102
Sabana Grande, P.R. B2 104a
Sabanalarga, Col. B4 86
Sabana Llana, P.R. B3 104a
Sabang, Indon. J2 48
Sabang, Indon. C11 50
Sabarei, Kenya D7 66
Sābari, stm., India C5 53
Sābarmati, stm., India G4 54
Sab'atayn, Ramlat as-, sand, Yemen F6 56
Sabbioneta, Italy E7 22
Şāberī, Hāmūn-e, l., Asia C9 56
Sabetha, Ks., U.S. E2 120
Sabhā, Libya B2 62
Sabidana, Jabal, mtn., Sudan D7 62
Sabie, S. Afr. D10 70
Sabiè, stm., Afr. D10 70
Sabile, Lat. C5 10
Sabina, Oh., U.S. E2 114
Sabina, hist. reg., Italy H9 22
Sabinal, Tx., U.S. E8 130
Sabinal, stm., Tx., U.S. E8 130
Sabinal, Cayo, i., Cuba B9 102
Sabiñánigo, Spain B10 20
Sabinas, Mex. B8 100
Sabinas, stm., Mex. B8 100
Sabinas, stm., Mex. B9 100
Sabinas Hidalgo, Mex. B8 100
Sabine, stm., U.S. G5 122
Sabine Bay, b., Can. A17 140
Sabine Lake, l., U.S. H5 122
Sabine Pass, strt., U.S. H5 122
Sabinópolis, Braz. J4 88
Şabiote, Spain F7 20
Šabla, Blg. F15 26
Sable, Cape, c., N.S., Can. G11 110
Sable, Cape, pen., Fl., U.S. K4 116
Sable Island, i., N.S., Can. G16 110
Sablūkah, Shallāl as- (Sixth Cataract), wtfl, Sudan D6 62
Šablykino, Russia H18 10
Sabor, stm., Port. C4 20
Sabou, Burkina G4 64
Sabrina Coast, cst., Ant. B16 81
Şabyā, Sau. Ar. F5 56
Sabyin, Mya. C2 48
Sabzevār, Iran B8 56
Sac, stm., Mo., U.S. G4 120
Sacaton, Az., U.S. J5 132
Sac City, Ia., U.S. B3 120
Săcele, Rom. D12 26
Sachayoj, Arg. C6 92
Sachsen, state, Ger. F9 16
Sachsen (Saxony), hist. reg., Ger. D5 16
Sachsen-Anhalt, state, Ger. D7 16
Şachs Harbour, N.T., Can. B14 140
Šack, Bela. G10 10
Sackets Harbor, N.Y., U.S. E13 112
Sackville, N.B., Can. E12 110
Saco, Me., U.S. G6 110
Saco, stm., U.S. F5 110
Sacramento, Braz. J2 88
Sacramento, Ca., U.S. E4 134
Sacramento, stm., Ca., U.S. E4 134
Sacramento Mountains, mts., N.M., U.S. E10 98
Sacramento Valley, val., Ca., U.S. D3 134
Sacramento Wash, stm., Az., U.S. H2 132
Sacred Heart, Mn., U.S. G3 118
Sádaba, Spain B9 20
Şa'dah, Yemen F5 56
Sadaik Taung, mtn., Mya. E4 48
Sada-misaki, c., Japan F4 40
Sada-misaki-hantō, pen., Japan F5 40
Sadang, stm., Indon. E11 50
Sa Dao, Thai. I5 48
Sadda, Pak. B3 54
Saddle Mountain, mtn., Co., U.S. C3 128
Saddle Mountain, mtn., Or., U.S. E3 136
Saddle Peak, mtn., India F7 46
Sa Dec, Viet. G7 48
Sādiqābād, Pak. D3 54
Sadiya, India C8 46
Sadlers, St. K./N. C2 105a
Sado, i., Japan A11 40
Sado, stm., Port. F2 20
Sado-kaikyō, strt., Japan B11 40
Sadowara, Japan G4 40
Şādri, India F4 54
Šadrinsk, Russia C10 32
Sädvaluspen, Swe. C7 8
Saegertown, Pa., U.S. C5 114
Şaerluojia Hu, l., China B11 54
Šafárikovo, Slov. H16 16
Säffle, Swe. G5 8
Saffron Walden, Eng., U.K. I13 12
Safi, Mor. C3 64
Safīd Kūh, Selseleh-ye, mts., Afg. C9 56
Safonovo, Russia D22 8
Safonovo, Russia E16 10
Safranbolu, Tur. B15 28
Saga, China D10 54
Saga, Japan F3 40
Saga, state, Japan F3 40
Sagae, Japan A13 40
Sagaing, Mya. B2 48
Sagaing, state, Mya. A2 48
Sagamihara, Japan D12 40
Sagami-nada, b., Japan D12 40
Saganaga Lake, l., N.A. C7 118
Saganoseki, Japan F4 40
Saganthit Kyun, i., Mya. F4 48
Sāgar, India D2 53
Sāgar, India G7 54
Sagara, Japan E11 40
Sagaranten, Indon. G5 50
Sagavanirktok, stm., Ak., U.S. C10 140
Sagay, Phil. E4 52
Sage, Mount, mtn., Br. Vir. Is. e8 104b
Sage Creek, stm., Mt., U.S. B16 136
Sagerton, Tx., U.S. A8 130
Saginaw, Mi., U.S. E6 112
Saginaw, stm., Mi., U.S. E5 112
Saginaw Bay, b., Mi., U.S. E6 112
Sağkaya, Tur. A6 58
Sagleipie, Lib. H3 64
Şaglek Bay, b., Nf., Can. F13 141
Sagonar, Russia D16 32
Şagu, Rom. C8 26
Saguache, Co., U.S. C2 128
Saguache Creek, stm., Co., U.S. C2 128
Sagua de Tánamo, Cuba B10 102
Sagua la Grande, Cuba A7 102
Saguaro National Park, p.o.i., Az., U.S. K5 132
Saguenay, stm., Qc., Can. B7 110
Sagunt, Spain E10 20
Sagunto see Sagunt, Spain E10 20
Sāgwāra, India G4 54
Sa'gya, China D12 54
Sahagún, Col. C4 86
Sahagún, Spain B5 20
Sahalin, ostrov, i., Russia F17 34
Sahalinskij zaliv, b., Russia F17 34
Sahara, des., Afr. E5 64
Sahāranpur, India C6 54
Saharsa, India F11 54
Sahel see Sudan, reg., Afr. E4 62
Sāhibganj, India F11 54
Sāhīwāl, Pak. C4 54
Şāhīwāl, Pak. C4 54
Şahovskaja, Russia D18 10
Şahrisabz, Uzb. G11 32
Şahtinsk, Kaz. E12 32
Şahtjorsk, Russia G17 34
Šahty, Russia E6 32
Sahuaripa, Mex. A4 100
Sahuarita, Az., U.S. L5 132
Sahuayo de José María Morelos, Mex. E7 100
Şahunja, Russia H22 8
Šahy, Slov. H14 16
Sai Buri, Thai. I5 48
Sai Buri, stm., Thai. I5 48
Saidor, Pap. N. Gui. b4 79a
Saidpur, Bngl. F12 54
Saidu, Pak. C11 56
Saigō, Japan C6 40
Saigon see Thanh Pho Ho Chi Minh, Viet. G8 48
Saijō, Japan F6 40
Şaiki, Japan G4 40
Šaim, Russia B10 32
Saimaa, l., Fin. F13 8
Sainte Agathe, Mb., Can. E16 124
Sainte-Agathe-des-Monts, Qc., Can. D2 110
Saint-Agrève, Fr. D10 18
Saint Alban's, Nf., Can. j22 107a
Saint Albans, Eng., U.K. J12 12
Saint Albans, Vt., U.S. F3 110
Saint Albans, W.V., U.S. F4 114
Saint Albert, Ab., Can. C17 138
Saint Aldhelm's Head, c., Eng., U.K. K10 12
Saint-Alexis-des-Monts, Qc., Can. D3 110
Saint-Amand-Mont-Rond, Fr. H11 14
Saint-André-Avellin, Qc., Can. E1 110
Saint Andrew, Barb. n8 105d
Saint Andrew, Mount, mtn., St. Vin. o11 105e
Saint Andrews, N.B., Can. E9 110
Saint Andrews, Scot., U.K. E10 12
Saint Andrews, S.C., U.S. D5 116
Sainte-Anne, Guad. h6 105c
Sainte-Anne, Mart. I7 105c
Sainte Anne, Lac, l., Ab., Can. C16 138
Sainte-Anne-de-Beaupré, Qc., Can. C5 110
Sainte-Anne-de-Madawaska, N.B., Can. C8 110
Sainte-Anne-des-Monts, Qc., Can. A10 110
Sainte-Anne-du-Lac, Qc., Can. D1 110
Saint Ann's Bay, Jam. i13 104d
Saint-Anselme, Qc., Can. D6 110
Saint Ansgar, Ia., U.S. H5 118
Saint Anthony, Nf., Can. i22 107a
Saint Anthony, Id., U.S. G15 136
Saint Arnaud, Austl. K4 76
Saint Augustin, Qc., Can. i22 107a
Saint Augustine, Fl., U.S. G4 116
Saint Austell, Eng., U.K. K8 12
Saint-Avold, Fr. E15 14
Saint-Barthélemy, i., Guad. B2 105a
Saint-Basile, N.B., Can. C8 110
Saint Bathans, Mount, mtn., N.Z. G3 80
Saint Bees Head, c., Eng., U.K. G9 12
Saint-Boniface-de-Shawinigan, Qc., Can. D3 110
Saint-Bonnet, Fr. E11 18
Saint Brides Bay, b., Wales, U.K. J7 12
Saint-Brieuc, Fr. F6 14
Saint-Brieuc, Baie de, b., Fr. F6 14
Saint Catharines, On., Can. E10 112
Saint Catherine, Mount, vol., Gren. q10 105e
Saint Catherines Island, i., Ga., U.S. E4 116
Saint Catherine's Point, c., Eng., U.K. K11 12
Saint-Céré, Fr. E7 18
Saint-Chamond, Fr. D10 18
Saint Charles, Id., U.S. A5 132
Saint Charles, Il., U.S. C9 120
Saint Charles, Mi., U.S. E5 112
Saint Charles, Mn., U.S. H6 118
Saint Charles, Mo., U.S. F7 120
Saint Charles Mesa, Co., U.S. C4 128
Saint Christopher (Saint Kitts), i., St. K./N. C2 105a
Saint Christopher and Nevis see Saint Kitts and Nevis, ctry., N.A. C2 105a
Saint Clair, Mi., U.S. B3 114
Saint Clair, Mo., U.S. F6 120
Saint Clair, stm., N.A. B3 114
Saint Clair, Lake, l., N.A. B3 114
Saint Clair Shores, Mi., U.S. B3 114
Saint-Claud, Fr. D6 18
Saint Claude, Mb., Can. E15 124
Saint-Claude, Fr. C11 18
Saint-Claude, Guad. h5 105c
Saint Cloud, Fl., U.S. H4 116
Saint Cloud, Mn., U.S. F4 118
Sainte-Croix, Qc., Can. D5 110
Saint Croix, i., V.I.U.S. g10 104c
Saint Croix, stm., N.A. E9 110
Saint Croix, stm., U.S. G6 118
Saint Croix Falls, Wi., U.S. F6 118
Saint Croix Island National Monument, p.o.i., Me., U.S. E10 110
Saint-Cyr, stm., Qc., Can. A1 110
Saint David, Az., U.S. L6 132
Saint David's, Wales, U.K. J7 12
Saint David's Head, c., Wales, U.K. J7 12
Saint David's Island, i., Ber. k16 104e
Saint-Denis, Fr. E11 14
Saint-Denis, Reu. i10 69a
Saint-Dié, Fr. F15 14
Saint-Dizier, Fr. F13 14
Saint-Donat-de-Montcalm, Qc., Can. D2 110
Saint Edward, Ne., U.S. F15 126
Saint Elias, Cape, c., Ak., U.S. E11 140
Saint Elias, Mount, mtn., N.A. C2 106
Saint Elias Mountains, mts., N.A. D12 140
Saint-Élie, Fr. Gu. C7 84
Saint Elmo, Il., U.S. E9 120
Saint-Étienne, Fr. D10 18
Saint-Étienne-du-Rouvray, Fr. E10 14
Saint-Eugène, Qc., Can. B4 110
Saint-Eustache, Qc., Can. E2 110
Saint-Fabien, Qc., Can. B8 110
Saint-Félicien, Qc., Can. B4 110
Saint-Félix-de-Valois, Qc., Can. D3 110
Saint-Florent-sur-Cher, Fr. G11 14
Saint-Flour, Fr. D9 18
Sainte-Foy, Qc., Can. D5 110
Sainte-Foy-la-Grande, Fr. E6 18
Saint Francis, Ks., U.S. B7 128
Saint Francis, Wi., U.S. I11 118
Saint Francis, stm., N.A. C7 110
Saint Francis, stm., U.S. C8 122
Saint Francis, Cape, c., S. Afr. I7 70
Saint Francis Bay, b., S. Afr. I7 70
Saint Francisville, Il., U.S. F10 120
Saint Francisville, La., U.S. G7 122
Saint-François, Guad. h6 105c
Saint-François, stm., Qc., Can. D4 110
Saint-François, Lac, l., Can. E2 110
Saint-François, Lac, res., Qc., Can. E5 110
Saint-Gabriel, Can. B8 110
Saint-Gabriel-de-Gaspé, Qc., Can. B12 110
Saint-Gall see Sankt Gallen, Switz. C6 22
Saint-Gaudens, Fr. F6 18
Sainte Genevieve, Mo., U.S. G7 120
Saint George, Austl. G7 76
Saint George, Ber. k16 104e
Saint George, N.B., Can. E10 110
Saint George, On., Can. E9 112
Saint George, Ut., U.S. F3 132
Saint George, Cape, c., Fl., U.S. H13 122
Saint George, Point, c., Ca., U.S. B1 134
Saint George Island, i., Fl., U.S. H14 122
Saint-Georges, Qc., Can. D4 110
Saint-Georges, Qc., Can. D6 110
Saint-Georges, Fr. Gu. C7 84
Saint George's, Gren. q10 105e
Saint George's Bay, b., Nf., Can. j22 107a
Saint Georges Bay, b., N.S., Can. E15 110
Saint George's Channel, strt., Eur. J7 12
Saint George's Channel, strt., Pap. N. Gui. a5 79a
Saint-Gilles-Croix-de-Vie, Fr. H6 14
Saint Gotthard Pass see San Gottardo, Passo del, p., Switz. D5 22
Saint Helena, Ca., U.S. E3 134
Saint Helena, dep., Afr. H5 60
Saint Helena Bay see Sint Helenabaai, b., S. Afr. H3 70
Saint Helens, Eng., U.K. H10 12
Saint Helens, Or., U.S. E4 136
Saint Helens, Mount, vol., Wa., U.S. D4 136
Saint Helier, Jersey E6 14
Saint-Hilaire-du-Harcouët, Fr. F7 14
Saint-Hyacinthe, Qc., Can. E4 110
Saint Ignace Island, i., On., Can. C11 118
Saint Ignatius, Guy. F12 86
Saint Ignatius, Mt., U.S. C12 136
Saint-Isidore, N.B., Can. C11 110
Saint Ives, Eng., U.K. K7 12
Saint James, Mi., U.S. C4 112
Saint James, Mn., U.S. G4 118
Saint James, Mo., U.S. G6 120
Saint James, Cape, c., B.C., Can. E4 106
Saint James Islands, is., V.I.U.S. e7 104b
Saint-Jean, Guad. B2 105a
Saint-Jean, Lac, res., Qc., Can. B4 110
Saint Jean Baptiste, Mb., Can. E16 124
Saint-Jean-d'Angély, Fr. C5 18
Saint-Jean-de-Luz, Fr. F4 18
Saint-Jean-de-Maurienne, Fr. D12 18
Saint-Jean-du-Gard, Fr. E9 18
Saint-Jean-Port-Joli, Qc., Can. C6 110
Saint-Jean-sur-Richelieu, Qc., Can. E3 110
Saint-Jérôme, Qc., Can. E3 110
Saint Jo, Tx., U.S. H11 128
Saint Joe, stm., Id., U.S. C11 136
Saint John, N.B., Can. E10 110
Saint John, N.D., U.S. F14 124
Saint John, Wa., U.S. C9 136
Saint John, i., V.I.U.S. e8 104b
Saint John, stm., N.A. E10 110
Saint John, Cape, c., Nf., Can. E19 106
Saint John's, Antig. f4 105b
Saint John's, Nf., Can. j23 107a
Saint Johns, Az., U.S. I7 132
Saint Johns, Mi., U.S. E5 112
Saint Johns, stm., Fl., U.S. G4 116
Saint Johnsbury, Vt., U.S. F4 110
Saint Joseph, Dom. j6 105c
Saint Joseph, Il., U.S. D9 120
Saint Joseph, Mi., U.S. F3 112
Saint Joseph, Mn., U.S. F4 118
Saint Joseph, Mo., U.S. E3 120
Saint Joseph, stm., U.S. G3 112
Saint Joseph, stm., U.S. G5 112
Saint Joseph, Lake, l., On., Can. E12 106
Saint-Joseph-de-Beauce, Qc., Can. D6 110
Saint Joseph Island, i., On., Can. B6 112
Saint-Jovite, Qc., Can. D2 110
Saint-Julien-en-Born, Fr. E4 18
Sainte-Julienne, Qc., Can. E3 110
Saint-Junien, Fr. D6 18
Saint Just, P.R. B4 104a
Saint Kilda, i., Scot., U.K. D4 12
Saint Kitts see Saint Christopher, i., St. K./N. C2 105a
Saint Kitts and Nevis, ctry., N.A. C2 105a
Saint-Lambert, Qc., Can. E3 110
Saint Landry, La., U.S. G6 122
Saint Laurent, Mb., Can. D16 124
Saint-Laurent (Saint Lawrence), stm., N.A. B8 110
Saint-Laurent du Maroni, Fr. Gu. E7 84
Saint Lawrence, Austl. D7 76
Saint Lawrence (Saint-Laurent), stm., N.A. E8 110
Saint Lawrence, Gulf of, b., Can. F18 106
Saint Lawrence Island, i., Ak., U.S. D5 140
Saint-Léandre, Qc., Can. B9 110
Saint-Léonard, N.B., Can. C9 110
Saint-Lô, Fr. E7 14
Saint Louis, Sk., Can. B8 124
Saint-Louis, Guad. i6 105c
Saint-Louis, Sen. F1 64
Saint Louis, Mi., U.S. E5 112
Saint Louis, Mo., U.S. F7 120
Saint Louis, stm., U.S. E6 118
Saint-Louis, Lac, l., Qc., Can. E3 110
Saint-Louis de Kent, N.B., Can. D12 110
Saint Louis Park, Mn., U.S. G5 118
Saint-Loup-sur-Semouse, Fr. G14 14
Sainte-Luce, Mart. I7 105c
Saint Lucia, ctry., N.A. m6 105c
Saint Lucia, Cape, c., S. Afr. F11 70
Saint Lucia, Lake, l., S. Afr. E11 70
Saint Lucia Channel, strt., N.A. I6 105c
Saint Lucia Game Reserve, S. Afr. F11 70
Saint Lucie Canal, can., Fl., U.S. J5 116
Saint Magnus Bay, b., Scot., U.K. n18 12a
Saint-Malo, Fr. F7 14
Saint-Malo, Golfe de, b., Fr. F6 14
Saint-Marc, Haiti C11 102
Saint-Marc, Canal de, strt., Haiti C11 102
Saint-Marc-des-Carrières, Qc., Can. D4 110
Sainte-Marie, Mart. k7 105c
Sainte Marie, Nosy, i., Madag. D9 68
Saint Maries, Id., U.S. C10 136
Saint Marks, stm., Fl., U.S. F1 116
Saint-Martin (Sint Maarten), i., N.A. A1 105a
Saint-Martin, Cap, c., Mart. k6 105c
Saint Martin, Lake, l., Mb., Can. C15 124
Saint Martins, N.B., Can. E11 110
Saint Martinville, La., U.S. G7 122
Saint Mary, Mo., U.S. G8 120
Saint Mary, stm., N.A. G18 138
Saint Mary Peak, mtn., Austl. H2 76
Saint Mary Reservoir, res., Ab., Can. G17 138
Saint Marys, Austl. n14 77a
Saint Marys, Ak., U.S. D7 140
Saint Marys, Ga., U.S. F4 116
Saint Marys, Ks., U.S. E1 120
Saint Marys, Pa., U.S. C7 114
Saint Marys, W.V., U.S. E4 114
Saint Mary's, i., Eng., U.K. L6 12
Saint Marys, stm., U.S. H5 112
Saint Marys, stm., U.S. F4 116
Saint Mary's Bay, b., Nf., Can. j23 107a
Saint Marys Bay, b., N.S., Can. F10 110
Saint Marys City, Md., U.S. F9 114
Saint-Mathieu, Fr. D6 18
Saint Matthew Island, i., Ak., U.S. D5 140
Saint Matthews, Ky., U.S. F12 120
Saint-Maurice, stm., Qc., Can. D4 110
Sainte-Maxime, Fr. F12 18
Saint Meinrad, In., U.S. F11 120
Saint Michael, Ak., U.S. D7 140
Saint Michaels, Md., U.S. F9 114
Saint-Michel-des-Saints, Qc., Can. D2 110
Saint-Mihiel, Fr. F14 14
Saint Moritz see Sankt Moritz, Switz. D6 22
Saint-Nazaire, Fr. G6 14
Saint-Nicolas see Sint-Niklaas, Bel. C12 14
Saint-Omer, Fr. D11 14
Saintonge, hist. reg., Fr. D5 18
Saint-Pacôme, Qc., Can. C7 110
Saint-Pamphile, Qc., Can. D7 110
Saint Paris, Oh., U.S. D2 114
Saint-Patrice, Lac, l., Qc., Can. B12 112
Saint Paul, Ab., Can. B19 138
Saint-Paul, Reu. i10 69a
Saint Paul, In., U.S. E12 120
Saint Paul, Ks., U.S. G2 120
Saint Paul, Mn., U.S. G5 118
Saint Paul, Va., U.S. H3 114
Saint Paul, stm., Lib. H2 64
Saint-Paul, Île, i., Afr. M10 142
Saint Paul Island, i., Ak., U.S. E6 140
Saint Paul's, St. K./N. C2 105a
Saint Pauls, N.C., U.S. B7 116
Saint Paul's Point, c., Pit. c28 78k
Saint Peter, Mn., U.S. G4 118
Saint Peter Port, Guern. E6 14
Saint Peters, N.S., Can. E16 110
Saint Peters Bay, P.E., Can. D14 110
Saint Petersburg see Sankt-Peterburg, Russia A13 10
Saint Petersburg, Fl., U.S. I3 116
Saint-Pierre, Mart. k6 105c
Saint-Pierre, Reu. i10 69a
Saint-Pierre, St. P./M. j22 107a
Saint Pierre, i., Sey. k12 69b
Saint-Pierre, Lac, l., Qc., Can. D3 110
Saint Pierre and Miquelon, dep., N.A. j22 107a
Saint Pierre-Jolys, Mb., Can. E16 124
Saint-Pierre-sur-Dives, Fr. E8 14
Saint-Pol-sur-Ternoise, Fr. D11 14
Saint-Pons-de-Thomières, Fr. F8 18
Saint-Prime, Qc., Can. B4 110
Saint-Prosper-de-Dorchester, Qc., Can. D6 110
Saint-Quentin, N.B., Can. C9 110
Saint-Quentin, Fr. E12 14
Saint-Raphaël, Fr. F12 18
Saint-Raymond, Qc., Can. D5 110
Saint Regis Falls, N.Y., U.S. F2 110
Saint-Rémy-de-Provence, Fr. F10 18
Saint Robert, Mo., U.S. G5 120
Saint-Roch-de-Mékinac, Qc., Can. D3 110
Saint-Romuald, Qc., Can. D5 110
Sainte-Rose-du-dégelis see Dégelis, Can. C8 110
Sainte Rose du Lac, Mb., Can. C14 124
Saintes, Fr. D5 18
Saint-Savin, Fr. H9 14
Saint-Siméon, Qc., Can. C6 110
Saint Simons Island, Ga., U.S. E4 116
Saint Simons Island, i., Ga., U.S. E4 116
Saintes-Maries-de-la-Mer, Fr. F10 18
Saint Stephen, S.C., U.S. C6 116
Sainte-Thérèse-de-Blainville, Qc., Can. E3 110
Saint Thomas, On., Can. F8 112
Saint Thomas, N.D., U.S. F16 124
Saint Thomas, i., V.I.U.S. e7 104b
Saint-Tite, Qc., Can. D4 110
Saint-Trond see Sint-Truiden, Bel. D14 14
Saint-Tropez, Fr. F12 18
Saint-Ubalde, Qc., Can. D4 110
Saint-Urbain-de-Charlevoix, Qc., Can. C6 110
Saint-Valéry-en-Caux, Fr. E9 14
Saint-Vallier, Fr. D10 18
Sainte-Véronique, Qc., Can. D2 110
Saint Vincent, Mn., U.S. C1 118
Saint Vincent, i., St. Vin. o11 105e
Saint-Vincent, Baie de, b., N. Cal. n15 79d
Saint Vincent, Gulf, b., Austl. J2 76
Saint Vincent and the Grenadines, ctry., N.A. p10 105e
Saint Vincent Passage, strt., N.A. m7 105c
Saint-Vith, Bel. D14 14
Saint Walburg, Sk., Can. E9 106
Saint-Yrieix-la-Perche, Fr. D7 18
Saint-Yvon, Qc., Can. A12 110
Saipan, i., N. Mar. Is. B5 72
Saiqi, China H8 42
Saitama, state, Japan C12 40
Saito, Japan G4 40
Sai Yok National Park, p.o.i., Thai. E4 48
Sajama, Nevado, mtn., Bol. C3 90
Sajanogorsk, Russia D16 32
Şajat, Turkmen. B9 56
Šajman, Taj. B11 56
Sajószentpéter, Hung. A7 26
Sak, stm., S. Afr. G5 70
Sa Kaeo, Thai. F6 48
Sakai, Japan E8 40
Sakaide, Japan E6 40
Sakaiminato, Japan D6 40
Sakakawea, Lake, res., N.D., U.S. G12 124
Sakala, Pulau, i., Indon. G10 50
Sakami, stm., Qc., Can. E15 106
Sakami, Lac, l., Qc., Can. E15 106
Sakania, D.R.C. G5 66
Sakaraha, Madag. E7 68
Sakarya, Tur. C13 28
Sakarya, state, Tur. C13 28
Sakarya (Sangarius), stm., Tur. B13 28
Sakata, Japan A12 40
Sakawa, Japan F6 40
Sakchu-ŭp, Kor., N. D6 38
Sakété, Benin H5 64
Sakhalin see Sahalin, ostrov, i., Russia F17 34
Sakhnin, Isr. F6 58
Şakht Sar, Iran B7 56
Šakiai, Lith. E6 10
Sakiet Sidi Youssef, Tun. H2 24
Sakishima-shotō, is., Japan G9 36
Sakon Nakhon, Thai. D6 48
Sakrand, Pak. E2 54
Saks, Al., U.S. D13 122
Sakti, India H9 54
Saku, Japan C11 40
Sakuma, Japan D10 40
Sakurai, Japan E8 40
Şal, i., C.V. k10 65a
Šal'a, Slov. H13 16
Sala, Swe. F7 8
Salaberry-de-Valleyfield, Qc., Can. E2 110
Salacgrīva, Lat. C7 10
Sala Consilina, Italy D9 24
Salada, Laguna, l., Mex. F5 98
Saladas, Arg. D8 92
Saladillo, Arg. G8 92
Saladillo, stm., Arg. D6 92
Saladillo Dulce, Arroyo, stm., Arg. E7 92
Salado, stm., Arg. D4 92
Salado, stm., Arg. E7 92
Salado, stm., Arg. I5 92
Salado, stm., Arg. G9 92
Salado, stm., Cuba B9 102
Salado, stm., Mex. B9 100
Salado, stm., N.M., U.S. I9 132
Salaga, Ghana H4 64
Salairskij krjaž, mts., Russia D14 32
Şălaj, state, Rom B10 26
Šalakuša, Russia E19 8
Salal, Chad E3 62
Şalālah, Oman F7 56
Şalālah, Sudan C7 62
Salamanca, Chile E2 92
Salamanca, Mex. E8 100
Salamanca, Spain D5 20
Salamanca, N.Y., U.S. F11 112
Salamanca, co., Spain D4 20
Salamanga, Moz. E11 70
Salamat, Bahr, stm., Chad F3 62
Salamina, Col. E4 86
Salamína, Grc. F6 28
Salamína, i., Grc. F6 28
Salamis, hist., N. Cyp. C4 58
Salamīyah, Syria C8 58
Salamonie, stm., In., U.S. H4 112
Salantai, Lith. D4 10
Salaquí, Col. D3 86
Salaquí, stm., Col. D3 86
Salas, Peru E2 84
Salas de los Infantes, Spain B7 20
Salatiga, Indon. G7 50
Salavat, Russia D9 32
Salaverry, Peru E2 84
Salawati, i., Indon. F9 44
Salāya, India G2 54
Sala y Gómez, Isla, i., Chile L28 142
Sala y Gomez Ridge, unds. L29 142
Şalbani, India G11 54
Šalčininkai, Lith. F8 10
Salcombe, Eng., U.K. K9 12
Saldaña, Spain B6 20
Saldaña, stm., Col. F4 86
Saldanha, S. Afr. H3 70
Saldungaray, Arg. I7 92
Saldus, Lat. D5 10
Sale, Austl. L6 76
Salé, Mor. C3 64
Sale Creek, Tn., U.S. B13 122
Saleh, Teluk, b., Indon. H10 50
Salehard, Russia A11 32
Salem, India F4 53
Salem, Monts. D3 105a
Salem, Ar., U.S. H6 120
Salem, Il., U.S. F9 120
Salem, Ia., U.S. D6 120
Salem, Ma., U.S. B15 114
Salem, Mo., U.S. G6 120
Salem, N.H., U.S. B14 114
Salem, N.J., U.S. E10 114
Salem, N.Y., U.S. G3 110
Salem, Oh., U.S. D5 114
Salem, Or., U.S. F3 136
Salem, S.D., U.S. D15 126
Salem, Va., U.S. G5 114
Salem, W.V., U.S. E5 114
Salemi, Italy G6 24
Salem Upland, plat., Mo., U.S. G6 120
Salentina, Penisola, pen., Italy D12 24
Salerno, Italy D8 24
Salerno, Golfo di, b., Italy D8 24
Salers, Fr. D8 18
Salgar, Col. D4 86
Salgótarján, Hung. A6 26
Salgueiro, Braz E6 88
Salher, mtn., India H4 54
Sali, Cro. G12 22
Salida, Co., U.S. C3 128
Salihli, Tur. E11 28
Salihorsk, Bela. H10 10
Salima, Mwi. C5 68
Salimbatu, Indon. B10 50
Salin, Mya. B2 48
Salina, Ks., U.S. C11 128
Salina, Ut., U.S. E5 132
Salina Cruz, Mex. G11 100
Salina Point, c., Bah. A10 102
Salinas, Braz. I4 88
Salinas, Ec. I1 86
Salinas, Mex. G5 130
Salinas, P.R. C3 104a
Salinas, Ca., U.S. G4 134
Salinas, stm., Braz. I4 88
Salinas, stm., N.A. D2 102
Salinas, stm., Ca., U.S. G4 134
Salinas, Pampa de las, pl., Arg. E4 92
Salinas de Hidalgo, Mex. D8 100
Salinas Pueblo Missions National Monument, p.o.i., N.M., U.S. G2 128
Salinas Victoria, Mex. I7 130
Saline, Mi., U.S. B2 114
Saline, stm., Ar., U.S. D6 122
Saline, stm., Ar., U.S. C4 122
Saline, stm., Ks., U.S. C11 128
Saline Bayou, stm., La., U.S. E6 122
Saline Lake, l., La., U.S. F6 122
Salines, Cap de ses, c., Spain E14 20
Salines, Point, c., Gren. r10 105e
Salines, Pointe des, c., Mart. I7 105c
Salinópolis, Braz. D8 84
Salipolo, Indon. E11 50
Salisbury, Austl. J2 76
Salisbury, Eng., U.K. J11 12
Salisbury, Md., U.S. F10 114
Salisbury, Mo., U.S. E5 120
Salisbury, N.C., U.S. I5 114
Salisbury, Pa., U.S. E6 114
Salisbury see Harare, Zimb. D5 68
Salisbury Island, i., Nu., Can. C15 106
Salisbury Plain, pl., Eng., U.K. J11 12
Salish Mountains, mts., Mt., U.S. B12 136
Salitpa, Al., U.S. F10 122
Salitre, stm., Braz. E5 88
Şalkhad, Syria F7 58
Salles-Curan, Fr. E8 18
Sallisaw, Ok., U.S. B4 122
Salluit, Qc., Can. C15 106
Salmi, Russia F14 8
Salmo, B.C., Can. G13 138
Salmon, stm., B.C., Can. B8 138
Salmon, stm., N.B., Can. D11 110
Salmon, stm., Id., U.S. E10 136
Salmon, Middle Fork, stm., Id., U.S. E12 136
Salmon, South Fork, stm., Id., U.S. E11 136
Salmon Arm, B.C., Can. F11 138
Salmon Falls Creek, stm., U.S. H12 136
Salmon Gums, Austl. F4 74
Salmon Peak, mtn., Tx., U.S. E7 130
Salmon River Mountains, mts., Id., U.S. F12 136
Salmon Valley, B.C., Can. B8 138
Salo, Fin. F10 8
Salò, Italy E7 22
Salome, Az., U.S. J3 132
Salomon, Cap, c., Mart. I6 105c
Salon-de-Provence, Fr. F11 18
Salonga, Parc National de la, p.o.i., D.R.C. E4 66
Salonika see Thessaloníki, Grc. C6 28
Salonika, Gulf of see Thermaïkós Kólpos, b., Grc. C6 28
Salonta, Rom. C8 26
Salor, stm., Spain E4 20
Salpaussel'kja, mts., Eur. B3 32
Sal Rei, C.V. k10 65a
Salsacate, Arg. E5 92
Salsipuedes, Canal, strt., Mex. A2 100
Sal'sk, Russia E6 32
Salsomaggiore Terme, Italy F6 22
Salt, stm., Az., U.S. J4 132
Salt, stm., Mo., U.S. E6 120
Salt, Middle Fork, stm., Mo., U.S. E5 120
Salt, North Fork, stm., Mo., U.S. E5 120
Salta, Arg. B5 92
Salta, state, Arg. D4 90
Saltanovka, Russia H17 10
Saltash, Eng., U.K. K8 12
Salt Basin, l., Tx., U.S. C2 130
Salt Cay, i., Bah. m18 104f
Saltcoats, Sk., Can. C11 124
Salt Creek, stm., Il., U.S. D8 120
Saltee Islands, is., Ire. I6 12
Saltfjellet Svartisen Nasjonalpark, p.o.i., Nor. C6 8
Saltillo, Mex. C8 100
Saltillo, Tn., U.S. B10 122
Salt Lake City, Ut., U.S. C4 132
Salto, Arg. G7 92
Salto, Ur. E9 92
Salto del Guairá, Para. A10 92
Salto Grande, Embalse, res., S.A. E8 92
Salton City, Ca., U.S. J9 134
Salton Sea, l., Ca., U.S. J10 134
Salto Santiago, Represa de, res., Braz. B11 92
Saltspring Island, i., B.C., Can. H7 138
Saltville, Va., U.S. H4 114
Saluda, Va., U.S. G9 114
Saluda, stm., S.C., U.S. B4 116
Salûm, Egypt A5 62
Sālūmbar, India F5 54
Sālūr, India B6 53
Saluzzo, Italy F4 22
Salvador, Braz. G6 88
Salvador, El see El Salvador, ctry., N.A. F3 102
Salvador, Lake, l., La., U.S. H8 122
Salvatierra, Mex. E8 100
Salviac, Fr. E7 18
Salween (Nu) (Khong) (Thanlwin), stm., Asia E8 46
Salyan, Azer. B6 56
Salyān, Nepal D9 54
Salyer, Ca., U.S. C2 134
Salyersville, Ky., U.S. G2 114
Salzach, stm., Eur. B9 22
Salzburg, Aus. C10 22
Salzburg, state, Aus. C10 22
Salzgitter, Ger. D6 16
Salzkammergut, reg., Aus. C10 22
Salzwedel, Ger. D7 16
Samacá, Col. E5 86
Samacèvičy, Bela. G14 10
Samagaltaj, Russia D16 32
Samah, Libya B3 62
Samales Group, is., Phil. G3 52
Samalga Pass, strt., Ak., U.S. g25 140a
Samal Island, i., Phil. G5 52
Sāmalkot, India C6 53
Samâlût, Egypt J1 58
Samaná, Dom. Rep. C13 102
Samāna, India C5 54

Name — Map Ref. — Page

Samaná, Bahía de, b., Dom. Rep. C13 102
Samaná, Cabo, c., Dom. Rep. C13 102
Samana Cay, i., Bah. A11 102
Samandağı, Tur. B6 58
Samaniego, Col. G3 86
Samaqua, stm., Qc., Can. A4 110
Samar, i., Phil. E5 52
Samara, Russia D8 32
Samara, stm., Russia D8 32
Samarai, Pap. N. Gui. c5 79a
Samaria, Id., U.S. A4 132
Samaria Gorge see Samariás, Farángi, val., Grc. H6 28
Samariapo, Ven. E8 86
Samariás, Farángi (Samaria Gorge), val., Grc. H6 28
Samarinda, Indon. D10 50
Samarka, Russia B10 38
Samarkand, Uzb. G11 32
Sāmarrā', Iraq C5 56
Samastīpur, India F10 54
Samaúna, Braz. E5 84
Samba Caju, Ang. B2 68
Sambaíba, Braz. D3 88
Sambalpur, India H9 54
Sambar, Tanjung, c., Indon. E7 50
Sambas, Indon. C6 50
Sambava, Madag. C9 68
Şambayat, Tur. A9 58
Sambhal, India D7 54
Sāmbhar, India E5 54
Sāmbhar Lake, l., India E5 54
Sambir, Ukr. G19 16
Sambit, Pulau, i., Indon. C11 50
Sambito, stm., Braz. D5 88
Samboja, Indon. D10 50
Sâmbor, Camb. F7 48
Samborombón, stm., Arg. G9 92
Samborombón, Bahía, b., Arg. G9 92
Sambre, stm., Eur. D12 14
Sambre à l'Oise, Canal de la, can., Fr. E12 14
Sambriāl, Pak. B5 54
Samch'ŏk, Kor., S. B2 40
Sam Chom, Khao, mtn., Thai. H4 48
Same, Tan. E7 66
Sam Ford Fiord, b., Nu., Can. A16 106
Samfya, Zam. C4 68
Samka, Mya. B3 48
Samnangjin, Kor., S. D1 40
Sam Ngao, Thai. D4 48
Samoa, ctry., Oc. g12 79c
Samoa Islands, is., Oc. h12 79c
Samo Alto, Chile E2 92
Samobor, Cro. E12 22
Samoded, Russia E19 8
Samokov, Blg. G10 26
Sámos, i., Grc. F9 28
Samoset, Fl., U.S. I3 116
Samosir, Pulau, i., Indon. B1 50
Samothrace see Samothráki, i., Grc. C8 28
Samothráki, Grc. C8 28
Samothráki (Samothrace), i., Grc. C8 28
Sampacho, Arg. F5 92
Sampanahan, Indon. E10 50
Sampang, Indon. G8 50
Sampit, Indon. E8 50
Sampit, stm., Indon. E8 50
Sampit, Teluk, b., Indon. E8 50
Sampwe, D.R.C. F5 66
Sam Rayburn Reservoir, res., Tx., U.S. F4 122
Samro, ozero, l., Russia B11 10
Sam Son, Viet. C7 48
Samsun, Tur. A4 56
Samsu-ŭp, Kor., N. D7 38
Samtown, La., U.S. F6 122
Samuhú, Arg. C7 92
Samui, Ko, i., Thai. H5 48
Samundri, Pak. C4 54
Samut Prakan, Thai. F5 48
Samut Sakhon, Thai. F5 48
Samut Songkhram, Thai. F5 48
San, Mali G3 64
San (Xan), stm., Asia F8 48
San, stm., China E8 42
San (Syan), stm., Eur. F18 16
Saña, Peru E2 84
Şan'ā', Yemen F5 56
Sana, stm., Bos. E3 26
Sanaa see Şan'ā', Yemen F5 56
Sanabu, Egypt K1 58
Sanaga, stm., Cam. D2 66
San Agustín, Arg. E5 92
San Agustín, Arg. I8 92
San Agustín, Mex. C1 130
San Agustin, Cape, c., Phil. G6 52
Sanak Islands, is., Ak., U.S. F7 140
San Alberto, Mex. G6 130
San Ambrosio, Isla, i., Chile H7 82
Sanana, Pulau, i., Indon. F8 44
Sānand, India G4 54
Sanandaj, Iran B6 56
San Andreas, Ca., U.S. E5 134
San Andrés, Col. F7 102
San Andrés, Isla de, i., Col. F7 102
San Andres Mountains, mts., N.M., U.S. H2 128
San Andrés Sajcabajá, Guat. E2 102
San Andrés Tuxtla, Mex. F11 100
San Andrés y Providencia, state, Col. F7 102
Sananduva, Braz. C12 92
San Angelo, Tx., U.S. C7 130
San Antero, Col. C4 86
San Antonio, Arg. D5 92
San Antonio, Chile F2 92
San Antonio, Col. F4 86
San Antonio, N.M., U.S. F2 128
San Antonio, N.M., U.S. J9 132
San Antonio, Tx., U.S. E9 130
San Antonio, Ur. E9 92
San Antonio, stm., Tx., U.S. F10 130
San Antonio, Cabo, pen., Arg. H9 92
San Antonio, Cabo de, c., Cuba B5 102
San Antonio, Lake, res., Ca., U.S. H4 134
San Antonio, Mount, mtn., Ca., U.S. I8 134
San Antonio, Punta, c., Mex. B3 100
San Antonio Abad see Sant Antoni de Portmany, Spain F12 20
San Antonio Bay, b., Tx., U.S. F11 130
San Antonio de Bravo, Mex. D3 130
San Antonio de La Paz see San Antonio, Arg. D5 92
San Antonio de los Baños, Cuba A6 102
San Antonio de los Cobres, Arg. B4 92
San Antonio del Táchira, Ven. D5 86
San Antonio de Tamanaco, Ven. C8 86
San Antonio el Grande, Mex. F2 130
San Antonio Mountain, mtn., N.M., U.S. E2 128
San Antonio Oeste, Arg. H4 90
Sanatorium, Ms., U.S. F9 122
San Augustine, Tx., U.S. F4 122
San Augustin Pass, p., N.M., U.S. K10 132
Sanāw, Yemen F7 56
Sanāwad, India G6 54
San Bartolomeo in Galdo, Italy C9 24
San Benedetto del Tronto, Italy H10 22
San Benedetto Po, Italy E7 22
San Benedicto, Isla, i., Mex. F3 100
San Benito, Tx., U.S. H10 130
San Benito, stm., Ca., U.S. G4 134
San Benito Mountain, mtn., Ca., U.S. G5 134
San Bernard, stm., Tx., U.S. E12 130
San Bernardino, Ca., U.S. I8 134
San Bernardino Mountains, mts., Ca., U.S. I9 134
San Bernardino Strait, strt., Phil. D5 52
San Bernardo, Chile F2 92
San Bernardo, Islas de, is., Col. C3 86
San Bernardo del Viento, Col. C3 86
Sanbe-yama, vol., Japan D5 40
San Blas, Mex. E6 100
San Blas, Mex. B4 100
San Blas, Cape, c., Fl., U.S. H13 122
San Blas, Golfo de, b., Pan. H8 102
San Blas, Serranía de, mts., Pan. H8 102
San Borja, Bol. B3 90
Sanborn, Ia., U.S. H3 118
Sanborn, N.D., U.S. H15 124
San Bruno, Ca., U.S. F3 134
San Buenaventura, Bol. B3 90
San Buenaventura, Mex. B8 100
San Buenaventura see Ventura, Ca., U.S. I6 134
San Carlos, Chile H2 92
San Carlos, Mex. C9 100
San Carlos, Mex. A8 100
San Carlos, Nic. G5 102
San Carlos, Phil. E4 52
San Carlos, Phil. C3 52
San Carlos, Az., U.S. J6 132
San Carlos, Ca., U.S. F3 134
San Carlos, Ur. G10 92
San Carlos, Ven. C7 86
San Carlos, stm., C.R. G5 102
San Carlos, stm., Ven. C7 86
San Carlos Centro, Arg. E7 92
San Carlos de Bariloche, Arg. H2 90
San Carlos de Bolívar, Arg. H7 92
San Carlos de Guaroa, Col. F5 86
San Carlos del Zulia, Ven. C5 86
San Carlos de Río Negro, Ven. G8 86
San Carlos Reservoir, res., Az., U.S. J6 132
San Cataldo, Italy G7 24
San Cayetano, Arg. I8 92
Sancha, stm., China H1 42
Sanchahe, China B7 38
Sanchenglong, China B4 38
San Ciro de Acosta, Mex. E9 100
San Clemente, Spain E8 20
San Clemente, Ca., U.S. J8 134
San Clemente Island, i., Ca., U.S. K7 134
San Cristóbal, Arg. E7 92
San Cristóbal, Dom. Rep. C12 102
San Cristóbal, Ven. D5 86
San Cristobal, i., Sol. Is. f9 79b
San Cristóbal, Bahía, b., Mex. B1 100
San Cristóbal, Isla, i., Ec. i12 84a
San Cristóbal, Volcán, vol., Nic. F4 102
San Cristóbal de las Casas, Mex. G12 100
Sancti Spíritus, Cuba A8 102
Sancy, Puy de, mtn., Fr. D8 18
Sand, Nor. G2 8
Sand, stm., Ab., Can. B19 138
Sand, stm., S. Afr. F8 70
Sand, stm., S. Afr. C9 70
Sandai, Indon. D7 50
Sandakan, Malay. H2 52
Sândăn, Camb. F8 48
Sandaré, Mali G2 64
Sand Arroyo, stm., U.S. D7 128
Sanday, i., Scot., U.K. B10 12
Sandefjord, Nor. G4 8
Sanderson, Tx., U.S. D5 130
Sandersville, Ga., U.S. D3 116
Sandersville, Ms., U.S. F9 122
Sand Fork, W.V., U.S. F5 114
Sand Hill, stm., Mn., U.S. D2 118
Sand Hills, hills, Ne., U.S. F11 126
Sāndi, India E8 54
Sandia, Peru F4 84
San Diego, Ca., U.S. K8 134
San Diego, Tx., U.S. G9 130
San Diego, Cabo, c., Arg. J3 90
San Diego Aqueduct, aq., Ca., U.S. J8 134
Sandıklı, Tur. E13 28
Sandīla, India E8 54
Sandilands Village, Bah. m18 104f
Sand Key, i., Fl., U.S. I3 116
Sand Lake, l., On., Can. A4 118
Sandnes, Nor. G1 8
Sandoa, D.R.C. F4 66
Sandomierz, Pol. F17 16
Sandoná, Col. G3 86
San Donà di Piave, Italy E9 22
Sandovo, Russia B19 10
Sandoway, Mya. C2 48
Sandown, Eng., U.K. K11 12
Sand Point, Ak., U.S. E7 140
Sandpoint, Id., U.S. B10 136
Sandringham, Austl. E2 76
Sandspit, B.C., Can. E4 106
Sand Springs, Ok., U.S. A2 122
Sand Springs, Tx., U.S. B6 130
Sandstone, Austl. E3 74
Sandstone, Mn., U.S. E5 118
Sandu Ao, b., China H8 42
Sandusky, Mi., U.S. E7 112
Sandusky, Oh., U.S. C3 114
Sandvika, Nor. G4 8
Sandviken, Swe. F7 8
Sandwich, Eng., U.K. J14 12
Sandwich Bay, b., Nmb. C2 70
Sandwick, B.C., Can. G5 138
Sandwīp Island, i., Bngl. G13 54
Sandy, Or., U.S. E4 136
Sandy, Ut., U.S. C5 132
Sandy Bay Mountain, mtn., Me., U.S. E6 110
Sandy Cape, c., Austl. E9 76
Sandy Cape, c., Austl. n12 77a
Sandy Creek, stm., Austl. I5 76
Sandy Hook, Ky., U.S. F2 114
Sandy Hook, spit, N.J., U.S. D12 114
Sandykači, Turkmen. B9 56
Sandy Lake, l., On., Can. E12 106
Sandy Point, c., Trin. r13 105f
Sandy Point Town, St. K./N. C2 105a
Sandy Springs, Ga., U.S. C1 116
Sandžak, reg., Yugo. F6 26
San Elizario, Tx., U.S. C1 130
San Enrique, Arg. G7 92
San Estanislao, Para. B9 92
San Esteban, Isla, i., Mex. A2 100
San Esteban de Gormaz, Spain C7 20
San Felipe, Chile F2 92
San Felipe, Col. G8 86
San Felipe, Mex. F5 98
San Felipe, Mex. E8 100
San Felipe, Ven. B7 86
San Felipe, Cayos de, is., Cuba B6 102
San Felipe Nuevo Mercurio, Mex. C7 100
San Felipe Pueblo, N.M., U.S. F2 128
San Felíu de Guixols see Sant Feliu de Guíxols, Spain C14 20
San Félix, Isla, i., Chile H6 82
San Fernando, Chile G2 92
San Fernando, Mex. C9 100
San Fernando, Mex. F6 130
San Fernando, Phil. B2 52
San Fernando, Phil. C3 52
San Fernando, Spain H4 20
San Fernando, Trin. s12 105f
San Fernando, Ca., U.S. I7 134
San Fernando de Apure, Ven. D8 86
San Fernando de Atabapo, Ven. E8 86
San Fernando del Valle de Catamarca, Arg. D4 92
Sånfjällets Nationalpark, p.o.i., Swe. E5 8
Sanford, Co., U.S. D2 128
Sanford, Fl., U.S. H4 116
Sanford, Me., U.S. G6 110
Sanford, N.C., U.S. A6 116
Sanford, Tx., U.S. F7 128
Sanford, stm., Austl. E3 74
Sanford, Mount, vol., Ak., U.S. D11 140
San Francisco, Arg. E6 92
San Francisco, El Sal. F3 102
San Francisco, Ca., U.S. F3 134
San Francisco, stm., Arg. B5 92
San Francisco, stm., U.S. J8 132
San Francisco, Paso de, p., S.A. C3 92
San Francisco Bay, b., Ca., U.S. F3 134
San Francisco Creek, stm., Tx., U.S. E5 130
San Francisco de Borja, Mex. B5 100
San Francisco de Horizonte, Mex. I4 130
San Francisco del Chañar, Arg. D5 92
San Francisco del Oro, Mex. B5 100
San Francisco del Rincón, Mex. E7 100
San Francisco de Macorís, Dom. Rep. C12 102
San Francisco de Mostazal, Chile F2 92
San Gabriel, Ec. G3 86
San Gabriel Chilac, Mex. F10 100
San Gabriel Mountains, mts., Ca., U.S. I8 134
Sangamankanda Point, c., Sri L. H5 53
Sangamner, India B1 53
Sangamon, stm., Il., U.S. D7 120
Sangar, Russia D14 34
Sangasanga-dalam, Indon. D10 50
San Gavino Monreale, Italy E2 24
Sangay, vol., Ec. I2 86
Sangay, Parque Nacional, p.o.i., Ec. H3 86
Sange, D.R.C. F5 66
Sangeang, Pulau, i., Indon. H11 50
Sanger, Ca., U.S. G6 134
Sanger, Tx., U.S. H11 128
Sângera, Mol. B15 26
Sangerhausen, Ger. E7 16
San Germán, P.R. B1 104a
Sangerville, Me., U.S. E7 110
Sanggan, stm., China A6 42
Sanggau, Indon. C7 50
Sangha, stm., Afr. E3 66
Sanghar, Pak. E2 54
Sangihe, Kepulauan, is., Indon. E7 44
Sangihe, Pulau, i., Indon. E8 44
San Gil, Col. D5 86
Sangilen, hrebet, mts., Russia D17 32
San Gimignano, Italy G7 22
San Giovanni in Fiore, Italy E10 24
San Giovanni in Persiceto, Italy F8 22
San Giovanni Rotondo, Italy C9 24
San Giovanni Valdarno, Italy G8 22
Sangiyn Dalay nuur, l., Mong. B4 36
Sangju, Kor., S. F8 38
Sangkapura, Indon. F8 50
Sângkê, stm., Camb. F6 48
Sangkulirang, Indon. C10 50
Sāngli, India C2 53
Sangmélima, Cam. D2 66
Sāngole, India C2 53
Sangolquí, Ec. H2 86
San Gorgonio Mountain, mtn., Ca., U.S. I9 134
San Gottardo, Passo del, p., Switz. D5 22
Sangre de Cristo Mountains, mts., U.S. E3 128
San Gregorio, Arg. G6 92
Sangre Grande, Trin. s12 105f
Sangro, stm., Italy H11 22
Sangrūr, India C5 54
Sangsang, China D11 54
Sangue, stm., Braz. F6 84
Sangutane, stm., Moz. C11 70
Sangya, China C13 54
San Hipólito, Punta, c., Mex. B1 100
Sanhu, China H6 42
Sânhûr, Egypt I1 58
Sanibel Island, i., Fl., U.S. J3 116
San Ignacio, Arg. C10 92
San Ignacio, Mex. D8 100
San Ignacio, Mex. B2 100
San Ignacio, Para. C9 92
San Ignacio, Isla, i., Mex. C4 100
San Ignacio, Laguna, b., Mex. B2 100
San Ignacio de Moxo, Bol. B3 90
San Ignacio de Velasco, Bol. C4 90
San Isidro, Arg. D5 92
San Isidro, Arg. G8 92
San Isidro del General, C.R. H5 102
San Jacinto, Col. C4 86
San Jacinto, Ca., U.S. J9 134
San Jacinto Peak, mtn., Ca., U.S. J9 134
San Jaime, Arg. E8 92
San Javier, Arg. C10 92
San Javier, Arg. E8 92
San Javier, Bol. C4 90
San Javier, Chile G2 92
San Javier, Mex. H8 130
San Javier, Ur. F8 92
San Javier, stm., Arg. E8 92
Sanjay National Park, p.o.i., India G8 54
San Jerónimo, Guat. E2 102
Sanjiang, China I3 42
Sanjō, Japan B11 40
San Joaquín, Bol. B4 90
San Joaquín, stm., Bol. B4 90
San Joaquin, stm., Ca., U.S. E4 134
San Joaquín de Omaguas, Peru D3 84
San Joaquin Valley, val., Ca., U.S. G5 134
San Jorge, Arg. E6 92
San Jorge, stm., Col. C4 86
San Jorge, Bahía de, b., Mex. F6 98
San Jorge, Golfo, b., Arg. I3 90
San Jorge Island, i., Sol. Is. e8 79b
San José, C.R. H5 102
San José, Mex. F7 130
San Jose, Phil. E3 52
San Jose, Ca., U.S. F4 134
San Jose, Il., U.S. D8 120
San Jose, N.M., U.S. F3 128
San José, Ven. q19 104g
San Jose, stm., N.M., U.S. I9 132
San José, Cerro, mtn., Mex. H2 130
San José, Isla, i., Mex. C3 100
San José, Isla, i., Pan. H8 102
San José, Laguna, b., P.R. B3 104a
San José de Bácum, Mex. B3 100
San José de Batuc, Mex. A3 100
San José de Chiquitos, Bol. C4 90
San José de Feliciano, Arg. E8 92
San José de Guanipa, Ven. C9 86
San José de Jáchal, Arg. E3 92
San José de la Popa, Mex. H7 130
San José de las Lajas, Cuba A6 102
San José del Cabo, Mex. D4 100
San José del Guaviare, Col. F5 86
San José de Mayo, Ur. G9 92
San José de Ocuné, Col. E6 86
San José de Tiznados, Ven. C8 86
San Jose Island, i., Tx., U.S. G11 130
San Juan, Arg. E3 92
San Juan, Mex. E3 130
San Juan, P.R. B3 104a
San Juan, state, Arg. E3 92
San Juan, stm., Arg. F4 92
San Juan, stm., Col. E3 86
San Juan, stm., Mex. H8 130
San Juan, stm., N.A. G5 102
San Juan, stm., U.S. F6 132
San Juan, stm., Ven. B10 86
San Juan, Cabezas de, c., P.R. B4 104a
San Juan, Cabo, c., Arg. J4 90
San Juan Basin, bas., N.M., U.S. G8 132
San Juan Bautista, Mex. H6 130
San Juan Bautista, Para. C9 92
San Juan Bautista see Sant Joan de Labritja, Spain E12 20
San Juan Bautista, Ca., U.S. G4 134
San Juan Creek, stm., Ca., U.S. H5 134
San Juan de Colón, Ven. C5 86
San Juan de Guadalupe, Mex. C7 100
San Juan de la Maguana, Dom. Rep. C12 102
San Juan del Norte, Nic. G6 102
San Juan de los Cayos, Ven. B7 86
San Juan de los Morros, Ven. C8 86
San Juan del Río, Mex. C6 100
San Juan del Río, Mex. E8 100
San Juan del Sur, Nic. G4 102
San Juan de Micay, stm., Col. F3 86
San Juan de Payara, Ven. D8 86
San Juan de Sabinas, Mex. G6 130
San Juanico, Mex. B2 100
San Juan Islands, is., Wa., U.S. B3 136
San Juanito, Isla, i., Mex. E5 100
San Juan Mountains, mts., Co., U.S. C9 98
San Juan Nepomuceno, Col. C4 86
San Juan Nepomuceno, Para. C9 92
San Justo, Arg. E7 92
Sankarani, stm., Afr. G3 64
Sankeshwar, India C2 53
Sankh, stm., India G10 54
Sankheda, India G4 54
Sankosh, stm., Asia E13 54
Sankt Anton am Arlberg, Aus. C7 22
Sankt Gallen, Switz. C6 22
Sankt Goarshausen, Ger. F3 16
Sankt Ingbert, Ger. G3 16
Sankt Michel see Mikkeli, Fin. F12 8
Sankt Moritz, Switz. D6 22
Sankt-Peterburg (Saint Petersburg), Russia A13 10
Sankt Peter-Ording, Ger. B4 16
Sankt Pölten, Aus. B12 22
Sankt Veit an der Glan, Aus. D11 22
Sankt-Vith see Saint-Vith, Bel. D14 14
Sankt Wendel, Ger. G3 16
Sankuru, stm., D.R.C. E4 66
San Lázaro, Cabo, c., Mex. C2 100
San Leandro, Ca., U.S. F3 134
San Leonardo, Mex. G3 130
Şanlıurfa (Urfa), Tur. A9 58
Şanlıurfa, state, Tur. A9 58
San Lorenzo, Arg. D8 92
San Lorenzo, Arg. F7 92
San Lorenzo, Bol. D4 90
San Lorenzo, Ec. G2 86
San Lorenzo, Mex. C7 100
San Lorenzo, P.R. B4 104a
San Lorenzo, stm., Mex. C5 100
San Lorenzo, Cabo, c., Ec. H1 86
San Lorenzo, Isla, i., Mex. A2 100
San Lorenzo, Monte (Cochrane, Cerro), mtn., S.A. I2 90
San Lorenzo de la Parrilla, Spain E8 20
Sanlúcar de Barrameda, Spain H4 20
San Lucas, Bol. D3 90
San Lucas, Mex. D3 100
San Lucas, Cabo, c., Mex. D4 100
San Luis, Arg. F4 92
San Luis, Cuba B10 102
San Luis, Guat. D3 102
San Luis, Co., U.S. D3 128
San Luis, Ven. B7 86
San Luis, state, Arg. F5 92
San Luís, Laguna, l., Bol. B4 90
San Luis, Sierra de, mts., Arg. F5 92
San Luis Creek, stm., Co., U.S. C3 128
San Luis de la Paz, Mex. E8 100
San Luis Gonzaga, Mex. C3 100
San Luis Gonzaga, Bahía, b., Mex. G5 98
San Luis Jilotepeque, Guat. E3 102
San Luis Obispo, Ca., U.S. H5 134
San Luis Potosí, Mex. D8 100
San Luis Potosí, state, Mex. D8 100
San Luis Reservoir, res., Ca., U.S. F4 134
San Luis Río Colorado, Mex. E5 98
San Luis Valley, val., Co., U.S. D3 128
San Manuel, Arg. H8 92
San Manuel, Az., U.S. K6 132
San Marcial, stm., Mex. A3 100
San Marcos, Col. C4 86
San Marcos, Mex. G9 100
San Marcos, Tx., U.S. E9 130
San Marcos, Isla, i., Mex. B2 100
San Marino, S. Mar. G9 22
San Marino, ctry., Eur. G9 22
San Martín, Arg. D5 92
San Martín, Arg. F3 92
San Martín, Col. F5 86
San Martín, stm., Bol. B4 90
San Martin, sci., Ant. B34 81
San Martín, Lago (O'Higgins, Lago), l., S.A. I2 90
San Martín de los Andes, Arg. H2 90
San Martino di Castrozza, ngh., Italy D8 22
San Mateo, Mex. G1 130
San Mateo see Sant Mateu del Maestrat, Spain D10 20
San Mateo, Ca., U.S. F3 134
San Mateo, Fl., U.S. G4 116
San Mateo, N.M., U.S. H9 132
San Matías, Bol. C5 90
San Matías, Golfo, b., Arg. H4 90
Sanmen, China G9 42
Sanmenhsia see Sanmenxia, China D4 42
Sanmenxia, China D4 42
San Miguel, Ec. H2 86
San Miguel, El Sal. F3 102
San Miguel, Mex. A8 100
San Miguel, Pan. H8 102
San Miguel, stm., Bol. B4 90
San Miguel, stm., S.A. G3 86
San Miguel, stm., Co., U.S. E8 132
San Miguel, Golfo de, b., Pan. H8 102
San Miguel de Allende, Mex. E8 100
San Miguel de Cruces, Mex. C6 100
San Miguel del Monte, Arg. G8 92
San Miguel de Salcedo, Ec. H2 86
San Miguel de Tucumán, Arg. C4 92
San Miguel Island, i., Ca., U.S. I5 134
Sanming, China H7 42
San Miniato, Italy G7 22
Sannār, Sudan E6 62
Sannicandro Garganico, Italy I12 22
San Nicolás, Peru G2 84
San Nicolas, Phil. A3 52
San Nicolás de los Arroyos, Arg. F7 92
San Nicolás de los Garza, Mex. C8 100
San Nicolas Island, i., Ca., U.S. J6 134
Sânnicolau Mare, Rom. C7 26
Sannieshof, S. Afr. E7 70
Sannikova, proliv, strt., Russia B16 34
Sano, Japan C12 40
Sanok, Pol. G18 16
Sânon, stm., Fr. F15 14
San Pablo, Phil. C3 52
San Pablo Bay, b., Ca., U.S. E3 134
San Pasqual, Punta, c., Mex. C3 100
San Pedro, Arg. B5 92
San Pedro, Arg. C5 92
San Pedro, Arg. F8 92
San Pedro, Chile F2 92
San Pedro, Col. C4 86
San-Pédro, C. Iv. I3 64
San Pedro, Neth. Ant. A1 105a
San Pedro, state, Para. B9 92
San Pedro, stm., Mex. F8 98
San Pedro, stm., Mex. G2 130
San Pedro, stm., N.A. D2 102
San Pedro, stm., N.A. K6 132
San Pedro, Punta, c., Chile B2 92
San Pedro, Volcán, vol., Chile D3 90
San Pedro Carchá, Guat. E2 102
San Pedro de Jujuy see San Pedro, Arg. B5 92
San Pedro de las Colonias, Mex. C7 100
San Pedro del Gallo, Mex. C6 100
San Pedro del Paraná, Para. C9 92
San Pedro de Macorís, Dom. Rep. C13 102
San Pedro de Ycuamandiyú, Para. B9 92
San Pedro Peaks, mtn., N.M., U.S. G10 132
San Pedro Sula, Hond. E3 102
San Pedro Tabasco, Mex. D2 102
San Pellegrino Terme, Italy E6 22
San Pietro, Isola di, i., Italy E2 24
San Pitch, stm., Ut., U.S. D5 132
Sanquhar, Scot., U.K. F9 12
Sanquianga, Parque Nacional, p.o.i., Col. F2 86
San Quintín, Cabo, c., Mex. F4 98
San Rafael, Arg. G3 92
San Rafael, Chile G2 92
San Rafael, Mex. C8 100
San Rafael, Ca., U.S. E3 134
San Rafael, N.M., U.S. H8 132
San Rafael, Ven. B6 86
San Rafael, stm., Mex. F5 98
San Rafael, stm., Ut., U.S. E6 132
San Rafael del Norte, Nic. F4 102
San Rafael Swell, plat., Ut., U.S. E6 132
San Ramón, Arg. C5 92
San Ramón, Bol. B4 90
San Ramón de la Nueva Orán, Arg. D4 90
San Remo, Italy G4 22
San Rodrigo, stm., Mex. F6 130
San Roque, Arg. D8 92
San Roque, Punta, c., Mex. B1 100
San Saba, Tx., U.S. C9 130
San Saba, stm., Tx., U.S. C9 130
San Salvador, Arg. E8 92
San Salvador, El Sal. F3 102
San Salvador, i., Bah. C10 96
San Salvador de Jujuy, Arg. A5 92
Sansanné-Mango, Togo G5 64
San Sebastián, P.R. B1 104a
San Sebastián see Donostia, Spain A9 20
San Sebastián, Bahía, b., Arg. J3 90
Sansepolcro, Italy G9 22
San Severo, Italy I12 22
Sansha, China H9 42
San Simon, Az., U.S. K7 132
San Simon, stm., Az., U.S. K7 132
San Simon Wash, stm., Az., U.S. K4 132
Sanski Most, Bos. E3 26
San Solano, Arg. E4 92
Sans-Souci, hist., Haiti C11 102
Santa, stm., Peru E2 84
Santa Adélia, Braz. K1 88
Santa Amalia, Spain E4 20
Santa Ana, Bol. B3 90
Santa Ana, Ec. H1 86
Santa Ana, El Sal. E3 102
Santa Ana, Mex. F7 98
Santa Ana, Mex. C8 100
Santa Ana, Ca., U.S. J8 134
Santa Ana, Ven. C9 86
Santa Ana del Alto Beni, Bol. C3 90
Santa Anna, Tx., U.S. C8 130
Santa Bárbara, Chile H2 92
Santa Barbara, Col. E4 86
Santa Bárbara, Hond. E3 102
Santa Bárbara, Mex. B6 100
Santa Barbara, Ca., U.S. I6 134
Santa Bárbara, Ven. D6 86
Santa Barbara Channel, strt., Ca., U.S. I6 134
Santa Barbara Island, i., Ca., U.S. J7 134
Santa Catalina, Gulf of, b., Ca., U.S. J7 134
Santa Catalina, Isla, i., Mex. C3 100
Santa Catalina Island, i., Ca., U.S. J7 134
Santa Catarina, Mex. C8 100
Santa Catarina, Mex. L10 134
Santa Catarina, state, Braz. C12 92
Santa Catarina, Ilha de, i., Braz. C13 92
Santa Cecília, Braz. C12 92
Santa Clara, Col. I7 86
Santa Clara, Cuba A7 102
Santa Clara, Ca., U.S. F3 134
Santa Clara, Ut., U.S. F3 132
Santa Clara, stm., Ca., U.S. I7 134
Santa Clarita, Ca., U.S. I7 134
Santa Clotilde, Peru D3 84
Santa Coloma de Farners, Spain C13 20
Santa Coloma de Farnés see Santa Coloma de Farners, Spain C13 20
Santa Comba, Spain A2 20
Santa Cruz, Braz. J5 88
Santa Cruz, Braz. D8 88
Santa Cruz, C.R. G5 102
Santa Cruz, Phil. C2 52
Santa Cruz, Phil. D4 52
Santa Cruz, Phil. C3 52
Santa Cruz, Ca., U.S. G3 134
Santa Cruz, state, Arg. I2 90
Santa Cruz, stm., Arg. J3 90
Santa Cruz, stm., N.A. J4 132
Santa Cruz, Isla, i., Ec. i11 84a
Santa Cruz Cabrália, Braz. I6 88
Santa Cruz de la Sierra, Bol. C4 90
Santa Cruz del Quiché, Guat. E2 102
Santa Cruz del Sur, Cuba B9 102
Santa Cruz de Mudela, Spain F7 20
Santa Cruz do Capibaribe, Braz. D7 88
Santa Cruz do Piauí, Braz. D5 88
Santa Cruz do Rio Pardo, Braz. L1 88
Santa Cruz do Sul, Braz. D11 92
Santa Cruz Island, i., Ca., U.S. J6 134
Santa Cruz Islands, is., Sol. Is. E7 72
Santa Elena, Arg. E8 92
Santa Elena, Ec. I1 86
Santa Elena, Mex. B7 100
Santa Elena, Bahía de, b., Ec. H1 86
Santa Elena, Cabo, c., C.R. G4 102
Santa Eufemia, Spain F6 20
Santa Eulalia, Spain D9 20
Santa Eulalia del Río see Santa Eulària del Riu, Spain E12 20
Santa Eulària del Riu, Spain E12 20
Santa Fe, Arg. E7 92
Santa Fe, Spain G7 20
Santa Fe, N.M., U.S. F3 128
Santa Fe, state, Arg. D7 92
Santa Fe, stm., Fl., U.S. G3 116
Santa Fe Baldy, mtn., N.M., U.S. F3 128
Santa Fe de Bogotá, Col. E4 86
Santa Fe de Minas, Braz. I3 88
Santa Fé do Sul, Braz. D6 90
Santa Filomena, Braz. E3 88
Sant'Agata di Militello, Italy F8 24
Santa Gertrudis, Mex. G2 130
Santa Helena, Braz. B3 88
Santa Helena de Goiás, Braz. G7 84
Santai, China F1 42
Santa Inês, Braz. G5 88
Santa Inés, Bahía, b., Mex. B3 100
Santa Inés, Isla, i., Chile J2 90
Santa Isabel, Arg. H4 92
Santa Isabel, P.R. C3 104a
Santa Isabel, i., Sol. Is. e8 79b
Santa Isabel, stm., Mex. F1 130
Santa Isabel, Pico de, mtn., Eq. Gui. I6 64
Santa Isabel Creek, stm., Tx., U.S. G8 130
Santa Juliana, Braz. J2 88
Santal, Baie du, b., N. Cal. m16 79d
Santa Lucía, Arg. D8 92
Santa Lucía, Ur. G9 92
Santa Lucia Range, mts., Ca., U.S. G4 134
Santaluz, Braz. F6 88
Santa Luzia, Braz. D7 88
Santa Magdalena, Arg. G6 92
Santa Magdalena, Isla, i., Mex. C2 100
Santa Margarita, Ca., U.S. H5 134
Santa Margarita, Isla, i., Mex. C2 100
Santa Margherita Ligure, Italy F6 22
Santa María, Arg. C4 92
Santa Maria, Braz. D10 92
Santa María, Mex. F6 130
Santa Maria, Ca., U.S. I5 134
Santa Maria, i., Vanuatu j16 79d
Santa Maria, stm., Braz. E10 92
Santa María, stm., Mex. F9 98
Santa María, stm., Mex. E8 100
Santa Maria, stm., Az., U.S. I3 132
Santa María, Bahía, b., Mex. C4 100
Santa María, Cabo, c., Ur. G10 92
Santa Maria, Cabo de, c., Ang. C1 68
Santa Maria, Cabo de, c., Port. H3 20
Santa María, Isla, i., Chile H1 92
Santa María, Isla, i., Ec. i11 84a
Santa María, Laguna de, l., Mex. F9 98
Santa María Asunción Tlaxiaco, Mex. G10 100
Santa Maria Capua Vetere, Italy C7 24
Santa María Colotepec, Mex. H10 100
Santa Maria da Boa Vista, Braz. E5 88
Santa Maria da Vitória, Braz. G3 88
Santa Maria de Itabira, Braz. J4 88
Santa María del Oro, Mex. C6 100
Santa María del Río, Mex. E8 100
Santa Maria di Leuca, Capo, c., Italy E12 24
Santa Maria do Suaçuí, Braz. J4 88
Santa María la Real de Nieva, Spain C6 20
Santa Marinella, Italy H8 22
Santa Marta, Col. B4 86
Santa Marta, Cabo de, c., Ang. C1 68
Santa Marta, Ciénaga Grande, b., Col. B4 86
Santa Mónica, Mex. F7 130
Santa Monica, Ca., U.S. I7 134
Santa Monica Bay, b., Ca., U.S. J7 134
Santan, Indon. D10 50
Santana, Braz. G3 88
Santana, Coxilha de (Santa Ana, Cuchilla de), hills, S.A. E10 92
Santana, Ilha de, i., Braz. B4 88
Santana da Boa Vista, Braz. E11 92
Santana do Ipanema, Braz. E7 88
Santana do Livramento, Braz. E9 92

Name	Map Ref.	Page
Santander, Col.	F3	86
Santander, Phil.	F4	52
Santander, Spain	A7	20
Santander, state, Col.	D5	86
Santander Jiménez, Mex.	C9	100
Sant'Andrea, Isola, i., Italy	D11	24
Santanghu, China	C3	36
Santanilla, Islas, is., Hond.	D6	102
Sant'Antine, Nuraghe, hist., Italy	D2	24
Sant'Antioco, Italy	E2	24
Sant'Antioco, Isola di, i., Italy	E2	24
Sant Antoni de Portmany, Spain	F12	20
Santanyí, Spain	E14	20
Santa Paula, Ca., U.S.	I6	134
Santaquin, Ut., U.S.	D5	132
Santa Quitéria, Braz.	C5	88
Santa Quitéria do Maranhão, Braz.	B4	88
Santarcangelo di Romagna, Italy	F9	22
Santarém, Braz.	D7	84
Santarém, Port.	E2	20
Santarém, state, Port.	E2	20
Santaren Channel, strt., Bah.	C9	96
Santa Rita, Braz.	D8	88
Santa Rita, Col.	G5	86
Santa Rita, Hond.	E3	102
Santa Rita, Mex.	G7	130
Santa Rita, Mt., U.S.	B14	136
Santa Rita, Ven.	B6	86
Santa Rosa, Arg.	H5	92
Santa Rosa, Braz.	H2	88
Santa Rosa, Braz.	C10	92
Santa Rosa, Col.	F7	86
Santa Rosa, Ec.	D2	84
Santa Rosa, Ca., U.S.	E3	134
Santa Rosa, Tx., U.S.	H10	130
Santa Rosa, Ven.	C7	86
Santa Rosa, Ven.	D7	86
Santa Rosa, Mount, hill, Guam	i10	78c
Santa Rosa Beach, Fl., U.S.	G12	122
Santa Rosa de Copán, Hond.	E3	102
Santa Rosa del Conlara, Arg.	F5	92
Santa Rosa de Leales, Arg.	C5	92
Santa Rosa de Osos, Col.	D4	86
Santa Rosa de Sucumbíos, Ec.	G3	86
Santa Rosa de Viterbo, Col.	E5	86
Santa Rosa Island, i., Ca., U.S.	J5	134
Santa Rosalía, Mex.	B2	100
Santa Rosalía, Mex.	H9	130
Santa Rosalía, Ven.	C7	86
Santa Rosa Wash, stm., Az., U.S.	K5	132
Šantarskie ostrova, is., Russia	E16	34
Santa Sylvina, Arg.	C7	92
Santa Teresa, Braz.	J5	88
Santa Teresa, Mex.	C9	100
Santa Teresa, stm., Braz.	G1	88
Santa Teresa, Embalse de, res., Spain	D5	20
Santa Teresa, Fortaleza de, hist., Ur.	F11	92
Santa Uxía, Spain	B1	20
Santa Vitória do Palmar, Braz.	F11	92
Santee, Ca., U.S.	K8	134
Santee, stm., S.C., U.S.	C6	116
Santee Dam, dam, S.C., U.S.	C5	116
Sant'Eufemia, Golfo di, b., Italy	F9	24
Sant Feliu de Guíxols, Spain	C14	20
Santhià, Italy	E5	22
Santiago, Braz.	D10	92
Santiago, Chile	F2	92
Santiago, Mex.	D4	100
Santiago, Pan.	H7	102
Santiago, Para.	C9	92
Santiago, i., C.V.	I10	65a
Santiago, stm., Mex.	C6	100
Santiago, stm., S.A.	D2	84
Santiago, Isla, i., Ec.	i11	84a
Santiago de Compostela, Spain	B2	20
Santiago de Cuba, Cuba	C9	102
Santiago del Estero, Arg.	C5	92
Santiago del Estero, state, Arg.	C5	92
Santiago de los Caballeros, Dom. Rep.	C12	102
Santiago Island, i., Phil.	B2	52
Santiago Ixcuintla, Mex.	E6	100
Santiago Jamiltepec, Mex.	G10	100
Santiago Larre, Arg.	G8	92
Santiago Papasquiaro, Mex.	C6	100
Santiago Peak, mtn., Ca., U.S.	J8	134
Santiago Peak, mtn., Tx., U.S.	E4	130
Santiaguillo, Laguna, l., Mex.	C6	100
Santiam Pass, p., Or., U.S.	F5	136
Säntis, mtn., Switz.	C6	22
Santisteban del Puerto, Spain	F7	20
Sant Joan de Labritja, Spain	E12	20
Sant Jordi, Golf de, b., Spain	D11	20
Sant Mateu del Maestrat, Spain	D10	20
Santo Amaro, Braz.	G6	88
Santo Amaro, Braz.	B4	88
Santo André, Braz.	L2	88
Santo Ângelo, Braz.	D10	92
Santo Antão, i., C.V.	k10	65a
Santo Antônio, Braz.	D8	88
Santo António, S. Tom./P.	I6	64
Santo Antônio, stm., Braz.	I3	88
Santo Antônio, stm., Braz.	F1	88
Santo Antônio da Patrulha, Braz.	D12	92
Santo Antônio de Jesus, Braz.	G6	88
Santo Antônio de Pádua, Braz.	K4	88
Santo Antônio do Amparo, Braz.	K3	88
Santo Antônio do Içá, Braz.	D4	84
Santo Augusto, Braz.	C11	92
Santo Domingo, Cuba	C8	96
Santo Domingo, Dom. Rep.	C13	102
Santo Domingo, Mex.	D8	100
Santo Domingo, Mex.	C2	100
Santo Domingo, Mex.	I3	130
Santo Domingo, Ven.	D5	86
Santo Domingo de la Calzada, Spain	B7	20
Santo Domingo de los Colorados, Ec.	H1	86
Santo Domingo Pueblo, N.M., U.S.	F2	128
Santo Domingo Tehuantepec, Mex.	G11	100
Santo Domingo Zanatepec, Mex.	G11	100
Santo Estêvão, Braz.	G6	88
Santo / Malo, state, Vanuatu	j16	79d
San Tomé, Ven.	C9	86
Santo Onofre, stm., Braz.	G4	88
Santorini see Thíra, i., Grc.	G8	28
Santos, Braz.	L2	88
Santos Dumont, Braz.	K4	88
Santo Tirso, Port.	C2	20
Santo Tomás, Mex.	L9	134
Santo Tomás, Punta, c., Mex.	L9	134
Santo Tomé, Arg.	E7	92
Santo Tomé, Arg.	D9	92
San Vicente de Alcántara, Spain	E3	20
San Vicente de Baracaldo see Barakaldo, Spain	A8	20
San Vicente del Caguán, Col.	F4	86
San Vincente, Arg.	D5	92
San Vincenzo, Italy	G7	22
San Vito, Capo, c., Italy	F6	24
Sanya, China	L3	42
Sanyati, stm., Zimb.	D4	68
Sanyō, Japan	E4	40
Sanyuan, China	D3	42
Sanzao Dao, i., China	K5	42
Sanza Pombo, Ang.	B2	68
São Benedito, Braz.	C5	88
São Benedito do Rio Preto, Braz.	B3	88
São Bento, Braz.	B3	88
São Bento do Norte, Braz.	C7	88
São Bento do Sul, Braz.	C13	92
São Bento do Una, Braz.	E7	88
São Borja, Braz.	D10	92
São Caetano do Sul, Braz.	L2	88
São Carlos, Braz.	L2	88
São Cristóvão, Braz.	F7	88
São Domingos, Braz.	G2	88
São Domingos, Braz.	C11	92
São Domingos, Gui.-B.	G1	64
São Domingos do Maranhão, Braz.	C3	88
São Felipe, Braz.	H5	88
São Félix de Balsas, Braz.	D3	88
São Francisco, Braz.	H3	88
São Francisco, stm., Braz.	E6	88
São Francisco, stm., Braz.	H5	88
São Francisco, Baía de, b., Braz.	C13	92
São Francisco, Ilha de, i., Braz.	C13	92
São Francisco de Assis, Braz.	D10	92
São Francisco de Goiás, Braz.	H1	88
São Francisco de Paula, Braz.	D12	92
São Francisco do Maranhão, Braz.	D4	88
São Francisco do Sul, Braz.	C13	92
São Gabriel, Braz.	F5	88
São Gabriel, Braz.	E10	92
São Gabriel da Palha, Braz.	J5	88
São Gabriel de Goiás, Braz.	H2	88
São Gonçalo do Sapucaí, Braz.	K3	88
São Gonçalo dos Campos, Braz.	G6	88
Sao Hill, Tan.	F7	66
São Jerônimo, Braz.	E12	92
São Jerônimo da Serra, Braz.	A12	92
São João da Aliança, Braz.	H2	88
São João da Barra, Braz.	K5	88
São João da Boa Vista, Braz.	L2	88
São João de Cortês, Braz.	B3	88
São João Del Rei, Braz.	K3	88
São João do Araguaia, Braz.	C1	88
São João do Jaguaribe, Braz.	C6	88
São João do Piauí, Braz.	E4	88
São João dos Patos, Braz.	D4	88
São Joaquim, Braz.	D12	92
São Joaquim, Parque Nacional de, p.o.i., Braz.	D13	92
São Joaquim da Barra, Braz.	K1	88
São José, Braz.	C13	92
São José, stm., Braz.	J5	88
São José da Laje, Braz.	E7	88
São José das Piranhas, Braz.	D6	88
São José de Anauá, Braz.	G11	86
São José do Cedro, Braz.	C11	92
São José do Egito, Braz.	D7	88
São José do Gurupi, Braz.	A2	88
São José do Mipibu, Braz.	D8	88
São José do Peixe, Braz.	D4	88
São José do Rio Preto, Braz.	K1	88
São José dos Campos, Braz.	L3	88
São José dos Pinhais, Braz.	B13	92
São Leopoldo, Braz.	D12	92
São Lourenço, Braz.	L3	88
São Lourenço, Pantanal de, sw., Braz.	C5	90
São Lourenço do Sul, Braz.	E12	92
São Luís, Braz.	B3	88
São Luís do Curu, Braz.	B6	88
São Luís do Quitunde, Braz.	E8	88
São Luís Gonzaga, Braz.	D10	92
São Manuel, Braz.	L1	88
São Manuel, stm., Braz.	E6	84
São Marcos, stm., Braz.	I2	88
São Marcos, Baía de, b., Braz.	B3	88
São Mateus, Braz.	J6	88
São Mateus, Braço Norte, stm., Braz.	J5	88
São Mateus do Sul, Braz.	B12	92
São Miguel, Braz.	D6	88
São Miguel, i., Port.	C3	20
São Miguel do Araguaia, Braz.	F7	84
São Miguel d'Oeste, Braz.	C11	92
São Miguel do Guamá, Braz.	A2	88
São Miguel dos Campos, Braz.	E7	88
São Miguel do Tapuio, Braz.	C5	88
Saona, Isla, i., Dom. Rep.	C13	102
Saône, stm., Fr.	C10	18
Saône-et-Loire, state, Fr.	C10	18
Saoner, India	H7	54
São Nicolau, i., C.V.	k10	65a
São Nicolau, stm., Braz.	C5	88
São Paulo, Braz.	L2	88
São Paulo, state, Braz.	D7	90
São Paulo de Olivença, Braz.	D4	84
São Paulo do Potengi, Braz.	C7	88
São Pedro do Piauí, Braz.	C4	88
São Pedro do Sul, Port.	D2	20
São Raimundo das Mangabeiras, Braz.	D3	88
São Raimundo Nonato, Braz.	E4	88
São Romão, Braz.	I3	88
São Roque, Braz.	L2	88
São Roque, Cabo de, c., Braz.	C8	88
São Sebastião, Braz.	L3	88
São Sebastião, Ilha de, i., Braz.	L3	88
São Sebastião, Ponta, c., Moz.	C12	70
São Sebastião do Paraíso, Braz.	K2	88
São Sepé, Braz.	E11	92
São Simão, Braz.	K2	88
São Simão, Represa de, res., Braz.	C7	90
São Timóteo, Braz.	G4	88
São Tomé, Braz.	C7	88
São Tomé, S. Tom./P.	I6	64
São Tomé, i., S. Tom./P.	I6	64
São Tomé, Cabo de, c., Braz.	L5	88
São Tomé, Pico de, mtn., S. Tom./P.	I6	64
Sao Tome and Principe, ctry., Afr.	I6	64
Saoura, Oued, stm., Alg.	D4	64
São Valério, stm., Braz.	F1	88
São Vicente, Braz.	M2	88
São Vicente, i., C.V.	k9	65a
São Vicente, Cabo de, c., Port.	H1	20
Sapanca, Tur.	C13	28
Sape, Selat, strt., Indon.	H11	50
Sapele, Nig.	H6	64
Sapelo Island, i., Ga., U.S.	E4	116
Sápes, Grc.	B8	28
Şapitwa, mtn., Mwi.	D6	68
Šapki, Russia	A14	10
Šapkina, stm., Russia	C26	8
Sapockin, Bela.	G6	10
Sappa Creek, stm., U.S.	A9	128
Sappa Creek, South Fork, stm., Ks., U.S.	B8	128
Sappho, Wa., U.S.	B2	136
Sapporo, Japan	C14	38
Sap Songkhla, Thale, l., Thai.	I5	48
Saptakośī, stm., Nepal	E11	54
Sapudi, Pulau, i., Indon.	G9	50
Sapulpa, Ok., U.S.	A2	122
Sapwe, D.R.C.	G5	66
Saqqâra, Egypt	I2	58
Saqqâra, Pyramides de (Step Pyramid), hist., Egypt	I1	58
Saqqez, Iran	B6	56
Saraana, Baie, b., Qc., Can.	B1	110
Sarāb, Iran	B6	56
Saraburi, Thai.	E5	48
Saracura, stm., Braz.	G5	88
Saraféré, Mali	F4	64
Saragosa, Tx., U.S.	C4	130
Saragossa see Zaragoza, Spain	C10	20
Sarāi Naurang, Pak.	B3	54
Saraipāli, India	H9	54
Sarajevo, Bos.	F5	26
Saraji, Austl.	D7	76
Sarakhs, Iran	B9	56
Saraktaš, Russia	D9	32
Saraland, Al., U.S.	G10	122
Saran', Kaz.	E12	32
Saran, Gunung, mtn., Indon.	D7	50
Saranac, Mi., U.S.	F4	112
Saranac, stm., N.Y., U.S.	F3	110
Saranda see Sarandë, Alb.	E13	24
Sarandë, Alb.	E13	24
Sarandi, Braz.	C11	92
Sarandí del Yi, Ur.	F10	92
Sarandí Grande, Ur.	F9	92
Sarangani Bay, b., Phil.	H5	52
Sarangani Islands, is., Phil.	H5	52
Sarangani Strait, strt., Phil.	H5	52
Sārangarh, India	H9	54
Sārangpur, India	G6	54
Saranpaul', Russia	B10	32
Saransk, Russia	D6	32
Saraphi, Thai.	C4	48
Sarapul, Russia	C8	32
Sarāqib, Syria	C7	58
Sarare, stm., Ven.	D6	86
Sarasota, Fl., U.S.	3	116
Sarata, Ukr.	C16	26
Saratoga, Ca., U.S.	F3	134
Saratoga, Tx., U.S.	G4	122
Saratoga, Wy., U.S.	B10	132
Saratoga Springs, N.Y., U.S.	G2	110
Saratov, Russia	D7	32
Saratov Reservoir see Saratovskoe vodohranilišče, res., Russia	D7	32
Saratovskoe vodohranilišče, res., Russia	D7	32
Sarāvān, Iran	D9	56
Saravan, Laos	E8	48
Saravena, Col.	D5	86
Sarawak, state, Malay.	B8	50
Sarawak, hist. reg., Malay.	E5	44
Saray, Tur.	B10	28
Saraya, Gui.	G2	64
Sarayevo see Sarajevo, Bos.	F5	26
Sarayköy, Tur.	F11	28
Sarayönü, Tur.	E15	28
Sarbāz, Iran	D9	56
Sarcelle, Passe de la, strt., N. Cal.	n16	79d
Sarcidano, reg., Italy	E3	24
Sarcoxie, Mo., U.S.	G3	120
Sārda (Mahākālī), stm., Asia	D8	54
Sardah, Bngl.	F12	54
Sardārpur, India	G5	54
Sardārshahr, India	D5	54
Sardegna, state, Italy	D4	24
Sardegna (Sardinia), i., Italy	D3	24
Sardinata, Col.	H11	102
Sardinia see Sardegna, state, Italy	D4	24
Sardinia see Sardegna, i., Italy	D3	24
Sardis, Al., U.S.	E12	122
Sardis, Ga., U.S.	D4	116
Sardis, Tn., U.S.	B10	122
Sardis, hist., Tur.	E10	28
Sardis Lake, res., Ms., U.S.	C9	122
Şardis Lake, res., Ok., U.S.	C3	122
Šardonem', Russia	E21	8
Sarek, mtn., Swe.	C7	8
Sareks Nationalpark, p.o.i., Swe.	C7	8
Sar-e Pol, Afg.	B10	56
Sarepta, La., U.S.	E5	122
Sargent, Ga., U.S.	D14	122
Sargent, Ne., U.S.	F13	126
Sargodha, Pak.	B4	54
Sarh, Chad	F3	62
Sārī, Iran	B7	56
Saria, i., Grc.	H10	28
Sarıgöl, Tur.	E11	28
Sarıkaya, Tur.	E15	28
Sarikei, Malay.	B7	50
Sarina, Austl.	C7	76
Sariñena, Spain	C10	20
Sariska Tiger Reserve, India	E6	54
Sarita, Tx., U.S.	G10	130
Sariwŏn, Kor., N.	E6	38
Şarıyar Barajı, res., Tur.	D14	28
Šarja, Russia	G21	8
Sark, i., Guern.	E6	14
Şarkand, Kaz.	E13	32
Šarkaŭščyna, Bela.	E10	10
Şarkikaraağaç, Tur.	E14	28
Şarköy, Tur.	C10	28
Şarles, N.D., U.S.	F15	124
Šarlyk, Russia	D9	32
Sarmi, Indon.	F10	44
Sarmiento, Arg.	I3	90
Särna, Swe.	F5	8
Sarnia, On., Can.	F7	112
Sarno, Italy	D8	24
Sarolangun, Indon.	E3	50
Saronic Gulf see Saronikós Kólpos, b., Grc.	F6	28
Saronikós Kólpos, b., Grc.	F6	28
Saronno, Italy	E6	22
Saros Körfezi, b., Tur.	C9	28
Sárospatak, Hung.	A8	26
Sarowbī, Afg.	C10	56
Sarpsborg, Nor.	G4	8
Sarralbe, Fr.	E15	14
Sarre (Saar), stm., Eur.	E15	14
Sarrebourg, Fr.	F16	14
Şarreguemines, Fr.	E16	14
Šarscin, Bela.	H14	10
Sartang, stm., Russia	C15	34
Sartell, Mn., U.S.	F4	118
Sartène, Fr.	H14	18
Sarthe, state, Fr.	G9	14
Sarthe, stm., Fr.	G8	14
Saruhanlı, Tur.	E10	28
Sárvár, Hung.	B3	26
Sárvíz, can., Hung.	C5	26
Saryg-Sep, Russia	D17	32
Sarykamyšskoe ozero, l., Asia	A8	56
Sarykopa, ozero, l., Kaz.	E10	32
Şaryozek, Kaz.	F13	32
Šarypovo, Russia	C15	32
Sarysu, stm., Kaz.	E11	32
Sary-Taš, Kyrg.	G12	32
Sarzana, Italy	F6	22
Sasabeneh, Eth.	F8	62
Sasaginnigak Lake, l., Mb., Can.	C17	124
Sasakwa, Ok., U.S.	C2	122
Sasamungga, Sol. Is.	d7	79b
Sāsarām, India	F9	54
Sasayama, Japan	D8	40
Sásd, Hung.	C5	26
Sasebo, Japan	F2	40
Saseginaga, Lac, l., Qc., Can.	A11	112
Saskatchewan, state, Can.	E9	106
Saskatchewan, stm., Can.	E10	106
Saskatoon, Sk., Can.	B7	124
Saskylah, Russia	B11	34
Sasolburg, S. Afr.	E8	70
Sasovo, Russia	D6	32
Saspamco, Tx., U.S.	E9	130
Sassafras, Ky., U.S.	G2	114
Sassafras Mountain, mtn., U.S.	A3	116
Sassandra, C. Iv.	I3	64
Sassandra, stm., C. Iv.	I3	64
Sassari, Italy	D2	24
Sassnitz, Ger.	B9	16
Sasso Marconi, Italy	F8	22
Sassuolo, Italy	F7	22
Sasyk, ozero, l., Ukr.	D16	26
Sasykkol', ozero, l., Kaz.	E14	32
Satadougou, Mali	G2	64
Satah Mountain, vol., B.C., Can.	D6	138
Sata-misaki, c., Japan	H3	40
Satāna, India	H5	54
Sátão, Port.	D3	20
Sātāra, India	C1	53
Satara Ruskamp, S. Afr.	D10	70
Satélite, Mex.	C1	130
Satellite Beach, Fl., U.S.	H5	116
Satengar, Pulau, i., Indon.	G10	50
Satevó, Mex.	G1	130
Satevó, stm., Mex.	G1	130
Satilla, stm., Ga., U.S.	E4	116
Sátiro Dias, Braz.	F6	88
Şatīt (Tekezē), stm., Afr.	E7	62
Šatki, Russia	I20	8
Satluj see Sutlej, stm., Asia	C5	54
Satna, India	F8	54
Sátoraljaújhely, Hung.	A8	26
Sātpura Range, mts., India	H6	54
Satsuma-hantō, pen., Japan	H3	40
Satsunan-shotō, is., Japan	k19	39a
Sattahip, Thai.	F5	48
Satui, Indon.	E9	50
Satu Mare, Rom.	B9	26
Satu Mare, state, Rom.	B10	26
Şatun, Thai.	I4	48
Šatura, Russia	I18	8
Saturnino M. Laspiur, Arg.	E6	92
Satyamangalam, India	F3	53
Sauce, Arg.	E8	92
Sauce Corto, Arroyo, stm., Arg.	H7	92
Saucier, Ms., U.S.	G9	122
Saucillo, Mex.	A6	100
Sauđárkrókur, Ice.	k30	8a
Saudi Arabia, ctry., Asia	E5	56
Sauerland, reg., Ger.	E4	16
Saueruiná, stm., Braz.	F6	84
Saugatuck, Mi., U.S.	F3	112
Saugeen, stm., On., Can.	D8	112
Saugerties, N.Y., U.S.	B12	114
Saugstad, Mount, mtn., B.C., Can.	D4	138
Saujil, Arg.	D4	92
Sauk, stm., Mn., U.S.	F4	118
Sauk Centre, Mn., U.S.	F3	118
Sauk City, Wi., U.S.	H9	118
Sauk Rapids, Mn., U.S.	F4	118
Saukville, Wi., U.S.	E1	112
Saül, Fr. Gu.	C7	84
Sauldre, Canal de la, can., Fr.	B8	18
Saulgau, Ger.	I5	16
Saulieu, Fr.	G13	14
Sault aux Cochons, stm., Qc., Can.	A7	110
Sault-de-Vaucluse, Fr.	E11	18
Saulteaux, stm., Ab., Can.	B16	138
Sault Sainte Marie, On., Can.	B5	112
Sault Sainte Marie, Mi., U.S.	B5	112
Saumarez Reef, rf., Austl.	C9	76
Saumlaki, Indon.	G9	44
Saumur, Fr.	G8	14
Saunders Island, i., Falk. Is.	J4	90
Saunders Island, i., S. Geor.	K12	82
Sauquoit, N.Y., U.S.	B10	114
Saurimo, Ang.	B3	68
Sausar, India	H7	54
Sausu, Indon.	D12	50
Sautar, Ang.	C2	68
Sauteurs, Gren.	q10	105e
Sauveterre-de-Guyenne, Fr.	E5	18
Sauwald, for., Aus.	B10	22
Sauzal, Mex.	C1	130
Sava, stm., Eur.	F16	22
Savai'i, i., Samoa	g11	79c
Savalou, Benin	H5	64
Savanna, Il., U.S.	B7	120
Savanna, Ok., U.S.	C3	122
Savannah, Ga., U.S.	D4	116
Savannah, Tn., U.S.	B10	122
Savannah, stm., U.S.	D4	116
Savannah River Plant, sci., S.C., U.S.	C4	116
Savannah Sound, Bah.	K9	116
Savannakhét, Laos	D7	48
Savanna-la-Mar, Jam.	i12	104d
Savant Lake, On., Can.	A8	118
Savant Lake, l., On., Can.	A8	118
Sāvantvādi, India	D1	53
Savanūr, India	D2	53
Savaştepe, Tur.	D10	28
Savè, Benin	H5	64
Save (Sabi), stm., Afr.	E5	68
Sāveh, Iran	B7	56
Savelugu, Ghana	H4	64
Savenay, Fr.	G7	14
Saverdun, Fr.	F7	18
Savigliano, Italy	F4	22
Savino-Borisovskaja, Russia	E21	8
Savinskij, Russia	E19	8
Şavissik, Grnld.	B13	141
Šavnik, Yugo.	G6	26
Savoie, state, Fr.	D12	18
Savoie, hist. reg., Fr.	D12	18
Savo Island, i., Sol. Is.	e8	79b
Savona, B.C., Can.	F10	138
Savona, Italy	F5	22
Savonlinna, Fin.	F13	8
Savoy, Tx., U.S.	D2	122
Savoy see Savoie, hist. reg., Fr.	D12	18
Savran', Ukr.	A17	26
Savusavu Bay, b., Fiji	p19	79e
Savu Sea see Sawu, Laut, Indon.	G7	44
Sawah, Indon.	B9	50
Sawahlunto, Indon.	D2	50
Sawāi Mādhopur, India	E6	54
Sawākin, Sudan	D7	62
Sawankhalok, Thai.	D4	48
Sawara, Japan	D13	40
Sawata, Japan	A11	40
Sawatch Range, mts., Co., U.S.	B2	128
Sawdā', Jabal, mtn., Sau. Ar.	F5	56
Sawdā', Jabal as-, hills, Libya	A4	62
Sawdā', Qurnat as-, mtn., Leb.	D7	58
Sawdirī, Sudan	E5	62
Şawqirah, Oman	F8	56
Şawqirah, Dawhat, b., Oman	F8	56
Sawtooth National Recreation Area, p.o.i., Id., U.S.	F12	136
Sawu, Laut (Savu Sea), Indon.	G7	44
Sawu, Pulau, i., Indon.	H7	44
Sawyer, Mi., U.S.	G3	112
Sawyer, N.D., U.S.	F12	124
Saxby, stm., Austl.	B3	76
Saxon, Wi., U.S.	E8	118
Saxony see Sachsen, state, Ger.	F9	16
Saxony see Sachsen, hist. reg., Ger.	D5	16
Saxony-Anhalt see Sachsen-Anhalt, state, Ger.	D7	16
Saxton, Pa., U.S.	D7	114
Say, Niger	G5	64
Sayan Mountains, mts., Asia	D17	32
Sayaxché, Guat.	D2	102
Şaydā (Sidon), Leb.	E6	58
Şaydā, state, Leb.	E6	58
Sayhūt, Yemen	F7	56
Sayil, hist., Mex.	B3	102
Saylac, Som.	B8	66
Saylūn, Khirbat (Shiloh), hist., W.B.	F6	58
Saynshand, Mong.	C7	36
Sayram Hu, l., China	F14	32
Sayre, Ok., U.S.	F9	128
Sayre, Pa., U.S.	C9	114
Sayreville, N.J., U.S.	D11	114
Sayward, B.C., Can.	F5	138
Saywūn, Yemen	F6	56
Saza, Japan	F2	40
Sazan, i., Alb.	D13	24
Şba, Alg.	D4	64
Ščadryn, Bela.	H12	10
Scafell Pike, mtn., Eng., U.K.	G9	12
Scalea, Italy	E9	24
Scammon Bay, Ak., U.S.	D6	140
Scandia, Ks., U.S.	B11	128
Scanlon, Mn., U.S.	E6	118
Scapa Flow, b., Scot., U.K.	C9	12
Scapegoat Mountain, mtn., Mt., U.S.	C14	136
Ščapino, Russia	E20	34
Şcappoose, Or., U.S.	E3	136
Ščara, stm., Bela.	G8	10
Scarborough, St. K./N.	C2	105a
Scarborough, Trin.	r13	105f
Scarborough, Eng., U.K.	G12	12
Scarborough, ngh., On., Can.	E10	112
Scărişoara, Rom.	F11	26
Scarp, i., Scot., U.K.	C5	12
Şcawfell Island, i., Austl.	C7	76
Šćedro, Otok, i., Cro.	G13	22
Ščekino, Russia	F20	10
Ščelkovo, Russia	E20	10
Şceptre, Sk., Can.	D4	124
Ščerbakovo, Russia	C21	34
Ščerbakty, Kaz.	D13	32
Ščerbinka, Russia	E20	10
Schaffhausen, Switz.	C5	22
Schaffhouse see Schaffhausen, Switz.	C5	22
Schärding, Aus.	B10	22
Schefferville, Qc., Can.	E17	106
Scheinfeld, Ger.	G6	16
Schelde, stm., Eur.	C13	14
Schell Creek Range, mts., Nv., U.S.	D2	132
Schenectady, N.Y., U.S.	B11	114
Schenevus Creek, stm., N.Y., U.S.	B11	114
Schertz, Tx., U.S.	E9	130
Schiedam, Neth.	C13	14
Schiermonnikoog, i., Neth.	C2	16
Schiltigheim, Fr.	F16	14
Schio, Italy	E8	22
Schkeuditz, Ger.	E8	16
Schladming, Aus.	C10	22
Schlater, Ms., U.S.	D8	122
Schleiden, Ger.	F2	16
Schleswig, Ger.	B5	16
Schleswig, Ia., U.S.	B2	120
Schleswig-Holstein, state, Ger.	B6	16
Schlitz, Ger.	F5	16
Schlüchtern, Ger.	F5	16
Schmölln, Ger.	F8	16
Schneeberg, Ger.	F8	16
Schneeberg, mtn., Ger.	F7	16
Schneverdingen, Ger.	C5	16
Schœlcher, Mart.	k6	105c
Schofield, Wi., U.S.	G9	118
Schoharie, N.Y., U.S.	B11	114
Schoharie Creek, stm., N.Y., U.S.	B11	114
Schönebeck, Ger.	D7	16
Schongau, Ger.	I6	16
Schopfheim, Ger.	I3	16
Schorndorf, Ger.	H5	16
Schouten, Kepulauan, is., Indon.	F10	44
Schouten Island, i., Austl.	o14	77a
Schouten Islands, is., Pap. N. Gui.	a3	79a
Schramberg, Ger.	H4	16
Schreiber, On., Can.	C11	118
Schriever, La., U.S.	H8	122
Schrobenhausen, Ger.	H7	16
Schulenburg, Tx., U.S.	E11	130
Schultz Lake, l., Nu., Can.	C11	106
Schuyler, Va., U.S.	G7	114
Schuylkill, stm., Pa., U.S.	D10	114
Schuylkill Haven, Pa., U.S.	D9	114
Schwabach, Ger.	G7	16
Schwaben, hist. reg., Ger.	H5	16
Schwäbische Alb, mts., Ger.	H5	16
Schwäbisch Gmünd, Ger.	H5	16
Schwäbisch Hall, Ger.	G5	16
Schwabmünchen, Ger.	H6	16
Schwandorf in Bayern, Ger.	G7	16
Schwaner, Pegunungan, mts., Indon.	D8	50
Schwarzach im Pongau, Aus.	C10	22
Schwarzwald (Black Forest), mts., Ger.	H4	16
Schwatka Mountains, mts., Ak., U.S.	C8	140
Schwaz, Aus.	C8	22
Schwechat, Aus.	B13	22
Schwedt, Ger.	C10	16
Schweinfurt, Ger.	F5	16
Schweizer Nationalpark, p.o.i., Switz.	D7	22
Schweizer-Reineke, S. Afr.	E7	70
Schwerin, Ger.	C7	16
Schweriner See, l., Ger.	C7	16
Schwyz, Switz.	C5	22
Sciacca, Italy	G6	24
Scicli, Italy	H8	24
Scilly, Isles of, is., Eng., U.K.	L6	12
Scio, Oh., U.S.	D4	114
Scio, Or., U.S.	F4	136
Şcioto, stm., Oh., U.S.	E3	114
Šćit, mtn., Bos.	E4	26
Scobey, Mt., U.S.	F8	124
Scone, Austl.	I8	76
Scooba, Ms., U.S.	E10	122
Scordia, Italy	G8	24
Scoresby Land, reg., Grnld.	C21	141
Scoresbysund (Ittoqqortoormiit), Grnld.	C21	141
Scoresby Sund, strt., Grnld.	C21	141
Scotia, N.Y., U.S.	B12	114
Scotia Ridge, unds.	N8	144
Scotia Sea	K10	82
Scotland, On., Can.	E9	112
Scotland, S.D., U.S.	D15	126
Scotland, Tx., U.S.	H10	128
Scotland, state, U.K.	E8	12
Scotlandville, La., U.S.	G7	122
Scotsburn, N.S., Can.	E14	110
Scott, Sk., Can.	B5	124
Scott, Ms., U.S.	D7	122
Scott, stm., Ca., U.S.	B3	134
Scott, Cape, c., B.C., Can.	F2	138
Scott, Mount, mtn., Or., U.S.	H4	136
Scott Base, sci., Ant.	C22	81
Scott City, Mo., U.S.	G8	120
Scott Coast, cst., Ant.	C20	81
Scottdale, Pa., U.S.	D6	114
Scott Island, i., Ant.	B23	81
Scott Islands, is., B.C., Can.	F2	138
Scott Peak, mtn., Id., U.S.	F14	136
Scott Reef, rf., Austl.	B4	74
Scottsbluff, Ne., U.S.	F9	126
Scotts Bluff National Monument, p.o.i., Ne., U.S.	F9	126
Scottsboro, Al., U.S.	C12	122
Scottsdale, Austl.	n13	77a
Scottsdale, Az., U.S.	J5	132
Scotts Head, c., Dom.	j6	105c
Scotts Hill, Tn., U.S.	B10	122
Scottsville, Ky., U.S.	H11	120
Scottville, Mi., U.S.	E3	112
Scourie, Scot., U.K.	C7	12
Scout Lake, Sk., Can.	E8	124
Scranton, N.D., U.S.	A9	126
Scranton, Pa., U.S.	C10	114
Screven, Ga., U.S.	E3	116
Scribner, Ne., U.S.	J2	118
Şcrub Island, i., Anguilla	A2	105a
Ščuče, Russia	C10	32
Ščučinsk, Kaz.	D12	32
Ščučyn, Bela.	G7	10
Scugog, Lake, l., On., Can.	D11	112
Scunthorpe, Eng., U.K.	H12	12
Şcutari, Lake, l., Eur.	H16	22
Ščytkavičy, Bela.	G10	10
Seabrook, Lake, l., Austl.	F3	74
Seaford, De., U.S.	F10	114
Seaforth, On., Can.	E8	112
Seahorse Point, c., Nu., Can.	C15	106
Sea Islands, is., U.S.	E5	116
Sea Isle City, N.J., U.S.	E11	114
Seal, stm., Mb., Can.	D11	106
Seal, Cape, c., S. Afr.	I6	70
Sea Lake, Austl.	J4	76
Sealark Channel, strt., Sol. Is.	e9	79b
Seal Cays, is., T./C. Is.	B12	102
Seale, Al., U.S.	E13	122
Sealevel, N.C., U.S.	B9	116
Seal Island, i., N.S., Can.	G10	110
Sealy, Tx., U.S.	H2	122
Seara, Braz.	C11	92
Searcy, Ar., U.S.	B7	122
Searles Lake, l., Ca., U.S.	H8	134
Searsport, Me., U.S.	F7	110
Seaside, Ca., U.S.	G4	134
Seaside, Or., U.S.	D3	136
Seaside Park, N.J., U.S.	E11	114
Seattle, Wa., U.S.	C4	136
Sebago Lake, l., Me., U.S.	G6	110
Se Bai, stm., Thai.	E7	48
Sebakung, Indon.	D10	50
Sebangan, Teluk, b., Indon.	E8	50
Sebangka, Pulau, i., Indon.	C4	50
Sebastian, Tx., U.S.	H10	130
Sebastian, Cape, c., Or., U.S.	A1	134
Sebastián Vizcaíno, Bahía, b., Mex.	A1	100
Sebastopol, Ca., U.S.	E3	134
Sebastopol, Ms., U.S.	E9	122
Şebec Lake, l., Me., U.S.	E7	110
Šebekino, Russia	D5	32
Seben, Tur.	C14	28
Sebeş, Rom.	D10	26
Sebes Körös (Crişul Repede), stm., Eur.	B8	26
Sebewaing, Mi., U.S.	E6	112
Sebež, Russia	D11	10
Sebino see Iseo, Lago d', l., Italy	E6	22
Sebnitz, Ger.	F10	16
Sebree, Ky., U.S.	G10	120
Sebring, Fl., U.S.	I4	116
Sebuku, Indon.	A10	50
Sebuku, Teluk, b., Indon.	A11	50
Sebuyau, Malay.	C7	50
Secchia, stm., Italy	F7	22
Sechura, Peru	E1	84
Sechura, Desierto de, des., Peru	E1	84
Seclantás, Arg.	B4	92
Sečovská Polianka, Slov.	H17	16
Section, Al., U.S.	C13	122
Security, Co., U.S.	C4	128
Seda, China	E5	36
Seda, Lith.	D5	10
Sedah, Indon.	B4	74
Sedalia, Ab., Can.	C3	124
Sedalia, Mo., U.S.	F4	120
Sedan, Fr.	E13	14
Sedanovo, Russia	C18	32
Sedayu, Indon.	G8	50
Seddon, Kap, c., Grnld.	B14	141
Sedel'nikovo, Russia	C13	32
Séderon, Fr.	E11	18
Sedgewick, Ab., Can.	D19	138
Sedgwick, Co., U.S.	G10	126
Sedgwick, Ks., U.S.	D11	128
Sédhiou, Sen.	G1	64
Sedlčany, Czech Rep.	G10	16
Sedom (Sodom), hist., Isr.	G6	58
Şedro Woolley, Wa., U.S.	B4	136
Šeduva, Lith.	E6	10
Seehausen, Ger.	D7	16
Seeheim, Nmb.	E3	70
Seeis, Nmb.	C3	70
Seekoei, stm., S. Afr.	G7	70
Seeley Lake, Mt., U.S.	C13	136
Seelyville, In., U.S.	E10	120
Sées, Fr.	F9	14
Seesen, Ger.	E6	16
Sefadu, S.L.	H2	64
Seferihisar, Tur.	E9	28
Segama, stm., Malay.	A11	50
Segamat, Malay.	K6	48
Ségbana, Benin	G5	64
Segeri, Indon.	F11	50
Segesta, hist., Italy	G6	24
Segeža, Russia	E15	8
Segorbe, Spain	E10	20

Name — Map Ref. — Page

Ségou, Mali G3 64
Segovary, Russia E20 8
Segovia, Spain D6 20
Segovia, co., Spain C6 20
Segozero, ozero, l., Russia E15 8
Segre, stm., Eur. H6 18
Seguam Island, i., Ak., U.S. g24 140a
Séguédine, Niger E7 64
Séguéla, C. Iv. H3 64
Segui, Arg. E7 92
Seguin, Tx., U.S. E10 130
Segundo, stm., Arg. E6 92
Seguntur, Indon. C10 50
Segura, stm., Spain F10 20
Segura, Sierra de, mts., Spain G8 20
Sehithwa, Bots. B6 70
Sehore, India G6 54
Sehwan, Pak. D10 56
Seibert, Co., U.S. B6 128
Seikpyu, Mya. B2 48
Seiland, i., Nor. A10 8
Seiling, Ok., U.S. E9 128
Seim, stm., Eur. D4 32
Seinäjoki, Fin. E10 8
Seine, stm., Mb., Can. E17 124
Seine, stm., On., Can. C6 118
Seine, stm., Fr. E9 14
Seine, Baie de la, b., Fr. E8 14
Seine, Bay of the see Seine, Baie de la, b., Fr. E8 14
Seine-et-Marne, state, Fr. F12 14
Seine-Maritime, state, Fr. E9 14
Seixal, Port. F1 20
Seixas, Ponta do, c., Braz. D8 88
Sejmčan, Russia D19 34
Sejny, Pol. B19 16
Sekayam, stm., Indon. C7 50
Sekayu, Indon. E3 50
Sekeladi, Indon. E3 50
Seki, Azer. A6 56
Seki, Japan D9 40
Sekiu, Wa., U.S. B2 136
Sekoma, Bots. D6 70
Sekondi, Ghana I4 64
Seksna, Russia A21 10
Selagskij, mys, c., Russia B23 34
Selama, Malay. J5 48
Selangor, state, Malay. K5 48
Selaru, Pulau, i., Indon. G9 44
Selatan, Tanjung, c., Indon. F9 50
Selatpanjang, Indon. C3 50
Selawik, Ak., U.S. C8 140
Selawik Lake, l., Ak., U.S. C7 140
Selayar, Pulau, i., Indon. G12 50
Selayar, Selat, strt., Indon. F12 50
Selb, Ger. F8 16
Selbusjøen, l., Nor. E4 8
Selby, Eng., U.K. H11 12
Selby, S.D., U.S. B12 126
Selbyville, De., U.S. F10 114
Sel'co, Russia E19 8
Sel'co, Russia G17 10
Selçuk, Tur. F10 28
Seldovia, Ak., U.S. D9 140
Selebi-Phikwe, Bots. C9 70
Selečnja, Russia H17 10
Selehov, Russia D18 32
Selemdža, stm., Russia F14 34
Selemdžinsk, Russia F15 34
Selenduma, Russia F10 34
Selenge, D.R.C. E3 66
Selenge, stm., Asia G9 34
Selenicë, Alb. D13 24
Selennjah, stm., Russia C16 34
Sélestat, Fr. F16 14
Seleznëvo, Russia F13 8
Selfoss, Ice. I29 8a
Selfridge, N.D., U.S. A11 126
Sel'gon, Russia G16 34
Sélibabi, Maur. F2 64
Seliger, ozero, l., Russia C15 10
Seligman, Az., U.S. H4 132
Selihova, zaliv, b., Russia D20 34
Selimbau, Indon. C8 50
Selinsgrove, Pa., U.S. D8 114
Selinunte, hist., Italy G6 24
Selišče, Russia D16 10
Seližarovo, Russia D16 10
Selkirk, Mb., Can. D17 124
Selkirk, Scot., U.K. F10 12
Selkirk Mountains, mts., N.A. F13 138
Sellers, S.C., U.S. B6 116
Sellersburg, In., U.S. F12 120
Selles-sur-Cher, Fr. G10 14
Selm, Ger. E3 16
Selma, Al., U.S. E11 122
Selma, Ca., U.S. G6 134
Selma, N.C., U.S. A7 116
Selmer, Tn., U.S. B10 122
Selmont, Al., U.S. E11 122
Selon', stm., Russia B13 10
Selong, Indon. H10 50
Selva, Arg. D6 92
Selvagens, Ilhas, is., Port. C1 64
Selvas, for., Braz. D8 84
Selway, stm., Id., U.S. D11 136
Selwyn, Austl. C3 76
Selwyn, Passage, strt., Vanuatu k16 79d
Selwyn Lake, l., Can. D10 106
Selwyn Mountains, mts., Can. C4 106
Selwyn Range, mts., Austl. C3 76
Seman, stm., Alb. D13 24
Semangka, Teluk, b., Indon. F4 50
Semara, W. Sah. D2 64
Semarang, Indon. G7 50
Semarang, Kenohan, l., Indon. D10 50
Sembakung, stm., Indon. B10 50
Semcy, Russia H16 10
Semenanjung Malaysia, hist. reg., Malay. K6 48
Semenov, Russia H21 8
Semeru, Gunung, vol., Indon. H8 50
Semey see Semipalatinsk, Kaz. D13 32
Semežava, Bela. H10 10
Semichi Islands, is., Ak., U.S. g21 140a
Semiluki, Russia D5 32
Semily, Czech Rep. F11 16
Seminary, Ms., U.S. F9 122
Seminoe Reservoir, res., Wy., U.S. A9 132
Seminole, Ok., U.S. B2 122
Seminole, Tx., U.S. B5 130
Seminole, Lake, res., U.S. G14 122
Seminole Draw, stm., U.S. B5 130
Semiozërnoe, Kaz. D10 32
Semipalatinsk, Kaz. D13 32
Semitau, Indon. C7 50
Semizbuga, Kaz. D13 32
Semliki, stm., Afr. D6 66
Semnän, Iran B7 56
Semois, stm., Eur. E13 14
Semonaiha, Russia D14 32
Sempora, Malay. H1 50
Semuda, Indon. E8 50
Semža, Russia C21 8
Sên, stm., Camb. F7 48
Sena, Bol. B3 90
Senador Canedo, Braz. I1 88
Senador Pompeu, Braz. C6 88
Senaki, Geor. F6 32
Sena Madureira, Braz. E4 84
Senanga, Zam. D3 68
Senanayake Samudra, res., Sri L. H5 53
Senath, Mo., U.S. H7 120

Senatobia, Ms., U.S. C8 122
Senber, Kaz. E11 32
Sendai, Japan H3 40
Sendai, Japan A13 40
Sendelingsdrif, Nmb. F3 70
Sendhwa, India H5 54
Sendurjana, India H7 54
Senduruhan, Indon. D7 50
Seneca, Il., U.S. C9 120
Seneca, Ks., U.S. E1 120
Seneca, Mo., U.S. H3 120
Seneca, S.C., U.S. B3 116
Seneca, Mount, mtn., N.Y., U.S. B7 114
Seneca Falls, N.Y., U.S. B9 114
Seneca Lake, l., N.Y., U.S. B8 114
Senegal, ctry., Afr. G2 64
Sénégal, stm., Afr. F2 64
Senekal, S. Afr. F8 70
Senetosa, Capu di (Senetosa, Punta di), c., Fr. H14 18
Senetosa, Punta di see Senetosa, Capu di, c., Fr. H14 18
Senftenberg, Ger. E10 16
Sengés, Braz. B13 92
Sênggê, stm., China B8 54
Senhor do Bonfim, Braz. F5 88
Senica, Slov. H13 16
Senigallia, Italy G10 22
Senirkent, Tur. E13 28
Senise, Italy D10 24
Senja, i., Nor. B7 8
Senkaku-shotō, is., Japan F9 36
Senköy, Tur. B7 58
Senkursk, Russia E20 8
Senlis, Fr. E11 14
Senmonorom, Camb. F8 48
Senneterre, Qc., Can. F15 106
Senoia, Ga., U.S. D14 122
Senquar, Tur. B16 28
Sens, Fr. F12 14
Senta, Yugo. D7 26
Sentarum, Danau, l., Indon. C7 50
Sentinel, Ok., U.S. F9 128
Sentinel Butte, mtn., N.D., U.S. A8 126
Senyavin Islands, is., Micron. C6 72
Seo de Urgel see La Seu d'Urgell, Spain B12 20
Seonāth, stm., India G7 54
Seoni, India G7 54
Seoni Mālwa, India G6 54
Seoul see Sŏul, Kor., S. F7 38
Sepanjang, Pulau, i., Indon. G9 50
Sepasu, Indon. C10 50
Sepik, stm., Pap. N. Gui. a3 79a
Sepopol, Pol. B17 16
Sept-Îles, Qc., Can. E17 106
Sepúlveda, Spain C7 20
Seputih, stm., Indon. F4 50
Sequatchie, stm., Tn., U.S. B13 122
Sequillo, stm., Spain C5 20
Sequim, Wa., U.S. B3 136
Sequoia National Park, p.o.i., Ca., U.S. G7 134
Šerabad, Uzb. B10 56
Serafimovič, Russia E6 32
Seraing, Bel. D14 14
Seram (Ceram), i., Indon. F8 44
Seram, Laut (Ceram Sea), Indon. F8 44
Serang, Indon. G5 50
Serasan, Pulau, i., Indon. B6 50
Serasan, Selat, strt., Indon. B6 50
Serayevo see Sarajevo, Bos. F5 26
Serbeulangit, Pegunungan, mts., Indon. K3 48
Serbia see Srbija, state, Yugo. E7 26
Serdo, Eth. E8 62
Serdobsk, Russia D6 32
Séré'ama, Mont, mtn., Vanuatu i16 79d
Serebrjansk, Kaz. E14 32
Serebrjanye Prudy, Russia F21 10
Sered', Slov. H13 16
Seredejskij, Russia F18 10
Serëdka, Russia B11 10
Seremban, Malay. K5 48
Serengeti National Park, p.o.i., Tan. E6 66
Serengka, Indon. D7 50
Serenje, Zam. C5 68
Seret (Siret), stm., Eur. A12 26
Sergač, Russia I21 8
Sergeevka, Kaz. D11 32
Sergeevka, Russia C10 38
Sergeja Kirova, ostrova, is., Russia A5 34
Sergen, Tur. B10 28
Sergiev Posad, Russia D21 10
Serginskij, Russia B10 32
Sergipe, state, Braz. F7 88
Sergozero, ozero, l., Russia C17 8
Seria, Bru. A9 50
Serian, Malay. C7 50
Seribudolok, Indon. B1 50
Seridó, stm., Braz. D7 88
Sérifos, i., Grc. F7 28
Serik, Tur. G14 28
Serinyol, Tur. B7 58
Serkin, stm., Italy E6 22
Serkovo, Russia A15 32
Šerlovaja Gora, Russia F12 34
Serov, Russia C10 32
Serowe, Bots. C8 70
Serpejsk, Russia F17 10
Serpentine Lakes, l., Austl. E5 74
Serpents Mouth, strt. C11 86
Ser'puhov, Russia F20 10
Serra, Braz. K5 88
Serra Branca, Braz. D7 88
Serra da Canastra, Parque Nacional da, p.o.i., K2 88
Serra da Capivara, Parque Nacional da, p.o.i., Braz. E4 88
Serra de Outes, Spain B2 20
Serra do Navio, Braz. C7 84
Serra do Salitre, Braz. J2 88
Serra dos Órgãos, Parque Nacional da, p.o.i., Braz. L4 88
Serrana, Braz. K2 88
Serrana Bank see Serrana, Cayo de, unds., Col. E7 102
Serrania de la Neblina, Parque Nacional, p.o.i., Ven. G8 86
Serranilla, Banco see Serranilla, Cayo de, unds., Col. E8 102
Serranilla, Cayo de, unds., Col. E8 102
Serranilla Bank see Serranilla, Cayo de, unds., Col. E8 102
Serrano, Banco see Serrana, Cayo de, unds., Col. E7 102
Serra Talhada, Braz. E6 88
Serres, Fr. E11 18
Sérres, Grc. B6 28
Serrezuela, Arg. E4 92
Serrinha, Braz. F6 88
Serrita, Braz. D6 88

Sertânia, Braz. E7 88
Sertãozinho, Braz. K1 88
Serui, Indon. F10 44
Serule, Bots. B8 70
Seruti, Pulau, i., Indon. D6 50
Seruwai, Indon. J4 48
Sêrxü, China E4 36
Seryševo, Russia F14 34
Sesayap, stm., Indon. B10 50
Sesayap Lama, Indon. B10 50
Seseganaga Lake, l., On., Can. A8 118
Sese Islands, is., Ug. E6 66
Sesfontein, Nmb. D1 68
Sesheke, Zam. D3 68
Sesia, stm., Italy E5 22
Sesibu, Indon. A10 50
Sesia Aurunca, Italy C7 24
Sestao, Spain A7 20
Sestri Levante, Italy F6 22
Šestroreck, Russia F14 8
Šešupė, stm., Eur. F5 10
Šeta, Lith. E7 10
Sete Barras, Braz. B13 92
Sete Cidades, Parque Nacional de, p.o.i., Braz. C5 88
Sete Lagoas, Braz. J3 88
Sete Quedas, Parque Nacional de, p.o.i., Braz. A11 92
Sete Quedas, Salto das (Guairá, Salto del), wtfl, S.A. B10 92
Seth Ward, Tx., U.S. G7 128
Seto, Japan D10 40
Seto-naikai (Inland Sea), Japan E5 40
Seton Portage, B.C., Can. F8 138
Settat, Mor. C3 64
Setté Cama, Gabon E1 66
Sette-Daban, hrebet, mts., Russia D16 34
Shandong Bandao (Shantung Peninsula), pen., China C9 42
Settlers, S. Afr. D9 70
Setúbal, Port. F1 20
Setúbal, Baía de, b., Port. F2 20
Seul, Lac, l., On., Can. A6 118
Seul Choix Point, c., Mi., U.S. C4 112
Seulimeum, Indon. J2 48
Sevan, Lake see Sevana Lich, l., Arm. A6 56
Sevana Lich, l., Arm. A6 56
Sevastopol', Ukr. G15 6
Sevelevskaja, Russia F20 8
Seven Persons, Ab., Can. E3 124
Seven Sisters Peaks, mtn., B.C., Can. B2 138
Seventy Mile House, B.C., Can. E9 138
Severn, stm., On., Can. E12 106
Severn, stm., U.K. J10 12
Severnaja Dvina (Northern Dvina), stm., Russia E19 8
Severnaja Osetija, state, Russia F6 32
Severnaja Sos'va, stm., Russia B10 32
Severnaja Zemlja, is., Russia B12 30
Severna Park, Md., U.S. E9 114
Severnoe, Russia C13 32
Severnye uvaly, hills, Russia C7 32
Severnyj Ural, mts., Russia B9 32
Severnyj Shuiku, res., China I6 42
Severočeský, state, Czech Rep. F9 16
Severodvinsk (Molotovsk), Russia D18 8
Severo-Jenisejskij, Russia B16 32
Severo-Kuril'sk, Russia F20 34
Severomoravský, state, Czech Rep. G13 16
Severomorsk, Russia B15 8
Severo-Sibirskaja nizmennost' (North Siberain Lowland), pl., Russia B6 34
Severoural'sk (Severouralsk), Russia B9 32
Severo-Zadonsk, Russia F21 10
Severy, Ks., U.S. D12 128
Sevettijärvi, Fin. B13 8
Sevier, stm., Ut., U.S. D4 132
Sevier, East Fork, stm., Ut., U.S. F5 132
Sevier Desert, des., Ut., U.S. D4 132
Sevier Lake, l., Ut., U.S. D3 132
Sevierville, Tn., U.S. I2 114
Sevilla, Col. E4 86
Sevilla (Seville), Spain G5 20
Sevilla, co., Spain G5 20
Seville see Sevilla, Spain G5 20
Seville, Fl., U.S. G4 116
Sevlievo, Blg. F12 26
Sewani, India D5 54
Seward, Ak., U.S. D10 140
Seward, Ne., U.S. G15 126
Seward, Pa., U.S. D7 114
Seward Peninsula, pen., Ak., U.S. C7 140
Sexsmith, Ab., Can. A12 138
Sextín, stm., Mex. B6 100
Seybaplaya, Mex. C2 102
Seychelles, ctry., Afr. k12 69b
Seychelles, is., Sey. k13 69b
Seydişehir, Tur. F14 28
Seydisfjördur, Ice. k32 8a
Seyhan (Sarus), stm., Tur. A6 58
Seyhan Baraji, res., Tur. A6 58
Seymour, S. Afr. H8 70
Seymour, Ct., U.S. C12 114
Seymour, In., U.S. F12 120
Seymour, Mo., U.S. G5 120
Seymour, Tx., U.S. H9 128
Seymour, Wi., U.S. D11 112
Sežana, Slvn. E10 22
Sezze, Italy C7 24
Sfântu Gheorghe, Rom. D12 26
Sfântu Gheorghe, Brațul, stm., Rom. E16 26
Sfântu Gheorghe, Ostrovul, i., Rom. D16 26
Sfax, Tun. C7 64
's-Gravenhage (The Hague), Neth. B13 14
Sha, stm., China H7 42
Sha, stm., China E6 42
Shabeelle (Shebelē Wenz, Wabē), stm., Afr. E5 66
Shabunda, D.R.C. E5 66
Shabwah, Yemen E19 16
Shache (Yarkant), China B12 56
Shackleton Ice Shelf, ice, Ant. B14 81
Shackleton Range, mts., Ant. D2 81
Shadrinsk, Russia C10 32
Shady Cove, Or., U.S. A3 134
Shady Grove, Fl., U.S. F2 116
Shadyside, Oh., U.S. E5 114
Shageluk, Ak., U.S. D8 140
Shag Rocks, r., S. Geor. J8 90
Shāhābād, India C5 54
Shāhābād, India E7 54
Shāhāda, India H5 54
Shah Alam, Malay. K5 48
Shahdol, India G8 54
Shahe, China J3 42
Shahe, China C6 42
Shahezhen, China A7 42

Shāhjahānpur, India E7 54
Shāh Kot, Pak. C4 54
Shāhpur, India C3 53
Shāhpur, Pak. D2 54
Shāhpura, India D8 54
Shāhpura, India E5 54
Shāhpura, India F5 54
Shahr-e Kord, Iran C7 56
Shaighālu, Pak. C2 54
Shājāpur, India G6 54
Shakawe, Bots. D3 68
Shaker Heights, Oh., U.S. G8 112
Shakespeare Island, i., On., Can. B10 118
Shaki, Nig. H5 64
Shakotan-hantō, pen., Japan C14 38
Shaktoolik, Ak., U.S. D7 140
Shala, Lake see Shala Hāyk', l., Eth. F7 62
Shala Hāyk', l., Eth. F7 62
Shalalth, B.C., Can. F8 138
Shaler Mountains, mts., Can. A8 106
Shallowater, Tx., U.S. H6 128
Shaluli Shan, mts., China E4 36
Shām, Jabal ash-, mtn., Oman E8 56
Shamattawa, Mb., Can. D12 106
Shambe, Sudan F6 62
Shambu, Eth. F7 62
Shāmli, India D6 54
Shamokin, Pa., U.S. D9 114
Shamrock, Fl., U.S. G2 116
Shamrock, Tx., U.S. F8 128
Shamva, Zimb. D5 68
Shancheng, China C2 42
Shandan, China D5 36
Shandī, Sudan D6 62
Shandong, state, China C7 42
Shandong Bandao (Shantung Peninsula), pen., China C9 42
Shand uul, mtn., Mong. C5 36
Shangani, Zimb. A9 70
Shangani, stm., Zimb. D4 68
Shangbahe, China F6 42
Shangcheng, China F6 42
Shang'iu see Shangqiu, China D6 42
Shangchuan Dao, i., China K5 42
Shanggao, China C7 36
Shanggui, China D6 42
Shanghai, China F9 42
Shanghai, state, China I4 38
Shanghai Shih see Shanghai, state, China I4 38
Shanghang, China I7 42
Shanghe, China C7 42
Shangjao see Shangrao, China G7 42
Shangjin, China J3 42
Shangqing, China I8 42
Shangqiu, China D6 42
Shangqiu, China D6 42
Shangrao, China G7 42
Shangshui, China E6 42
Shangxian, China E3 42
Shangyi, China A6 42
Shangying, China B7 38
Shangyou Shuiku, res., China I6 42
Shangzhi, China B8 38
Shangzhi, China B8 38
Shanhaiguan see Shanhaiguan, China A8 42
Shanhetun, China B7 38
Shankou, China K3 42
Shannon, Il., U.S. B8 120
Shannon, Ms., U.S. C10 122
Shannon, Ø, i., Grnld. B22 141
Shannontown, S.C., U.S. C5 116
Shanshan, China C3 36
Shansi see Shanxi, state, China B5 42
Shantar Islands see Santarskie ostrova, is., Russia E16 34
Shāntipur, India G12 54
Shantou, China J7 42
Shantung see Shandong, state, China C7 42
Shantung Peninsula see Shandong Bandao, pen., China C9 42
Shanwei, China J6 42
Shanxi, state, China B5 42
Shanxian, China D7 42
Shanyang, China E3 42
Shanyin, China B5 42
Shaoguan, China I5 42
Shaoshan see Shaoxing, China G9 42
Shaoshing see Shaoxing, China G9 42
Shaokuan see Shaoguan, China I5 42
Shaoleng, stm., China C3 38
Shaowu, China H7 42
Shaoxing, China G9 42
Shaoyang, China H4 42
Shaqqā, Syria F7 58
Shaqrā', Sau. Ar. D6 56
Shaqrā', Yemen G6 56
Shara, gora, mtn., Asia A5 56
Shari-dake, mtn., Japan C16 38
Sharin Gol, Mong. B6 36
Sharjah see Ash-Shāriqah, U.A.E. D8 56
Shark Bay, b., Austl. E2 74
Sharktooth Mountain, mtn., B.C., Can. D5 106
Sharm el-Sheikh, Egypt K5 58
Sharon, N.D., U.S. G16 124
Sharon, Tn., U.S. H9 120
Sharon, Wi., U.S. B9 120
Sharpe, Lake, res., S.D., U.S. C12 126
Sharpsville, Pa., U.S. C5 114
Shashe, stm., Afr. B9 70
Shashemenē, Eth. F7 62
Shashi, China F5 42
Shasi see Shashi, China F5 42
Shasta, Ca., U.S. C3 134
Shasta, Mount, vol., Ca., U.S. B3 134
Shasta Lake, res., Ca., U.S. C3 134
Shāti', Wādī ash-, stm., Libya B2 62
Shats'kyi Pryrodnyi Natsional'nyi Park, p.o.i., Ukr. E19 16
Shattuck, Ok., U.S. E8 128
Shaunavon, Sk., Can. E5 124
Shaw, Ms., U.S. D8 122
Shaw, China C2 36
Shawinigan, Qc., Can. D4 110
Shawinigan-Sud, Qc., Can. D4 110
Shawnee, Oh., U.S. E3 114
Shawnee, Ok., U.S. B2 122
Shawneetown, Il., U.S. G9 120
Shawville, Qc., Can. C13 112
Shaxian, China H7 42
Shayang, China F5 42
Shaykh Miskīn, Syria F7 58
Shaykh 'Uthmān, Yemen G6 56

Shchūchinsk see Ščučinsk, Kaz. D12 32
She, stm., China F6 42
Shebeele Werz, Wabē (Shabeelle), stm., Afr. C8 66
Sheberghān, Afg. B10 56
Sheboygan, Wi., U.S. E2 112
Sheboygan, stm., Wi., U.S. E1 112
Sheboygan Falls, Wi., U.S. E1 112
Shechem, hist., W.B. F6 58
Shedin Peak, mtn., B.C., Can. D5 106
Sheelin, Lough, l., Ire. H5 12
Sheenjek, stm., Ak., U.S. C11 140
Sheep Mountain, mtn., Az., U.S. K2 132
Sheerness, Eng., U.K. J13 12
Sheet Harbour, N.S., Can. F14 110
Sheffield, N.Z. F4 80
Sheffield, Eng., U.K. H11 12
Sheffield, Al., U.S. C11 122
Sheffield, Il., U.S. C8 120
Sheffield, Pa., U.S. C6 114
Shegaon, India H6 54
Sheho, Sk., Can. C10 124
Shehong, China F1 42
Sheikhpura, India F10 54
Shekhūpura, Pak. C4 54
Shekki see Zhongshan, China J5 42
Shelagyote Peak, mtn., B.C., Can. D5 106
Shelbina, Mo., U.S. E5 120
Shelburne, N.S., Can. G11 110
Shelburne, On., Can. D9 112
Shelburne Falls, Ma., U.S. B13 114
Shelby, Ia., U.S. C2 120
Shelby, Mi., U.S. E3 112
Shelby, Ms., U.S. D8 122
Shelby, Mt., U.S. B15 136
Shelby, N.C., U.S. A4 116
Shelbyville, Il., U.S. E9 120
Shelbyville, In., U.S. E12 120
Shelbyville, Mo., U.S. E5 120
Shelbyville, Tn., U.S. B12 122
Shelbyville, Lake, res., Il., U.S. E8 120
Sheldon, Ia., U.S. H3 118
Sheldon, Mo., U.S. G3 120
Sheldon, Tx., U.S. H3 122
Shelek see Cilik, Kaz. F13 32
Shelikhov, Gulf of see Selihova, zaliv, b., Russia D20 34
Shelikof Strait, strt., Ak., U.S. E9 140
Shell, stm., Mb., Can. C12 124
Shellbrook, Sk., Can. A7 124
Shell Creek, stm., Ne., U.S. F15 126
Shelley, B.C., Can. C8 138
Shellharbour, Austl. J8 76
Shell Lake, Wi., U.S. F7 118
Shellman, Ga., U.S. F14 122
Shellmouth Dam, dam, Mb., Can. D12 124
Shell Rock, Ia., U.S. B5 120
Shell Rock, stm., U.S. I6 118
Shellsburg, Ia., U.S. B5 120
Shelton, Ct., U.S. C12 114
Shelton, Ne., U.S. G14 126
Shemogue, N.B., Can. D12 110
Shemonaiha see Semonaiha, Kaz. D14 32
Shenandoah, Ia., U.S. D2 120
Shenandoah, Pa., U.S. D9 114
Shenandoah, Va., U.S. F7 114
Shenandoah, stm., Va., U.S. E8 114
Shenandoah, North Fork, stm., Va., U.S. F7 114
Shenandoah, South Fork, stm., Va., U.S. F7 114
Shenandoah National Park, p.o.i., Va., U.S. F7 114
Shenchi, China B4 42
Shendam, Nig. H6 64
Shenge, S.L. H2 64
Shengli Liedao, is., China I5 38
Shengxian, China G9 42
Shengze, China F9 42
Shenjing, China J5 42
Shenqiu, China E6 42
Shensi see Shaanxi, state, China E3 42
Shenton, Mount, mtn., Austl. E4 74
Shenxian, China C6 42
Shenyang (Mukden), China D5 38
Shenzhen, China J6 42
Sheoganj, India F4 54
Sheopur, India F6 54
Shepard, Ab., Can. E17 138
Shepherd, Mi., U.S. E5 112
Shepherd, state, Vanuatu k17 79d
Shepherd, Îles, is., Vanuatu k17 79d
Shepherdstown, W.V., U.S. E7 114
Shepherdsville, Ky., U.S. F12 120
Shepparton, Austl. K5 76
Sheppey, Isle of, i., Eng., U.K. J13 12
Sheqi, China E5 42
Sherard, Cape, c., Nu., Can. C10 141
Sherard Osborn Fjord, b., Grnld. A14 141
Sherborne, Eng., U.K. K10 12
Sherbro Island, i., S.L. H2 64
Sherbrooke, N.S., Can. E14 110
Sherbrooke, Qc., Can. E4 110
Sherburn, Mn., U.S. H4 118
Sherburne, N.Y., U.S. B10 114
Sheridan, Ar., U.S. C6 122
Sheridan, In., U.S. H3 112
Sheridan, Or., U.S. E3 136
Sheridan, Wy., U.S. C6 126
Sherman, N.Y., U.S. B6 114
Sherman, Tx., U.S. D2 122
Sherman Mills, Me., U.S. E8 110
Sherman Mountain, mtn., Ar., U.S. I4 120
Sherman Station, Me., U.S. E8 110
Sherpur, Bngl. F12 54
Sherpur, Bngl. F13 54
Sherridon, Mb., Can. E10 106
Sherrill, N.Y., U.S. B10 114
Shertallai, India G3 53
's-Hertogenbosch, Neth. C14 14
Sherwood, Ar., U.S. C6 122
Sherwood, Oh., U.S. C1 114
Sherwood Park, Ab., Can. C17 138
Sherwood Shores, Tx., U.S. D9 130
Shesh Gāv, Afg. B2 54
Shetland Islands, is., Scot., U.K. n17 12a
Shetrunji, stm., India H3 54
Sheyang, China E9 42
Sheyenne, N.D., U.S. G15 124
Sheyenne, stm., N.D., U.S. H16 124
Shibām, Yemen F6 56
Shibata, Japan B12 40
Shibīn el-Kôm, Egypt H1 58
Shibing, China H2 42
Shibukawa, Japan C12 40
Shibushi, Japan H4 40
Shickley, Ne., U.S. G15 126
Shidao, China C9 42
Shidian, China F4 36
Shidler, Ok., U.S. E12 128
Shiga, state, Japan D9 40

Shigezhuang, China B6 42
Shigouyi, China C2 42
Shiguaigou, China A4 42
Shihch'i see Zhongshan, China J5 42
Shihchiazhuang see Shijiazhuang, China C6 42
Shihkiachwang see Shijiazhuang, China C6 42
Shijiazhuang, China C6 42
Shijiu Hu, l., China F8 42
Shikārpur, India D2 53
Shikārpur, Pak. E2 54
Shikohābād, India E7 54
Shikoku, i., Japan F6 40
Shikoku-sanchi, mts., Japan F6 40
Shikotsu-ko, l., Japan C14 38
Shiliguri, India E12 54
Shillelagh, Ire. I6 12
Shillington, Pa., U.S. H13 112
Shillong, India F13 54
Shiloh, Oh., U.S. I5 112
Shiloh see Saylūn, Khirbat, hist., W.B. F6 58
Shilong, China J5 42
Shima, Japan E9 40
Shimabara, Japan G3 40
Shimada, Japan E11 40
Shimane, state, Japan D5 40
Shimbiris, mtn., Som. B9 66
Shimen, China G4 42
Shimian, China F5 36
Shimizu, Japan D11 40
Shimla, India C6 54
Shimminato, Japan C10 40
Shimoda, Japan E11 40
Shimodate, Japan C13 40
Shimoga, India E2 53
Shimonoseki, Japan F3 40
Shimono-shima, i., Japan E2 40
Shin, Loch, l., Scot., U.K. C8 12
Shinano, stm., Japan B11 40
Shindand, Afg. C9 56
Shingbwiyang, Mya. C8 46
Shingū, Japan F9 40
Shingū, Japan E7 40
Shingwidzi, S. Afr. C10 70
Shingwidzi (Singuédeze), stm., Afr. C10 70
Shinji-ko, l., Japan D5 40
Shinjō, Japan A13 40
Shinyanga, Tan. E6 66
Shiocton, Wi., U.S. G10 118
Shiogama, Japan A14 40
Shiojiri, Japan C10 40
Shiono-misaki, c., Japan F8 40
Shioya-zaki, c., Japan C13 40
Shiping, China G5 36
Shiping, China G2 42
Shipka Pass see Šipčenski Prohod, p., Blg. G12 26
Shipman, Va., U.S. G7 114
Shippegan, N.B., Can. C12 110
Shippensburg, Pa., U.S. D8 114
Shiprock, N.M., U.S. G8 132
Ship Rock, stm., U.S. G8 132
Ship Rock, mtn., N.M., U.S. I6 118
Shipshaw, Qc., Can. B5 110
Shipu, China G9 42
Shiquan, China E3 42
Shirahama, Japan D12 40
Shirakawa, Japan B13 40
Shīrāz, Iran D7 56
Shirbīn, Egypt G2 58
Shiretoko-misaki, c., Japan B16 38
Shir Kūh, mtn., Iran C7 56
Shirley, In., U.S. I4 112
Shiroishi, Japan B13 40
Shirone, Japan B11 40
Shirpur, India H5 54
Shīrvān, Iran B8 56
Shishaldin Volcano, vol., Ak., U.S. F7 140
Shishi, China I8 42
Shishmaref, Ak., U.S. C6 140
Shitang, China H9 42
Shiv, India E3 54
Shively, Ky., U.S. F12 120
Shivpuri, India F6 54
Shivta, Horvot (Subeita), hist., Isr. H5 58
Shivwits Plateau, plat., Az., U.S. G3 132
Shiwu, China C6 38
Shizhu, China G3 42
Shizugawa, Japan A14 40
Shizui, China C6 38
Shizunai, Japan C15 38
Shizuoka, Japan E11 40
Shizuoka, state, Japan D11 40
Shkodra see Shkodër, Alb. B13 24
Shkodër, Alb. B13 24
Shkotovo, Russia C10 40
Shoal, stm., Fl., U.S. G12 122
Shoal Creek, stm., Mo., U.S. E4 120
Shoalhaven, stm., Austl. J8 76
Shoal Lake, l., Can. B3 118
Shoals, In., U.S. F11 120
Shoalwater Bay, b., Austl. D8 76
Shōbara, Japan E6 40
Shōdo-shima, i., Japan E7 40
Sholinganur, India E4 53
Shorāpur, India C3 53
Shoreacres, B.C., Can. G13 138
Shorewood, Wi., U.S. E2 112
Shorkot, Pak. C4 54
Shortland Island, i., Sol. Is. d6 79b
Shortland Islands, is., Sol. Is. d6 79b
Shoshone, Id., U.S. H12 136
Shoshone, stm., Wy., U.S. D22 126
Shoshone, South Fork, stm., Wy., U.S. G17 136
Shoshone Lake, l., Wy., U.S. F15 136
Shoshone Mountains, mts., Nv., U.S. E8 134
Shoshone Peak, mtn., Nv., U.S. G9 134
Shoshone Range, mts., Nv., U.S. C9 134
Shoshong, Bots. D4 70
Shostka, Ukr. D4 32
Shouchang, China G8 42
Shouguang, China C7 42
Shouxian, China E7 42
Shouyang, China C5 42
Show Low, Az., U.S. I6 132
Shpola, Ukr. G4 32
Shqipëria see Albania, ctry., C14 24
Shreve, Oh., U.S. D4 114
Shreveport, La., U.S. E5 122
Shrewsbury, Eng., U.K. I10 12
Shri Dūngargarh, India D4 54
Shri Mohangarh, India E3 54
Shrirāmpur, India G12 54
Shropshire see Salop, co., Eng., U.K. I10 12
Shu see Chu, stm., Asia F11 32
Shu, stm., China D7 42
Shuajingsi, China E5 36
Shuangcheng, China B7 38
Shuangfeng, China H5 42
Shuanggou, China D7 42
Shuangji, stm., China D5 42
Shuangliao, China C5 38
Shuangpai, China I4 42

Name	Map Ref.	Page
Shuangshutai, China	C4	38
Shuangyang, China	C6	38
Shuangyashan, China	B11	36
Shubrā el-Kheima, Egypt	H1	58
Shubuta, Ms., U.S.	F10	122
Shucheng, China	F7	42
Shuibatang, China	G2	42
Shuiji, China	H8	42
Shuijingtang, China	G2	42
Shuikoushan, China	H5	42
Shuitou, China	I8	42
Shuiye, China	C5	42
Shujāābād, Pak.	D3	54
Shujālpur, India	G6	54
Shuksan, Mount, mtn., Wa., U.S.	B5	136
Shulan, China	B7	38
Shulaps Peak, mtn., B.C., Can.	F8	138
Shule, China	B12	56
Shule, stm., China	C4	36
Shumagin Islands, is., Ak., U.S.	F7	140
Shunchang, China	H7	42
Shunde, China	J5	42
Shungnak, Ak., U.S.	C8	140
Shunyi, China	A7	42
Shuqualak, Ms., U.S.	E10	122
Shurkhua, Mya.	A1	48
Shurugwi, Zimb.	D5	68
Shūshtar, Iran	C6	56
Shuswap, stm., B.C., Can.	F12	138
Shuswap Lake, l., B.C., Can.	F11	138
Shuwak, Sudan	E7	62
Shuyak Island, i., Ak., U.S.	E9	140
Shuyang, China	D8	42
Shwangliao see Liaoyuan, China	C6	38
Shwebo, Mya.	A2	48
Shwegun, Mya.	D3	48
Shwegyin, Mya.	D3	48
Shymkent see Symkent, Kaz.	F11	32
Shyok, India	A7	54
Shyok, stm., Asia	B4	46
Si, stm., China	D7	42
Sia, Indon.	G9	44
Siāhān Range, mts., Pak.	D9	56
Siak, stm., Indon.	C2	50
Siak Sri Indrapura, Indon.	C3	50
Siālkot, Pak.	B5	54
Siam see Thailand, ctry., Asia	E5	48
Siam, Gulf of see Thailand, Gulf of, b., Asia	G5	48
Sian see Xi'an, China	D3	42
Siangtan see Xiangtan, China	H5	42
Sianów, Pol.	B12	16
Siantan, Pulau, i., Indon.	B4	50
Siapa, stm., Ven.	G9	86
Siargao Island, i., Phil.	F6	52
Siasconset, Ma., U.S.	C15	114
Siasi, Phil.	H3	52
Siasi Island, i., Phil.	H3	52
Siaškotan, ostrov, i., Russia	G19	34
Šiau, Pulau, i., Indon.	E7	44
Siauliai, Lith.	E6	10
Sibay, Lake, l., S. Afr.	E11	70
Šibenik, Cro.	G12	22
Siberia see Sibir', reg., Russia	C12	34
Siberut, Pulau, i., Indon.	D1	50
Sibi, Pak.	D10	56
Sibigo, Indon.	K2	48
Sibir', reg., Russia	C12	34
Sibircevo, Russia	B10	38
Sibirjakova, ostrov, i., Russia	B4	34
Sibiti, Congo	E2	66
Sibiu, Rom.	D11	26
Sibiu, state, Rom.	D11	26
Sibley, Ia., U.S.	H3	118
Sibley, La., U.S.	E5	122
Sibley, Ms., U.S.	F7	122
Sibley Peninsula, pen., On., Can.	C10	118
Sibolga, Indon.	C1	50
Sibsāgar, India	C7	46
Sibu, Malay.	B7	50
Sibuguey Bay, b., Phil.	G4	52
Sibut, C.A.R.	C3	66
Sibutu Island, i., Phil.	H2	52
Sibutu Passage, strt., Asia	H2	52
Sibuyan Island, i., Phil.	D4	52
Sibuyan Sea, Phil.	D4	52
Sicapoo, Mount, mtn., Phil.	B3	52
Siccus, stm., Austl.	H2	76
Sichang see Xichang, China	F5	36
Si Chon, Thai.	H4	48
Sichuan, state, China	E5	36
Sichuan Pendi, bas., China	F1	42
Sichuanzhai, China	E5	36
Sicilia (Sicily), i., Italy	F8	24
Sicilia (Sicily), i., Italy	G7	24
Sicilia see Sicilia, state, Italy	F8	24
Sicily see Sicilia, i., Italy	G7	24
Sicily, Strait of, strt.	G5	24
Sicily Island, La., U.S.	F7	122
Sicuani, Peru	F3	84
Sidareja, Indon.	G6	50
Sidas, Indon.	C5	50
Siddhapur, India	G4	54
Siddipet, India	B4	53
Sidéradougou, Burkina	G4	64
Siderno, Italy	F10	24
Siderópolis, Braz.	D13	92
Sideros, Ákra, c., Grc.	H9	28
Sidhauli, India	E8	54
Sidhi, India	F8	54
Sīdi Barrāni, Egypt	A5	62
Sidi bel Abbès, Alg.	B4	64
Sidi-Ifni, Mor.	D2	64
Siding Spring Mountain, mtn., Austl.	H7	76
Sidirókastro, Grc.	B6	28
Sidi Sālim, Egypt	G1	58
Sidlaghatta, India	E3	53
Sidley, Mount, mtn., Ant.	C28	81
Sidmouth, Eng., U.K.	K9	12
Sidnaw, Mi., U.S.	E10	118
Sidney, B.C., Can.	H7	138
Sidney, Il., U.S.	D9	120
Sidney, Mt., U.S.	G9	124
Sidney, Ne., U.S.	F10	126
Sidney, N.Y., U.S.	B10	114
Sidney, Oh., U.S.	D1	114
Sidney Lanier, Lake, res., Ga., U.S.	B2	116
Sidon see Saydā, Leb.	E6	58
Sidon, Ms., U.S.	D8	122
Sidra, Gulf of see Surt, Khalīj, b., Libya	A3	62
Sidrolândia, Braz.	D6	90
Siedlce, state, Pol.	D18	16
Siedlce, Pol.	D17	16
Siegburg, Ger.	F3	16
Siegen, Ger.	F4	16
Siemianowice Śląskie, Pol.	F15	16
Siĕmpang, Camb.	E8	48
Siĕmréab, Camb.	F6	48
Siena, Italy	G8	22
Sienyang see Xianyang, China	D3	42
Sieradz, Pol.	D13	16
Sieradz, state, Pol.	E14	16
Sieraków, Pol.	D12	16
Sierpc, Pol.	D15	16
Sierra Blanca, Tx., U.S.	C2	130
Sierra Blanca Peak, mtn., N.M., U.S.	H3	128
Sierra Chica, Arg.	H7	92
Sierra Colorada, Arg.	H3	90
Sierra Gorda, Chile	D3	90
Sierra Leone, ctry., Afr.	H2	64
Sierra Mojada, Mex.	G4	130
Sierra Nevada see Nevada, Sierra, mts., Ca., U.S.	F6	134
Sierra Nevada, Parque Nacional, p.o.i., Mex.	C6	86
Sierra Vista, Az., U.S.	L6	132
Sierre, Switz.	D4	22
Siesta Key, Fl., U.S.	I3	116
Sifnos, i., Grc.	F7	28
Sifton Villanueva, Mex.	G7	130
Sig, Russia	D16	8
Sigatoka, Fiji	q18	79e
Sigep, Indon.	D1	50
Sighetu Marmaţiei, Rom.	B10	26
Sighişoara, Rom.	C11	26
Siglan, Russia	E19	34
Sigli, Indon.	J2	48
Siglufjördur, Ice.	j30	8a
Sigmaringen, Ger.	H5	16
Signal Mountain, Tn., U.S.	B13	122
Signal Mountain, mtn., Vt., U.S.	F4	110
Signy, sci., Ant.	B36	81
Sigourney, Ia., U.S.	C5	120
Sigsig, Ec.	D2	84
Siguanea, Ensenada de la, b., Cuba	B6	102
Siguatepeque, Hond.	E3	102
Sigüenza, Spain	C8	20
Siguiri, Gui.	G3	64
Sigulda, Lat.	C7	10
Sigurd, Ut., U.S.	E5	132
Siguri Falls, wtfl, Tan.	F7	66
Sihabuhabu, Dolok, mtn., Indon.	B1	50
Sihanoukville see Kâmpóng Saôm, Camb.	G6	48
Sihŏr, India	H3	54
Sihorā, India	G8	54
Sihote-Alin', mts., Russia	E17	30
Sihtovo, Russia	E15	10
Sihui, China	J5	42
Siirt, Tur.	B5	56
Sija, Russia	E19	8
Sijunjung, Indon.	D2	50
Sikandarābād, India	D6	54
Sikanni Chief, stm., B.C., Can.	D6	106
Sikao, Thai.	I4	48
Sikar, India	E5	54
Sikasso, Mali	G3	64
Sikeston, Mo., U.S.	H8	120
Sikhote-Alin Mountains see Sihote-Alin', mts., Russia	E17	30
Sikiang see Xi Jiang, China	J5	42
Sikinos, i., Grc.	G8	28
Sikkim, state, India	E12	54
Sikonge, Tan.	F6	66
Sikotan, ostrov (Shikotan-tō), i., Russia	C17	33
Siktjah, Russia	B13	34
Sikuati, Malay.	G1	52
Sikyón, hist., Grc.	F5	28
Sil, stm., Spain	B3	20
Šila, Russia	E7	34
Silalė, Lith.	E5	10
Silao, Mex.	E8	100
Silchar, India	F14	54
Šile, Tur.	B12	28
Siler City, N.C., U.S.	I6	114
Sileru, stm., India	C5	53
Silesia see hist. reg., Eur.	F13	16
Sileţteniz, ozero, l., Kaz.	D12	32
Siletz, Or., U.S.	F3	136
Siletz, stm., Or., U.S.	F3	136
Silgadhī, Nepal	D8	54
Silghāt, India	E14	54
Silhouette, i., Sey.	j13	69g
Siliana, Tun.	H3	24
Siliana, Oued, stm., Tun.	I3	24
Siling Co, l., China	C12	54
Silistra, Blg.	E14	26
Silivri, Tur.	B11	28
Šiljan, i., Swe.	F6	8
Šilka, Russia	F12	34
Šilka, stm., Russia	F12	34
Silkeborg, Den.	H3	8
Sillamäe, Est.	A10	10
Sillem Island, i., Nu., Can.	A16	106
Sillian, Aus.	D9	22
Sillon de Talbert, pen., Fr.	F5	14
Silsbee, Tx., U.S.	G4	122
Silton, Sk., Can.	D9	124
Siluas, Indon.	C6	50
Šilutė, Lith.	E4	10
Silvânia, Braz.	I1	88
Silvassa, India	H4	54
Silver, Tx., U.S.	B7	130
Silver Bank Passage, strt., N.A.	B12	102
Silver Bell, Az., U.S.	K5	132
Silver City, N.M., U.S.	K8	132
Silver City, N.C., U.S.	B6	115
Silver Creek, Ms., U.S.	F9	122
Silver Creek, stm., Az., U.S.	I6	132
Silver Creek, stm., Or., U.S.	G7	136
Silverdale, Wa., U.S.	C4	136
Silver Lake, Ks., U.S.	E2	120
Silver Lake, Mn., U.S.	G4	118
Silver Lake, Wi., U.S.	F1	112
Silver Lake, l., Or., U.S.	G5	136
Silver Lake, l., Or., U.S.	G5	136
Silver Spring, Md., U.S.	E8	114
Silver Star Mountain, mtn., Wa., U.S.	E4	136
Silverthrone Mountain, vol., B.C., Can.	E4	138
Silverton, B.C., Can.	G13	138
Silverton, Co., U.S.	F9	132
Silverton, Tx., U.S.	G7	128
Silvi, Italy	H11	22
Silvia, Col.	F3	86
Silvies, stm., Or., U.S.	G7	136
Simanovsk, Russia	F14	34
Simao, China	A5	48
Simão Dias, Braz.	F6	88
Simav, Tur.	D11	28
Simav, stm., Tur.	C11	28
Simbach, Ger.	H8	16
Simcoe, On., Can.	F9	112
Simcoe, Lake, l., On., Can.	D10	112
Simdega, India	G10	54
Simeonovski, mys, c., Russia	F21	34
Simeulue, Pulau, i., Indon.	K2	48
Simferopol', Ukr.	G15	6
Simikot, Nepal	C8	54
Similkameen, stm., N.A.	G11	138
Simiti, Col.	D4	86
Simi Valley, Ca., U.S.	I7	134
Simla see Shimizu, Japan	D11	40
Simla, Co., U.S.	B4	128
Simmern, Ger.	G4	16
Simmie, Sk., Can.	E5	124
Simms, Mt., U.S.	C15	136
Simnas, Lith.	F7	10
Simoca, Arg.	C5	92
Simões, Braz.	D5	88
Simojärvi, l., Fin.	C12	8
Simojovel, Mex.	G12	100
Simon, Lac, l., Qc., Can.	E1	110
Simon, stm., Ab., Can.	A12	138
Simonoseki see Shimonoseki, Japan	F3	40
Simonstad see Simon's Town, S. Afr.	I4	70
Simon's Town, S. Afr.	I4	70
Simoom Sound, B.C., Can.	F4	138
Simpang, Indon.	D3	50
Simpang-kiri, stm., Indon.	K3	48
Simplon Pass, p., Switz.	D4	22
Simplón, Iran	D8	56
Simpson Desert, des., Austl.	D7	74
Simpson Island, i., On., Can.	C11	118
Simpson Peninsula, pen., Nu., Can.	B13	106
Simpson Strait, strt., Nu., Can.	B11	106
Simpsonville, S.C., U.S.	B3	116
Simrishamn, Swe.	I6	8
Simsonbaai, Neth. Ant.	A1	105a
Simunjan, Malay.	C7	50
Simušir, ostrov, i., Russia	G19	34
Sīna, stm., India	B2	53
Sinabang, Indon.	K3	48
Sinabung, Gunung, vol., Indon.	K4	48
Sinai (Sinai Peninsula), pen., Egypt	J4	58
Sinai, Mount, stm., Mex.	G8	98
Sinai, Mount see Mûsa, Gebel, mtn., Egypt	J5	58
Sinai, Mount, vol., Gren.	q10	105e
Sisaba, mtn., Tan.	D12	26
Sinai Peninsula see Sinai, pen., Egypt	J4	58
Sinajana, Guam	j10	78c
Sinaloa, state, Mex.	C5	100
Sinaloa, stm., Mex.	C5	100
Sinamaica, Ven.	B6	86
Sinan, China	H3	42
Sinanpaşa, Tur.	E13	28
Sināwin, Libya	A2	62
Sincan, Tur.	D15	28
Sincé, Col.	B2	84
Sincelejo, Col.	C4	86
Sinch'ang-ŭp, Kor., N.	D8	38
Sin-ch'ŏn, Kor., N.	E6	38
Sinclair, Wy., U.S.	B9	132
Sinclair, Lake, res., Ga., U.S.	C2	116
Sinclair Mills, B.C., Can.	B9	138
Sind, state, Pak.	F2	54
Sind, stm., India	F7	54
Sindañgan, Phi.	F4	52
Sindangbarang, Indon.	G5	50
Sindara, Gabon	E2	66
Sindelfingen, Ger.	H4	16
Sindhnūr, India	D3	53
Sindhulī Mādhi, Nepal	E10	54
Sindingale, Mya.	C2	48
Sindor, Russia	B8	32
Sines, Port.	G2	20
Sinfra, C. Iv.	H3	64
Singalamwe, Nmb.	D3	68
Singapore, Sing.	C3	50
Singapore, ctry., Asia	L6	48
Singapore, Strait of, strt., Asia	C4	50
Singaraja, Indon.	H9	50
Sing Buri, Thai.	E5	48
Singen, Ger.	I4	16
Singida, Tan.	E6	66
Singitic Gulf see Ayíou Órous, Kólpos, b., Grc.	C6	28
Singkaling Hkämti, Mya.	C3	46
Singkang, Indon.	F11	50
Singkawang, Indon.	C5	50
Singkep, Pulau, i., Indon.	D4	50
Singkil, Indon.	K3	48
Singkuang, Indon.	C1	50
Singleton, Austl.	I8	76
Singleton, Mount, mtn., Austl.	E3	74
Singuédeze (Shingwidzi), stm., Afr.	C10	70
Sinhung, Kor., N.	D7	38
Sining see Xining, China	D5	36
Sinj, Cro.	G13	22
Sinjai, Indon.	F12	50
Sinjah, Sudan	E6	62
Sinjār, Iraq	B5	56
Sinjil, West Bank	F6	58
Sinjaja, stm., Eur.	D11	10
Sinjaja, stm., Eur.	D14	34
Sinjuga, Russia	E12	34
Sinkat, Sudan	D7	62
Sinkiang see Xinjiang, state, China	A5	46
Sinnamahoning, Pa., U.S.	C7	114
Sinnamary, Fr. Gu.	B7	84
Sinnar, India	B2	53
Sinnūris, Egypt	I1	58
Sinnyŏng, Kor., S.	C1	40
Sinoe, Lacul, l., Rom.	E15	26
Sinop, Tur.	A4	56
Sinop, Braz.	F6	84
Sinsheim, Ger.	G4	16
Sinsiang see Xinxiang, China	D5	42
Sinskoe, Russia	D14	34
Sintang, Indon.	C7	50
Sint Christoffelberg, hill, Neth. Ant.	p21	104g
Sint Eustatius, i., Neth. Ant.	B1	105a
Sint Helenabaai, b., S. Afr.	H3	70
Sint Kruis, Neth. Ant.	p21	104g
Sint Maarten (Saint-Martin), i., N.A.	A1	105a
Sint Nicolaas, Aruba	p20	104g
Sint-Niklaas, Bel.	C12	14
Sintra, Port.	F1	20
Sint-Truiden, Bel.	D14	14
Sinŭiju, Kor., N.	D6	38
Sió, stm., Hung.	C5	26
Siocon, Phil.	G4	52
Siófok, Hung.	C5	26
Sion, Switz.	D4	22
Sioraparuk, Grnld.	B12	141
Sioux Center, Ia., U.S.	H2	118
Sioux City, Ia., U.S.	B1	120
Sioux Falls, S.D., U.S.	H2	118
Sioux Lookout, On., Can.	A6	118
Sioux Narrows, On., Can.	B4	118
Sioux Rapids, Ia., U.S.	B2	120
Sipalay, Phil.	F4	52
Sipan, Otok, i., Cro.	H14	22
Sípapo, stm., Ven.	E8	86
Siparia, Trin.	s12	105f
Šipčenski Prohod (Shipka Pass), p., Blg.	G12	26
Sipicyno, Russia	F22	8
Siping, China	C6	38
Sipiwesk Lake, l., Mb., Can.	D11	106
Sipura, Pulau, i., Indon.	E1	50
Siqueira Campos, Braz.	A12	92
Siquia, stm., Nic.	F5	102
Siquijor, Phil.	F4	52
Siquijor Island, i., Phil.	F4	52
Siquirres, C.R.	G6	102
Sira, India	E3	53
Sira, Russia	D16	32
Sira, stm., Nor.	G2	8
Siracusa, Italy	G9	24
Sirāhā, Nepal	E11	54
Sirājganj, Bngl.	F12	54
Sir Bani Yās, i., U.A.E.	E7	56
Sir Douglas, Mount, mtn., Can.	E15	138
Sir Edward Pellew Group, is., Austl.	C7	74
Sirik, Tanjong, c., Malay.	B7	50
Sirikit Reservoir, res., Thai.	D5	48
Sirino, Monte, mtn., Italy	D9	24
Sir James MacBrien, Mount, mtn., N.T., Can.	C4	106
Sīrjān, Iran	D8	56
Sirkeli, Tur.	C15	28
Sirocina, Bela.	E12	10
Sirohi, India	F4	54
Sirokovo, Russia	C17	32
Sironj, India	F6	54
Sirpur, India	B5	53
Sīrrī, Jazīreh-ye, i., Iran	D7	56
Sirsa, India	D5	54
Sir Sandford, Mount, mtn., B.C., Can.	E13	138
Sirsi, India	D2	53
Sirsilla, India	B4	53
Sirte, Gulf of see Surt, Khalīj, b., Libya	A3	62
Sir Timothy's Hill, hill, St. K./N.	C2	105a
Sīrvan, stm., Mex.	G8	98
Sirvintos, Lith.	E7	10
Sir Wilfrid Laurier, Mount, mtn., B.C., Can.	D11	138
Sisaba, mtn., Tan.	E6	66
Sishen, S. Afr.	E6	70
Sishilijie, China	J7	42
Sishui, China	D7	42
Sisib Lake, l., Mb., Can.	E14	124
Sisimiut see Holsteinsborg, Grnld.	D15	141
Siskiyou Pass, p., Or., U.S.	A3	134
Sisseton, S.D., U.S.	F1	118
Sīstān, reg., Asia	C9	56
Sister Bay, Wi., U.S.	C2	112
Sisters, Or., U.S.	F5	136
Sistersville, W.V., U.S.	E5	114
Sīt, stm., Russia	B20	10
Sitāmarhi, India	E10	54
Sitāpur, India	E8	54
Siteia, Grc.	H9	28
Siteki, Swaz.	E10	70
Si Thep, hist., Thai.	E5	48
Sithonía, pen., Grc.	C6	28
Sitidgi Lake, l., N.T., Can.	B4	106
Sítio d'Abadia, Braz.	H2	88
Sitka, Ak., U.S.	E12	140
Sitkalidak Island, i., Ak., U.S.	E9	140
Sittard, Neth.	C14	14
Sitten see Sion, Switz.	D4	22
Sittoung, stm., Mya.	C3	48
Sittwe, Mya.	D7	46
Siuri, India	G11	54
Siuslaw, stm., Or., U.S.	G3	136
Sivaganga, India	G4	53
Sivakāsi, India	G4	53
Sivaki, Russia	F14	34
Sivas, Tur.	B4	56
Šiveluč, vulkan, vol., Russia	E21	34
Siverek, Tur.	B4	56
Siverskij, Russia	A12	10
Sivrihisar, Tur.	D14	28
Sīwah, Egypt	C5	62
Siwalik Range, mts., India	C6	54
Siwān, India	E10	54
Sixian, China	E7	42
Sixth Cataract see Sablūkah, Shallāl as-, wtfl, Sudan	D6	62
Sizuoka see Shizuoka, Japan	E11	40
Sjælland, i., Den.	I4	8
Sjamža, Russia	F19	8
Sjarheevič, Bela.	G10	10
Sjas', stm., Russia	A15	10
Sjas'stroj, Russia	F15	8
Sjenica, Yugo.	F7	26
Sjuzikozero, Russia	F17	8
Skærfjorden, b., Grnld.	B22	141
Skaftafell Nasjonalpark, p.o.i., Ice.	k31	8a
Skagafjördur, b., Ice.	j31	8a
Skagen, Den.	H4	8
Skagerrak, strt., Eur.	H3	8
Skagit, stm., N.A.	H8	138
Skagway, Ak., U.S.	E12	140
Skála, Grc.	F5	28
Skaistkalne, Lat.	D7	10
Skalistyj Golec, gora, mtn., Russia	E12	34
Skałka, l., Pol.	C8	8
Skanderborg, Den.	H3	8
Skäne, state, Swe.	H5	8
Skardu, Pak.	B12	56
Skarszewy, Pol.	B14	16
Skarżysko-Kamienna, Pol.	E16	16
Skaudvilė, Lith.	E5	10
Skeena, stm., B.C., Can.	B1	138
Skeena Crossing, B.C., Can.	A3	138
Skeena Mountains, mts., B.C., Can.	D5	106
Skegness, Eng., U.K.	H13	12
Skei, Nor.	F2	8
Skellefteå, Swe.	D9	8
Skellefteälven, stm., Swe.	D8	8
Skellytown, Tx., U.S.	F7	128
Skerryvore, i., Scot., U.K.	E6	12
Ski, Nor.	G4	8
Skiatook, Ok., U.S.	H1	120
Skibbereen, Ire.	J3	12
Skidal', Bela.	G7	10
Skiddaw, mtn., Eng., U.K.	G9	12
Skidmore, Tx., U.S.	F10	130
Skien, Nor.	G3	8
Skierniewice, state, Pol.	D16	16
Skierniewice, Pol.	D16	16
Skikda, Alg.	B6	64
Skilak Lake, l., Ak., U.S.	D9	140
Skipton, Eng., U.K.	H10	12
Skíros, Grc.	E7	28
Skjáltandafljót, stm., Ice.	k31	8a
Skjern, Den.	I3	8
Skobeleva, pik, mtn., Asia	B11	56
Skofja Loka, Slvn.	D11	22
Skoganvarri see Skoganvarre, Nor.	B11	8
Skokie, Il., U.S.	F2	112
Skŏn, Camb.	F7	48
Skópelos, i., Grc.	D6	28
Skopin, Russia	D5	32
Skopje see Skopje, Mac.	A4	28
Skopje, Mac.	A4	28
Skövde, Swe.	G5	8
Skovorodino, Russia	F13	34
Skowhegan, Me., U.S.	F7	110
Skownan, Mb., Can.	C14	124
Skrunda, Lat.	C5	10
Skrudaliena, Lat.	E9	10
Skukuza, S. Afr.	D10	70
Skull Valley, Az., U.S.	I4	132
Skuna, stm., Ms., U.S.	D9	122
Skunk, stm., Ia., U.S.	D6	120
Skuodas, Lith.	D4	10
Skuratovskij, Russia	F20	10
Skwierzyna, Pol.	D11	16
Skye, Island of, i., Scot., U.K.	D6	12
Skyland, N.C., U.S.	A3	116
Skyring, Península, pen., Chile	I1	90
Skyring, Seno, strt., Chile	J2	90
Skyros, i., Grc.	E7	28
Slabada, Bela.	G11	10
Slagelse, Den.	I4	8
Slagnäs, Swe.	D8	8
Slamet, Gunung, vol., Indon.	G6	50
Slancy, Russia	A11	10
Slaney, stm., Ire.	H6	12
Slănic, Rom.	D12	26
Slano, Cro.	H14	22
Slaný, Czech Rep.	F10	16
Slater, Ia., U.S.	C4	120
Slater, Mo., U.S.	E4	120
Slatina, Cro.	E14	22
Slatina, Rom.	E12	26
Slaughter, La., U.S.	G7	122
Slaunae, Bela.	F12	10
Slautnoe, Russia	D22	34
Slave, stm., Can.	C8	106
Slave Coast, cst., Afr.	H5	64
Slave Lake, Ab., Can.	A16	138
Slavgorod, Russia	D13	32
Slavjanka, Russia	C9	38
Slavjansk-na-Kubani, Russia	E5	32
Slavkoviči, Russia	C12	10
Slavonia see Slavonija, hist. reg., Cro.	E14	22
Slavonija, hist. reg., Cro.	E14	22
Slavonski Brod, Cro.	E15	22
Slavsk, Russia	E4	10
Stawno, Pol.	B12	16
Slayton, Mn., U.S.	G3	118
Sleaford, Eng., U.K.	H12	12
Sledge, Ms., U.S.	C8	122
Sledzjuki, Bela.	G13	10
Sleeper Islands, is., Nu., Can.	D14	106
Sleeping Bear Dunes National Lakeshore, p.o.i., Mi., U.S.	D3	112
Sleepy Eye, Mn., U.S.	G4	118
Sleśin, Pol.	D14	16
Slidell, La., U.S.	G9	122
Slide Mountain, mtn., N.Y., U.S.	B11	114
Sliema, Malta	I8	24
Slievekimalta, mtn., Ire.	I4	12
Sligeach see Sligo, Ire.	G4	12
Sligo, Ire.	G4	12
Sligo, Pa., U.S.	C6	114
Sligo, state, Ire.	G4	12
Sligo Bay, b., Ire.	G4	12
Slinger, Wi., U.S.	H10	118
Slino, ozero, l., Russia	C16	10
Slippery Rock, Pa., U.S.	C5	114
Slissel'burg, Russia	A13	10
Slīteres Rezervāts, Lat.	C5	10
Sljudjanka, Russia	D18	32
Sloan, Nv., U.S.	H1	132
Slobodka, Ukr.	B16	26
Slobodskoj, Russia	C8	32
Slobozia, Mol.	C16	26
Slobozia, Rom.	E14	26
Slobozia, Rom.	F12	26
Slocan, B.C., Can.	G13	138
Slocan Lake, l., B.C., Can.	G13	138
Slocomb, Al., U.S.	F13	122
Slonim, Bela.	G8	10
Slough, Eng., U.K.	J12	12
Slovakia, ctry., Eur.	H14	16
Slovenia, ctry., Eur.	E11	22
Slovenske rudohorie, mts., Slov.	H15	16
Slov'jans'k, Ukr.	E5	32
Słowiński Park Narodowy, p.o.i., Pol.	B13	16
Słubice, Pol.	D10	16
Sluč, stm., Bela.	G10	10
Sluknov, Czech Rep.	E10	16
Słupca, Pol.	D13	16
Słupia, stm., Pol.	B13	16
Słupsk (Stolp), Pol.	B13	16
Słupsk, state, Pol.	B13	16
Slutsk see Sluck, Bela.	G10	10
Smålandsfarvandet, b., Den.	I4	8
Smalininkai, Lith.	E5	10
Smallwood Reservoir, res., Nf., Can.	E18	106
Smabuka, Bela.	E13	10
Smarhon', Bela.	F9	10
Smederevo, Yugo.	E7	26
Smela see Smila, Ukr.	E16	6
Smeralda, Costa, cst., Italy	C3	24
Smethport, Pa., U.S.	C7	114
Smidovič, Russia	G15	34
Smidta, poluostrov, pen., Russia	F17	32
Smila, Ukr.	E4	32
Smiley, Sk., Can.	A16	138
Smiley, Tx., U.S.	E10	130
Smiltene, Lat.	C8	10
Smith, Ab., Can.	A16	138
Smith, stm., U.S.	H5	114
Smith, stm., Mt., U.S.	C15	136
Smith Arm, b., N.T., Can.	B6	106
Smith Bay, b., Ak., U.S.	B10	141
Smith Bay, b., Ak., U.S.	B9	140
Smith Canyon, val., Co., U.S.	D5	128
Smithers, B.C., Can.	B3	138
Smithfield, S. Afr.	G8	70
Smithfield, N.C., U.S.	A7	116
Smithfield, Ut., U.S.	B5	132
Smith Island see Sumisu-jima, i., Japan	E13	36
Smith Island, i., N.C., U.S.	C8	116
Smith Mountain Lake, res., Va., U.S.	G6	114
Smith Point, c., N.S., Can.	E13	110
Smiths, Al., U.S.	E13	122
Smiths Falls, On., Can.	D13	112
Smiths Grove, Ky., U.S.	G11	120
Smithton, Austl.	n12	77a
Smithville, Ga., U.S.	E1	116
Smithville, Tn., U.S.	I11	120
Smithville, Tx., U.S.	D10	130
Smoke Creek Desert, des., Nv., U.S.	C6	134
Smokey, Cape, c., N.S., Can.	D16	110
Smoky, stm., Ab., Can.	A12	138
Smoky Hill, stm., U.S.	B12	128
Smoky Hill, North Fork, stm., U.S.	B7	128
Smoky Lake, Ab., Can.	B18	138
Smøla, i., Nor.	E2	8
Smolensk, Russia	E16	6
Smolenskaja oblast', co., Russia	F15	10
Smoljan, Blg.	H11	26
Smoot, Wy., U.S.	H16	136
Smoothrock Lake, l., On., Can.	A9	118
Smorodovka, Russia	C12	10
Smyrna see Izmir, Tur.	E10	28
Smyrna, De., U.S.	E10	114
Smyrna, Ga., U.S.	D14	122
Smyrna, Tn., U.S.	I11	120
Smythe, Mount, mtn., B.C., Can.	D6	106
Snæfell, mtn., Ice.	k32	8a
Snaefell, mtn., I. of Man	G8	12
Snæfellsness, pen., Ice.	k28	8a
Snag, Yk., Can.	C3	106
Snake, stm., Yk., Can.	B4	106
Snake, stm., U.S.	D8	136
Snake, stm., Ne., U.S.	E11	126
Snake Creek, stm., S.D., U.S.	B14	126
Snake River Plain, pl., Id., U.S.	G13	136
Snake Valley, val., U.S.	D3	132
Snares Islands, is., N.Z.	H2	80
Snåsavatnet, l., Nor.	D4	8
Sneads, Fl., U.S.	G13	122
Sneedville, Tn., U.S.	H2	114
Sneek, Neth.	A14	14
Sněžka, mtn., Czech Rep.	F11	16
Sniardwy, Jezioro, l., Pol.	C17	16
Sniatyn, Ukr.	A12	26
Snina, Slov.	G18	16
Snipe Lake, l., Ab., Can.	A14	138
Snjadin, Bela.	H11	10
Snøhetta, mtn., Nor.	E3	8
Snohomish, Wa., U.S.	C4	136
Snoqualmie Pass, p., Wa., U.S.	C5	136
Snøtinden, mtn., Nor.	C5	8
Snov, stm., Eur.	H15	10
Snover, Mi., U.S.	E7	112
Snowbird Lake, l., N.T., Can.	C10	106
Snowdon, mtn., Wales, U.K.	H8	12
Snowdonia National Park, p.o.i., Wales, U.K.	I8	12
Snowflake, Az., U.S.	I6	132
Snow Hill, Md., U.S.	F10	114
Snow Hill, N.C., U.S.	A8	116
Snow Lake, Mb., Can.	E10	106
Snowmass Mountain, mtn., Co., U.S.	D9	132
Snow Mountain, mtn., Ca., U.S.	D3	134
Snowtown, Austl.	I2	76
Snowy Mountain, mtn., N.Y., U.S.	G2	110
Snowy Mountains, mts., Austl.	K7	76
Snowy River National Park, p.o.i., Austl.	K6	76
Snŭöl, Camb.	F8	48
Snyder, Ok., U.S.	G10	128
Snyder, Tx., U.S.	B7	130
Soacha, Col.	E4	86
Soalala, Madag.	D8	68
Soap Lake, Wa., U.S.	C7	136
Soavinandriana, Madag.	D8	68
Sobaek-sanmaek, mts., Kor., S.	C1	40
Soběslav, Czech Rep.	G10	16
Sobinka, Russia	I19	8
Sobradinho, Represa de, res., Braz.	E5	88
Sobral, Braz.	B5	88
Sobrance, hist. reg., Spain	B10	20
Sochaczew, Pol.	D16	16
Soch'e see Shache, China	B12	56
Soči, Russia	F5	32
Société, Archipel de la (Society Islands), is., Fr. Poly.	E11	72
Society Hill, S.C., U.S.	B6	116
Society Islands see Société, Archipel de la, is., Fr. Poly.	E11	72
Soco, stm., Dom. Rep.	C13	102
Socompa, Paso (Socompa, Portezuelo de), p., S.A.	B3	92
Socompa, Portezuelo de (Socompa, Paso), p., S.A.	B3	92
Soconusco, Sierra de see Madre de Chiapas, Sierra, mts., N.A.	G12	100
Socorro, Col.	D5	86
Socorro, N.M., U.S.	I10	132
Socorro, Isla, i., Mex.	F3	100
Socotra see Suquţrā, i., Yemen	G7	56
Soc Trang, Viet.	H8	48
Socuéllamos, Spain	E8	20
Soda Creek, B.C., Can.	D8	138
Soda Lake, l., Ca., U.S.	H9	134
Sodankylä, Fin.	C12	8
Soda Springs, Id., U.S.	H15	136
Söderhamn, Swe.	F7	8
Södermanland, state, Swe.	G7	8
Södertälje, Swe.	G7	8
Sodo, Eth.	F7	62
Sodom see Sedom, hist., Isr.	G6	58
Sodus, N.Y., U.S.	E12	112
Sodwana Bay National Park, p.o.i., S. Afr.	E11	70
Soe, Indon.	G7	44
Soekmekar, S. Afr.	C9	70
Soest, Ger.	E4	16
Soest, Neth.	B14	14
Sofala, Moz.	B12	70
Sofala, state, Moz.	B12	70
Sofia see Sofija, Blg.	G10	26
Sofija (Sofia), Blg.	G10	26
Sofija, state, Blg.	G10	26
Sofijsk, Russia	F16	34
Sofporog, Russia	D14	8
Sofronovo, Russia	F20	8
Sogamoso, Col.	E5	86
Sogamoso, stm., Col.	D5	86
Soganlı, stm., Tur.	C15	28
Sogcho see Sŏkch'o, Kor., S.	A1	40
Sogda, Russia	F16	34
Sögel, Ger.	D3	16
Sogn og Fjordane, state, Nor.	F2	8
Sogod, Phil.	E5	52
Sogo Nur, l., China	C5	36
Sogŭksan-do, i., Kor., S.	H7	38
Sogožа, stm., Russia	B22	10
Sögütlü, Tur.	C13	28
Sog Xian, China	E3	36
Sohâg, India	D6	54
Sohano, Pap. N. Gui.	D6	79a
Sohar see Şuḩār, Oman	E8	56
Sohng Gwe, Khao, mtn., Asia	D4	48
Söhrewād, Iran	C6	56
Soignies, Bel.	D12	14
Soissons, Fr.	E12	14
Sojana, Russia	D20	8
Sojna, Russia	F4	34
Sojosŏn-man, b., Kor., N.	E6	38
Sokal', Ukr.	A1	40
Sŏkch'o, Kor., S.	A1	40
Söke, Tur.	F10	28

Name	Map Ref.	Page
Sokele, D.R.C.	F4	66
Sokodé, Togo	H5	64
Sokol, Russia	G19	8
Sokol, Russia	B14	34
Sokółka, Pol.	C19	16
Sokolov, Czech Rep.	F8	16
Sokorŏw Małopolski, Pol.	F18	16
Sokone, Sen.	G1	64
Sokoto, Nig.	G5	64
Sokoto, stm., Nig.	G5	64
Sokyriany, Ukr.	A14	26
Sol, Costa del, cst., Spain	H5	20
Sola, Vanuatu	i16	79c
Solacolu, Rom.	E13	26
Solai, Kenya	D7	66
Solan, India	C6	54
Solana, Fl., U.S.	J3	116
Solânea, Braz.	D8	88
Solano, Phil.	B3	52
Solāpur, India	C2	53
Solca, Rom.	B12	26
Sol'cy, Russia	B13	10
Solda Gölü, l., Tur.	F12	28
Sol de Julio, Arg.	D6	92
Soldiers Grove, Wi., U.S.	H8	118
Soldotna, Ak., U.S.	D9	140
Soledad, Col.	B4	86
Soledad, Ca., U.S.	G4	134
Soledad, Ven.	C10	86
Soledad, Picacho, mtn., Mex.	B5	100
Soledad Díez Gutiérrez, Mex.	D8	100
Soledade, Braz.	D11	92
Soledad Pass, p., Ca., U.S.	I7	134
Solen, N.D., U.S.	A12	126
Solenzara, Fr.	H15	18
Soleure see Solothurn, Switz.	C4	22
Solihull, Eng., U.K.	I11	12
Solikamsk, Russia	C9	32
Sol'-Ileck, Russia	D8	32
Soliman, Tun.	H4	24
Solingen, Ger.	E3	16
Solís de Mataojo, Ur.	G10	92
Sollefteå, Swe.	E7	8
Sollentuna, Swe.	G7	8
Sóller, Spain	E13	20
Solnečnogorsk, Russia	D19	10
Sologne, reg., Fr.	G10	14
Sologoncy, Russia	C11	34
Solok, Indon.	D2	50
Solomennoe, Russia	F16	8
Solomon, Az., U.S.	K7	132
Solomon, stm., Ks., U.S.	B11	128
Solomon, North Fork, stm., Ks., U.S.	B10	128
Solomon, South Fork, stm., Ks., U.S.	B10	128
Solomon Islands, unds.	J18	142
Solomon Islands, ctry., Oc.	D7	72
Solomon Islands, is., Oc.	d7	79b
Solomon Sea, Oc.	D6	72
Solomon's Pools see Sulaymān, Birak, hist., W.B.	G5	58
Solon, China	B9	36
Solon, Ia., U.S.	C6	120
Solon, Me., U.S.	F7	110
Solothurn, Switz.	C4	22
Soloveckie ostrova, is., Russia	D16	8
Solov'evsk, Russia	F12	34
Solov'evsk, Russia	F13	34
Solsona, Spain	C12	20
Šolta, Otok, i., Cro.	G13	22
Solţānābād, Iran	B8	56
Soltau, Ger.	C5	16
Solvang, Ca., U.S.	I5	134
Solvay, N.Y., U.S.	A9	114
Sol'vyčegodsk, Russia	F22	8
Solway Firth, b., U.K.	G9	12
Solwezi, Zam.	C4	68
Solza, Russia	D18	8
Sōma, Japan	B13	40
Soma, Tur.	D10	28
Somabhula, Zimb.	D4	68
Somalia, ctry., Afr.	D9	66
Somali Basin, unds.	I8	142
Somaliland see Somalia, ctry., Afr.	D9	66
Somali Republic see Somalia, ctry., Afr.	D9	66
Sombo, Ang.	B3	68
Sombor, Yugo.	D6	26
Sombrerete, Mex.	D7	100
Sombreretillo, Mex.	H7	130
Sombrero Channel, strt., India	G7	46
Sombrio, Braz.	D13	92
Sombrio, Lagoa do, l., Braz.	D13	92
Somdari, India	F4	54
Somerset, Austl.	n12	77a
Somerset, Co., U.S.	E9	132
Somerset, Ky., U.S.	G13	120
Somerset, Oh., U.S.	E3	114
Somerset, Pa., U.S.	D6	114
Somerset, Tx., U.S.	E9	130
Somerset East, S. Afr.	H7	70
Somerset Island, i., Nu., Can.	A12	106
Somerset West, S. Afr.	I4	70
Somers Point, N.J., U.S.	E11	114
Somersworth, N.H., U.S.	G5	110
Somerton, Az., U.S.	K2	132
Somerville, N.J., U.S.	D11	114
Somerville, Tn., U.S.	B9	122
Somerville, Tx., U.S.	G2	122
Somerville Lake, res., Tx., U.S.	D11	130
Someş (Szamos), stm., Eur.	B9	26
Somino, Russia	A17	10
Somme, state, Fr.	D11	14
Somme, stm., Fr.	E11	14
Somme, Baie de la, b., Fr.	D10	14
Sommen, l., Swe.	H6	8
Sömmerda, Ger.	E7	16
Somogy, state, Hung.	C4	26
Somosierra, Puerto de, p., Spain	C7	20
Somosomo, Fiji	p20	79e
Somosomo Strait, strt., Fiji	p19	79e
Somoto, Nic.	F4	102
Somovo, Russia	H17	10
Somport, Col du (Somport, Puerto de), p., Eur.	G5	18
Somport, Puerto de (Somport, Col du), p., Eur.	G5	18
Sompuis, Fr.	F13	14
Son, stm., India	F10	54
Sonāmarg, India	A5	54
Sonāmukhi, India	G11	54
Sŏnch'ŏn-ŭp, Kor., N.	E6	38
Sønderborg, Den.	I3	8
Sønderjylland, state, Den.	I3	8
Sondershausen, Ger.	E6	16
Søndre Strømfjord, Grnld.	D15	141
Sondrio, Italy	D6	22
Sonepur, India	H9	54
Song, Nig.	H7	64
Song, Thai.	C5	48
Song Bay Hap Cua, b., Viet.	H7	48
Song Cau, Viet.	F9	48
Song Da see Black, stm., Asia	D9	46
Songea, Nor.	G3	8
Songea, Tan.	G7	66
Song Hong see Red, stm., Asia	D9	46
Songhua, stm., China	B11	36
Songhua Hu, res., China	C7	38
Songjiang, China	F9	42

Name	Map Ref.	Page
Songjŏng, Kor., S.	G7	38
Sŏngju, Kor., S.	D1	40
Songkhla, Thai.	I5	48
Songkhram, stm., Thai.	D6	48
Songlinba, China	I6	42
Sŏngnam, Kor., S.	F7	38
Sŏngnim, Kor., N.	E6	38
Songpan, China	E5	36
Song Phi Nong, Thai.	E4	48
Songtao, China	G3	42
Songxi, China	H8	42
Songxian, China	D4	42
Sonid Youqi, China	C7	36
Sonid Zuoqi, China	C7	36
Sonīpat, India	D6	54
Son La, Viet.	B6	48
Sonmiāni, Pak.	D10	56
Sonmiāni Bay, b., Pak.	D10	56
Sonneberg, Ger.	F7	16
Sonningdale, Sk., Can.	B6	124
Sono, stm., Braz.	I3	88
Sono, stm., Braz.	E1	88
Sonora, Ca., U.S.	E3	134
Sonora, Ca., U.S.	F5	134
Sonora, Tx., U.S.	D7	130
Sonora, stm., Mex.	G7	98
Sonora, state, Mex.	G7	98
Sonora, stm., Mex.	G7	98
Sonora, Desierto de, des., N.A.	F6	98
Sonoyta, Mex.	F6	98
Sonqor, Iran	C6	56
Sŏnsan, Kor.	C1	40
Sonseca, Spain	E6	20
Sonsón, Col.	E4	86
Sonsonate, El Sal.	F3	102
Sonsorol Islands, is., Palau	D9	44
Sonstraal, S. Afr.	E6	70
Son Tay, Viet.	B7	48
Sonthofen, Ger.	I6	16
Soochow see Suzhou, China	F9	42
Sooke, B.C., Can.	H7	138
Sooner Lake, res., Ok., U.S.	A1	122
Sopchoppy, Fl., U.S.	G14	122
Soperton, Ga., U.S.	D3	116
Sopki, Russia	C13	10
Sopot, Pol.	B14	16
Sop Pong, Laos	A6	48
Sopron, Hung.	B3	26
Sopur, India	A5	54
Sora, Italy	I10	22
Sorada, India	I10	54
Sorata, Bol.	C3	90
Sorbhog, India	E13	54
Sorel, Qc., Can.	D3	110
Sorell, Cape, c., Austl.	o12	77a
Serfold, Nor.	C6	8
Sorgues, Fr.	E10	18
Soria, Spain	C8	20
Soria, co., Spain	C8	20
Soriano, Ur.	F8	92
Sørli, Nor.	D5	8
Soro, India	H11	54
Soro, Monte, mtn., Italy	G8	24
Soroca, Mol.	A15	26
Sorocaba, Braz.	L2	88
Soročinsk, Russia	D8	32
Soroco, P.R.	B4	104a
Soroco, at., Micron.	C5	72
Soroni, India	E7	54
Sorong, Indon.	F9	44
Sororó, stm., Braz.	C1	88
Sorot', stm., Russia	C12	10
Soroti, Ug.	D6	66
Sørøya, i., Nor.	A10	8
Sorrento, Italy	D8	24
Sorrento, La., U.S.	G8	122
Sorris-Sorris, Nmb.	B2	70
Sor Rondane Mountains, mts., Ant.	C7	81
Sorsk, Russia	D16	32
Sorso, Italy	D2	24
Sorsogon, Phil.	D4	52
Sort, Spain	B12	20
Sortandy, Kaz.	D12	32
Sortavala, Russia	F14	8
Sør-Trøndelag, state, Nor.	E4	8
Sŏrve neem, c., Est.	C4	10
Sos del Rey Católico, Spain	B9	20
Soskovo, Russia	H18	10
Sosna, stm., Russia	H21	10
Sosneado, Cerro, mtn., Arg.	G3	92
Sosnovec, Russia	D15	8
Sosnovka, Kaz.	D13	32
Sosnovka, Russia	C19	8
Sosnovo-Ozërskoe, Russia	F11	34
Sosnovskoe, Russia	I20	8
Sosnovyj Bor, Russia	A11	10
Sosnowiec, Pol.	F15	16
Sos'va, Russia	B10	32
Sotkamo, Fin.	D13	8
Soto, Mex.	F1	130
Soto la Marina, Mex.	D9	100
Soto la Marina, Barra, i., Mex.	C10	100
Sotra see Store Sotra, i., Nor.	F1	8
Sotteville-lès-Rouen, Fr.	E9	14
Souanké, Congo	D2	66
Soubré, C. Iv.	H3	64
Soudan, Austl.	D7	74
Souderton, Pa., U.S.	D10	114
Soufrière, St. Luc.	m6	105c
Soufrière, vol., Guad.	h5	105c
Soufrière, vol., St. Vin.	o11	105e
Soufrière Hills, vol., Monts.	d3	105a
Souillac, Fr.	E7	18
Sŏul (Seoul), Kor., S.	F7	38
Soulac-sur-Mer, Fr.	D4	18
Sound, The, strt., Eur.	I5	8
Sounding Creek, stm., Ab., Can.	E19	138
Sounding Lake, l., Ab., Can.	B3	124
Sources, Mont-aux- (Phofung), mtn., Afr.	F9	70
Soure, Braz.	D8	84
Sour el Ghozlane, Alg.	H14	20
Souris, Mb., Can.	E13	124
Souris, stm., N.A.	E13	124
Souris, stm., U.S.	G4	124
Sousa, Braz.	D6	88
Sousel, Port.	F3	20
Sousse, Tun.	I4	24
South, stm., S. Afr.	H6	70
South, stm., N.C., U.S.	B7	116
South America, cont.	G9	4
Southampton, On., Can.	D8	112
Southampton, Eng., U.K.	K11	12
Southampton, N.Y., U.S.	D13	114
Southampton, Cape, c., Nu., Can.	C13	106
Southampton Island, i., Nu., Can.	C14	106
South Andaman, i., India	F7	46
South Anna, stm., Va., U.S.	G8	114
South Australia, state, Austl.	E6	74
South Australian Basin, unds.	M15	142
South Baldy, mtn., N.M., U.S.	J9	132
South Bank, B.C., Can.	C5	138
South Bay, Fl., U.S.	J5	116
South Bay, b., Nu., Can.	C14	106
South Bay, b., On., Can.	C8	112

Name	Map Ref.	Page
South Baymouth, On., Can.	C7	112
South Bend, In., U.S.	G3	112
South Bend, Wa., U.S.	D3	136
South Bohemia see Jihočeský kraj, state, Czech Rep.	G10	16
South Borneo see Kalimantan Selatan, state, Indon.	E9	50
South Boston, Va., U.S.	H6	114
Southbridge, N.Z.	F5	80
Southbridge, Ma., U.S.	B13	114
South Brookfield, N.S., Can.	F11	110
South Bruny Island, i., Austl.	o13	77a
South Burlington, Vt., U.S.	F3	110
South Carolina, state, U.S.	C5	116
South Celebes see Sulawesi Selatan, state, Indon.	E11	50
South Charleston, W.V., U.S.	F4	114
South China Basin, unds.	H14	142
South China Sea, Asia	H15	30
South Dakota, state, U.S.	C12	126
South Downs, hills, Eng., U.K.	K12	12
South East, state, Bots.	D7	70
South East Cape, c., Austl.	o13	77a
Southeast Indian Ridge, unds.	N12	142
Southeast Pacific Basin, unds.	P25	142
South East Point, c., Austl.	L6	76
Southend-on-Sea, Eng., U.K.	J13	12
Southern, state, Bots.	D7	70
Southern see HaDarom, state, Isr.	H5	58
Southern Alps, mts., N.Z.	F4	80
Southern Bug see Pivdennyy Buh, stm., Ukr.	A17	26
Southern Cook Islands, is., Cook Is.	E10	72
Southern Cross, Austl.	F3	74
Southern Ghāts, mts., India	G3	53
Southern Indian Lake, l., Mb., Can.	D10	106
Southern Ocean	N13	142
Southern Pines, N.C., U.S.	A6	116
South Esk, stm., Austl.	n13	77a
South Fabius, stm., Mo., U.S.	E6	120
South Fallsburg, N.Y., U.S.	C11	114
Southfield, Mi., U.S.	B2	114
South Fiji Basin, unds.	L20	142
South Foreland, c., Eng., U.K.	J14	12
South Fork, Co., U.S.	F10	132
South Fulton, Tn., U.S.	H8	120
Southgate, Mi., U.S.	B2	114
South Georgia, i., S. Geor.	J9	90
South Georgia and the South Sandwich Islands, dep., S.A.	K11	82
South Grand, stm., Mo., U.S.	F3	120
South Hātia Island, i., Bngl.	G13	54
South Haven, Mi., U.S.	F3	112
South Henderson, N.C., U.S.	H7	114
South Henik Lake, l., Nu., Can.	C11	106
South Hero, Vt., U.S.	F3	110
South Hill, Village, Anguilla	A1	105a
South Holston Lake, res., U.S.	H3	114
South Honshu Ridge, unds.	G16	142
South Houston, Tx., U.S.	H3	122
South Indian Basin, unds.	O12	142
South Indian Lake, Mb., Can.	D11	106
South International Falls, Mn., U.S.	C5	118
South Island, i., N.Z.	G5	80
South Konkan Hills, hills, India	C1	53
South Korea see Korea, South, ctry., Asia	G8	38
South Lake Tahoe, Ca., U.S.	E5	134
Southland, N.C., U.S.	H7	128
Southlawn, Il., U.S.	E8	120
South Llano, stm., Tx., U.S.	D8	130
South Loup, stm., Ne., U.S.	F13	126
South Lyon, Mi., U.S.	F6	112
South Magnetic Pole, misc. cult.	B18	81
South Manitou Island, i., Mi., U.S.	C3	112
South Miami, Fl., U.S.	K5	116
South Milwaukee, Wi., U.S.	F2	112
South Moravia see Jihomoravský kraj, state, Czech Rep.	G12	16
South Nahanni, stm., N.T., Can.	C5	106
South Nation, stm., On., Can.	C14	112
South Negril Point, c., Jam.	i12	104d
South Ogden, Ut., U.S.	B5	132
South Orkney Islands, is., Ant.	B36	81
South Paris, Me., U.S.	F6	110
South Pass, p., Wy., U.S.	E4	126
South Pekin, Il., U.S.	D8	120
South Pittsburg, Tn., U.S.	B13	122
South Platte, stm., U.S.	F11	126
South Point, c., Barb.	n8	105d
South Pole, misc. cult., Ant.	D1	81
Southport (Gold Coast), Austl.	F9	76
Southport, Austl.	o13	77a
Southport, Eng., U.K.	H9	12
Southport, N.C., U.S.	C7	116
South Portland, Me., U.S.	G6	110
South Range, Mi., U.S.	D10	118
South River, On., Can.	C10	112
South Ronaldsay, i., Scot., U.K.	C10	12
South Sandwich Islands, is., S. Geor.	K11	82
South Sandwich Trench, unds.	N11	144
South Saskatchewan, stm., Can.	A8	124
South Shetland Islands, is., Ant.	B35	81
South Sioux City, Ne., U.S.	I2	118
South Skunk, stm., Ia., U.S.	C5	120
South Slocan, B.C., Can.	G13	138
South Sound, b., Br. Vir. Is.	e9	104b
South Spicer Island, i., Nu., Can.	B15	106
South Sulphur, stm., Tx., U.S.	D3	122
South Sumatra see Sumatera Selatan, state, Indon.	E4	50
South Taranaki Bight, b., N.Z.	D5	80
South Tasman Rise, unds.	N17	142
South Thompson, stm., B.C., Can.	F11	138
South Torrington, Wy., U.S.	E8	126
South Uist, i., Scot., U.K.	D5	12
South Umpqua, stm., Or., U.S.	G3	136
South Ventana Cone, mtn., U.S.	G4	134
South Vietnam see Vietnam, ctry., Asia	E9	48
South West Africa see Namibia, ctry., Afr.	E2	70
South West Cape, c., Austl.	o12	77a
South West Cape, c., N.Z.	H2	80

Name	Map Ref.	Page
South West City, Mo., U.S.	H3	120
Southwest Harbor, Me., U.S.	F8	110
Southwest Indian Ridge, unds.	M8	142
Southwest Miramichi, stm., N.B., Can.	D10	110
Southwest National Park, p.o.i., Austl.	o12	77a
Southwest Pacific Basin, unds.	M23	142
Southwest Point, c., Bah.	K8	116
South Whitley, In., U.S.	G4	112
South Wichita, stm., Tx., U.S.	H9	128
South Windham, Me., U.S.	G6	110
Southwold, Eng., U.K.	I14	12
Soutpansberg, mts., S. Afr.	C9	70
Sovata, Rom.	C11	26
Sovetsk, Russia	G20	10
Sovetsk, Russia	E4	10
Sovetsk, Russia	C7	32
Sovetskaja Gavan', Russia	G17	34
Sovetskij, Russia	F13	8
Sovpole, Russia	D20	8
Sowa Pan, pl., Bots.	B7	70
Soweto, S. Afr.	E8	70
Sŏya-misaki, c., Japan	B14	38
Soyang-chŏsuji, res., Kor., S.	F7	38
Soyo, Ang.	B1	68
Sož, stm., Eur.	H13	10
Sozimskij, Russia	C8	32
Sozopol, Blg.	G14	26
Spa, Bel.	D14	14
Spain, ctry., Eur.	E7	20
Spalding, Sk., Can.	B9	124
Spalding, Eng., U.K.	I12	12
Spanish, On., Can.	B7	112
Spanish, stm., On., Can.	B8	112
Spanish Fork, Ut., U.S.	C5	132
Spanish Point, c., Ber.	k15	104e
Spanish Sahara see Western Sahara, dep., Afr.	E2	64
Spanish Town, B. Vir. Is.	e9	104b
Spanish Town, Jam.	i13	104d
Spánta, Ákra, c., Grc.	H6	28
Sparkman, Ar., U.S.	D6	122
Sparks, Nv., U.S.	D6	134
Sparland, Il., U.S.	C8	120
Sparlingville, Mi., U.S.	F7	112
Sparrows Point, Md., U.S.	E9	114
Sparta see Spárti, Grc.	F5	28
Sparta, Ga., U.S.	C2	116
Sparta, Il., U.S.	F8	120
Sparta, Ky., U.S.	F13	120
Sparta, N.J., U.S.	C11	114
Sparta, N.C., U.S.	H4	114
Sparta, Tn., U.S.	I12	120
Sparta, Wi., U.S.	H8	118
Spartanburg, S.C., U.S.	B4	116
Spárti, Grc.	F5	28
Spartivento, Capo, c., Italy	F2	24
Spartivento, Capo, c., Italy	G10	24
Spas-Klepiki, Russia	I19	8
Spassk-Dal'nij, Russia	B10	38
Spearfish, S.D., U.S.	C8	126
Spearville, Ks., U.S.	D9	128
Spednic Lake, l., N.A.	E9	110
Speedway, In., U.S.	I3	112
Speightstown, Barb.	n8	105d
Speikkogel, mtn., Aus.	C12	22
Speke Gulf, b., Tan.	E6	66
Spencer, Ia., U.S.	H3	118
Spencer, In., U.S.	E11	120
Spencer, N.C., U.S.	I5	114
Spencer, W.V., U.S.	E4	114
Spencer, Wi., U.S.	G8	118
Spencer, Cape, c., Austl.	G7	74
Spencer, Cape, c., N.B., Can.	E11	110
Spencer Gulf, b., Austl.	F7	74
Spences Bridge, B.C., Can.	F9	138
Speos (Rock Tombs), hist., Egypt	K1	58
Sperrin Mountains, mts., U.K.	F6	12
Spétses, i., Grc.	F6	28
Spey, stm., Scot., U.K.	D9	12
Speyer, Ger.	G4	16
Spezia see La Spezia, Italy	F6	22
Spezzano Albanese, Italy	E10	24
Sphinx see Abū el-Hul, hist., Egypt	I1	58
Spickard, Mo., U.S.	D4	120
Spilimbergo, Italy	D9	22
Spillville, Ia., U.S.	A5	120
Spindale, N.C., U.S.	A4	116
Spires see Speyer, Ger.	G4	16
Spirit Lake, Ia., U.S.	H3	118
Spirit River, Ab., Can.	D7	106
Spiro, Ok., U.S.	B4	122
Spišská Nová Ves, Slov.	H16	16
Spitsbergen, i., Nor.	B4	30
Spitsbergen Bank, unds.	B5	142
Spittal an der Drau, Aus.	D10	22
Split, Cro.	G13	22
Split Lake, res., Mb., Can.	D11	106
Spogi, Lat.	D9	10
Spokane, Wa., U.S.	C9	136
Spokane, stm., U.S.	C8	136
Spoleto, Italy	H9	22
Spoon, stm., Il., U.S.	D7	120
Spooner, Wi., U.S.	F7	118
Sporava, Bela.	H8	10
Spornoe, Russia	D19	34
Spotsylvania, Va., U.S.	F8	114
Sprague, Wa., U.S.	D5	44
Spratly Islands, is., Asia	F7	136
Spray, Or., U.S.	F7	136
Spree, stm., Ger.	E10	16
Spremberg, Ger.	E10	16
Spring, stm., Ar., U.S.	H6	120
Spring, stm., Ar., U.S.	H5	120
Spring, South Fork, stm., S. Geor.	H6	120
Springbok, S. Afr.	F3	70
Spring City, Tn., U.S.	B14	122
Spring City, Ut., U.S.	D5	132
Spring Creek, stm., Austl.	D3	76
Spring Creek, stm., N.D., U.S.	G11	124
Spring Creek, stm., S.D., U.S.	C8	134
Springdale, Nf., Can.	j22	107a
Springdale, Ut., U.S.	F4	132
Springdale, Wa., U.S.	B9	136
Springe, Ger.	D5	16
Springer, N.M., U.S.	I7	132
Springerville, Az., U.S.	I7	132
Springfield, Fl., U.S.	G13	122
Springfield, Ga., U.S.	D4	116
Springfield, Il., U.S.	E8	120
Springfield, Ma., U.S.	B13	114
Springfield, Mn., U.S.	G4	118
Springfield, Oh., U.S.	E2	114
Springfield, Or., U.S.	F4	136
Springfield, S.D., U.S.	A5	130
Springfield, S.D., U.S.	E14	126
Springfield, Tn., U.S.	H10	120
Springfontein, S. Afr.	G7	70
Spring Glen, Ut., U.S.	D5	132
Spring Green, Wi., U.S.	A7	120
Spring Grove, Mn., U.S.	H7	118
Springhill, N.S., Can.	E12	110
Springhill, La., U.S.	D5	122
Spring Hope, N.C., U.S.	I7	114
Springhouse, B.C., Can.	E8	138

Name	Map Ref.	Page
Spring Lake, N.C., U.S.	A7	116
Springs, S. Afr.	E9	70
Springsure, Austl.	E7	76
Springvale, Austl.	D3	76
Springvale, Me., U.S.	G6	110
Spring Valley, Il., U.S.	J9	118
Spring Valley, N.Y., U.S.	C11	114
Spring Valley, Wi., U.S.	G6	118
Spring Valley, val., Nv., U.S.	D2	132
Springview, Ne., U.S.	E13	126
Springville, Al., U.S.	D12	122
Springville, Ut., U.S.	G7	134
Springville, Ut., U.S.	C5	132
Sproat Lake, l., B.C., Can.	G5	138
Spruce Grove, Ab., Can.	C17	138
Spruce Knob, mtn., W.V., U.S.	F6	114
Spruce Mountain, mtn., Az., U.S.	I4	132
Spruce Pine, Al., U.S.	C11	122
Spruce Pine, N.C., U.S.	I3	114
Spulico, Capo, c., Italy	E10	24
Spurfield, Ab., Can.	A16	138
Spurger, Tx., U.S.	G4	122
Spurn Head, c., Eng., U.K.	H13	12
Spuzzum, B.C., Can.	G9	138
Squamish, B.C., Can.	G7	138
Squamish, stm., B.C., Can.	F7	138
Squam Lake, l., N.H., U.S.	G5	110
Square Lake, l., Me., U.S.	D8	110
Squatec, Qc., Can.	C8	110
Squaw Cap Mountain, mtn., N.B., Can.	C10	110
Squaw Peak, mtn., Ca., U.S.	C12	136
Squalax, B.C., Can.	F11	138
Squillace, Golfo di, b., Italy	F10	24
Squinzano, Italy	D12	24
Sragen, Indon.	G7	50
Srbija (Serbia), state, Yugo.	E7	26
Srbobran, Yugo.	D6	26
Srě Âmběl, Camb.	G6	48
Sredinnyj hrebet, mts., Russia	E20	34
Sredna Gora, mts., Blg.	G11	26
Sredne Kujto, ozero, l., Russia	D14	8
Srednekolymsk, Russia	C19	34
Srednerusskaja vozvyšennost', plat., Russia	D5	32
Srednesibirskoe ploskogor'e (Central Siberian Uplands), plat., Russia	C10	34
Srednij Ural, mts., Russia	C9	32
Srednij Vasjugan, Russia	C13	32
Srednjaja Olëkma, Russia	E13	34
Srem, Pol.	D13	16
Srě Môăt, Camb.	F8	48
Sremska Mitrovica, Yugo.	E6	26
Sremski Karlovci, Yugo.	D6	26
Srêng, stm., Camb.	F6	48
Srêpôk, stm., Camb.	F8	48
Sretensk, Russia	F12	34
Sri Aman, Malay.	C7	50
Sri Jayawardenepura (Kotte), Sri L.	H5	53
Srīkākulam, India	B6	53
Srī Kālahasti, India	E4	53
Sri Lanka, ctry., Asia	G5	53
Srīnagar, India	A5	54
Srīrampur, India	B2	53
Srīrangam, India	F4	53
Srīvardhan, India	B1	53
Srīvilliputtūr, India	G3	53
Środa Śląska, Pol.	E12	16
Środa Wielkopolska, Pol.	D13	16
Sseu-tch'ouan see Sichuan, state, China	E5	36
Ssup'ing see Siping, China	C6	38
Staaten, stm., Austl.	C8	74
Stacyville, Ia., U.S.	H6	118
Stade, Ger.	C5	16
Stadl-Paura, Aus.	B10	22
Stadskanaal, Neth.	A16	14
Stadtallendorf, Ger.	F5	16
Stadtoldendorf, Ger.	D5	16
Stafford, Eng., U.K.	I10	12
Stafford, Ks., U.S.	D10	128
Stafford Springs, Ct., U.S.	C13	114
Staffordsville, Ky., U.S.	G14	120
Stagen, Indon.	E10	50
Staines, Eng., U.K.	J12	12
Staked Plain see Estacado, Llano, pl., U.S.	H6	128
Stakhanov, Ukr.	E5	32
Stalać, Yugo.	F8	26
Stalingrad see Volgograd, Russia	E6	32
Stalowa Wola, Pol.	F18	16
Stamford, Austl.	C4	76
Stamford, Eng., U.K.	I12	12
Stamford, Ct., U.S.	C12	114
Stamford, N.Y., U.S.	B11	114
Stamford, Tx., U.S.	B8	130
Stamford, Lake, res., Tx., U.S.	A8	130
Stamps, Ar., U.S.	D5	122
Stanardsville, Va., U.S.	F7	114
Stanberry, Mo., U.S.	D3	120
Stancionno-Ojašinskij, Russia	C14	32
Standard, Ab., Can.	E18	138
Standerton, S. Afr.	E9	70
Standish, Mi., U.S.	E6	112
Stanfield, Or., U.S.	E7	136
Stanford, Ky., U.S.	G13	120
Stanford, Mt., U.S.	C16	136
Stanger, S. Afr.	F10	70
Stanislaus, stm., Ca., U.S.	F5	134
Stanley, Austl.	n12	77a
Stanley, N.B., Can.	D10	110
Stanley, Falk. Is.	J5	90
Stanley, N.C., U.S.	A4	116
Stanley, N.D., U.S.	F11	124
Stanley, Wi., U.S.	G7	118
Stanley Falls, wtfl, D.R.C.	D4	66
Stanley Reservoir, res., India	F3	53
Stanleyville see Kisangani, D.R.C.	D5	66
Stanovoe nagor'e, mts., Russia	E11	34
Stanovoj hrebet, mts., Russia	E14	34
Stanovoy Mountains see Stanovoe nagor'e, mts., Russia	E11	34
Stanthorpe, Austl.	G8	76
Stanton, Ky., U.S.	G2	114
Stanton, Mi., U.S.	E5	112
Stanton, Ne., U.S.	F15	126
Stanton, N.D., U.S.	G12	124
Stanton, Tn., U.S.	B5	122
Stantonsburg, N.C., U.S.	A8	116
Stanwood, Wa., U.S.	B4	136
Staples, Mn., U.S.	E4	118
Stapleton, Al., U.S.	G11	122
Staporków, Pol.	E16	16
Star, Ms., U.S.	E8	122
Star, N.C., U.S.	A6	116
Starachowice, Pol.	E17	16
Staraja Rudnja, Bela.	H13	10
Staraja Russa, Russia	B14	10
Stara Pazova, Yugo.	D7	26
Stara Zagora, Blg.	G12	26
Starbuck, Mb., Can.	E16	124
Starbuck, Wa., U.S.	D8	136
Starbuck, i., Kir.	D11	72
Star City, Ar., U.S.	D7	122
Star City, Sk., Can.	B9	124
Star City, W.V., U.S.	E6	114
Stargard Szczeciński, Pol.	C11	16
Stargo, Az., U.S.	J7	132
Star Harbour, b., Sol. Is.	f10	79b
Starica, Russia	D17	10

Name	Map Ref.	Page
Stari Grad, Cro.	G13	22
Starij Rjad, Russia	B17	10
Stari Vlah, reg., Yugo.	F7	26
Starke, Fl., U.S.	G3	116
Starkville, Ms., U.S.	D10	122
Starnberg, Ger.	H7	16
Starnberger See, l., Ger.	I7	16
Starodub, Russia	H15	10
Staroe Rahino, Russia	B15	10
Starogard Gdański, Pol.	C14	16
Starokozache, Ukr.	C16	26
Star Peak, mtn., Nv., U.S.	C7	134
Start Point, c., Eng., U.K.	K9	12
Starya Darohi, Bela.	G11	10
Staryj Medved', Russia	B13	10
Staryj Oskol, Russia	D5	32
Stary Sącz, Pol.	G16	16
Stassfurt, Ger.	E7	16
State College, Pa., U.S.	D7	114
State Line, Ms., U.S.	F10	122
Stateline, Nv., U.S.	E5	134
Staten Island see Estados, Isla de los, i., Arg.	J4	90
State Road, N.C., U.S.	H4	114
Statesboro, Ga., U.S.	D4	116
Statesville, N.C., U.S.	I5	114
Staţtłon, Il., U.S.	E8	120
Staunton, Va., U.S.	F6	114
Staunton see Roanoke, stm., U.S.	H8	114
Stavanger, Nor.	G1	8
Stave Lake, l., B.C., Can.	F17	138
Stavely, Ab., Can.	F17	138
Stavern, Ukr.	G18	16
Stavropol', Russia	F6	32
Stawell, Austl.	K4	76
Stawell, stm., Austl.	C4	76
Stawiszyn, Pol.	E14	16
Stayner, On., Can.	D9	112
Steamboat Springs, Co., U.S.	C10	132
Stearns, Ky., U.S.	H13	120
Stebark, Pol.	C16	16
Steele, Mo., U.S.	H8	120
Steele, N.D., U.S.	H14	124
Steele, Mount, mtn., Wy., U.S.	B9	132
Steels Point, c., Norf. I.	y25	78i
Steelville, Mo., U.S.	G6	120
Steenby Inlet, b., Nu., Can.	A15	106
Steenwijk, Neth.	B15	14
Steep Rock, Mb., Can.	C15	124
Stefanie, Lake, l., Afr.	G7	62
Stefansson Island, i., Nu., Can.	A9	106
Stefan Vodă, Rom.	E14	26
Stege, Den.	B8	16
Stehekin, Wa., U.S.	B6	136
Steiermark, state, Aus.	C11	22
Steinach, Aus.	C8	22
Steinbach, Mb., Can.	E17	124
Steinfurt, Ger.	D3	16
Steinhausen, Nmb.	B4	70
Steinkjer, Nor.	D4	8
Stekljanka, Russia	G19	8
Stella, S. Afr.	E7	70
Stellarton, N.S., Can.	E14	110
Stellenbosch, S. Afr.	H4	70
Stelvio, Parco Nazionale dello, p.o.i., Italy	D7	22
Stelvio, Passo dello, p., Italy	D7	22
Stendal, Ger.	C5	10
Stende, Lat.	C5	10
Stephen, Mn., U.S.	C2	118
Stephens, Ar., U.S.	D5	122
Stephens, Port, b., Austl.	I9	76
Stephens City, Va., U.S.	E7	114
Stephens Creek, Austl.	G3	76
Stephens Lake, res., Mb., Can.	D11	106
Stephenville, Nf., Can.	j22	107a
Stephenville, Tx., U.S.	B9	130
Step Pyramid see Saqqâra, Pyramides de, hist., Egypt	I2	58
Steptoe Valley, val., Nv., U.S.	D2	132
Stepurino, Russia	D18	10
Steréa Ellás, state, Grc.	E5	28
Sterkstroom, S. Afr.	G8	70
Sterling, Co., U.S.	A5	128
Sterling, Il., U.S.	C8	120
Sterling, Ks., U.S.	C10	128
Sterling, Mi., U.S.	D5	112
Sterling, Ne., U.S.	D1	120
Sterling City, Tx., U.S.	C7	130
Sterlington, La., U.S.	D6	122
Sterlitamak, Russia	D9	32
Šternberk, Czech Rep.	G13	16
Sterzing see Vipiteno, Italy	D8	22
Stettin see Szczecin, Pol.	C10	16
Stettler, Ab., Can.	D18	138
Steubenville, Oh., U.S.	D5	114
Stevenage, Eng., U.K.	J12	12
Stevenson, Al., U.S.	C13	122
Stevenson Entrance, strt., Ak., U.S.	E9	140
Stevens Pass, p., Wa., U.S.	C5	136
Stevens Peak, mtn., Id., U.S.	C11	136
Stevens Point, Wi., U.S.	G9	118
Stevensville, Mi., U.S.	F3	112
Stevensville, Mt., U.S.	D12	136
Stewardson, Il., U.S.	E9	120
Stewart, B.C., Can.	D4	106
Stewart, stm., Yk., Can.	C3	106
Stewart, Isla, i., Chile	J2	90
Stewart Island, i., N.Z.	H3	80
Stewartstown, Pa., U.S.	E9	114
Stewart Valley, Sk., Can.	D6	124
Stewartville, Mn., U.S.	H6	118
Steyerberg, Ger.	D4	16
Steyr, Aus.	B11	22
Steytlerville, S. Afr.	H7	70
Stickney, S.D., U.S.	D14	126
Stiene, Lat.	C7	10
Stif, Alg.	B6	64
Stigler, Ok., U.S.	B3	122
Stih, hora, mtn., Ukr.	A10	26
Stikine, stm., N.A.	D4	106
Stikine Ranges, mts., B.C., Can.	D4	106
Stilbaai, S. Afr.	I5	70
Stillfontein, S. Afr.	E8	70
Stilis, Grc.	E5	28
Stillhouse Hollow Lake, res., Tx., U.S.	D10	130
Stillwater, B.C., Can.	G6	138
Stillwater, Mn., U.S.	F6	118
Stillwater, Ok., U.S.	A1	122
Stillwell, Ok., U.S.	B4	122
Stînca-Costeşti, Lacul, res., Eur.	B14	26
Stine Mountain, mtn., Mt., U.S.	E13	136
Stinking Water Creek, stm., Ne., U.S.	G11	126
Stinnett, Tx., U.S.	F7	128
Stip, Mac.	B5	28
Stirling, On., Can.	D12	112
Stirling, Scot., U.K.	E9	12
Stirling City, Ca., U.S.	D4	134
Stirrat, W.V., U.S.	G15	120
Stjernøya, i., Nor.	A9	8
Stobi, hist., Mac.	B4	28
Stockach, Ger.	I5	16
Stockbridge, Ga., U.S.	C1	116
Stockbridge, Mi., U.S.	B1	114
Stockdale, Tx., U.S.	E10	130
Stockerau, Aus.	B13	22

Name	Map Ref.	Page
Stockholm, Swe.	G8	8
Stockholm, Me., U.S.	C8	110
Stockholm, state, Swe.	G8	8
Stockport, Eng., U.K.	H10	12
Stockton, Al., U.S.	G11	122
Stockton, Ca., U.S.	F4	134
Stockton, Il., U.S.	B8	120
Stockton, Ks., U.S.	B9	128
Stockton, Mo., U.S.	G4	120
Stockton-on-Tees, Eng., U.K.	G11	12
Stockton Plateau, plat., Tx., U.S.	D5	130
Stockton Reservoir, res., Mo., U.S.	G4	120
Stockton Springs, Me., U.S.	F8	110
Stœng Trêng, Camb.	F9	48
Stoffberg, S. Afr.	D9	70
Stojba, Russia	F15	34
Stoke-on-Trent, Eng., U.K.	I11	12
Stokes Point, c., Austl.	n11	77a
Stolberg, Ger.	F2	16
Stolbovo, Russia	H17	10
Stolbovoj, ostrov, i., Russia	B16	34
Stoneboro, Pa., U.S.	C5	114
Stone Harbor, N.J., U.S.	E11	114
Stonehaven, Scot., U.K.	E10	12
Stonehenge, Austl.	E4	76
Stonehenge, hist., Eng., U.K.	J11	12
Stone Mountain, Ga., U.S.	C1	116
Stone Mountain, mtn., Vt., U.S.	F5	110
Stoner, B.C., Can.	C8	138
Stoneville, N.C., U.S.	H6	114
Stonewall, Mb., Can.	D16	124
Stonewall, Ms., U.S.	E10	122
Stonewall, Ok., U.S.	C2	122
Stoney Creek, On., Can.	E10	112
Stonington, Me., U.S.	F8	110
Stonington, Ms., U.S.	E8	120
Stony Creek, stm., Ca., U.S.	D3	134
Stony Lake, l., Mb., Can.	D11	106
Stony Lake, l., On., Can.	D12	112
Stony Plain, Ab., Can.	C16	138
Stony Point, N.C., U.S.	I4	114
Stony Rapids, Sk., Can.	D9	106
Stony River, Ak., U.S.	D8	140
Stopnica, Pol.	F16	16
Stora Lulevatten, l., Swe.	C8	8
Storavan, l., Swe.	D8	8
Stord, i., Nor.	G1	8
Storebælt, strt., Den.	I4	8
Store Koldewey, i., Grnld.	B22	141
Støren, Nor.	E4	8
Store Sotra, i., Nor.	F1	8
Storkerson Bay, b., N.T., Can.	B14	140
Storkerson Peninsula, pen., Nu., Can.	A9	106
Storlien, Swe.	E5	8
Storm Bay, b., Austl.	o13	77a
Storm Lake, Ia., U.S.	B2	120
Stornoway, Scot., U.K.	C6	12
Storozhynets', Ukr.	A12	26
Storrs, Ct., U.S.	C13	114
Storsjøen, l., Nor.	F4	8
Storsjön, l., Swe.	E5	8
Storthoaks, Sk., Can.	E12	124
Storuman, Swe.	D7	8
Storuman, l., Swe.	D6	8
Storvindeln, l., Swe.	D7	8
Storvreta, Swe.	F7	8
Story City, Ia., U.S.	B4	120
Stosch, Isla, i., Chile	I1	90
Stoubcy, Bela.	G9	10
Stoughton, Ca., U.S.	E10	124
Stoughton, Ma., U.S.	B14	114
Stoughton, Wi., U.S.	B8	120
Stœŭng, stm., Camb.	F7	48
Stow, Oh., U.S.	C4	114
Stowe, Vt., U.S.	F4	110
Stowell, Tx., U.S.	H4	122
Stowmarket, Eng., U.K.	I14	12
Stoyoma Mountain, mtn., B.C., Can.	G9	138
Stradella, Italy	E6	22
Stradeč, Bela.	I6	10
Strahan, Austl.	o12	77a
Stralsund, Ger.	B9	16
Strand, S. Afr.	I4	70
Stranraer, Scot., U.K.	G8	12
Strasbourg, Sk., Can.	C9	124
Strasbourg, Fr.	F16	14
Strasburg, Ger.	C9	16
Strasburg, N.D., U.S.	A12	126
Strasburg, Oh., U.S.	D4	114
Strasburg, Va., U.S.	E9	114
Strǎşeni, Mol.	B15	26
Stratford, On., Can.	E8	112
Stratford, N.Z.	D6	80
Stratford, Ca., U.S.	G6	134
Stratford, Ct., U.S.	C12	114
Stratford, Ia., U.S.	B4	120
Stratford, Ok., U.S.	C2	122
Stratford, Wi., U.S.	G8	118
Stratford-upon-Avon, Eng., U.K.	I11	12
Strathalbyn, Austl.	J2	76
Strathclair, Mb., Can.	D13	124
Strathgordon, Austl.	o12	77a
Strathmore, N.S., Can.	D15	110
Strathmore, Ab., Can.	E17	138
Strathmore, val., Scot., U.K.	E9	12
Strathroy, On., Can.	F8	112
Stratton, Co., U.S.	B8	128
Stratton, Me., U.S.	E6	110
Stratton, Ne., U.S.	A7	128
Straubing, Ger.	H8	16
Strausberg, Ger.	D9	16
Strawberry, stm., Ar., U.S.	H6	120
Strawberry, stm., Ut., U.S.	C6	132
Strawberry Mountain, mtn., Or., U.S.	F8	136
Strawberry Reservoir, res., Ut., U.S.	C5	132
Strawn, Tx., U.S.	B9	130
Streaky Bay, b., Austl.	F6	74
Streatham, B.C., Can.	C4	138
Streator, Il., U.S.	C9	120
Středočeský, state, Czech Rep.	G10	16
Stredoslovenský Kraj, state, Slov.	H15	16
Streeter, N.D., U.S.	A13	126
Streetsboro, Oh., U.S.	C4	114
Streetsville, On., Can.	E10	112
Strehaia, Rom.	E10	26
Strelka-Čunja, Russia	B18	32
Strel'na, Russia	C18	8
Strêžsin'yo, Russia	G22	8
Strickland, stm., Pap. N. Gui.	b3	79a
Strimon, Gulf of see Strymonikós Kólpos, b., Grc.	C6	28
Strjama, stm., Blg.	G11	26
Strode, Arg.	H4	90
Strofádes, i., Grc.	F3	28
Stromboli, Isola, i., Italy	F9	24
Strome, Ab., Can.	D18	138
Stromeferry, Scot., U.K.	D7	12
Strömstad, Swe.	G4	8
Strömsund, Swe.	E6	8
Strong City, Ks., U.S.	C12	128
Stronghurst, Il., U.S.	D7	120
Stronsay, i., Scot., U.K.	B10	12
Stropkov, Slov.	G17	16
Stroud, Austl.	I8	76
Stroud, Eng., U.K.	J10	12
Stroud, Ok., U.S.	B2	122
Stroudsburg, Pa., U.S.	D10	114
Struga, Mac.	B3	28
Strumble Head, c., Wales, U.K.	I7	12
Strumica, Mac.	B5	28
Strunino, Russia	D21	10
Struthers, Oh., U.S.	C5	114
Stryi, stm., Ukr.	H19	16
Stryker, Mt., U.S.	B12	136
Stryker, Oh., U.S.	G5	112
Strykόw, Pol.	E15	16
Strymonikós Kólpos (Strimon, Gulf of), b., Grc.	C6	28
Strzegom, Pol.	F12	16
Strzelce Krajeńskie, Pol.	D11	16
Strzelce Opolskie, Pol.	F14	16
Strzelecki Creek, stm., Austl.	G3	76
Strzelecki Desert, des., Austl.	F3	76
Strzelecki National Park, p.o.i., Austl.	n13	77a
Strzelin, Pol.	F12	16
Strzyżów, Pol.	G17	16
Stuart, Fl., U.S.	I5	116
Stuart, Ne., U.S.	E14	8
Stuart, Va., U.S.	H5	114
Stuart, stm., B.C., Can.	B7	138
Stuart Island, i., Ak., U.S.	D7	140
Stuart Lake, l., B.C., Can.	B5	138
Stuarts Draft, Va., U.S.	G6	114
Studen Kladenec, Jazovir, res., Blg.	H12	26
Stuie, B.C., Can.	D4	138
Stupino, Russia	D21	10
Stura di Demonte, stm., Italy	F4	22
Sturge Island, i., Ant.	B21	81
Sturgeon, stm., On., Can.	B9	112
Sturgeon, stm., Mi., U.S.	E10	118
Sturgeon Bay, Wi., U.S.	D2	112
Sturgeon Bay, b., Mb., Can.	B15	124
Sturgeon Falls, On., Can.	B10	112
Sturgeon Lake, l., Ab., Can.	A13	138
Sturgeon Lake, l., On., Can.	D11	112
Sturgeon Lake, l., On., Can.	A7	118
Sturgis, Sk., Can.	C11	124
Sturgis, Ky., U.S.	G10	120
Sturgis, Mi., U.S.	G4	112
Sturgis, S.D., U.S.	C9	126
Šturovo, Slov.	I14	16
Sturt, Mount, mtn., Austl.	G3	76
Sturtevant, Wi., U.S.	F2	112
Sturt National Park, p.o.i., Austl.	G3	76
Sturt Stony Desert, des., Austl.	G3	76
Stuttgart, Ger.	H5	16
Stutterheim, S. Afr.	H7	70
Stuttgart, Ar., U.S.	C7	122
Styr, stm., Eur.	H9	10
Styria see Steiermark, state, Aus.	C11	22
Šu, Kaz.	F12	32
Suaçuí Grande, stm., Braz.	J4	88
Sual, Malay.	B8	50
Suaita, Col.	D5	86
Suapure, stm., Ven.	D8	86
Suaqui Grande, Mex.	A4	100
Subah, Indon.	G6	50
Subang, Indon.	G5	50
Subansiri, stm., Asia	D14	54
Subarkuduk, Kaz.	E9	32
Subarnarekha, stm., India	G11	54
Sŭbăt, stm., Sudan	F6	62
Subate, Lat.	D8	10
Subei, China	D3	36
Subeita see Shivta, Horvot, hist., Isr.	H5	58
Subiaco, Italy	I10	22
Sublette, Ks., U.S.	D8	128
Sublett Range, mts., Id., U.S.	H14	136
Subotica, Yugo.	C6	26
Sucarnoochee, stm., U.S.	E10	122
Succotah, hist., Egypt	H3	58
Suceava, Rom.	B13	26
Suceava, state, Rom.	B12	26
Suchou see Suzhou, China	F9	42
Süchow see Suzhou, China	D7	42
Sucio, stm., Col.	D3	86
Sucre, Bol.	C3	90
Sucre, Col.	C4	86
Sucre, state, Col.	C4	86
Sucre, state, Ven.	B10	86
Sucuaro, Col.	E7	86
Sucumbíos, state, Ec.	H3	86
Sucuriju, Braz.	C8	84
Sucurú, stm., Braz.	C6	84
Sud, state, N. Cal.	m16	79d
Sud, Canal du, strt., Haiti	C11	102
Suda, stm., Russia	A20	10
Sudan, Tx., U.S.	G6	128
Sudan, ctry., Afr.	E5	62
Sudan, reg., Afr.	E4	62
Sudbišči, Russia	H20	10
Sudbury, On., Can.	B8	112
Sudbury, Eng., U.K.	I13	12
Sudd see As-Sudd, reg., Sudan	F6	62
Sudetes, mts., Eur.	F11	16
Sudogda, Russia	H19	8
Sudomskaja vozvyšennost', plat., Russia	C12	10
Sudost', stm., Eur.	H16	10
Südtirol see Trentino-Alto Adige, state, Italy	D8	22
SudØroy, i., Far. Is.	n34	8b
Sue, stm., Sudan	F5	62
Sueca, Spain	E10	20
Suez see El-Suweis, Egypt	I3	58
Suez, Gulf of see Suweis, Khalīg el-, b., Egypt	J4	58
Suez Canal see Suweis, Qanâ el-, can., Egypt	H3	58
Suffield, Ab., Can.	D2	124
Suffolk, Va., U.S.	H9	114
Sufu see Kashi, China	B12	56
Sugar Island, l., Id., U.S.	G15	136
Sugar Hill, Ga., U.S.	B1	116
Sugar Land, Tx., U.S.	B5	112
Sugarloaf, Tx., U.S.	H3	122
Sugarloaf Mountain, mtn., Me., U.S.	E6	110
Sugarloaf Point, c., Austl.	I9	76
Suğla Gölü, l., Tur.	F14	28
Sugut, stm., Malay.	G1	52
Suhai Hu, l., China	G16	32
Suhār, Oman	E8	56
Sühbaatar, Mong.	A6	36
Suhindol, Blg.	F12	26
Suhiniči, Russia	F18	10
Suhodol'skij, Russia	G21	10
Suhona, stm., Russia	F21	8
Suhoverkovo, Russia	D18	10
Suhumi, Geor.	F6	32
Suhāj, Egypt	B6	62
Suhut, Tur.	E13	28
Suái-Miçu, stm., Braz.	F7	84
Suichang, China	H8	42
Suide, China	C4	42
Suifu see Yibin, China	F5	36
Suihua, China	B10	36
Suijiang, China	F5	36
Suileng, China	B10	36
Suining, China	E7	42
Suining, China	F1	42
Suipacha, Arg.	G8	92
Suiping, China	E5	42
Suippes, Fr.	E13	14
Suir, stm., Ire.	I5	12
Suixi, China	E7	42
Suiyang, China	B9	38
Suiyang, China	H2	42
Suizhongdian, China	E5	42
Suizhou, China	F5	42
Suja, Russia	H19	8
Suja, stm., Russia	E15	8
Sujāngarh, India	D5	54
Sujāwal, Pak.	F2	54
Sukabumi, Indon.	G5	50
Sukadana, Indon.	D6	50
Sukadana, Indon.	F4	50
Sukadana, Teluk, b., Indon.	D6	50
Sukagawa, Japan	B13	40
Sukamara, Indon.	E7	50
Sukaraja, Indon.	E7	50
Sukau, Malay.	A11	50
Sukhothai, Thai.	D4	48
Sukkertoppen (Maniitsoq), Grnld.	D15	141
Sukkozero, Russia	E14	8
Sukkur, Pak.	E2	54
Sukoharjo, Indon.	G7	50
Sukromi'na, Russia	D17	10
Sukses, Nmb.	B3	70
Sukumo, Japan	G5	40
Sukunka, stm., B.C., Can.	A9	138
Sul, Baía, b., Braz.	C13	92
Sula, i., Nor.	F1	8
Sula, stm., Russia	C23	8
Sula, Kepulauan (Sula Islands), is., Indon.	F8	44
Sulaimān Range, mts., Pak.	C3	54
Sula Islands see Sula, Kepulauan, is., Indon.	F8	44
Sulawesi (Celebes), i., Indon.	F7	44
Sulawesi Selatan, state, Indon.	E11	50
Sulawesi Tengah, state, Indon.	D12	50
Sulawesi Tenggara, state, Indon.	E12	50
Sulaymān, Birak (Solomon's Pools), hist., W.B.	G5	58
Sulcis, reg., Italy	E2	24
Sulechów, Pol.	D11	16
Sulęcin, Pol.	D11	16
Sulejówek, Pol.	D17	16
Sulen, Mount, mtn., Pap. N. Gui.	a3	79a
Suleyani, Ghana	H4	64
Suļģarvi, Russia	E15	8
Suligmussalmi, Fin.	D13	8
Sulingen, Ger.	D4	16
Sulitelma, mtn., Eur.	C7	8
Sullana, Peru	D1	84
Sulligent, Al., U.S.	D10	122
Sullivan, Il., U.S.	E9	120
Sullivan, In., U.S.	E10	120
Sullivan Lake, l., Ab., Can.	E18	138
Sulmona, Italy	H10	22
Sulphur, La., U.S.	G5	122
Sulphur, Ok., U.S.	C2	122
Sulphur, stm., U.S.	D5	122
Sulphur Springs, Tx., U.S.	D3	122
Sulphur Springs Draw, stm., U.S.	H3	128
Sulphur Springs Valley, val., Az., U.S.	L7	132
Sultan, Wa., U.S.	C5	136
Sultan Alonto, Lake, l., Phil.	G5	52
Sultandağı, Tur.	E14	28
Sultanhisar, Tur.	F11	28
Sultan Kudarat, Phil.	G5	52
Suluq, Libya	A4	62
Sulu Archipelago, is., Phil.	H3	52
Sulu Chi, l., China	C11	54
Sulu Sea, Asia	G8	50
Sulūq, Libya	A4	62
Sulzbach-Rosenberg, Ger.	G7	16
Sulzberger Bay, b., Ant.	C25	81
Sumadija, reg., Yugo.	E7	26
Sumangat, Tanjong, c., Malay.	G1	52
Sumatera (Sumatra), i., Indon.	E3	44
Sumatera Barat, state, Indon.	D2	50
Sumatera Selatan, state, Indon.	E4	50
Sumatera Utara, state, Indon.	K4	48
Sumatra see Sumatera, i., Indon.	E3	44
Sumba, Far. Is.	n34	8b
Sumba, i., Indon.	H11	50
Sumba, Selat, strt., Indon.	H11	50
Sumbawa, i., Indon.	H10	50
Sumbawa Besar, Indon.	H10	50
Sumbawanga, Tan.	F6	66
Sumbe, Ang.	C1	68
Sumburgh Head, c., Scot., U.K.	o18	12a
Sumé, Braz.	D7	88
Sumedang, Indon.	G5	50
Sümeg, Hung.	B4	26
Sumen, Blg.	F13	26
Sumenep, Indon.	G8	50
Sumerlja, Russia	D6	32
Sumisu-jima (Smith Island), i., Japan	E13	36
Šumjači, Russia	G15	10
Summerfield, Fl., U.S.	G3	116
Summerfield, N.C., U.S.	H6	114
Summer Lake, l., Or., U.S.	H6	136
Summerland, B.C., Can.	G11	138
Summerside, P.E.I., Can.	D13	110
Summersville, Mo., U.S.	G6	120
Summerton, S.C., U.S.	C5	116
Summerville, Ga., U.S.	C13	122
Summerville, S.C., U.S.	C5	116
Summit, S.D., U.S.	F1	118
Summit Lake, l., B.C., Can.	B8	138
Summit Mountain, mtn., Nv., U.S.	D9	134
Sumner, Ia., U.S.	B5	120
Sumner, Wa., U.S.	C4	136
Šumperk, Czech Rep.	G13	16
Sumprabum, Indon.	C8	46
Sumqayıt, Azer.	A6	56
Sumter, S.C., U.S.	C5	116
Sumy, Ukr.	D4	32
Sün, stm., Mt., U.S.	C14	136
Sunāmganj, Bngl.	F13	54
Sunburst, Mt., U.S.	B14	136
Sunbury, Austl.	K5	76
Sunbury, Pa., U.S.	D9	114
Suncho Corral, Arg.	C6	92
Sunch'ŏn, Kor., S.	G7	38
Sunch'ŏn-ŭp, Kor., N.	EE	38
Sun City, Az., U.S.	J4	132
Suncook, N.H., U.S.	G5	110
Sunda, Selat (Sunda Strait), strt., Indon.	G4	50
Sundance, Wy., U.S.	C8	126
Sundarbans, reg., Asia	H12	54
Sundargarh, India	G9	54
Sunda Shelf, unds.	I13	142
Sunda Strait see Sunda, Selat, strt., Indon.	G4	50
Sundays, stm., S. Afr.	H7	70
Sunde, Nor.	G1	8
Sunderland, Eng., U.K.	G11	12
Sundown, On., Can.	H5	128
Sundridge, On., Can.	C10	112
Sundsvall, Swe.	E7	8
Sunflower, Ms., U.S.	D8	122
Sunflower, Mount, mtn., Ks., U.S.	B7	128
Sungaianyar, Indon.	E10	50
Sungaibareh, Indon.	D2	50
Sungaigerung, Indon.	C3	50
Sungai Kolok, Thai.	I5	48
Sungaipenuh, Indon.	D2	50
Sungai Petani, Malay.	J5	48
Sungaipinang, Indon.	D8	50
Sungairotan, Indon.	E4	50
Sungari see Songhua, stm., China	B11	36
Sungari Reservoir see Songhua Hu, res., China	C7	38
Sungchiang see Songjiang, China	F9	42
Sungguminasa, Indon.	F11	50
Sungsang, Indon.	E4	50
Sunland Park, N.M., U.S.	L10	132
Sunne, Swe.	G5	8
Sunnynook, Ab., Can.	E19	138
Sunnyside, Ut., U.S.	D6	132
Sunnyside, Wa., U.S.	D7	136
Sunnyslope, Ab., Can.	E17	138
Sunnyvale, Ca., U.S.	F3	134
Sun Prairie, Wi., U.S.	A8	120
Sunrise, Fl., U.S.	J5	116
Sunrise, Wy., U.S.	E8	126
Sunrise Manor, Nv., U.S.	G1	132
Sunset, La., U.S.	G6	122
Sunset, Tx., U.S.	H11	128
Sunset Country, reg., Austl.	J3	76
Sunset Crater National Monument, p.o.i., Az., U.S.	H5	132
Sunshine, Austl.	K5	76
Sunsar-Hajata, hrebet, mts., Russia	D17	34
Sunwu, China	B10	36
Sunwui see Jiangmen, China	J5	42
Sunyani, Ghana	H4	64
Suoarvi, Russia	E15	8
Suomussalmi, Fin.	D13	8
Suō-nada, Japan	F4	40
Suordah, Russia	C15	34
Suoyarvi, Russia	D10	86
Supai, India	E15	54
Superi see La Merced, Arg.	D5	92
Superior, Az., U.S.	J5	132
Superior, Mt., U.S.	C12	136
Superior, Wi., U.S.	E6	118
Superior, Wy., U.S.	B7	132
Superior, Laguna, b., Mex.	G11	100
Superior, Lake, l., N.A.	B10	108
Supetar, Cro.	G13	22
Suphan Buri, Thai.	E4	48
Suphan Buri, stm., Thai.	E5	48
Suponevo, Russia	G17	10
Suqian, China	E8	42
Suq Suwayq, Sau. Ar.	E8	42
Suquṭrā (Socotra), i., Yemen	G7	56
Sur, Oman	E8	56
Sūr (Tyre), Leb.	E6	58
Sur, Point, c., Ca., U.S.	G4	134
Sura, stm., Russia	C7	32
Surabaya, Indon.	G8	50
Surakarta, Indon.	G7	50
Sürän, Syria	C7	58
Surany, Slov.	H14	16
Surat, Austl.	F7	76
Surat Thani, Thai.	H4	48
Suratgarh, India	D5	54
Surazh, Bela.	E13	10
Surendranagar, India	G3	54
Surf City, N.J., U.S.	E11	114
Surfers Paradise, Austl.	G9	76
Surgères, Fr.	C5	18
Surgoinsville, Tn., U.S.	H3	114
Surgut, Russia	B12	32
Suri, India	G11	54
Surigao, Phil.	F5	52
Surin, Thai.	E6	48
Surinam, ctry., S.A.	C6	84
Surin Islands see Surin, Mu Ko, is., Thai.	H3	48
Surkhob, stm., Taj.	B11	56
Surovikino, Russia	E6	32
Surrency, Ga., U.S.	E3	116
Surrey, N.D., U.S.	F12	124
Surry, Va., U.S.	G9	114
Sursee, Switz.	C5	22
Surt, Libya	A3	62
Surt, Khalīj (Sidra, Gulf of), b., Libya	A3	62
Surtanāhu, Pak.	E2	54
Surtsey, i., Ice.	l29	8a
Surup, Pap. N. Gui.	b3	79a
Suruga-wan, b., Japan	E11	40
Surumu, stm., Braz.	F11	86
Susak, Otok, i., Cro.	F11	22
Susami, Japan	F9	40
Susanville, Ca., U.S.	C5	134
Susitna, stm., Ak., U.S.	D9	140
Susong, China	D9	42
Suspiro del Moro, Puerto, p., Spain	G7	20
Susquehanna, Pa., U.S.	C10	114
Susquehanna, stm., U.S.	F9	114
Susquehanna, West Branch, stm., U.S.	C8	114
Susques, Arg.	D3	90
Sussex, N.B., Can.	E11	110
Sussex, N.J., U.S.	C11	114
Sussex, Va., U.S.	H8	114
Susuman, Russia	D18	34
Susurluk, Tur.	D11	28
Susuzmüsellim, Tur.	B9	28
Sušvė, stm., Lith.	E6	10
Sutak, India	B7	54
Sutherland, S. Afr.	H5	70
Sutherland, Ia., U.S.	A2	120
Sutherlin, Or., U.S.	G3	136
Sutjeska Nacionalni Park, p.o.i., Bos.	F5	26
Sutlej (Langqén) (Satluj), stm., Asia	D3	54
Sutter Buttes, mtn., Ca., U.S.	D4	134
Sutter Creek, Ca., U.S.	E5	134
Sutton, Ak., U.S.	D10	140
Sutton, W.V., U.S.	F5	114
Sutton, Monts see Green Mountains, mts., N.A.	G4	110
Sutton in Ashfield, Eng., U.K.	H11	12
Sutton West, On., Can.	D10	112
Suttor, stm., Austl.	C6	76
Sutwik Island, i., Ak., U.S.	E8	140
Suure-Jaani, Est.	B8	10
Suur Munamägi, hill, Est.	C9	10
Suur Pakri, i., Est.	A6	10
Suva, Fiji	q19	79e
Suvadiva Atoll, at., Mald.	i12	46a
Suvarlı, Tur.	A8	58
Suvasvesi, l., Fin.	E12	8
Suvorov, Russia	F19	10
Suwa, Japan	C11	40
Suwałki, Pol.	B18	16
Suwałki, state, Pol.	B18	16
Suwannaphum, Thai.	E6	48
Suwannee, stm., U.S.	G2	116
Suwanose-jima, i., Japan	k19	39a
Suwarrow, at., Cook Is.	E10	72
Suweis, Khalīg el- (Suez, Gulf of), b., Egypt	J4	58
Suweis, Qanâ el- (Suez Canal), can., Egypt	H3	58
Suwŏn, Kor., S.	F7	38
Suzak, Kaz.	F11	32
Suzaka, Japan	C11	40
Suzdal', Russia	H19	8
Suzhou, China	F9	42
Suzhou, China	E7	42
Suzigou, China	A10	42
Suzuka, Japan	E9	40
Suzu-misaki, c., Japan	B10	40
Suzun, Russia	D14	32
Suzzara, Italy	F7	22
Svalbard, dep., Eur.	B6	30
Svaliava, Ukr.	A10	26
Svapa, stm., Russia	H18	10
Svappavaara, Swe.	C9	8
Svärdsjö, Swe.	F6	8
Svartenhuk, pen., Grnld.	C15	141
Svartisen, ice, Nor.	C5	8
Svataj, Russia	C19	34
Svay Riêng, Camb.	G7	48
Svedala, Swe.	I5	8
Švédasai, Lith.	E8	10
Švegsjön, l., Swe.	E5	8
Švékšna, Lith.	E4	10
Svelvik, Nor.	G4	8
Svenčionėliai, Lith.	E8	10
Svenčionys, Lith.	F8	10
Svendborg, Den.	A6	16
Sventoji, l., Russia	D3	10
Sventoji, stm., Lith.	E7	10
Sverdlovsk see Ekaterinburg, Russia	C10	32
Sverdrup, ostrov, i., Russia	B4	34
Sverdrup Channel, strt., Nu., Can.	A6	141
Sverdrup Islands, is., Nu., Can.	B5	141
Sveti Nikole, Mac.	B4	28
Svetlahorsk, Bela.	H12	10
Svetlaja, Russia	B12	36
Svetlogorsk, Russia	F2	10
Svetlograd, Russia	E6	32
Svetlyj, Russia	D10	32
Svetlyj, Russia	E12	34
Svetogorsk, Russia	F13	8
Svetozarevo, Yugo.	F8	26
Svidník, Slov.	G17	16
Svilengrad, Blg.	H13	26
Svínoy, i., Far. Is.	m34	8b
Svir, Bela.	F9	10
Svir', stm., Russia	F16	8
Svirica, Russia	F15	8
Svirsk, Russia	D18	32
Svislač, stm., Bela.	G11	10
Svištov, Blg.	F12	26
Svit, Slov.	G16	16
Svitavy, Czech Rep.	G12	16
Svjatoj Nos, mys, c., Russia	B18	8
Svjatoj Nos, mys, c., Russia	B17	34
Svobodnyj, Russia	F14	34
Svolvær, Nor.	B6	8
Svratka, stm., Czech Rep.	G12	16
Swabia see Schwaben, hist. reg., Ger.	H5	16
Swain Reefs, rf., Austl.	C9	76
Swainsboro, Ga., U.S.	D3	116
Swains Island, i., Am. Sam.	E9	72
Swakop, stm., Nmb.	C2	70
Swakopmund, Nmb.	C2	70
Swale, stm., Eng., U.K.	G11	12
Swan, stm., Ab., Can.	B13	124
Swan, stm., Austl.	A15	138
Swanage, Eng., U.K.	K11	12
Swanee see Suwannee, stm., U.S.	G2	116
Swan Hill, Austl.	J4	76
Swan Hills, Ab., Can.	B15	138
Swan Islands see Santanilla, Islas, is., Hond.	D6	102
Swan Lake, l., Mb., Can.	B13	124
Swan Lake, l., Mn., U.S.	G4	118
Swannanoa, N.C., U.S.	I3	114
Swan Peak, mtn., Mt., U.S.	C13	136
Swanquarter, N.C., U.S.	A9	116
Swan Range, mts., Mt., U.S.	C13	136
Swan Reach, Austl.	J2	76
Swan River, Mb., Can.	B12	124
Swansboro, N.C., U.S.	B8	116
Swansea, Wales, U.K.	J8	12
Swanton, Vt., U.S.	F3	110
Swanville, Mn., U.S.	F4	118
Swart-Mfolozi, stm., S. Afr.	F10	70
Swartz Creek, Mi., U.S.	F6	112
Swarzędz, Pol.	D13	16
Swāt, stm., Pak.	A3	54
Swatow see Shantou, China	J7	42
Swaziland, ctry., Afr.	E10	70
Sweden, ctry., Eur.	D6	8
Swedish Knoll, mtn., Ut., U.S.	D5	132
Sweeny, Tx., U.S.	E12	130
Sweers, Ia., U.S.	A1	116
Sweet Grass, Mt., U.S.	A15	136
Sweet Grass Hills, hills, Mt., U.S.	B15	136
Sweet Home, Or., U.S.	F4	136
Sweet Springs, Mo., U.S.	E10	130
Sweetwater, Tn., U.S.	A1	116
Sweetwater, Tx., U.S.	B7	130
Sweetwater, stm., Wy., U.S.	F5	126
Swellendam, S. Afr.	H5	70
Świdnica, Pol.	F12	16
Świdnik, Pol.	E18	16
Świdwin, Pol.	C11	16
Świebodzice, Pol.	F11	16
Świebodzin, Pol.	D11	16
Świecie, Pol.	C14	16
Świerzawa, Pol.	E11	16
Świętokrzyski Park Narodowy, p.o.i., Pol.	F16	16
Swift Current, Sk., Can.	D6	124
Swift Current Creek, stm., Sk., Can.	D6	124
Swinburne, Cape, c., Nu., Can.	A11	106
Swindle Island, i., B.C., Can.	D2	138
Swindon, Eng., U.K.	J11	12
Swinford, Ire.	H4	12
Świnoujście (Swinemünde), Pol.	C9	16
Switzerland, ctry., Eur.	C14	18
Swords, Ire.	H6	12
Syalah, Russia	C13	34
Syan (San), stm., Eur.	F18	16
Sycamore, Ga., U.S.	E2	116
Sycamore, Il., U.S.	C9	120
Sycamore, Oh., U.S.	D2	114
Sydenham, stm., On., Can.	F7	112
Sydney, Austl.	I8	76
Sydney, N.S., Can.	D16	110
Sydney Bay, b., Norf. I.	y25	78i
Sydney Lake, l., On., Can.	A4	118
Sydney Mines, N.S., Can.	D16	110
Syčy, Bela.	H12	10
Syke, Ger.	D4	16
Sykesville, Pa., U.S.	C8	114
Syktyvkar, Russia	B8	32
Sylacauga, Al., U.S.	D12	122
Sylhet, Bngl.	F13	54
Syloga, Russia	E20	8
Sylt, i., Ger.	B4	16
Sylva, N.C., U.S.	A2	116
Sylvan Grove, Ks., U.S.	C10	128
Sylvania, Ga., U.S.	D4	116
Sylvania, Oh., U.S.	C2	114
Sylvan Lake, l., Ab., Can.	D16	138
Sylvan Pass, p., Wy., U.S.	F16	136
Sylvester, Ga., U.S.	E2	116
Sylvester, Tx., U.S.	B7	130
Sym, Russia	B15	32
Syme see Sými, i., Grc.	G10	28
Sými, i., Grc.	G10	28
Symkent, Kaz.	F11	32
Synevir, Ukr.	A10	26
Syowa, sci., Ant.	C9	81
Syracuse, Ks., U.S.	C7	128
Syracuse, Ne., U.S.	D1	120
Syracuse, N.Y., U.S.	A9	114
Syracuse, Ut., U.S.	A10	56
Syr Darya (Syrdar'ja), stm., Asia	F11	32
Syria, ctry., Asia	B4	56
Syriam, Mya.	D3	48
Syrian Desert (Shām, Bādiyat ash-), des., Asia	C4	56
Syrna, i., Grc.	G9	28
Sýros, i., Grc.	F7	28
Sysmä, Fin.	F11	8
Sysola, stm., Russia	B8	32
Syt'kovo, Russia	D16	10
Syväri, i., Fin.	E13	8
Syzran', Russia	D7	32
Szabolcs-Szatmár-Bereg, state, Hung.	A9	26
Szamos (Someş), stm., Eur.	B9	26
Szamotuły, Pol.	D12	16
Szarvas, Hung.	C7	26
Szczawnica, Pol.	G16	16
Szczecin (Stettin), Pol.	C10	16
Szczecin, state, Pol.	C12	16
Szczecinek, Pol.	C13	16
Szczytno, Pol.	C16	16
Szechwan see Sichuan, state, China	E5	36
Szechwan Basin see Sichuan Pendi, bas., China	F1	42
Szeged, Hung.	C7	26
Szeghalom, Hung.	B8	26
Székesfehérvár, Hung.	B5	26
Szekszárd, Hung.	C5	26
Szentendre, Hung.	B5	26
Szentes, Hung.	C7	26
Szeping see Siping, China	C6	38
Szerencs, Hung.	A8	26
Szob, Hung.	B5	26
Szolnok, Hung.	B7	26
Szombathely, Hung.	B3	26
Szprotawa, Pol.	E11	16
Szubin, Pol.	C13	16
Szypliszki, Pol.	B19	16

T

Name	Map Ref.	Page
Taal, Lake, l., Phil.	D3	52
Tábara, Spain	C5	20
Tabar Islands, is., Pap. N. Gui.	a5	79a
Tabarka, Tun.	H2	24
Tabasco, state, Mex.	D6	96
Tabelbala, Alg.	D4	64
Taber, Ab., Can.	G18	133
Tabernes de Valldigna see Tavernes de la Valldigna, Spain	E10	20
Tabira, Braz.	D7	88
Tablas de Daimiel, Parque Nacional de las, p.o.i., Spain	E7	20
Tablas Island, i., Phil.	D4	52
Tablas Strait, strt., Phil.	D3	52
Tablat, Alg.	H14	20
Table Mountain, mtn., Az., U.S.	K6	132
Table Rock, Ne., U.S.	D1	120
Table Rock Lake, res., U.S.	H4	120
Table Top, mtn., Az., U.S.	K4	132
Tablones, P.R.	B4	104a
Taboi, Mount, hill, St. Vin.	p11	105e
Tábor, Czech Rep.	G10	16
Tabor, Russia	B19	34
Tabor, Ia., U.S.	D2	120
Tabor City, N.C., U.S.	B7	116
Tabou, Ci.	I3	64
Tabrīz, Iran	B6	56
Tabuaeran, at., Kir.	C11	72
Tabūk, Sau. Ar.	J7	58
Tabūk, Phil.	B3	52
Tabuleiro do Norte, Braz.	C6	88
Tabwémasana, Mont, mtn., Vanuatu	j16	79d
Tacámbaro de Codallos, Mex.	F8	100
Tacaná, Volcán, vol., N.A.	H12	100
Tacañitas, Arg.	D6	92
Taché, Lac, l., N.T., Can.	C7	106
Tacheng, China	A1	42
Tachichitte, hills, Mex.	B6	100
Tachie, stm., B.C., Can.	B6	138
Tacloban, Phil.	E5	52
Tacna, Peru	G4	84
Tacoma, Wa., U.S.	C4	136
Taconic Range, mts., U.S.	B12	114
Tacuarembó, Ur.	E9	92
Tacuari, stm., Ur.	F11	92
Tacutu (Takutu), stm., S.A.	F11	86
Tademaït, Plateau du, plat., Alg.	D5	64
Tădepallegudem, India	C5	53
Tadjemout, Alg.	C5	64
Tadjerouine, Tun.	I2	24
Tadotsu, Japan	E7	40
Tadoule Lake, l., Mb., Can.	D11	106
Tadoussac, Qc., Can.	B7	110

Name	Map Ref.	Page
Tādpatri, India	D4	53
T'aean, Kor., S.	F7	38
T'aebaek-sanmaek, mts., Asia	F8	38
Taech'ŏn, Kor., S.	F7	38
Taedong-gang, stm., Kor., N.	E6	38
Taegu, Kor., S.	D1	40
Taejin, Kor., S.	C2	40
Taejŏn, Kor., S.	F7	38
Taeng, stm., Thai.	C4	48
Tafahi, i., Tonga	E9	72
Tafalla, Spain	B9	20
Tafanlieh, Tai.	J9	42
Tafassâsset, Oued, stm., Afr.	E6	64
Tafassasset, Ténéré du, des., Niger	E7	64
Taféa, state, Vanuatu	I17	79d
Tafelberg, hill, Neth. Ant.	p22	104g
Tafí Viejo, Arg.	C5	92
Tafo, Ghana	H4	64
Taft, Ca., U.S.	H6	134
Taft, Tx., U.S.	F10	130
Taftān, Kūh-e, vol., Iran	D9	56
Taga, Samoa	g11	79c
Tagajō, Japan	A14	40
Taganrog, Russia	E5	32
Tagânt, reg., Maur.	F2	64
Tagawa, Japan	F3	40
Tagaytay, Phil.	C3	52
Tagbilaran, Phil.	F4	52
Tage, Pap. N. Gui.	b3	79a
Tagish Lake, l., Can.	C3	106
Tagliamento, stm., Italy	E9	22
Taglio di Po, Italy	E9	22
Taguatinga, Braz.	G2	88
Taguke, China	B10	54
Tagula Island, i., Pap. N. Gui.	B10	74
Tagum, Phil.	G5	52
Tagus (Tajo) (Tejo), stm., Eur.	E2	20
Tahakopa, N.Z.	H3	80
Tahan, Gunong, mtn., Malay.	J6	48
Tahat, mtn., Alg.	E6	64
Tahiataš, Uzb.	F9	32
Tahifet, Alg.	E6	64
Tahiryuak Lake, l., N.T., Can.	A8	106
Tahiti, i., Fr. Poly.	v23	78h
Tahiti-Faaa, Aéroport International de, Fr. Poly.	v21	78h
Tahkuna nina, c., Est.	A5	10
Tahlequah, Ok., U.S.	I3	120
Tahoe, Lake, l., U.S.	E5	134
Tahoe City, Ca., U.S.	D5	134
Tahoe Lake, l., Nu., Can.	A8	106
Tahoka, Tx., U.S.	A6	130
Tahoua, Niger	F5	64
Tahquamenon, stm., Mi., U.S.	B4	112
Tahta, Egypt	L2	58
Tahta, Russia	E6	32
Tahta-Bazar, Turkmen.	B9	56
Tahtaköprü, Tur.	D12	28
Tahtamygda, Russia	F13	34
Tahtsa Lake, res., B.C., Can.	C3	138
Tahtsa Peak, mtn., B.C., Can.	C3	138
Tahuata, i., Fr. Poly.	s18	78g
Tahulandang, Pulau, i., Indon.	E7	44
Tahuna, Indon.	E8	44
Tai'an, China	C7	42
Taiarapu, Presqu'île de, pen., Fr. Poly.	w22	78h
Taibai Shan, mtn., China	E2	42
Taibilla, Sierra de, mts., Spain	F8	20
Taibus Qi, China	C8	36
Taicang, China	F9	42
T'aichou see Taizhou, China	E8	42
T'aichung, Tai.	I9	42
Taieri, stm., N.Z.	G4	80
Taigu, China	C5	42
Taihang Shan, mts., China	C5	42
Taihape, N.Z.	D6	80
Taihe, China	H6	42
Taihe, China	E6	42
Taihezhen, China	B5	38
T'aihsien see Taizhou, China	E8	42
Taihu, China	F7	42
Tai Hu, l., China	F9	42
Taikang, China	D6	42
Taikou, China	F4	42
Tailai, China	B9	36
Tai Lake see Tai Hu, l., China	F9	42
Tailem Bend, Austl.	J2	76
Taimba, Russia	B17	32
T'ainan, Tai.	J8	42
Taínaro, Ákra, c., Grc.	G5	28
Taining, China	H7	42
Taiobeiras, Braz.	H4	88
T'aipei, Tai.	I9	42
T'aipeihsien, Tai.	I9	42
Taiping, China	J2	42
Taiping, Malay.	J5	48
Taipingdian, China	E4	42
Taipu, Braz.	C8	88
Tais, Indon.	F3	50
Taisha, Japan	D5	40
Taishan, China	J5	42
Tai Shan see Yuhuang Ding, mtn., China	C9	42
Taishun, China	H8	42
Taitao, Península de, pen., Chile	I2	90
T'aitung, Tai.	J9	42
Taivalkoski, Fin.	D12	8
Taiwan, ctry., Asia	J9	42
Taiwan Strait, strt., Asia	I8	42
Taixian, China	E9	42
Taixing, China	E9	42
Taiyiba, Isr.	F6	58
Taiyuan, China	C5	42
Taizhao, China	D14	54
Taizhou, China	E8	42
Taizi, stm., China	D5	38
Tajbola, Russia	B15	8
Tajga, Russia	C15	32
Tajgonos, mys, c., Russia	D21	34
Tajgonos, poluostrov, pen., Russia	D21	34
Tajikistan, ctry., Asia	B11	56
Tajima, Japan	B12	40
Tajimi, Japan	D10	40
Tajique, N.M., U.S.	G2	128
Tajitos, Mex.	F6	98
Tāj Mahal, hist., India	E7	54
Tajmura, stm., Russia	B18	32
Tajmyr, ozero, l., Russia	B9	34
Tajmyr, poluostrov, pen., Russia	B7	34
Tajšet, Russia	C17	32
Tajumulco, Volcán, vol., Guat.	E2	102
Tajuña, stm., Spain	D7	20
Tak, Thai.	D4	48
Takachu, Bots.	C5	70
Takahagi, Japan	C13	40
Takahashi, Japan	E6	40
Takahe, Mount, mtn., Ant.	C29	81
Takaka, N.Z.	E5	80
Takakkaw Falls, wtfl, B.C., Can.	E14	138
Takalar, Indon.	F11	50
Takamatsu, Japan	E7	40
Takanabe, Japan	G4	40
Takaoka, Japan	C9	40
Takasago, Japan	E7	40
Takasaki, Japan	C11	40
Takatsuki, Japan	E8	40
Ta-kaw, Mya.	B4	48
Takayama, Japan	C10	40
Takefu, Japan	D9	40
Takenake, China	A8	54
Takengon, Indon.	J3	48
Takeo, Japan	F3	40
Take-shima, is., Asia	B4	40
Taketa, Japan	G4	40
Takêv, Camb.	G7	48
Takhatpur, India	G8	54
Takhli, Thai.	E5	48
Takhta-Bazar see Tahta-Bazar, Turkmen.	B9	56
Takijuq Lake, l., Nu., Can.	B8	106
Takikawa, Japan	C14	38
Takla Lake, l., B.C., Can.	A5	138
Takla Landing, B.C., Can.	D5	106
Takla Makan Desert see Taklimakan Shamo, des., China	G14	32
Taklimakan Shamo (Takla Makan Desert), des., China	G14	32
Takolekaju, Pegunungan, mts., Indon.	E11	50
Taksimo, Russia	F10	34
Taku, Japan	F3	40
Takuan, Mount, vol., Pap. N. Gui.	d6	79b
Takum, Nig.	H7	64
Takutea, i., Cook Is.	E11	72
Takutu (Tacutu), stm., S.A.	F11	86
Talačyn, Bela.	F12	10
Talagang, Pak.	B4	54
Talagante, Chile	F2	92
Talaimannar, Sri L.	G4	53
Talāja, India	H4	54
Talak, reg., Niger	F6	64
Tālāla, India	H3	54
Talang, Gunung, vol., Indon.	D2	50
Talangbetutu, Indon.	E4	50
Talangpadang, Indon.	F4	50
Talangrimbo, Indon.	E4	50
Talara, Peru	D1	84
Talas, Kyrg.	F12	32
Talasea, Pap. N. Gui.	b4	79a
Tal'at al-Jamā'ah, Rujm, mtn., Jord.	H6	58
Talata Mafara, Nig.	G6	64
Talaud, Kepulauan (Talaud Islands), is., Indon.	E8	44
Talaud Islands see Talaud, Kepulauan, is., Indon.	E8	44
Talavera de la Reina, Spain	D5	20
Talawanta, Austl.	B3	76
Talawdī, Sudan	E6	62
Talayan, Phil.	G5	52
Talbotton, Ga., U.S.	E14	122
Talbragar, stm., Austl.	I7	76
Talca, Chile	G2	92
Talcahuano, Chile	H1	92
Tālcher, India	H10	54
Talco, Tx., U.S.	D3	122
Taldom, Russia	D20	10
Taldykorgan, Kaz.	F13	32
Taldyqorghan see Taldykorgan, Kaz.	F13	32
Talence, Fr.	E5	18
Talent, Or., U.S.	A3	134
Talgar, Kaz.	F13	32
Talghar see Talgar, Kaz.	F13	32
Talhār, Pak.	F2	54
Taliabu, Pulau, i., Indon.	F7	44
Talibon, Phil.	E5	52
Talibong, Ko, i., Thai.	I4	48
Talica, Russia	C10	32
Talien see Dalian, China	B9	42
Tālīkota, India	C3	53
Taliparamba, India	E2	53
Talisay, Phil.	E4	52
Taliwang, Indon.	H10	50
Talkeetna, Ak., U.S.	D9	140
Talkeetna Mountains, mts., Ak., U.S.	D10	140
Talla, Egypt	J1	58
Talladega, Al., U.S.	D12	122
Tallahala Creek, stm., Ms., U.S.	F9	122
Tallahassee, Fl., U.S.	F1	116
Tallahatchie, stm., Ms., U.S.	D8	122
Tallangatta, Austl.	K6	76
Tallapoosa, Ga., U.S.	D13	122
Tallapoosa, stm., U.S.	E12	122
Tallard, Fr.	E11	18
Tallassee, Al., U.S.	E12	122
Tall as-Sulṭān, hist., Gaza	G6	58
Tall Bīsah, Syria	D7	58
Tallinn, Est.	G11	8
Tallmadge, Oh., U.S.	C4	114
Tall Rif'at, Syria	B8	58
Tallulah, La., U.S.	E7	122
Talmage, Ca., U.S.	D2	134
Talmage, Ne., U.S.	K2	118
Tal'menka, Russia	D14	32
Talnah, Russia	C6	34
Taloda, India	H5	54
Taloga, Ok., U.S.	E10	128
Talok, Indon.	C11	50
Tāloqān, Afg.	B10	56
Talovka, Russia	F7	32
Taloyoak, Nu., Can.	B12	106
Talquin, Lake, res., Fl., U.S.	G14	122
Talsi, Lat.	C5	10
Taltal, Chile	B2	92
Taltson, stm., N.T., Can.	C8	106
Talu, Indon.	C1	50
Taluk, Indon.	D2	50
Talumphuk, Laem, c., Thai.	H5	48
Talvikjulja, Russia	B13	8
Talwood, Austl.	G7	76
Tama, Arg.	E4	92
Tama, Ia., U.S.	C5	120
Tamalameque, Col.	C5	86
Tamale, Ghana	H4	64
Tamalea, Indon.	E11	50
Tamalpais, Mount, mtn., Ca., U.S.	F3	134
Tamana, Japan	G3	40
Tamana, Mount, hill, Trin.	s12	105f
Tamanaco, stm., Ven.	C9	86
Tamaniquá, Braz.	I9	86
Taman Negara, p.o.i., Malay.	J6	48
Tamano, Japan	E6	40
Tamanquaré, Ilha, i., Braz.	H9	86
Tamapatz, Mex.	E9	100
Tamar, stm., Austl.	n13	77a
Tamarac, stm., Mn., U.S.	C2	118
Tamaroa, Il., U.S.	F8	120
Tamási, Hung.	C5	26
Tamaulipas, state, Mex.	C9	100
Tamazulapan del Progreso, Mex.	G9	100
Tamazunchale, Mex.	E9	100
Tambacounda, Sen.	G2	64
Tambakboyo, Indon.	G7	50
Tamba-kōchi, plat., Japan	D8	40
Tambangsawah, Indon.	E3	50
Tambara, Moz.	D5	68
Tāmbaram, India	E5	53
Tambej, Russia	B3	34
Tambelan, Kepulauan, is., Indon.	C5	50
Tamberías, Arg.	E3	92
Tambo, stm., Austl.	K6	76
Tambohorano, Madag.	D7	68
Tambolongang, Pulau, i., Indon.	G12	50
Tambora, Gunung, vol., Indon.	H10	50
Tamboril, Braz.	C5	88
Tamboryacu, stm., Peru	H4	86
Tambov, Russia	D6	32
Tambre, stm., Spain	B2	20
Tambu, Teluk, b., Indon.	C11	50
Tambunan, Malay.	H1	52
Tambura, Sudan	F5	62
Tâmchekket, Maur.	F2	64
Tame, Col.	D6	86
Tameapa, Mex.	C5	100
Tâmega, stm., Port.	C3	20
Tamel Aike, Arg.	I2	90
Tamenghest, Alg.	E6	64
Tamenghest, Oued, stm., Alg.	E5	64
Tamga, Russia	B10	38
Tamgak, Adrar, mtn., Niger	F6	64
Tamiahua, Mex.	E10	100
Tamiahua, Laguna de, l., Mex.	E10	100
Tamiami Canal, can., Fl., U.S.	K4	116
Tamil Nādu, state, India	F4	53
Tamiš (Timiș), stm., Eur.	D7	26
Tâmîya, Egypt	I1	58
Tamkūhi, India	E10	54
Tam Ky, Viet.	E9	48
Tammerfors see Tampere, Fin.	F10	8
Tammisaari, Fin.	G10	8
Tamms, Il., U.S.	G8	120
Tampa, Fl., U.S.	I3	116
Tampa Bay, b., Fl., U.S.	I3	116
Tampang, Indon.	F4	50
Tampaon, stm., Mex.	E9	100
Tampere (Tammerfors), Fin.	F10	8
Tampico, Mex.	D10	100
Tampico, Il., U.S.	C8	120
Tampin, Malay.	K6	48
Tamsagbulag, Mong.	B8	36
Tamshiyacu, Peru	D3	84
Tamsweg, Aus.	C10	22
Tamu, Mya.	D7	46
Tamuning, Guam	i10	78c
Tamworth, Austl.	H8	76
Tamworth, Eng., U.K.	I11	12
Tana (Teno), stm., Eur.	B12	8
Tana, stm., Kenya	D8	66
Tana, Lake see T'ana Hāyk', l., Eth.	E7	62
Tanabe, Japan	F8	40
Tanabi, Braz.	K1	88
Tana bru, Nor.	A12	8
Tanacross, Ak., U.S.	D11	140
Tanafjorden, b., Nor.	A13	8
Tanaga Island, i., Ak., U.S.	g23	140a
T'ana Hāyk', l., Eth.	E7	62
Tanahbala, Pulau, i., Indon.	F2	44
Tanahgrogot, Indon.	D10	50
Tanahjampea, Pulau, i., Indon.	G12	50
Tanahmasa, Pulau, i., Indon.	F2	44
Tanahmerah, Indon.	G10	44
Tanah Merah, Malay.	J6	48
Tanahputih, Indon.	C2	50
Tanakeke, Pulau, i., Indon.	F11	50
Tanakpur, India	D7	54
Tanami Desert, des., Austl.	C5	74
Tan An, Viet.	G8	48
Tanana, Ak., U.S.	C9	140
Tanana, stm., Ak., U.S.	D10	140
Tananarive see Antananarivo, Madag.	D8	68
Tanbar, Austl.	E3	76
Tan Chau, Viet.	G7	48
Tanch'ŏn-ŭp, Kor., N.	D8	38
Tancítaro, Pico de, mtn., Mex.	F7	100
Tanda, Egypt	K1	58
Tānda, India	E9	54
Tānda, India	C5	54
Tandag, Phil.	F6	52
Tandaltī, Sudan	E6	62
Țăndărei, Rom.	E14	26
Tandil, Arg.	H8	92
Tando Ādam, Pak.	F2	54
Tando Allāhyār, Pak.	F2	54
Tandou Lake, l., Austl.	I3	76
Tandula Tank, res., India	H8	54
Tandun, Indon.	C2	50
Tāndūr, India	C3	53
Tanega-shima, i., Japan	I9	38
Tanezrouft, des., Afr.	E4	64
Tang, stm., China	E7	42
Tang, stm., China	E5	42
Tang, stm., China	B6	42
Tanga, Russia	F11	34
Tanga, Tan.	F7	66
Tangail, Bngl.	F12	54
Tanga Islands, is., Pap. N. Gui.	a5	79a
Tanga Langua, c., Gren.	q10	105e
Tanganyika see Tanzania, ctry., Afr.	F6	66
Tanganyika, Lake, l., Afr.	F6	66
Tangarana, stm., Peru	I4	86
Tangarare, Sol. Is.	e8	79b
Tanger (Tangier), Mor.	B3	64
Tangerang, Indon.	G5	50
Tangerhütte, Ger.	D7	16
Tangermünde, Ger.	D7	16
Tanggu, China	B7	42
Tanggulashan, China	A14	54
Tanggula Shan, mts., China	E3	36
Tanggula Shankou, p., China	B13	54
Tanghe, China	E5	42
Tangi, Pak.	A3	54
Tangier, N.S., Can.	F14	110
Tangier see Tanger, Mor.	B3	64
Tangier, Va., U.S.	G10	114
Tangipahoa, stm., U.S.	G8	122
Tangjiagou, China	F7	42
Tangkou, China	F8	42
Tangmai, China	E4	36
Tango-hantō, pen., Japan	D8	40
Tangra Yumco, l., China	C11	54
Tangshan, China	B8	42
Tangtou, China	D8	42
Tangyan, Mya.	A4	48
Tangyin, China	D6	42
Tangyuan, China	B10	36
Tanhoj, Russia	F10	34
Taniantaweng Shan, mts., China	F4	36
Tanigawa-dake, mtn., Japan	C11	40
Tanimbar, Kepulauan, is., Indon.	G9	44
Tanintharyi, state, Mya.	F3	48
Tanis, hist., Egypt	H2	58
Tanjay, Phil.	F4	52
Tanjung, Indon.	H10	50
Tanjung, Indon.	E9	50
Tanjungbalai, Indon.	B1	50
Tanjungbatu, Indon.	C3	50
Tanjungbatu, Indon.	B11	50
Tanjungkarang-Telukbetung, Indon.	F4	50
Tanjunglabu, Indon.	E5	50
Tanjungpandan, Indon.	E5	50
Tanjungpinang, Indon.	C4	50
Tanjungpura, Indon.	K4	48
Tanjungraja, Indon.	E4	50
Tanjungredep, Indon.	B10	50
Tanjungselor, Indon.	B10	50
Tanjunguban, Indon.	C4	50
Tānk, Pak.	B3	54
Tankwa, stm., S. Afr.	H5	70
Tanna, i., Vanuatu	I17	79d
Tannenberg see Stębark, Pol.	C16	16
Tanner, Mount, mtn., B.C., Can.	G12	138
Tannu-Ola, hrebet, mts., Asia	D16	32
Tannūrah, Ra's, c., Sau. Ar.	D7	56
Tanon Strait, strt., Phil.	E4	52
Tanout, Niger	F6	64
Tanquinho, Braz.	G6	88
Tanshui, Tai.	I9	42
Tanta, Egypt	H2	58
Tan-Tan, Mor.	D2	64
Tantoyuca, Mex.	E9	100
Tanuku, India	C5	53
Tanvald, Czech Rep.	F11	16
Tanyang, Kor., S.	C1	40
Tanzania, ctry., Afr.	F6	66
Tao'er, stm., China	B5	38
Taohuazhen, China	A6	42
Taole, China	B2	42
Taonan, China	B5	38
Taongi, at., Marsh. Is.	B7	72
Taormina, Italy	G9	24
Taos, Mo., U.S.	F5	120
Taos, N.M., U.S.	E3	128
Taos Pueblo, N.M., U.S.	E3	128
Taoudenni, Mali	E4	64
Taounate, Mor.	C4	64
Taourirt, Mor.	C4	64
Taoyuan, China	G4	42
Taoyüan, Tai.	I9	42
Tapa, Est.	G11	8
Tapachula, Mex.	H12	100
Tapaga, Cape, c., Samoa	h12	79c
Tapah, Malay.	J5	48
Tapajós, stm., Braz.	D6	84
Tapaktuan, Indon.	K3	48
Tapalqué, Arg.	H7	92
Tapauá, stm., Braz.	E4	84
Tapejara, Braz.	D12	92
Taperoá, Braz.	D7	88
Tapes, Braz.	E12	92
Tapeta, Lib.	H3	64
Taphan Hin, Thai.	D5	48
Taphoen, stm., Thai.	E4	48
Tāpi, stm., India	H4	54
Ta Pi, stm., Thai.	H4	48
Tapiche, stm., Peru	E3	84
Tapini, Pap. N. Gui.	b4	79a
Taplan National Park, p.o.i., Thai.	E6	48
Tāplejungg, Nepal	E11	54
Tappen, N.D., U.S.	H14	124
Tapuae-o-Uenuku, mtn., N.Z.	E5	80
Tapuio, stm., Braz.	C3	88
Tapul Group, is., Phil.	H3	52
Tapun, Mya.	C2	48
Tapuruquara, Braz.	H9	86
Taqāṭu' Hayyā, Sudan	D7	62
Taquara, Braz.	D12	92
Taquaras, Ponta das, c., Braz.	C13	92
Taquari, stm., Braz.	D12	92
Taquari Novo, stm., Braz.	C5	90
Taquaritinga, Braz.	K1	88
Tar, stm., N.C., U.S.	I8	114
Tara, Austl.	F8	76
Tara, Russia	C12	32
Tara, stm., Eur.	G16	22
Tara, stm., Russia	C13	32
Taraba, stm., Nig.	H7	64
Tarabuco, Bol.	C3	90
Ṭarābulus (Tripoli), Leb.	D6	58
Ṭarābulus (Tripoli), Libya	A2	62
Ṭarābulus (Tripolitania), hist. reg., Libya	A2	62
Taraclia, Mol.	D15	26
Tarago, Austl.	J7	76
Taraira (Traíra), stm., S.A.	H7	86
Taraju, Indon.	G6	50
Tarakan, Indon.	B10	50
Tarakan, Pulau, i., Indon.	B10	50
Taralga, Austl.	J7	76
Tara Nacionalni Park, p.o.i., Yugo.	F6	26
Tārānagar, India	D5	54
Taranaki, Mount (Egmont, Mount), vol., N.Z.	D6	80
Tarancón, Spain	D8	20
Taranto, Italy	D11	24
Taranto, Golfo di, b., Italy	E10	24
Tarapoto, Peru	E2	84
Taraquá, Braz.	G7	86
Tarare, Fr.	D10	18
Tarariras, Ur.	G9	92
Tarāsa Dwīp, i., India	G7	46
Tarascon, Fr.	F10	18
Tarascon-sur-Ariège, Fr.	G7	18
Tarasovo, Russia	C19	32
Tarat, Alg.	D6	64
Tarata, Bol.	C3	90
Taratakbuluh, Indon.	C2	50
Tarauacá, stm., Braz.	E3	84
Taravao, Isthme de, isth., Fr. Poly.	v22	78h
Tarawa, at., Kir.	C8	72
Tarawera, N.Z.	D7	80
Tarazona, Spain	C9	20
Tarbagataj, hrebet, mts., Asia	E14	32
Tarbagatay Shan see Tarbagataj, hrebet, mts., Asia	E14	32
Tarbela Reservoir, res., Pak.	A4	54
Tarbert, Scot., U.K.	D6	12
Tarbes, Fr.	F6	18
Tarboro, N.C., U.S.	I8	114
Tarbū, Libya	B3	62
Tarcoola, Austl.	F6	74
Tardoki-Jani, gora, mtn., Russia	G16	34
Taree, Austl.	H9	76
Tareja, Russia	B7	34
Tärendö, Swe.	C10	8
Tarentum, Pa., U.S.	D6	114
Tarfa, Wadi el-, stm., Egypt	J2	58
Tarfaya, Mor.	D2	64
Targhee Pass, p., U.S.	F15	136
Tărgovište, Blg.	F13	26
Târgoviște, Rom.	E12	26
Târgu Bujor, Rom.	D14	26
Târgu Frumos, Rom.	B14	26
Târgu Jiu, Rom.	D10	26
Târgu Mureș, Rom.	C11	26
Târgu-Neamț, Rom.	B13	26
Târgu Ocna, Rom.	C13	26
Târgu Secuiesc, Rom.	D12	26
Tarifa, Spain	H5	20
Tarifa, Punta de, c., Spain	H5	20
Tarija, Bol.	D4	90
Tarikere, India	E2	53
Tarim, stm., China	F14	32
Tarim Pendi, bas., China	F12	30
Taritatu, stm., Indon.	F10	44
Tarkastad, S. Afr.	G8	70
Tarkio, Mo., U.S.	D2	120
Tarkio, stm., U.S.	D2	120
Tarko-Sale, Russia	B13	32
Tarkwa, Ghana	H4	64
Tarlac, Phil.	C3	52
Tarm, Den.	I3	8
Tarma, Peru	F2	84
Tarn, state, Fr.	F8	18
Tarn, stm., Fr.	F7	18
Tärnaby, Swe.	D6	8
Tarnak, stm., Afg.	B1	54
Târnava Mare, stm., Rom.	C11	26
Târnăveni, Rom.	C11	26
Tarn-et-Garonne, state, Fr.	F7	18
Tarnobrzeg, Pol.	F17	16
Tarnobrzeg, state, Pol.	F17	16
Tarnogród, Pol.	F18	16
Târnova, Mol.	A14	26
Tarnów, Pol.	G16	16
Tarnów, state, Pol.	G16	16
Tarnowskie Góry, Pol.	F14	16
Taro, Sol. Is.	d7	79b
Taro, stm., Italy	F7	22
Taron, Pap. N. Gui.	a5	79a
Tarong, Austl.	F8	76
Taroom, Austl.	E7	76
Taroudannt, Mor.	C3	64
Ta Roun, Co, mtn., Viet.	D8	48
Tarpon Springs, Fl., U.S.	H3	116
Tarquinia, Italy	H8	22
Tarra, stm., S.A.	C5	86
Tarrafal, C.V.	k10	65a
Tarragona, Spain	C12	20
Tarragona, co., Spain	D11	20
Tarraleah, Austl.	o13	77a
Tarrasa see Terrassa, Spain	C13	20
Tàrrega, Spain	C12	20
Tárrega see Tàrrega, Spain	C12	20
Tarsus, Tur.	B5	58
Tartagal, Arg.	D4	90
Tartu, Est.	G12	8
Ṭarṭūs, Syria	D6	58
Ṭarṭūs, state, Syria	D7	58
Tarum, stm., Indon.	G5	50
Tarumirim, Braz.	J5	88
Tarumizu, Japan	H3	40
Tarutao, Ko, i., Thai.	I4	48
Tarutao National Park, p.o.i., Thai.	I4	48
Tarutino, Russia	E19	10
Tarutung, Indon.	B1	50
Tarvisio, Italy	D10	22
Tarzan, Tx., U.S.	B6	130
Taşağıl, Tur.	B2	58
Tasāwah, Libya	B2	62
Tasbuget, Kaz.	F11	32
Taseeva, stm., Russia	C16	32
Taseevo, Russia	C17	32
Taseko Lakes, l., B.C., Can.	E7	138
Taseko Mountain, mtn., B.C., Can.	E7	138
Tāsgaon, India	C2	53
Tashi Gang Dzong, Bhu.	E13	54
Tashk, Daryācheh-ye, l., Iran	D7	56
Tasikmalaya, Indon.	G5	50
Tåsinge, i., Den.	B6	16
Taškent, Uzb.	F11	32
Taškepri, Turkmen.	B9	56
Taš-Kumyr, Kyrg.	F12	32
Tasman Basin, unds.	N18	142
Tasman Bay, b., N.Z.	E5	80
Tasmania, state, Austl.	n13	77a
Tasmania, i., Austl.	o13	77a
Tasman Peninsula, pen., Austl.	o13	77a
Tasman Sea, Oc.	G7	72
Tășnad, Rom.	B9	26
Tassialouc, Lac, l., Qc., Can.	D16	106
Taštagol, Russia	D15	32
Tastiota, Mex.	A3	100
Tata, Hung.	B5	26
Tata, Mor.	D3	64
Tatabánya, Hung.	B5	26
Tatarbunary, Ukr.	D16	26
Tatarija, state, Russia	C8	32
Tatarinka, Russia	E16	10
Tatarsk, Russia	C13	32
Tatarskij proliv, strt., Russia	G17	34
Tatarskoe-Maklakovo, Russia	I21	8
Tatarstan see Tatarija, state, Russia	C8	32
Tatar Strait see Tatarskij proliv, strt., Russia	G17	34
Tate, Ga., U.S.	B1	116
Tate, stm., Austl.	A4	76
Tateyama, Japan	E12	40
Tate-yama, vol., Japan	C10	40
Tathlina Lake, l., N.T., Can.	C7	106
Tatlayoko Lake, B.C., Can.	E6	138
Tatlayoko Lake, l., B.C., Can.	E6	138
Tatlow, Mount, mtn., B.C., Can.	E7	138
Tatnam, Cape, c., Mb., Can.	D12	106
Tatranský Narodný Park, p.o.i., Slov.	G15	16
Tatrzański Park Narodowy, p.o.i., Pol.	G15	16
Tatsuno, Japan	E7	40
Tatsuno, Japan	D10	40
Tatuí, Braz.	L1	88
Tatum, N.M., U.S.	H5	128
Tatum, Tx., U.S.	E4	122
Tat'ung see Datong, China	A5	42
Tatvan, Tur.	B5	56
Tau, Am. Sam.	h13	79c
Tau, Nor.	G1	8
Tau, i., Am. Sam.	h13	79c
Tauá, Braz.	C5	88
Taubaté, Braz.	L3	88
Tauberbischofsheim, Ger.	G5	16
Taučik, Kaz.	F8	32
Taujskaja guba, b., Russia	E18	34
Taumarunui, N.Z.	D6	80
Taumaturgo, Braz.	E3	84
Taum Sauk Mountain, mtn., Mo., U.S.	G7	120
Taungbon, Mya.	E3	48
Taungdwingyi, Mya.	B2	48
Taunggyi, Mya.	B3	48
Taungnyo Range, mts., Mya.	E3	48
Taungup, Mya.	C2	48
Taungup Pass, p., Mya.	C2	48
Taunsa, Pak.	C3	54
Taunton, Eng., U.K.	J9	12
Taunton, Ma., U.S.	C14	114
Taupo, N.Z.	D6	80
Taupo, Lake, l., N.Z.	D7	80
Tauragė, Lith.	E5	10
Tauranga, N.Z.	C7	80
Taurianova, Italy	F9	24
Taurisano, Italy	E12	24
Tauroa Point, c., N.Z.	B5	80
Taurus Mountains see Toros Dağları, mts., Tur.	A3	58
Tautira, Fr. Poly.	v23	78h
Tavan-Bogdo-Ula, gora, mtn., Asia	E15	32
Tavares, Braz.	D7	88
Tavas, Tur.	F12	28
Tavastehus see Hämeenlinna, Fin.	F10	8
Tavda, Russia	C11	32
Tavda, stm., Russia	C11	32
Tavernes de la Valldigna, Spain	E10	20
Tavernier, Fl., U.S.	K5	116
Taveuni, i., Fiji	p20	79e
Taviano, Italy	E11	24
Tavira, Port.	G3	20
Tavistock, On., Can.	E9	112
Tavistock, Eng., U.K.	K8	12
Tavolara, Isola, i., Italy	D3	24
Tavoliere, reg., Italy	C9	24
Tavolžan, Kaz.	D13	32
Tavor, Har, mtn., Isr.	F6	58
Tavoy Point, c., Mya.	F3	48
Tavşanlı, Tur.	D12	28
Tavua, Fiji	p18	79e
Tawaeli, Indon.	D11	50
Tawakoni, Lake, res., Tx., U.S.	E2	122
Tawas City, Mi., U.S.	D6	112
Tawau, Malay.	A10	50
Tawīla, Gezira, is., Egypt	K4	58
Tawitawi Group, is., Phil.	H3	52
Tawitawi Island, i., Phil.	H2	52
Ṭawkar, Sudan	D7	62
Taxco de Alarcón, Mex.	F8	100
Taxkorgan Tajik Zizhixian, China	B12	56
Tay, stm., Scot., U.K.	E9	12
Tay, Firth of, b., Scot., U.K.	E9	12
Tay, Loch, l., Scot., U.K.	E8	12
Tayabamba, Peru	E2	84
Tayabas Bay, b., Phil.	D3	52
Tayan, Indon.	C7	50
Taylor, Az., U.S.	I6	132
Taylor, Ne., U.S.	F13	126
Taylor, Tx., U.S.	D10	130
Taylor, Mount, mtn., N.M., U.S.	H9	132
Taylors, S.C., U.S.	B3	116
Taylorsville, Ky., U.S.	F12	120
Taylorsville, Ms., U.S.	F9	122
Taylorsville, N.C., U.S.	I4	114
Taylorville, Il., U.S.	E8	120
Taymā', Sau. Ar.	K9	58
Taymouth, N.B., Can.	D10	110
Taymyr Peninsula see Tajmyr, poluostrov, pen., Russia	B7	34
Tay Ninh, Viet.	G8	48
Taytay, Phil.	E2	52
Tayu, Indon.	G7	50
Taz, stm., Russia	A14	32
Taza, Mor.	C4	64
Tazewell, Tn., U.S.	H2	114
Tazewell, Va., U.S.	G4	114
Tazin, stm., Can.	C8	106
Tazin Lake, l., Sk., Can.	D9	106
Tazovskaja guba, b., Russia	A13	32
Tazovskij, Russia	A13	32
Tazovskij poluostrov, pen., Russia	C4	34
Tbessa, Alg.	B6	64
Tbilisi, Geor.	F6	32
Tchaourou, Benin	H5	64
Tchentlo Lake, l., B.C., Can.	A5	138
Tchesinkut Lake, l., B.C., Can.	B5	138
Tchibanga, Gabon	E2	66
Tcho-kiang see Zhejiang, state, China	G8	42
Tchollíré, Cam.	C2	66
Tchula, Ms., U.S.	D8	122
Tczew, Pol.	B14	16
Té, stm., Camb.	F8	48
Teá, stm., Braz.	H9	86
Teaca, Rom.	C11	26
Teaehoa, c., Fr. Poly.	s18	78g
Teague, Tx., U.S.	F2	122
Teahupoo, Fr. Poly.	w22	78h
Te Anau, Lake, l., N.Z.	G2	80
Teapa, Mex.	G12	100
Te Awamutu, N.Z.	C6	80
Teba, Spain	H5	20
Tebakang, Malay.	C7	50
Tebicuary, stm., Para.	C9	92
Tebicuary-mí, stm., Para.	C9	92
Tebingtinggi, Indon.	B1	50
Tebingtinggi, Indon.	E3	50
Tebingtinggi, Pulau, i., Indon.	C3	50
Tébourba, Tun.	H3	24
Téboursouk, Tun.	H3	24
Tecalitlán, Mex.	F7	100
Tecate, Mex.	K9	134
Techirghiol, Rom.	E15	26
Techlé, W. Sah.	E2	64
Techou see Dezhou, China	C7	42
Tecka, Arg.	H2	90
Tecka, stm., Arg.	H2	90
Tecomán, Mex.	F7	100
Tecopa, Ca., U.S.	H9	134
Tecpan de Galeana, Mex.	G8	100
Tecuala, Mex.	D6	100
Tecuci, Rom.	D14	26
Tecumseh, Ok., U.S.	B2	122
Tedžen, Turkmen.	B9	56
Tedžen (Harīrūd), stm., Asia	B9	56
Teec Nos Pos, Az., U.S.	G7	132
Teeli, Russia	D16	32
Tees, stm., Eng., U.K.	G11	12
Teeswater, On., Can.	D8	112
Tefé, Braz.	D5	84
Tefé, stm., Braz.	D4	84
Tefenni, Tur.	F12	28
Tegal, Indon.	G6	50
Tégama, reg., Niger	F6	64
Tegéa, hist., Grc.	F5	28
Tegineneng, Indon.	F4	50
Tegucigalpa, Hond.	E4	102
Tegul'det, Russia	C15	32
Tehachapi, Ca., U.S.	H7	134
Tehachapi Pass, p., Ca., U.S.	H7	134
Tehek Lake, l., Nu., Can.	C12	106
Tehrān (Teheran), Iran	B7	56
Tehrathum, Nepal	E11	54
Tehuacán, Mex.	F10	100
Tehuantepec, Golfo de, b., Mex.	H11	100
Tehuantepec, Gulf of see Tehuantepec, Golfo de, b., Mex.	H11	100
Tehuantepec, Isthmus of see Tehuantepec, Istmo de, isth., Mex.	G11	100
Tehuantepec, Istmo de, isth., Mex.	G11	100
Teignmouth, Eng., U.K.	K9	12
Teixeira, Braz.	D7	88
Teixeira Pinto, Gui.-B.	G1	64
Tejakula, Indon.	H9	50
Tejkovo, Russia	H19	8
Tejon Pass, p., Ca., U.S.	I7	134
Tejupilco de Hidalgo, Mex.	F8	100
Tekamah, Ne., U.S.	C1	120
Tekapo, Lake, l., N.Z.	F4	80
Tekax, Mex.	B3	102
Teke, Tur.	B12	28
Teke Burnu, c., Tur.	E9	28
Tekeli, Kaz.	F13	32
Tekezē (Satīt), stm., Afr.	E7	62
Tekirdağ, Tur.	C10	28
Tekirdağ, state, Tur.	B10	28
Tekkali, India	B7	53
Tekoa, Wa., U.S.	C9	136
Tekonsha, Mi., U.S.	B1	114
Te Kuiti, N.Z.	D6	80
Tel, stm., India	A6	53
Tela, Hond.	E4	102
Telaopengsha Shan, mtn., China	C11	54
Telavi, Geor.	F7	32
Tel Aviv-Jaffa see Tel Aviv-Yafo, Isr.	F5	58
Tel Aviv-Yafo, Isr.	F5	58
Telč, Czech Rep.	G11	16
Teleckoe, ozero, l., Russia	D15	32
Telefomin, Pap. N. Gui.	b3	79a
Telegraph Creek, B.C., Can.	D4	106
Telêmaco Borba, Braz.	B12	92
Telemark, state, Nor.	G3	8
Telembí, stm., Col.	G2	86
Telén, Arg.	H5	92
Telen, stm., Indon.	C10	50
Telenești, Mol.	B15	26
Teleno, mtn., Spain	B4	20
Teleorman, state, Rom.	E12	26
Teleorman, stm., Rom.	E12	26
Telescope Point, c., Gren.	q10	105e
Telese, Italy	C8	24
Telford, Eng., U.K.	I10	12
Télimélé, Gui.	G2	64
Telire, stm., C.R.	H6	102
Teljo, Jabal, mtn., Sudan	E5	62
Telkwa, B.C., Can.	B3	138
Tell Basta, hist., Egypt	H2	58
Tell City, In., U.S.	G11	120
Tell El-Amarna, hist., Egypt	K1	58
Tellel Rub, hist., Egypt	H2	58
Teller, Ak., U.S.	C6	140

Name | Map Ref. | Page

Tellicherry, India F2 53
Tellier, Arg. I3 90
Tello, Col. F4 86
Telluride, Co., U.S. F9 132
Tel Megiddo, hist., Isr. F6 58
Telmen nuur, l., Mong. B4 36
Teloloapan, Mex. F8 100
Telos see Tílos, i., Grc. G10 28
Telsen, Arg. H3 90
Telšiai, Lith. E5 10
Teltow, Ger. D9 16
Telukbayur, Indon. D2 50
Telukbayur, Indon. B10 50
Telukdalem, Indon. L3 48
Teluk Intan, Malay. K5 48
Tema, Ghana H5 64
Temagami, Lake, l., On., Can. A9 112
Temaju, Pulau, i., Indon. C6 50
Te Manga, mtn., Cook Is. a26 78j
Temangga, Indon. C7 50
Tematangi, at., Fr. Poly. F12 72
Temax, Mex. B3 102
Tembeling, stm., Malay. J6 48
Tembenči, stm., Russia A17 32
Tembesi, stm., Indon. D3 50
Tembilahan, Indon. D3 50
Temblador, Ven. C10 86
Temblor Range, mts., Ca., U.S. H6 134
Teme, stm., Eng., U.K. I10 12
Temecula, Ca., U.S. J8 134
Temelli, Tur. D15 28
Temengor, Tasik, res., Malay. J5 48
Temetiu, mtn., Fr. Poly. s18 78g
Temir, Kaz. E9 32
Temirtau, Kaz. D12 32
Témiscaming, Qc., Can. B10 112
Témiscamingue, Lac (Timiskaming, Lake), res., Can. B10 112
Témiscouata, Lac, l., Qc., Can. C7 110
Tëmkino, Russia E17 10
Temora, Austl. J6 76
Temosachic, Mex. A5 100
Tempe, Az., U.S. J5 132
Tempe, Danau, l., Indon. F12 50
Tempino, Indon. D3 50
Tempio Pausania, Italy D2 24
Temple, Tx., U.S. C10 130
Templi, Valle dei, hist., Italy G7 24
Templin, Ger. C9 16
Tempoal, stm., Mex. E9 100
Tempoal de Sánchez, Mex. E9 100
Tempy, Russia D20 10
Temuco, Chile G2 90
Temwen, i., Micron. m12 78d
Tena, Ec. H3 86
Tenabo, Mex. B2 102
Tenaha, Tx., U.S. F4 122
Tena Kourou, mtn., Burkina G4 64
Tenāli, India C5 53
Tenasserim, Mya. F4 48
Tendaho, Eth. E8 62
Tende, Col de, p., Eur. E13 18
Ten Degree Channel, strt., India G7 46
Tendō, Japan A13 40
Ténenkou, Mali G3 64
Ténéré, des., Niger F7 64
Ténès, Alg. H12 20
Ténès, Cap, c., Alg. H12 20
Teng, stm., Mya. B3 48
Tengah, Kepulauan, is., Indon. G10 50
Tengchong, China G4 36
Tenggara, Nusa (Lesser Sunda Islands), is., Indon. G6 44
Tenggara Celebes see Sulawesi Tenggara, state, Indon. E12 50
Tenggarong, Indon. D10 50
Tengger Shamo, des., China D5 36
Tenghilan, Malay. G1 52
Tengiz, ozero, l., Kaz. D11 32
Tengréla, C. Iv. G3 64
Tengtiao (Na), stm., Asia A6 48
Tengxian, China J4 42
Tengxian, China D7 42
Tenkāsi, India G3 53
Tenke, D.R.C. G5 66
Tenkeli, Russia B17 34
Tenkiller Ferry Lake, res., Ok., U.S. B4 122
Tenkodogo, Burkina G4 64
Tennant Creek, Austl. C6 74
Tennessee, state, U.S. D10 108
Tennessee, stm., U.S. A11 122
Tennille, Ga., U.S. D3 116
Teno, Chile G2 92
Teno (Tana), stm., Eur. B12 8
Tenom, Malay. A9 50
Tenos see Tínos, Grc. F8 28
Tenos see Tínos, i., Grc. F8 28
Tenosique, Mex. D2 102
Tenryū, Japan E10 40
Tenryū, stm., Japan E10 40
Tensas, stm., La., U.S. F7 122
Tensed, Id., U.S. C10 136
Ten Sleep, Wy., U.S. C5 126
Tenterfield, Austl. G8 76
Ten Thousand Islands, is., Fl., U.S. K4 116
Tentolomatinan, Gunung, mtn., Indon. E7 44
Teocaltiche, Mex. E7 100
Teodelina, Arg. G7 92
Teófilo Otoni, Braz. I5 88
Teo Lakes, l., Sk., Can. C4 124
Teotihuacán, hist., Mex. F9 100
Tepa, Indon. G8 44
Tepalcatepec, Mex. F7 100
Tepebaşı, Tur. B3 58
Tepehuanes, Mex. C6 100
Tepehuanes, stm., Mex. C6 100
Tepeji de Ocampo, Mex. E9 100
Tepelenë, Alb. D13 24
Tepic, Mex. E6 100
Teplice, Czech Rep. F9 16
Tepoca, Bahía de, b., Mex. F6 98
Tepoca, Punta, c., Mex. G6 98
Ter, stm., Spain B14 20
Téra, Niger G5 64
Tera, stm., Spain C4 20
Teradomari, Japan B11 40
Teraina, i., Kir. C11 72
Teramo, Italy H10 22
Terbuny, Russia H21 10
Terceira, i., Port. C3 60
Tercero, stm., Arg. F6 92
Terdal, India C2 53
Terek, stm., Russia G18 6
Terempa, Indon. B5 50
Terengganu, state, Malay. J6 48
Terengganu, stm., Malay. J6 48
Terenos, Braz. D6 90
Teresina, Braz. C4 88
Teresópolis, Braz. L4 88
Terespol, Pol. D19 16
Terevaka, Cerro, mtn., Chile e29 78l
Tergüün Bogd uul, mtn., Mong. C5 36
Teriang, stm., Malay. K6 48
Teriberka, Russia B16 8
Terihi, i., Fr. Poly. t19 78g
Terlingua, Tx., U.S. E4 130
Terlingua Creek, stm., Tx., U.S. E4 130
Termas del Arapey, Ur. E9 92
Termas de Río Hondo, Arg. C5 92
Termez, Uzb. B10 56
Termini Imerese, Italy G7 24
Termini Imerese, Golfo di, b., Italy F7 24
Terminillo, Monte, mtn., Italy H9 22
Términos, Laguna de, b., Mex. C2 102
Termoli, Italy H11 22
Termonde see Dendermonde, Bel. C12 14
Ternej, Russia B12 38
Terneuzen, Neth. C12 14
Terni, Italy H9 22
Ternitz, Aus. C12 22
Ternopil', Ukr. F14 6
Terpenija, mys, c., Russia G17 34
Terpenija, zaliv, b., Russia G17 34
Terra Alta, W.V., U.S. E6 114
Terra Bella, Ca., U.S. H6 134
Terrace, B.C., Can. B2 138
Terracina, Italy C7 24
Terra Cotta Army (Qinshihuang Mausoleum), hist., China D3 42
Terral, Ok., U.S. H11 128
Terralba, Italy E2 24
Terra Santa, Braz. D6 84
Terrassa, Spain C13 20
Terrebonne Bay, b., La., U.S. H8 122
Terre-de-Bas, Guad. i5 105c
Terre-de-Haut, Guad. i5 105c
Terre-de-Haut, i., Guad. i5 105c
Terre Haute, In., U.S. E10 120
Terrell, Tx., U.S. E2 122
Terre-Neuve see Newfoundland, state, Can. B17 110
Territoire du Yukon see Yukon, state, Can. B3 106
Territoires du Nord-Ouest see Northwest Territories, state, Can. B10 106
Terry, Ms., U.S. E8 122
Terry, Mt., U.S. A7 126
Terschelling, i., Neth. A14 14
Terskej-Alatau, hrebet, mts., Kyrg. F13 32
Teruel, Col. F4 86
Teruel, Spain D9 20
Teruel, co., Spain D10 20
Terujak, Indon. J3 48
Tervola, Fin. C11 8
Terzaghi Dam, dam, B.C., Can. F8 138
Tes, stm., Asia D16 32
Tescott, Ks., U.S. B11 128
Teseney, Erit. D7 62
Teshekpuk Lake, l., Ak., U.S. B9 140
Teshio, Japan B14 38
Teshio, stm., Japan B15 38
Teslin, Yk., Can. C4 106
Teslin, stm., Can. C4 106
Teslin Lake, l., Can. C4 106
Tësovo, Russia E17 10
Tësovo-Netyl'skij, Russia B13 10
Tësovskij, Russia B13 10
Tessalit, Mali E5 64
Tessaoua, Niger G6 64
Testa, Capo, c., Italy C3 24
Testour, Tun. H3 24
Tetachuck Lake, res., B.C., Can. C4 138
Tete, Moz. D5 68
Tête Jaune Cache, B.C., Can. D11 138
Tetepare Island, i., Sol. Is. e7 79b
Teterow, Ger. C8 16
Tetica, mtn., Spain G8 20
Teton, Id., U.S. G15 136
Teton, stm., Id., U.S. G15 136
Teton, stm., Mt., U.S. C15 136
Tetonia, Id., U.S. G15 136
Teton Range, mts., Wy., U.S. G16 136
Tetouan, Mor. B4 64
Tetovo, Mac. A4 28
Tetufera, Mont, mtn., Fr. Poly. v22 78h
Teuco, stm., Arg. D4 90
Teulada, Italy F2 24
Teulada, Capo, c., Italy F2 24
Teulon, Mb., Can. D16 124
Teutoburger Wald, hills, Ger. D4 16
Teuva, Fin. E9 8
Tevere (Tiber), stm., Italy H9 22
Teverya, Isr. F6 58
Te Waewae Bay, b., N.Z. H2 80
Tewah, Indon. D8 50
Tewantin-Noosa, Austl. F9 76
Tewkesbury, Eng., U.K. I11 12
Texada Island, i., B.C., Can. G6 138
Texana, Lake, res., Tx., U.S. F11 130
Texarkana, Ar., U.S. D4 122
Texarkana, Tx., U.S. D4 122
Texas, Austl. G8 76
Texas, state, U.S. E8 108
Texas City, Tx., U.S. H4 122
Texel, i., Neth. A13 14
Texhoma, Ok., U.S. E7 128
Texico, N.M., U.S. G5 128
Texoma, Lake, res., U.S. H11 128
Teyateyaneng, Leso. F8 70
Teywarah, Afg. C9 56
Teziutlán, Mex. F10 100
Tezpur, India E14 54
Tezzeron Lake, l., B.C., Can. B6 138
Tha, stm., Laos B5 48
Tha-anne, stm., Nu., Can. C11 106
Thabana-Ntlenyana, mtn., Leso. F9 70
Thabaung, Mya. D2 48
Thabazimbi, S. Afr. D8 70
Thabyu, Mya. E4 48
Thagyettaw, Mya. F3 48
Thai Binh, Viet. B8 48
Thailand, ctry., Asia E5 48
Thailand, Gulf of, b., Asia G5 48
Thai Nguyen, Viet. B7 48
Thak, Pak. B3 54
Thal, Pak. B3 54
Thala, Tun. I2 24
Thal Desert, des., Pak. C3 54
Thalfang, Ger. G2 16
Tha Li, Thai. D5 48
Thalia, Tx., U.S. H9 128
Thālith, Ash-Shallāl ath- (Third Cataract), wtfl, Sudan D6 62
Thalwil, Switz. C5 22
Thames, N.Z. C6 80
Thames, stm., On., Can. F8 112
Thames, stm., Eng., U.K. J13 12
Thames, Firth of, b., N.Z. C6 80
Thamesford, On., Can. E8 112
Thamesville, On., Can. F7 112
Thāna, India B1 53
Thandaung, Mya. C3 48
Thangoo, Austl. C4 74
Thangool, Austl. E8 76
Thanh Hoa, Viet. C7 48
Thanh Pho Ho Chi Minh (Saigon), Viet. G8 48
Thanjāvūr, India F4 53
Thann, Fr. B12 18
Thap Than, stm., Thai. E4 48
Tharabwin West, Mya. F4 48
Tharād, India F3 54
Thar Desert (Great Indian Desert), des., Asia D3 54
Thargomindah, Austl. F5 76
Tharrawaddy, Mya. D2 48
Tha Sala, Thai. H4 48
Thásos, Grc. C7 28
Thásos, i., Grc. C7 28
Thásos, hist., Grc. C7 28
Thaton, Mya. D3 48
Tha Tum, Thai. E6 48
Thau, Bassin de, l., Fr. F9 18
Thaungyin (Moei), stm., Asia D3 48
Thaya (Dyje), stm., Eur. H12 16
Thayawthadangyi Kyun, i., Mya. F3 48
Thayer, Ks., U.S. G2 120
Thayer, Mo., U.S. H6 120
Thayetchaung, Mya. F4 48
Thayetmyo, Mya. C2 48
Thazi, Mya. B3 48
Thebes see Thíva, Grc. E6 28
The Bottom, Neth. Ant. B1 105a
The Cheviot, mtn., Eng., U.K. F10 12
The Dalles, Or., U.S. E5 136
Thedford, Ne., U.S. E12 126
The Father see Ulawun, Mount, vol., Pap. N. Gui. b5 79a
The Fens, reg., Eng., U.K. I12 12
The Fishing Lakes, l., Sk., Can. D10 124
The Granites, hill, Austl. D6 74
The Hague see 's-Gravenhage, Neth. B12 14
The Heads, c., Or., U.S. H2 136
Theinkun, Mya. G4 48
The Lakes National Park, p.o.i., Austl. L6 76
The Little Minch, strt., Scot., U.K. D6 12
Thelon, stm., Can. C11 106
The Lynd, Austl. B5 76
The Minch, strt, Scot., U.K. D6 12
Thenia, Alg. H14 20
Theodore, Austl. E8 76
Theodore, Sk., Can. C10 124
Theodore, Al., U.S. G10 122
Theodore Roosevelt National Park North Unit, p.o.i., N.D., U.S. G10 124
Theodore Roosevelt National Park South Unit, p.o.i., N.D., U.S. G10 124
The Pas, Mb., Can. E10 106
Thepha, Thai. I5 48
The Pinnacle, hill, Mo., U.S. E6 120
The Rand see Witwatersrand, mts., S. Afr. D8 70
Theresa Creek, stm., Austl. D6 76
The Rhins, pen., Scot., U.K. G7 12
Thermaïkós Kólpos (Salonika, Gulf of), b., Grc. C6 28
Thermopolis, Wy., U.S. D4 126
Thermopylae see Thermopýles, hist., Grc. E5 28
Thermopýles (Thermopylae), hist., Grc. E5 28
The Rock, Austl. J6 76
The Rockies, mtn., Wa., U.S. D4 136
The Rope, clf, Pit. c28 78k
Thesiger Bay, b., N.T., Can. B15 140
The Slot see New Georgia Sound, strt., Sol. Is. e8 79b
Thessalía, state, Grc. D5 28
Thessalía, hist. reg., Grc. D5 28
Thessalon, On., Can. B6 112
Thessaloníki (Salonika), Grc. C6 28
Thessaly see Thessalía, hist. reg., Grc. D5 28
Thetford, Eng., U.K. I13 12
Thetford Mines, Qc., Can. D5 110
Theunissen, S. Afr. F8 70
The Valley, Anguilla A1 105a
The Village, Ok., U.S. F11 128
The Wash, b., Eng., U.K. I13 12
The Weald, reg., Eng., U.K. J13 12
Thibodaux, La., U.S. H8 122
Thief Lake, l., Mn., U.S. C3 118
Thief River Falls, Mn., U.S. C2 118
Thiene, Italy E8 22
Thiers, Fr. D9 18
Thiès, Sen. G1 64
Thika, Kenya E7 66
Thimphu, Bhu. E12 54
Thingvallavatn, l., Ice. k29 8a
Thingvellir, Ice. k29 8a
Thingvellir Nasjonalpark, p.o.i., Ice. k29 8a
Thio, N. Cal. m16 79d
Thionville, Fr. E15 14
Thíra, Grc. G8 28
Thíra (Santorini), i., Grc. G8 28
Third Cataract see Thālith, Ash-Shallāl ath-, wtfl, Sudan D6 62
Thiruvananthapuram see Trivandrum, India G3 53
Thiruvārūr, India F4 53
Thistilfjördur, b., Ice j32 8a
Thíva, Grc. E6 28
Thiviers, Fr. D6 18
Thjórsá, stm., Ice k30 8a
Thohoyandou, S. Afr. C10 70
Thoi Binh, Viet. H7 48
Thomas, Ok., U.S. F10 128
Thomas, W.V., U.S. E6 114
Thomaston, Al., U.S. E11 122
Thomaston, Ga., U.S. D1 116
Thomaston, Me., U.S. F7 110
Thomasville, Ga., U.S. F2 116
Thomasville, N.C., U.S. I5 114
Thompson, Mb., Can. D11 106
Thompson, Ia., U.S. H4 118
Thompson, N.D., U.S. D1 118
Thompson, stm., B.C., Can. F9 138
Thompson, stm., U.S. E4 120
Thompson Falls, Mt., U.S. C11 136
Thompson Peak, mtn., Ca., U.S. B3 134
Thomsen, stm., N.T., Can. B16 140
Thomson, Ga., U.S. C3 116
Thomson, Il., U.S. C7 120
Thomson, stm., Austl. E4 76
Thongwa, Mya. D3 48
Thonon-les-Bains, Fr. C12 18
Thonotosassa, Fl., U.S. H3 116
Thonze, Mya. D2 48
Thorhild, Ab., Can. B17 138
Thórisvatn, l., Ice. k30 8a
Thorlákshöfn, Ice. l29 8a
Thornaby-on-Tees, Eng., U.K. G11 12
Thornbury, On., Can. D9 112
Thorndale, Tx., U.S. D10 130
Thornton, Co., U.S. B4 128
Thornton, Tx., U.S. F2 122
Thorntonville, Tx., U.S. C4 130
Thorp, Wi., U.S. G8 118
Thorsby, Ab., Can. C16 138
Thorshavn see Tórshavn, Far. Is. n34 8b
Thórshöfn, Ice. j32 8a
Thouars, Fr. H8 14
Thoune see Thun, Switz. D4 22
Thousand Lake Mountain, mtn., Ut., U.S. E5 132
Thousand Oaks, Ca., U.S. I7 134
Thousand Ships Bay, b., Sol. Is. e8 79b
Thousand Springs Creek, stm., U.S. B2 132
Thrace, hist. reg., Eur. H13 26
Thrakikó Pélagos, Grc. C8 28
Three Forks, Mt., U.S. E15 136
Three Gorges Dam, dam, China F4 42
Three Hills, Ab., Can. E17 138
Three Hummock Island, i., Austl. n12 77a
Three Kings Islands, is., N.Z. B5 80
Three Mile Plains, N.S., Can. F12 110
Three Points, Cape, c., Ghana I4 64
Three Rivers, Mi., U.S. G4 112
Three Rivers, Tx., U.S. F9 130
Three Sisters, mtn., Or., U.S. F5 136
Three Sisters Islands, is., Sol. Is. f10 79b
Three Springs, Austl. E3 74
Thrissur see Trichūr, India F3 53
Throssel, Lake, l., Austl. E4 74
Thu, Cu Lao, i., Viet. G9 48
Thuan Chau, Viet. B6 48
Thu Dau Mot, Viet. G8 48
Thuin, Bel. D13 14
Thule (Qaanaaq), Grnld. B12 141
Thun, Switz. D4 22
Thun Chang, Thai. C5 48
Thunder Bay, On., Can. C9 118
Thunder Bay, b., On., Can. C9 118
Thunderbird, Lake, res., Ok., U.S. F11 128
Thunderbolt, Ga., U.S. D4 116
Thunder Butte Creek, stm., S.D., U.S. B10 126
Thunder Creek, stm., Sk., Can. D7 124
Thuner See, l., Switz. D4 22
Thung Salaeng Luang National Park, p.o.i., Thai. D5 48
Thung Wa, Thai. I4 48
Thüringen, state, Ger. F7 16
Thüringer Wald, mts., Ger. F6 16
Thuringia see Thüringen, state, Ger. F7 16
Thurles, Ire. I5 12
Thurmont, Md., U.S. E8 114
Thursday Island, Austl. B8 74
Thurso, Scot., U.K. C9 12
Thurston Island, i., Ant. C31 81
Thusis, Switz. D6 22
Thylungra, Austl. F4 76
Thyolo, Mwi. D5 68
Thysville see Mbanza-Ngungu, D.R.C. F3 66
Tiachiv, Ukr. A10 26
Tianchang, China E8 42
Tiandeng, China J2 42
Tiandong, China J2 42
Tian'e, China I2 42
Tiangang, China C7 38
Tianguá, Braz. B5 88
Tianjin (Tientsin), China B7 42
Tianjin, state, China B7 42
Tianjun, China D4 36
Tianlin, China I2 42
Tian Ling, mtn., China B8 38
Tianmen, China F5 42
Tianqiaoling, China C8 38
Tianshifu, China D6 38
Tianshui, China D1 42
Tiantai, China G9 42
Tiantang, China J4 42
Tianwangsi, China F8 42
Tianyang, China J2 42
Tianzhen, China A6 42
Tianzhu, China D5 36
Tianzhu, China H3 42
Tiarei, Fr. Poly. v22 78h
Tiaro, Austl. E9 76
Tiassalé, C. Iv. H4 64
Ti'avea, Samoa g12 79c
Tibagi, stm., Braz. A12 92
Tibal-og, Phil. G5 52
Tibasti, Sarīr, des., Libya C3 62
Tibati, Cam. C2 66
Tibbie, Al., U.S. F10 122
Tiber see Tevere, stm., Italy H9 22
Tiberias, Lake see Kinneret, Yam, l., Isr. F6 58
Tibesti, mts., Afr. C3 62
Tibet see Xizang, state, China B5 46
Tibet, Plateau of see Qing Zang Gaoyuan, plat., China B6 46
Tiblawan, Phil. G6 52
Tibnīn, Leb. E6 58
Tibooburra, Austl. G4 76
Tiburón, Cabo, c. C3 86
Tiburón, Isla, i., Mex. G6 98
Tiča, Jazovir, res., Blg. F13 26
Ticao Island, i., Phil. D4 52
Tîchît, Maur. F3 64
Ticino, stm., Eur. D14 18
Tickfaw, stm., U.S. G8 122
Ticonderoga, N.Y., U.S. G3 110
Ticul, Mex. B3 102
Tidioute, Pa., U.S. C6 114
Tidiquin, Jbel, mtn., Mor. C4 64
Tidjikja, Maur. F2 64
Tiébissou, C. Iv. H3 64
T'ienling see Tieling, China C5 38
Tiel, Neth. C14 14
Tieli, China B10 36
Tieling, China C5 38
Tielt, Bel. C12 14
Tiémé, C. Iv. H3 64
T'ienching see Tianjin, China B7 42
Tien Giang see Mekong, stm., Asia F9 46
Tien Shan, mts., Asia F13 32
T'ienshui see Tianshui, China D1 42
Tientsin see Tianjin, China B7 42
Tientsin see Tianjin, state, China B7 42
Tien Yen, Viet. B8 48
Tie Plant, Ms., U.S. D9 122
Tierp, Swe. F7 8
Tierra Amarilla, Chile C2 92
Tierra Blanca, Mex. F10 100
Tierra Blanca, Mex. G3 130
Tierra Blanca Creek, stm., U.S. G6 128
Tierra de Campos, reg., Spain C5 20
Tierra del Fuego, Arg. J3 90
Tierra del Fuego, i., S.A. J3 90
Tiétar, stm., Spain E5 20
Tietê, Braz. L2 88
Tietê, stm., Braz. D6 90
Tiéti, N. Cal. m15 79d
Tiffany Mountain, mtn., Wa., U.S. B7 136
Tiffin, Oh., U.S. C2 114
Tifton, Ga., U.S. E2 116
Tiga, Île, i., N. Cal. m16 79d
Tigalda Island, i., Ak., U.S. F7 140
Tigapuluh, Pegunungan, mts., Indon. D3 50
Tighina, Mol. C16 26
Tigil', Russia E20 34
Tignall, Ga., U.S. C3 116
Tignish, P.E., Can. D12 110
Tigoda, stm., Russia A14 10
Tigre, Col. F7 86
Tigre, stm., Peru D2 84
Tigre, stm., Ven. C10 86
Tigris (Dicle) (Dijlah), stm., Asia C5 56
Tiguentourine, Alg. D6 64
Tihany, hist., Hung. C4 26
Tihert, Alg. B5 64
Tihon, Russia G22 8
Tihookeanskij, Russia C10 38
Tihoreck, Russia E6 32
Tihua see Ürümqi, China C2 36
Tihuatlán, Mex. E10 100
Tihvin, Russia A16 10
Tijuana, Mex. K8 134
Tijuana, stm., N.A. K9 134
Tijucas, Braz. C13 92
Tijucas do Sul, Braz. B13 92
Tijuco, stm., Braz. J1 88
Tikal, hist., Guat. D3 102
Tikal, Parque Nacional, p.o.i., Guat. D3 102
Tikrīt, Iraq C5 56
Tikša, Russia D15 8
Tikšeozero, ozero, l., Russia C14 8
Tiksi, Russia B14 34
Tiladummati Atoll, at., Mald. h12 46a
Tilburg, Neth. C14 14
Tilbury, On., Can. F7 112
Tilcha, Austl. G3 76
Tilden, Il., U.S. F8 120
Tilden, Ne., U.S. E15 126
Tilden, Tx., U.S. F9 130
Tilhar, India D7 54
Tilimsen, Alg. C4 64
Tilin, Mya. B2 48
Tillabéri, Niger G5 64
Tilley, Ab., Can. F19 138
Tillia, Niger F5 64
Tillmans Corner, Al., U.S. G10 122
Tillson, N.Y., U.S. C11 114
Tillsonburg, On., Can. F9 112
Tílos, i., Grc. G10 28
Tilpa, Austl. H5 76
Tilton, N.H., U.S. G5 110
Tiltonsville, Oh., U.S. D5 114
Tima, Egypt L2 58
Timaná, Col. G3 86
Timanskij krjaž, hills, Russia B8 32
Timaru, N.Z. G4 80
Timbalier Bay, b., La., U.S. H8 122
Timbaúba, Braz. D8 88
Timbavati Game Reserve, S. Afr. D10 70
Timbedgha, Maur. F3 64
Timber Lake, S.D., U.S. B11 126
Timbiras, Braz. C4 88
Timbó, Braz. C13 92
Timbo, Lib. H3 64
Timbuktu see Tombouctou, Mali F4 64
Timétrine, Mali F4 64
Timétrine, mts., Mali F4 64
Timimoun, Alg. D5 64
Timirist, Râs, c., Maur. F1 64
Timirjazevo, Russia E4 10
Timiș, state, Rom. D8 26
Timiș (Tamiš), stm., Eur. D7 26
Timiskaming, Lake (Témiscamingue, Lac), res., Can. B10 112
Timișoara, Rom. D8 26
Timmendorfer Strand, Ger. B7 16
Timmins, On., Can. F14 106
Timmonsville, S.C., U.S. B6 116
Timms Hill, mtn., Wi., U.S. F8 118
Timna' see Mikhrot Timna', hist., Isr. I5 58
Timok, stm., Eur. E9 26
Timon, Braz. C4 88
Timor, i., Indon. G8 44
Timor Sea K15 142
Timošino, Russia H21 8
Timotes, Ven. C6 86
Timpanogos Cave National Monument, p.o.i., Ut., U.S. C5 132
Timpton, stm., Russia E14 34
Timšer, Russia B9 32
Tims Ford Lake, res., Tn., U.S. B12 122
Tina, stm., S. Afr. G9 70
Tîna, Khalîg el- (Pelusium Bay), b., Egypt G3 58
Tinaca Point, c., Phil. H5 52
Tinambung, Indon. E11 50
Tinapagee, Austl. G5 76
Tinaquillo, Ven. C7 86
Tindivanam, India E4 53
Tindouf, Alg. D3 64
Tineba, Pegunungan, mts., Indon. D12 50
Tineg, stm., Phil. B3 52
Ting, stm., China I7 42
Tinggi, Pulau, i., Malay. K7 48
Tingha, Austl. G8 76
Tinghert, Ḥamādat (Tinghert, Plateau du), plat., Afr. D7 64
Tinghert, Plateau du (Tinghert, Ḥamādat), plat., Afr. D6 64
Tinghsien see Dingxian, China B6 42
Tinglev, Den. B5 16
Tingo María, Peru E2 84
Tingri, China D11 54
Tingri see Dinggyê, China D11 54
Tinguiririca, Volcán, vol., Chile G2 92
Tinharé, Ilha de, i., Braz. G6 88
Tinh Bien, Viet. G7 48
Tinian, i., N. Mar. Is. B5 72
Tinjar, stm., Malay. B9 50
Tínos, Grc. F8 28
Tínos, i., Grc. F8 28
Tinsley, Ms., U.S. E8 122
Tinsukia, India C8 46
Tintagel, B.C., Can. B5 138
Tintina, Arg. C6 92
Tintinara, Austl. J3 76
Tio, Erit. E8 62
Tiobrad Árann see Tipperary, Ire. I4 12
Tioga, N.D., U.S. F11 124
Tiojala, Fin. F10 8
Tioman, Pulau, i., Malay. K7 48
Tionesta, Pa., U.S. C6 114
Tipasa, Alg. H13 20
Tipitapa, Nic. F4 102
Tippecanoe, stm., In., U.S. H3 112
Tipperary, Ire. I4 12
Tipperary, state, Ire. I5 12
Tipton, Ca., U.S. G6 134
Tipton, Ia., U.S. C6 120
Tipton, Mo., U.S. F5 120
Tipton, Ok., U.S. G9 128
Tipton, Mount, mtn., Az., U.S. H2 132
Tiptonville, Tn., U.S. H8 120
Tip Top Mountain, mtn., On., Can. F13 106
Tiptūr, India E3 53
Tiputini, stm., Ec. H4 86
Tīra, Isr. F5 58
Tīrān, i., Sau. Ar. K5 58
Tiran, Strait of, strt. K5 58
Tirana see Tiranë, Alb. C13 24
Tiranë, Alb. C13 24
Tirano, Italy D7 22
Tiraspol, Mol. C16 26
Tire, Tur. E10 28
Tiree, i., Scot., U.K. E6 12
Tirich Mīr, mtn., Pak. B11 56
Tirna, stm., India B3 53
Tírnavos, Grc. D5 28
Tirodi, India H7 54
Tirol, state, Aus. C8 22
Tiros, Braz. J3 88
Tirso, stm., Italy E2 24
Tīrthahalli, India E2 53
Tiruchchirāppalli, India F4 53
Tiruchengodu, India F3 53
Tirukkalukkunram, India E5 53
Tirukkovilūr, India F4 53
Tiruliai, Lith. E6 10
Tirunelveli, India G3 53
Tirupati, India E4 53
Tiruppattūr, India E4 53
Tiruppur, India F3 53
Tirūr, India F2 53
Tirutturaippūndi, India F4 53
Tiruvalla, India G3 53
Tiruvannāmalai, India E4 53
Tirūvottiyūr, India E5 53
Tiruvur, India C5 53
Tisa (Tisza) (Tysa), stm., Eur. D7 26
Tisaiyanvilai, India G3 53
Tisdale, Sk., Can. B9 124
Tishomingo, Ok., U.S. C2 122
Tisīyah, Syria F7 58
Tiskilwa, Il., U.S. C8 120
Tisovec, Slov. H15 16
Tīsta, stm., Asia F12 54
Tisza (Tisa) (Tysa), stm., Eur. C7 26
Tiszaföldvár, Hung. C7 26
Tiszaújváros, Hung. B7 26
Tiszavasvári, Hung. A8 26
Titaf, Alg. D4 64
Tit-Ary, Russia B14 34
Titicaca, Lake, l., S.A. G4 84
Titilāgarh, India H9 54
Titonka, Ia., U.S. H4 118
Titov Veles, Mac. B4 28
Titran, Nor. E2 8
Tittabawassee, stm., Mi., U.S. E5 112
Tittmoning, Ger. H8 16
Titule, D.R.C. D5 66
Titusville, Fl., U.S. H5 116
Titusville, Pa., U.S. C6 114
Tiuni, India C6 54
Tivaouane, Sen. F1 64
Tiverton, Eng., U.K. K9 12
Tivoli, Italy I9 22
Tivoli, Tx., U.S. F11 130
Tiyās, Syria D8 58
Tizimín, Mex. B3 102
Tizi-Ouzou, Alg. B5 64
Tizmant el-Zawâya, Egypt I1 58
Tiznados, stm., Ven. C8 86
Tiznit, Mor. D3 64
Tjörn, i., Swe. G4 8
Tjukalinsk, Russia C12 32
Tjul'gan, Russia D9 32
Tjumen', Russia C10 32
Tjung, stm., Russia D13 34
Tjuva-Guba, Russia B15 8
Tlacotalpan, Mex. F11 100
Tlacotepec, Mex. G9 100
Tlahualilo de Zaragoza, Mex. B7 100
Tlalnepantla, Mex. F9 100
Tlaltenango de Sánchez Román, Mex. E7 100
Tlapaneco, stm., Mex. G9 100
Tlaquepaque, Mex. E7 100
Tlaxcala, state, Mex. F9 100
Tlaxcala de Xicohténcatl, Mex. F9 100
Tłuszcz, Pol. D17 16
Tmassah, Libya B3 62
Tnâot, stm., Camb. G7 48
Toa Alta, P.R. B3 104a
Toa Baja, P.R. B3 104a
Toachi, stm., Ec. H2 86
Toahayana, Mex. B5 100
Toamasina, Madag. D8 68
Toba, Japan E9 40
Toba, Danau, l., Indon. K4 48
Tobago, i., Trin. r13 105f
Toba Inlet, b., B.C., Can. F6 138
Toba Kākar Range, mts., Pak. C10 56
Tobarra, Spain F9 20
Tobas, Arg. D6 92
Toba Tek Singh, Pak. C4 54
Tobejuba, Isla, i., Ven. C11 86
Tobermorey, Austl. D7 74
Tobermory, On., Can. C8 112
Tobermory, Scot., U.K. E6 12
Tobias, Ne., U.S. G15 126
Tobias Barreto, Braz. F6 88
Tobin, Mount, mtn., Nv., U.S. C8 134
Tobique, stm., N.B., Can. C9 110
Toboali, Indon. E5 50
Tobol, Kaz. D10 32
Tobol, stm., Asia C11 32
Toboli, Indon. D12 50
Tobol'sk, Russia C11 32
Toboso, Phil. E4 52
Tobruk see Ṭubruq, Libya A4 62
Tobseda, Russia B25 8
Tobyhanna, Pa., U.S. C10 114
Tobyš, stm., Russia C24 8
Tocantínia, Braz. E1 88
Tocantinópolis, Braz. D2 88
Tocantins, state, Braz. F8 84
Tocantins, stm., Braz. D8 84
Tocantins, stm., Braz. F1 88
Tocantinzinho, stm., Braz. H1 88
Tochcha Lake, l., B.C., Can. B5 138
Tochigi, Japan C12 40
Tochigi, state, Japan C12 40
Tochio, Japan B12 40
Toco, Trin. s13 105f
Tocoa, Hond. E5 102
Toconao, Chile D3 90
Tocopilla, Chile D2 90
Tocuco, stm., Ven. C5 86
Tocumwal, Austl. J5 76
Tocuyo, stm., Ven. B7 86
Tocuyo de la Costa, Ven. B7 86
Toda Rāisingh, India E5 54
Todi, Italy H9 22
Todos os Santos, Baia de, b., Braz. G6 88
Todos Santos, Bol. C3 90
Todos Santos, Mex. D3 100
Todos Santos, Bahía de, b., Mex. L8 134
Tofino, B.C., Can. G5 138
Toga, i., Vanuatu i16 79d
Togi, Japan B9 40
Togiak, Ak., U.S. E7 140
Togian, Kepulauan, is., Indon. F7 44
Togo, ctry., Afr. H5 64
Togtoh, China A4 42
Togučin, Russia C14 32
Togur, Russia C14 32
Togwotee Pass, p., Wy., U.S. G15 136
Tōhaku, Japan D6 40
Tohiea, Mont, mtn., Fr. Poly. v20 78h
Tohopekaliga, Lake, l., Fl., U.S. H4 116
Tohtamyš, Taj. B11 56
Toi-misaki, c., Japan H4 40
Toiyabe Range, mts., Nv., U.S. D8 134
Tōjō, Japan E6 40
Tojtepa, Uzb. F11 32
Tok, Ak., U.S. D11 140
Tokachi, stm., Japan C15 38
Tokachi-dake, vol., Japan C15 38
Tokaj, Hung. A8 26
Tōkamachi, Japan B11 40
Tokara-kaikyō, strt., Japan j19 39a
Tokara-rettō, is., Japan k19 39a
Tokat, Tur. A4 56
Tŏkchŏk-kundo, is., Kor., S. F6 38
Tokelau, dep., Oc. D9 72

Name	Map Ref.	Page
Tokko, Russia	D12	34
Tokma, Russia	C19	32
Tokmak, Kyrg.	F13	32
Tokoro, stm., Japan	C15	38
Tokoroa, N.Z.	D6	80
Tok-to, is., Asia	B4	40
Toktogul, Kyrg.	F12	32
Tokuno-shima, i., Japan	I19	39a
Tokur, Russia	F15	34
Tokushima, Japan	E7	40
Tokushima, state, Japan	F7	40
Tokuyama, Japan	E4	40
Tokwe, stm., Zimb.	B10	70
Tōkyō, Japan	D12	40
Tōkyō, state, Japan	D12	40
Tokyo Bay see Tōkyō-wan, b., Japan	D12	40
Tōkyō-daigaku-uchūkūkan-kenkyūsho, sci., Japan	H4	40
Tōkyō-wan, b., Japan	D12	40
Tôlañaro, Madag.	F8	68
Tolbo, Mong.	B3	36
Toledo, Braz.	B11	92
Toledo, Col.	D5	86
Toledo, Phil.	E4	52
Toledo, Spain	E6	20
Toledo, Il., U.S.	E9	120
Toledo, Oh., U.S.	C2	114
Toledo, Or., U.S.	F3	136
Toledo, co., Spain	E6	20
Toledo, Montes de, mts., Spain	E6	20
Toledo Bend Reservoir, res., U.S.	F4	122
Tolentino, Italy	G10	22
Toli, China	B1	36
Toliara, Madag.	E7	68
Tolima, state, Col.	E4	86
Tolima, Nevado del, vol., Col.	E4	86
Tolitoli, Indon.	C12	50
Toljatti, Russia	D7	32
Tol'ka, Russia	B14	32
Tolleson, Az., U.S.	J4	132
Tolloche, Arg.	B6	92
Tolmači, Russia	C18	10
Tolmezzo, Italy	D10	22
Tolmin, Slvn.	D10	22
Tolna, state, Hung.	C5	26
Tolo, Teluk, b., Indon.	F7	44
Tolosa, Spain	A8	20
Tolstoj, mys, c., Russia	E20	34
Tolti, Pak.	A6	54
Tolú, Col.	C4	86
Toluca, Il., U.S.	D8	120
Toluca, Nevado de, vol., Mex.	F9	100
Toluca de Lerdo, Mex.	F9	100
Tolybaj, Kaz.	D10	32
Tom', stm., Russia	C14	32
Tomah, Wi., U.S.	H8	118
Tomahawk, Wi., U.S.	F9	118
Tomakomai, Japan	C14	38
Tomanivi, mtn., Fiji	p19	79e
Tomar, Port.	E2	20
Tomari, Russia	G17	34
Tomás Gomensoro, Ur.	E9	92
Tomasine, stm., Qc., Can.	B13	112
Tomaszów Lubelski, Pol.	F19	16
Tomaszów Mazowiecki, Pol.	E15	16
Tombador, Serra do, plat., Braz.	F6	84
Tomball, Tx., U.S.	G3	122
Tombigbee, stm., U.S.	F10	122
Tombos, Braz.	K5	88
Tombouctou (Timbuktu), Mali	F4	64
Tombstone, Az., U.S.	L6	132
Tombstone Mountain, mtn., Yk., Can.	C3	106
Tombua, Ang.	D1	68
Tom Burke, S. Afr.	C9	70
Tomé, Chile	H1	92
Tomé-Açu, Braz.	B1	88
Tomelilla, Swe.	I5	8
Tomelloso, Spain	E8	20
Tomichi Creek, stm., Co., U.S.	C2	128
Tomini, Indon.	C12	50
Tomini, Teluk, b., Indon.	F7	44
Tomioka, Japan	C11	40
Tommot, Russia	E14	34
Tomo, stm., Col.	E7	86
Tompkins, Sk., Can.	D5	124
Tompkinsville, Ky., U.S.	H12	120
Tompo, Indon.	C12	50
Tom Price, Austl.	D3	74
Tomptokan, Russia	E15	34
Tomsk, Russia	C15	32
Toms River, N.J., U.S.	E11	114
Tonalá, Mex.	G12	100
Tonami, Japan	C9	40
Tonantins, Braz.	I7	86
Tonantins, stm., Braz.	I7	86
Tonasket, Wa., U.S.	B7	136
Tonawanda, N.Y., U.S.	B6	114
Tonbo, Mya.	C2	48
Tonbridge, Eng., U.K.	J13	12
Tondano, Indon.	E8	44
Tønder, Den.	B4	16
Tondi, India	G4	53
Tone, stm., Japan	D13	40
Tonekābon, Iran	B7	56
Tonga, ctry., Oc.	E9	72
Tongaat, S. Afr.	F10	70
Tong'an, China	I7	42
Tonganoxie, Ks., U.S.	E2	120
Tonga Ridge, unds.	K21	142
Tongariro National Park, p.o.i., N.Z.	D6	80
Tongatapu, state, Tonga	o14	78e
Tongatapu, i., Tonga	n13	78e
Tonga Trench, unds.	L21	142
Tongbai, China	E5	42
Tongbai Shan, mts., China	E5	42
Tongbei, China	B10	36
Tongcheng, China	F7	42
Tongchuan, China	D3	42
Tongde, China	D5	36
Tongeren, Bel.	D14	14
Tongguan, China	G5	42
Tongguan, China	D3	42
Tonghai, China	G5	36
Tonghe, China	B10	36
Tonghua, China	D6	38
Tongjiang, China	B11	36
Tongjiang, China	F2	42
Tongjosŏn-man, b., Kor., N.	E7	38
Tongliang, China	G1	42
Tongliao, China	C4	38
Tongling, China	F7	42
Tongling, China	J3	42
Tonglu, China	G8	42
Tongnae, Kor., S.	D2	40
Tongnan, China	F1	42
Tongo, Austl.	H4	76
Tongoa, i., Vanuatu	k17	79d
Tongoy, Chile	E2	92
Tongren, China	D5	36
Tongren, China	H3	42
Tongres see Tongeren, Bel.	D14	14
Tongsa Dzong, Bhu.	E13	54
Tongtian, stm., China	E4	36
Tongue, Scot., U.K.	C8	12
Tongue, stm., U.S.	A7	126
Tongue of the Ocean, unds.	C9	96
Tongwei, China	D1	42
Tongxian, China	B7	42
Tongxin, China	C1	42
Tongxu, China	D6	42
Tongyu, China	B5	38
Tongzi, China	G2	42
Tonj, Sudan	F5	62
Tonk, India	E5	54
Tonkawa, Ok., U.S.	E11	128
Tonkin see Bac Phan, hist. reg., Viet.	A7	48
Tonkin, Gulf of, b., Asia	C8	48
Tônlé Sab, Bœng, l., Camb.	F6	48
Tonle Sap see Tônlé Sab, Bœng, l., Camb.	F6	48
Tonneins, Fr.	E6	18
Tonopah, Nv., U.S.	E8	134
Tonoshō, Japan	E7	40
Tonosí, Pan.	D1	86
Tonotha, Bots.	B8	70
Tons, stm., India	F8	54
Tønsberg, Nor.	G4	8
Tonstad, Nor.	G2	8
Tonto Creek, stm., Az., U.S.	I5	132
Tonto National Monument, p.o.i., Az., U.S.	J5	132
Toodyay, Austl.	F3	74
Tooele, Ut., U.S.	C4	132
Toogoolawah, Austl.	F9	76
Toomsboro, Ga., U.S.	D2	116
Toora-Hem, Russia	D17	32
Toowoomba, Austl.	F8	76
Topeka, Ks., U.S.	E2	120
Top Hill, hill, Gren.	q11	105e
Topia, Mex.	C5	100
Topki, Russia	C15	32
Topko, gora, mtn., Russia	E16	34
Topley, B.C., Can.	B4	138
Toplița, Rom.	C12	26
Topocalma, Punta, c., Chile	G1	92
Topol'čany, Slov.	H14	16
Topolobampo, Mex.	C4	100
Topolovățu Mare, Rom.	D8	26
Toporok, Russia	B16	10
Topozero, ozero, l., Russia	D14	8
Toppenish, Wa., U.S.	D6	136
Topsa, Russia	E20	8
Top Springs, Austl.	C6	74
Tor, Eth.	F6	62
Torbalı, Tur.	E10	28
Torbat-e Ḩeydarīyeh, Iran	B8	56
Torbat-e Jām, Iran	B9	56
Torbrook, N.S., Can.	F12	110
Torch Lake, l., Mi., U.S.	C4	112
Tordesillas, Spain	C5	20
Töre, Swe.	C10	8
Torgau, Ger.	E8	16
Torhout, Bel.	C12	14
Toribulu, Indon.	D11	50
Torino (Turin), Italy	E4	22
Torit, Sudan	G6	62
Tormes, stm., Spain	C5	20
Torna, Russia	B20	8
Torna, mtn., India	B1	53
Torneälven (Tornionjoki), stm., Eur.	C10	8
Torneträsk, l., Swe.	B8	8
Torngat Mountains, mts., Can.	F13	141
Tornillo, Tx., U.S.	C1	130
Tornionjoki (Torneälven), stm., Eur.	C10	8
Tornquist, Arg.	I6	92
Toro, Spain	C5	20
Toro, mtn., Mex.	F6	100
Toro, Lago del, l., Chile	J2	90
Toro, Punta, c., Chile	F1	92
Törökszentmiklós, Hung.	B7	26
Torom, Russia	F16	34
Toronto, On., Can.	E10	112
Toronto, Ks., U.S.	G1	120
Toronto, S.D., U.S.	G2	118
Toropec, Russia	D14	10
Tororo, Ug.	D6	66
Toros Dağları (Taurus Mountains), mts., Tur.	A3	58
Torosozero, Russia	E18	8
Toroume, hill, Cook Is.	b26	78j
Torquay, Sk., Can.	E10	124
Torquay (Torbay), Eng., U.K.	K9	12
Torrance, Ca., U.S.	J7	134
Torrão, Port.	F2	20
Torreblanca, Spain	D11	20
Torre del Greco, Italy	D8	24
Torredonjimeno, Spain	G6	20
Torrejoncillo, Spain	E4	20
Torrejón de Ardoz, Spain	D7	20
Torrejón-Tiétar, Embalse de, res., Spain	E5	20
Torrelavega, Spain	A6	20
Torremolinos, Spain	H6	20
Torrens, Lake, l., Austl.	F7	74
Torrens Creek, Austl.	C5	76
Torrens Creek, stm., Austl.	D5	76
Torrent, Arg.	D9	92
Torrent, Spain	E10	20
Torrente see Torrent, Spain	E10	20
Torrenueva, Spain	F7	20
Torreón, Mex.	C7	100
Torre Pellice, Italy	F4	22
Torreperojil, Spain	F7	20
Torres, Braz.	D13	92
Torres, Îles, is., Vanuatu	i16	79d
Torres Islands see Torres, Îles, is., Vanuatu	i16	79d
Torres Strait, strt., Oc.	b3	79a
Torres Vedras, Port.	E1	20
Torrevella, Spain	G10	20
Torrevieja see Torrevella, Spain	G10	20
Torridon, Scot., U.K.	D7	12
Torrijos, Spain	D6	20
Torrington, Ct., U.S.	C12	114
Torrington, Wy., U.S.	E8	126
Torröjen, l., Swe.	E5	8
Torsa (Amo), stm., Asia	E12	54
Torsby, Swe.	F5	8
Tórshavn (Thorshavn), Far. Is.	n34	8b
Tortola, i., Br. Vir. Is.	e8	104b
Tórtolas, Cerro de las (Las Tórtolas, Cerro), mtn., S.A.	D2	92
Tortona, Italy	F5	22
Tortorici, Italy	F8	24
Tortosa, Spain	D11	20
Tortosa, Cap de, c., Spain	D11	20
Tortue, Île de la, i., Haiti	B11	102
Tortuga Island see Tortue, Île de la, i., Haiti	B11	102
Tortuguero, Laguna, b., P.R.	B2	104a
Toruń, Pol.	C14	16
Toruń, state, Pol.	C15	16
Torup, Swe.	H5	8
Toržok, Russia	C17	10
Torzym, Pol.	D11	16
Tosa, Japan	F6	40
Tosa-shimizu, Japan	G5	40
Tosa-wan, b., Japan	F6	40
Tosca, S. Afr.	D6	70
Toscana, state, Italy	G8	22
Toses, Collada de, p., Spain	B12	20
Tosno, Russia	A13	10
Toson Hu, l., China	D4	36
Tosontsengel, Mong.	B4	36
Tostado, Arg.	D7	92
Tõstamaa, Est.	G10	8
Tosu, Japan	F3	40
Totana, Spain	G9	20
Toteng, Bots.	B6	70
Totiyas, Som.	D8	66
Tot'ma, Russia	F20	8
Totness, Sur.	B6	84
Totoya, i., Fiji	q20	79e
Tottenham, Austl.	I6	76
Tottenham, On., Can.	D10	112
Tottori, Japan	D7	40
Tottori, state, Japan	D6	40
Touba, C. Iv.	H3	64
Toubkal, Jebel, mtn., Mor.	C3	64
Touchet, stm., Wa., U.S.	D8	136
Touchwood Lake, l., Ab., Can.	B19	138
Toudao, stm., China	C7	38
Touggourt, Alg.	C6	64
Touho, N. Cal.	m15	79d
Toul, Fr.	F14	14
Touliu, Tai.	J9	42
Toulon, Fr.	F11	18
Toulon-sur-Arroux, Fr.	H13	14
Toulouse, Fr.	F7	18
Toumodi, C. Iv.	H3	64
Tounassine, Hamada, des., Alg.	D3	64
Toungo, Nig.	H7	64
Toungoo, Mya.	C3	48
Touraine, hist. reg., Fr.	G9	14
Tourcoing, Fr.	D11	14
Touriñan, Cabo, c., Spain	A1	20
Tournai, Bel.	D12	14
Tournon, Fr.	D10	18
Tournus, Fr.	H13	14
Touros, Braz.	C8	88
Tours, Fr.	G9	14
Toussidé, Pic, vol., Chad	C3	62
Touws, stm., S. Afr.	H5	70
Toužim, Czech Rep.	F9	16
Tovar, Ven.	C6	86
Tovarkovskij, Russia	G21	10
Tovuz, Azer.	A6	56
Tow, Tx., U.S.	D9	130
Towada, Japan	D14	38
Towanda, Ks., U.S.	D12	128
Towanda, Pa., U.S.	C9	114
Tower, Mn., U.S.	D6	118
Tower City, Pa., U.S.	D9	114
Tower Hill, Austl.	D5	76
Tower Hill, Il., U.S.	E9	120
Towerhill Creek, stm., Austl.	C5	76
Towla, Mount, mtn., Zimb.	B9	70
Town and Country, Wa., U.S.	C9	136
Town Hill, hill, Ber.	k16	104e
Townsend, Mt., U.S.	D15	136
Townshend Island, i., Austl.	D8	76
Townsville, Austl.	B6	76
Towson, Md., U.S.	E9	114
Towuti, Danau, l., Indon.	F7	44
Toyah, Tx., U.S.	C4	130
Toyah Creek, stm., Tx., U.S.	D4	130
Toyama, Japan	C10	40
Toyama, state, Japan	C10	40
Toyama-wan, b., Japan	C10	40
Tōyo, Japan	F6	40
Tōyō, Japan	F7	40
Toyohashi, Japan	E10	40
Toyokawa, Japan	E10	40
Toyonaka, Japan	E8	40
Toyooka, Japan	D7	40
Toyosaka, Japan	B12	40
Toyota, Japan	D10	40
Toyoura, Japan	E3	40
Tozeur, Tun.	C6	64
Trabzon, Tur.	A4	56
Tracadie, N.B., Can.	C12	110
Tracy, Qc., Can.	E3	110
Tracy, Ca., U.S.	F4	134
Tracy City, Tn., U.S.	B13	122
Tradewater, stm., Ky., U.S.	G10	120
Traer, Ia., U.S.	B5	120
Trafalgar, Cabo, c., Spain	H4	20
Traíd, Spain	D9	20
Tráighlí see Tralee, Ire.	I3	12
Traiguén, Chile	I1	92
Trail, B.C., Can.	G13	138
Traill Ø, i., Grnld.	C21	141
Traipu, Braz.	E7	88
Traíra (Taraira), stm., S.A.	H7	86
Trairi, Braz.	B6	88
Trakai, Lith.	F7	10
Tralee, Ire.	I3	12
Trá Lí see Tralee, Ire.	I3	12
Trammel, Va., U.S.	G3	114
Tramperos Creek (Punta de Agua Creek), stm., U.S.	E5	128
Tramping Lake, l., Sk., Can.	B5	124
Tra My, Viet.	E9	48
Trăn, Blg.	G9	26
Tranås, Swe.	G6	8
Trancas, Arg.	C5	92
Tranco de Beas, Embalse de, res., Spain	F8	20
Trang, Thai.	I4	48
Trangan, Pulau, i., Indon.	G9	44
Trang Dinh, Viet.	A8	48
Trani, Italy	C10	24
Tran Ninh see Xiangkhoang, Plateau de, plat., Laos	C6	48
Tranqueras, Ur.	E9	92
Transantarctic Mountains, mts., Ant.	D30	81
Transkei, hist. reg., S. Afr.	G8	70
Transylvania, hist. reg., Rom.	C10	26
Transylvanian Alps see Carpații Meridionali, mts., Rom.	D11	26
Trapani, Italy	F6	24
Trapper Peak, mtn., Mt., U.S.	E12	136
Traralgon, Austl.	L6	76
Trârza, reg., Maur.	F1	64
Trasimeno, Lago, l., Italy	G9	22
Trás-os-Montes, hist. reg., Port.	C3	20
Trat, Thai.	F6	48
Traun, Aus.	B11	22
Traun, stm., Aus.	B11	22
Traunstein, Ger.	I8	16
Travellers Lake, l., Austl.	I4	76
Traverse, Lake, res., U.S.	F2	118
Traverse City, Mi., U.S.	D4	112
Tra Vinh, Viet.	H8	48
Travis, Lake, l., Tx., U.S.	D10	130
Travnik, Bos.	E4	26
Trayning, Austl.	F3	74
Trbovlje, Slvn.	D12	22
Třebíč, Czech Rep.	G11	16
Trebinje, Bos.	G5	26
Trebišov, Slov.	H17	16
Treblinka, Pol.	D18	16
Trece Martires, Phil.	C3	52
Tregosse Islets, is., Austl.	A8	76
Tregubovo, Russia	B14	10
Treinta y Tres, Ur.	F10	92
Trélazé, Fr.	G8	14
Trelew, Arg.	H3	90
Trelleborg, Swe.	I5	8
Tremadog Bay, b., Wales, U.K.	I8	12
Tremblant, Mont, mtn., Qc., Can.	D2	110
Trembleur Lake, l., B.C., Can.	B5	138
Tremiti, Isole, is., Italy	H12	22
Tremont, Il., U.S.	K9	118
Tremonton, Ut., U.S.	B4	132
Tremp, Spain	B11	20
Trempealeau, Wi., U.S.	G7	118
Trenche, stm., Qc., Can.	B4	110
Trenčín, Slov.	H14	16
Trenel, Arg.	G5	92
Trêng, Camb.	F6	48
Trenggalek, Indon.	H7	50
Trenque Lauquen, Arg.	G6	92
Trent, stm., On., Can.	D12	112
Trent, stm., Eng., U.K.	H12	12
Trente et Un Milles, Lac des, l., Qc., Can.	B13	112
Trentino-Alto Adige, state, Italy	D8	22
Trento (Trent), Italy	D7	22
Trenton, N.S., Can.	E14	110
Trenton, On., Can.	D12	112
Trenton, Fl., U.S.	G3	116
Trenton, Ga., U.S.	C13	122
Trenton, Mo., U.S.	D4	120
Trenton, Ne., U.S.	A8	128
Trenton, N.J., U.S.	D11	114
Trenton, N.C., U.S.	A8	116
Trentwood, Wa., U.S.	C9	136
Trepassey, Nf., Can.	j23	107a
Tres Algarrobos, Arg.	G6	92
Tres Arroyos, Arg.	I7	92
Três Corações, Braz.	K3	88
Três Coroas, Braz.	D12	92
Três de Maio, Braz.	C10	92
Tres Esquinas, Col.	G4	86
Três Lagoas, Braz.	D6	90
Tres Lagos, Arg.	I2	90
Tres Lomas, Arg.	H6	92
Três Marias, Braz.	J3	88
Tres Marías, Islas, is., Mex.	E5	100
Três Marias, Represa de, res., Braz.	J3	88
Tres Montes, Península, pen., Chile	I1	90
Tres Montosas, mtn., N.M., U.S.	I9	132
Tres Palos, Laguna, l., Mex.	G9	100
Três Passos, Braz.	C11	92
Tres Picos, Cerro, mtn., Arg.	I6	92
Três Pontas, Braz.	K3	88
Tres Puntas, Cabo, c., Arg.	I3	90
Três Rios, Braz.	L4	88
Tres Vírgenes, Volcán de las, vol., Mex.	B2	100
Tres Zapotes, hist., Mex.	F11	100
Tretten, Nor.	F4	8
Treuchtlingen, Ger.	H6	16
Treuenbrietzen, Ger.	D8	16
Treviglio, Italy	E6	22
Treviso, Italy	E9	22
Trevorton, Pa., U.S.	D9	114
Trgovište, Yugo.	G9	26
Triabunna, Austl.	o13	77a
Triberg, Ger.	H4	16
Tribugá, Ensenada de, b., Col.	E3	86
Tribune, Sk., Can.	E10	124
Tribune, Ks., U.S.	C7	128
Tricarico, Italy	D10	24
Tricase, Italy	E12	24
Trichonída, Límni, l., Grc.	E4	28
Trichūr, India	F3	53
Tri County Supply Canal, can., Ne., U.S.	G12	126
Trida, Austl.	I5	76
Trident Peak, mtn., Nv., U.S.	B7	134
Trier, Ger.	G2	16
Trieste (Trst), Italy	E10	22
Trieste, Gulf of, b., Eur.	E10	22
Triglav, mtn., Slvn.	D10	22
Triglavski narodni park, p.o.i., Slvn.	D10	22
Trigueros, Spain	G4	20
Tríkala, Grc.	D4	28
Trikora, Puncak, mtn., Indon.	F10	44
Trilby, Fl., U.S.	H3	116
Triman, Pak.	D2	54
Trincheras, Mex.	F7	98
Trincomalee, Sri L.	G5	53
Trindade, Braz.	I1	88
Trindade, i., Braz.	H12	82
Třinec, Czech Rep.	G14	16
Trinidad, Bol.	B3	90
Trinidad, Col.	E6	86
Trinidad, Cuba	B8	102
Trinidad, Co., U.S.	D4	128
Trinidad, Tx., U.S.	E2	122
Trinidad, Ur.	F9	92
Trinidad, i., Trin.	s13	105f
Trinidad, Isla, i., Arg.	I7	92
Trinidad and Tobago, ctry., N.A.	s13	105f
Trinity, Tx., U.S.	G3	122
Trinity, stm., Ca., U.S.	C2	134
Trinity, stm., Tx., U.S.	D13	130
Trinity, Elm Fork, stm., Tx., U.S.	H11	128
Trinity, South Fork, stm., Ca., U.S.	C2	134
Trinity, West Fork, stm., Tx., U.S.	H11	128
Trinity Bay, b., Nf., Can.	j23	107a
Trinity Bay, b., Tx., U.S.	H4	122
Trinity Islands, is., Ak., U.S.	E9	140
Trinity Peak, mtn., Nv., U.S.	C7	134
Trinity Site, hist., N.M., U.S.	H2	128
Trino, Italy	E5	22
Tripa, stm., Indon.	J3	48
Trípoli, Grc.	F5	28
Tripoli see Țarābulus, Leb.	D6	58
Tripoli see Țarābulus, Libya	A2	62
Tripoli, Ia., U.S.	I6	118
Tripolis, hist., Tur.	F12	28
Tripp, S.D., U.S.	D15	126
Tripura, state, India	G13	54
Tristan da Cunha Group, is., St. Hel.	J4	60
Tristao, Îles, is., Gui.	G2	64
Triste, Spain	B10	20
Triste, Golfo, b., Ven.	B7	86
Tri Ton, Viet.	G7	48
Triumph, La., U.S.	H9	122
Trivandrum, India	G3	53
Trnava, Slov.	H13	16
Trobriand Islands, is., Pap. N. Gui.	b5	79a
Trogir, Cro.	G13	22
Troia, Italy	C9	24
Troick, Russia	D10	32
Troickoe, Russia	D15	32
Troickoe, Russia	G16	34
Troicko-Pečorsk, Russia	B9	32
Troina, Italy	G8	24
Troisdorf, Ger.	F2	16
Trois-Pistoles, Qc., Can.	B7	110
Trois Pitons, Morne, vol., Dom.	j6	105c
Trois-Rivières, Qc., Can.	D4	110
Trois-Rivières, Guad.	i5	105c
Trojan, Blg.	G11	26
Trojanova Tabla, hist., Yugo.	E9	26
Trollhättan, Swe.	G5	8
Trombetas, stm., Braz.	C6	84
Troms, state, Nor.	B8	8
Tromsø, Nor.	B8	8
Trona, Ca., U.S.	H8	134
Tronador, Cerro, mtn., S.A.	H2	90
Trondheim, Nor.	E4	8
Trondheimsfjorden, b., Nor.	E4	8
Troödos, Cyp.	D3	58
Troodos Mountains, mts., Cyp.	D3	58
Troon, Scot., U.K.	F8	12
Trophy Mountain, vol., B.C., Can.	E11	138
Tropic, Ut., U.S.	F4	132
Tropojë, Alb.	B14	24
Troškūnai, Lith.	E7	10
Trosna, Russia	H18	10
Trotuș, stm., Rom.	C13	26
Troup, Tx., U.S.	E3	122
Trout, La., U.S.	F6	122
Trout, stm., N.T., Can.	C6	106
Trout Creek, Mi., U.S.	E9	118
Trout Creek Pass, p., Co., U.S.	C3	128
Trout Lake, l., N.T., Can.	C6	106
Trout Lake, l., On., Can.	E12	106
Troutville, Va., U.S.	G6	114
Trouville-sur-Mer, Fr.	E9	14
Trowbridge, Eng., U.K.	J10	12
Troy, Al., U.S.	F13	122
Troy, Id., U.S.	D10	136
Troy, Mo., U.S.	F7	120
Troy, N.H., U.S.	B13	114
Troy, N.Y., U.S.	B12	114
Troy, N.C., U.S.	A6	116
Troy, Oh., U.S.	D1	114
Troy, Pa., U.S.	C9	114
Troy, Tn., U.S.	H8	120
Troy, Tx., U.S.	C10	130
Troy see Truva, hist., Tur.	D9	28
Troyes, Fr.	F13	14
Troy Peak, mtn., Nv., U.S.	E1	132
Trst see Trieste, Italy	E10	22
Trstená, Slov.	G15	16
Truax, Sk., Can.	E8	124
Trubč'evsk, Russia	H16	10
Truchas, N.M., U.S.	E3	128
Truchas Peak, mtn., N.M., U.S.	E3	128
Trucial States see United Arab Emirates, ctry., Asia	E7	56
Truckee, Ca., U.S.	D5	134
Truckee, stm., U.S.	D6	134
Trud, Russia	C16	10
Trujillo, Col.	E3	86
Trujillo, Hond.	E4	102
Trujillo, Peru	E2	84
Trujillo, Spain	E5	20
Trujillo, Ven.	C6	86
Trujillo, state, Ven.	C6	86
Trujillo Alto, P.R.	B4	104a
Truk Islands see Chuuk, is., Micron.	C6	72
Truman, Mn., U.S.	H4	118
Trumann, Ar., U.S.	B8	122
Trumansburg, N.Y., U.S.	B9	114
Trumbull, Ct., U.S.	C12	114
Trumbull, Mount, mtn., Az., U.S.	G3	132
Trundle, Austl.	I6	76
Trung Phan (Annam), hist. reg., Viet.	D8	48
Truro, N.S., Can.	E13	110
Truro, Eng., U.K.	K7	12
Trusan, stm., Malay.	A9	50
Truscott, Tx., U.S.	H9	128
Trușeni, Mol.	B15	26
Truth or Consequences, N.M., U.S.	J9	132
Trutnov, Czech Rep.	F11	16
Truva (Troy), hist., Tur.	D9	28
Truxton Wash, stm., Az., U.S.	H3	132
Truyère, stm., Fr.	E8	18
Tryduby, Ukr.	A17	26
Tryon, Ne., U.S.	F12	126
Tryon, N.C., U.S.	A3	116
Trzcianka, Pol.	C12	16
Trzciel, Pol.	D11	16
Trzebiatów, Pol.	B11	16
Trzebinia, Pol.	F15	16
Trzebnica, Pol.	E13	16
Tsagaannuur, Mong.	E15	32
Tsaidam Basin see Qaidam Pendi, bas., China	D3	36
Tsala Apopka Lake, l., Fl., U.S.	H3	116
Tsamkong see Zhanjiang, China	K4	42
Ts'anghsien see Cangzhou, China	B7	42
T'sangwu see Wuzhou, China	J4	42
Tsaratanana, Madag.	D8	68
Tsaratanana, mts., Madag.	C8	68
Tsau, Bots.	E3	68
Tsavo, Kenya	E7	66
Tsaydaychuz Peak, mtn., B.C., Can.	C4	138
Tsebrykove, Ukr.	B17	26
Tses, Nmb.	D4	70
Tsetserleg, Mong.	B5	36
Tsévié, Togo	H5	64
Tshabong, Bots.	D6	70
Tshane, Bots.	D5	70
Tshela, D.R.C.	E2	66
Tshidilamolomo, S. Afr.	D7	70
Tshikapa, D.R.C.	F4	66
Tshofa, D.R.C.	F5	66
Tshuapa, stm., D.R.C.	E4	66
Tshumbe (Chiumbe), stm., Afr.	B3	68
Tsiafajavona, vol., Madag.	D8	68
Tsiigehtchic, N.T., Can.	B4	106
Tsimlyansk Reservoir see Cimljanskoe vodohranilišče, res., Russia	E6	32
Tsinan see Jinan, China	C7	42
Tsineng, S. Afr.	E6	70
Tsinghai see Qinghai, state, China	D4	36
Tsingkiang see Qingjiang, China	E8	42
Tsingtao see Qingdao, China	C9	42
Tsingyuan see Baoding, China	B6	42
Ts'in-hai see Qinghai, state, China	D4	36
Tsining see Jining, China	D7	42
Tsinling Shan see Qin Ling, mts., China	E3	42
Tsintsabis, Nmb.	D2	68
Tsiombe, Madag.	F8	68
Tsipa see Cipa, stm., Russia	F11	34
Tsiribihina, stm., Madag.	D7	68
Tsiroanomandidy, Madag.	D8	68
Tsitsihar see Qiqihar, China	B9	36
Tsna see Cna, stm., Russia	D6	32
Tsomo, stm., S. Afr.	H8	70
Tsomog, Mong.	B6	36
Tsu, Japan	E9	40
Tsubame, Japan	B11	40
Tsuchiura, Japan	C13	40
Tsugaru-kaikyō, strt., Japan	D14	38
Tsukumi, Japan	F4	40
Tsukushi-sanchi, mts., Japan	F3	40
Tsumeb, Nmb.	D2	68
Tsumkwe, Nmb.	D3	68
Tsuni see Zunyi, China	H2	42
Tsuruga, Japan	D9	40
Tsurugi-san, mtn., Japan	F7	40
Tsuruoka, Japan	A12	40
Tsushima, is., Japan	E2	40
Tsushima-kaikyō (Eastern Channel), strt., Japan	F2	40
Tsuyama, Japan	D7	40
Tswaane, Bots.	C6	70
Ttruchchendūr, India	G4	53
Tua, D.R.C.	E3	66
Tua, stm., Port.	C3	20
Tua, Tanjung, c., Indon.	F4	50
Tua Chua, Viet.	B6	48
Tual, Indon.	G9	44
Tuam, Ire.	H4	12
Tuamotu, Îles, is., Fr. Poly.	E12	72
Tuamotu Archipelago see Tuamotu, Îles, is., Fr. Poly.	E12	72
Tuamotu Ridge, unds.	K24	142
Tuanan, Indon.	E9	50
Tuangku, Pulau, i., Indon.	K3	48
Tuapse, Russia	F5	32
Tuasivi, Cape, c., Samoa	g11	79c
Tuba, Russia	C18	32
Tuba, stm., Russia	D16	32
Tubac, Az., U.S.	L5	132
Tuban, Indon.	G8	50
Tubarão, Braz.	D13	92
Ṭūbās, W.B.	F6	58
Tübingen, Ger.	H4	16
Ṭubruq, Libya	A4	62
Tubuai, i., Fr. Poly.	F12	72
Tucacas, Ven.	B7	86
Tucano, Braz.	F6	88
Tucheng, China	G2	42
Tuchów, Pol.	G17	16
Tuckerman, Ar., U.S.	B7	122
Tuckerton, N.J., U.S.	E11	114
Tučkovo, Russia	E19	10
Tucson, Az., U.S.	K5	132
Tucumán, state, Arg.	C5	92
Tucumcari, N.M., U.S.	F5	128
Tucunuco, Arg.	E3	92
Tucupido, Ven.	C9	86
Tucupita, Ven.	C11	86
Tucuruí, Braz.	D8	84
Tucuruí, Represa de, res., Braz.	D8	84
Tudela, Phil.	F4	52
Tudela, Spain	B9	20
Tudmur (Palmyra), Syria	D9	58
Tufānganj, India	E12	54
Tufi, Pap. N. Gui.	b4	79a
Tugela, stm., S. Afr.	F10	70
Tug Fork, stm., U.S.	G3	114
Tuggerah Lake, b., Austl.	I8	76
Tuguegarao City, Phil.	B3	52
Tugur, Russia	F16	34
Tuhai, stm., China	C7	42
Tuhuangba, China	F3	42
Tui, Spain	B2	20
Tuibo, China	C7	38
Tuira, stm., Pan.	D3	86
Tujmazy, Russia	D8	32
Tukangbesi, Kepulauan, is., Indon.	G7	44
Tukituki, stm., N.Z.	D7	80
Tukosméra, Mont, mtn., Vanuatu	I17	79d
Tūkrah, Libya	A4	62
Tuktoyaktuk, N.T., Can.	B4	106
Tukums, Lat.	D6	10
Tukuringra, hrebet, mts., Russia	F14	34
Tukuyu, Tan.	F6	66
Tula, Mex.	D9	100
Tula, Russia	F20	10
Tulach Mhór see Tullamore, Ire.	H5	12
Tulaghi, Sol. Is.	e8	79b
Tulancingo, Mex.	E9	100
Tulangbawang, stm., Indon.	F4	50
Tulare, Ca., U.S.	G6	134
Tulare, S.D., U.S.	C14	126
Tulare Lake Bed, reg., Ca., U.S.	G6	134
Tulare Lake Canal, can., Ca., U.S.	G6	134
Tularosa, N.M., U.S.	H2	128
Tularosa Valley, bas., N.M., U.S.	E9	98
Tulbagh, S. Afr.	H4	70
Tulcán, Ec.	G3	86
Tulcea, Rom.	D15	26
Tulcea, state, Rom.	D15	26
Tulelake, Ca., U.S.	B4	134
Tule Lake, l., Ca., U.S.	B4	134
Tulemalu Lake, l., Nu., Can.	C11	106
Tule Valley, val., Ut., U.S.	D3	132
Tuli, Zimb.	B9	70
Tuliszków, Pol.	D14	16
Tulita, N.T., Can.	C5	106
Ṭūlkarm, W.B.	F6	58
Tullahoma, Tn., U.S.	B12	122
Tullamore, Ire.	H5	12
Tulle, Fr.	D7	18
Tullibigeal, Austl.	I6	76
Tulln, Aus.	B13	22
Tullos, La., U.S.	F6	122
Tullus, Sudan	E4	62
Tully, Austl.	A5	76
Tulsa, Ok., U.S.	H2	120
Tulsequah, B.C., Can.	D4	106
Tul'skaja oblast', co., Russia	G20	10
Tuluá, Col.	E3	86
Tulum, Mex.	B4	102
Tulum, hist., Mex.	B4	102
Tulun, Russia	D18	32
Tulungagung, Indon.	H7	50
Tulungselapan, Indon.	E4	50
Tuma, stm., Nic.	F5	102
Tumacacori National Historical Park, p.o.i., Az., U.S.	L5	132
Tumaco, Col.	G2	86
Tumaco, Rada de, b., Col.	G2	86
Tuman-gang (Tumen), stm., Asia	C8	38
Tumanskij, Russia	D24	34
Tumany, Russia	D20	34
Tumbarumba, Austl.	J6	76
Tumbes, Peru	D1	84
Tumbes, Punta, c., Chile	H1	92
Tumbler Ridge, B.C., Can.	A10	138
Tumen, China	C8	38
Tumen (Tuman-gang), stm., Asia	C8	38
Tumeremo, Ven.	D11	86
Tumiritinga, Braz.	J5	88
Tumkūr, India	E3	53
Tumoteqi, China	A4	42
Tumpat, Malay.	I6	48
Tumsar, India	H7	54
Tumtum, Wa., U.S.	C9	136
Tumu, Ghana	G4	64
Tumuc-Humac Mountains, mts., S.A.	C6	84
Tumut, Austl.	J7	76
Tun, stm., Thai.	D4	48
Tunapuna, Trin.	s12	105f
Tunari, Cerro, mtn., Bol.	C3	90
Tunas de Zaza, Cuba	B8	102
Tunchang, China	L3	42
T'unch'i see Huangshan, China	G8	42
Tunduru, Tan.	G7	66
Tundža, stm., Eur.	G13	26
Tungabhadra, stm., India	D3	53
Tungabhadra Reservoir, res., India	D2	53
Tungaru, Sudan	E6	62
T'ungchou see Tongxian, China	B7	42
T'ungch'uan see Tongchuan, China	D3	42
Tung Hai see East China Sea, Asia	F9	36
T'unghsien see Tongxian, China	B7	42
T'unghua see Tonghua, China	D6	38
Tunghwa see Tonghua, China	D6	38
Tungkal, stm., Indon.	D3	50
Tungku, Malay.	A11	50
Tungla, Nic.	F5	102
T'ungliao see Tongliao, China	C4	38
Tungsha Tao (Pratas Island), i., Tai.	K7	42
Tungshih, Tai.	I9	42
Tungsten, N.T., Can.	C5	106
Tungurahua, state, Ec.	H2	86
Tungurahua, vol., Ec.	H2	86
Tuni, India	C6	53
Tunia, stm., Col.	G5	86
Tunis, Tun.	H4	24
Tunis, Golfe de, b., Tun.	G4	24
Tunis, Gulf of see Tunis, Golfe de, b., Tun.	G4	24
Tunisia, ctry., Afr.	C6	64
Tunisie see Tunisia, ctry., Afr.	C6	64

Name	Map Ref.	Page
Tunja, Col.	E5	86
Tunkhannock, Pa., U.S.	C9	114
Tunliu, China	C5	42
Tunnel Hill, Ga., U.S.	C13	122
Tunnelton, W.V., U.S.	E6	114
Tunnsjøen, l., Nor.	D5	8
Tuntum, Braz.	C3	88
Tunu see Østgrønland, state, Grnld.	C18	141
Tununak, Ak., U.S.	D6	140
Tunuyán, Arg.	F3	92
Tunuyán, stm., Arg.	F4	92
Tunxi, China	G8	42
Tuo, stm., China	G1	42
Tuo, stm., China	E7	42
Tuobalage, China	C12	54
Tuobuja, Russia	D13	34
Tuoj-Haja, Russia	B20	32
Tuokusidawan Ling, mtn., China	A6	46
Tuolumne, can., Ca., U.S.	F5	134
Tuong Duong, Viet.	C7	48
Tuotuo, stm., China	A13	54
Tupã, Braz.	D6	90
Tupaciguara, Braz.	J1	88
Tupanciretã, Braz.	D10	92
Tuparro, stm., Col.	E7	86
Tupelo, Ms., U.S.	C10	122
Tupelo, Ok., U.S.	C2	122
Tupik, Russia	F13	34
Tupinambarana, Ilha, i., Braz.	D6	84
Tupiraçaba, Braz.	H1	88
Tupiza, Bol.	D3	90
Tupper Lake, N.Y., U.S.	F2	110
Tupungato, Cerro, mtn., S.A.	F2	92
Tuquan, China	B9	36
Túquerres, Col.	G3	86
Tura, India	F13	54
Tura, Russia	B18	32
Tura, stm., Russia	C11	32
Turabah, Sau. Ar.	E5	56
Turaiyūr, India	F4	53
Turan, Russia	D16	32
Ṭurāq al-ʿIlab, hills, Syria	E9	58
Turau, Bela.	H10	10
Turbaco, Col.	B4	86
Turbat, Pak.	D9	56
Turbo, Col.	C3	86
Turčasovo, Russia	E18	8
Turda, Rom.	C10	26
Turek, Pol.	D14	16
Turfan see Turpan, China	C2	36
Turfan Depression see Turpan Pendi, depr., China	C2	36
Turgaj, Kaz.	E10	32
Turgaj, stm., Kaz.	E10	32
Turgajskaja ložbina, reg., Kaz.	D10	32
Turgajskoe plato, plat., Kaz.	D10	32
Turgay see Turgaj, stm., Kaz.	E10	32
Turginovo, Russia	D18	10
Turgoš, Russia	A18	10
Turgutlu, Tur.	E10	28
Türi, Est.	B8	10
Turia (Túria), stm., Spain	D9	20
Túria (Turia), stm., Spain	D9	20
Turiaçu, Braz.	A3	88
Turiaçu, stm., Braz.	B3	88
Turimiquire, Cerro, mtn., Ven.	B10	86
Turin, Ab., Can.	F18	138
Turin see Torino, Italy	E4	22
Turinsk, Russia	C10	32
Turka, Ukr.	G19	16
Turkana, Lake see Rudolf, Lake, l., Afr.	D7	66
Turkestan, Kaz.	F11	32
Turkestanskij hrebet, mts., Asia	B10	56
Túrkeve, Hung.	B7	26
Turkey, ctry., Asia	B3	56
Turkey, stm., Ia., U.S.	I7	118
Turkey Creek, stm., Ne., U.S.	K2	118
Turkish Republic of Northern Cyprus see Cyprus, North, ctry., Asia	C4	58
Turkmenbaši, Turkmen.	B7	56
Turkmenia see Turkmenistan, ctry., Asia	B8	56
Turkmenistan, ctry., Asia	B8	56
Türkoğlu, Tur.	A7	58
Turks and Caicos Islands, dep., N.A.	A12	102
Turks Island Passage, strt., T./C. Is.	B12	102
Turks Islands, is., T./C. Is.	B12	102
Turku (Åbo), Fin.	F9	8
Turku ja Pori, state, Fin.	F10	8
Turkwel, stm., Kenya	D7	66
Turley, Ok., U.S.	H2	120
Turlock, Ca., U.S.	F5	134
Turmalina, Braz.	I4	88
Turmantas, Lith.	E9	10
Turnagain, stm., B.C., Can.	D5	106
Turneffe Islands, is., Belize	D4	102
Turner, Mt., U.S.	F5	124
Turner, Or., U.S.	F4	136
Turners Falls, Ma., U.S.	B13	114
Turnhout, Bel.	C13	14
Turnov, Czech Rep.	F11	16
Turnu Măgurele, Rom.	F11	26
Turnu Roşu, Pasul, p., Rom.	D11	26
Turočak, Russia	D15	32
Turon, Ks., U.S.	D10	128
Turpan, China	C2	36
Turpan Pendi (Turfan Depression), depr., China	C2	36
Turquino, Pico, mtn., Cuba	C9	102
Turrell, Ar., U.S.	B8	122
Turret Peak, mtn., Az., U.S.	I5	132
Turtle, stm., Mb., Can.	D14	124
Turtle-Flambeau Flowage, res., Wi., U.S.	E8	118
Turtle Islands, is., S.L.	H2	64
Turtle Lake, N.D., U.S.	G13	124
Turtle Lake, Wi., U.S.	F6	118
Turu, stm., Russia	B18	32
Turuhan, stm., Russia	A14	32
Turuhansk, Russia	C6	34
Turvo, Braz.	D13	92
Turvo, stm., Braz.	K1	88
Turwi, stm., Zimb.	B10	70
Turzovka, Slov.	G14	16
Tuscaloosa, Al., U.S.	D11	122
Tuscaloosa, Lake, res., Al., U.S.	D11	122
Tuscany see Toscana, state, Italy	G8	22
Tuscarora Mountain, mts., Pa., U.S.	D8	114
Tuscola, Tx., U.S.	B8	130
Tuscumbia, Al., U.S.	C11	122
Tuscumbia, Mo., U.S.	F5	120
Tuskegee, Al., U.S.	E13	122
Tustumena Lake, l., Ak., U.S.	D9	140
Tutaev, Russia	C22	10
Tuticorin, India	G4	53
Tutin, Yugo.	F7	26
Tutóia, Braz.	B4	88
Tutoko, Mount, mtn., N.Z.	G3	80
Tutrakan, Blg.	E13	26
Tuttle, N.D., U.S.	G14	124
Tuttle Creek Lake, res., Ks., U.S.	B12	128
Tutuala, Indon.	G8	44
Tutuila, i., Am. Sam.	h12	79c
Tutupaca, Volcán, vol., Peru	G3	84
Tutwiler, Ms., U.S.	C8	122
Tutzing, Ger.	I7	16
Tuul, stm., Mong.	B6	36
Tuva, state, Russia	D16	32
Tuvalu, ctry., Oc.	D8	72
Tuvuca, i., Fiji	p20	79e
Ṭuwayq, Jabal, mts., Sau. Ar.	E6	56
Tuxford, Sk., Can.	D8	124
Tuxpan, Mex.	E6	100
Tuxpan de Rodríguez Cano, Mex.	E10	100
Tuxtepec, Mex.	F10	100
Tuxtla Gutiérrez, Mex.	G12	100
Túy see Tui, Spain	B2	20
Tuy, stm., Ven.	B8	86
Tuyen Hoa, Viet.	D8	48
Tuyen Quang, Viet.	B7	48
Tuy Hoa, Viet.	F9	48
Tuyün see Duyun, China	H2	42
Ṭuyūr, Burj aṭ-, hill, Sudan	C5	62
Tuz, Iraq	C5	56
Tuz Gölü, l., Tur.	B3	56
Tuzigoot National Monument, p.o.i., Az., U.S.	I4	132
Tuzla, Bos.	E5	26
Tuzly, Ukr.	D17	26
Tvardiţa, Mol.	C15	26
Tver' (Kalinin), Russia	D18	10
Tverca, stm., Russia	D18	10
Tverskaja oblast', co., Russia	D16	10
Tweed, On., Can.	D12	112
Tweed, stm., U.K.	F10	12
Tweed Heads, Austl.	G9	76
Twee Rivieren, S. Afr.	E5	70
Twelve Mile Lake, l., Sk., Can.	E7	124
Twenthekanaal, can., Neth.	B15	14
Twentynine Palms, Ca., U.S.	I9	134
Twin Buttes, mtn., Or., U.S.	F4	136
Twin Buttes Reservoir, res., Tx., U.S.	C7	130
Twin City, Ga., U.S.	D3	116
Twin Falls, Id., U.S.	H12	136
Twin Lakes, Ga., U.S.	F2	116
Twin Lakes, Wi., U.S.	B9	120
Twinsburg, Oh., U.S.	C4	114
Twisp, Wa., U.S.	B6	136
Twitchell Reservoir, res., Ca., U.S.	H5	134
Twitya, stm., N.T., Can.	C5	106
Two Butte Creek, stm., Co., U.S.	D6	128
Twofold Bay, b., Austl.	K7	76
Two Harbors, Mn., U.S.	D7	118
Two Medicine, stm., Mt., U.S.	B14	136
Two Rivers, Wi., U.S.	D2	112
Tybee Island, Ga., U.S.	D5	116
Tychy, Pol.	F14	16
Tyczyn, Pol.	G18	16
Tye, Tx., U.S.	B8	130
Tygda, Russia	F14	34
Tyler, Mn., U.S.	G2	118
Tyler, Tx., U.S.	E3	122
Tylertown, Ms., U.S.	F8	122
Tylihul, stm., Ukr.	B17	26
Tylihul's'kyi lyman, l., Ukr.	B17	26
Tym, stm., Russia	C14	32
Tymovskoe, Russia	F17	34
Tynda, Russia	E13	34
Tyndall, S.D., U.S.	D15	126
Tyndaris, hist., Italy	F8	24
Tynemouth, Eng., U.K.	F11	12
Tynset, Nor.	E4	8
Tyre see Ṣūr, Leb.	E6	58
Tyrifjorden, l., Nor.	F3	8
Tyrma, Russia	F15	34
Tyrma, stm., Russia	F15	34
Tyrone, Ok., U.S.	E7	128
Tyrrell, Lake, l., Austl.	J4	76
Tyrrhenian Sea, Eur.	G11	6
Tysa (Tisa) (Tisza), stm., Eur.	A10	26
Tysnesøya, i., Nor.	F1	8
Tysse, Nor.	F1	8
Tytuvėnai, Lith.	E6	10
Ty Ty, Ga., U.S.	E2	116
Tyva see Tuva, state, Russia	D16	32
Tzaneen, S. Afr.	C9	70
Tzekung see Zigong, China	F5	36
Tzeliutsing see Zigong, China	F5	36
Tzucacab, Mex.	B3	102
Tzukung see Zigong, China	F5	36
Tzupo see Boshan, China	C7	42
Tzupo see Zibo, China	C8	42

U

Name	Map Ref.	Page
Uatumã, stm., Braz.	D6	84
Uauá, Braz.	E6	88
Uaupés, Braz.	H8	86
Uaupés (Vaupés), stm., S.A.	G7	86
Uaxactún, hist., Guat.	D3	102
Ubá, Braz.	K4	88
Ubagan, stm., Kaz.	D10	32
Ubaidullaganj, India	G6	54
Ubaitaba, Braz.	H6	88
Ubajara, Parque Nacional de, p.o.i., Braz.	B5	88
Ubangi (Oubangui), stm., Afr.	E3	66
Ubatã, Braz.	H6	88
Ubaté, Col.	E5	86
Ubatuba, Braz.	L3	88
Ube, Japan	F4	40
Úbeda, Spain	F7	20
Uberaba, Braz.	J2	88
Uberlândia, Braz.	J1	88
Überlingen, Ger.	I5	16
Ubiña, Peña, mtn., Spain	B4	20
Ubl'a, Slov.	H18	16
Ubly, Mi., U.S.	E7	112
Ubombo, S. Afr.	E11	70
Ubon Ratchathani, Thai.	E7	48
Ubrique, Spain	H5	20
Ubundu, D.R.C.	E5	66
Učaly, Russia	D9	32
Učami, Russia	B17	32
Učaral, Kaz.	E14	32
Ucayali, stm., Peru	D3	84
Uchinoura, Japan	H4	40
Uchiura-wan, b., Japan	C14	38
Uchiza, Peru	E2	84
Uchoa, Braz.	K1	88
Uckermark, reg., Ger.	C9	16
Ucon, Id., U.S.	G15	136
Učur, stm., Russia	E15	34
Uda, stm., Russia	C17	32
Uda, stm., Russia	F15	34
Udagamandalam, India	F3	53
Udaipur, India	F4	54
Udalguri, India	E13	54
Udall, Ks., U.S.	D11	128
Udamalpet, India	F3	53
Udankudi, India	G4	53
Udaquiola, Arg.	H8	92
Udaypur, Nepal	E11	54
Uddevalla, Swe.	G4	8
Uddjaur, l., Swe.	D8	8
Udgīr, India	B3	53
Udhampur, India	B5	54
Udimskij, Russia	F21	8
Udine, Italy	D10	22
Udmurtia see Udmurtija, state, Russia	C8	32
Udmurtija, state, Russia	C8	32
Udokan, hrebet, mts., Russia	E12	34
Udomlja, Russia	C17	10
Udon Thani, Thai.	D6	48
Udskaja guba, b., Russia	F16	34
Udskoe, Russia	F15	34
Udupi, India	E2	53
Udža, Russia	B12	34
Ueckermünde, Ger.	C10	16
Ueda, Japan	C11	40
Uele, stm., D.R.C.	D4	66
Uelen, Russia	C26	34
Uel'kal', Russia	C25	34
Uelzen, Ger.	C6	16
Ueno, Japan	E9	40
Uere, stm., D.R.C.	D5	66
Uetersen, Ger.	C5	16
Ufa, Russia	D9	32
Ufa, stm., Russia	C9	32
Uffenheim, Ger.	G6	16
Ugab, stm., Nmb.	E2	68
Uganda, ctry., Afr.	D6	66
Ugărčin, Blg.	F11	26
Ugarit, hist., Syria	C6	58
Ugashik, Ak., U.S.	E8	140
Uglegorsk, Russia	G17	34
Uglekamensk, Russia	C10	38
Uglič, Russia	C21	10
Ugljan, Otok, i., Cro.	F12	22
Ugodiči, Russia	C22	10
Ugodskij Zavod, Russia	E19	10
Ugra, stm., Russia	F18	10
Uherské Hradiště, Czech Rep.	G13	16
Uherský Brod, Czech Rep.	H13	16
Uhlenhorst, Nmb.	C3	70
Uhra, stm., Russia	B22	10
Uhta, Russia	F18	8
Uhta, Russia	B8	32
Uíge, Ang.	B1	68
Uil, Kaz.	E8	32
Uinebona, stm., Ven.	E10	86
Uinta Mountains, mts., Ut., U.S.	C6	132
Uiraúna, Braz.	D6	83
Uisŏng, Kor., S.	C1	40
Uitenhage, S. Afr.	H7	70
Uithuizermeeden, Neth.	A15	14
Uj, stm., Asia	D10	32
Ujandina, stm., Russia	C17	34
Ujar, Russia	C16	32
Ujelang, at., Marsh. Is.	C7	72
Újfehértó, Hung.	B8	26
Ujhāni, India	D7	54
Uji, Japan	E8	40
Uji-guntō, is., Japan	H2	40
Ujiji, Tan.	E5	66
Ujjain, India	G5	54
Ujung, Indon.	G12	50
Ujunggenteng, Indon.	G5	50
Ujungkulon National Park, p.o.i., Indon.	G4	50
Ujungpandang (Makasar), Indon.	F11	50
Uk, Russia	C17	32
Uka, Russia	E21	34
Ukara Island, i., Tan.	E6	66
Ukerewe Island, i., Tan.	E6	66
Ukiah, Ca., U.S.	D2	134
Uki Ni Masi Island, i., Sol. Is.	f9	79b
Ukmergė, Lith.	E7	10
Ukraine, ctry., Eur.	F15	6
Ukui, Indon.	D3	50
Ukyr, Russia	G10	34
Ula, Bela.	E12	10
Ulaanbaatar, Mong.	B6	36
Ulaangom, Mong.	G7	34
Ulan, Austl.	I7	76
Ulan Bator see Ulaanbaatar, Mong.	B6	36
Ulan Buh Shamo, des., China	A2	42
Ulan-Burgasy, hrebet, mts., Russia	F10	34
Ulanów, Pol.	F18	16
Ulansuhai Nur, l., China	A3	42
Ulan-Ude, Russia	F10	34
Ulawa Island, i., Sol. Is.	e9	79b
Ulawun, Mount (The Father), vol., Pap. N. Gui.	b5	79a
Ulchin, Kor., S.	B2	40
Ulcinj, Yugo.	H6	26
Ulco, S. Afr.	F7	70
Uldz, stm., Asia	B8	36
Uleåborg see Oulu, Fin.	D11	8
Ulen, Mn., U.S.	D2	118
Ulety, Russia	F11	34
Ulëz, Alb.	C13	24
Ulhāsnagar, India	B1	53
Ul'ianovka, Ukr.	A17	26
Uliastay, Mong.	B4	36
Ulindi, stm., D.R.C.	E5	66
Ulja, Russia	E17	34
Uljanovo, Russia	G18	10
Uljanovsk, Russia	D7	32
Ul'kan, Russia	C19	32
Ulla, stm., Spain	B2	20
Ulladulla, Austl.	J8	76
Ullin, Il., U.S.	G8	120
Ullŭng-do, i., Kor., S.	B3	40
Ulm, Ger.	H5	16
Ulm, Mt., U.S.	C15	136
Ulmarra, Austl.	G9	76
Ulmeni, Rom.	D13	26
Ulónguè, Moz.	C5	68
Ulsan, Kor., S.	D2	40
Ulster, hist. reg., Eur.	G5	12
Ulster Canal, can., Eur.	G5	12
Ulu, Indon.	E8	44
Ulu, Russia	D14	34
Ulúa, stm., Hond.	E3	102
Ulubat Gölü, l., Tur.	C11	28
Uluborlu, Tur.	E13	28
Uluçınar, Tur.	B6	58
Uludağ, mtn., Tur.	C12	28
Uludağ Yarımdası Milli Parkı, p.o.i., Tur.	C12	28
Ulukışla, Tur.	A5	58
Ulul, i., Micron.	C5	72
Ulungur, stm., China	B2	36
Ulungur Hu, l., China	B2	36
Ulunhan, Russia	F11	34
Uluru (Ayers Rock), mtn., Austl.	E6	74
Ulutau, gory, mts., Kaz.	E11	32
Ulverston, Eng., U.K.	G9	12
Ulverstone, Austl.	n12	77a
Ulysses, Ks., U.S.	D7	128
Uma, China	F13	34
Umán, Mex.	B3	102
Umanak, Grnld.	C15	141
Umanak Fjord, b., Grnld.	C15	141
Umargãon, India	H4	54
Umaria, India	G8	54
Umarizal, Braz.	D7	88
Umarkot, Pak.	F2	54
Umatac, Guam	j9	78c
Umatilla, Fl., U.S.	H4	116
Umatilla, Or., U.S.	E7	136
Umatilla, stm., Or., U.S.	E7	136
Umatilla, Lake, res., U.S.	E4	136
Umba, Russia	C16	8
Umbertide, Italy	G9	22
Umboi Island, i., Pap. N. Gui.	b4	79a
Umbria, state, Italy	G9	22
Umbukul, Pap. N. Gui.	a4	79a
Umbuzero, ozero, l., Russia	C16	8
Umeå, Swe.	E9	8
Umeälven, stm., Swe.	D8	8
Umfolozi Game Reserve, S. Afr.	F10	70
Umfors, Swe.	C6	8
Umfreville Lake, res., On., Can.	A3	118
Umkomaas, S. Afr.	G10	70
Umm al-Arānib, Libya	B2	62
Umm al-Jimāl, Khirbat, hist., Jord.	F7	58
Umm al-Qaywayn, U.A.E.	D8	56
Umm as-Sa'd, hist., Syria	E7	58
Umm Bel, Sudan	E5	62
Umm Durmān (Omdurman), Sudan	D6	62
Umm el Fahm, Isr.	F6	58
Umm Lajj, Sau. Ar.	D4	56
Umm Mitmam, sand, Egypt	H3	58
Umm Omeiyid, Râs, mtn., Egypt	K3	58
Umm Ruwābah, Sudan	E6	62
Umm Sayyālah, Sudan	E6	62
Umnak Island, i., Ak., U.S.	g25	140a
Umpqua, stm., Or., U.S.	G3	136
Umpulo, Ang.	C2	68
'Umrān, Yemen	F5	56
Umraniye, Tur.	D14	28
Umred, India	H7	54
Umreth, India	G4	54
Umtata, S. Afr.	G9	70
Umuarama, Braz.	A11	92
Umzingwani, stm., Zimb.	B9	70
Umzinto, S. Afr.	G10	70
Una, Braz.	H6	88
Una, India	H3	54
Una, stm., Eur.	E13	22
Unac, stm., Bos.	E3	26
Unadilla, Ga., U.S.	D2	116
Unadilla, N.Y., U.S.	B10	114
Unaí, Braz.	I2	88
Unalakleet, Ak., U.S.	D7	140
Unalaska, Ak., U.S.	F6	140
Unalaska Island, i., Ak., U.S.	F6	140
Unare, stm., Ven.	C9	86
'Unayzah, Sau. Ar.	D5	56
Uncia, Bol.	C3	90
Uncompahgre Peak, mtn., Co., U.S.	E9	132
Uncompahgre Plateau, plat., Co., U.S.	E8	132
Unden, l., Swe.	G5	8
Underberg, S. Afr.	F9	70
Undva nina, c., Est.	B4	10
Uneča, Russia	H15	10
Uneiuxi, stm., Braz.	H9	86
Unga Island, i., Ak., U.S.	E7	140
Ungava, Péninsule d', pen., Qc., Can.	D16	106
Ungava Bay, b., Can.	D17	106
Ungava Peninsula see Ungava, Péninsule d', pen., Qc., Can.	D16	106
Ungch'ŏn, Kor., S.	D1	40
Unggi-ŭp, Kor., N.	C9	38
Ungheni, Mol.	B14	26
União, Braz.	C4	88
União dos Palmares, Braz.	E7	88
Unicoi, Tn., U.S.	H3	114
Uniejów, Pol.	D14	16
Unimak Island, i., Ak., U.S.	F7	140
Unimak Pass, strt., Ak., U.S.	F6	140
Unini, stm., Braz.	H11	86
Unión, Arg.	G5	92
Unión, Para.	B9	92
Union, Ia., U.S.	B4	120
Union, La., U.S.	G8	122
Union, N.J., U.S.	D11	114
Union, Or., U.S.	E9	136
Union, S.C., U.S.	B4	116
Union, Wa., U.S.	C3	136
Union, W.V., U.S.	G5	114
Union Bay, B.C., Can.	G6	138
Union City, Ga., U.S.	D14	122
Union City, Mi., U.S.	F4	112
Union City, Oh., U.S.	D1	114
Union City, Pa., U.S.	C6	114
Union City, Tn., U.S.	H8	120
Unión de Reyes, Cuba	A7	102
Unión de Tula, Mex.	E7	100
Union Flat Creek, stm., U.S.	D9	136
Union Grove, Wi., U.S.	F1	112
Union Island, i., St. Vin.	p10	105e
Union Point, Ga., U.S.	C2	116
Union Springs, Al., U.S.	E13	122
Uniontown, Al., U.S.	E11	122
Uniontown, Ky., U.S.	G10	120
Uniontown, Pa., U.S.	E6	114
Unionville, Mi., U.S.	E6	112
United, Pa., U.S.	D6	114
United Arab Emirates, ctry., Asia	E7	56
United Arab Republic see Egypt, ctry., Afr.	B5	62
United Kingdom, ctry., Eur.	D8	6
United States, ctry., N.A.	C10	102
Unity, Sk., Can.	B4	124
Universal City, Tx., U.S.	E9	130
University, Ms., U.S.	C9	122
University City, Mo., U.S.	F7	120
University Park, N.M., U.S.	K10	132
University Park, Tx., U.S.	E2	122
Unjha, India	G4	54
Unnão, India	E8	54
Uno, Canal Numero, can. Arg.	H9	92
Unquillo, Arg.	E5	92
Unst, i., Scot., U.K.	n19	12a
Unstrut, stm., Ger.	E7	16
Unža, stm., Russia	G21	8
Unzen-dake, vol., Japan	G3	40
Uong Bi, Viet.	B8	48
Uozu, Japan	C10	40
Upa, stm., Russia	G20	10
Upanema, Braz.	C7	88
Upata, Ven.	C10	86
Upemba, Lac, l., D.R.C.	F5	66
Upernavik, Grnld.	C14	141
Upía, stm., Col.	E5	86
Upington, S. Afr.	F5	70
Upland, Ne., U.S.	A10	128
Upleta, India	H3	54
Upolu, i., Samoa	h11	79c
Upolu Point, c., Hi., U.S.	C6	78a
Upper Arlington, Oh., U.S.	D2	114
Upper Arrow Lake, l., B.C., Can.	F13	138
Upper Austria see Oberösterreich, state, Aus.	B10	22
Upper Blackville, N.B., Can.	D10	110
Upper Darby, Pa., U.S.	E10	114
Upper Egypt see El-Saʿîd, hist. reg., Egypt	J2	58
Upper Fraser, B.C., Can.	B8	138
Upper Ganga Canal (Upper Ganges Canal), can., India	D6	54
Upper Iowa, stm., U.S.	H7	118
Upper Kapuas Mountains, mts., Asia	C8	50
Upper Klamath Lake, l., Or., U.S.	H5	136
Upper Lake, Ca., U.S.	D3	134
Upper Lake, l., Ca., U.S.	B5	134
Upper Manitou Lake, l., On., Can.	B5	118
Upper Musquodoboit, N.S., Can.	E14	110
Upper Red Lake, l., Mn., U.S.	C4	118
Upper Sandusky, Oh., U.S.	D2	114
Upper Takutu-Upper Essequibo, state, Guy.	F12	86
Upper Trajan's Wall, misc. cult., Mol.	C15	26
Upper Volta see Burkina Faso, ctry., Afr.	G4	64
Uppsala, Swe.	G7	8
Uppsala, state, Swe.	F7	8
Upshi, India	B6	54
Upton, Ky., U.S.	G12	120
Urabá, Golfo de, b., Col.	C3	86
Uracoa, Ven.	C10	86
Uraj, Russia	B10	32
Urakawa, Japan	C15	38
Ural, stm.	E8	32
Ural Mountains see Ural'skie gory, mts., Russia	C9	32
Ural'sk, Kaz.	D8	32
Ural'skie gory (Ural Mountains), mts., Russia	C9	32
Urana, Austl.	J6	76
Urandangi, Austl.	D7	74
Urangan, Austl.	E9	76
Urania, La., U.S.	F6	122
Uranium City, Sk., Can.	D9	106
Uraricaá, stm., Braz.	F10	86
Uraricoera, Braz.	F11	86
Uraricoera, stm., Braz.	F11	86
Ura-Tjube, Taj.	B10	56
Uravakonda, India	D3	53
Uravan, Co., U.S.	E8	132
Urawa, Japan	D12	40
Urbana, Ar., U.S.	D6	122
Urbana, Il., U.S.	D9	120
Urbana, Oh., U.S.	D2	114
Urbandale, Ia., U.S.	C4	120
Urbania, Italy	G9	22
Urbino, Italy	G9	22
Urcos, Peru	F3	84
Urdinarrain, Arg.	F8	92
Urdžar, Kaz.	E14	32
Ure, stm., Eng., U.K.	G11	12
Urèčča, Bela.	H10	10
Uren', Russia	H21	8
Ureña, Ven.	D5	86
Ures, Mex.	G7	98
Ureshino, Japan	F2	40
Urewera National Park, p.o.i., N.Z.	D7	80
Urgenč, Uzb.	F10	32
Urho Kekkosen kansallispuisto, p.o.i., Fin.	B12	8
Uriah, Al., U.S.	F11	122
Uriah, Mount, mtn., N.Z.	E4	80
Uribante, stm., Ven.	D6	86
Uribe, Col.	F4	86
Uribia, Col.	B5	86
Urich, Mo., U.S.	F4	120
Urickij, Kaz.	D11	32
Urique, stm., Mex.	B5	100
Urjung-Haja, Russia	B11	34
Urjupinsk, Russia	D6	32
Urla, Tur.	E9	28
Urlaţi, Rom.	D13	26
Urlings, Antig.	f4	105b
Urmia see Orūmīyeh, Iran	B6	56
Urmia, Lake see Orūmīyeh, Daryācheh-ye, l., Iran	B6	56
Uromi, Nig.	H6	64
Uroševac, Yugo.	G8	26
Urrao, Col.	D3	86
Ursa, Il., U.S.	D6	120
Uruaçu, Braz.	H1	88
Uruapan, Mex.	L9	134
Uruapan del Progreso, Mex.	F7	100
Urubamba, Peru	F3	84
Urubamba, stm., Peru	F3	84
Urubaxi, stm., Braz.	H9	86
Urubu, stm., Braz.	D6	84
Urubu, stm., Braz.	F1	88
Uruburetama, Braz.	B6	88
Urucará, Braz.	D6	84
Urucu, stm., Braz.	D5	84
Uruçuca, Braz.	H6	88
Uruçuí, Serra da, hills, Braz.	E3	88
Urucuia, stm., Braz.	I3	88
Uruçui-preto, stm., Braz.	E3	88
Uruguai (Uruguay), stm., S.A.	F8	92
Uruguaiana, Braz.	D9	92
Uruguay, ctry., S.A.	F10	92
Uruguay (Uruguai), stm., S.A.	F8	92
Urumchi see Ürümqi, China	C2	36
Ürümqi, China	C2	36
Urup, ostrov, i., Russia	G19	34
Urupês, Braz.	K1	88
Urutaí, Braz.	I1	88
Uruwira, Tan.	F6	66
Urziceni, Rom.	E13	26
Uržum, Russia	C7	32
Usa, Japan	F4	40
Usa, stm., Russia	A9	32
Uşak, Tur.	E12	28
Uşak, state, Tur.	E12	28
Ušaki, Russia	A13	10
Usakos, Nmb.	B2	70
Usborne, Mount, mtn., Falk. Is.	J5	90
Uščerpe, Russia	H14	10
U.S. Department of Energy Hanford Site, sci., Wa., U.S.	D7	136
Usedom, i., Eur.	B10	16
Ushant see Ouessant, Île d', i., Fr.	F3	14
Ushashi, Tan.	E6	66
Ushtobe see Uštobe, Kaz.	E13	32
Ushuaia, Arg.	J3	90
Usingen, Ger.	F4	16
Usinsk, Russia	A9	32
Usk, Wa., U.S.	B9	136
Usk, stm., Wales, U.K.	J9	12
Uslar, Ger.	E5	16
Usmas ezers, l., Lat.	C4	10
Usole, Russia	C9	32
Usole-Sibirskoe, Russia	D18	32
Uspallata, Arg.	F3	92
Uspanapa, stm., Mex.	G11	100
Ussuri (Wusuli), stm., Asia	C11	36
Ussurijsk, Russia	C10	38
Ust'-Barguzin, Russia	F10	34
Ust'-Belaja, Russia	C23	34
Ust'-Bolšereck, Russia	F20	34
Ust'-Čaun, Russia	C23	34
Ust'-Chorna, Ukr.	A10	26
Ust'-Cil'ma, Russia	D25	8
Uste, Russia	G18	8
Uster, Switz.	C5	22
Ustica, Isola di, i., Italy	F7	24
Ust'-Ilimsk, Russia	C18	32
Ust'-Ilimskoe vodohranilišče, res., Russia	C18	32
Ústí nad Labem, Czech Rep.	F10	16
Ústí nad Orlicí, Czech Rep.	G12	16
Ust'-Išim, Russia	C12	32
Ustja, stm., Russia	F21	8
Ust'-Javron'ga, Russia	E21	8
Ustjuckoe, Russia	B18	10
Ustjužna, Russia	B19	10
Ustka, Pol.	B12	16
Ust'-Kamčatsk, Russia	E21	34
Ust'-Kamenogorsk, Kaz.	E14	32
Ust'-Koksa, Russia	D15	32
Ust'-Kujda, Russia	B16	34
Ust'-Kulom, Russia	B8	32
Ust'-Kut, Russia	C19	32
Ust'-Lyža, Russia	A9	32
Ust'-Maja, Russia	D15	34
Ust'-Man'ja, Russia	B10	32
Ust'-Nera, Russia	D17	34
Ust'-Njukža, Russia	E13	34
Uštobe, Kaz.	E13	32
Ust'-Omčug, Russia	D18	34
Ust'-Ordynskij, Russia	D18	32
Ust'-Ozërnoe, Russia	C15	32
Ust'-Pinega, Russia	D19	8
Ust'-Reki, Russia	E22	8
Ustroń, Pol.	G14	16
Ust'-Sumy, Russia	D14	32
Ust'-Tym, Russia	D24	6
Ust'-Ulagan, Russia	D15	32
Ust'-Urgal, Russia	F15	34
Ust-Urt Plateau, plat., Asia	F9	32
Ust-Vyjskaja, Russia	E22	8
Usu, China	C1	36
Usuki, Japan	F4	40
Usulután, El Sal.	F3	102
Usumacinta, stm., N.A.	D2	102
Usumbura see Bujumbura, Bdi.	E5	66
Ušumun, Russia	F14	34
Usvjaty, Russia	E13	10
Utah, state, U.S.	D5	132
Utah Lake, l., Ut., U.S.	C5	132
Utata, Russia	D18	32
Ute, Ia., U.S.	B2	120
Ute Creek, stm., N.M., U.S.	F5	128
Utegi, Tan.	E6	66
Utena, Lith.	E8	10
Utete, Tan.	F7	66
Uthai Thani, Thai.	E4	48
Uthal, Pak.	D10	56
U Thong, Thai.	E4	48
Utiariti, Braz.	F6	84
Utica, Ks., U.S.	C8	128
Utica, Mi., U.S.	F6	112
Utica, Ms., U.S.	E8	122
Utica, N.Y., U.S.	E14	112
Utica, Oh., U.S.	D3	114
Utica see Utique, hist., Tun.	G3	24
Utiel, Spain	E9	20
Utila, Isla de, i., Hond.	D4	102
Utinga, stm., Braz.	G5	88
Utique (Utica), hist., Tun.	G3	24
Uto, Japan	G3	40
Utopia, Tx., U.S.	E8	130
Utorgoš, Russia	B13	10
Utraula, India	E9	54
Utrecht, Neth.	B14	14
Utrecht, S. Afr.	E10	70
Utrera, Spain	G5	20
Utrik, at., Marsh. Is.	B7	72
Utroja, stm., Eur.	D10	10
Utsunomiya, Japan	C12	40
Uttamapālaiyam, India	G3	53
Uttaradit, Thai.	D4	48
Uttarkāshi, India	C7	54
Uttar Pradesh, state, India	E7	54
Utuado, P.R.	B2	104a
Utukok, stm., Ak., U.S.	C7	140
Utupua, i., Sol. Is.	E7	72
Uulu, Est.	B7	10
Uusimaa, state, Fin.	F11	8
Uvá, stm., Col.	F7	86
Uvalda, Ga., U.S.	D3	116
Uvalde, Tx., U.S.	E8	130
Uvaravičy, Bela.	H13	10
Uvarovo, Russia	D6	32
Uvdal, Nor.	F3	8
Uvinza, Tan.	F6	66
Uvira, D.R.C.	E5	66
Uvs Lake see Uvsu-Nur, ozero, l., Asia	F7	34
Uvsu-Nur, ozero, l., Asia	F7	34
Uvworé, c., Vanuatu	I17	79d
Uwa, Japan	F5	40
Uwajima, Japan	F5	40
Uwayl, Sudan	F5	62
Uxbridge, On., Can.	D10	112
Uxmal, hist., Mex.	B3	102
Uyo, Nig.	H6	64
Uyuni, Bol.	D3	90
Uyuni, Salar de, pl., Bol.	D3	90
Uzbekistan, ctry., Asia	E10	30
Uzda, Bela.	G10	10
Uzerche, Fr.	D7	18
Uzgen, Kyrg.	F12	32
Uzhhorod, Ukr.	A9	26
Užice, Yugo.	F6	26
Uzlovaja, Russia	F20	10
Üzümlü, Tur.	G12	28
Uzun Ada, i., Tur.	E9	28
Uzunköprü, Tur.	B9	28
Uzunkuduk, Uzb.	F11	32
Užur, Russia	C16	32
Užventis, Lith.	E5	10

V

Name	Map Ref.	Page
Vaal, stm., S. Afr.	F7	70
Vaaldam, res., S. Afr.	E8	70
Vaalwater, S. Afr.	D8	70
Vaasa (Vasa), Fin.	E9	8
Vaasa, state, Fin.	E10	8
Vabalninkas, Lith.	D7	10
Vác, Hung.	B6	26
Vacacaí, stm., Braz.	E11	92
Vacaria, Braz.	D12	92
Vacaria, stm., Braz.	I4	88
Vacaville, Ca., U.S.	E4	134
Vaccarès, Étang de, l., Fr.	F10	18
Vache, Île à, i., Haiti	C11	102
Vad, Russia	I21	8
Vadakara see Badagara, India	F2	53
Vădeni, Rom.	D14	26
Vadnagar, India	G4	54
Vado, N.M., U.S.	K10	132
Vadodara (Baroda), India	G4	54
Vado Ligure, Italy	F5	22
Vadsø, Nor.	A13	8
Vaduz, Liech.	C6	22
Vaga, stm., Russia	F20	8
Vågåmo, Nor.	F3	8
Vágar, i., Far. Is.	m34	8b
Vaghena Island, i., Sol. Is.	d7	79b
Vah, stm., Russia	B13	32
Váh, stm., Slov.	H13	16
Vahsel, Cape, c., S. Geor.	J9	90
Vaiden, Ms., U.S.	D9	122
Vaigai, stm., India	G4	53
Vaigat, strt., Grnld.	C15	141
Vaijāpur, India	B2	53
Vaikam, India	G3	53
Väike-Maarja, Est.	A9	10
Vail, Co., U.S.	D10	132
Vail, Ia., U.S.	B2	120
Vaimali, Vanuatu	k17	79d
Vaippār, stm., India	G4	53
Vaison-la-Romaine, Fr.	E11	18
Vaitahu, Fr. Poly.	s18	78g
Vākhān, hist. reg., Afg.	B11	56
Valaam, Russia	F14	8
Valadeces, Mex.	H9	130
Valandovo, Mac.	B5	28
Valašské Meziříčí, Czech Rep.	G13	16
Valatie, N.Y., U.S.	B12	114
Vâlcea, state, Rom.	E11	26
Vălčedrăm, Blg.	F10	26
Valcheta, Arg.	H3	90
Valdagno, Italy	E8	22
Valdai Hills see Valdajskaja vozvyšennost', hills, Russia	C15	10
Valdaj, Russia	E16	8
Valdaj, Russia	B16	10
Valdajskaja vozvyšennost' (Valdai Hills), hills, Russia	C15	10
Valdarno, val., Italy	G8	22
Val-de-Cães, Braz.	A1	88
Valdecañas, Embalse de, res., Spain	E5	20
Valdemarsvik, Swe.	G7	8
Valdepeñas, Spain	F7	20
Valderaduey, stm., Spain	C5	20
Valdés, Península, pen., Arg.	H4	90
Val-des-Bois, Qc., Can.	C14	112
Valdez, Ak., U.S.	D10	140
Valdivia, Chile	G2	90

Name	Map Ref.	Page
Valdivia, Col.	D4	86
Valdobbiadene, Italy	E8	22
Val-d'Oise, state, Fr.	E10	14
Val-d'Or, Qc., Can.	F15	106
Valdosta, Ga., U.S.	F2	116
Valdoviño see Aviño, Spain	A2	20
Vale, Or., U.S.	G9	136
Valemount, B.C., Can.	D11	138
Valença, Braz.	L4	88
Valença, Braz.	G6	88
Valença, Port.	B2	20
Valença do Piauí, Braz.	D4	88
Valence, Fr.	E10	18
Valencia, Phil.	F5	52
València, Spain	E10	20
Valencia, Ven.	B7	86
València, state, Spain	E10	20
València, co., Spain	E10	20
Valencia, Golf de b., Spain	E10	20
Valencia, Golfo de see València, Golf de b., Spain	E10	20
Valencia, Gulf of see València, Golf de b., Spain	E10	20
Valencia, Lago de i., Ven.	B8	86
Valencia de Alcántara, Spain	E3	20
Valencia de Don Juan, Spain	B5	20
Valencia Island, i., Ire.	J2	12
Valenciennes, Fr.	D12	14
Valente, Braz.	F6	88
Valentin, Russia	C11	38
Valentine, Ne., U.S.	E12	126
Valentine, Tx., U.S.	D3	130
Valenza, Italy	F5	22
Valera, Ven.	C6	86
Valga, Est.	H12	8
Valiente, Peninsula, pen., Pan.	H7	102
Valili, mtn., Fiji	p19	79e
Valjevo, Yugo.	E6	26
Valkeakoski, Fin.	F11	8
Valkenswaard, Neth.	C14	14
Valkininkas, Lith.	F7	10
Valladares, Mex.	B7	130
Valladolid, Mex.	B13	102
Valladolid, Spain	C6	20
Valladolid, co., Spain	C6	20
Vall de Uxó see La Vall d'Uixó, Spain	E10	20
Valle, Lat.	D7	10
Vallecillo, Mex.	H7	130
Valle d'Aosta, state, Italy	E4	22
Valle de Allende, Mex.	H2	130
Valle de la Pascua, Ven.	C8	86
Valle del Cauca, state, Col.	F3	86
Valle del Rosario, Mex.	G1	130
Valle de Olivos, Mex.	B5	100
Valle de Santiago, Mex.	E8	100
Valledupar, Col.	B5	86
Vallée d'Aoste see Valle d'Aosta, state, Italy	E4	22
Valle Edén, Ur.	E9	92
Vallegrande, Bol.	C4	90
Valle Hermoso, Mex.	C10	100
Vallejo, Ca., U.S.	E3	134
Vallenar, Chile	B2	92
Valle Redondo, Mex.	K9	134
Valletta, Malta	I8	24
Valley, Al., U.S.	E13	122
Valley, Ne., U.S.	C1	120
Valley, Wa., U.S.	B9	136
Valley, stm., Mb., Can.	C13	124
Valley Bend, W.V., U.S.	F6	114
Valley City, N.D., U.S.	H16	124
Valley East, On., Can.	B8	112
Valley Falls, Ks., U.S.	E2	120
Valley Farms, Az., U.S.	K5	132
Valley Head, Al., U.S.	C13	122
Valley Mills, Tx., U.S.	C10	130
Valley of the Kings, hist., Egypt	B6	62
Valley Springs, S.D., U.S.	H2	118
Valley Station, Ky., U.S.	F12	120
Valleyview, Ab., Can.	A13	138
Valley View, Tx., U.S.	H11	128
Vallimanca, Arroyo, stm., Arg.	H7	92
Vallorbe, Switz.	D3	22
Valls, Spain	C12	20
Valmeyer, Il., U.S.	F7	120
Valmiera, Lat.	C8	10
Valoria la Buena, Spain	C6	20
Valožyn, Bela.	F9	10
Vālpārai, India	F3	53
Valparaíso, Chile	F2	92
Valparaíso, Mex.	D7	100
Valparaiso, Fl., U.S.	G12	122
Valparaiso, In., U.S.	G2	112
Valparaíso, Ne., U.S.	F16	126
Valparaíso, state, Chile	F2	92
Valréas, Fr.	E10	18
Vals, stm., S. Afr.	E8	70
Vals, Tanjung, c., Indon.	G10	44
Valsbaai see False Bay, b., S. Afr.	I4	70
Valtimo, Fin.	E13	8
Valujki, Russia	D5	32
Valverde del Camino, Spain	G4	20
Valyncy, Bela.	E11	10
Vamori Wash, stm., Az., U.S.	L5	132
Van, Tur.	B5	56
Van, Lake see Van Gölü, l., Tur.	B5	56
Vanadzor, Arm.	A5	56
Vanajavesi, l., Fin.	F10	8
Van Alstyne, Tx., U.S.	D2	122
Vananda, B.C., Can.	G8	138
Vanavara, Russia	B16	32
Van Bruyssel, Qc., Can.	C4	110
Van Buren, Ar., U.S.	B4	122
Van Buren, Me., U.S.	C8	110
Vanceboro, Me., U.S.	E9	110
Vanceburg, Ky., U.S.	F2	114
Vancouver, B.C., Can.	G8	138
Vancouver, Wa., U.S.	E4	136
Vancouver Island, i., B.C., Can.	G4	138
Vancouver Island Ranges, mts., B.C., Can.	G5	138
Vandalia, Il., U.S.	F8	120
Vandalia, Mo., U.S.	E6	120
Vandalia, Oh., U.S.	E1	114
Vandavāsi, India	E4	53
Vanderbijlpark, S. Afr.	E8	70
Vanderbilt, Tx., U.S.	F11	130
Vanderhoof, B.C., Can.	B6	138
Vanderkloof Dam, res., S. Afr.	F7	70
Vanderlin Island, i., Austl.	C7	74
Vandervoort, Ar., U.S.	C4	122
Van Diemen Gulf, b., Austl.	B6	74
Vandry, Qc., Can.	C3	110
Vandžiogala, Lith.	E6	10
Vanegas, Mex.	D8	100
Vänern, l., Swe.	G5	8
Vänersborg, Swe.	G5	8
Vangaindrano, Madag.	E8	68
Van Gölü, l., Tur.	B5	56
Vangunu Island, i., Sol. Is.	e8	79b
Van Horn, Tx., U.S.	C3	130
Van Horne, Ia., U.S.	B5	120
Vanier, On., Can.	C14	112
Vanikolo, i., Sol. Is.	E7	72
Vanimo, Pap. N. Gui.	a3	79a
Vanino, Russia	G17	34
Vānīvilāsa Sāgara, res., India	E3	53
Vāniyambādi, India	E4	53
Vankarem, Russia	C25	34
Vankleek Hill, On., Can.	E2	110
Van Lear, Ky., U.S.	G3	114
Vanna, i., Nor.	A8	8
Vännäs, Swe.	E8	8
Vanndale, Ar., U.S.	B8	122
Vannes, Fr.	G6	14
Van Ninh, Viet.	F9	48
Van Phong, Vung, b., Viet.	F9	48
Van Phong Bay see Van Phong, Vung, b., Viet.	F9	48
Van Reenen, S. Afr.	F9	70
Van Rees, Pegunungan, mts., Indon.	F10	44
Vanrhynsdorp, S. Afr.	G4	70
Vansant, Va., U.S.	G3	114
Vansittart Island, i., Nu., Can.	B14	106
Vanskoe, Russia	B19	10
Vanthali, India	H3	54
Vanua Balavu, i., Fiji	p20	79e
Vanua Lava, i., Vanuatu	i16	79d
Vanua Levu, i., Fiji	p19	79e
Vanuatu (New Hebrides), ctry., Oc.	k16	79d
Van Wert, Oh., U.S.	D1	114
Van Wyksdorp, S. Afr.	H5	70
Van Zylsrus, S. Afr.	E6	70
Vao, N. Cal.	n16	79d
Var, state, Fr.	F12	18
Var, stm., Fr.	F13	18
Varada, stm., India	D2	53
Varallo, Italy	E5	22
Vārānasi (Benares), India	F9	54
Varandej, Russia	A9	32
Varangerfjorden, b., Nor.	A14	8
Varangerhalvøya, pen., Nor.	A13	8
Varano, Lago di, l., Italy	C11	22
Varaždin, Cro.	D13	22
Varazze, Italy	F5	22
Varberg, Swe.	H5	8
Vardak, state, Afg.	A2	54
Vardar (Axiós), stm., Eur.	B5	28
Varel, Ger.	C4	16
Varela, Arg.	G4	92
Vārena, Lith.	F7	10
Varennes-sur-Allier, Fr.	C9	18
Varese, Italy	E5	22
Vărfurile, Rom.	C9	26
Vargem, Riacho da, stm., Braz.	E6	88
Vargem Grande, Braz.	B3	88
Varginha, Braz.	K3	88
Varkallai, India	G3	53
Varkaus, Fin.	E12	8
Värmeln, l., Swe.	G5	8
Värmland, state, Swe.	G5	8
Varna, Blg.	F14	26
Varna, Russia	D10	32
Varna, state, Blg.	F14	26
Värnamo, Swe.	H6	8
Varniai, Lith.	E5	10
Varnjany, Bela.	F9	10
Varnsdorf, Czech Rep.	F10	16
Varnville, S.C., U.S.	D4	116
Várpalota, Hung.	B5	26
Värska, Est.	C10	10
Varvarin, Yugo.	F8	26
Várzea Alegre, Braz.	D6	88
Várzea da Palma, Braz.	I3	88
Várzea Grande, Braz.	G6	84
Varzino, Russia	B17	8
Vas, state, Hung.	B3	26
Vasa see Vaasa, Fin.	E9	8
Vasai, India	E3	46
Vasalemma, Est.	A7	10
Vasco, País see Euskal Herriko, state, Spain	A8	20
Vashkivtsi, Ukr.	A12	26
Vashkivtsi, Ukr.	A14	26
Vashon Island, i., Wa., U.S.	C4	136
Vasilevichy, Bela.	H12	10
Vasil'evskij Moh, Russia	C18	10
Vasilikã, Grc.	C6	28
Vasjugan, stm., Russia	C13	32
Vaška, stm., Russia	D21	8
Vaskelovo, Russia	F14	8
Vaslui, Russia	C14	26
Vaslui, state, Rom.	C14	26
Vass, N.C., U.S.	A6	116
Vassar, Mi., U.S.	E6	112
Västerås, Swe.	G7	8
Västerbotten, state, Swe.	D8	8
Västernorrland, state, Swe.	E7	8
Västervik, Swe.	H7	8
Västmanland, state, Swe.	G7	8
Vasto, Italy	H11	22
Västra Götaland, state, Swe.	G5	8
Vasvár, Hung.	B3	26
Vatan, Fr.	G10	14
Vatican see Vatican City, ctry., Eur.	I9	22
Vatican City, ctry., Eur.	I9	22
Vaticano, Capo, c., Italy	F9	24
Vatnajökull, ice, Ice.	k31	8a
Vatomandry, Madag.	D8	68
Vatra Dornei, Rom.	B12	26
Vättern, l., Swe.	G6	8
Vatu-i-ra Channel, strt., Fiji	p19	79e
Vatukoula, Fiji	p18	79e
Vauclin, Montagne du, mtn., Mart.	k7	105c
Vaucluse, state, Fr.	F11	18
Vaucouleurs, Fr.	F14	14
Vaughan, On., Can.	E10	112
Vaughn, N.M., U.S.	G3	128
Vaukavysk, Bela.	G7	10
Vaupés, state, Col.	G6	86
Vaupés (Uaupés), stm., S.A.	G6	86
Vavaʻu, i., Tonga	79	64
Vavoua, C. Iv.	H3	64
Vavuniya, Sri L.	G5	53
Växjö, Swe.	H6	8
Vaza-barris, stm., Braz.	F6	88
Vazante, Braz.	J2	88
Vazuza, stm., Russia	E16	10
Vazuzskoe vodohranilišče, res., Russia	E16	10
Veazie, Me., U.S.	F8	110
Veblen, S.D., U.S.	B15	126
Vechta (Vechte), stm., Eur.	B15	14
Vechta, Ger.	A4	16
Vechte (Vecht), stm., Eur.	B15	14
Vecpiebalga, Lat.	C8	10
Vecsés, Hung.	B6	26
Veddige, Swe.	H4	8
Vedea, Arg.	G7	92
Vednoe, Russia	C19	10
Veedersburg, In., U.S.	H2	112
Veenendaal, Neth.	C14	14
Vega, i., Nor.	D4	8
Vega Alta, P.R.	B3	104a
Vega Baja, P.R.	B3	104a
Vegreville, Ab., Can.	C18	138
Veguita, N.M., U.S.	I10	132
Veinticinco de Mayo, Arg.	D7	84
Veiros, Braz.	D7	84
Vejen, Den.	I3	8
Veile, Lith.	E6	10
Vejer de la Frontera, Spain	H5	20
Vejle, Den.	I3	8
Vejle, state, Den.	H3	8
Vela Luka, Cro.	H13	22
Velardeña, Mex.	C7	100
Velas, Cabo, c., C.R.	G4	102
Velázquez, Ur.	G10	92
Velden, Ger.	H8	16
Vel'e, Russia	C17	10
Velebit, mts., Cro.	F11	22
Veleka, stm., Blg.	G14	26
Velenje, Slvn.	D11	22
Veles, Mac.	B4	28
Velešina, Bela.	F11	10
Vélez, Col.	D5	86
Vélez-Málaga, Spain	H6	20
Vel'gija, Russia	B17	10
Velhas, stm., Braz.	I3	88
Velikaja, stm., Russia	C11	10
Velikaja, stm., Russia	D23	34
Velikaja Kema, Russia	B12	38
Velika Morava, stm., Yugo.	E8	26
Velikie Luki, Russia	D13	10
Velikij Ustjug, Russia	F21	8
Velikij Vitorog, mtn., Bos.	E4	26
Velikoe, Russia	G17	8
Velikoe, ozero, l., Russia	C19	10
Velikovisočnoe, Russia	C25	8
Veliko Tărnovo, Blg.	F12	26
Veli Lošinj, Cro.	F11	22
Vélingara, Sen.	G2	64
Veliž, Russia	E14	10
Vel'ké Kapušany, Slov.	H18	16
Velké Meziříčí, Czech Rep.	G12	16
Vella Gulf, strt., Sol. Is.	d7	79b
Vella Lavella, i., Sol. Is.	d7	79b
Vellār, stm., India	F4	53
Velletri, Italy	I9	22
Vellore, India	E4	53
Velma, Ok., U.S.	G11	128
Vel'sk, Russia	F20	8
Velten, Ger.	D9	16
Velva, N.D., U.S.	F13	124
Velyka Mykhailivka, Ukr.	B16	26
Velykodolyns'ke, Ukr.	C17	26
Velykoplos'ke, Ukr.	C16	26
Velykyi Bychkiv, Ukr.	B11	26
Velykyi Kuialnyk, stm., Ukr.	B17	26
Venadillo, Col.	E4	86
Venado Tuerto, Arg.	F6	92
Venafro, Italy	C8	24
Venâncio Aires, Braz.	D11	92
Vence, Fr.	F13	18
Venda, hist. reg., S. Afr.	C10	70
Vendas Novas, Port.	F2	20
Vendée, state, Fr.	C4	18
Vendéen, Bocage, reg., Fr.	C4	18
Vendôme, Fr.	G10	14
Vendrell see El Vendrell, Spain	C12	20
Veneta, Laguna, b., Italy	E9	22
Venetie, Ak., U.S.	C10	140
Veneto, state, Italy	E8	22
Venev, Russia	F21	10
Venézia (Venice), Italy	E9	22
Venezuela, ctry., S.A.	B4	84
Venezuela, Golfo de, b., S.A.	A3	84
Venezuela, Gulf of see Venezuela, Golfo de b., S.A.	A3	84
Venezuelan Basin, unds.	G7	144
Vengerovo, Russia	C13	32
Venganga, India	D1	53
Veniaminof, Mount, vol., Ak., U.S.	E8	140
Venice see Venézia, Italy	E9	22
Venice, Fl., U.S.	I3	116
Venice, La., U.S.	H9	122
Venice, Gulf of, b., Eur.	E9	22
Vénissieux, Fr.	D10	18
Venkatagiri, India	E4	53
Venlo, Neth.	C15	14
Venosa, Italy	C9	24
Venoste, Alpi (Ötztaler Alpen), mts., Eur.	D7	22
Venray, Neth.	C15	14
Venta, stm., Eur.	C4	10
Ventanas, Ec.	H2	86
Ventersdorp, S. Afr.	E8	70
Venterstad, S. Afr.	G7	70
Ventimiglia, Italy	G4	22
Ventotene, Isola, i., Italy	D7	24
Ventspils, Lat.	C4	10
Ventura, stm., Ven.	E8	86
Ventura, Ca., U.S.	I6	134
Ventura, N.D., U.S.	B13	126
Venustiano Carranza, Mex.	G12	100
Venustiano Carranza, Presa, res., Mex.	B8	100
Vera, Arg.	D7	92
Vera, Spain	G9	20
Vera, Cape, c., Nu., Can.	B8	141
Veracruz, Mex.	F10	100
Veracruz, state, Mex.	F10	100
Veranópolis, Braz.	D12	92
Veravāl, India	H3	54
Verbania, Italy	E5	22
Verbano see Maggiore, Lago, l., Eur.	C14	18
Verbeek, Pegunungan, mts., Indon.	E12	50
Verbilki, Russia	D20	10
Vercelli, Italy	E5	22
Vercors, reg., Fr.	E11	18
Verde, stm., Braz.	F6	84
Verde, stm., Braz.	F4	88
Verde, stm., Braz.	J1	88
Verde, stm., Braz.	H1	88
Verde, stm., Braz.	D4	90
Verde, stm., Mex.	E7	100
Verde, stm., Az., U.S.	J5	132
Verde, Cape, c., Bah.	A10	102
Verde Grande, stm., Braz.	H4	88
Verden, Ger.	D5	16
Verde Pequeno, stm., Braz.	H4	88
Verdi, Nv., U.S.	D5	134
Verdigris, stm., U.S.	E13	128
Verdon, stm., Fr.	F12	18
Verdun, Fr.	E14	14
Verdun, Qc., Can.	E3	110
Verdun-sur-Garonne, Fr.	E7	18
Verdun-sur-Meuse, Fr.	E14	14
Vereeniging, S. Afr.	E9	70
Veregin, Sk., Can.	C11	124
Vereja, Russia	E19	10
Verešćagino, Russia	B15	32
Vergemont Creek, stm., Austl.	D4	76
Vergennes, Vt., U.S.	F3	110
Verhnedneprovskij, Russia	B16	32
Verhneimbatsk, Russia	B15	32
Verhnemulomskoe vodohranilišče, res., Russia	B14	8
Verhnetulomskij, Russia	B14	8
Verhneural'sk, Russia	D9	32
Verhnij Baskunčak, Russia	E7	32
Verhnij Most, Russia	C11	10
Verhnij Ufalej, Russia	C10	32
Verhnjaja Amga, stm., Russia	E14	34
Verhnjaja Angara, stm., Russia	E11	34
Verhnjaja Salda, Russia	C10	32
Verhnjaja Tojma, Russia	E21	8
Verhnjaja Tura, Russia	C9	32
Verhojansk, Russia	C15	34
Verhojanskij hrebet (Verkhoyansk Mountains), mts., Russia	C14	34
Verhopuje, Russia	F19	8
Verhove, Russia	H20	8
Verigin see Veregin, Sk., Can.	C11	124
Verín, Spain	C3	20
Veríssimo, Braz.	J1	88
Verkhivka, Ukr.	A11	26
Verkhoyansk Mountains see Verhojanskij hrebet, mts., Russia	C14	34
Vermelho, stm., Braz.	E2	88
Vermelho, stm., Braz.	E8	88
Vermenton, Fr.	G12	14
Vermilion, Ab., Can.	C19	138
Vermilion, Oh., U.S.	C3	114
Vermilion, stm., Ab., Can.	C19	138
Vermilion, stm., Mn., U.S.	C6	118
Vermilion, b., La., U.S.	H7	122
Vermilion Lake, l., On., Can.	A6	118
Vermilion Lake, l., Mn., U.S.	D5	118
Vermilion Pass, p., Can.	E14	138
Vermillion, S.D., U.S.	E16	126
Vermillion, stm., S.D., U.S.	E15	126
Vermillion, East Fork, stm., S.D., U.S.	D15	126
Vermont, Il., U.S.	D7	120
Vermont, state, U.S.	F3	110
Vernal, Ut., U.S.	C7	132
Verndale, Mn., U.S.	E3	118
Verneuil, Fr.	F9	14
Vernon, B.C., Can.	F11	138
Vernon, Fr.	E10	14
Vernon, Al., U.S.	D10	122
Vernon, Ct., U.S.	C13	114
Vernon, In., U.S.	F12	120
Vernon, Tx., U.S.	G9	128
Vernon, Ut., U.S.	C4	132
Vernonia, Or., U.S.	E3	136
Vernon River, P.E., Can.	D13	110
Vero Beach, Fl., U.S.	I5	116
Véroia, Grc.	C5	28
Verona, On., Can.	D13	112
Verona, Italy	E8	22
Verona, Ms., U.S.	C10	122
Verónica, Arg.	G9	92
Versailles, Fr.	F11	14
Versailles, Il., U.S.	E7	120
Versailles, Ky., U.S.	F13	120
Versailles, Oh., U.S.	D1	114
Veršino-Darasunskij, Russia	F12	34
Veršino-Šahtaminskij, Russia	F12	34
Vertedero, P.R.	B3	104a
Vertentes, Cuba	B8	102
Verulam, S. Afr.	F10	70
Verviers, Bel.	D14	14
Verwoerd Reservoir see Gariep Dam, res., S. Afr.	G7	70
Vescovato, Fr.	G15	18
Veselí nad Lužnicí, Czech Rep.	G10	16
Veselyj Jar, Russia	C11	38
Vescie, Monte, mtn., Italy	D9	24
Vesoul, Fr.	G15	14
Vespasiano, Braz.	J4	88
Vesta, C.R.	H6	102
Vest-Agder, state, Nor.	G2	8
Vestavia Hills, Al., U.S.	D12	122
Vesterålen, is., Nor.	B6	8
Vestfjorden, b., Nor.	C5	8
Vestfold, state, Nor.	G4	8
Vestgrønland (Kitaa), state, Grnld.	D16	141
Vestsjælland, state, Den.	I4	8
Vestvågøya, i., Nor.	B5	8
Vesúvio (Vesuvius), vol., Italy	D8	24
Vesuvius see Vesuvio, vol., Italy	D8	24
Veszprém, Hung.	B4	26
Veszprém, state, Hung.	B4	26
Vésztő, Hung.	C8	26
Vetapālem, India	D5	53
Vetju, Russia	E24	8
Vetlanda, Swe.	H6	8
Vetluga, Russia	C7	32
Vetluga, stm., Russia	H21	8
Vetlužskij, Russia	G21	8
Vetlužskij, Russia	H21	8
Vetrişoaia, Rom.	C15	26
Vetschau, Ger.	E9	16
Veurne, Bel.	C11	14
Vevey, Switz.	D3	22
Veynes, Fr.	E11	18
Vézère, stm., Fr.	D7	18
Viacha, Bol.	C3	90
Viadana, Italy	F7	22
Viale, Arg.	E8	92
Viamão, Braz.	E12	92
Viamonte, Arg.	F6	92
Vian, Ok., U.S.	B4	122
Viana, Braz.	B3	88
Viana do Bolo, Spain	C3	20
Viana do Castelo, Port.	C1	20
Viana do Castelo, state, Port.	C2	20
Viangchan (Vientiane), Laos	D6	48
Viareggio, Italy	G7	22
Vibank, Sk., Can.	D10	124
Viborg, Den.	H3	8
Viborg, S.D., U.S.	D15	126
Viborg, state, Den.	H3	8
Vibo Valentia, Italy	F10	24
Vic, Spain	C13	20
Vícam, Mex.	B3	100
Vicebsk, Bela.	E11	10
Vicebsk, state, Bela.	E11	10
Vicente Guerrero, Presa, res., Mex.	D9	100
Vicenza, Italy	E8	22
Vich see Vic, Spain	C13	20
Vichada, state, Col.	E7	86
Vichadero, Ur.	E10	92
Vichra, stm., Russia	F14	10
Vichuquén, Chile	G1	92
Vichy, Fr.	C9	18
Vici, Ok., U.S.	E9	128
Vicksburg, Ms., U.S.	E8	122
Viçosa, Braz.	K4	88
Viçosa do Ceará, Braz.	B5	88
Vic-sur-Cère, Fr.	E8	18
Victor, Id., U.S.	G15	136
Victor, Ia., U.S.	C5	120
Victor Harbor, Austl.	J2	76
Victoria, Arg.	E7	92
Victoria, B.C., Can.	H7	138
Victoria, P.E., Can.	D13	110
Victoria, Chile	I1	92
Victoria see Labuan, Malay.	A9	50
Victoria see Rabat, Malta	H8	24
Victoria, Sey.	k13	69b
Victoria, Ks., U.S.	C9	128
Victoria, Tx., U.S.	F11	130
Victoria, Va., U.S.	G7	114
Victoria, state, Austl.	K4	76
Victoria, Lake, l., Afr.	E6	66
Victoria, Chutes see Victoria Falls, wtfl, Afr.	D4	68
Victoria, Lake, l., Austl.	I3	76
Victoria, Mount, mtn., Pap.	b4	79a
Victoria Falls, wtfl, Afr.	D4	68
Victoria Fjord, b., Grnld.	A16	141
Victoria Harbour, On., Can.	D10	112
Victoria Island, i., Can.	A8	106
Victoria Land, reg., Ant.	C20	81
Victoria Nile, stm., Afr.	D6	66
Victoria Peak, mtn., Belize	D3	102
Victoria Peak, mtn., B.C., Can.	F4	138
Victoria River Downs, Austl.	C6	74
Victorias, Phil.	E4	52
Victoria Strait, strt., Nu., Can.	B10	106
Victoriaville, Qc., Can.	D5	110
Victoria West, S. Afr.	G6	70
Victorica, Arg.	H5	92
Victorville, Ca., U.S.	I8	134
Vičuga, Russia	H19	8
Vicuña, Chile	E2	92
Vicuña Mackenna, Arg.	F5	92
Vidalia, Ga., U.S.	D3	116
Vidalia, La., U.S.	F7	122
Vidal Ramos, Braz.	C13	92
Videira, Braz.	C12	92
Vidigueira, Port.	F3	20
Vidin, Blg.	F9	26
Vidisha, India	G6	54
Vidor, Tx., U.S.	G4	122
Vidoy, i., Far. Is.	m34	8b
Vidra, Rom.	E13	26
Vidsel, Swe.	D9	8
Vidzeme, hist. reg., Lat.	C8	10
Viedma, Arg.	H4	90
Viedma, Lago, l., Arg.	I2	90
Vieille Case, Dom.	i6	105c
Viejo, Cerro, mtn., Peru	D2	84
Viella, Spain	B11	20
Vienna see Wien, Aus.	B13	22
Vienna, Ga., U.S.	D2	116
Vienna, Il., U.S.	G9	120
Vienna, Mo., U.S.	F5	120
Vienna, W.V., U.S.	E4	114
Vienna see Wien, state, Aus.	B13	22
Vienna Woods see Wienerwald, mts., Aus.	B13	22
Vienne, Fr.	D10	18
Vienne, state, Fr.	C6	18
Vienne, stm., Fr.	C6	18
Vientiane see Viangchan, Laos	D6	48
Vieques, P.R.	B5	104a
Vieques, Aeropuerto, P.R.	B5	104a
Vieques, Isla de, i., P.R.	B5	104a
Vieremä, Fin.	E12	8
Vierwaldstätter See (Lucerne, Lake of), l., Switz.	D5	22
Vierzon, Fr.	G11	14
Viesca, Mex.	C7	100
Vieste, Italy	I13	22
Vietnam, ctry., Asia	E9	48
Viet Tri, Viet.	B7	48
Vieux-Fort, Guad.	i22	107a
Vieux-Fort, St. Luc.	m7	105c
Vieux-Fort, Pointe du, c., Guad.	i5	105c
Vieux-Habitants, Guad.	h5	105c
Vievis, Lith.	F7	10
Vigala, Est.	B7	10
Vigan, Phil.	B3	52
Vigevano, Italy	E5	22
Vigía Airport, St. Luc.	F7	22
Vignola, Italy	F7	22
Vigo, Spain	B2	20
Vigo, Ría de, est., Spain	B1	20
Vihāri, Pak.	D4	54
Vihorevka, Russia	C18	32
Vihowa, Pak.	C3	54
Vihren, mtn., Blg.	H10	26
Viinijärvi, Fin.	E13	8
Viivikonna, Est.	A10	10
Vijāpur, India	G4	54
Vijayawāda, India	C5	53
Vikārābād, India	C3	53
Viking, Ab., Can.	C19	138
Vikna, i., Nor.	D4	8
Vikramasingapuram, India	G3	53
Vikulovo, Russia	C12	32
Vila da Ribeira Brava, C.V.	k10	65a
Vila de Sena, Moz.	D5	68
Vila do Bispo, Port.	G1	20
Vila do Conde, Port.	C2	20
Vila Fontes, Moz.	D6	68
Vilafranca del Panadés see Vilafranca del Penedès, Spain	C12	20
Vilafranca del Penedès, Spain	C12	20
Vila Franca de Xira, Port.	F2	20
Vilagarcía de Arousa, Spain	B1	20
Vila Gamito, Moz.	C5	68
Vilaine, stm., Fr.	C10	10
Vilaka, Lat.	C10	10
Vilāni, Lat.	D9	10
Vilanculo, Moz.	B12	70
Vila Nova de Famalicão, Port.	C2	20
Vilanova i la Geltrú, Spain	C12	20
Vila Real, Port.	C3	20
Vila-real, Spain	E10	20
Vila Real, state, Port.	C3	20
Vila Velha, Braz.	K5	88
Vila Verde, Port.	C2	20
Vilcabamba, Cordillera de, mts., Peru	F3	84
Vilejka, Bela.	F9	10
Vilelas, Bela.	C6	92
Vilhelmina, Swe.	D7	8
Vilhena, Braz.	F5	84
Vília (Néris), stm., Eur.	E8	10
Viljandi, Est.	G11	8
Viljui, stm., Russia	D13	34
Viljujsk, Russia	D14	34
Viljujskoe vodohranilišče, res., Russia	B20	32
Vilkaviškis, Lith.	F6	10
Vil'kickogo, ostrov, i., Russia	A19	34
Vil'kickogo, proliv, strt., Russia	A9	34
Vilkija, Lith.	E6	10
Villa Abecia, Bol.	D3	90
Villa Ana, Arg.	D8	92
Villa Ángela, Arg.	C7	92
Villa Atamisqui, Arg.	D6	92
Villa Bella, Bol.	B3	90
Villa Berthet, Arg.	C7	92
Villa Bruzual, Ven.	C7	86
Villacañas, Spain	E7	20
Villa Carlos Paz, Arg.	E5	92
Villacarrillo, Spain	F7	20
Villacastín, Spain	D6	20
Villach, Austria	D10	22
Villacidro, Italy	E2	24
Villa Clara, Arg.	E8	92
Villa Concepción del Tío, Arg.	E6	92
Villa Constitución, Arg.	F7	92
Villa Coronado, Mex.	B6	100
Villa de Arista, Mex.	D8	100
Villa de Cos, Mex.	D7	100
Villa del Río, Spain	F6	20
Villa Dolores, Arg.	F4	92
Villa Flores, Mex.	G12	100
Villa Florida, Para.	C9	92
Villa Frontera see Frontera, Mex.	B6	100
Villa General Roca, Arg.	F4	92
Villa Gesell, Arg.	H9	92
Villagrán, Mex.	C9	100
Villa Grove, Il., U.S.	E9	120
Villaguay, Arg.	E8	92
Villa Guerrero, Mex.	F9	100
Villa Hayes, Para.	B9	92
Villahermosa, Mex.	G12	100
Villa Hidalgo, Mex.	H3	130
Villa Huidobro, Arg.	G5	92
Villa Insurgentes, Mex.	C3	100
Villajoyosa see La Vila Joiosa, Spain	F10	20
Villa Juárez, Mex.	B3	100
Villa Krause, Arg.	E3	92
Villalba, P.R.	B3	104a
Villalba see Villalba, Spain	A3	20
Villaldama, Mex.	B8	100
Villalón, Arg.	E5	92
Villalonga, Arg.	G4	90
Villalpando, Spain	C5	20
Villa Mainero, Mex.	C9	100
Villa María, Arg.	F6	92
Villamartín, Spain	H5	20
Villa Mazán, Arg.	D4	92
Villa Media Agua, Arg.	E3	92
Villa Mercedes, Arg.	F5	92
Villa Montes, Bol.	D4	90
Villa Nueva, Arg.	G4	92
Villa Nueva, Col.	B5	86
Villanueva, N.M., U.S.	F3	128
Villanueva de Córdoba, Spain	F6	20
Villanueva de la Serena, Spain	F5	20
Villanueva de la Sierra, Spain	D4	20
Villanueva de los Infantes, Spain	F7	20
Villanueva del Río y Minas, Spain	G4	20
Villanueva y Geltrú see Vilanova i la Geltrú, Spain	C12	20
Villa Ocampo, Arg.	D8	92
Villa Ocampo, Mex.	H2	130
Villa Oliva, Para.	B8	92
Villa Pérez, P.R.	B2	104a
Villapinzón, Col.	E5	86
Villarcayo, Spain	B7	20
Villa Regina, Arg.	G3	90
Villa Reynolds, Arg.	F5	92
Villa Rica, Ga., U.S.	D14	122
Villarreal see Vila-real, Spain	E10	20
Villarrica, Para.	B9	92
Villarrobledo, Spain	E8	20
Villarrubia de los Ojos, Spain	E7	20
Villa San Giovanni, Italy	F9	24
Villa Santa Rita de Catuna, Arg.	E4	92
Villasayas, Spain	C8	20
Villa Serrano, Bol.	C4	90
Villasis, Phil.	C3	52
Villa Unión, Arg.	D3	92
Villa Unión, Arg.	D6	92
Villa Unión, Mex.	D5	100
Villa Valeria, Arg.	G5	92
Villavicencio, Col.	E5	86
Villaviciosa de Córdoba, Spain	F5	20
Villazón, Bol.	D3	90
Villefranche-de-Rouergue, Fr.	E8	18
Villefranche-sur-Saône, Fr.	C10	18
Villena, Spain	F10	20
Villeneuve-sur-Lot, Fr.	E6	18
Villeneuve-sur-Yonne, Fr.	F12	14
Ville Platte, La., U.S.	G6	122
Villers-Cotterêts, Fr.	E12	14
Villerupt, Fr.	E14	14
Villeta, Col.	E4	86
Villeurbanne, Fr.	D10	18
Villiers, S. Afr.	E9	70
Villingen-Schwenningen, Ger.	H4	16
Villisca, Ia., U.S.	D3	120
Villmanstrand see Lappeenranta, Fin.	F12	8
Vilnius, Lith.	F8	10
Vilsbiburg, Ger.	H8	16
Vilshofen, Ger.	H9	16
Viluppuram, India	E4	53
Vilvorde see Vilvoorde, Bel.	D13	14
Vimmerby, Swe.	H6	8
Vimperk, Czech Rep.	G9	16
Vina, Ca., U.S.	D3	134
Viña, stm., Cam.	C2	66
Viña del Mar, Chile	F2	92
Vinalhaven, Me., U.S.	F8	110
Vinalhaven Island, i., Me., U.S.	F8	110
Vinaròs, Spain	D11	20
Vincennes, In., U.S.	F10	120
Vincennes Bay, b., Ant.	B15	81
Vincent, Al., U.S.	D12	122
Vinces, Ec.	H2	86
Vindelälven, stm., Swe.	D8	8
Vindeln, Swe.	D8	8
Vinderup, Den.	H3	8
Vineland, N.J., U.S.	E10	114
Vineyard Haven, Ma., U.S.	C15	114
Vineyard Sound, strt., Ma., U.S.	C15	114
Vinh, Viet.	C7	48
Vinh Long, Viet.	G8	48
Vinh Yen, Viet.	B7	48
Vinita, Ok., U.S.	H2	120
Vinkovci, Cro.	E15	22
Vinnytsia, Ukr.	A16	26
Vinson Massif, mtn., Ant.	C32	81
Vintilă Vodă, Rom.	D13	26
Vinton, Ia., U.S.	B5	120
Vinton, Va., U.S.	G6	114
Viola, Il., U.S.	C7	120
Vioolsdrif, S. Afr.	F3	70
Vir, Otok, i., Cro.	F11	22
Virac, Phil.	D5	52
Viramgām, India	G4	54
Virārajendrapet, India	E3	53
Virbalis, Lith.	F5	10
Virden, Mb., Can.	E13	124
Virden, Il., U.S.	E8	120
Virden, N.M., U.S.	K8	132
Vire, Fr.	F8	14
Virgem da Lapa, Braz.	I4	88
Virgenes, Cabo, c., S.A.	J3	90
Virgin, stm., U.S.	F2	132
Virgin Gorda, i., Br. Vir. Is.	e9	104b
Virginia, S. Afr.	F8	70
Virginia, Ire.	H6	12
Virginia, Mn., U.S.	D6	118
Virginia, state, U.S.	G7	114
Virginia Beach, Va., U.S.	H10	114
Virginia City, Mt., U.S.	E14	136
Virginia City, Nv., U.S.	D6	134
Virginia Falls, wtfl, N.T., Can.	C5	106
Virgin Islands, dep., N.A.	h14	96a
Virgin Islands, is., N.A.	e7	104b
Virgin Islands National Park, p.o.i., V.I.U.S.	e7	104b
Virgin Passage, strt., N.A.	e8	104a
Virje, Cro.	D13	22
Viroqua, Wi., U.S.	H7	118
Virovitica, Cro.	E14	22

Name	Map Ref.	Page
Virrat, Fin.	E10	8
Virtaniemi, Fin.	B13	8
Virtsu, Est.	G10	8
Virú, Peru	E2	84
Virudunagar, India	G3	53
Virunga, Parc National de, p.o.i., D.R.C.	D5	66
Viru-Nigula, Est.	A9	10
Virvytė, stm., Lith.	D5	10
Vis see Visrivier, stm., Nmb.	E3	70
Vis, stm., S. Afr.	G5	70
Vis, Otok, i., Cro.	G13	22
Visale, Sol. Is.	e8	79b
Visalia, Ca., U.S.	G6	134
Visayan Islands, is., Phil.	E4	52
Visayan Sea, Phil.	E4	52
Visby, Swe.	H8	8
Viscount, Sk., Can.	C8	124
Viscount Melville Sound, strt., Can.	B11	94
Višegrad, Bos.	F6	26
Viseu, Port.	D3	20
Viseu, state, Port.	D3	20
Vishākhapatnam, India	C6	53
Visnagar, India	G4	54
Višneva, Bela.	F9	10
Visoko, Bos.	E5	26
Visokoi Island, i., S. Geor.	K12	82
Visp, Switz.	D4	22
Visrivier, stm., Nmb.	E3	70
Vista, Ca., U.S.	J8	134
Vistina, Russia	A10	32
Vistula see Wisła, stm., Pol.	B14	16
Vistula Lagoon, b., Eur.	B16	16
Vita, Mb., Can.	E17	124
Vita, stm., Col.	E7	86
Viterbo, Italy	H8	22
Viti see Fiji, ctry., Oc.	E8	72
Viti Levu, i., Fiji	p19	79e
Vitim, Russia	E11	34
Vitim, stm., Russia	E12	34
Vitimskoe ploskogor'e, plat., Russia	F11	34
Vitinja, p., Blg.	G10	26
Vítkov, Czech Rep.	G13	16
Vitória, Braz.	D7	84
Vitória, Braz.	K5	88
Vitoria see Gasteiz, Spain	B8	20
Vitória da Conquista, Braz.	H5	88
Vitória de Santo Antão, Braz.	E8	88
Vitória do Mearim, Braz.	B3	88
Vitorino Freire, Braz.	C3	88
Vitré, Fr.	F7	14
Vitry-le-François, Fr.	F13	14
Vitteaux, Fr.	G13	14
Vittoria, Italy	H8	24
Vittorio Veneto, Italy	D9	22
Viveiro, Spain	A3	20
Viver see Viveiro, Spain	A3	20
Vivi, stm., Russia	D8	34
Vivian, La., U.S.	E4	122
Vizcaíno, Desierto de, des., Mex.	B2	100
Vizcaya see Bizkaiko, co., Spain	A8	20
Vize, Tur.	B10	28
Vizianagaram, India	B6	53
Vizille, Fr.	D11	18
Vizinga, Russia	B7	32
Vjalikaja Mašćanica, Bela.	G12	10
Vjalikija Radvaničy, Bela.	H7	10
Vjaseja, Bela.	G10	10
Vjatka, stm., Russia	C8	32
Vjatskije Poljany, Russia	C8	32
Vjazemskij, Russia	G15	34
Vjaz'ma, Russia	E17	10
Vjazniki, Russia	H20	8
Vjazyn', Bela.	F10	10
Vjosës (Aóös), stm., Eur.	D13	24
Vlaardingen, Neth.	C13	14
Vladeasa, Vârful, mtn., Rom.	C9	26
Vladičin Han, Yugo.	G8	26
Vladikavkaz, Russia	F6	32
Vladimir, Russia	H18	8
Vladimirskaja oblast', co., Russia	I19	8
Vladimirskij Tupik, Russia	E16	10
Vladivostok, Russia	C9	38
Vlasenica, Bos.	E5	26
Vlasotince, Yugo.	G9	26
Vlasovo, Russia	B16	34
Vlieland, i., Neth.	A13	14
Vlissingen, Neth.	C12	14
Vlora see Vlorë, Alb.	D13	24
Vlorë, Alb.	D13	24
Vltava (Moldau), stm., Czech Rep.	F10	16
Vnukovo, Russia	E20	10
Vöcklabruck, Aus.	C10	22
Vo Dat, Viet.	G8	48
Vodla, stm., Russia	F17	8
Vodlozero, ozero, l., Russia	F17	8
Vodosalma, Russia	D14	8
Voël, stm., S. Afr.	H7	70
Voghera, Italy	F6	22
Voh, N. Cal.	m15	79d
Vohimena, Tanjona, c., Madag.	F8	68
Vohipeno, Madag.	E8	68
Võhma, Est.	G11	8
Voi, Kenya	E7	66
Voinești, Rom.	B14	26
Vonjama, Lib.	H3	64
Voiron, Fr.	D11	18
Voitsberg, Aus.	C12	22
Vojmsjön, l., Swe.	D6	8
Vojnica, Russia	D14	8
Vojvodina, co., Yugo.	D7	26
Volcano, Hi., U.S.	D6	78a
Volcano Islands see Kazan-rettō, is., Japan	G18	30
Volčha, Russia	D14	32
Volda, Nor.	E2	8
Volga, S.D., U.S.	G2	118
Volga, stm., Russia	E7	32
Volga-Baltic Canal see Volgo-Baltijskij kanal, can., Russia	G17	8
Volgodonsk, Russia	E6	32
Volgograd, Russia	E6	32
Volgograd Reservoir see Volgogradskoe vodohranilišče, res., Russia	E7	32
Volgogradskoe vodohranilišče, res., Russia	D7	32
Volhov, Russia	A15	10
Volhov, stm., Russia	G14	8
Volissós, Grc.	E8	28
Völklingen, Ger.	G2	16
Volksrust, S. Afr.	E9	70
Volčanka, Russia	B7	34
Volodarsk, Kaz.	D11	32
Voloe, Russia	F17	10
Vologda, Russia	A22	10
Vologodskaja oblast', co., Russia	A22	10
Volokolamsk, Russia	D18	10
Volonga, Russia	C22	8
Vólos, Grc.	D5	28
Volos, Gulf of see Pagasitikós Kólpos, b., Grc.	D5	28
Vološka, Russia	F19	8
Volosovo, Russia	A12	10
Volot, Russia	C13	10
Volovo, Russia	G21	10
Vol'sk, Russia	D7	32
Volta, stm., Ghana	H5	64
Volta Blanche (White Volta), stm., Afr.	G4	64
Volta Lake, res., Ghana	H4	64
Volta Noire (Black Volta) (Mouhoun), stm., Afr.	G4	64
Volta Redonda, Braz.	L3	88
Volterra, Italy	G7	22
Vol'teva, Russia	D21	8
Voltri, ngh., Italy	F5	22
Volturno, stm., Italy	C8	24
Vólvi, Límni, l., Grc.	C6	28
Volyn', co., Ukr.	E20	16
Volžsk, Russia	C7	32
Volžskij, Russia	E6	32
Vonavona Island, i., Sol. Is.	e7	79b
Vonda, Sk., Can.	B7	124
Vondanka, Russia	G22	8
Vondrozo, Madag.	E8	68
Von Frank Mountain, mtn., Ak., U.S.	D8	140
Vopnafjördur, Ice.	k32	8a
Vopnafjördur, b., Ice.	k32	8a
Vorarlberg, state, Aus.	C6	22
Vorau, Aus.	C12	22
Vorderrhein see Rein Anterior, stm., Switz.	D6	22
Vordingborg, Den.	I4	8
Vóreio Aigaío, state, Grc.	D8	28
Vórioi Sporádhes, is., Grc.	D6	28
Vórios Evvoïkós Kólpos, b., Grc.	E5	28
Vorkuta, Russia	A10	32
Vormsi, i., Est.	G10	8
Vorobevo, Russia	C13	32
Voroncov, Mol.	B16	26
Voroncovo, Russia	C11	10
Voronež, Russia	D5	32
Voronežskaja oblast', co., Russia	H21	10
Voronja, stm., Russia	B16	8
Voronok, Russia	H15	10
Voronovo, Russia	E5	34
Vorpommern, hist. reg., Ger.	C9	16
Vorsma, Russia	H20	8
Varterkaka Nunatak, mtn., Ant.	C8	81
Võrtsjärv, l., Est.	G12	8
Võru, Est.	H12	8
Vosburg, S. Afr.	G6	70
Vosges, state, Fr.	F15	14
Vosges, mts., Fr.	F15	14
Voskresensk, Russia	E21	10
Voskresenskoe, Russia	C20	10
Voskresenskoe, Russia	B21	10
Voss, Nor.	F2	8
Vostočno-Kounradskij, Kaz.	E13	32
Vostočno-Sibirskoe more, Russia	B20	34
Vostočnyj Sajan, mts., Russia	D17	32
Vostok, i., Kir.	E11	72
Vostok, sci., Ant.	C15	81
Votice, Czech Rep.	G10	16
Votkinsk, Russia	C8	32
Votuporanga, Braz.	D7	90
Vouga, stm., Port.	D2	20
Vouziers, Fr.	E13	14
Voyageurs National Park, p.o.i., Mn., U.S.	C6	118
Voyeykov Ice Shelf, ice, Ant.	B17	81
Vože, ozero, l., Russia	F18	8
Vožega, Russia	F19	8
Voznesene, Russia	F18	8
Vozroždenija, ostrov, i., Asia	E9	32
Vraca, Blg.	F10	26
Vradíyivka, Ukr.	B17	26
Vrancea, state, Rom.	D13	26
Vrangelja, ostrov (Wrangel Island), i., Russia	B24	34
Vranje, Yugo.	G8	26
Vratsa see Vraca, Blg.	F10	26
Vrbas, Yugo.	D6	26
Vrbas, stm., Bos.	E4	26
Vrbovec, Cro.	E13	22
Vrchlabí, Czech Rep.	F11	16
Vrede, S. Afr.	E9	70
Vredenburg, S. Afr.	H3	70
Vredenburgh, Al., U.S.	F11	122
Vredenburg-Saldanha see Vredenburg, S. Afr.	H3	70
Vredendal, S. Afr.	G4	70
Vriddhāchalam, India	F4	53
Vrindāvan, India	E6	54
Vršac, Yugo.	D8	26
Vrútky, Slov.	G14	16
Vryburg, S. Afr.	E7	70
Vryheid, S. Afr.	E10	70
Vsetín, Czech Rep.	G13	16
Vsevidof, Mount, mtn., Ak., U.S.	F6	140
Vučitrn, Yugo.	G7	26
Vukovar, Cro.	E16	22
Vulcan, Ab., Can.	F17	138
Vulcan, Rom.	D10	26
Vulcănești, Mol.	D15	26
Vulcano, Isola, i., Italy	F8	24
Vuisino see Bolsena, Lago di, l., Italy	H9	22
Vung Tau, Viet.	G8	48
Vunidawa, Fiji	p19	79e
Vunisea, Fiji	q18	79e
Vuohijärvi, l., Fin.	F11	8
Vuyyūru, India	C5	53
Vyāra, India	H4	54
Vyborg (Viipuri), Russia	F13	8
Vyčegda, stm., Russia	B7	32
Vyčegodskij, Russia	F22	8
Východočeský, state, Czech Rep.	F11	16
Východoslovenský Kraj, state, Slov.	H17	16
Vygoniči, Russia	G16	10
Vygozero, ozero, l., Russia	E16	8
Vyksa, Russia	I20	8
Vynohradiv, Ukr.	A10	26
Vypolzovo, Russia	C16	10
Vyrica, Russia	A13	10
Vyšgorodok, Russia	C11	10
Vyškov, Czech Rep.	G12	16
Vyšneol'šanoe, Russia	H20	10
Vyšnevolockoe vodohranilišče, res., Russia	C16	10
Vyšnij Voločok, Russia	C16	10
Vysokaja Gora, Russia	C7	32
Vysoké Mýto, Czech Rep.	G12	16
Vysokinči, Russia	F19	10
Vysokoe, Russia	D17	10
Vysokogornyj, Russia	G16	34
Vysokovsk, Russia	D19	10
Vytebet', stm., Russia	G18	10
Vytegra, Russia	F17	8
Vyzhnytsia, Ukr.	A12	26

W

Name	Map Ref.	Page
Wa, Ghana	G4	64
Waal, stm., Neth.	C14	14
Waalwijk, Neth.	C14	14
Wabag, Pap. N. Gui.	b3	79a
Wabakimi Lake, l., On., Can.	A8	118
Wabamun, Ab., Can.	C16	138
Wabamun Lake, l., Ab., Can.	C15	138
Wabana, Nf., Can.	j23	107a
Wabasca, stm., Ab., Can.	D7	106
Wabasca-Desmarais, Ab., Can.	D8	106
Wabash, In., U.S.	H4	112
Wabash, stm., U.S.	F9	120
Wabasha, Mn., U.S.	G6	118
Wabasso, Mn., U.S.	G3	118
Wabeno, Wi., U.S.	F10	118
Wabera, Eth.	F8	62
Wabowden, Mb., Can.	E11	106
Wabrzeźno, Pol.	C14	16
Wabu Hu, l., China	E7	42
Waccamaw, stm., U.S.	C7	116
Waccamaw, Lake, l., N.C., U.S.	B7	116
Wachapreague, Va., U.S.	G10	114
Wachau, reg., Aus.	B12	22
Wacissa, Fl., U.S.	F2	116
Waco, Tx., U.S.	C10	130
Waco Lake, res., Tx., U.S.	C10	130
Waconda Lake, res., Ks., U.S.	B10	128
Wadayama, Japan	D7	40
Wad Bandah, Sudan	E5	62
Wadbilliga National Park, p.o.i., Austl.	K7	76
Waddenzee, strt., Neth.	A14	14
Waddington, N.Y., U.S.	D14	112
Waddington, Mount, mtn., B.C., Can.	E5	138
Wadena, Sk., Can.	C10	124
Wadena, Mn., U.S.	E3	118
Wadesboro, N.C., U.S.	B5	116
Wādī as-Sīr, Jord.	G6	58
Wādī Halfā', Sudan	C6	62
Wadley, Al., U.S.	D13	122
Wadley, Ga., U.S.	D3	116
Wad Madanī, Sudan	E6	62
Wadowice, Pol.	G15	16
Wadsworth, Nv., U.S.	D6	134
Wadsworth, Oh., U.S.	C4	114
Wafangdian, China	B9	42
Wageningen, Neth.	C14	14
Wager Bay, b., Nu., Can.	B13	106
Wagga Wagga, Austl.	J6	76
Wagin, Austl.	F3	74
Waging am See, Ger.	I8	16
Wagner, S.D., U.S.	D14	126
Wagner, Ok., U.S.	I2	120
Wagon Mound, N.M., U.S.	F4	128
Wagontire Mountain, mtn., Or., U.S.	G7	136
Wagrien, reg., Ger.	B6	16
Wagrowiec, Pol.	D13	16
Waha, Libya	B4	62
Wahai, Indon.	F8	44
Wāh Cantonment, Pak.	B4	54
Wahiawa, Hi., U.S.	B3	78a
Wahpeton, N.D., U.S.	E2	118
Wahran (Oran), Alg.	B4	64
Wai, India	B1	53
Waialua, Hi., U.S.	B3	78a
Waianae, Hi., U.S.	B3	78a
Waiau, N.Z.	F5	80
Waiau, stm., N.Z.	G2	80
Waiau, stm., N.Z.	F5	80
Waiblingen, Ger.	H5	16
Waidhofen an der Thaya, Aus.	B12	22
Waidhofen an der Ybbs, Aus.	C11	22
Waigeo, Pulau, i., Indon.	E9	44
Waihi, N.Z.	C6	80
Waikabubak, Indon.	H11	50
Waikato, N.Z.	C6	80
Waikelo, Indon.	H11	50
Waikerie, Austl.	J2	76
Wailuku, Hi., U.S.	C5	78a
Waimate, N.Z.	G4	80
Waimea, Hi., U.S.	A2	78a
Wainganga, stm., India	H7	54
Waingapu, Indon.	H12	50
Waini, stm., Guy.	D12	86
Wainunu Bay, b., Fiji	p19	79e
Wainwright, Ab., Can.	B3	124
Wainwright, Ak., U.S.	B7	140
Waipukurau, N.Z.	E7	80
Wairarapa, Lake, l., N.Z.	E6	80
Wairau, stm., N.Z.	E5	80
Wairoa, N.Z.	D7	80
Wairoa, stm., N.Z.	B6	80
Waitaki, stm., N.Z.	G4	80
Waitara, N.Z.	D6	80
Waitemata, N.Z.	C6	80
Waite Park, Mn., U.S.	F4	118
Waitotara, N.Z.	D6	80
Waitsburg, Wa., U.S.	D8	136
Waiwo, Indon.	F9	44
Wajima, Japan	B9	40
Wajir, Kenya	D8	66
Waka, D.R.C.	D4	66
Waka, Eth.	F7	62
Wakarusa, In., U.S.	G3	112
Wakasa-wan, b., Japan	D8	40
Wakatipu, Lake, l., N.Z.	G3	80
Wakaw, Sk., Can.	B8	124
Wakayama, Japan	E8	40
Wakayama, state, Japan.	F8	40
WaKeeney, Ks., U.S.	B9	128
Wakefield, Eng., U.K.	H11	12
Wakefield, Ks., U.S.	B11	128
Wakefield, Ne., U.S.	E15	126
Wakefield, Mi., U.S.	E8	118
Wake Forest, N.C., U.S.	H7	114
Wakema, Mya.	D2	48
Waki, Japan	E7	40
Wakis, Pap. N. Gui.	b5	79a
Wakita, Ok., U.S.	E10	128
Wakkanai, Japan	B14	38
Wakomata Lake, l., On., Can.	B6	112
Wakonda, S.D., U.S.	E15	126
Waku Kungo, Ang.	C2	68
Walachia, hist. reg., Rom.	E11	26
Walaklae, stm., Indon.	F12	50
Walawe, stm., Sri L.	H5	53
Wałbrzych, state, Pol.	F12	16
Walcha, Austl.	H8	76
Walcott, Lake, res., Id., U.S.	H13	136
Wałcz, Pol.	C12	16
Waldbröl, Ger.	F3	16
Walden, Co., U.S.	C10	132
Waldheim, Sk., Can.	B7	124
Waldkirchen, Ger.	H9	16
Waldmünchen, Ger.	G8	16
Waldo, Fl., U.S.	G3	116
Waldoboro, Me., U.S.	F7	110
Waldorf, Md., U.S.	F9	114
Waldport, Or., U.S.	F2	136
Waldron, In., U.S.	E12	120
Waldron, Ar., U.S.	C4	122
Waldshut-Tiengen, Ger.	I4	16
Waldviertel, reg., Aus.	B12	22
Wales, state, U.K.	I9	12
Wales Island, i., Nu., Can.	B13	106
Walewale, Ghana	G4	64
Walgett, Austl.	G6	76
Walgreen Coast, cst., Ant.	C30	81
Walhachin, B.C., Can.	F10	138
Walhalla, N.D., U.S.	F15	124
Walhalla, S.C., U.S.	B2	116
Walhalla, hist., Ger.	G8	16
Walker, Ia., U.S.	B6	120
Walker, stm., Nv., U.S.	D7	134
Walker Bay, b., S. Afr.	I4	70
Walker Lake, l., Nv., U.S.	E7	134
Walkerton, On., Can.	D8	112
Walkerton, In., U.S.	G3	112
Walkertown, N.C., U.S.	H5	114
Walkerville, Mt., U.S.	D14	136
Wall, S.D., U.S.	D10	126
Wallace, Id., U.S.	C11	136
Wallace, Ne., U.S.	G11	126
Wallace, N.C., U.S.	B7	116
Wallaceburg, On., Can.	F7	112
Wallal Downs, stm., Austl.	C4	74
Wallam Creek, stm., Austl.	G8	76
Wallangarra, Austl.	G8	76
Wallaroo, Austl.	K4	76
Wallasey, Eng. U.K.	H9	12
Walla Walla, Wa., U.S.	D8	136
Wallingford, Ct., U.S.	C13	114
Wallingford, Vt., U.S.	G4	110
Wallis, Tx., U.S.	H2	122
Wallis, îles, is., Wal./F.	E9	72
Wallis and Futuna, dep., Oc.	E9	72
Wallisville Lake, res., Tx., U.S.	H4	122
Wall Lake, Ia., U.S.	I3	118
Wallowa, Or., U.S.	E9	136
Wallowa, stm., Or., U.S.	E9	136
Walls of Jericho National Park, p.o.i., Austl.	n3	77a
Walnut, Il., U.S.	C8	120
Walnut, Ia., U.S.	C2	120
Walnut, Ms., U.S.	C10	122
Walnut, N.C., U.S.	I3	114
Walnut, stm., Ks., U.S.	D11	128
Walnut Canyon National Monument, p.o.i., Az., U.S.	H5	132
Walnut Cove, N.C., U.S.	H5	114
Walnut Creek, stm., Ks., U.S.	C9	128
Walnut Grove, Mn., U.S.	G3	118
Walnut Grove, Ms., U.S.	E9	122
Walnut Ridge, Ar., U.S.	H7	120
Walnut Springs, Tx., U.S.	B10	130
Walpole, Austl.	G3	74
Walpole, N.H., U.S.	G4	110
Walsall, Eng., U.K.	I11	12
Walsenburg, Co., U.S.	D4	128
Walsh, Ab., Can.	E3	124
Walsh, stm., Austl.	A5	76
Walsrode, Ger.	D5	16
Walterboro, S.C., U.S.	D5	116
Walters, Ok., U.S.	G10	128
Waltershausen, Ger.	F6	16
Walthall, Ms., U.S.	D9	122
Walthill, Ne., U.S.	B1	120
Walton, In., U.S.	H3	112
Walton, N.S., Can.	E13	110
Walton, N.Y., U.S.	B10	114
Walvisbaai see Walvis Bay, Nmb.	C2	70
Walvis Bay (Walvisbaai), Nmb.	C2	70
Walvis Bay, b., Nmb.	C2	70
Walvis Ridge, unds.	K14	144
Walworth, Wi., U.S.	B9	120
Wamba, D.R.C.	D5	66
Wamba, Nig.	H6	64
Wamba (Uamba), stm., Afr.	F3	66
Wampú, Hond.	E5	102
Wampú, stm., Hond.	E5	102
Wampum, Pa., U.S.	D5	114
Wamsutter, Wy., U.S.	B9	132
Wanaka, N.Z.	G3	80
Wanaka, Lake, l., N.Z.	G3	80
Wan'an, China	H6	42
Wanapa, Neth. Ant.	p23	104g
Wanapitei, stm., On., Can.	B9	112
Wanapitei Lake, l., On., Can.	B8	112
Wanbaoshan, China	B6	38
Wanbi, Austl.	J3	76
Wanblee, S.D., U.S.	D11	126
Wanchese, N.C., U.S.	I10	114
Wandel Hav, Grnld.	A22	141
Wandering, stm., Ab., Can.	A18	138
Wanfoxia, China	C4	36
Wang, stm., Thai.	D4	48
Wanganui, N.Z.	D6	80
Wangaratta, Austl.	K6	76
Wangcun, China	C7	42
Wangdu Phodrang, Bhu.	E12	54
Wangerooge, i., Ger.	C4	16
Wang Noi, Thai.	E5	48
Wang Yang, b., China	F9	42
Wangqing, China	C8	38
Wangtai, China	H7	42
Wangyehmiao see Horqin Youyi Qianqi, China	B9	36
Wanhsien see Wanxian, China	F3	42
Wani, India	A4	53
Wanie-Rukula, D.R.C.	D5	66
Wanigela, Pap. N. Gui.	b4	79a
Wanipigow, stm., Can.	C18	124
Wänkäner, India	G3	54
Wanneroo, Austl.	F3	74
Wannian, China	G7	42
Wanparti, India	C4	53
Wantan, China	F4	42
Wanxian, China	F3	42
Wanyuan, China	E2	42
Wanzai, China	H6	42
Wanzleben, Ger.	D7	16
Wapakoneta, Oh., U.S.	D1	114
Waparucka, stm., Can.	C2	112
Wapato, Wa., U.S.	D6	136
Wapello, Ia., U.S.	C6	120
Wapiti, stm., Can.	A12	138
Wappingers Falls, N.Y., U.S.	C12	114
Wapsipinicon, stm., U.S.	J8	118
War, W.V., U.S.	G4	114
Warangal, India	B4	53
Wārāseoni, India	H7	54
Waratah Bay, b., Austl.	L5	76
Warburg, Ger.	E4	16
Warburton, Austl.	K5	76
Warburton, stm., Austl.	F3	76
Warburton Bay, b., N.T., Can.	C8	106
Warden, S. Afr.	E9	70
Wardha, India	H7	54
Wardha, stm., India	H7	54
Ward Hill, hill, Scot., U.K.	C9	12
Wardlow, B.C., Can.	F19	138
Wardner, B.C., Can.	G15	138
Wardsweli Draw, stm., U.S.	B5	130
Ware, Ma., U.S.	B13	114
Wareham, Eng., U.K.	K10	12
Waremme, Bel.	D14	14
Waren, Indon.	F10	44
Warenda, stm., Austl.	E3	76
Warendorf, Ger.	E3	16
Ware Shoals, S.C., U.S.	B3	116
Wargla, Alg.	C6	64
Warin Chamrap, Thai.	E7	48
Warman, Sk., Can.	B7	124
Warmandi, Indon.	F9	44
Warmbad, Nmb.	F4	70
Warmbad, S. Afr.	D9	70
Warm Baths see Warmbad, S. Afr.	D9	70
Warminster, Eng., U.K.	J10	12
Warminster, Pa., U.S.	D10	114
Warm Springs, Ga., U.S.	E14	122
Warm Springs, Or., U.S.	F5	136
Warnemünde, ngh., Ger.	B7	16
Warner, Ab., Can.	G18	138
Warner, N.H., U.S.	G5	110
Warner Lakes, l., Or., U.S.	H6	136
Warner Mountains, mts., U.S.	B5	134
Warner Peak, mtn., Or., U.S.	A6	134
Warner Robins, Ga., U.S.	D2	116
Warnow, stm., Ger.	B7	16
Warra, Austl.	F8	76
Warracknabeal, Austl.	K4	76
Warragul, Austl.	L5	76
Warrawagine, Austl.	D4	74
Warrego, stm., Austl.	G5	76
Warren, Ar., U.S.	D6	122
Warren, In., U.S.	H4	112
Warren, Mi., U.S.	B2	114
Warren, Mn., U.S.	C2	118
Warren, Oh., U.S.	C5	114
Warren, Pa., U.S.	C6	114
Warrens, Wi., U.S.	G8	118
Warrensburg, Mo., U.S.	F4	120
Warrenton, S. Afr.	F7	70
Warrenton, Mo., U.S.	F6	120
Warrenton, N.C., U.S.	H7	114
Warrenton, Or., U.S.	D2	136
Warri, Nig.	H6	64
Warrington, Eng., U.K.	H10	12
Warrington, Fl., U.S.	G11	122
Warrior, Al., U.S.	D12	122
Warrnambool, Austl.	L4	76
Warroad, Mn., U.S.	C3	118
Warrumbungle National Park, p.o.i., Austl.	H7	76
Warsaw see Warszawa, Pol.	D16	16
Warsaw, Il., U.S.	D6	120
Warsaw, In., U.S.	G4	112
Warsaw, Ky., U.S.	F13	120
Warsaw, Mo., U.S.	F4	120
Warsaw, N.Y., U.S.	B7	114
Warsaw, N.C., U.S.	A7	116
Warspite, Ab., Can.	B18	138
Warszawa (Warsaw), Pol.	D16	16
Warszawa, state, Pol.	D16	16
Warta, Pol.	E14	16
Warta, stm., Pol.	D11	16
Wartburg, Tn., U.S.	H13	120
Wartrace, Tn., U.S.	B12	122
Warud, India	H7	54
Warwick, Austl.	G9	76
Warwick, Eng., U.K.	I11	12
Warwick, R.I., U.S.	C14	114
Warwick Channel, strt., Austl.	B7	74
Wasaga Beach, On., Can.	D10	112
Wasagu, Nig.	G6	64
Wasatch Range, mts., Ut., U.S.	C5	132
Wasbank, S. Afr.	F10	70
Wascana Creek, stm., Sk., Can.	D9	124
Wasco, Ca., U.S.	H6	134
Wasco, Or., U.S.	E6	136
Waseca, Mn., U.S.	G5	118
Wasgomuwa National Park, p.o.i., Sri L.	H5	53
Washademoak Lake, l., N.B., Can.	E11	110
Washburn, Il., U.S.	D8	120
Washburn, N.D., U.S.	G12	124
Washburn, Wi., U.S.	E7	118
Washburn, Mount, mtn., Wy., U.S.	F16	136
Washburn Lake, l., Nu., Can.	A9	106
Washington, D.C., U.S.	E9	114
Washington, Ga., U.S.	C3	116
Washington, Ia., U.S.	C6	120
Washington, In., U.S.	F10	120
Washington, Ks., U.S.	B11	128
Washington, La., U.S.	G6	122
Washington, Mo., U.S.	F6	120
Washington, N.C., U.S.	A8	116
Washington, N.J., U.S.	D11	114
Washington, Pa., U.S.	D5	114
Washington, Ut., U.S.	F3	132
Washington, Va., U.S.	F7	114
Washington, state, U.S.	C6	136
Washington, Mount, mtn., N.H., U.S.	F5	110
Washington Court House, Oh., U.S.	E2	114
Washington Island, i., Wi., U.S.	C3	112
Washington Land, reg., Grnld.	A12	141
Washington Terrace, Ut., U.S.	B4	132
Washita, stm., U.S.	G12	128
Washow Bay, b., Can.	C17	124
Washpool National Park, p.o.i., Austl.	G9	76
Washtucna, Wa., U.S.	D8	136
Wasian, Indon.	F9	44
Wasilków, Pol.	C19	16
Wasior, Indon.	F9	44
Waskada, Mb., Can.	E13	124
Waskaganish, Qc., Can.	E15	106
Waskahigan, stm., Ab., Can.	B13	138
Waskom, Tx., U.S.	E4	122
Wassamu, Japan	B15	38
Wassenaar, Neth.	C14	14
Wasserburg, Ger.	I8	16
Wasseralfingen, Ger.	H6	16
Wassy, Fr.	F13	14
Watampone, Indon.	F12	50
Watansoppeng, Indon.	F11	50
Watatic, Mount, mtn., Ma., U.S.	B14	114
Watauga, stm., U.S.	C9	122
Waterberge, mts., S. Afr.	D8	70
Waterbury, Ct., U.S.	C12	114
Waterbury, Vt., U.S.	F4	110
Waterford (Port Lairge), Ire.	I5	12
Waterford, Ca., U.S.	F5	134
Waterford, Wi., U.S.	B9	120
Waterhen Lake, l., Mb., Can.	B14	124
Water Island, i., V.I.U.S.	e7	104b
Waterloo, Aust.	C5	74
Waterloo, Bel.	D13	14
Waterloo, On., Can.	E9	112
Waterloo, Qc., Can.	E4	110
Waterloo, Al., U.S.	C10	122
Waterloo, Il., U.S.	F7	120
Waterloo, Ia., U.S.	B5	120
Waterloo, N.Y., U.S.	B8	114
Waterloo, Wi., U.S.	A9	120
Waterproof, La., U.S.	F7	122
Watersmeet, Mi., U.S.	E9	118
Waterton-Glacier International Peace Park, p.o.i., N.A.	B13	136
Waterton Lakes National Park, p.o.i., Ab., Can.	G16	138
Watertown, N.Y., U.S.	E14	112
Watertown, S.D., U.S.	C15	126
Waterval Boven, S. Afr.	D10	70
Water Valley, Ms., U.S.	C9	122
Waterville, N.S., Can.	E12	110
Waterville, Ks., U.S.	B12	128
Waterville, Me., U.S.	F7	110
Waterville, Oh., U.S.	C2	114
Waterville, Wa., U.S.	C6	136
Waterville, N.Y., U.S.	B12	114
Watford, Eng., U.K.	J12	12
Watford City, N.D., U.S.	G10	124
Wathena, Ks., U.S.	E2	120
Watkins Glen, N.Y., U.S.	B9	114
Watkinsville, Ga., U.S.	C2	116
Watling Island see San Salvador, i., Bah.	C10	96
Watonga, Ok., U.S.	F10	128
Watrous, Sk., Can.	C8	124
Watsa, D.R.C.	D5	66
Watseka, Il., U.S.	H2	112
Watsikengo, D.R.C.	E4	66
Watson, Sk., Can.	B9	124
Watson Lake, Yk., Can.	C5	106
Watsonville, Ca., U.S.	G4	134
Watt Mountain, vol., Dom.	j6	105c
Watts Bar Lake, res., Tn., U.S.	B14	122
Watts Mills, S.C., U.S.	B4	116
Wattwil, Switz.	C5	22
Watubela, Kepulauan, is., Indon.	F9	44
Watzmann, mtn., Ger.	I8	16
Waubay Lake, l., S.D., U.S.	B15	126
Wauchope, Austl.	D6	74
Wauchula, Fl., U.S.	I4	116
Wauconda, Wa., U.S.	B7	136
Waugh, Mb., Can.	B3	118
Waukara, Bukit, mtn., Indon.	I2	76
Waukaringa, Austl.	I2	76
Waukarlycarly, Lake, l., Austl.	D4	74
Waukegan, Il., U.S.	F2	112
Waukesha, Wi., U.S.	A9	120
Waukon, Ia., U.S.	H7	118
Waunakee, Wi., U.S.	A8	120
Wauneta, Ne., U.S.	G11	126
Waupaca, Wi., U.S.	H10	118
Waupun, Wi., U.S.	G11	128
Waurika, Ok., U.S.	G11	128
Waurika Lake, res., Ok., U.S.	G10	128
Wausa, Ne., U.S.	E15	126
Wausau, Wi., U.S.	G9	118
Wauseon, Oh., U.S.	C1	114
Wautoma, Wi., U.S.	G9	118
Wauwatosa, Wi., U.S.	E1	112
Wauzeka, Wi., U.S.	A7	120
Wave Hill, Austl.	C6	74
Waverly, Ia., U.S.	B5	120
Waverly, Mo., U.S.	E4	120
Waverly, Ne., U.S.	D11	116
Waverly, N.Y., U.S.	B9	114
Waverly, Oh., U.S.	E2	114
Waverly, Tn., U.S.	H10	120
Waverly, Va., U.S.	G8	114
Waverly Hall, Ga., U.S.	E14	122
Wāw, Sudan	F5	62
Wawa, On., Can.	B14	106
Wawa, Nig.	H5	64
Wawa, stm., Nic.	E5	102
Wāw al-Kabīr, Libya	B3	62
Wawanesa, Mb., Can.	E14	124
Waxahachie, Tx., U.S.	B11	130
Waxhaw, N.C., U.S.	B5	116
Way, Lake, l., Austl.	E4	74
Waya, i., Fiji	p18	79e
Waycross, Ga., U.S.	E3	116
Wayland, Ia., U.S.	C6	120
Wayland, Ky., U.S.	G3	114
Wayland, Mi., U.S.	F4	112
Waylyn, S.C., U.S.	D6	116
Wayne, Ab., Can.	E18	138
Wayne, Mi., U.S.	B2	114
Wayne, Ne., U.S.	E15	126
Wayne, N.J., U.S.	D11	114
Wayne, W.V., U.S.	F3	114
Wayne City, Il., U.S.	F9	120
Waynesboro, Ms., U.S.	F10	122
Waynesboro, Pa., U.S.	E8	114
Waynesboro, Tn., U.S.	B11	122
Waynesboro, Va., U.S.	F6	114
Waynesburg, Pa., U.S.	E5	114
Waynesville, N.C., U.S.	A3	116
Waynoka, Ok., U.S.	E10	128
Wāzah Khwāh, Afg.	B2	54
Wazīrābād, Pak.	B5	54
Wda, stm., Pol.	C14	16
We, N. Cal.	m16	79d
We, Pulau, i., Indon.	j2	48
Weatherford, Ok., U.S.	F10	128
Weatherford, Tx., U.S.	B10	130
Weatherly, Pa., U.S.	D10	114
Weaubleau, Mo., U.S.	G4	120
Weaver Lake, l., Mb., Can.	B17	124
Weaverville, Ca., U.S.	C3	134
Weaverville, N.C., U.S.	A3	116
Webb, Sk., Can.	D5	124
Webb, Ms., U.S.	D8	122
Webbwood, On., Can.	B7	112
Weber, stm., Ut., U.S.	B5	132
Weber City, Va., U.S.	H3	114
Webster, Ab., Can.	A12	138
Webster, Fl., U.S.	H3	116
Webster, Ma., U.S.	B14	114
Webster, N.Y., U.S.	B8	114
Webster, S.D., U.S.	B15	126
Webster City, Ia., U.S.	B4	120
Weda, Indon.	E8	44
Weddell Island, i., Falk. Is.	J4	90
Weddell Sea, Ant.	B36	81
Wedderburn, Austl.	K4	76
Wedgeport, N.S., Can.	G11	110
Wedowee, Al., U.S.	D13	122
Weed, Ca., U.S.	B3	134
Weems, Va., U.S.	G9	114
Weenen, S. Afr.	F10	70
Weeping Water, Ne., U.S.	D1	120
Weert, Neth.	C14	14
Wee Waa, Austl.	H7	76
Węgorzewo, Pol.	B17	16
Węgrów, Pol.	D17	16
Wei, stm., China	D3	42
Wei, stm., China	C5	42
Weichang, China	A7	42
Weichuan, China	D7	42
Weida, Ger.	F8	16
Weiden in der Oberpfalz, Ger.	G8	16
Weifang, China	C8	42
Weihai, China	C10	42
Weihaiwei see Weihai, China	C10	42
Weihe, China	B8	38
Weilburg, Ger.	F4	16
Weilheim, Ger.	I7	16
Weimar, Ger.	E7	16
Weimar, Tx., U.S.	E11	130
Weinan, China	D3	42
Weinheim, Ger.	G4	16
Weipa, Austl.	B8	74
Weippe, Id., U.S.	D11	136
Weir, Ks., U.S.	D14	128
Weir, Ms., U.S.	D9	122
Weir, stm., Austl.	G7	76
Weirton, W.V., U.S.	D5	114
Weisburd, Arg.	C6	92
Weiser, Id., U.S.	F10	136
Weiser, stm., Id., U.S.	F10	136
Weisner Mountain, mtn., Al., U.S.	C13	122
Weissenburg in Bayern, Ger.	G7	16
Weissenfels, Ger.	E7	16
Weiss Lake, res., Al., U.S.	C13	122
Weisswasser, Ger.	E10	16
Weitra, Aus.	B11	22
Weixi, China	F4	36

Name	Map Ref.	Page
Weixian, China	C6	42
Weiyuan, stm., China	A5	48
Weiz, Aus.	C12	22
Wejherowo, Pol.	B14	16
Wekoewa Punt, c., Neth. Ant.	p23	104g
Welaka, Fl., U.S.	G4	116
Welch, Ok., U.S.	H2	120
Welch, Tx., U.S.	B5	130
Welcome, Mn., U.S.	H4	118
Weldiya, Eth.	E7	62
Weldon, Sk., Can.	A8	124
Weldon, Il., U.S.	D9	120
Weldon, stm., U.S.	D4	120
Weleetka, Ok., U.S.	B2	122
Welk'ītē, Eth.	F7	62
Welkom, S. Afr.	E8	70
Welland, On., Can.	F10	112
Welland, stm., Eng., U.K.	I12	12
Wellborn, Fl., U.S.	F3	116
Wellborn, Tx., U.S.	G2	122
Wellesley Islands, is., Austl.	C8	74
Wellingborough, Eng., U.K.	I12	12
Wellington, Austl.	I7	76
Wellington, On., Can.	E12	112
Wellington, N.Z.	E6	80
Wellington, S. Afr.	H4	70
Wellington, Eng., U.K.	K9	12
Wellington, Co., U.S.	G7	126
Wellington, Mo., U.S.	E4	120
Wellington, Oh., U.S.	C3	114
Wellington, Tx., U.S.	G8	128
Wellington, Ut., U.S.	D6	132
Wellington, Isla, i., Chile	I2	90
Wellington Bay, b., Nu., Can.	B9	106
Wellington Channel, strt., Nu., Can.	B7	141
Wellman, Ia., U.S.	C6	120
Wellman, Tx., U.S.	A5	130
Wells, Eng., U.K.	J10	12
Wells, Mi., U.S.	C2	112
Wells, Mn., U.S.	H5	118
Wells, N.Y., U.S.	G2	110
Wells, Tx., U.S.	F3	122
Wells, Lake, l., Austl.	E4	74
Wells, Mount, hill, Austl.	C5	74
Wellsboro, Pa., U.S.	C8	114
Wellsburg, Ia., U.S.	B4	120
Wellsburg, W.V., U.S.	D5	114
Wellsford, N.Z.	C6	80
Wells-next-the-Sea, Eng., U.K.	I13	12
Wellston, Oh., U.S.	E3	114
Wellsville, Ks., U.S.	C13	128
Wellsville, Mo., U.S.	E6	120
Wellsville, N.Y., U.S.	B8	114
Wellsville, Oh., U.S.	D5	114
Wellton, Az., U.S.	K2	132
Wels, Aus.	B10	22
Welsford, N.B., Can.	E10	110
Welshpool, Wales, U.K.	I9	12
Welwyn Garden City, Eng., U.K.	J12	12
Wembley, Ab., Can.	A11	138
Wena, D.R.C.	E4	66
Wenatchee, Wa., U.S.	C6	136
Wenatchee Mountains, mts., Wa., U.S.	C6	136
Wenceslau Braz, Braz.	L1	88
Wenchang, China	L4	42
Wencheng, China	H8	42
Wenchi, Ghana	H4	64
Wenchou see Wenzhou, China	F9	36
Wenchow see Wenzhou, China	F9	36
Wendell, Id., U.S.	H12	136
Wenden, Az., U.S.	J3	132
Wendeng, China	C10	42
Wendover, Ut., U.S.	C2	132
Weng, stm., China	I6	42
Weng'an, China	H2	42
Wenling, China	G9	42
Wenlock, stm., Austl.	B8	74
Wenquan, China	E14	32
Wenshan, China	A7	48
Wenshang, China	D7	42
Wenshui, China	C4	42
Wenshui, China	G2	42
Wensleydale, val., Eng., U.K.	G11	12
Wentworth, Austl.	J3	76
Wentworth, S.D., U.S.	G2	118
Wenxi, China	D4	42
Wenxian, China	D5	42
Wenzhou, China	F9	36
Wepener, S. Afr.	F8	70
Werda, Bots.	D6	70
Werdau, Ger.	F8	16
Werder, Ger.	D8	16
Wernadinga, Austl.	B2	76
Wernigerode, Ger.	E6	16
Werra, stm., Ger.	E5	16
Werribee, Austl.	K5	76
Werrikimbe National Park, p.o.i., Austl.	H9	76
Werris Creek, Austl.	H8	76
Wertheim, Ger.	G5	16
Wesel, Ger.	E2	16
Weser, stm., Ger.	C4	16
Weskan, Ks., U.S.	C7	128
Weslaco, Tx., U.S.	H10	130
Weslemkoon Lake, l., On., Can.	C12	112
Wesley, Dom.	i6	105c
Wesleyville, Pa., U.S.	B5	114
Wessel, Cape, c., Austl.	B7	74
Wessel Islands, is., Austl.	B7	74
Wessington, S.D., U.S.	C14	126
Wessington Springs, S.D., U.S.	C14	126
West, Ms., U.S.	D9	122
West, Tx., U.S.	C10	130
West Allis, Wi., U.S.	B9	120
West Antarctica, reg., Ant.	D30	81
Westbank, B.C., Can.	G11	138
West Bank, dep., Asia	F6	58
West Bay, N.S., Can.	E15	110
West Bay, b., Tx., U.S.	E12	130
West Bend, Ia., U.S.	B3	120
West Bend, Wi., U.S.	E1	112
West Bengal, state, India	G11	54
West Blocton, Al., U.S.	D11	122
West Bohemia see Západočeský kraj, state, Czech Rep.	G9	16
West Borneo see Kalimantan Barat, state, Indon.	D7	50
West Branch, Ia., U.S.	C6	120
Westbridge, B.C., Can.	G11	138
West Bromwich, Eng., U.K.	I11	12
Westbrook, Me., U.S.	G6	110
Westbrook, Mn., U.S.	G3	118
Westbrook, Tx., U.S.	B6	130
West Burlington, Ia., U.S.	D6	120
West Burra, i., Scot., U.K.	n18	12a
Westby, Austl.	J6	76
Westby, Wi., U.S.	H8	118
West Cache Creek, stm., Ok., U.S.	G10	128
West Caicos, i., T./C. Is.	B11	102
West Cape, c., N.Z.	G2	80
West Cape Howe, c., Austl.	G3	74
West Carlisle, Tx., U.S.	H6	128
West Caroline Basin, unds.	I16	142
West Chester, Pa., U.S.	E10	114
Westchester Station, N.S., Can.	E13	110
Westcliffe, Co., U.S.	C3	128
West Columbia, S.C., U.S.	B4	116
West Columbia, Tx., U.S.	H3	122
West Cote Blanche Bay, b., La., U.S.	H7	122
West Des Moines, Ia., U.S.	C4	120
West Dolores, stm., Co., U.S.	F8	132
West Elk Peak, mtn., Co., U.S.	E9	132
West End, Ar., U.S.	C6	122
West End, N.C., U.S.	A6	116
Westerland, Ger.	B4	16
Westerly, R.I., U.S.	C14	114
Western, state, Sol. Is.	e7	79b
Western, stm., Austl.	D4	76
Western Australia, state, Austl.	D4	74
Western Cape, state, S. Afr.	H5	70
Western Channel, strt., Asia	E2	40
Western Desert, des., Egypt	B5	62
Western Division, state, Fiji	p18	79e
Western Dvina (Daugava) (Zahodnjaja Dzvina) (Zapadnaja Dvina), stm., Eur.	D7	10
Western Ghāts, mts., India	E3	46
Westernport, Md., U.S.	E6	114
Western Sahara, dep., Afr.	E2	64
Western Samoa see Samoa, ctry., Oc.	g12	79c
Western Sayans see Zapadnyj Sajan, mts., Russia	D16	32
Western Shore, N.S., Can.	F12	110
Westerschelde, est., Neth.	C12	14
Westerstede, Ger.	C3	16
Westerville, Oh., U.S.	D3	114
Westerwald, mts., Ger.	F3	16
West European Basin, unds.	D12	144
West Falkland, i., Falk. Is.	J4	90
West Fargo, N.D., U.S.	E1	118
Westfield, Il., U.S.	E9	120
Westfield, In., U.S.	H3	112
Westfield, Ma., U.S.	H4	110
Westfield, N.J., U.S.	D11	114
Westfield, Pa., U.S.	C8	114
Westfield, Wi., U.S.	H9	118
West Fork, Ar., U.S.	I3	120
West Frankfort, Il., U.S.	G9	120
West Friese Eilanden, is., Neth.	A14	14
West Frisian Islands see West Friese Eilanden, is., Neth.	A14	14
Westgate, Austl.	F6	76
West Grand Lake, res., Me., U.S.	E8	110
West Hamlin, W.V., U.S.	F3	114
West Hartford, Ct., U.S.	C13	114
West Haven, Ct., U.S.	C13	114
West Helena, Ar., U.S.	C8	122
Westhoff, Tx., U.S.	E10	130
Westhope, N.D., U.S.	F12	124
West Ice Shelf, ice, Ant.	B13	81
West Indies, is.	C7	82
West Java see Jawa Barat, state, Indon.	G5	50
West Jefferson, N.C., U.S.	H4	114
West Jordan, Ut., U.S.	C4	132
West Kettle, stm., B.C., Can.	G11	138
West Kingston, R.I., U.S.	C14	114
West Lafayette, In., U.S.	H2	112
Westlake, La., U.S.	G5	122
Westland National Park, p.o.i., N.Z.	F3	80
West Laramie, Wy., U.S.	F7	126
West Lebanon, In., U.S.	H2	112
West Liberty, Ky., U.S.	G2	114
West Liberty, Oh., U.S.	D2	114
Westlock, Ab., Can.	B16	138
West Lorne, On., Can.	F8	112
Westmeath, state, Ire.	H5	12
West Memphis, Ar., U.S.	B8	122
Westminster, Co., U.S.	B3	128
Westminster, Md., U.S.	E9	114
West Monroe, La., U.S.	E6	122
Westmoreland, Ks., U.S.	B12	128
Westmoreland, Tn., U.S.	H11	120
Westmorland, Ca., U.S.	J10	134
West Nicholson, Zimb.	B9	70
West Nishnabotna, stm., Ia., U.S.	C2	120
West Nueces, stm., Tx., U.S.	E7	130
West Nusa Tenggara see Nusa Tenggara Barat, state, Indon.	G10	50
Weston, Id., U.S.	A4	132
Weston, Mo., U.S.	E3	120
Weston, Oh., U.S.	C2	114
Weston, Or., U.S.	E8	136
Weston, W.V., U.S.	E5	114
Weston-super-Mare, Eng., U.K.	J9	12
West Orange, Tx., U.S.	G5	122
Westover, Tn., U.S.	B10	122
West Palm Beach, Fl., U.S.	J5	116
West Palm Beach Canal, can., Fl., U.S.	J5	116
West Pensacola, Fl., U.S.	G11	122
Westphalia, Ks., U.S.	F2	120
West Plains, Mo., U.S.	H6	120
West Point, Ga., U.S.	E13	122
West Point, Ia., U.S.	D6	120
West Point, Ky., U.S.	F11	120
West Point, Ms., U.S.	D10	122
West Point, Ne., U.S.	J2	118
West Point, N.Y., U.S.	C11	114
West Point, Va., U.S.	G9	114
West Point Lake, res., U.S.	D13	122
West Poplar (Poplar, West Fork), stm., N.A.	F8	124
Westport, N.S., Can.	F10	110
Westport, On., Can.	D13	112
Westport, Ire.	H3	12
Westport, Ct., U.S.	C12	114
Westport, In., U.S.	E12	120
Westport, Or., U.S.	D3	136
Westpunt, c., Aruba	o19	104g
West Quoddy Head, c., Me., U.S.	F10	110
Westray, i., Scot., U.K.	B9	12
West Richland, Wa., U.S.	D7	136
West Road, stm., B.C., Can.	C7	138
West Rutland, Vt., U.S.	G3	110
West Salem, Il., U.S.	F9	120
West Salem, Oh., U.S.	D3	114
West Shoal Lake, l., Mb., Can.	D16	124
West Siberian Plain see Zapadno-Sibirskaja ravnina, pl., Russia	B12	32
West Slovakia see Západoslovenský Kraj, state, Slov.	H14	16
West Spanish Peak, mtn., Co., U.S.	D4	128
West Sumatra see Sumatera Barat, state, Indon.	D2	50
West Terre Haute, In., U.S.	E10	120
West Union, Ia., U.S.	B6	120
West Union, Oh., U.S.	F2	114
West Unity, Oh., U.S.	C1	114
West Valley City, Ut., U.S.	C4	132
West Vancouver, B.C., Can.	G7	138
Westville, N.S., Can.	E14	110
Westville, In., U.S.	G3	112
West Virginia, state, U.S.	F5	114
West Walker, stm., U.S.	E6	134
West Warwick, R.I., U.S.	C14	114
West Webster, N.Y., U.S.	E12	112
Westwold, B.C., Can.	F11	138
Westwood, Ca., U.S.	C5	134
Westwood Lakes, Fl., U.S.	K5	116
West Wyalong, Austl.	I6	76
West Yellowstone, Mt., U.S.	F15	136
Wetar, Pulau, i., Indon.	G8	44
Wetar, Selat, strt., Indon.	G8	44
Wetaskiwin, Ab., Can.	C17	138
Wete, Tan.	E7	66
Wethersfield, Ct., U.S.	C13	114
Wetmore, Ks., U.S.	E2	120
Wetumpka, Al., U.S.	E12	122
Wetzlar, Ger.	F4	16
Wewahitchka, Fl., U.S.	G13	122
Wewak, Pap. N. Gui.	a3	79a
Wewoka, Ok., U.S.	B2	122
Wexford, Ire.	I6	12
Wexford, state, Ire.	I6	12
Weyburn, Sk., Can.	E10	124
Weymontachie, Qc., Can.	C3	110
Weymouth, N.S., Can.	F10	110
Weymouth, Eng., U.K.	K10	12
Weymouth, Ma., U.S.	B15	114
Whakatane, N.Z.	C7	80
Whangarei, N.Z.	B6	80
Whapmagoostui, Qc., Can.	D15	106
Wharfe, stm., Eng., U.K.	H11	12
Wharton, W.V., U.S.	G4	114
Wharton Basin, unds.	K12	142
Wharton Lake, l., Nu., Can.	C10	106
Whataroa, N.Z.	F4	80
What Cheer, Ia., U.S.	C5	120
Whatley, Al., U.S.	F11	122
Wheatland, Ca., U.S.	D4	134
Wheatland, Ia., U.S.	C7	120
Wheatley, On., Can.	F7	112
Wheatley, Ar., U.S.	C7	122
Wheaton, Il., U.S.	C9	120
Wheaton, Md., U.S.	E8	114
Wheat Ridge, Co., U.S.	B3	128
Wheeler, Ms., U.S.	C10	122
Wheeler, Tx., U.S.	F8	128
Wheeler, stm., Qc., Can.	D17	106
Wheeler Lake, res., Al., U.S.	C11	122
Wheeler Peak, mtn., Nv., U.S.	D2	132
Wheeler Peak, mtn., N.M., U.S.	E3	128
Wheeling, W.V., U.S.	D5	114
Wheelwright, Arg.	F7	92
Wheelwright, Ky., U.S.	G3	114
Whidbey Island, i., Wa., U.S.	B4	136
Whiskey Peak, mtn., Wy., U.S.	E5	126
Whistler, B.C., Can.	F8	138
Whitakers, N.C., U.S.	H8	114
Whitby, On., Can.	E11	112
Whitby, Eng., U.K.	G12	12
Whitchurch, Eng., U.K.	H10	12
Whitchurch-Stouffville, On., Can.	E10	112
White, Ga., U.S.	C14	122
White, stm., N.A.	C2	106
White, stm., U.S.	C7	122
White, stm., U.S.	D13	126
White, stm., U.S.	C7	132
White, stm., Az., U.S.	J6	132
White, stm., In., U.S.	F10	120
White, stm., Nv., U.S.	F1	132
White, stm., Tx., U.S.	H7	128
White, stm., Wa., U.S.	C5	136
White, East Fork, stm., In., U.S.	F10	120
White, Lake, l., Austl.	D5	74
White Bay, b., Nf., Can.	i22	107a
White Bear Lake, Mn., U.S.	F6	118
White Bluff, Tn., U.S.	H10	120
White Butte, mtn., N.D., U.S.	A9	126
White Castle, La., U.S.	G7	122
White City, Ks., U.S.	C12	128
White Cliffs, Austl.	H4	76
Whitecourt, Ab., Can.	B15	138
White Deer, Tx., U.S.	F7	128
Whiteface, stm., Mn., U.S.	D6	118
Whiteface Mountain, mtn., N.Y., U.S.	F3	110
Whitefield, N.H., U.S.	F5	110
Whitefish, Mt., U.S.	B12	136
Whitefish Bay, Wi., U.S.	A10	120
Whitefish Bay, b., On., Can.	B4	118
Whitefish Bay, b., N.A.	B5	112
Whitefish Lake, l., Ab., Can.	B18	138
Whitefish Lake, l., N.T., Can.	C9	106
Whitefish Point, Mi., U.S.	B4	112
Whitefish Point, c., Mi., U.S.	B4	112
White Hall, Ar., U.S.	C6	122
White Hall, Il., U.S.	E7	120
Whitehall, Mi., U.S.	E3	112
Whitehall, N.Y., U.S.	G3	110
Whitehall, Wi., U.S.	G7	118
Whitehaven, Eng., U.K.	G9	12
Whitehorse, Yk., Can.	C4	106
White House, Tn., U.S.	H11	120
Whitehouse, Tx., U.S.	E3	122
White Island, i., Nu., Can.	B13	106
White Island, i., N.Z.	C7	80
White Lake, S.D., U.S.	D14	126
White Lake, Wi., U.S.	F10	118
White Lake, l., On., Can.	C13	112
White Lake, l., La., U.S.	H6	122
Whitemark, Austl.	n13	77a
White Mountain Peak, mtn., Ca., U.S.	F7	134
White Mountains, mts., N.H., U.S.	F5	110
Whitemouth, stm., Mb., Can.	E18	124
Whitemouth Lake, l., Mb., Can.	E18	124
Whitemud, stm., Mb., Can.	D15	124
White Nile (Abyaḍ, Al-Bahr al-), stm., Afr.	E6	62
White Oak, Tx., U.S.	E4	122
White Oak Creek, stm., Tx., U.S.	D3	122
White Otter Lake, l., On., Can.	B6	118
White Pigeon, Mi., U.S.	G4	112
Whitepine, Mt., U.S.	C11	136
White Pine, Tn., U.S.	H2	114
White Plains, N.Y., U.S.	C12	114
White Plains, N.C., U.S.	H5	114
Whiteriver, Az., U.S.	J6	132
White River, S.D., U.S.	D12	126
White River Junction, Vt., U.S.	G4	110
White Rock, B.C., Can.	G8	138
White Russia see Belarus, ctry., Eur.	E14	6
Whitesail Lake, res., B.C., Can.	C3	138
Whitesand, stm., Sk., Can.	C11	124
White Sands National Monument, p.o.i., N.M., U.S.	B1	130
Whitesboro, Tx., U.S.	D2	122
White Sea see Beloe more, Russia	D18	8
White Settlement, Tx., U.S.	B10	130
White Springs, Fl., U.S.	F3	116
White Sulphur Springs, Mt., U.S.	D16	136
White Sulphur Springs, W.V., U.S.	G5	114
Whitesville, Ky., U.S.	G11	120
Whiteville, N.C., U.S.	B7	116
Whiteville, Tn., U.S.	B9	122
White Volta (Volta Blanche), stm., Afr.	G4	64
Whitewater, Mt., U.S.	F6	124
Whitewater, Wi., U.S.	B9	120
Whitewater, stm., U.S.	E13	120
Whitewater Baldy, mtn., N.M., U.S.	J8	132
Whitewater Creek, stm., N.A.	F6	124
Whitewater Lake, l., Mb., Can.	E13	124
White Woman Creek, stm., U.S.	C7	128
Whitewood, Austl.	C4	76
Whitewood, Sk., Can.	D11	124
Whitewood, S.D., U.S.	C9	126
Whithorn, Jam.	i12	104d
Whithorn, Scot., U.K.	G8	12
Whiting, Ia., U.S.	B1	120
Whiting, Ks., U.S.	E2	120
Whitley City, Ky., U.S.	H13	120
Whitman, Ma., U.S.	B15	114
Whitmire, S.C., U.S.	B4	116
Whitmore Mountains, mts., Ant.	D31	81
Whitney, On., Can.	C11	112
Whitney, Lake, res., Tx., U.S.	C10	130
Whitney, Mount, mtn., Ca., U.S.	G7	134
Whitney Point, N.Y., U.S.	B9	114
Whitsunday Island, i., Austl.	C7	76
Whittemore, Ia., U.S.	A3	120
Whittemore, Mi., U.S.	D6	112
Whittle, Cap, c., Qc., Can.	i22	107a
Whittlesea, Austl.	K5	76
Whittlesey, Mount, hill, Wi., U.S.	E8	118
Whitwell, Tn., U.S.	B13	122
Wholdaia Lake, l., N.T., Can.	C9	106
Whyalla, Austl.	F7	74
Whycocomagh, N.S., Can.	E15	110
Wiang Phan, Thai.	B4	48
Wiarton, On., Can.	D8	112
Wichian Buri, Thai.	E5	48
Wichita, Ks., U.S.	D11	128
Wichita, stm., Tx., U.S.	G10	128
Wichita Falls, Tx., U.S.	H10	128
Wick, Scot., U.K.	C9	12
Wickenburg, Az., U.S.	J4	132
Wickepin, Austl.	F3	74
Wickett, Tx., U.S.	C5	130
Wickham, Austl.	D3	74
Wickiup Reservoir, res., Or., U.S.	G5	136
Wickliffe, Ky., U.S.	H8	120
Wicklow, Ire.	H6	12
Wicklow, state, Ire.	H7	12
Wicklow Head, c., Ire.	I7	12
Wicklow Mountains, mts., Ire.	H6	12
Widgeegoara Creek, stm., Austl.	F6	76
Więcbork, Pol.	C13	16
Wieleń, Pol.	D12	16
Wieliczka, Pol.	F16	16
Wielkopolska, reg., Pol.	E13	16
Wielkopolski Park Narodowy, p.o.i., Pol.	D12	16
Wieluń, Pol.	E14	16
Wien (Vienna), Aus.	B13	22
Wien, state, Aus.	B13	22
Wiener Neustadt, Aus.	C13	22
Wienerwald, mts., Aus.	B13	22
Wieprz, stm., Pol.	E18	16
Wieprza, stm., Pol.	B12	16
Wieprz-Krzna, Kanał, can., Pol.	E19	16
Wierden, Neth.	D2	16
Wiergate, Tx., U.S.	F5	122
Wieruszów, Pol.	E14	16
Wierzyca, stm., Pol.	B14	16
Wiesbaden, Ger.	F4	16
Wiesloch, Ger.	G4	16
Wigan, Eng., U.K.	H10	12
Wiggins, Co., U.S.	A4	128
Wiggins, Ms., U.S.	G9	122
Wight, Isle of, i., Eng., U.K.	K11	12
Wigtown, Scot., U.K.	G8	12
Wilbur, Wa., U.S.	C8	136
Wilburton, Ok., U.S.	C3	122
Wilcannia, Austl.	H4	76
Wilcox, Sk., Can.	D9	124
Wilcox, Ne., U.S.	A9	128
Wildcat Creek, stm., In., U.S.	H3	112
Wildcat Hill, mtn., Sk., Can.	A11	124
Wild Coast, cst., S. Afr.	H9	70
Wilder, Id., U.S.	G9	136
Wilderness of Judaea (Midbar Yehuda), des., Asia	G6	58
Wildhay, stm., Ab., Can.	C13	138
Wildhorse Creek, stm., U.S.	G10	126
Wild Horse Lake, l., Mt., U.S.	B17	136
Wild Rice, stm., Mn., U.S.	D2	118
Wild Rice, stm., N.D., U.S.	H17	124
Wildrose, N.D., U.S.	F10	124
Wild Rose, Wi., U.S.	G9	118
Wildwood, Ab., Can.	C15	138
Wildwood, N.J., U.S.	F11	114
Wilge, stm., S. Afr.	E9	70
Wilhelm, Mount, mtn., Pap. N. Gui.	b3	79a
Wilhelmina Gebergte, mts., Sur.	C6	84
Wilhelmshaven, Ger.	C4	16
Wilhelmstal, Nmb.	B3	70
Wilkerson Pass, p., Co., U.S.	B3	128
Wilkes-Barre, Pa., U.S.	C10	114
Wilkesboro, N.C., U.S.	H4	114
Wilkes Land, reg., Ant.	C16	81
Wilkie, Sk., Can.	B5	124
Willacoochee, Ga., U.S.	E2	116
Willamette, stm., Or., U.S.	E4	136
Willamette, Middle Fork, stm., Or., U.S.	G4	136
Willamina, Or., U.S.	E3	136
Willandra Billabong Creek, stm., Austl.	I5	76
Willandra National Park, p.o.i., Austl.	I5	76
Willapa Bay, b., Wa., U.S.	D2	136
Willard, Mo., U.S.	G4	120
Willard, Oh., U.S.	C3	114
Willard, Ut., U.S.	B4	132
Willard, Punta, c., Mex.	A2	100
Willcox, Az., U.S.	K7	132
Willcox Playa, l., Az., U.S.	K7	132
Willemstad, Neth. Ant.	p22	104g
Willeroo, Austl.	C6	74
William, Mount, mtn., Austl.	K4	76
William Bill Dannelly Reservoir, res., Al., U.S.	E11	122
Williams, Ca., U.S.	D3	134
Williams, Ia., U.S.	I5	118
Williams, Mn., U.S.	C3	118
Williams, stm., Austl.	C3	76
Williamsburg, Ia., U.S.	C5	120
Williamsburg, Ky., U.S.	H1	114
Williamsburg, Va., U.S.	G9	114
Williams Lake, B.C., Can.	D8	138
Williamson, N.Y., U.S.	E12	112
Williamson, W.V., U.S.	G3	114
Williamson, stm., Or., U.S.	H5	136
Williamson, Mount, mtn., Ca., U.S.	G7	134
Williamsport, Pa., U.S.	C8	114
Williamston, Mi., U.S.	F5	112
Williamston, S.C., U.S.	B3	116
Williamstown, Ky., U.S.	F1	114
Williamstown, N.J., U.S.	E11	114
Williamstown, W.V., U.S.	E4	114
Williamsville, Il., U.S.	L9	118
Willikies, Antig.	f4	105b
Willimantic, Ct., U.S.	C13	114
Willingboro, N.J., U.S.	D10	114
Willis, Tx., U.S.	G3	122
Willis Group, is., Austl.	C10	74
Williston, Fl., U.S.	G3	116
Williston, N.D., U.S.	F10	124
Williston, S.C., U.S.	C4	116
Williston Lake, res., B.C., Can.	D6	106
Willits, Ca., U.S.	D2	134
Willmar, Mn., U.S.	F3	118
Willoughby, Oh., U.S.	C4	114
Willoughby Bay, b., Antig.	f4	105b
Willow, Ak., U.S.	D10	140
Willow, stm., B.C., Can.	C8	138
Willowbrook, Sk., Can.	C10	124
Willow Bunch, Sk., Can.	E8	124
Willow Bunch Lake, l., Sk., Can.	E8	124
Willow Creek, Ca., U.S.	C2	134
Willow Creek, Mt., U.S.	E15	136
Willow Creek, stm., Ab., Can.	F17	138
Willow Creek, stm., Or., U.S.	F9	136
Willow Creek, stm., Or., U.S.	E7	136
Willow Lake, S.D., U.S.	C15	126
Willow Lake, l., N.T., Can.	C7	106
Willowmore, S. Afr.	H6	70
Willowra, Austl.	D6	74
Willow Reservoir, res., Wi., U.S.	F9	118
Willows, Ca., U.S.	D3	134
Willow Springs, Mo., U.S.	H6	120
Willowvale, S. Afr.	H9	70
Wills Creek, stm., Austl.	D2	76
Wills Point, Tx., U.S.	E2	122
Wilmar, Ar., U.S.	D6	122
Wilmer, Al., U.S.	G10	122
Wilmer, Tx., U.S.	E2	122
Wilmette, Il., U.S.	F2	112
Wilmington, De., U.S.	E10	114
Wilmington, N.C., U.S.	B7	116
Wilmington, Oh., U.S.	E2	114
Wilmington, Vt., U.S.	H4	110
Wilmore, Ky., U.S.	G13	120
Wilmot, S.D., U.S.	F2	118
Wilpattu National Park, p.o.i., Sri L.	G4	53
Wilsall, Mt., U.S.	D16	136
Wilson, Austl.	H2	76
Wilson, Ar., U.S.	B8	122
Wilson, La., U.S.	G7	122
Wilson, N.Y., U.S.	E11	112
Wilson, N.C., U.S.	I8	114
Wilson, Ok., U.S.	G11	128
Wilson, Tx., U.S.	H7	128
Wilson, stm., Austl.	F4	76
Wilson, Cape, c., Nu., Can.	B14	106
Wilson, Mount, mtn., Az., U.S.	H2	132
Wilson, Mount, mtn., Ca., U.S.	I7	134
Wilson, Mount, mtn., Co., U.S.	F8	132
Wilson Lake, res., Al., U.S.	C11	122
Wilson Lake, res., Ks., U.S.	C10	128
Wilsons Promontory, pen., Austl.	L6	76
Wilsons Promontory National Park, p.o.i., Austl.	L6	76
Wilsonville, Ne., U.S.	A8	128
Wilton, Eng., U.K.	J11	12
Wilton, Me., U.S.	F6	110
Wilton, N.H., U.S.	B14	114
Wilton, Wi., U.S.	H8	118
Wilton, stm., Austl.	B6	74
Wiluna, Austl.	E4	74
Wimauma, Fl., U.S.	I3	116
Wimberley, Tx., U.S.	D9	130
Winamac, In., U.S.	G3	112
Winburg, S. Afr.	F8	70
Winchendon, Ma., U.S.	B13	114
Winchester, On., Can.	C14	112
Winchester, Eng., U.K.	J11	12
Winchester, Il., U.S.	E7	120
Winchester, In., U.S.	H5	112
Winchester, Ky., U.S.	G1	114
Winchester, Tn., U.S.	B12	122
Winchester, Va., U.S.	E7	114
Wind, stm., Yk., Can.	B3	106
Wind, stm., Wy., U.S.	D4	126
Wind Cave National Park, p.o.i., S.D., U.S.	D9	126
Winder, Ga., U.S.	B2	116
Windermere, B.C., Can.	F15	138
Windermere, Eng., U.K.	G10	12
Windfall, Ab., Can.	B14	138
Windhoek, Nmb.	C3	70
Windigo, stm., Qc., Can.	C3	110
Windom, Mn., U.S.	H3	118
Windorah, Austl.	E4	76
Window Rock, Az., U.S.	H7	132
Wind River Peak, mtn., Wy., U.S.	E3	126
Wind River Range, mts., Wy., U.S.	D3	126
Windsor, Austl.	I8	76
Windsor, N.S., Can.	E12	110
Windsor, On., Can.	F6	112
Windsor, Qc., Can.	E5	110
Windsor, Eng., U.K.	J12	12
Windsor, Ca., U.S.	E3	134
Windsor, Ct., U.S.	C13	114
Windsor, Il., U.S.	E9	120
Windsor, Mo., U.S.	F4	120
Windsor, N.C., U.S.	I9	114
Windsor, Va., U.S.	H9	114
Windsor Forest, Ga., U.S.	E4	116
Windsor Locks, Ct., U.S.	C13	114
Windthorst, Tx., U.S.	H10	128
Windward, Gren.	p11	105e
Windward Islands, is., N.A.	k6	105c
Windward Passage, strt., N.A.	C11	102
Windy Peak, mtn., Co., U.S.	C2	128
Winfield, Al., U.S.	D11	122
Winfield, Ks., U.S.	D12	128
Winfield, Mo., U.S.	E7	120
Winfield, W.V., U.S.	F4	114
Wing, N.D., U.S.	G13	124
Wingate, N.C., U.S.	B5	116
Wingham, Austl.	H9	76
Wingham, On., Can.	E8	112
Wingo, Ky., U.S.	H9	120
Winisk, On., Can.	D13	106
Winisk, stm., On., Can.	E13	106
Winisk Lake, l., On., Can.	E13	106
Wink, Tx., U.S.	C4	130
Winkana, Mya.	E4	48
Winkelman, Az., U.S.	K6	132
Winkler, Mb., Can.	E16	124
Winlock, Wa., U.S.	D3	136
Winneba, Ghana	H4	64
Winnebago, Mn., U.S.	H4	118
Winnebago, Ne., U.S.	B1	120
Winnebago, stm., Ia., U.S.	H5	118
Winnebago, Lake, l., Wi., U.S.	G10	118
Winneconne, Wi., U.S.	G10	118
Winnemucca, Nv., U.S.	B8	134
Winnemucca Lake, l., Nv., U.S.	C6	134
Winner, S.D., U.S.	D13	126
Winnetka, Il., U.S.	F2	112
Winnett, Mt., U.S.	H5	124
Winnibigoshish, Lake, res., Mn., U.S.	D4	118
Winnie, Tx., U.S.	H4	122
Winning, Austl.	D2	74
Winnipeg, Mb., Can.	E16	124
Winnipeg, stm., Can.	E11	106
Winnipeg, Lake, l., Mb., Can.	E11	106
Winnipeg Beach, Mb., Can.	D17	124
Winnipegosis, Mb., Can.	C13	124
Winnipegosis, Lake, l., Mb., Can.	B13	124
Winnipesaukee, Lake, l., N.H., U.S.	G5	110
Winnsboro, S.C., U.S.	B4	116
Winnsboro, Tx., U.S.	E3	122
Winnsboro Mills, S.C., U.S.	B4	116
Winona, Ks., U.S.	B7	128
Winona, Mn., U.S.	G7	118
Winona, Ms., U.S.	D9	122
Winona, Mo., U.S.	G6	120
Winooski, stm., Vt., U.S.	F4	110
Winschoten, Neth.	A15	14
Winschoterdiep, can., Neth.	A15	14
Winsen, Ger.	C6	16
Winslow, Az., U.S.	H6	132
Winslow, In., U.S.	F10	120
Winslow, Me., U.S.	F7	110
Winsted, Mn., U.S.	G4	118
Winston, Fl., U.S.	H3	116
Winston, Or., U.S.	G3	136
Winston-Salem, N.C., U.S.	H5	114
Winter, Wi., U.S.	F8	118
Winter Garden, Fl., U.S.	H4	116
Winter Harbor, Me., U.S.	F8	110
Winter Harbour, B.C., Can.	F2	138
Winterhaven, Ca., U.S.	K2	132
Winter Haven, Fl., U.S.	I4	116
Winter Island, i., Nu., Can.	B14	106
Winter Park, Fl., U.S.	H4	116
Winters, Ca., U.S.	E3	134
Winters, Tx., U.S.	C8	130
Winterset, Ia., U.S.	C4	120
Winterswijk, Neth.	B15	14
Winterthur, Switz.	C5	22
Winterville, Ga., U.S.	C2	116
Winterville, Ms., U.S.	D7	122
Winthrop, Me., U.S.	F7	110
Winthrop, Wa., U.S.	B6	136
Winthrop Harbor, Il., U.S.	F2	112
Wintinna, Austl.	E6	74
Winton, Austl.	D4	76
Winton, N.Z.	H3	80
Winton, N.C., U.S.	H8	114
Wirātnagar, Nepal	E11	54
Wīrganj, Nepal	E10	54
Wisbech, Eng., U.K.	I12	12
Wiscasset, Me., U.S.	G7	110
Wisconsin, state, U.S.	G9	118
Wisconsin, stm., Wi., U.S.	I8	118
Wisconsin Dells, Wi., U.S.	H9	118
Wisconsin Dells, misc. cult., Wi., U.S.	H9	118
Wisconsin Rapids, Wi., U.S.	G8	118
Wisdom, Mt., U.S.	E13	136
Wise, Va., U.S.	G3	114
Wiseman, Ak., U.S.	C9	140
Wishek, N.D., U.S.	A13	126
Wishram, Wa., U.S.	E5	136
Wisła, Pol.	G14	16
Wisła (Vistula), stm., Pol.	B14	16
Wiślany, Mierzeja, spit, Eur.	B15	16
Wisłok, stm., Pol.	F18	16
Wisłoka, stm., Pol.	F17	16
Wismar, Ger.	C7	16
Wisner, La., U.S.	F7	122
Wister, Ok., U.S.	C4	122
Wisznice, Pol.	E19	16
Witbank, S. Afr.	D9	70
Witham, stm., Eng., U.K.	H12	12
Withlacoochee, stm., U.S.	F2	116
Witkowo, Pol.	D13	16
Wit-Mfolozi, stm., S. Afr.	F10	70
Witney, Eng., U.K.	J11	12
Wit Nossob, stm., Nmb.	C4	70
Witsand, S. Afr.	I5	70
Witt, Il., U.S.	E8	120
Wittenberg, Wi., U.S.	G9	118
Wittenberge, Ger.	C7	16
Wittenburg, Ger.	C6	16
Wittenoom, Austl.	D3	74
Wittingen, Ger.	D6	16
Wittlich, Ger.	G2	16
Wittmund, Ger.	C3	16
Wittstock, Ger.	C8	16
Witu Islands, is., Pap. N. Gui.	a5	79a
Witvlei, Nmb.	C4	70
Witwatersrand, mts., S. Afr.	D8	70
Witzenhausen, Ger.	E5	16
Wiżajny, Pol.	B18	16
Wkra, stm., Pol.	C15	16
Wleń, Pol.	E11	16
Włocławek, Pol.	D15	16
Włocławek, state, Pol.	D14	16
Włoszczowa, Pol.	F15	16
Woburn, Ma., U.S.	B14	114
Wodonga, Austl.	K6	76
Wodzisław Śląski, Pol.	F14	16
Wokam, Pulau, i., Indon.	G10	44
Woking, Eng., U.K.	J12	12
Wokingham Creek, stm., Austl.	C4	76
Wolbrom, Pol.	F15	16
Wolcott, In., U.S.	D10	120
Wolcott, N.Y., U.S.	E13	112
Wolcottville, In., U.S.	G4	112
Woleai, at., Micron.	C5	72
Wolf, stm., U.S.	B9	122
Wolf, stm., Ms., U.S.	G9	122
Wolf, stm., Wi., U.S.	G10	118
Wolf, Volcán, vol., Ec.	h11	84a
Wolfach, Ger.	H4	16
Wolf Creek, Or., U.S.	H3	136
Wolf Creek, stm., U.S.	E9	128
Wolf Creek, stm., Mt., U.S.	C17	136
Wolf Creek Pass, p., Co., U.S.	F10	132
Wolf Creek Reservoir, res., Ks., U.S.	F2	120
Wolfeboro, N.H., U.S.	G5	110
Wolfe Island, i., On., Can.	D13	112
Wolfen, Ger.	E8	16
Wolfenbüttel, Ger.	D6	16
Wolfenden, Mount, mtn., B.C., Can.	F3	138
Wolfforth, Tx., U.S.	H6	128
Wolfhagen, Ger.	E4	16
Wolf Lake, Mi., U.S.	E3	112
Wolf Lake, l., Ab., Can.	B20	138
Wolf Point, Mt., U.S.	F8	124
Wolfratshausen, Ger.	I7	16
Wolf Rock, r., Eng., U.K.	L7	12
Wolfsberg, Aus.	D11	22
Wolfsburg, Ger.	D6	16
Wolfville, N.S., Can.	E12	110
Wolgast, Ger.	B9	16
Woliński Park Narodowy, p.o.i., Pol.	C10	16
Wollaston Lake, l., Sk., Can.	D10	106
Wollaston Peninsula, pen., Can.	B7	106
Wollemi National Park, p.o.i., Austl.	I7	76
Wollongong, Austl.	J8	76
Wołomin, Pol.	D17	16
Wołów, Pol.	E12	16
Wolseley, Sk., Can.	D10	124
Wolsey, S.D., U.S.	C14	126
Wolverhampton, Eng., U.K.	I10	12
Wolverton, Eng., U.K.	I11	12
Wonarah, Austl.	C7	74
Wondai, Austl.	F8	76
Wonderland, Ca., U.S.	C4	134
Wondinong, Austl.	E3	74
Wonewoc, Wi., U.S.	H8	118
Wŏnju, Kor., S.	F7	38
Wonogiri, Indon.	G7	50
Wonosari, Indon.	H7	50
Wonosobo, Indon.	G6	50
Wŏnsan, Kor., N.	E7	38
Wonthaggi, Austl.	L5	76
Wood, S.D., U.S.	D12	126

Name	Map Ref.	Page
Wood, stm., Ne., U.S.	G13	126
Wood, Mount, mtn., Mt., U.S.	E17	136
Woodall Mountain, hill, Ms., U.S.	C10	122
Woodbine, Ga., U.S.	F4	116
Woodbine, Ia., U.S.	C2	120
Woodbridge, Eng., U.K.	I14	12
Woodbridge, Va., U.S.	F8	114
Woodburn, Or., U.S.	E4	136
Woodbury, Ga., U.S.	E14	122
Woodbury, N.J., U.S.	E10	114
Woodbury, Tn., U.S.	I11	120
Woodhull, Il., U.S.	C7	120
Woodlake, Ca., U.S.	G6	134
Wood Lake, Ne., U.S.	E12	126
Woodland, Ca., U.S.	E4	134
Woodland, Me., U.S.	E9	110
Woodland, N.C., U.S.	H8	114
Woodland Park, Co., U.S.	C3	128
Woodridge, Mb., Can.	E17	124
Wood River, Il., U.S.	F7	120
Wood River, Ne., U.S.	G14	126
Woodroffe, Mount, mtn., Austl.	E6	74
Woodruff, Az., U.S.	I6	132
Woodruff, S.C., U.S.	B3	116
Woodruff, Wi., U.S.	F9	118
Woods, Lake, l., Austl.	C6	74
Woods, Lake of the, l., N.A.	B3	118
Woodsboro, Tx., U.S.	F10	130
Woodsfield, Oh., U.S.	E4	114
Woods Hole, Ma., U.S.	C15	114
Woodside, Austl.	L6	76
Woodson, Tx., U.S.	A8	130
Woodstock, Austl.	D3	76
Woodstock, N.B., Can.	D9	110
Woodstock, On., Can.	E9	112
Woodstock, Eng., U.K.	J11	12
Woodstock, Il., U.S.	B9	120
Woodstock, N.Y., U.S.	B11	114
Woodstock, Vt., U.S.	G4	110
Woodsville, N.H., U.S.	F4	110
Woodville, N.Z.	E6	80
Woodville, Al., U.S.	C12	122
Woodville, Ga., U.S.	C2	116
Woodville, Ms., U.S.	F7	122
Woodville, Oh., U.S.	G6	112
Woodville, Tx., U.S.	G4	122
Woodward, Ok., U.S.	E9	128
Woody, stm., Can.	B12	124
Woody Head, c., Austl.	G9	76
Woolmarket, Ms., U.S.	G9	122
Woomera, Austl.	F7	74
Woonsocket, R.I., U.S.	B14	114
Woonsocket, S.D., U.S.	C14	126
Woorabinda, Austl.	E7	76
Wooramel, Austl.	E2	74
Wooramel, stm., Austl.	E2	74
Wooster, Oh., U.S.	D3	114
Worcester, S. Afr.	H4	70
Worcester, Eng., U.K.	I10	12
Worcester, Ma., U.S.	B14	114
Worden, Mt., U.S.	A4	126
Wörgl, Aus.	C9	22
Workington, Eng., U.K.	G9	12
Worksop, Eng., U.K.	H11	12
Worland, Wy., U.S.	C5	126
Worms, Ger.	G4	16
Worthing, Eng., U.K.	K12	12
Worthington, In., U.S.	E11	120
Worthington, Mn., U.S.	H3	118
Worthington, Oh., U.S.	D3	114
Worthington Peak, mtn., Nv., U.S.	E1	132
Wotho, at., Marsh. Is.	B7	72
Wotu, Indon.	E12	50
Wouhnta, Nic.	F6	102
Wounded Knee, S.D., U.S.	D10	126
Wounded Knee Creek, stm., S.D., U.S.	D10	126
Wowan, Austl.	D8	76
Wowoni, Pulau, i., Indon.	F7	44
Woy Woy, Austl.	I8	76
Wrangel Island see Vrangelja, ostrov, i., Russia	B24	34
Wrangell, Ak., U.S.	E13	140
Wrangell, Cape, c., Ak., U.S.	g21	140a
Wrangell Mountains, mts., Ak., U.S.	D11	140
Wrath, Cape, c., Scot., U.K.	C8	12
Wrens, Ga., U.S.	C3	116
Wrentham, Ab., Can.	G18	138
Wrexham, Wales, U.K.	H10	12
Wright, Mount, mtn., Mt., U.S.	B14	136
Wright City, Mo., U.S.	F6	120
Wright Patman Lake, res., Tx., U.S.	D4	122
Wrightson, Mount, mtn., Az., U.S.	L6	132
Wrightstown, Wi., U.S.	D1	112
Wrightsville, Ga., U.S.	D3	116
Wrightsville Beach, N.C., U.S.	B8	116
Wrigley, N.T., Can.	C6	106
Wrigley, Tn., U.S.	I10	120
Wrocław (Breslau), Pol.	E13	16
Wrocław, state, Pol.	E13	16
Wrong Lake, l., Mb., Can.	B17	124
Wrottesley, Cape, c., N.T., Can.	B15	140
Wroxton, Sk., Can.	C12	124
Września, Pol.	D13	16
Wschowa, Pol.	E12	16
Wu, stm., China	H3	42
Wu, stm., China	G2	42
Wu, stm., China	H4	42
Wu, stm., China	G7	42
Wu, stm., China	I5	42
Wubu, China	C4	42
Wuchang, China	B7	38
Wuchang Hu, l., China	F7	42
Wuchin see Changzhou, China	F8	42
Wuchou see Wuzhou, China	J4	42
Wuchow see Wuzhou, China	J4	42
Wuchuan, China	K4	42
Wuchuan, China	A4	42
Wuchung see Wuzhong, China	C2	42
Wuda, China	B2	42
Wudaoliang, China	D3	36
Wudi, China	C7	42
Wuding, China	F5	36
Wuding, stm., China	C4	42
Wudu, China	E5	36
Wufeng, China	F4	42
Wugang, China	H4	42
Wugong, China	D2	42
Wugong Shan, mts., China	H5	42
Wuhai, China	B2	42
Wuhan (Hankow), China	F6	42
Wuhsi see Wuxi, China	F9	42
Wuhsing see Huzhou, China	F9	42
Wuhu, China	F8	42
Wuhua, China	J6	42
Wuhuanchi, China	C4	38
Wüjang, China	B7	54
Wujia, stm., China	A3	42
Wujiangdu, China	H2	42
Wukang, China	F8	42
Wukari, Nig.	H6	64
Wukeshu, China	B7	38
Wulateqianqi, China	A3	42
Wuliang Shan, mts., China	G5	36
Wulong, China	G2	42
Wuluhan, Indon.	H8	50
Wulumuch'i see Ürümqi, China	C2	36
Wuluo, China	H3	42
Wuming, China	J3	42
Wundwin, Mya.	B2	48
Wunnummin Lake, l., On., Can.	E13	106
Wunstorf, Ger.	D5	16
Wupatki National Monument, p.o.i., Az., U.S.	H5	132
Wuppertal, Ger.	E3	16
Wuppertal, S. Afr.	H4	70
Wuqi, China	C3	42
Wuqia, China	B12	56
Wuqiang, China	B6	42
Wurno, Nig.	G6	64
Würzburg, Ger.	G5	16
Wurzen, Ger.	E8	16
Wushan, China	F3	42
Wusheng, China	F2	42
Wushenqi, China	B3	42
Wushi, China	J4	42
Wusih see Wuxi, China	F9	42
Wusuli (Ussuri), stm., Asia	B11	36
Wutai, China	B5	42
Wutai Shan, mtn., China	B5	42
Wutong, China	I3	42
Wutongqiao, China	F5	36
Wutsin see Changzhou, China	F8	42
Wut'ungch'iao see Wutongqiao, China	F5	36
Wutungkiao see Wutongqiao, China	F5	36
Wuvulu Island, i., Pap. N. Gui.	a3	79a
Wuwei, China	D5	36
Wuwei, China	F7	42
Wuxi, China	F9	42
Wuxi, China	F3	42
Wuxiang, China	C5	42
Wuyang, China	H4	42
Wuyi, China	G8	42
Wuyi Shan, mts., China	H7	42
Wuyuan, China	A3	42
Wuyuan, China	G7	42
Wuzhai, China	B4	42
Wuzhi Shan (Wuzhi Peak), mtn., China	L3	42
Wuzhong, China	C2	42
Wuzhou, China	J4	42
Wyaconda, Mo., U.S.	D6	120
Wyandotte, Mi., U.S.	B2	114
Wyandra, Austl.	F5	76
Wyangala, Lake, res., Austl.	J7	76
Wyatt, Mo., U.S.	H8	120
Wycheproof, Austl.	K4	76
Wye, stm., U.K.	J10	12
Wyeville, Wi., U.S.	G8	118
Wyk, Ger.	B4	16
Wykoff, Mn., U.S.	H6	118
Wylie, Lake, res., U.S.	A4	116
Wymark, Sk., Can.	D6	124
Wymondham, Eng., U.K.	I13	12
Wymore, Ne., U.S.	K2	118
Wyndham, Austl.	C5	74
Wyndmere, N.D., U.S.	E1	118
Wynne, Ar., U.S.	B8	122
Wynnewood, Ok., U.S.	G11	128
Wynniatt Bay, b., Can.	A8	106
Wynona, Ok., U.S.	E12	128
Wynot, Ne., U.S.	E15	126
Wynyard, Austl.	n12	77a
Wynyard, Sk., Can.	C9	124
Wyodak, Wy., U.S.	C7	126
Wyoming, On., Can.	F7	112
Wyoming, Ia., U.S.	B6	120
Wyoming, Mi., U.S.	F4	112
Wyoming, state, U.S.	E5	126
Wyoming Peak, mtn., Wy., U.S.	H16	136
Wyong, Austl.	I8	76
Wyperfield National Park, p.o.i., Austl.	J3	76
Wyśmierzyce, Pol.	E16	16
Wysokie Mazowieckie, Pol.	D18	16
Wyszków, Pol.	D17	16
Wytheville, Va., U.S.	H4	114
X		
Xaafuun, Raas, c., Som.	B10	66
Xàbia, Spain	F11	20
Xaidulla, China	A4	46
Xainza, China	C12	54
Xai-Xai, Moz.	D11	70
Xalapa (Jalapa), Mex.	F10	100
Xalin, Som.	C9	66
Xam (Chu), stm., Asia	B7	48
Xambioá, Braz.	D1	88
Xambrê, stm., Braz.	A11	92
Xam Nua, Laos	B7	48
Xá-Muteba, Ang.	B2	68
Xan (San), stm., Asia	E8	48
Xangongo, Ang.	D2	68
Xankändi, Azer.	B6	56
Xánthi, Grc.	B7	28
Xanxerê, Braz.	C11	92
Xapecó, stm., Braz.	C11	92
Xapuri, Braz.	F4	84
Xar Moron, stm., China	C3	38
Xàtiva, Spain	F10	20
Xau, Lake, pl., Bots.	B7	70
Xavantina, Braz.	D6	90
Xaxim, Braz.	C11	92
Xcalak, Mex.	C4	102
X-Can, Mex.	B4	102
Xelva, Spain	E9	20
Xenia, Oh., U.S.	E2	114
Xepenehe, N. Cal.	m16	79d
Xhumo, Bots.	B7	70
Xi, stm., China	J5	42
Xiachuan Dao, i., China	K5	42
Xiagaixin, China	A5	48
Xiamen (Amoy), China	I7	42
Xi'an (Sian), China	D3	42
Xianfeng, China	G3	42
Xiang, stm., China	G5	42
Xiangcheng, China	E5	42
Xiangfan, China	F4	42
Xianggang (Hong Kong), China	J6	42
Xiangkhoang, Laos	C6	48
Xiangkhoang, Plateau de (Tran Ninh), plat., Laos	C6	48
Xiangning, China	D4	42
Xiangride, China	D4	36
Xiangshan, China	G9	42
Xiangtan, China	H5	42
Xiangxiang, China	H5	42
Xiangyin, China	G5	42
Xiangyuan, China	C5	42
Xiangzhou, China	J3	42
Xianju, China	G9	42
Xianshui, stm., China	B9	46
Xiantao, China	F5	42
Xianyang, China	D3	42
Xianyang, China	G8	42
Xianyou, China	I8	42
Xiao, stm., China	G8	42
Xiaochengzi, China	C5	38
Xiaogan, China	F5	42
Xiaoguai, China	B1	36
Xiao Hinggan Ling (Lesser Khingan Range), mts., China	B10	36
Xiaojin, China	E5	36
Xiaojiu, China	B7	38
Xiaoluan, stm., China	D2	38
Xiaopingyang, China	J3	42
Xiaoshan, China	F9	42
Xiaoxian, China	D7	42
Xiaoyi, China	C4	42
Xiapu, China	H9	42
Xiawa, China	C4	38
Xiaxian, China	D4	42
Xibo, stm., China	D3	38
Xichang, China	F5	36
Xichong, China	F1	42
Xicoténcatl, Mex.	D9	100
Xié, stm., Braz.	G8	86
Xifei, stm., China	E7	42
Xifeng, China	C6	38
Xifeng, China	H2	42
Xigazê, China	D12	54
Xihan, stm., China	D1	42
Xihe, China	F5	42
Xiheying, China	B6	42
Xihua, China	E6	42
Xiji, China	D1	42
Xiliao, stm., China	C5	38
Xilin, China	D11	54
Xilinhot, China	C2	38
Ximakou, China	F5	42
Ximalin, China	A6	42
Ximiao, China	C5	36
Xin, stm., China	G7	42
Xin'an, China	C6	38
Xin'anjiang Shuiku, res., China	G8	42
Xinavane, Moz.	D11	70
Xin Barag Youqi, China	B8	36
Xin Barag Zuoqi, China	B8	36
Xinbin, China	D6	38
Xincai, China	E6	42
Xinchang, China	G9	42
Xincheng, China	G6	36
Xincheng, China	B6	42
Xindu, China	I4	42
Xinfeng, China	I6	42
Xinfeng Shuiku, res., China	J6	42
Xing'an, China	I4	42
Xingcheng, China	A9	42
Xingguo, China	H6	42
Xinghai, China	D4	36
Xinghe, China	A5	42
Xinghua, China	E8	42
Xinglong, China	D1	42
Xingren, China	F6	36
Xingrenbu, China	C1	42
Xingtai, China	C6	42
Xingtang, China	B6	42
Xingu, stm., Braz.	D7	34
Xingxian, China	B4	42
Xingyi, China	F5	36
Xinhe, China	C6	42
Xinhua, China	H4	42
Xinhui, China	J5	42
Xining, China	D5	36
Xinji, China	C6	42
Xinjiang, China	D4	42
Xinjiang, state, China	A5	46
Xinjin, China	E5	36
Xinjin, China	B9	42
Xinjiulong (New Kowloon), China	J6	42
Xinkai, stm., China	C5	38
Xinli, China	B7	38
Xinlitun, China	D5	38
Xinmin, China	C5	38
Xinning, China	H4	42
Xinshao, China	H4	42
Xintian, China	I5	42
Xinwen, China	D7	42
Xinxian, China	B5	42
Xinxian, China	F6	42
Xinxiang, China	D5	42
Xinxing, China	C8	38
Xinyang, China	E6	42
Xinye, China	E5	42
Xinyi, China	D8	42
Xinyu, China	H6	42
Xinzhou, China	L3	42
Xiongyuecheng, China	A9	42
Xiping, China	E6	42
Xiping, China	G8	42
Xiqing Shan, mts., China	E5	36
Xique-Xique, Braz.	F4	88
Xırdalan, Azer.	A6	56
Xishanqiao, China	F8	42
Xisha Qundao (Paracel Islands), is., China	B5	50
Xishui, China	F6	42
Xiti, China	B9	54
Xiu, stm., China	G6	42
Xi Ujimqin Qi, China	B2	38
Xiushui, China	G6	42
Xiuyan, China	A10	42
Xiva, Spain	E10	20
Xixabangma Feng, mtn., China	D10	54
Xixi, China	H8	42
Xixian, China	E6	42
Xixiang, China	E2	42
Xixona, Spain	F10	20
Xiyang, China	C5	42
Xizang (Tibet), state, China	B5	46
Xizi, China	D3	38
Xochicalco, hist., Mex.	F9	100
Xochistlahuaca, Mex.	G9	100
Xu, stm., China	H7	42
Xuancheng, China	F8	42
Xuan'en, China	F3	42
Xuang, stm., Laos	B6	48
Xuanhan, China	F2	42
Xuanhua, China	A6	42
Xuanwei, China	F5	36
Xuchang, China	D5	42
Xun, stm., China	J4	42
Xungru, China	D10	54
Xunwu, China	I6	42
Xupu, China	H4	42
Xúquer see Júcar, stm., Spain	E10	20
Xuwen, China	K4	42
Xuyi, China	E8	42
Xuyong, China	G1	42
Xuzhou, China	D7	42
Xylókastro, Grc.	E5	28
Y		
Yaak, Mt., U.S.	B11	136
Yaan, China	E5	36
Yaapeet, Austl.	J3	76
Yablonovy Range see Jablonovyj hrebet, mts., Russia	F11	34
Yabluniv, Ukr.	A12	26
Yabrīn, Sau. Ar.	E6	56
Yabucoa, P.R.	B4	104a
Yabuli, China	B8	38
Yacambu, Parque Nacional, p.o.i., Ven.	C7	86
Yacata, i., Fiji	p20	79e
Yacheng, China	L3	42
Yachi, stm., China	H2	42
Yaco see Iaco, stm., S.A.	F4	84
Yacuiba, Bol.	D4	90
Yacyretá, Isla, i., Para.	C9	92
Yādgīr, India	C3	53
Yadkin, stm., N.C., U.S.	H4	114
Yadkinville, N.C., U.S.	H5	114
Yadong, China	E12	54
Yafran, Libya	A2	62
Yagasa Cluster, i., Fiji	q20	79e
Yagoua, Cam.	B3	66
Yagradagzê Shan, mtn., China	D4	36
Yaguajay, Cuba	A8	102
Yaguarón (Jaguarão), stm., S.A.	F11	92
Yaguas, stm., S.A.	I6	86
Yahe, China	B9	38
Yahk, B.C., Can.	G14	138
Yahualica, Mex.	E7	100
Yai, Khao, mtn., Thai.	E4	48
Yainax Butte, mtn., Or., U.S.	A4	134
Yaita, Japan	C12	40
Yaitopya see Ethiopia, ctry., Afr.	F7	62
Yaizu, Japan	E11	40
Yajiang, China	E5	36
Yakacık, Tur.	E7	58
Yakeshi, China	E9	36
Yakima, Wa., U.S.	D6	136
Yakima, stm., Wa., U.S.	D7	136
Yakmach, Pak.	D9	56
Yako, Burkina	G4	64
Yakoma, D.R.C.	D4	66
Yakumo, Japan	C14	38
Yaku-shima, i., Japan	I9	38
Yakutat Bay, b., Ak., U.S.	E11	140
Yakutia see Jakutija, state, Russia	D14	34
Yala, Thai.	I5	48
Yalahau, Laguna de, b., Mex.	B4	102
Yale, B.C., Can.	G9	138
Yale, Mi., U.S.	E7	112
Yale, Ok., U.S.	A2	122
Yale, Mount, mtn., Co., U.S.	C2	128
Yalgoo, Austl.	E3	74
Yalinga, C.A.R.	C4	66
Yalobusha, stm., Ms., U.S.	D9	122
Yalong, stm., China	E5	36
Yalova, Tur.	C12	28
Yalpuh, ozero, l., Ukr.	D15	26
Yalu (Amnok-kang), stm., Asia	D7	38
Yalu, stm., China	D6	38
Yalvaç, Tur.	E14	28
Yamaga, Japan	F3	40
Yamagata, Japan	A13	40
Yamagata, state, Japan	A13	40
Yamaguchi, Japan	E4	40
Yamaguchi, state, Japan	E4	40
Yamal Peninsula see Jamal, poluostrov, pen., Russia	B2	34
Yamanaka, Japan	C9	40
Yamanashi, state, Japan	D11	40
Yamasaki, Japan	D7	40
Yamaska, stm., Qc., Can.	E4	110
Yamatengwumulu, China	D4	36
Yamba, Austl.	G9	76
Yambio, Sudan	G5	62
Yamdena, Pulau, i., Indon.	G9	44
Yame, Japan	F3	40
Ya Men, b., China	J5	42
Yamethin, Mya.	B3	48
Yamma Yamma, Lake, l., Austl.	F3	76
Yamoussoukro, C. Iv.	H4	64
Yampa, stm., Co., U.S.	C8	132
Yampil', Ukr.	A15	26
Yamsay Mountain, mtn., Or., U.S.	H5	136
Yamuna, stm., India	F8	54
Yamzho Yumco, l., China	D13	54
Yan, stm., China	C4	42
Yan, stm., Sri L.	G5	53
Yanac, Austl.	K3	76
Yanagawa, Japan	F3	40
Yanai, Japan	F5	40
Yanam, India	C6	53
Yan'an, China	C3	42
Yanbu' al-Bahr, Sau. Ar.	E4	56
Yanceyville, N.C., U.S.	H5	114
Yanchang, China	C3	42
Yancheng, China	E9	42
Yanchi, China	C2	42
Yanco Creek, stm., Austl.	J5	76
Yanda Creek, stm., Austl.	H5	76
Yandama Creek, stm., Austl.	G3	76
Yandé, Île, i., N. Cal.	m14	79d
Yandina, Sol. Is.	e8	79b
Yandoon, Mya.	D2	48
Yanfolila, Mali	G3	64
Yang, stm., Thai.	D7	48
Yangambi, D.R.C.	D4	66
Yan'gang, China	I7	42
Yangbajain, China	C13	54
Yangcheng, China	D5	42
Yangchiang see Yangjiang, China	K4	42
Yangchou see Yangzhou, China	E8	42
Yangchow see Yangzhou, China	E8	42
Yangch'üan see Yangquan, China	C5	42
Yangchun, China	J4	42
Yangdachengzi, China	B6	38
Yanggao, China	A5	42
Yanghexi, China	G3	42
Yangjiang, China	K4	42
Yangkü see Taiyuan, China	C5	42
Yangliuqing, China	B7	42
Yangon (Rangoon), Mya.	D2	48
Yangon, state, Mya.	D3	48
Yangpingguan, China	E1	42
Yangquan, China	C5	42
Yangriwan, China	F4	42
Yangsan, Kor., S.	D2	40
Yangshan, China	I5	42
Yangshuo, China	I4	42
Yangtze see Chang, stm., China	F8	36
Yangtze see Jinsha, stm., China	F5	36
Yangxian, China	E2	42
Yangxin, China	G6	42
Yangyang, Kor., S.	A1	40
Yangyuan, China	A5	42
Yangzhou, China	E8	42
Yanhe, China	G3	42
Yanji, China	C8	38
Yanji, China	C8	38
Yanjiadian, China	B9	42
Yankeetown, Fl., U.S.	G3	116
Yankton, S.D., U.S.	E15	126
Yanqi, China	C2	36
Yanqing, China	A6	42
Yanshou, China	B8	38
Yantabulla, Austl.	G5	76
Yantai, China	C9	42
Yantan, China	G9	42
Yanting, China	F1	42
Yantongshan, China	C6	38
Yanyuan, China	F5	36
Yanzhou, China	D7	42
Yao, Chad	E3	62
Yaoundé, Cam.	D2	66
Yaoxian, China	D3	42
Yao Yai, Ko, i., Thai.	I4	48
Yap, i., Micron.	C4	72
Yapacana, Parque Nacional, p.o.i., Ven.	F8	86
Yapacaní, Bol.	C4	90
Yapen, Pulau, i., Indon.	F10	44
Yapen, Selat, strt., Indon.	F10	44
Yappar, stm., Austl.	B4	76
Yaque del Norte, stm., Dom. Rep.	C12	102
Yaqui, stm., Mex.	G8	98
Yaquina, stm., Or., U.S.	F3	136
Yaracuy, state, Ven.	B7	86
Yaraka, Austl.	E5	76
Yardımcı, Tur.	A10	58
Yardımcı Burnu, c., Tur.	G13	28
Yarí, stm., Col.	H5	86
Yariga-take, mtn., Japan	C10	40
Yarīm, Yemen	G5	56
Yaring, Thai.	I5	48
Yaritagua, Ven.	B7	86
Yarkand see Shache, China	B12	56
Yarkand see Yarkant, stm., China	G13	32
Yarkant see Shache, China	B12	56
Yarkant, stm., China	G13	32
Yarloop, Austl.	F3	74
Yarmouth, N.S., Can.	G10	110
Yarmouth, Me., U.S.	G6	110
Yarmu, Pap. N. Gui.	a3	79a
Yarram, Austl.	L6	76
Yarraman, Austl.	F9	76
Yarrawonga, Austl.	K5	76
Yarumal, Col.	D4	86
Yasawa Group, is., Fiji	p18	79e
Yashiro-jima, i., Japan	F5	40
Yasinia, Ukr.	A11	26
Yasothon, Thai.	E6	48
Yass, Austl.	J7	76
Yasugi, Japan	D6	40
Yasuní, stm., Ec.	H3	86
Yasuni, Parque Nacional, p.o.i., Ec.	H4	86
Yata, stm., Bol.	B3	90
Yatağan, Tur.	F11	28
Yaté, N. Cal.	n16	79d
Yates City, Il., U.S.	D7	120
Yathkyed Lake, l., Nu., Can.	C11	106
Yating, China	I2	42
Yatsuga-take, mtn., Japan	D11	40
Yatsuo, Japan	C10	40
Yatsushiro, Japan	G3	40
Yatsushiro-kai, b., Japan	G3	40
Yatuá, stm., Ven.	G8	86
Yauca, Peru	G3	84
Yauco, P.R.	B2	104a
Yautepec, Mex.	F9	100
Yavarí (Javari), stm., S.A.	D3	84
Yavaros, Mex.	B4	100
Yavatmāl, India	H7	54
Yaví, Cerro, mtn., Ven.	E9	86
Yavita, Ven.	F8	86
Yaviza, Pan.	H9	102
Yavoriv, Ukr.	G19	16
Yavuzeli, Tur.	A8	58
Yaw, stm., Mya.	B2	48
Yawatahama, Japan	F5	40
Yaxchilán, hist., Mex.	D2	102
Yayladağı, Tur.	C7	58
Yayuan, China	D7	38
Yazd, Iran	C7	56
Yazoo, stm., Ms., U.S.	E8	122
Yazoo City, Ms., U.S.	E8	122
Ybbs an der Donau, Aus.	B12	22
Yding Skovhøj, hill, Den.	I3	8
Ýdra (Hydra), i., Grc.	F6	28
Ye, Mya.	E3	48
Yebyu, Mya.	E4	48
Yecheng, China	B12	56
Yech'ŏn, Kor., S.	C1	40
Yecla, Spain	F9	20
Yedashe, Mya.	C3	48
Yedi Göller Milli Parkı, p.o.i., Tur.	B14	28
Yedseram, stm., Nig.	G7	64
Yeeda, Austl.	C4	74
Yeghegnador, Arm.	B6	56
Yei, Sudan	G6	62
Yeji, China	F6	42
Yela Island, i., Pap. N. Gui.	B10	74
Yelarbon, Austl.	G8	76
Yell, i., Scot., U.K.	n18	12a
Yellandu, India	C5	53
Yellow see Huang, stm., China	D8	36
Yellow, stm., Wi., U.S.	G8	118
Yellow, stm., Wi., U.S.	F7	118
Yellow Grass, Sk., Can.	E9	124
Yellowhead Pass, p., Can.	D12	138
Yellow House Draw, stm., Tx., U.S.	H3	122
Yellowknife, N.T., Can.	C8	106
Yellowknife, stm., N.T., Can.	C8	106
Yellow Sea, Asia	G5	38
Yellowstone, stm., U.S.	B7	108
Yellowstone, Clarks Fork, stm., U.S.	B3	126
Yellowstone Falls, wtfl, Wy., U.S.	F16	136
Yellowstone Lake, l., Wy., U.S.	F16	136
Yellowstone National Park, Wy., U.S.	F16	136
Yellowstone National Park, p.o.i., U.S.	F16	136
Yellowtail Dam, dam, Mt., U.S.	B4	126
Yellville, Ar., U.S.	H5	120
Yelverton Bay, b., Nu., Can.	A9	141
Yemen, ctry., Asia	F6	56
Yenagoa, Nig.	H6	64
Yenangyaung, Mya.	B2	48
Yenanma, Mya.	C2	48
Yen Bai, Viet.	B7	48
Yench'eng see Yancheng, China	E9	42
Yenchi see Yanji, China	C8	38
Yenda, Austl.	J6	76
Yendéré, Burkina	G4	64
Yendi, Ghana	H4	64
Ye-ngan, Mya.	B3	48
Yengisar, China	B12	56
Yengo National Park, p.o.i., Austl.	I8	76
Yenice, Tur.	A6	58
Yenice, stm., Tur.	B15	28
Yenicekale, Tur.	A7	58
Yenierenköy, N. Cyp.	C5	58
Yenimehmetli, Tur.	D15	28
Yenipazar, Tur.	C13	28
Yenişehir, Tur.	C12	28
Yenisey see Enisej, stm., Russia	C6	34
Yenshuichen, Tai.	J9	42
Yentai see Yantai, China	C9	42
Yeola, India	H5	54
Yeo Lake, l., Austl.	E4	74
Yeovil, Eng., U.K.	K10	12
Yepachic, Mex.	A4	100
Yeppoon, Austl.	D8	76
Yerevan (Erivan), Arm.	A5	56
Yerington, Nv., U.S.	E6	134
Yerköy, Tur.	B3	56
Yerlisu, Tur.	C9	28
Yermo, Ca., U.S.	I9	134
Yerupaja, Nevado, mtn., Peru	F2	84
Yerushalayim (Jerusalem), Isr.	G6	58
Yesa, Embalse de, res., Spain	B9	20
Yeşildere, Tur.	A4	58
Yeşilköy, Tur.	C11	28
Yeşiltepe, Tur.	A3	58
Yeso, N.M., U.S.	G4	128
Yetman, Austl.	G8	76
Yetti, reg., Afr.	D3	64
Ye-u, Mya.	A2	48
Yeu, Île d', i., Fr.	H6	14
Yevlax, Azer.	A6	56
Yexian, China	E5	42
Yexian, China	C8	42
Yeywa, Mya.	B3	48
Ygatimí, Para.	B10	92
Yguazú, stm., Para.	B10	92
Yhú, Para.	B10	92
Yi, stm., China	B6	42
Yi, stm., China	D8	42
Yi, stm., China	D5	42
Yi, stm., Ur.	F10	92
Yi'allaq, Gebel, mtn., Egypt	H4	58
Yi'an, China	B10	36
Yibin, China	F5	36
Yibug Caka, l., China	B11	54
Yichang, China	F4	42
Yicheng, China	F5	42
Yichuan, China	D5	42
Yichuan, China	C3	42
Yichuan see Yinchuan, China	B2	42
Yichun, China	B10	36
Yichun, China	H6	42
Yidie, China	C4	42
Yidu, China	C8	42
Yidu, China	F4	42
Yifeng, China	G6	42
Yığılca, Tur.	C14	28
Yilan, China	B10	36
Yilaxi, China	C7	38
Yiliang, China	F5	36
Yilong, China	F2	42
Yin, stm., Mya.	B2	48
Yinbaing, Mya.	D3	48
Yinchuan, China	B2	42
Ying, stm., China	E6	42
Yingcheng see Yingchengzi, China	B6	38
Yingcheng, China	F5	42
Yingchengzi, China	B6	38
Yingde, China	I5	42
Yingjin, stm., China	C3	38
Yingkou, China	A10	42
Yingkou, China	A9	42
Yingpan, China	I2	42
Yingshang, China	E6	42
Yingshouyingzi, China	A7	42
Yingtan, China	G7	42
Yining, China	F14	32
Yinjiang, China	G3	42
Yinkeng, China	H6	42
Yinmatu, stm., China	D2	38
Yinnyein, Mya.	D3	48
Yin Shan, mts., China	C6	36
Yi'ong, stm., China	E3	36
Yirga'Alem, Eth.	F7	62
Yirol, Sudan	F6	62
Yishan, China	I3	42
Yishui, China	D8	42
Yisuhe, China	H5	42
Yitong, stm., China	C6	38
Yitulihe, China	A9	36
Yiwu, China	G8	42
Yiwu, China	A5	48
Yixian, China	D4	38
Yixing, China	F8	42
Yixun, stm., China	D2	38
Yiyang, China	G5	42
Yiyang, China	D4	42
Yiyang, China	G7	42
Yiyuan, China	C8	42
Yizhang, China	I5	42
Yli-Kitka, l., Fin.	C13	8
Ylivieska, Fin.	D11	8
Ymer Ø, i., Grnld.	C21	141
Ynykčanskij, Russia	D16	34
Yoakum, Tx., U.S.	E10	130
Yocona, stm., Ms., U.S.	C9	122
Yog Point, c., Phil.	C5	52
Yogyakarta, Indon.	G7	50
Yogyakarta, state, Indon.	H7	50
Yoho National Park, p.o.i., B.C., Can.	E14	138
Yōka, Japan	D7	40
Yokadouma, Cam.	D2	66
Yōkaichi, Japan	D9	40
Yokkaichi, Japan	D9	40
Yoko, Cam.	C2	66
Yokoate-jima, i., Japan	k19	39a
Yokohama, Japan	D12	40
Yokosuka, Japan	D12	40
Yokote, Japan	E14	38
Yola, Nig.	H7	64
Yolombo, D.R.C.	E4	66
Yom, stm., Thai.	D5	48
Yonago, Japan	D6	40
Yoncalla, Or., U.S.	G3	136
Yonezawa, Japan	B12	40
Yong'an, China	I7	42
Yongchang, China	D5	36
Yongcheng, China	D7	42
Yŏngch'ŏn, Kor., S.	D1	40
Yongchuan, China	G1	42
Yongding, China	I7	42
Yongding, stm., China	A6	42
Yŏngdŏk, Kor., S.	C2	40
Yŏngdong, Kor., S.	F7	38
Yongfeng, China	H6	42
Yonggi, Kor., S.	C1	40
Yongi, China	C7	38
Yŏngil-man, b., Kor., S.	C2	40
Yŏngju, Kor., S.	C1	40
Yongkang, China	G9	42
Yongle, stm., China	H5	42
Yongnian, China	C6	42
Yongning, China	J3	42
Yongning, China	B1	42
Yongping, China	F4	36
Yongren, China	F5	36
Yongshan, China	F5	36
Yongshou, China	D2	42
Yongtai, China	I8	42
Yŏngwŏl, Kor., S.	B1	40
Yongxing, China	B4	42
Yongxing, China	H5	42
Yongxiu, China	G6	42
Yŏngyang, Kor., S.	C2	40
Yongzhou, China	H4	42
Yonibana, S.L.	H2	64
Yonkers, N.Y., U.S.	D12	114
Yonne, state, Fr.	G12	14
Yonne, stm., Fr.	F12	14
Yopal, Col.	E5	86
Yopurga, China	B12	56
York, Austl.	F3	74
York, Eng., U.K.	H11	12
York, Al., U.S.	E10	122
York, N.D., U.S.	F14	124
York, Pa., U.S.	E9	114
York, S.C., U.S.	A4	116
York, Cape, c., Austl.	B8	74
York, Kap, c., Grnld.	B12	141
Yorke Peninsula, pen., Austl.	F7	74
Yorketown, Austl.	G7	74
York Factory, Mb., Can.	D12	106
Yorkshire Dales National Park, p.o.i., Eng., U.K.	G10	12
York Sound, strt., Austl.	B4	74
Yorkton, Sk., Can.	C11	124
Yorktown, Tx., U.S.	E10	130
Yorktown, Va., U.S.	G9	114
Yorkville, Il., U.S.	J10	118
Yorkville, N.Y., U.S.	E14	112
Yoro, Hond.	E4	102
Yoron-jima, i., Japan	I19	39a
Yosemite National Park, p.o.i., Ca., U.S.	F6	134
Yosemite Village, Ca., U.S.	F6	134
Yoshii, stm., Japan	E7	40
Yösöbulag see Altay, Mong.	B4	36
Yos Sudarso, Pulau, i., Indon.	G10	44
Yŏsu, Kor., S.	G7	38
You, stm., China	G6	36
You, stm., China	G4	42
Youanmi, Austl.	E3	74
Youghal, Ire.	J5	12
Young, Austl.	J7	76
Young, Sk., Can.	C8	124
Young, Az., U.S.	I5	132
Young, Ur.	F9	92
Younghusband Peninsula, pen., Austl.	K2	76
Young Island, i., Ant.	B21	81
Youngs Rock, r., Pit.	c28	78k
Youngstown, Ab., Can.	C2	124
Youngstown, N.Y., U.S.	E10	112
Youngstown, Oh., U.S.	C5	114
Youngsville, La., U.S.	G6	122
Youngsville, N.C., U.S.	H7	114
Yountville, Ca., U.S.	E3	134

Name	Map Ref.	Page
Youssoufia, Mor.	C3	64
Youxian, China	H5	42
Youyang, China	G3	42
Yŏyang-ni, Kor., S.	B1	40
Yozgat, Tur.	B3	56
Ypres see Ieper, Bel.	D11	14
Ypsilanti, Mi., U.S.	B2	114
Yreka, Ca., U.S.	B3	134
Ysabel Channel, strt., Pap. N. Gui.	a4	79a
Ystad, Swe.	I5	8
Ytterhogdal, Swe.	E6	8
Yu, stm., China	J3	42
Yuam, stm., Thai.	C3	48
Yuan see Red, stm., Asia	D9	46
Yuan, stm., China	H6	42
Yuan, stm., China	G4	42
Yuanling, China	G4	42
Yuanmou, China	F5	36
Yuantan, China	J5	42
Yuanyang, China	D5	42
Yuasa, Japan	E8	40
Yuba City, Ca., U.S.	D4	134
Yūbari, Japan	C15	38
Yucaipa, Ca., U.S.	I8	134
Yucatán, state, Mex.	B3	102
Yucatán, Península de (Yucatan Peninsula), pen., N.A.	C3	102
Yucatan Channel, strt., N.A.	B4	102
Yucatan Peninsula see Yucatán, Península de, pen., N.A.	C3	102
Yucca, Az., U.S.	I2	132
Yucca Mountain, mtn., Nv., U.S.	G9	134
Yucca Valley, Ca., U.S.	I9	134
Yucheng, China	C7	42
Yuci, China	C5	42
Yudu, China	I6	42
Yuechi, China	F2	42
Yueqing, China	G9	42
Yuexi, China	F5	36
Yueyang, China	G5	42
Yufa, China	B7	42
Yugan, China	G7	42
Yugoslavia, ctry., Eur.	F7	26
Yuhebu, China	C3	42
Yuhuan Dao, i., China	G9	42
Yuhuang Ding, mtn., China	C9	42
Yukon, Ok., U.S.	F11	128
Yukon, state, Can.	B3	106
Yukon, stm., N.A.	D7	140
Yukon Flats, sw., Ak., U.S.	C11	140
Yukuhashi, Japan	F3	40
Yuli, China	F15	32
Yüli, Tai.	J9	42
Yulin, China	B3	42
Yulin, China	J3	42
Yulin, China	L3	42
Yuma, Az., U.S.	K2	132
Yuma, Co., U.S.	A6	128
Yuma, Bahía de, b., Dom. Rep.	C13	102
Yumare, Ven.	B7	86
Yumbel, Chile	H1	92
Yumbo, Col.	F3	86
Yumen, China	D4	36
Yumt uul, mtn., Mong.	C4	36
Yun, stm., China	F5	42
Yuna, stm., Dom. Rep.	C13	102
Yunak, Tur.	E14	28
Yunan, China	J4	42
Yuncheng, China	D4	42
Yuncheng, China	D6	42
Yungay, Chile	H2	92
Yungchi see Jilin, China	C7	38
Yungchia see Wenzhou, China	F9	36
Yungning see Nanning, China	J3	42
Yunkai Dashan, mts., China	J4	42
Yun Ling, mts., China	F4	36
Yunnan, state, China	G5	36
Yunnanfu see Kunming, China	F5	36
Yunta, Austl.	I2	76
Yunwu Shan, mtn., China	A7	42
Yunxi, China	E4	42
Yunxian, China	E4	42
Yunxiao, China	I7	42
Yunyang, China	F3	42
Yunyang see Yunxian, China	E4	42
Yunzalin, stm., Mya.	D3	48
Yuping, China	H3	42
Yuqing, China	H2	42
Yurimaguas, Peru	E2	84
Yuriria, Laguna de, l., Mex.	E8	100
Yuruá see Juruá, stm., S.A.	D4	84
Yuruarí, stm., Ven.	D11	86
Yurubi, Parque Nacional, p.o.i., Ven.	B7	86
Yurungkax, stm., China	A5	46
Yuscarán, Hond.	F4	102
Yûsef, Bahr (Yūsuf, Baḥr), can., Egypt	K1	58
Yushan, China	G8	42
Yü Shan, mtn., Tai.	J9	42
Yushanzhen, China	G3	42
Yushu, China	E4	36
Yushu, China	B7	38
Yutian, China	B7	42
Yutian, China	A5	46
Yuty, Para.	C9	92
Yütz'u see Yuci, China	C5	42
Yuxian, China	B6	42
Yuxian, China	B5	42
Yuxian, China	D5	42
Yuyao, China	F9	42
Yuzawa, Japan	E14	38
Yvelines, state, Fr.	F10	14
Yverdon-les-Bains, Switz.	D3	22
Ywathagyi, Mya.	A2	48

Z

Name	Map Ref.	Page
Zaandam see Zaanstad, Neth.	B13	14
Zaanstad, Neth.	B13	14
Zabalac', Bela.	G7	10
Zăbalț, Rom.	C8	26
Zabīd, Yemen	G5	56
Žabinka, Bela.	H6	10
Ząbkowice Śląskie, Pol.	F12	16
Žabljak, Yugo.	F6	26
Żabno, Pol.	F16	16
Zābol, Iran	C9	56
Zābol, state, Afg.	C1	54
Zabolotiv, Ukr.	A12	26
Zabor''e, Bela.	E12	10
Zabore, Russia	F15	10
Zabory, Russia	E15	10
Zabrze, Pol.	F14	16
Zabyčanne, Bela.	G14	10
Zacapa, Guat.	E3	102
Zacapu, Mex.	F8	100
Zacatecas, Mex.	D7	100
Zacatecas, state, Mex.	D7	100
Zacatlán, Mex.	F10	100
Zacoalco de Torres, Mex.	E7	100
Zacualtipan, Mex.	E9	100
Zadar (Zara), Cro.	F12	22
Zadetkale Kyun, i., Mya.	G3	48
Zadetkyi Kyun, i., Mya.	H3	48
Zadoi, China	B8	46
Za'farâna, well, Egypt	I3	58
Zafer Burnu, c., N. Cyp.	C5	58
Zafirovo, Blg.	F13	26
Zafra, Spain	F4	20
Żagań, Pol.	E11	16
Žagare, Lith.	D6	10
Zagazig, Egypt	H2	58
Zaghouan, Tun.	H4	24
Zaghouan, Jebel, mtn., Tun.	H4	24
Zagora, Mor.	C3	64
Zagórz, Pol.	G18	16
Zagreb, Cro.	E12	22
Zāgros, Kūhhā-ye, mts., Iran	C7	56
Zagros Mountains see Zāgros, Kūhhā-ye, mts., Iran	C7	56
Za'gya, stm., China	B13	54
Zāhedān, Iran	D9	56
Zahīrābād, India	C3	53
Zaḥlah, Leb.	E6	58
Zahnitkiv, Ukr.	A15	26
Zahrebetnoe, Russia	B17	8
Žailma, Kaz.	D10	32
Zaire see Congo, Democratic Republic of the, ctry., Afr.	E4	66
Zaïre see Congo, stm., Afr.	F2	66
Zaječar, Yugo.	F9	26
Zajsan, Kaz.	E14	32
Zajsan, ozero, l., Kaz.	E14	32
Zaka, Zimb.	B10	70
Zakamensk, Russia	F9	34
Zakarpattia, co., Ukr.	A10	26
Zakhidnyy Buh (Bug) (Buh), stm., Eur.	D17	16
Zakliczyn, Pol.	G16	16
Zakopane, Pol.	G16	16
Zakouma, Chad	E3	62
Zakroczym, Pol.	D16	16
Zákynthos, Grc.	F3	28
Zákynthos, i., Grc.	F3	28
Zala, state, Hung.	C3	26
Zala, stm., Hung.	C4	26
Zalaegerszeg, Hung.	C3	26
Zalamea de la Serena, Spain	F5	20
Zalantun, China	B9	36
Zalari, Russia	D18	32
Zalaszentgrót, Hung.	C4	26
Zalău, Rom.	B10	26
Zalese, Russia	F4	10
Zalim, Sau. Ar.	E5	56
Zalingei, Sudan	E4	62
Zaltyr, Kaz.	D12	32
Žaludok, Bela.	G7	10
Zama, Ms., U.S.	E9	122
Zamakh, Yemen	F6	56
Zamantı, stm., Tur.	A6	58
Zambeze, stm., Afr.	C3	68
Zambezi, Zam.	C3	68
Zambezi, stm., Afr.	D5	68
Zambezi Escarpment, clf, Zimb.	D4	68
Zambia, ctry., Afr.	C4	68
Zamboanga, Phil.	G3	52
Zamboanga Peninsula, pen., Phil.	G3	52
Zambrów, Pol.	C18	16
Žambyl, Kaz.	F12	32
Žambyl, Kaz.	E12	32
Zamežnaja, Russia	D24	8
Zami, stm., Mya.	D4	48
Zamora, Ec.	D2	84
Zamora, Spain	C5	20
Zamora, co., Spain	C5	20
Zamora de Hidalgo, Mex.	F7	100
Zamość, Pol.	F19	16
Zamość, state, Pol.	F19	16
Zanaga, Congo	E2	66
Žanatas, Kaz.	F11	32
Záncara, stm., Spain	E8	20
Zanda, China	C7	54
Zanesville, Oh., U.S.	E3	114
Zanjān, Iran	B6	56
Zanjón, Arg.	C5	92
Žannetty, ostrov, i., Russia	A20	34
Zante see Zákynthos, i., Grc.	F3	28
Zanthus, Austl.	F4	74
Zanzibar, Tan.	F7	66
Zanzibar, i., Tan.	F7	66
Zanzibar Channel, strt., Tan.	F7	66
Zaostrove, Russia	F14	8
Zaō-zan, vol., Japan	A13	40
Zaozërnyj, Russia	C16	32
Zaozhuang, China	D7	42
Zap, N.D., U.S.	G12	124
Zapadnaja Dvina, Russia	D15	10
Zapadna Morava, stm., Yugo.	F8	26
Zapadno-Sibirskaja ravnina (West Siberian Plain), pl., Russia	B12	32
Zapadnyj hrebet, mts., Russia	F17	34
Zapadnyj Sajan, mts., Russia	D16	32
Západočeský kraj, state, Czech Rep.	G9	16
Západoslovenský Kraj, state, Slov.	H14	16
Zapala, Arg.	G2	90
Zapata, Tx., U.S.	H8	130
Zapata, Península de, pen., Cuba	A7	102
Zapatoca, Col.	D5	86
Zapatosa, Ciénaga de, l., Col.	C5	86
Zapljuse, Russia	B12	10
Zapole, Russia	B12	10
Zapoljarnyj, Russia	B14	8
Zapopan, Mex.	E7	100
Zaporizhzhia, Ukr.	E5	32
Zapovednyj, Russia	C10	38
Zaprudnja, Russia	D20	10
Zaqatala, Azer.	A6	56
Zaragoza, Mex.	A8	100
Zaragoza, Mex.	C1	130
Zaragoza (Saragossa), Spain	C10	20
Zaragoza, co., Spain	C9	20
Zarajsk, Russia	F21	10
Zaranj, Afg.	C9	56
Zarasai, Lith.	E9	10
Zárate, Arg.	G8	92
Zarautz, Spain	A8	20
Zarauz see Zarautz, Spain	A8	20
Zaraza, Ven.	C9	86
Zareče, Russia	E21	8
Zarečensk, Russia	C14	8
Zarghūn Shahr, Afg.	C10	56
Zaria, Nig.	G6	64
Żarki, Pol.	F15	16
Žarma, Kaz.	E14	32
Zărnești, Rom.	D12	26
Žarsuat, Kaz.	E12	32
Zarubino, Russia	C9	38
Zarumilla, Peru	D1	84
Żary, Pol.	E11	16
Zarzaïtine, Alg.	D6	64
Zarzal, Col.	E4	86
Zasa, Lat.	D8	10
Zāskār, stm., India	B6	54
Zāskār Mountains, mts., Asia	B7	54
Zaslaue, Bela.	F10	10
Zastava, Russia	G22	8
Zasule, Russia	D22	8
Žatec, Czech Rep.	F9	16
Zatyshshya, Ukr.	B16	26
Zavalla, Tx., U.S.	F4	122
Zave, Zimb.	D5	68
Zavet, Blg.	F13	26
Zavodoukovsk, Russia	C11	32
Zavodovski Island, i., S. Geor.	K12	82
Zavolžsk, Russia	H20	8
Zawadzkie, Pol.	F14	16
Zawiercie, Pol.	F15	16
Zāwiyat al-Mukhaylá, Libya	A4	62
Zaydābād, Afg.	A2	54
Zaysan see Zajsan, Kaz.	E14	32
Zaysan, Lake see Zajsan, ozero, l., Kaz.	E14	32
Zayü, stm., China	C8	46
Zayzan see Zajsan, Kaz.	E14	32
Zaza, stm., Cuba	B8	102
Zaza, Presa, res., Cuba	B8	102
Zbąszynek, Pol.	D11	16
Zbraslav, Czech Rep.	G10	16
Žd'ár nad Sazavou, Czech Rep.	G11	16
Ždiar, Slov.	G16	16
Zduńska Wola, Pol.	E14	16
Zearing, Ia., U.S.	B4	120
Zeballos, B.C., Can.	G4	138
Zebedelia, S. Afr.	D9	70
Zebulon, Ga., U.S.	C1	116
Zedang, China	D13	54
Zeebrugge, Bel.	C11	14
Zeehan, Austl.	n12	77a
Zeeland, Mi., U.S.	F4	112
Zeeland, N.D., U.S.	B13	126
Zeerust, S. Afr.	D7	70
Zefat, Isr.	F6	58
Zehdenick, Ger.	D9	16
Zeil, Mount, mtn., Austl.	D6	74
Zeist, Neth.	B14	14
Zeitz, Ger.	E8	16
Zeja, Russia	F14	34
Zeja, stm., Russia	F14	34
Zejskoe vodohranilišče, res., Russia	F14	34
Zelee, Cape, c., Sol. Is.	e9	79b
Zelenoborskij, Russia	C14	8
Zelenogorsk, Russia	F13	8
Zelenograd, Russia	D20	10
Zelenogradsk, Russia	F3	10
Zelenokumsk, Russia	F6	32
Železinka, Kaz.	D13	32
Železnodorožnyj, Russia	F4	10
Železnodorožnyj, Russia	B8	32
Železnogorsk, Russia	H18	10
Železnogorsk-Ilimskij, Russia	C18	32
Zelienople, Pa., U.S.	D5	114
Zella-Mehlis, Ger.	F6	16
Zell am See, Aus.	C9	22
Zell am Ziller, Aus.	C8	22
Zèl'va, Bela.	G7	10
Želva, Lith.	E8	10
Zemaitijos nacionalnis parkas, p.o.i., Lith.	D4	10
Zembin, Bela.	F11	10
Zembra, Île, i., Tun.	G4	24
Zémio, C.A.R.	C4	66
Zempoala, hist., Mex.	F10	100
Zemun, Yugo.	E7	26
Zeng, stm., China	J5	42
Zenica, Bos.	E4	26
Zenon Park, Sk., Can.	A10	124
Zentsūji, Japan	E6	40
Zenza do Itombe, Ang.	B1	68
Zephyr, Tx., U.S.	C9	130
Zephyrhills, Fl., U.S.	H3	116
Zepu, China	B12	56
Zeravšan, stm., Asia	B10	56
Zeravšanskij hrebet, mts., Asia	B10	56
Zerbst, Ger.	D8	16
Żerków, Pol.	D13	16
Zerqan, Alb.	C14	24
Žešart, Russia	E23	8
Zeulenroda, Ger.	F7	16
Zeven, Ger.	C5	16
Zevenaar, Neth.	E2	16
Zeytinbağı, Tur.	C11	28
Žezdy, Kaz.	E11	32
Zêzere, stm., Port.	E2	20
Žezkazgan, Kaz.	E11	32
Zgierz, Pol.	E15	16
Zgorzelec, Pol.	E11	16
Zhabuchaka Hu, l., China	C9	54
Zhakou, China	F5	42
Zhambyl see Žambyl, Kaz.	F12	32
Zhang, stm., China	I6	42
Zhang, stm., China	C5	42
Zhangaözen see Novyj Uzen', Kaz.	F8	32
Zhangaqazaly see Novokazalinsk, Kaz.	F10	32
Zhangbei, China	A6	42
Zhangguangcai Ling, mts., China	B8	38
Zhanghuang, China	K3	42
Zhangjiakou, China	A6	42
Zhangping, China	I7	42
Zhangpu, China	I7	42
Zhangqiu, China	C7	42
Zhangshuping, China	F4	42
Zhangwu, China	C5	38
Zhangye, China	D5	36
Zhangzhou, China	I7	42
Zhanjiang, China	K4	42
Zhanyu, China	B5	38
Zhao'an, China	J7	42
Zhaodong, China	A7	38
Zhaojue, China	C9	46
Zhaoping, China	I4	42
Zhaoqing, China	J5	42
Zhaotong, China	F5	36
Zhaoxing, China	B11	36
Zhaoyuan, China	B10	36
Zhari Namco, l., China	C10	54
Zharma see Žarma, Kaz.	E14	32
Zhaxi Co, l., China	B10	54
Zhaxigang, China	B7	54
Zhayyq see Ural, stm.	E8	32
Zhecheng, China	D6	42
Zhegu, China	D13	54
Zhejiang, state, China	G8	42
Zhelin, China	F9	42
Zhem see Emba, stm., Kaz.	E9	32
Zhenbeikou, China	B2	42
Zheng'an, China	G2	42
Zhengding, China	B6	42
Zhenghe, China	H8	42
Zhenglan Qi, China	C8	36
Zhengning, China	D3	42
Zhengyang, China	E6	42
Zhengzhou, China	D5	42
Zhenhai, China	G9	42
Zhenjiang, China	E8	42
Zhenlai, China	B9	36
Zhenning, China	H1	42
Zhenping, China	E5	42
Zhentou, stm., China	E6	42
Zhenxiong, China	F5	36
Zhenyu, China	H9	42
Zhenyuan, China	H3	42
Zhenyuan, China	D2	42
Zherong, China	H8	42
Zhetiqara see Džetygara, Kaz.	D10	32
Zhijiang, China	H3	42
Zhixia, China	G8	42
Zhob, Pak.	C2	54
Zhob, stm., Pak.	C10	56
Zhongba, China	C5	46
Zhongdian, China	F4	36
Zhongning, China	C1	42
Zhongpingchang, China	F3	42
Zhongshan, China	J5	42
Zhongshan, China	I4	42
Zhongshan, sci., Ant.	B12	81
Zhongtiao Shan, mts., China	D4	42
Zhongwei, China	C1	42
Zhongxian, China	F3	42
Zhongxiang, China	F5	42
Zhongyaozhan, China	F14	34
Zhoucun, China	C7	42
Zhouning, China	H8	42
Zhoushan Dao, i., China	F9	42
Zhoushan Qundao, is., China	F10	42
Zhouzhi, China	D3	42
Zhuanghe, China	B10	42
Zhuanglang, China	D1	42
Zhucang, China	H2	42
Zhucheng, China	D8	42
Zhuhe, China	G5	42
Zhuji, China	G9	42
Zhujia Jian, i., China	G10	42
Zhujiang Kou, est., Asia	J5	42
Zhumadian, China	E5	42
Zhuolu, China	A6	42
Zhuozhou, China	B6	42
Zhuozi, China	A5	42
Zhushan, China	E4	42
Zhuxi, China	E3	42
Zhuzhou, China	H5	42
Zhytomyr, Ukr.	E14	6
Zi, stm., China	C8	42
Zi, stm., China	G4	42
Ziārat, Pak.	C10	56
Žiar nad Hronom, Slov.	H14	16
Zibo, China	C8	42
Zichang, China	C3	42
Ziębice, Pol.	F13	16
Zielona Góra, Pol.	E11	16
Zielona Góra, state, Pol.	D11	16
Zierikzee, Neth.	C12	14
Ziesar, Ger.	D8	16
Zifta, Egypt	H2	58
Žigalovo, Russia	D19	32
Žigansk, Russia	C13	34
Zigong, China	F5	36
Zigui, China	F4	42
Ziguinchor, Sen.	G1	64
Zihuatanejo, Mex.	G8	100
Ziiyang, China	E3	42
Zijin, China	J6	42
Zikhron Ya'aqov, Isr.	F5	58
Žilaja Tambica, Russia	E17	8
Žilina, Slov.	G14	16
Žilino, Russia	F4	10
Zillah, Libya	B3	62
Zillertaler Alpen (Aurine, Alpi), mts., Eur.	C8	22
Zilupe, Lat.	D11	10
Zilwaukee, Mi., U.S.	E6	112
Zima, Russia	D18	32
Zimapán, Mex.	E9	100
Zimbabwe, ctry., Afr.	D4	68
Zimbabwe Ruins, hist., Zimb.	B10	70
Zimi, S.L.	H2	64
Zimnicea, Rom.	F12	26
Zimonino, Russia	G14	10
Zinder, Niger	G6	64
Zinga Mulike, Tan.	F7	66
Zinnik see Soignies, Bel.	D12	14
Zion, Il., U.S.	F2	112
Zion National Park, p.o.i., Ut., U.S.	F4	132
Zionsville, In., U.S.	I3	112
Zipaquirá, Col.	E5	86
Zirbitzkogel, mtn., Aus.	C11	22
Žirjatino, Russia	G16	10
Žirovnice, Czech Rep.	G11	16
Zitong, China	F1	42
Zittau, Ger.	F10	16
Ziway, Lake see Ziway Hāyk', l., Eth.	F7	62
Ziway Hāyk', l., Eth.	F7	62
Zixi, China	G7	42
Ziya, stm., China	B7	42
Ziyuan, China	I4	42
Žizdra, stm., Russia	F19	10
Zizhong, China	G1	42
Zizhou, China	C3	42
Žižica, Russia	D14	10
Žižickoe, ozero, l., Russia	D14	10
Zlaté Moravce, Slov.	H14	16
Zlatoust, Russia	C9	32
Zlatoustovsk, Russia	F15	34
Zlín, Czech Rep.	G13	16
Zlīṭan, Libya	A2	62
Žlobin, Bela.	H13	10
Złoczew, Pol.	E14	16
Złotoryja, Pol.	E11	16
Złotów, Pol.	C13	16
Zlynka, Russia	H14	10
Zmeinogorsk, Russia	D14	32
Żmigród, Pol.	E12	16
Zmiïnyi, ostriv, i., Ukr.	D17	26
Znamenka, Russia	F17	10
Znamensk, Russia	F4	10
Znamenskoe, Russia	C12	32
Żnin, Pol.	D13	16
Znojmo, Czech Rep.	H12	16
Zoar, S. Afr.	H5	70
Žodzina, Bela.	F11	10
Zoétélé, Cam.	D2	66
Zogang, China	F4	36
Žohova, ostrov, i., Russia	A19	34
Zohreh, stm., Iran	C7	56
Zolotaja Gora, Russia	F14	34
Žolymbet, Kaz.	D12	32
Zomba, Mwi.	D6	68
Zonguldak, Tur.	B14	28
Zonguldak, state, Tur.	B15	28
Zonza, Fr.	H15	18
Zorita, Spain	E5	20
Zorra, Arroyo de la, stm., Mex.	E6	130
Zouar, Chad	C3	62
Zouérat, Maur.	E2	64
Zoug see Zug, Switz.	C5	22
Zouxian, China	D7	42
Zovka, Russia	B11	10
Zrenjanin, Yugo.	D7	26
Žuantobe, Kaz.	F11	32
Zuata, stm., Ven.	C9	86
Zubaydīyah, Jabal az-, mtn., Syria	E8	58
Zubovo, Russia	F17	8
Zudáñez, Bol.	C4	90
Zuera, Spain	C10	20
Zufar (Dhofar), reg., Oman	F7	56
Zug, Switz.	C5	22
Zugdidi, Geor.	F6	32
Zuger See, l., Switz.	C5	22
Zugspitze, mtn., Eur.	I6	16
Zújar, stm., Spain	F5	20
Žukopa, Russia	D15	10
Žukovka, Russia	G16	10
Žukovskij, Russia	E21	10
Zuli, stm., China	D1	42
Zulia, state, Ven.	C5	86
Zulia, stm., S.A.	C5	86
Zululand, hist. reg., S. Afr.	F10	70
Zumbo, Moz.	D5	68
Zumbrota, Mn., U.S.	G6	118
Zungeru, Nig.	H6	64
Zunhua, China	A7	42
Zuni, stm., U.S.	I7	132
Zuni Pueblo, N.M., U.S.	H8	132
Zunyi, China	H2	42
Zuo, stm., China	J2	42
Zuodeng, China	J2	42
Zuomuchedong Hu, l., China	D12	54
Zuoyun, China	A5	42
Žuravičy, Bela.	G13	10
Zurich, On., Can.	E8	112
Zürich (Zurigo), Switz.	C5	22
Zurich, Lake see Zürichsee, l., Switz.	C5	22
Zürichsee, l., Switz.	C5	22
Zurigo see Zürich, Switz.	C5	22
Zurmi, Nig.	G6	64
Zuša, stm., Russia	G19	10
Žut, Otok, i., Cro.	G12	22
Zutphen, Neth.	B15	14
Zuwārah, Libya	A2	62
Zuwayzā, Jord.	G6	58
Zvenigorod, Russia	E19	10
Zvezdec, Blg.	G14	26
Zvezdnyj, Russia	C19	32
Zvishavane, Zimb.	B9	70
Zvolen, Slov.	H15	16
Zwedru, Lib.	H3	64
Zweibrücken, Ger.	G3	16
Zweisimmen, Switz.	D4	22
Zwickau, Ger.	F8	16
Zwierzyniec, Pol.	F18	16
Zwoleń, Pol.	E17	16
Zwolle, Neth.	B14	14
Zwolle, La., U.S.	F5	122
Żyrardów, Pol.	D16	16
Zyrjanka, Russia	C19	34
Zyrjanovsk, Kaz.	E14	32
Zyrjanskoe, Russia	C15	32
Zyryan see Zyrjanovsk, Kaz.	E14	32
Žytkavičy, Bela.	H10	10
Żywiec, Pol.	G15	16